Travel Discount Coupon

This coupon entitles you to special discounts
when you book your trip through the

TRAVEL NETWORK®
RESERVATION SERVICE

Hotels ♦ Airlines ♦ Car Rentals ♦ Cruises
All Your Travel Needs

Here's what you get: *

♦ A discount of $50 USD on a booking of $1,000** or
more for two or more people!

♦ A discount of $25 USD on a booking of $500** or more
for one person!

♦ Free membership for three years, and 1,000 free miles
on enrollment in the unique Travel Network Miles-to-
Go® frequent-traveler program. Earn one mile for
every dollar spent through the program. Redeem
miles for free hotel stays starting at 5,000 miles. Earn
free roundtrip airline tickets starting at 25,000 miles.

♦ Personal help in planning your own, customized trip.

♦ Fast, confirmed reservations at any property
recommended in this guide, subject to availability.***

♦ Special discounts on bookings in the U.S. and around
the world.

♦ Low-cost visa and passport service.

♦ Reduced-rate cruise packages and special car rental
programs worldwide.

Visit our website at http://www.travelnetwork.com/Frommer
or call us globally at 201-567-8500, ext. 55. In the U.S., call
toll-free at 1-888-940-5000, or fax 201-567-1838. In Canada,
call at 1-905-707-7222, or fax 905-707-8108. In Asia, call
60-3-7191044, or fax 60-3-7185415.

* To qualify for these travel discounts, at least a portion of your trip must
include destinations covered in this guide. No more than one coupon discount
may be used in any 12-month period, for destinations covered in this guide.
Cannot be combined with any other discount or promotion.
**These are U.S. dollars spent on commissionable bookings.
***A $10 USD fee, plus fax and/or phone charges, will be added to the cost of
bookings at each hotel not linked to the reservation service. Customers must
approve these fees in advance. If only hotels of this kind are booked, the traveler(s)
must also purchase roundtrip air tickets from Travel Network for the trip.

Valid until December 31, 1999. Terms and conditions of the Miles-to-
Go® program are available on request by calling 201-567-8500, ext 55.

CBB234

W9-ARN-325

Frommer's®
2nd Edition

CARIBBEAN
FROM $60 A DAY

The Ultimate Guide to Low-cost Travel

by Darwin Porter and Danforth Prince

Macmillan • USA

ABOUT THE AUTHORS

A native of North Carolina, **Darwin Porter** was a bureau chief for the *Miami Herald* when he was 21 and later worked in television advertising. A veteran travel writer, he is the author of numerous best-selling Frommer's guides. He is assisted by **Danforth Prince,** formerly of the Paris bureau of the *New York Times.*

They have traveled widely in the Caribbean for years, and are also the authors of *Frommer's Caribbean Cruises,* the most candid and up-to-date guide to cruise vacations on the market. In this guide, they share their secrets and discoveries with you.

MACMILLAN TRAVEL

A Simon & Schuster Macmillan Company
1633 Broadway
New York, NY 10019

Find us online at **http://www.frommers.com** or
on America Online at Keyword: **Frommers.**

ISBN 0-02-861668-5
ISSN 1082-5053

Editor: Robin Michaelson
Special thanks to Suzanne Jannetta
Production Editor: John Carroll
Design by Michele Laseau
Digital Cartography by Roberta Stockwell and Ortelius Design

SPECIAL SALES

Bulk purchases (10+ copies) of Frommer's travel guides are available to corporations at special discounts. The Special Sales Department can produce custom editions to be used as premiums and/or for sales promotion to suit individual needs. Existing editions can be produced with custom cover imprints such as corporate logos. For more information write to: Special Sales, Simon & Schuster, 1633 Broadway, New York, NY 10019.

Manufactured in the United States of America

Contents

1 **Choosing the Perfect Island:
The Best of the Caribbean from $60 a Day   1**

1 The Best Destinations for Low-Cost Vacations   1

2 The Best Beaches   4

3 The Best Snorkeling   5

4 The Best Dive Sites   5

5 The Best Golf Courses—with Greens Fees That Won't
Break the Bank   6

6 The Best Adventures That Deliver Bang for Your Buck   7

7 The Friendliest Islands   8

8 The Best Experiences You Can Have for Free
(or Almost)   9

9 The Best Destinations for Serious Shoppers
Who Insist on Bargains   10

10 The Best Reasonably Priced Honeymoon Resorts   12

11 The Best Family Resorts (for Parents Who Don't Want
to Blow the Kids' College Fund)   12

12 The Best Camping   13

13 The Best Places to Get Away from It All Without
Spending a Fortune   13

14 The Best Authentic Dining   14

15 The Best Places for Sunset Cocktails   15

16 The Best Nightspots Without Sky-High
Cover Charges   16

2 **Getting to Know the Caribbean   17**

1 The Islands in Brief   17

★ *Which Island Is for You?*   20

2 From Salsa to Reggae: The Musical Heritage
of the Caribbean   23

3 A Taste of the Islands   25

3 **Planning an Affordable Trip to the Caribbean   32**

1 Visitor Information, Entry Requirements, Customs
& Money   32

★ *What Things Cost in the Caribbean*   35

★ *The U.S. Dollar & The British Pound*   36

2 When to Go   36

3 40 Money-Saving Tips 37

4 Finding the Best Airfare 40

5 Cruises That Don't Cost a Fortune 42

6 Terrific Deals on Packages & Tours 48

7 Getting the Best Value Out of Your
Accommodations 50

8 Getting Married in the Caribbean 52

9 Tips for Travelers with Special Needs 55

4   The Cayman Islands   58

★ *Fast Facts: The Cayman Islands* 60

1 Grand Cayman 61

★ *Into the Deep: Submarine Dives* 70

2 Cayman Brac 74

3 Little Cayman 76

5   Puerto Rico   78

★ *Fast Facts: Puerto Rico* 82

1 San Juan 83

2 Dorado 105

3 Highlights in Northwestern Puerto Rico 105

4 Aguadilla 106

5 Rincón 107

6 Mayagüez 109

7 Boquerón & Cabo Rojo 111

8 Ponce 113

9 Exploring Northeastern Puerto Rico 116

★ *El Yunque Tropical Rain Forest* 117

10 Palmas del Mar 119

11 Island Drives 120

★ *Driving Tour 1: The Rain Forests
& Beaches of the East* 121

★ *Driving Tour 2: Karst Country / West & South Coasts* 124

12 Vieques 130

13 Culebra 134

6   The U.S. Virgin Islands   136

★ *Fast Facts: The U.S. Virgin Islands* 138

1 St. Thomas 139

2 St. John 162

★ *This Island Was Made for Hiking* 173

3 St. Croix 176

7 The British Virgin Islands 199

★ *Fast Facts: The British Virgin Islands* 200

1 Anegada 202

2 Jost Van Dyke 203

3 Tortola 205

★ *The Wreck of the* Rhône *& Other Top Dive Sites* 216

4 Virgin Gorda 218

8 The Dominican Republic 225

★ *Fast Facts: The Dominican Republic* 228

1 Santo Domingo 229

★ *His Name Was Rubi, He Was a Playboy* 233

2 Barahona Peninsula 242

3 La Romana & Altos de Chavón 244

4 Puerto Plata 248

5 Sosúa 253

6 Samaná 257

9 The British Leeward Islands 260

1 Antigua & Barbuda 260

★ *Fast Facts: Antigua* 261

2 Montserrat 277

★ *Fast Facts: Montserrat* 279

3 St. Kitts 285

★ *Fast Facts: St. Kitts* 286

★ *Into the Volcano* 296

4 Nevis 298

★ *Fast Facts: Nevis* 300

10 The Dutch Windwards in the Leewards 308

1 St. Maarten 308

★ *Fast Facts: St. Maarten* 312

2 St. Eustatius 324

★ *Fast Facts: St. Eustatius* 326

   3 Saba   332

★ *Fast Facts: Saba*   333

★ *Exploring an Underwater Wonderland*   339

11   Jamaica   341

★ *Fast Facts: Jamaica*   346

★ *Catch a Fire: Jamaica's Reggae Festivals*   352

   1 Montego Bay   349

   2 Negril   361

   3 Falmouth   370

   4 Runaway Bay   372

   5 Ocho Rios   374

   6 Port Antonio   383

   7 Kingston   388

★ *Climbing the Blue Mountain*   392

   8 Mandeville   395

   9 The South Coast   397

12   The French West Indies   400

   1 Martinique   401

★ *Fast Facts: Martinique*   405

★ *Begin the Beguine*   415

   2 Guadeloupe   425

★ *Fast Facts: Guadeloupe*   428

★ *Joe vs. the Volcano*   445

   3 St. Martin   453

★ *Fast Facts: St. Martin*   456

13   The British Windwards   466

   1 Dominica   466

★ *Fast Facts: Dominica*   469

   2 St. Lucia   479

★ *Fast Facts: St. Lucia*   482

★ *Rare Birds & Other Critters*   490

   3 St. Vincent   496

★ *Fast Facts: St. Vincent*   498

★ *Joe vs. the Volcano, Part II*   505

   4 The Grenadines   508

   5 Grenada   513

★ *Fast Facts: Grenada*   514

14   Barbados   532

★ *Fast Facts: Barbados*   534

1 Bargain Places to Stay   537

2 Where to Eat   543

3 Beaches, Water Sports & Other Outdoor Pursuits   548

4 Exploring the Island   551

5 Shopping   559

6 Barbados After Dark   561

★ *The Joints Are Still Jumping at Dawn:*
   Where to Find the Best Local Watering Holes   562

15   Trinidad & Tobago   564

★ *Fast Facts: Trinidad & Tobago*   564

1 Trinidad   566

★ *A Swirl of Color & Sound: The Carnival of Trinidad*   575

2 Tobago   579

16   The Dutch Leewards   590

1 Aruba   590

★ *Fast Facts: Aruba*   593

2 Bonaire   606

★ *Fast Facts: Bonaire*   609

★ *Coastal Reef Diving*   616

3 Curaçao   621

★ *Fast Facts: Curaçao*   622

List of Maps

The Caribbean Islands   2

The Cayman Islands   59

Puerto Rico   81

Old San Juan   95

St. Thomas   141

St. John   163

St. Croix   179

The British Virgin
   Islands   201

The Dominican
   Republic   227

Antigua   263

Barbuda   276

Montserrat   279

St. Kitts   287

Nevis   299

St. Maarten   311

St. Eustatius   325

Saba   333

Jamaica   344

Montego Bay   350

Ocho Rios   377

Martinique   403

Guadeloupe   427

St. Martin   455

Dominica   467

St. Lucia   481

St. Vincent and
   the Grenadines   497

Grenada   515

Barbados   535

Trinidad   567

Tobago   581

Aruba   591

Bonaire   607

Curaçao   623

AN INVITATION TO THE READER

In researching this book, we discovered many wonderful places—hotels, restaurants, shops, and more. We're sure you'll find others. Please tell us about them, so we can share the information with your fellow travelers in upcoming editions. If you were disappointed with a recommendation, we'd love to know that, too. Please write to:

Darwin Porter & Danforth Prince
Frommer's Caribbean on $60 a Day, 2nd Edition
Macmillan Travel
1633 Broadway
New York, NY 10019

AN ADDITIONAL NOTE

Please be advised that travel information is subject to change at any time—and this is especially true of prices. We therefore suggest that you write or call ahead for confirmation when making your travel plans. The authors, editors, and publisher cannot be held responsible for the experiences of readers while traveling. Your safety is important to us, however, so we encourage you to stay alert and be aware of your surroundings. Keep a close eye on cameras, purses, and wallets, all favorite targets of thieves and pickpockets.

WHAT THE SYMBOL MEANS

✪ Frommer's Favorites

Hotels, restaurants, attractions, and entertainment you should not miss.

The following abbreviations are used for credit cards:

AE	American Express	MC	MasterCard
DC	Diners Club	V	Visa
DISC	Discover		

The following abbreviations are used in hotel listings:

MAP (Modified American Plan) usually means room, breakfast, and dinner, unless the room rate has been quoted separately, and then it means only breakfast and dinner.

AP (American Plan) includes your room plus three meals.

CP (Continental Plan) includes room and a light breakfast.

EP (European Plan) means room only.

Choosing the Perfect Island: The Best of the Caribbean from $60 a Day

You can hike through national parks and scuba dive along underwater mountains. But perhaps your idea of the perfect Caribbean vacation is to plunk yourself down on a beach and do nothing at all. This guide will show you the best of the islands, and prove to you that memorable vacations don't have to cost a fortune. In this chapter, we'll share an opinionated list of our favorite finds and bargains to help you start planning.

For a thumbnail portrait of each island, see "The Islands in Brief" in chapter 2.

1 The Best Destinations for Low-Cost Vacations

Some islands, such as pricey St. Barts or Anguilla, are best left to the rich and famous. If you're not a movie star who commands $18 to $25 million per picture, here are some lovely, less expensive options.

- **Puerto Rico:** You can go for broke in Puerto Rico, that's for sure, but you can also find incredible bargains. Ignore those ritzy resorts: Puerto Rico is filled with B&Bs, small inns, and even government-run paradors out in the countryside where you can stay for just a fraction of the price you'd pay along the Condado in San Juan. There's terrific dining at inexpensive roadside kiosks, small cafes, and little family-run dining rooms frequented by locals. See chapter 5.
- **The Dominican Republic:** Canadians, whose dollar is weaker in the Caribbean than the Yankee buck, have long flocked to this island nation for its sun, sand, and bargains. It's one of the cheapest destinations in the West Indies. And new resort areas are under development, including the peninsula at Samaná and the Barahona Peninsula, each charging resort prices you haven't seen in 25 years. See chapter 8.
- **St. Eustatius:** Called "Statia" for short, this Dutch-held island is for escapists on a lean budget. It's sleepy, it's undiscovered—and that means great bargains for you. You'll just have to forgo white sandy beaches for some gray or black sandy ones. It's filled with terrific hiking trails and wonderful dive sites that line the coast; the islanders are friendly; and you can find mom-and-pop hotels charging prices "the way they were." See chapter 10.

The Caribbean Islands

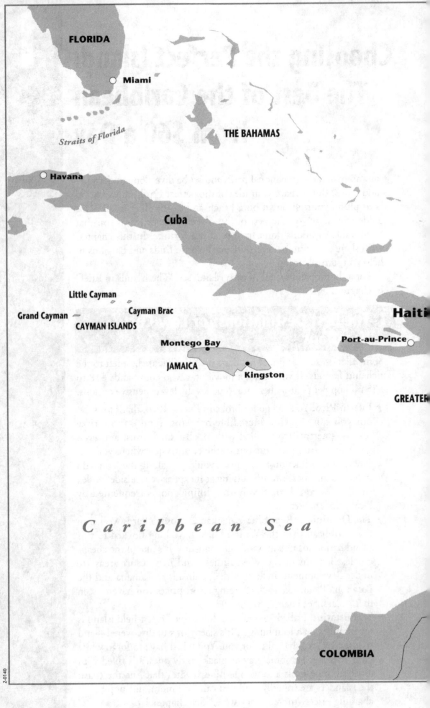

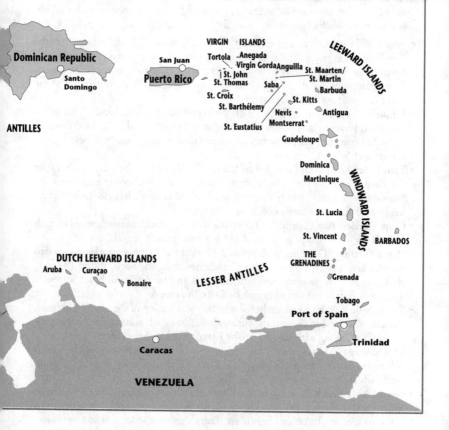

Atlantic

Ocean

TURKS AND CAICOS ISLANDS

Dominican Republic

Santo
Domingo

ANTILLES

San Juan

Puerto Rico

VIRGIN   ISLANDS

Tortola   Anegada
          Virgin Gorda Anguilla St. Maarten/
     St. John   St. Martin
St. Thomas   Saba
                                 Barbuda
St. Croix
     St. Barthélemy   St. Kitts
              Nevis   Antigua
     St. Eustatius   Montserrat

              Guadeloupe

LEEWARD ISLANDS

              Dominica
              Martinique

                   St. Lucia

                   St. Vincent   BARBADOS
              THE
              GRENADINES
                        Grenada

WINDWARD ISLANDS

DUTCH LEEWARD ISLANDS
Aruba   Curaçao   LESSER ANTILLES
              Bonaire

                              Tobago
                   Port of Spain

     Caracas   Trinidad

VENEZUELA

0 ━━━━━ 200 mi
        320 km

N

3

- **Saba:** Along with Statia, this, too, is a Dutch-held island, but it's like none other in the Caribbean. Only 5 square miles, it's not everyone's cup of tea. But if you can forgo beaches, this volcanic island, ringed with steep cliffs, offers some of the finest diving in the Caribbean. And the hiking is terrific, too. On this beautiful island, the hotels are some of the most affordable in the Caribbean. See chapter 10.
- **Jamaica:** Sure, there's a long list of posh resorts and pricey all-inclusives. But beyond these guarded compounds exists another Jamaica, where the prices are as appealing as a frosty Red Stripe beer. Jamaica is riddled with small inns, and new resort areas are being developed, including along the south coast around Treasure Beach, east of Negril on the long road to Kingston. Even such normally tony areas as Montego Bay are filled with affordable B&Bs and small inns. See chapter 11.
- **Dominica:** This island nation with a British/French-Créole flavor has rugged mountains and lush forests. But it lacks great beaches, which has hindered its development as a resort. That lack of a tourist boom is good news for bargain hunters. If you enjoy lush settings and landscapes, Dominica is for you. The locals are among the friendliest hosts in the West Indies. See chapter 13.

2 The Best Beaches

Good beaches can be found on virtually every island of the Caribbean, with the possible exception of Saba (which has rocky shores) and Dominica.

- **Seven Mile Beach** (Grand Cayman): It's really about 5^1/$_2$ miles long, but the 7-mile label has stuck. And who cares? Lined with condos and plush resorts, this beach is known for its array of water sports and its translucent aquamarine waters. Australian pines dot the background, and the average winter temperature of the water is a perfect 80°F. See chapter 4.
- **Luquillo Beach** (Puerto Rico): This crescent-shaped public beach, with white sands and towering palms, lies 30 miles east of San Juan and is the local favorite. It also has tent sites and picnic facilities. Coral reefs protect the crystal-clear lagoon. See chapter 5.
- **Trunk Bay** (St. John): Protected by the U.S. National Park Service, this is one of the Caribbean's most popular beaches. A favorite with cruise-ship passengers, it's known for its underwater trail, where markers guide snorkelers along the reef lying just off the white sandy beach. See chapter 6.
- **Cane Garden Bay** (Tortola): One of the more spectacular stretches of beach, it extends for 1^1/$_2$ miles of white sand and is a favorite with joggers. See chapter 7.
- **Playa Grande** (Dominican Republic): One of the Caribbean's least crowded beaches and one of the best, Playa Grande lies along the north shore. The long stretch of sand is powdery, and farther west is another beautiful beach at Sosúa, with calm waters and lots of tourist facilities. See chapter 8.
- **Seven-Mile Beach** (Jamaica): In the northwestern section of the island, this beach stretches for 7 miles. Not for the conservative, the beach also contains some nudist "patches" along with bare-all Booby Island offshore. See chapter 11.
- **Le Diamant** (Martinique): This bright white sandy beach stretches for about 6^1/$_2$ miles, much of it undeveloped. It faces a rocky offshore island, Diamond Rock, which has uninhabited shores. See chapter 12.
- **Grand Anse Beach** (Grenada): This 2-mile stretch of sand is reason enough to go to Grenada. Although the island has some 45 beaches, most with white sand, this is the pick of the litter, and rightly so. There's enough space and so few visitors that you'll likely find a spot just for yourself. The sugar-white sands of Grand Anse extend into deep waters far offshore. See chapter 13.

3 The Best Snorkeling .

St. Croix, St. John, and St. Thomas are among the top five favorite places to snorkel in the Caribbean.

- **Stingray City** (Grand Cayman): Stingray City has been called the best 12-foot dive (or snorkel) site in the world. In these shallow depths in Grand Cayman's North Sound, more than 30 southern Atlantic stingrays swim freely with snorkelers and divers. See chapter 4.
- **Buck Island Reef National Monument** (St. Croix): More than 250 species of fish, as well as a variety of sponges, corals, and crustaceans, have been recorded at this 850-acre island and reef system, 2 miles off St. Croix's north shore. The reef is strictly protected by the National Park Service. See chapter 6.
- **Cane Bay** (St. Croix): One of the island's best diving and snorkeling sites is off this breezy north-shore beach. On a clear day, you can swim out 150 yards and see the Cane Bay Wall, which drops off dramatically to deep waters below. Multicolored fish and elkhorn and brain coral thrive here. See chapter 6.
- **Trunk Bay** (St. John): This self-guided 225-yard-long trail has large underwater signs that identify species of coral and other items of interest. There are freshwater showers, changing rooms, equipment rentals, and a lifeguard on duty. See chapter 6.
- **Leinster Bay** (St. John): With easy access from land or sea, Leinster Bay offers calm, clear, and uncrowded waters, with an abundance of sea life. See chapter 6.
- **Haulover Bay** (St. John): A favorite with locals, this small bay is rougher than Leinster and is often deserted. The snorkeling is dramatic, with ledges, walls, nooks, and sandy areas set close together. At this spot, only about 200 yards separate the Atlantic Ocean from the Caribbean Sea. See chapter 6.
- **Magens Bay** (St. Thomas): On the north shore, Coki Point offers year-round snorkeling, especially around the ledges near Coral World's underwater tower, a favorite with cruise-ship passengers. See chapter 6.
- **Buccoo Reef** (Tobago): The shallow, sun-flooded waters off the South American coastline nurture enormous colonies of marine life. Buccoo Reef on Tobago offers many opportunities for snorkeling, and many local entrepreneurs take snorkeling enthusiasts out for junkets on various sailing craft. See chapter 15.
- **Bonaire:** Right from their hotels, snorkelers can wade from the shore to the reefs and view an array of coral, including elkhorn barrier, fire and leaf corals, and a range of colorful fish, such as redlip blennies, jewelfish, and parrot fish. The reefs just off Klein Bonaire and Washington/Slagbaai National Park receive rave reviews. See chapter 16.
- **Curaçao Underwater Park** (Curaçao): In contrast to Curaçao's sterile terrain, the marine life that rings the island is rich and spectacular. The best-known snorkeling sites stretch for 12½ miles along Curaçao's southern coastline—the Curaçao Underwater Park. Sunken shipwrecks, gardens of coral, and millions of fish are your reward. See chapter 16.

4 The Best Dive Sites

Scuba diving, as everyone knows, is hardly cheap. But if it's your primary reason for visiting the Caribbean, look for a diver's package to get the best deal. Many resorts, including those on Bonaire and the Cayman Islands (the best spots for divers), offer packages that include your room, meals, and limited scuba diving.

If diving is only a sometimes passion for you, you can stay at a budget hotel and visit a local dive operator. Most one-tank dives cost $45 to $55, with two-tank dives costing $65 to $75. These prices can vary widely, however. A full certification course can range from $300 to $450.

- **The Cayman Islands:** Grand Cayman has been called "the best known dive destination in the Caribbean—if not the world," by *Skin Diver* magazine. There are 34 dive operations on Grand Cayman (plus five more on Little Cayman, and three on Cayman Brac). A full range of professional dive services is available, including equipment sales, rentals, and repairs; instruction at all levels; underwater photography, video schools, and processing services. Stingray City has become Grand Cayman's most famous dive (and snorkel) site.

  On Little Cayman, **Sam McCoy's Diving and Fishing Lodge** (☎ 800/626-0496) offers reasonable dive packages that usually include all meals. This resort attracts divers who pursue the sport with a passion. See chapter 4.

- **St. Croix:** Increasingly known as a top diving destination, St. Croix hasn't overtaken Grand Cayman yet, but it has a lot going for it. Beach dives, reef dives, wreck dives, nighttime dives, wall dives—it's all here. But none can compete with the underwater trails of the national park at Buck Island, lying off St. Croix's "mainland." Other sites include the drop-offs and coral canyons at Cane Bay and Salt River. Davis Bay is the location of the 12,000-foot-deep Puerto Rico Trench, the fifth-deepest body of water on earth.

  In Christiansted, the **Hotel Caravelle** (☎ 345/773-0687) offers discounts if you book your accommodations and several dive outings simultaneously. See chapter 6.

- **Virgin Gorda:** Many divers plan their entire vacations around exploring the famed wreck of the RMS *Rhône*, off Salt Island. This royal mail steamer, which went down in 1867, is the most celebrated dive site in the Caribbean. See chapter 7.

- **Saba:** Islanders can't brag about Saba's beaches, but the waters around the island are blessed with some of the Caribbean's richest marine life. It's one of the premier diving locations in the Caribbean, with 38 official dive sites. The unusual setting includes underwater lava flows, black-sand bottoms, very large strands of black coral, millions of fish, and underwater mountaintops.

  The **Saba Deep Dive Center** (☎ 599/4-63347), one of the best-organized dive outfitters anywhere, offers an assortment of lodgings, many of them affordable choices with charm and a sense of Saban history as part of the package. See chapter 10.

- **Bonaire:** Here local license plates read "A Diver's Paradise." The highly accessible reefs that surround Bonaire have never suffered from exploitation, poaching, or pollution, and the island's environmentally conscious dive industry will ensure they never do. For the first-timer to the certified diver, the island is one of the world's top underwater environments—it's a underwater mountain created from volcanic eruptions. Diving is possible 24 hours a day.

  Captain Don's Habitat Dive Shop (☎ 800/327-6709) offers some of the most all-around reasonable packages that combine accommodations, meals, and diving. See chapter 16.

5 The Best Golf Courses—with Greens Fees That Won't Break the Bank

When you see the price of greens fees in the Caribbean, you may want to wait to tee off until you return home. But if you're like many golfers, your passion for the game means that you're willing to splurge to play on a top course. So in the chapters that follow, we've listed the courses designed by some of the world's most famous golf architects, including Robert Trent Jones (Jr. and Sr.), Pete Dye, Gary Player, and others. In addition, we've found some worthwhile courses where you can play without going broke.

- **Bahia Beach Plantation Golf Course** (Puerto Rico; ☎ 787/256-5600): Puerto Rico is the golfing capital of the West Indies, and you'll find its least expensive course only a 30-minute drive east of San Juan. On this 18-hole, par-72 golf course, the fairways are lined either with palm trees or mangrove swamps—and it's a honey of a spot for tee-off time. See chapter 5.
- **Playa Dorado** (Dominican Republic; ☎ 809/320-4340): Normally, playing one of the courses designed by Robert Trent Jones Sr. or Jr. means paying for the privilege and prestige. But there is an exception or two, including this par-72, 18-hole course, a real champion, at Playa Dorado on the north coast of the Dominican Republic. Greens fees are the most reasonable in the Caribbean. If you don't want to play 18 holes, you play 9 holes for less, before enjoying the beach (which is absolutely free). See chapter 8.
- **Royal St. Kitts Golf Club** (St. Kitts; ☎ 809/465-8339): If you hop over to St. Kitts's neighbor, Nevis, you'll need to win the lottery to play its newly fabled course. But if you stick to St. Kitts, you can play a reasonable game at a reasonable price. This 18-hole, par-72 championship course spreads across 160 acres. You'll have a great game in a scenic setting, designed around seven beautiful ponds. See chapter 9.
- **Ironshore Golf & Country Club** (Montego Bay, Jamaica; ☎ 809/953-2800): Montego Bay is home to some of the world's most legendary courses, notably the championship tee-off spots at Tryall and Half Moon. However, the resort also boasts this excellent, well-manicured, privately owned 18-hole, par-72 golf course. It's not as ritzy as its famous neighbors, but it's quite playable, and the prices are a lot easier on the wallet. See chapter 11.
- **Golf de l'Impératrice-Joséphine** (Martinique; ☎ 0596-68-32-81): Robert Trent Jones Sr. created this splendid 18-holer on Martinique, the island's only course. Rolling hills and scenic vistas sweeping down to the sea make for a bucolic setting, and the greens fees are unexpectedly reasonable even though this is a relatively high-priced island. See chapter 12.

6 The Best Adventures That Deliver Bang for Your Buck

- **Spending a Day on Buck Island** (off St. Croix): Legendary throughout the Caribbean for its underwater life, Buck Island is riddled with a network of hiking trails. On this 300-acre island surrounded by 550 acres of underwater coral gardens, the snorkeling possibilities are stunning. A circular underwater trail on the island's easternmost side has arrow markers to guide viewers along the inner reef. The elkhorn coral here are among the most massive specimens in the world. See chapter 6.
- **Hiking the Blue Mountains** (Jamaica): Unlike many of its neighboring islands, Jamaica offers mountain peaks of up to 7,402 feet. The flora, fauna, waterfalls, and panoramas have attracted increasing numbers of hikers and hillclimbers. The Jamaica Alternative Tourism Camping and Hiking Association includes three separate tour operators. Foremost among these is **SENSE Adventures Ltd.,** P.O. Box 216, Kingston 7, Jamaica (☎ 809/927-2097; fax 809/929-6967), which offers individually designed backpacking tours of the Blue Mountains and canoe trips along its rivers. Most of the expeditions use the Maya Lodge, a rustic but clean and comfortable 15-acre base from which hiking tours depart. All-inclusive packages

cost $55 to $90 per person per day, depending on the number of participants. See chapter 11.

- **Exploring Lush, Luxuriant Guadeloupe:** The mountainous terrain of Basse-Terre island is extraordinarily beautiful. Although the island's coastline is lined with beach resorts and fishing villages, the mountainous interior is a sparsely inhabited region devoted almost completely to a French national forest, Le Parc Naturel de Guadeloupe. Near the park's southernmost boundary stands the 4,812-foot volcanic peak, La Soufrière. The park contains more than 200 miles of hiking trails, allowing physically fit hikers to visit a wealth of gorges, ravines, rivers, and (at points north of La Soufrière) some of the highest waterfalls in the Caribbean. See chapter 12.

- **Trekking to a Boiling Lake** (Dominica): The highlight of Dominica National Park, this solfatara lake is like a large cauldron of steaming gray-blue water—a flooded fumarole. It's the world's second-largest boiling lake. Getting here is part of the fun, as it's a real arduous climb. The trail (which you should follow only with a guide) takes you through Gtitgou Gorge and along forested mountains until you reach the aptly named Valley of Desolation. After that, it's a rough valley crossing until you ascend to the mysterious lake on the far side. The trick is not to fall through the thin crust that blankets the hot, steaming lava below! See chapter 13.

- **Going Deep into Harrison's Cave** (Barbados): If you can explore only one cave in the Caribbean, make it this one. Open to the public since 1981, these limestone caverns are a fairy-tale world of stalagmites, subterranean streams, and stalactites—everything reaching its crescendo with a 40-foot waterfall. Harrison's, the premier attraction of Barbados, is one of the finest cave systems in the world. See chapter 14.

- **Discovering the Greatest Sight in the Avian World** (Trinidad): The Caroni Swamp National Park, spread across 40 square miles in Trinidad, is without equal in the Caribbean. Home of the national bird of Trinidad & Tobago, the scarlet ibis, this is the world's premier site for birders. Even *Audubon* magazine agrees. Beginning in the late afternoon, fire-engine–red birds arrive by the thousands, settling into roost for the night. As if this weren't enough, snowy egrets and herons fly in to join them in their slumber. The birds arrive in such vast numbers that they look like flaming scarlet and white Christmas tree decorations. See chapter 15.

7 The Friendliest Islands

A few islands are plagued with racial tensions and violent crime, and visitors may not feel welcome. In particular, Jamaica's portside cities (especially Ocho Rios, Kingston, and Montego Bay) are known for crowds of hawkers and peddlers who aggressively pressure tourists to buy unwanted souvenirs. St. Thomas and St. Croix are not very welcoming either, and also have crime problems. And both Puerto Rico and the Dominican Republic are populous enough to have an urban atmosphere where some visitors might feel anonymous. Locals are pretty jaded about the hordes of tourists who arrive each year.

So, with these caveats expressed, let's proceed to friendlier oases.

- **St. John:** St. John remains an unspoiled and relatively safe destination. The locals aren't as jaded about tourism as they are on St. Thomas, and in most places you'll receive a genuine welcome. Many places appreciate your business and want you to return, so they make you feel welcome. See chapter 6.

- **Virgin Gorda:** Many locals leave their houses and cars unlocked (though we don't recommend that you become that casual). But, it's the lazy, peaceful life here. Visitors are welcomed into most places with a smile. See chapter 7.
- **Nevis:** Nevis has a small, intimate feeling. Most accommodations are charming and historic inns, with a British tradition of good manners. See chapter 9.
- **Montserrat:** The friendly, churchgoing people of this underpopulated, lush island have lovely manners and clipped British accents. See chapter 9.
- **Saba:** The residents here refer to their island as the "Unspoiled Caribbean Queen," because there are no beaches, casinos, or large hotels, and only a handful of bars. The population of 1,200 shy but cautiously friendly residents follow traditions that were established by the Dutch settlers who first arrived in the 1600s. You'll be very safe here, but will be expected to behave with dignity and respect for island traditions. See chapter 10.
- **Grenada / St. Vincent / The Grenadines:** The islands of the southern Caribbean are English-speaking, music-loving outposts. Locals can be warm and welcoming to North Americans. See chapter 13.
- **Bonaire:** With a tiny population of about 11,000 souls, Bonaire has a small-town atmosphere with a pace slow enough for the most diehard escapist. Residents are usually curious about off-islanders. See chapter 16.

8 The Best Experiences You Can Have for Free (or Almost)

- **Boating Over to Monkey Island** (off Palmas del Mar Resort, Humacao, Puerto Rico): Reached from the marina at Palmas del Mar, the 39-acre islet of Cayo Santiago lies off the eastern shore of Puerto Rico. A boat, the *Shagrada,* takes snorkelers and the merely curious over to see an island colony of rhesus monkeys whose ancestors were brought here from India in 1938 for study. Many significant breakthroughs in human medicine have been attributed to observing the behavioral patterns of these rambunctious primates. Passengers aren't allowed to actually go on the island, but you can see the monkeys on the shore, swinging through the trees, playing the mating game, nursing their young, or just going bananas. See chapter 5.
- **Diving off Mona Island** (Mayagüez, Puerto Rico): Surrounded by some of the most beautiful coral reefs in the Caribbean, Mona Island has the most pristine, extensive, and well-developed reefs in Puerto Rican waters. The tropical marine ecosystem around Mona includes patch reefs, black coral, spore and groove systems, underwater caverns, deep-water sponges, fringing reefs, and algae reefs. The lush environment attracts octopuses, lobster, queen conch, rays, barracuda, snapper, jack, grunt, angelfish, trunkfish, filefish, butterfly fish, dolphin, parrot fish, tuna, flying fish, and more. The crystal waters afford exceptional horizontal vision for 150 to 200 feet as well as good views down to the shipwrecks that mark the site—including some Hispanic galleons. Five different species of whales visit the island's offshore waters. Instead of booking an expensive tour, negotiate with a local fisherman to take you over for a look. See chapter 5.
- **Floating Over to "Treasure Island":** Norman Island, south of Tortola and east of St. John, is accessible only by boat. The island has serviced the needs of smugglers and ruffians since the 1600s, when pirates used its hillocks to spot Spanish galleons to plunder. Legend has it that this was the island that inspired Robert

Louis Stevenson's *Treasure Island,* first published in 1883. In a dinghy, you can row into the southernmost cave on the island—with bats overhead and phosphorescent patches. This is where Stevenson's Mr. Fleming, according to legend, took his precious treasure. It was reported that in 1750, treasure from the sunken *Nuestra Señora* was recovered here. The island has a series of other caves whose bottoms are filled with seawater teeming with marine life. Intrepid hikers climb through scrubland to the island's central ridge, Spy Glass Hill, to appreciate the panoramic view of the land and sea, though hiking trails are either nonexistent or poorly maintained. See chapter 7.

- **Enjoying Jamaica's People to People Program:** Tell the Jamaica Tourist Board (see chapter 11 for contact information) what your interests are—butterflies, reggae, Bible studies, sailing, whatever—and they'll pair you up with Jamaican families who will, without fuss or bother, spend a few hours with you, including you in the normal routine of their lives. Almost 700 Jamaican families participate. There's no cost, but a small gift as a gesture of appreciation is always welcome. Many lasting friendships have formed as a result of this program.
- **Rafting on the Río Grande** (Port Antonio, Jamaica; ☎ **809/993-2778**): Until the late actor Errol Flynn discovered what fun it was, rafting on this river was simply a means of transporting bananas. Now it's the most amusing sport in Jamaica. Propelled by stout bamboo poles, you're guided down the river for 8 miles, viewing a lush backdrop of coconut palms and banana plantations. You're even taken through the Tunnel of Love. See chapter 11.
- **Exploring Two Unspoiled Islands near Guadeloupe:** Marie-Galante (named by Columbus in 1493) and the Iles des Saintes are rarely visited islands near the coast of Guadeloupe. They preserve a raffish, seafaring atmosphere you might have found in Marseille during the 1930s. Come to sunbathe, explore by bike, and savor the seclusion. See chapter 12.
- **Calling on the Once-Hostile Caribs** (Dominica): The Carib Indian Reservation, along the eastern coast of Dominica, is home to the once-hostile tribe for whom the Caribbean is named. Reviled by the Spanish invaders because of their cannibalism, the Caribs now live peacefully in half a dozen villages, the largest of which are Bataka, Sineku, and Salybia. See chapter 13.

9 The Best Destinations for Serious Shoppers Who Insist on Bargains

Since the American government allows U.S. citizens to take (or send) home more duty-free goods from the U.S. Virgin Islands than from other ports of call, the U.S. Virgin Islands remain the shopping bazaar of the Caribbean. U.S. citizens may carry home $1,200 worth of goods untaxed, as opposed to only $400 worth of goods from most islands in the Caribbean. (The only exception to this rule is Puerto Rico, where any purchase, regardless of the amount, can be carried tax-free back to the U.S. mainland.)

- **Cayman Islands:** You can buy tax-free goods at a daunting collection of malls and minimalls throughout Grand Cayman. Most of these are along the highway that parallels Seven Mile Beach; you'll need a car to shop around. There are also many stores in George Town, which you can explore on foot, poking in and out of some large emporiums in your search for bargains. See chapter 4.
- **Puerto Rico:** U.S. citizens don't have to pay any duty on anything—yes, anything—bought in Puerto Rico. Jewelry and watches abound, often at competitive prices, especially in the island's best-stocked area, Old San Juan. Also of great

interest are such Puerto Rican handcrafts as charming papier-mâché carnival masks. See chapter 5.

- **St. Thomas:** Many of its busiest shops are in restored warehouses that were originally built in the 1700s. Charlotte Amalie, the capital, is a shopper's town. However, despite all the fanfare, real bargains are hard to come by. Regardless, the island attracts hordes of cruise-ship passengers on a sometimes frantic hunt for bargains, real or imagined. The number of stores in Charlotte Amalie is staggering—they're stocked with more merchandise than can be found anywhere else in the entire Caribbean. Look for two local publications, *This Week* and *Best Buys;* either might steer you to the type of low-cost merchandise you're seeking. If at all possible, try to avoid shopping when more than one cruise ship is in port—the shopping district is a madhouse on those days. See chapter 6.

- **St. Croix:** This island is the poor stepchild of St. Thomas. But still, there's much to interest the "born-to-shop" visitor here, and merchandise has never been more wide-ranging than it is today. Even though most cruise ships call at Frederiksted, a colorful but isolated town near the island's western tip, most shops are in Christiansted, the island's capital. You'll see many of the same shops and chains on St. Croix that you would find on St. Thomas. Prices are about the same, but the crowds aren't nearly as bad here. See chapter 6.

- **Dominican Republic:** The island's best buys include handcrafts, amber from Dominican mines, and the distinctive pale-blue semiprecious gemstone known as larimar. However, the amber you buy from a streetside vendor might be nothing more than orange-colored transparent plastic, so buy only from well-established shops. Other charming souvenirs might include a Dominican rocking chair (remember the one JFK used to sit in?), which is sold boxed, in pieces. Shopping malls and souvenir stands abound in Santo Domingo, in Puerto Plata, and along the country's northern coast. See chapter 8.

- **Jamaica:** The shopping was better in the good old days before new taxes added a 10% surcharge. Despite that, Jamaica offers a wealth of desirable goods, including flavored rums, Jamaican coffees, handcrafts (such as woodcarvings, woven baskets, and sandals), original paintings and sculpture, and cameras, wristwatches, and VCRs. Unless you're a glutton for handmade souvenirs (available on every beach and street corner), you'd be wise to limit most of your purchases to bona fide merchants and stores. See chapter 11.

- **Barbados:** Bajan shops seem to specialize in all things English. Merchandise includes bone china from British and Irish manufacturers, china, wristwatches, jewelry, and perfumes. Bridgetown's Broad Street is the shopping headquarters of the island, although there are malls along the congested southwestern coast. Except for cigarettes and tobacco, duty-free items can be hauled off by any buyer as soon as they're paid for. Duty-free status is extended to anyone showing a passport or ID and an airline ticket with a date of departure from Barbados. See chapter 14.

- **Aruba:** The wisest shoppers on Aruba are the cost-conscious souls who have carefully checked the prices of comparable goods before leaving home. Duty is relatively low (only 3.3%). Much of the European china, jewelry, perfumes, wristwatches, and crystal has a disconcerting habit of reappearing everywhere, so after you determine exactly which brand of watch or china you want, you can comparison-shop. See chapter 16.

- **Curaçao:** Curaçao has been a mercantile center since the 1700s. In the island's capital, tidy and prosperous Willemstad, hundreds of merchants will be only too happy to cater to your needs. A handful of malls lie on Willemstad's outskirts, but most shops are clustered within a few blocks of the center of town. During seasonal sales, goods might be up to 50% less than comparable prices in the States;

most of the year, you'll find luxury goods (porcelain, crystal, watches, and gemstones) priced at about 25% less than in the States. Technically, you'll pay import duties on virtually everything you buy, but rates are so low that you might not even notice. See chapter 16.

10 The Best Reasonably Priced Honeymoon Resorts

More and more couples are exchanging their vows in the Caribbean. Many resorts will arrange everything from the preacher to the flowers, so we've included in the following list some resorts that provide wedding services. For more information about weddings on some of the more popular Caribbean islands, see "Getting Married in the Caribbean" in chapter 3.

- **Villa Blanca** (St. Thomas; ☎ 809/776-0749): Villa Blanca, in Charlotte Amalie, was the former home of the heiress to the Dodge fortune. Now it's the honeymoon bargain of the island, with 12 guest rooms, each with a private balcony and a kitchenette. The "Honeymoon Hideaway" package, for 8 days and 7 nights, costs $875 per couple in winter and only $575 per couple from mid-April to mid-December, including welcome drinks, a bottle of champagne, and flowers. See chapter 6.
- **The Copper and Lumber Store** (Antigua; ☎ 809/460-1058): For honeymooners, the hotel offers four Georgian suites overlooking English Harbour, with fine Chippendale and Queen Anne reproductions, kitchens, and ceiling fans. Newlyweds are provided with round-trip transfers between the airport and the hotel, a bottle of champagne, a flower arrangement, breakfast on the first morning, and the choice of an afternoon or evening cruise on the inn's 55-foot yacht. Check to see if honeymoon packages are offered when you plan to visit. See chapter 9.
- **Jake's** (Calabash Bay, Jamaica; ☎ 809/965-0552): If you're looking for the perfect honeymoon hideaway, make it Jake's, a 3-hour drive east of Montego Bay's airport. On a cliff by the sea, you can live in a compound of flamboyant colored cottages that offer a lot of pizzazz for little money. It's offbeat, and it's just plain fun, mon. What to do in this sleepy backwater? Swim, eat, sleep, snorkel, and do whatever honeymooners do. If you get bored, you can walk up to a cafe called "Trans Love" and catch up on the latest gossip between the rasta men and their girlfriends. See chapter 11.
- **Harmony Marina Suites** (St. Lucia; ☎ 758/452-8756): The honeymoon package for a 7-night/8-day stay starts at $1,620 per couple from mid-April to mid-December, whereas winter rates are several hundred dollars more. The property has eight honeymoon suites that include double Jacuzzis, four-poster beds, white rattan furniture, and wet bars. The package includes fresh flowers, a fruit basket, a bottle of champagne, a candlelit dinner, and a romantic sunset cruise. See chapter 13.

11 The Best Family Resorts (for Parents Who Don't Want to Blow the Kids' College Fund)

- **Maho Bay** (St. John; ☎ 800/392-9004 or 809/776-6226): At the edge of a great beach, you'll stay in a network of tent-cottages, with communal showers and a sense of the great outdoors that children adore. See chapter 6.
- **Mango Bay Resort** (Virgin Gorda; ☎ 809/495-5672): On the western shore, little villas open right onto the beach, and each has its own fully equipped kitchen (including a dishwasher), plus maid service. Shaded by palm trees and surrounded

by wide terraces, the villas can be configured to accommodate both large and small families. An ideal family hideaway. See chapter 7.

- **Falmouth Harbour Beach Apartments** (Antigua; ☎ **268/460-1094**): For the family that wants to get away from it all, these snug nests with kitchenettes open onto a private white sandy beach ideal for beginning swimmers. Each apartment has its own full-length verandah for outdoor dining and lounging. The units are among the best values on Antigua. See chapter 9.
- **Islander Hotel** (St. Lucia; ☎ **800/223-9815** in the U.S., or 758/452-8757): This Spartan motel was built in 1985 by a local entrepreneur who didn't worry too much about architectural finesse. But a beautiful beach with very gentle surf lies a few steps away, and many of the units contain modest kitchenettes. With a brood in tow, you'll definitely save money if you opt to cook for yourself. See chapter 13.

12 The Best Camping

- **Cinnamon Bay Campground** (St. John; ☎ **800/539-9998**): Directly on the beach, this National Park Service campground is the most complete in the Caribbean. Sleeping in tents, cottages, or bare sites, you're surrounded by thousands of acres of tropical foliage. You can get up in the morning and take a running leap into the warm waters off Cinnamon Bay Beach before breakfast. Bare-siters can make use of a picnic table and grill. There are ample facilities, including a cafeteria, water sports, and bathhouses. See chapter 6.
- **Maho Bay** (St. John; ☎ **800/392-9004**): At Maho Bay you can camp close to nature—in style and comfort. Its three-room tent cottages are linked by boardwalks and ramps that lead to the beach. Electric lamps, propane stoves, bathhouses, barbecue areas, water sports, a commissary, even a restaurant—it's all here. See chapter 6.
- **Brewers Bay Campground** (Tortola; ☎ **809/494-3463**): At one of the prime snorkeling sites in the BVI, this campground offers you a choice—either a bare site or a prepared one. It's fairly basic here, but it's a safe, clean location. See chapter 7.
- **Anegada Beach Campground** (Anegada; ☎ **809/495-9466**): On this remote island you can wander along miles of secluded beaches. At this campground, you get simple accommodations with flush toilets and outdoor showers. There's even a restaurant, although cookout areas are available if you want to barbecue. A cottage is offered for rent. See chapter 7.
- **White Bay Campground** (Jost Van Dyke; ☎ **809/495-9312**): At Little Harbour, on this practically deserted island (a former pirate's stamping ground), you get both tent and bare-site options. Running water and flush toilets are available as are cookout areas. You can wander endlessly without encountering another soul at times. See chapter 7.

13 The Best Places to Get Away from It All Without Spending a Fortune

- **La Casa del Francés** (Vieques, off the coast of Puerto Rico; ☎ **809/741-3751**): This house was built in 1905 as the headquarters of a sugar plantation. Since the 1950s it's been an eccentric but very appealing hideaway, though it's not for everyone. The house includes a collection of primitive art objects scattered amid dozens of potted plants and climbing vines. See chapter 5.

- **La Sagesse Nature Center** (Grenada; ☎ 809/444-6458): Even though you're near the airport, the opportunities for exploring the glories of nature are almost unlimited. Trails wind through the neighboring landscape, and ample opportunities for bird-watching are within an easy walk. See chapter 13.
- **Papillote Wilderness Retreat** (Dominica; ☎ 809/448-2287): It's situated in the heart of the Papillote Forest, one of the wildest and least-explored rain forests in the Caribbean. If frequent rain showers don't bother you (and it rains a lot in this incessantly lush region of Dominica), Papillote might provide a suitable escape at a surprisingly reasonable price. See chapter 13.
- **Blanchisseuse Beach Resort** (Trinidad; ☎ 809/628-3731): This place lies in the heart of 28 acres of rain forest. You can swim in freshwater springs or in the lagoons of swift-flowing rivers, watch (from afar) the beaches where leatherback turtles lay their eggs, and eat grilled fish caught by local fishers. It costs only $32.50 a day, per person, double occupancy. See chapter 15.

14 The Best Authentic Dining

- **Eunice's Terrace** (St. Thomas; ☎ 809/775-3975): It's not the most scenic place on the island, but people flock here anyway for the most authentic Créole dishes on St. Thomas. Pineapple-coconut-fried shrimp, herb-stuffed lobster, callaloo soup, funghi (something like polenta), and plantain are dished out in generous portions—and everything's finished off with sweet potato pie. One or two of Eunice's Queen Mary rum punches will sail you off happily into the afternoon. See chapter 6.
- **Cosmo's Seafood Restaurant & Bar** (Negril, Jamaica; ☎ 809/957-4330): At a laid-back bohío bordering the beach, Cosmo Brown makes Jamaica's best conch soup. His eatery may be rustic, but it's the place to find authentic Jamaican flavor and escape the hotel restaurants with their bland international fare. Fresh fish is your best bet here and on some nights you can get lobster, curried or grilled. See chapter 11.
- **Double V Jerk Centre** (Ocho Rios, Jamaica; ☎ 809/974-5998): Although jerk pork seasonings are now sold in American supermarkets, the most authentic taste is still found in Jamaica. At this alfresco place, where you're served a frosty Red Stripe beer the moment you arrive at the door, you can feast on this fiery and crispy dish. If you don't like pork, then you can ask for the equally delectable jerk chicken. See chapter 11.
- **Chez Mally Edjam** (Martinique; ☎ 0596-78-51-18): It's said that Martinique chefs serve the Caribbean's zestiest cuisine. If you'd like to find out for yourself, head to this little dive where you'll encounter a virtuosa cook. On the island's northernmost tip, the home is modest—but not the meals. The Créole dishes here are delicacies, everything from stuffed land crab with hot seasoning to the best pork curry on the island. Save room for one of her original confitures, tiny portions of fresh island fruit such as guava preserved in vanilla syrup. See chapter 12.
- **Mamma's** (Grenada; ☎ 809/440-1459): Mamma used to welcome visitors with one of her rum punches and tasty regional cuisine. And we're really talking regional here. When Mamma could get them, she served armadillo or manicou (possum), or even monkey. Regrettably, Mamma isn't with us any more, but daughter Cleo learned all her culinary secrets. Try her fresh seafood such as octopus or crayfish, her callaloo soup, or one of her curries. See chapter 13.

- **Koko's** (Barbados; ☎ 246/424-4557): This casual road stop offers some of the most authentic dishes on island. Overlooking the sea at Prospect, it lures with such delights as *koq-ka-doo,* which is banana-stuffed chicken dished up with rum sauce. Or else try shrimp kristo, which is stuffed into the squashlike "boat" of a christophine. The "ketch" of the day is generally appetizing, as are such delights as crab fritters, and island rabbit in a ginger-flavored sauce seasoned with tamarind for more zest and bite. See chapter 14.
- **Jemma's Seaview Kitchen** (Tobago; ☎ 809/440-1459): Mrs. Jemma Sealey will feed you well after squeezing some fresh orange or pineapple juice to settle your stomach. She doesn't put on airs—she just serves up the most authentic Tobagonian cuisine on the island. Tucked away on the beach, her place is cheap, good, and may be permanently etched in your memory, especially after you try her kingfish steak dipped in batter and accompanied with a spicy sweet sauce. On some nights, she might serve you a lobster if she has them, or perhaps crab and dumplings. See chapter 15.
- **Golden Star** (Curaçao; ☎ 599/9-654795): It's nothing but a down-home roadside diner, but it's got authentic Antillean grub—all that good stuff like *tia chiki* (goat stew), well-seasoned grilled conch, shrimp Créole, and *keshi yena* (baked Gouda cheese stuffed with spicy meat filling). See chapter 16.

15 The Best Places for Sunset Cocktails

- **The Bar at Paradise Point** (St. Thomas; ☎ 809/777-4540): Head here for your sundowner, and get the bartender to serve you his specialty: a "Painkiller." Sometimes a one-man steel band is on hand to serenade the sunset watchers, who, after a few of those Painkillers, don't know if the sun has set or not. See chapter 6.
- **Admiral's Inn** (Antigua; ☎ 268/460-1027): At one of the most atmospheric inns in the Caribbean, you can enjoy your cocktail and watch the sun go down over the loveliest harbor in the West Indies. After the sun sets, you can always play a game of English darts with whatever crew has arrived at the dockyard. See chapter 9.
- **Rick's Cafe** (Negril, Jamaica; ☎ 809/957-0380): Rick's is the premier sunset-watching spot in the Caribbean, almost rivaling the docks at Key West. Watching sunsets here is quite a ritual. The rowdy crowd even toasts Mother Nature with lethal rum drinks, followed by shouts and laughter. Some even applaud at her "handiwork" in getting the sun to set so spectacularly. After the "performance," the rum flows all night. See chapter 11.
- **Frangipani Hotel** (Bequia, the Grenadines; ☎ 809/458-3255): Any of the watering holes along Admiralty Bay would be lovely for a sundowner, although we give this hotel the edge, since it's where the locals go. A lot of yachties gather here, some of whom fly the skull and crossbones flag. Often you can hear steel bands playing along the shore, and the whole place becomes festive, making you want to linger long after the sun has disappeared. See chapter 13.
- **John Moore Bar** (Barbados; ☎ 246/422-2258): On the waterfront, this is the most famous little bar on Barbados. It's the social center of the island, so you can catch up on the latest gossip while enjoying a rum punch. See chapter 14.
- **Karel's Beach Bar** (Bonaire; ☎ 599/7/8434): Join the diving set at this Tahitian-styled alfresco bar perched above the sea on stilts right in the center of town. The convivial crowd starts gathering around five o'clock, and on weekends a local band entertains, making it a great place to linger. See chapter 16.

16 The Best Nightspots Without Sky-High Cover Charges

- **Palm Court** (in El San Juan Hotel, Isla Verde, Puerto Rico; ☎ 809/791-1000): This is the most beautiful bar in the Caribbean (but not for sunset watching, as it's enclosed). And when you walk through the elegant lobby, you'll feel quite posh. But drink prices are reasonable and you can hear live music on many nights emanating from the adjoining El Chico Bar. There's no finer place for drinking in San Juan. See chapter 5.

- **Greenhouse** (Charlotte Amalie, St. Thomas; ☎ 809/774-7998): If you must be in Charlotte Amalie at night (there are safer places to be), head here for drinking, dining, and perhaps listening to some of the best music on the island, either live or recorded. What's even better are the two-for-one happy hours including a generous free buffet Monday through Saturday. There's only a modest cover charge when live bands play. See chapter 6.

- **Blue Moon** (St. Croix; ☎ 809/772-2222): This is the hottest dive on the island, holding forth in the capital, Christiansted. Thursday and Friday are the best nights to show up. It's hip and it's fun—and it also offers good bistro-type food. Live entertainment is often featured, and a convivial crowd—a happy mix of locals and visitors—shows up. See chapter 6.

- **Bomba's Surfside Shack** (Tortola; ☎ 809/495-4148): For uninhibited nightlife, this joint, covered with Day-Glo graffiti, rocks until the early hours. Built from the flotsam of a junkyard, it's fun, funky, and wild. The all-you-can-eat barbecue (on some nights) and the live reggae music keep the joint jumping until the early hours. See chapter 7.

- **Kaiser's Café** (Negril, Jamaica; ☎ 809/957-4070): After having your sundowner at Rick's Café, head for this hot, hot spot where you'll hear live reggae concerts most nights. Even some of the exhibitionistic crowd from the resort, Hedonism II, don their togas and head here for a night of uninhibited fun and revelry. If you want dinner, try the catch of the day grilled in butter sauce. See chapter 11.

Getting to Know the Caribbean

Golden beaches shaded by palm trees and crystalline waters teeming with colorful sea creatures—it's all just a few hours' flight from the east coast of the United States. Dubbed the "Eighth Continent of the World," the Caribbean islands have an amazing variety of terrain that ranges from thick rain forests to haunting volcanoes, from white- to black-sand beaches. Spicy food, spicier music, and the gentle, leisurely lifestyle of the islands draw millions of visitors each year, all hoping to find the perfect place in the sun. We'll help you choose yours in the pages that follow.

1 The Islands in Brief

ANTIGUA (British Leewards)   Antigua claims to have a different lovely beach for each day of the year. Some British traditions (including a passion for cricket) linger on, though this nation became independent in 1981; its British legacy means that you can see some of the most interesting historic naval sites in the world on Antigua. The island has a population of 80,000, mostly descended from the African slaves of plantation owners. Though there are many conservative but very glamorous resorts, we've found some affordable accommodations with charming island atmosphere. Antigua is politically linked to the sparsely inhabited and largely undeveloped island of Barbuda, about 30 miles north. See chapter 9.

ARUBA (Dutch Leewards)   Until its beaches were "discovered" in the late 1970s, Aruba was an almost-forgotten outpost of Holland, mostly valued for its oil refineries and salt factories. Today it's favored for its unique terrain—an almost lunar landscape of desert, plus spectacular beaches where you can bask under constant sunshine. There's an almost total lack of racial tensions, though its population of 70,000 is culturally diverse, with roots in Holland, Portugal, Spain, Venezuela, India/Pakistan, and Africa. A building boom in the 1980s has transformed this island into a pale version of Las Vegas (this is one of the islands most noted for casinos) and created some of the most aggressive marketing campaigns in Caribbean history. Unfortunately, it's next to impossible to find real budget accommodations, though we've scouted out a few for you. See chapter 16.

BARBADOS   Cosmopolitan Barbados has the densest population of any island in the Caribbean, a sports tradition that avidly pursues cricket, and many stylish, medium-sized hotels. Its topography varies from rolling hills and savage waves on the eastern (Atlantic) coast, to densely populated flatlands and sheltered beaches in the southwest. Barbados is generally an expensive destination. See chapter 14.

BONAIRE   Bonaire is the place to be for serious divers and birders. The landscape is as dry and inhospitable as anything you'll find in the Caribbean, and the beaches aren't the best, but there's a wealth of rich marine life along the island's miles of off-shore reefs. There's little nightlife or shopping here; most visitors come for diving or nature. A terrific destination for cost-conscious travelers. See chapter 16.

BRITISH VIRGIN ISLANDS   Still a British Crown Colony, this lushly forested archipelago contains about 50 mountainous islands (depending on how many rocks, cays, and uninhabited islets you want to include). A superb venue for sailing, the BVI is less densely populated, is less developed, and has fewer social problems than its neighbors in the U.S. Virgin Islands. Tortola is the main island, followed in importance by Virgin Gorda. See chapter 7.

CAYMAN ISLANDS   This is a grouping of three islands near the southern coast-line of Cuba. Flat and prosperous, this tiny nation is dependent on Britain for its economic survival, and attracts millionaire expatriates from all over because of its lenient tax and banking laws. The landscapes aren't as lush and lovely as others in the Caribbean—these islands are covered with scrubland and swamp, but they do have great beaches and world-class diving. Many of these beaches are lined with upscale (and horrendously expensive) private homes and condominiums, but we've found some affordable places to stay. See chapter 4.

CURAÇAO (Dutch Leewards)   Since much of the island's surface is an arid desert that grows only cactus, its canny Dutch settlers ruled out farming and developed Curaçao into one of the Dutch Empire's busiest trading posts. Until the post–World War II collapse of the oil refineries, Curaçao was a thriving mercantile society with a capital (Willemstad) that somewhat resembled Amsterdam. Tourism began to de-velop here during the 1980s, and many new hotels—usually in the Dutch colonial style—have been built. Overall, Curaçao is more than just a tourist mecca: It's a well-defined society in its own right. See chapter 16.

DOMINICA (British Windwards)   An English-speaking island set midway between Guadeloupe and Martinique, Dominica (Doh-mi-*nee*-kah) is the largest and most mountainous island of the Windwards. A mysterious, rarely visited land of waterfalls, rushing streams, and rain forests, it has only a few beaches, which are mainly lined with black volcanic sand. Some 82,000 people live here, including 2,000 remaining descendants of the Carib Indians. Dominica is one of the poorest islands in the Caribbean, with the misfortune of lying directly in the hurricane belt. But if you like the offbeat and unusual, you may find this the most fascinating island in the Caribbean, with beautiful, lush landscapes to explore—and it's one of the best bargain destinations. See chapter 13.

DOMINICAN REPUBLIC   Occupying the eastern two-thirds of Hispaniola (the island shared with Haiti), this mountainous country is the second-largest in the Caribbean, and boasts gorgeous beaches. An endless series of military dictatorships once wreaked havoc on its social fabric, but today there's a more favorable political climate. The D.R. offers some of the least expensive vacation options in the entire Caribbean, though there are some drawbacks: The contrast between the wealth of foreign tourists and the poverty of locals is especially obvious here, and it's not the safest of the islands. Its crowded capital is Santo Domingo, with a population of two million. The island offers lots of Hispanic color, wonderful merengue music, and many opportunities to dance, drink, and party. See chapter 8.

GRENADA (British Windwards)   The southernmost nation of the Windward Islands, Grenada (Gre-*nay*-dah) is one of the lushest in the Caribbean. Extravagantly fertile, it's one of the largest producers of spices in the Western Hemisphere, a result of a gentle climate, volcanic soil, and a corps of good-natured islanders. There's a lot of very appealing local color on Grenada, particularly since the political troubles of the 1980s seem to have ended. The beaches are white and sandy, and the populace (a mixture of English expatriates and islanders of African descent) is friendly. Once a British Crown Colony but now independent, the island nation incorporates two smaller landmasses—Carriacou and Petit Martinique, neither of which has very many tourist facilities. Grenada's capital, St. George's, is one of the most raffishly charming towns in the Caribbean. See chapter 13.

GUADELOUPE (French West Indies)   It isn't as sophisticated or cosmopolitan as the two outlying islands (Saint Barthélemy and the French sector of St. Martin) over which it holds administrative authority. Despite that, there's a lot of natural beauty in this *département* of France. With a relatively low population density (only 340,000 people live here, mostly along the coast), butterfly-shaped Guadeloupe is actually two distinctly different volcanic islands separated by a narrow saltwater strait, the rivière Salée. It's ideal for scenic drives and Créole color, offering any Francophile an unusual insight into the French colonial world. See chapter 12.

JAMAICA   A favorite of North American honeymooners, Jamaica is a mountainous island rising abruptly from the sea 90 miles south of Cuba and about 100 miles west of Haiti. One of the most densely populated nations in the Caribbean, with a vivid sense of its own identity, Jamaica has a tragic history rooted in slavery, and today a legacy of poverty and political turbulence remains. Yet despite that poverty and a regrettable increase in crime and harassment of tourists by vendors in such resort areas as Ocho Rios, Jamaica is one of the most successful black democracies in the world. The island is large enough to allow the more or less peaceful coexistence of all kinds of people, including everything from expatriate English aristocrats to dyed-in-the-wool Rastafarians. Overall, Jamaica is a fascinating island, with a vibrant culture, a rich musical heritage, and an astounding diversity of landscapes. Many super-expensive resorts line its lovely beaches, fenced off and isolated from the life of the island, but there are countless bargains to be had, too, and we'll round them up for you in chapter 11.

MARTINIQUE (French West Indies)   One of the most exotic French-speaking destinations in the Caribbean, Martinique was once the site of a settlement that was demolished by volcanic activity (St. Pierre, which is now only a pale shadow of a once-thriving city). Like Guadeloupe and St. Barts, Martinique is legally and culturally French (certainly many islanders drive with a Gallic panache—read: very badly), although many Créole customs and traditions continue to flourish. The beaches are beautiful, the Créole cuisine is full of flavor and flair, and the island has lots of tropical charm. See chapter 12.

MONTSERRAT (British Leewards)   This tiny, pear-shaped "Emerald Isle," 27 miles southeast of Antigua, is a British Crown Colony that is periodically endangered by volcanic activity. Montserrat has fertile volcanic soil and beaches of both black and white sand. Its population numbers only 12,500 residents, most of African descent. Unless you rent one of the island's private villas, tourist facilities are limited, although clean and tidy. See chapter 9.

Which Island is for You?

Island	Vacation Costs	All-Inclusive Resorts	Beaches	Above-Average Food	Campgrounds	Casinos	Condo/Villa Rentals	Family-Friendly	Cruise-Ship Port	Deluxe Resorts
Anguilla	$$$$	✔	✔	✔			✔			✔
Antigua	$$$	✔	✔	✔		✔		✔	✔	✔
Aruba	$$	✔	✔	✔		✔	✔	✔	✔	✔
Barbados	$$$	✔	✔	✔			✔	✔	✔	✔
Barbuda	$$$$		✔	✔						✔
Bonaire	$$		✔							
Cayman Islands	$$$	✔	✔	✔			✔	✔	✔	✔
Curaçao	$$		✔			✔			✔	✔
Dominica	$									
Dominican Republic	$	✔	✔			✔		✔	✔	✔
Grenada	$$		✔					✔	✔	✔
The Grenadines	$$	✔	✔							✔
Guadeloupe	$$	✔	✔	✔	✔	✔			✔	
Iles des Saintes/M. Galante	$$		✔	✔						
Jamaica	$$	✔	✔	✔	✔		✔	✔	✔	✔
Martinique	$$$	✔	✔	✔	✔	✔			✔	✔
Montserrat	$$		✔							
Nevis	$$$		✔	✔						✔
Puerto Rico	$		✔	✔	✔	✔	✔	✔	✔	✔
Saba	$									
St. Barthélemy	$$$$		✔	✔			✔			✔
St. Croix	$$		✔	✔			✔	✔	✔	✔
St. Eustatius	$		✔							
St. John	$$$		✔	✔	✔		✔	✔		✔
St. Kitts	$$	✔	✔			✔		✔		✔
St. Lucia	$$	✔	✔					✔	✔	✔
St. Martin/Sint Maarten	$$$	✔	✔	✔		✔	✔	✔	✔	✔
St. Thomas	$$	✔	✔	✔			✔	✔	✔	✔
St. Vincent	$		✔							
Tobago	$$		✔							✔
Tortola	$$		✔		✔		✔	✔	✔	✔
Trinidad	$		✔							
Virgin Gorda	$$$	✔	✔	✔	✔			✔		✔

Golf	Hiking	Historic Sites	Mountainous Terrain	Music/Entertainment Nightlife	Nonstop Flights from U.S.	Public Transport	Rain Forest	Romantic Getaways	Sailing	Scenic Beauty	Scuba Diving/Snorkeling	Secret Hideaways	Shopping	Verdant & Lush Terrain	Very Dry Climate
	✔			✔	✔			✔							
✔	✔	✔			✔			✔	✔	✔	✔	✔			
✔	✔	✔	✔					✔		✔		✔			
✔	✔	✔		✔	✔	✔			✔	✔		✔			
	✔			✔	✔			✔							
	✔			✔						✔				✔	
✔	✔	✔	✔			✔		✔		✔					
	✔	✔	✔	✔	✔					✔		✔		✔	
	✔	✔	✔			✔	✔			✔		✔		✔	
✔	✔	✔	✔	✔	✔	✔				✔		✔	✔	✔	
✔	✔	✔	✔		✔	✔	✔	✔	✔	✔	✔	✔		✔	
	✔	✔	✔		✔			✔							
✔	✔	✔	✔		✔	✔		✔	✔	✔			✔		
	✔			✔											
✔	✔	✔	✔	✔	✔	✔	✔	✔	✔	✔	✔	✔	✔	✔	
✔	✔	✔	✔	✔			✔	✔		✔	✔			✔	
✔	✔	✔							✔				✔		
✔	✔	✔	✔					✔		✔		✔		✔	
✔	✔	✔	✔	✔	✔	✔	✔	✔	✔	✔	✔	✔	✔	✔	
	✔		✔							✔	✔	✔		✔	
✔	✔	✔	✔			✔		✔							
✔	✔	✔		✔			✔	✔		✔	✔	✔		✔	
	✔														
	✔	✔	✔					✔	✔	✔	✔	✔		✔	
✔	✔	✔								✔		✔			
✔	✔		✔		✔		✔	✔		✔		✔		✔	
✔	✔	✔	✔			✔				✔		✔			
✔	✔	✔	✔	✔	✔			✔				✔			
	✔		✔						✔					✔	
✔	✔			✔	✔		✔								
	✔		✔			✔			✔	✔	✔	✔		✔	
	✔			✔	✔	✔	✔			✔				✔	
	✔		✔			✔		✔	✔	✔	✔	✔		✔	

PUERTO RICO   Home to 3.3 million Spanish-speaking people, the Commonwealth of Puerto Rico is under the jurisdiction of the United States. It's one of the most urban islands of the Caribbean, with glittering casinos, lots of traffic, a relatively high crime rate, and a more-or-less comfortable mixture of Latin and U.S. cultures. The island's interior is filled with ancient volcanic mountains and lush rain forest; the coastline is ringed with sandy beaches. San Juan, the island's 16th-century capital, contains beautifully preserved Spanish colonial neighborhoods, and the Condado, its beach strip of high-rise hotels, which evokes Miami Beach. Outside of the glitzy resorts are many charming and reasonably priced places to stay, lots of wonderful down-home restaurants, and a host of affordable adventures. See chapter 5.

SABA (Dutch Windwards in the Leewards)   Saba is a cone-shaped extinct volcano that rises abruptly and steeply from the watery depths of the Caribbean. There are no beaches to speak of, but the local Dutch- and English-speaking populace has traditionally made a living from fishing, trade, and needlework rather than tourism. Visitors usually come to Saba to dive (which is expensive, but worth it), to visit the rain forest (which is free), and to totally get away from it all. Hotel choices are limited, often designed in the traditional Saban style of stone foundations terraced into sloping hillsides with white walls and red roofs. See chapter 10.

ST. EUSTATIUS (known as Statia; Dutch Windwards in the Leewards)   Today the island is among the poorest in the Caribbean, with 8 square miles of arid landscape, beaches that have strong and sometimes dangerous undertows, a population of around 1,700 people, and a sleepy capital, Oranjestad. The island is very committed to maintaining its political and fiscal links to the Netherlands. See chapter 10.

ST. KITTS & NEVIS (British Leewards)   These two islands form a single nation although they're separated by a 2-mile strait. St. Kitts (also known as St. Christopher, with 68 square miles) and Nevis (with 36 square miles) both enjoyed some of the richest sugarcane economies of the plantation age, and the boiling rooms and great houses have in many cases been transformed into quaint inns. Both islands possess a very appealing, small-scale charm. See chapter 9.

ST. LUCIA (British Windwards)   St. Lucia (*Loo*-sha) is the second-largest of the Windward Islands. A volcanic island with lots of rainfall and great natural beauty, it has both white and black sandy beaches, bubbling sulfur springs, and panoramic mountain scenery. Most tourism is concentrated on the island's northwestern tip, near the capital (Castries), but the arrival of up to 200,000 visitors a year has inevitably altered St. Lucia's old agrarian lifestyle throughout the island. Nevertheless, it remains a beautiful and welcoming place. See chapter 13.

SINT MAARTEN / ST. MARTIN (Dutch Windwards in the Leewards/French West Indies)   This "twin nation" of 37 square miles has been divided between the Dutch (St. Maarten) and the French (St. Martin) since 1648. Regardless of how you spell it, it's the same island, although each side of the unguarded border is quite different. The Dutch side contains the island's major airport, and more shops and tourist facilities; St. Martin, whose capital is Marigot, has some of the poshest hotels and the best food on the island. Both sides of the island are modern, urban, and proudly international. Each suffers from traffic jams, a lack of parking space in the capitals, tourist-industry burnout (especially on the Dutch side), and a disturbing increase in crime. See chapters 10 and 12.

ST. VINCENT & THE GRENADINES (British Windwards)   Despite its natural beauty, this mini-archipelago has only recently emerged from obscurity. It has always been known to divers and yachties, who find its north-to-south string of cays and coral islets some of the most panoramic sailing regions in the world. St. Vincent is by far the largest and most fertile island in the country. Its capital is the sleepy, some-what dilapidated town of Kingstown. Stretching like a pearl necklace to the south of St. Vincent are some 32 neighbor islands called the Grenadines. These include the boat-building community of Bequia and chic Mustique. Less densely populated islands in the chain include the tiny outposts of Mayreau, Canouan, Palm Island, and Petit St. Vincent, whose sun-blasted surfaces were for the most part covered with scrub until around the late 1960s, when hotel owners planted groves of palms and hardwood trees. See chapter 13.

TRINIDAD & TOBAGO   The southernmost of the West Indies, this two-island nation lies just 7 miles off the coast of Venezuela. Trinidad is the most industrial island in the Caribbean, with oil deposits and a polyglot population derived from India, Pakistan, Venezuela, Africa, and Europe. Known for its calypso music and carnivals, Trinidad is one of the most culturally distinct nations in the Caribbean. It has a rich artistic tradition, a bustling capital (Port-of-Spain), and exotic flora and fauna.

About 20 miles northeast of Trinidad, tiny Tobago is calmer and less heavily forested, with a rather dull capital (Scarborough) and a spectacular array of white-sand beaches. Whereas Trinidad seems to consider tourism as only one of many viable industries, Tobago is absolutely dependent on it. For details on both islands, see chapter 15.

U.S. VIRGIN ISLANDS   Formerly Dutch possessions, these islands became part of the United States in 1917. St. Croix is the largest and flattest of the U.S. Virgins, whereas St. Thomas and St. John are more mountainous. St. Thomas and, to a lesser degree, St. Croix offer all the diversions, facilities, and amusements you'd find on the U.S. mainland, including bars, restaurants, and lots of modern resort hotels. St. Thomas is sometimes referred to as the shopping mall of the Caribbean, and crowds of cruise-ship visitors frequently pass through. Much of the surface of St. John is devoted to a national park, a gift from Laurance Rockefeller. All three islands offer sailing, snorkeling, and unspoiled vistas. Crime is on the increase, however—an unfortunate fly in the ointment of what would otherwise be a corner of paradise. See chapter 6.

2 From Salsa to Reggae: The Musical Heritage of the Caribbean

The gutsy, aggressive beat of African music was brought in with the slave ships—it drowned out the harpsichord music wafting from the master's house soon enough. Over the years, it spawned many musical forms, including calypso and reggae, which usually spring to mind for most people when the music of the Caribbean is mentioned.

The major "music islands" of the Caribbean are Jamaica and Puerto Rico, and to a lesser extent the Dominican Republic, Trinidad, and Barbados.

The best time to enjoy the music and dancing of the Caribbean is during **carnival.** On islands with strong Roman Catholic ties, this is similar to Mardi Gras in New Orleans. For some islands, carnival lasts from Epiphany (January 6) to Ash Wednesday, with parades and dancing in the streets, especially on each Sunday before Lent. On other islands, festivals, fiestas, and special days (many held in summer) take the place of carnival. For example, Barbados holds a festival celebrating the end of the sugarcane harvest.

At least some of the instruments used in traditional Puerto Rican music had their origins with the Taíno peoples. Most noteworthy is the *guicharo,* or *guiro,* a notched, hollowed-out gourd whose form was almost directly adapted from pre-Columbian days. At least four different stringed instruments were adapted from the six-string Spanish classical guitar: the *requinto,* the *bordonua,* the *cuatro,* and the *tiple,* each of which produces a unique tone and pitch. The most popular of these is the cuatro, a guitarlike instrument with 10 strings (arranged into five pairs). Also used on the island are such percussion instruments as *tambours* (hollowed tree trunks covered with stretched-out animal skin), *maracas* (gourds filled with pebbles or dried beans and mounted on handles), and a host of different drums whose original designs were brought from Africa by the island's slaves. All these instruments have a place in a rich variety of folk music with roots in the cultural melting pot of the island's Spanish, African, and native Taíno traditions.

The major music coming out of Puerto Rico now is **salsa,** literally translated as the "sauce" that makes parties happen. Originally developed in the Puerto Rican community of New York, it draws heavily on the musical roots of the Cuban and the African-Caribbean experience. Highly danceable, its rhythms are hot, urban, sophisticated, and very compelling. Salsa bands employ a huge array of percussion instruments, including maracas, bongos, timbales, conga drums, and claves—and, to add the *jíbaro* (hillbilly) touch, a clanging cow bell. Of course, it also takes a bass, a horn section, a chorus, and a lead vocalist to get the combination right.

The roots of Jamaica's unique **reggae** music can be found in an early form of Jamaican music called *mento,* brought to the island from Africa by slaves and reminiscent of the rhythm and blues that in the mid–20th century swept across North America. It was usually accompanied by hip-rolling dances known as bubbling, with highly suggestive lyrics to match.

In the late 1950s Jamaican musicians combined boogie-woogie with rhythm and blues to form a short-lived but vibrant music named **ska.** It was the politicization of ska by Rastafarians that led to the creation of reggae.

Sometimes referred to as the heartbeat of Jamaica, reggae is the island's most distinctive musical form, as closely linked to Jamaica as soul is to Detroit, jazz to New Orleans, and blues to Chicago. The term *reggae* is best defined as "coming from the people." It has influenced the music of international stars like the Rolling Stones, Eric Clapton, and Paul Simon. Most notably, it propelled onto the world scene a street-smart kid from Kingston named Bob Marley. Today the recording studios of Kingston churn out hundreds of reggae albums every year.

One of the most recent adaptations of reggae is **soca,** which is more upbeat and less politicized. Aficionados say that reggae makes you think, while soca makes you dance. The music is fun, infectious, and spontaneous, perfect for partying, and often imbued with the humor and wry attitudes of Jamaican urban dwellers.

After 1965, the influx of Jamaican immigrants to the potboiling pressures of North America's ghettos had a profound influence on popular music. Such Jamaican-born stars as Clive Campbell, combining the Jamaican gift for the spoken word with reggae rhythms and high electronic amplification, developed the roots of what eventually became known as **rap.**

Some purists point out that **calypso** music is really a product of Trinidad, though it remains very popular in Jamaica (and also Barbados). Calypso, which originated on Trinidad, is a mixture—basically African but with African-Spanish rhythms, English verses, and traces of French structure. The words to calypso tunes were originally (and sometimes still are) spontaneous improvisations based on all sorts of subjects—love, sex, politics, whatever.

3 A Taste of the Islands

Chefs throughout the Caribbean prepare a presentable American and continental cuisine, but in recent years, even the kitchens of the deluxe hotels have placed a greater emphasis on local dishes. We've had many memorable meals in the cheap, authentic, local spots on each island—you really don't have to splurge in a so-called gourmet restaurant at some deluxe resort to savor the best flavors of the islands, and we'll share some terrific finds with you.

And what's on the menu? Well, first off, you'll enjoy an abundance of fruit in the islands. Most breakfasts include a platter of freshly sliced fruit. Coconut is used in everything from breads to soups. Soursop ice cream appears on some menus, and guava might turn up in anything from juice to cheese. Papaya is called paw paw, and it will most often be your melon choice at breakfast. Mango is ubiquitous, used not only in chutney but also in drinks and desserts. The avocado, most often called "pears," is used in fresh seafood salads and often stuffed with fresh crabmeat.

By now, most visitors know that plantain (which is similar to a banana but red in color) is not eaten raw. It's usually served as a cooked side dish, the way Americans serve french fries. Puerto Ricans eat dried plantains, called tostones, instead of potato chips. Plantains can also be served mashed or boiled, and they turn up in many desserts, especially when mixed with coconut and pineapple.

Two staples of the Caribbean islands have always been rice and pigeon peas. Balls of cornmeal, called fungi, often accompany a salt-pork main dish known as mauffay. Sometimes these cornmeal concoctions will appear on the menus of local restaurants as coo coo.

One of the most common vegetables in the islands is christophine (sometimes called foo foo), a green, prickly gourd that tastes somewhat like zucchini. Breadfruit, introduced to the islands by Captain Bligh (of *Bounty* fame) is green and round and used like a potato. Potatoes and yams are also local favorites. The leaflike callaloo is one of the best-known vegetables in the West Indies. It's like spinach and is often served with crab, salt pork, and fresh fish (with floating fungi as a garnish).

In a true local restaurant in the Caribbean, you'll see hot peppers placed on the table. (Be sparing.) A selection of hot-pepper pastes is called sambal.

And of course, aside from tropical fruit, seafood is the staple of island cuisine. Throughout the islands, warm-water **lobster** is the king of the sea and the most sought after—and most expensive—main course to order. The "catch of the day" is most likely to be **red snapper** or **grouper,** but could also be shark or barracuda.

We urge you to be cautious in eating **barracuda,** which have been known to contain copper deposits. Fish caught north of Antigua and also along the Cayman Islands and Cuba are said to be at risk, though the barracuda in south-lying Barbados are fine and usually very healthy. **Dolphin** may also appear on the menu, but—never fear—this dolphin is a fish, not Flipper.

Distilled easily from sugarcane, **rum** played a major role in the history of the West Indies. Today the rusted machinery and tumbledown ruins of distilleries are tourist stops on dozens of Caribbean islands.

While **planter's punch** is the most popular drink in the islands, the average bar in the Caribbean is likely to offer a bewildering array of rum-based drinks. *One word of caution though:* Be alert to your limits, especially if you're driving. Sure, these frosty drinks are pastel-colored and come with cute umbrellas, but they'll get you drunk on very short notice because of their elevated sugar content as well as the hot climate.

Don't think that the only **beer** you'll be able to find will **be imported** from Milwaukee or Holland. Of course, Heineken is ubiquitous, as is **Amstel, especially** in the Dutch islands, but Red Stripe from Jamaica is a famous local **brand.**

Water is generally safe throughout the islands, but many tourists **get sick from** drinking it simply because it's different from the water they're accustomed **to. If it's** available, order bottled water.

SPECIALTIES OF THE ISLANDS

ANTIGUA & BARBUDA   At most restaurants and in most resorts catering **to** tourists, you get typical American or continental fare. But look for local food, which tends to be spicy, with sauces often based on Créole recipes or East Indian curry dishes—that means pepperpot stew, spareribs, curried goat, and the like. A British heritage lingers in some of the island's blander dishes. If fresh seafood is on the menu, go for it.

ARUBA   A few of Aruba's restaurants serve *rijstaffel,* the Indonesian "rice table," or *nasi goreng,* a mini-rijstaffel. In addition, many Chinese restaurants operate in Oranjestad. Aruban specialties are beginning to appear on menus. Although we don't always find them suited to the tropics, these include *keshi yena,* Edam cheese filled with a mixture of chicken or beef and flavored with onions, pickles, tomatoes, olives, and raisins. *Sopito de pisca* is a savory fish chowder made with a bouquet of spices. *Funchi,* like a cornmeal pudding of the Deep South, accompanies many regional dishes. *Pastechi* is a meat-stuffed turnover, and *cala* is a bean fritter.

BARBADOS   The famous flying fish appears on every menu, and when prepared right, it's a delicacy—moist and succulent, nutlike in flavor, approaching the subtlety of brook trout. Bajans boil it, steam it, bake it, stew it, fry it, and stuff it.

Try the sea urchin, or *oursin,* which you may have already sampled on Martinique and Guadeloupe. Bajans often call these urchins "sea eggs." Crab-in-the-back is another specialty, as is *langouste,* the Barbadian lobster. Dolphin and salt fish cakes are other popular items. Yams, sweet potatoes, and eddoes (similar to yams) are typical vegetables. Luscious Barbadian fruits include papaya, passionfruit, and mango.

If you hear that any hotel or restaurant is having a *cohobblopot* (or more commonly, a Bajan buffet), head right over! This is a Barbadian term that means to "cook up," and it inevitably will produce an array of local dishes.

BONAIRE   Bonaire's food is generally acceptable, though nearly everything has to be imported. Your best bet is fresh-caught fish and an occasional *rijstaffel,* the traditional Indonesian "rice table," or local dishes. Popular foods are conch cutlet or stew, pickled conch, red snapper, tuna, wahoo, dolphin, fungi (a thick cornmeal pudding), rice, beans, *sate* (marinated meat with curried mayonnaise), goat stew, and Dutch cheeses.

BRITISH VIRGIN ISLANDS   The food is relatively simple and straightforward, with fresh fish the best item on the menu. Most other items, including meat and poultry, are shipped in frozen. In most major restaurants and hotels, American or continental cuisine prevails. For a taste of the islands, seek out the local dives (we recommend several good bets in that chapter). Locals give colorful names to the various fish brought home for dinner, everything from "ole wife" to "doctors." "Porgies and grunts," along with yellowtail, kingfish, and bonito, show up on many tables. Fish is usually boiled in a lime-flavored brew seasoned with hot peppers and herbs, and is commonly served with a Créole sauce of peppers, tomatoes, and onions, among other ingredients. Salt fish and rice is another low-cost dish, the fish flavored with onion, tomatoes, garlic, and green pepper.

Conch Créole is a tasty brew, flavored with onions, garlic, spices, hot peppers, and salt pork. A favorite local dish is chicken and rice, made with Spanish peppers. Curried goat, the longtime "classic" West Indian dinner, is made with herbs, including cardamom pods and onions. The famous johnnycakes that accompany many of these fish and meat dishes are fried in deep fat or baked.

CAYMAN ISLANDS   American and continental cooking predominate, although there is also a cuisine known as Caymanian, which features specialties made from turtle. (Environmental groups in the States consider this species to be endangered; however, in the Cayman Islands it is bred for food, as opposed to being caught in the wild at sea.) Fresh fish is the star, and conch is used in many ways. Local lobster is in season from late summer through January. Since most restaurants have to rely on imported ingredients, prices tend to be high.

CURAÇAO   The basic cuisine is Dutch, but there are many specialty items, particularly Latin American and Indonesian. The cuisine strikes many visitors as heavy for the tropics, so you may want to have a light lunch and order the more filling concoctions, such as *rijstaffel,* in the evening. You'll want to finish your meals with Curaçao, the orange-based liqueur that made the island famous.

Ertwensoep, the well-known Dutch pea soup, is a popular dish, as is *keshi yena,* which is Edam cheese stuffed with meat and then baked. *Funchi,* a cornmeal pudding, accompanies many local dishes. *Sopito,* fish soup often made with coconut water, is an especially good local dish, and conch is featured in curries and many other dishes.

DOMINICA   The local delicacy is the fine flesh of the *crapaud* (a frog), called "mountain chicken." Freshwater crayfish is another specialty, as is *tee-tee-ree,* fried cakes made from tiny fish. Stuffed crab back is usually a delight—the backs of red and black land crabs are stuffed with delicate crabmeat and Créole seasonings. The fresh fruit juices of the island are lovely, and no one lets a day go by without at least one rum punch.

DOMINICAN REPUBLIC   The national dish is *sancocho,* a thick stew made with meats (maybe seven kinds), vegetables, and herbs, especially marjoram. Another national favorite is *chicharrones de pollo,* pieces of fried chicken and fried green bananas flavored with pungent spices. One of the most typical dishes is *la bandera* (the flag), made with red beans, white rice, and stewed meat. Johnnycakes and *mangu,* a plaintainlike dish, are frequently eaten. Johnnycakes can be bought on the street corner or at the beach, but you must ask for them as *vaniqueques.*

A good local beer is called Presidente. Wines are imported, so prices tend to run high. Dominican coffee compares favorably with that of Colombia and Brazil.

GRENADA   We've found food on Grenada better than on the other British Windward Islands. Many of the chefs are European or European trained, and local cooks are also on hand to prepare Grenadian specialties, such as conch (called *lambi* here), lobster, callaloo soup (with greens and crab), and soursop or avocado ice cream. Turtle steaks appear on many menus, although this is an endangered species. The national dish, called "oil down," consists of breadfruit and salt pork covered with dasheen leaves and steamed in coconut milk (it's not the favorite of every visitor). Some 22 kinds of fish, including fresh tuna, dolphin, and barracuda, are caught off the island's shores, and most are good for eating. Naturally, the spices of the island, such as nutmeg, are used plentifully. Meals are often served family style in an open-air setting with a view of the sea.

GUADELOUPE   The Créole cuisine of Guadeloupe is similar to Martinique's, and we think it's the best in the Caribbean. The island's chefs have been called "seasoned sorcerers." Having African roots, Créole cooking is based on seafood. Out in the country, every cook has his or her own herb garden, since the cuisine makes great use of herbs and spices. Except in the major hotels, most restaurants are family run, offering real homemade cooking. Best of all, you usually get to dine alfresco.

Stuffed, stewed, skewered, or broiled spiny lobsters, as well as clams, conchs, oysters, and octopus are presented to you with French taste and subtlety. Every good chef knows how to make *colombo*, a spicy rich stew of poultry, pork, or beef served with rice, herbs, sauces, and a variety of seeds. Another Créole favorite is calalou (callaloo in English), a soup flavored with savory herbs. Yet another traditional French Caribbean dish is *blaff*, fresh seafood poached in clear stock and usually seasoned with hot peppers.

JAMAICA   There is great emphasis on seafood. Rock lobster appears on every menu—grilled, thermidor, cold, hot. *Saltfish and ackee,* the national dish, is a concoction of salt cod and a brightly colored vegetable that tastes something like scrambled eggs. *Escovitch* (marinated fish) is usually fried and then simmered in vinegar with onions and peppers. Curried mutton and goat are popular, as is pepperpot stew, all highly seasoned.

Jerk pork is found in country areas, where it's barbecued slowly over wood fires until crisp and brown. Rice and peas (really red beans) are usually served with onions, spices, and salt pork. Vegetables are exotic: breadfruit, imported by Captain Bligh in 1723; callaloo, rather like spinach, used in pepperpot soup; *cho-cho,* served boiled or stuffed; and green bananas and plantains, fried or boiled and served with almost everything. Then there's pumpkin, which goes into a soup or is served on the side, boiled and mashed with butter. Sweet potatoes appear with main courses, but there's also a sweet-potato pudding made with sugar and coconut milk, flavored with cinnamon, nutmeg, and vanilla.

You'll come across dishes with really odd names: *stamp and go* are saltfish cakes eaten as appetizers; *dip and fall back* is a salty stew with bananas and dumplings; and *rundown* is mackerel cooked in coconut milk, often eaten for breakfast. For the really adventurous, *manish water,* a soup made from goat offal and tripe, is said to increase virility. *Patties* (meat pies)—the best on the island are at Montego Bay—are another staple snack. Boiled corn, roast yams, roast saltfish, fried fish, soups, and fruits are all sold at roadside stands.

Tea is used to describe any nonalcoholic drink in Jamaica, a tradition dating back to plantation days. *Fish tea* is actually a bowl of hot soup made from freshly caught fish. *Skyjuice,* a favorite on hot afternoons, is sold by street vendors from not-always-sanitary carts. It consists of shaved ice with sugar-laden fruit syrup and is sold in small plastic bags with a straw. Coconut water is a refreshing drink, especially when you stop to have a local vendor chop open a fresh coconut.

Rum punches are everywhere, and the local beer is Red Stripe. The island produces many liqueurs, the most famous being Tía Maria, made from coffee beans. *Bellywash,* the local name for limeade, will supply the extra liquid you may need to counteract the heat. Blue Mountain coffee is the best, but tea, cocoa, and milk are usually available to round off a meal.

MARTINIQUE   See Guadeloupe, above.

MONTSERRAT   Some of the best fruits and vegetables in the Caribbean are grown in the rich, volcanic soil of Montserrat. The island is known for its tomatoes, carrots, and mangoes. *Goat water* (a mutton stew) is the most popular local dish. Another island specialty is *mountain chicken,* otherwise known as frogs' legs.

PUERTO RICO   Although Puerto Rican cooking has similarities to Cuban, Spanish, and Mexican cuisine, it has its own unique style, using such indigenous ingredients as cilantro, papaya, cacao, nispero, apio, plantains, and yampee.

Lunch and dinner generally begin with sizzling hot appetizers such as *bacalaitos* (crunchy cold fritters), *surullitos* (sweet, plump cornmeal fingers), and *empanadillas* (crescent-shaped turnovers filled with lobster, crab, conch, or beef). Next, a bowl of steaming *asopao* (a hearty gumbo soup with rice and chicken or shellfish) may be followed by *lechón asado* (roast suckling pig), *pollo en vino dulce* (succulent chicken in wine), or *bacalao* (dried salted cod mixed with various roots and tubers and fried). No matter the selection, main dishes are served with salted *tostones* (deep-fried plantains, or green bananas) and plentiful portions of rice and beans.

The aroma that wafts from kitchens throughout Puerto Rico comes from adobo and sofrito—blends of herbs and spices that give many of the native foods their distinctive taste and color. *Adobo,* made from peppercorns, oregano, garlic, salt, olive oil, and lime juice or vinegar, is rubbed into meats before they are roasted. *Sofrito,* a potpourri of onions, garlic, and peppers browned in olive oil or lard and colored with *achiote* (annatto seeds), imparts a bright yellow color to the island's rice, soups, and stews. Dessert is usually *flan* (custard) or perhaps *nisperos de batata* (sweet-potato balls made with coconut, cloves, and cinnamon), or guava jelly and *queso blanco* (white cheese).

SABA   No one visits for the food. Caribbean and continental dishes prevail, and there are no really outstanding local dishes. Most of the food is imported.

ST. EUSTATIUS   This Dutch island is not written up in gourmet cookbooks. Most of the food is imported, and restaurants are adequate, not exciting. Some restaurants make a stab at preparing a French cuisine with generally frozen ingredients. Local bistros serve some regional cooking such as stewed conch, salt fish with johnnycakes, or curried goat.

ST. KITTS & NEVIS   On St. Kitts, most guests eat at their hotels, but the island has a number of good restaurants where you can find spiny lobster, crab back, pepperpot stew, breadfruit, and curried conch. The drink of the island is CSR (Cane Spirit Rothschild), a pure sugarcane liqueur developed by Baron Edmond de Rothschild. Islanders mix it with Ting, a bubbly grapefruit soda.

On Nevis, the local food is good. Suckling pig is roasted with many spices, and eggplant is used in a number of tasty ways, as is avocado. (You may see turtle on some menus, but remember that this is an endangered species.)

ST. LUCIA   It's best to dine in one of St. Lucia's little character-loaded restaurants (we'll make suggestions in that chapter). The local food is excellent and reflects the years of French and British occupation. St. Lucia's marketplace offers the ingredients for local dishes, including callaloo soup (fresh greens, dumplings, and salted beef), *pouile dudon* (a sweet, zesty chicken dish), and breadfruit cooked on open hot coals. Pumpkin soup, flying fish, lobster, and *tablette* (a coconut sugar candy that resembles white coral) round out the menu choices.

SINT MAARTEN / ST. MARTIN   This island, part Dutch, part French, has a truly excellent cuisine, in spite of its heavy reliance on imported ingredients. Here you'll find classic French cuisine, as well as American and continental, with a touch of West Indian spice and flavors. All the French classics are served, including frogs' legs and escargots, but Caribbean offerings, inspired by Martinique, include *crabes farcis* (stuffed crab), *blaff* (seafood poached and seasoned with peppers), and curried *colombo* (a stew with chicken, mutton, or goat). Nearby Anguilla supplies a never-ending basket of spiny lobsters, the most delectable dish on the island. Dutch specialties are rare, although there's plenty of tasty Dutch beer. A lot of good French wine, served either by the bottle or the carafe, is also shipped into the island.

ST. VINCENT & THE GRENADINES   Most dining takes place in the hotels, although there is a scattering of local bistros serving such West Indian food as local fish Créole style and callaloo soup. But mostly locals try to serve what they've heard foreigners like, including frozen steak flown in from Chicago, frozen shrimp from South America, and frozen french fries from who-knows-where. Local bartenders take pride in the variety of their rum punches as well as their lethal effects.

TRINIDAD & TOBAGO   The food on these islands is as varied and cosmopolitan as the islanders themselves. Red-hot curries testify to Trinidad's strong East Indian influence, and some Chinese dishes are about as good here as any you'll find in Hong Kong. Créole and Spanish fare, as well as French, are also to be enjoyed. A typical savory offering is a *rôti,* a king-size crêpe, highly spiced and filled with chicken, shellfish, or meat. Of course, you may prefer to skip such local delicacies as opossum stew and fried armadillo. Naturally, your fresh rum punch will have a dash of Angostura Bitters. On Trinidad, there's a tendency to deep-fry everything—you can avoid this by careful menu selections.

Tobago has fewer dining choices than Trinidad. On Tobago, your best bet is local fish dishes, such as stuffed kingfish in Créole sauce. Local crayfish is also good, and lobster appears on some menus, perhaps stuffed into a crêpe. One island favorite that appears frequently is seafood casserole with ginger wine. Some typical Tobago dishes include baby shark marinated in lime and rum and conch stewed with coconut and rum.

U.S. VIRGIN ISLANDS   Although a lot of the food is imported and frozen (often from Miami or Puerto Rico), St. Thomas, and to a lesser extent St. Croix and St. John, serve some of the finest American and continental cuisine in the Caribbean. A whole range of ethnic restaurants exist too, including Chinese and Mexican. Italian food is commonplace.

The most famous soup of the islands is kallaloo, or *callaloo,* made in an infinite number of ways from a leafy green vegetable similar to spinach. This soup is flavored with salt beef, pig mouth, pig tail, ham bone, fresh fish, crabs, or perhaps conch, along with okra, onions, and spices. Many soups are sweetened with sugar, and putting fruits in soups is common. The classic *red-bean soup,* made with pork or ham, various spices, and tomatoes, is sugared to taste. Tannia soup is made from the root of the so-called Purple Elephant Ear. Salt-fat meat and ham, along with tomatoes, onions, and spices, are added to the tannias.

Souse is an old-time favorite made with the feet, head, and tongue of the pig, and flavored with a lime-based sauce and various spices. Salt-fish salad is traditionally served on Holy Thursday or Good Friday, as well as at other times. It's made with boneless salt fish, potatoes, onions, boiled eggs, and an oil-and-vinegar dressing. *Herring gundy* is an old-time island favorite made with salt herring, potatoes, onions, sweet and hot green peppers, olives, diced beets, raw carrots, herbs, and boiled eggs.

Seasoned rice is popular with Virgin Islanders, who often serve several starches at one meal. Most often rice is flavored with ham or salt pork, tomatoes, garlic, onion, and shortening. *Fungi* is a simple cornmeal dumpling that can be made more interesting with the addition of various ingredients, such as okra. Sweet fungi becomes a dessert, with sugar, milk, cinnamon, and raisins.

Okra (often spelled ochroe in the islands) is a mainstay vegetable, often accompanying beef, fish, or chicken. It's fried in an iron skillet after being flavored with hot pepper, tomatoes, onions, garlic, and bacon fat or butter. *Accra,* another popular dish, is made with okra, black-eyed peas, salt, and pepper. It's dropped into boiling fat and fried until golden brown. The classic vegetable dish—some families serve it every night—is peas and rice, made with pigeon peas flavored with ham or salt meat, onion, tomatoes, herbs, and sometimes slices of pumpkins.

For dessert, *sweet-potato pone* is a classic, made with sugar, eggs, butter, milk, salt, cinnamon, raisins, and chopped almonds. The exotic fruits of the islands lend themselves to various homemade ice creams, including mango. Orange-rose sherbet is made by pounding rose petals into a paste and flavoring it with sugar and orange juice. Guava ice cream is a delectable flavor, as are soursop, banana, and papaya. Sometimes dumplings are served for dessert, made with guava, peach, plum, gooseberry, or cherry, and certainly apple.

3 Planning an Affordable Trip to the Caribbean

This chapter is designed to provide most of the nuts-and-bolts information you'll need before setting off on your island escape. We'll show you how to save money when booking your trip, and how to scout out the best airfares and cruise bargains.

1 Visitor Information, Entry Requirements, Customs & Money

VISITOR INFORMATION

All the major islands have tourist representatives who will supply information before you go; we list each one in the "Fast Facts" section of the individual island chapters. The **Caribbean Tourism Organization,** 20 E. 46th St., New York, NY 10017 (☎ **212/682-0435**), can also provide general information.

A good travel agent can also provide information, but make sure the agent is a member of the American Society of Travel Agents (ASTA). If you have a complaint, contact **ASTA Consumer Affairs,** 1101 King St., Alexandria, VA 22314 (☎ **703/706-0387**).

You may also want to get in touch with the U.S. State Department for background bulletins. Contact the Superintendent of Documents, **U.S. Government Printing Office,** Washington, DC 20402 (☎ **202/512-1800**). A free catalog of books and background notes is available. Background bulletins are offered for many Caribbean nations, including Antigua and Barbados, the Dominican Republic, Grenada, Jamaica, St. Lucia, St. Kitts and Nevis, St. Vincent and the Grenadines, and Trinidad and Tobago.

If you have Internet access, "City.net" (**http://www.city.net/regions/caribbean/**) is a great site that will point you toward a wealth of Caribbean travel information on the Web. One of the best Caribbean sites it lists is "Caribbean-On-Line" (**http://www.webcom.com/earleltd/**), a series of virtual guidebooks full of information on hotels, restaurants, and shopping, along with sights and detailed maps of the islands and their major towns and ports. The site also includes links to travel agents and cruise lines that are on the Web.

ENTRY REQUIREMENTS

Even though the Caribbean islands are, for the most part, independent nations and thereby classified as international destinations, passports are not generally required, though we recommend carrying them anyway. You'll certainly need identification, and a passport is the best form for speeding you through Customs and Immigration. Other acceptable documents include an ongoing or return ticket, plus a current voter registration card or a birth certificate (the original or a copy that has been certified by the U.S. Department of Health). You will also need some photo ID, such as a driver's license or an expired passport; however, driver's licenses are not acceptable as a sole form of ID. Visas are usually not required, but some countries may require you to fill out a tourist card (see the individual island chapters for details).

Before leaving home, make two copies of your documents, including your passport and your driver's license, your airline ticket, and any hotel vouchers. If you're on medication, you should also make copies of prescriptions.

CUSTOMS

Each island has specific requirements that will be detailed in the destination chapters that follow. Generally, you're permitted to bring in items intended for your personal use, including tobacco, cameras, film, and a limited supply of liquor— usually 40 ounces. Here's what you can bring home from the islands:

U.S. CUSTOMS   The U.S. government generously allows $1,200 worth of duty-free imports every 30 days from the U.S. Virgin Islands; those who go over their exemption are taxed at 5% rather than the usual 10%. The limit is $400 for such international destinations as the French islands of Guadeloupe and Martinique, and $600 for many other islands. If you visit only Puerto Rico, you don't have to go through Customs at all, since the island is a U.S. commonwealth.

Joint Customs declarations are possible for members of a family traveling together. For instance, if you are a husband and wife with two children, your purchases in the U.S. Virgin Islands become duty free up to $4,800! Unsolicited gifts can be sent to friends and relatives at the rate of $100 per day from the U.S. Virgin Islands (or $50 a day from the other islands). U.S. citizens, or returning residents at least 21 years of age, traveling directly or indirectly from the U.S. Virgin Islands, are allowed to bring in free of duty 1,000 cigarettes, 5 liters of alcohol, and 100 cigars (but not Cuban cigars). Duty-free limitations on articles from other countries are generally 1 liter of alcohol, 200 cigarettes, and 200 cigars.

Collect receipts for all purchases made abroad. Sometimes merchants suggest a false receipt to undervalue your purchase. *Warning:* You could be involved in a sting operation—the merchant might be an informer to U.S. Customs. You must also declare on your Customs form the nature and value of all gifts received during your stay abroad. It's prudent to carry proof that you purchased expensive cameras or jewelry on the U.S. mainland. If you purchased such an item during an earlier trip abroad, you should carry proof that you have previously paid Customs duty on the item.

If you use any medication containing controlled substances or requiring injection, carry an original prescription or note from your doctor.

For more specifics, write to the **U.S. Customs Service,** P.O. Box 7407, Washington, DC 20044 (☎ **202/927-6724**), and request the free pamphlet *Know Before You Go.*

CANADIAN CUSTOMS   Canada allows its citizens a $300 exemption, and they are allowed to bring back duty free 200 cigarettes, 2.2 pounds of tobacco, 40 imperial ounces of liquor, and 50 cigars. In addition, they are allowed to mail gifts to Canada from abroad at the rate of $60 a day, provided they are unsolicited and aren't alcohol or tobacco (write on the package: "Unsolicited gift, under $60 value").

All valuables should be declared on Form Y-38 before your departure from Canada, including serial numbers, as in the case, of, for example, expensive foreign cameras you already own. *Note:* The $300 exemption can be used only once a year and only after an absence of at least 7 days.

For clarification, write for the booklet *I Declare,* issued by **Revenue Canada,** 2265 St. Laurent Blvd., Ottawa, K1G 4K3 (☎ **800/461-9999** or 613/993-0534).

BRITISH CUSTOMS On returning from the Caribbean, if you either arrive directly in the U.K. or via a port in another EU country where you did not pass through Customs controls with all your baggage, you must go through U.K. Customs and declare any goods in excess of the allowances, which are: 200 cigarettes or 100 cigarillos or 50 cigars or 250 grams of tobacco; 2 liters of still table wine and 1 liter of spirits or strong liqueurs over 22% volume, or 2 liters of fortified or sparkling wine or other liqueurs, or 2 liters of additional still table wine; 60cc/ml of perfume; and £145 worth of all other goods, including gifts and souvenirs. (No one under 17 years of age is entitled to a tobacco or drinks allowance.) Only go through the Green "nothing to declare" channel if you're sure that you have no more than the Customs allowances and no prohibited or restricted goods.

For further details on U.K. Customs, contact **HM Customs and Excise Office,** Dorset House, Stamford Street, London SE1 9PY (☎ **0171/202-4510**).

MONEY

CASH/CURRENCY The U.S. dollar is widely accepted on many of the islands, and is the legal currency of the U.S. Virgin Islands, the British Virgin Islands, and Puerto Rico. Many islands use the Eastern Caribbean dollar, even though your hotel bill will most likely be presented in U.S. dollars. French islands use the French franc, although many hotels often quote their prices in U.S. dollars. For details, see "Fast Facts" in the individual island chapters.

TRAVELER'S CHECKS **American Express** (☎ **800/221-7282** in the U.S. and Canada) is one of the largest issuers of traveler's checks. If you're a member of AAA, you can avoid commission fees by purchasing checks at AAA offices. Also, the commission fee is waived for holders of gold and platinum American Express cards who get their traveler's checks through the American Express service number (☎ **800/553-6782**).

Citicorp (☎ **800/645-6556** in the U.S. and Canada, or 813/623-1709, collect, from anywhere else in the world), is another major issuer.

Thomas Cook (☎ **800/223-7373** in the U.S. and Canada, or 609/987-7300, collect, from anywhere else in the world) issues MasterCard traveler's checks, and **Interpayment Services** (☎ **800/221-2426** in the U.S. or Canada, or 212/858-8500, collect, from anywhere else in the world) sells Visa traveler's checks.

CREDIT & CHARGE CARDS Credit and charge cards are widely used in the Caribbean. Visa and MasterCard predominate, although American Express and, to a lesser extent, Diners Club and Discover, are also popular. We've noted which cards are accepted at each hotel and restaurant recommended throughout this book.

ATM NETWORKS Plus, Cirrus, and other automated-teller machine networks operate in the Caribbean. Before departing, check to see if your PIN (Personal Identification Number) must be reprogrammed for use at Caribbean ATMs to withdraw money on either your ATM or credit card. ATMs are found in such places as Puerto Rico and St. Thomas; however, don't count on this service being available at one of the remote islands such as Mustique in the Grenadines.

What Things Cost in the Caribbean

	Local Phone Call	Avg Double Room	Avg Lunch	Avg Dinner	Coffee	Film
Antigua	10¢	$70	$5	$15	$1	$10
Aruba	25¢	$60	$10	$15	75¢	$9
Barbados	25¢	$110	$15	$25	$1.25	$10
Bonaire	10¢	$65	$12	$20	$1	$8
British Virgins	25¢	$80	$6	$10	60¢	$8
Cayman Islands	10¢	$95	$6	$12	$1	$6.25
Curaçao	25¢	$105	$20	$25	$1	$20.40
Dominica	25¢	$65	$15	$25	$1	$10
Dominican Republic	25¢	$50	$10	$12	60¢	$7
Granada	free	$50	$8	$8	$1.50	$7-$9
Guadeloupe	40¢	$110	$20	$30	$1.25	$8
Jamaica	10¢	$80	$5	$10	$1	$9
Martinique	40¢	$110	$20	$30	$1.25	$8
Montserrat	5¢	$62	$9	$15	$1.50	$9.60
Nevis/St. Kitts	25¢	$75	$5	$10	$1.50	$7
Puerto Rico	10¢	$75	$15	$20	55¢	$8
Saba	14¢	$125	$10	$15	$1	$7
St. Eustatius	25¢	$100	$12	$15	$1	$6.50
St. Lucia	10¢	$125	$10	$20	$1	$6
St. Maarten	30¢	$120	$10	$20	$1	$6
St. Martin	20¢	$80	$10	$25	$3	$5
St. Vincent	15¢	$80	$8	$15	75¢	$9
Trinidad/ Tobago	23¢	$75	$12	$15	50¢	$7
U.S. Virgin Islands	25¢	$65	$8	$20	50¢	$9

Always determine what the frequency limits for withdrawals and cash advances are on your bank or credit card. For locations of **Cirrus** abroad, call ☎ **800/424-7787.** For **Plus** usage abroad, dial ☎ **800/843-7587.** ATMs give a better exchange rate than banks, but some ATMs exact a service charge on every transaction.

MONEYGRAMS   If you find yourself out of money, a new wire service provided by American Express can help you tap willing friends and family for emergency funds. Through **MoneyGram,** 6200 S. Quebec St. (P.O. Box 5118), Englewood, CO 80155 (☎ **800/926-9400**), money can be sent around the world in less than 10 minutes. Senders should call AMEX to learn the address of the closest outlet that

The U.S. Dollar & the British Pound

The U.S. dollar is commonly used throughout the Caribbean, except on the French islands of Martinique and Guadeloupe. It is widely accepted even on islands that print their own currency. British travelers will want to convert their pounds sterling into dollars, even for use on islands that are British Crown Colonies.

International exchange rates fluctuate, so the rates given in the table below (based on £1 = $1.60) may not be the same when you travel to the Caribbean. This table should only be used as a guide.

U.S.$	U.K.£	U.S.$	U.K.£
.25	.16	15.00	9.38
.50	.31	20.00	12.50
.75	.47	25.00	15.63
1.00	.625	50.00	31.25
2.00	1.25	75.00	46.88
3.00	1.88	100.00	62.50
4.00	2.50	150.00	93.75
5.00	3.13	200.00	125.00
6.00	3.75	250.00	156.25
7.00	4.38	300.00	187.50
8.00	5.00	350.00	218.75
9.00	5.63	400.00	250.00
10.00	6.25	500.00	312.50

handles MoneyGrams. Cash, credit/charge card, or the occasional personal check (with ID) are acceptable forms of payment. AMEX's fee for the service is $10 for the first $300 with a sliding scale for larger sums. The service includes a short telex message and a 3-minute phone call from sender to recipient. The beneficiary must present a photo ID at the outlet where the money is received.

2 When to Go

THE CLIMATE

The temperature variations in the Caribbean are surprisingly slight, averaging between 75° and 85° Fahrenheit in both winter and summer, although it can get really chilly, especially in the early morning and at night. The Caribbean winter is usually like a perpetual May. Overall, the mid-80s prevail throughout most of the region, and trade winds make for comfortable days and nights, even without air-conditioning.

The humidity and bugs can be a problem here year-round. However, more mosquitoes come out during the rainy season, which traditionally occurs in the autumn.

HURRICANES The curse of Caribbean weather, the hurricane season lasts—officially, at least—from June 1 to November 30. But there's no cause for panic. Satellite forecasts give adequate warnings so that precautions can be taken.

To get a weather report before you go, call the nearest branch of the National Weather Service, listed in your phone directory under the "U.S. Department of Commerce." You can also call Weather Trak; for the telephone number for your particular area, call ☎ **900/370-8725** (a taped message gives you the three-digit access code for the place you're interested in; the call costs 75¢ for the first minute and 50¢ for each additional minute).

THE HIGH SEASON & THE OFF-SEASON

The Caribbean has become a year-round destination. The "season" runs roughly from mid-December to mid-April. Hotels charge their highest prices during the peak winter period, which is generally the driest season; however, it can be a wet time in mountainous areas, and you can expect showers especially in December and January on Martinique, Guadeloupe, Dominica, St. Lucia, on the north coast of the Dominican Republic, and in northeast Jamaica.

For a winter vacation, make reservations 2 to 3 months in advance—or earlier for trips at Christmas and in February.

The off-season in the Caribbean—roughly from mid-April to mid-December (although this varies from hotel to hotel)—amounts to a summer sale. In most cases, hotels, inns, and condos slash rates to 20% to 60% off their winter tariffs.

Dollar for dollar, you'll spend less money by renting a summer house or self-sufficient unit in the Caribbean than you would on Cape Cod, Fire Island, Laguna Beach, or the coast of Maine. Sailing and water sports are better too, because the West Indies are protected from the Atlantic on their western shores, which border the calm Caribbean Sea.

Because there's such a drastic difference in high-season and low-season rates at most hotels, we've included both on every property we review. You'll see the incredible savings you can enjoy if your schedule is flexible enough to wait a couple of months for your fun in the sun!

3 40 Money-Saving Tips

AIRFARES

1. Ask about air/land packages. Particularly in the Caribbean, a week's stay at even a top-of-the-line hostelry is often much cheaper if it's arranged as part of a package booked with your airfare. The savings might make a stay at an expensive hotel completely affordable.

2. Fly standby. Though the major carriers don't offer standby fares any more, some smaller carriers still do—notably BWIA and the lesser-known airlines (see "Getting There" in the individual island chapters for the names and phone numbers of these small carriers). Standby fares are usually disguised today as "special promotion fares" or "last-minute departures." Use these terms—not "standby"—when calling an airline. These low fares can sometimes be locked in up to an hour before departure, but only in off-peak travel times.

3. Make sure you're flying into the right airport. On some islands, such as St. Lucia, you can rack up substantial transfer costs by flying into the wrong airport. Whenever an island has more than one international airport, be sure to figure out its position in relation to your hotel and plan your incoming flight accordingly. Taxi costs across the length of a mountainous island can total more than $60.

4. Fly off-season. Airfares plummet from April to late June and from mid-September until about 10 days before Christmas.

ACCOMMODATIONS

5. Find out what "extras" are included in the hotel price. A moderately priced hotel that tacks on charges for everything from beach chairs to snorkel equipment may

wind up costing you more than a luxury hotel that includes these extras in its price. And be sure to ask what taxes and surcharges might be tacked on to your final bill.

6. Find out if airport transfers are included in a hotel's price.

7. If you're traveling off-season, don't always assume that a large hotel will cost more than an inn with a limited number of amenities. Especially during off-season promotions, a megaresort might be more generous with discounts, add-ons, and packages.

8. Know that an oceanfront room will cost more than a room without a view. Can you live without seeing the blue waters from your window?

9. If you're traveling with kids, consider housing up to two of your children in your room with you on foldaway beds. Many places offer free accommodations to anyone under 12, under 16, or (in some cases) under 18. We've noted these policies on every hotel we review.

10. Rent an apartment or villa, especially if you're traveling in a group of four or more, that has kitchen facilities so you can cook for yourself.

11. Look for the "window" that comes during the slow month of January, following right after New Year's, when many hotels slash their rates because of a slowdown in post-holiday business. Sometimes these discounts even match off-season rates!

12. If a hotel is not on the beach, find out if there's a charge to get there. The hotel rates may be lower, but will you wind up spending a lot of time and money to get to the sands every day?

13. In small B&Bs and guest houses, rooms without private bath, although they often have a sink with hot and cold running water, will sometimes save you an average of 40% off the regular rate.

14. Ask if a hotel charges extra for paying with a credit or charge card. Although this is against the bylaws of such lenders as American Express, hoteliers often do it anyway. If you're penalized for plastic, consider bringing enough cash (or, better yet, traveler's checks).

15. If you're an avid golfer, tennis player, or scuba diver, shop around for the best packages without all the frilly stuff.

16. Consider camping. It's not always available on all islands, but on those where it is (St. John's, for example), it may be the way to go.

17. Check the surcharge for either local or long-distance calls, which can be an astonishing 40%. Make your calls outside at a pay phone or the post office.

18. Determine if breakfast is included in the rates, as an extra daily charge can make a big difference in your final bill.

19. If you're going to spend at least a week at a resort, ask about a discount. If they're not full, some hotels might give you the seventh night free.

20. Book the MAP (Modified American Plan), including breakfast and dinner, if it looks good. It'll save big ones over the à la carte menu.

DINING

21. Scan advertisements in local tourist guides and newspapers publicizing specialty buffets and special discounts on meals.

22. Sample local foods, like fresh fish, chicken, fruit, and vegetables. Most other food is imported at a high cost, and arrives frozen to boot.

23. Stick to rum-based drinks—the island favorite—and watch out for those high price tags on imported booze such as scotch.

24. In most cases, the fixed-price menu or daily specials might be a third cheaper than ordering à la carte.

OUTDOOR ACTIVITIES

25. Instead of high-priced sporting activities such as golf, parasailing, horseback riding, and scuba diving, consider hiking or snorkeling instead, or take a walk in a nature preserve. And, of course, the beach provides you with free amusement all day long!

NIGHTLIFE

26. Scan the local press for reggae concerts, community groups sponsoring "bashes" (all reasonable in price), charity bazaars, whatever. There's always something going on in the Caribbean, and you can learn about island life, too.

27. Hit a bar at happy hour, usually from 5 to 6:30 or even 7pm, when drinks are traditionally discounted 20% to 50%.

SHOPPING

28. Before you leave home, stop by your local discount shops to check the latest prices. Only then can you comparison shop to determine whether you're getting a bargain in a Caribbean discount outlet.

29. Don't be afraid to haggle. Savvy shoppers pride themselves in almost never paying retail for anything. If you think the price is too high, make a lower offer. Sometimes you'll get yes for an answer.

30. If you're traveling as a family, submit a joint declaration to Customs—that is, combine the duty allowance of all members of your group into one bulk package. Even a child gets a duty-free allowance ranging from $400 to $1,200, depending on the island.

31. Buy handcrafted arts and crafts, which in most cases are duty free regardless of the amount you paid.

32. Remember that Puerto Rico has the same tariff barriers as the U.S. mainland. You can take home as many bargains as you find here without paying duty.

33. U.S. Customs allows you to take back home duty free $600 worth of merchandise (per family member) from such islands as Jamaica and Barbados, but only $400 from such islands as St. Barts and Martinique (because these islands are technically part of France).

34. The best deal of all is the U.S. Virgin Islands (St. Thomas, St. Croix, and St. John) where you can bring back $1,200 in duty-free purchases. If you go over the limit, you're charged at a flat rate of 5% up to $1,000 rather than the usual 10% imposed on goods from other countries.

35. Save your big purchases for so-called "duty free" islands as opposed to those that have a heavy sales tax.

TRANSPORTATION

36. Think about whether you can skip a rental car altogether. You might not be as mobile, but your hotel might offer minivan transport that will get you to shops, a local beach, and snorkeling facilities.

37. Renting a local taxi for a day's outing might work out to be less expensive than an entire week's rental of a car. See all the sights over a 1- or 2-day period, and plan to relax close to your hotel on other days.

38. If you do want to rent a car, weekly rentals are more cost-efficient (on a day-to-day basis) than a single day's rental.
39. Rent bikes to get around. Although bicycles are definitely *not* recommended for nighttime use (Caribbean roads are notoriously dark at night), they can be an invigorating and efficient mode of transportation.
40. Stay at a hotel in Charlotte Amalie, Christiansted, Montego Bay, or Puerto Rico's Condado or Isla Verde. With dozens of restaurants, bars, and nightclubs nearby, you'll almost never need a car.

4 Finding the Best Airfare

You shouldn't have to pay a regular fare to the Caribbean. Why? There are so many deals out there—in both summer and winter—that you can certainly find a discount fare. That's especially true if you're willing to plan on the spur of the moment: If a flight is not fully booked, an airline will discount tickets to try to fill it up.

If you fly in summer, spring, and fall, you're guaranteed substantial reductions on airfares to the Caribbean. You can also ask if it's cheaper to fly Monday through Thursday. And don't forget to consider air-and-land packages, which offer considerably reduced rates.

Most airlines charge different fares according to the season. Peak season, which is winter in the Caribbean, is most expensive; basic season, in the summer, offers the lowest fares. Shoulder season refers to the spring and fall months in between. Most airlines also offer promotional fares, which carry stringent requirements like advance purchase, minimum stay, and cancellation penalties; the most common is the APEX fare. Land arrangements (prebooking of hotel rooms) are often tied in with promotional fares offered by airlines.

SERIOUS MONEY-SAVING STRATEGIES

BUCKET SHOPS (CONSOLIDATORS) A bucket shop acts as a clearinghouse for blocks of tickets that airlines discount and consign during normally slow periods of air travel. In the case of the Caribbean, that usually means from mid-April to mid-December.

Tickets are sometimes—but not always—discounted 20% to 35%. Terms of payment can vary, from anywhere from 45 days prior to departure to the last minute. Discounted tickets can also be purchased through regular travel agents, who usually mark up the ticket 8% to 10%, maybe more, thereby greatly reducing your savings.

A survey conducted of flyers who use consolidator tickets voiced only one major complaint: You can't arrange for an advance seat assignment. The survey revealed that most flyers received a savings off the regular price. But—and here's the hitch—many flyers reported no savings at all, as the airlines will sometimes match the consolidator ticket with a promotional fare. The situation is a bit tricky and calls for some careful investigation on your part to determine just how much you're saving.

Bucket shops abound from coast to coast. Look for their ads in your local newspaper's travel section. One of the biggest U.S. consolidators is **Travac,** 2601 E. Jefferson St., Orlando, FL 32803 (☎ **800/TRAV**-800 or 407/896-0014), with another office at 989 Ave. of the Americas, New York, NY 10018 (☎ **212/563-3303**).

In New York, try **TFI Tours International,** 34 W. 32nd St., 12th Floor, New York, NY 10001 (☎ **800/745-8000,** or 212/736-1140 in New York State). This tour company offers services to 177 cities worldwide.

In the Midwest, contact **Travel Avenue,** 10 S. Riverside Plaza, Suite 1404, Chicago, IL 60606 (☎ **800/333-3335** or 312/876-1116), whose tickets are often cheaper than most shops, and it charges the customer only a $25 fee on international tickets.

Also in the Midwest, try **TMI (Travel Management International),** 1129 E. Wayzata Blvd., Wayzata, MN 55391 (☎ **800/245-3672** in the U.S.), which offers a wide variety of discounts, including youth fares, student fares, and access to other kinds of air-related discounts as well.

CHARTER FLIGHTS   Many major carriers offer charter flights at rates that are sometimes 30% (or more) off the regular airfare. There are some drawbacks, however. Advance booking of up to 45 days or more may be required, and there are hefty cancellation penalties, although you can take out insurance against emergency cancellations. Also, you must depart and return on your scheduled dates—if you're not on the plane, you can kiss your money good-bye.

One reliable charter-flight operator is **Council Charter,** run by the Council on International Educational Exchange, 205 E. 42nd St., New York, NY 10017 (☎ **800/800-8222** or 212/661-0311), which arranges charter seats on regularly scheduled aircraft.

Travac, 2601 E. Jefferson St., Orlando, FL 32803 (☎ **800/TRAV-800** or 407/896-0014), also offers seats on charter flights. You can also contact their New York office at 989 Ave. of the Americas, New York, NY 10018 (☎ **212/563-3303**).

REBATORS   To confuse the situation even more, rebators have also begun to compete in the low-airfare market. These outfits pass along to the passenger part of their commission, although many assess a fee for their services. They're not the same as travel agents, but they sometimes offer roughly similar services, such as discounted land arrangements, including hotels and car rentals. Most rebators offer discounts averaging anywhere from 10% to 25%, plus a $25 handling charge.

Travel Avenue, 10 S. Riverside Plaza, Suite 1404, Chicago, IL 60606 (☎ **800/333-3335** or 312/876-1116), offers upfront cash rebates on every airline ticket over $300 it sells. Also available are tour and cruise fares, plus hotel bookings.

Another major rebater is **The Smart Traveller,** 3111 SW 27th Ave. (P.O. Box 330010), Miami, FL 33133 (☎ **800/448-3338** or 305/443-3544), which also offers discounts on packaged tours.

TRAVEL CLUBS   Travel clubs supply an unsold inventory of tickets offering discounts in the usual range of 20% to 60%. After you pay an annual fee, you are given a "hot line" number to call to find out what discounts are available. Some discounts become available a few days in advance of actual departure, some a week in advance, and some as much as a month. Of course, you're limited to what's available, so you have to be flexible. Some of the best of these clubs include:

Moment's Notice, 7301 New Utrecht Ave., Brooklyn, NY 11204 (☎ **718/234-6295**), charges $25 per year for membership, which allows spur-of-the-moment participation in discounted air-and-land packages to all Caribbean islands. Members can call the hot line (☎ **718/873-0908**) to learn what options are available. Most of the company's best-valued tours depart from JFK, LaGuardia, and Newark airports.

Travelers Advantage, 3033 S. Parker Rd., Suite 900, Aurora, CO 80014 (☎ **800/TEL-TRIP**), features a 3-month trial offer for $1 and an annual membership for $49. This includes the HalfPrice HotelCard, granting you 50% off regular published room rates at more than 3,000 participating hotels both foreign and domestic. Travelers

Advantage is a full-service travel agency. For membership information, call ☎ **800/ 548-1116.**

Another club, **Encore Travel Club,** 4501 Forbes Blvd., Lanham, MD 20706 (☎ **800/638-8976** in the U.S.), charges $49.95 a year for membership, which offers up to 50% discounts at more than 4,000 hotels. It also offers discounts on airfares, cruises, and car rentals through its volume purchase plans. Membership includes a travel package outlining the company's many services, and use of a toll-free phone number for advice and information.

5   Cruises That Don't Cost a Fortune

Except for peak-season cruises between Christmas and New Year's, forget the prices listed in the cruise-line brochures. Overcapacity and fierce competition have ushered in the age of the discounted fare. There are great bargains out there, enough at times to baffle even the most experienced cruise-line travel specialists. These low prices make cruising the Caribbean a viable option.

Don't succumb to sticker shock the moment you're quoted a rate for your cruise, because the price you'll pay adds up to a great value—an all-inclusive vacation package. Included are accommodations, as many as eight (!) meals a day, a packed roster of activities, free use of facilities, as well as cabaret, jazz performances, dance bands, and discos. It also includes stops at ports of call that otherwise you'd have to reach (and pay for) by airplane.

Cruises typically cost less than comparable land-based vacations. The key word, of course, is "comparable." If you stay at a Motel 6 and eat only at the local burger joint, you'll do better on land.

Almost everything is included in the cruise price. But know before you go that even the sweetest cruise-related deal will contain its share of hidden extras, and if you're not careful, you might get some unpleasant surprises when you eventually pay your piper. You'll have to pay extra for your bar and wine tabs, some shore excursions, gambling, tips, the exorbitant cost of any ship-to-shore phone calls or faxes, any special pampering (hairdressers, manicurists/pedicurists, massages, and/or skin treatments), purchases in the shipboard boutiques and at the ports of call, and medical treatments in the ship's infirmary. There will also be the question of **port charges,** which most cost-conscious cruise outfits limit to no more than $65 per person (but be sure to ask when you book). Other extra costs? There's always shopping as well as pretrip incidentals, such as airport or port parking fees, and trip or flight insurance.

BOOKING A CRUISE FOR THE BEST PRICE

How should you book your cruise and get to the port of embarkation before the good times roll? It's best to use a travel agent, particularly one who specializes in cruises. He or she will be likely to match you with a cruise line whose priorities and style are compatible with you, and also steer you toward any of the special promotions that come and go as frequently as Caribbean rainstorms. And to get to the port on time, many cruise lines offer deals including airfare from the airport nearest you into the one closest to the cruise-departure point. It's possible to purchase your air ticket on your own and book your cruise ticket separately, but in most cases you'll save money by combining the fares into a package deal.

Here are some travel agencies to consider: **Ambassador Tours,** 120 Montgomery St., Suite 400, San Francisco, CA 94104 (☎ **800/989-9000** or 415/981-5678); **Cruises, Inc.,** 5000 Campuswood Dr. E., Syracuse, NY 13057 (☎ **800/854-0500** or 315/463-9695); **Cruises of Distinction, Inc.,** 2750 S. Woodward Ave.,

Bloomfield Hills, MI 48304 (☎ **800/634-3445** or 810/332-3030); **Cruise Fairs of America,** Century Plaza Towers, 2029 Century Park E., Suite 950, Los Angeles, CA 90067 (☎ **800/456-4FUN** or 310/556-2925); **Kelly Cruises,** 1315 W. 22nd St., Suite 105, Oak Brook, IL 60521 (☎ **800/837-7447** or 708/990-1111); and **Hartford Holidays Travel,** 626 Willis Ave., Williston Park, NY 11596 (☎ **800/ 828-4813**). These companies stay tuned to last-minute price wars brewing between such low-budget contenders as Dolphin, Premier, and Commodore, and such middle-bracket, mid-priced operators as Carnival, Royal Caribbean, Princess, and Holland America. Sales pop up all the time, because these megaships simply aren't economically feasible for the cruise lines if they don't operate near peak capacity.

You're likely to sail from Miami, which has become the cruise capital of the world. Other departure ports include San Juan, Port Everglades, and (via the Panama Canal) Los Angeles.

DISCOUNT CRUISE LINES

The lines listed below, if you catch them during off-season and book a relatively small, simple cabin, are known for some of the lowest rates in the Caribbean cruise industry. For much more detailed information, including specific information about saving money and reviews of each individual ship, pick up a copy of *Frommer's Caribbean Cruises & Ports of Call '98.*

American Canadian Caribbean (☎ 800/556-7450 or 401/247-0955) draws tremendous repeat business—not only for its low prices, but because it offers some of the most exotic itineraries in the Caribbean. Its vessels aren't old, and from a marine engineering point of view, they're technically very sophisticated. But they're far less glamorous than most of the other liners and don't have a huge list of facilities. In other words, they're ships more than floating hotels. With this line, the destination is more important than the activities and diversions aboard the ship. Cruises are 7- to 12-day excursions through complicated shoals, near remote Caribbean landmasses where larger ships cannot go. At least one of the company's three ships spends part of its winter cruising around The Bahamas, the Virgin Islands, the Panama Canal, and the coasts of Central America.

Carnival Cruise Lines (☎ 800/438-6744 or 305/599-2600), with some of the biggest and most brightly decorated ships afloat, is the richest, boldest, brashest, and most successful mass-market cruise line in the world. Eight of its megavessels depart from Florida or Caribbean ports that include Miami, Tampa, New Orleans, and San Juan, and four of them specialize in 7-day tours that include stopovers in the Virgin Islands, Aruba, San Juan, Guadeloupe, Grenada, Grand Cayman, and Jamaica. In 1998, Carnival launched the super-megaship *Destiny,* which at 101,000 tons was the largest cruise ship in the world. Most cruises—especially during summer—offer good value, last 3 to 7 nights, and feature nonstop activities. Think of these cruises as floating theme parks, loaded with whimsy, full of crowds, and with lots of emphasis on Atlantic City–style partying. Lots of single passengers opt for this line, and the average on-board age is a relatively youthful 42.

Celebrity Cruises (☎ 800/437-3111 or 305/262-8322) maintains five newly built, medium- to large-sized ships offering cruises of between 7 and 17 nights. Ports of call include Key West, San Juan, Grand Cayman, Ocho Rios, Antigua, and Curaçao, among others. Celebrity is unpretentious but classy, a notch above mass-market, but with pricing that's relatively competitive. Accommodations are roomy and well equipped, and its cuisine is among the best of its competitors.

Costa Cruise Lines (☎ 800/462-6782 or 305/358-7325), the U.S.-based branch of a cruise line that has thrived in Italy for about a century, maintains hefty to megasized vessels that are newer than many others afloat. Two of these offer virtually identical jaunts through the western and eastern Caribbean on alternate weeks, departing from Fort Lauderdale. Ports of call on the eastern Caribbean itineraries of both vessels include St. Thomas, Serena Cay (a private island known for its beaches off the coast of the Dominican Republic), Grand Cayman, Jamaica, and in some cases, Key West and Cozumel. The ships—*CostaRomantica* and *CostaVictoria*—have an Italian ambience; pizza parties by the pool are frequent. Prices, though not rock-bottom, tend to remain competitive.

If you like what you might have seen at a land-based Club Med, you'll appreciate **Club Med Cruises** (☎ 800/4-LE-SHIP), which seem like summer camp for adults. Its vessels are the largest cruise ships with sails, but frankly, those sails are in use less often than you might hope for. You're more likely to motor between such ports of call as St. Barts, St. Kitts, St. Lucia, and scattered ports in the Virgin Islands and Venezuela. The staff is both French- and English-speaking, and the atmosphere is lighthearted. The cuisine is not the gourmet fare you might expect from a French company, but it's pretty good and the servings are certainly more than generous. You may not find the bargains here you'd get from other lines that have older ships, but a sense of relaxed permissiveness justifies the extra expense for some travelers.

The only ship of **Commodore Cruise Line** (☎ 800/237-5361 or 954/967-2100) is solid and seaworthy, but much less competitive than many of the newer vessels being launched by more upscale lines. Passengers who embark for jaunts through the western Caribbean usually spend 3 full days at sea, visiting ports in Jamaica, the Cayman Islands, and Honduras. The ship has a relative lack of state-of-the-art facilities, but its low rates make a Caribbean cruise possible for many first-time cruisers without a lot of cash.

Dolphin Cruise Lines (☎ 800/222-1003 or 305/358-5122) has three ships offering low-cost, relatively glitter-free cruises on much-renovated older vessels with somewhat outmoded amenities. Nothing is particularly fancy, but no one seems to mind in view of the good values. Cruise bargain-hunters and retirees often make up the passenger list. *SeaBreeze* spends more time in the eastern Caribbean than its shipmates, making regular stops on alternate weeks in Puerto Rico and the U.S. Virgin Islands, usually with 3 days at sea in between.

Holland America Line–Westours (☎ 800/426-0327 or 206/281-3535) is the most high-toned of the mass-market cruise lines, with eight respectably hefty and good-looking ships. Cruises, which stop at deepwater, relatively mainstream ports throughout the Caribbean, last for an average of 7 days. They usually offer solid value, with very few jolts or surprises, and an overall sense of squeaky-clean thrift and value. Expect a solid, well-grounded clientele of mature travelers on board who expect (and get) a lot for their dollar. Cruise stopovers, among others, include Key West, Grand Cayman, St. Maarten, St. Lucia, Curaçao, Barbados, and St. Thomas. Late-night revelers and serious partyers might want to book cruises on other lines such as Carnival.

Norwegian Cruise Line (☎ 800/327-7030 or 305/445-0866) appeals to all ages and income levels, with Scandinavian officers, an international staff, and a pervasive modern-Viking theme. Two of the company's five ships (the relatively informal *Seaward* and the line's dignified flagship, *Norway*) make it a point to stop in St. Thomas as part of circuits that encompass visits to such other points as Santo Domingo, St. Lucia, and St. Kitts. Others focus on visits to NCL's private Bahamian island, Great Stirrup Cay, plus St. Maarten, St. Kitts, and St. Lucia. One of the ships (*Seaward*) is based in San Juan, which places passengers sooner within the heart of Caribbean action than vessels that depart from south Florida. The company's largest ship and corporate symbol (the *Norway*) offers the best amenities and services.

NCL isn't at all shy about pricing some of its inside cabins, during some slow seasons, at around $15 per person per day, without airfare. To qualify for this rate, you might have to travel with two or three companions in a cabin for three or four, but with the line's snappy roster of shipboard activities and themes, it's doubtful that you'll spend a lot of time in your cabin anyway.

Princess Cruises (☎ **800/421-0522** or 310/553-1770) has at least five members of its far-flung fleet sailing in Caribbean and Bahamian waters. The company is one of the very few in the world offering luxury accommodations and upscale service aboard megaships whose cruises last for 7 to 11 days. These usually carry a smaller number of passengers than similarly sized vessels at less elegant lines. Despite the company's upscale image, look for deep discounts during slow seasons.

Royal Caribbean Cruise Line (☎ **305/539-6000**) leads the industry in the development of megaships—and that means they've got to pack those ships so they'll be hyper-competitive, even if they have to offer discount rates. Most of this company's dozen or so vessels weigh in at around 73,000 tons, are among the largest of any line afloat, and boast floating hardware that's more impressive than that of many national navies. It's a mainstream, mass-market line, and its offerings have been fine-tuned through years of experience. The line encourages a house-party theme that's somehow a bit less frenetic than what you'll find aboard Carnival cruises. The company is well run, and there are enough on-board activities to suit virtually any taste and age level. Though accommodations and accoutrements are more than adequate, they're not upscale, and cabins aboard some of the line's older vessels tend to be a bit more cramped than the industry norm. Using either Miami or San Juan as their home port, RCCL ships call regularly at St. Thomas, San Juan, Ocho Rios, St. Maarten, Grand Cayman, and Curaçao. RCCL is the only cruise line in the business that owns, outright, two tropical beaches whose sands and water-sports facilities are the focus of many of the company's cruises.

Royal Olympic Cruises (☎ **800/872-6400** or 212/397-6400), formed in 1995 from a merger between Sun Lines and Epirotiki Cruises, is a well-respected Greek shipping line that operates the only Greek-registered ship in the Caribbean, the comfortable and well-maintained but aging *Stella Solaris*. Most stops at Caribbean ports (Trinidad, St. Vincent, Bequia, Barbados, and Curaçao) are configured as visits en route to either the Amazon or the Panama Canal. Despite the age of the ship, its many restorations and the cheerfulness of one of the best staffs of any vessel afloat make this a consistently popular ship. Pricing aboard this line is iffy—depending mostly on seasonal or special promotions, and whether you opt for one of the smallest and least fancy cabins. Nonetheless, a Greek/Caribbean cruise can be less expensive than you might have imagined, and the exotic nature of the company's itineraries make it a tempting choice.

Seawind Cruises (☎ **800/356-5566** or 305/573-3222) operates only one ship, the seaworthy but not particularly glamorous *Seawind Crown,* the only major cruise ship based in the southern Caribbean port of Aruba. This large ship carries only 624 passengers, allowing lots of room for wandering and relaxing. Most of its cruises last 7 nights, and focus on southern Caribbean islands that are too far from south Florida to be efficiently visited by most major cruise ships. They include Trinidad and Tobago, as well as Martinique, Curaçao, and St. Lucia. The line is adept at arranging land-based holidays, sometimes at incredibly low rates, either before or after a cruise, at hotels on Aruba, St. Lucia, or Martinique.

Tall Ship Adventures (☎ **800/662-0090** or 303/755-7983) has only one ship—a tall-masted, bare-boned reconfiguration of a circa-1917 schooner that was originally built to carry copper ore from the coast of Chile to the Baltic ports of Germany.

Today, after extensive refittings, it carries aficionados of sailing ships on meandering trips through the Virgin Islands. It focuses more intently on the scattered islets of the BVI than any other cruise line, spending most of its winter exploring such relatively remote outposts as Peter Island, Norman Island, Cooper Island, Marina Cay, Long Bay, and sites on or slightly offshore from Virgin Gorda. Cruises last a week, begin and depart from Roadtown, on Tortola, and seem rather like an unpretentious but invigorating fraternity-party experience.

Windjammer Barefoot Cruises (☎ **800/327-2601** or 305/672-6453) are similar in ambience to the above-mentioned Tall Ship Adventures, but this outfit operates seven sailing ships, most of which are faithful renovations of antique schooners or sail-driven private yachts. Although they encourage participants to double and triple up, and in some cases, even share dormitory-style accommodations with up to six berths, most have illustrious antecedents, including stints as the private getaway ships of sometimes notorious billionaires or wanna-bes. They're proud of being the least expensive and least formal outfit afloat; few passengers ever bring more than sneakers, T-shirts, shorts, and a bathing suit for their time aboard. The armada goes to rarely visited islands, with special emphasis on the Virgin Islands and the Grenadines. If you're looking for something a bit more staid, consider the fleet's durable but not-very-exciting supply ship, *Amazing Grace,* a freighter-style vessel that carries provisions and supplies for the company's other (sailing) ships. Stops for this vessel include virtually everything between Freeport, The Bahamas, and Trinidad, and are covered within a span of 13 days.

MORE WAYS TO CUT CRUISE COSTS

Here are some more suggestions to save money when you're negotiating your cruise package.

REPOSITIONING CRUISES   You can get good deals on "repositioning cruises," which occur when ships leave one destination to sail south to the Caribbean. These cruises tend to have lower costs per mile traversed than those solely in the Caribbean. But there will be fewer stops at ports of call, and your cruise will include long stretches of time exclusively at sea.

BACK-TO-BACK CRUISES   When you can't decide where in the Caribbean you want to cruise, consider taking a "back-to-back" cruise—two cruises, one right after another. You'll be on the same ship, but you'll be visiting different ports on the second phase of your journey. And you'll sail with a different set of passengers.

Cruise lines offer big discounts to passengers who book what is in essence a double cruise. Some offer a third week free if you're already combining 2 weeks together, whereas others grant a flat discount of up to 50% on your second cruise. Carnival, for example, offers back-to-back discounts combining 4-day cruises to Cozumel and Key West with 3-day cruises to The Bahamas. Your back-to-back scheduling can combine an almost unlimited number of cruises of long or short duration.

SAIL-AND-STAY PROMOTIONS   Cruises are now departing from ports of embarkation that are tourist attractions in their own right. You might want to explore Miami or drive to Walt Disney World from Port Canaveral or spend a few days in San Juan.

Many cruise lines negotiate group discounts at hotels for passengers interested in prolonging their vacation. These packages usually include transportation from the docks to the hotel (after a cruise) or from the hotel to the ship (before the cruise).

UNADVERTISED SPECIALS   Most passengers don't know that cruise lines often advertise different prices for the same cruise in different American cities. Fares advertised in Atlanta, for example, might not be promoted or advertised in New York. These lower fares are known in the business as "unadvertised regional specials."

How can you, a New Yorker or Chicagoan, get the same discount available to a passenger from Los Angeles or Atlanta? Contact **Cruises of Distinction,** 2750 S. Woodward, Bloomfield Hills, MI 48304 (☎ **800/634-3445** or 810/332-2020). A discount broker that stays on top of unadvertised or underpublicized specials, it can book a cruise on virtually any ship anywhere in the world. Established clients of the agency receive a roster of mailings sent out to the agency, but if you're a neophyte and tell a phone representative there what line you prefer and what some of your preferences are, chances are that you'll be added to one or another of the firm's mailing lists for future sales promoted by one or another of the Caribbean's cruise lines.

TWO-FERS   Promotions called "two-fers"—2-for-1 deals that let you bring a companion free—come and go like hurricane winds, so if you see one, it's worth considering. A cruise specialist should know if some cut-rate discount for two is being offered at the time you plan to sail. (These deals don't happen during the peak winter season in the Caribbean.)

You'll have to negotiate these two-fers carefully, and compare them with various air/sea packages to see if you're indeed getting a discounted deal. If airfare is included for both of you, then go for it. But if airfare has to be booked separately, compare the cost of a two-fer without airfare to an air/sea package for two to see which one is the better deal.

DISCOUNTS FOR A THIRD OR FOURTH PASSENGER   If you're willing to be a bit crowded in your room and have some very good friends you'd like to cruise with, you can save money by sharing your cabin with a third or fourth passenger. Many lines, especially those with older ships, still offer cabins that can house a total of three or four passengers. Depending on the season and their special promotions, many lines—especially those with older ships that struggle to compete with the new crop of megaships being launched—will offer a massively discounted rate for the third and/or fourth passenger sharing a cabin with two passengers paying a *regular* fare. For example, sailings aboard three members of NCL's fleet (*Norway, Dreamward,* and *Windward*) offer per diem rates in deluxe inside cabins on sailings during November and early December at a daily per-person rate of $57 for the first two occupants, and an almost embarrassingly low $14.30 daily rate for third or fourth occupants. Port taxes and airfare, naturally, are additional, but at these rates it's more expensive to stay at home. Per diem rates on somewhat more prestigious, better-accessorized ships, such as Princess Cruises *Star Princess,* are also worth a second look. If four occupants share a communal inside cabin, the daily per-person rate on some November sailings goes as low as $108 for each of the four occupants, not including airfare and port charges.

GROUP BOOKINGS   Travel agents are especially good at coordinating widely scattered members of a group that plans to travel together. Many lines offer reduced rates to groups of 10 passengers or more, making cruise ships appropriate for family reunions and the like. Discounts for this type of group travel can be significant, but are wholly determined by the cruise line and seasonal demand at the time.

Some high-volume cruise agencies may be able to team you up with a "group" the agency is booking aboard a certain ship—ask about the possibility. Unlike group travel on land, shipboard groups are not herded about as a community and, of course, have individual cabins.

AVOIDING THE SINGLE PENALTY   When booking a cabin, you'll pay a premium for traveling alone. Most ships impose a supplement of between 125% and

200% of the per-person price for single occupancy of a double cabin. To avoid this penalty, you could let the cruise line match you with a (same-sex) stranger in a shared cabin. Some devoted party lines like Carnival will put up to four single cruisers in a quad cabin at bargain-basement prices. You'll lose your privacy, but you'll love the price: around $275 per person for 3 days, $395 for 4 days, and $650 for a week.

You could also tap into the "singles" and "senior singles" phone network run by **The Cruise Line, Inc.,** 150 NW 168th St., North Miami Beach, FL 33169 (☎ **800/777-0707**). When you call this number, you'll hear information geared to general passenger needs before you get to information pertinent to the solo traveler.

SENIOR CITIZEN DISCOUNTS   The cruise industry offers more discounts to seniors (usually defined as anyone 55 years or older) than almost any targeted group. So don't keep your age a secret. Membership in any of dozens of clubs, such as the AAA or AARP, can afford discounts of anywhere from 5% to 50%. Always ask when you're booking.

The nonprofit **National Council of Senior Citizens,** 1331 F St. NW, Washington, DC 20004 (☎ **202/347-8800**), charges $12 per person or couple, for which you receive 11 issues annually of a newsletter that's devoted partly to travel tips, including cruises. Membership benefits include discounts on hotels, motels, and auto rentals.

These tour operators also keep on top of cruise industry discounts, and in some cases, configure blocks of cabins aboard selected cruise ships that are sold, for the most part, to established clients composed mostly of mature travelers. **Grand Circle Travel** (☎ **800/221-2610** or 617/350-7500) offers experiences aboard such ships as Celebrity's *Meridien* where most of the clients will be like-minded senior citizens looking for competitive prices and a special understanding of their priorities and needs. For a free booklet entitled *101 Tips for the Mature Traveler,* write to Grand Circle Travel, 347 Congress St., Boston, MA 02110. Under the same administration is an outfit geared to more adventurous forms of travel for groups that almost never exceed 16 participants: **Overseas Adventure Co.,** 625 Mount Auburn St., Cambridge, MA 02138 (☎ **800/221-0814**).

REPEAT PASSENGER PROGRAMS   If you've cruised before and are considering booking on the same line, be sure to ask what discounts might be available for repeat passengers. Cruise lines try to hold on to passengers by coddling them with perks—maybe champagne and flowers in the cabin, cabin upgrades, cocktail receptions with the ship's officers, and price incentives. Some lines, including Cunard, offer a frequent flyer–type program with "sailing miles" that are redeemable for cabin upgrades or discounted cruises. Other lines offer free trip-cancellation and medical insurance.

IT NEVER HURTS TO ASK   It's amazing what can happen if you imply that you can't book a cruise unless the deal is sweetened. So just ask for a complimentary cabin upgrade, free shore excursions, or free wine with dinner on your anniversary, or free or discounted lodging at a company-owned hotel before or after your cruise. It never hurts to ask.

6 Terrific Deals on Packages & Tours

One of the best ways to save money on your Caribbean vacation is booking a package. Some package deals only include airfare and hotel accommodations, usually at much lower prices than what you'd pay if you'd booked each component yourself.

In some cases, they might include minivan, bus, or taxi transfers between the airport and your hotel. And if you specifically request it, the package might also include optional add-ons, such as reduced prices on scuba lessons or sailing excursions. Packages to the Caribbean are peddled through every travel agency in the world.

To save time comparing the price and value of all the package tours out there, consider calling **TourScan, Inc.,** P.O. Box 2367, Darien, CT 06820 (☎ **800/ 962-2080** or 203/655-8091). Every season the company computerizes the contents of travel brochures containing about 10,000 different vacations at 1,600 hotels in the Caribbean, The Bahamas, and Bermuda. TourScan selects the best-value vacation at each hotel and condo. Two catalogs are printed each year, which list a choice of hotels on most of the Caribbean islands, in all price ranges. Write to TourScan for their catalogs costing $4 each, the price of which is credited to any TourScan vacation.

Another good deal might be a combined land-and-air package offered by one of the major U.S. carriers. Call their toll-free numbers: **American Airlines Fly-Away Vacations** (☎ **800/433-7300**) or **Delta's Dream Vacations** (☎ **800/872-7786**). **TWA Getaway Vacations** (☎ **800/GETAWAY**) specializes only in cruises, and **United Airlines Vacations** (☎ **800/328-6877**) features only San Juan.

Other tour operators include the following:

Caribbean Concepts Corp., 575 Underhill Blvd., Syosset, NY 11791 (☎ **800/ 423-4433** or 516/496-9800), offers low-cost air-and-land packages to the islands, including apartments, hotels, villas, and condo rentals, plus local sightseeing (which can be arranged separately).

Caribbean Travel Naturally, P.O. Box 897, Lutz, FL 33549 (☎ **800/462-6833** or 813/948-1303), offers clothing-optional tours at nudist resorts and cruises through the West Indies.

The best diving cruises are packaged by **Oceanic Society Expeditions,** Fort Mason Center, Building E, San Francisco, CA 94123 (☎ **800/326-7491** or 415/ 441-1106). Whale-watching jaunts and some research-oriented trips are also a feature. Another specialist in this field is **Tropical Adventures,** 111 Second Ave. N., Seattle, WA 98109 (☎ **800/247-3483** or 206/441-3483). Its packages to Saba are a diver's dream.

AIB Tours, 2500 NW 79th Ave., Suite 211, Miami, FL 33122 (☎ **800/ 242-8687,** or 305/715-0056 in Florida), offers tours to Aruba, Bonaire, and Curaçao.

Nature lovers prefer **Ecosummer Expeditions,** 1516 Duranleau St., Vancouver, B.C., Canada V6H 3S4 (☎ **800/465-8884** or 604/669-7741).

Renaissance Vacations, 2655 Lejeune Rd., Suite 400, Coral Gables, FL 33134 (☎ **800/874-0027**), offers deals to Ocho Rios (Jamaica), St. Thomas, Santo Domingo, and Grenada. **Horizon Tours,** 1010 Vermont Ave. NW, Suite 202, Washington, DC 20005 (☎ **888/SUN-N-SAND** or 202/393-8390), specializes in good deals for all-inclusive resorts in The Bahamas, Jamaica, Aruba, Puerto Rico, Antigua, and St. Lucia.

Club Med, Club Med Sales, P.O. Box 4460, Scottsdale, AZ 85261-4460 (☎ **800/258-2633**), has various all-inclusive options throughout the Caribbean and the Bahamas.

Globus, 5301 S. Federal Circle, Littleton, CO 80123 (☎ **800/851-0728,** ext. 518), gives escorted island-hopping expeditions to three or four islands, focusing on the history and culture of the West Indies.

Finally, advertising more packages to The Bahamas and the Caribbean than any other agency is **Liberty Travel,** with offices in many states, including 69 Spring St., Ramsey, NJ 07446 (☎ **201/934-3500**).

PACKAGES FOR BRITISH TRAVELERS   Package tours can be booked through **British Virgin Islands Holidays,** 11–13 Hockerill St., Bishop's Stortford, Herts CM23 2DH (☎ **01279/656111**). This company is the major booking agent for all the important hotels in the B.V.I. Stays can be arranged in more than one hotel if you'd like to visit more than one island. The company also offers staffed yacht charters and bareboat charters.

   Caribbean Connection, Concorde House, Forest Street, Chester CH1 1QR (☎ **01244/341131**), offers all-inclusive packages (airfare and hotel) to the Caribbean and customizes tours for independent travel. Other Caribbean specialists operating out of England include: **Kuoni Travel,** Kuoni House, Dorking, Surrey RH5 4AZ (☎ **01306/740888**); and **Caribtours,** 161 Fulham Rd., London SW3 6SN (☎ **0171/581-3517**), a small, very knowledgeable outfit that focuses on Caribbean travel and tailors individual itineraries.

7 Getting the Best Value Out of Your Accommodations

UNDERSTANDING THE RATES   Nearly all islands charge a government tax on hotel rooms, usually $7^1/_2$%, but that rate varies from island to island. This tax mounts quickly, so ask if the rate you're quoted includes this room tax. Sometimes the room tax depends on the quality of the hotel, relatively low for a guest house but steeper for a first-class resort. Determine the tax before you accept the rate.

   Furthermore, most hotels routinely add 10% to 12% for "service," even if you didn't like the service or didn't see much evidence of it. That means that with tax and service, some bills are 17% or even 25% higher than originally quoted to you! Naturally, you need to determine just how much the hotel, guest house, or inn plans to add to your bill at the end of your stay.

   That's not all. Some hotels slip in little hidden extras that mount quickly. For example, it's common for many establishments to quote rates that include a continental breakfast. Should you prefer ham and eggs added to the order, that will mean extra charges. Sometimes if you request special privileges, such as extra towels for the beach or laundry done in a hurry, surcharges mount. It pays to watch those extras.

WHAT THE ABBREVIATIONS MEAN   Rate sheets often have these classifications that we've also used in this guide:

   MAP (Modified American Plan) usually means room, breakfast, and dinner, unless the room rate has been quoted separately, and then it means only breakfast and dinner.

   CP (Continental Plan) includes room and a light breakfast.

   EP (European Plan) means room only.

   AP (American Plan) includes your room plus three meals a day.

HOTELS & RESORTS   Many budget travelers skip the big hotels and resorts because of their "impossible" prices. However, there are so many deals going on, even in winter, that some investigation might yield surprises. A savvy travel agent can help. Some hotels are often quite flexible about their rates, and many offer discounts and upgrades whenever they have a big block of rooms to fill and few reservations. The smaller hotels and inns are not as likely to be as generous in coming forth with discounts, much less upgrades. Even if you book into one of these bigger hotels, ask for the cheaper rooms—that is, those that don't open directly onto the ocean. Caribbean hoteliers charge dearly for the view alone.

ALL-INCLUSIVE RESORTS   The promises are persuasive: "Forget your cash, put your plastic away." Presumably, everything's all paid for in advance at an "all-inclusive" resort. But is it?

The all-inclusives have a reputation for being expensive, and many of them are, especially the giant SuperClubs of Jamaica or even the Sandals properties (unless you book in a slow period or off-season).

In the 1990s, so many competitors have entered the all-inclusive game that the term means different things to the various resorts using that form of marketing. The ideal all-inclusive is just that—a place where everything, even drinks and water sports, is included. But in the most narrow sense it means a room and three meals a day, with drinks, sports, cigarettes, whatever, appearing as extra charges. Of course, when booking it's important to ask and to understand exactly what's included in your so-called all-inclusive. Water-sports programs and offerings vary greatly at the various resorts. Extras might include options for horseback riding or sightseeing on the island.

The all-inclusive market is geared to the active traveler who likes to participate in organized entertainment, a lot of sports, and workouts at fitness centers, and who also likes a lot of food and drink.

If you're single or gay, avoid Sandals. If you have young children, stay away from Hedonism II in Negril, Jamaica, which lives up to its name. Even some Club Meds are targeted more for singles and couples, although many now aggressively pursue the family market. Some Club Meds have Mini Clubs, Baby Clubs, and Teen Clubs at some of its properties, at least during holiday and summer seasons.

This guide doesn't review the high-priced all-inclusives, but does preview the resorts possible for the traveler on a budget—for example, only one Sandals in Jamaica (see Montego Bay in chapter 11) falls in the price range of the budget traveler. Forget Jamaica's SuperClubs—consider one of the Jack Tar Villages, including those in Jamaica (Montego Bay), the Dominican Republic (north coast), and St. Kitts instead. The Pineapple resort on Antigua is at least moderate in price, a good splurge choice, and most Club Meds fall within the moderate (if not budget) range.

The trick is to look for that special deal and to travel in off-peak periods, which doesn't always mean just from mid-April to mid-December. Discounts are often granted during certain slow periods—called "windows"—for hotels, most often after the New Year's holiday. If you want a winter vacation at an all-inclusive, choose the month of January—not February or the Christmas holidays, when prices are at their all-year high.

One good deal might be Club Med's "Wild Card," geared to singles, couples, and families. Reservations must be made 2 or more weeks prior to departure. One week prior to departure, Club Med advises passengers which "village" on which island they're going to. If this uncertainty doesn't bother you, you can save $150 to $300 per weekly package. The complete per-person Wild Card cost for a week's package is a flat $999, while two adults and two children pay $2,999. Each package includes round-trip air transportation from New York, double-occupancy accommodations, all meals with complimentary wine and beer (other alcoholic drinks extra), use of all sports facilities except scuba (extra charges), nightly entertainment, and other recreational activities such as boat rides, snorkeling expeditions, and picnics. For more information call ☎ **800/CLUB-MED.**

Consult a good travel agent for other good deals that might be available.

GUEST HOUSES   An entirely different type of accommodation is the guest house, where most of the Antilleans themselves stay when they travel. In the Caribbean, the term *guest house* can mean anything. Sometimes so-called guest houses are really like simple motels built around swimming pools. Others are small individual cottages, with their own kitchenettes, constructed around a main building in which you'll often find a bar and a restaurant serving local food. Some are surprisingly comfortable, often with private baths and swimming pools. You may or may not have air-conditioning.

For value, the guest house can't be topped. You can always journey over to a big beach resort and use its seaside facilities for only a small charge, perhaps no more than $4. Although bereft of frills, the guest houses we've recommended are clean and safe for families or single women. The cheapest ones are not places where you'd want to spend time, because of their simple, modest furnishings.

COOKING FOR YOURSELF   Particularly if you're a family or a group of friends, a "housekeeping holiday" can be one of the least expensive ways to vacation in the Caribbean. Accommodations with kitchens are now available on nearly all the islands. Some are individual cottages you can rent, others are housed in one building, and some are private homes rented when the owners are away. Many self-catering places have maid service included in the rental, and you're given fresh linen as well.

In the simpler rentals, doing your own cooking and laundry or even your own maid service may not be your idea of a good time in the sun, but it saves money—a lot of money.

The disadvantages to many of these self-catering cottages is that they're in inaccessible places, which may mean you'll need a car. Public transportation on any island in the Caribbean is simply inadequate, if it exists at all.

You have to approach these rental properties with a certain sense of adventure and a do-it-yourself independence. These rentals are not for everybody, but they can make a Caribbean vacation possible for families or other groups on a tight budget.

For a list of agencies to arrange rentals, refer to the hotel sections of the individual island chapters.

PRIVATE APARTMENTS, EFFICIENCIES & COTTAGES   There are lots of private apartments for rent, either with or without maid service. This is more of a no-frills option than a villa or condo. The apartments may not be in buildings with swimming pools, and they may not have a front desk to help you.

Cottages are the most freewheeling way to stay. Most are fairly simple; many open onto a beach, whereas others may be clustered around a communal swimming pool. Many contain no more than a simple bedroom with a small kitchen and bath. For the peak winter season, reservations should be made at least 5 or 6 months in advance.

Dozens of agents throughout the United States and Canada offer these types of rentals; we've noted some in the destination chapters that follow. You can also write to local tourist offices for good suggestions.

Travel experts agree that savings, especially for a family of three to six people, or two or three couples, can range from 50% to 60% of what a hotel would cost. If there are only two in your party, these savings don't apply. However, groceries are sometimes priced 35% to 60% higher than the average on the U.S. mainland because nearly all foodstuffs have to be imported. Even so, preparing your own food will be a lot cheaper than dining at restaurants.

8 Getting Married in the Caribbean

If you yearn to take the plunge on a sun-dappled island, here are some wedding basics on the islands:

ANTIGUA   There is a 24-hour waiting period for marriages on Antigua. A couple appears at the Ministry of Justice in the capital of St. John to complete and sign a declaration before a marriage coordinator and pays a $150 license fee. The coordinator will arrange for a marriage officer to perform a civil ceremony at any of Antigua's hotels or another place the couple selects. The fee for the marriage officer is $50. Several hotels and resorts offer wedding/honeymoon packages. For more information on civil or religious wedding ceremonies, contact the **Antigua Department of Tourism,** 610 Fifth Ave., Suite 311, New York, NY 10020 (☎ 212/541-4117).

ARUBA   Civil weddings are possible on Aruba only if one of the partners is an Aruban resident. However, couples can arrange Roman Catholic, Protestant, and Jewish weddings on the island. For more information about planning a wedding on Aruba, contact the **Aruba Tourism Authority,** 1000 Harbor Blvd., Weehawken, NJ 08707 (☎ 800/TO-ARUBA or 201/330-0800).

BARBADOS   Couples can now marry the same day they arrive on Barbados, but must first obtain a marriage license from the **Ministry of Home Affairs** (☎ 246/228-8950). Bring either a passport, or a birth certificate and photo ID, $50 (U.S.) in fees, and $12.50 for the revenue stamp that can be obtained at the local post office, a letter from the authorized officiant who will perform the service, plus proof, if applicable, of pertinent deaths or divorces of any former spouse(s). A Roman Catholic wedding on Barbados carries additional requirements. For more information, contact the **Barbados Tourism Authority,** 800 Second Ave., New York, NY 10017 (☎ 800/221-9831 or 212/986-6516).

BONAIRE   The bride and/or groom must have a temporary residency permit, obtained by writing a letter to the governor of the Island Territory of Bonaire, Wilhelminaplein 1, Kralendijk, Bonaire, N.A. The letter, submitted within 2 months of departure for Bonaire, should request permission to marry on Bonaire, apply for temporary residency, as well as inform the governor of your arrival and departure dates and the date you wish to marry. The partner who applies for residency must be on island for 7 days prior to the wedding. A special dispensation must be issued by the governor if there is less than a 10-day time period between the announcement of the marriage and getting married. In addition, send three passport photos, copies of the bride's and groom's passports, birth certificates, and proof of divorce or in the case of widows and widowers, the death certificate of the deceased spouse.

If you desire, you can arrange your wedding on Bonaire through **Multro Travel and Tours,** Attn: Mrs. Marvel Tromp, Kaya Amazon 27B (P.O. Box 237), Bonaire, N.A. (☎ 599/7-8334; fax 599/7-8834), or check with the hotel where you're planning to stay. Some hotels arrange weddings on special request. For further information, contact the **Bonaire Tourist Office** (☎ 800/826-6247 or 212/956-5911).

BRITISH VIRGIN ISLANDS   There is no requirement of island residency, but a couple must apply for a license at the attorney general's office, and must stay in the B.V.I. for 3 days while the application is processed. Present a passport or original birth certificate and photo identification, plus certified proof of your marital status, plus any divorce or death certificates that apply to any former spouse(s). Two witnesses must accompany the couple. The fee is $110. Marriages can be performed by the local registrar or by the officiant of your choice. Contact the Registrar's Office, P.O. Box 418, Road Town, Tortola, B.V.I. (☎ 809/494-3701 or 809/494-3492).

CAYMAN ISLANDS   Visitors must first arrange for a marriage officer prior to arriving in the Cayman Islands in order to name the individual who will be officiating on the application. The application for a special marriage license, which costs $200, can be obtained from the **Deputy Secretary's Office,** Third Floor, Government Administration Building, George Town (☎ **345/949-7900**). There is no waiting period. Present a birth certificate plus the embarkation/disembarkation cards issued by the island's immigration authorities, along with divorce decrees or proof of a spouse's death (if applicable). Complete wedding services and packages are offered by **Cayman Weddings of Grand Cayman,** which is owned and operated by Caymanian marriage officers Vernon and Francine Jackson. For more information, contact them at P.O. Box 678, Grand Cayman (☎ **345/949-8677;** fax 345/949-8237). A brochure, **Getting Married in the Cayman Islands,** is available from Government Information Services, Broadcasting House, Grand Cayman (☎ **345/949-8092;** fax 345/949-5936).

CURAÇAO   Couples must be on-island 2 days before applying for a marriage license, for which there is a 14-day waiting period. Passport, birth certificate, return ticket, and divorce papers (if applicable) are required. The fee is subject to change, so check in advance. For further information, call the **Curaçao Tourist Board,** 475 Park Ave. S., Suite 2000, New York, NY 10016 (☎ **212/683-7660;** fax 212/683-9337).

JAMAICA   In high season, some Jamaican resorts witness several weddings a day. Many of the larger Jamaican resorts can arrange for an officiant, a photographer, and even the wedding cake and champagne. Some resorts, however, will even throw in your wedding with the cost of your honeymoon at the hotel. Both the Jamaican Tourist Board and your hotel will assist you with the paperwork. Participants must reside on Jamaica for 24 hours before the ceremony. Bring birth certificates and affidavits saying you've never been married before, or, if you've been divorced, bring copies of your divorce papers, or in the case of widows and widowers, a copy of the deceased spouses' death certificate. The cost of the license and stamp duty is $200. The cost of the ceremony can range from $50 to $200, depending on how much legwork you want to do yourself. You may apply in person at the **Ministry of National Security and Justice,** 12 Ocean Blvd., Kingston, Jamaica (☎ **809/922-0080**).

PUERTO RICO   There are no residency requirements. You'll need parental consent if either party is under 18. Blood tests are required, although a test conducted within 10 days of the ceremony on the U.S. mainland will suffice. A doctor in Puerto Rico must sign the license after conducting an examination of the bride and groom. For complete details, contact the **Commonwealth of Puerto Rico Health Department,** Demographic Register, 171 Quisaueya St., Hato Rey, PR 00917 (☎ **787/767-9120**).

ST. LUCIA   Both parties must have remained on the island for 48 hours prior to the ceremony. Present your passport or birth certificate, plus (if either participant has been widowed or divorced) proof of death or divorce from the former spouse(s). Before the ceremony it usually takes about 2 days to process all the paperwork. Fees run around $150 for a lawyer (one is usually needed for the application to the governor-general), $25 for the registrar to perform the ceremony, and $37.75 for the stamp duty and the license. Some resorts and vacation properties also offer wedding packages that include all the necessary arrangements for a single fee. For more information, contact the **St. Lucia Tourist Board,** 820 Second Ave., 9th Floor, New York, NY 10017 (☎ **212/867-2950;** fax 212/370-7867).

U.S. VIRGIN ISLANDS   No blood tests or physical examinations are necessary, but there is a $25 license fee, a $25 notarized application, and an 8-day waiting period, which is sometimes waived, depending on circumstances. Civil ceremonies before a judge of the territorial court cost $200 each; religious ceremonies performed by clergy are equally valid. Fees and schedules for church weddings must be negotiated directly with the officiant. More information is available from the **U.S. Virgin Islands Division of Tourism,** 1270 Ave. of the Americas, New York, NY 10020 (☎ 212/332-2222).

The guide *Getting Married in the U.S. Virgin Islands* is distributed by U.S.V.I. tourism offices; it gives information on all three islands, including wedding planners, places of worship, florists, and limousine services. The guide also provides a listing of island accommodations that offer in-house wedding services.

Couples can apply for a marriage license for St. Thomas or St. John by contacting the **Territorial Court of the Virgin Islands,** P.O. Box 70, St. Thomas, USVI 00804 (☎ 809/774-6680). For weddings on St. Croix, applications are available by contacting the Territorial Court of the Virgin Islands, Family Division, P.O. Box 929, Christiansted, St. Croix, USVI 00821 (☎ 809/778-9750).

9 Tips for Travelers with Special Needs

FOR TRAVELERS WITH DISABILITIES   You can obtain a free copy of **"Air Transportation of Handicapped Persons,"** published by the U.S. Department of Transportation. Write for Free Advisory Circular No. AC12032, Distribution Unit, U.S. Department of Transportation, Publications Division, 3341Q 75th Ave., Landover, MD 20785. Only written requests are accepted.

For names and addresses of operators of tours specifically for visitors with disabilities, and other relevant information, contact the **Society for the Advancement of Travel for the Handicapped (SATH),** 347 Fifth Ave., Suite 610, New York, NY 10016 (☎ 212/447-7284; fax 212/725-8253). Yearly membership dues in the society are $45, $25 for senior citizens and students. Send a self-addressed, stamped envelope and $5. SATH will also provide you with hotel/resort accessibility for Caribbean destinations.

The **Information Center for Individuals with Disabilities,** Fort Point Place, 27-43 Wormwood Place, Boston, MA 02210 (☎ 617/727-5540, or 800/462-5015 in Massachusetts), is another good source. It has lists of travel agents who specialize in tours for persons with disabilities, and provides travel-tip fact sheets for Caribbean destinations.

For people who are blind or visually impaired, the best source is the **American Foundation for the Blind,** 11 Penn Plaza, Suite 300, New York, NY 10001 (☎ 800/232-5463 to order information kits and supplies, or 212/502-7600). It acts as a referral source for travelers and can offer advice on the transport and border formalities for seeing-eye dogs.

One of the best organizations serving the needs of persons with disabilities is **Flying Wheels Travel,** 143 West Bridge (P.O. Box 382), Owatoona, MN 55060 (☎ 800/535-6790 or 507/451-5005). It offers customized, all-inclusive vacation packages in the Caribbean.

For a $25 annual fee, consider joining **Mobility International USA,** P.O. Box 10767, Eugene, OR 97440 (☎ 541/343-1284 voice & TDD). It answers questions on various destinations and also offers discounts on its programs, videos, and publications. Its quarterly newsletter, *Over the Rainbow,* provides information on Caribbean hotel chains, accessibility, and transportation.

Tips for British Travelers with Disabilities   The **Royal Association for Disability and Rehabilitation (RADAR),** Unit 12, City Forum, 250 City Rd., London, ECIV 8AF (☎ 0171/250-3222), publishes holiday "fact packs"—three in all, which sell for £2 each or all three for £5. The first one provides general information, including planning and booking a holiday, insurance, finances, and useful organization and holiday providers. The second outlines transportation available when going abroad and equipment for rent. The third deals with specialized accommodations.

FOR GAY & LESBIAN TRAVELERS   Some of the islands are more gay-friendly than others. These would include all the U.S. possessions—notably Puerto Rico, the "gay capital of the Caribbean," which offers an array of gay guest houses, nightclubs, bars, and discos. To a lesser extent, much of St. Thomas, St. John, and St. Croix are welcoming, though they have nowhere near the number of gay-oriented establishments as Puerto Rico.

The French islands—St. Barts, St. Martin, Guadeloupe, and Martinique—are technically an extension of mainland France, and the French have always regarded homosexuality with a certain blasé tolerance. The Dutch islands of Aruba, Bonaire, and Curaçao are quite conservative, so discretion is suggested.

Gay life is fairly secretive in many of the sleepy islands of the Caribbean. There are even some islands with repressive laws, including Jamaica and Barbados. Homosexuality is illegal on Barbados, and there is often a lack of tolerance here in spite of the large number of gay residents and visitors. Jamaica is the most homophobic island in the Caribbean, with harsh anti-gay laws, even though there's a large local gay population. One local advised that it's not smart for a white gay man to wander the streets of Jamaica at night.

Many all-inclusive resorts, notably the famous Sandals of Jamaica, have discriminatory policies. Although Sandals started off welcoming "any two people in love," they quickly switched to allowing only male-female couples. Gays are excluded from their love nests. However, not all all-inclusives practice such blatant discrimination.

Men can order *Spartacus,* the international gay guide ($32.95), or *Odysseus, The International Gay Travel Planner,* an annually published guide to international gay accommodations ($25). Both lesbians and gay men might want to pick up a copy of *Gay Travel A to Z* ($16), which specializes in general information, as well as listings of bars, hotels, restaurants, and places of interest for gay travelers throughout the world. These books and others are available from **Giovanni's Room,** 1145 Pine St., Philadelphia, PA 19107 (☎ **215/923-2960**).

Our World, 1104 N. Nova Rd., Suite 251, Daytona Beach, FL 32117 (☎ **904/441-5367**), is a magazine devoted to options and bargains for gay and lesbian travel worldwide. It costs $35 for 10 issues. *Out and About,* 8 W. 19th St., Suite 401, New York, NY 10011 (☎ **800/929-2268**), has been hailed for its "straight" reporting about gay travel. It profiles the best gay or gay-friendly hotels, restaurants, gyms, clubs, and other places, with coverage of destinations throughout the world. The cost is $49 a year for 10 information-packed issues, plus four events calendars. It aims for the more upscale gay male and lesbian traveler. Both these publications are also available at most gay and lesbian bookstores.

The **International Gay Travel Association (IGTA),** P.O. Box 4974, Key West, FL 33041 (☎ **800/448-8550**), encourages gay and lesbian travel worldwide. With around 1,200 member agencies, it specializes in networking, providing the information travelers would need for an individual traveler to link up with the appropriate gay-friendly service organization or tour specialist. It offers quarterly newsletters, marketing mailings, and a membership directory that's updated four times a year. Travel agents who are IGTA members will be tied into this organization's vast information resources.

FOR SENIORS   Write for a free booklet called **101 Tips for the Mature Traveler,** available from Grand Circle Travel, 347 Congress St., Suite 3A, Boston, MA 02210 (☎ **800/221-2610** or 617/350-7500). This tour operator offers extended vacations, escorted programs, and cruises that feature unique learning experiences for seniors at competitive prices.

SAGA International Holidays, 222 Berkeley St., Boston, MA 02116 (☎ **800/343-0273**), books travelers who are 50 plus on cruises to the Caribbean, offering them good value. Medical insurance is included in the net price of the cruise-ship booking.

Information on travel for seniors is also available from the **National Council of Senior Citizens,** 8401 Colesville Rd., Suite 1200, Silver Spring, MD 20910 (☎ **301/578-8800**). A nonprofit organization, the council charges a membership fee of $13 per couple for which you receive a monthly newsletter and membership benefits, including travel services, discounts on hotels, motels, and auto rentals, and also supplemental medical insurance.

Mature Outlook, P.O. Box 9390, Des Moines, IA 50306-9519 (☎ **800/336-6330**), is a travel organization for people more than 50 years of age. Members are offered discounts at ITC-member hotels and will receive a bimonthly magazine. Annual membership of $14.95 entitles its members to discounts on selected auto rentals and restaurants and in some cases discounted merchandise from Sears Roebuck Co.

4 The Cayman Islands

Don't go to the Cayman Islands expecting fast-paced excitement. Island life focuses on the sea. Snorkelers will find a paradise, beach lovers will relish the powdery sands of Seven Mile Beach—but party-hungry travelers in search of urban thrills might be disappointed.

The Caymans, 480 miles due south of Miami, consist of three islands: Grand Cayman, Cayman Brac, and Little Cayman. Despite its name, Grand Cayman is only 22 miles long and 8 miles across at its widest point. The other islands are considerably smaller, of course, and contain very limited tourist facilities, in contrast to well-developed Grand Cayman. George Town on Grand Cayman is the capital, and is therefore the hub of government, banking, and shopping.

English is the official language of the islands, although it's often spoken with an English slur mixed with an American southern drawl and a lilting Welsh accent.

The Cayman Islands tend to be expensive (the cost of living is about 20% higher than in the United States), but with careful planning you can make a trip here affordable, although there are a lot of cheaper places to visit in the Caribbean. The key is advance planning and traveling between mid-April and mid-December when prices are 20% to 40% lower. Winter vacations in the Caymans can be pricey affairs.

But in the past few years several low-cost or moderately priced lodgings have opened. Many of the inexpensive places have provisions for cooking simple meals, and if you shop the supermarkets you'll cut costs further. Because so much food has to be imported from the U.S. mainland, restaurant tabs are high. It's estimated that restaurant prices in the Caymans are second only to the high-priced French islands such as St. Barts and Martinique. We've included tips on how to save on dining costs in "Where to Eat," below.

GETTING THERE

The Cayman Islands are easily accessible. Flying time from Miami is 1 hour 20 minutes; from Houston, 2 hours 45 minutes; from Tampa, 1 hour 40 minutes; and from Atlanta, 3 hours 35 minutes. Only a handful of nonstop flights are available from the heartland of North America to Grand Cayman, so many visitors use Miami as their gateway.

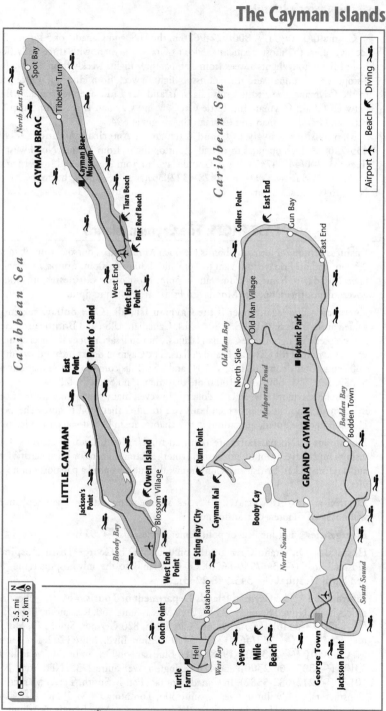

Airport ✈ Beach ⚓ Diving 🤿

Caribbean Sea

CAYMAN BRAC

North East Bay
Spot Bay
Tibbetts Turn
Cayman Brac Museum
Tiara Beach
Brac Reef Beach
West End
West End Point

LITTLE CAYMAN

East Point
Point o' Sand
Jackson's Point
Owen Island
Blossom Village
Bloody Bay
West End Point

Caribbean Sea

GRAND CAYMAN

Colliers Point
East End
Gun Bay
East End
Old Man Bay
Old Man Village
North Side
Malportas Pond
Botanic Park
Bodden Bay
Bodden Town
Rum Point
Sting Ray City
Cayman Kai
Booby Cay
North Sound
South Sound
Conch Point
Batabano
Turtle Farm
Hell
West Bay
Seven Mile Beach
George Town
Jacksson Point

N

0   3.5 mi
    5.6 km

2-0211

Cayman Airways (☎ 800/422-9626 in the U.S. and Canada, or 345/949-2311 locally) offers the most frequent service to Grand Cayman, with three daily flights from Miami, four flights a week from Tampa, three flights weekly from Atlanta (with a stopover in Tampa), and three nonstop flights a week from Houston. Once you're in the Caymans, the airline's subsidiary, **Island Air Ltd.,** operates frequent flights between Grand Cayman and Little Cayman and Cayman Brac. Round-trip fares between Grand Cayman and Cayman Brac begin at $94.

Many visitors also fly to Grand Cayman on **American Airlines** (☎ 800/433-7300), which operates three daily nonstop flights from Miami. **Northwest Airlines** (☎ 800/447-4747) flies to Grand Cayman from Detroit, and from Memphis via Miami. **US Airways** (☎ 800/428-4322) operates one daily flight from Charlotte, N.C., to Grand Cayman.

FAST FACTS: The Cayman Islands

Business Hours Normally, **banks** are open Monday to Thursday from 9am to 2:30pm and on Friday from 9am to 1pm and 2:30 to 4:30pm. **Shops** are usually open Monday to Saturday from 9am to 5pm. Most **other businesses,** including government offices, operate Monday to Friday from 9am to 5pm.

Currency The legal tender is the **Cayman Islands (C.I.) dollar,** currently valued at $1.25 U.S. ($1 U.S. = 80¢ C.I.). Canadian, U.S., and British currencies are accepted throughout the Cayman Islands, but you'll save money if you exchange your U.S. dollars for Cayman Island dollars. The Cayman dollar breaks down into 100 cents. Coins come in 1¢, 5¢, 10¢, and 25¢. Bills come in denominations of $1, $5, $10, $25, $50, and $100 (note that there is no $20 C.I. bill).

Most hotels quote rates in U.S. dollars. However, many restaurants quote prices in Cayman Islands dollars, which leads you to think that food is much cheaper. Unless otherwise noted, quotations in this chapter are in U.S. dollars, rounded off.

Documents No passports are required for U.S. or Canadian citizens, but visitors must have proof of citizenship (voter registration card or birth certificate) and a return ticket. British and Commonwealth subjects need a passport but not a visa.

Electricity It's 110 volts AC, 60 cycles, so American and Canadian appliances will not need adapters or transformers.

Emergencies For medical or police emergencies, dial ☎ **911.**

Hospitals On Grand Cayman, the only hospital is **George Town Hospital,** Hospital Road (☎ 345/949-8600). On Cayman Brac, the only hospital is the 18-bed **Faith Hospital** (☎ 345/948-2243).

Information The **Cayman Islands Department of Tourism** has the following offices in the United States: 9525 W. Bryn Mawr, Suite 160, Rosemont, IL 60018 (☎ 847/678-6446); Two Memorial City Plaza, 820 Gessner, Suite 170, Houston, TX 77024 (☎ 713/461-1317); 3440 Wilshire Blvd., Suite 1202, Los Angeles, CA 90010 (☎ 213/738-1968); 6100 Blue Lagoon Dr., Suite 150, Miami, FL 33126 (☎ 305/266-2300); and 420 Lexington Ave., Suite 2733, New York, NY 10170 (☎ 212/682-5582). In Canada, contact Earl B. Smith, Travel Marketing Consultants, 234 Eglinton Ave. E., Suite 306, Toronto, ON M4P 1K5 (☎ 416/485-1550). In the United Kingdom, the contact is Cayman Islands, 6 Arlington St., London, SW1A 1RE (☎ 0171/491-7771).

Taxes   A government tourist tax of 10% is added to your hotel bill. Also, a departure tax of $8 C.I. ($10) is collected when you leave the Caymans.

Telephone   The Cayman Islands are no longer part of the 345 Caribbean area code. Now the **area code** for the Cayman Islands is **345.** If you're calling within the Cayman Islands, omit the area code and dial all seven digits.

Time   Eastern standard time is in effect all year—daylight saving time is not observed.

Tipping   Many restaurants add a 10% to 15% charge in lieu of tipping. Hotels also add a 10% service charge to your bill.

1 Grand Cayman

The largest of the three islands and a real diving mecca, Grand Cayman is one of the hottest tourist destinations in the Caribbean. With more than 500 banks, its capital, George Town, is the offshore banking center of the Caribbean. Retirees are drawn to the peace and tranquillity of this British Crown Colony, site of a major condominium development. Almost all the Cayman Islands' population of 32,000 live on Grand Cayman. The civil manners of the locals reflect their British heritage.

GETTING AROUND

BY TAXI   All arriving flights are met by taxis. The rates are fixed by the director of civil aviation (☎ **345/949-7811**); typical one-way fares from the airport to Seven Mile Beach range from $10 to $12. Taxis (which can hold five people) will also take visitors on around-the-island tours. **Cayman Cab Team** (☎ **345/947-1173**) and **Holiday Inn Taxi Stand** (☎ **345/947-4491**) offer 24-hour service.

BY RENTAL CAR   If you want to rent a car, you'll find **Marshall's Rent-a-Car,** Owen Roberts Drive (at the airport; ☎ **345/949-7821**), usually cheaper than Hertz, Avis, and Budget. This local agent rents Toyotas, Chevrolets, Mazdas, and Nissans— all economy-size cars. The rate for most cars is $40 per day, dropping to $30 per day off-season, with unlimited mileage. The best-value deal: an off-season weekly rental of an economy car for $180 a week. You can also arrange to have a car picked up at the branch office along West Bay Drive (Seven Mile Beach). If Marshall can't hook you up, then try one of the old reliables: **Cico Avis** (☎ **800/527-0700** in the U.S. or 345/949-2468), **Ace Hertz** (☎ **800/654-3131** in the U.S. or 345/949-7861), and **Budget** (called Budget Rent-a-Car) (☎ **800/527-0700** or 345/949-8223). All three have offices at the airport. Each will issue the mandatory Cayman Islands driving permit for $5 (U.S.). All three require that reservations be made between 6 and 36 hours before pickup. At Avis, drivers must be at least 21 and at Hertz, 25. Budget requires that drivers be between 25 and 70 years old. All three require a valid driver's license and either a valid credit or charge card or a large cash deposit.

Remember to drive on the left and to reserve your car as far in advance as possible, especially in midwinter.

BY MOTORCYCLE OR BICYCLE   **Soto Scooters, Ltd.,** Seven Mile Beach (☎ **345/945-4652**), located at Coconut Place, offers Honda Elite scooters for $25 daily, or bicycles for $15 daily. It also offers Jeep and car rentals from $44 per day.

ESSENTIALS

The **Department of Tourism** is at the Pavilion Building, Cricket Lane (P.O. Box 67), George Town, Grand Cayman, B.W.I. (☎ **345/949-0623**). The best-located pharmacy is **Cayman Drug,** Kirk Freeport Centre, Panton Street (☎ **345/ 949-2597**) in George Town, open Monday to Saturday from 8:30am to 5:30pm. Also in George Town, the **post office** and **Philatelic Bureau** is on Edward Street (☎ **345/949-2474**), open Monday to Friday from 8:30am to 5pm and on Saturday from 8:30am to noon; a branch counter at the General Post Office and Philatelic Office at the Seven Mile Beach Post Office keeps the same hours. These offices sell the postage stamps for which the Cayman Islands are famous. These bureaus sell mainly stamps of recent issue, with a very limited supply of back issues.

WHERE TO STAY

True budget travelers will rent an apartment or condominium (shared with friends or families), so they can cut costs by cooking their own meals. Divers will want to find hotels or small resorts that include a half day's dive in their tariffs. Hotels, unlike many Caymanian restaurants, generally quote prices to you in U.S. dollars.

DOUBLES FOR LESS THAN $75 (WINTER) / $65 (OFF-SEASON)

✪ **Adam's Guest House.** Melmac Ave., George Town, Grand Cayman, B.W.I. ☎ **345/ 949-2512.** Fax 345/949-0919. 3 rms, 1 apt. A/C TV. Winter, $65 single; $75 double; $170 apt. Off-season, $55 single; $65 double; $150 apt. Year-round, $170 apt for four; $10 per person extra (up to a maximum of six). V (accepted only for room deposit; pay with cash or traveler's checks).

Tom and Olga Adam advertise their guest house as "the best at the lowest." While it may not be the best, this place is among the best values on the island. This 1950s-style West Indian ranch bungalow is located in a residential area a mile south of the capital of George Town, which is a long 4-mile haul from Seven Mile Beach. However, there's excellent snorkeling at Smith Cove Bay, only about a 10-minute walk away, and scuba-diving facilities—five different outfits—lie within a 5-minute stroll. For a restaurant and bar, you can stroll over to the Seaview Hotel, about 5 minutes away. A supermarket and a drugstore are also nearby, as are some breakfast places.

Each no-frills room has a private entrance, twin beds, a private bath, ceiling fans, and a compact refrigerator, along with a microwave and TV. The two-bedroom apartment, which can hold up to six, is ideal for families.

The Enterprise Bed & Breakfast. Selkirk Dr., Red Bay (P.O. Box 246, Savannah), Grand Cayman, B.W.I. ☎ **345/947-6009.** Fax 345/947-6010. 8 rms. A/C TV. Year-round, $63.80 single or double. Extra person $12. Rates include American breakfast. AE, MC, V (accepted for deposit only).

A 6-minute drive from the airport, this two-story white frame house is about a 10-minute ride from the sands of Seven Mile Beach. It's better to have a car if you stay here. A very helpful staff will welcome you and explain nearby options for diving, fishing, and snorkeling. The rooms are simply but comfortably furnished, containing such extras as a small refrigerator, kitchenette, bar sink, and microwave. There's a laundry nearby, and baby-sitting can be arranged if sufficient notice is given.

The place is definitely for *Star Trek* buffs, as pictures and posters of the cast and crew decorate the B&B—hence, its name. Naturally, videos of all *Star Trek* shows and movies are shown as well. No smoking.

DOUBLES FOR LESS THAN $100 (WINTER) / $80 (OFF-SEASON)

Ambassador's Inn. P.O. Box 1789, Grand Cayman, B.W.I. ☎ **800/648-7748** in the U.S. and Canada, or 345/949-7577. Fax 345/949-7050. 18 rms. A/C TV TEL. Winter (3-night minimum), $80 single; $90 double. Off-season, $70 single; $80 double. One or two children 11 and under stay free in parents' room. AE, MC, V.

This small, family-owned property conveys the feeling of the Caymans of long ago. It's a pink-walled concrete building beside an impossibly rocky beach—since many guests come here for the diving and snorkeling (and not for the beach life), no one seems to mind. Each accommodation, simplicity itself, has a ceiling fan, maid service, and radio.

Its location near Smith Cove guarantees privacy; you'll be removed from the frenzy of the more crowded (and much more expensive) beaches to the north. There's a freshwater pool and dive shop on the premises and an unpretentious restaurant (and bar) serving an American-style breakfast and lunch. You can grill your dinner on the outdoor barbecue.

✪ **Erma Eldemire's Guest House.** S. Church St. (P.O. Box 482), George Town, Grand Cayman, B.W.I. ☎ **345/949-5387.** Fax 345/949-6987. 5 rms, 3 apts. A/C. Winter, $80 single; $90 double; $100 apt. Off-season, $70 single; $80 double; $90 apt. No credit cards.

This casual and friendly place is owned by an old-time Caymanian, now in her 80s, who established the first guest house on the island. No one knows the island better than dear Mrs. Eldemire, who will not only regale you with tall tales of Caymanian life but might also share her recipe for coconut jelly. About a mile from the center of George Town and half a mile from the snorkeling favorite, Smith Cove Beach, this rambling West Indian ranch-style house offers bedrooms and studio apartments. The place is simple yet comfortable and suitable for families. Each room can take an extra guest at only $10 per night. Each unit has a private bath, air-conditioning, and a ceiling fan. Guests also have access to a refrigerator, toaster oven, hotplate, and coffeemaker. The apartments have their own kitchenettes, with maid service Monday to Saturday.

Within walking distance are dive sites, a snorkeling area, the "Cove" (a white sandy beach with crystal-clear water), and a number of restaurants. Seven Mile Beach lies 2 miles away, and the house is 3 miles from the airport. Families or groups might want to use the barbecue pit and the picnic table in the garden. A launderette is nearby. Across the street is a restaurant where you can order breakfast for $5.

Seaview Hotel. S. Church St., George Town, Grand Cayman, B.W.I. ☎ **345/945-0558.** Fax 345/945-0559. 15 rms. A/C. Winter, $85 single; $95 double. Off-season, $65 single; $75 double. Extra person $10. Children 11 and under stay free in parents' room. AE, MC, V.

As its name indicates, this seafront property lies on the south side of George Town, about a 10-minute walk from the downtown area or a 10-minute walk to the beach at Smith Cove. By car, it's about a 2- to 3-minute drive to Seven Mile Beach. One of the island's oldest properties, the hotel, built in 1951, still retains the somewhat dull look of that era. Under new management, it's being improved and upgraded, but is still a tin-roofed wooden hotel. Bright Caribbean fabrics have enlivened some rooms, and 10 accommodations face the ocean in a central verandah style. The on-site pool is large and inviting, and there's also an inside restaurant and bar, offering three meals a day, with rather excellent seafood. Boat dives can be arranged.

BEST BUDGET DIVE RESORTS

Coconut Harbour. S. Church St., George Town, Grand Cayman, B.W.I. ☎ **800/552-6281** in the U.S., or 345/949-7468. Fax 345/949-7117. 35 rms. A/C TV TEL. Winter, $338–$383 per person. Off-season, $312.50–$348.50 per person. Rates include 3-night package with 2 two-tank dives, plus continental breakfast. AE, MC, V.

This resort property just south of George Town, with a friendly staff and a convivial crowd, offers one of the best-value package deals for divers. There's excellent diving right offshore, and on site is a full-service dive shop operated by Parrots Landing (which you might check out even if you don't stay here). The clean and comfortable rooms, with kitchenettes, are furnished in a plain Florida-motel style. Upper rooms have balconies overlooking the sea, and lower accommodations open onto patios. There's daily housekeeping. The hotel operates an open-air bar, a good place for a drink, and a rather standard restaurant open until 10pm. There's also a large pool.

Sunset House. S. Church St. (P.O. Box 479), George Town, Grand Cayman, B.W.I. ☎ **800/ 854-4767** in the U.S., or 345/949-7111. Fax 345/949-7101. 59 rms. A/C TV TEL. Winter, $125– $195 single; $135–$205 double; $145–$215 triple; $155–$225 quad. Off-season, $100–$165 single; $110–$175 double; $120–$185 triple; $130–$195 quad. Children 11 and under stay free in parents' room. AE, DC, MC, V.

Of the many homey inns catering to divers, this is another good deal, although it's a better value if you're willing to team up in a triple or a quad instead of a single or double. However, some of the standard rooms are too small, and the furnishings are a bit frayed. Called a place "for divers by divers," it lies south of George Town on the Ironshore, a craggy limestone shoreline about an 8-minute walk from the beach at Smith Cove. The five light-pink concrete buildings are informally but thoughtfully managed. Many rooms have two doubles or two king-size beds along with a balcony or patio, and a refrigerator can be rented for another $5 a day. The hotel offers two pools—one freshwater, the other saltwater—plus a Jacuzzi. On the premises are a dive shop and the Cathy Church photo school. The Seaharvest restaurant is decidedly informal, serving standard fare, and the thatched-roof seaside "My Bar" is a drinking haven for divers. Even if you're not a guest, it's one of the best places on the island to go for a sundowner.

VILLA & CONDO RENTALS

Grand Cayman offers a wide choice of condominiums and villas and renting one can cut your accommodation costs considerably. Most are owned as second or third homes (or purely as untaxed investments) by absentee owners, and are available for short-term rentals by qualified vacationers.

Most places have some kind of kitchen or kitchenette as well as a washing machine and dryer (or access to coin-operated laundry facilities on-site). Some even have barbecue grills in the garden area, so you can stock up at a grocery store for a cookout. You may be able to arrange maid service. Or you can go for a bare-boned rental, even bringing from home your own sheets and towels.

There's no shortage of real-estate agents or management firms to show you the ropes. One of the best-known rental agencies is **Hospitality World Ltd.,** P.O. Box 30123, Grand Cayman, B.W.I. (☎ **800/232-1034** in the U.S., or 345/949-3458; fax 345/949-7054). It handles rentals for at least 14 condominium complexes on Grand Cayman, plus a handful of other developments on Little Cayman and Cayman Brac. Its offerings include the Seaview Hotel, set beside the respectable but not-very-glamorous neighborhood of South Sound. Winter rates for a double are as little as $89 per day, with a third person paying only $10 extra per day. Between April and mid-December, the bargains are better, with single, double, or triple occupancy of a unit priced at a mere $65 a day. And you can stay in a newer condo with nice amenities set directly beside Seven Mile Beach for not that much more: In winter, six people can share a condo with a kitchen and nearby laundry facilities for only $325 a day (around $54 per person). Off-season, the same unit rents for $200 a day.

Other well-recommended firms offer a different pool of condo rentals. These include **Reef House Ltd. Property Management,** P.O. 1540, Grand Cayman, B.W.I. (☎ 345/949-7093), and **Scales & Company Ltd.,** P.O. Box 1103, Grand Cayman, B.W.I. (☎ **345/947-4325**). Ask a rental agent when a condo is at its cheapest.

For more great deals, you can contact the following condo and villa rentals yourself. Try the **Grape Tree Cocoplum** (☎ **800/635-4824** in the U.S. and Canada, or 345/949-5640), **The Retreat at Rum Point** (☎ **345/947-9135**), or the **Victoria House Apartments** (☎ **345/947-4233**).

Calypso Cove. West Bay, Grand Cayman, B.W.I. ☎ **345/949-3730.** 7 units. A/C TV TEL. Winter, $100–$125 studio; $145 one-bedroom unit; $200 two-bedroom unit. Off-season, $65–$95 studio; $105 one-bedroom unit; $140 two-bedroom unit. Children 11 and under stay free in parents' room. MC, V.

Just a dozen or so steps from the northernmost fringe of Seven Mile Beach, this guest house run by Sonia and Leif Barkinge is often booked by airline employees stopping over on Grand Cayman. They know what a good bargain it is on this high-priced island. It's a condo facility, in two pink concrete-block buildings in West Bay, with three studios for two, two one-bedroom units for up to four, and two two-bedroom/two-bath units housing as many as six. The two-bedroom units are each equipped with a washer and dryer. All accommodations have full kitchens, ceiling fans, and front and back patios, and are furnished in standard style with various combinations of twin, queen-size, and king-size beds and sofa sleepers. The place has recently been upgraded, and maid service is available for an additional fee. There is no pool, restaurant, or bar on the premises, but a number of places are within walking distance.

BEST OFF-SEASON BETS

The best way to save money on Grand Cayman is to schedule your visit in spring, summer, or autumn, when the most luxurious accommodations are reasonably priced. Prices are more reasonable between mid-April and mid-December, and quite low during the not-very-popular months of May and October.

Morritt's Tortuga Club. East End (P.O. Box 496GT), Grand Cayman, B.W.I. ☎ **800/447-0309** in the U.S., or 345/947-7449. Fax 345/947-7669. 145 condos. A/C TV. Winter, $175–$205 studio; $230–$295 one-bedroon apt; $295–$375 two-bedroom townhouse; $325–$405 two-bedroom penthouse. Off-season, $145–$155 studio; $160–$180 one-bedroom apt; $225–$250 two-bedroom townhouse; $255–$280 two-bedroom penthouse. AE, DC, MC, V.

With its verandahs and beachfront position on the East End, this three-story condo cluster opens onto 8 secluded acres beside the sea. Off-season, double rooms rent for around $72.50 per person, but you'll pay even less if you share an accommodation for three (under $55 per person) or four (under $40 per person). There's a seafront restaurant for burgers, grilled fish, and salads, but you can buy groceries and cook in your own kitchen.

Pan-Cayman. West Bay Rd. (P.O. Box 440GT), Grand Cayman, B.W.I. ☎ **345/947-4002.** Fax 345/945-4011. 10 condos. A/C TV TEL. Winter, $305 two-bedroom apt; $390 three-bedroom apt. Off-season, $165–$185 two-bedroom apt; $245 three-bedroom apt. Additional person $35–$45 extra. DISC, MC, V.

Its design is a modern, tropical adaptation of a Georgian building, and the location, beside Seven Mile Beach, is quite desirable. Between April and early December, you can rent a condo with kitchen for $82.50 and up per person for two, from $55 for three, and from $41.50 per person for four to six. Contrast these rates with midwinter highs of as much as $305 for a two-bedroom unit, and you'll appreciate the seasonal savings. Maid service is part of the rental cost.

Silver Sands. West Bay Rd. (P.O. Box 205GT), Grand Cayman, B.W.I. ☎ **800/327-8777** in the U.S., or 345/949-3343. Fax 345/949-1223. 19 condos. A/C TV. Winter, $360–$370 two-bedroom apt; $440 three-bedroom apt. Off-season, $205–$210 two-bedroom apt; $290 three-bedroom apt. Additional person $20 extra. Children 10 and under stay free in parents' unit. Minimum stay 7 nights in winter, 3 nights in off-season. AE, MC, V.

On Seven Mile Beach, this property boasts a swimming pool and tennis courts. Divided into eight buildings of three stories each, Silver Sands is large enough to offer plenty of available accommodations throughout the off-season at favorable rates. A three-bedroom unit breaks down to a per-person price of $145 for two, under $72 for four, and $48 for six. One or two children under 12 stay free in their parents' room. Laundry facilities are on the premises, and you can feed an army in the in-house kitchen.

Sleep Inn Hotel. West Bay Rd. (P.O. Box 30111), Grand Cayman, B.W.I. ☎ **345/949-9111.** Fax 345/949-6699. 115 rms, 6 suites. A/C TV TEL. Winter, $115–$185 double; $155–$195 junior suite for two. Children 12 and under stay free in parents' room. AE, DC, DISC, MC, V.

Even during high season, when doubles cost from $155 for two, this hotel is one of the least expensive recommendable hotels on Grand Cayman. The Sleep Inn is the closest hotel on Seven Mile Beach to downtown George Town. During off-season, it's a rock-bottom bargain, with singles from $95, doubles from $53 per person, and quads from $36 per person. There are no cooking facilities, but since this is quite close to the burger joints and sandwich shops of George Town, no one seems to mind.

WHERE TO EAT

Make sure you understand which currency the menu is printed in. If it's not written on the menu, ask the waiter if the prices are in U.S. dollars or Cayman Island dollars, as this will make a big difference when you get your final bill.

Savvy travelers for years have gone to the huge all-you-can-eat buffet breakfast served at the **Holiday Inn Grand Cayman,** West Bay Road (☎ **345/947-4444**). Ask to be directed to the Verandah Dining Room. There, for only $8 C.I. ($10), you can fortify yourself almost for the whole day with dish after dish, including tropical fruits. The buffet is served Monday to Saturday from 7 to 11am and on Sunday from 7am to 2pm. There's also a nightly all-you-can-eat dinner buffet from 6 to 9pm for only $15.50 to $26.95 C.I. ($19.40 to $33.70), with barbecues on Wednesday and Saturday.

One of the best places for breakfast is the **Wholesome Bakery & Café,** North Church Street (☎ **345/949-7064**). It's also a good bet if you're planning a picnic as it does an excellent takeout. Breakfast prices range from $2.45 to $3.45 C.I. ($3.10 to $4.30), with overstuffed sandwiches going for $1.75 to $3.50 C.I. ($2.20 to $4.40). Throughout the day you can order main courses for $3.45 to $5.45 C.I. ($4.30 to $6.80). Place your order at the counter. Open Monday to Friday from 6:30am to 7pm, Saturday from 6:30am to 6pm, and Sunday from 6:30am to 4pm.

✪ **Big Daddy's Restaurant and Sports Bar.** West Bay Rd. ☎ **345/949-8511.** Reservations recommended at dinner. Main courses $4.95–$14.50 C.I. ($6.20–$18.15). AE, MC, V. Mon–Sat 8–11am, noon–4pm, and 5–10pm; Sun 4pm–midnight. INTERNATIONAL.

This bustling, big-windowed emporium of food and drink is set on the upper level of a concrete-sided building; look for the liquor store on the ground floor. One part of the restaurant is devoted to a woodsy, nautically decorated bar area, where TV screens broadcast either CNN or the day's big game. Three separate dining areas, more or less isolated from the activity at the bar, serve well-prepared food. Dishes include morning omelets, deli sandwiches, half-pound burgers, garlic shrimp, T-bone steaks, barbecued ribs, fresh catch of the day, country-fried steak, and such pasta dishes as fettuccine Alfredo.

Billy's Place. N. Church St., George Town. ☎ **345/949-0470.** Main courses $8–$19 C.I. ($10–$23.75); lunch $6–$17 C.I. ($7.50–$21.25). AE, DISC, MC, V. Mon–Fri 10:30am–10pm, Sun 5:30–10pm. JAMAICAN/CARIBBEAN/INDIAN.

Don't come here if you feel like dressing up and hitting the town. But if you like to stay in your T-shirt and shorts and enjoy the laid-back island style, this is the local favorite. A pink-and-blue house in the Kirk Shopping Center with flowers on both sides and a garden and fountain in front, it's the creation of Jamaican-born Billy MacLaren, a real raconteur. He wanders through the restaurant making sure everything is running smoothly, but he only sits with people he knows. While calypso and reggae rock in the background, you can check out the menu.

The Indian curries are the best on the island, as are the Jamaican-inspired jerk dishes such as chicken and pork. He even serves the island's only "jerk" pizza. Try one of the Indian pakoras (vegetable fritters) or tandoori chicken or shrimp. There's very little difference between the lunch and dinner menus except the prices.

Champion House. Eastern Ave. ☎ **345/949-2190.** Reservations recommended. Soups $2–$4 C.I. ($2.50–$5); main courses $5–$6 C.I. ($6.30–$7.50). No credit cards. Sun–Thurs 11:30am–midnight, Fri–Sat 11:30am–3am. WEST INDIAN.

The Champion House has two grades of restaurants; this particular location is the least expensive. Here you'll get down-home West Indian food such as curried goat and chicken, stewed beef, peppered steak, and barbecued beef and ribs. There's also a variety of fresh seafood, but the West Bay location has a greater selection. The casual and friendly atmosphere has a certain quaint charm about it.

✪ Chicken! Chicken! In the West Shore Centre, West Bay Rd., along Seven Mile Beach. ☎ **345/945-2290.** Reservations not accepted. Main courses $6.95–$9.95 C.I. ($8.70–$12.40); lunch specials $4.50–$5.95 C.I. ($5.65–$7.45). AE, MC, V. Daily 11am–10pm. CHICKEN.

The chicken is marinated in a sauce of lemon, lime, rosemary, parsley, garlic, and thyme and served with fresh vegetables. The dinners include your choice of two side dishes, including garlic-and-herb potatoes, wild-mushroom pilaf, sweet tarragon carrots, potato salad, spinach pesto pasta, and coleslaw. For a slightly different taste, this restaurant serves two kinds of chicken salad (one with ginger, oranges, soy sauce, and water chestnuts). For a finish they include the congo square, a chocolate brownie smothered in chocolate, coffee, and rum. This enterprise also offers fixed-price feasts for four or more people, including one for eight for $36.95 C.I. ($46.20).

✪ Corita's Copper Kettle. In Dolphin Center. ☎ **345/949-7078.** Reservations required. Main courses $8–$15; lunch $7–$8.50; Sun buffet $8. No credit cards. Mon–Sat 7:30am–4pm, Sun 7:30am–3pm. WEST INDIAN/AMERICAN.

This place is generally packed in the mornings when diners can enjoy not only a full American breakfast but also a wide selection of West Indian breakfast specialties. Included are green bananas served with fried dumplings, fried flying fish, and Corita's Special (ham, melted cheese, egg, and jelly all presented on a fried fritter). For lunch, the menu varies from salads to chicken and beef along with conch, turtle, or lobster prepared as burgers or served up in a hearty stew. On Sunday, Corita's offers a buffet laden with a mixture of local West Indian and American fare.

Crocodile Rock Café. In Falls Centre, West Bay Rd. (just north of the Holiday Inn Grand Cayman). ☎ **345/947-5288.** Main courses $6.95–$13.95 C.I. ($8.70–$17.40); lunch $4.95–$7.95 C.I. ($6.20–$9.90). MC, V. Mon–Fri 6:30am–10pm, Sat–Sun 7am–10pm. AMERICAN/INTERNATIONAL.

Formerly Eats Diner, this restaurant has changed ownership and now has a Hard Rock Cafe atmosphere, with a bright pink-and-blue interior. It serves hearty fare at reasonable prices. Lunch features salads, sandwiches, and burgers. Dinner spotlights stir-fries including Szechuan teriyaki and mix-and-match pastas (a selection of five with the choice of seafood, tomato, pesto, Alfredo, or meat sauce). Other dishes include black-bean soup, coconut shrimp, and rum-garlic shrimp. Breakfast can also be ordered, including eggs, toast, bacon, fruit juice, and coffee for $5.95 C.I. ($7.40).

Eats Café. In the Cayman Falls Shopping Center, West Bay Rd. ☎ **345/947-5288.** Main courses $4.95–$15 C.I. ($6.20–$18.75); lunch $4.95–$6.95 C.I. ($6.20–$8.70). AE, MC, V. Daily 6:30am–11pm. AMERICAN.

With a name like "Eats," you expect to do just that. And you will at this lively little spot, which is very casual and draws a good local crowd. It's located in a dull shopping center, in a brown wooden structure in front of the Hotel Westin. Inside, there's more dull brown, but the food is just fine. Many folks file in for breakfast and even come back for lunch, which is the usual fare of burgers and fries, pastas, fish and chips, and grilled chicken with various toppings. Dinner is hardly gourmet, but you get generally well-prepared platters of beef, chicken, and shrimp in generous portions.

Golden Pagoda. West Bay Rd., along Seven Mile Beach. ☎ **345/949-5475.** Reservations recommended in winter. Main courses $6–$19.50; lunches $7–$18.50 AE, MC, V. Mon–Fri 11:30am–2:30pm and 6–10pm, Sat–Sun 6–10pm. CHINESE.

Craving Chinese? This friendly restaurant is located in front of the Radisson Resort Grand Cayman on West Bay Road. When you see the sign TAKEE OUTEE, you've found it! In front is a fountain with a modest garden and a small, red bridge that leads to the front door. One house specialty is the mango chicken, a stir-fry dish with mango chutney, water chestnuts, and green peppers. The Hakka-style cooking features such fare as Mongolian beef, butterfly shrimp, Kung Pao chicken, and (the dish that the locals love) sweet-and-sour chicken.

☺ Liberty's West Bay. Reverend Blackman Rd., West Bay. ☎ **345/949-3226.** Main courses $7.50–$19.95 C.I. ($9.40–$24.95); lunch $7.50–$14.95 C.I. ($9.40–$18.70). MC, V. Daily 11am–10pm. CAYMANIAN.

Visitors rarely find this local dive in the center of the West Bay shopping area, but it offers some of the best values on the island, especially at its all-you-can-eat dinner buffets on Wednesday, Friday, and Sunday night, which cost $14.95 C.I. ($18.70). The place is a real dollar-stretcher, and a local patron told us that the food was "real he-man." Presumably by that he meant such regional fare as codfish and ackee (the national dish of Jamaica), curried goat, and zesty oxtail, the latter a might greasy but good. On many nights a "seafood feast" is offered up, with lobster, shrimp, and the local catch. At lunch you might opt for burgers and sandwiches.

WORTH A SPLURGE

Crow's Nest Restaurant. South Sound. ☎ **345/949-9366.** Reservations recommended. Main courses $11.95–$21.95 C.I. ($14.95–$27.45). AE, MC, V. Mon–Sat 11:30am–2pm and 5:30–10pm, Sun 5:30–10pm. CARIBBEAN.

With a boardwalk and terrace jutting onto the sands, this informal restaurant has a view of both Sand Cay and a nearby lighthouse. It's on the island's southwesternmost tip, a 4-minute drive from George Town. The restaurant is one of those places that evoke the Caribbean "the way it used to be." There's no pretense here—you get good, honest Caribbean cookery featuring grilled seafood. Try a daily special or perhaps sweet, tender Caribbean lobster. Other dishes include grilled tuna steak with ackee or Jamaican chicken curry with roast coconut. For dessert, try the banana toffee pie, if it's available.

BEACHES, WATER SPORTS & OUTDOOR PURSUITS

What they lack in nightlife, the Caymans make up for in water sports—fishing, swimming, waterskiing, and diving are among the finest in the Caribbean. *Skin Diver* magazine has written that "Grand Cayman has become the largest single island in the Caribbean for dive tourism." Coral reefs and coral formations encircle the islands and are filled with lots of marine life—which scuba divers are forbidden to disturb, by the way.

It's easy to dive close to shore, so boats aren't necessary, but there are plenty of boats and scuba facilities available. On certain excursions, we recommend a trip with a qualified divemaster. There are many dive shops for rentals, but they won't rent you scuba gear or supply air unless you have a card from one of the national diving schools, such as NAUI or PADI. Hotels also rent diving equipment to their guests, as well as arrange snorkeling and scuba-diving trips.

Universally regarded as the most up-to-date and best-equipped water-sports facility in the Cayman Islands, **Red Sail Sports** maintains its headquarters at the Hyatt Regency Grand Cayman, West Bay Road (☎ **800/255-6425** or 345/949-8745). Other locations are at the Westin Casuarina (☎ **345/949-8732**) and at Rum Point (☎ **345/947-9203**). They have a wide range of offerings, from deep-sea fishing to sailing, diving, and more. Red Sail can also arrange waterskiing for $75 per half hour (the cost can be divided among several people) and parasailing at $45 per ride.

What follows are the best options for a gamut of outdoor activities, arranged by subject.

BEACHES One of the finest in the Caribbean, Grand Cayman's ✪ **Seven Mile Beach,** which begins north of George Town, has sparkling white sands with Australian pines in the background. Beaches on the **east and north coasts** are also fine, as they're protected by an offshore barrier reef. In winter, the average water temperature is 80° Fahrenheit; it rises to 85° in summer.

FISHING Grouper and snapper are most plentiful for those who bottom-fish along the reef. Deeper waters turn up barracuda and bonito. The flats on Little Cayman are said to offer the best bonefishing in the world. Unfortunately, the costs for charter boats and experienced guides tend to be prohibitive, unless you can hook up with a party and go fishing with several other fishers.

GOLF It's not cheap, but it's the only game on the island. The **Britannia Golf Club,** next to the Hyatt Regency on West Bay Road (☎ **345/949-8020**), was designed by Jack Nicklaus and is unique in that it incorporates three different courses in one: a 9-hole championship layout, an 18-hole executive setup, and a Cayman course. The last was designed for play with the Cayman ball, which goes about half the distance of a regulation ball. The Britannia charges $50 to $80 for greens fees in season, $40 to $65 off-season. Cart rentals are $15 to $25; club rentals, $25.

SAILING **Red Sail Sports** (see above) rents 16-foot Prindle Cats for $40 per hour, depending on the time of day. One of the best-designed sailing catamarans in the Caribbean is berthed in a canal a short walk from the water-sports center. Some 65 feet in length, with an aluminum mast 75 feet tall, it's fast, stable, and exhilarating. A 10am-to-2pm sail to Stingray City, with snorkeling equipment and lunch included in the price of $60.50 per person, leaves once daily.

SCUBA DIVING Established in 1957, the best-known and best dive operation in the Cayman Islands is **Bob Soto's Diving Ltd.** (☎ **345/949-2022,** or 800/262-7686

Into the Deep: Submarine Dives

So scuba diving's not enough for you? You want to see the real undiscovered depths of the ocean? On Grand Cayman, you can take the *Atlantis* reef dive. It's expensive, but it's a unique way to go underwater—and it might be the highlight of your trip.

One of the island's most popular attractions is the ***Atlantis XI,*** Goring Avenue (☎ **800/887-8571** or 345/949-8296), a submersible that's 65 feet long, weighs 80 tons, and was built at a cost of $3 million to carry 48 passengers. You can view the reefs and colorful tropical fish through the 26 large viewpoints 2 feet in diameter, as it cruises at a depth of 100 feet through the maze of coral gardens at a speed of 1½ knots; a guide keeps you informed.

There are three types of dives. The premier dive, *Atlantis* Odyssey, features such high-tech extras as divers communicating with submarine passengers by wireless underwater phone and moving about on underwater scooters. This dive, operated both day and night, costs $82. On the *Atlantis* Expedition dive, you'll experience the reef and see the famous Cayman Wall; this dive lasts 55 minutes and costs $72. The *Atlantis* Discovery, costing $55, lasts 40 minutes and introduces viewers to the marine life of the Caymans. Children 4 to 12 are charged half price (no children under 4 allowed). *Atlantis XI* dives Monday to Saturday, and reservations are recommended 24 hours in advance.

to make reservations). Owned by Ron Kipp, the operation includes full-service dive shops at Treasure Island, the SCUBA Centre on North Church Street, and Soto's Coconut in the Coconut Place Shopping Centre. A full-day resort course, designed to teach the fundamentals of scuba to beginners who know how to swim, costs $90: The morning is spent in the pool and the afternoon is a one-tank dive from a boat. All necessary equipment is included. Certified divers can choose from a wide range of one-tank ($40 to $45) and two-tank ($60 to $65) boat dives daily on the west, north, and south walls, plus shore diving from the SCUBA Centre. Nondivers can take advantage of daily snorkel trips ($20), including Stingray City. The staff is helpful and highly professional.

Red Sail Sports (see above) offers beginners' scuba diving as well as excursions for the experienced. A two-tank morning dive includes exploration of two different dive sites at depths ranging from 50 to 100 feet, and costs $66. Beginners can take a daily course that costs $99 per person.

EXPLORING THE ISLAND

The capital, **George Town,** can easily be explored in an afternoon; stop by for its restaurants and shops (and banks!)—not sights. The town does offer a clock monument to King George V and the oldest government building in use in the Caymans today, the post office on Edward Street. Stamps sold here are avidly sought by collectors.

The island's premier museum, the **Cayman Islands National Museum,** Harbor Drive, in George Town (☎ **345/949-8368**), is in a much-restored clapboard-sided antique building directly on the water. (The verandah-fronted building served until recently as the island's courthouse.) The formal exhibits include a collection of Caymanian artifacts collected by Ira Thompson beginning in the 1930s. Today the museum incorporates a gift shop, theater, cafe, and more than 2,000 items portraying the natural, social, and cultural history of the Caymans. Admission is $4 C.I. ($5) for adults and $2 C.I. ($2.50) for children 7 to 12 and senior citizens, free for children 6 and under. It's open Monday to Friday from 9am to 5pm and on Saturday from 10am to 2pm (last admission is half an hour prior to closing).

Elsewhere on the island, you might **go to Hell!** That's at the north end of West Bay Beach, a jagged piece of rock named Hell by a former commissioner. There the postmistress will stamp "Hell, Grand Cayman" on your postcard to send back to the States.

The ✪ **Cayman Turtle Farm,** Northwest Point (☎ **345/949-3894**), is the only green sea-turtle farm of its kind in the world, and is also, with some 250,000 visitors annually, the most popular land-based tourist attraction in the Caymans. Once the islands had a multitude of turtles in the surrounding waters (which is why Columbus called the islands "Las Tortugas"), but today these creatures are sadly few in number (practically extinct elsewhere in the Caribbean), and the green sea turtle has been designated an endangered species. You cannot bring turtle products into the United States. The turtle farm has a twofold purpose: to provide the local market with edible turtle meat and to replenish the waters with hatchling and yearling turtles. Visitors today can look at 100 circular concrete tanks in which these sea creatures can be observed in every stage of development; the hope is that one day their population in the sea will regain its former status. Turtles here range in size from 6 ounces to 600 pounds. At a snack bar and restaurant, you can sample turtle dishes. The turtle farm is open daily from 8:30am to 5pm. Admission is $6 for adults, $3 for children 6 to 12, free for children 5 and under.

At **Botabano,** on the North Sound, fishers tie up with their catch, much to the delight of photographers. You can buy lobster (in season), fresh fish, even conch. A large barrier reef protects the sound, which is surrounded on three sides by the island and is a mecca for diving and sports fishing.

If you're driving, you might want to go along **South Sound Road,** which is lined with pines and, in places, old wooden Caymanian houses. After leaving the houses behind, you'll find good spots for a picnic.

On the road again, you reach **Bodden Town,** once the largest settlement on the island. At Gun Square, two cannons commanded the channel through the reef. They are now stuck muzzle-first into the ground.

On the way to the **East End,** just before Old Isaac Village, you'll see the onshore sprays of water shooting up like geysers. These are called "blowholes," and they sound like the roar of a lion.

Later, you'll spot the fluke of an anchor sticking up from the ocean floor. As the story goes, this is a relic of the famous "Wreck of the Ten Sails" in 1788. A modern wreck can also be seen—the *Ridgefield,* a 7,500-ton Liberty ship from New England, which struck the reef in 1943.

Old Man Bay is reached by a road that opened in 1983. From here you can travel along the north shore of the island to **Rum Point,** which has a good beach and is a fine place to end the tour. After visiting Rum Point, you can head back toward Old Man Village, where you can go south along a cross-island road through savannah country that will eventually lead you west to George Town.

The offshore waters of Grand Cayman are home to one of the most unusual (and ephemeral) underwater attractions in the world, ✪ **Stingray City.** Set in the sun-flooded, 12-foot-deep waters of North Sound, about 2 miles east of the island's northwestern tip, the site originated in the mid-1980s when local fishers cleaned their catch and dumped the offal overboard. They quickly noticed scores of stingrays (which usually eat marine crabs) feeding on the debris, a phenomenon that quickly attracted local divers and marine zoologists. Today, between 30 and 50 relatively tame stingrays hover in the waters around the site for daily handouts of squid and bally-hoo from increasing hordes of amateur snorkelers and scuba enthusiasts.

Interestingly, most of the stingrays that feed here are females, the males preferring to remain in deeper waters offshore. To capitalize on the phenomenon, about half a dozen entrepreneurs lead expeditions from points along Seven Mile Beach, traveling around the landmass of Conch Point to the feeding grounds. One well-known outfit is **Treasure Island Divers** (☎ **800/872-7552** or 345/949-4456), which charges divers $45 and snorkelers $25. Trips are made on Monday, Wednesday, Friday, and Sunday at 1:30pm.

Be warned that stingrays possess deeply penetrating and viciously barbed stingers capable of inflicting painful damage to anyone who mistreats them. (Above all, the divers say, never try to grab one by the tail.) Despite the dangers, divers and snorkelers seem amazingly adept at feeding, petting, and stroking the velvet surfaces of these batlike creatures and avoiding unpleasant incidents.

An annual event, **Cayman Islands Pirates' Week** is held in late October. It's a national festival with cutlass-bearing pirates and sassy wenches storming George Town, capturing the governor, thronging the streets, and staging a costume parade. The celebration, which is held throughout the islands, pays tribute to the nation's past and its cultural heritage. For the exact dates, contact the Pirates Week Festival Administration (☎ **345/949-5078**).

On 60 acres of rugged wooded land off Frank Sound Road, North Side, the **Queen Elizabeth II Botanic Park** (☎ **345/947-9462**) offers visitors a 1-hour walk through wetland, swamp, dry thicket, mahogany trees, orchids, and bromeliads. The trail is eight-tenths of a mile long. You'll likely see hickatees, the fresh-water turtles found only on the Caymans and in Cuba. Occasionally you'll spot the rare Grand Cayman parrot, or if not that, perhaps the anole lizard, with its cobalt-blue throat pouch. Even rarer is the endangered blue iguana. There are six rest stations with visitor information along the trail. The park is open daily from 7:30am to 5:30pm. Admission is $2.50 for adults, $1 for children, free for children 5 and under.

In 1996, a visitor center opened here, with changing exhibitions, plus a canteen for food and refreshments. It's set in a botanic park adjacent to the woodland trail and includes a heritage garden with a re-creation of a traditional Cayman home, garden, and farm; a floral garden with 1^1/$_2$ acres of flowering plants, and a 2-acre lake with three islands, home to many native birds.

One of the newest attractions in the Cayman Islands is the **Mastic Trail,** a restored 200-year-old footpath through a 2-million-year-old woodland area in the heart of the island. The trail lies west of Frank Sound Road, about a 45-minute drive from the heart of George Town. Named for the majestic mastic tree, the trail showcases the reserve's natural attractions, including a native mangrove swamp, traditional agriculture, and an ancient woodland area—home to the largest variety of native plant and animal life found in the Cayman Islands. Guided tours, lasting 2^1/$_2$ hours and limited to eight participants, are offered Monday to Friday at 8:30am and at 3pm, and again on Saturday at 8:30am. Reservations are required, and the cost is $25 C.I. ($31.25) per person. The hike is not recommended for children under 6, the elderly, or persons with physical disabilities. Wear comfortable, sturdy shoes and carry water and insect repellent. For reservations, call ☎ **345/949-1996** Monday to Friday from 10am to 3pm.

SHOPPING

The free-port shopping in George Town encompasses silver, china, crystal, Irish linen, French perfumes, British woolen goods, and such local crafts as black-coral jewelry and thatch-woven baskets. But there aren't any real bargains. Don't purchase turtle products—they cannot be brought into the United States.

Artifacts Ltd. Harbour Dr., George Town. ☎ **345/949-2442.**

The premier outlet on the island for back issues of some of the rare stamps issued by the Cayman government, this shop is managed by Charles Adams, one of the country's philatelic authorities. Stamps range in price from 17¢ to $900, and inventory includes the rare War Tax Stamp issued during World War II. Other items for sale include antique Dutch and Spanish coins unearthed from underwater shipwrecks, enameled boxes, and antique prints and maps. The shop lies on the harborfront of George Town, across from the landing dock for cruise-ship tenders.

English Shoppe. Harbour Dr. (in front of the cruise-ship landing), George Town. ☎ **345/949-2457.**

Watches, black- and pink-coral jewelry, and 14- and 18-karat jewelry are priced in U.S. dollars. One section of the shop sells fine jewelry, the other souvenirs.

The Jewelry Centre. Fort St., George Town. ☎ **345/949-0070.**

A virtual department store, this outlet has the island's largest selection of jewelry, with many items at more reasonable prices than those at the jewelry boutiques. In a two-story building in the town center, it contains six departments specializing in loose and set diamonds, gold (sold as chains or as ornaments, including coins found in shipwrecks offshore), black coral, colored gemstones, and caymanite, the pinkish-brown striated rock found only on the Caymans.

Kirk Freeport Plaza. Cardinal Ave. and Panton St., George Town. ☎ **345/949-7477.**

The largest store of its kind on the Caymans, Kirk Freeport Plaza contains a treasure trove of gold jewelry, watches, china, crystal, perfumes, and cosmetics. The store holds a Cartier franchise, with items priced 15% to 35% below suggested retail prices Stateside. Also stocked are crystal and porcelain from Wedgwood, Waterford, Lladró, and Baccarat, priced 30% to 50% less than recommended retail prices Stateside.

Pure Art. S. Church St., George Town. ☎ **345/949-9133.**

The Cayman Islands are not known for their handcrafts as is Jamaica. But if you'd like some local souvenirs, this is your best bet for art and crafts. One room is devoted to original art, including locally produced Christmas ornaments. Another room sells art prints and note cards, and the shop also carries carvings, ceramics, thatch work, and baskets, plus pottery from the Bodden Town primary school (made by the youngsters there). Tin art is also displayed, as are other handcrafted household items.

Sunflower Boutique. South Church St. ☎ **345/949-4090.**

This unusual boutique, established some quarter of a century ago in a two-story building beside the waterfront, sells hand-painted skirts and blouses; T-shirts and shorts for men and women; jewelry fashioned from black, pink, and white coral; an assortment of gift items; and Caribbean paintings. It's directly on the waterfront in the center of George Town.

Tropical Trader Market & Bazaar. Edward St. ☎ **345/949-6538.**

In an island of overpriced art galleries, you can pick up some typical Caymanian scenes here, not only paintings, but drawings and prints as well, for $15 and up. Local artists painted many of the island scenes in watercolors. The outlet is a true bazaar, selling gold, silver, and black coral jewelry (the latter among the most inexpensive on the island). You can also purchase watches by Anne Klein, Casio, and Swiss Army, plus Tommy Bahama men's sports clothing. Bags and luggage by Kipling and Tumi are also sold.

GRAND CAYMAN AFTER DARK

The Cracked Conch. West Bay Rd., near Turtle Bay Farm. ☎ **345/947-5217.**

This popular seafood restaurant, known for its conch fritters and conch chowder, is also becoming known as a nightspot. It offers karaoke and also shows classic dive films. Its happy hour, with free hors d'oeuvres, Tuesday to Friday evenings is a great deal.

Lone Star Bar & Grill. West Bay Rd. ☎ **345/945-5175.**

At this transplanted corner of the Texas Panhandle, you can enjoy juicy hamburgers in the dining room or head immediately for the bar in back. Here, beneath murals of Lone Star beauties, you can watch several sports events simultaneously on 15 different TV screens and sip lime and strawberry margaritas. Monday and Thursday are fajita nights, all-you-can-eat affairs, and Tuesday is all-you-can-eat lobster. There's a new volleyball court.

The Planet. West Bay Rd. ☎ **345/949-7169.** Cover $4 Tues and Thurs, $5 Wed and Fri–Sat.

About a block inland from West Bay Road, adjacent to the island's only cinema, this dance club is the island's largest dance floor with the biggest indoor stage and four bars dispensing reasonably priced drinks along with bar food. The mix of locals and tourists form a wide age range—from 18 to 50. Thursday is retro music night, with tunes from the 1970s. Monday night is devoted to watching football games and there's no cover.

Ten Sails Pub and Coconuts Comedy Club. In the Holiday Inn Grand Cayman, West Bay Rd. ☎ **345/947-4444.** Cover: Pub, none during the day; comedy club, $12 C.I. ($15), plus a two-drink minimum.

During the day, this place functions as an English-style pub. Several nights a week, however, the premises are transformed into the comedy club Coconuts, with comedic talents imported from all over the world. After the show, you can try your talents at a karaoke platform. Murals of swashbuckling pirates and their treasure adorn the walls. A few steps from the pub's entrance, beside the hotel pool, a local musician and his band play island music throughout the evening.

2 Cayman Brac

The "middle" island of the Caymans is Cayman Brac, a piece of limestone and coral-based land 12 miles long and a mile wide, about 89 miles east-northeast of Grand Cayman. It was given the name Brac (Gaelic for bluff) by 17th-century Scottish fishers who settled here. The bluff for which the island was named is a towering limestone plateau rising to 140 feet above the sea, covering the eastern half of Cayman Brac. Caymanians refer to the island simply as Brac, and its 1,400 inhabitants, a hospitable bunch of people, are called Brackers.

The big attraction of the bluff is the more than 170 caves honeycombing its limestone height. In the early 18th century, the Caymans were occupied by pirates, and Edward Teach, the infamous Blackbeard, is supposed to have spent quite a bit of time around Cayman Brac. Some of the caves are at the bluff's foot; others can be reached only by climbing over jagged limestone rock. One of the biggest caves is Great Cave, with a number of chambers. Harmless fruit bats cling to the roofs of the caverns.

On the south side of the bluff, you won't see many people, and the only sounds are the sea crashing against the lavalike shore. The island's herons and wild green parrots are seen here. Most of the Brackers live on the north side, many in traditional wooden seaside cottages, some built by the island's pioneers. The islanders must all have green thumbs, as attested to by the variety of flowers, shrubs, and fruit trees in many of the yards. On Cayman Brac, you'll see poinciana trees, bougainvillea, Cayman orchids, croton, hibiscus, aloe, sea grapes, cactus, and coconut and cabbage palms. The gardeners grow cassava, pumpkins, breadfruit, yams, and sweet potatoes.

There are no actual towns on the island—only settlements, such as Stake Bay (the "capital"), Spot Bay, the Creek, Tibbitt's Turn, the Bight, and West End, where the airport is located.

GETTING THERE

Flights from Grand Cayman to Cayman Brac are operated on **Cayman Airways** (☎ **800/422-9626** in the U.S., or 345/949-2311). The airline uses relatively large 737 jets carrying 122 passengers each. There is an evening flight here, plus a morning return. The round-trip cost is $99 per person for a day trip, or $154 for a flight that includes an overnight stopover.

WHERE TO STAY

The two major resorts on the island, Brac Reef Beach Resort and Divi Tiara Beach Resort, are pretty high-priced. However, there is one simple place—the Brac Airport Inn—where you can stay without breaking the bank on Cayman Brac. (Then you can have a drink or dinner at the more expensive resorts, or eat near the airport!) The best buy is the pizzeria in the shopping center. Even cheaper than the Brac Airport Inn is a room in a private home. However, this is a sometime thing. You have to inquire about who's offering rooms when you arrive at the airport.

Brac Airport Inn. P.O. Box 56, Cayman Brac, Cayman Islands, B.W.I. ☎ **345/948-1323.** Fax 345/948-1207. 4 rms. A/C TV. Year-round, $105 single or double. AE, MC, V. Free parking.

This hotel was conceived and designed as part of the only shopping center on Cayman Brac. It might not be suited to everyone's beachgoing fantasy, as it's in a landlocked setting 1 1/2 miles from the sea. But budget travelers sometimes opt for a relatively simple lodging here, then commute to the island's legendary beach and scuba facilities. Technically, guests can enjoy the dining, drinking, and sports facilities of the larger (and better-equipped) Brac Reef Beach Resort, which manages this place. You can arrange dining for around $36 a day (MAP) at the Brac Reef Beach Resort. The bedrooms (each with a radio and ceiling fan) are above the shops, and usually cost around 15% less than equivalent accommodations in more upscale locations.

WHERE TO EAT

Captain's Table. Brac Caribbean Beach Village, Stake Bay. ☎ **345/948-2265.** Reservations recommended. Main courses $11.25–$22.50; lunch from $12. MC, V. Daily 11:30am–3pm and 6–9:30pm. AMERICAN.

The decor is Caribbean cliché, vaguely nautical with oars over and around the bar and pieces of boats forming the restaurant's entryway. In the same building as a scuba shop and the reception desk, the restaurant offers both indoor and air-conditioned seating, along with outside dining by the pool. Begin with a captain's cocktail of shrimp and lobster or perhaps conch fritter, then follow with one of the soups such as black bean. Main dishes include everything from the catch of the day, often served pan-fried, to barbecue ribs. At lunch, you can order burgers and sandwiches.

FUN ON & OFF THE BEACH

The biggest lure to Cayman Brac is the variety of **water sports**—swimming, fishing, snorkeling, and some of the world's best diving and exploration of coral reefs. There are undersea walls on both the north and south sides of the island, with stunning specimens lining their sides. The best dive center is **Peter Hughes Dive Tiara** at the Divi Tiara Beach Resort (☎ **800/367-3484** or 345/945-1553).

History buffs might check out the **Cayman Brac Museum,** in the former Government Administration Building, Stake Bay (☎ **345/948-2622**), which has an interesting collection of Caymanian antiques, including pieces rescued from shipwrecks and items from the 18th century. Open Monday to Friday from 9am to noon and 1 to 4pm, Saturday from 9am to noon, and Sunday from 1 to 4pm. Admission is free.

3 Little Cayman

The smallest of the Cayman Islands is cigar-shaped Little Cayman, 10 miles long and about a mile across at its widest point. It lies about 75 miles northeast of Grand Cayman and some 5 miles from Cayman Brac. The entire island is coral and sand.

The islands of the Caymans are mountaintops of the long-submerged Sierra Maestra Range, which runs north and into Cuba. Coral formed layers over the underwater peaks, eventually forming the islands. Beneath Little Cayman's Bloody Bay is one of the mountain's walls—a stunning sight for snorkelers and scuba divers.

The island seems to have come into its own now that fishing and diving have taken center stage; this is a near-perfect place for such pursuits. The waters around the little island were hailed by the late Philippe Cousteau as one of the three finest diving spots in the world. Fine bonefishing is available just offshore, and a brackish inland pool can be fished for tarpon. Even if you don't dive or fish, you can row 200 yards off Little Cayman to isolated and uninhabited Owen Island, where you can swim from the sandy beach and picnic by a blue lagoon.

There may still be pirate treasure buried on the island, but it's in the dense interior of what is now the largest bird sanctuary in the Caribbean. Little Cayman is also home to a unique species of lizard that predates the iguana.

Blossom Village, the island's "capital," is on the southwest coast.

GETTING THERE

Most visitors fly from Grand Cayman to Little Cayman. **Cayman Airways** (☎ **800/ 949-0241** in the U.S., or 345/949-5252 on Grand Cayman) is the reservations agent for Island Air, a charter company that charges $149 (U.S.) round-trip.

WHERE TO STAY

Paradise Resort. P.O. Box 30, Little Cayman, Cayman Islands, B.W.I. ☎ **345/948-0001.** Fax 345/948-0002. 12 rms. A/C. Winter, $130 single; $150 double; $160 triple. Off-season, $120 single; $130 double; $140 triple. Children 11 and under stay free in parents' room. AE, MC, V.

On this high-priced little island, this resort on the beach is your best deal, and it's also the best choice if you're traveling with family (baby-sitting can be arranged). The style is typically Caymanian, with gingerbread decoration, metal roofs, and porches front and back. Guests prepare their own meals. Bordering the sea are six duplex cottages, each divided into two one-bedroom units. Pullout couches in the living room easily accommodate extra guests, and in addition to air-conditioning, there are ceiling fans. The resort is on the island's south side, near the little airport from which pickup is provided free. A grocery store, boutique, two auto rentals, and a liquor store are all within walking distance, and Paradise Resort offers free bikes. On premise is the best affordable restaurant on the island, the Hungry Iguana (see below). Diving is arranged through Paradise Divers. Its two-tank dive at $70 is the island's best value.

Sam McCoy's Diving and Fishing Lodge. Little Cayman. (Send written inquiries to P.O. Box 1725GT, Grand Cayman, Cayman Islands, B.W.I.) ☎ **800/626-0496** in the U.S. and Canada, or 345/948-4526. Fax 345/949-6821. 8 rms. A/C. Dive packages, $483.10 for 3 nights/2 days, and $1,206.70 for 7 nights/6 days, per person, double occupancy. Rates include all meals and all dives. AE, MC, V.

Set on the island's northwestern shore, this hotel reflects the personalities of Sam McCoy and his family, who include their guests in many aspects of their day-to-day lives. There's not really a bar or restaurant in the traditional sense; rather, you'll pour your own drinks (usually from your own bottle) or drink at a beach bar that rises from the sands of Bloody Bay a short walk from the hotel. Light snacks and simple platters are offered at outdoor tables near the main lodge with Sam and his gang, many of whom are associated in one way or another with diving operations on the reefs offshore. The bedrooms are ultra-simple, with few adornments other than beds, a table and chair, and a ceiling fan. Maid service is included in the price. There's a pool on the premises, but most visitors opt for dips in the wide blue sea instead, usually taking part in any of the wide choice of scuba explorations offered by Sam and his staff. (Jackson Beach lies nearby.) Picnics can be arranged to the offshore sands of Owens Cay. This is a place built by divers, and intended for divers, even those with children in tow.

WHERE TO EAT

Birds of Paradise. At Little Cayman Resort. ☎ **345/948-1033.** Reservations recommended for dinner. Dinner $25 C.I. ($31.25); lunch $15 C.I. ($18.75); breakfast $12 C.I. ($15). AE, MC, V. Daily 7:30–8:30am, 12:30–1:30pm, and 6:30–7:30pm. AMERICAN/CONTINENTAL.

The best buffet dinners on the island—the kind your parents might have enjoyed back in the golden 1950s or 1960s—are served at this little spot that caters primarily to hotel guests, but welcomes outsiders. The best night to show up is Tuesday, which features the island's most generous barbecue spread—all the ribs, fish, and Jamaican-inspired jerk chicken you'd want. On other nights, try the prime rib, fresh fish Caribbean style (your best bet), or chicken either Russian style (Kiev) or French style (Cordon Bleu). There's a freshly made salad bar, and homemade desserts are yummy, especially the key lime pie. At night, opt for an outdoor table under the stars.

The Hungry Iguana. Paradise Resort. ☎ **345/948-0007.** Reservations recommended. Dinner $13.95–$17.95 C.I. ($17.45–$22.45); lunch $3.25–$6.75 C.I. ($4.05–$8.45). AE, MC, V. Daily noon–9:30pm. (Bar, Mon–Fri noon–1am, Sat–Sun noon–midnight.) AMERICAN/CARIBBEAN.

At the beach, you'll spot this place immediately with its mammoth iguana mural. The island's tastiest dishes are served here, a winning combination of standard American fare along with some zesty flavors from the islands south of here. It's the most macho place on the island, especially the sports bar with its satellite TV in the corner, a sort of TGI Friday's atmosphere. Lunch is the usual burgers and fries along with some well-stuffed sandwiches. We always prefer the grilled chicken salad. Dinner gets a little more elaborate—there's usually a special meat dish of the day, depending on the market (supplies are shipped in once a week by barge). Try one of the seafood platters. The chef always seems willing to prepare you a steak as you like it. Marinated shrimp with rémoulade is a tasty choice as well. To go local, sample the marinated conch salad.

5 Puerto Rico

No one has ever suffered from boredom on Puerto Rico, which offers a vast array of activities and entertainment. It has hundreds of beaches, a mind-boggling array of water sports, acres of golf courses, miles of tennis courts, and casinos galore. It has more discos than any other place in the Caribbean, and shopping bargains to equal those of St. Thomas.

Lush, verdant Puerto Rico is only half the size of New Jersey and is located some 1,000 miles southeast of the tip of Florida. With 272 miles of Atlantic and Caribbean coastline, and a culture dating back 2,000 years, Puerto Rico is a formidable attraction. Old San Juan is its greatest historic center, with 500 years of recorded history, as reflected in its restored Spanish colonial architecture.

It's also a land of contrasts. There are 79 cities and towns on Puerto Rico, each with a unique charm and flavor. The countryside is dotted with centuries-old coffee plantations, sugar estates still in use, foreboding caves, and enormous boulders with mysterious petroglyphs carved by the Taíno peoples (original settlers of the island). You can travel along colorful but often narrow and steep roads, and meandering mountain trails leading out to tropical settings. Travelers on a budget, and those who want to see the *real* Puerto Rico, will want to explore some of these back roads, leaving San Juan, especially the high-priced Condado Beach area, behind.

Of all the islands in the Caribbean, Puerto Rico is perhaps the very best choice for budget travelers, with inexpensive *paradores* (government-sponsored inns), small guest houses, local little inns, and mom-and-pop restaurants, many of which overlook the sea. Any number of restaurants serve fresh fish and native Puerto Rican dishes. Following in the Spanish tradition, Puerto Rico also has the *café*, where you can enjoy a cup of coffee as well as a *comida criolla* (local dinner). Sometimes a dinner will cost only $12, or even less, at a roadside kiosk.

In this chapter, we start out in San Juan, and then move west, counterclockwise around the island, until we reach Ponce. Then we'll turn our attention to attractions east of San Juan, and head clockwise around the island. Keep in mind that you can base yourself at one hotel and still do a lot of exploring elsewhere if you don't mind driving for a couple of hours. It's possible to branch out and see a lot of the island even if you're staying in San Juan.

GETTING THERE

Puerto Rico is by far the most accessible of the Caribbean islands, with frequent airline service. **American Airlines** (☎ 800/433-7300) has designated San Juan as its hub for the entire Caribbean. American offers 39 nonstop daily flights to San Juan from Baltimore, Boston, Chicago, Dallas–Fort Worth, Hartford, Miami, Newark, New York (JFK), Orlando, Philadelphia, Tampa, Fort Lauderdale, and Washington (Dulles), plus flights to San Juan from both Montréal and Toronto with changes in Chicago or Miami. There are at least two daily flights from Los Angeles to San Juan that touch down in Dallas or Miami.

Delta (☎ 800/221-1212) has four daily nonstop flights from Atlanta Monday to Friday, nine nonstop on Saturday, and seven nonstop on Sunday. It also offers one daily nonstop flight to San Juan from Orlando. Flights into Atlanta from around the world are frequent, with excellent connections from points throughout Delta's network in the South and Southwest.

United Airlines (☎ 800/241-6522) has daily nonstop flights from Chicago to San Juan. United offers connecting service from most major U.S. cities. **Northwest** (☎ 800/447-4747) has daily connecting flights via Detroit to San Juan and one daily nonstop flight from Detroit. It also has Saturday and Sunday nonstop service from Memphis and Minneapolis to San Juan.

TWA (☎ 800/892-4141) has three daily nonstop flights in winter from New York to San Juan, dropping down to two off-season. There are also daily nonstop flights from St. Louis to San Juan in winter, but none in summer. US Airways (☎ 800/428-4322) also competes, with one weekly direct flight from Baltimore to San Juan.

Smaller airlines competing include **Carnival** (☎ 800/824-7386), a Florida-based airline wholly owned by the Carnival Group of cruise-line fame. This line offers a nonstop flight from New York to Aguadilla and Ponce, and connecting flights through New York's JFK and Newark. It also has flights from Miami and Los Angeles to San Juan.

Tower Air (☎ 800/221-2500, or 800/452-5531 in New York State) has a nonstop flight from New York to San Juan every day except Tuesday and Saturday.

British travelers can take a **British Airways** (☎ 800/247-9297) Sunday flight direct from London to San Juan; **Lufthansa** (☎ 800/645-3880) passengers can fly on Saturday (one weekly flight) from Frankfurt to San Juan via Condor (a subsidiary operating the flight); and **Iberia** (☎ 800/772-4642) has two weekly flights from Madrid to San Juan, leaving on Thursday and Sunday.

GETTING AROUND THE ISLAND

FLIGHTS WITHIN PUERTO RICO   American Eagle (☎ 787/749-1747) flies from Luís Muñoz Marín International Airport to Mayagüez, which can be your gateway to the west of Puerto Rico. Most round-trip fares are between $69 and $130. For information about air connections to the offshore islands of Vieques and Culebra, see sections 12 and 13, below.

PUBLIC TRANSPORTATION   *Públicos* are cars or minibuses that provide low-cost transportation and are designated with the letters "P" or "PD" following the numbers on their license plates. They run to all the main towns of Puerto Rico, including Mayagüez and Ponce. Passengers are dropped off and picked up along the way. Rates are set by the Public Service Commission. Públicos usually operate during daylight hours and depart from the main plaza (central square) of a town.

Information about público routes between San Juan and Mayagüez is available from **Lineas Sultana,** calle Esteban González 898, Urbanización Santa Rita, Rio Piedras (☎ 787/765-9377). Information about público routes between San Juan and Ponce is available from **Choferes Unidos de Ponce** (☎ 787/764-0540). Fares vary according to whether or not the público will make a detour to pick up or drop off a passenger at a specific locale. If you want to deviate from the predetermined routes, you'll pay more than if you wait for a público beside the main highway. Fares from San Juan to Mayagüez range from $10 to $25; from San Juan to Ponce, from $18 to $20. Although prices of públicos are low, the routes are slow, with frequent stops, an often erratic routing, and lots of inconvenience.

RENTAL CARS   Some local rental-car agencies may tempt you with slashed prices, but if you're planning to tour the island, you won't find any local branches should you run into car trouble. And some of the agencies advertising low-cost deals don't take credit or charge cards and want cash in advance. You also have to watch out for hidden extras and the insurance problems that sometimes proliferate among the smaller and not-very-well-known firms.

So if you're planning to do much touring, you may want to stick to the reliables: **Avis** (☎ 800/331-2112 or 787/791-2500), **Budget** (☎ 800/527-0700 or 787/791-3685), and **Hertz** (☎ 800/654-3001 or 787/791-0840). However, local companies often rent cars at much lower prices, so it pays to shop around. Try **Charlie Car Rental,** Isla Verde Avenue, km 0.7, Carolina, in San Juan (☎ 800/289-1227 or 787/728-2418); or **L & M Car Rental,** calle Los Angeles, Carolina (☎ 800/666-0807 or 787/725-8461), in San Juan.

Distances are often posted in kilometers rather than in miles (a kilometer is 0.62 mile), but speed limits are in miles per hour. Be careful driving, because car theft is high on Puerto Rico.

SIGHTSEEING TOURS

If you want to see more of the island, but you don't want to rent a car or manage the inconveniences of public transportation, perhaps an organized tour is for you. **Castillo Sightseeing Tours & Travel Services,** calle Laurel 2413, Punta La Marias, Santurce (☎ 787/791-6195 or 787/726-5752), offers some of the best and least expensive tours, undercutting some of the bigger operators. Using six air-conditioned service buses, it operates tours that pick up passengers at their hotels as an added convenience.

One of the most popular half-day tours departs most days of the week between 8:30 and 9am, lasts 4 to 5 hours, and costs $25 per person. Departing from San Juan, it tours along the northeastern part of the island to El Yunque rain forest.

The company also offers a city tour of San Juan that departs daily at 1 or 1:30pm. The 4-hour trip costs $25 per person, and includes a stop at the Bacardi rum factory, where you're treated to a rum drink.

For a day excursion to the best islands, beaches, reefs, and snorkeling in the area, contact **Capt. Jack Becker,** Villa Marina Yachting, Fajardo (☎ 787/860-0861). Captain Jack, a long-ago native of Washington, D.C., and a longtime resident of Puerto Rico, takes two to six passengers at a time on his sailboat. Participants appreciate the sun, the reefs, and the marine life such a tour makes visible. Before departure, guests are directed to a nearby delicatessen, where they can buy drinks and a package lunch. The price for a trip is $45 per person, and the trip lasts from 10am to 3:30pm. Reservations can be made at any hour.

Puerto Rico

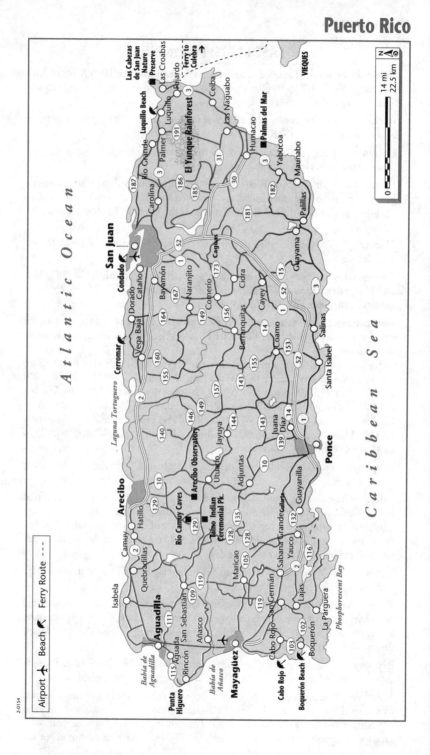

81

FAST FACTS: Puerto Rico

American Express　American Express–related services are at 1035 Ashford Ave., Condado (☎ 787/725-0960). Open Monday to Friday from 9am to 5pm and Saturday from 9 to 11:30am.

Banks　Major U.S. banks have branches in San Juan, and are open Monday to Friday from 8:30am to 2:30pm.

Currency　The U.S. dollar is the coin of the realm. Canadian currency is accepted by some big hotels in San Juan, although reluctantly.

Documents　Since Puerto Rico is part of the United States, American citizens do not need a passport or visa. Canadians, however, should carry some form of identification, such as a birth certificate. Citizens of the United Kingdom should have a passport.

Electricity　The electricity is 110 volts AC, as it is in the continental United States and Canada.

Emergencies　In San Juan in an emergency, call the local **police** (☎ 787/343-2020), **fire department** (☎ 787/343-2330), **ambulance** (☎ 787/343-2550), or **medical assistance** (☎ 787/754-3535).

Information　Out in the island, it's best to go to the local city hall for tourist data. Ask for a copy of *Qué Pasa,* the official visitors' guide containing much useful information.

For information before you leave home, contact one of the following **Puerto Rico Tourism Company** offices: 575 Fifth Ave., New York, NY 10017 (☎ **800/ 223-6530** or 212/599-6262); 3575 W. Cahuenga Blvd., Suite 405, Los Angeles, CA 90068 (☎ **213/874-5991**); or 901 Ponce de Leon Blvd., Suite 604, Coral Gables, FL 33134 (☎ **800/815-7391** or 305/445-9112). In Canada you can stop by 41–43 Colbourne St., Suite 301, Toronto, ON M5E 1E3 (☎ **800/667-0394** or 416/368-2680), for information.

Language　English is understood in most of San Juan. Out in the island, Spanish is still *número uno.*

Safety　Use common sense and take precautions. Muggings have been reported on the Condado and Isla Verde beaches in San Juan, so you might want to skip that moonlit stroll on the beach. The countryside of Puerto Rico is safer than San Juan, but caution is always the rule. Avoid small and narrow little country roads and isolated beaches, either night or day.

Taxes　There's a government tax of 7% in regular hotels or 9% in hotels with casinos. There's no airport departure tax.

Time　Puerto Rico is on Atlantic standard time year-round, making it 1 hour ahead of eastern standard time. In winter, when it's noon in Miami, it's 1pm in San Juan. But from April until late October (during daylight saving time on the East Coast), Puerto Rico and the East Coast keep the same time.

Tipping　Some hotels add a 10% service charge to your bill. If they don't, you're expected to tip for services rendered. Tip as you would in the United States.

Weather　Puerto Rico is cooler than most of the other Caribbean islands because of its northeast trade winds. Sea, land, and mountain breezes also help keep the temperatures at a comfortable level. The climate is fairly stable all year, with an average temperature of 76° Fahrenheit. The only variants are found in the mountain regions, where the temperature fluctuates between 66° and 76°, and on the north coast, where the temperature ranges from 70° to 80°.

1 San Juan

San Juan, the capital of Puerto Rico, is a major city—actually an urban sprawl of several municipalities that lie along the island's north coast. Its architecture ranges from classic colonial buildings that recall the Spanish empire to modern beachfront hotels reminiscent of Miami Beach.

ESSENTIALS

ARRIVING   If you're not traveling on a package deal that includes transfers to your hotel, you'll see lots of options after landing at the San Juan airport. A wide variety of vehicles refer to themselves as *limosinas* (their Spanish name).

One outfit with a sign-up desk in the arrivals hall of the international airport, near the American Airlines arrival facilities, is the **Airport Limousine Service** (☎ 787/791-4745). It offers minivan transport from the airport to various neighborhoods of San Juan for prices that are lower than for similar routings offered by taxis. Whenever 8 to 10 passengers can be accumulated, the fare for transport, with luggage, to any hotel in Isla Verde is $2.50 per person; to the Condado, $3 per person; and to Old San Juan, $3.50 per person.

ORIENTATION   San Juan breaks down into several divisions: **San Juan Island,** containing the city center and the old walled city (Old San Juan); **Santurce,** a large peninsula that's linked to San Juan Island by causeway; **Condado,** a narrow peninsula that stretches between San Juan Island and Santurce; **Puerto de Tierra,** the section east of Old San Juan that contains many government buildings; **Miramar,** a lagoonfront section south of the Condado; and **Isla Verde,** which is detached from the rest of San Juan by an isthmus.

VISITOR INFORMATION   Tourist information is available at the **Luís Muñoz Marín Airport** (☎ 787/791-1014). Another office is at **La Casita,** Pier 1, Old San Juan (☎ 787/722-1709).

FAST FACTS   One of the most centrally located **drugstores** is the Puerto Rico Drug Co., calle San Francisco 157 (☎ 787/725-2202), in Old San Juan; it's open Monday to Friday from 7am to 9:30pm, Saturday from 8am to 9:30pm, and Sunday from 8:30am to 7:30pm. **Walgreen's,** 1130 Ashford Ave., Condado (☎ 787/725-1510), is a 24-hour pharmacy. In a **medical emergency,** call ☎ 787/721-2116. There's a 24-hour emergency room at **Ashford Memorial Community Hospital,** 1451 Ashford Ave. (☎ 787/721-2160).

GETTING AROUND

BY TROLLEY   The best way to save your feet in Old San Juan is to board one of the free open-air trolleys that slowly make their way through the narrow, often cobblestone, old streets. You can board a trolley at any point along its route, or go to the marina or La Puntilla for departures.

BY BUS   The **Metropolitan Bus Authority** (☎ 787/767-7979) operates buses in the greater San Juan area. Bus stops are marked by upright metal signs or yellow posts, reading PARADA. Bus terminals in San Juan are in the dock area and at plaza de Colón. A typical fare is 25¢ to 50¢. Call for more information about routes and schedules.

BY FERRY   The *Agua Expreso* (☎ 787/751-7055) connects the old town of San Juan with the industrial and residential communities of Hato Rey and Cataño, across the bay. Ferries depart daily every 30 minutes from 6am to 9pm. The one-way fare is 75¢ to Hato Rey (till 6:40pm) and 50¢ to Cataño (till 8pm). Departures are from the San Juan Terminal at the pier in Old San Juan. However, avoid rush hours, as locals who work in town use this ferry connection by the hundreds. Rides last about 20 minutes. Call for more information.

BY TAXI   Taxis are the most expensive way to get around. Operated by the **Public Service Commission** (☎ 787/756-1919), taxis are metered in San Juan—or should be. The initial charge is $1, plus 10¢ for each one-tenth of a mile and 50¢ for every suitcase. A minimum fare is $3. Call the PSC to request information or report any irregularities. **Taxi Turisticos** is a fleet designed especially for visitors; taxis are painted white with an official logo on their doors. Their rates, ranging between $6 and $16, are fixed, and these cabs go between Old San Juan and the Condado, or to Isla Verde.

GREAT DISCOUNTS THROUGH THE LELOLAI VIP PROGRAM

For $10, the cost of membership in Puerto Rico's ✪ **LeLoLai VIP** (Value in Puerto Rico), visitors can enjoy the equivalent of up to $200 in travel benefits. Admission to folkloric shows and discounts on guided tours of historic sites and natural attractions, as well as on lodgings, meals, shopping, sports activities, and more, add up to significant savings.

The *paradores puertorriqueños,* the island's network of modestly priced country inns, give cardholders 10% to 20% lower room rates Monday to Thursday. Discounts of 10% to 20% are offered at many restaurants, from San Juan's toniest hotels to several *mesones gastronómicos,* government-sanctioned restaurants out on the island serving Puerto Rican fare. Shopping discounts are offered at many stores and boutiques and, best yet, 10% to 20% discounts at many island attractions.

The card also entitles you to free admission to folkloric musical shows, including *Noches de Puerto Rico* on Thursday at 10pm (adults only) at the Sands Hotel Casino & Beach Resort. The pass also works for another show, *Jolgorio* at the Caribe Terrace of the Caribe Hilton on Wednesday at 8:30pm. For more information about this card, call ☎ 787/723-3125.

WHERE TO STAY

Most hotels lie in Condado and Isla Verde, areas out by the airport that border the beach. Or you can stay in Old San Juan—but factor in the cost of daily transportation to the beach if that's where you want to go.

All hotel rooms in Puerto Rico are subject to a 7% to 9% tax, which is *not* included in the rates listed in this chapter. Most hotels also impose a 10% service charge.

DOUBLES FOR LESS THAN $30 IN OLD SAN JUAN

Hotel Central. Calle San José 202, Old San Juan, PR 00901. ☎ **787/722-2751.** 60 rms. Year-round, $20–$30 single or double. AE, V. Bus: M2 or M3.

This is one of the most unusual hotels in the historic heart of Old San Juan, but it's definitely not for everyone. Its fans compare it to the kind of weather-beaten, run-down hotel that has staggered through revolutions, civil wars, and the changing tides of fashion. In fact, few other hotels on Puerto Rico will give you such a strong sense of nostalgia as will this battered remnant of another time. Originally built in the 1930s, and maintained by the same family ever since, it lies adjacent to the Old Town's plaza de Armas. Although the pleasures and distractions of the city's historic core lie all around the hotel, don't expect amenities of any kind in the accommodations.

Rooms have ceiling fans, minimalist (and rather old) furnishings, and private bathrooms. A somewhat dingy cafeteria on the premises serves simple platters at lunch and dinner to local office workers. The nearest beach is a 20-minute ride away.

DOUBLES FOR LESS THAN $80 (WINTER) / $55 (OFF-SEASON)

On the Condado

✪ At Wind Chimes Inn. Calle Taft 53, Condado, San Juan, PR 00911. ☎ **800/946-3244** or 787/727-4153. Fax 787/726-5321. 12 rms, 1 suite. A/C TV TEL. Winter, $65–$75 double; from $85 suite. Off-season, $55–$65 double; $75 suite. Rates include continental breakfast. AE, DC, DISC, MC, V. Bus: M8, A7, T1, or 2.

This restored and renovated Spanish manor, 1 short block from the beach and 3¹/₂ miles from the airport, is one of the best Puerto Rican guest houses on the Condado. Upon entering a tropical patio, you'll find tile tables surrounded by palm trees and bougainvillea. There's plenty of space on the deck and a covered lounge for relaxing, socializing, and eating breakfast. Dozens of decorative wind chimes add melody to the daily breezes. The rooms offer a choice of size, beds, and kitchens; all contain ceiling fans and air-conditioning.

Casa del Caribe. Calle Caribe 57, San Juan, PR 00907. ☎ **787/722-7139.** Fax 787/725-3995. 9 rms. A/C TV TEL. Winter, $50–$65 single; $65–$85 double. Off-season, $45–$65 single; $55–$75 double. Rates include continental breakfast. AE, DISC, MC, V. Bus: A7, T1, or 2.

Don't expect the Ritz, but if you're looking for a bargain on the Condado, this is it. Formerly known as Casablanca, this renovated guest house lies in the heart of the Condado. Built in the 1940s, it was later expanded, then totally refurbished with a tropical decor late in 1995. A very Puerto Rican ambience has been created, with emphasis on Latin hospitality and comfort. On a shady side street just off Ashford Avenue, behind a wall and garden, you'll discover Casa del Caribe's wraparound verandah. The cozy guest rooms have ceiling fans and air-conditioners, and most rooms feature original Puerto Rican art. The front porch is a social center for guests. You can also cook out at a barbecue area. The beach is a 2-minute walk away, and the hotel is also within walking distance of some megaresorts with their glittering casinos.

Embassy Condado. 1126 Seaview, Condado, San Juan, PR 00907. ☎ **787/725-2400.** 13 rms, 1 suite. A/C TV. Winter, $65–$115 single or double; $145 suite. Off-season, $45–$85 single or double; $100–$120 suite. Extra person $15. AE, MC, V. Bus: A7 or 10.

This two-story guest house sits about a block inland from the sands of Condado Beach. Surrounded by a residential neighborhood, on a quiet dead-end street, it offers a relaxed atmosphere—you could live in a swimsuit or shorts for your entire stay. The all-white bedrooms have rattan furniture and tropical accessories. Each has a kitchenette or access to one. The hotel features a rooftop sun deck, and a restaurant (across the road), which offers a view directly over the beach. Maid service is included, and baby-sitters can be arranged.

In Isla Verde

Green Isle / Casa Mathiesen. Calle Uno 36, Villamar, Isla Verde, PR 00979. ☎ **800/ 677-8860** in the U.S., or 787/726-4330. Fax 787/268-2415. 44 rms. A/C TV TEL. Winter, $69–$74 single or double. Off-season, $55–$65 single or double. AE, DC, MC, V. Bus: A7, M7, or T1.

Small, unassuming, and somewhat battered by the tropical sun and the roar of the nearby traffic, this hotel stands across the busy avenue from the beach used by the larger and much more expensive Sands Hotel. Each of the simple, low-slung accommodations contains its own kitchenette, and simple, summery furniture that was upgraded in 1996. There's a small swimming pool on the premises, although most residents prefer the nearby sea. No meals are served on site, but dozens of inexpensive hamburger joints are nearby.

In Ocean Park

Beach Buoy Inn. 1853 McLeary, Ocean Park, San Juan, PR 00911. ☎ **800/221-8119** or 787/728-8119. Fax 787/268-0037. 11 rms, 4 efficiencies. A/C TV. Winter, $60–$70 single or double; $75 efficiency. Off-season, $50–$60 single or double; $60 efficiency. Children 11 and under stay free in parents' room. Rates include continental breakfast. AE, MC, V.

About a block from the beach, this B&B deserves to be better known. Its rooms are not decorated as nicely as those at the At Wind Chimes, but they're clean and decent; the efficiencies have two double beds each. The staff is especially helpful and friendly. The rooms have color cable TVs, although many guests gather around the large TV in the lounge to watch basketball and football games. The accommodations are affordable and unpretentious, and there's parking on the premises. Some units have small refrigerators, and there's daily maid service. Although this place is a comfortable, snug nest, it's short on amenities: no restaurant, no bar, no pool, but many of these features are available nearby. You can enjoy breakfast outdoors on the patio if you wish.

In Santurce

Arcade Inn. 8 Taft St., Santurce, Condado, PR 00911. ☎ **787/725-0668.** Fax 787/728-7525. 18 rms, 2 suites. A/C TV. Winter, $50 single; $60–$65 double; $75 suite. Off-season, $45 single; $55 double; $60–$75 suite. DC, MC, V. Bus: A7.

This simple, no-frills hotel has attracted families with their children and college students traveling in groups since the 1960s. It's a stucco-covered building with vaguely Spanish colonial detailing on a residential street lined with similar buildings. The accommodations each contain a small refrigerator and simple, slightly battered furniture. There's no swimming pool and very few amenities on site, but the beach is quite close.

DOUBLES FOR LESS THAN $110 (WINTER) / $80 (OFF-SEASON)

In Old San Juan

Gallery Inn at Galería San Juan. Calle Norzagaray 204–206, San Juan, PR 00901. ☎ **787/722-1808.** Fax 787/724-7360. 9 rms, 13 suites. Year-round, $95–$300 double; $200–$350 suite. Rates include continental breakfast. AE, MC, V. Bus: A7, T1, or 21.

Though most of the rates above are too high for this category, we suggest booking one of the least expensive doubles here—even the cheapest units are fairly roomy and attractively furnished. This hotel's location and ambience is unbeatable. Set on a hilltop in the old town, with a sweeping sea view, this unusual hotel contains a maze of verdant courtyards. In the 1700s it was the home of an aristocratic Spanish family. Today it's one of the most whimsically bohemian hotels in the Caribbean. All courtyards and rooms are adorned with hundreds of sculptures, silk-screens, or original paintings, usually for sale. There are three free parking spaces, plus parking on the street. The nearest beach is a 20-minute ride away, though.

On the Condado

Condado Lagoon Days Inn. Calle Clemenceau 6, Condado, San Juan, PR 00907. ☎ **800/858-7407** or 787/721-0171. Fax 787/724-4356. 48 rms, 2 suites. A/C TV TEL. Winter, $85 single; $95 double; $150 suite. Off-season, $75 single; $90 double; $140 suite. Children stay free in parents' room. AE, DC, MC, V. Bus: A7 or 10.

Rising seven stories above a residential neighborhood across the street from Condado Beach is this family-oriented hotel, whose rooms were remodeled in 1996. There's a small swimming pool on the premises, and a modest coffee shop near the lobby. Each unit benefits from room service and maid service. Baby-sitters can be arranged. The accommodations are small, and not particularly imaginative in their decor, but usually contain queen-size beds and a small refrigerator. Some rooms have sofas that convert into beds for children. Although there are few frills on the premises, the bars, restaurants, and facilities of the Condado neighborhood are within walking distance.

✪ **El Canario by the Lagoon Hotel.** Calle Clemenceau 4, Condado, San Juan, PR 00907. ☎ **800/533-2649** in the U.S., or 787/722-5058. Fax 787/723-8590. 40 rms. A/C TV TEL. Winter, $95 single; $100–$110 double. Off-season, $75 single; $80–$90 double. Rates include continental breakfast and morning newspaper. AE, DC, DISC, MC, V. Bus: A7 or M2.

A European-style hotel, El Canario is in a quiet residential neighborhood just a short block from Condado Beach. The attractive but small rooms all have their own balconies, and the hotel has a guest laundry and an in-house tour desk. A relaxing informal atmosphere prevails.

Tanama Princes Hotel. 1 Joffre St., Condado, San Juan, PR 00907. ☎ **and fax 787/724-4160.** 115 rms. A/C TV TEL. Winter, $75 single; $85 double. Off-season, $65 single; $75 double. Children 12 and under stay free in parents' room. AE, DC, DISC, MC, V. Bus: T1.

Even as we speak, this hotel is slated for a major expansion. It started out at 57 rooms, but at the time of your visit the room count may have grown to 115. A seven-story white-painted structure, it has a desirable Condado location, without the towering prices of the grand resorts along the beach. Tanama is about a 5-minute walk from the beach, and is convenient to Old San Juan (10 minutes) and the airport (20 minutes). Most accommodations come with two double beds (ideal for families) and ceiling fans. Many open onto balconies with water views. It's a relatively easy walk over to one of the Condado casinos or to water-sports activities on the beach. A fairly good restaurant serves a nouvelle cuisine nightly, or you can walk to many nearby restaurants.

In Isla Verde

Casa de Playa Beach Hotel. Ave. Isla Verde 86, Isla Verde, San Juan, PR 00979. ☎ **800/916-2272** or 787/728-9779. Fax 787/727-1334. 18 rms, 4 suites. A/C TV TEL. Winter, $80 single; $90 double; from $120 suite. Off-season, $60 single; $70 double; from $90 suite. Children 9 and under stay free in parents' room. Rates include continental breakfast. AE, DC, DISC, MC, V. Bus: M4 or T1.

Jutting out over the sand on the mile-long Isla Verde beach, one of Puerto Rico's finest, this bargain oasis is a find. If you're less interested in being in the center of San Juan than you are in spending time on the beach, check out this modest choice. The hotel consists of two two-story peach-colored buildings, with a porch around the second floor and a small garden in front. Some rooms have small refrigerators. Standard but inexpensive Italian food is served at a beach bar and restaurant. The staff will try to arrange baby-sitting. The hotel doesn't have everything—no pool, no room service—but the price is hard to beat in Isla Verde.

In Ocean Park

✪ **Hostería del Mar.** 1 Tapia St., Ocean Park, Santurce, San Juan, PR 00911. ☎ **787/727-3302.** Fax 345/268-0772. 8 rms, 4 apts. Winter, $85 single; $107–$160 double; $175 apt. Off-season, $54 single; $74–$96 double; $125 apt. Children 11 and under stay free in parents' room. AE, MC, V.

Lying a few blocks from the Condado casinos are the white walls of this distinctive landmark. It's located between Isla Verde and Condado in a residential seaside community that's popular with locals looking for beach action on weekends. The rates are a little high for this category, but ask for one of the least expensive units. The hotel boasts ocean-view rooms with balconies from its second floor. On the floor below, the rooms open onto patios. The bedroom style is invitingly tropical, with wicker furniture, pastel prints, and ceiling fans. There's no pool, but a full-service restaurant is known for its vegetarian, macrobiotic, and Puerto Rican plates, all freshly made. The place is simple, yet with its own elegance, and the hospitality is warm. Aficionados of small, select Caribbean inns would like to keep this one a secret.

Número Uno Guest House. Calle Santa Ana 1, Ocean Park, San Juan, PR 00911. ☎ **787/ 726-5010.** Fax 787/727-5482. 12 rms. A/C. Winter, $70–$120 single; $85–$135 double. Off-season, $55–$90 single; $70–$105 double. Rates include continental breakfast. AE, MC, V.

In a prestigious residential neighborhood at the edge of the high-rise glitter of Isla Verde, this small and recently renovated hotel has a well-trained, English-speaking staff. There's a garden with palmettos and a swimming pool, easy access to a sandy beach, and all the distractions of several megaresorts relatively close at hand. The accommodations have wicker or rattan furniture. There's a bar and a very good restaurant on the premises, serving a Caribbean fusion cuisine. The owners can direct you to water-sports emporiums for scuba, waterskiing, sailing excursions, or whatever.

WORTH A SPLURGE

Best Western Hotel Pierre. 105 de Diego Ave., Condado, San Juan, PR 00914. ☎ **800/ 334-7234** or 787/721-1200. Fax 787/721-3118. 184 rms. A/C TV TEL. Winter, $123–$142 single; $133–$152 double. Off-season, $106–$116 single; $116–$126 double. Children 11 and under stay free in parents' room. Rates include continental breakfast. AE, DC, DISC, MC, V.

If you'd like to stay in a big high-rise hotel with conveniences and services, choose the "Lucky Pierre." This hotel has long been one of the capital's major bargains. It's 4 blocks from the beach and an easy drive to most major San Juan attractions, if you rent a car. It's a small resort, with a large swimming pool, deck, and poolside lanai, in a setting of palm trees. The bedrooms, although hardly grand, have recently been remodeled. Kids are welcomed here, and baby-sitting can be arranged. Two restaurants, Metropol and La Petite, are moderately priced and serve a respectable cuisine. On-site services include laundry and valet, a beauty and barber shop, secretarial services, and room service from 5pm to midnight.

GAY-FRIENDLY PLACES TO STAY

As the gay capital of the Caribbean, San Juan offers a number of gay guest houses, catering both to gay men and lesbians, although primarily men. Here's the pick of the lot. Lesbians will find a welcoming environment at the Hostería del Mar (see above).

Atlantic Beach Hotel. 1 Vendig St., Condado, San Juan, PR 00907. ☎ **787/721-6900.** Fax 787/721-6917. 37 rms. A/C TV TEL. Winter, $75–$110 single; $90–$125 double; $140 triple. Off-season, $60–$90 single; $75–$105 double; $120 triple. AE, DC, DISC, MC, V. Bus: A7, M7, or T1.

On Condado Beach, this establishment is proud of its status as the best-known gay hotel on Puerto Rico. The five-story hotel, with vaguely art deco styling, is a friendly refuge, mostly for men. The bedrooms are outfitted with tropical fabrics and accessories, and rattan furnishings. There's a simple snack-style bar and restaurant on the premises, with a Sunday-afternoon tea dance attracting many of the city's gay men.

Ocean Walk. 1 Atlantic Place, Condado, San Juan, PR 00911. ☎ **800/468-0615** or 787/ 728-0855. Fax 787/728-6434. 40 rms, 5 apts with kitchenette. TV TEL. Winter, $55 single; $75–$105 double; $120–$140 apt. Off-season, $40 single; $50–$70 double; $75–$90 apt. AE, DISC, MC, V. Bus: A7, 7, T1, or 2.

Built in the 1950s, this hotel caters to a mostly gay male clientele from all over the world. The accommodations are in three low-rise Spanish colonial–style buildings that ring the edges of a sun deck and swimming pool. The beach is quite close, and on the premises are a bar and a simple restaurant that's open daily for breakfast and lunch. The accommodations are basic but comfortable, summery, and airy, either with air-conditioning or ceiling fans.

BEST OFF-SEASON BETS

Some of the more expensive hostelries, such as those on beach-bordering Isla Verde—site of some of the leading high-rise resorts—lower their rates substantially from mid-April to mid-December. Here are some of the best places to find off-season bargains.

Empress Oceanfront. 2 Amapola St., Isla Verde, San Juan, PR 00913. ☎ **800/678-0757** in the U.S., or 787/791-3083. Fax 787/791-1423. 30 rms. A/C TV TEL. Winter, $148–$168 double. Off-season, $88–$128 double. AE, DC, DISC, MC, V. Bus: T1 stops half a mile from the hotel.

Set on 2^1/$_2$ acres of rocky headlands jutting out from the coastline of a residential neighborhood of Isla Verde, this four-story pink-sided hotel has an enclosed swimming pool terrace and one of the most sweeping views of San Juan. The bedrooms are airy and comfortable, and Sonny's Oceanfront Place for Ribs is one of the best budget restaurants in the area. Another restaurant, Shangrila, is open only in winter. Off-season, rates drop substantially, with singles for $68 and doubles for $88 to $128.

Travelodge. Ave. Isla Verde (P.O. Box 6007, Loiza Station), Santurce, San Juan, PR 00914. ☎ **800/468-2028** or 787/728-1300. Fax 809/268-0637. 88 rms, 2 suites. A/C TV TEL. Winter, $137 double; $175 suite. Off-season, $91 double; $160 suite. AE, MC, V.

Rising eight floors above the busy traffic of Isla Verde, this member of a national chain offers comfortable bedrooms in spite of the rather bland furnishings. It's across from two of the most expensive hotels on Puerto Rico, El San Juan and the Sands. The beaches in front of these deluxe properties are excellent, with white sands, although there's an on-site swimming pool at the Travelodge. There's a bar and a restaurant, the Country Kitchen, on the premises. The off-season rates are $83 for a single, $91 for a double, and $160 for a suite.

WHERE TO EAT
IN OLD SAN JUAN

Butterfly People Café. Calle Fortaleza 152. ☎ **787/723-2432.** Reservations not required. Main courses $5.50–$9.50. AE, DC, MC, V. Mon–Sat 11am–5pm. Bus: A7, T1, or 2. CONTINENTAL/AMERICAN.

This butterfly venture with gossamer wings (see "Shopping," below) is on the second floor of a restored mansion in Old San Juan. Next to the world's largest gallery devoted to butterflies, you can dine in the cafe, which overlooks a patio and has 15 tables inside. The cuisine is tropical and light European fare made with fresh ingredients. You might begin with gazpacho or vichyssoise, follow with quiche or a daily special, and finish with chocolate mousse or the tantalizing raspberry chiffon pie with fresh raspberry sauce. Wherever you look, framed butterflies will delight you.

Café Berlin. Calle San Francisco 407. ☎ **787/722-5205.** Main courses $3.75–$15.95. AE, MC, V. Daily 9am–11pm. Bus: A7, T1, or 21. INTERNATIONAL/VEGETARIAN.

This indoor-outdoor cafe-style restaurant overlooking plaza de Colón is a beloved favorite of locals. No one is quite sure how it got its name, as this cafe is not German; instead, it's known for its vegetarian dishes, including a specialty, an eggplant tofu sandwich with the works. You can also order chicken and turkey dishes as well, along with a delectable mahimahi. Salmon, shrimp, and most definitely quiche appear on the menu. You can make up various combinations of dishes. The cafe specializes in fresh bread, used in its tasty lunch sandwiches. You can also drop in for breakfast to sample homemade pastries.

El Patio de Sam. Calle San Sebastián 102. ☎ **787/723-1149.** Reservations not required. Main courses $7.95–$21.95. AE, DC, CB, DISC, MC, V. Sun–Thurs 11am–midnight, Fri–Sat 11am–1:30am. Bus: A7, T1, or 2. AMERICAN/PUERTO RICAN.

Located across from the Iglesia de San José, this popular gathering spot for American expatriates, newspeople, and shopkeepers is known for having the best burgers in San Juan. Even though the dining room is not outdoors, it has been transformed into a patio. You'll swear you're dining alfresco. Every table is placed near a cluster of potted plants, and canvas panels and awnings cover the skylight. For a satisfying lunch, try the black-bean soup, followed by the burger platter, and topped off with a key lime tart. Some other menu items have not met with favor among many readers, who have written us that the food was overpriced and the service confused. Nevertheless, this place remains Old Town's most popular dining room. There's live entertainment Monday to Saturday, with a guitarist playing Spanish music some nights and a classical pianist other nights.

Hard Rock Cafe. Calle Recinto Sur 253. ☎ **787/724-7625.** Reservations not required. Main courses $5.95–$15.95. AE, MC, V. Daily 11am–midnight. (Bar, daily 11am–2am.) Bus: A7, T1, or 2. AMERICAN.

Filled with rock 'n' roll memorabilia, this cafe lies in a historic district of the old town, serving a "classic" American cuisine against a backdrop of loud rock music. Between drinks and burgers, diners check out the collection of artifacts ranging from a wig worn by Elton John to a jacket worn by John Lennon. Throughout the day well-stuffed sandwiches and juicy burgers are served, along with fajitas, barbecued chicken, pork ribs, or even the catch of the day. The chili will set you ablaze. There's even a selection of salads. This is the most frequented dining spot in the old town, with a gift shop selling Hard Rock Cafe merchandise.

✪ La Bombonera. Calle San Francisco 259. ☎ **787/722-0658.** Reservations recommended. Main courses $5.75–$15.90. AE, MC, V. Daily 7:30am–8pm. Bus: M2, M3, or T1. PUERTO RICAN.

This favorite was established in 1902, and ever since it has been offering homemade pastries and endless cups of coffee in a traditional colonial decor. Its sandwiches are some of the best in town. For decades it was a rendezvous for the island's literati and for old San Juan families, but now it has been discovered by tourists. The authentic food is inexpensive. Regional dishes include rice with squid, roast leg of pork, and seafood asopao. For dessert, you might select an apple, pineapple, or prune pie, or one of the many types of flan. Service is polite, if a bit rushed, and the place fills up quickly at lunchtime.

La Mallorquina. Calle San Justo 207. ☎ **787/722-3261.** Reservations not accepted at lunch, recommended at dinner. Main courses $13.95–$29.95. AE, MC, V. Mon–Sat 11:30am–10pm. Bus: A7, T1, or 2. PUERTO RICAN.

San Juan's oldest restaurant was founded in 1848 and is in a three-story, glassed-in courtyard with arches and antique wall clocks. Even if you've already eaten, you might want to have a drink at the old-fashioned wooden bar. The chef specializes in the most typical Puerto Rican rice dish—asopao. You can have it with either chicken, shrimp, or lobster and shrimp. Arroz con pollo is almost as popular. Begin with garlic soup or gazpacho. Other recommended main dishes are grilled pork chops with fried plantain, beef tenderloin Puerto Rican style, and assorted seafood stewed in wine. Lunch is busy, and dinners are sometimes quiet. The food seems little changed over the decades; visit here for tradition rather than innovation.

NoNo's. Calle San Sebastián 100 (at calle Cristo). ☎ **787/725-7819.** Hamburgers and main courses $3.50–$10.95. AE, MC, V. Daily 11am–9pm. (Bar, daily 11am–4am.) Bus: A7, T1, or 2. AMERICAN/FAST FOOD.

In the heart of Old San Juan, NoNo's brings Stateside food to those eager for a taste of the salads, mozzarella sticks, three-decker sandwiches, chicken-fried steaks, hamburgers (here called NoNo burgers), and onion rings they've been missing. You'll sit beneath a beamed ceiling in one of San Juan's oldest buildings, near a large and accommodating bar where folks seem only peripherally interested in the food.

IN CONDADO

The Condado is generally an expensive place to dine. However, the elegant **Capriccio,** in the Condado Plaza Hotel, 999 Ashford Ave. (☎ **787/721-1000**), features early-bird specials from noon to 6:30pm daily. Everything on the menu, except seafood dishes and drinks, is half price, and all the choices are excellent. Major credit cards are accepted.

Caruso. 1104 Ashford Ave., Condado. ☎ **787/723-6876.** Reservations not required. Main courses $6.75–$30; lunch platters $5–$10. AE, DC, MC, V. Daily noon–11pm. Bus A7. ITALIAN.

Its decor and the brisk efficiency of its staff might remind you of a neighborhood trattoria in New York City, and in fact it's become the preferred neighborhood restaurant of many Condado residents who hail from New York. It's one of the most popular places around for pasta, partly because of its low prices and partly because of its simple but down-to-earth food. Menu items include shrimp scampi, filet mignon, veal piccata, veal marsala, and grilled fish of the day.

Mona's Mexican Restaurant. 1015 Ashford Ave. ☎ **787/728-0140.** Reservations not accepted. Main courses $4.50–$16.50. AE, DISC, MC, V. Daily 11:30am–midnight. Bus: A7 or 2. MEXICAN.

Occupying pleasant premises in the residential neighborhood of Ocean Park not far from the big resorts of Isla Verde, this restaurant re-creates Old Mexico in a tropical setting. Consider enjoying a tart margarita at the ample bar area before heading to your table. Specialties include all that's Tex-Mex—chimichangas, carnitas, enchiladas, tacos, burritos, and nachos.

✪ **Oasis.** 1043 Ashford Ave. ☎ **787/724-2005.** Reservations not required. Main courses $6.50–$32. AE, DC, MC, V. Daily noon–3pm and 6–11pm. Bus: A7, T1, or 2. CUBAN/INTERNATIONAL.

This lone budget restaurant manages to hold its own along an expensive Condado beachfront strip where prices are sometimes lethal. Most dishes here are very reasonable in price, except shellfish. It's really a family-style dining room that has a large array of "Cuban Créole" dishes, along with international specialties and Puerto Rican regional fare. The tables in back open onto views of the ocean.

Caldo gallego, that richly flavored soup of beans and greens, with meat and sausage, is a hearty opener, followed by any number of main courses, perhaps stuffed Cornish game hen, oxtails in a Créole sauce, breaded red snapper filet, or lobster asopao. Paella is another specialty (for at least two diners). Good value, good food (and plenty of it), and an informal, relaxed atmosphere keep this place going year after year.

Tony Roma's. In the Condado Plaza Hotel, 999 Ashford Ave. ☎ **787/721-1000,** ext. 2123. Reservations not accepted. Main courses $7.50–$17.95. AE, DC, MC, V. Daily noon–midnight. Bus: A7. BARBECUE.

Efficient and unpretentious, this is Puerto Rico's busiest branch of an international chain. It's one of the least expensive restaurants in the Condado, and it's a fine choice if you're in the mood for spicy barbecued food (the honey barbecue is not as fiery).

Via Appia. 1350 Ashford Ave., Condado. ☎ **787/725-8711.** Pizza $8.95–$14.95; main courses $8.95–$14.95. AE, MC, V. Daily 11am–midnight. Bus: A7. ITALIAN.

A favorite of *sanjuaneros* visiting Condado for the day, Via Appia offers food that's sometimes praiseworthy rather than merely passable. Its pizzas are the best in the neighborhood. Savory pasta dishes, including baked ziti, lasagne, and spaghetti with several of your favorite sauces, are also prepared. All of this can be washed down with sangría. During the day, freshly made salads or sandwiches are also available.

IN ISLA VERDE

✪ **Metropol.** Ave. Isla Verde. ☎ **787/791-4046.** Main courses $11–$15. AE, MC, V. Daily 11am–7pm. CUBAN / PUERTO RICAN / INTERNATIONAL.

This is part of a restaurant chain known for serving the island's best Cuban food, although the chefs prepare a much wider range of dishes. Metropol is the happiest blend of Cuban and Puerto Rican food we've ever discovered. The black-bean soup is among the island's finest, served in the classic Havana style with a side dish of rice and chopped onions. Endless garlic bread accompanies most dinners, likely to include Cornish game hen stuffed with Cuban rice and beans or perhaps marinated steak topped with a fried egg (reportedly Castro's favorite). Smoked chicken or chicken fried steak are also heartily recommended; portions are huge. Plaintains, yucca, and all that good stuff accompany most dishes. Finish with a choice of thin or firm custard.

Panadería España Repostería. Centro Villamar, Isla Verde. ☎ **787/727-3860.** Reservations not accepted. Sandwiches $3–$5. AE, DISC, MC, V. Daily 6am–10pm. Bus: A7, M7, or T1. SANDWICHES/COFFEES.

These writers believe that whenever a restaurant becomes famous for one item, it's worth walking across town just to sample it. That's the case with the Panadería España, which is said to make the Puerto Rican capital's definitive Cuban sandwich— a cheap meal in itself for budget travelers. Consisting of sliced baked pork packed in crusty bread, it's about the only thing offered except for drinks and coffee dispensed from behind a much-used bar. There's also an assortment of gourmet items from Spain, which are arranged as punctuation marks on shelves set against an otherwise all-white decor. The place has been serving simple breakfasts, drinks, coffee, and Cuban sandwiches virtually every day, in very much the same format, since it opened around 1970.

✪ **Repostería Kassalta.** Calle McLeary 1966. ☎ **787/727-7340.** Reservations not accepted. Full American breakfast $3.75–$4.50; soups $4.50; sandwiches $2.25–$5.25. MC, V. Daily 6am–10pm. Bus: T1. SPANISH/PUERTO RICAN.

This is the most famous of the cafeteria/bakery/delicatessens of San Juan because of its reasonable prices and eat-in and take-out foods. It lies in a commercial neighborhood 4 miles east of Old San Juan. When you get there, you'll enter a cavernous room flanked with modern sun-flooding windows and glass-fronted display cases, which, depending on the season, will be filled with meats, sausages, and pastries appropriate to the forthcoming holiday.

At one end of the room, patrons line up to place their order at a cash register, then carry their selections, cafeteria style, to one of the many tables. It helps to know Spanish. Among the selections offered are steaming bowls of the best caldo gallego in Puerto Rico. (Served in thick earthenware bowls; laden with collard greens, potatoes, and sausage slices; and accompanied with hunks of bread, this soup makes a meal in itself.) Also popular are Cuban sandwiches (made with sliced pork, cheese, and fried bread), steak sandwiches, octopus salad, and an assortment of omelets.

Sonny's Oceanfront Place for Ribs. In the Empress Oceanfront Hotel, 2 Amapola St. ☎ **787/791-3083.** Reservations not required. Main courses $8.95–$14.95. AE, DC, DISC, MC, V. Daily 8am–11pm. Bus: T1. AMERICAN.

This restaurant overlooks the sea and the hotel's terraced swimming pool. The cuisine is unpretentious and guaranteed to satisfy hunger pangs for American fare. You can order burgers, barbecued ribs, pastas, chicken, omelets, and steak. Swordfish can be grilled, broiled, or fried and brushed with lemon.

Village Bake Shop. 105 de Diego Ave. ☎ **787/724-8566.** Pastas $12.95–$15.95; sandwiches $7.95–$8.95. AE, MC, V. Wed–Sat 7:30am–6pm, Sun 7:30am–5pm. INTERNATIONAL.

At first the prices seem a bit high, but one plate of pasta is a meal unto itself. The bake shop also features the area's most well-stuffed sandwiches. Incidentally, you might want to stock up on some of its excellent and freshly baked pastries to take back to your room.

WORTH A SPLURGE

✪ **Pamela's.** In the Número Uno Guest House, calle Santa Ana 1, Ocean Park. ☎ **787/ 726-5010.** Reservations recommended. Main courses $14–$18. AE, MC, V. Mon–Sat noon–3pm and 7–10pm, Sun 11:30am–2:30pm and 7–10pm. CARIBBEAN FUSION.

At this previously recommended guest house in Ocean Park, you would hardly expect to encounter one of the finest chefs in the Caribbean, Pamela Hope Yahn. But that's what you get at Pamela's—that and some of the finest cuisine served in San Juan. Previously Ms. Yahn was at the famous Ottley's Plantation on the island of St. Kitts. For starters, we'd recommend her stuffed shrimp with a ginger mousse or one of her delectable and original soups—perhaps spiced South American turkey, corn, and potato, served with an aji sauce, avocado, and sour cream. For a main dish, the red snapper with baked stuffed mango, hearts of palm, and both portabello and button mushrooms represents Caribbean dining at its finest. You might also opt for the Jamaican-style roast loin of pork with candied ginger, dark rum, cloves, lime, and garlic, accompanied by nutmeg-scented sweet potatoes. The desserts are equally yummy.

PICNICS

Puerto Rico is usually ideal for picnicking year-round. The best place to fill a picnic basket is the **Repostería Kassalta** (see "Ocean Park," earlier in this chapter)—a cafeteria/bakery/deli with lots of goodies. Puerto Rican families often come here to order delicacies for their Sunday outings. The best places for a picnic are **Muñoz Marín Park,** along Las Américas Expressway, west of avenida Piñero, and the **Botanical Gardens** operated by the University of Puerto Rico in the Río Piedras section.

BEACHES, WATER SPORTS & OUTDOOR PURSUITS IN & AROUND SAN JUAN

BEACHES   With some 300 miles of coastline, both Atlantic and Caribbean, Puerto Rico obviously has plenty of beaches. Some, such as Luquillo, are overcrowded, especially on Saturday and Sunday. Others are practically deserted. If you find that secluded, hidden beach of your dreams, proceed with caution. On unguarded beaches you'll have no way to protect yourself or your valuables should you be approached by a robber or mugger, which has been known to happen. For more information about the island's many beaches, call the **Department of Sports and Recreation** (☎ 787/722-1551).

Beaches in Puerto Rico are open to the public, although you will be charged for parking and for use of *balneario* facilities, such as lockers and showers. The public beaches on the north shore of San Juan at **Ocean Park** and **Park Barbosa** are good, and can be reached by bus. **Luquillo,** on the north coast, is some 30 miles east of San Juan. Public beaches shut down on Monday; if Monday is a holiday, the beaches are open for the holiday but close the next day, Tuesday. Beach hours are 9am to 5pm in winter, to 6pm off-season. All three of these have changing rooms and showers; Luquillo also has picnic tables. You don't have to buy picnic supplies in San Juan if you're heading for Luquillo. You can follow the local families and stop by the food kiosks strung along the road leading to the beach, where you can get root vegetable croquettes stuffed with chicken or seafood, cigar-shaped pastries filled with meat, or crisp salt-cod fritters, along with cold beer.

GOLF   For just about the most inexpensive golf near San Juan, head for the ✪ **Bahia Beach Plantation Golf Course** (☎ 787/256-5600), lying at km 4.2, Highway 187, Rio Grande. Within a 30-minute drive east of San Juan, closer to the capital than any other major golf course, this 18-hole, par-72 course charges greens fees of $60 for 18 holes, including use of a golf cart. Clubs can be rented for between $15 and $35 a set.

SCUBA/SNORKELING   The continental shelf, which surrounds Puerto Rico on three sides, contributes to an abundance of coral reefs, caves, sea walls, and trenches for scuba diving and snorkeling.

In San Juan, the best-recommended option for underwater diving is **Karen Vega's Carib Aquatic Adventures,** P.O. Box 9024278, San Juan Station, San Juan, PR 00902 (☎ 787/724-1882). Most of its activities revolve around its main office in the rear lobby of the Radisson Normandie Hotel. The company offers diving certification from both PADI and NAUI as part of 40-hour courses priced at $465 each. A resort course for first-time divers costs $100. Also offered are kayak rentals (single or double) at $17 or $34 per hour, windsurfing (see below), and a choice of short, local excursions in San Juan or full-day diving expeditions to various reefs off the east coast of Puerto Rico.

TENNIS   In San Juan, the **Caribe Hilton & Casino,** calle Los Rosales (☎ 787/ 721-0303), and the **Condado Plaza Hotel & Casino,** 999 Ashford Ave. (☎ 787/ 721-1000), have tennis courts. Also there's a **public court** at the old navy base, Isla Grande, Miramar. The entrance is from avenida Fernández Juncos at Stop 11.

WINDSURFING   The sheltered waters of the Condado Lagoon in San Juan are a favorite spot. It's easy to find a shop renting windsurfing equipment and offering instruction. One of the best places in San Juan to go windsurfing is at **Karen Vega's Carib Aquatic Adventures,** with its main branch in San Juan's Radisson Normandie Hotel (☎ 787/724-1882). Rentals cost $25 per hour, with a lesson costing $45.

STEPPING BACK IN TIME: EXPLORING THE HISTORIC SIGHTS

The streets are narrow and teeming with traffic, but a walk through Old San Juan— in Spanish, El Viejo San Juan—is like a stroll through five centuries of history. You can do it in less than a day. In a 7-square-block historic-landmark area in the westernmost part of the city you can see many of Puerto Rico's chief historical sightseeing attractions, and do some shopping along the way.

The Spanish moved to Old San Juan in 1521, and the city founded here was to play an important role as Spain's bastion of defense in the Caribbean. Once the city was called Puerto Rico (Rich Port), as the whole island was once called San Juan.

Old San Juan

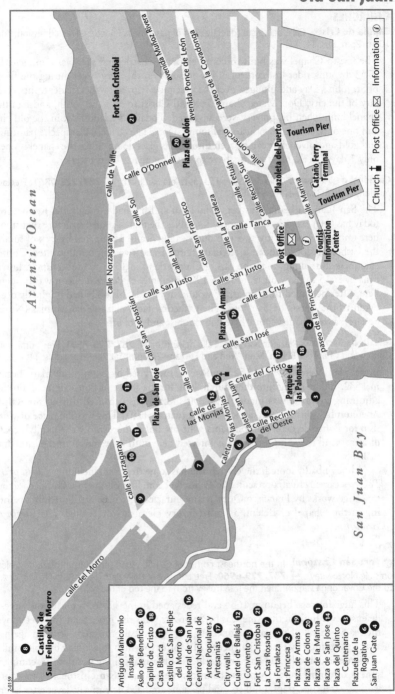

Atlantic Ocean

San Juan Bay

Castillo de
San Felipe del Morro

Fort San Cristóbal

Plaza de Colón

Plaza de Armas

Plaza de San José

Parque de
las Palomas

calle del Morro
calle Norzagaray
calle de Valle
calle Sol
calle Norzagaray
calle San Sebastián
calle Sol
calle San Justo
calle Luna
calle San Justo
calle San Francisco
calle La Fortaleza
calle O'Donnell
avenida Muñoz Rivera
avenida Ponce de León
paseo de la Covadonga
calle Comercio
calle Tetuán
calle Recinto Sur
calle Marina
calle Tanca
calle San José
calle La Cruz
calle del Cristo
calle de
las Monjas
caleta de las Monjas
caleta San Juan
calle Recinto
del Oeste
paseo de la Princesa

Plazoleta del Puerto
Tourism Pier
Cataño Ferry
Terminal
Tourism Pier
Tourist
Information
Center
Post Office

Church   Post Office   Information

Antiguo Manicomio
Insular 9
Asilo de Beneficias 10
Capillo de Cristo 18
Casa Blanca 11
Castillo de San Felipe
del Morro 8
Catedral de San Juan 16
Centro Nacional de
Artes Populares y
Artesanías 17
City walls 3
Cuartel de Ballajá 12
El Convento 15
Fort San Cristóbal 21
La Casa Rosada 7
La Fortaleza 5
La Princesa 2
Plaza de Armas 19
Plaza de Colon 20
Plaza de la Marina 1
Plaza de San Jose 14
Plaza del Quinto
Centenario 13
Plazuela de la
Rogativa 6
San Juan Gate 4

2-0159

95

CHURCHES

Capilla de Cristo. Calle del Cristo (directly west of paseo de la Princesa). Free admission. Tues 10am–2pm. Bus: T1.

The Cristo Chapel was built to commemorate what legend says was a miracle. In 1753 a young rider lost control of his horse down this very street during the fiesta of St. John's Day and plunged over the precipice. Moved by the accident, the secretary of the city, Don Mateo Pratts, invoked Christ to save the youth, and had the chapel built when his prayers were answered. Today it's a landmark in the old city and one of its best-known historical monuments. The chapel's Campèche paintings and gold and silver altar can be seen through its glass doors. Since the chapel is open only 1 day a week, most visitors have to settle for a view of its exterior.

Catédral de San Juan. Calle del Cristo 153 (at caleta San Juan). ☎ **787/722-0861.** Free admission. Daily 8:30am–4pm. Bus: T1.

The San Juan Cathedral was begun in 1540 and has had a rough life. Restoration today has been extensive, so it hardly resembles the thatch-roofed structure that stood here until 1529, when it was wiped out by a hurricane. Hampered by lack of funds, the cathedral slowly added a circular staircase and two adjoining vaulted Gothic chambers. But along came the earl of Cumberland in 1598 to loot it, and a hurricane in 1615 to blow off its roof. In 1908 the body of Ponce de León was brought here. After he'd died from an arrow wound in Florida, his body had originally been taken to the Iglesia de San José. The cathedral faces plaza de las Monjas (Nuns' Square), a tree-shaded spot where you can rest and cool off.

Iglesia de San José. Plaza de San José, Calle del Cristo. ☎ **787/725-7501.** Free admission. Church and Chapel of Belém, Mon–Wed and Fri 7am–2:30pm, Sat 7am–1pm. Bus: T1.

Initial plans were drawn in 1523 and work, supervised by Dominican friars, began in 1532. Before going into the church, look for the statue of Ponce de León on the adjoining plaza. It was made from British cannons captured during Sir Ralph Abercromby's unsuccessful attack on San Juan in 1797. This was the place of worship for Ponce de León's descendants, who are buried here under the family's coat-of-arms. And the conquistador was interred here until his removal to the cathedral in 1908.

Although badly looted, the church still has some treasures, including *Christ of the Ponces*, a carved crucifix presented to Ponce de León; four oils by José Campèche; and two large works by Francisco Oller. Many miracles have been attributed to a painting in the Chapel of Belém, a 15th-century Flemish work called *The Virgin of Bethlehem*.

FORTS

✪ **Fort San Cristóbal.** In the northeast corner of Old San Juan (uphill from plaza de Colón on calle Norzagaray). ☎ **787/729-6960.** Free admission. Daily 9am–5pm. Bus: T1, M3, or A7 to the Covadonga station; then the free trolley from to the top of the hill.

This huge fortress, begun in 1634 and redesigned in the 1770s, is one of the largest defenses ever built in the Americas by Spain. Its walls rise more than 150 feet above the sea, a marvel of military engineering. San Cristóbal protected San Juan against attackers coming by land, a partner to El Morro, to which it is joined by half a mile of monumental walls and bastions studded with cannon-firing positions. A complex system of tunnels and dry moats connects the center of San Cristóbal to its "outworks"—trenches, traps, bunkers, and bastions arranged defensively, layer after layer, over a 27-acre site. You'll get the idea if you look at a scale model on display. Be sure to see the Garita del Diablo, the Devil's Sentry Box, one of the oldest parts of San

Cristóbal's defenses and famous in Puerto Rican legend. The devil himself, it is said, would snatch away sentinels on this lonely post at the edge of the sea. Check at the guard house near the fort's entrance for the daily schedule of special activities and fort tours led by park rangers.

☼ **Castillo San Felipe del Morro.** At the end of calle Norzagaray. ☎ **787/729-6960.** Free admission. Daily 9am–5pm. Bus: T1 or M3.

Called El Morro, this fort stands on a rocky promontory dominating the entrance to San Juan Bay. Ordered built in 1539, the original fort was a round tower, which can still be seen deep inside the lower levels of the castle. More walls and cannon-firing positions were added, and by 1787 the fortification attained the complex design we see today. This fortress was attacked repeatedly by both the English and the Dutch. The National Park Service protects the fortifications of Old San Juan, which have been declared a World Heritage Site by the United Nations. With some of the most dramatic views in the Caribbean, El Morro is an intriguing labyrinth of dungeons, barracks, vaults, lookouts, and ramps. A video in English and Spanish is shown. The nearest parking is the underground facility beneath the Quincentennial Plaza at the Ballajá Barracks on calle Norzagaray.

Fort San Jerónimo. East of the Caribe Hilton, at the entrance to Condado Bay. ☎ **787/724-1844.** Free admission. Wed–Sat 9am–3pm. Bus: T1.

Completed in 1608, this fort was damaged in the English assault of 1797. Reconstructed in the closing year of the 18th century, it has now been taken over by the Institute of Puerto Rican Culture. To see the inside, you must call the Caribe Hilton; security here will open the gate.

OTHER HISTORIC SIGHTS

The **city walls** around San Juan were built in 1630 to protect the town against both European invaders and Caribbean pirates. The thickness of the walls averages 20 feet at the base and 12 feet at the top, with an average height of 40 feet. Between Fort San Cristóbal and El Morro, bastions were erected at frequent intervals. You can start seeing the walls from your approach from San Cristóbal on your way to El Morro. Take bus T1.

San Juan Gate, calle San Francisco and calle Recinto Oeste, built around 1635, just north of La Fortaleza, was the main gate and entry point into San Juan—that is, if you arrived by ship in the 18th century. The gate is the only one remaining of the several entries to the old walled city. Take bus T1.

Plazuela de la Rogativa, caleta de las Monjas, basks in legend. In 1797 the British across San Juan Bay at Santurce held the old town under siege. However, that same year they mysteriously sailed away. Later the commander claimed he feared that the enemy was well prepared behind those walls—he apparently saw many lights and believed them to be reinforcements. Some people claim that those lights were torches carried by women in a *rogativa* (religious procession) as they followed their bishop. A handsome statue of a bishop, trailed by a trio of torch-bearing women, was donated to the city on its 450th anniversary. Take bus T1.

El Arsenal. La Puntilla. ☎ **787/724-5949.** Free admission. Wed–Sun 8:30am–4:30pm. Bus: T1.

The Spaniards used shallow craft to patrol the lagoons and mangroves in and around San Juan. Needing a base for these vessels, they constructed El Arsenal, and it was at this same base that they, so to speak, staged their last stand, flying the Spanish colors until the final Spaniard was removed in 1898, at the end of the Spanish-American War. Exhibitions are held in the building's three galleries.

La Fortaleza. Calle Fortaleza, overlooking San Juan Harbor. ☎ **787/721-7000,** ext. 2211. Free admission. Garden tours (conducted in English and Spanish) given Mon–Fri every hour 9am–4pm. Bus: T1.

The office and residence of the governor of Puerto Rico is the oldest executive mansion in continuous use in the Western Hemisphere, and it has served as the island's seat of government for more than three centuries. Yet its history goes back farther, to 1553 when construction began for a fortress to protect San Juan's Spanish settlers during raids by Carib tribesmen and pirates. The original medieval towers remain, but as the edifice was subsequently enlarged into a palace, other modes of architecture and ornamentation were also incorporated, including baroque, Gothic, neoclassical, and Arabian. La Fortaleza has been designated a national historic site by the U.S. government. Informal but proper attire is required.

Casa Blanca. Calle San Sebastián 1. ☎ **787/724-4102.** Admission $1 adults, 50¢ children. Tues–Sat 9am–noon and 1–4:30pm. Bus: T1.

Ponce de León never lived here, although construction of the house (built in 1521) sometimes is attributed to him. The house was erected 2 years after the explorer's death, and work was ordered by his son-in-law, Juan García Troche. Descendants of the explorer lived in the house for about $2^{1}/_{2}$ centuries until the Spanish government took it over in 1779. This historic residence now houses two museums. On the first floor, the Juan Ponce de León Museum is furnished with antiques, paintings, and artifacts from the 16th through the 18th century. On the second floor, the Taíno Indian Ethno-Historic Exhibit opens with a series of 16th-century European maps of the known world, reproductions of famous paintings of Columbus, and charts of his voyage. Taíno life is depicted through artifacts, ceremonial objects, everyday articles, and a model of a native village.

Alcaldía (City Hall). Calle San Francisco. ☎ **787/724-7171,** ext. 3070. Free admission. Tours by appointment Mon–Fri 9am–3pm. Closed holidays. Bus: T1.

The City Hall, with its double arcade flanked by two towers resembling Madrid's City Hall, was constructed in stages from 1604 to 1789. Still in use, this building is more than a historic site—it's a unique place full of monuments and legends.

Casa de los Contrafuertes (House of the Buttresses). Plaza de San José, calle San Sebastián 101. ☎ **787/724-5477.** Free admission. Tues–Sat 8:30am–4:30pm. Bus: T1.

Adjacent to the Museo de Pablo Casals, this building, which has thick buttresses, is believed to be the oldest residence remaining in El Viejo San Juan. The complex also contains a **pharmacy museum,** which existed in the 19th century in the town of Cayey. Upstairs you'll find a **graphic arts museum,** displaying prints and paintings by local artists.

MUSEUMS: FROM THE TAÍNOS TO CASALS

Museo de las Americas. Cuartel de Ballajá. ☎ **787/724-5052.** Free admission. Tues–Fri 10am–4pm, Sat–Sun 11am–5pm.

One of San Juan's major new museums, the Museo de las Americas showcases the artisans of North, South, and Central America, featuring everything from carved figureheads from New England whaling ships to dugout canoes carved by Carib Indians in Dominica. Also on display are paintings by artists from throughout the Spanish-speaking world, some of which are for sale.

Museo de Pablo Casals. Plaza de San José, calle San Sebastián 101. ☎ **787/723-9185.** Admission $1 adults, 50¢ children. Tues–Sat 9:30am–5:30pm. Bus: T1.

Adjacent to the Iglesia de San José, this museum is devoted to the memorabilia that the cellist, conductor, and composer Pablo Casals left to the people of Puerto Rico. The maestro's cello is here, along with a library of videotapes (played upon request) of some of his festival concerts. This small 18th-century house also contains manuscripts and photographs of Casals. The annual Casals Festival, held during the first 2 weeks of June, draws worldwide interest and attracts some of the greatest performing artists.

Museo de Arte e Historia de San Juan. Calle Norzagaray 150. ☎ **787/724-1875.** Free admission. Mon–Fri 8am–noon and 1–4pm, Sat 9am–noon and 1–5pm. Bus: T1 to the Old San Juan terminal; then a free trolley car to the museum.

Located in a historic Spanish colonial building at the corner of calle MacArthur, this is a contemporary cultural center today. In the mid–19th century it was the city's main marketplace. Local art is displayed in the east and west galleries, and audiovisual materials reveal the city's history. Sometimes major cultural events are staged in the museum's large courtyard. English- and Spanish-language audiovisual shows are presented Monday to Friday every hour on the hour from 9am to 4pm.

Museum of the University of Puerto Rico. Ave. Ponce de León, Recinto de Río Piedras. ☎ **787/764-0000,** ext. 2452. Free admission. Mon–Fri 9am–4:30pm, Sat–Sun 9am–4pm. Take the bus marked RÍO PIEDRAS from plaza de Colón in Old San Juan to stop 36.

Here you'll find good collections of paintings by Puerto Rican artists, including Francisco Oller and José Campèche, the first important artist of the country (18th century). There's also a large collection of pre-Columbian Puerto Rican native artifacts from the Ingeri, sub-Taíno, and Taíno civilizations. In the museum's temporary exhibition hall you can see contemporary art exhibits.

HORSE RACING

Great thoroughbreds and outstanding jockeys compete all year at **El Comandante,** avenida 65 de Infantería, Route 3, km 15.3, at Canovanas (☎ **787/724-6060**), Puerto Rico's only racetrack, a 20-minute drive east of the center of San Juan. Post time varies from 2:15 to 2:45pm on Monday, Wednesday, Thursday, Friday, and Sunday. A restaurant is open on race days from 12:30 to 4:30pm. Entrance to the clubhouse costs $3 per person, although no admission is charged for the grandstand. Telephone for luncheon reservations; most credit and charge cards are accepted.

SHOPPING

U.S. citizens don't pay duty on items brought back to the United States. And you can still find great bargains on Puerto Rico, where the competition among shopkeepers is fierce. Even though the U.S. Virgin Islands are duty free, many readers report finding far lower prices on many items in San Juan than on St. Thomas.

The streets of the **Old Town,** such as calle San Francisco and calle del Cristo, are the major venues for shopping. Note, however, that most stores in Old San Juan are closed Sunday.

Native handcrafts can be good buys. Look for *santos* (hand-carved wooden religious figures), needlework, straw work, ceramics, hammocks, guayabera shirts for men, papier-mâché fruit and vegetables, and paintings and sculptures by Puerto Rican artists.

The biggest and most modern shopping plaza in the Caribbean Basin is **Plaza Las Americas,** located in the financial district of Hato Rey, right off the Las Americas Expressway. The complex, with its fountains and advanced architecture, has more than 200 mostly upscale shops.

BEACHWEAR

W. H. Smith. In the Condado Plaza Hotel, 999 Ashford Ave. ☎ **787/721-1000,** ext. 2094.

This outlet sells mostly women's clothing, everything from bathing suits and beach attire to jogging suits. For men, there are shorts, bathing suits, and jogging suits. There's also a good selection of books and maps.

BOOKS

Bell, Book & Candle. 102 de Diego Ave., Santurce. ☎ **787/728-5000.**

This large general-interest bookstore carries fiction and classics in both Spanish and English, plus a huge selection of postcards. It's the best bookstore in Santurce.

The Book Store. Calle San José 255. ☎ **787/724-1815.**

This is the leading bookstore in the old town, with the largest selection of titles. It sells a number of books on Puerto Rican culture and also sells good touring maps of the island.

BUTTERFLIES (MOUNTED)

Butterfly People. Calle Fortaleza 152. ☎ **787/723-2432.**

Butterfly People is a gallery and cafe in a handsomely restored building in Old San Juan. Butterflies, sold here in artfully arranged boxes, range from $20 for a single mounting. The butterflies are preserved and treated naturally and will last forever. The dimensional artwork is sold in limited editions and can be shipped worldwide. The majority of these butterflies come from farms around the world, some of the most beautiful coming from the densest tropical regions of Indonesia, Malaysia, and New Guinea.

CIGARS

Gillies & Woodward. Calle San Justo 253. ☎ **787/725-5280.**

Right in the heart of Old San Juan this shop carries the increasingly fashionable cigar made from home-grown tobacco. Frankly, these cigars aren't the level of a true Havana cigar, but they're the second-best thing—and you can bring them back to the States. Also available are flowers, souvenirs, and the best of Puerto Rican coffees.

COFFEE & HOT SAUCES

Spicy Caribbee. Calle Cristo 154. ☎ **787/725-4690.**

This store sells the finest of Puerto Rican coffee beans for about $10 per pound. It also offers moderately priced island handcrafts, plus other products from around the world, along with hot sauces and cookbooks featuring Puerto Rican recipes.

FACTORY OUTLETS

London Fog. Calle del Cristo 156. ☎ **787/722-4334.**

The last thing you need in steamy San Juan is a winter overcoat or parka, but the prices at this factory outlet of London Fog are usually so low that a purchase is often well worth it. Prices are between 30% and 35% less than for equivalent garments on the U.S. mainland. Men's, women's, and children's garments are displayed on two floors of a colonial house.

Polo Ralph Lauren Factory Store. Calle del Cristo 201. ☎ **787/722-2136.**

It's as stylish and carefully orchestrated as anything you'd expect from one of North America's leading clothiers. Even better, its prices are 35% to 40% less than the cost of equivalent garments sold retail on the U.S. mainland. You can find even greater discounts on irregular or slightly damaged garments. The store occupies two floors of a pair of colonial buildings, with one upstairs room devoted to home furnishings.

GIFTS & HANDCRAFTS

Anaiboa. Calle San Francisco 100. ☎ **787/724-8017.**

Anaiboa occupies a cubbyhole that opens onto a pedestrians-only stretch adjacent to calle del Cristo. Run by a married team of artists, it sells one-of-a-kind artifacts including ceramic boxes, hatracks, mirrors, serving trays, and small-scale furniture accented with whimsical drawings of faces, plants, and animals. Many objects sell for as little as $15.

Bared & Sons. Calle Fortaleza 265 (at calle San Justo). ☎ **787/724-4811.**

Now in its fourth decade, this is the main outlet of a chain of at least 20 upper-bracket jewelry stores on Puerto Rico. There's a worthy inventory of gemstones, gold, diamonds, and wristwatches on the street level that does a thriving business with cruise-ship passengers. But the real value of this store lies one floor up, where a monumental collection of porcelain and crystal is packed, in claustrophobic proximity, for display. It's a great source for hard-to-get and discontinued patterns (priced at around 20% less than at equivalent outlets Stateside) from Christofle, Royal Doulton, Wedgwood, Limoges, Royal Copenhagen, Lalique, Baccarat, and Daum.

De Aguadilla a San Juan. Calle de la Cruz 265 (at plaza de Armas). ☎ **787/722-0578.**

This shop has one of the best collections of inexpensively priced Puerto Rican crafts—wood carvings and pottery, but also hats and baskets. Its specialty is Puerto Rican lace, which is becoming increasingly rare.

El Artesano. Calle Fortaleza 314. ☎ **787/721-6483.**

Here you'll find Mexican and Peruvian icons of the Virgin Mary; charming depictions of fish and Latin American birds in terra-cotta and brass; all kinds of woven goods; painted cupboards, chests, and boxes; and mirrors and Latin dolls.

Galería Bóveda. Calle del Cristo 209. ☎ **787/725-0263.**

This long narrow space is crammed with exotic jewelry, clothing, wall hangings, and elaborately detailed masks from Sri Lanka, Ghana, India, and Thailand. Most of the clothing is designed for women.

M. Rivera. Calle del Cristo 107. ☎ **787/724-1004.**

Señor Rivera is the person to seek out if you're a collector of miniature houses—in this case in the Spanish style. They're made of hydrastone, then painted and glazed. The houses can be hung or placed on tables. Señor Rivera's designs are based on replicas of old houses still standing in San Juan and country homes in other parts of Puerto Rico. Prices start at $15.

Olé. Calle Fortaleza 105. ☎ **787/724-2445.**

Even if you don't buy anything, you can still learn a lot about the crafts displayed here. Practically everything that isn't made on Puerto Rico comes from South America, and all is artistically displayed in a high-ceilinged room decorated clear to the top. If you want a straw hat from Ecuador, hand-beaten Chilean silver, Christmas ornaments, or Puerto Rican *santos,* this is the place to buy them.

Puerto Rican Arts & Crafts. Calle Fortaleza 204. ☎ **787/725-5596.**

In a colonial building is this unique store, which is the premier outlet on the island for authentic artifacts from Puerto Rico. Here you'll find modern contemporary ceramics to traditional crafts such as hand-carved *santos*. Of particular interest are the papier-mâché carnival masks from the south-coast town of Ponce, whose grotesque and colorful features are originally made to chase away evil spirits.

JEWELRY

The Gold Ounce. Plaza los Muchachos, calle Fortaleza 201. ☎ **787/724-3102.**

This is the direct factory outlet for the oldest jewelry factory on Puerto Rico, the Kury Company. Most of the output is shipped Stateside. Don't expect a top-notch jeweler here: Many of the pieces are replicated in endless repetition. But don't overlook the place for 14-karat-gold ornaments. Some of the designs are charming, and prices are about 20% less than at retail stores on the North American mainland.

200 Fortaleza. Calle Fortaleza 200 (at calle de la Cruz). ☎ **787/723-1989.**

Known as a leading place to find bargains on fine jewelry in Old San Juan, this shop has 14-karat Italian gold chains and bracelets that are measured, fitted, and sold by weight. You can purchase watches or beautiful gems in modern settings in both 14- and 18-karat gold.

Vergina Gallery. Calle del Cristo 202. ☎ **787/721-0592.**

The most exotic jewelry emporium in San Juan, this is the only outlet in the Caribbean showcasing the neo-Byzantine and ancient Greek designs of Zolotos, one of Greece's most spectacular jewelers. Most of the pieces are made of hammered 18- and 22-karat gold, inset with colorful glittering gemstones. There's also an inventory of streamlined platinum jewelry from Germany, and worthy reproductions of medieval Greek and Russian icons, priced from $10.

Yas Mar. Calle Fortaleza 205. ☎ **787/724-1377.**

This shop sells convincing, glittering fake diamonds for those who don't want to wear the real thing. It also stocks real diamond chips, emeralds, sapphires, and rubies.

LINENS

The Linen House. Calle Fortaleza 250. ☎ **787/721-4219.**

This unpretentious store specializes in napery, bed linens, and lace. Inventories include embroidered shower curtains selling for around $35 each, and lace doilies, bun warmers, placemats, and tablecloths that seamstresses took weeks to complete. Some astonishingly beautiful items are available for around $30 each. The aluminum/pewter serving dishes have strikingly beautiful Spanish colonial designs. Prices here are sometimes 40% lower than on the North American mainland.

SAN JUAN AFTER DARK
THE PERFORMING ARTS

Qué Pasa, the official visitor's guide to Puerto Rico, lists cultural events, including music, dance, theater, film, and art exhibits.

Centro de Bellas Artes. Ave. Ponce de León 22. ☎ **809/724-4747.** Tickets $12–$60, depending on the show; 50% discounts for seniors. Bus: 1.

In the heart of Santurce, the Performing Arts Center contains the Festival Hall, Drama Hall, and the Experimental Theater. Some events here will be of interest only to those who speak Spanish; others attract an international audience.

El Teatro. In El Centro, at the Condado Beach Trio, Ashford Ave. ☎ **787/722-8433.** Admission $28 (but price can vary). Bus: A7.

In San Juan's convention center, this room is known for having the most spectacular show revues in San Juan. Usually these are in the *Olé Latino* style, with colorful costumes, Latin music, and dancing. A "taste of the tropics" is promised and ultimately delivered. Call to find out what's happening at the time of your visit. Shows are at 9pm Monday to Wednesday and Saturday, and at both 9 and 10pm on Friday. Friday-night shows include LeLoLai at 9pm and Olé Latino at 10pm.

Teatro Tapía. Ave. Ponce de León. ☎ **787/722-0407.** Tickets $10–$30.

Standing across from plaza de Colón, this theater was built about 1832. In 1976 a restoration returned the theater to its original look. Much of Puerto Rican theater history is connected with the Tapía, named after the island's first prominent playwright, Alejandro Tapía y Rivera (1826–82). Various productions—some musical—are staged here throughout the year and include drama, dances, and cultural events. You'll have to call the box office (open Monday to Friday from 9am to 4pm).

THE CLUB & MUSIC SCENE

Amadeus Disco. In El San Juan Hotel & Casino, Isla Verde Ave., Isla Verde. ☎ **787/791-1000.** Cover $8 Wed–Thurs and Sun, $10 Fri–Sat.

Its conservative art deco interior welcomes the rich and beautiful, the merely rich, and the gaggle of onlookers pretending to be both. The Amadeus Disco is in the most exciting hotel in San Juan, so a visit here could be combined with a stop in the adjacent casino and a gawk at the best-decorated lobby on Puerto Rico. The duplex area has one of the best sound systems in the Caribbean.

Egypt. Ave. Roberto H. Todd 1. ☎ **787/725-4664.** Cover (including one or two drinks) $5–$10.

This busy nightclub attracts young, upwardly mobile singles. There's a well-worn dance floor, although many visitors come only for drinks at the long and very accommodating bar. The decor is inspired by ancient Egypt. There's live music every Thursday and usually on Friday. The club is on two floors: normally one devoted to disco, the other to Latin music. No jeans are allowed on Thursday, Friday, or Saturday. The transformation from a bar to a crowded disco usually occurs around 9pm.

Laser. Calle de la Cruz 251. ☎ **787/725-7581.** Cover $8–$10.

Set in the heart of the old town, this disco attracts a mostly straight crowd. You can wander around the three floors of its historic premises, listening to whatever music happens to be hot in New York, with lots of additional Latino merengue and salsa thrown in as well. Laser is officially open Thursday, Friday, and Saturday, but also opens when cruise ships pull into port.

THE BAR SCENE

Fiesta Bar. In the Condado Plaza Hotel & Casino, 999 Ashford Ave. ☎ **787/721-1000.**

This bar attracts a healthy mixture of local residents who mingle with hotel guests. The margaritas are appropriately salty, the rhythms are hot and Latin, and the lack of a cover charge helps you forget any losses you might have suffered in the nearby casinos.

Maria's. Calle del Cristo 204. No phone.

Here you'll be served some of the coolest and most refreshingly original drinks in the capital—a banana, pineapple, or chocolate frost; an orange, papaya, or lime freeze; or a mixed-fruit frappé. The students, TV personalities, writers, and models who gather here also enjoy Mexican dishes, such as chili with cheese, tacos, or enchiladas.

⭐ **Palm Court.** In El San Juan Hotel, Isla Verde Ave., Isla Verde. ☎ **787/791-1000.**

This is the most beautiful bar on the island—perhaps in the entire Caribbean. Set amid russet-colored marble and Italian mahogany, and designed as an oval that wraps around a sunken bar area, it offers a view of one of the world's largest chandeliers and an undeniable sense of style. After 9pm Monday to Saturday, live music emanates from an adjoining room (El Chico Bar).

Shannon's Irish Pub. Calle Bori 496, Río Piedras. ☎ **787/281-8466.**

Ireland and its ales meet the tropics at this pub with a Latin accent. A sports bar, it's the regular watering hole of many university students, a constant supplier of high-energy rock 'n' roll and 10 TV monitors. There's live music Wednesday to Sunday—everything from rock to jazz to Latin. There are pool tables, and a simple cafe serves inexpensive lunches Monday to Friday.

Violeta's. Calle Fortaleza 56. ☎ **787/723-6804.**

Stylish, comfortable, and urban, Violeta's occupies the ground floor of a 200-year-old beamed house 2 blocks from the landmark Gran Hotel Convento. Sometimes a pianist performs at the oversize grand piano. An open courtyard in back provides additional seating.

HOT NIGHTS IN GAY SAN JUAN

The Barefoot Bar. Calle Vendig 2. ☎ **787/724-7230.**

This, along with the bar at the Atlantic Beach Hotel, just across the street, is the most tuned-in gay bar on Puerto Rico. The blue building has a terrace that extends out over the beach shared by the Marriott Hotel, almost next door. Simple lunches, consisting mostly of sandwiches and salads, are served from noon till around 4pm; after that the food service ends in favor of drinking and dialogues.

The Beach Bar. In the Atlantic Beach Hotel, calle Vendig 1. ☎ **787/721-6900.**

Its indoor/outdoor format, and its position adjacent to a terrace that extends out over the beach, are roughly equivalent to the facilities at the Barefoot Bar, just across the street. Together, they form a complex of bars and terraces that appeal to a mostly male and mostly gay clientele. A restaurant in the hotel serves breakfast and lunch.

Cups. Calle San Mateo 1, Santurce. ☎ **787/268-3570.**

This Latino tavern is the only place in San Juan that caters to gay women. Although music plays, it's conducive to quiet conversation over beer or wine.

Krash. 1257 Ave. Ponce de León, Santurce. ☎ **787/722-1131.** No cover Wed–Thurs and Sun, $10 (including two free drinks) Fri–Sat.

Any gay male employed by any of the cruise lines that dock in San Juan's harbor overnight will almost invariably head for the flashing lights and up-to-date music of Puerto Rico's largest and busiest gay disco. It was renovated in 1996 into an ancient Greek/Egyptian motif, and occupies two levels of a building in an urban neighborhood in the Santurce district. Rum-based drinks, merengue, and whatever music is favored in New York are popular, and most of the flirting, dancing, and dialogues here begin after around 10:30pm. Open Wednesday to Sunday from 9pm to 5am.

CASINOS

Casinos are one of the island's biggest draws. Many visitors come here on package deals and stay at one of the posh hotels at Condado or Isla Verde, just to gamble.

You can try your luck at the **Caribe Hilton** (one of the better ones), the **Condado Beach Trio, El San Juan Hotel & Casino** on Isla Verde Avenue, and the **Condado Plaza Hotel & Casino.** You don't have to flash a passport or pay admission, as in

European casinos. The **Radisson Ambassador Plaza Hotel and Casino** is another deluxe hotel noted for its casino action. There's another casino at the **Dutch Inn Hotel & Casino,** avenida Condado 55. Recently open is a casino at the **Holiday Inn Crowne Plaza Hotel and Tropical Casino** on Route 187.

The island's largest casino is the elegant **Sands Casino** at the Sands Hotel & Casino Beach Resort on Isla Verde Avenue at Isla Verde. Open from noon to 4am daily, this 10,000-square-foot gaming facility offers 207 slot machines, 16 blackjack tables, three dice tables, four roulette wheels, and a minibaccarat table.

The best casinos "out on the island" are those at the **Hyatt Regency Cerromar Beach** and **Hyatt Dorado Beach.** In fact, you can drive to either of these from San Juan to enjoy their nighttime diversions. There's also a casino at **Palmas del Mar** and yet another at the **Ponce Hilton and Casino.**

Most casinos are open daily from 1 to 4pm and again from 8pm to 4am. Jackets for men are sometimes requested.

2 Dorado

The name itself evokes a kind of magic. Along the north shore of Puerto Rico, about a 40-minute drive (22 miles) west of the capital, a world of luxury resorts and villa complexes unfolds. The big properties of the Hyatt Dorado Beach Hotel and Hyatt Regency Cerromar Beach Hotel sit on the choice white sandy beaches here. These properties cost far more than even our most generous budget allows, but you can still spend a day in the area, enjoying the white sandy beaches.

An unpretentious local place serving a good Puerto Rican cuisine is **El Malecón,** Route 693, km 8.2 (☎ **787/796-1645**), located in a small shopping center. It has a cozy family ambience and is especially popular on weekends. The chef is best with fresh seafood.

There's wonderful golf here, but it's very expensive. (We mention it because we know that golfers sometimes like to splurge on the top courses, though.) You'll find 72 holes of golf at the **Hyatt Resorts Puerto Rico** at Dorado (☎ **787/796-1234**). If you're determined to play one of the Hyatt courses, make it the north or south course and you'll pay $120 for greens fees for 18 holes. The east and west courses are even pricier.

If you want to windsurf or enjoy other water sports, the best place on the island's north shore is along the well-maintained beachfront of the Hyatt Dorado Beach Hotel. Here, **Lisa Penfield Watersports** (☎ **787/796-1234,** ext. 3768, or 787/796-2188) offers board rentals at $60 per half day. A kayaking/snorkeling trip, lasting 1½ hours, costs $45. Two-tank boat dives go for $119 per person. Waverunners can be rented for $55 per half hour, or a Sunfish for $50 an hour.

3 Highlights in Northwestern Puerto Rico

Dubbed "an ear to heaven," the **Arecibo Observatory** (☎ **787/878-2612**) contains the world's largest and most sensitive radar/radiotelescope. The telescope features a 20-acre dish or radio mirror set in an ancient sinkhole. It's 1,000 feet in diameter and 167 feet deep, and allows scientists to examine the ionosphere, the planets, and the moon with powerful radar signals and to monitor natural radio emissions from distant galaxies, pulsars, and quasars. It's being used by scientists as part of the Search for Extraterrestrial Intelligence (SETI). This research effort speculates that advanced civilizations elsewhere in the universe might also communicate via radio waves. The 10-year, $100-million search for life in space was launched on October 12, 1992, the 500-year anniversary of the New World's discovery by Columbus.

Unusually lush vegetation flourishes under the giant dish—ferns, wild orchids, and begonias. Assorted creatures like mongooses, lizards, and dragonflies have also taken refuge there. Suspended in outlandish fashion above the dish is a 600-ton platform that resembles a space station.

Free self-guided tours are available at the observatory Tuesday to Friday from 2 to 3pm and on Sunday from 1 to 4:30pm. There's a souvenir shop on the grounds. The observatory lies a 90-minute drive west of San Juan, outside the town of Arecibo. From Arecibo, it's a 35-minute drive via routes 22, 134, 635, and 625 (the site is signposted).

✪ **Río Camuy Cave Park** is 1 hour and 20 minutes west of San Juan on Route 129, at km 18.9 (☎ **787/898-3100**), and contains the third-largest underground river in the world. It runs through a network of caves, canyons, and sinkholes that have been cut through the island's limestone base over the course of millions of years. Known to the pre-Columbian Taíno peoples, the caves came to the attention of speleologists in the 1950s. They were opened to the public in 1986.

Visitors first see a short film about the caves, then descend into the caverns in open-air trolleys. The trip takes you through a 200-foot-deep sinkhole and a chasm where tropical trees, ferns, and flowers flourish, along with birds and butterflies. The trolley then goes to the entrance of Clara Cave of Epalme, one of 16 in the Camuy caves network, where visitors begin a 45-minute walk, viewing the majestic series of rooms rich in stalagmites, stalactites, and huge natural "sculptures" formed over the centuries. The park has added the Tres Pueblos Sinkhole and the Spiral Sinkhole to its slate of attractions.

The caves are open Tuesday to Sunday from 8am to 4pm. Tickets are $10 for adults, $7 for children 2 to 12; senior citizens pay $5. Parking is $2. For more information, phone the park.

4 Aguadilla

While big-spenders rush east from San Juan to pricey deluxe resorts, true budget travelers head for the west of Puerto Rico where the living's easy, the beaches are among the island's finest, and the hotels and restaurants are often a bargain.

Reached along the north-coast road (Rte. 2), Aguadilla is about 2 to 2¹⁄₂ hours from the capital, depending on traffic (Sunday traffic is the worse). As you travel here, you'll be following in the footsteps of Columbus, who stepped onto Puerto Rican soil somewhere along the northern half of this coast during his 1493 voyage.

The area around Aguadilla is known for its beaches, which are shaded by coconut palms extending along northwestern Puerto Rico from Rincón (see below) to the calm Crash Boat Beach north of Aguadilla. Other beaches are found around Borinquen Point, site of the former Ramey Air Force Base, now a civilian area being developed for tourism. From Punta Borinquen (its Spanish name), beaches stretch all the way to Isabela, which lies west of Quebradillas.

Be warned that waters off these beaches can be rough, especially from December to April. Although swimming isn't that great, the beaches draw windsurfers from around the world.

WHERE TO STAY

Hacienda El Pedregal. Aguadilla Bay, off Rte. 111 (P.O. Box 4719), Aguadilla, PR 00605. ☎ and fax **787/891-6068.** 27 rms. A/C TEL. Year-round, $53.50 single; $69.55 double; $61 for room with one large and one small bed. Extra person $10; children 11 and under stay free in parents' room. AE, MC, V.

At the highest point in Aguadilla, with the beach a 5-minute car ride away, this hacienda was the site of a former estate house. Now converted to receive guests, it consists of two white concrete-block and stucco buildings—one facing the ocean. The bedrooms are simply but immaculately furnished, most (but not all) with phone. Some rooms have balconies with a water view. The hacienda evokes a Puerto Rican parador. The open-air restaurant and bar is reasonably priced, serving standard Puerto Rican fare (three meals a day). There are two swimming pools, one for adults, the other for children. There's a large parking area. Locals often hold weddings here on the green lush grounds.

SHOPPING

Aguadilla is the center of Puerto Rico's tiny lace-making industry, a craft imported here many centuries ago by immigrants from Spain, Holland, and Belgium.

El Hoz de Anero, Shopping Center B & M, Gate 5 near Ramey in Aguadilla (☎ 787/890-4690), carries Puerto Rican *santos* (saint figurines), including the nativity and three kings. Prices, of course, depend on the size and material used, but start at $50. Wall hangings showing scenes from life in San Juan or Aguadilla are also featured, as are candle holders, picture frames, and hand-painted ceramic figures (not necessarily of local origin).

5 Rincón

At the island's westernmost point, Rincón, 6 miles north of Mayagüez, has one of the most exotic beaches on the island, which draws surfers from around the world. In and around this small fishing village are some unique accommodations.

If you rent a car at the San Juan airport, it will take approximately $2^1/_2$ hours to drive here via the busy northern Route 2, or 3 hours via the scenic mountain route (no. 52) to the south. We recommend the southern route through Ponce.

In addition, there are five flights each weekday, and three each on Saturday and Sunday, from San Juan to Mayagüez on **American Eagle** (☎ 800/433-7300). These flights take 45 minutes. From the Mayagüez airport, Rincón is a 30-minute drive to the north on Route 2 (go left or west at the intersection with Route 115). Round-trip fares range from $69 to $130 per person.

WHERE TO STAY

J. B. Hidden Village Hotel. Bo. Piedras Blancas, Sector Villarrubia, Aguada, PR 00602. ☎ **787/868-8686.** Fax 787/268-8701. 31 rms, 7 semisuites. A/C TV TEL. Year-round, $59.85 single; $77 double; $93–$130 semisuite. AE, MC, V.

Named after the initials of its owners (Julio Bonilla, his wife, Jinnie, and their son, Julio Jr.), this clean and isolated hotel opened in 1990. Located half a mile east of nearby Aguada, on a side street running off Route 4414, it's nestled into a valley between three forested hillsides and is almost invisible from the road outside. It offers a quiet and simple refuge to vacationers who enjoy exploring the area's many different beaches. There's a restaurant on the premises with a view looking out over a neighboring ravine, a small swimming pool, and a bar. Each bedroom offers views of the pool.

The Lazy Parrot. 413 Punta (P.O. Box 430), Rincón, PR 00677. ☎ **787/823-5654.** Fax 787/823-0224. 7 rms. A/C TV. Year-round, $60 single; $65 double. Extra person $5. AE, DISC, MC, V.

This is an extensively remodeled, family-run inn set in a residential neighborhood within a half-mile walk or drive to at least half a dozen different beaches. Originally built as a private home, the Lazy Parrot was converted into a guest house in 1989. The peach-colored accommodations have recently been upgraded. The rooms have small refrigerators, and one room, with a bunk-bed arrangement, is ideal for families. Most of the clientele are families or retired people seeking a safe, clean beach accommodation at a good price. A pool is scheduled to be installed at some point during the lifetime of this edition.

Even if you don't stay here, you may want to patronize the Lazy Parrot Restaurant, which offers good views from its main dining room, where your best bet is the catch of the day. It's more romantic at a table in the candlelit floral garden, where the coquí (tree frog), hummingbird, wild parrot, and butterflies can be seen year-round. The Sea Glass Bar is a popular local rendezvous point.

Parador Villa Antonio. Rte. 115, km 12.3 (P.O. Box 68), Rincón, PR 00677. ☎ **800/ 443-0266** in the U.S., or 787/823-2645. Fax 787/823-3380. 55 apts. A/C TV TEL. $74.90–$107 single or double. AE, DC, MC, V. From Rincón, take Rte. 2 to Rte. 22 and stay on 22 until you see the sign HATILLO-ARECIBO; at this point, bear left and get back on Rte. 2 and stay on it until you see a sign, ANASCO #109 LEFT, RINCÓN #115 RIGHT; take Rte. 115 until you reach El Bambino Restaurant; after passing the restaurant, take a hard left and in about 200 feet make a right turn.

Ilia and Hector Ruíz offer apartments by the sea in this privately owned and run parador. The beach outside is nice, but we've seen litter here; it's not kept as clean as it should be by the local authorities. Facilities include a children's playground, games room, two tennis courts, and a swimming pool. Surfing and fishing can be enjoyed just outside your front door, and you can bring your catch right into your cottage and prepare a fresh seafood dinner in your own kitchenette (there's no restaurant). Be aware that the air-conditioning doesn't work properly here, and in general better maintenance is needed. Room prices are based on the view, not the size.

Sea Beach Breezes. Fisherman's Walk, Sea Beach Rincón, PR 00677. ☎ **787/823-5389** or 212/988-3525. Fax 212/639-9690. 3 apts. TV. Year-round, $400 per week one-bedroom apt; $500 per week two-bedroom apt. Weekend rate, $75 daily one-bedroom apt; $100 daily two-bedroom apt. No credit cards.

These apartments are a good value. The complex consists of two two-bedroom apartments and one one-bedroom unit, all with fully equipped kitchens (microwave ovens), color TV, and full linen service. The interiors are simply yet tastefully decorated, and all apartments open onto ocean views. The complex is on a private beach and has a beachside gazebo for outdoor cooking and entertaining, although several restaurants dishing up a regional cuisine are nearby. Available nearby are scuba diving and snorkeling, golf and tennis, world-class windsurfing, casino gambling, boat cruises, and even whale watching.

WHERE TO EAT

The Black Eagle. Rte. 413, km 1.0 interio, Barrio Ensenada. ☎ **787/823-3510.** Main courses $10–$18. AE, MC, V. Daily 11am–11pm. STEAKS/SEAFOOD.

This restaurant one of the best in the neighborhood, serving up enormous portions of fresh seafood dishes at inexpensive prices. It's in an isolated black-and-white house adjacent to the beach, about a quarter of a mile north of the center of Rincón, close to the Black Eagle marina (with which it's not associated). In the wood-paneled dining room, you might begin your meal with a house special Black Eagle, a deceptively potent pink-colored cocktail. Menu items include lobster or shrimp cocktails, a 32-ounce porterhouse steak (the restaurant's trademark dish), grilled lobster, pan-fried conch, asopao of lobster or shrimp, and a traditional version of *mofongo criollo,* a hearty, typically Puerto Rican plantain dish in the Créole style. All main courses come with salad, bread, and vegetables.

HITTING THE BEACH & THE LINKS

One of Puerto Rico's most outstanding beaches, comparable to the finest surfing spots in the world, is at **Punta Higuero,** on Route 413 near Rincón. In the winter months especially, uninterrupted Atlantic swells, with perfectly formed waves averaging 5 to 6 feet in height, roll shoreward, and rideable swells sometimes reach 15 to 25 feet.

The **Punta Borinquén Golf Club** (☎ 787/890-2987), at Aguadilla, the former Ramey Air Force Base, has an 18-hole public course, open daily from 7am to 7pm. Greens fees are $10 for an all-day pass, plus an additional $10 for use of an electric cart.

6 Mayagüez

Puerto Ricans have nicknamed their third-largest city the "Sultan of the West." This port city, not architecturally remarkable, was once the needlework capital of the island. There are still craftspeople who do fine embroidery.

Mayagüez is the honeymoon capital of Puerto Rico. The tradition dates from the 16th century, when, it is said, local fathers in need of husbands for their daughters (because of the scarcity of eligible young men) kidnapped young Spanish sailors who stopped here for provisions en route to South America.

American Eagle (☎ 800/433-7300) flies six times daily throughout the year between San Juan and Mayagüez. The flight takes 25 minutes, although there are often ground delays. The round-trip fare ranges from $69 to $130.

If you rent a car at the San Juan airport, it will take approximately 2$^1/_2$ hours to drive to Mayagüez via the busy northern Route 2, or 3 hours via the scenic mountain Route 52 to the south.

WHERE TO STAY

Hotel Parador El Sol. Calle Santiago Riera Palmer, 9 Este, Mayagüez, PR 00680. ☎ **787/ 834-0303.** Fax 787/265-7567. 52 rms. A/C TV TEL. Year-round, $50 single; $60 double; $70 triple. Rates include continental breakfast. AE, MC, V.

This concrete building from 1970 provides reasonable and hospitable accommodations, although it's far more geared to business travelers than to tourists. It's located 2 blocks from the landmark plaza del Mercado in the heart of the city and is central to the shopping district and to all western-region transportation and highways. Furnishings are no frills in the seven-floor restored hotel, but it offers up-to-date facilities, including cable TV, a restaurant, and a swimming pool.

✪ **Parador Hacienda Juanita.** Rte. 105, km 23.5 (P.O. Box 777), Maricao, PR 00606. ☎ **800/443-0266** in the U.S. for reservations only, or 787/838-2550. Fax 787/838-2551. 21 rms. $64 single; $72 double. Children 11 and under stay free in parents' room. AE, MC, V.

Named after one of its long-ago owners, a matriarch named Juanita, this parador was originally constructed in 1836 as part of a coffee plantation. It's situated in relative isolation, surrounded by only a few neighboring buildings and the jungle, 2 miles west of the village of Maricao, beside Route 105 heading to Mayagüez. The pink-stucco house has a long verandah and a living room that's decorated with antique tools and artifacts of the coffee industry. The Luís Rivera family welcomes visitors and serves drinks and meals in their restaurant. There's a swimming pool, billiards table, and Ping-Pong table. The rooms are simple and rural, with ceiling fans, rocking chairs, and rustic furniture. None has a phone, TV, or air-conditioning; with the cool temperatures in this high-altitude place, no one really needs air-conditioning.

WHERE TO EAT

El Castillo. In the Best Western Mayagüez Resort & Casino, Rte. 104. ☎ **787/831-7575.** Main courses $12–$25; breakfast buffet $11.25; buffet lunch (Mon–Sat) $14; brunch buffet (Sun) $21.95. AE, MC, V. Daily 6:30am–11pm. INTERNATIONAL.

This is the most professionally managed large-scale dining room in western Puerto Rico; it's the premier restaurant in the largest hotel and casino in this part of the island. Budget travelers might not be able to stay here, but you can certainly take advantage of the reasonably priced dining. The copious lunchtime buffet is the town's best dining value. Dinners are à la carte only. The food here has real flavor—it isn't your typical bland hotel fare.

La Casona de Juanita. In the Parador Hacienda Juanita, Rte. 105, km 23.5. ☎ **787/838-2550.** Main courses $7.50–$19.95. AE, MC, V. Sun–Thurs 8am–8pm, Fri–Sat 8am–10pm. PUERTO RICAN.

You'll find some of the best food and the most reasonable prices in the area at this previously reviewed parador. The regional cuisine is prepared with flair and zest. The chef makes at least three regional soups daily (the menu is the same for lunch or dinner); our favorite is the shrimp and rice. Look for the daily special or else ask for one of the regular house specialties—corned beef and sweet banana pie, Puerto Rican–style beef stew, or local chicken, which can be breaded, fried, or roasted. Everything is served with rice, beans, and fried plantains. For dessert, make it guava shells with a native white cheese or homemade pumpkin custard pudding.

SURFING, TROPICAL GARDENS & MORE

BEACHES   Along the western coastal bends of Route 2, north of Mayagüez, lie the best surfing **beaches** in the Caribbean. Surfers from as far away as New Zealand come to ride the waves. You can also check out panoramic **Punta Higuero** beach, nearby on Route 413, near Rincón.

South of Mayagüez is **Boquerón Beach,** one of the island's best.

GOLF   For golfers, the **Best Western Mayagüez Resort & Casino** at Mayagüez (☎ 787/831-7575) makes arrangements for guests to play at a nine-hole course at a nearby country club.

OTHER ATTRACTIONS   The chief sight is the **Tropical Agriculture Research Station** (☎ 787/831-3435). At the administration office, ask for a free map of the tropical gardens, which contain one of the largest collections of tropical species useful to people, including cacao, fruit trees, spices, timbers, and ornamentals. It's on Route 65, between Post Street and Route 108, adjacent to the University of Puerto Rico at Mayagüez campus and across the street from the **Parque de los Próceres** (Patriots' Park). The grounds are open free, Monday to Friday from 7am to 4pm.

Mayagüez might also be the jumping-off point for a visit to ✪ **Mona Island,** "the Galápagos of the Caribbean," which enjoys many legends of pirate treasure and is known for its white-sand beaches and marine life. Accessible only by private boat, the island is virtually uninhabited, except for two policemen and a director of the institute of natural resources. The island attracts hunters seeking pigs and wild goats, along with big-game fishers. But mostly it's intriguing to anyone who wants to escape civilization. Playa Sardinera on Mona Island was a nesting ground of pirates. On one side of the island, Playa de Pajaros, there are caves where the Taíno people left their mysterious hieroglyphs. Camping is available at $1 per night. Everything needed, including water, must be brought in, and everything, including garbage, must be taken out. For further information, call the **Puerto Rico Department of Natural Resources** (☎ 787/724-3724).

7 Boquerón & Cabo Rojo

Boquerón is Puerto Rico's Cape Cod, lying in the southwestern corner of the island, and reached by heading south from Mayagüez along Route 102 (becoming 103) for 45 minutes or so, depending on traffic. Once a tiny fishing village, Boquerón is now a center of tacky restaurants and low-cost beachside inns. It is, in fact, the cheapest place on Puerto Rico to go for a beachside vacation. It's not an elegant resort like Palmas del Mar, but Puerto Ricans, along with a scattering of foreign visitors, like the funky, often raffish, atmosphere of this laid-back retreat.

The big draw is the white sandy beach, stretching for some 2 miles. Beach umbrellas aren't necessary because the palm trees bordering the beach offer shade. Vacationers come here to go fishing, sailing, waterskiing, windsurfing, or scuba diving. Deep-sea enthusiasts will find several dive shops scattered along the beach offering 3- to 5-day packages.

Boquerón has several restaurants known for their fresh fish and seafood (although they're not strong on fruit and vegetables, except for plantains, rice and beans). But you can eat well without going to a restaurant. At various beach shacks you can purchase fresh oysters, a local delicacy. They're shucked right on the spot, and locals douse them with hot sauce. You can also purchase skewers of chicken. For another local delicacy—sold at various stands—finish off with the incredibly delicious maize ice cream, made with sweet corn and dusted with paprika (don't knock it until you've tried it).

Sleepy Boquerón is part of the municipality of Cabo Rojo. An additional attraction is the **Boquerón Lagoon,** a refuge for ducks and other birds. You can also shop here for crafts at various kiosks in the area.

Directly south of Boquerón is the fishing and resort community at **El Combate Beach.** This area is the headquarters for the U.S. Fish and Wildlife's Caribbean refuges. A visitors' center provides information about regional wildlife refuges and local bird-watching trails.

A coastal mangrove forest and a salt farm sprawl along the southwest tip of the island. You can drive along a dirt road trenched with potholes to the "end of the line," where the 19th-century Spanish colonial **Cabo Rojo Lighthouse** awaits you. A former pirate hangout, this section—called Punta Jagüey—is one of the most beautiful spots in the Caribbean, if you don't mind the rough ride to it. The lighthouse's squat hexagonal blue tower is now boarded up. But few come here just to view the lighthouse. Once here, you're treated to Puerto Rico's most panoramic view of the rugged coast and an inner lagoon with bays on either sides. It's worth the detour.

WHERE TO STAY AT BOQUERÓN

At the tiny fishing village of Boquerón (now a vacation and water-sports center), the government of Puerto Rico offers beachside cabañas that sleep up to six, which is one of the best values on the island for those seeking a holiday by the sea. Arrangements can be made by calling or contacting **Centro Vacacional Boquerón** (☎ 787/722-1551;** fax 787/722-0090). Beachside cabañas sleeping up to six rent for only $32.10 per night during the week, rising to $53.50 on Friday and Saturday (no credit cards). The cabañas have two bedrooms, a bath, and a kitchen, although they're sparsely furnished. At this price, you even have to provide your own bed linen and cooking utensils.

Parador Boquemar. 101 Rte. 307, Boquerón, PR 00622. ☎ **800/933-2158** or 787/851-2158. Fax 787/851-7600. 64 rms. A/C TV. Year-round, $65 single; $65–$75 double. AE, MC, V. From either Mayagüez or San Germán, take Rte. 102 into Cabo Rojo and then Rte. 100 south; turn right onto Rte. 101 and the hotel will be 2 blocks from the beach.

Parador Boquemar, built in the late 1980s, lies near Boquerón Beach (one of the best bathing beaches on the island) in the southwest corner of the island, between Mayagüez and Ponce. There's also a swimming pool, popular with Puerto Rican families, in back of the hotel. The Boquemar rents comfortable bedrooms with modern furnishings and has a well-known restaurant (see below).

WHERE TO STAY AT CABO ROJO

Combate Guest House. Playa el Combate, Cabo Rojo, PR 00623. ☎ **787/254-0001** or 787/747-0384. 19 rms. A/C TV. Winter, $35 single; $40–$50 double, triple, or quad; $75 room for up to eight. Summer, $42 single; $48–$50 double, triple, or quad; $95 room for up to eight. Children 11 and under stay free in parents' room. No credit cards.

A bit funky, frayed and tattered in parts, this hotel is recommended for its "end of the world" location off Route 301 in the southwestern corner of Puerto Rico. It's for beach buffs who don't mind roughing it a bit. The somewhat barebone rooms are mainly for sleeping, as guests spend most of their days on the beach. Two concrete and wood buildings shelter the hotel. Some of the accommodations contain small kitchens. There's also a large patio with showers, chairs, tables, cooking facilities, and a refrigerator for sharing. Although there's no restaurant on site, several are within walking distance. The facility is undergoing remodeling and may have improved by the time of your visit. Summer is the high season here, unlike most of Puerto Rico.

Hotel Joyuda Beach. Rte. 102, km 11.7, Cabo Rojo, PR 00623. ☎ **787/851-5650.** Fax 787/255-3750. 41 rms. A/C TV TEL. Year-round, $70–$85 single or double. Two children 11 and under stay free in parents' room. AE, DISC, MC, V. Follow Rte. 102 south of Mayagüez to Joyuda.

On the beach in scenic Cabo Rojo, this 1989 hotel offers comfortably furnished and air-conditioned bedrooms, with such amenities as private baths and room service. It's a good center for touring such attractions as El Combate Beach and the Cabo Rojo Wildlife Refuge. Tennis and golf are just 5 minutes away, and sportfishing charters can also be arranged, as well as windsurfing and canoeing. The hotel is often a favorite of Puerto Rican honeymooners. Its restaurant is open only on Saturday and Sunday.

WHERE TO EAT

✪ **Casona de Serafín.** Punta Arena Joyuda, Rte. 102, km 9. ☎ **787/851-0068.** Reservations required for Sun meals. Main courses $19.50–$24.50. AE, MC, V. Daily 11:30am–11pm. Drive 3 miles south on Rte. 102. PUERTO RICAN.

Set in a modest concrete building beside the highway and sporting a clean stucco-and-tile interior, this restaurant offers fresh seafood and well-prepared Puerto Rican platters. Seafood, brought in fresh every day, is served in such concoctions as lobster parmigiana, red snapper in Spanish sauce, a zarzuela of shellfish, three versions of asopao, and a number of shrimp preparations. There also are filet mignons and flank steaks from a charcoal brazier. It's a splurge, but it's one of our favorites.

La Cascada. At the Parador Boquemar, 101 Rte. 307. ☎ **787/851-2158.** Main courses $9.50–$15.75. AE, MC, V. Mon–Thurs 7:30am–noon and 4–8:30pm, Fri–Sun 7am–9pm. PUERTO RICAN.

Known for its fresh seafood, this place is especially popular with San Juan families who flock to the beaches here on weekends and always schedule a dinner at La Cascada. The staff here has their good days and bad days, and service is among the slowest along the coast, but you can often get such good-tasting fresh fish that you're willing to suffer the inconvenience. The red snapper can be broiled or fried and often is memorable. Begin with one of the salads, perhaps made of conch or octopus, then proceed deeper into the menu, perhaps ordering a rice stew with lobster or shrimp in a chili sauce. The meat dishes—shipped in frozen—are not noteworthy in any way, although the chicken stew isn't bad. Specialties include the chef's special rice with seafood and vegetables blended or mashed green plantain stuffed with seafood, including lobster and shrimp.

8 Ponce

Puerto Rico's second-largest city, Ponce—called the "Pearl of the South"—was named after Loíza Ponce de León, grandson of Juan Ponce de León. Today it's Puerto Rico's principal shipping port on the Caribbean. The city is well kept and attractive, as reflected by its many plazas, parks, and public buildings. There is something in its lingering air that suggests a provincial Mediterranean town. Look for the *rejas* (framed balconies) of the handsome colonial mansions.

Maps and information can be found at the **tourist office,** on the second floor of the Citibank Building on plaza de las Delicias (☎ **787/841-8160**).

GETTING THERE

Ponce lies 75 miles southwest of San Juan and is reached by Route 52. There is no bus service between the two cities.

American Eagle (☎ **800/433-7300**) flies twice a day between San Juan and Ponce (a 40-minute flight) for $69 to $90 round-trip.

WHERE TO STAY

Days Inn. Rte. 1, km 123.5, Mercedita, Ponce, PR 00715. ☎ **800/329-7466** or 787/841-1000. Fax 787/841-2560. 117 rms, 3 suites. A/C TV TEL. Year-round, $94.50 single or double; $119.50 suite. AE, DC, MC, V.

A 15-minute drive east of Ponce on Highway 52, opposite the Interamerican University, this hotel has modest bedrooms that are conservative and comfortable. The prices appeal to families. The facilities include a courtyard swimming pool, a children's wading pool, a Jacuzzi, a coin-operated laundry, an international restaurant, a bar/disco, and ice and vending machines for sodas and snacks.

Mary Lee's by the Sea. Rte. 333, km 6.7 (P.O. Box 394), Guánica, PR 00653. ☎ **787/821-3600.** 9 units (with kitchens). Year-round, $110 suite; $120–$130 one-bedroom apt; $140–$150 two-bedroom house; $160–$200 three-bedroom house. Extra person $10. Taxes extra. No credit cards.

Owned and operated by Michigan-born Mary Lee Alvarez, a fiercely independent former resident of Cuba and a self-described "compulsive decorator," this is an informal collection of cottages, seafront houses, and apartments located beside the coastal highway 4 miles east of Guánica. Two of the buildings are California-style houses; the rest are a confusing medley of other structures built since the 1970s. The entire compound is landscaped with flowering shrubs, trees, and vines.

To the north is the Guánica National Forest, a well-known sanctuary for birds and wildlife, designated an International Biosphere Reserve. Picnic areas, trails, and campsites are found throughout the reserve. The hotel sits next to sandy beaches and a handful of uninhabited offshore cays. For the benefit of its nature-watching guests, the hotel maintains about half a dozen rental boats with putt-putt motors, two different waterside sun decks, and several kayaks. A single visit by a maid each week is included in the price, although for an extra fee guests can arrange to have a maid come in every day. Each unit includes a modern kitchen, an outdoor barbecue pit, and a sense of privacy.

Don't come here looking for nighttime activities or enforced conviviality: The place is quiet, secluded, and appropriate only for low-key vacationers seeking privacy and isolation with a companion and/or with nature. There isn't a bar or restaurant here, and there aren't any formally organized activities on the premises.

Melía. Calle Cristina 2, Ponce, PR 00731. ☎ **787/842-0260.** Fax 787/841-3602. 78 rms. A/C TV TEL. Year-round, $65–$80 single; $70–$85 double. Rates include continental breakfast. AE, DC, MC, V. Parking $3.

A city hotel with southern hospitality, the Melía—which has no connection with other hotels in the world bearing the same name—often attracts businesspeople. The location is a few steps away from Our Lady of Guadalupe Cathedral and from the Parque de Bombas (the red-and-black firehouse). The lobby floor and all stairs are covered with Spanish tiles of Moorish design. The desk clerks speak English. The rooms are comfortably furnished; most have a balcony facing either busy calle Cristina or the old plaza. Breakfast is served on a rooftop terrace with a good view of Ponce, and the restaurant on site is independently run. You can park your car in the lot nearby.

WHERE TO EAT

✪ **El Ancla.** Ave. Hostos Final 9, Playa Ponce. ☎ **787/840-2450.** Main courses $5.95–$35. AE, DC, MC, V. Sun–Thurs 11am–10pm, Fri–Sat 11am–midnight. PUERTO RICAN/SEAFOOD.

This place ranks among the best restaurants of Ponce. Much of its appeal derives from its location south of the city on soaring piers that extend from the rocky coastline out over the surf. As you dine, the sound of the sea rises from beneath your feet. Specialties, made with the catch of the day, might include red snapper served with a pumpkin flan, dorado in a tomato-brandy sauce, seafood casserole, and broiled lobster. Steak, veal, and chicken dishes are also available. The dishes have real Puerto Rican zest and flavor.

Lupita's Mexican Restaurant. Calle Isabel 60. ☎ **787/848-8808.** Reservations required on weekends. Main courses $7–$26. AE, DC, MC, V. Sun–Thurs 11am–10pm, Fri–Sat 11am–2am. MEXICAN/PUERTO RICAN.

Set in a 19th-century building and its adjoining courtyard, a short walk from Ponce's main square, this is the creative statement of Hector de Castro. The specialties include tortilla soup, taco salads, grilled lobster tail with tostones, seafood fajitas, and burritos, tacos, and enchiladas with a wide choice of fillings. Some standard Puerto Rican dishes are offered as well. On Friday from 8pm to midnight a mariachi band will probably provide entertainment.

WORTH A SPLURGE

La Montserrate. Sector Las Cucharas, Rte. 82. ☎ **787/841-2740.** Main courses $14–$29. AE, DC, MC, V. Daily 10am–10pm. PUERTO RICAN/SEAFOOD.

Beside the seafront, in a residential neighborhood about 4 miles west of the town center, this restaurant draws a loyal clientele from the surrounding houses. A culinary institution in Ponce, it occupies a large, airy, modern building divided into two different dining areas. The first of these is slightly more formal than the next. Most visitors, however, head for the large room in back, where windows on three sides encompass a view of some offshore islands.

Specialties, concocted from the catch of the day, might include octopus salad, four different kinds of asopao, a whole red snapper in Créole sauce, or (for diners who've already had their fill of seafood) a selection of different steaks and grills. The Velásquez family are the congenial owners.

⊙ **Mark's at the Melía.** In the Melía Hotel, calle Cristina. ☎ **787/842-0260.** Reservations recommended. Main courses $8–$21; lunch $12–$18. AE, DC, MC, V. Tues–Sat noon–3pm and 6–11pm. INTERNATIONAL.

The hot new restaurant excitement in Ponce is generated by Mark and Melody French who took over what was a rather dull restaurant in this landmark hotel. This elegantly appointed setting provides a showcase for chef Mark's classical cookery with fresh local ingredients and Melody's expertise in wine and service. At lunch you can be tantalized by tostone skins with plantains, or tempura jumbo shrimp with an Oriental salad. Soups are likely to feature cream of pumpkin, followed by such main dishes as corn-crusted red snapper with a yucca purée. At night you get the best French signature dishes in Ponce, including roast rack of lamb with a mint crust, country veal chop flavored with horseradish, and duck breast with summer berries. Spectacular desserts include vanilla flan layered with rum sponge cake and topped with caramelized banana or a crisp filo with mascarpone cheese and a warm mango compôte.

SEEING THE SIGHTS

A $40-million restoration project is restoring more than 1,000 buildings to their original turn-of-the-century charm. Here architectural styles combine neoclassical with "Ponce Créole" and later art deco to give Ponce its distinctive ambience.

Any of the Ponceños will direct you to their ⊙ **Museo de Arte de Ponce,** avenida Las Americas 25 (☎ 787/848-0505), which has the finest collection of European and Latin American art in the Caribbean. Among the nearly 400 paintings, sculptures, and other artwork on display are exceptional pre-Raphaelite and Italian baroque paintings. The building was designed by Edward Durell Stone and has been called the "Parthenon of the Caribbean." It's open daily from 10am to 5pm. Adults pay $4; children 11 and under are charged $2.

Most visitors head for the **Parque de Bombas,** plaza de las Delicias (☎ 787/ 284-3338), the main plaza of Ponce. This fantastic old black-and-red firehouse was built for a fair in 1883. Open Wednesday to Monday from 9:30am to 6pm.

Around from the firehouse, the trail will lead to the **Cathedral of Our Lady of Guadalupe,** calle Concordia / calle Unión (☎ 787/842-0134). Designed by the architects Francisco Porrato Doría and Francisco Trublard in 1931, featuring a pipe organ installed in 1934, it remains an important place for prayer. The cathedral is open Monday to Friday from 6am to 3:30pm and on Saturday and Sunday from 6am to noon and 3 to 8pm.

El Museo Castillo Serrallés, El Vigía 17 (☎ 787/259-1774), the largest and most imposing building in Ponce, was built high on a hilltop above town by the Serrallés family (owners of a local rum distillery) during the 1930s. This is one of the architectural gems of Puerto Rico and the best evidence of the wealth produced by the turn-of-the-century sugar boom. Guides will escort you through the Spanish Revival house, where Moorish and Andalusian details include panoramic courtyards, a baronial dining room, and terraced gardens. It's open Tuesday to Sunday from 10am to 5pm. Admission is $3 for adults, $2 for senior citizens over 65, and $1.50 for students and children 11 and under.

The oldest cemetery in the Antilles, excavated in 1975, is near Ponce on Route 503 at km 2.7. The **Tibes Indian Ceremonial Center** (☎ 787/840-2255) contains some 186 skeletons, dating from A.D. 300, as well as pre-Taíno plazas from A.D. 700. Bordered by the Portugués River, the museum is open Wednesday to Sunday from 9am to 4pm. Admission is $2 for adults and $1 for children. Guided tours in English and Spanish are conducted through the grounds. Shaded by trees are seven rectangular ball courts and two dance grounds. The arrangements of stone points on the dance grounds, in line with the solstices and equinoxes, suggest a pre-Columbian Stonehenge. A re-created Taíno village includes not only the museum but also an exhibition hall where you can see a documentary about Tibes; you can also visit the cafeteria and souvenir shop.

The **Hacienda Buena Vista,** Route 10, km 16.8 (☎ 787/284-7020), is a 30-minute drive north of Ponce. Built in 1833, it preserves an old way of life, with its whirring waterwheels and artifacts of 19th-century farm production. Once it was one of the most successful plantations on Puerto Rico, producing coffee, corn, and citrus. The rooms of the hacienda have been furnished with authentic pieces from the 1850s. Two-hour tours are conducted Wednesday to Sunday at 8:30am, 10:30am, 1:30pm (the only English tour), and 3:30pm. Reservations are required; contact the Conservation Trust of Puerto Rico (☎ 787/722-5882 Monday to Friday; otherwise, call the hacienda directly). Tours cost $5 for adults, $2 for children. The hacienda lies in the small town of Barrio Magüeyes, on Route 10 from Ponce to Adjuntas.

SHOPPING

If you feel a yen for shopping, head for the **Fox-Delicias Mall,** at the intersection of calle Reina Isabel and plaza de Las Delicias, the city's most innovative shopping center. Among the many interesting stores here is **Regalitos y Algo Mas,** located on the upper level, which specializes in unusual gifts from around Puerto Rico. Look especially for the Christmas tree ornaments, crafted from wood, metal, colored porcelain, or bread dough, and for the exotic dolls.

9 Exploring Northeastern Puerto Rico

Now that we've covered the western portion of Puerto Rico, we'll begin heading east from San Juan. From the capital, Route 3 leads toward the fishing town of Fajardo, where you'll turn north to Las Croabas, about 31 miles from the capital.

You'll be near ✪ **Luquillo Beach,** one of the island's best and most popular public stretches of sand.

In the Luquillo Mountains east of San Juan is another favorite escape from the capital—**El Yunque,** a tropical forest teeming with hundreds of species of plant and animal life (see box, below).

WHERE TO STAY & EAT AT CEIBA (NEAR EL YUNQUE)

Casa Cubuy. Rte. 191, km 22 (P.O. Box 721), Rio Blanco, PR 00744. ☎ **787/874-6221.** 5 rms. Year-round, $65 single; $75 double. Rates include American breakfast. AE, MC, V.

Most guests come to Casa Cubuy for the proximity to El Yunque, Puerto Rico's 28,000-acre tropical rain forest where one may spot the endangered Puerto Rican parrot. This is a tranquil establishment meant mainly for the ecotourist. The rooms are decorated in a tropical motif offering clean and relaxed surroundings. The owner, Marianne Kavanaugh, serves healthy meals at very reasonable prices: $10 for lunch or $12.50 for dinner. For those days you're in the mood for the beach, you can visit Playa de Naguabo, 20 minutes away, for a day of fun in the sun.

Ceiba Country Inn. Rd. no. 977, km 1.2 (P.O. Box 1067), Ceiba, PR 00735. ☎ **787/885-0471.** 9 rms. A/C TEL. Year-round, $60 single; $70 double. Extra person $5. Rates include breakfast. AE, DISC, MC, V. Free parking.

If you're looking for an escape from the hustle and bustle of everyday life, then this is the place for you. This small well-maintained bed-and-breakfast is located on the

In case you want to see the world.

At American Express, we're here to make your journey a smooth one. So we have over 1,700 travel service locations in over 120 countries ready to help. What else would you expect from the world's largest travel agency?

do more

AMERICAN EXPRESS

Travel

http://www.americanexpress.com/travel

In case you want to be welcomed there.

We're here to see that you're always welcomed at establishments everywhere. That's why millions of people carry the American Express® Card – for peace of mind, confidence, and security, around the world or just around the corner.

do more

AMERICAN
EXPRESS

Cards

And just in case.

We're here with American Express® Travelers Cheques
and Cheques *for Two*.® They're the safest way to carry
money on your vacation and the surest way to get a
refund, practically anywhere, anytime.

Another way we help you...

do more

AMERICAN
EXPRESS

Travelers
Cheques

El Yunque Tropical Rain Forest

Some 25 miles east of San Juan lies El Yunque, the only tropical forest in the U.S. National Forest system. It was given national park status by President Theodore Roosevelt. With 28,000 acres, it's said to contain some 240 tree species (only half a dozen of which are found on the mainland United States). In this world of cedars and satinwood (draped in tangles of vines), you'll hear chirping birds, see wild orchids, and perhaps hear the song of the tree frog, the coquí. The entire forest is a bird sanctuary and may be the last retreat of the rare Puerto Rican parrot.

El Yunque is situated high above sea level, and the peak of El Toro rises to 3,532 feet. You can be fairly sure you'll be showered upon, as more than 100 billion gallons of rain falls here annually. But the showers are brief and there are lots of shelters.

El Yunque offers a number of walking and hiking trails. One such trail is the rugged "El Toro," which passes through four different forest systems en route to Pico El Toro, the highest peak in the forest. El Yunque Trail leads to three of the recreation area's most spectacular lookouts, and the Big Tree Trail is an easy walk to panoramic La Mina Falls. Just off the main road is La Coca Falls, a sheet of water cascading down mossy cliffs.

Nearby, the Sierra Palm Interpretive Service Center offers maps and information and arranges for guided tours of the forest.

A 45-minute drive southeast from San Juan (near the intersection of Route 3 and Route 191), El Yunque is a popular half-day or full-day outing. Major hotels provide guided tours. For more information about the park, call the **rangers' office** (☎ 787/887-2875).

easternmost part of Puerto Rico near the Roosevelt Roads U.S. naval base, and to reach this little haven in the mountains you must rent a car. El Yunque is only 15 miles away. Housed in a large old family home, the rooms, located on the bottom floor, all have private baths; two also have small refrigerators. The rooms are decorated in a tropical motif with flowered murals on the walls painted by a local artist. For a quiet evening cocktail, you may want to visit the small lounge on the second floor.

TO THE LIGHTHOUSE: EXPLORING LAS CABEZAS DE SAN JUAN NATURE RESERVE

Better known as **El Faro** or "The Lighthouse," this preserve in the northeastern corner of the island, north of Fajardo off Route 987, is one of the most beautiful and important areas on Puerto Rico—a number of different ecosystems flourish in the vicinity.

Surrounded on three sides by the Atlantic Ocean, the 316-acre site encompasses forestland, mangroves, lagoons, beaches, cliffs, offshore cays, and coral reefs. El Faro serves as a research center for the scientific community. It's home to a vast array of flora and fauna, including sea turtles and other endangered species.

The nature reserve is open Wednesday to Sunday; reservations are required, so call before going. For reservations throughout the week, call ☎ 787/722-5882; for reservations on Saturday and Sunday, call ☎ 787/860-2560 (reservations on weekends can be made only on the day of your intended visit). Admission is $5 for adults, $2 for children 11 and under, and $2.50 for seniors. Guided tours are conducted at 9:30am, 10am, 10:30am, and 2pm (in English at 2pm).

CAGUAS

Located 20 miles south of San Juan, Caguas is the largest city in the interior and the focal point of the broad and fertile Turabo Valley. Ringed by mountain peaks, the city has a population of around 120,000, many of whom commute to work in San Juan. The city was named after Caguax, the 16th-century Taíno chief who ruled the valley during the Spanish conquest and whose peacemaking efforts eventually led, according to legend, to his conversion to Christianity. The town's central square, plaza Palmer, with its 19th-century cathedral, is quite charming.

FAJARDO

This small and sleepy town was established as a supply depot for the many pirates who plied the nearby waters. Today a host of private yachts bob at anchor in its harbor, and the many offshore cays provide naturalists with secluded beaches. From Fajardo, ferryboats make choppy but frequent runs to the offshore islands of Vieques and Culebra (see later in this chapter). Close by are the coral-bordered offshore islands, the most popular being Icacos, a favorite among snorkelers and divers. To get there, take Route 3 from the eastern outskirts of San Juan all the way to Fajardo.

WHERE TO STAY & EAT IN FAJARDO

Parador La Familia. Rte. 987, km 42, Las Croabas, Fajardo, PR 00648. ☎ **787/863-1193.** Fax 787/850-5345. 28 rms. A/C TV TEL. $66.35 single; $77.05 double. AE, DC, DISC, MC, V.

This parador (certainly not the best in the chain) is located near the beach in this northeastern fishing village. The building is modern and undistinguished, and readers have complained about the laid-back style of management, but it's a popular little favorite among many islanders. Only one room opens onto a balcony. Ask to look at your room before checking in. Facilities include private parking, two swimming pools (one for adults and another for children), a cocktail lounge, and a cafeteria serving breakfast only.

Mon's Mexican Restaurant. Rte. 3, km 53. ☎ **787/860-6300.** Main courses $4.50–$16.50. AE, DISC, MC, V. Tues–Fri 6pm–midnight, Sat–Sun 11:30am–2pm and 6pm–midnight. MEXICAN.

A branch of this restaurant on San Juan's Condado became so popular that its owners decided to extend their zesty cuisine to the east coast of Puerto Rico. Here in a new setting Old Mexico is re-created. A full array of Tex-Mex specialties is served—chimichangas, carnitas, enchiladas, tacos, burritos, and nachos. You've had it all before, and probably in better versions. But Mona's does provide change-of-pace dining in a town not known for its gastronomy.

CAMPING

There are some three dozen camping sites that are located in parks ranging from Luquillo Beach to El Yunque National Forest. Tent sites are available at about $4 per person, although it's also possible to rent *casetas* (tiny cottages), lean-tos, huts, and even small trailers. Costs average $20 per night. Don't expect luxury; these are barebone and rustic. Sometimes a cold shower might be offered; at other times there's no running water or even a toilet. As such, these are recommended only for the most rugged campers. For more information about the designated areas for camping, contact the **Department of Natural Resources** (☎ 787/724-3724) or the **Recreation Department** (☎ 787/722-1771).

10 Palmas del Mar

Called the "Caribbean side of Puerto Rico," the residential resort community of Palmas del Mar lies on the island's southeastern shore, 45 miles from San Juan, outside the town of Humacao, about an hour's drive from the San Juan airport.

You'll find plenty to do: golf, tennis, scuba diving, sailing, deep-sea fishing, horseback riding, whatever. Hiking on the resort's grounds is another favorite activity. There's a forest preserve with giant ferns, orchids, and hanging vines. There's even a casino. In fact, the resort has one of the most action-packed sports programs in the Caribbean.

The Humacao Regional Airport is 3 miles from the northern boundary of Palmas del Mar. Its 2,300-foot strip will accommodate private planes; no regularly scheduled airline currently serves the Humacao airport.

WHERE TO STAY

Lying on 2,700 acres, **Palmas del Mar,** P.O. Box 2020, Humacao, PR 00791 (☎ **800/468-3331** in the U.S., or 787/852-6000), is a former coconut plantation including a stretch of the Caribbean coastline. Guests are housed in villas built around a marina, the beach, a tennis complex, and a championship golf course. You have a choice of either rooms or villas, depending on your space needs. In the same complex are some privately owned condominium homes that the owners make available to guests when they're not living in them. In addition to the villas, guests can stay at the luxurious Palmas Inn or the Candelero Hotel. Most guests book in Palmas del Mar on a package plan, such as a golf package.

However, prices are high here. If you're an off-season traveler between mid-April and mid-December, you can take advantage of discounts at the Candelero Hotel.

Candelero Hotel. Palmas del Mar (P.O. Box 2020), Humacao, PR 00791. ☎ **800/468-3331** or 787/852-6000. Fax 787/852-6320. 101 rms. A/C TV TEL. Winter, $192–$211 single or double. Off-season, $138 single or double. MAP $55 per person extra in winter, $34.50 off-season. AE, DC, MC, V.

The rooms here come in a variety of sizes, some with king-size beds. High cathedral ceilings accentuate the roominess that's further extended by patios on the ground floor. The main dining spot is Las Garzas. The beach and golf course are near at hand.

WHERE TO EAT

The resort restaurants tend to be expensive, but you can find a number of places serving reasonably priced snacks and meals daily from 9:30am to 5pm. At any of these places you can have a light meal for $12, maybe less if you want only a hamburger.

The least expensive dining spots on the grounds include **El Coquí Bar & Grille,** a colorful Caribbean-style beach hut that's a family favorite. Located on Candelero Beach, adjacent to the children's play area and a miniature golf course, it offers light snack fare and beach libations.

Beach Bohío is the Palmas del Mar beach party headquarters. Directly on Candelero Beach, it features live calypso music, exotic tropical drinks, snacks, and fresh grilled items.

The **Crosscourt Counter** offers patio dining overlooking Court Number 8. The menu focuses on light and healthy eating, with 75% of the main courses being vegetarian. Crosscourt also specializes in refreshing fruit and yogurt smoothies, the ideal pick-me-up after a grueling game of tennis.

ACTIVE SPORTS, ON & OFF THE WATER

Nonguests of the Palmas del Mar resorts can still use these hotel facilities, but should call ahead first.

GOLF   The **Golf Club** at Palmas del Mar (☎ 787/852-6000, ext. 54) is one of the leading courses on Puerto Rico. On the southeast coast, it has a par-72, 6,803-yard layout designed by Gary Player. Crack golfers consider holes 11 to 15 the toughest five successive holes in the Caribbean. The pro shop is open daily from 7am to 5pm.

HORSEBACK RIDING   The **Equestrian Center** at Palmas del Mar (☎ 787/852-6000, ext. 12721) has 42 horses, including English hunters for jumping, plus a variety of trail rides and instruction at all levels of ability. The land set aside for equestrian pursuits abuts the resort's airstrip and is bounded on one side by a stream. Trail rides skirt this creek and follow paths through the coconut plantation and jungle. A trail ride costs $22 per person for 1 hour and $40 for 2 hours.

SCUBA DIVING   The **Coral Head Divers & Water Sports Center,** P.O. Box 10246, Humacao, PR 00792 (☎ 800/635-4529 in the U.S., or 787/850-7208), operates out of a building on the harbor at the Palmas del Mar Resort. The dive center owns two fully equipped boats, measuring 26 and 48 feet. The center offers daily two-tank open-water dives for certified divers, plus snorkeling trips to Monkey Island and Vieques. The two-tank dive includes tanks, weights, and computer at $75. A snorkeling trip to Monkey Island includes use of equipment and a beverage at $45 per person. A scuba resort lesson costs $45.

TENNIS   The **Tennis Center** at Palmas del Mar (☎ 787/852-6000, ext. 51), the largest in the Caribbean, features 20 courts. Court fees are $18 per hour during the day and $22 at night. Special tennis packages are available, including accommodations. Call for more information.

PALMAS DEL MAR AFTER DARK

The hot nightspot in Palmas del Mar is the **Palm Terrace Restaurant & Lounge,** near the casino. Here guests can drink and dance to the latest rhythms Wednesday to Sunday from 8pm to 2am (perhaps later on Friday and Saturday). The $7 minimum includes your first drink.

The **casino** in the Palmas del Mar complex, near the Palmas Inn (☎ 787/852-6000, ext. 10142), is near the reception area. It has 12 blackjack tables, two roulette wheels, a craps table, and dozens of slot machines. The casino is open daily from 6pm year-round: Sunday to Thursday to 2am and Friday and Saturday to 3am. Under Puerto Rican law, drinks cannot be served in a casino, but you can enjoy one in the Palm Terrace Lounge.

11 Island Drives

Puerto Rico is a relatively small island, barely 100 miles long and about 35 miles wide, but there is a wide variety of natural scenery. From your car you can see terrain ranging from the rain forests and lush mountains of El Yunque to the lime deposits of the north and the arid stretches along the south shore, where irrigation is necessary and cacti grow wild. Seasonal changes also transform the landscape: In November the sugarcane fields are in bloom, and in January and February the flowering trees along the roads are covered with red and orange blossoms. Springtime brings delicate pink flowers to the Puerto Rican oak and deep-red blossoms to the African tulip tree, whereas summer is a flamboyant time when the roadsides seem to be on fire with blooming flowers.

Puerto Rico has colorful but often narrow and steep roads. While driving on mountain roads, blow your horn before every turn; this will help to avoid an accident. Commercial road signs are forbidden, so make sure that you take along a map and this guide to keep you abreast of restaurants, hotels, and possible points of interest. There are white roadside markers noting distances in kilometers (1 kilometer is equal to 0.62 miles) in black lettering. Speed limits are given in miles per hour.

Two programs that have helped the Puerto Rico Tourism Company successfully promote Puerto Rico as "The Complete Island" are the *paradores puertorriqueños* and the *mesones gastronómicos.*

The *paradores puertorriqueños* are a chain of privately owned and operated country inns under the auspices of the Commonwealth Development Company. These hostelries are easily identified by the Taíno grass hut that appears in the signs and logos of each one. The Puerto Rico Tourism Company started the program in 1973, modeling it after Spain's parador system, although it's a poor cousin. Each parador is situated in a historic or particularly beautiful spot. They vary in size, but all share the virtues of affordability, hospitable staffs, and high standards of cleanliness.

The paradores are also known for their food—each serves Puerto Rican cuisine of excellent quality, with meals starting at $15. There are now paradores at locations throughout the island, many within an easy drive of San Juan. For reservations or further information, contact the **Paradores Puertorriqueños Reservation Office,** P.O. Box 902-3960, Old San Juan Station, San Juan, PR 00902 (☎ **800/443-0266** in the mainland U.S., 800/981-7575 in Puerto Rico, or 787/721-2884 in San Juan).

As you tour the island, you'll find few well-known restaurants, except for those in major hotels. However, there are plenty of roadside places and simple taverns. If you long for authentic island cuisine, you can rely on *mesones gastronómicos* (gastronomic inns). This established dining "network," sanctioned by the Puerto Rico Tourism Company, highlights restaurants recognized for excellence in preparing and serving Puerto Rican specialties at modest prices. Mesón gastronómico status is limited to restaurants outside the San Juan area that are close to major island attractions.

What follows are two driving tours of the Puerto Rican countryside. The first will take you to the lush tropical forests and sandy beaches of eastern Puerto Rico, the second to the subterranean sights of Karst Country and on to the west and south coasts. They're both extended tours—the first takes approximately 2 days to complete and the second approximately 6 days—but Puerto Rico's small size and many roads will give you many places to pick up or leave the tour. In fact, there are several points in the tours where we give you the opportunity to cut your tour short and head back to San Juan.

DRIVING TOUR 1
The Rain Forests & Beaches of the East

Start: San Juan.
Finish: San Juan.
Time: Allow approximately 2 days, although you may wish to stay longer at places along the way.
Best times: Any sunny day Monday to Friday.
Worst times: Saturday and Sunday, when the roads are often impossibly crowded.

This tour will take you through some of Puerto Rico's most spectacular natural scenery, including El Yunque rain forest and Luquillo Beach. You'll travel through the small towns of Trujillo Alto, Gurabo, Fajardo, Naguabo, Humacao, Yabucoa, San Lorenzo, and Caguas before returning to San Juan.

From the center of San Juan, go to Río Piedras and take Route 3 (avenida 65 de Infantería, named after the Puerto Rican regiment that fought in World War II and the Korean War). Turn south onto Route 181 toward Trujillo Alto, then take Route 851 up to Route 941. At the end of the valley you can spot the:

1. **Lake of Loíza.** Houses can be seen nestled on the surrounding hills. You may even see local farmers *(jíbaros)* riding horses laden with produce going to or from the marketplace. The lake is surrounded by mountains. Your next stop is:

2. **Gurabo.** This is tobacco country, and you'll know that you're nearing the town from the sweet aroma enveloping it (tobacco smells sweet before it's harvested). Part of the town of Gurabo is set on the side of a mountain and the streets consist of steps.

   Leave the town by heading east on Route 30. Near Juncos, turn left onto Route 185 north, follow it up through Lomas, and then get on Route 186 south. This road offers views of the ocean beyond the mountain and valleys. At this point you'll be driving on the lower section of the Caribbean National Forest; the vegetation is dense, and you'll be surrounded by giant ferns. The brooks descending from the mountains become small waterfalls on both sides of the road. At about 25 miles east of San Juan is:

3. **El Yunque.** Consisting of about 28,000 acres, it's the only tropical forest in the U.S. National Forest system. It contains some 240 different tree species native to the area (only half a dozen of these are found on the mainland United States). In this world of cedars and satinwood (draped in tangles of vines), you'll hear chirping birds, see wild orchids, and perhaps hear the song of the tree frog—the *coquí*. The entire forest is a bird sanctuary and may be the last retreat of the rare Puerto Rican parrot.

   El Yunque is situated high above sea level, and the peak of El Toro is at 3,532 feet. You can be fairly sure you'll be showered upon, since more than 100 billion gallons of rain falls here annually. However, the showers are brief and there are many shelters.

   Continue driving on Route 186 through Benítez and El Verde until you reach Route 986. Turn south and drive until you reach Route 191, which will take you to the:

4. **Sierra Palma Visitor Center.** Located at km 11.6 on Route 191, the center is open daily from 9:30am to 5pm. Guides here give lectures and show slides; groups, if they make arrangements in advance, can go on guided hikes. Since the center has no working telephone, call the Administrative Headquarters of the **El Yunque Ranger District** (☎ 787/887-2875) for information about the area.

   To make your way back, backtrack on Route 191 until you reach Route 3. Five miles east from the intersection is:

5. **Luquillo Beach.** About 30 miles east of San Juan, edged by a vast coconut grove, this crescent-shaped beach is not only the best on Puerto Rico but also one of the finest in the Caribbean. You pay $1 to enter with your car, and you can rent a locker, take a shower, and use the changing rooms to put on your suit. Luquillo Beach becomes rather crowded on weekends, so if possible go on a weekday when you'll have more sand to yourself. Picnic tables are available.

   The beach is open Tuesday to Sunday from 9am to 5pm; it's closed Monday (if Monday is a holiday, the beach will shut on Tuesday that week instead). Before entering the beach, you may want to stop at one of the roadside thatched huts that sell Puerto Rican snacks and pick up the makings for a picnic.

Not far from the beach is the Parador Martorell, where you can spend a restful night at the seaside (see "Where to Stay Along the Way," at the end of this tour).

From Luquillo, return to Route 3 east until the first exit to Fajardo, where you make a left onto Route 194. At the traffic light at the corner of the Monte Brisas Shopping Center, turn left; stay on this road until the next traffic light and turn right. Continue on this road until it intersects with Route 987. Turn left onto Route 987 and continue until you reach the entrance to:

6. **Las Cabezas de San Juan Nature Reserve,** better known as El Faro (The Lighthouse), one of the most beautiful and important areas of the island—unique because of the number of different ecological communities that flourish here.

Surrounded on three sides by the Atlantic Ocean, the 316-acre site encompasses forest land, mangroves, lagoons, beaches, cliffs, offshore cays, and coral reefs. El Faro serves as a research center for the scientific community. Home to a vast array of flora and fauna (such as sea turtles and other endangered species), including abundant and varied underwater life, it's an important spawning ground for fish and crustaceans, and for shore and migratory birds.

The nature reserve is open Friday to Sunday; since reservations are required, call ☎ 787/722-5882 before going. Admission is $5 for adults, $2 for children 11 and under (parking included). Guided tours, lasting 2 to 2¹/₂ hours, are scheduled four times daily: at 9:30am, 10am, 10:30am, and 2pm.

After visiting the reserve, you can take the same road back to Route 3 and then follow the highway signs into:

7. **Fajardo.** This fishing port was hotly contested during the Spanish-American War. Sailors and fishers are attracted to the shores of Fajardo and nearby Las Croabas, which has a lot of fish restaurants. If you have time, you can take a very satisfying trip by ferry from Fajardo to either Vieques or Culebra, small islands off the Puerto Rican coast that make urban troubles seem far, far away (see below).

Continue south on Route 3, following the Caribbean coastline. At Cayo Lobos, just off the Fajardo port, the Atlantic meets the Caribbean. Here the vivid colors of the Caribbean seem subdued compared to those of the ocean.

Go through the town of Ceiba, near the Roosevelt Navy Base, until you reach:

8. **Naguabo Beach.** Here you can have coffee and *pastelillos de chapin* (pastry turnovers that were actually used as tax payments during Spanish colonial days). At km 70.9 of Route 3, take a brief detour to the town of Naguabo and enjoy the town plaza's scented, shady laurel trees, imported from India.

Continue south along Route 3, going through Humacao and its sugarcane fields. When the cane blooms during November and December, the tops of the fields change colors according to the time of day. Humacao itself isn't of much interest, but it has a balneario-equipped beach with changing facilities, lockers, and showers. From here you can detour to the sprawling resort of:

9. **Palmas del Mar.** This is a sun-and-sports paradise; see section 10 for more details.

After this stopover, you can continue along Route 3 through Yabucoa, nestled amid some hills. The view along the road opens up at Cerro La Pandura, a mountain from which there's a panoramic outlook over giant boulders onto the Caribbean.

At the town of Maunabo, leave Route 3 for Route 181, which passes through the mountains to San Lorenzo. Here, Route 183 will lead you to Caguas, where you may choose between the scenic tour (Route 1) or the speedy highway (Route 52) back into San Juan.

WHERE TO STAY ALONG THE WAY

Parador Martorell. 6A Ocean Dr., Luquillo, PR 00773. ☎ **787/889-2710.** 11 rms, 7 with bath. A/C TV. $65 single or double without bath, $75 single or double with bath; $107 family room for four with bath. Rates include breakfast. MC, V. At km 36.2 along Rte. 3, turn toward the shore, then turn left and drive 4 short blocks.

Back in 1800 the Martorell family came to Puerto Rico from Spain and fell in love with the island. Today their descendants own and operate this Luquillo parador near the island's most impressive beach. When you arrive at the parador, you'll find it surrounded by locked iron gates (the neighborhood isn't considered safe at night). The rooms are rather dour and you may not want to stay more than 1 night. The real reason to recommend the place is not so much for its charm, but for its location near Luquillo Beach, which has shady palm groves, crescent beaches, coral reefs for snorkeling and scuba diving, and a surfing area. Try to see your bedroom before checking in.

DRIVING TOUR 2
Karst Country/West & South Coasts

Start: San Juan.
Finish: San Juan.
Time: Between 2 and 6 days, depending on how much of the itinerary you want to complete; the tour could run longer if you spend extra time out at some of the stops along the way.
Best times: Monday to Friday, any sunny day.
Worst times: Saturday and Sunday, when the roads are overcrowded with drivers from San Juan.

This tour begins with a foray into the famous karst district of Puerto Rico. Along the way, you'll see the Taíno Indian Ceremonial Ball Park, Pagan Pagan's Cave, Río Camuy Cave Park, and Arecibo Observatory. You will then emerge from the island's interior to begin a roundabout tour of the west and south coasts, taking in Guajataca Beach, Mayagüez, San Germán, Phosphorescent Bay, Ponce, Coamo, and numerous other towns and attractions.

Starting out from San Juan, take Route 2 west through the town of Manatí, after which you'll pass the pineapple region. At km 57.9 turn left at Cruce Dávila and follow Route 140 south to the village of Florida. At km 25.5 you'll find a coffee cooperative where, during harvest time, the beans are processed, ground, and packed. At km 30.7, turn right toward the:

1. **Hacienda Rosas.** A coffee plantation, interesting at all times, is especially so from September to December or January, when groups of pickers walk under the bushes and gather the crimson beans while other workers process the yield.

    Shortly thereafter, you may leave Route 140 for Route 141, which will take you on an interesting detour to:

2. **Jayuya.** This village in the middle of the Cordillera Central is home to the Parador Hacienda Gripiñas, a former coffee plantation where you can avail yourself of a very authentic and unique glimpse of the old days (see "Where to Stay & Eat Along the Way," at the end of this tour).

    If you decide to make this restful side trip, pick up the trail again by returning on Route 141 to Route 140, then travel west on Route 140 until you pass Lake Caonillas. Here, turn onto Route 111 west, and you'll soon reach the town of:

3. Utuado. A small mountain town, Utuado boasts the Parador La Casa Grande, with accommodations, a restaurant, a swimming pool, and a good place to stop after a day's touring (see "Where to Stay & Eat Along the Way," at the end of this tour).

From Utuado, continue west on Route 111 to km 12.3, where you'll find the:

4. Taíno Indian Ceremonial Ball Park. Archeologists have dated this site to approximately two centuries before Europe's discovery of the New World. It is believed that the Taíno chief Guarionex gathered his subjects on this site to celebrate rituals and practice sports. Set on a 13-acre field surrounded by trees are some 14 vertical monoliths with colorful petroglyphs, all arranged around a central sacrificial stone monument. The ball complex also includes a museum, open daily from 9am to 5pm; admission is free. There's also a gallery, Herencia Indigena, where visitors can purchase Taíno relics at very reasonable prices, including the sought-after *Cemis* (Taíno idols) and figures of the famous little frog, the coquí.

Continue next on Route 111 to the town of Lares, then turn onto Route 129 north. Drive about 3½ miles, then turn right onto Route 4456, and you'll soon reach the:

5. Río Camuy Cave Park. Río Camuy, the third-largest underground river in the world, runs through a network of caves, canyons, and sinkholes that have been cut through the island's limestone base over the course of millions of years. The caves, known to both the pre-Columbian Taíno peoples and local Puerto Rican farmers, came to the attention of speleologists in the 1950s. Developed by the Puerto Rico Land Administration, they were opened to the public in 1987.

Gardens in the focal point of the park surround buildings where tickets can be purchased. Visitors first see a short film about the caves, then descend to where open-air trolleys carry them on the downward journey to the actual caves. The trip takes you through a 200-foot-deep sinkhole, a chasm where tropical trees, ferns, and flowers flourish, supporting many birds and butterflies. The trolley then goes to the entrance of Empalme Cave, one of the 16 in the Camuy Caves network, where visitors begin a 45-minute cave walk, viewing the majestic series of rooms rich in stalagmites, stalactites, and huge sculptures carved out and built up through the centuries. In 1989 the park opened Tres Pueblos Sinkhole, measuring 650 feet in diameter with a depth of 400 feet—room enough to accommodate all of San Juan's El Morro Fortress. Tres Pueblos lies on the boundaries of the Camuy, Hatillo, and Lares municipalities. In Tres Pueblos, visitors can walk along two platforms: one on the Lares side facing the town of Camuy and the other on the Hatillo side overlooking Tres Pueblos Cave and the Río Camuy.

The caves are open Tuesday to Sunday from 8am to 4pm. Tickets are $10 for adults ($5 for seniors), $7 for children 2 to 12, free for children under 2. Parking is $2. For more information, phone the park at ☎ **787/898-3100.**

For more spelunking, drive to km 13.6 of Route 129. Here, take Route 489 south to La Cueva de la Luz (Cave of Light). From here, continue on Route 489 to the Barrio Aibonito, Pagan sector. If you're not sure of your whereabouts, ask anyone to help you find:

6. La Cueva de Pagan Pagan (Pagan Pagan's Cave). A narrow road will lead you to a general store where you can receive directions to Pagan. Only the agile and those who like to explore should venture inside the cave. The cave is lit by daylight, but the floor is rough and irregular. (It's advisable to wear slacks and good walking shoes here.) There are no bats in the cave. Inside, a stone vessel contains fresh water that some believe has rejuvenating qualities. Other caves in this area have not been explored fully, but relics from the native peoples have been found in some of them.

A short drive from Pagan Pagan's Cave is the:

7. Arecibo Observatory. To get here, backtrack on Route 489 to Route 635; then turn right and travel east for a short distance until you reach Route 625. Turn right and take this road to the observatory.

Arecibo Observatory, also called the National Astronomy and Ionosphere Center of Cornell University, has the world's largest and most sensitive radar/radiotelescope. Unusually lush vegetation flourishes under the giant dish, benefiting from the filtered sunlight and rain. There are ferns, grasses, and other plants such as wild orchids and begonias. Creatures such as mongooses, lizards, frogs, dragonflies, and an occasional bird have taken refuge under the dish. Suspended in outlandish fashion above the dish is a 600-ton platform similar in design to a bridge. Hanging as it does in midair, it resembles a space station.

The observatory (☎ 787/878-2612) is open for self-guided tours Tuesday to Friday from 2 to 3pm and on Sunday from 1 to 4pm. There's a souvenir shop on the grounds.

When you're ready to leave the observatory, follow routes 625 and 635 back out to Route 129 and consider the time of day and your own inclinations when deciding whether to head south to one of the paradores in Utuado or Jayuya; head north to Arecibo and Route 2, the main north-coast highway, where you can turn toward attractions and accommodations to the west; or return to San Juan.

Going west on Route 2 from Arecibo, the next stop on the tour is:

8. Quebradillas. Beautiful Guajataca Beach and two paradores are only a 15-mile trip from Arecibo along Route 2 in the vicinity of this small town near the sea. Guajataca is fine for sunning and collecting shells, but a *playa peligrosa* (dangerous for swimming unless you're a strong swimmer) warns swimmers. Parador El Guajataca and Parador Vistamar are located fairly close to each other (see "Where to Stay & Eat Along the Way," at the end of this tour).

From Quebradillas, take Route 113 south to Route 119, which will bring you to the artificial Guajataca Lake. Follow the lake's shoreline for about 2¹/₂ miles and turn left at km 19 to Route 455; you'll soon cross a bridge spanning the Guajataca River, which runs through the lush mountains.

Return to Route 119, which you follow west to San Sebastián. Here, take Route 109 across coffee plantations through the town of Añasco and on to Route 2, where you turn south and head for:

9. Mayagüez. For a complete discussion of where to stay and eat and what to see in the environs of this western port city, see section 6.

When you're ready to leave Mayagüez, continue southeast along Route 2 until you reach:

10. San Germán. This town, a little museum piece, was founded in 1512 and destroyed by the French in 1528. Rebuilt in 1570, it was named after Germain de Foix, the second wife of King Ferdinand of Spain. Gracious old-world-style buildings line the streets, and flowers brighten the patios as they do in Seville. San Germán is the site of the Parador Oasis (see "Where to Stay & Eat Along the Way," at the end of this tour).

On a knoll at one end of the town stands the chapel of:

11. Porta Coeli (Gate of Heaven). Dating from 1606, this is the oldest church in the New World. Restored by the Institute of Puerto Rican Culture, it contains a museum of religious art with a collection of ancient *santos*, the carved figures of saints that have long been a major branch of Puerto Rican folk art. Admission is free; it's open Tuesday to Sunday from 9am to noon and 2 to 4:30pm. Guided tours (☎ 787/892-5845) are offered Wednesday to Saturday.

Easily accessible from either Mayagüez or San Germán via Route 102 to Route 100 south is:

12. **Boquerón Beach.** This is one of Puerto Rico's best bathing beaches, and there's a parador with a good restaurant only 2 blocks away.

From San Germán, take Route 320 to Route 101 into Lajas, where Route 116 will lead to Route 304, which will take you to:

13. **La Parguera.** There are two paradores in this small fishing village, the Parador Villa Parguera and the Parador Posada Porlamar (see "Where to Stay & Eat Along the Way," at the end of this tour). If you have the good fortune to find yourself in La Parguera on a moonless night, we recommend going to:

14. **Phosphorescent Bay.** A boat leaves Villa Parguera pier nightly from 7:30pm to 12:30am, depending on the demand, and heads for this small bay to the east of La Parguera. Here, a pitch-black night will facilitate a show, since you can see fish leave a luminous streak on the water's surface and watch the boat's wake glimmer in the dark. This phenomenon is produced by a large colony of dinoflagellates, a microscopic form of marine life that produces sparks of chemical light when their nesting is disturbed. However, it should be noted that an opening to the sea and the inevitable pollution have reduced the dinoflagellate population. A few sparkles—and that's about all you get.

To travel on, take Route 304 up to Route 116 and drive west through Ensenada. At Guánica, you may turn south and follow Route 333 out to Caña Gorda Beach for lunch or a swim. While here, look for the cacti that flourish in this unusually dry region. Back on Route 116, drive north to Palomas, where you can take Route 2 into:

15. **Ponce.** A complete discussion of the many interesting eateries, inns, and sights in this old colonial city can be found in section 8.

When you're ready to leave Ponce, take Route 1 east in the direction of Guayama. At the town of Santa Isabel, you may want to take an interesting detour north along Route 153 to:

16. **Coamo.** Along the way to this town, you'll see signs pointing to the Baños de Coamo. Legend has it that these hot springs were the Fountain of Youth sought by Ponce de León. It is believed that the Taíno peoples, during pre-Columbian times, held rituals and pilgrimages here as they sought health and well-being. For more than 100 years (1847–1958) the site was a center for rest and relaxation for Puerto Ricans as well as visitors, some on their honeymoons, others in search of the curative powers of the geothermal springs, which lie about a 5-minute walk from Parador Baños de Coamo (see "Where to Stay & Eat Along the Way," at the end of this tour).

Return to Route 1, driving east onto Route 3 and on into:

17. **Guayama.** The small town of Guayama is green and beautiful, with steepled churches and one of the finest museums around, the Museo Cautino. The old mansion is a showplace of fine turn-of-the-century furnishings and pictures of the prize horses for which the Guayama area is famous. Just minutes from town is Arroyo Beach, a tranquil place to spend an afternoon.

To begin the final leg back to San Juan, take Route 15 north. If you travel this road in either spring or summer, you'll be surrounded by the brilliant colors of flowering trees.

At km 17.1, in Jajome, you can see the governor's former summer palace, an ancient building now restored and enlarged as a roadside inn. Continue on Route 15, then take Route 1, which goes directly back to the capital.

WHERE TO STAY & EAT ALONG THE WAY

At Jayuya

✪ **Parador Hacienda Gripinas.** Rte. 527, km 2.5 (P.O. Box 387), Jayuya, PR 00664. ☎ **787/ 828-1717.** Fax 787/828-1719. 20 rms. Year-round, $55.50 single; $66.20 double. AE, MC, V. From Jayuya, head east via Rte. 144; at the junction with Rte. 527, go south for 1¹/₂ miles.

A former coffee plantation about 2¹/₂ hours from San Juan, in the very heart of the Cordillera Central (Central Mountain Range), the parador is reached by a long, narrow, and curvy road. This home-turned-inn is a delightful blend of the hacienda of days gone by and the conveniences of today. The plantation's ambience is found everywhere—ceiling fans, splendid gardens, hammocks on a porch gallery, and more than 20 acres of coffee-bearing bushes. You'll taste the home-grown product when you order the inn's aromatic brew.

The restaurant features Puerto Rican and international cuisine. You can swim in the pool, soak up the sun, or enjoy the nearby sights. Boating and plenty of fishing are just 30 minutes away at Lake Caonillas.

At Utuado

Parador La Casa Grande. P.O. Box 616, Caonillas, Utuado, PR 00761. ☎ **787/894-3939.** Fax 787/894-3900. 20 rms. Year-round, $60 single or double. AE, MC, V. From Utuado, head south via Rte. 111 until you reach Rte. 140; then head west until you come to the intersection with Rte. 612 and follow 612 south for about half a mile.

Parador La Casa Grande lies in the district of Caonillas Barrios, in the mountainous heartland of the island, about 2¹/₂ hours from San Juan. Situated on 107 acres of a former coffee plantation, it has a restaurant with both Puerto Rican and international specialties. The inn is better than ever now that it's been taken over by Steven and Marlene Weingarten. A former court reporter, she is a gourmet cook, and Steven was an attorney in New York. The bedrooms are attractively decorated with private baths and balconies. There's also a bar and a swimming pool.

At Quebradillas

Parador el Guajataca. Rte. 2, km 103.8 (P.O. Box 1558), Quebradillas, PR 00742. ☎ **787/ 895-3070.** Fax 787/895-3589. 38 rms. A/C TV TEL. Year-round, $72–$77 single; $75–$80 double. AE, DC, MC, V. From Quebradillas, continue northwest on Rte. 2 for 1 mile (the parador is signposted).

Originally built in the 1930s as a two-room guest house, this place was gradually expanded over the years. It lies along the north coast 70 miles west of San Juan. Service, hospitality, and the natural beauty surrounding El Guajataca—plus modern conveniences and a family atmosphere—add up to a good visit. The parador is set on a rolling hillside that reaches down to the surf-beaten beach. Each room is like a private villa with its own entrance and private balcony opening onto the turbulent Atlantic. There are two swimming pools (one for adults, another for children), plus a playground for children.

Room service is available, but meals are more enjoyable in the glassed-in dining room where all the windows face the sea. Dinner is an experience, with a cuisine that blends Créole and international specialties. A local musical group plays for dining and dancing on weekend evenings.

Parador Vistamar. 6205 Rte. 113N (P.O. Box T-38), Quebradillas, PR 00678. ☎ **787/ 895-2065.** Fax 787/895-2294. 55 rms. A/C TV TEL. Year-round, $70–$90.95 single or double. Up to two children 12 and under stay free in parents' room. AE, DC, MC, V. At Quebradillas, head northwest on Rte. 2, then go left at the junction with Rte. 113 for half a mile.

High atop a mountain, overlooking greenery and a seascape in the Guajataca area, this 1970s parador, one of the largest on Puerto Rico, sits like a sentinel surveying the scene. There are gardens and intricate paths carved into the side of the mountain where you can enjoy the fragrance of the tropical flowers. Or you may choose to search for the calcified fossils that abound on the carved mountainside. For a unique experience, visitors can try their hand at freshwater fishing in the only river on Puerto Rico with green waters, just down the hill from the hotel. Flocks of rare tropical birds are frequently seen in the nearby mangroves.

A short drive from the hotel will bring you to the Punta Borinquén Golf Course. Tennis courts are just down the hill from the inn itself. Sightseeing trips to the nearby Arecibo Observatory—the largest radar/radiotelescope in the world—and to Monte Calvario (a replica of Mount Calvary) are available. Another popular visit is to the plaza in Quebradillas, where you can tour the town in a horse-driven coach. Back at the hotel, prepare yourself for a typical Puerto Rican dinner, or choose from the international menu, in the dining room with its view of the ocean.

At San Germán

Parador El Oasis. Calle Luna 72, San Germán, PR 00683. ☎ **787/892-1175.** Fax 787/892-1156. 52 rms. A/C TV TEL. Year-round, $52–$54 single; $58–$60 double. Extra person $10. Children 11 and under stay free in parents' room. AE, DC, DISC, MC, V.

Although not state-of-the-art, this three-story hotel possesses some reminders of Spanish colonial charm. If you'd like to anchor into this quaint old town, far removed from the beaches, it's the most suitable oasis. A three-story building constructed around a pool and patio area, the hotel some 200 years ago used to be a family mansion. With its peppermint-pink walls and white wicker furniture, there is some of the old grace left. Right off the lobby, the older rooms show the wear and tear of the years but are still preferred by some. The more modern rooms in the back are without character—plain, functional, clean, but more spacious than the older units. Three of the accommodations have private balconies. In the center of town, the standard restaurant has a full bar and serves three reasonably priced meals a day. There's also a small gym and sauna.

At La Parguera

Parador Posada Porlamar. Rte. 304 (P.O. Box 405), La Parguera, Lajas, PR 00667. ☎ **787/899-4015.** 27 rms. A/C. Year-round, $55 single; $65 double. AE, MC, V. Drive west along Rte. 2 until you reach the junction of Rte. 116; then head south along Rte. 116 and Rte. 304.

Life in a simple fishing village plus all the modern conveniences you want in a vacation are what you'll find at this "Guest House by the Sea" in the La Parguera section of Lajas, in the southwestern part of the island. The area is famous for its Phosphorescent Bay and good fishing, especially for snapper. The guest house, built in 1960, is near several fishing villages and other points of interest. If you like to collect seashells, you can beachcomb. Other collectors' items found here are fossilized crustacea and marine plants. If you want to fish, you can rent a boat at the nearby villages, and you can even cook your catch in a communal kitchen. The inn has added a swimming pool and a dive shop, and can also arrange snorkeling, kayaking, waterskiing, and boat rides.

Parador Villa Parguera. 304 Main St. (P.O. Box 273), La Parguera, Lajas, PR 00667. ☎ **787/899-7777.** Fax 787/899-6040. 62 rms. A/C TV TEL. Sun–Thurs, $81–$92 single or double. Fri–Sat (including half board), $299 double-occupancy packages for 2 days. Two children 9 and under stay free in parents' room. AE, DC, MC, V. Drive west along Rte. 2 until you reach the junction with Rte. 116; then head south along Rte. 116 and Rte. 304.

Although the water in the nearby bay is too polluted for swimming, guests can still enjoy a view of the water and the swimming pool. Situated on the southwestern shore of Puerto Rico, this parador is known for its seafood dinners (the fish is not caught in the bay), its comfortable rooms, and its location next to the phosphorescent waters of one of the coast's best-known bays. The dining room offers daily specials, as well as such chef's favorites as filet of fish stuffed with lobster and shrimp. The rooms are furnished in a simple modern style. Because the inn is popular with the residents of San Juan on weekends, there's a special weekend package for a 2-night minimum stay: $299 covers the price of the double room, welcome drinks, breakfasts, dinners, and dancing with a free show.

At Coamo

Parador Baños de Coamo. P.O. Box 540, Coamo, PR 00769. ☎ **787/825-2186.** Fax 787/825-4739. 48 rms. A/C TV TEL. Year-round, $64.20 single; $74.90 double. AE, DC, MC, V. From Rte. 1, turn onto Rte. 153 at Santa Isabel; then turn left onto Rte. 546 and drive west for 1 mile.

The spa at Baños de Coamo features a parador offering hospitality in the traditional Puerto Rican style, although this place has a somewhat Mexican atmosphere. The buildings range from a lattice-adorned, two-story motel unit with wooden verandahs to a Spanish colonial pink stucco building housing the restaurant. The cuisine here is both Créole and international, and the coffee Baños style is a special treat. The bedrooms draw a mixed reaction from visitors, so ask to see your prospective room before deciding to stay here.

Coamo is inland on the south coast, about a 90-minute drive from San Juan; swimming is limited to an angular pool, but you can easily drive to a nearby public beach in about 20 minutes.

12 Vieques

About 6 miles east of the big island of Puerto Rico lies Vieques (Bee-*ay*-kase), an island about twice the size of Manhattan with some 8,000 inhabitants and scores of palm-lined white-sand beaches. Since World War II, some two-thirds of the 21-mile-long island has belonged to the United States military forces. Much of the government-owned land is now leased for cattle grazing, and when there are no military maneuvers the public can visit the beaches, which are sometimes restricted. Being allowed use of the land does not, however, totally cover local discontent and protest at the presence of the navy and marine corps personnel on the island.

GETTING THERE

The **Puerto Rico Port Authority** (☎ 787/863-0852) operates two ferryboats a day that sail from the eastern port of Fajardo to Vieques in a travel time of about 45 to 60 minutes each way. The round-trip fare is $4 for adults, $2 for children 14 and under. Tickets on the morning ferry leaving on Saturday and Sunday sell out quickly, requiring passengers to be in line at the ticket window in Fajardo before 8am to be certain of a seat on the 9:30am boat. Otherwise, they must wait until the 3pm ferry. In Vieques call ☎ 787/741-8331 for more information.

Vieques Airlink (☎ 787/722-3736) operates flights from Isla Grande Airport in San Juan. Five flights leave throughout the day, taking 20 minutes. Service from San Juan is also provided by **Isla Nena Airlines** (☎ 787/791-5110).

GETTING AROUND

Public cabs or vans called **públicos** transport people around the island. **Island Car Rental,** Route 201, in Florida (☎ 787/741-1666), is one of the two largest car-rental companies on the island, with an inventory of stripped-down Suzukis that usually offer dependable, barebone transport to many of the island's beautiful but hard-to-reach beaches.

WHERE TO STAY

Bananas. P.O. Box 1300, Barrio Esperanza, Vieques, PR 00765. ☎ **787/741-8700.** 8 rms, 1 suite. Year-round, $45–$60 single or double; $60 suite. AE, MC, V.

Located on the beach east of the U.S. Naval Reservation, and best known for its bar and restaurant, this guest house also has simple, clean, and comfortable rooms, some recently renovated. Each has a ceiling fan, and three rooms and the suite are air-conditioned with their own screened-in porches.

The real heart of the place, however, is the pleasant verandah restaurant. You can choose from deli sandwiches, burgers, grilled Caribbean lobster, such local fish as snapper and grouper, plus homemade desserts. The restaurant and bar are open Sunday to Thursday from noon to 10pm. On Friday and Saturday, food is served from noon to 1am, and the bar remains open until 3am. Breakfast isn't served, although you can order food at other places nearby.

✪ **Crow's Nest Guest House.** P.O. Box 1521, Barrio Florida, Vieques, PR 00765. ☎ **787/741-0033.** Fax 787/741-1294. 12 rms. Year-round, $50–$75 single or double. AE, MC, V.

Liz O'Dell, one of the most hospitable innkeepers on Vieques, runs this inviting little lodge on 5 hilltop acres with ocean views, with the nearest beach a 5-minute car ride from the property. There's also a pool on site. Hers is one of the best oases of value on island. Each of her units comes with a kitchenette, and all are housed in a pair of two-story buildings separated by a large patio and gardens overlooking the ocean. The rooms are decorated in a typical Caribbean motif with sitting areas, ceiling fans, and reading lights over the beds. All but two have air-conditioning. There's no TV in the rooms, although there is a set in the lounge and another in the bar. The guest house operates a good restaurant, serving Puerto Rican and international dishes at breakfast and dinner. This is an adult retreat, and children are discouraged. Two locals will take you out fishing, and 2-hour horseback rides through the hills can be arranged.

✪ **La Casa del Francés.** P.O. Box 458, Barrio Esperanza, Vieques, PR 00765. ☎ **787/741-3751.** Fax 787/741-2330. 18 rms. Winter, $99 single or double. Off-season, $75 single or double. MAP (available in winter only) $20 per person extra. AE, MC, V.

La Casa del Francés is about a 15-minute drive southeast of Isabel Segunda, just north of the center of Esperanza, east of the U.S. Naval Reservation. Set in a field near the southern coastline, it has columns and an imposing facade that rise from the landscape surrounding it. In the 1950s it was acquired by Irving Greenblatt, who installed a swimming pool and, with his partner, Frank Celeste, transformed 18 of its high-ceilinged bedrooms into old-fashioned hotel rooms as an R&R oasis for his executives. Many rooms enjoy access to the sweeping two-story verandahs ringing the white facade.

However, note that readers have had mixed reactions to this inn. Some praise it, while others have complained. If you don't like the personality of Mr. Greenblatt (and many readers don't), you really won't fit in here.

The $15 fixed-price dinners are attended by many island residents who enjoy the Italian, barbecue, or Puerto Rican buffets presented beneath a 200-year-old mahogany tree.

New Dawn Caribbean Retreat & Guest House. P.O. Box 1512, Calla 995, Obo Pilon, Vieques, PR 00765. ☎ **787/741-0495.** 6 rms in guest house, 6 bunks in dormitory (for women), 1 two-story cottage, 1 two-bedroom apt. Year-round, $40 single; $50 double; $18 per person in bunkhouse; tent platforms for campers $10 per person; $425 per week cottage; $475 per week apt. No credit cards.

This retreat attracts primarily women who like to rough it a bit. This place where hurricanes have come to call is the personal statement of Gail Burchard, former flight attendant, restaurant owner, charter-boat mate, and mother of two. She carved this place out of the wilderness, along with the help of some enthusiastic female carpentry students. On 5 acres of hillside dotted with such flowering plants as hibiscus and bougainvillea, the main house is completely tropical, with Guatemalan textiles and woven palm lamp shades. Large decks with swings and hammocks encourage R&R. There are six rather basic private rooms (each with a loft) plus a women's bunkhouse, containing two bunk beds and two single beds. If you'd like to camp on the grounds, bring your own tent.

The rooms are very basic and open to breezes. Other cooling is by either ceiling or wall-mounted fans. The main house has a deck all around the second floor. A restaurant is open in winter, serving "summer camp" fare for breakfast and dinner. A picnic lunch can be provided upon request. The two-story wooden cottage includes a kitchen, private bath, and deck, sleeping up to four, and the two-bedroom apartment in a concrete house can also sleep four. The retreat lies about 3 miles from the nearest good beach. Sometimes an entire group will book the property.

Sea Gate. P.O. Box 747, Vieques, PR 00765. ☎ and fax **787/741-4661.** 12 rms, 4 suites. TV. Year-round, $35–$55 single; $40 double; $65 suite for two. Rates include breakfast. No credit cards.

This simple guest house was established on 2 isolated acres of hilltop land in 1979, and since then has grown into a compound of about five different buildings. It's cooler here than in properties at lower elevations because of its position exposed to the prevailing winds. The bedrooms are white, with steel-framed or wooden furniture, a radio, a minifridge, and a ceiling fan, and each has a terrace or balcony and wooden lounge chairs. Views from most look down over Vieques' harborfront. The sands of Gringo Beach lie within a 20-minute walk. There's no bar or restaurant, but the owners are friendly and articulate, and will direct you to the handful of dining options available on the island.

Trade Winds Guesthouse. Flamboyan 107C (P.O. Box 1012), Barrio Esperanza, Vieques, PR 00765. ☎ **787/741-8666.** 11 rms, 2 studios. Year-round, $45–$60 single; $55–$70 double; $75–$85 studio. Minimum 3-night deposit by check or money order required. AE, MC, V.

Along the shore on the south side of the island east of the U.S. Naval Reservation, in the fishing village of Esperanza, this oceanside guest house offers 13 units, four of them air-conditioned with terraces. The others have ceiling fans, and some also have terraces. The open-air restaurant overlooks the ocean.

Water's Edge Guest House. P.O. Box 1374, Isabel Segunda, Vieques, PR 00765. ☎ **787/741-1128.** Fax 787/741-0690. 9 rms, 2 suites, 1 villa. A/C TV. Winter, $64.20–$80.25 single or double; $96.30 suite; $1,800 per week villa. Off-season, $53.50–$69.55 single or double; $85.60 suite; $1,600 per week villa. Children 11 and under stay free in parents' room. AE, MC, V.

Just north of town, this is one of the best-appointed guest houses on island. Built of adobe cinderblock, stucco, and terra-cotta tile, it's a two-story building in a Mexican hacienda design style overlooking the water. There's a second-floor deck for ocean-facing rooms. All the rooms are tastefully furnished with ceiling fans and a small refrigerator. A good beach is only a few steps away and there's a swimming pool on site. The villa, rented only by the week, has a full kitchen. The setting is lush, on well-landscaped grounds with large palm trees and colorful tropical plants.

WHERE TO EAT

La Campesina. La Hueca. ☎ **787/741-1239.** Reservations recommended. Main courses $10–$18. MC, V. Tues–Sun 6–10pm. Closed Oct. INTERNATIONAL.

Consciously designed to reflect indigenous dwellings, this unusual and excellent restaurant was built a few steps from one of the richest archeological deposits of Taíno artifacts in the Caribbean. It's located on the southwestern end of the island (follow the coast road from Esperanza) in the untrammeled fishing village of La Hueca.

In a room lined with baskets and weavings amid trailing vines of jasmine and flickering candles, you can enjoy a cuisine of distinctly tropical or uniquely Puerto Rican flair. Fresh herbs such as cilantro, tasty varieties of local vegetables, and fruits such as papaya, mango, and tamarind served in relishes and pastries, complement the menu. Nightly specials might include avocado rémoulade, conch fritters, lobster ravioli, local fish, and great steak.

Trade Winds. Flamboyan 107C, Barrio Esperanza. ☎ **787/741-8666.** Reservations recommended. Meals $9.95–$14.50. AE, MC, V. Mon–Sat 7:30–10am and 6–9:30pm, Sun 7:30–11am and 6–9:30pm. STEAK/SEAFOOD.

You'll find this restaurant at the ocean esplanade on the south side of the island in the fishing village of Esperanza (its guest house was reviewed above). It features the Topside Bar for relaxing with drinks with a view of the water, and the Upper Deck for open-air dining. Menu items include several shrimp dishes, Jamaican jerk beef, and fresh fish daily. The chef's specialty is Carmen's piñon, made with layers of sweet plantains, tomato sauce, green beans, spiced beef, and mozzarella. A pasta of the day is also featured, served with a house or Caesar salad. Included in the price of a main dish are bread and butter, a salad, two fresh vegetables, and a choice of rice or potato.

THE BEST BEACHES

On the south coast, **Esperanza,** once a center for the island's sugarcane industry, now a pretty little fishing village, lies near **Sun Bay (Sombe) public beach.** Sun Bay is a magnificent government-run crescent of sand. The fenced area has picnic tables, a bathhouse, and a parking lot. Admission is $1 per car.

Few of the island's 40-some beaches have even been named, but most have their loyal supporters—loyal, that is, until too many people learn about them, in which case the devotees can always find another good spot. The U.S. Navy named some of the strands, such as **Green Beach,** a beautiful clean stretch at the island's west end. **Red and Blue Beaches,** also with navy nomenclature, are great jumping-off points for snorkelers. Other popular beaches are **Navia, Half Moon, Orchid,** and **Silver,** but if you continue along the water, you may find your own nameless secluded cove with a fine strip of sand. **Mosquito Bay,** sometimes called Phosphorescent Bay because it glows with phosphorescence on moonless nights, is a short way east of Esperanza. Less well known than the handful of other phosphorescent bays scattered throughout the Caribbean, the one at Vieques is in some ways the most vivid. The luminosity filling its waters is a function of millions of microorganisms— technically known as dinoflagellata—which thrive on the roots of red mangrove trees.

Those who decide to swim off the side of the boat are amazed at the way the whorls of churning water created by their moving bodies seem to come alive with an eerie glow. The ideal time to tour is on a cloudy, moonless night, and you should wear a bathing suit. **18E North** (☎ **787/741-8600**) runs tours on powerboats from Esperanza, and **Sharon Grasso** (☎ **787/741-3751**), aboard her *Luminosa I* and *Luminosa II,* operates trips leaving from La Casa del Francés (see "Where to Stay," above). Trips are not offered around the time of the full moon. Trips usually cost $15 per person.

13 Culebra

A tranquil little island, Culebra lies in a mini-archipelago of 24 chunks of land, rocks, and cays in the sea, halfway between Puerto Rico and St. Thomas, U.S. Virgin Islands. Just 7 miles long and 3 miles wide, with nearly 2,000 residents, the inviting little island is in U.S. territorial waters belonging to Puerto Rico, 18 miles away. This little-known year-round vacation spot in what was once called the Spanish Virgin Islands was settled as a Spanish colony in 1886, but like Puerto Rico and Vieques, it became part of the United States after the Spanish-American War in 1898. In fact, Culebra's only town, **Dewey,** was named for Adm. George Dewey, American hero of that war, although the locals call the fishing village **Puebla.**

For a long time, beginning in 1909, Culebra was used by the U.S. Navy as a gunnery range, and it even became a practice bomb site in World War II. In 1975, after years of protest over military abuse of the island's environment, the navy withdrew from Culebra, with the understanding that the island be kept as a nature preserve and habitat for the many rare species of birds, turtles, and fish that abound there.

GETTING THERE

From the port of Fajardo, the **Puerto Rico Port Authority** operates one or two ferryboats a day (depending on the day of the week) from the Puerto Rican mainland to Culebra, taking about an hour each way. The round-trip fare is $4.50 for adults, $2.25 for children 14 and under. For information and reservations, call ☎ 787/742-3161 on Culebra or ☎ 787/863-0705 in Fajardo.

Flamenco Airways, Inc. (☎ 787/725-7707 in San Juan), flies to Culebra four times daily from both San Juan's Isla Grande Airport and from the Fajardo Airport. The round-trip fare is $60 per person. **Carib Air** (☎ 800/981-0212 or 787/791-1240), located in Terminal B at Luís Muñoz Marín International Airport, flies four times a day to Culebra. A round-trip from here costs $75.

WHERE TO STAY

Club Seabourne. Fulladoza Rd. (P.O. Box 357), Culebra, PR 00775. ☎ **787/742-3169.** Fax 787/742-3176. 15 units. A/C. $95–$105 clubhouse double; $105 crow's nest; $115 studio villa; $125 cottage. Rates include continental breakfast. AE, MC, V. From Dewey, follow Fulladoza Rd. along the south side of the bay for 1¹/₂ miles.

Across the road from an inlet, about an 8-minute drive from town, is a concrete-and-wooden structure set in a garden of crotons and palms, lying at the mouth of one of the island's best harbors, Ensenada Honda. One of the island's few bonafide hotels, it offers eight villas, two cottages, one crow's nest, and four rooms inside the clubhouse. All units contain small refrigerators. The two cottages have two bedrooms and full kitchen facilities. Dive packages and water sports can be arranged at the office. The hotel has a large freshwater swimming pool and a 90-foot dock.

Coral Island Guest House. Calle Pedro 2 (P.O. Box 396), Culebra, PR 00775. ☎ **787/742-3177.** 5 rms, 3 with bath; 1 apt. Year-round, $40 single without bath; $45 double without bath; $90 two-bedroom apt. MC, V.

This is the oldest guest house on the island and is located on the south-central end surrounded on three sides by a canal, a lagoon, and Sardine Bay. These simple accommodations are decorated with a nautical theme. A restaurant specializing in Puerto Rican fare is downstairs, and guests can expect to spend $8 for a meal. You can also rent sailboats, rowboats, and snorkeling equipment directly from the guest house.

Flamenco Resort & Fishing Club. Pedro Marquez 10, Flamenco Beach (P.O. Box 183), Culebra, PR 00645. ☎ **787/742-3144.** 29 units. A/C. Winter, $95 studio; $115 one-bedroom suite; $160 two-bedroom suite. Off-season, $85 studio; $105 one-bedroom suite; $150 two-bedroom suite. MC, V.

This is the only guest house or hotel near the white sands of one of the region's best beaches, Flamenco Beach. Each unit has its own kitchen. The accommodations are arranged around spacious sitting rooms much like those in an informal beach house. The owner has studio apartments suitable for two and one-bedroom apartments also suitable for two. You can opt to take day trips on a sailboat to one of the nearby islands, go snorkeling, and make fishing expeditions.

WHERE TO EAT

Club Seabourne. Fulladoza Rd. ☎ **787/742-3169.** Reservations recommended. Main courses $4.75–$20. AE, MC, V. Daily 8–11am and 6–10pm. From Puebla, follow Fulladoza Rd. along the south side of the bay for 1¹/₂ miles. CARIBBEAN.

There are those who consider this the only bona fide restaurant on the island. Overlooking Fulladoza Bay, the club's dining room features fresh lobster, shrimp, snapper, grouper, conch, steaks, and the occasional Puerto Rican specialty. It also has a large patio with a nightly happy hour.

OUTDOOR FUN: SAILING, BEACHES & MORE

The **Culebra School of Sailing,** Bahía Mosquito, Mosquito Bay (☎ 787/742-3136), is owned and operated by Hugh Callum with the able assistance of his sister, Shirley Frowick. Sailing lessons and day sailing trips are available at $50 per person, including lunch. Also offered are fishing trips, windsurfing, and evening sails on either a 27-foot sloop or a 42-foot ketch. This, the island's only sailing school and rental agency, is operated out of the Callum's home on 5 acres of land on Mosquito Bay; since the location is remote, Hugh or Shirley will pick up guests in town. They also offer rooms to rent in their guest house. Their B&B offers comfortable accommodations in two separate guest cabins for up to six guests (larger family groups can usually be helped). The smaller cabin rents for $50 per night double; the larger, for $75 per night.

The four tracts of the **Culebra Wildlife Refuge,** plus 23 other offshore islands, are managed by the U.S. Fish and Wildlife Service. Culebra is one of the most important turtle-nesting sites in the Caribbean. Large seabird colonies, notably terns and boobies are seen.

Culebra's white-sand **beaches** (especially **Flamenco Beach**), the clear waters, and long coral reefs invite swimmers, snorkelers, and scuba divers. The landscape ranges from scrub and cactus to poincianas, frangipanis, and coconut palms.

Culebrita, which means "Little Culebra," is a mile-long coral-isle satellite of Culebra, known for its hilltop lighthouse, the oldest in the West Indies, or so it's said. A favorite goal of boaters and a venue for kayaking, it possesses one of Puerto Rico's better beaches on its north side. The islet is also known for its "nature's aquariums" or tide pools.

6 The U.S. Virgin Islands

The U.S. Virgin Islands are known for their sugar-white beaches, which are among the finest in the world. The most developed island in the chain is **St. Thomas,** which has the largest concentration of shopping in the Caribbean in its capital, Charlotte Amalie. With a population of some 50,000, tiny St. Thomas isn't exactly a secluded tropical retreat; you'll hardly have its beaches to yourself. The place abounds in bars and restaurants, including fast-food joints, and has a vast selection of hotels in all price ranges, making it a great place for the budget traveler.

St. Croix is bigger, but more tranquil. A favorite with cruise-ship passengers (as is St. Thomas), St. Croix touts its shopping and has more stores than most islands in the Caribbean, especially in and around Christiansted, although it's not the shopping mecca Charlotte Amalie is. Its major attraction is Buck Island, a national park that lies offshore. The place is peppered with small inexpensive inns and condo, apartment, and villa rentals.

St. John, the smallest of the three islands, is also the most beautiful and the least developed. Lying a few miles east of St. Thomas, it has only two big hotels, but is known for its campgrounds. There are also several low-cost inns and a number of condo and villa rentals. Some two-thirds of the island is a national park. Even if you visit only for the day while based on St. Thomas, you'll want to sample the island's dream beach, Trunk Bay.

The U.S. Virgin Islands lie in two bodies of water: St. John is entirely in the Atlantic Ocean, St. Croix is entirely in the Caribbean Sea, and St. Thomas separates the Atlantic and the Caribbean. These islands enjoy one of the most perfect year-round climates in the world. They lie directly in the belt of the subtropical, easterly trade winds. At the eastern end of the Greater Antilles and the northern tip of the Lesser Antilles, the U.S. Virgins are some 60 miles east of Puerto Rico and 1,100 miles southeast of Miami.

For much of late 1995 and early 1996, St. Thomas seemed to be visited more by carpenters than by tourists. Hurricane Marilyn struck in mid-September 1995; with winds of 140 to 150 m.p.h., it dealt a devastating blow to the island, shutting down most of its hotels. Since St. Thomas's economy is almost wholly tourist-based, this was a major disaster. Hotels rushed to bounce back from the blow.

Some were able to open in time for the winter season of 1995 and 1996; others announced opening dates in 1996. Even in 1997 some properties had not fully recovered from the devastating effects of Marilyn.

St. Croix, which still has lingering memories of Hurricane Hugo's destruction of 1989, escaped Marilyn with far less damage and bounced back quickly, picking up the lost business from St. Thomas. St. John sustained damage in part but also recovered quickly, with some notable exceptions here and there.

GETTING THERE

Nonstop flights to the U.S. Virgin Islands from either New York or Atlanta usually take $3^3/4$ and $3^1/2$ hours, respectively. The flight time between St. Thomas and St. Croix is only 20 minutes. Flying to San Juan from mainland cities and changing planes may save you money over the APEX nonstop fare.

American Airlines (☎ 800/433-7300) offers frequent service into St. Thomas and St. Croix from the U.S. mainland, with five daily flights from New York to St. Thomas. Summer flights can vary. Passengers originating in other parts of the world are usually routed to St. Thomas through American's hubs in Miami or San Juan, both of which offer nonstop service (often several times a day) to St. Thomas. Connections from Los Angeles or San Francisco to either St. Thomas or St. Croix are usually made through New York, San Juan, or Miami. American can also arrange discount packages that include both airfare and hotel. Flights from Puerto Rico to the U.S. Virgin Islands are on American's partner, **American Eagle** (☎ 800/433-7300), which has about 10 to 15 flights daily.

Delta (☎ 800/221-1212) offers two daily nonstop flights between Atlanta and St. Thomas, the first departing in the morning and the second in the afternoon. The latter flight also provides an air link to St. Croix. **TWA** (☎ 800/221-2000) flies into San Juan two or three times daily nonstop from JFK. A flight from St. Louis touches down at JFK before going to Puerto Rico. In San Juan, connections are made to St. Thomas. **US Airways** has two flights from Baltimore to St. Thomas daily—one nonstop from Baltimore, the other originating in Philadelphia and stopping in Baltimore before flying on to St. Thomas.

BY BOAT St. Thomas's capital, Charlotte Amalie, is one of the busiest cruise-ship ports in the Caribbean. St. Thomas maintains no ferry connections to St. Croix, some 40 miles to the south.

If you're already in the British Virgin Islands and want to visit St. Thomas, there's a well-traveled route by boat between Charlotte Amalie and Tortola, the capital of the BVI. The trip takes 45 minutes and costs $19 one-way or $35 round-trip. The principal carriers based on Tortola making the run to St. Thomas include **Smith's Ferry** (☎ 809/775-7292) and **Native Son** (☎ 809/774-8685).

St. Thomas is also linked by boat to St. John, its neighbor island, some 3 to 5 miles away (depending on where you measure from). Ferries depart from Red Hook on the East End of St. Thomas and reach St. John (or rather, its capital of Cruz Bay) in about 20 minutes; the cost is $3 one-way. For complete ferry schedules, call ☎ 809/776-6282.

A new ferry service from St. Thomas to Puerto Rico, with a stop in St. John, is available once every two weeks—maybe more if demand merits it. The 2-hour trip from Puerto Rico to Charlotte Amalie costs $60 one-way, including ground transportation to the San Juan airport or Condado. For more information, call ☎ 809/776-6282.

FAST FACTS: The U.S. Virgin Islands

Currency   The **U.S. dollar** is the unit of currency in the Virgin Islands.

Customs   Every U.S. resident can bring home $1,200 worth of duty-free purchases, including a gallon of alcoholic beverages per adult. If you go over the $1,200 limit, you pay a flat 5% duty, up to an additional $1,000. You can also mail home an unlimited amount in gifts valued at up to $100 per day, which you don't have to declare. (At other spots in the Caribbean, U.S. citizens are limited to $400 or $600 worth of duty-free merchandise and a single bottle of liquor.)

Documents   U.S. and Canadian citizens are required to present some proof of citizenship to enter the Virgin Islands—say, a voter registration card or a birth certificate. A passport is not strictly required, but carrying one is a good idea.

Driving   Remember to *drive on the left.* This comes as a surprise to many visitors, who expect that U.S. driving practices will hold here. Speed limits are 20 m.p.h. in towns, 35 m.p.h. outside.

Electricity   It's the same as on the mainland: 120 volts AC, 60 cycles. No transformer, adapter, or converter is needed.

Information   Before you go, contact the **U.S. Virgin Islands Division of Tourism,** 1270 Ave. of the Americas, New York, NY 10020 (☎ **212/332-2222;** fax 332-2223). Branch offices are at 225 Peachtree St. NE, Suite 760, Atlanta, GA 30303 (☎ **404/688-0906;** fax 404/525-1102); 500 N. Michgan Ave., Suite 2030, Chicago, IL 60611 (☎ **312/670-8784;** fax 312/670-8788); 900 17th St. NW, Suite 500, Washington, DC 20006 (☎ **202/293-3707;** fax 202/785-2542); 2655 Le Jeune Rd., Suite 907, Coral Gables, FL 33134 (☎ **305/442-7200;** fax 305/445-9044); and 3460 Wilshire Blvd., Los Angeles, CA 90010 (☎ **213/739-0138;** fax 213/739-2005).

Mail   The Virgin Islands are part of the U.S. Postal System, so postage rates are the same as on the mainland.

Safety   The U.S. Virgin Islands have more than their share of crime. St. John is safer than St. Thomas or St. Croix. But even on St. John there is crime, usually stolen possessions that were left unattended. Travelers should exercise extreme caution both day and night when wandering the backstreets of Charlotte Amalie on St. Thomas and both Christiansted and Frederiksted on St. Croix—muggings are commonplace in those districts. Avoid night strolls or drives along quiet roads. Never go walking on the beaches at night.

Time   The U.S. Virgins are on Atlantic standard time year-round, which places the islands an hour ahead of eastern standard time. When it's 6am in the Virgin Islands, it's still 5am in Florida. When the U.S. mainland goes on daylight saving time, Virgin Island clocks and those on the East Coast record the same time.

Tipping   As a general rule, it's customary to tip 15%. Some hotels add a 10% to 15% surcharge to cover service. When in doubt, ask.

Water   There's ample water for showers and bathing in the Virgin Islands, but you're asked to conserve. Hotels will supply you with all your drinking water. Many visitors drink the local tap water with no harmful after effects. Others, more prudent or with more delicate stomachs, should stick to bottled water.

Weather   From November through February, temperatures average about 77° Fahrenheit. The average temperature divergence is 5° to 7°. Sometimes in August the temperature peaks in the high 80s, but the subtropical breezes keep it comfortably cool in the shade. The temperature in winter may drop into the low 60s, but this happens rarely.

1 St. Thomas

One of the two busiest cruise-ship harbors in the West Indies, St. Thomas is the second largest of the U.S. Virgins; it's about 40 miles north of St. Croix. St. Thomas, with the U.S. Virgins' capital at Charlotte Amalie, is about 12 miles long and 3 miles wide. The capital is also the shopping center of the Caribbean. Hotels on the north side of St. Thomas face the Atlantic and those on the south side front the calmer Caribbean.

St. Thomas is a boon for cruise-ship shoppers, who flood Main Street, the shopping center, basically 3 to 4 blocks long in the center of town. However, this center, which gets very crowded, is away from all beaches, major hotels, most restaurants, and entertainment facilities. At a hotel "out on the island," you can still find the seclusion you may be seeking.

If you're visiting in August, make sure you carry along mosquito repellent.

GETTING AROUND

BY BUS   St. Thomas has the best public transportation of any island in the U.S. chain. Administered by the government, they're called **Vitran buses,** and, depending on their route, service Charlotte Amalie, its outlying neighborhoods, and the countryside as far away as Red Hook. Vitran stops are found at reasonable intervals beside each of the most important traffic arteries on St. Thomas. Among the most visible are those that line the edges of Veterans Drive in the capital. You rarely have to wait more than 30 minutes during the day, and they run between 5:30am and 10:30pm. A one-way ride costs 75¢ within Charlotte Amalie, $1 for rides from Charlotte Amalie into its outer neighborhoods. Although you won't be delivered door to door, and might have to walk some distance to your final destination, it's still a comfortable (usually air-conditioned) form of transport. For information about Vitran buses, their stops, and their schedules, call ☎ **809/774-5678.**

BY VAN OR MINIBUS   Less structured, and more erratic, are the **"taxi vans,"** a miniflotilla of privately owned vans or minibuses that make unscheduled stops along major traffic arteries of the island. Charging the same rates as the Vitran buses, and operated by a frequently changing cast of local entrepreneurs, they may or may not have their end destination written on a cardboard sign displayed on the windshield. They tend to be less comfortable than Vitran buses and not as well maintained, but some residents sometimes opt for a ride if one happens to arrive near a Vitran stop at a convenient moment and is headed in the right direction. If in doubt, it's much better to stick to the Vitran buses.

BY TAXI   The chief means of transport is the taxi, which is unmetered; agree with the driver on the charges before you get into the car. For 24-hour radio-dispatched service, call ☎ **809/774-7457.** Many taxis transport 8 to 12 passengers in vans to multiple destinations.

BY RENTAL CAR   St. Thomas has a high accident rate: Many visitors are not used to driving on the left, the hilly terrain shelters blind curves and entrance ramps, and some drivers unwisely drive after too many drinks. In many cases, the roads are narrow and the lighting is poor.

Because of these factors, collision-damage insurance is strongly recommended. It costs $13 or $14 per day extra, but be alert to the fact that even if you purchase it, you still might be responsible for a whopping deductible if you have an accident. It pays to ask lots of questions about insurance coverage and your financial responsibilities before you rent. The minimum age requirements for drivers at many companies is 25.

Instead of calling Hertz or Avis, you can often save money by renting from a local agency, although vehicles sometimes aren't as well maintained. Try **ABC Rentals,** 30 Havenside, across from the cruise-ship dock (☎ **800/524-2080** or 809/776-1222), which keeps a fleet of such cars as Suzuki Sidekicks, Jeep Wranglers, and Chrysler Neons. In winter, the cheapest rentals begin at $61.95 per day. However, in the off-season, they offer discounted specials.

The former Thrifty car rental is now **Paradise Car Rental,** in the Windward Passage Hotel courtyard, near the waterfront in Charlotte Amalie (☎ **809/775-7282**). Prices here fluctuate throughout the year, so you'll have to call and see what's currently available. Off-season tariffs usually begin at $55 per day for a fleet of cars likely to include Ford Tempos and Chevrolet Sprints. You might also check with **Dependable Car Rental,** 3901 B Altona, behind the Bank of Nova Scotia and the Medical Arts Complex (☎ **800/522-3076** or 809/774-2253), which will pick up prospective renters at the airport or their hotel. It has attractive winter rates usually beginning at $54.95 per day, lowered off-season to $49.95 per day.

A final choice is the aptly named **Discount Car Rental,** 14 Content, outside the airport on the main highway (☎ **809/776-4858**), which grants drivers a 12% discount on rivals' rates. Its rates are usually among the most reasonable on the island, beginning at $39.95 per day in winter, lowered to $32.95 per day off-season. The firm closely monitors prices charged at Budget, Hertz, and Avis, and then undercuts them.

ESSENTIALS

American Express is represented on St. Thomas by the **Caribbean Travel Agency, Inc. / Tropic Tours,** 9716 Estate Thomas, Suite 1 (☎ **809/774-1855**), a 5-minute drive east of Charlotte Amalie's center, opposite the entrance to the Havensight Shopping Mall. **St. Thomas Hospital,** the largest on the island with the best-equipped emergency room, is at 48 Sugar Estate, Charlotte Amalie (☎ **809/776-8311**), a 5-minute drive east of the town's commercial center. Radio **weather reports** can be heard at 8:30am and 7:30pm on 99.5 FM. There's a **Visitors Center** in St. Thomas at Emancipation Square (☎ **809/774-8784**).

WHERE TO STAY

Nearly every beach has its own hotel. St. Thomas may have more quaint inns than anyplace else in the Caribbean. There's an 8% government hotel tax.

If you're interested in a condo rental, contact **Paradise Properties of St. Thomas,** P.O. Box 9395, St. Thomas, USVI 00801 (☎ **809/775-3115**), which currently represents six condo complexes. Rental units range from studio apartments to four-bedroom villas suitable for up to eight people. Each has a fully equipped kitchen. A minimum stay of 3 days is required in any season, and 7 nights around Christmas.

Sometimes even better deals can be had at **Calypso Realty,** P.O. Box 12178, St. Thomas, USVI 00802 (☎ **800/747-4858** or 809/774-1620). It's especially noted for its offerings at discounted prices from April until mid-December. It features apartments, houses, and villa rentals, the apartments being cheaper, of course. A studio overlooking Pillsbury Sound often goes for $90 per night off-season or $110 per night in winter. Another source to check is **McLaughlin Anderson Vacations Ltd.,** 100 Blackbeard's Hill, St. Thomas, USVI 00802 (☎ **800/666-6246** or 809/776-0635),

St. Thomas

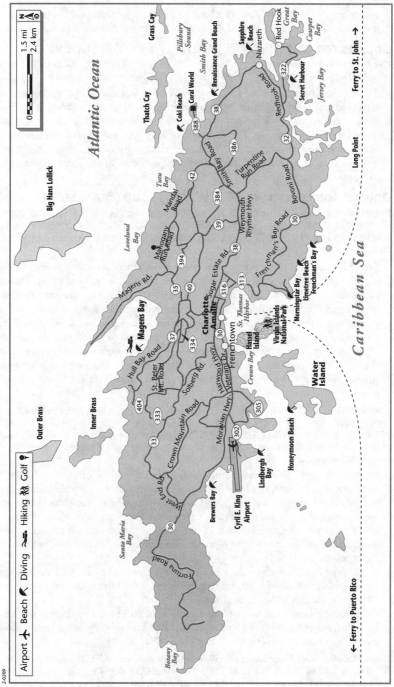

which has rentals not only on St. Thomas but on St. John and St. Croix as well. A one-bedroom villa begins at $1,250 per week in winter, with off-season discounts.

DOUBLES FOR LESS THAN $75 (WINTER) / $60 (OFF-SEASON)

Bayside Inn & Fitness Center. 7140 Bolongo, St. Thomas, USVI 00802. ☎ **800/524-4746** or 809/693-2600. Fax 809/775-3298. 6 rms. A/C TV TEL. Year-round, $65 double. AE, MC, V.

The Bayside Inn is a restored 19th-century West Indian manor that was completely renovated and converted into a fitness center in early 1993. Guests staying in the inn's quiet, comfortable rooms are just steps away from Bolongo Beach, where beach and scuba facilities are available. The Bayside Inn is the ideal way to combine relaxation, fitness, and fun into one vacation. Facilities include a dry sauna, a weight room, and cardiovascular equipment such as treadmills and stationary bikes. There's also a swimming pool.

DOUBLES FOR LESS THAN $100 (WINTER) / $80 (OFF-SEASON)

Bunkers' Hill Hotel. 7 Commandant Gade, Charlotte Amalie, St. Thomas, USVI 00802. ☎ **809/774-8056.** Fax 809/774-3172. 15 rms, 3 suites. A/C TV TEL. Winter, $80 single; $90 double; $95 suite. Off-season, $59 single; $69 double; $79 suite. Rates include continental breakfast. AE, MC, V.

We really only recommend this guest house if the others previously recommended are fully booked (as is often the case). There are far safer places to be on St. Thomas than this district, so caution is advised—especially at night. This clean and centrally located guest lodge is suitable for anyone who will sacrifice some comfort, such as putting up with street noises, for economy's sake. At this laid-back informal place, guests share a communal kitchen. Four rooms have balconies, and some offer a view of the lights of Charlotte Amalie and the sea. In spite of some minor improvements, the furnishings are simple and often threadbare. On the premises is a deli serving soups, sandwiches, and drinks. The closest beach is Lindbergh Bay, a 15-minute drive away.

Danish Chalet Inn. 9E–9J Nordsidevej (Solberg Rd.) (P.O. Box 4319), Charlotte Amalie, St. Thomas, USVI 00803. ☎ **800/635-1531** in the U.S. and Canada, or 809/774-5764. Fax 809/777-4886. 11 rms, 6 with bath. TEL. Winter, $75 single or double without bath, $85–$95 single or double with bath. Off-season, $70 single or double without bath, $80–$90 single or double with bath. Rates include continental breakfast. MC, V.

Set high above Charlotte Amalie on the western edge of the cruise-ship harbor, a 5-minute walk to the harborfront, this trio of buildings sits on a steeply inclined acre of land dotted with tropical shrubs and bougainvillea, behind a facade of lattices and modern verandas. The heart and soul of the place is the panoramic terrace, which has a 180° view over the cruise ships and an honor bar. The bedrooms are neat, clean, and colorful, all but the cheapest of which contain refrigerators and air-conditioning; the others have ceiling fans.

Much of this hotel's business stems from its willingness to accept 1-night guests (many other small island hotels insist on bookings of several nights), making it popular with sailing buffs and senior citizens.

The establishment has no swimming pool, but it does have a semisecluded Jacuzzi spa. The nearest beaches are Morningstar and Beachcomber, about a 4-minute drive away. Only breakfast is served.

Hotel Mafolie. 7091 Estate Mafolie, Mafolie Hill, Charlotte Amalie, St. Thomas, USVI 00802. ☎ **800/225-7035** or 809/774-2790. Fax 809/774-4091. 18 rms, 4 minisuites. A/C TV. Winter, $87 single; $97 double; $135 minisuite for up to four. Off-season, $70 single; $80 double; $105 minisuite. Children 11 and under stay free in parents' room; children 12 and over $15 each. AE, MC, V.

An old favorite, with plenty of fans and only a few detractors, the Mafolie enjoys a tranquil location with a panoramic view of the harbor (often filled with cruise ships). Perched about 850 feet over Charlotte Amalie, it has bounced back into operation after Hurricane Marilyn devastated the place. Now with major renovations, it's much better than before. A sprawling guest house–type hotel, it attracts honeymooners. The ambience is not the stuff of dreamy postcards, but the rooms are comfortably furnished, with a rather uninspired decor. Cooling is not only by air-conditioning but also by ceiling fans. Its once-touted restaurant is gone with the wind, but there's still a pool bar where breakfast is served. A shuttle transports visitors to Magens Bay, about a 5-minute ride.

Island View Guesthouse. 11-C Contant (P.O. Box 1903), Charlotte Amalie, St. Thomas, USVI 00803. ☎ **800/524-2023** for reservations only, or 809/774-4270. Fax 809/774-6167. 15 rms, 13 with bath; 1 suite. TV TEL. Winter, $60 single without bath, $90 single with bath; $65 double without bath, $95 double with bath; $115 suite. Off-season, $45 single without bath, $70 single with bath; $50 double without bath, $75 double with bath; $95 suite. Rates include continental breakfast. AE, MC, V. From the airport, turn right onto Rte. 30; then cut left and continue to the unmarked Scott Free Rd., where you go left and look for the sign.

The Island View is located in a steeply inclined neighborhood of private homes and villas about a 7-minute drive west of Charlotte Amalie and a 20-minute drive from the nearest beach at Magens Bay. Set 545 feet up Crown Mountain, it has sweeping views over Charlotte Amalie and the harbor. Family owned and managed, it was originally built in the 1960s as a private home. Enlarged in 1989, it contains main-floor rooms (two without private bath) and some poolside rooms, plus six units in a recent addition (three with kitchens and all with balconies). The bedrooms are cooled by breezes and fans, and the newer ones have optional air-conditioning. A self-service open-air bar on the gallery operates on the honor system.

Doubles For Less Than $120 (Winter) / $80 (Off-Season)

Galleon House. Government Hill (P.O. Box 6577), Charlotte Amalie, St. Thomas, USVI 00804. ☎ **800/524-2052** in the U.S., or 809/774-6952. Fax 809/774-6952. 14 rms, 12 with bath. A/C TV TEL. Winter, $59 single without bath, $109 single with bath; $69 double without bath, $119 double with bath. Off-season, $49 single without bath, $69 single with bath; $59 double without bath, $79 double with bath. Rates include continental breakfast. AE, DISC, MC, V.

At the east end of Main Street, about a block from the main shopping section of Charlotte Amalie, Galleon House is reached after a difficult climb, especially in sweltering heat. Nevertheless, its rates are among the most competitive in town, if you don't mind a place operated without state-of-the-art maintenance and a staff attitude that many readers have complained about.

Nevertheless, it's an acceptable choice if your demands aren't too high. You walk up a long flight of stairs to reach a concrete terrace doubling as the reception area. The rooms are scattered in several hillside buildings, each with a ceiling fan, cable TV with HBO, and so-so air-conditioning. There's a small freshwater pool and a sundeck. Breakfast is served on a veranda overlooking the harbor, and Magens Beach is 15 minutes by car or taxi from the hotel.

Villas & Condos

Sea Horse Cottages. Nazareth Bay (P.O. Box 302312), Charlotte Amalie, St. Thomas, USVI 00803. ☎ **809/775-9231.** 15 cottages. Winter, $125 cottage for two; $140 cottage for four. Off-season, $60–$80 cottage for two; $100 cottage for four. Extra person $12.50. No credit cards.

The family-run Sea Horse overlooks Nazareth Bay on the southeastern side of the island near Red Hook, a commercial area where guests can go to restaurants and grocery stores. The Sea Horse has steps leading down the hillside from the pool to a tanning platform and a cove for swimming and snorkeling. The rooms contain teak furniture, twin beds, and shuttered windows. The airport is 9 miles away, but with the traffic the car ride may take about 45 minutes. Baby-sitting is not difficult to arrange, and guests who enjoy water sports are sent to Secret Harbour nearby.

Best Off-Season Bets

From mid-April to mid-December, St. Thomas is more of a bargain than in winter. All hotels lower their rates, some considerably. The best deals—outside of some cut-rate package—might be at one of the following hotels:

Blackbeard's Castle. Blackbeard's Hill (P.O. Box 6041), Charlotte Amalie, St. Thomas, USVI 00801. ☎ **800/344-5771** in the U.S., or 809/776-1234. Fax 809/776-4321. 18 rms, 3 junior suites, 3 full suites. A/C TV TEL. Winter, $140 double; $170 junior suite for two; $190 full suite for two. Off-season, $95 double; $120 junior suite for two; $145 full suite for two. Rates include continental breakfast. AE, DC, DISC, MC, V. From the airport, turn right onto Rte. 30; when you get to Rte. 35, take a left turn and travel for a half mile until you see the sign pointing left to the hotel.

This genuinely charming inn enjoys one of the island's finest views of Charlotte Amalie and its harbor, thanks to its perch high on a hillside above the town. Legend says that Blackbeard himself lived in a tower on this site. Each bedroom has a semisecluded veranda, a flat-weave Turkish kilim, terra-cotta floors, simple furniture, and a private bath. Guests enjoy the swimming pool and many consider the hotel's restaurant one of the best on the island. The best deal off-season is on the rooms, which in winter rent for $112 single and $140 double. However, off-season, a single drops to only $75 and a double to $95.

✪ **Hotel 1829.** Kongens Gade (P.O. Box 1567), Charlotte Amalie, St. Thomas, USVI 00804. ☎ **800/524-2002** in the U.S., or 809/776-1829. Fax 809/776-4313. 14 rms. A/C MINIBAR TV TEL. Winter, $90–$180 double; from $230 suite. Off-season, $70–$130 double; from $165 suite. Rates include continental breakfast. AE, DISC, MC, V.

Built by a French sea captain for his bride, this place is the most famous "inn of character" on St. Thomas. It's a 15-minute ride from Magens Beach. Danish and African labor completed the structure in 1829—hence the name. After a major renaissance, this once-decaying historic site has become one of the leading small hotels in the Caribbean. It has entertained the likes of Mikhail Baryshnikov in its often small rooms, which are nevertheless beautifully designed and comfortable. Singles in winter range from $70 to $170, with doubles costing $90 to $180. Off-season, singles are priced at $50 to $120; doubles, at $70 to $130.

Worth a Splurge

✪ **The Admiral's Inn.** Villa Olga (P.O. Box 306162), Frenchtown, Charlotte Amalie, St. Thomas USVI 00802. ☎ **809/774-1376.** Fax 809/774-8010. 12 rms. A/C TV TEL. Winter, $99–$149 single or double. Off-season, $79–$109 single or double. Children 11 and under stay free in parents' room. Rates include continental breakfast. AE, DISC, MC, V.

Set on a peninsula in Frenchtown near the western entrance to Charlotte Amalie's harbor, this beachfront hotel, which attracts yachties and divers, provides modern lodging in a relaxed setting with both harbor and oceanfront views. The secluded yet central location is just a short walk from town. Units sit on a landscaped hillside. The freshwater pool was terraced into the slope and has a large sundeck and flowering borders. The beach and saltwater pool lie a few paces from the lanai-style ocean-view units. Full breakfasts and light lunches are available, and the poolside bar remains open for guests throughout the morning and afternoon. Dinner is served at the Chart House Restaurant nearby.

Carib Beach Resort. 70-C Lindbergh Bay, St. Thomas, USVI 00801. ☎ **800/792-2747.** Fax 809/777-4131. 66 rms. A/C TV. Winter, $109–$119 single; $119–$149 double. Off-season, $79–$89 single; $89–$129 double. Children 11 and under stay free in parents' room. AE, MC, V.

Only about a 3-minute walk from Lindbergh Bay with its good beach, this Best Western hotel is recommendable for its affordable air-conditioned ocean-view rooms with private terraces. It's not the fanciest place on the island, but is preferred to its sibling, the Emerald Beach, another Best Western. The bedrooms are not large but are adequately comfortable, although somewhat dated in decor. All rooms have refrigerators but no kitchen facilities, and there's no room service. The accommodations are in pink-and-blue concrete structures—one two story, another three story—with five cottages closer to the sea. There's a well-patronized pool, plus a restaurant and bar. Dinner is served only in winter; otherwise, guests are shuttled free to the Emerald Beach Resort.

Island Beachcomber Hotel. P.O. Box 302579, Lindbergh Bay, St. Thomas, USVI 00803. ☎ **800/982-9898** or 809/774-5250. Fax 809/774-5615. 47 rms. A/C TV TEL. Winter, $125–$140 single; $130–$145 double. Off-season, $95–$110 single; $100–$115 double. Children $20 extra. AE, DC, DISC, MC, V.

Near the airport, this rather standard hostelry has long been known for its affordable rates on pricey St. Thomas. A beach-party atmosphere prevails, even though the inn attracts a slightly older crowd. Many guests are 1-nighters staying over between yacht charters. There's a Tahiti aura to the place, with tropical foliage, bird cages, bridges, and thatched umbrellas. The inn received a lot of publicity and budget traveler business when *Caribbean Travel & Life* rated it as one of the 10 most affordable properties in the West Indies. The inn has been run by the same family for some four decades and enjoys a faithful clientele. The bedrooms are clean and well maintained, although their furnishings are a bit shopworn. Each of the accommodations has a small refrigerator, plus a patio or porch. Attracting locals as well as visitors, a decent beachfront restaurant serves a reasonably priced although standard cuisine. The beach bar can be fun if the crowd's right. Lounge chairs and rafts are free to guests. There's a free shuttle to town.

✪ Villa Blanca. 4 Raphune Hill, Rte. 38, Charlotte Amalie, St. Thomas, USVI 00801. ☎ **809/776-0749.** Fax 809/779-2661. 16 rms. TV. Winter, $105–$125 single; $115–$135 double. Off-season, $75–$95 single; $75–$85 double. AE, DC, MC, V.

Small, intimate, and charming, this small-scale hotel lies $1^1/2$ miles east of Charlotte Amalie on 3 secluded acres of hilltop land, which is some of the most panoramic on the island. Originally built in 1953 as the private home of Christine Cromwell, heiress to the Dodge fortune, its main building served as the private home of its present owner, Blanca Terrasa Smith, between 1973 and 1985. After the death of her husband, Mrs. Smith added a 12-bedroom annex in her garden and opened her grounds to paying guests.

Each room contains a ceiling fan and/or air-conditioning, a well-equipped kitchenette, and a private balcony or terrace with sweeping views either eastward to St. John or westward to Puerto Rico and the harbor of Charlotte Amalie. No meals are served, but nonetheless a homelike and caring ambience prevails. On the premises are a freshwater swimming pool and a large covered patio. The closest beach is Morningstar Bay, about a 20-minute drive away.

Villa Santana. Denmark Hill, St. Thomas, USVI 00802. ☎ and fax **809/776-1311.** 7 suites. TV TEL. Winter, $125–$195 suite for one or two. Off-season, $85–$135 suite for one or two. AE.

This all-suite property was built by Gen. Antonio Lopez de Santa Anna of Mexico in the 1850s and offers a panoramic view of Charlotte Amalie and the St. Thomas harbor. It's a 5-minute walk from the shopping district in Charlotte Amalie and a 15-minute drive to Magens Beach. This unique country villa can accommodate guests at La Mansion, the former library of the general; La Terraza, originally the general's wine cellar; La Cocina de Santa Anna, once the central kitchen for the entire estate; La Casa de Piedra, once the bedroom of the general's most trusted attaché; and in La Torre, the old pump house that has been converted into a modern lookout tower. All rooms have fully equipped kitchens, televisions, telephones, private baths, and ceiling fans. The Mexican decor features clay tiles, rattan furniture, and stonework. The property includes a pool, sundeck, and small garden with hibiscus and bougainvillea.

WHERE TO EAT

The cuisine on St. Thomas is among the top in the entire West Indies. But prices, unfortunately, are high, and many of the best spots can only be reached by taxi. With a few exceptions, the finest and most charming restaurants aren't in Charlotte Amalie, but are out on the island. But the town does offer the best options for budget travelers.

If you're in a villa, apartment, or condo rental, patronize the Pueblo supermarkets. You'll find them across from the Havensight Mall (where the cruise ships dock), at the Sub Base, and also at the Lockhart Gardens and Four Winds shopping centers.

IN CHARLOTTE AMALIE

✪ **Bumpa's.** 38-A Waterfront. ☎ **809/776-5674.** Reservations not accepted. Main courses $4–$6.50. No credit cards. Daily 7am–6pm. Closed Sept. AMERICAN.

This deli-style, open-air joint is on the second level of a little old West Indian house with a canvas-roof porch offering a panoramic view of the harbor. Don't get your hopes up; it isn't that special, but it's an ideal choice for a good, filling, and low-priced breakfast or lunch. The shopping hordes find this a favorite refueling stop. The cook prepares a fresh soup for lunch, and you can also get sandwiches and freshly made salads. Many patrons stop in just to order Ben & Jerry's ice cream, one of the homemade pies, or a refreshing lemonade on a hot day.

Cafesito. 21 Queens Charter. ☎ **809/774-9574.** Main courses $5–$20. AE, MC, V. Daily 11am–11pm. SPANISH.

Right on the waterfront, this is one of the most festive choices for dining. It's located in an old Danish building with a high ceiling and pithy Spanish quotations on the walls. Wooden tables with wrought-iron chairs are placed in the courtyard. The menu is essentially the same at lunch and dinner, except for the daily specials. Even if every dish doesn't merit an ¡olé!, many are quite good, and there's an energetic geniality about the place. Dishes include *torre de pollo*, a pastry tower stuffed with chicken, fresh mushrooms, and roast pappers. Franko's chicken is a tasty choice, as is the big plate of grilled calamari. Classic guitar music is a feature on Wednesday nights, along with a steel band that also plays on Thursday, Friday, and Sunday.

Diamond Barrel. 18 Norre Gade. ☎ **809/774-5071.** Main courses $7–$20. AE, MC, V. Daily 6am–6pm. AMERICAN/WEST INDIAN.

This popular local eatery and hangout is active throughout the day. The decor (what there is of it) is appropriately nautical, with rattan pieces and murals of sealife.

Breakfast is fairly standard fare, but at lunch you can sample some good regional dishes, including the catch of the day and various chicken dishes. You might begin with the oxtail soup or whatever's in the kettle that day. If you want to go really local, opt for the stewed mutton or the pickled pigs' feet, although you might settle more happily for the salmon patties. On site is a bakery providing fresh pastries and other baked goods.

✪ **Gladys's Café.** Royal Dane Mall. ☎ **809/774-6604.** Reservations required for parties of four or more. Main courses $6.95–$12.95; breakfast $2.95–$5.95. AE, MC, V. Mon–Thurs and Sat 6:30am–4pm, Fri 6:30am–midnight, Sun 8am–2pm. WEST INDIAN / AMERICAN.

Antigua-born Gladys Isles worked at the Palm Passage restaurant for years as a waitress, but when she developed a following that demanded so much of her time, she decided to open her own place. It has been a hit ever since. Gladys is a warm, gracious woman who makes a visit here all the more special. Gladys's Café is housed in a 1700 pump house with a stonework courtyard that has a well (one of only three on the island) in the middle. Considering the portions, quality, and price, her breakfast is the best value in town. The lunch offerings are various sandwiches, salads, and fresh seafood, including an excellent swordfish and dumplings. The house specialty is the hot chicken salad made with pieces of sautéed breasts with red-wine vinegar, pine nuts, and dill weed, all nestled on a bed of lettuce. Dinner is served only on Friday when a popular jazz band plays from 8pm to midnight. Try a local lobster, or else shrimp, fresh pasta, fresh fish, or perfectly done steaks.

Greenhouse. Veterans Dr. ☎ **809/774-7998.** Main courses $9.95–$19.95; breakfast $3.95–$4.95. AE, DISC, MC, V. Daily 8am–2am. AMERICAN/CARIBBEAN.

Fronted with big sunny windows, this waterfront restaurant attracts cruise-ship passengers who have shopped and need a place to drop. The food is not the island's best, but it's perfectly satisfying if you're not too demanding. A breakfast menu of eggs, sausages, and bacon segues into the daily specialties, including much American fare and some Jamaican-inspired dishes. A pretty good freshly grilled mahimahi is served here with a Florida key lime ginger butter and Jamaican jerk, or you might order a delectable specialty such as barbecued pork ribs, again with Jamaican jerk seasoning. Happy hour is daily from 4:30 to 7pm. This is one of the safest places to be in Charlotte Amalie after dark.

Hard Rock Cafe. In International Plaza, the Waterfront, Queen's Quarter. ☎ **809/777-5555.** Reservations not accepted. Main courses $7.95–$16.95. AE, MC, V. Mon–Sat 10am–9pm, Sun 10am–3pm. AMERICAN.

Occupying the second floor of a pink-sided mall whose big windows overlook the ships moored in Charlotte Amalie's harbor, this restaurant is a member of the international chain that defines itself as the "Smithsonian of Rock 'n' Roll." Entire walls are devoted to the memorabilia of John Lennon, Eric Clapton, Bob Marley, and others. Throughout most of the day the place functions as a restaurant, serving barbecued meats, salads, sandwiches, burgers (including a well-flavored veggie burger), fresh fish, steaks, and the best fajitas in the Virgin Islands. On Friday and Saturday nights a live band performs, at which time a small dance floor gets busy and the bar trade picks up considerably.

✪ **Little Bopeep.** Barber Plaza. ☎ **809/774-1959.** Reservations not accepted. Main courses $5.50–$11.95. AE, MC, V. Mon–Sat 7:30–11am (take-out only) and 11:30am–4pm. WEST INDIAN.

This little tavern serves up some of the best West Indian food on the island. Some critics like it better than Eunice's Terrace (see below). The menu changes daily, and no one puts on any airs. Reservations aren't taken—just show up. Breakfast is strictly take-out, but it's the least expensive morning meal in town. You can order—to go—meat patties and sandwiches such as egg, bacon, and cheese. Lunch—the only main meal of the day served—gets more intriguing and a lot spicier, with jerk chicken (a secret recipe), curried chicken, and curried conch. Fried plantains accompany most dishes. Centrally located in a brick building, it offers a very plain interior, as you'd expect.

Pizza Amore. 18 Estate Thomas. ☎ **809/774-2822.** Meals $2–$20. No credit cards. Mon–Sat 11am–8pm, Sun 11am–5pm. PIZZA/SANDWICHES.

This small pizzeria is decorated with an Italian motif including posters of different Italian coffees and wines. The booths, tables, and chairs are all made from maple, and the floor is brick. They serve New York–style pizza with a wide range of topping choices. They also offer salads and sandwiches—salami, ham, and heros on French loaves. Round out your meal with an espresso and cappuccino.

Randy's Wine Bar & Bistro. In Al Cohen's Plaza, 4002 Raphune Hill. ☎ **809/777-3199.** Main courses $14.95–$24.95; lunch $4.95–$6.95. AE, MC, V. Bistro, daily 9am–1am; deli, daily 9am–5pm. CONTINENTAL.

This is a local oddity, catering to deli devotees (usually from New York), cigar aficionados, and bistro fans. As one local customer, who goes here every day, said to us, "It's anything you want it to be." The on-site store sells a good selection of wines, along with the standard liquors and cigars. If you don't like the bistro wine list, you can purchase a wine from the store and bring it into the bistro, although you'll pay a $5 corkage fee. The deli serves the usual sandwiches and salads (some quite good), while the bistro dishes up a quite delectable cuisine, especially if you stick to the fresh fish, steak, and lobster. Look for one of the daily specials such as pork tenderloin in a Dijon mustard sauce.

Tickles Dockside Pub. Crown Bay Marina. ☎ **809/776-1595.** Main courses $8–$15; lunch $6–$10. DC, V. Daily 6am–10pm. AMERICAN.

Tickles is dedicated to the concept of fun, comfort, and reasonably priced food in a friendly atmosphere. Diners at this open-air restaurant can sit back and relax while watching the sailboats and cruise ships on the water. The menu offers a simple American fare of burgers, including a chicken burger, and sandwiches, like the renowned Reuben made with your choice of ham, turkey, or corned beef, grilled with Tickles's own special Russian dressing, Swiss cheese, and sauerkraut. Start off with a plate of "gator eggs" (lightly breaded jalapeño peppers stuffed with cheese) or maybe the "sweet lips" (strips of sweet, fried chicken in the shape of lips served with a honey-mustard sauce). If you're in the mood for seafood, you may want to try the fish-and-chips, beer battered white fish fried and served with Swiss-fried potatoes.

Zorba's Cafe. 1854 Hus, Government Hill. ☎ **809/776-0444.** Main courses $9.95–$18.95; lunch $5.95–$9.95. AE, MC, V. Mon–Thurs 10:30am–3:30pm and 6–10pm, Fri–Sat 10:30am–3:30pm and 6–10:30pm, Sun 6–10pm. GREEK.

If you're in the mood for Greek food, this is the place to go. Jimmy Boukas is the owner of this casual, friendly establishment located in a 19th-century building in the heart of Charlotte Amalie. Guests may sit out on the courtyard surrounded by banana and palm trees. We highly recommend the spaniko pita (spinach-and-feta pie), the moussaka (eggplant casserole), and the gyros, but be sure to save room for the homemade baklava.

AT FRENCHTOWN

Between the harbor and the airport on the outskirts of Charlotte Amalie, you'll find the **Frenchtown Deli,** in the Frenchtown Mall (☎ 809/776-7211), open Monday to Saturday from 10am to 8pm, serving sandwiches for $4 to $6.50. House-baked breads, fresh salads, and beer, soda, and wine are also sold. It's a good place to stock up on supplies if you have a rented place with a kitchenette, or you'd like the makings of a picnic.

Hook, Line & Sinker. 2 Honduras, Frenchtown. ☎ **809/776-9708.** Main courses $11.95–$18.95; lunch from $10; brunch (Sun) $6.95–$9.95. AE, MC, V. Mon–Sat 7–10am, 11:30am–4pm, and 6–10pm; Sun 10am–2:30pm. AMERICAN.

Both locals and visitors flock to this rendezvous, where they get friendly service, good food at reasonable prices, and a panoramic view of the harbor. The setting evokes a New England seaport village, and the restaurant has a pitched roof and skylights, along with wraparound French doors and windows. A *Cheers*-like crowd frequents the bar. Breakfast, except for Sunday brunch, is the standard old menu, but at lunch you can try everything from a Caesar salad to various grilled chicken dishes. The dinner menu is usually a delight, with such dishes as a not-bad bouillabaisse, an almond-crusted yellowtail, and a particularly good pineapple-lemon chicken. The pastas are well prepared, and there are plenty of extras, such as freshly made soups of the day and conch fritters.

IN RED HOOK

Duffy's Love Shack. 650 Red Hook Plaza, Rte. 38. ☎ **809/779-2080.** Main courses $9.25–$14. No credit cards. Daily 11am–2am. AMERICAN/WEST INDIAN.

This is a fun and happening place if you like to mingle with the locals. As the evening wears on, the customers become the entertainment, often dancing on tables or forming conga lines. Yes, it also serves food, a standard American cuisine given Caribbean flair and flavor. The restaurant is open-air with lots of bamboo and a thatched roof over the bar—in other words, the quintessential island look. Even the menu appears on a bamboo stick like an old-fashioned fan. Start with a Caribbean eggroll or black-bean cakes, then roll on to cowboy steak or voodoo pineapple chicken (in a hot garlic-and-pineapple sauce). Surf and turf here translates as jerk tenderloin and mahimahi. After 10pm, the stove-pot cookery is dropped and a late-night menu appears, mostly sandwiches. The bar business is huge, and the bartender is known for his lethal rum drinks.

East Coast. In Red Hook Plaza, Rte. 38. ☎ **809/775-1919.** Main courses $6.75–$21.75. AE, MC, V. Daily 5:30–11pm. (Bar, daily 4:30pm–4am.) CARRIBBEAN.

Every night local and Stateside sports fans cram into the East Coast to cheer on their favorite teams (playing on the TV). What's not readily apparent is that the adjacent restaurant serves very good meals. Put your name on the list and then enjoy a beer at the bar while waiting for a table. You can dine in a denlike haven or on an outdoor terrace in back. A different fish of the day is prepared the way you like it: grilled, baked, or broiled. The selections might include tuna, wahoo, dolphin, swordfish, or snapper. The last is best in a garlic-cream sauce. The kitchen also turns out Cajun shrimp and their famous "Coast burgers."

Grateful Deli & Coffee Shop. 6500 Red Hook Plaza, Suite 125. ☎ **809/775-5160.** Sandwiches and burgers $2.95–$6.95. AE, MC, V. Mon–Sat 7am–5pm, Sun 7:30am–3pm. AMERICAN DELI.

Across from the ferry dock, this is the most affordable joint for a breakfast or dinner. The breakfast menu isn't just the usually dull ham 'n' eggs order, but includes such delectable offerings as "designer omelets" and glazed waffles served with strawberries and whipped cream. Sometimes you can get low-cost regional fare here at lunch, including stewed chicken with rice or vegetable lasagne, even pumpkin or black-bean soup. But most guests show up for one of the sandwiches, which are Red Hook's, or even the island's, finest—everything from Black Forest ham with Saga bleu cheese to a triple-decker club with pastrami, corned beef, and Swiss cheese.

Señor Pizza. Red Hook (across from the St. John ferry dock). ☎ **809/775-3030.** Pizza $1.75 (slice) to $18 (supreme). No credit cards. Daily 11am–9pm. PIZZA.

Red Hook's best pizzas are served here; the generous slices are practically a lunch unto themelves. If you're staying in a place nearby, the staff will deliver, or else you can settle into one of the on-site picnic tables. If you're not in the mood for pizza, try one of the tasty calzones.

Wok & Roll. 6200 Smith Bay, Red Hook. ☎ **809/775-6246.** Main courses $3.75–$9. No credit cards. Mon–Thurs 11am–10pm, Fri–Sat 11am–10:30pm, Sun 5–10pm. CHINESE.

Across from the dock for the ferry to St. John, this small Chinese restaurant, above which is the Warehouse Bar, is housed in a cinder-block building with a blue roof. A patio seats about 25 people, but the majority of the business is take-out. The restaurant serves typical Asian dishes such as chow mein and sweet-and-sour pork along with such specials as Shanghai spring rolls, shrimp in a lobster sauce, and Hong Kong lo mein. The famous dish at this place is the crab Rangoon, which is said to be like no other.

EN ROUTE TO THE EAST END

Poll's Mexican Restaurant. 4125 Anna's Retreat, at Tillett Gardens. ☎ **809/775-4550.** Reservations recommended. Main courses $5.95–$13.95. AE, MC, V. Mon–Sat 11:30am–9:30pm. MEXICAN.

It's a bit of an offbeat adventure to dine at this open-air restaurant with a Mexican theme of florid colors, flowers, and local art on the walls. Its setting is right in the Tillet Gardens where silk screening is produced, lying on Route 38 east, opposite the Four Winds Shopping Plaza on the road to the East End beaches. For lunch, everyone's favorite is a sizzling fajita, made to order with your choice of shrimp, fish, chicken, or steak. Five different burritos are also featured, including one for vegetarians. Burgers, of course, appear on the menu, but the reason to go is to sample the Mexican specialties, including a chile relleno plate (the green chili peppers are stuffed with Monterey jack cheese). Children's plates, including tacos and cheese quesadillas or enchiladas, are also dished up, along with some juicy, meaty smoked ribs with a fiery Texas barbecue sauce.

AT BOLONGO & COWPET BAYS

✪ **Cunningham's Restaurant & Beach Bar.** In the Anchorage Condos (next to the St. Thomas Yacht Club), Cowpet Bay. ☎ **809/779-2212.** Reservations recommended for dinner. Main courses $4.50–$8.50. AE, DISC, MC, V. Daily 11am–10pm. Closed 2 weeks in Sept. AMERICAN.

If you're staying in the East End (highly likely) and looking for that picture-postcard waterfront dive (with affordable prices), be sure to check out this place. The pink-and-aqua with wicker decor may be a cliché, but this open-air spot has real island flair. On a clear day, you can see St. John and Tortola. In the evening, the staff gets a little fancier and hauls out the pink tablecloths. Homemade soups are a specialty at lunch, followed by "killer" burgers, freshly made salads, and daily specials. Dinners here are more elaborate, with fresh or frozen seafood, succulent pastas, plus the usual array of beef and chicken dishes. If the chef's in the right mood, he might poach you some shrimp and flavor it with Sambuca. He also does a mean blackened fish. Although the menu is basically American, it roams the world for inspiration. Save room for the yummy desserts—everything from chocolate thunder to banana-walnut cake.

Iggie's Restaurant. At the Bolongo Bay Beach Club, Bolongo Bay, 50 Estate Bolongo (Rte. 30). ☎ **809/775-1800.** Burgers and sandwiches $7.95–$9.95; main courses $9.95–$15.95. AE, MC, V. Daily noon–3pm and 6:30–10pm. AMERICAN.

Sports fans and others patronize this action-packed seaside place—with giant TVs broadcasting the latest games, it's the island's best sports bar and grill. To make things even livelier, karaoke sing-alongs are staged, when anyone who wants to can grab his or her 15 minutes of fame. The place has "indestructible" furniture, lots of electronic action, and an aggressively informal crowd. Bring the kids along; no one will mind if they make a ruckus. The menu is geared to such kid favorites as burgers, oversized sandwiches, and pastas. Adults ease their pain by ordering such sudsy tropical drinks as Iggie's Queen (coconut cream, crème de Noya, and rum) or the "Ultimate Kamikazi," the ingredients of which are a secret.

ON THE NORTH COAST

✪ **Eunice's Terrace.** 66–67 Smith Bay, Rte. 38. ☎ **809/775-3975.** Reservations not accepted. Main courses $5.25–$18.95. AE, MC, V. Mon–Sat 11am–10pm, Sun 5–10pm. WEST INDIAN / AMERICAN.

A 30-minute taxi ride east of the airport, just east of the Coral World turnoff, is one of the best-known local restaurants, which went from a simple shack to a modern building. A collection of West Indian locals and tourists crowd into its confines for generous platters of savory island food. A popular drink concoction is the "Queen Mary" (tropical fruits laced with dark rum). This little restaurant made news around the world in January 1997 when President Clinton, along with Hillary, dined here. They both shared a conch appetizer; he then opted for a local fish ("ole wife") whereas the First Lady preferred the grilled vegetable plate. Dinner specialties include conch fritters, broiled or fried fish (especially dolphin), sweet-potato pie, and a number of specials usually served with fungi, rice, or plantains. On the lunch menu are fishburgers, sandwiches, and such daily specials as Virgin Islands doved pork or mutton. (Doving, pronounced "*dough*-ving," involves baking sliced meat while basting it with a combination of its own juices, tomato paste, Kitchen Bouquet, and island herbs.) Key lime pie is a favorite dessert.

IN & AROUND THE SUB BASE

Barnacle Bill's. At the Crown Bay Marina, 16 Sub Base. ☎ **809/774-7444.** Main courses $3–$15. AE, MC, V. Mon–Sat 11:30am–midnight. INTERNATIONAL.

Established by the hardworking entrepreneur Bill Grogan, this restaurant is best known as a bar with live music. Its fans, however, also enjoy its view of one of the island's best marinas (Crown Point) and its food, which includes some of the best pizzas on St. Thomas. The main-dish portions, large and well prepared, include everything from steaks to lobsters, with lots of burgers, sandwiches, pastas, and salads as well. The setting is a pastel-colored clapboard house with lots of outdoor terraces and decks overlooking the yachts moored in the nearby marina.

Texas Pit BBQ. Sub Base. ☎ **809/776-9579.** Main courses $5–$9; combination platters $15. No credit cards. Daily 6am–midnight. BARBECUE.

The owners hail from Texas, where they know not only how to barbecue but how to make a fiery sauce to wake up your palate . . . and everything else. This is just a take-away stand with no place to sit and eat, but locals flock to this waterfront hole. The place has been around for some 15 years, and in spite of hurricanes is still going strong. Chicken, tender ribs, or Texas-style beef are dished up in cowboy-size portions, along with the usual accompaniments of rice, cole slaw, and potato salad.

One resident nearby pronounced the ribs here the island's best, but we're still sampling other places before coming up with a final verdict.

✪ **Victor's Hide Out.** 103 Sub Base (off Rte. 30). ☎ **809/776-9379**. Reservations recommended. Main courses $9.95–$29.95. AE, MC, V. Mon–Sat 11:30am–3:30pm and 5:30–10pm, Sun 5:30–10pm. SEAFOOD/CARIBBEAN.

Victor's is operated by Victor Sydney, who comes from Montserrat. You never know who's going to show up here—maybe Bill Cosby, perhaps José Feliciano. Victor's has some of the best local dishes on the island, but first you must find it, as it's truly a place to hide out. If you're driving, call for directions; otherwise, take a taxi. On a hilltop perch, the large, airy restaurant serves fresh lobster prepared Montserrat style (that is, in a creamy sauce) or grilled in the shell. You might also ask for a plate of juicy barbecued ribs. For dessert, try the coconut, custard, or apple pie.

PICNIC FARE & WHERE TO EAT IT

Because of the dozens of restaurants and beachside cabañas selling hamburgers and beer, many would-be picnickers tend to forgo advance picnic arrangements in favor of a quick beachside bite followed by a snooze on Bay Beach, Drake's Seat, and any of the secluded high-altitude panoramas along the island's western end.

You can, however, create a successful picnic with the culinary expertise of **The Cream and Crumb Shop,** Building 6, Havensight Mall (☎ **809/774-2499**). Located at the point where most cruise ships dock for daytime excursions onto St. Thomas, this cheerful modern shop is easy to miss amid the crush of tax-free jewelers and perfume shops that surround it. The shop sells some of the best pizza on the island ($3 a slice), although more practical for take-out might be one of the thickly layered deli sandwiches ($4.75 to $6.95), or salads such as shrimp, chicken, potato, or crabmeat. You can also get freshly baked pastries, four different kinds of yogurt (piña colada is perfect), and 18 different flavors of deliciously fattening ice cream. Open Monday to Saturday from 6:30am to 6pm.

BEACHES, WATER SPORTS & OTHER OUTDOOR PURSUITS

BEACHES   Chances are, you'll be staying right on the beach, or very close to one, and this is where you'll anchor for most of your stay. All the beaches in the Virgin Islands are public, and most lie anywhere from 2 to 5 miles from Charlotte Amalie.

The North Side   Less than a mile long, ✪ **Magens Bay** lies between two mountains 3 miles north of the capital. One of the world's most beautiful beaches, it charges $1 for adults and $1 per car. Changing facilities are available, and snorkeling gear, lounge chairs, paddle boats, and kayaks can be rented. There is no public transportation to reach it; from Charlotte Amalie, take Route 35 north all the way. The beach is terribly crowded on cruise-ship days, but the crowds thin in the midafternoon. The gates to the beach are open daily from 6am to 6pm (after 4pm, you'll need insect repellent to protect yourself from mosquitoes and sand flies).

In the northeast near Coral World, **Coki Beach** also gets crowded when cruise ships are in port. Snorkelers and scuba divers are attracted to this popular beach, with its abundance of reef fish. Pickpockets frequent this beach as well, so protect your valuables. Concessions at the beach can arrange everything from waterskiing to parasailing—not just snorkeling. The East End Vitran bus runs to Smith Bay, letting you off at the gate to Coral World and Coki Beach.

Also on the north side is the **Renaissance Grand Beach Resort,** one of the island's most beautiful. Many water sports are available at this beach, which opens onto Smith Bay and is near Coral World. The beach lies right off Smith Bay Road (Rte. 38), east of Charlotte Amalie.

The South Side   On the south side near the Frenchman's Reef Hotel, **Morningstar** lies about 2 miles east of Charlotte Amalie. This is where you can wear your most daring swimwear. Or you can rent sailboats, sailboards, snorkeling equipment, and lounge chairs. The beach is reached by a cliff-front elevator at Frenchman's Reef. There's no public transportation to the beach, but it's only a short taxi ride from Charlotte Amalie.

Set against a backdrop of sea grape trees and shady palms, **Limetree** lures those who want a serene spot to sunbathe. You can rent snorkeling gear, lounge and beach chairs, and towels. Cool drinks are served, including a Limetree green piña colada. There's no public transportation, but the beach can easily be reached by taxi from Charlotte Amalie.

One of the island's most popular beaches, **Brewers Bay** lies in the southwest part of the island, near the University of the Virgin Islands. Light meals and drinks are served along the beach. It's not good for snorkeling, however. From Charlotte Amalie, take the Fortuna bus heading west and get off at the edge of Brewers Bay, across from the Reichhold Center, the cultural center of St. Thomas.

Near the airport, **Lindbergh Beach** has a lifeguard, toilet facilities, and a bath-house. It, too, lies on the Fortuna bus route heading west from Charlotte Amalie.

The East End   Small and special, **Secret Harbour** lies near a number of condos whose owners frequent the beach. It's often crowded on weekends. The snorkeling near the rocks here is great. No public transportation stops here, but it's an easy taxi ride east of Charlotte Amalie in the direction of Red Hook.

One of the finest beaches on St. Thomas is ✪ **Sapphire Beach,** popular with windsurfers. A large reef is located close to the fine, white-coral-sand shore, and there are good views of offshore cays and St. John. It's set against the backdrop of the Doubletree Sapphire Beach Resort & Marina, where you lunch or order drinks. You can rent snorkeling gear and lounge chairs. To reach Sapphire Beach, take the East End bus from Charlotte Amalie via Red Hook and get off at the entrance to Sapphire Bay.

GOLF   On the north shore, **Mahogany Run,** Mahogany Run Road (☎ **800/ 253-7103** or 809/775-6006), is an 18-hole, par-70 course. This beautiful course rises and drops like a roller coaster on its journey to the sea where cliffs and crashing sea waves are the ultimate hazards at the 13th and 14th holes. Greens fees are $85 for 18 holes, reduced to $70 in the late afternoon, depending on the daylight available. Carts cost $15 year-round.

KAYAK TOURS   **Virgin Island Ecotours** (☎ **809/779-2155** for information) offers 2 1/2-hour kayak trips through a mangrove lagoon on the southern coastline. The tour, which costs $50 per person, is led by professional naturalists who allow enough time for 30 minutes of snorkeling.

SCUBA & SNORKELING   With 30 spectacular reefs just off St. Thomas, the U.S. Virgins are rated as one of the "most beautiful areas in the world" by *Skin Diver* magazine.

The **St. Thomas Diving Club,** 7147 Bolongo Bay (☎ **800/538-7348** or 809/ 776-2381), is a full-service PADI five-star IDC center, the best on the island. An open-water certification course, including four scuba dives, costs $330. An advanced open-water certification course, including five dives that can be accomplished in 2 days, goes for $275. Every Thursday, participants are taken on an all-day scuba excursion that includes a two-tank dive to the wreck of the RMS *Rhône* in the British Virgin Islands, costing $110. You can also enjoy local snorkeling for $25.

Dive In, in the Doubletree Sapphire Beach Resort and Marina, Smith Bay Road, Route 36 (☎ **809/775-6100**), is a well-recommended and complete diving center offering some of the finest diving services in the U.S. Virgin Islands, including professional instruction (beginner to advanced), daily beach and boat dives, custom dive packages, underwater photography and videotapes, snorkeling trips, and a full-service PADI dive center. An introductory course costs $55. Certified divers can enjoy a two-dive morning trip for $70 or a one-dive afternoon trip at $50. Evening dives cost $55. Serious divers can purchase a six-dive pass for $185.

TENNIS   Your best bet for great tennis on the island is the **Wyndham Sugar Bay Beach Club,** 6500 Estate Smith Bay (☎ 809/777-7100), which has the Virgin Islands' first stadium tennis court, seating 220, plus six additional Laykold courts lit at night. There's also a pro shop.

Another good resort for tennis is the **Bolongo Beach Resort,** Bolongo Bay (☎ 809/775-1800), which has two tennis courts that are lit until 10pm. It is free to members and hotel guests *only.*

At **Marriott's Frenchman's Reef Tennis Courts** (☎ 809/776-8500, ext. 444), there are four courts lit until 10pm. Nonguests pay $10 per half hour per court.

WINDSURFING   This increasingly popular sport is available at the major resort hotels and at some public beaches, including Brewers Bay, Morningstar Beach, and Limetree Beach. The **Renaissance Grand Beach Resort,** Smith Bay Road, Route 38 (☎ 809/775-1510), is the major hotel offering windsurfing. If you're a nonresident, the cost is $35 per hour.

SEEING THE SIGHTS

IN CHARLOTTE AMALIE   The color and charm of a real Caribbean waterfront town come vividly to life in the capital of St. Thomas, Charlotte Amalie, where most visitors begin their sightseeing on the small island. In days of yore, seafarers from all over the globe flocked to this old-world Danish town, as did pirates and members of the Confederacy, who used the port during the American Civil War. St. Thomas was also the biggest slave market in the world.

The old warehouses once used for storing pirate goods still stand and, for the most part, house today's shops. In fact, the main streets (called "Gade" here in honor of their Danish heritage) are now a virtual shopping mall and are usually packed. Sandwiched among these shops are a few historic buildings, most of which can be covered on foot in about 2 hours. Before starting your tour, stop off in the so-called Grand Hotel, near Emancipation Park. No longer a hotel, it contains, along with shops, a **visitor center,** Tolbod Gade 1 (☎ 809/774-8784), that's open Monday to Friday from 8am to 5pm and on Saturday from 8am to noon.

Most visitors explore Charlotte Amalie to shop rather than to look at historic buildings; however, they can't miss **Fort Christian** (☎ 809/776-4566), dating from 1672 and dominating the center of town. Named after the Danish king Christian V, the structure has been everything from a governor's residence to a jail. The fort was a police station, court, and jail until 1983 (in 1977, it became a national historic landmark). The museum demonstrates the history of the island culture and its people, including the Danish settlement. Cultural workshops and turn-of-the-century furnishings are just some of the exhibits. A museum shop features local crafts, maps, and prints. Admission free, the fort is open Monday to Friday from 8:30am to 4:30pm, Saturday from 9:30am to 4pm, and Sunday from noon to 2pm.

The **Seven Arches Museum,** Government Hill (☎ 809/774-9295), is an 18th-century Danish house that has been restored to its original condition and furnished with West Indian antiques. You can walk through the yellow ballast arches and visit the great room with its view of the busiest harbor in the Caribbean. The admission of $5 includes a cold tropical drink served in a walled garden filled with flowers. It's open Tuesday to Saturday from 10am to 3pm or by appointment.

The **St. Thomas Synagogue,** or Beracha Veshalom U'Gemilut Hasidim (Blessing and Peace and Loving Deeds), Synagogue Hill (☎ **809/774-4312**), is the oldest synagogue in continuous use under the American flag and the second oldest in the Western Hemisphere. It still maintains the tradition of sand on the floor, commemorating the exodus from Egypt. Erected in 1833 by Sephardic Jews, it was built of local stone along with ballast brick from Denmark and mortar made of molasses and sand. It's open to visitors Monday to Friday from 9am to 4pm. The synagogue is reached by a steep climb from Main Street up to Krystal Gade.

ELSEWHERE ON THE ISLAND   West of Charlotte Amalie, Route 30 (Veterans Drive) will take you to **Frenchtown** (turn left at the sign to the Admirals Inn). This was settled by a French-speaking people who were uprooted when the Swedes invaded and took over their homeland on St. Barts. They were known for wearing *cha-chas,* or straw hats. Some of the people who live here today are the direct descendants of those long-ago immigrants.

This colorful village, many of whose residents engage in fishing, contains several interesting restaurants and taverns. Now that Charlotte Amalie has been deemed a dangerous place to be at night, Frenchtown has picked up the business, and it's the best choice for nighttime dancing, entertainment, and drinking.

The number-one tourist attraction of St. Thomas—destroyed by Hurricane Marilyn in 1995—is a 20-minute drive from downtown off Route 38. It's being rebuilt after the hurricane and should be fully functional some time in 1997. The ✪ **Coral World Marine Park & Underwater Observatory,** 6450 Coki Point (☎ **809/775-1555**), is a marine complex that features a three-story underwater observation tower 100 feet offshore. Through windows you'll see sponges, fish, coral, and other underwater life in its natural state. In the Marine Gardens Aquarium, saltwater tanks display everything from sea horses to sea urchins. An 80,000-gallon reef tank features exotic marine life of the Caribbean; another tank is devoted to sea predators, with circling sharks and giant moray eels, among other creatures. Entrance is through a waterfall of cascading water.

The latest addition to the park is a semisubmersible submarine that lets you enjoy the panoramic view and the "down under" feeling of a submarine without truly submerging. Coral World's guests can take advantage of adjacent Coki Beach for snorkel rental, scuba lessons, or simply swimming and relaxing. Lockers and showers are available.

Also included in the marine park are the Tropical Terrace Restaurant, duty-free shops, and a tropical nature trail. Activities include daily fish and shark feedings and exotic bird shows. The complex is open daily from 9am to 6pm. Admission is $16 for adults and $10 for children, but these prices are subject to change in 1997.

The **Paradise Point Tramway** (☎ **809/774-9809**) affords visitors a dramatic view of the Charlotte Amalie harbor with a ride to a 697-foot peak, although you'll pay dearly for the privilege. The tramway operates four cars, each with a 10-person capacity, for the 15-minute round-trip ride. The tramways, similar to those used at ski resorts, haul customers from the Havensight area to Paradise Point, where riders disembark to visit shops and the popular restaurant and bar. The tramway runs daily from 9am to 5pm, costing $10 per person round-trip. Children travel for half price.

The **Estate St. Peter Greathouse Botanical Gardens,** 6A St. Peter Mountain Rd., at the corner of Route 40 and Barrett Hill Road (☎ **809/774-4999**), consists of 11 acres set at the foot of volcanic peaks on the northern rim of the island. It's laced with self-guided nature walks that will acquaint you with some 200 varieties of West Indian plants and trees, including an umbrella plant from Madagascar. From a panoramic deck, you can see some 20 of the Virgin Islands, including Hans Lollick, an uninhabited island between Thatched Cay and Madahl Point. The house itself is worth a visit, its interior filled with art by locals. It's open daily from 9am to 5pm, charging an admission of $8 for adults and $4 for children, which is rather steep for what you get.

ON NEARBY WATER ISLE   The fourth-largest of the U.S. Virgins, with 500 acres of land, Water Isle is only half a mile long. Visitors head out here to spend the day on **Honeymoon Beach,** where they swim, snorkel, sail, waterski, or just sunbathe on the palm-shaded beach and order lunch or a drink from the beach bar.

The process of transferring Water Isle to the U.S.V.I. government is underway. An agreement has been signed to turn about 50 acres of the property over to the government. Under the agreement, some $3 million will be spent cleaning up the island. About 430 acres of the island, currently owned by the U.S. Department of the Interior, still remains to be transferred.

Water Isle is often visited via private boat from the St. Thomas mainland as a kind of escapist holiday for Virgin Islanders. You can take one of the public **ferryboats** maintained by **Launch with Larry** (☎ **809/775-8071** or 809/779-6807). Priced at $3 per person each way ($5 each way for evening passages), it runs between the Crown Bay Marina (part of St. Thomas's submarine base) from a pier opposite Tickles Restaurant. It departs from St. Thomas every day at 6:45, 7:15, and 8am; noon; and 2, 4, 5, and 6pm, with a return to St. Thomas scheduled for approximately 30 minutes later. On Monday, Friday, and Saturday nights, there are additional departures from St. Thomas at 9 and 10pm, with a return from Water Isle to St. Thomas 30 minutes later.

If you happen to miss any of these departures, the ferryboat operator will sometimes schedule private departures for a minimum price of $20 for up to four passengers. Getting information about departure times of the individual boats is somewhat awkward (leave a beeper message with Launch with Larry and hope for a return call). Although not associated with the ferryboat, the reception staff at the **Limestone Reef,** Water Isle's only hotel (☎ **809/774-2148**), can also provide data and information about ferryboat transit between Water Isle and St. Thomas.

. . . & UNDER THE SEA   A major attraction is the *Atlantis* **submarine** (☎ **809/ 776-5650**), which takes you on a 1-hour voyage to depths of 90 feet, unfolding a world of exotic marine life. You'll gaze on coral reefs and sponge gardens through 2-foot windows on the air-conditioned sub, which carries 30 passengers. You take a surface boat from the West Indies Dock, right outside Charlotte Amalie, to the submarine, which lies near Buck Island (the St. Thomas version, not the more famous Buck Island near St. Croix). The fare is $72 per person; children 4 to 12 are charged $27, and teens (13 to 17) are charged $36. Children 3 and under are not permitted. The *Atlantis* operates daily from November to April and Tuesday to Saturday from May to October. Reservations are imperative. Hours and days vary depending on the arrival of cruise ships. For tickets, go to the Havensight Shopping Mall, Building 6, or call for reservations.

SHOPPING

Shoppers not only have the benefits of St. Thomas's liberal duty-free allowances, but they'll also find well-known brand names at savings of up to 40% off Stateside prices.

However, to find true value you often have to plow through a lot of junk. Many items offered for sale—binoculars, stereos, watches, cameras—can be matched in price at your hometown discount store. Therefore, you need to know the prices back home to determine if you're in fact making a savings.

Most shops, some of which occupy former pirate warehouses, are open Monday to Saturday from 9am to 5pm, regular business hours, and some stay open later. Nearly all stores close on Sunday and major holidays—unless a cruise ship is in port. Friday is the biggest cruise-ship visiting day at Charlotte Amalie (one day we counted eight at one time)—so try to avoid shopping then.

Nearly all the major shopping on St. Thomas is located along the harbor of Charlotte Amalie. Cruise-ship passengers mainly shop at the **Havensight Mall,** where they disembark, at the eastern edge of Charlotte Amalie. The principal shopping street is called **Main Street** or Dronningens Gade (its old Danish name). North of this street is another merchandise-loaded street called **Back Street** or Vimmelskaft.

Many shops are also spread along the **Waterfront Highway** (also called Kyst Vejen). Between these major streets or boulevards are a series of side streets, walkways, and alleys, all filled with shops. Major shopping streets are Tolbod Gade, Raadets Gade, Royal Dane Mall, Palm Passage, Storervaer Gade, and Strand Gade.

All the major stores on St. Thomas are located by number on an excellent map in the publication *St. Thomas This Week,* distributed free to all arriving plane and boat passengers.

If you want to combine a little history with shopping, go into the courtyard of the old **Pissarro Building,** entered through an archway off Main Street. The impressionist painter lived here as a child, and the old apartments have been turned into a warren of interesting shops.

It's illegal for most street vendors to ply their trades outside a designated area called **Vendors Plaza,** at the corner of Veterans Drive and Tolbod Gade. Hundreds converge at 7:30am, remaining there usually no later than 5:30pm, Monday to Saturday. (Very few remain in place on Sunday, unless a cruise ship is scheduled to arrive.)

When you completely tire of French perfumes and Swiss watches, head for **Market Square** as it's called locally, or more formally, Rothschild Francis Square. Here under a Victorian tin roof, locals with machetes will slice open fresh coconuts for you so you can drink the milk, and women wearing bandannas will sell akee, cassava, or breadfruit they harvested themselves.

ART GALLERIES & FINE CRAFTS

Camille Pissarro Building Art Gallery. In the Caribbean Cultural Centre, 14 Dronningens Gade. ☎ **809/774-4621.**

In the house where Camille Pissarro was born in 1830, this art gallery—reached by climbing stairs—honors the illustrious painter. Three high-ceilinged and airy rooms display available Pissarro paintings. Many prints and note cards of local artists are also available. The gallery also sells original batiks, alive in vibrant colors.

✪ **Jim Tillett Art Gallery & Silk Screen Print Studio.** At Tillett Gardens, 4126 Anna's Retreat, Tutu. ☎ **809/775-1929.** Take Rte. 38 east from Charlotte Amalie.

Since 1959, Tillett Gardens, once an old Danish farm, has been the island's arts and crafts center. Including an art gallery and a screen-printing studio, this tropical compound is a series of buildings housing arts-and-crafts studios, galleries, and an outdoor garden restaurant and bar. Prints in the galleries start as low as $10. The famous Tillett maps on fine canvas are priced from $30. There are even daily iguana feedings.

BOOKS

Dockside Bookshop. In the Havensight Mall (Building VI). ☎ **809/774-4937.**

Need something to read on the beach? The best supply of books is found at this store near the cruise-ship dock, east of Charlotte Amalie. The shop has a selection on island lore, light and serious reading choices, and everything from photo books to plants and animals.

ELECTRONICS

✪ **Royal Caribbean.** 33 Main St. ☎ **809/776-4110.**

This is the largest camera and electronics store in the Caribbean. This store and its outlets carry Nikon, Minolta, Pentax, Canon, and Panasonic products. It's a good source for watches, including such brand names as Seiko, Movado, Corum, Fendi, and Zodiac. It also has a complete collection of Philippe Charriol watches, jewelry, and leather bags, and a wide selection of Mikimoto pearls, 14- and 18-karat jewelry, and Lladró figurines.

There are additional branches at 23 Main St. (☎ **809/776-5449**) and in Havensight Mall (☎ **809/776-8890**).

FASHION

Coki. In Compass Point Marina. ☎ **809/775-6560.**

Coki of St. Thomas has a factory $1^1/_2$ miles from Red Hook amid a little restaurant row, so you might want to combine a gastronomic tour with a shopping expedition. From the factory's expansive cutting board come some of the most popular varieties of shoulder tote bags in the Virgin Islands. These include pieces of canvas and elegant cotton prints converted to beach bags, zip-top bags, and draw-string bags. All Coki bags are 100% cotton, stitched with polyester sailmaker's thread.

Cosmopolitan, Inc. Drakes Passage and the waterfront. ☎ **809/776-2040.**

Its shoe salon features Bally of Switzerland, and Bally handbags are a popular addition. In swimwear, it offers one of the island's best selections of Gottex of Israel for women and Gottex, Hom, Lahco of Switzerland, and Fila for men. A men's wear section offers Paul & Shark from Italy, and Burma Bibas sports shirts. The shop also features ties by Gianni Versace and Pancaldi of Italy (for at least 30% less than the U.S. mainland price), and Nautica sportswear for men discounted by 10%.

FRAGRANCES

Tropicana Perfume Shoppe. 2 Main St. ☎ **800/233-7948** or 809/774-0010.

This store at the beginning of Main Street is billed as the largest perfumery in the world, and it offers all the famous names in perfumes, skin care, and cosmetics. It carries Lancôme and La Prairie, among other products. Men will also find Europe's best colognes and aftershave lotions here.

GIFTS

✪ **A. H. Riise Gift & Liquor Stores.** 37 Main St. at the A. H. Riise Gift & Liquor Mall (perfume and liquor branch stores at the Havensight Mall). ☎ **800/524-2037** or 809/776-2303.

St. Thomas's oldest outlet for luxury items such as jewelry, crystal, china, and perfumes is still the largest. It also offers the widest sampling of liquors and liqueurs on the island. Everything is displayed in a 19th-century Danish warehouse, extending from Main Street to the waterfront. The store boasts a collection of fine jewelry and watches from Europe's leading craftspeople, including Vacheron Constantin, Bulgari,

Omega, and Gucci, as well as a wide selection of Greek gold, platinum, and precious gemstone jewelry.

Imported cigars are stored in a climate-controlled walk-in humidor. Delivery to cruise ships and the airport is free. A. H. Riise offers a vast selection of fragrances for both men and women, along with the world's best-known names in cosmetic products. Featured in the china and crystal department are Waterford, Lalique, Baccarat, and Rosenthal, among others. Specialty shops in the complex sell Caribbean gifts, books, clothing, food, art prints, note cards, and designer sunglasses.

Caribbean Marketplace. In the Havensight Mall (Building III). ☎ **809/776-5400.**

The island's best selections of Caribbean handcrafts are found here, including Sunny Caribbee products—a vast array of condiments ranging from spicy peppercorns to nutmeg mustard. There's also a wide selection of Sunny Caribbee's botanical products. Other items range from steel-pan drums from Trinidad to wooden Jamaican jigsaw puzzles, from Indonesian batiks to bikinis from the Cayman Islands. Don't expect very attentive service.

Down Island Traders. Veterans Dr. ☎ **809/776-4641.**

The aroma of spices will lead you to these markets, which have Charlotte Amalie's most attractive array of spices, teas, seasonings, candies, jellies, jams, and condiments, most of which are packaged from natural Caribbean products. The owner carries a line of local cookbooks, as well as silk-screened T-shirts and bags, Haitian metal sculpture, handmade jewelry, Caribbean folk art, and children's gifts.

Little Switzerland. 5 Main St. ☎ **809/776-2010.**

A branch of this shop seems to appear on virtually every island in the Caribbean. Its concentration of watches, including Omega and Rolex, are topped by no one. But it also sells a wide variety of other objects as well, including cuckoo clocks and music boxes. Its china, especially the Royal Worcester and Rosenthal collection, is outstanding, as are its crystal and jewelry. It also maintains the official outlets for Hummel, Lladró, and Swarovski figurines. There are several other branches of this store on the island, especially at the Havensight Mall, but the main store has the best selection.

JEWELRY

Blue Carib Gems and Rocks. 2 Back St. (behind Little Switzerland). ☎ **809/774-8525.**

For a decade, the owners scoured the Caribbean for gemstones—these stones have been brought directly from the mines to you. The raw stones are cut, polished, and then fashioned into jewelry by the lost-wax process. On one side of the premises, you can see the craftspeople at work, and on the other, view their finished products. A lifetime guarantee is given on all handcrafted jewelry. Since the items are locally made, they're duty free and not included in the $1,200 Customs exemption.

✪ Cardow Jewelers. 39 Main St. ☎ **809/776-1140.**

Often called the Tiffany's of the Caribbean, Cardow Jewelers boasts the largest selection of fine jewelry in the world. This fabulous shop, where more than 20,000 rings are displayed, offers savings because of its worldwide direct buying, large turnover, and duty-free prices. Unusual and traditional designs are offered in diamonds, emeralds, rubies, sapphires, and Brazilian stones, as well as pearls. Cardow has a whole wall of Italian gold chains, and also features antique-coin jewelry. The Treasure Cove has cases of fine gold jewelry all priced under $200.

Colombian Emeralds International. In the Havensight Mall. ☎ **809/774-2442.**

The Colombian Emeralds stores are renowned throughout the Caribbean for offering the finest collection of Colombian emeralds, both set and unset. Here you buy direct from the source, cutting out the middleperson, which can mean significant savings for you. In addition to jewelry, the shop stocks fine watches. There's another outlet on Main Street.

H. Stern Jewellers. In the Havensight Mall. ☎ **800/524-2024** or 809/776-1223.

This international jeweler is one of the most respected in the world, with some 175 outlets. In a world of fake jewelry and fake everything, it's good to know that there's still a name you can count on. It's a leading competitor on the island to Cardow (see above). Colorful gem and jewel creations are offered at Stern's locations on St. Thomas—there are two on Main Street, this one at the Havensight Mall, and branches at Marriott's Frenchman's Reef. Stern gives worldwide guaranteed service, including a 1-year exchange privilege.

Irmela's Jewel Studio. In the Old Grand Hotel, at the beginning of Main St. ☎ **800/524-2047** or 809/774-5875.

Irmela's has made a name for itself in the highly competitive jewelry business on St. Thomas. Here the jewelry is unique, custom-designed by Irmela, and handmade by her studio or imported from around the world. Irmela has the largest selection of cultured pearls in the Caribbean, including freshwater Biwa, South Sea, and natural-color black Tahitian pearls. Choose from hundreds of clasps and pearl necklaces. Irmela has a large selection of unset stones.

LEATHER

The Leather Shop, Inc. 1 Main St. ☎ **809/776-0290.**

Here you'll find the best selection from Italian designers such as Fendi, Longchamp, De Vecchi, Furla, and Il Bisonte. There are many styles of handbags, belts, wallets, briefcases, and attaché cases. Some of these items are very expensive, of course, but there is less expensive merchandise like backpacks, carry-ons, and Mola bags from Colombia. If you're looking for a bargain, ask them to direct you to the outlet store on Back Street, selling closeouts at prices that are sometimes 50% off U.S. mainland tags.

LINENS

The Linen House. In the A. H. Riise Mall, 37 Main St. ☎ **809/774-1668.**

The Linen House is the best store for linens in the West Indies. You'll find a wide selection of placemats, decorative tablecloths, and many hand-embroidered goods, much of it handmade in China.

   Other branches are at the Havensight Mall (☎ **809/774-0868**), and 7A Royal Dane Mall (☎ **809/774-8117**).

MALLS

Mountain Top. Rte. 33. ☎ **809/774-2400.**

Set near the center of the island, this modern shopping mall—a bit too tourist-tacky for us—contains only about a dozen shops, but many people come as much for the view as for the merchandise. Boutiques sell everything from beachwear to island-inspired prints and engravings, as well as jams, jellies, and local crafts. There's an observation platform with a view over the rest of the island.

ST. THOMAS AFTER DARK
THE PERFORMING ARTS

Reichhold Center for the Arts. University of the Virgin Islands, 2 John Brewer's Bay. ☎ **809/ 693-1550.** Tickets $12–$40.

This artistic center, the premier venue in the Caribbean, lies west of Charlotte Amalie. Call the theater or check with the tourist office to see what's on at the time of your visit. The lobby displays a frequently changing free exhibit of paintings and sculptures by Caribbean artists. A Japanese-inspired amphitheater is set into a natural valley, with seating space for 1,196. The smell of gardenias adds to the beauty of the performances. Several different repertory companies of music, dance, and drama perform here. Performances begin at 8pm (call the theater to check).

THE BAR, CLUB & MUSIC SCENE

The Bar at Paradise Point. Paradise Point. ☎ **809/777-4540.**

Any savvy insider will tell you to head here for your sunset watching. It's located 740 feet above sea level across from the cruise-ship dock, providing excellent photo ops and panoramic sunset views. There's a tram you can ride up the hill. Get the bartender to serve you a "Painkiller" (his specialty). You might want two. Sometimes a one-man steel band is on hand to serenade the sunset watchers, who after a few of those painkillers don't know if the sun has set or not. You can also order inexpensive food here, such as barbecued ribs, hot dogs, and hamburgers, beginning at $4. Happy hour with discounted drinks begins at 5pm, with no set cut-off time.

Barnacle Bill's. At the Crown Bay Marina, in the Sub Base. ☎ **809/774-7444.** No cover.

A restaurant during the day, this is one of the most desirable nightclubs on St. Thomas in the evening. Beginning around 9pm a parade of local and imported musical talent plays to full houses until at least 1am. Although the bar is open nightly, live music is presented only January to March, Thursday to Saturday. The beer is cheap.

Cabaña Lounge. Blackbeard's Castle, Blackbeard's Hill. ☎ **809/776-1234.**

This lounge is one of the friendliest and most *simpatico* places to gather on St. Thomas any night but Monday from 5pm until 10pm. Your hosts, Bob Harrington and Henrique Konzen, provide a limited but choice menu—nothing over $12—and an inviting atmosphere. On some nights, activities—games, a movie night, even an Ides of March toga party—are planned. After Hurricane Marilyn destroyed much of the property, this bar and pool area was converted into the Cabaña.

Epernay. Rue de St. Barthélemy, Frenchtown. ☎ **809/774-5348.**

Adjacent to Alexander's Restaurant, this stylish watering hole with a view of the ocean adds a touch of Europe to the neighborhood. You can order glasses of at least six different brands of champagne, and vintage wines by the glass. Appetizers cost $6 to $10 and include sushi and caviar. You can also order main courses, plus tempting desserts, such as chocolate-dipped strawberries.

✪ **Greenhouse.** Veterans Dr. ☎ **809/774-7998.** No cover Thurs–Tues, $5 (including the first drink) Wed.

Set directly on the waterfront, this bar and restaurant is one of the few nightspots we recommend in Charlotte Amalie. You can park nearby and walk to the entrance. Each night a different entertainment is featured, ranging from reggae to disco. Wednesday night is the "big blast."

Iggie's Bolongo. At the Bolongo Beach Resort, 7150 Bolongo. ☎ **809/779-2844.**

During the day, Iggie's functions as an informal open-air restaurant serving hamburgers, sandwiches, and salads. After dark, however, it turns into an entertainment venue featuring karaoke and occasional live entertaiment. Call to find out what's happening.

Larry's Hideaway. 10 Hull Bay. ☎ **809/777-1898.**

This place has a laid-back, casual atmosphere and many local fans, who especially like to hide-away here on lazy Sunday afternoons. It used to have live music on Sunday (and may again some time in the future), but Hurricane Marilyn caused a lot of damage when it swept through here. The atmosphere is still funky, and it's a cheap place to eat if you devour the hot dogs and hamburgers served until 4pm. After 5pm, you can order affordable main courses in the restaurant, including the catch of the day and the chef's pork stew.

Mackenzie's Harbour Pub & Tap Room. At the American Yacht Harbour, Red Hook. ☎ **809/779-2261.**

Many savvy locals regard this pub and tap room as their "local," frequenting it almost every night. Music is on the stereo, and there's never a cover charge. Happy hour with reduced drinks is daily from 4 to 7pm. It also serves wings and batter-dipped vegetables at this time. The setting is lively. If you'd like a cheap meal here, try the chef's Irish stew or order a big plate of spaghetti.

Turtle Rock Bar. In the Mangrove Restaurant at the Wyndham Sugar Bay Beach Club, 6500 Estate Smith Bay. ☎ **809/777-7100.** No cover.

Located a few minutes' drive west of Red Hook, this popular bar presents live music, steel bands, and karoake. There's space to dance, but most patrons just sway and listen to the steel-pan bands that play from 2pm to closing every night, or the more elaborate bands that play on Tuesday, Sunday, and some other nights. Thursday night is karoake (for those of you who simply must—or those of you who want to stay away). If you're hungry, burgers, salads, steaks, and grilled fish are available at the Mangrove Restaurant a few steps away. There's no cover, and happy hour (when most drinks are half price) is 4 to 6pm every night.

Walter's. 3 Trompeter Gade. ☎ **809/774-5025.** No cover Sun–Thurs, $3 Fri–Sat.

Dimly and rather flatteringly lit, this two-level watering hole attracts locals—often gay men—in season, drawing more off-island visitors in winter. Located about 100 yards from the island's famous synagogue, in a clapboard town house built around 1935, Walter's cellar bar features an intimate atmosphere with music from the 1950s, 1960s, and 1970s.

2 St. John

The smallest and least populated of the U.S. Virgin Islands, St. John is known for its lush, unspoiled beauty. More than half its land, as well as its shoreline, was set aside and protected in 1956 as the Virgin Islands National Park.

Ringed by a rocky coastline, crescent-shaped bays, and white-sand beaches, the island contains an array of bird and wildlife that's the envy of ornithologists and zoologists around the world. Miles of serpentine hiking trails lead to spectacular views and the ruins of 18th-century Danish plantations. Mysterious geometric petroglyphs incised into boulders and cliffs can be pointed out by island guides; of unknown age and origin, the figures have never been deciphered.

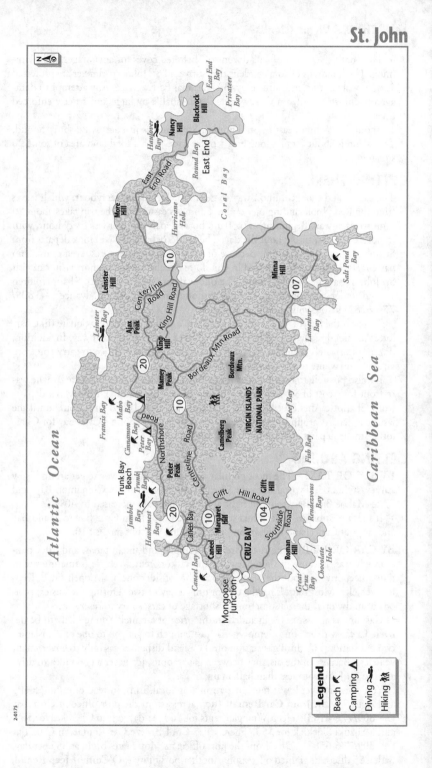

Legend
Beach ⏜
Camping ▲
Diving ⟋
Hiking 🚶

Atlantic Ocean

Caribbean Sea

East End Bay
Privateer Bay
Haulover Bay
Nancy Hill
Blackrock Hill
East End
Round Bay
More Hill
Coral Bay
Hurricane Hole
Salt Pond Bay
Leinster Hill
Minna Hill
107
Leinster Bay
Ajax Peak
Centerline Road
King Hill Road
King Hill
Lameshur Bay
Bordeaux Mtn. Road
Bordeaux Mtn.
Mamey Peak
10
20
VIRGIN ISLANDS NATIONAL PARK
Reef Bay
Francis Bay
Maho Bay
Cinnamon Bay
Peter Bay
Northshore Road
Camelberg Peak
Fish Bay
Trunk Bay Beach
Trunk Bay
Peter Peak
Centerline Road
Jumbie Bay
Hawksnest Bay
20
Caneel Bay
Gifft Hill
Gifft Hill Road
Rendezvous Bay
Margaret Hill
10
104
Caneel Bay
Caneel Hill
CRUZ BAY
Southside Road
Chocolate Hole
Roman Hill
Great Cruz Bay
Mongoose Junction

2-0175

The boating set seeks out its dozens of sheltered coves for anchorages and swimming. The hundreds of coral gardens that surround St. John's perimeter are protected as rigorously as the land surface by the National Park Service. Any attempt to damage or remove coral from these waters is punishable by large and strictly enforced fines.

About 3 to 5 miles east of St. Thomas, St. John lies just across Pillsbury Sound. The island is about 7 miles long and 3 miles wide, with a total land area of some 20 square miles.

GETTING THERE

The easiest and most common way to get to St. John is by **ferryboat,** which leaves from the Red Hook landing pier on St. Thomas's eastern tip; the trip takes about 20 minutes each way. Beginning at 6:30am, boats depart more or less every hour, with minor exceptions, throughout the day. The last ferry back to Red Hook departs from St. John's Cruz Bay at 11pm. Because of such frequent departures, even cruise-ship passengers, temporarily anchored in Charlotte Amalie for only a short visit, can visit St. John for a quickie island tour. The one-way fare is $3 for adults, $1 for children 10 and under. Schedules can change without notice, so call in advance (☎ 809/ 776-6282) before your intended departure.

To reach the ferry, take the Vitran bus from a point near Market Square (in Charlotte Amalie) directly to Red Hook. The cost is $1 per person each way. In addition, dozens of privately owned taxis will be willing to negotiate a price to carry you from virtually anywhere to the docks at Red Hook.

It's also possible to board a boat for St. John directly at the Charlotte Amalie waterfront for a cost of $7 each way. The ride takes 45 minutes. The ferryboat departs from Charlotte Amalie at 9am and continues at intervals of 1 or 2 hours until the last boat departs around 7pm. (The last boat to leave St. John's Cruz Bay for Charlotte Amalie departs at 5:15pm.)

GETTING AROUND

BY BUS OR TAXI The most popular and least expensive way to get around is by **surrey-style taxi.** Typical fares are $3 to Trunk Bay, $3.50 to Cinnamon Bay, and $7 to Mahoe Bay. Between midnight and 6am, fares are increased by 40%.

It's also possible to use the **bus** service, which runs from Cruz Bay to Maho Bay and stops at Caneel and Cinnamon bays. The one-way bus fare is $10.

BY CAR OR JEEP The roads are undeveloped and uncluttered, and offer panoramic vistas. Because of these views, many visitors rent a vehicle (sometimes with four-wheel drive) to tour the island. You might consider one of the open-sided, Jeep-like vehicles. Most renters need a car for only a day or two. During the busiest periods of midwinter, there's sometimes a shortage of cars, so try to reserve early.

Gasoline is almost never included in the price of a rental. You're likely to be delivered a car with an almost-empty tank, just enough to get you to one of the island's two gas stations. (A third gas station on the island dispenses gas only to government vehicles.) Because of the distance between gas stations, it's never a good idea to drive around St. John with less than half a tank of gas.

You can often get lower rates by patronizing local firms, instead of calling Hertz and Avis. Try **St. John Car Rental, Inc.,** across from the post office in Cruz Bay (☎ 809/776-6103); a Jeep Wrangler rents for $60 per day, a Jeep Cherokee for $65, and a Suzuki Sidekick for $55. There's also **Cool Breeze Car Rental,** in Cruz Bay (☎ 809/776-6588), across from the post office; its winter rates begin at $55 per day, with a $5 discount granted off-season. Another possibility is **O'Connor Jeep Rental,** in Cruz Bay (☎ 809/776-6343), 3 blocks up from the ferry dock at the Texaco station. Its rentals also begin at $55 per day in winter, lowered by 10% off-season.

ESSENTIALS

In an emergency, call ☎ 915 for the **police,** ☎ 921 to report a **fire,** or ☎ 922 for a **medical emergency;** otherwise, go to **St. John Myrah Keating Smith Community Health Clinic,** 3B Sussanaberg (☎ 809/693-8900). A leading drugstore is **St. John Drugcenter, Inc.,** in the Boulon Shopping Center, Cruz Bay (☎ 809/ 776-6353), which also sells film. The **Visitors Center** at St. John is at Cruz Bay (☎ 809/776-6450).

WHERE TO STAY

The choice of accommodations on St. John is limited, and that's how most people would like to keep it. And except for the campgrounds recommended below, the tabs at most of the establishments here are far beyond the pocketbook of the average traveler. If you'll settle for just the minimum necessities, the following places will provide a low-cost holiday on St. John. These are places merely "to bunk."

GUEST HOUSES

Doubles for Less than $95 (Winter) / $75 (Off-Season)

The Cruz Inn. P.O. Box 566, Cruz Bay, St. John, USVI 00831. ☎ 800/666-7688 in the U.S., or 809/693-8688. Fax 809/693-8590. 2 studios, 4 suites, 4 apts. Winter, $75 studio; $90 suite; $95–$105 apt. Off-season, $65 studio; $75 suite; $85–$95 apt. Rates include continental breakfast. AE, DISC, MC, V.

This is hardly the most refined or elegant accommodation on St. John, but it has its admirers who seek clean, reasonably comfortable accommodations at a fair price. Overlooking Enighed Pond, the inn is on par with Raintree Inn and is a bit rustic. Cruz Inn recently finished remodeling, and now all its rooms have a private bath. The studios and suites also have a refrigerator and are air-conditioned, whereas all the apartments have kitchenettes and two are also air-conditioned. In the main building are three two-bedroom suites and one of the studios. The Papaya Suite is airy with a wraparound deck; this unit sleeps up to six. Lying a few blocks from the Cruz Bay Dock, the inn has a convivial bar, a low-cost restaurant serving standard food, and an outdoor deck.

✪ **The Inn at Tamarind Court.** South Shore Rd. (P.O. Box 350), Cruz Bay, St. John, USVI 00831. ☎ 800/221-1637 or 809/776-6378. Fax 809/776-6722. 20 rms, 13 with bath; 1 apt; 2 suites. Winter, $48 single without bath; $88 double with bath; $118 apt; $138 suite. Off-season, $38 single without bath; $68 double with bath; $98 apt; $118 suite. Rates include continental breakfast. AE, DISC, MC, V.

Right outside Cruz Bay but still within walking distance of the ferryboat dock, this modest establishment consists of a small hotel (where the no-smoking rooms have been renovated) and an even simpler West Indian inn. Baths at the inn are shared, while in the hotel all rooms have private bath. The establishment's social life revolves around its courtyard bar. From the hotel, you can walk to shuttles taking you to the beaches; the staff will advise.

The Raintree Inn. P.O. Box 566, Cruz Bay, St. John, USVI 00831. ☎ 800/666-7449 or 809/ 693-8590. Fax 809/693-8590. 8 rms, 3 efficiencies. A/C TEL. Winter, $87–$92 single or double; $133.20 efficiency. Off-season, $70–$80 single or double; $111.60 efficiency. 3-day minimum stay in efficiencies. AE, DISC, MC, V.

One block from the ferry stop, next to the Catholic church, the Raintree Inn has simple no-smoking double rooms, some with high ceilings. Linen, towels, and soap are supplied upon request. Three rooms have full kitchens, and two twins are in a carpeted loft. A small deck is attached. The inn adjoins a reasonably priced restaurant next door, The Fish Trap (see "Where to Eat," below). Laundry service is available on the premises.

CAMPGROUNDS

✪ **Cinnamon Bay Campground.** P.O. Box 720, Cruz Bay, St. John, USVI 00831. ☎ **800/ 539-9998** in the U.S., or 809/776-6330. Fax 809/776-6458. 126 units, none with bath. Winter, $95–$105 cottage for one or two; $75 tent site; $17 bare site. Off-season, $63–$68 cottage for one or two; $48 tent site; $17 bare site (5-day minimum). Extra person $15. AE, MC, V.

Established by the National Park Service in 1964, this campground is the most complete in the Caribbean. The site is directly on the beach, and thousands of acres of tropical vegetation surround you. Life is simple here, and you have a choice of three different ways of sleeping: tents, cottages, and bare sites. At the bare campsites, nothing is provided except general facilities. The canvas tents are 10 by 14 feet with a floor, and a number of facilities are offered, including all cooking equipment. Even your linen is changed weekly. The cottages are 15 by 15 feet, a screened room with two concrete walls and two screen walls. They contain four twin beds, and two cots can be added; cooking facilities are also supplied. Lavatories and showers are in separate buildings nearby. Camping is limited to a 2-week period in any given year. Near the road is a camp center office, with a grocery and a cafeteria (dinners for $15).

Concordia Eco-Tents. 20–27 Estate Concordia, Coral Bay, St. John, USVI 00830. Reservations taken in New York at ☎ **800/392-9004** or 212/472-9453. Fax 212/861-6210. 5 tent-cottages. Winter, $95 tent for one or two. Off-season, $60 tent for one or two. Extra person $20 in winter, $15 off-season. MC, V.

The Eco-Tents are the newest addition to Stanley Selengut's celebrated Concordia development project on the southern tip of St. John. Overlooking Salt Pond Bay and Ram Head Point, these solar- and wind-powered tent cottages combine sustainable technology with some of the most spectacular views on the island. The light framing, fabric walls, and large screened-in windows also lend a "tree house" atmosphere to the guests' experience.

Being on the windward side of the island means that the tent-cottages enjoy natural ventilation from the cooling trade winds. There are two twin beds in each bedroom, one or two twin mattresses on a loft platform, and a queen-size futon in the living room area, so the tent-cottages can sleep up to six people comfortably. Each kitchen comes equipped with a running-water sink, propane stove, and cooler. In addition, each Eco-Tent has a private shower and composting toilet.

Built into the hillside, surrounded by hundreds of acres of pristine national park land, the secluded location requires guests to arrange for their own rental vehicle. Beaches, hikes, and the shops and restaurants of Coral Bay are only a 10-minute drive from the property.

✪ **Maho Bay.** P.O. Box 310, Cruz Bay, St. John, USVI 00831. ☎ **800/392-9004**, 212/ 472-9453 in New York City, or 809/776-6226. Fax 809/776-6504, or 212/816-6210 in New York City. 114 tent-cottages, none with bath. Mid-Dec to Apr, $95 tent-cottage for one or two (minimum stay of 7 nights required). May to mid-Dec, $60 tent-cottage for one or two (no minimum stay). Extra occupant $15. MC, V.

Maho Bay is an interesting concept in ecology vacationing, where you camp close to nature, but with considerable comfort. Defined as a deluxe campground, an 8-mile drive northeast from Cruz Bay, it's set on a hillside above the beach surrounded by the Virgin Islands National Park. To preserve the existing ground cover, all 114 tent-cottages are on platforms above a thickly wooded slope. Utility lines and pipes are hidden under wooden boardwalks and stairs.

The tent cottages are covered with canvas and screens. Each unit has two movable twin beds, a couch, electric lamps and outlets, a dining table, chairs, a propane stove, and an ice chest (cooler). That's not all—you're furnished linen, towels, and cooking and eating utensils. There's a store where you can buy supplies. You can do your own cooking or eat at the camp's outdoor restaurant. Guests share communal bathhouses.

Maho Bay has an open-air Pavilion Restaurant, which always serves breakfast and dinner. The Pavilion also functions as an amphitheater and community center where various programs are featured. The camp has an excellent water-sports program.

HOUSEKEEPING UNITS

Villa vacations are on the rise on St. John. These private homes and condos deliver spaciousness and comfort, as well as privacy, and come with fully equipped kitchens, dining areas, bedrooms, and such amenities as VCRs and patio grills. Rentals go from large multiroom resort homes to simply decorated one-bedroom condos. Villa rentals year-round typically run from about $1,200 to $2,000 per week, an affordable option for multiple couples or families looking for a large house. Condos generally range from $105 to $360 per night per unit. For information on privately owned villas and condos on St. John, call ☎ **800/USVI-INFO.** You can also try **Caribbean Villas & Resort Management** (☎ **800/338-0987** in the U.S., or 809/776-6152) or **Villa Portfolio Management** (☎ **800/858-7989** or 809/693-9100).

Jadan Cottages. P.O. Box 84, Cruz Bay, St. John, USVI 00831. ☎ **809/779-6423.** Fax 809/779-4323. 2 cottages, both with bath and kitchen. Winter, $150 per day or $875–$1,050 per week for two. Off-season, $125 per day or $600–$875 per week for two. Additional bedroom suitable for two guests $350 extra per week. No credit cards.

These cottages are within a 10-minute walk of the settlement of Cruz Bay, and although they lie near one another, each unit has ample amounts of privacy thanks to screens of verdant jasmine. The larger of the two cottages (Mampoo Cottage) can be enlarged if a renter arranges for the use of a satellite bedroom, which is reached via a covered breezeway. Both buildings are maintained with pride and care by the Jadans. Each has kitchen facilities, ceiling fans, white tile floors, simple summery furniture, a deliberately rustic decor that includes teakwood furniture, and panoramic views over Cruz Bay. Neither of these accommodations could ever be considered ultra-luxurious, but if their costs are shared by four occupants during off-season, the per-day rate works out to a most reasonably priced holiday. The rooms lie a 5-minute walk to Frank Bay, a rather rocky beach but a very private one. Also on the property is a four-story observation deck from which you can look out over the other U.S. Virgin Islands and can even see some of the British Virgin Islands.

Serendi Vacation Condos. P.O. Box 293, Cruz Bay, St. John, USVI 00830. ☎ and fax **809/776-6646.** 10 apts, all with kitchenette. TEL. Winter, $105 studio apt for one or two; $155 one-bedroom apt for two. Off-season, $85 studio apt for one or two; $110 one-bedroom apt for two. Extra person $20; children 3–10 $10 each; children 2 and under stay free in their parents' apt. MC, V.

Its angular lines and concrete verandas are shielded by masses of shrubbery. Set on sloping land on a hillside above Cruz Bay, it contains slightly dated furniture, concrete latticework, and a kitchenette in each unit. Each unit has a ceiling fan, radio, and terrace or balcony. Maid service is usually not included as part of a rental here. Tennis courts and water sports are nearby. A gas-heated barbecue grill on the grounds is available for the use of guests. Costs here are especially attractive for vacationers who include extra guests in their plans.

WORTH A SPLURGE

Estate Concordia Studios. 20–27 Estate Concordia, Coral Bay, St. John, USVI 00830. ☎ **800/392-9004** in the U.S. and Canada, or 212/472-9453 in New York City. Fax 212/861-6210 in New York City. 9 studios, 5 eco-tents. Winter, $135–$190 studio for one or two; $95 eco-tents for two. Off-season, $95–$150 studio for one or two; $60 eco-tents for two. Extra person $15. MC, V.

Opened in 1993, this enviromentally correct, 51-acre development project was widely praised for its integration with the local ecosystem. The elevated structures were designed to coexist with the stunning southern edge of St. John. Nestled on a low cliff above a salt pond, surrounded by hundreds of acres of pristine national park, the secluded location is recommended for those with a rental vehicle. Each building was designed to protect mature trees, and is connected to its neighbors with boardwalks. The nine studios are contained in six postmodern cottages. Each comes with a kitchen, bathroom, balcony, and ceiling fan. Some units have an extra bedroom or a larger-than-expected private bathroom. A newer addition are five eco-tents, which are solar- and wind-powered, with large screened-in windows to create a "tree house" atmosphere. There are two twin beds in each room, one or two twin mattresses on a loft platform, and a queen-size fold-out couch, allowing the tent-cottages to sleep 5 or 6 comfortably. Each kitchen comes with a stove and a running-water sink. Each tent has a toilet and private shower.

Estate Concordia also features a hillside swimming pool and guest laundry facilities. On-site management assists with activity suggestions.

Frank Bay Bed & Breakfast. P.O. Box 408, Cruz Bay, St. John, USVI 00831. ☎ **800/561-7290** or 809/693-8617. 3 rms, 1 with bath. Winter, $130 single or double without or with bath. Off-season, $100 single or double without or with bath. DISC.

A 3-minute stroll from the town ferry, Michele O'Keefe and Joshlynn Crosley have opened this winning B&B in a secluded spot great for swimming and snorkeling. The location is on Frank Bay, in an old estate set on extensive grounds blooming with bougainvillea and wild orchids. Guests enjoy a continental breakfast on a veranda overlooking the bay. Personal attention is the hallmark of the place. The guest rooms are simply furnished with Bali batiks. The Bougainvillea Room, with a bay view, has a queen-size bed, ceiling fan, and large screened windows to take advantage of the trade winds. The Shade Room has a double bed and is air-conditioned. Both these units share a bath, whereas the Garden Room has extra privacy and a private bath, along with an outdoor patio and a minirefrigerator.

✪ **Harmony.** P.O. Box 310, Cruz Bay, St. John, USVI 00831. ☎ **800/392-9004** in the U.S. and Canada, 212/472-9453 in New York City, or 809/776-6226. Fax 809/776-6504, or 212/861-6210 in New York City. 12 studios. Winter, $150–$180 studio for one or two. Off-season, $95–$125 studio for one or two. Extra person $25. 7-night minimum stay in winter. MC, V.

Built on a hillside above the Maho Bay Campground, this is a small-scale cluster of 12 luxury studios in six two-story houses with views sweeping down to the sea. Designed to combine both ecological technology and comfort, it's one of the few resorts in the Caribbean to operate exclusively on sun and wind power. Most of the building materials are derived from recycled materials, including reconstituted plastic and glass containers, newsprint, old tires, and scrap lumber. The managers and staff are committed to offering educational experiences as well as the services of a small-scale resort. Guests are asked to share their experience of living in an ecologically sensitive resort. They are taught to operate a user-friendly computer telling them how their unit's energy is being spent, and to give their assessments of the experimental appliances, furnishings, and supplies.

Studios contain queen-size sleep sofas and/or twin beds, tile bathrooms, kitchenettes, dining area, and an outdoor terrace. Guests can walk a short distance downhill to the restaurant, grocery store, and water-sports facilities at the Maho Bay campground.

WHERE TO EAT

✪ **Café Roma.** Cruz Bay. ☎ **809/776-6524.** Main courses $8–$17. MC, V. Daily 5–10pm. ITALIAN.

Diners climb a flight of steps to reach this restaurant in the center of Cruz Bay. You might arrive early and have a strawberry colada, then enjoy a standard pasta, veal, seafood, or chicken dish. On most evenings, there are 30 to 40 vegetarian items on the menu, much better than most restaurants. The owner claims with good reason that his pizzas are the best on the island, praised by New Yorkers and Chicagoans who know their pizza. Ask for the white pizza. This is not a place for great finesse in the kitchen, but it's a long-standing favorite, and has pleased a lot of diners seeking casual, informal meals. Italian wines are sold by the glass or bottle, and you can end the evening with an espresso.

The Fish Trap. In the Raintree Inn, Cruz Bay. ☎ **809/693-9994.** Reservations accepted only for parties of six or more. Main courses $7.95–$22.95. AE, DISC, MC, V. Tues–Fri 11am–3pm and 4:30–9:30pm, Sat–Sun 10:30am–2:30pm and 4:30–9:30pm. SEAFOOD.

The Fish Trap attracts both locals and vacationers. It's known for its wide selection of fresh fish, but it also caters to the vegetarian and burger crowd. In the midst of coconut palms and banana trees, most diners begin with an appetizer, such as seared scallops with stir-fried vegetables. We recently enjoyed a herb-crusted snapper with a Dijon-tarragon-cream sauce. On another occasion, blackened swordfish with roasted red pepper aïoli was a crowd-pleaser, or you might try grilled fish and shrimp with papaya and kiwi salsa. In other words, it's not another fish-and-chips joint.

The Lime Inn. In the Lemon Tree Mall, Konges Gade, Cruz Bay. ☎ **809/776-6425.** Reservations recommended. Main courses $6.25–$20; lunch $3.95–$9.95. AE, MC, V. Mon–Fri 11:30am–3pm and 5:30–10pm, Sat 5:30–10pm. Closed 3 weeks in July. SEAFOOD.

This lively open-air restaurant is at the Lemon Tree Mall in the heart of Cruz Bay. It's known for its fresh grilled Caribbean-style lobster. Diners can enjoy grilled seafood ranging from shrimp to the fresh catch of the day. If you're not in the mood for seafood, try one of the daily chicken and pasta specials or one of the grilled steaks. For a combination of both land and sea, the Lime Inn offers a tender grilled filet mignon stuffed with crabmeat. The most popular night of the week here is Wednesday when the Lime Inn offers an all-you-can-eat, peel-and-eat shrimp feast for $17.95.

Luscious Licks. Cruz Bay. ☎ **809/693-8400.** Reservations not accepted. Main courses $5–$8. No credit cards. Mon–Sat 10am–4pm. VEGETARIAN/VEGAN.

Located on the eastern side of the island at Cruz Bay, next to Mongoose Junction, this eatery offers open-air dining with a view of the water. The walls are appointed with small chalkboards, which have various quotations and pithy everyday sayings written on them. The menu offers a varied selection of vegetarian dishes from soups, such as split pea, to the house specialty, the stroller—a flour tortilla filled with hummus, bean sprouts, carrots, avocado, broccoli, tahini, and yogurt. Diners may enjoy the pita sandwiches with fillings ranging from Swiss cheese to hummus, tabbouleh, or marinated tofu. Your drink comes from the vegetable and fruit juice bar. For a finish, try a selection from the ice-cream bar located off the patio, featuring Ben and Jerry's creamy concoctions.

Seabreeze Café. 4F Little Plantation, on Salt Pond Rd., Coral Bay. ☎ **809/693-5824.** Main courses $9–$12; standard breakfast $2.25; lunch specials $3–$6; Sun brunch $5.25. No credit cards. Mon–Sat 6:30am–2am, Sun 9am–2am. AMERICAN / WEST INDIAN.

This local hangout, which keeps the longest hours on the island, is in a green concrete building in the country and has a patio where you can watch the ocean and mountains. Dinner service technically stops after 9pm, but if you speak sweetly to the bartender, she might feed you. Most of the food is American, but with West Indian overtones. It's really standard fare, but the price is right, and there's plenty of local color. Breakfast often attracts workers heading for their jobs. At lunch, you get the usual burgers, plus steak sandwiches. Fresh fish dishes, depending on what's available, appear on the dinner menu. Pizzas are often served, and Sunday is usually Mexican night with live music.

✪ Shipwreck Landing. 34 Freeman's Ground, Rte. 107, Coral Bay. ☎ **809/693-5640.** Reservations requested. Main courses $9.75–$15.25; lunch from $10. AE, MC, V. Daily 11am–10pm. (Bar, daily 11am–11pm.) SEAFOOD/CONTINENTAL.

Eight miles east of Cruz Bay on the road to Salt Pond Beach, Shipwreck Landing is run by Pat and Dennis Rizzo. You dine amid palms and tropical plants on a veranda overlooking the sea. The intimate bar specializes in tropical frozen drinks. Lunch isn't ignored here; there's a lot more than sandwiches, salads, and burgers—say, a pan-seared blackened snapper in Cajun spices or conch fritters to get you going. The chef shines brighter at night though, offering a pasta of the day along with such specialties as a rather tantalizing Caribbean blackened shrimp. A lot of the fare is routine, including New York strip steak and fish and chips, but the grilled mahimahi in lime butter is worth the trip. Live music is featured on Friday, Saturday, and Sunday.

Tamarind Court. South Shore Rd. ☎ **809/776-6378.** Main courses $6.75–$10.75; breakfast from $3. AE, DISC, MC, V. Daily 7–11am and 3–9pm. AMERICAN/SUSHI.

On the east end of Cruz Bay, diners enjoy meals amid a setting of palm trees and tropical flowers in a courtyard with a small fountain. This is one of the few places on island where sushi is featured; you can order such delights as flying fish, eel, nigiri, salmon roe, and smoked salmon. Otherwise, the menu is fairly ordinary except for some of the best burgers on the island—served on poppy-seed buns. Your best bet is the Cruz Bay chicken breast, grilled or blackened. You can always stop in for breakfast, ordering everything from steak and eggs to a burrito, as well as Belgium waffles with strawberries and cream. Live music is presented on Friday nights from 6:30 to 9:30pm with happy hour from 5 to 7pm, featuring $1 rum drinks.

✪ Vie's Snack Shack. East End Rd. ☎ **809/693-5033.** Main courses $4.95–$6.50. No credit cards. Tues–Sat 10am–5pm, but call first! WEST INDIAN.

Vie's, located 12½ miles east of Cruz Bay, looks like little more than a plywood-sided hut. Nonetheless, its charming and gregarious owner is known as one of the best local chefs on St. John—her garlic chicken is famous. She also serves conch fritters, johnnycakes, island-style beef pâtés, and coconut and pineapple tarts. Don't leave without a glass of homemade limeade made from home-grown limes. The place is open most days, but as Vie says, "Some days, we might not be here at all"—so you'd better call before you head out.

Woody's Seafood Saloon. Cruz Bay. ☎ **809/779-4625.** Reservations not accepted. Main courses $7.95–$15; lunch $5–$7.95. No credit cards. Mon–Thurs 11am–1am, Fri–Sun 11am–2am. SEAFOOD/AMERICAN.

Just 50 yards from the ferry dock, this local dive and hangout at Cruz Bay is more famous for its different beers on tap than for its cuisine. A mix of local fishers, taxi drivers, tour guides, aimless on-island drifters, and an occasional husband and wife show up here to sample the spicy conch fritters and mingle with the islanders. Shrimp appears in various styles, and you can usually order fresh fish and other dishes, including blackened shark, drunken shellfish, and mussels and clams steamed in beer. But fancy cookery is just not the style of this place. You can always get a burger here, reggae on Wednesday, and, as a patron said, "a little bit of everything and anything" on a Saturday night.

WORTH A SPLURGE

Mongoose Restaurant and Deli. Mongoose Junction. ☎ **809/693-8677.** Reservations required in winter. Main courses $13.95–$18.95; lunch from $12. AE, MC, V. Daily 8–10pm. (Bar, daily 8am–10pm.) CARIBBEAN.

Because of the strong vertical lines and the 25-foot ceiling, some visitors compare the soaring interior design here to a large Japanese birdcage. The restaurant is set among trees and built above a stream. Some guests perch at the open-centered bar for a drink and sandwich, while others sit on an adjacent deck where a canopy of trees filters the tropical sunlight. The bar offers more than 20 varieties of frothy island-inspired libations.

Lunches include soups, well-stuffed sandwiches, salad platters, burgers, and pastas. Dinner is more formal, with such specialties as grilled steaks, fresh catch of the day, surf and turf, seafood Créole, and island fish cakes. This establishment's Sunday brunch is mobbed with St. Johnians, who make eggs Benedict the most popular dish.

✪ **Pusser's.** Wharfside Village, Cruz Bay. ☎ **809/693-8489.** Reservations recommended. Main courses $9.95–$24.95. AE, MC, V. Daily 11am–3pm and 6–10pm. INTERNATIONAL/ CARIBBEAN.

A double-decker air-conditioned store and pub in Cruz Bay, Pusser's overlooks the harbor and is near the ferry dock. These stores are unique in the Caribbean, and they serve Pusser's Rum, a blend of five West Indian rums that the Royal Navy has served to its men for three centuries. You can choose from three bars: the Beach Bar (where you can enjoy food while still in your bathing suit), the Oyster Bar (the main dining area), and the Crow's Nest. The same food is served at each bar. Here you can enjoy traditional English fare, including steak and ale. Try the jerk tuna filet, the jerk chicken with a tomato-basil sauce over penne, or the spaghetti with lobster cooked in rum, wine, lemon juice, and garlic. Caribbean lobster is the eternal favorite, or else you might be seized with island fever and order the chicken Tropical (coconut-encrusted, pan-seared, and served up with a rum-and-banana sauce with macadamia nuts). Finish with Pusser's famous "mud pie." The food is satisfying, competent, and not a lot more—but after all that Pusser rum, who can judge?

BEACHES, WATER SPORTS & OTHER OUTDOOR PURSUITS

St. John offers some of the best snorkeling, scuba diving, swimming, fishing, hiking, sailing, and underwater photography in the Caribbean. The island is known for its coral-sand beaches, winding mountain roads, trails past old bush-covered sugarcane plantations, and hidden coves.

BEACHES The best one, hands down, is ✪ **Trunk Bay,** the biggest attraction on St. John and a beach collector's find. To miss its great white sweep would be like touring Europe and skipping Paris. Trouble is, even though it's a beautiful stretch of sand, the word is out. It's likely to be overcrowded, and there are pickpockets. The beach has lifeguards and offers rentals, such as snorkel gear. Beginning snorkelers in particular are attracted to its underwater trail near the shore. Both taxis and "safari buses" to Trunk Bay meet the ferry as it docks at Cruz Bay from Red Hook on St. Thomas.

At Trunk Bay, you can take the ✪ **National Park Underwater Trail** (☎ 809/776-6201). The trail stretches for 650 feet and identifies what you see, everything from false coral to colonial anemones. You'll pass lavender sea fans and schools of silversides. Equipment rental costs $4, and rangers are on hand to provide information.

Caneel Bay, the stamping ground of the rich and famous, has seven beautiful beaches on its 170 acres. Among them is **Hawksnest Beach,** a little gem of white sand beloved by St. Johnians. The beach is a bit narrow and windy, but beautiful, as filmmakers long ago discovered. Close to the road are barbecue grills, and there are portable toilets. Safari buses and taxis from Cruz Bay will take you along North Shore Road.

The campgrounds of Cinnamon Bay and Maho Bay (see above) have their own beaches, where forest rangers sometimes have to remind visitors to put their swimming trunks back on. Snorkelers find good reefs here, and changing rooms and showers are available.

Salt Pond Bay is known to locals but often missed by visitors. The bay here is tranquil and there are no facilities. The Ram Head Trail beginning here and winding for a mile leads to a panoramic belvedere overlooking the bay.

TENNIS   There are two public courts at Cruz Bay near the fire station. They are lit until 10pm, and are available on a first-come, first-served basis. Regrettably, maintenance is not state of the art.

WATER SPORTS GALORE   The most complete line of water sports available on St. John is offered at the **Cinnamon Bay Watersports Center** on Cinnamon Bay Beach (☎ 809/776-6330). For the adventurous, there's windsurfing, kayaking, and sailing.

The windsurfing here is some of the best anywhere, for either the beginner or the expert. High-quality equipment is available for all levels, even for kids. You can rent a board at $15 an hour; a 2-hour introductory lesson costs $40.

Want to paddle to a secluded beach, explore a nearby island with an old Danish ruin, or jump overboard anytime you like for snorkeling or splashing? Then try a sit-on-top kayak; one- and two-person kayaks are available for rent at $10 to $17 per hour.

You can also sail away in a 12- or 14-foot Hobie monohull sailboat, renting for $20 to $30 per hour.

Snorkeling equipment can be rented from the Watersports Beach Shop for $7.

Divers can ask about scuba packages at **Low Key Watersports,** Wharfside Village (☎ 800/835-7718 or 809/693-8999). All wreck dives are two-tank/two-location dives. A one-tank dive costs $55 per person, with night dives going for $65. Snorkel tours are also available at $25 per person, and parasailing at $50. The center uses its own custom-built dive boats and also offers and specializes in water-sports gear, including masks, fins, snorkels, and "dive skins." It also arranges day sailing charters, kayaking tours, and deep-sea sport fishing.

Cruz Bay Watersports, P.O. Box 252, Palm Plaza, St. John, USVI 00831 (☎ 800/835-7730 or 809/76-6234), is a PADI and NAUI five-star diving center on St. John. Certifications can be arranged through a divemaster, starting at $225. Certification classes start daily, as well as two-tank reef dives with all the dive gear for $68. Beginner single dives are $65, and wreck dives (Wednesday and Friday), night dives, and dive packages are available at accommodations that range from

This Island Was Made for Hiking

St. John's **Virgin Island National Park** is laced with a wide choice of clearly marked trails. However, we suggest a tour by Jeep first, just to get your bearings, or setting out with someone familiar with the island. At the visitor center at Cruz Bay, ask for a free trail map of the park.

At least 20 of these trails originate from designated points along either North Shore Road (Route 20) or from points along the island's main east-to-west artery, Centerline Road (Route 10). Each is marked at its starting point with a preplanned itinerary; the walks last from 10 minutes to 2 hours.

Another series of hikes traversing the more arid eastern section of St. John originate at clearly marked points along the island's southeastern tip off Route 107. Many of the trails cross the grounds of 18th-century plantations, often circumnavigating ruined schoolhouses, rum distilleries, molasses factories, and Great Houses, many of them verdantly overgrown with encroaching vines and trees.

One of our favorite tours requires only about a half-mile stroll (about 30 minutes round-trip, not including stops) and departs from clearly marked points along the island's north coast, near the junction of Routes 10 and 20. Identified by the National Park Service as **trail no. 10 (The Annaberg Historic Trail),** this self-guided tour goes by partially restored ruins of an 18th-century house overlooking the island's north coast. Signs along the way give historical and botanical data.

If you want to prolong your experience, **trail no. 11 (The Leinster Bay Trail)** begins near the point where trail no. 10 ends. Following the edge of Watermelon Bay, it leads past mangrove swamps and coral inlets rich with plant and marine life. Markers identify some of the plants and animals.

The **U.S. National Park Service** (☎ **809/776-6330** or 809/776-6201) provides a number of free ranger-led activities in the park. One of the most popular is the 2¹/₂-mile Reef Bay hike. A park ranger leads the hike down the Reef Bay Trail interpreting the natural and cultural history along the way. Included is a stop at the only known petroglyphs on the island and a tour of the sugar mill ruins. Reservations are required for this hike and can be made by phone. Visitors are encouraged to stop by the Cruz Bay Visitor Center where you can pick up the park brochure, which includes a map of the park, and the *Virgin Islands National Park News,* which has the latest information on activities in the park.

budget to first class. Snorkel tours are available daily for $35, as well as trips to the British Virgin Islands (bring your passport).

SEEING THE SIGHTS

The best way to see St. John in a nutshell, and rather quickly, is to take a 2-hour taxi tour. The cost is $30 for one or two passengers, or $12 per person for three or more riders. Almost any taxi at Cruz Bay will take you on these tours, or you can call **Virgin Island Taxi** (☎ 809/774-4550). For complaints, problems, or information, you can also call the **Taxi Commission** (☎ 809/776-8294).

Many visitors like to spend a lot of time at **Cruz Bay,** where the ferry docks. In this West Indian village, there are interesting bars, restaurants, boutiques, and pastel-painted houses. It's pretty sleepy, but it's relaxing after the fast pace of St. Thomas. The **Elaine Ione Sprauve Museum** (☎ 809/776-6359) at Cruz Bay isn't big, but it does contain some local artifacts, and it will teach you some of the history of the island. It's at the public library and can be visited Monday to Friday from 9am to 5pm; admission is free.

Most cruise-ship passengers dart through Cruz Bay and head for the island's biggest attraction, the ✪ **Virgin Islands National Park** (☎ **809/776-6201**). But before going to the park, you may want to stop at the visitor center at Cruz Bay, which is open daily from 8am to 4:30pm. Here you'll see some exhibits and learn more about what you can see in the park. Established in 1956 to preserve significant natural and cultural values, the park totals 12,624 acres, including submerged lands and water adjacent to St. John.

If time is limited, try to visit the **Annaberg Ruins,** Leinster Bay Road, where the Danes maintained a thriving plantation and sugar mill after 1718. It's located off North Shore Road east of Trunk Bay on the north shore. The Annaberg Historic Trail leads you around the ruined buildings of the best-preserved plantation on St. John. The walk around the grounds takes about 30 minutes, and on certain days of the week (dates vary) guided walks of the area are given by park rangers.

✪ **Trunk Bay** is one of the world's most beautiful beaches. It's also the site of one of the world's first marked underwater trails (bring your mask, snorkel, and fins). It lies to the east of Cruz Bay along North Shore Road. Beware of pickpockets.

Fort Berg (also called Fortsberg), at Coral Bay, dating from 1717, played a disastrous role during the 1733 slave revolt, when soldiers at the fort crushed the rebellion. The fort may be restored as a historic monument.

SHOPPING

Compared to St. Thomas it isn't much, but what's here is interesting. The boutiques and shops of Cruz Bay are individualized and quite special. Most shops are clustered at **Mongoose Junction,** in a woodsy area beside the roadway about a 5-minute walk from the ferry dock. We've already recommended restaurants in this complex (see "Where to Eat," above), and it also houses shops of merit.

Before you set sail for St. Thomas, you'll want to visit **Wharfside Village,** just a few steps from the ferry-departure point on the waterfront, opening onto Cruz Bay. Here in this complex of courtyards, alleys, and shady patios is a mishmash of all sorts of boutiques, along with some restaurants, fast-food joints, and bars.

Bamboula. Mongoose Junction. ☎ **809/693-8699.**

Bamboula has an unusual and very appealing collection of gifts from such destinations as Guatemala, Haiti, India, Indonesia, and Central Africa. Its exoticism is unexpected and very pleasant.

The Canvas Factory. Cruz Bay. ☎ **809/776-6196.**

The Canvas Factory produces its own handmade, rugged, and colorful canvas bags in the "factory" at Mongoose Junction. The products range from sailing hats to handsome luggage to an extensive line of islandmade 100% cotton clothing.

The Clothing Studio. Mongoose Junction. ☎ **809/776-6585.**

The Caribbean's oldest hand-painted–clothing studio has been in operation since 1978. You can watch talented artists create original designs on fine tropical clothing, including swimwear, and daytime and evening clothing, for babies, women, and men.

Coconut Coast Studios. Frank Bay. ☎ **809/776-6944.**

A 5-minute stroll from the heart of Cruz Bay (follow along the waterfront bypassing Gallows Point) will lead you to the studio of Elaine Estern and Lucinda Schutt. They are the best watercolorists on the island. Especially known for her Caribbean landscapes, Elaine is the official artist of Westins Resort and Lucinda for Caneel Bay. Note cards begin at $8, with unmatted prints costing $15 and up.

Donald Schnell Studio. Mongoose Junction. ☎ **809/776-6420.**

In this working studio and gallery, Mr. Schnell and his assistants feature one of the finest collections of handmade pottery, sculpture, and blown glass in the Caribbean. The staff can be seen working daily and are especially noted for their rough-textured coral work. Water fountains are a specialty item, as are house signs. The coral pottery dinnerware is unique and popular. The studio will mail works all over the world. Go in and discuss any particular design you may have in mind—they enjoy designing to please customers.

Fabric Mill. Mongoose Junction. ☎ **809/776-6194.**

This shop features silk-screened and batik fabrics from around the world. Vibrant rugs and bed, bath, and table linens add the perfect touch to your home. Whimsical soft sculpture, sarongs, scarves, and handbags are also made in this studio shop.

Pusser's of the West Indies. Wharfside Village, Cruz Bay. ☎ **809/693-8489.**

This link in a famous chain was previously recommended for food and drink. The store offers a large collection of classically designed old-world travel and adventure clothing along with unusual accessories. It's a unique shopping trip for the island. Clothing for women, men, and children is displayed, along with T-shirts carrying Pusser's emblem. Nautical paintings and antiques from all over are also displayed.

R and I Patton Goldsmithing. Mongoose Junction. ☎ **809/776-6548.**

On the island since 1973, this is one of the oldest tourist businesses here, and three-quarters of the merchandise is made on St. John. It has a large selection of island-designed jewelry in sterling silver, gold, and precious stones. Also featured are the works of goldsmiths from outstanding American studios, plus Spanish coins.

ST. JOHN AFTER DARK

Compared to St. Thomas, there's not much going on here after dark. Most people are content to have a long leisurely dinner and then head for bed. The locals hit their favorite watering holes. Sometimes there are island events, such as a fish fry—ask the tourist office.

Among the popular bars of Cruz Bay, **Pusser's** (see above) at Wharfside Vilage has the most convivial atmosphere. The **Caneel Bay Bar,** at Caneel Bay (☎ **809/776-6111**), presents live music nightly from 8:30 to 11pm. The most popular drinks include a Cool Caneel (local rum with sugar, lime, and anisette) and the house trademark, a Plantation Freeze (lime and orange juice with three different kinds of rum, bitters, and nutmeg).

All the places recommended above are very touristy. If you'd like to go where the locals go for drinking and gossiping, try **JJ's Texas Coast Café,** Cruz Bay (☎ **809/776-6908**), a real local dive lying across the park from the ferry dock. Your Texan host, JJ Gewels, makes everybody feel welcome—at least if he likes you. The Tex-Mex food here is the island's best, and the margaritas are lethal.

Another Cruz Bay hot spot is the aptly named **Bad Art Bar** (☎ **809/693-8666**). Whoever selected this funky art had no taste at all, unless you're the type to go for a velvety Elvis (several locals claim to have spotted him on St. John, especially when they've had one drink too many). Find yourself a day-glo table and devour one of the frozen drink specials, especially the "Witches Tit" and "Busted Nut." Live entertainment is presented 2 nights a week, and if you go between 6 and 8pm daily, you can order two-for-one frozen drink specials. The location is above the Purple Door Restaurant.

Also at Cruz Bay, check out the action at **Fred's** (☎ 809/776-6363), which brings in island bands on Wednesday, Friday, and Sunday nights. The island's most laid-back bar, it's also the best place to go to dance, at least on those nights. It's just a little hole-in-the-wall and can get crowded fast. It's located across from the Lime Inn.

The best sports bar on the island is **Skinny Legs,** Emmaus, Coral Bay, beyond the fire station (☎ 809/779-4892). This shack of tin and wood serves the best hamburgers on St. John. The chili dogs aren't bad either. The yachting crowd likes to hang out here. There's a satellite dish to televise major sporting events. Live music is presented at least once a week; otherwise it's the dartboard or horseshoe pits for you.

As a final option, check out the **Sea Breeze,** 4F Little Plantation, on Salt Pond Road, Coral Bay (☎ 809/693-5824), where you can not only drink and enjoy live entertainment but can order three meals a day. Each night a different chef demonstrates his or her specialties. A local dive and popular hangout, this place is very laid-back.

3 St. Croix

Even though seven different flags have flown over St. Croix, it's the nearly 2 1/2 centuries of Danish influence that still permeates the island and its architecture.

At the east end of St. Croix, which, incidentally, is the easternmost point of the United States, the terrain is rocky and arid. The west end is lusher, with a rain forest of mango and mahogany, tree ferns, and dangling lianas. Rolling hills and upland pastures characterize the area lying between the two extremes. African tulips are just one of the species of flowers that add a splash of color to the landscape, which is dotted with stately towers that once supported grinding mills. The island is 84 square miles.

St. Croix has some of the best beaches in the Virgin Islands, and ideal weather. It doesn't have the nightlife of St. Thomas, nor would its permanent residents want that.

GETTING THERE

See "Getting There" at the beginning of the chapter for details on flights to St. Croix. It's possible to take the *Fast Cat* (☎ 809/773-3278), a catamaran that goes from St. Thomas to St. Croix three times a day, costing $50 round-trip for adults and $30 for children 11 and under. One-way passage is $25 for adults and $15 for children. It's cheaper than flying.

GETTING AROUND

BY BUS   Air-conditioned buses run between Christiansted and Frederiksted about every 40 minutes daily between 5:30am and 9pm. Beginning at Tide Village, to the east of Christiansted, buses go along Route 75 to the Golden Rock Shopping Center. Then they make their way to Route 70, with stopovers at the Sunny Isle Shopping Center, La Reine Shopping Center, St. George Village Botanical Garden, and Whim Plantation Museum, before reaching Frederiksted. Bus service is also available from the airport to either of the two towns. Fares are $1, 55¢ for senior citizens. For more **information,** call ☎ 809/773-7746.

BY BIKE   **St. Croix and Tours,** 5035 Cotton Valley, Christiansted (☎ 809/ 773-5004), rents 21-speed mountain bikes that are suitable for the rugged terrain. It also features two bike tours: a Rainforest Mountain Bike Tour for the experienced rider, covering 14 to 18 miles of tropical forests and scenic hillsides; and the less strenuous Coastal Bike Tour, centered around the island's natural beauty. Call for more information.

BY TAXI   At Alexander Hamilton Airport you'll find official taxi rates posted. Per-person rates require a minimum of two passengers; a single person is charged double the posted fares. Expect to pay about $10 for one or two riders from the airport to Christiansted and about $8.50 for one or two from the airport to Frederiksted. As the cabs are unmetered, agree on the rate before you get in.

The **St. Croix Taxicab Associations** (☎ **809/778-1088**) offer door-to-door service.

BY RENTAL CAR   Okay, we're warning you: The roads are often disastrous. Sometimes the government smooths them out before the big season begins.

Car-rental rates on St. Croix are reasonable. However, because of the island's higher-than-usual accident rate (which is partly because many tourists aren't used to driving on the left), insurance costs are higher than on the mainland. **Budget** (☎ **888/227-3359** or 809/778-9636), **Hertz** (☎ **800/654-3001** or 809/778-1402), and **Avis** (☎ **800/331-2112**) all maintain their headquarters at the island's airport, with kiosks near the baggage-claim areas.

However, you'll generally be quoted lower rates by **Caribbean Jeep & Car,** 2152 Hospital St. in Christiansted (☎ **809/773-4399**). They keep a fleet of vehicles such as Chevrolet Cavaliers and Sprints, with charges ranging from $35 to $40 per day.

ESSENTIALS

The **American Express** service representative is Southerland, Chandler's Wharf, Gallows Bay (☎ **800/260-2682** or 809/773-9500). For medical care, try the **St. Croix Hospital,** 6 Diamond Bay, Christiansted (☎ **809/778-6311**). The **Visitors Center** at St. Croix is in the Old Scalehouse at the waterfront, Christensted (☎ **809/773-0495**).

WHERE TO STAY

All rooms are subject to an 8% hotel room tax, which is *not* included in the rates given below.

If you're interested in a villa or condo rental, contact **Island Villas, Property Management Rentals,** 6 Company St., Christiansted, St. Croix, USVI 00820 (☎ **800/626-4512** or 809/773-8821; fax 809/773-8823), which offers some of the best-value properties on St. Croix. The outfit specializes in villa and condo rentals, really private residences with pools; many are on the beach. One-bedroom units begin at $1,200 per week.

DOUBLES FOR LESS THAN $50 (WINTER) / $36 (OFF-SEASON)

In Christiansted

Club Comanche. 1 Strand St., Christiansted, St. Croix, USVI 00820. ☎ **800/524-2066** or 809/773-0210. 40 rms, 4 suites, 1 mill. A/C TV TEL. Winter, $49.50-$85.50 single or double; $108 suite; $126 mill. Off-season, $36-$64 single or double; $76 suite; $88 mill. AE, DC, V.

Right on the Christiansted waterfront, this is a famous old West Indian inn, based around a 250-year-old Danish-inspired main house, once the home of Alexander Hamilton. Extensively remodeled over the years, some of its bedrooms have slanted ceilings with carved four-poster beds, old chests, and mahogany mirrors. The public areas have a faux W. Somerset Maugham aura, or at least Sydney Greenstreet. Reached by a covered bridge, a more modern addition passes over a shopping street to the waterside. Some rooms are at poolside or harborfront buildings. Since accommodations come in such a wide range of styles and sizes, your opinion of this place is likely to be influenced entirely by your room assignment. The place always draws mixed reactions. The most romantic unit, preferred by honeymooners, is in a mill on the grounds. The club also offers the most popular restaurant in Christiansted. Four minutes by ferry will take you to the beach at Hotel on the Cay.

DOUBLES FOR LESS THAN $85 (WINTER) / $75 (OFF-SEASON)

In Christiansted

Danish Manor Hotel. 2 Company St., Christiansted, St. Croix, USVI 00820. ☎ **800/524-2609** in the U.S., or 809/773-1377. Fax 809/773-1913. 34 rms, 2 suites. A/C TV. Winter, $59–$105 single; $69–$115 double; $115–$150 suite. Off-season, $49–$79 single; $59–$89 double; $89–$110 suite. Rates include continental breakfast. AE, DC, DISC, MC, V.

Built around an old Danish courtyard and a freshwater pool, right in the heart of town between King Street and Queen Street, this compound combines the very old and the very new. The hotel was erected on the site of a Danish West Indies Company's counting house. An L-shaped three-story addition stands in the rear, with spacious rooms with air-conditioning, ceiling fans, and cable TV with HBO. All units overlook the courtyard dominated by an ancient mahogany tree. The entrance to the courtyard is through old arches. You can park in a public lot off King Street. The hotel has a courtyard for guests where cool drinks and wine coolers are available, and the popular Italian/seafood restaurant, Tutto Bene, fronts the hotel. Guests can swim at the beach in Christiansted Harbor, about a 4-minute ferry ride from the hotel.

✪ **Kronegade Inn.** 1112 Western Suburb, Christiansted, St. Croix, USVI 00820. ☎ **809/692-9590.** Fax 809/692-9591. 12 suites. A/C TV TEL. Winter, $85 suite for one or two; $107 two-bedroom suite. Off-season, $75 suite for one or two; $95 two-bedroom suite. AE, MC, V.

Opened in 1994, this small inn in Christiansted offers a certain "down-home" charm at reasonable rates. Some guests call it the "best kept secret in Christiansted." The inn offers 12 suites or apartments, each with full kitchen, air-conditioning, TV, phone, radio, and ceiling fan. The nearest beach is at the offshore Hotel on the Cay, a 4-minute ferry ride away, where Kronegade guests are allowed to use the beach and facilities. The decor is in a tropical motif with white rattan furnishings. The inn doesn't offer food service, but a number of restaurants and cafes are nearby.

DOUBLES FOR LESS THAN $110 (WINTER) / $85 (OFF-SEASON)

In Christiansted

✪ **Holger Danske.** 1200 King Cross St., Christiansted, St. Croix, USVI 00821. ☎ **800/528-1234** or 809/773-3600. Fax 809/773-8828. 44 rms. A/C TV TEL. Winter, $89–$130 single; $94–$140 double. Off-season, $64–$110 single; $69–$130 double. AE, DC, DISC, MC, V.

This is one of the best bets in town for the budget traveler. Freshly remodeled and refurbished, right in the heart of Christiansted, it's a Best Western hotel. The inn provides pleasantly furnished accommodations, each with cable TV, air-conditioning, a private furnished balcony, and a refrigerator. Some units also offer efficiency kitchens. It has a pool patio and a garden path walkway, but only the superior rooms open onto the harbor and its offshore cay. Water sports and other activities are near at hand, as are a bevy of shops and restaurants. The nearest beach is a 4-minute ferry ride away.

King Christian Hotel. 59 King's Wharf (P.O. Box 3619), Christiansted, St. Croix, USVI 00822. ☎ **800/524-2012** in the U.S., or 809/773-2285. Fax 809/773-9411. 39 rms. A/C TV TEL. Winter, $95 economy single, $130 superior single; $100 economy double, $140 superior double.

St. Croix

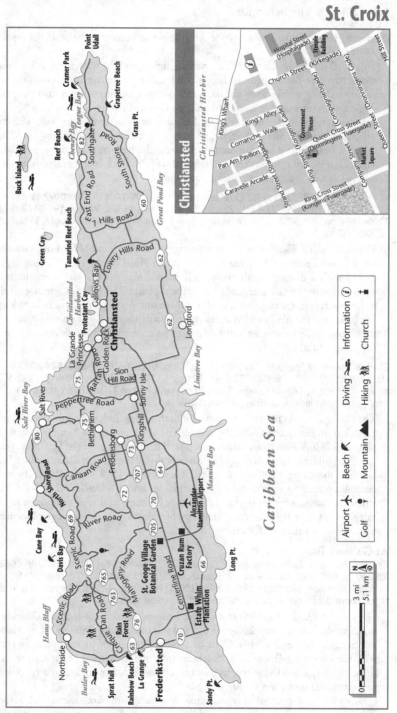

Christiansted

Christiansted Harbor

Hospital Street (Hospitalgade)
Steeple Building
Church Street (Kirkegade)

King's Wharf
King's Alley
Comanche Walk
Pan Am Pavilion
Caravelle Arcade
Strand Street (Strandgade)
King Street (Kongens Gade)
Government House
Queen Cross Street (Dronningens Tvaergade)
Queen Street (Dronningens Gade)
Hill Street
Market Square
Company Street
King Cross Street (Kongens Tvaergade)

Point Udall
Cramer Park
Grapetree Beach
Reef Beach
Chenay Bay
Teague Bay
82
Southgate
South Shore Road
Grass Pt.
60
Great Pond Bay
7 Hills Road
East End Road
Tamarind Reef Beach
Green Cay
Lowry Hills Road
62
Gallows Bay
Christiansted Harbor
Protestant Cay
Christiansted
Longford
62
La Grande Princesse
Golden Rock
Rattan Road
Sion Hill Road
Sunny Isle
Limetree Bay
75
Peppertree Road
Salt River
80
75
Bethlehem
Fredensborg
Kingshill
73
Canaan Road
707
64
72
70
705
Alexander Hamilton Airport
Manning Bay
River Road
69
Scenic Road
78
765
Mahogany Road
763
St. George Village Botanical Garden
Cruzan Rum Factory
66
Estate Whim Plantation
70
Hans Bluff
Northside
Scenic Road
Creque Dan Road
Rain Forest
63
76
La Grange
Rainbow Beach
Sprat Hall
Butler Bay
Frederiksted
Sandy Pt.
Long Pt.

Buck Island
Green Cay
Davis Bay
Cane Bay

Caribbean Sea

Airport ✈   Beach 🏖   Diving 🤿   Information ⓘ
Golf ⛳   Mountain ⛰   Hiking 🥾   Church ✝

3 mi
5.1 km
0

N

2-0202

Off-season, $80 economy single, $100 superior single; $85 economy double, $107 superior double. AE, DC, DISC, MC, V.

This hotel is right in the heart of everything, directly on the waterfront. All its front rooms have two double beds, bathroom, cable color TV, refrigerator, room safe, and private balcony overlooking the harbor. No-frills economy-wing rooms have two single beds or one double and a bath, but no view or balcony.

You can relax on the sundeck or shaded patio, or in the freshwater pool. The staff will make arrangements for golf, tennis, horseback riding, and sightseeing tours, and there's a beach just a few hundred yards across the harbor, reached by ferry. Mile Mark Charters water-sports center offers daily trips to Buck Island's famous snorkeling trail as well as a complete line of water sports.

King's Alley Hotel. 57 King St., Christiansted, St. Croix, USVI 00820. ☎ **800/843-3574** or 809/773-0103. Fax 809/773-4431. 23 rms, 12 suites. A/C TV TEL. Winter, $99–$148 single; $109–$134 double; $158 suite. Off-season, $74–$99 single; $79–$104 double; $115 suite. AE, DC, MC, V.

The King's Alley Hotel stands at water's edge, near Christiansted Harbor's yacht basin, a 4-minute ferry ride to the nearest beach at Hotel on the Cay. The inn is furnished with a distinct Mediterranean flair, and many of its rooms overlook its swimming-pool terrace surrounded by tropical plants. The galleries opening off the bedrooms are almost spacious enough for entertaining. All rooms have twin or king-size beds, and the newly added suites contain four-posters. Right outside your door are boutiques and restaurants. Breakfast can be ordered if you walk over to one of the nearby cafes.

✪ **Pink Fancy.** 27 Prince St., Christiansted, St. Croix, USVI 00820. ☎ **800/524-2045** in the U.S., or 809/773-8460. Fax 809/773-6448. 12 rms. A/C TV TEL. Winter, $90 single; $90–$120 double. Off-season, $65–$75 single; $65–$90 double. Children 11 and under stay free in parents' room. Rates include continental breakfast. AE, MC, V.

The Pink Fancy was restored and turned into this small, unique private hotel located 1 block from the Annapolis Sailing School. The oldest part of the four-building complex is a 1780 Danish town house, now one of the historic places of St. Croix. Years ago the building was a private club for wealthy planters. Fame came when Jane Gottlieb, the Ziegfeld Follies star, opened it as a hotel in 1948. In the 1950s, the hotel became a mecca for writers and artists, including, among others, Noël Coward. The efficiency rooms, with ceiling fans, are in four buildings clustered around the swimming pool. Other than the complimentary breakfast and a 24-hour complimentary bar, you're on your own for meals.

At Gallows Bay
✪ **Hilty House.** Questa Verde Rd. (P.O. Box 26077), Gallows Bay, St. Croix, USVI 00824. ☎ and fax **809/773-2594.** 4 rms, 2 cottages. Winter, $85 single; $110 double; $115–$135 cottage. Off-season, $70 single; $95 double; $100–$110 cottage. 3-night minimum stay in cottages. Room rates include continental breakfast. No credit cards.

Jacquie and Hugh Hoare-Ward own this bed-and-breakfast, which is housed in a building that's more than 200 years old and was once a rum distillery. Hilty House is located on the east side of St. Croix on a hilltop surrounded by mountains and hills with the airport 7 miles away, a 15-minute ride, and the nearest beach a 10-minute drive away. Upon arriving, guests pass through a shaded courtyard to a set of iron gates that lead to the inn's gardens.

The plantation-style house is beautifully appointed with hand-painted Italian tiles. The interior includes a high-ceilinged living room and an enormous fireplace that houses a spit. The master bedroom is the most lavish room, with a four-poster bed

ove 0-800-99-0011

the springtime.

Every country has its own AT&T Access Number which makes

calling from France and other countries really easy. Just dial

the AT&T Access Number for the country you're calling from

and we'll take it from there. And be sure to charge your calls

on your AT&T Calling Card. It'll help you avoid outrageous

phone charges on your hotel bill and save you up to 60%.*

0-800-99-0011 is a great place to visit any time of year,

especially if you've got these two cards. So please take the

attached wallet card of worldwide AT&T Access Numbers.

AT&T Direct™ Service

How to call internationally from overseas

1. Just dial the AT&T Access Number for the country you are calling from.
2. Dial the phone number you're calling.
3. Dial the calling card number listed above your name.

AT&T Access Numbers

France	0-800-99-0011
Germany	0130-0010
Italy	172-1011
Philippines	105-11
Saudi Arabia	1-800-10

AT&T True Choice™ Calling Card

836 000 6780 1111
T BOFFA

International Number 891288 327 926 730 3   Auth. Code 50

All you need for the
fastest, clearest connections home.

and sunken shower over which hangs a chandelier. There are also two self-catering cottages that can be rented with a required minimum stay of 3 nights. The Danish Kitchen, one of the cottages, has a covered porch, television, and telephone.

A continental breakfast is included in the room rates only, not the cottage rates, and dinner, which has a set price of $25 and is comprised of a three-course meal, is usually just served on Monday night. Guests may enjoy taking a swim in the large pool, which is decorated with hand-painted tile. The atmosphere is very homey and the place gives off a warm feeling. No children under 12 are accepted, and no more than three people are allowed in a room.

At Frederiksted

The Frederiksted. 20 Strand St., Frederiksted, St. Croix, USVI 00840. ☎ **800/595-9519** in the U.S., or 809/772-0500. 40 rms. A/C TV TEL. Winter, $85–$95 single; $95–$105 double. Off-season, $75–$85 single; $85–$95 double. AE, DC, MC, V.

For those who'd like to stay in the "second city" of St. Croix, historic Frederiksted, this contemporary four-story inn is the answer. It's located in the center of Frederiksted, about a 10-minute ride from the airport. Much of the activity takes place in the outdoor tiled courtyard, where guests enjoy drinks and listen to live music on Friday and Saturday nights. There's also a small swimming pool here. The average-size bedrooms, a bit tattered, are done in a tropical motif of pastels and are equipped with small refrigerators for drinks as well as a wet bar. The best (and most expensive) bedrooms are those with an ocean view, even though subject to street noise. A full breakfast is served at the poolside patio, and the bar is popular in the evening, as guests order rum punches. The nearest beach is Dorch Beach, a 1-mile walk or a 5-minute drive from the hotel along the water.

On the Beach Resort. Frederiksted Beach (P.O. Box 1908), Frederiksted, St. Croix, USVI 00841. ☎ **800/524-2018** or 809/772-1205. Fax 809/772-1757. 20 rms. Winter, $90–$110 single or double. Off-season, $50–$105 single or double. Rates include continental breakfast. AE, MC, V.

The best-known gay hotel on St. Croix, this small place lies half a mile from the town's shopping and dining facilities. Catering to both gay men and lesbians, or anyone else for that matter, the hotel offers comfortably furnished bedrooms, all with kitchenettes, private baths, and chamber service. The hotel's original owner, Bill Owens, has returned to manage the place. There are two freshwater swimming pools, a hot tub, and a beachfront patio. The resort's restaurant is one of the best in Frederiksted.

COTTAGES ON THE WATER

Cottages by the Sea. P.O. Box 1697 (no street address), Frederiksted, St. Croix, USVI 00841-1697. ☎ **800/323-7252** or 809/772-1753. Fax 809/772-1753. 20 cottages, 2 villas. A/C TV. Winter, $95–$115 cottage for one or two; $165–$175 villa for four. Off-season, $70–$95 cottage for one or two; $125–$140 villa for four. Extra person $20 in winter, $15 off-season. AE, DISC, MC, V.

These isolated cottages are located on the water right outside Frederiksted about 6 miles from the airport. The enterprise was launched with 4 cottages back in the late 1970s and has increased to 20. The owners, Pat and Mac McFee, like to keep it quiet so no children under the age of 8 are allowed. Some cottages are made of cinder blocks, and others are wood. The timeworn interiors include paneling, and all cottages have air-conditioning, TVs, and private patios. There are big patios out front where the guests can grill their dinners. Water sports have to be arranged elsewhere, but guests are welcome to go snorkeling in the waters just outside the grounds. Some families return year after year.

CONDOS

In general, condominiums are rented at half or a third the going hotel rates, and if you wait until after April 15, prices are even lower.

Cane Bay Reef Club. P.O. Box 1407, Kingshill, St. Croix, USVI 00851. ☎ **800/253-8534** in the U.S., or 809/778-2966. Fax 809/778-2966. 9 suites. Winter, $140–$180 suite for one or two. Off-season, $90–$115 suite for one or two. Extra person $15. AE, MC, V.

This is one of the little gems of the island, offering large suites, each with a living room, a full kitchen, a bedroom, a bath, and a balcony overlooking the water. The decor is breezy tropical, with cathedral ceilings, overhead fans, and Chilean tiles. The location is on the north shore of St. Croix, about a 20-minute taxi ride from Christiansted, fronting the rocky Cane Bay Beach near the Waves at Cane Bay. Guests enjoy the pool, and local rum drinks are served at the patio bar.

WORTH A SPLURGE

Sprat Hall Plantation. Rte. 63 (P.O. Box 695), Frederiksted, St. Croix, USVI 00841. ☎ **800/843-3584** or 809/772-0305. 17 units, all with bath. A/C TV. Winter, $110–$120 single; $120–$130 double; $150 suite; $170 cottage; $150 Great House room. Off-season, $90–$100 single; $100–$110 double; $130 suite; $160 cottage; $130 Great House room. AE, DC, MC, V.

This resort, 1 mile north of Frederiksted, is the oldest plantation Great House (and the only French-built plantation house left intact) in the Virgin Islands. Dating from St. Croix's French occupation of 1650 to 1690, it's set on 20 acres of grounds, with private white sandy beaches. The plantation has room for about 40 people, depending on how many guests use the cottage units, which all have radios.

The units in the Great House have been designated for nonsmokers because of the value of the antiques contained inside. An annex was originally built in the 1940s. Within it, each unit has simple furnishings and a view of the sea. If you prefer your Caribbean living old-fashioned and homey, with a sense of the region's historic origins, you should insist on a room in the Great House. Compared to the rest of the shabbily genteel property, the cottages aren't very romantic, but they have been re-modeled and refurnished with queen-size beds.

You can be assured of good food, either at the Beach Restaurant during the lunch hour or in the Sprat Hall Restaurant. Clients are requested to dress with decorum—no jeans or T-shirts, please. Only guests of the hotel and/or their invited guests can attend dinners here.

On the grounds is a worthwhile equestrian stable (see "Beaches, Water Sports & Other Pursuits," below). The Hurd and Young family run the operation, and offer hiking and bird-watching, as well as snorkeling, swimming, and shore fishing. Jetskiing and waterskiing can be arranged.

WHERE TO EAT
IN & AROUND CHRISTIANSTED

Anabelle's Tea Room. 51-ABC Company St. ☎ **809/773-3990.** Reservations recommended. Sandwiches, salads, and platters $6.50–$12. No credit cards. Mon–Sat 9am–3pm. INTERNATIONAL.

It occupies a quiet gingerbread courtyard filled with tropical plants, and is surrounded with clapboard buildings whose iron railings evoke New Orleans. Don't expect grand cuisine—what you get is a shady place to rest your feet, a warm welcome from Anna Deering or a member of her staff, a sense of Cruzan history, and a simple but refreshing assortment of sandwiches, salads, soups, and platters. Dolphin (the fish) in herb-flavored butter sauce, Cubano or "Lazy Virgin" sandwiches ("all vegetables and cheese, with no meat"), and conch Créole are ongoing favorites.

Blue Moon. 17 Strand St. ☎ **809/772-2222.** Main courses $14–$18.50. AE, DISC, MC, V. Tues–Sun 11am–2pm and 6–10pm. (Bar, Tues–Sun 5pm–2am.) Closed Aug to mid-Sept. INTERNTIONAL/CAJUN.

The best little bistro in Christiansted becomes a hot, hip spot on Thursday and Friday nights when it offers entertainment. A favorite of all visiting jazz musicians, the bistro is in a 200-year-old stone house on the waterfront. For 10 years, it's been going strong, building up a savvy local following. Tourists have now discovered but not ruined it. It's decorated with funky, homemade art of the States, including a garbage-can–lid restaurant sign. It has a very casual, cafelike atmosphere. Begin wth the "lunar pie," with feta cheese, cream cheese, onions, mushrooms, and celery in phyllo pastry. Or else opt for the artichoke-and-spinach dip. This could be followed by the catch of the day, or on occasion, Maine lobster. The clams served in garlic sauce are also from Maine. Vegetarians opt for the spinach fettuccine, and there's the usual array of steak and chicken dishes. Save room for the yummy guava pie.

The Bombay Club. 5A King St. ☎ **809/773-1838.** Reservations recommended. Main courses $10–$18. AE, MC, V. Mon–Fri 11am–10pm, Sat–Sun 6–10pm. INTERNATIONAL.

The owners have managed to squeeze much miscellany into what has become one of the most enduring restaurants in Christiansted. It's concealed from the street by the brick foundations of an 18th-century planter's town house. You enter through a low stone tunnel and eventually find yourself near its bar and the courtyard that contains many of its tables. The food, while not overly fancy, is plentiful, flavorful, and reasonably priced. Menu items include the catch of the day, regional dishes such as conch, veal dishes, beef filet, and pasta.

✪ Camille's Café. 53B Company St. (at Queen Cross St.). ☎ **809/773-2985.** Main courses $10.95–$15.95; fixed-price dinner $15.95. MC, V. Mon–Sat 7:30am–3pm and 5–10pm. MEDITERRANEAN.

Across from Government House, Camille's, a wine bar, serves New York deli–type food during the day, along with a selection of Mediterranean dishes at dinner. It's one of the best dining values in town, especially its fixed-price dinner. Salads are featured, or you might begin with a homemade soup. The dinner menu includes such dishes as fresh fish, filet mignon, prime rib, lobster, and chicken. The place is a neighborhood enclave of convivial locals. Its brick walls and beamed ceilings were originally part of an 18th-century guest house.

Cheeseburgers in Paradise. 67 Southgate. ☎ **809/773-1119.** Main courses $6.50–$8.50. MC, V. Daily 11am–10:30pm (bar open later). WEST INDIAN.

Three miles outside of Christiansted, this restaurant isn't owned by Jimmy Buffett, but makes the best burgers on island. You get almost a half pound of meat with all the fixin's. A margarita accompanies many a burger plate. Cheeseburgers aren't all: you get an array of burritos, freshly made salads, a tasty grilled chicken sandwich, and daily specials. The pizza oven is heated up on Thursday. Dinners run the gamut from barbecued ribs to stir-fry. The fresh fish dishes are excellent, and the chef has a winning way with chicken. He cooks a big prime rib on Saturday. Live music is presented Thursday to Sunday.

Comanche Club. 1 Strand St. ☎ **809/773-2665.** Reservations recommended. Main courses $8.95–$16.95; lunch from $12. AE, MC, V. Mon–Sat 11:30am–2:30pm and 6–11pm. WEST INDIAN/CONTINENTAL.

One of the island's most popular restaurants, Comanche is relaxed yet elegant. The specialties are eclectic—there's everything from fish and conch chowder to shark cakes. Each night a different special is featured. There's also a good selection of

Cruzan dishes—one for every night of the week. Salads and a cold buffet are traditionally featured; the Comanche curries have won over devotees. Island fish are generally sautéed with lemon butter and capers; typical West Indian dishes include conch Créole with fungi. You can also order standard international dishes such as filet mignon in a béarnaise sauce.

Harbormaster Restaurant. At the Hotel on the Cay, Protestant Cay. ☎ **809/773-2035.** Main courses $5.75–$15.50; breakfast from $2.75. AE, DC, MC, V. Tues 7am–5pm and 7–10:30pm, Wed–Mon 7am–5pm. AMERICAN.

A 4-minute ferry ride across the harbor from Christiansted, this is where guests at the local town inns head for a day at the beach (it's the nearest best beach). While here, you don't want to go back into Christiansted for lunch, so this hotel has wisely decided to accommodate its many day visitors by offering this quite acceptable restaurant. The cookery is not the island's best, but it's good. Of course, you get the usual array of salad platters, sandwiches, omelets, and burgers. But many main dishes are more elaborate and appealing, especially the grilled filet of dolphin (or swordfish); the conch in a lemon, garlic, and butter sauce; and the barbecued ribs. The chef also prepares a good dinner but only 1 night a week.

The Hideaway. At the Hibiscus Beach Hotel, La Grande Princesse. ☎ **809/773-4042.** Reservations recommended. Main courses $10–$20; lunch $6–$10. AE, MC, V. Daily 7am–10pm. AMERICAN.

Three miles west of Christiansted, this open-air restaurant fronts one of the island's best beaches. Even if you don't go here for dinner, you might want to patronize it at lunch. It's a true hideaway, known for serving one of the island's best breakfasts, including all that good stuff like eggs Benedict or salmon with sour cream. The chef also makes one of the island's best omelets. At lunch, you get the usual burgers and sandwiches, as well as hot main-dish spcialties. At night, the menu is considerably upgraded, based on the market that day. You can usually get fresh fish prepared as you like it, along with lobster (sometimes available). The baby back ribs are a winner, and chicken and beef are prepared in interesting ways. On Wednesday, it's beach barbecue time.

✪ **Luncheria.** In the Apothecary Hall Courtyard, 2111 Company St. ☎ **809/773-4247.** Main courses $5–$6.75. No credit cards. Mon–Fri 11am–9pm, Sat noon–9pm. MEXICAN/CUBAN/PUERTO RICAN.

In a historic courtyard in the center of town, this Mexican restaurant offers some of the best dining values on the island. You get the usual tacos, tostadas, burritos, nachos, and enchiladas. Specialties include chicken fajitas, enchiladas verde, and arroz con pollo (spiced chicken with brown rice). Daily specials feature both low-calorie and vegetarian choices, and the chef's refried beans are lard free. Whole-wheat tortillas are offered. Check the board for daily specials, and know that the salsa bar is complimentary, ranging from mild to hot sauce, plus jalapeños. More recently some Cuban and Puerto Rican dishes have appeared on the menu, including a zesty chicken curry, black-bean soup, and roast pork. The bartender makes the island's best margaritas. However, the $1 cheapo version is referred to as "ethyl" or "jet fuel" by locals.

Marina Bar & Grill. At the Kings Landing Yacht Club. ☎ **809/773-0103.** Main courses $5.50–$10. AE, MC, V. Daily 7am–9pm. CARIBBEAN/CONTINENTAL.

Some in-the-know boaters head here for their morning pick-me-up, a great, spicy Bloody Mary to get their blood circulating. You can join them for breakfast, which is rather standard fare, with bagels, muffins, and eggs as you like them. Lunch is also a bit standard; many opt for one of the burgers, even a veggie burger. The best bet is one of the daily specials. In the evening the menu perks up, and fresh fish is the best item to order. Your dinner is often accompanied by steel drum music. If you show up Monday night you can get in on the crab races. Locals are fond of dining here, sitting on the waterfront watching the seaplane land. On site is a more upscale restaurant, Taste of Asia, open daily from 11am to 11pm.

Nolan's Tavern. 5A Estate St. Peter, Christiansted East. ☎ **809/773-6660.** Reservations recommended only for groups of six or more. Burgers $7–$8.50; main courses $12.75–$16.25. AE, DISC, MC, V. Daily 5–9pm. (Bar, daily 3pm–midnight.) INTERNATIONAL / WEST INDIAN.

It's the first place people in the know think of when you ask them for a warm, cozy, Antillean tavern with absolutely no social pretentions. It lies 2 miles east of Christiansted's harborfront, across from the capital's most visible elementary school, the Pearl B. Larsen School. Your host is Nolan Joseph, a Trinidad-born chef who makes a special point of welcoming guests and offering "tasty food and good service." No one will mind if you stop in just for a drink. Mr. Joseph, referred to by some diners as "King Conch," prepares the mollusk in at least half a dozen ways, including versions with curry, Créole sauce, and garlic-pineapple sauce. Reportedly, he experimented for 3 months to perfect a means of tenderizing the tough mollusk without artificial chemicals. His ribs are also tasty. Like Sinatra, he prepares them "my way." Many guests come here to fill up on his steak, ribs, and chicken.

Stixx on the Waterfront. 39 Strand St. ☎ **809/773-5157.** Reservations recommended. Main courses $10–$30; lunches from $5.50; all-you-can-eat Sun brunch $10. AE, MC, V. Daily 7am–10pm. INTERNATIONAL/AMERICAN.

This rustic eatery is located on the waterfront in downtown Christiansted. This two-story establishment at the Pan Am Pavilion has a deck that extends out over the harbor. It has been said that this restaurant sells more lobster than anyone else on the island, thus making it the house specialty. The menu is varied from chicken to seafood. Stixx is also known for its stuffed mushrooms, the swordfish served with a mango salsa, and grilled vegetables over angel-hair pasta with surf-and-turf specials once or twice a week.

Tommy & Susan's Taverna. In the Apothecary Hall Courtyard, Company St. ☎ **809/773-8666.** No reservations accepted. Main courses $6.75–$8.25. No credit cards. Daily 11:30am–2:30pm. MEDITERRANEAN/ GREEK/ WEST INDIAN.

This local hangout is a good and inexpensive place for lunch if you're spending the day shopping in Christiansted. The food doesn't exactly explode with color and flavor, but it's quite good. A wide variety of cuisines is offered, happily blending the Mediterranean and the Caribbean. Dining is in air-conditioned rooms or else in the courtyard with an open-air porch for sunlovers and smokers. The pastas are quite decent, including some in a pesto sauce. A variety of soups are homemade daily, and you can also get some of the town's best sandwiches. Light beer and white wine are served.

IN & AROUND FREDERIKSTED

The Last Hurrah. 57 King St. (at Hill St.). ☎ **809/772-5225.** Reservations not accepted. Main courses $5.50–$6.50. No credit cards. Mon–Fri 11am–3pm. (Bar, Tues–Sun 4pm–2am.) AMERICAN.

For a touch of Hollywood, head for this little open-air bistro, beloved by locals. One of the newest restaurants to open here, it feeds you well and inexpensively. It's not great, but it's satisfying—particularly the prices. At lunch, munch on burgers, a homemade soup and salad, buffalo wings, or a big helping of lasagne. Look for the daily specials such as a meatloaf sandwich or crab cakes. At happy hour on weekdays from 5 to 7pm, you get two drinks for one. On Saturday, they clear the patio for dancing to a DJ's music. Live entertainment is presented once a month—on one recent occasion, a drag show with strippers.

Pier 69. 69 King St. ☎ **809/772-0069.** Reservations not accepted. Sandwiches and platters $4.25–$17. AE, DC, DISC, MC, V. Mon–Thurs 10am–midnight, Fri–Sun 10am–4pm. AMERICAN/CARIBBEAN.

Although it will serve you a worthy but unfussy platter of food, this place is far more interesting for its resemblance to a funky bar in New York's Greenwich Village than for its reputation as a culinary citadel. New York–born Unise Tranberg is the earth-mother/matriarch of the place, whose heart and soul is a warm and somewhat battered combination of a 1950s living room with a nautical bar sheathed in varnished tropical woods. Regardless of when you arrive, someone will probably be deep into his or her second or third drink, so if you imbibe a bit you won't be alone. Counterculture fans from Christiansted make this their preferred hangout, sometimes opting for a mango colada or a lime lambada. If you're stepping off a ship and want something to eat, menu items include the predictable salads, sandwiches, and platters, ranging from the American to the Caribbean in their inspiration.

Sprat Hall Beach Restaurant. Rte. 63. ☎ **809/772-5855.** Lunch $7–$15. No credit cards. Daily 9am–4pm (hot food 11:30am–2:30pm). CARIBBEAN.

One mile north of Frederiksted, this is an informal spot on the western coast of St. Croix near Sprat Hall Plantation. It's the best place on the island to combine lunch and a swim. The restaurant has been in business since 1948, feeding both locals and visitors. Try such local dishes as conch chowder, pumpkin fritters, tannia soup, and the fried fish of the day. These dishes have authentic island flavor, perhaps more so than any other place on the island. If you'd like more standard fare, they also do salads and burgers. The bread is home-baked daily. The place is directed by Cruzan-born Joyce Merwin Hurd and her husband, Jim, who charge $2 for use of the showers and changing rooms.

Vel's. 16A King St. ☎ **809/772-2160.** Main courses $6.50–$10. No credit cards. Mon–Sat 11am–8:30pm. PUERTO RICAN / WEST INDIAN.

Savvy local foodies, even the island governor, will steer you to this place if you're seeking down-home West Indian cookery. Val, a native of Puerto Rico, is the owner, and she does her own cooking. Does she ever know how to rattle those pots and pans. She also prepares a daily special; perhaps it'll be her classic arroz con pollo (chicken and rice) at the time of your visit. She does a real tasty pork, as well as a savory beef stew, and somehow gets the best fish caught on the island. She also prepares a "mean" conch. The place is so popular that some residents from St. Thomas come over here just to dine.

BEACHES, WATER SPORTS & OTHER PURSUITS

BEACHES   Beaches are the big attraction. The drawback is that getting to them from Christiansted, center of most of the hotels, isn't always easy. It can also be expensive, especially if you want to go back and forth every day of your stay. Of course, you can always rent one of those housekeeping condos right on the water.

In Christiansted, if you want to beach it, head for the **Hotel on the Cay.** You'll have to take a 4-minute ferry ride to this palm-shaded island.

Cramer Park, at the northeastern end of the island, is a special public park operated by the Department of Agriculture. Lined with sea-grape trees, the beach also has a picnic area, a restaurant, and a bar. We highly recommend **Davis Bay** and **Cane Bay** as the type of beaches you'd expect to find on a Caribbean island—palms, white sand, and good swimming and snorkeling. Cane Bay adjoins Route 80 on the north shore. Snorkelers and divers are attracted to this beach, with its rolling waves, coral gardens, and drop-off wall. No reefs guard the approach to Davis Beach, which draws bodysurfers but doesn't have changing facilities. It's off South Shore Road (Route 60), in the vicinity of the Carambola Beach Resort.

Windsurfers like **Reef Beach,** which opens onto Teague Bay along Route 82, East End Road, a half-hour ride from Christiansted. Food can be ordered at Duggan's Reef. On Route 63, a short ride north of Frederiksted, **Rainbow Beach** lures people with its white sand and ideal snorkeling conditions. In the vicinity, also on Route 63, about 5 minutes north of Frederiksted, **La Grange** is another good beach. Lounge chairs can be rented, and there's a bar nearby.

At the ✪ **Cormorant Beach Club,** about 5 miles west of Christiansted, some 1,200 feet of white sands are shaded by palm trees. Since a living reef lies just off the shore, snorkeling conditions are ideal. **Grapetree Beach** offers about the same footage of clean white sand on the eastern tip of the island (Route 60). Follow South Shore Road to reach it. Water sports are popular here.

Two more beaches on St. Croix include **Buccaneer Beach,** 2 miles west of Christiansted, and **Sandy Point,** directly south of Frederiksted, the largest beach in all the U.S. Virgin Islands. Its waters are shallow and calm, perfect for swimming. Jutting out from southwestern St. Croix like a small peninsula, Sandy Point is reached by taking the Melvin Evans Highway (Route 66) west from the Alexander Hamilton Airport.

GOLF St. Croix has the best golfing in the U.S. Virgins. The ✪ **Carambola Golf Course** (☎ 809/778-0747), on the northeast side of St. Croix, was designed by Robert Trent Jones Sr., who called it "the loveliest course I ever designed." The course looks like a botanical garden with its bamboo, saman trees, and palms. Greens fees are $77 per person for a day in winter ($47.50 in summer), which allows you to play as many holes as you like. Rental of a golf cart is mandatory at $12.50 per 18 holes.

The other major course, at the **Buccaneer** (☎ 809/773-2100, ext. 738), 2 miles east of Christiansted, is a challenging 5,810-yard, 18-hole course. Nonguests who reserve pay $40 greens fees, and carts rent for $14.

A final course is the **Reef,** at the island's east end at Teague Bay (☎ 809/773-8844), a 3,100-yard, 9-hole course, charging greens fees of $10 to $14, with carts renting for $5 to $8.

HIKING The **St. Croix Environmental Association,** 6 Company St. (☎ 809/773-1989), in Christiansted, offers regularly scheduled hikes from December to March. In addition to in-season hikes, their programs include lectures, slide shows, and films on environmental issues. Prices for events vary, and contributions are accepted.

HORSEBACK RIDING Specializing in nature tours, **Paul and Jill's Equestrian Stables,** Sprat Hall Plantation, Route 58 (☎ 809/772-2880), is the largest equestrian stable in the Virgin Islands. Set on the sprawling grounds of the island's oldest plantation Great House, it's operated by Paul Wojcie and his wife, Jill Hurd, one of the daughters of the establishment's original founders. The stables are known throughout the Caribbean for the quality of the horses and the scenic trail rides through the forests, past ruins of abandoned 18th-century plantations and sugar mills, to the tops of the hills of St. Croix's western end. All tours are accompanied by the operators, who give running commentaries on island fauna, history, and riding techniques. Beginners and experienced riders alike are welcome.

A 2-hour trail ride costs $50 per person. Tours usually depart daily in winter at 10am and 4pm, and off-season at 5pm, with slight variations according to demand. Reservations at least a day in advance are important.

TENNIS Some authorities rate the tennis at the **Buccaneer** (☎ 809/773-2100, ext. 736) as the best in the West Indies. This hotel offers a choice of eight courts, two lit for night games, all open to the public. Nonguests pay $12 per person per hour; however, you must call to reserve a court. There's also a pro shop.

A notable selection of courts is also found at the **Carambola Golf Club** (☎ 809/778-0747), which has five clay courts, two of which are lit for night games. Open to the public, it charges $25 per hour for nonguests. You must call to reserve.

WATER SPORTS Sponge life, black-coral trees (the finest in the West Indies), and steep drop-offs into water near the shoreline have made St. Croix a diver's goal.

Buck Island, with an underwater visibility of more than 100 feet, is the site of the nature trail of the underwater national monument, and it's the major diving destination (see "A Side Trip to Buck Island: Unspoiled Nature & World-Class Snorkeling," at the end of this chapter). All the minor and major agencies offer scuba and snorkeling tours to Buck Island. St. Croix is home to the largest living reef in the Caribbean, including the fabled north-shore wall that begins in 25 to 30 feet of water and drops—sometimes straight down—to 13,200 feet. There are 22 moored sites, allowing the dive boats to tie up without damaging the reef. Favorite scuba-diving sites include the historic **Salt River Canyon,** the gorgeous coral gardens of **Scotch Banks,** and **Eagle Ray,** the latter so named because of the rays that cruise along the wall there. **Pavilions** is yet another good dive site, with a virgin coral reef that's in pristine shape.

Dive St. Croix, 59 King's Wharf (☎ 800/523-DIVE in the U.S., or 809/773-3434), operates the 38-foot dive boat *Reliance.* The staff offers complete instructions from resort courses through full certification, as well as night dives. A resort course is $75, with a two-tank dive going for $70. Scuba trips to Buck Island are offered for $65, and dive packages begin at $190 for six dives.

V. I. Divers Ltd., in the Pan Am Pavilion on Christiansted's waterfront (☎ 800/544-5911 or 809/773-6045), is the oldest (1971) and one of the best dive operations on the island. In fact, *Rudales Scuba Diving* magazine rated its staff as among the top 10 worldwide. A full-service PADI five-star facility, it offers daily two-tank boat dives, guided snorkeling trips to Green Cay, night dives, and a full range of scuba-training programs from introductory dives through divemaster. Introductory dives, which require no experience, are $95 for a two-tank dive, including all instruction and equipment. The outfitter offers a 6-dive package for $195 and a 10-dive package for $295. A two-tank or beach dive is priced at $75, with night dives going for $55. A 2-hour guided snorkel tour costs $25, or $35 for the boat snorkeling trip to Green Cay.

WINDSURFING The best place for this increasingly popular sport is the **St. Croix Water Sports Center** (☎ 809/773-7060), located on a small offshore island in Christiansted Harbor and part of the Hotel on the Cay. It gives lessons and is open daily from 9am to 5pm in winter or 10am to 5pm off-season. Windsurfer rentals are $25 per hour. It also offers two-seater Sea Doos for $50 for 30 minutes, plus parasailing at $50 per person, even snorkeling equipment at $12 per day.

EXPLORING THE RAIN FOREST

Unlike the rest of St. Croix, a verdant parcel in the island's western district is covered with dense forest, a botanical landscape very different from the scrub-covered hills covering other parts of the island. Set amid the sparsely populated terrain of the island's northwestern corner, north of Frederiksted, the area grows thick with ma-hogany trees, kapok (silk-cotton) trees, turpentine (red-birch) trees, samaan (rain) trees, and all kinds of ferns and vines. In many cases, sweet limes, mangoes, hog plums, and breadfruit trees, which have sown themselves in the wild since the days of the district's plantations, intersperse themselves among the forest's larger trees. The bird life includes crested hummingbirds, pearly-eyed thrashers, green-throated caribs, yellow warblers, and perky but drably camouflaged banana quits.

Although technically the district is not a tropical rain forest, it's known by virtu-ally everyone as the Rain Forest. How best to experience its botanical charms? Some visitors opt to drive along Route 76 (also known as Mahogany Road, and arguably the most mysterious road on St. Croix), stopping their car beside any of the footpaths that meander off to either side of the highway into dry riverbeds and glens on either side. (It's advisable to stick to the best-worn of the foot trails to avoid losing your way, and retrace your steps after a few moments after admiring the local botany).

Equally feasible is to hike beside those highways of the island's western sector where few cars ever venture. Three of the most viable include Creque Dam Road (rtes. 58/78), Scenic Road (Rte. 78); and Western Scenic Road (rtes. 63/78). Consider begin-ning your trek near the junction of Creque Dam Road and Scenic Road. (Though passable by cars, it's likely you'll see only a few along these roads during your entire walking tour.)

Your trek will cover a broad triangular swath, beginning at the above-mentioned junction, heading north and then west along Scenic Road. First the road will rise, then descend toward the coastal lighthouse of the island's extreme northwestern tip, Hamm's Bluff. Most trekkers will decide to retrace their steps after about 45 min-utes of northwesterly trekking, returning to their parked cars after admiring the land and seascapes. Real diehards, however, will continue trekking all the way to the coast-line, then head south along the coastal road (Butler Bay Road), then head east along Creque Dam Road to their parked cars at the junction of Creque Dam Road and Scenic Road. Embark on this longer expedition only if you're really prepared for a prolonged trek (about 5 hours) and some serious nature-watching.

SEEING THE SIGHTS
IN CHRISTIANSTED

The picture-book harbor town of the Caribbean, Christiansted is an old Danish port, handsomely restored—or at least in the process of being restored. On the northeastern shore of the island, on a coral-bound bay, the town is filled with Danish buildings erected by prosperous merchants in the booming 18th century. These red-roofed structures are often washed in pink, ocher, or yellow. Arcades over the sidewalks make ideal shaded colonnades for shoppers. **Government House**—in fact, the whole area around the harborfront—has been designated a historic site and is looked after by the National Park Service.

You can begin at the **visitors' bureau** (☎ **809/773-0495**), a yellow-sided build-ing with a cedar-capped roof near the harborfront. It was originally built as the Old Scalehouse in 1856 to replace a similar, older structure that burned down. In its hey-day, all taxable goods leaving and entering the harbor were weighed here. The scales that once stood could accurately weigh barrels of sugar and molasses up to 1,600 pounds each.

Another major attraction is the **Steeple Building** (☎ **809/773-1460**) or Church of Lord God of Sabaoth, which was completed in 1753 as St. Croix's first Lutheran church. It, too, stands near the harborfront, reached by going along Hospital Street.

It was embellished with a steeple in 1794–96, and today houses exhibits relating to island history and culture. The building was deconsecrated in 1831, and has served at various times as a bakery, a hospital, and a school. Admission is $2, which also includes admission to Fort Christiansvaern (see below). It's usually open Monday to Friday from 9:30am to noon and 1 to 3pm.

Overlooking the harbor, **Fort Christiansvaern** (☎ 809/773-1460) is the best-preserved colonial fortification in the Virgin Islands. The fort is maintained as a historic monument by the National Park Service. Its original four-pronged star-shaped design was in accordance with the most advanced military planning of its era. The fort is also the site of the St. Croix Police Museum, which traces police work on the island from the late 1800s to the present. Photos, weapons, and artifacts create the police force's past. It's open Monday to Thursday from 8am to 5pm and on Friday and Saturday from 9am to 5pm. Admission is included in the ticket to the Steeple Building (see above).

Relocated from Frederiksted, the **St. Croix Aquarium,** in the Caravelle Arcade, 38 Strand St. (☎ 809/773-8995), has expanded with many new exhibits. It houses some 40 species of marine animals and more than 100 species of invertebrates. A touch pond contains starfish, sea cucumbers, brittle stars, and pencil urchins. The aquarium is open Tuesday to Saturday from 11am to 4pm, charging $4.50 for adults and $2 for children.

The **Christiansted Apothecary Museum Exhibit,** Queens Cross Street (☎ 809/772-0598), is located in a building dating back to 1827. The Apothecary is fully stocked with all the medicine, supplies, and equipment needed to stock a pharmacy found on a small West Indian island in the late 19th century. It's open Monday to Saturday from 10am to 4pm, charging no admission.

IN FREDERIKSTED

This old Danish town at the western end of the island, about 17 miles from Christiansted, is a sleepy port town that comes to life only when a cruise ship docks at its shoreline. In 1994, a 1,500-foot pier opened to accommodate the largest cruise ships (the old pier had suffered damage from Hurricane Hugo in 1989). The pier facility is designed to accommodate two large cruise vessels and two mini–cruise vessels simultaneously.

Frederiksted was destroyed by a fire in 1879, and the citizens rebuilt it with wood frames and clapboards on top of the old Danish stone and yellow-brick foundations.

Most visitors begin their tour at russet-colored **Fort Frederik,** next to the cruise-ship pier (☎ 809/772-2021). Some historians claim that this was the first fort to sound a foreign salute to the U.S. flag, in 1776. It was here, on July 3, 1848, that Gov.-Gen. Peter von Scholten emancipated the slaves in the Danish West Indies. The fort, at the northern end of Frederiksted, has been restored to its 1840 look. You can explore the courtyard and stables, and an exhibit area has been installed in what was once the Garrison Room. Admission is $2, and it's open Monday to Friday from 8:30am to 4:30pm.

Just south of the fort, the Customs House is an 18th-century building with a 19th-century two-story gallery. Here you can go into the **visitors' bureau** (☎ 809/772-0357) and pick up a free map of the town.

Nearby, privately owned **Victoria House,** on Market Street, is a gingerbread-trimmed structure built after the fire of 1879.

Along the waterfront strand is the **Bellhouse,** once the Frederiksted Public Library. One of its owners, G. A. Bell, ornamented the steps with bells. The house today is an arts-and-crafts center and a nursery. Sometimes a local theater group presents dramas here.

The **Danish School,** on Prince Street, was adapted in the 1830s into a building designed by Hingelberg, a well-known Danish architect. Today it's the police station and Welfare Department.

Two churches are of interest: **St. Paul's Anglican Church,** 28 Prince St., was founded outside the port in the late 18th century; the present building dates from 1812. **St. Patrick's Catholic Church,** 5 Prince St., was built in the 1840s.

AROUND THE ISLAND: FROM NATURE RESERVES TO RUM FACTORIES

North of Frederiksted, you can drop in at Sprat Hall, the island's oldest plantation, or else continue along to the rain forest, which covers about 15 acres, including the 150-foot-high **Creque Dam.** The terrain is private property, but the owner lets visitors go inside to explore. Most visitors come here to see the jagged estuary of the northern coastline's **Salt River.** Salt River was where Columbus landed on November 14, 1493, the only known site where the explorer landed on what is now U.S. territory during any of his four expeditions. Marking the 500th anniversary of Columbus's arrival, then-President George Bush signed a bill creating the 912-acre **Salt River Bay National Historical Park and Ecological Preserve.** The land mass includes the site of the original Carib village explored by Columbus and his men, including the only ceremonial ball court ever discovered in the Lesser Antilles.

The park contains the largest mangrove forest in the Virgin Islands, sheltering many endangered animals and plants, plus an underwater canyon attracting scuba divers from around the world. The park today is virtually in a natural state, with a plaque indicating what it is.

At the Carib settlement, Columbus's men liberated several Taíno Indian women and children held as slaves. On the way back to their vessels, the Spaniards faced a canoe filled with hostile Caribs, armed with poison arrows. One Spanish soldier was killed, and perhaps six Caribs were either slain or captured. This is the first documented case of hostility between invading Europeans and the Native Americans. Sailing away, Columbus named this part of St. Croix "Cape of the Arrows."

The **St. Croix Environmental Association,** 3 Arawak Building, Gallows Bay (☎ 809/773-1989), conducts tours of the area and can be called for details. Tours cost $15 for adults, $12 for children 11 and under.

St. George Village Botanical Garden of St. Croix. 127 Estate St., Kingshill. ☎ **809/692-2874.** Admission $5 adults, $1 children 12 and under; donations welcome. Nov–May, daily 9am–5pm; June–Oct, Tues–Sat 9am–4pm.

Just north of Centerline Road, 4 miles east of Frederiksted at Estate St. George, is a veritable Eden of tropical trees, shrubs, vines, and flowers. Built around the ruins of a 19th-century sugarcane workers' village, the garden is a feast for the eye and the camera—from the entrance drive bordered by royal palms and bougainvillea to the towering kapok and tamarind trees. Restoration of the ruins is a continuing project. Two sets of workers' cottages provide space for a gift shop, rest rooms, a kitchen, and an office; these have been joined together with a Great Hall, which is used by the St. Croix community for various functions. Other completed projects include the superintendent's house, the blacksmith's shop, and various smaller buildings used for a library, a plant nursery, workshops, and storehouses.

Self-guided walking-tour maps are available at the entrance to the Great Hall.

Cruzan Rum Factory. West Airport Rd. (Rte. 64). ☎ **809/692-2280.** Admission $3. Tours given Mon–Fri 9–11:30am and 1–4:15pm.

This factory distills the famous Virgin Islands rum, which is considered by residents to be the finest in the world. Guided tours depart from the visitors' pavilion; call for reservations and information.

Estate Whim Plantation Museum. Centerline Rd. ☎ **809/772-0598.** Admission $5 adults, $1 children. Mon–Sat 10am–4pm.

About 2 miles east of Frederiksted, this museum was restored by the St. Croix Landmarks Society and is unique among the many sugar plantations whose ruins dot the island of St. Croix. This Great House is different from most in that it's composed of only three rooms. With 3-foot-thick walls made of stone, coral, and molasses, the house is said by some to resemble a luxurious European château.

Also on the museum's premises is a woodworking shop that features tools and techniques from the 18th century, the estate's original kitchen, a gift shop, and a reproduction of a typical town apothecary. The ruins of the plantation's sugar-processing plant, complete with a restored windmill, remain.

SHOPPING
IN CHRISTIANSTED

In Christiansted, where the core of our shopping recommendations are found, the emphasis is on hole-in-the-wall boutiques selling one-of-a-kind merchandise; hand-made items are strong. Of course the same duty-free stipulations, as outlined earlier, apply to your shopping selections on St. Croix.

Knowing that it can't compete with Charlotte Amalie, Christiansted has forged its own creative statement in its shops and has now become the "chic spot for merchandise" in the Caribbean. All the shops are easily compressed into half a mile or so. Most shops are open Monday to Saturday from 9am to 5pm.

Following the hurricanes of 1995, a major redevelopment of the waterfront at Christiansted was launched. The **King's Alley Complex** (☎ **809/778-8135**) opened as a pink-sided compound, filled with the densest concentration of shopping options on St. Croix. You might want to drop in—at least for some window shopping.

Caribbean Clothing Co. 41 Queen Cross St. ☎ **809/773-5012.**

Hip sports clothing by top-name U.S. designers in all the latest styles are sold at this outlet. They carry Calvin Klein, Guess?, Polo, and Dockers, among others. You get not only casual wear but some evening clothes for women. They also sell a small stock of shoes for both men and women, along with a good selection of jewelry, belts, scarves, and purses.

Colombian Emeralds. 43 Queen Cross St. ☎ **809/773-1928.**

Along with stunning emeralds, called "the rarest gemstone in the world," rubies and diamonds also dazzle here. The staff will show you the large range of 14-karat-gold jewelry, along with the best buys in watches, including Seiko quartz. Even though fake jewelry is peddled throughout the Caribbean, Colombian Emeralds is the genuine thing.

Crucian Gold. 57A Company St. ☎ **809/773-5241.**

In this small West Indian cottage, you encounter the unique gold creations of island-born Brian Bishop. He designs all the gold creations himself, although cheaper versions of his work come in sterling silver. The most popular item is the Crucian bracelet, which contains a "True Lovers' Knot" in its design. The outlet also sells hand-tied knots (bound in gold wire), rings, pendants, and earrings.

1870 Townhouse Shoppes. 52 King St. ☎ **809/778-8880.**

One of the best collections of reasonably priced beachwear is sold here, along with an extensive collection of casual clothing for women. Much of the merchandise is a mixed bag, ranging from African carved bowls and figures to Chinese pottery, even gold and silver jewelry (not local) for women.

Elegant Illusions Copy Jewelry. 55 King St. ☎ **809/773-2727.**

This branch of a hugely successful chain based in California sells convincing fake jewelry. The lookalikes range in price from $9, and include credible copies of the baroque and antique jewelry your great-grandmother might have worn.

Folk Art Traders. 1B Queen Cross St. ☎ **809/773-1900.**

Since 1985 the operators of this store have traveled throughout the Caribbean ("in the bush") to acquire a unique collection of local art and folk-art treasures—not only carnival masks, pottery, ceramics, and original paintings, but also hand-wrought jewelry. The wide-ranging assortment includes batiks from Barbados and high-quality iron sculpture from Haiti. There's nothing else like it in the Virgin Islands.

From the Gecko. 1233 Queen Cross St. ☎ **809/778-9433.**

This boutique will get you in a South Pacific mood, with its collection of sarongs and batiks. Many fashions for this boutique were created by local artists in hand-dyed silk and hand-painted cotton. The shop also carries a selection of gold and silver jewelry, also created by local artisans, as well as leather bags and others fashioned from hand-carved coconuts and calabash gourds.

Gone Tropical. 55 Company St. ☎ **809/773-4696.**

About 60% of the merchandise in this unique shop is made in Indonesia (usually Bali). Prices of new, semiantique, or antique sofas, beds, chests, tables, mirrors, and decorative carvings are the same (and sometimes less) than equivalent furniture you might have bought new at more conventional furniture stores. The store also sells worthy art objects and furniture (which can be shipped to wherever you want) ranging upward in price from $5. Gone tropical also sells jewelry, batiks, candles, and baskets.

Green Papaya. Caravelle Arcade no. 15, 38 Strand St. ☎ **809/773-8848.**

For home interiors, the shopkeepers here have assembled a unique collection of accessories, including picture frames, lighting fixtures, and baskets. There are two rooms, one displaying these wares, another dedicated to their new interior design service, with fabrics on display.

Harborside Market & Spirits. 59 King's Wharf. ☎ **809/773-8899.**

Here you'll find a great selection of duty-free liquors, wine, and beer. The shop is also conveniently located.

Java Wraps. In the Pan Am Pavilion, Strand St. ☎ **809/773-3770.**

Known for resortwear for women, men, and children, this shop is a kaleidoscope of colors and prints. You expect Dorothy Lamour, star of all those "Road" pictures, to appear at any minute. In fact, today's Dorothy (actually a local salesperson) demonstrates how to wrap and tie beach pareos and sarongs. Men's shirts are a collection of tropical and ethnic prints, and there's also a children's selection. The outlet also carries Javanese and Balinese art and antiquities.

Larimar. The Boardwalk / King's Walk. ☎ **809/692-9000.**

Everything sold in this shop is produced by the largest manufacturer of gold settings for larimar in the world. Discovered in the 1970s, larimar is a pale-blue pectolyte prized for its sky-blue color. It's produced from mines in only one mountain in the world, which is located in the southwestern edge of the Dominican Republic, near the Haitian border. Objects range from $25. Although other shops sell the stone in imaginative settings, this emporium has the widest selection.

Little Switzerland. 1108 King St. ☎ **809/773-1976.**

This place, with branches throughout the Caribbean, is the best source on the island for crystal, figurines, watches, china, perfume, flatware, and lots of fine jewelry. It specializes in all the big names, such as Paloma Picasso leather goods. For luxuries like a Rolex watch, an Omega, or heirloom crystal such as Lalique, Swarovski, and Baccarat, this is the place. Some items—at least a few—are said to sell for up to 30% less than on the U.S. mainland, but don't take anyone's word for that unless you've checked prices carefully.

Many Hands. In the Pan Am Pavilion, Strand St. ☎ **809/773-1990.**

Many Hands sells Virgin Islands handcrafts exclusively. The merchandise includes West Indian spices and teas, shellwork, stained glass, hand-painted china, pottery, and handmade jewelry. The collection of local paintings is intriguing, as is the year-round "Christmas tree."

Only in Paradise. 5 Company St. ☎ **809/773-0331.**

It's the largest store of its kind in Christiansted, filled with merchandise you might want as mementoes. The inventory includes cunningly crafted boxes, jewelry, and accessories for fashionable evenings out on the town. The outlet also sells a curious mix of leather products and lingerie. The taste is bourgeois and plush. Don't expect attentive service, however; the staff is inexperienced.

The Royal Poinciana. 1111 Strand St. ☎ **809/773-9892.**

This is the most interesting gift shop on St. Croix. In what looks like an antique apothecary, you'll find such Caribbean-inspired items as hot sauces ("fire water"), seasoning blends for gumbos, island herbal teas, Antillean coffees, and a scented array of soaps, toiletries, lotions, and shampoos. There's also a selection of museum-reproduction greeting cards and calendars. Also featured are educational but fun gifts for children.

St. Croix Perfume Center. 53 King St. ☎ **800/225-7031** or 809/773-7604.

Here you'll find the largest duty-free assortment of men's and women's fragrances on St. Croix, usually at 30% below U.S. mainland prices. For a minimum charge of $5 this store will ship perfumes anywhere in the world. The center recently added Iman cosmetics for women of color.

Sonya Ltd. 1 Company St. ☎ **809/778-8605.**

Sonya Hough is the matriarch of a cult following of local residents who wouldn't leave home without wearing one of her bracelets. She's most famous for her sterling-silver or gold (from 14- to 24-karat) interpretations of the C-clasp bracelet. Locals communicate discreet messages by how it's worn: If the cup of the "C" is turned toward your heart, it means you're emotionally committed. If the cup of the "C" is turned outward, it means you're available to whomever strikes your fancy. Prices range from $20 to $2,500. She also sells rings, earrings, and necklaces.

Urban Threadz / Tribal Threadz. 52C Company St. ☎ **809/773-2883.**

It's the most comprehensive clothing store in Christiansted's historic core, with a two-story, big-city scale and appeal that's different from the tropical-boutique aura of nearby T-shirt shops. It's the store where island residents prefer to shop, because of the clothing's hip, urban styles. Garments for men are on the street level, women's garments are upstairs, and the inventory includes everything from Bermuda shorts to lightweight summer blazers and men's suits. It carries Calvin Klein, Nautica, and Oakley, among others.

Violette Boutique. In the Caravelle Arcade, 38 Strand St. ☎ **809/773-2148.**

A small department store with many boutique areas carrying lines known worldwide, Violette includes many exclusive fragrances and hard-to-find toiletry items. It also has the latest in Cartier, Fendi, Pequignet, and Gucci. A wide selection of famous cosmetic names is featured, and Fendi has its own area for bags and accessories. A selection of gifts for children is also carried. Many famous brand names found here are located nowhere else on the island, but are definitely found elsewhere in the Caribbean.

Woolworth's. In the Sunny Isle Shopping Center, Centerline Rd. ☎ **809/778-5466.**

Although primarily a department store, this retail outlet contains the island's largest supply of duty-free liquor. Cruzan rum is in plentiful supply, along with a vast array of other brand-name liquors and liqueurs.

AROUND THE ISLAND

Land of Oz. King and Market sts., Frederiksted. ☎ **809/772-3003.**

This is the most enchanting store for children in the Virgin Islands. Variety is the keynote of this establishment, with emphasis on unusual items from around the world. That could mean games for both adults and children, ranging from chess to African wari. Puzzles, kites, education games, and various kits are sold—a whole store filled with neat stuff.

St. Croix Leap. Mahogany Rd., Rte. 76. ☎ **809/772-0421.**

On your tour of the island, especially if you're on western St. Croix near Frederiksted, stop off at St. Croix Leap for an offbeat adventure. In this open-air shop you can see stacks of rare and beautiful woods being fashioned into tasteful objects. It's a St. Croix Life and Environmental Arts Project, dedicated to the natural environment through manual work, conservation, and self-development. The end result is a fine collection of Cruzan mahogany serving boards, tables, wall hangings, and clocks. Sections of unusual pieces are crafted into functional objects that are a form of art.

St. Croix Leap is 15 miles from Christiansted, 2 miles up Mahogany Road from the beach north of Frederiksted. Large mahogany signs and sculptures flank the driveway. Visitors should bear to the right to reach the woodworking area and gift shop. The site is open daily from 7am to 5:30pm. For inquiries, write to Leap, P.O. Box 245, Frederiksted, USVI 00841-0245.

Whim Museum Store. In the Estate Whim Plantation Museum, east of Frederiksted on Centerline Rd. ☎ **809/772-0598.**

Offering a good selection of gifts and appealing to a wide age spectrum, this store has many imported items, but also many that are Cruzan made. Some were personally made for the store. And if you buy something, it all goes to a worthy cause: the upkeep of the museum and the grounds.

ST. CROIX AFTER DARK

St. Croix doesn't have the nightlife of St. Thomas, so to find the action you might have to hotel- or bar-hop or consult *St. Croix This Week.*

Try to catch a performance of the **Quadrille Dancers,** the cultural treat of St. Croix. Their dances are little changed since plantation days; the women wear long dresses, white gloves, and turbans, and the men are attired in flamboyant shirts, sashes, and tight black trousers. When you've learned their steps, you're invited to join the dancers on the floor. Ask at your hotel if and where they are performing.

THE PERFORMING ARTS

Island Center. Sunny Isle. ☎ **809/778-5272.** Tickets $5–$25.

This 1,100-seat amphitheater, half a mile north of Sunny Isle, continues to attract big-name entertainers to St. Croix. Its program is widely varied, ranging from jazz, nostalgia, and musical revues to Broadway plays. Consult *St. Croix This Week* or call the center to see what's being presented. The Caribbean Community Theatre and Courtyard Players perform regularly. Call for performance times.

THE CLUB & MUSIC SCENE

✪ **Blue Moon.** 17 Strand St. ☎ **809/772-2222.** No cover.

The hottest spot in Christiansted on Thursday and Friday is this little dive, which is also a good bistro. On Thursday pianist Bobby Page (the Bobby Short of St. Croix) takes over the keys, and on Friday a five-piece ensemble entertains. There's no cover. Stick around to try some of the food from the eclectic menu that ranges from the Bayou Country to Asia.

Hondo's Nightclub. 53 King St. ☎ **809/773-5855.** Cover $5.

Simply called "Hondo's" by the regulars, this local dive is a hot spot with mostly re-corded music. But they occasionally heat up with live reggae, calypso, Latino, and international. It's always party night here, and locals usually outnumber the tourists. Exercise caution going through the streets late at night to reach this joint.

The Marina Bar. In the King's Alley Hotel, King's Alley / The Waterfront. ☎ **809/773-0103.**

It occupies a panoramic position on the waterfront, on a shaded terrace overlooking the deep-blue sea and Protestant Cay. Although the place remains open throughout the day, the most appealing activities begin here around 5:30pm (right after the last seaplane departs for St. Thomas from a position nearby) and continues energetically until 8:30pm. Sunset-colored cocktails made with rum, mangos, bananas, papaya, and grenadine are the libations of choice. You can stave off hunger pangs with burgers, sandwiches, and West Indian–style platters. The bar has live entertainment most nights, usually steel bands. On Monday you can bet on crab races.

Mt. Pellier Hut Domino Club. Montpellier. ☎ **809/772-9914.**

Unique on the island, this club came into being as a battered snack shack established to serve players of a never-ending domino game. Gradually it grew into a drinking and entertainment center, although the game is still going strong. Today the bar offers a beer-drinking pig (Miss Piggy), and has a one-man band, Piro, who plays on Sunday. The bartender will also serve you a lethal rum-based Mamma Wanna.

The Terrace Lounge. In the Buccaneer, Rte. 82, Estate Shoys. ☎ **809/773-2100.** Cover $5.

Every night this lounge off the main dining room of one of St. Croix's most upscale hotels welcomes some of the Caribbean's finest entertainers, often including a full band.

The Wreck Bar. 5-AB Hospital St., Christiansted. ☎ **809/773-6092.**

The margaritas are "absolutely habit-forming," and the decor at this hole-in-the-wall is inspired directly by *Gilligan's Island,* with a retractable awning that extends over the open-air dance floor whenever it rains, and an indoor-outdoor space full of bamboo and thatch. The place has a sense of irreverent fun, especially when it offers live reggae.

A SIDE TRIP TO BUCK ISLAND: UNSPOILED NATURE & WORLD-CLASS SNORKELING

The crystal-clear water and the white coral sand of Buck Island, a satellite of St. Croix, are legendary. Slithering through its undergrowth in days of yore, you'd likely have run into Morgan, LaFitte, Blackbeard, or even Captain Kidd. Now the National Park Service has marked an underwater snorkeling trail. The park covers about 850 acres, including the land area, which has a sandy beach with picnic tables set out and pits for having your own barbecues, as well as rest rooms and a small changing room. There are two major underwater trails for snorkeling on the reef, plus many other labyrinths and grottoes for more serious divers. You can also take a hiking trail through the tropical vegetation that covers the island.

Only a third of a mile wide and a mile long, Buck Island lies only 1 1/2 miles off the northeastern coast of St. Croix. A barrier reef shelters many reef fish, including queen angelfish and the smooth trunkfish. The attempt to return the presently uninhabited Buck Island to nature has been successful—even the endangered brown pelicans are producing young here.

Small boats run between St. Croix and Buck Island. Snorkeling equipment is furnished. You head out in the morning, and nearly all charters allow 1 1/2 hours of snorkeling and swimming.

You can have a memorable ramble through sun-flooded and shallow waters off the rocky coastline. A couple of warnings, though: Bring protection from the sun's sometimes-merciless rays. And even more important, don't rush to touch every plant you see. The island's western edge has groves of poisonous machineel trees, whose leaves, bark, and fruit cause extreme irritation if they come into contact with human skin.

Circumnavigating the island on foot will take about 2 hours. Buck Island's trails meander from several points along its coastline to its sun-flooded summit, affording views over nearby St. Croix.

But the greatest attraction of Buck Island is its **underwater snorkeling trail,** which rings part of the island. With a face mask, swim fins, and a snorkel, you'll be treated to some of the most panoramic underwater views in the Caribbean. Plan on spending at least two-thirds of a day at this extremely famous ecological site.

Mile Mark Watersports, in the King Christian Hotel, 59 King's Wharf, Christiansted (☎ **809/773-2628**), has twice-daily tours of Buck Island. They offer two ways to reach the reefs. One is a half-day tour aboard a glass-bottom boat departing from the King Christian Hotel. Tours are given daily from 9:30am to 1pm and 1:30 to 5pm, and cost $35 per person; all snorkeling equipment is included. A more romantic journey is aboard one of the company's wind-powered sailboats, which, for $45 per person, offers the sea breezes and the thrill of wind power to reach the reef. A full-day tour, offered daily from 10am to 4pm on the company's 40-foot catamaran, can take up to 20 participants to Buck Island's reefs. Included in the tour are a West Indian barbecue picnic on the isolated sands of Buck Island's beaches and plenty of opportunities for snorkeling. The full-day tour costs $60.

Captain Heinz (☎ **809/773-3161** or 809/773-4041) is an Austrian-born skipper with some 22 years or more of sailing experience. His trimaran, *Teroro II,* leaves Green Cay Marina "H" Dock at 9am and 2pm, never filled with more than 24 passengers. The snorkeling trip costs $45 in the morning or $40 in the afternoon. All gear and safety equipment are provided. The captain is not only a skilled sailor but is also a considerate host. He will even take you around the outer reef, which the other guides do not, for an unforgettable underwater experience.

The British Virgin Islands 7

With their small bays and hidden coves, the British Virgin Islands are among the world's loveliest cruising grounds. Strung over the northeastern corner of the Caribbean, about 60 miles east of Puerto Rico, are some 40 islands, though that's including some small uninhabited cays or spits of land. Only a trio of the British Virgins are of any significant size: Virgin Gorda (the "Fat Virgin"), Tortola ("dove of peace"), and Jost Van Dyke. Other islands have such names as Fallen Jerusalem and Ginger. Norman Island is said to have been the inspiration for Robert Louis Stevenson's *Treasure Island*. On Deadman Bay, a rocky cay, Blackbeard marooned 15 pirates and a bottle of rum, which gave rise to the ditty.

There are predictions that mass tourism is on the way, but so far the British Virgins are still a paradise for escapists. According to a report we once read, the British Home Office listed them as "the least important place in the British Empire."

The good news for budget travelers is that you'll turn up any number of moderately priced or inexpensive hotels and restaurants here. Many of these places have recently opened, so in the pages that follow, we'll introduce you to hotels, inns, guest houses, restaurants, and taverns that, in many cases, are making their debut in any guidebook. You'll also find here some of the best camping grounds in the Caribbean, although those on St. John are still better.

GETTING THERE

BY PLANE There are no direct flights from New York to the British Virgin Islands, but you can make good connections from San Juan and St. Thomas to Beef Island/Tortola. (See chapter 5 on Puerto Rico and chapter 6 on the U.S. Virgin Islands for information on transportation to these islands.)

Your best bet to reach Beef Island/Tortola is to take **American Eagle** (☎ 800/433-7300 in the U.S.), which is viewed as the most reliable airline in the Caribbean and operates at least four daily trips from San Juan to Beef Island/Tortola.

Another choice, if you're on one of Tortola's neighboring islands, is the less reliable **Leeward Islands Air Transport (LIAT)** (☎ 284/462-0701). This Caribbean carrier flies to Tortola from St. Kitts, Antigua, St. Maarten, St. Thomas, and San Juan, in small planes. Reservations are made through travel agents or through the larger U.S.–based airlines that connect with LIAT hubs. The flying time to Beef Island/Tortola from San Juan is 35 minutes; from St. Thomas, 25 minutes; and from the most distant of the LIAT hubs (Antigua), 90 minutes, including stops on St. Kitts and one other island.

Beef Island, the site of the main airport for passengers arriving in the British Virgins, is connected to Tortola by the one-lane Queen Elizabeth Bridge.

BY FERRY You can travel from Charlotte Amalie (St. Thomas) by public ferry to West End and Road Town on Tortola, a 45-minute voyage along Drake's Channel through the islands. Services making this run include **Native Sun** (☎ 284/ 495-4617), **Smith's Ferry Service** (☎ 284/495-4495), and **Inter-Island Boat Services** (☎ 284/776-6597). The last specializes in a somewhat-obscure routing— that is, from St. John to West End on Tortola.

FAST FACTS: The British Virgin Islands

Bank Hours Banks are normally open Monday to Thursday from 9am to 2:30pm and on Friday from 9am to 2:30pm and 4:30 to 6pm.

Currency The **U.S. dollar** is the legal currency, much to the surprise of arriving Britishers who find no one willing to accept their pounds.

Documents U.S. and Canadian citizens need produce only an authenticated birth certificate or a voter registration card to enter the British Virgin Islands for a stay of up to 6 months, but they must possess return or ongoing tickets and show evidence of adequate means of support and prearranged accommodations during their stay. British citizens need a passport.

Electricity Your U.S.–made appliances can be used here, as the electricity is 110 volts AC, 60 cycles.

Information For more information on the British Virgin Islands before you leave home, contact the **British Virgin Islands Tourist Board** (☎ 800/835-8530 in the U.S. and Canada), 370 Lexington Ave., Suite 1605, New York, NY 10017 (☎ 212/696-0400 or 212/949-8254). On the West Coast, contact the B.V.I. Tourist Board, 1804 Union St., San Francisco, CA 94123 (☎ 415/775-0344; fax 415/775-2554). In the United Kingdom, contact the B.V.I. Tourist Board, 110 St. Martin's Lane, London, WC2N 4DY (☎ 0171/240-4259).

Laws Unlike some parts of the Caribbean, nudity is an offense punishable by law in the B.V.I. Drugs, their use or sale, are also strictly prohibited.

Medical Care Thirteen doctors practice on Tortola; **Peebles Hospital,** Porter Road, Road Town (☎ 284/494-3497), has X-ray and laboratory facilities. One doctor practices on Virgin Gorda. If you need them, your hotel will put you in touch with the islands' medical staff.

Safety Crime is rare here: In fact, the B.V.I. is one of the safest places in the Caribbean. But crime does exist, and you should take all the usual precautions you would anywhere. Don't leave items unattended on the beach.

Taxes A government tax of 7% is imposed on all hotel rooms. There's no sales tax. An $8 departure tax is collected from everyone leaving by air and $5 for those departing by sea.

Telephone Each phone number in the islands begins with 49. However, when you're here, omit the 49 to make local calls.

Time The islands operate on Atlantic standard time year-round. In the peak winter season, when it's 6am in the British Virgins, it's only 5am in Florida. However,

The British Virgin Islands

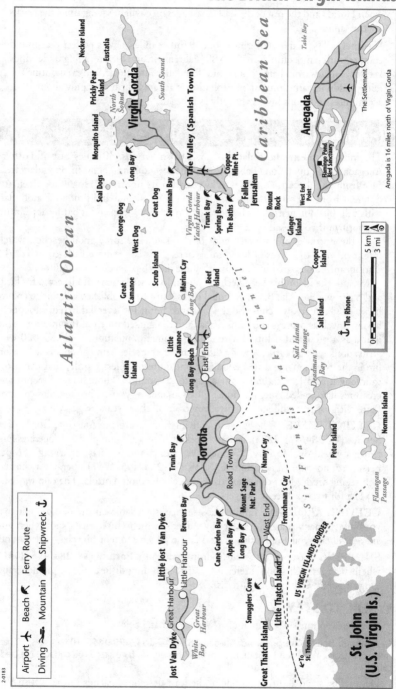

Airport ✈ | Beach 🏖 | Ferry Route - - -
Diving 🤿 | Mountain 🔺 | Shipwreck ⚓

Atlantic Ocean

Caribbean Sea

Necker Island
Eustatia
Prickly Pear Island
Mosquito Island
South Sound
North Sound
Virgin Gorda
Seal Dogs
Long Bay
The Valley (Spanish Town)
George Dog
West Dog
Great Dog
Savannah Bay
Copper Mine Pt.
Virgin Gorda Yacht Harbour
Trunk Bay
Spring Bay
The Baths
Fallen Jerusalem
Round Rock

Scrub Island
Great Camanoe
Marina Cay
Beef Island
Long Bay
Ginger Island

Guana Island
Little Camanoe
East End
Long Bay Beach
Cooper Island
Salt Island
⚓ The Rhone

Drake Channel
Salt Island Passage
Deadman's Bay
Sir Francis

Tortola
Trunk Bay
Road Town
Nanny Cay
Frenchman's Cay
West End
Mount Sage Nat. Park
Brewers Bay
Cane Garden Bay
Apple Bay
Long Bay
Smugglers Cove

Peter Island
Norman Island
Flanagan Passage

Little Jost Van Dyke
Little Harbour
Great Harbour
Jost Van Dyke
White Bay
Great Harbour
Little Thatch Island
Great Thatch Island

US VIRGIN ISLANDS BORDER
←To St. Thomas
St. John (U.S. Virgin Is.)

N
5 km
3 mi
0

Anegada
Table Bay
The Settlement
Flamingo Pond Bird Sanctuary
West End Point
Anegada is 16 miles north of Virgin Gorda

2-0183

when Florida and the rest of the East Coast goes on daylight saving time, the clocks are the same.

Weather   The islands, covering about 59 square miles, have a perfect year-round climate, with temperatures of 75° to 85° Fahrenheit, and the prevailing trade winds keep the islands from being too humid. Rainfall is infrequent, and even during the rainy season in early autumn, precipitation is generally heavy for only about 10 or 15 minutes and stops just as abruptly as it began.

1 Anegada

The most northerly and isolated of the British Virgins, 30 miles east of Tortola, Anegada has a population of about 250, none of whom has found the legendary treasure from the more than 500 wrecks lying off its notorious Horseshoe Reef. It's different from the other British Virgins in that it's a coral-and-limestone atoll, flat, with a 2,500-foot airstrip. Its highest point reaches 28 feet, and it hardly appears on the horizon if you're sailing to it.

At the northern and western ends of the island are some good beaches, which might be your only reason for coming here. This is a remote little corner of the Caribbean: Be prepared to put up with some hardships, such as mosquitoes.

Most of the island has been declared off-limits to settlement and reserved for birds and other wildlife. The B.V.I. National Parks Trust has established a flamingo colony in a bird sanctuary, which is also the protected home for several different varieties of heron as well as ospreys and terns. It has also designated much of the interior of the island as a preserved habitat for Anegada's animal population of some 2,000 wild goats, donkeys, and cattle. Among the endangered species being given a new lease on life is the rock iguana, a fierce-looking but quite-harmless reptile, that can grow to a length of 5 feet and a weight of up to 20 pounds. Though rarely seen, these creatures have called Anegada home for thousands of years. The environment they share with other wildlife has hardly changed in all those years.

GETTING THERE   The only carrier flying from Tortola to Anegada, **Gorda Aero Service** (☎ **284/495-2271**), uses six- to eight-passenger prop planes. It operates four times a week, on Monday, Wednesday, Friday, and Sunday, charging $56 per person round-trip. In addition, **Fly BVI** (☎ **284/495-1747**) operates a charter/sightseeing service between Anegada and Beef Island off Tortola. The one-way cost is $125 for two to three passengers.

GETTING AROUND   Limited taxi service is available on the island—not that you'll have many places to go. **Tony's Taxis,** which you'll easily spot when you arrive, will take you around the island. It's also possible to rent **bicycles**—ask around.

SHOPPING   You might want to drop in at **Pat's Pottery** (☎ **284/495-8031**), where islanders sell some interesting crafts, including dishes, plates, pitchers, and mugs in whimsical folk-art patterns.

WHERE TO STAY

Also see Neptune's Treasure under "Where to Eat," below.

✪ **Anegada Beach Campground.** Anegada, B.V.I. ☎ **284/495-9466.** 10 tent sites, 10 bare sites, 2 cottages. Year-round, $36 tent for two; $7 per person bare site; $100 cottage. No credit cards.

Despite its isolated setting on one of the least developed islands in the British Virgins, this campground boasts amenities that are usually not available at campgrounds on other, better-accessorized islands such as Tortola. It lies near waters with many snorkeling options, at the edge of about a dozen miles of secluded beachfront. For those who enjoy bare-boned living in a natural setting, this campsite contains a woodsy but relatively elaborate restaurant (which serves dinners priced at $14 to $30 each), access to cookout areas for budgeteers who want to barbecue, flush toilets, and outdoor showers whose privacy is assured by artfully woven palm fronds. For tent sites, the management provides a sponge-foam mattress, but campers usually bring their own pillows. The campsite also contains two breezy beach cottages for rent, equipped with a private kitchenette.

WHERE TO EAT

Neptune's Treasure. Between Pomato and Saltheap points, Anegada, B.V.I. ☎ **284/495-9439** or VHF Channel 16 or 68. Reservations not necessary. Breakfast from $7; sandwiches from $4; fixed-price meals $12–$30. AE, MC, V. Daily 8am–10pm. INTERNATIONAL.

Set near its own 24-slip marina, near the southern tip of the island in the same cluster of buildings that includes the more high-priced Anegada Reef Hotel, this raffishly appealing bar and restaurant is known to off-island yacht owners who make it a point to mingle with local residents. Dining is in a spacious indoor area whose focal point is a bar and lots of nautical memorabilia. The drink of choice is a Pink Whopee, composed of fruit juices and rum. The Soares family and their staff serve platters of swordfish, lobster, fish fingers, chicken, steaks, and ribs; dispense information about local snorkeling sites; and generally maintain order and something approaching a (low-key) party atmosphere.

They also maintain four simple bedrooms and about four tents for anyone looking for super-low-cost lodgings. Depending on the season, rooms with private bath rent for $45 to $55 single and $70 to $85 double. Tents share the plumbing facilities of the restaurant and go for $15 a night for one occupant, $25 a night for two. Continental breakfast is included in the rates, and discounts are offered for stays of a week or more.

2 Jost Van Dyke

This rugged island off the west side of Tortola was probably named for a Dutch settler. In the 1700s a Quaker colony settled here to develop sugarcane plantations. One of the colonists, William Thornton, won a worldwide competition to design the U.S. Capitol in Washington, D.C. Smaller islands surround the place, including Little Jost Van Dyke, the birthplace of Dr. John Lettsome, founder of the London Medical Society.

About 130 people live on the 4 square miles of this mountainous island. On the south shore, White Bay and Great Harbour are good beaches. While there are only a handful of places to stay, there are several dining choices, as it's a popular stopping-over point not only for the yachting set, but also for many cruise ships, including Club Med, Cunard, and often all-gay cruises. So you'll only experience the peace and tranquillity of yesteryear when the cruise ships aren't here.

GETTING THERE   Take the ferry from either St. Thomas or Tortola. (Be warned that departure times can vary widely throughout the year, and at times don't adhere very closely to the printed timetables.) Ferries from St. Thomas depart from Red Hook 3 days a week (Friday, Saturday, and Sunday) about twice a day. More convenient (and more frequent) are the daily ferryboat shuttles from Tortola's isolated West End. The latter departs three times a day on the 25-minute trip, and costs

$8 each way, $15 round-trip. Call the **Jost Van Dyke Ferryboat service** (☎ **284/ 494-2997**) for information about departures from any of the above-mentioned points. If all else fails, carefully negotiate a transportation fee with one of the handful of privately operated water taxis.

WHERE TO STAY

The ✪ **White Bay Campground** (☎ **284/495-9312** on Tortola) rents bare sites costing $15 for three people or equipped tent sites going for $35 for two. Facilities include showers and toilets.

Rudy's Mariner Inn. Great Harbour, Jost Van Dyke, B.V.I. ☎ **284/495-9282,** or 284/ 775-3558 in the U.S.V.I. 4 rms. Winter, $75–$125 single or double. Off-season, $55–$75 single or double. Rates include full board. DISC, MC, V.

About as simple as you'd like to get, this place is modesty itself, but it's got a lot of friends who like the hospitality of Rudy George, the owner. It's also one of the best places to eat on the island, with simply prepared and inexpensive food. (Conch always seems to be available, and a catch of the day is featured. Dinner is served daily.) Next to the boat dock at the west end of the harbor, this place is the social gathering point for much of the island: It's also a bar and nightclub of sorts and a ship's commissary. Some of the rooms open onto the water. There's snorkeling from the beach, and fishing and windsurfing can be arranged. It's a true West Indian inn.

WHERE TO EAT

Abe's by the Sea. Little Harbour. ☎ **284/495-9329.** Reservations recommended for groups of five or more. Dinner $12–$30; nightly barbecue $20. MC, V. Daily 8–11am, noon–3pm, and 7–10pm. Take the private motor launch or boat from Tortola; as you approach the east side of the harbor you'll see Abe's on your right. WEST INDIAN.

In this local bar and restaurant, sailors are satisfied with a menu of fish, lobster, conch, and chicken. Prices are low too, and it's money well spent, especially when a fungi band plays for dancing. For the price of the main course, you get peas and rice, coleslaw, plus dessert. On Wednesday night in season Abe's has a festive pig roast.

✪ **Foxy's Tamarind Bar.** Great Harbour. ☎ **284/495-9258.** Reservations recommended. Main courses $12–$35; lunch from $6. AE, MC, V. Daily 9am "until." WEST INDIAN.

Arguably the most famous bar in the B.V.I., this mecca of yachties and other boat people spins entirely around a sixth-generation Jost Van Dyke native, Philicianno ("Foxy") Callwood. He opened the place some three decades ago, and sailors and the world have been coming back ever since. A songwriter and entertainer, Foxy is part of the draw. He creates impromptu calypso—almost in the Jamaican tradition— around his guests. If you're singled out, he'll embarrass you, but all in good fun. He also plays the guitar and takes a profound interest in preserving the environment of his native island.

Thursday to Saturday a live band entertains. On other evenings, it's rock 'n' roll, perhaps reggae or soca. The food and drink aren't neglected either. Try his Painkiller Punch. During the day flying fish sandwiches, rôtis, and the usual burgers are served, but in the evening it might be freshly caught lobster, spicy steamed shrimp, or even grilled fish, depending on the catch of the day. No lunch is served on Saturday and Sunday.

✪ **Rudy's Mariner's Rendezvous.** Great Harbour. ☎ **284/495-9292.** Reservations required by 6:30pm. Dinner $12–$25. MC, V. Daily 7pm–midnight. WEST INDIAN.

Rudy's, at the western end of Great Harbour, serves good but basic West Indian food and plenty of it. The place looks and feels like a private home with a waterfront terrace for visiting diners. A welcoming drink awaits sailors and landlubbers alike, and the food that follows is simply prepared and inexpensive. Conch always seems to be available, and a catch of the day is featured.

3 Tortola

On the southern shore of this 24-square-mile island, **Road Town** is the capital of the British Virgin Islands. It's the seat of Government House and other administrative buildings, but it seems more like a village. The landfill at **Wickhams Cay,** a 70-acre town center development and marina in the harbor, has brought in a massive yacht-chartering business and has transformed the sleepy capital into more of a bustling center.

The entire southern coast of Tortola, including Road Town, is characterized by rugged mountain peaks. On the northern coast are white sandy beaches, banana trees, mangoes, and clusters of palms.

Beef Island, close to Tortola's eastern end, is the site of the main airport for passengers arriving in the British Virgins. The tiny island is connected to Tortola by the Queen Elizabeth Bridge, which the queen dedicated in 1966. The one-lane bridge spans the 300-foot channel that divides the little island from its bigger neighbor, Tortola. On the north shore of Beef Island is a good beach, Long Bay.

Because Tortola is the gateway to the British Virgin Islands, the information on how to get there is covered at the beginning of this chapter.

GETTING AROUND

BY BUS   Scato's Bus Service (☎ 284/494-2365) operates from the north end of the island to the west end, picking up passengers who hail it down. Fares for a trek across the island run $1 to $3.

BY TAXI   Taxis meet every arriving flight. Your hotel can also call a taxi. The fare from the Beef Island airport to Road Town is $15 for one to three passengers. A tour lasting 2¹/₂ hours costs $45 for one to three people. To call a taxi in Road Town, dial ☎ **284/494-2322;** on Beef Island, ☎ **284/495-2378.**

BY RENTAL CAR   We recommend that you reserve your rental car in advance, especially in winter. On Tortola, **Budget** is at 1 Wickhams Cay, Road Town (☎ **800/527-0700** in the U.S., or 284/494-5150). **Avis** maintains offices opposite the police headquarters in Road Town (☎ **800/331-2112** in the U.S., or 284/494-3322). **Hertz** (☎ **800/654-3001** in the U.S., or 284/495-4405) has offices outside Road Town, on the island's West End, near the ferryboat landing dock. Rental companies will usually deliver your car to your hotel. All three companies require a valid driver's license and a temporary B.V.I. driver's license, which the car-rental company can sell you; the cost is $10 and it's valid for 3 months.

Remember to *drive on the left.* Because the sinuous and narrow island roads are notoriously underilluminated, with few, if any, lines marking the shoulders, night-time driving can be disturbing. It's a good idea to rent a taxi to take you to that difficult-to-find restaurant or nightspot.

ESSENTIALS

To cash traveler's checks, try the **Bank of Nova Scotia,** Wickhams Cay (☎ **284/494-2526**), or **Barclays Bank,** Wickhams Cay (☎ **284/494-2171**), both near Road Town. The local **American Express** representative is Travel Plan Ltd., Waterfront Drive, Road Town (☎ **284/494-2347**). The **B.V.I. Tourist Board,** Road Town (☎**809/494-3134**), is near the ferry dock, just south of Wickhams Cay.

The best place for photographic needs is **Bolo's Brothers Department Store,** Wickhams Cay (☎ **284/494-2867**). It has some of the best supplies on the island (stock up here on film if you're going to one of the other islands) and features 1-hour developing service. If you need a drugstore, try **J. R. O'Neal Ltd.,** Main Street, Road Town (☎ **284/494-2292**); it's closed Sunday. Stock up here on any prescribed medicines or other supplies you'll need if you're planning visits to the other islands.

WHERE TO STAY

None of the island's hotels is as big, splashy, and all-encompassing as the hotels in the U.S. Virgin Islands, and that's just fine with many of the island's repeat clients. All rates are subject to a 10% service charge and a 7% government tax on the room.

DOUBLES FOR LESS THAN $60 (WINTER) / $55 (OFF-SEASON)

The Jolly Roger Inn. West End, Tortola, B.V.I. ☎ **284/495-4559.** Fax 284/495-4184. 5 rms, 2 with bath. Winter, $50 single without bath, $59 single with bath; $60 double without bath, $69 double with bath; $70 triple without bath, $79 triple with bath. Off-season, $40 single without bath, $49 single with bath; $45 double without bath, $60 double with bath; $50 triple without bath, $70 triple with bath. AE, MC, V. Closed Aug–Sept.

This small harborfront hotel is located at Soper's Hole, only 100 yards from the ferry dock for St. Thomas and St. John. The accommodations are clean and very simple. The small rooms have recently been refurbished with new draperies, bedspreads, and fresh paint, though only two have a private bath. In spite of the lack of air-conditioning, the rooms are breezy. The atmosphere is fun and casual and is definitely laid-back. The hotel can arrange sportfishing charters, sailing, or diving trips. For sailors the hotel also offers a dinghy dock, bag ice, and fax service. The beach at Smuggler's Cove is a 20- to 30-minute walk over the hill.

Sea View Hotel. P.O. Box 59, Road Town, Tortola, B.V.I. ☎ **284/494-2483.** Fax 284/494-4952. 24 rms, 5 suites, 5 efficiency apts. TV. Year-round, $44 single or double; $60–$65 suite for two; $100–$160 efficiency apt with kitchenette for four. MC, V.

Set at the western perimeter of Road Town, this concrete-sided modern guest house occupies a sloping site that affords a view over the boats bobbing at anchor in Road Town Harbour, but it's a 10-mile ride to the nearest beach. It's about as simple (and inexpensive) a hotel as you're likely to find, with few frills. The efficiency apartments contain a sitting room, a concrete-sided porch, ceiling fans, two bedrooms, and a modest kitchen. The smaller suites have air-conditioning, radios, and a minifridge. Only breakfast is served, but the bars, sandwich shops, and grocery stores of Road Town are a 5-minute walk away. Maid service and use of a small swimming pool are included in the price.

DOUBLES FOR LESS THAN $100 (WINTER) / $70 (OFF-SEASON)

Castle Maria. P.O. Box 206, Road Town, Tortola, B.V.I. ☎ **284/494-2553.** Fax 284/494-2111. 31 rms. A/C TV TEL. Winter, $70–$75 single; $85–$95 double; $96–$105 triple; $115–$130 quad. Off-season, $55–$60 single; $70–$75 double; $90–$99 triple; $100–$110 quad. MC, V.

The Hotel Castle Maria sits on a hill overlooking Road Town Harbour just a few minutes' walk from downtown. The lush, tropical garden out front is one of the best in the entire British Virgin Islands. An orchard produces avocados, mangoes, and bananas, which guests can enjoy. Some rooms have balconies, patios, and kitchenettes with a tropical decor. Facilities include a freshwater pool, a bar, and a restaurant that serves breakfast and dinner year-round. All the beaches are on the northern shores so guests must take a taxi to them.

✪ **Fort Burt Hotel.** P.O. Box 3380, Fort Burt, Road Town, Tortola, B.V.I. ☎ **284/494-2587.**
Fax 284/494-2002. 15 rms, 3 suites. A/C TV. Winter, $85–$110 single; $95–$120 double; $150–
$200 suite with kitchen, $275 suite with private pool but no kitchen. Off-season, $75–$100
single; $85–$110 double; $130–$180 suite with kitchen, $255 suite with private pool but no
kitchen. AE, MC, V.

Covered with flowering vines, Fort Burt rents rooms but devotes some of its energy
to its popular pub and restaurant (reviewed below). Built in 1960 on the ruins of a
17th-century Dutch fort, the rooms are set at a higher elevation than any others in
Road Town, offering views from their private terraces to the waterfront below.
Simple, sun-flooded, and cozy, they have a colonial charm and freewheeling conviviality. The suite rentals put this place in the expensive category, but the regular doubles
are spacious enough and have recently been refurbished. There's a pool on the
grounds, or in 3 minutes guests can walk to Garden Bay Beach or Smuggler's Cove
Beach.

Maria's by the Sea. P.O. Box 206, Road Town, Tortola, B.V.I. ☎ **284/494-2595.** Fax 284/
494-2420. 20 rms. A/C TV TEL. Winter, $85–$105 single; $95–$125 double. Off-season, $70–
$90 single; $85–$105 double. AE, MC, V.

This enterprise is centrally located in Road Town with a panoramic view of the
harbor, although it's a 10- to 15-minute drive to the nearest beach. The rooms are
decorated with rattan furniture and locally created murals. All rooms include a kitchenette, balcony, and private bath. The hotel has a freshwater pool, and water sports
can be arranged. This business also offers a bar and restaurant serving breakfast, lunch,
and dinner.

Rhymer's Beach Hotel. P.O. Box 570, Cane Garden Bay, Tortola, B.V.I. ☎ **284/495-4639.**
Fax 284/495-4820. 21 rms. A/C TV TEL. Winter, $75 single; $80 double. Off-season, $40 single;
$45 double. Extra person $10. AE, MC, V.

A low-slung pink-sided building, this comfortable, unpretentious miniresort sits next
to a white-sand beach on the island's north shore. The hotel's social center is a wide
ground-floor veranda where beach life and restaurant/bar orders merge into one
smoothly flowing ritual. The simple accommodations have ceiling fans and basic
kitchenettes. On the premises is a restaurant, a beauty salon, a general store/commis-
sary, and a boutique. Music lovers can head for the bar of the nearby Ole Works Inn,
where live music by island star Quito Rhymer is presented.

APARTMENT & VILLA RENTALS

Elizabeth Beach Resort. Elizabeth Beach, Tortola, B.V.I. ☎ **284/495-2877.** Fax 284/
495-2876. For reservations, contact Resorts Management, Inc., The Carriage House, 201¹/₂
E. 29th St., New York, NY 10016 (☎ **800/225-4255** or 212/696-4566). 3 villas, all with
kitchen. Winter, $250–$330 two-bedroom villa for up to seven; $320–$410 three-bedroom villa
for up to nine. Off-season, $170 two-bedroom villa for up to seven; $220 for three-bedroom
villa for up to nine. No credit cards.

Set on steeply sloping land a brisk walk above a sandy beach, at the base of a steeply
forested hillside, this is a collection of brown and white bungalow-style villas with
terra-cotta roofs and large verandas. On the isolated northern coast of Tortola, within
a 25-minute ride over winding roads from Road Town, it's a suitable refuge for escapists. Budgeteers appreciate the use of a Jeep (necessary for the rutted roads on this
side of Tortola), which comes with any rental at this complex. Up to nine occupants
can be lodged in any three-bedroom villa. In that case, the math works out to less
than $25 per person off-season.

Fort Recovery Estate. P.O. Box 239, Road Town, Tortola, B.V.I. ☎ **800/367-8455** or 284/
495-4354. Fax 284/495-4036. 17 units. A/C TV. Winter, $185–$295 villa for four; $486–$629

house for six to eight. Off-season, $125–$210 villa for four; $378–$429 house for six to eight. Extra person $25. Rates include continental breakfast. AE, MC, V.

Nestled in a small palm grove about 8 miles from Road Town, this enterprise faces the Sir Francis Drake Channel and offers villas and two houses. The property contains the remnants of an old Dutch Fort with the stone lookout tower still standing. The large house has an art gallery hallway and a large wraparound porch. The villas have living/dining areas, air-conditioned bedrooms, private baths, and sliding glass doors that open onto patios facing the ocean. Although there's no restaurant on the premises, guests can enjoy dinner selected from a well-chosen menu, with each course brought to the room by courteous waiters. The accommodations come with complimentary continental breakfasts; for guests staying 7 or more nights dinner is also complimentary, along with a boat trip. Baby-sitting (24-hour notice), yoga classes, and massages are available.

Icis Vacation Villas. P.O. Box 383, Road Town, Tortola, B.V.I. ☎ **284/494-6979.** Fax 284/494-6980. 3 efficiencies, 4 one-bedroom apts, 1 three-bedroom apt. A/C TV. Winter, $99–$115 efficiency; $159 one-bedroom apt; $260 three-bedroom apt. Off-season, $69–$79 efficiency; $89–$99 one-bedroom apt; $179 three-bedroom apt. Children 11 and under stay free in parents' unit. DC, DISC, MC, V.

Just yards from Brewers Bay with its good swimming, these apartment units, although rather basic, are spotlessly maintained. Doors open onto a patio or porch in three white-and-pink concrete buildings in a tropical setting with lots of foliage. The rooms are decorated in summery colors with both air-conditioning and ceiling fans. Room service is available upon request, and baby-sitting can be arranged. There are no room phones, but an on-site coin phone is available. The place is in a tranquil part of the island, and plans call for a swimming pool to be added.

Josiah Bay Cottages. P.O. Box 306, Road Town, Tortola, B.V.I. ☎ **284/494-6186.** Fax 284/494-2000. 7 units. Winter, $288 suite for two; $450 bungalow for two. Off-season, $216 suite for two; $336 bungalow for two. Rates are for 4 days and 3 nights. Extra person $30; children 11 and under $15 each. MC, V.

This well-designed cottage compound is located at the base of the steep and heavily forested hillsides of Tortola's northern coast, a 5-minute walk from the beach. Its focal point is a swimming pool ringed with terra-cotta tiles and parasols. Although there are a handful of substantial cottages on the premises, these are usually reserved for long-term visits by their absentee owners. Their presence, however, helps lend a welcome solidity to this resort, which charges relatively low rates for the red-roofed bungalows that are scattered throughout the garden. Each unit contains its own kitchenette; there's no restaurant or bar on site. Costs here are especially reasonable if shared by a family with young children in tow. Even in winter, in a bungalow shared by two, the per-person costs work out to less than $80 a day. Coupled with the ability to prepare your own meals, it's a decent bargain. Note that there's a 3-day minimum stay virtually all year.

Mongoose Apartments. P.O. Box 581, Cane Garden Bay, Tortola, B.V.I. ☎ **284/495-4421.** Fax 284/495-9721. 6 one-bedroom apts. Winter, $90 apt for one or two. Off-season, $70 apt for one or two. Extra person $20; children 12 and under $10. No credit cards.

Just minutes from the beach, in the Cane Garden Bay area, is one of the most reasonably priced apartment units on the island. All the apartments, although simply furnished, have a living room, kitchen and balcony, a twin sleeper couch in the living room, and ceiling fans. Two units have TV, although you'll have to rely on the office phone. The apartments are in a U-shaped two-story building. Some of the rooms open onto an ocean view. The good news is that the complex lies only 100 yards from the beach. There's no restaurant, but a number of eateries are close at hand. The owner Sandra Henley grows medicinal teas which guests are invited to try. Baby-sitting can be arranged.

Ronneville Cottages. P.O. Box 2652, Brewers Bay, Tortola, B.V.I. ☎ **809/494-3337.** 2 two-bedroom cottages, 1 three-bedroom/two-bath house. TV. Winter, $675 cottage per week; $725 house per week. Off-season, $425 cottage per week; $500 house per week. Extra person $25 year-round; children 2 and under stay free with parents. No credit cards.

If you'd like an inexpensive vacation for a week in the Brewers Bay area, this is a good choice, although the cottages are hardly romantic. They're designed for basic beach living; a beach bar serving burgers and the like is only a 5-minute walk away. The cottages are in white concrete structures on ground level, and everything is set in tropical foliage with lots of flowers. The units are clean and basic, with ceiling fans in the living rooms and standing fans in the bedrooms. Each unit has a porch or patio and TV. There's no pool, however, and no restaurant. But if you'd like some local cookery, the owner will prepare a dinner with sufficient notice.

CAMPING

✪ **Brewers Bay Campground.** Brewers Bay (P.O. Box 185), Road Town, Tortola, B.V.I. ☎ **284/494-3463.** 20 tents, 20 bare sites. Year-round, $35 tent for two; $8 bare site for two. No credit cards. A camp shuttle is sometimes available.

Most camping buffs appreciate this place, located 3 miles from Road Town, for its low costs and for its easy access to some of the best snorkeling off the coast of Tortola. Both tent and bare-site options are available, and both include access to cookout areas, showers with running water and flush toilets, and a simple beachfront bar selling sandwiches, hot dogs, and beer. Dinner can be provided with advance notice, and on Friday nights there's a communal fish fry, followed by a barbecue on Sunday night, each costing $8 per person. There's no on-site commissary, but shops in Road Town sell groceries and camping paraphernalia.

BEST OFF-SEASON BETS

Between mid-April and mid-December many hotels that might be out of your price range become more affordable. The best discounts are offered at the following properties:

The Moorings / Mariner Inn. Wickhams Cay (P.O. Box 139, Road Town), Tortola, B.V.I. ☎ **800/435-7289** in the U.S., or 284/494-2332. Fax 284/494-2226. 39 rms, 4 suites. A/C TEL. Winter, $170 double; $230 suite. Off-season, $95 double; $125 suite. Additional person $15 extra. AE, MC, V.

The Caribbean's only complete yachting resort is outfitted with at least 100 sailing yachts. Not surprisingly, the Mariner Inn, on the 8-acre resort, is a favorite with yachties. Each lanai-style hotel room has a kitchenette. When the winter boating crowd goes back to cooler waters in the north, summer discounts are available. That $155 single or $170 double is lowered to only $85 single and $95 double off-season.

Nanny Cay Resort & Marina. P.O. Box 281, Road Town, Tortola, B.V.I. ☎ **800/74-CHARMS** in the U.S., or 284/494-2512. Fax 284/494-0555. 42 studios. A/C TV TEL. Winter, $140–$255 studio for two. AE, MC, V.

On a 25-acre inlet adjoining a 180-slip marina, Nanny Cay lies 3 miles from the center of Road Town and 10 miles from the airport. All accommodations are studios with fully equipped kitchenettes. Standard studios have two double beds; deluxe studios are larger, with a sitting area and two queen-size beds. The units have ceiling fans along with private balconies opening onto a view of the water, marina, or gardens.

The hotel's Pegleg Landing Restaurant serves both lunch and dinner daily. In winter a single or double ranges from $140 to $255. However, off-season the simplest single or double goes for only $45, although you'd have to pay $195 for the more deluxe accommodations.

WORTH A SPLURGE

Ole Works Inn. P.O. Box 560, Cane Garden Bay, Tortola, B.V.I. ☎ **284/495-4837.** Fax 284/495-9618. 15 rms, 3 suites. A/C TEL. Winter, $100–$130 single; $140–$170 double; from $205 suite. Off-season, $50–$80 single; $60–$90 double; from $125 suite. Extra person $25; children 11 and under stay free in parents' room. Rates include breakfast. MC, V. Closed Sept.

Set inland from Cane Bay, this hotel occupies the historic premises of a 300-year-old sugar refinery. It's across the road from a white-sand beach known for its beauty, and has what might be one of the best musical venues on Tortola—the rustic indoor/outdoor restaurant/bar, Quito's Gazebo.

The accommodations are cramped but cozy, outfitted with angular furniture and pastel colors; many have water views. Each accommodation contains a small refrigerator and ceiling fan. The most romantic unit is the honeymoon suite in the venerable tower; it's larger than you'd expect. On the premises is a boutique-style art gallery showing watercolors by local artists and souvenirs, and a restaurant that serves West Indian/Caribbean cuisine as part of full meals priced at $15 to $25 per person for dinner.

The in-house bar is a magnet for lovers of modern calypso music, largely because it's supervised by the hotel owner Quito (Enriquito) Rhymer, who's the most famous living recording star ever produced on Tortola. Quito himself performs several times a week.

Sebastians on the Beach. Little Apple Bay (P.O. Box 441), West End, Tortola, B.V.I. ☎ **284/495-4212.** Fax 284/495-4466. 26 rms. Winter, $110 single; $120–$190 double. Off-season, $75–$140 single; $85–$150 double. Extra person $15; MAP $35 per person extra. AE, DISC, MC, V.

The hotel is located at Little Apple Bay, about a 15-minute drive from Road Town, on a long beach that offers some of the best surfing in the B.V.I. The rooms are housed in three buildings, with only one on the beach. All the floral-accented rooms come with rattan furniture and have small refrigerators and private baths, while six have air-conditioning, balconies, and porches. The restaurant overlooks the bay and offers an international menu. On Saturday and Sunday guests can enjoy live entertainment in the bar. The hotel features dive packages along with packages that include a MAP plan, a welcome cocktail, a dozen assorted postcards, a pictorial guide to the B.V.I., and a bottle of rum.

WHERE TO EAT

✪ Capriccio di Mare. Waterfront Dr., Road Town. ☎ **284/494-5369.** Reservations not accepted. Main courses $5–$12. No credit cards. Daily 8–10:30am and 11am–9pm. ITALIAN.

Small, casual, and laid-back, this local favorite was created by the owners of the upmarket Brandywine Bay restaurant in a moment of whimsy. It's the most authentic-looking Italian *caffè* in the Virgin Islands. When it opens for breakfast, many locals stop in for a refreshing Italian pastry along with a cup of cappuccino. You can come back for lunch or dinner. If it's evening, you might also order the mango Bellini, a variation of the famous cocktail served at Harry's Bar in Venice (which is made with fresh peaches). Begin with such appetizers as *tiapina* (flour tortillas with various toppings), and go on to such orders as fresh pastas with succulent sauces, the best pizza on the island, or even well-stuffed sandwiches. We prefer the pizza topped with freshly grilled eggplant. If you arrive on the right night, you might even be treated to lobster ravioli in a rosé sauce. Also try one of their freshly made salads: We go for the *insalata mista* with large, leafy greens and slices of fresh parmesan.

Flying Iguana. At the airport. ☎ **284/495-5277.** Main courses $12.50–$38; lunch $4–$12. MC, V. Daily 8:30am–10pm. WEST INDIAN.

Don't make a special trip here, but if you're in the vicinity this is a good luncheon spot. It also serves tasty dinners as well, most main courses costing $12 to $15, with large portions, a meal unto themselves. This open-air restaurant is painted in vivid Caribbean colors. At lunch order one of the iguana burgers (actually, made with beef), the conch chowder, or one of the spicy conch fritters, along with a selection of sandwiches and pasta. The kitchen shines brighter at dinner, with an array of steak and seafood dishes, filet mignon, and surf and turf. Puck, the chef and co-owner, will also prepare you his special duck.

Fort Burt Restaurant and Pub. Fort Burt, Road Town. ☎ **284/494-2587.** Reservations recommended for dinner. English breakfast $8.75; dinner platters $15–$25; lunch sandwiches and platters $5–$8.50. AE, MC, V. Daily 8–10am, noon–3pm, and 6–11pm. (Bar, daily 10am–midnight.) INTERNATIONAL.

This restaurant was built on rocks mortared together in the 17th century with lime and molasses by the Dutch and French. Lunches offer soups, salads, grilled fish, and sandwiches. Dinners are candlelit and more elaborate, with such dishes as fresh asparagus with aïoli sauce, conch fritters, shepherd's pie, pepper steak, and roast duck with orange-and-tarragon sauce. It's hardly the best food on the island, although quite passable. Chalk it up as a "local favorite."

Hungry Sailor Garden Café. Wickhams Cay II. ☎ **284/494-3885.** Reservations recommended. Main courses $10.50–$13.50. DC, MC, V. Mon–Fri 11:30am–2:30pm and 6:30–9pm, Sat–Sun 6:30–9pm. INTERNATIONAL.

Set amid a cluster of palm trees on the marina, this offshoot of the costlier Captain's Table offers patrons outdoor dining in an inviting atmosphere. For appetizers you can enjoy selections ranging from gazpacho to fried mozzarella to escargots. Also included is honey-dipped chicken, which is lightly coated with flour and deep-fried to a golden brown, then served with french fries on the side. For a lighter meal, you may want to try the Cajun chicken over a Caesar salad. For even more substantial appetites, the menu offers dolphin, served sautéed or grilled, along with grilled salmon and lobster. The cafe is not open for lunch, but the adjoining Captain's Table does offer lunch, costing $6 to $12.50. However, the Captain's Table becomes a bit pricey when it hauls out its dinner menu.

The Jolly Roger. West End. ☎ **284/495-4559.** Main courses $10.95–$18.50; pizzas from $10.25. AE, MC, V. Daily 7–10pm. Closed July–Aug. INTERNATIONAL/SEAFOOD.

The Jolly Roger is located close to the St. Thomas ferry dock and is a favorite watering hole for Tortola's resident yachties. The menu offerings range from burgers and signature pizzas to cracked conch and other island dishes such as rôti. Look for the seafood specials offered daily. The chef cooks island dishes with what he calls "an American twist." The house specialty is homemade key lime pie along with rum-fried banana. On Friday and Saturday nights guests can savor the Caribbean barbecue and on Friday they also can enjoy live music.

Marlene's. Wickhams Cay. ☎ **284/494-4634.** Pâtés $1.50–$2.50; main courses $6.50–$12; breakfast $2.50–$5. No credit cards. Mon–Sat 7:30am–6pm. WEST INDIAN.

This centrally located restaurant—really a take-out joint—is housed in a concrete structure. It provides casual dining with tropical overtones. Marlene's offers

West Indian pâtés—conch, swordfish, chicken, or beef wrapped in pastry dough, then baked or fried. Included among the local fare are rôtis and curries. If you're not in the mood for local creations, you can order baked chicken, steak, or seafood such as lobster and other shellfish. The desserts are made from scratch.

Midtown Restaurant. Main St., Road Town. ☎ **284/494-2764.** Main courses $6–$15. No credit cards. Mon–Sat 7am–10pm, Sun 7am–5pm. WEST INDIAN.

Set in the heart of Road Town, this hangout offers typical local fare such as curried chicken and mutton. The menu also includes soups ranging from conch to pea along with a boiled cow-foot soup for the more adventurous. Patrons may enjoy other fare including the stewed beef ribs, baked chicken, and a wide selection of fresh seafood, depending on the day's catch. Most dishes come with your choice of fungi, plantains, or Caribbean carrots.

✪ North Shore Shell Museum Bar & Restaurant. Main Rd., Carrot Bay. ☎ **284/495-4714.** Dinner $26; breakfast from $5; lunch $4.50–$10. No credit cards. Daily 7am–10pm. WEST INDIAN.

When Egberth and Mona Donovan, both chefs, got married, they naturally decided to open a restaurant to showcase their culinary talents. They have succeeded admirably, serving an authentic island cuisine. Mona learned from her mother, Mrs. Scatliffe, who is the most celebrated local chef in the B.V.I. On the ground floor of this two-story concrete house is a museum of sorts, mainly shells and stuff that washed up on the beach. You can skip it and head instead for the upstairs where good home-cookery awaits you.

If you're in the area for breakfast, by all means drop in to sample the pancakes. They're not your typical offerings, but made with coconut, guava, and mango, and they're delectable. At lunch you can sample typical island fare along with some spicy conch fritters. For dinner you can try what was good at the market that day. The best soursop daiquiri on the island will get you in the mood for the evening fare. Tuesday and Saturday are barbecue nights, with chicken, lobster, and ribs featured. After dining, patrons hang out for a hoedown, a music fest with such instruments as a ukulele, a washtub, or a gourd maraca.

Oliver's. Wickhams Cay I (at the traffic circle). ☎ **284/494-2177.** Main courses $10–$20; lunch $4–$11.95. AE, MC, V. Daily 8am–10pm. WEST INDIAN/CONTINENTAL.

If you're a foodie who likes to taste authentic flavor regardless of where you land, try this place. Its dishes have true island flavor and zest. It's better to stick to the local items and skip the so-called continental dishes. The walls of this West Indian–style restaurant are decorated with murals by local artists. On occasion someone will play light music on the baby grand. Many drop in for lunch to order the usual array of sandwiches, burgers, and salads. At night the menu is more elaborate. Try the grilled chicken with a tamarind sauce—it's a winner. Mahimahi, seafood combos (quite delectable), a stew of the day (often mutton or curried goat), and even such pricey dishes as filet mignon and lobster also tempt you.

Paradise Pub. Fort Burt Marina, Harbour Rd. ☎ **284/494-2608.** Reservations recommended. Main courses $8.50–$21. AE, MC, V. Mon–Sat 6am–10pm. INTERNATIONAL.

In a low-slung timbered building on a narrow strip of land between the coastal road and the southern edge of Road Town's harbor, this establishment has a grangelike interior and a rambling veranda built on piers over the water. Many of the island's sports teams celebrate here after their victories. The pub also attracts the island's "boat people." Available are more than 25 different kinds of beer. If you're here for a meal, you can order Bahamian fritters, Caesar or Greek salad, pasta, four kinds of steaks, and burgers. The chef also prepares a catch of the day, perhaps wahoo. Different nights of the week are devoted to theme dinners, including all-you-can-eat pasta night, prime rib night, even baby-back ribs night. Call to find out what the offerings are for the night of your visit. Happy hour with discounted drinks is 5 to 7pm Monday to Thursday and 11am to 7pm on Friday when hot wings and raw vegetable platters are offered.

✪ Pusser's Road Town Pub. Waterfront Dr. and Main St., Road Town. ☎ **284/494-3897.** Reservations recommended. Main courses $7–$20. AE, DISC, MC, V. Daily 10am–10pm. CARIBBEAN / ENGLISH PUB / MEXICAN.

Standing on the waterfront across from the ferry dock, Pusser's serves Caribbean fare, English pub grub, and good pizzas. This is not as fancy or as good as the Pusser's in the West End, but it's a lot more convenient and has faster service. The complete lunch and dinner menu includes English shepherd's pies and deli-style sandwiches. *Gourmet* magazine asked for the recipe for its chicken-and-asparagus pie. John Courage ale is on draft, but the drink to have here is the famous Pusser's Rum, the same blend of five West Indian rums that the Royal Navy has served to its men for more than 300 years. Thursday is nickel beer night.

There's also Pusser's Landing, in the West End, opening onto the water (☎ **284/ 495-4554**).

✪ Quito's Gazebo. Cane Garden Bay. ☎ **284/495-4837.** Main courses $12–$18; lunch platters, sandwiches, and salads $5–$10. AE, MC, V. Tues–Sun 11am–3pm and 6:30–9:30pm. (Bar, Tues–Sun 11am–midnight.) CONTINENTAL/WEST INDIAN.

Owned by Quito Rhymer, the island's most acclaimed musician, this is the most popular of the several restaurants located along the shoreline of Cane Bay. Quito himself performs after dinner several nights a week. Set directly on the sands of the beach, and designed like an enlarged gazebo, it serves frothy rum-based drinks (ask for the house version of a piña colada, or a Bushwacker made with four different kinds of rum). Lunch is served to a beach-loving crowd, and includes sandwiches, salads, and platters. Evening meals are more elaborate, and might feature conch or pumpkin fritters, mahimahi with a wine-butter sauce, a conch dinner with (Callwood) rum sauce, chicken rôti, and steamed local mutton served with a sauce of island tomatoes and pepper. Dishes have true island flavor and a lot of zest.

Rita's Restaurant. Round-A-Bout, Road Town. ☎ **284/494-6165.** Reservations not required. Breakfast $2.50–$8; lunch $10–$15. No credit cards. Mon–Sat 8am–5pm. WEST INDIAN/AMERICAN.

If you're looking for an inexpensive eatery with a touch of the island, then you may want to stop at Rita's for some local West Indian fare. The surroundings are simple, but the atmosphere is lively. Breakfast ranges from the standard American fare to local favorites such as fried fish or saltfish, which is chopped up with a variety of spices and sautéed in butter. Both are served with johnnycakes. The lunch menu includes pea soup, curried chicken, and stewed mutton. For those who want a taste of home, try the barbecued chicken and ribs, sandwiches, or that old standby, spaghetti and meatballs.

Rôti Palace. Abbot Hill, Road Town. ☎ **284/494-4196.** Main courses $6–$15. No credit cards. Mon–Sat 7am–9:30pm. INDIAN.

The best rôtis in the B.V.I. are served here—they're just as good as those in Port-of-Spain, Trinidad. These Indian-style turnovers are stuffed with such good things as potato and peas for vegetarians or curried chicken. Right on the old main street of the island's capital, this is primarily used as a luncheon stop, although it's also a good choice for an affordable dinner. The breakfast is standard, but the menu gets lively at lunch and dinner, with a wide selection of vegetables and local conch, along with lobster, beef, and chicken dishes, often spicy and tasty. Ginger beer or limeade, along with the usual juices and wines, might accompany your meal.

Scuttlebutt Bar and Grill. In the Prospect Reef Resort, Drake's Hwy. ☎ **284/494-3311.** Sandwiches, platters, and salads $4.50–$10.50. AE, MC, V. Daily 7am–1am. INTERNATIONAL/ CARIBBEAN.

This cafe's greatest asset is its location 1 mile west of the center of Road Town beside the smallest and most charming marina. Order your meal at the counter, then carry it to one of the picnic tables, which are sheltered from the sun but not from the breezes off the water. The simple setting here keeps prices down, and the food— especially breakfast—is plentiful and good. Specialties include beef crêpes and crabmeat salads, sandwiches, burgers, and a house drink that combines several kinds of rum into a lethal combination known as a Painkiller. The place is especially popular at breakfast, when eight different kinds of "rooster omelets" draw the yachters. Upstairs is a more expensive restaurant, Callaloo.

Spaghetti Junction. Waterfront Dr., Road Town. ☎ **284/494-4880.** Main courses $9.75– $23. AE, MC, V. Daily 6–11pm. Closed Sept–Oct. ITALIAN/SEAFOOD.

Boaters like this funky place. It's located near several marinas on the second floor of a blue-painted building designed to look like a poop deck. There's a nautical mural on the floor, and the gorilla in the toilet is a huge painting and a source of constant amusement. Although there's no formal entertainment, the bar remains open long after the food service has stopped, and there's occasional impromptu dancing late at night. The Italian dishes, although standard, are quite good, including the chicken or veal parmigiana. Beef marsala and several seafood items are also featured. We like the sun-dried tomatoes added to the Caesar salad—a nice touch.

The Tavern in the Town. Main St. (also entered from Waterfront Dr.), Road Town. ☎ **284/ 494-2790.** Main courses $14–$20; sandwiches and burgers $3.95–$7.75. No credit cards. Mon–Fri 11:30am–3pm and 5:30–9:30pm. (Bar, Mon–Fri 10:30am–closing; hours vary.) ENGLISH PUB.

Expatriates David and Jackie Cameron run this traditional English pub and beer garden in the center of Road Town. This is a warm and inviting place for either a drink, snack, or full meal. Be sure to check out the daily specials. Burgers are juicy quarter-pounders served on a toasted bun with fried onions and french fries, and you can also order from a selection of sandwiches. Appetizers range from a prawn cocktail to garlic mushrooms. The soup-of-the-day platter with a sandwich is a good value at $7.50. Main dishes are the traditional fish-and-chips, but you can also order honey-dipped chicken or fisherman's pie. You'll think you're back in Britain when you see "mushy" peas listed on the menu.

Virgin Queen. Fleming St., Road Town. ☎ **284/494-2310.** Reservations recommended. Main courses $7.50–$16.50; lunch $4.50–$11.50. No credit cards. Mon–Fri 11am–10pm, Sat 6:30– 10pm. WEST INDIAN / ENGLISH PUB.

Housed in a cinder-block building, this restaurant offers casual dining in simple surroundings modestly appointed with nautical pictures scattered throughout. The menu includes a wide spectrum of dishes ranging from local fare, such as curried chicken, to a more international offering of pastas, such as the fettuccine served with a tomato-basil sauce, and barbecued chicken and ribs. Included among the British specialties are shepherd's pie, bangers and mash, and a steak-and-ale pie. Although some dishes are on the pricey side, the portions are substantial and many dishes, along with the daily specials, are less than $8.

FUN ON & OFF THE BEACH

An organized tour may be your best way to see Tortola. **Travel Plan Tours,** Romasco Place, Wickhams Cay I, Road Town (☎ **284/494-2872**), will pick you up at your hotel (a minimum of four required), and take you on a 2¹/₂-hour tour of the island for $25 per person. The agent also offers 2¹/₂-hour snorkeling tours for $35 per person, and glass-bottom-boat tours, also 2¹/₂ hours, for $25 per person.

A **taxi tour** lasting 2¹/₂ hours costs $45 for one to three people. To call a taxi in Road Town, dial ☎ **284/494-2322;** on Beef Island, ☎ **284/495-2378.**

BEACHES   Beaches are rarely crowded on Tortola unless a cruise ship is docked. You can rent a car or a Jeep to reach these beaches, or else take a taxi (but arrange for it to return at an appointed time to pick you up). There's no public transportation.

The finest beach is ✪ **Cane Garden Bay** (see "A Side Trip to Cane Garden Bay," below), which some aficionados have compared favorably to the famous Magens Bay Beach on the north shore of St. Thomas. It's directly west of Road Town, up and down some steep hills, but it's worth the effort.

Surfers like **Apple Bay,** west of Road Town. A hotel here, Sebastians, caters to a surfing crowd. January and February are the ideal time for visits.

Brewers Bay, site of a campground, is northwest of Road Town. Both snorkelers and surfers are attracted to this beach.

Smugglers Cove is at the extreme western end of Tortola, opposite the offshore island of Great Thatch and very close to the American island of St. John, directly to the south. Snorkelers also like this beach, sometimes known as Lower Belmont Bay.

Long Bay Beach is on Beef Island, east of Tortola and the site of the major airport. This mile-long stretch of white sandy beach is reached by taking the Queen Elizabeth Bridge. Long Bay is approached by going along a dirt road to the left before you come to the airport. From Long Bay you'll have a good view of Little Camanoe, one of the rocky offshore islands around Tortola.

EXPLORING AN ANCIENT RAIN FOREST   No visit to Tortola is complete without a trip to ✪ **Mount Sage,** a national park rising to 1,780 feet. Here you'll find traces of a primeval rain forest, and you can enjoy a picnic while overlooking neighboring islets and cays. Go west from Road Town to reach the mountain.

Before you head out, stop by the tourist office and pick up a brochure called *Sage Mountain National Park.* It has a location map, directions to the forest (where there's a parking lot), and an outline of the main trails through the park.

Covering 92 acres, the park was established in 1964 to protect the remnants of Tortola's original forests not burned or cleared during the island's plantation era. From the parking lot, a trail leads to the main entrance to the park. The two main trails are the Rain Forest Trail and the Mahogany Forest Trail.

HORSEBACK RIDING   **Shadow's Ranch,** Todman's Estate (☎ **284/494-2262**), offers horseback rides through Mount Sage National Park or down to the shores of Cane Garden Bay. Call for details Monday to Saturday from 9am to 4pm. The cost is $25 per hour.

SAILING OFFSHORE   The B.V.I. is the headquarters of the **Offshore Sailing School,** at the Prospect Reef Resort, Road Town (☎ **284/494-3311**). The school offers sailing instruction year-round. For information before you go, write or contact Offshore Sailing School, 16731 McGregor Blvd., Fort Myers, FL 33908 (☎ **941/494-3311**).

The Wreck of the *Rhône* & Other Top Dive Sites

The one site in the British Virgin Islands that lures divers over from St. Thomas is the wreck of the ✪ **RMS *Rhône,*** which sank in 1867 near the western point of Salt Island. *Skin Diver* magazine called this "the world's most fantastic shipwreck dive." It teems with marine life and coral formations and was featured in the movie *The Deep.*

For the entry-level diver to those more experienced, **Baskin in the Sun,** a PADI five-star facility (☎ **800/233-7983** in the U.S., or 284/494-5854), is a good choice on Tortola. Baskin in the Sun has two locations: the Prospect Reef Resort, near Road Town, and Soper's Hole, at Tortola's West End. Baskin offers a "Half Day Scuba Diving" experience for $95 to give beginners a taste of diving under supervision. They cater to all experience levels. Daily trips are scheduled to such sites as the RMS *Rhône,* "Painted Walls" (an underwater canyon, the walls of which are formed of brightly colored coral and sponges) and the "Indians" (four pinnacle rocks sticking out of the water, which drivers trace down to coral reefs along the sea floor, 40 feet below the surface).

Underwater Safaris (☎ **800/537-7032** in the U.S., or 284/494-3235) takes you to all the best sites, including the RMS *Rhône,* "Spyglass Wall," and "Alice in Wonderland." Its offices, "Safari Base," are located in Road Town and its "Safari Cay" office lies on Cooper Island. Get complete directions and information when you call. The center, connected with the Moorings, offers a complete PADI and NAUI training facility. An introductory resort course and one dive costs $95, and an open-water certification, with 4 days of instruction and four open-water dives, goes for $385, plus $40 for the instruction manual.

SNORKELING   If you plan on snorkeling by yourself, exercise due caution and consider driving to **Marina Cay,** off Tortola's East End and known for its good snorkeling beach, or **Cooper Island,** across Sir Francis Drake Channel. Underwater Safaris (see box, above) leads dives and snorkel expeditions to both sites, weather permitting.

SHOPPING

Most of the shops are on Main Street, Road Town, on Tortola, but know that the British Virgins have no duty-free-port shopping. British goods are imported without duty, and the wise shopper will be able to find some good buys among these imported items, especially in English china. In general, store hours are 9am to 4pm Monday to Friday and 9am to 1pm on Saturday.

Caribbean Corner Spice House Co. Soper's Hole. ☎ **284/495-4498.**

Here you'll find the island's finest selection of spices and herbs, along with local handcrafts and botanical skin-care products, most which you'll find useful in the fierce sun. There's also a selection of Cuban cigars, but you'll have to smoke them on island, as U.S. Customs does not allow their importation.

Caribbean Fine Arts Ltd. Main St., Road Town. ☎ **284/494-4240.**

This store has one of the most unusual collections of art from the West Indies. It sells original watercolors and oils, limited-edition serigraphs and sepia photographs, and pottery and primitives.

Caribbean Handprints. Main St., Road Town. ☎ **284/494-3717.**

This store features island hand-prints, all hand-done by local craftspeople. It also sells colorful fabric by the yard.

Flamboyance. Soper's Hole. ☎ **284/495-4699.**

This is the best place to shop for duty-free perfume. Fendi purses are also sold here.

Fort Wines Gourmet. Main St., Road Town. ☎ **284/494-3036.**

For the makings of a picnic you'd have to fly to the mainland to top stocking up on provisions here. Sample its full line of Hediard pâté terrines along with a wide selection of chocolates, including some of the best from Paris. There's also an elegant showcase of glassware, lacquered boxes, and handmade Russian filigree items plated in 24-karat gold.

J. R. O'Neal. Upper Main St., Road Town. ☎ **284/494-2292.**

Across from the Methodist church, this decorative and home accessories store has an extensive collection of terra-cotta pottery, and wicker and rattan home furnishings, Mexican glassware, Dhurrie rugs, baskets, ceramics, fine crystal, china, and more.

Little Denmark. Main St., Road Town. ☎ **284/494-2455.**

This is your best bet for famous names in gold and silver jewelry and china: Spode and Royal Copenhagen. Here you'll find many of the well-known designs from Scandinavian countries. It also offers jewelry made in the B.V.I., and watches. The outlet also offers a large selection of fishing equipment. It also sells Cuban cigars, which you'll have to smoke before you go home.

Pusser's Company Store. Main St., Road Town. ☎ **284/494-2467.**

There's a long, mahogany-trimmed bar accented with many fine nautical artifacts and a Pusser's Store selling a proprietary line of Pusser's sports and travel clothing and upmarket gift items. Pusser's Rum is one of the best-selling items here, or perhaps you'd prefer a Pusser's ceramic flask as a memento.

Sunny Caribbee Herb and Spice Company. Main St., Road Town. ☎ **284/494-2178.**

This old West Indian building was the first hotel on Tortola, and its shop specializes in Caribbean spices, seasonings, teas, condiments, and handcrafts. You can buy two world-famous specialties here: West Indian hangover cure and Arawak love potion. A Caribbean cosmetics collection, Sunsations, is also available and includes herbal bath gels, island perfume, and sunshine lotions. With its aroma of spices permeating the air, this factory is an attraction in itself. There's a daily sampling of island products, something different every day—perhaps tea, coffee, sauces, or dips. Right next door is the Sunny Caribbee Gallery, featuring original paintings, prints, wood carvings, and hand-painted furniture, plus crafts from throughout the Caribbean. In the Sunny Caribbee Art Gallery, adjacent to the spice shop, you'll find an extensive collection of original art, prints, metal sculpture, and many other Caribbean crafts.

TORTOLA AFTER DARK

Ask around to find out which hotel might have entertainment on any given evening. Steel bands and fungi or scratch bands (African-Caribbean musicians who improvise on locally available instruments) appear regularly, and nonresidents are usually welcome. Pick up a copy of **Limin' Times,** an entertainment magazine listing what's happening locally; it's usually available at your hotel.

✪ **Bomba's Surfside Shack,** Cappoon's Bay (☎ 284/495-4148), is the oldest, most memorable, and most uninhibited nightlife venue on the island and sits on a 20-foot-wide strip of unpromising coastline near the West End. By anyone's standards this is the "junk palace" of the island; it's covered with Day-Glo graffiti and laced into a semblance of coherence with wire and rejected odds and ends of plywood, driftwood, and abandoned rubber tires. Despite its makeshift appearance, the shack has the electronic amplification systems to create a really great party. The place is at its wildest on Wednesday and Sunday nights, when there's live music and a $7 all-you-can-eat barbecue. Open daily from 10am to midnight (or later, depending on business).

The Moorings / Mariner Inn. Wickhams Cay. ☎ **284/494-2332.**

This inn contains the preferred watering hole for some upscale yacht owners, but drink prices are low. Open to a view of its own marina, and bathed in a dim and flattering light, the place is nautical and relaxed. A fungi band sometimes provides a backdrop to the socializing.

Spyhouse Bar. In the Treasure Isle Hotel, at the eastern end of Road Town. ☎ **284/494-2501.**

This popular bar is in a little house designed with Haitian gingerbread. The sunken bar on a terrace overlooks the swimming pool and faraway marina facilities of this popular hotel. Bar specialties include Treasure Island rum punch with dark rum, orange juice, strawberry syrup, and apricot brandy, and "Windstorm," made with Galiano, rum, fruit punch, and Seven-Up.

A SIDE TRIP TO CANE GARDEN BAY

If you've decided to risk everything and navigate the roller-coaster hills of the B.V.I., then head to Cane Garden Bay, one of the choicest pieces of real estate on the island, long ago discovered by the sailing crowd. Its white sandy beach with sheltering palms is a living cliché of Caribbean charm.

Rhymer's, Cane Garden Bay (☎ 284/495-4639), is the place to go for food and entertainment. Skippers of any kind of craft are likely to stock up on supplies here, but you can also order cold beer and refreshing rum drinks. If you're hungry, try the conch or whelk, or the barbecued spareribs. The beach bar and restaurant is open daily from 8am to 9pm and serves breakfast, lunch, and dinner. Main courses cost $12 to $20. On some nights a steel-drum band entertains the mariners. Ice and freshwater showers are available (and you can rent towels). Ask about renting Sunfish and Windsurfers. Major credit and charge cards are accepted.

4 Virgin Gorda

In 1493, on his second voyage to the New World, Columbus named this island Virgin Gorda, or "fat virgin" (from a distance, the island looks like a reclining woman with a protruding stomach). The second-largest island in the cluster of British Virgins, Virgin Gorda is 10 miles long and 2 miles wide, with a population of some 1,400. It's 12 miles east of Road Town and 26 miles from St. Thomas.

The island was a fairly desolate agricultural community until Laurance S. Rockefeller established the Little Dix Bay Hotel in the early 1960s, following his success with St. John and Caneel Bay in the 1950s. He envisioned a "wilderness beach," where privacy and solitude reign, and he literally put Virgin Gorda on the map. Other major hotels followed in the wake of Little Dix, but you can still find that privacy and solitude.

In 1971 the Virgin Gorda Yacht Harbour opened. Operated by the Little Dix Bay Hotel, it accommodates 120 yachts.

GETTING THERE   **Air St. Thomas** (☎ 284/776-2722) flies to Virgin Gorda daily from St. Thomas. The 40-minute flight costs $63 one-way, $129 round-trip.

Speedy's Fantasy (☎ 284/495-5240) operates a ferry service between Road Town and Virgin Gorda. Five ferries a day leave from Road Town Monday to Saturday, reduced to two on Sunday. The trip costs $10 one-way or $19 round-trip. From St. Thomas to Virgin Gorda there's service three times a week (on Tuesday, Thursday, and Saturday), costing $25 one-way or $45 round-trip.

GETTING AROUND   Independently operated open-sided **safari buses** run along the main road. Holding up to 14 passengers, these buses charge upwards from $3 per person to transport a passenger, say, from The Valley to The Baths.

If you'd like to rent a car, try one of the local firms, including **Mahogany Rentals,** The Valley, Spanish Town (☎ 284/495-5469), across from the yacht harbor. A representative will meet you at the airport or ferry dock and do the paperwork there. This company is the least expensive on the island, beginning at $41.75 daily for a Suzuki Samuari. An alternative choice is **Andy's Taxi and Jeep Rental** (☎ 284/495-5252), 7 minutes from the marina in Spanish Town. A representative here will also meet you at the airport of ferry dock for the paperwork. Rates begin at $45 daily year-round.

ESSENTIALS   The local **American Express** representative is Travel Plan Ltd., Virgin Gorda Yacht Harbour (☎ 284/495-5586).

WHERE TO STAY

Sometimes, particularly in the off-season, you can get a good deal on a villa rental. The best agency for that is **Virgin Gorda Villa Rentals Ltd.,** P.O. Box 63, The Valley, Virgin Gorda, B.V.I. (☎ 284/495-7421; fax 284/495-7367). The company manages villas throughout the island, most of which are quite expensive. A 5-night minimum stay is required off-season, a 7-night minimum in winter. About the cheapest weekly rentals in winter are $1,150 per week, dropping to $800 per week off-season—plus 19% tax.

DOUBLES FOR LESS THAN $85 (WINTER) / $70 (OFF-SEASON)

Oceanview Hotel. P.O. Box 66, Virgin Gorda, B.V.I. ☎ 284/495-5230. 12 rms. A/C TV TEL. Year-round, $85 single or double. AE, MC, V. Free parking.

This hotel is in a residential neighborhood at the edge of Virgin Gorda's largest settlement, site of the ferryboat arrivals from nearby Tortola. Small, simple, and family-operated, it offers sheetrock- or cinder block–sided rooms with ceiling fans, a sense of West Indian aesthetics, and very few frills. The nearest beach (Devil's Bay) is within a half mile, and many guests abandon their rather small rooms to spend many hours outdoors near the sea. The bars, restaurants, and launderettes of town are a short walk away. There's also a very plain bar and restaurant on the premises, serving dinners for around $17 per person.

The Wheelhouse. Spanish Town, Virgin Gorda, B.V.I. ☎ 284/495-5230. 12 rms. TV TEL. Winter, $85 single or double. Off-season, $70 single or double. AE, DISC, MC, V.

The Wheelhouse offers some of the lowest resort rates on the island. This cinder-block building is definitely no-frills, although it is conveniently located, near a shopping center and the Virgin Gorda Marina. The rooms are clean but simply furnished, often done in pastels with two single beds or a double bed. Children are welcome, and baby-sitting can be arranged. The rooms are on the second floor with a long porch front and back, and downstairs is an inexpensive restaurant and bar, serving local food. There's also a garden in back. There's no pool, and you're a 15-minute walk from the beach.

DOUBLES FOR LESS THAN $150 (WINTER) / $100 (OFF-SEASON)

✪ **Fischers Cove Beach Hotel.** The Valley (P.O. Box 60), Virgin Gorda, B.V.I. ☎ **284/ 495-5252.** Fax 284/495-5820. 12 rms, 8 studio cottages. A/C. Winter, $145–$150 single or double; $170–$180 studio cottage. Off-season, $100 single or double; $125–$135 studio cottage. MAP $40 per person extra. AE, MC, V.

There's swimming at your doorstep in this group of units nestled near the sandy beach of St. Thomas Bay. Erected of native stone, each cottage is self-contained, with one or two bedrooms and a combination living/dining room with a kitchenette. You can stock up on provisions at a food store near the grounds. There are 12 pleasant but simple rooms with views of Drake Channel. Each has its own private bath (hot and cold showers) and private balcony. Jeep rentals are available, as is a children's playground. Live entertainment is often presented.

✪ **Guavaberry Spring Bay Vacation Homes.** Spring Bay (P.O. Box 20), Virgin Gorda, B.V.I. ☎ **284/495-5227.** Fax 284/495-5283. 18 houses. Winter, $142 one-bedroom house for two; $200 two-bedroom house for four. Off-season, $95 one-bedroom house for two; $140 two-bedroom house for four. Extra person $15–$20. No credit cards.

Staying in one of these hexagonal white-roofed redwood houses built on stilts is like living in a treehouse, with screened and louvered walls to let in sea breezes. Each home, available for daily or weekly rental, has one or two bedrooms, and all have private baths, a small kitchenette, and a dining area. The hosts will show you to one of their unique vacation homes, each with its own elevated sun deck overlooking Sir Francis Drake Passage. Within a few minutes of the cottage colony is the beach at Spring Bay, and the Yacht Harbour Shopping Centre is 1 mile away. It's also possible to explore "The Baths" nearby.

The owners provide a complete commissary for guests, and tropical fruits can be picked in season or bought at local shops. They will make arrangements for day charters for scuba diving or fishing, and will also arrange for island Jeep tours and sailing.

Leverick Bay Resort & Marina. The Valley (P.O. Box 63), Virgin Gorda, B.V.I. ☎ **800/ 848-7081** in the U.S., 800/463-9396 in Canada, or 284/495-7421. Fax 284/495-7367. 16 rms, 4 condos. A/C TV TEL. Winter, $149 single or double. Off-season, $119 single or double. Extra person $36 in winter, $24 off-season. Condos (by the week only): Winter, from $1,600; off-season, from $1,190. AE, MC, V.

Set at the southern edge of the sheltered waters of Virgin Gorda's North Sound, this establishment offers a well-designed row of town house–style hotel rooms. The facade of each unit is painted a different pastel color, and the building is capped with an orange-red roof and fronted by three tiers of ocean-facing balconies. It's stylish, comfortable, and graced with touches of architectural gingerbread. The bedrooms are pastel-colored, breezy, and filled with original art, and have seafront balconies or verandas. A kidney-shaped pool punctuates the white sand of the beach. The site contains a food market, an art gallery, two small beaches (a larger beach at Savannah Bay is within a 10-minute drive), a gift shop, and its own restaurant and bar. Lunches cost under $10; dinners range from $15 to $25 each. A quartet of condo units are set in modern, red-roofed hexagons flanked on four sides by wraparound porches. A dive shop and marina facilities are on the premises, with surfers, kayaks, and sailboats for rent.

VILLA & CONDO RENTALS

✪ **Mango Bay Resort.** Mahoe Bay (P.O. 1062), Virgin Gorda, B.V.I. ☎ **800/223-6510** in the U.S., 800/424-5500 in Canada, or 284/495-5672. Fax 284/495-5674. 32 units (all with kitchen). A/C. Winter, $120–$168 efficiency studio for one or two; $215–$310 one-bedroom villa for two; $255–$506 two-bedroom villa for four; $384–$564 three-bedroom villa for six. Off-season, $99–$105 efficiency studio for one or two; $138–$249 one-bedroom villa for two; $184–$398 two-bedroom villa for four; $283–$412 three-bedroom villa for six. Extra person on foldaway couch $30–$55. No credit cards.

Set on lushly landscaped acres overlooking the scattered islets of Drake's Channel on the island's western shore, this is a well-designed compound of eight white-sided villas. It's a little pricey, but you get good value for your money. It offers what might be the most adaptable set of accommodations on the island, as doors can be locked or unlocked to divide or unify each villa into as many as four independent units. It's quite easy to invite another person along since the floor plans are flexible. Costs vary with the proximity of your unit to the nearby beach. Interiors are stylish yet simple, often dominated by the same turquoise as that of the seascape in front of you. Daily maid service is included. You can cook in, or else dine on site at the quite-good Georgio's Table, serving three meals a day. There's also a bar.

Paradise Beach Resort. P.O. Box 1105, Virgin Gorda, B.V.I. ☎ **800/225-4255** or 284/495-5871. Fax 284/495-5872. 2 studios, 5 suites. Winter, $125 studio for one or two; $230–$330 one-bedroom suite for two; $285–$390 two-bedroom suite for four; $410–$540 three-bedroom villa for six. Off-season, $85 studio for one or two; $140–$180 one-bedroom suite for two; $170–$220 two-bedroom suite for four; $260–$325 three-bedroom villa for six. Extra person $30; children 3 and under stay free in parents' room. No credit cards. Closed the first 2 weeks of Sept.

This beachfront complex was created by Italian designers who made ample use of marble, terra-cotta tile, and a breezy indoor-outdoor exposure to the sea. Bougainvillea and oleander climb up pergolas that shelter some of the amenities from too much direct exposure to the sun. If you stay here you're rather isolated, but the management will rent you a Jeep for $40 per day. Don't even consider this resort if you're looking for gregarious contact with lots of other tourists: It was designed "for the plucky" who prefer vacations as unstructured as possible, and who want to spend most of their holiday in their swimsuits. The design of each unit permits the combination of any two units into a three-bedroom "villa," which might be useful if you plan on bringing your own in-house menagerie.

BEST OFF-SEASON BET

✪ **The Olde Yard Inn.** The Valley (P.O. Box 26), Virgin Gorda, B.V.I. ☎ **800/653-9273**, 284/495-5544, or 284/633-7411. Fax 284/495-5986. 14 rms. Winter, $195 double; $220 triple; $245 quad. Off-season, $110 double; $130 triple; $150 quad. MAP $50 per person extra. Honeymoon packages available. AE, MC, V.

This little Caribbean inn 1 mile from the airport offers good value and is a charmer. Near the main house are two long bungalows with large renovated bedrooms, each with its own bath and patio. Scattered about are a few antiques and special accessories. A huge pool and Jacuzzi are part of the attractions, as are such facilities as tennis courts, a health club, and French-accented meals. Its winter rates are $145 in a single and up to $195 in a double, but off-season tariffs drop to just $90 single and $110 double.

WHERE TO EAT

The Crab Hole. The Valley. ☎ **284/495-5307.** Dinner $10–$15; lunch $6–$12. No credit cards. Daily 9am–10pm. Head south along the road to The Baths, and turn left at the sign to the Crab Hole. WEST INDIAN.

This is a clean and decent West Indian restaurant, far removed from the expense and glitter of such resorts as Little Dix Bay and Biras Creek Estate. The private home of Kenroy and Janet Millington built in 1986, it occupies the ground level of a concrete house surrounded by fields and other simple private dwellings. Order your food from the chalkboard posted above the bar. Don't expect too much—they have their good days and bad days here, depending on what the market turned up. You might get stewed whelk with a Créole sauce made from local spices or tomatoes, and perhaps stewed chicken—most definitely fried fish. Stewed oxtail is sometimes on the menu, and guests, often hotel workers in the area, drop in for a noonday hamburger.

Mad Dog. The Baths, The Country. ☎ **284/495-5830.** Sandwiches $4; piña coladas $3.50. No credit cards. Daily 10am–7pm. PIÑA COLADAS / SANDWICHES.

This is the most skillful and charming reconstruction of a West Indian cottage on Virgin Gorda. A wide veranda and the brightly painted 19th-century wooden timbers and clapboards create a cozy and convivial drink and sandwich bar where the piña coladas are absolutely divine. The owner and supervisor of this laid-back corner of heaven is London-born Colin McCullough, a self-described mad dog who sailed the B.V.I. for almost 30 years before establishing his domain here.

✪ **Pusser's Leverick Bay.** Leverick Bay, North Sound. ☎ **284/495-7369.** Reservations recommended. Main courses $12.95–$24.95; lunch $5.95–$13.95; pizzas from $4.95. AE, MC, V. Daily 8:30am–10pm. CONTINENTAL.

Scattered throughout this restaurant are glass cases containing ship models to add a nautical feel. Dark wooden beams and an antique English bar add just the right touch of quiet elegance. Although there are a few tables inside, the main dining area is on the deck overlooking North Sound. The menu selections range from the very simple to the more elaborate such as the roast duckling glazed with a guava-and-candied-lemon sauce. The real bargains here are the meals served up until 6pm, when dinner begins. The breakfasts are hearty, lunches are filling, and to beat those higher prices at night, opt for an early dinner of pizza, which is served from 11am to 6pm every day.

Teacher Ilma's. The Valley. ☎ **284/495-5355.** Reservations required for dinner; call before 3pm. Full meals $18–$25. No credit cards. Daily 12:30–2pm and 7–9:30pm. At Spanish Town, turn left at the main road past the entrance to the Fischers Cove Hotel; the sign to Teacher Ilma's is about 2 minutes ahead and to the right. WEST INDIAN.

Mrs. Ilma O'Neal, who taught youngsters at the island's public school for 43 years, began her restaurant by cooking privately for visitors and island construction workers. Main courses, which include appetizers, might be chicken, local goat meat, lobster, conch, pork, or fish (your choice of grouper, snapper, tuna, dolphin, swordfish, or triggerfish), followed by such desserts as homemade coconut, pineapple, or guava pie. Teacher Ilma emphasizes that her cuisine is not Créole but local in its origins and flavors.

Thelma's Hideout. The Valley. ☎ **284/495-5646.** Reservations required for dinner. Dinner $13–$15; lunch $8–$9. No credit cards. Daily 7–10am, 11:30am–2:30pm, and (only upon notification before 3pm) 6–10pm. (Bar, daily 11am–midnight.) WEST INDIAN.

Mrs. Thelma King, one of the most outspoken *grandes dames* of Virgin Gorda (who worked in Manhattan for many years before returning to her native B.V.I.), runs this convivial gathering place for the island's West Indian community. It's located in a concrete house whose angles are softened by ascending tiers of verandas. Food choices include grilled steaks, fish filets, and West Indian stews containing pork, mutton, or chicken. Limeade or mauby are available, but many clients stick to rum or beer. Live music is presented on Saturday night in winter, and every other Saturday off-season.

Top of the Baths. The Valley. ☎ **284/495-5497.** Dinner from $18; sandwiches, pizza, and salad plates $5–$12. AE, MC, V. Daily 8am–10pm. CARIBBEAN.

This aptly named green-and-white restaurant offers a patio with a swimming pool. Here locals gather to enjoy food they grew up on. At lunch you can order an array of appetizers, sandwiches, salad plates, and even pizza. You're invited to swim in the pool either before or after dining. At night the kitchen turns out good home-style cookery, including fresh fish, plus lobster, chicken, and steaks. Look for one of the daily specials. On Sunday a DJ entertains from 10am to 3pm, and occasional live music is presented.

SEEING THE SIGHTS: SALTWATER POOLS, BOULDER-STREWN PARKS & MORE

The northern side of Virgin Gorda is mountainous, with one peak reaching 1,370 feet. However, the southern half is flat, with large boulders appearing at every turn. The **best beaches** are The Baths, where giant boulders form a series of panoramic pools and grottoes flooded with sea water (nearby snorkeling is excellent). Neighboring The Baths is Spring Bay, one of the best of the island's beaches, with white sand, clear water, and good snorkeling. Trunk Bay is a wide sand beach reachable by boat or along a rough path from Spring Bay. Savannah Bay is a sandy beach north of Yacht Harbour, and Mahoe Bay, at the Mango Bay Resort, has a gently curving beach with vivid blue water.

Among the places of interest, **Coppermine Point** is the site of an abandoned copper mine and smelter. Because of loose rock formations it can be dangerous, so you should exercise caution if you explore it. Legend has it that the Spanish worked these mines in the 1600s; however, the only authenticated document reveals that the English sank the shafts in 1838 to mine copper.

You'll find ✪ **The Baths** on every visitor's list, and the area is known for its snorkeling. Equipment can be rented on the beach. These are a phenomenon of tranquil pools and caves formed by gigantic house-size boulders. As these boulders toppled over one another, they formed saltwater grottoes, suitable for exploring. The pools around The Baths are excellent for swimming.

Devil's Bay National Park can be reached by a trail from The Baths traffic circle. The walk to the secluded coral-sand beach takes about 15 minutes through a natural setting of boulders and dry coastal vegetation.

The Baths and surrounding areas are part of a proposed system of parks and protected areas for the B.V.I. The protected area encompasses 682 acres of land, including sites at Little Fort, Spring Bay, The Baths, and Devil's Bay on the east coast.

The best way to see the island if you're over for a day trip is to call Andy Flax at the Fischers Cove Beach Hotel (☎ **284/495-5252**). He runs the **Virgin Gorda Tours Association,** which will give you a tour of the island for about $20 per person. The tour leaves twice daily. You can be picked up at the ferry dock.

Kilbrides Underwater Tours is located at the Bitter End Resort at North Sound (☎ **800/932-4286** in the U.S., or 284/495-9638). Today Kilbrides offers the best diving in the B.V.I. at 15 to 20 dive sites, including the wreck of the ill-fated RMS *Rhône.* Prices range from $80 to $90 for a two-tank dive on one of the coral reefs. Fees include use of all necessary equipment, and videos of your dives are available.

HIKING IN VIRGIN GORDA PEAK NATIONAL PARK

Consider a trek up the stairs and hiking paths that crisscross Virgin Gorda's largest stretch of undeveloped land, the Virgin Gorda Peak National Park. To reach the best departure point for your uphill trek, drive north of The Valley on the only road leading to North Sound for about 15 minutes of very hilly drives (use of a four-wheel-drive vehicle is a very good idea). Stop at the base of the stairway leading steeply uphill. There's a sign pointing to the Gorda Peak National Park.

Depending on your speed, you'll embark on a trek of between 25 and 40 minutes to reach the summit of Gorda Peak, the highest point on the island, where views out over many scattered islets of the Virgin archipelago await you. There's a tower at the summit, which you can climb for enhanced views. Admire the flora and the fauna (birds, lizards, nonvenomous snakes) that you're likely to run across en route. Because the vegetation you'll encounter is not particularly lush, wear protection against the somewhat damaging rays of the intense noonday sun, and consider bringing a picnic as tables are scattered along the hiking trails.

SHOPPING

Your best bet is the **Virgin Gorda Craft Shop** at Yacht Harbour (☎ 284/495-5137), which has some good items crafted in straw. Some of the more upmarket hotels have boutiques to tempt you, notably the **Bitter End Yacht Club's Reeftique** (☎ 284/494-2745), with its selection of sport clothing, including sundresses and logowear. You can also purchase a hat here to protect you from the sun. You might also check out the **Boutique at Little Dix Bay** (☎ 284/495-5555), with its selection of locally produced crafts along with the inevitable T-shirts.

VIRGIN GORDA AFTER DARK

There isn't a lot of action at night, unless you want to make some of your own. The **Bath & Turtle Pub,** at Yacht Harbour (☎ 284/495-5239), brings in local bands for dancing. Most evenings in winter the **Bitter End Yacht Club** (☎ 284/494-2745) has live music. Call to see what's happening at the time of your visit.

Andy's Chateau de Pirate. At the Fischer's Cove Beach Hotel, The Valley. ☎ **284/495-5252.** No cover most nights, $5 Fri–Sun.

Solidly built on poured concrete in 1985, this sprawling, sparsely furnished local hangout has a simple stage, a very long bar, and huge oceanfront windows which almost never close. The complex also houses the Lobster Pot Restaurant, the Buccaneer Bar, and the nightclub EFX. The Lobster Pot is open from 7am to 10pm. The place is a famous showcase for the island's musical groups, which perform Wednesday to Sunday from 8pm to midnight; lots of people congregate to listen and kibitz.

The Dominican Republic 8

Called "the fairest land under heaven," the Dominican Republic has a surprisingly rich colonial heritage and attracts visitors to its white sandy beaches and mountain resorts. It's among the fastest-growing tourist destinations in the Caribbean.

It may be a fair land, but there's also grinding poverty here. The 54-mile-wide Mona Passage separates the República Dominicana from Puerto Rico, and many poverty-stricken citizens risk their lives across this channel every day hoping to slip into Puerto Rico and then illegally go on to the U.S. mainland. Some never make it. Crime, especially muggings and robbery of tourists, is on the rise. Yet the island holds such fascination that visitors often return.

The Dominican Republic is one of the cheapest places in the West Indies for the vacationer. Too many hotels, too few guests, along with underpaid workers, keep costs down. Package tours are considerably less expensive than "rack" rates or independent bookings. The American and the Canadian dollars are traded extremely favorably against the Dominican peso.

Often mistakenly thought of as "just another poorer Puerto Rico," the Dominican Republic has its own distinctive cuisine and heritage. Five centuries of culture and tradition converge here.

In the heart of the Caribbean archipelago, the country has an 870-mile coastline, about a third of which is given to magnificent beach. The average temperature is 77° Fahrenheit. August is the warmest month and January the coolest, although even then it's still warm enough to swim and enjoy the tropical sun. So why did it take so long for the Dominican Republic to be discovered by visitors? The answer is largely political. The country has been steeped in misery and bloodshed almost from the beginning, and it climaxed with the infamous reign of Rafael Trujillo and the civil wars that followed.

GETTING THERE

American Airlines (☎ 800/433-7300) offers the most frequent service—at least a dozen flights daily from points throughout North America to either Santo Domingo or Puerto Plata. Most flights to those cities from New York's JFK, Miami International, or San Juan's Luís Muñoz Marín airport are nonstop. Good connections are offered to the Dominican Republic from Boston, Chicago, and Los Angeles. Flights from New York's LaGuardia are usually routed through either Miami or San Juan.

If you're heading to one of the D.R.'s less prominent airports, your best bet will be aboard any of the flights that connect with affiliated local carrier **American Eagle** (☎ **800/433-7300**). Its small-scale (around 60-passenger) planes depart every day from San Juan (with connecting flights from Mayagüez) for airports throughout the Dominican Republic. These include Santo Domingo, Puerto Plata, La Romana, and Punta Cana.

Continental Airlines (☎ **800/525-0280** in the U.S.) flies daily from New Jersey's Newark airport to Santo Domingo. **TWA** (☎ **800/221-2000** in the U.S.) flies nonstop from New York's JFK every evening to Santo Domingo. **Carnival** (☎ **800/ 824-7386**) flies daily to Santo Domingo from Miami, Orlando, and New York.

The Dominican Republic is geared to mass tourism and offers all-inclusive packages for however many days you specify. These packages almost always save money over what you'd pay when booking your air travel and hotel accommodations yourself. American might be your best bet for this type of package.

A Traveler's Advisory: Arriving at Santo Domingo's Las Américas International Airport is confusing and chaotic. Customs officials tend to be rude and overworked, and give you a very thorough check! In addition, many readers have reported luggage being stolen. Beware of "porters" who offer to help. Hold on to your possessions carefully. Arrival at La Unión International Airport, 23 miles east of Puerto Plata on the north coast, is generally much easier, but be careful here too.

For information on flights into Casa de Campo / La Romana, see section 3 of this chapter.

GETTING AROUND

This is not always easy if your hotel is remote. The most convenient means of transport is provided by taxis, rental cars, *públicos* (multipassenger taxis), and *guaguas* (public buses).

BY PUBLIC TRANSPORTATION　*Públicos* are a kind of unmetered multipassenger taxi that travels on main thoroughfares and stops to pick up people waving from the side of the street. You must tell the driver your destination when you're picked up to make sure the público is going to your destination. Watch for cars with a white seal on the car's front door.

Public buses, often in the form of minivans or panel trucks, are called *guaguas*. They provide the same service as públicos, but they're more crowded. Larger **buses** provide service outside the towns. Bus travel is dirt-cheap, but beware of pickpockets.

BY TAXI　Taxis aren't metered, and determining the cost in advance (which you should do) may be difficult if you don't speak Spanish (the island's official language). Taxis can be hailed in the streets, and you'll find them at the major hotels and outside the airport as you emerge from Customs. The minimum fare in Santo Domingo is $6, but most drivers try to get more. Don't get into an unmarked street taxi. Many visitors, particularly in Santo Domingo, have been assaulted and robbed by doing just that.

BY RENTAL CAR　The best way to see the Dominican Republic is by car: Island buses tend to be erratic, hot, and overcrowded, and there's no rail transportation. Make sure that the car you rent has functioning seat belts.

Your Canadian or American driver's license is suitable documentation, along with a valid credit or charge card or a substantial cash deposit. And unlike many places in the Caribbean, *you drive on the right*. Be aware that, although the major highways are relatively clear of obstacles, the country's secondary roads, especially those in the

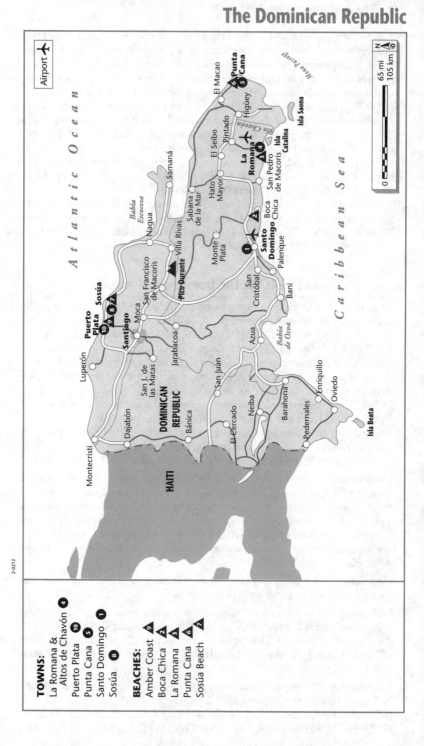

The Dominican Republic

TOWNS:

La Romana &
Altos de Chavón ④
Puerto Plata ⑩
Punta Cana ⑤
Santo Domingo ①
Sosúa ⑧

BEACHES:

Amber Coast ⑨
Boca Chica ②
La Romana ③
Punta Cana ⑥
Sosúa Beach ⑦

Airport ✈

Atlantic Ocean

Caribbean Sea

HAITI

DOMINICAN
REPUBLIC

Montecristi
Dajabón
Luperón
Puerto Plata
Sosúa ⑦ ⑧
⑩ ⑨ Santiago
Moca
San J. de
las Matas
Bánica
Jarabacoa
San Juan
El Cercado
Neiba
Azua
Bani
San
Cristóbal
Pedernales
Oviedo
Enriquillo
Barahona
*Bahía
de Ocoa*
Isla Beata
San Francisco
de Macorís
Pico Duarte
Villa Rivas
Nagua
Samaná
*Bahía
Escocesa*
Sabana
de la Mar
Monte
Plata
Hato
Mayor
El Seibo
Pintado
Higüey
El Macao
⑥ Punta
⑤ Cana
Isla Saona
Isla
Catalina
③ ④ La Romana
San Pedro
de Macorís
Boca
Chica
① Santo ②
Domingo
Palenque

N
65 mi
105 km
0

2-0212

227

east, are very potholed and rutted. Plan a generous amount of transit time between destinations and drive carefully. In addition, a policeman often flags you down alleging (often wrongly) that you committed some infraction. Many locals give the policeman $5 "for your children" and then are allowed to go on their way. In the D.R. low-paid policemen supplement their income by this form of *regalo* or gift.

The high accident and theft rate in recent years has helped raise the cost of car rentals substantially. Prices are always changing, so call around for last-minute quotations. You should fully understand your insurance coverage (or lack thereof). Your credit- or charge-card issuer may already provide you with this insurance; contact the issuer.

For reservations and more information, call the rental companies at least a week before your departure: **Avis** (☎ **800/331-1084** in the U.S.), **Budget** (☎ **800/527-0700** in the U.S.), and **Hertz** (☎ **800/654-3001** in the U.S.).

You might also try the biggest local car-rental outfit, **Nelly Rent-a-Car** (☎ **800/526-6684**), with locations in Santo Domingo at Paseo de Los Locutores 1 at Avenida Winston Churchill (☎ **809/544-1800**); and in Puerto Plata at Plaza Playa Dorado in the tourist zone (☎ **809/320-4888**).

FAST FACTS: The Dominican Republic

Currency   The Dominican monetary unit is the **peso (RD$),** made up of 100 **centavos.** Coin denominations are 5, 10, 25, and 50 centavos, and 1 peso. Bill denominations are RD$5, RD$10, RD$20, RD$50, RD$100, RD$500, and RD$1,000. Price quotations in this chapter appear sometimes in American and sometimes in Dominican currency, depending on the policy of the establishment— the use of any currency other than Dominican pesos is technically illegal, but few seem to bother with this mandate. As of this writing, you get about RD$13.20 to $1 U.S. Bank booths at the international airports and major hotels will change your currency into Dominican pesos at the rate of exchange prevailing in the free market. You'll be given a receipt for the amount of foreign currency you exchanged. You can present this at the Banco de Reservas booth at the airport when you're ready to leave to have any remaining pesos changed back into American dollars.

Documents   To enter the Dominican Republic, citizens of the United States and Canada need only proof of citizenship, such as a passport or an original birth certificate. However, citizens may have trouble returning home without a passport; a reproduced birth certificate is not acceptable. Upon your arrival at the airport, you must purchase a tourist card for $10 U.S. To avoid waiting in line in the Dominican Republic, purchase this at the airport counter when you check in for your flight to the island.

Electricity   The country uses 110 volts AC, 60 cycles, so adapters and transformers are usually not necessary for U.S. appliances.

Embassies   All embassies are in Santo Domingo, the national capital. The Embassy of the **United States** is on Calle Cesar Nicholas Penson (☎ **809/221-2171**), the Embassy of the **United Kingdom** is on Avenida 27 de Febrero (☎ **809/427-7111**), and the Embassy of **Canada** is at Ave. Máximo Gómez 30 (☎ **809/685-1136**).

Information   Before your trip, contact any of the following **Dominican Republic Tourist Information Centers:** 1501 Broadway, Suite 410, New York, NY 10036 (☎ **212/575-4966;** fax 212/575-5448); 2355 Salzedo St., Suite 307, Coral Gables, FL 33134 (☎ **305/444-4592**); and 2080 Crescent St., Montréal, PQ H3G 2B8

(☎ **800/563-1611** in Canada, or 514/499-1918; fax 514/499-1393). At the **information hot line** (☎ **800/752-1151**), operators can field questions on a wide range of subjects, from travel tips to money matters to festivals. Their information is usually very general—don't expect them to answer too many specifics.

Language   The official language is Spanish; many people also know some English.

Safety   The Dominican Republic has more than its fair share of crime (see "Getting There," above, for a warning about the airports). Avoid unmarked street taxis, especially in Santo Domingo; you could be targeted for assault and robbery. While strolling around the city you're likely to be accosted by hustlers selling various wares, and you can also be mugged. Pickpocketing is commonplace. Don't go walking in Santo Domingo after dark. Many locals will offer their services as a guide, and sometimes a loud refusal is not enough to shake their presence. Hiring an official guide from the tourist office can prevent this.

Taxes   A departure tax of $10 U.S. is assessed and must be paid in U.S. currency. The government imposes a 13% tax on hotel rooms, and 7% on food and beverages.

Time   It's Atlantic standard time throughout the country year-round. When New York and Miami are on eastern standard time and it's 6am, it's 7am in Santo Domingo. However, during daylight saving time, when it's noon on the East Coast mainland it's the same time in Santo Domingo.

Tipping and Service   In most restaurants and hotels a 10% service charge is added to your check. Most people usually add 5% to 10% more, especially if the service has been good.

Weather   The average temperature is 77° Fahrenheit. August is the warmest month and January the coolest month, although even then it's warm enough to swim.

1 Santo Domingo

Bartholomeo Columbus, brother of Christopher, founded the city of New Isabella (later renamed Santo Domingo) on the banks of the Ozama River on August 4, 1496, which makes it the oldest city in the New World. On the southeastern Caribbean coast, Santo Domingo—known as Ciudad Trujillo from 1936 to 1961—is the capital of the Dominican Republic. It has had a long, sometimes glorious, more often sad, history. At the peak of its power, Diego de Velázquez sailed from here to settle Cuba, Ponce de León went forth to discover and settle Puerto Rico and Florida, and Cortés was launched toward Mexico. The city today still reflects its long history—French, Haitian, and especially Spanish.

ESSENTIALS

In Santo Domingo, 24-hour drugstore service is provided by **San Judas Tadeo,** ave. Independencia 57 (☎ 809/689-2851). An emergency room operates at the **Centro Médico Universidad,** Ave. Máximo Gómez 68 (☎ 809/221-0171). To summon the **police,** phone ☎ **911.** For tourist information, see the **Secretary of Tourism,** Officinas Guberbamentales Building D, at the corner of Avenida Mexico and Avenida 30 de Marco (☎ 809/221-4600), in Santo Domingo.

WHERE TO STAY

Even the highest-priced hotels in Santo Domingo might be classified as medium-priced in most of the Caribbean. However, remember that taxes and service will be added to your bill, which will make the rates 23% higher. When making reservations, ask if these are included in the rates quoted—usually they aren't.

For better prices, you might consider a package deal arranged by **TourScan, Inc.,** P.O. Box 2367, Darien, CT 06820 (☎ **800/962-2080** or 203/665-8091). TourScan can inform you of package deals to 23 places in Santo Domingo and the same number in Puerto Plata, ranging from luxury resorts to simple inns. Some best-value air-and-hotel packages begin at $470 per person for 3 nights.

DOUBLES FOR LESS THAN $50

Apart-Hotel Plaza Florida. Ave. Bolívar 203 (Calle Armando Rodriguez), Santo Domingo, República Dominicana. ☎ **809/541-3957.** Fax 809/540-5582. 32 rms, all with kitchenette. A/C TV TEL. RD$525 ($39.40) single; RD$625 ($46.90) double. AE, MC, V.

Favored by business travelers from nearby Caribbean nations, this three-story hotel was built in 1978 in a modern commercial district near the larger (and more expensive) Hotel Commodoro. The accommodations, all with kitchenettes, are simple, airy, and clean, with few frills. The result resembles something like an apartment complex, where residents tend to stay longer than conventional tourists, usually preparing at least breakfast in their rooms. About half the units have small balconies. There are no bar or restaurant facilities on site.

Hotel Cervantes. Ave. Cervantes 202, Santo Domingo, República Dominicana. ☎ **809/ 688-2261.** Fax 809/686-5754. 179 rms. A/C TV TEL. Year-round, $36 single; $42.40–$62 double. Breakfast from $6 extra. AE, DC, MC, V.

Long a favorite among budget travelers, the family-oriented Cervantes, with a security guard on staff, offers comfortably furnished bedrooms with refrigerators. It may not have the most tasteful decor in Santo Domingo, but is nevertheless clean and efficient and has a pleasant staff. The hotel has a swimming pool and is also known for its Bronco Steak House. Street parking is available.

DOUBLES FOR LESS THAN $60

El Napolitano. Ave. George Washington 51 (between Calle Cambrunal and Calle del Número), Santo Domingo, República Dominicana. ☎ **809/687-1131.** Fax 809/687-6814. 72 rms. A/C TV TEL. Year-round, RD$800 ($60) single or double. AE, DC, MC, V.

El Napolitano is a safe haven and a good bargain along the Malecón, which is usually lively—and potentially dangerous—until the wee hours. Popular with Dominicans, the hotel rents comfortably furnished but simple units, many large enough for families. All accommodations open onto the sea. There's a swimming pool on the second floor.

The cafe is open 24 hours a day, as is room service, and the hotel also has a good restaurant specializing in seafood (especially lobster). There's a disco and a piano bar, plus a terrace casino, with both live and recorded music. If you like crowds, lots of action, and informality, El Napolitano may be for you.

✪ **Hostal Nicolás de Ovando.** Calle Las Damas 55 (at Calle Las Mercedes), Santo Domingo, República Dominicana. ☎ **809/686-9220.** Fax 809/221-4167. 43 rms. A/C TEL. Year-round, $60 single or double. Rates include American breakfast. Extra person $10. No credit cards.

In the shop-studded area of La Atarazana, in the old town, two 15th-century mansions have been converted into a *hostal* and named after the governor of Hispaniola, who lived here from 1502 to 1509. The structure is an example of a fortified house, with its own observation tower overlooking the Ozama River. Lying in the Colonial Zone, the *palacio* is the oldest hotel in the New World. This hotel is the best choice for those who want to be in the heart of the old city. The bedrooms are small, Spartan, and clean. The public rooms have heraldic tapestries, bronze mirrors, and colonial furnishings. The hotel was undergoing interior and exterior renovations at press time, so the design may change.

Hostal Nicolás Nader. Calle Admiral Luperón 251 (at Calle Duarte, 4 blocks west of calle Las Damas), Santo Domingo, República Dominicana. ☎ **809/687-6674.** Fax 809/687-7887. 9 rms. A/C. RD$625 ($46.90) single; RD$750 ($56.25) double. MC, V.

The family owners of this spacious but simply decorated hotel will proudly tell you that two former residents of this building were eventually elected president of the Dominican Republic. Originally a private house in the 1930s, it provides clean but exceptionally simple lodgings, with battered, old-fashioned furniture, some antiques. The guest rooms overlook either the street or a small Andalusian courtyard with cast-iron furniture. Breakfast is the only meal served.

Hotel Palacio. Calle Duarte 106 (at Calle Solomé Ureña), Santo Domingo, República Dominicana. ☎ **809/682-4730.** Fax 809/687-5535. 16 rms, all with kitchenette. A/C TV TEL. $53 single; $60 double. Children 12 and under stay free in parents' room. AE, MC, V.

This severely dignified stone-and-stucco building is a stripped-down reminder of the grander aspects of the city's colonial past. It lies in the heart of Santo Domingo's historic zone, 2 blocks from the cathedral. Built in the 1600s, it functioned as the family home of a former president of the Dominican Republic, Buenaventura Báez, and still retains its original iron balconies and high ceilings. In the early 1990s kitchenettes were added to each of the bedrooms, and simple, warm-weather furniture was added as part of its transformation into a hotel. Your fellow residents are likely to be visiting business travelers from other parts of the Latin Caribbean and tourists. There's a small gym, with its own Jacuzzi on the rooftop.

DOUBLES FOR LESS THAN $85

✪ **Hispaniola Hotel.** Ave. Independencia (at Ave. Abraham Lincoln), Santo Domingo, República Dominicana. ☎ **809/221-1511.** Fax 809/535-4050. 166 rms. A/C MINIBAR TV TEL. Year-round, $74 single; $84 double. Rates include American breakfast. AE, MC, V.

The Hispaniola has done an amazing Cinderella act and emerged from the shell of the Trujillo-era Hotel Pax into its present reincarnation. Now operated by Premier Resorts and Hotels, it was practically rebuilt. Located on 10 landscaped acres across from the deluxe Hotel Santo Domingo, it's a six-story structure with well-furnished bedrooms. The top-floor rooms, which are preferable, offer seaside views. The hotel's restaurant, La Piazzetta, serves Italian fare. The evening hot spots are the casino and the disco Neon 2002, which attracts many locals. In the thatched coffeehouse (a *bohío*) near the swimming pool, you can order breakfast, lunch, or drinks. Other amenities include room service, laundry, baby-sitting, a sauna, and a swimming pool. Guests can also use the facilities at the Hotel Santo Domingo, including tennis courts.

WORTH A SPLURGE

Capella Beach Renaissance Resort. Villas del Mar (Apdo. Postal 4750), Santo Domingo, República Dominicana. ☎ **800/HOTELS-1** in the U.S., or 809/526-1080. Fax 809/526-1088. 261 rms, 22 suites. A/C TV TEL. Winter, $105–$150 single or double; from $235 suite. Off-season, $85–$115 single or double; from $200 suite. AE, DC, MC, V.

Just 20 minutes from the International Airport of the Americas, this resort lies in the newly developed town of Villas del Mar. Architecturally, it resembles an exotic Andalusian town in southern Spain; it has its own beach, shared with Villas del Mar. The rooms have either a king-size or full-size bed, satellite TV, hair dryer, individually controlled air-conditioning, direct-dial phone, and room service. There are 35 no-smoking rooms and special accommodations for persons with disabilities.

The suites include six reserved for honeymooners, with private balconies, Jacuzzis, and sun decks. The best rooms are in the Renaissance club, which has extra service and amenities, including a complimentary continental breakfast.

There are three restaurants: Il Capellini, serving Italian fare; El Pescador, a seafood restaurant; and El Batey de la Costa, a buffet-style eatery. Facilities include two swimming pools with swim-up bars, a water-sports center, evening tennis, a Kid's club (ages 5 to 12), and a European spa facility.

Gran Hotel Lina. Aves. Máximo Gómez and 27 de Febrero, Santo Domingo, República Dominicana. ☎ **800/942-2461** or 809/563-5000. Fax 809/686-5521. 200 rms. A/C MINIBAR TV TEL. Year-round, $106 single; $111 double. Rates include breakfast. AE, DC, MC, V.

Rising 15 floors in the heart of the capital in a sterile cinder-block design, the Lina offers a wide range of services and facilities. All the rather plain rooms contain refrigerators and full-size beds; at least 30% of the accommodations overlook the Caribbean. The best rooms are on the 11th floor.

The hotel boasts one of the best-known restaurants in the Caribbean, a cafeteria and snack bar, and a nightclub. Services include 24-hour room service and laundry, and facilities include a swimming pool, Jacuzzi, solarium, gym, sauna, and shopping arcade.

Plaza Naco Hotel. In the Plaza Naco Mall, Ave. Presidente Gonzalez at Ave. Tiradentes (Apdo. Postal 30228), Santo Domingo, República Dominicana. ☎ **809/541-6226.** Fax 809/541-7251. 220 suites. A/C TV TEL. Year-round, $90–$100 junior suite for one or two; $130–$150 one-bedroom suite for up to four. Rates include breakfast. AE, MC, V.

An ideal accommodation for commercial travelers or for visitors seeking a lot of space and facilities, the Plaza Naco offers handsomely decorated accommodations equipped with computer safe-lock doors, guest safes, kitchenettes, dining rooms, and hair dryers.

There's a good restaurant and a cafeteria, plus a deli and minimarket. Those who want their own supplies for their suites can shop at the deli or the minimarket. Hotel guests are admitted free to the disco. There's also 24-hour room service, laundry, dry cleaning, bilingual secretarial and legal translation services, a rental-car desk, a tour desk, a sauna (with massage available), and a gym.

WHERE TO EAT

✪ **El Conuco.** Calle Casimiro de Moya 152. ☎ **809/221-3231.** Main courses RD$45–RD$150 ($3.40–$11.25). Daily noon–3pm and 7pm–2am. DOMINICAN/CRIOLLA.

Near the Jaragua Resort and Casino, close to the seafront avenue known as the Malecón, this well-managed and authentically Dominican restaurant celebrates, gastronomically and visually, the traditions of the Dominican Republic. Despite its urban location, it features many of the aesthetic traditions you'd have expected in the open countryside. (Indeed, its name translates as "the countryside.") Amid thatched roofs and potted and hanging plants, you'll find original paintings, hand-woven baskets, battered license plates from virtually every corner of the country, and occasional bouts of either live or recorded merengue music. Menu items include all the staples of the traditional Dominican kitchen, including *la bandera* (stewed beef served with rice and beans), fresh fish, spicy versions of grilled chicken, and different preparations of stewed codfish. There are four separate dining areas, some air-conditioned, others open-air.

Fonda La Atarazana. Calle Atarazana 5. ☎ **809/689-2900.** Main courses RD$95–RD$270 ($7.15–$20.25). AE, DC, MC, V. Daily 10am–1am. CREOLE/INTERNATIONAL.

His Name Was Rubi, He Was a Playboy

His nickname was Rubi, and he was widely reputed to be the world's greatest lover. A bow-legged polo player from the Dominican Republic, "Big Boy" Porfirio Rubirosa had a fatal charm that captured the hearts of countless women such as Joan Crawford and Zsa Zsa Gabor. Once described as "a tough guy with perfect manners," he even got two of the world's richest women, Doris Duke and Barbara Hutton (in that order) to marry him, although both marriages proved disastrous.

Although Rubirosa is largely unknown to today's generation, he was a media darling of the 1940s and 1950s. He was born the son of a general in the Dominican Republic, later moving with his family to Paris, where he was educated.

In 1930 the notorious dictator and strongman Gen. Rafael Trujillo took power in the the Dominican Republic, and Rubirosa was recruited into the army. In time the dictator, nicknamed "The Goat" because of his excesses, named Rubi his aide-de-camp. Flor de Oro (flower of gold), the nymphomaniac daughter of the dictator, met Rubirosa and was immediately attracted to him. Although Trujillo objected, they were married in 1932. Trujillo had many new jobs for his son-in-law, mainly arranging assassinations.

Regrettably, attempts to make a film of Rubi's life have never found financing. What an adventure story it would make! Although Rubi eventually divorced Flor de Oro, she had half the Dominican army to comfort her. Rubi ended up in France during the war, selling visas to wealthy Jewish people fleeing for their lives. The highest-paid movie star in France at the time was Danielle Darrieux, a known Nazi sympathizer. Rubi married her in 1942.

Years after the war the CIA released documents citing Rubi on its list of Nazi intelligence agents working in France. At the liberation of Paris, French Resistance fighters shot Rubi in his kidneys three times as he was driving in an automobile with his wife. He recovered, but it was never really known if the bullets were meant for him or for Danielle. When Rubi arrived with Danielle in Rome, a journalist showed up to interview him. Her name was Doris Duke, and she was the richest woman in the world. They were married in 1947 as he smoked a cigarette. After the divorce he married Barbara Hutton.

Rubi lived in the fast lane and died in the fast lane. The great Dominican playboy wrapped his Ferrari around a tree on the night of July 5, 1965. He'd been on a wild binge of drinking, womanizing, and nightclubbing in Paris. He was killed instantly. His young widow, Odile, was joined at his graveside by scores of mourning women.

This patio restaurant offers regional food in a colonial atmosphere, with night music for dancing and folklore festivals. Just across from the Alcázar, it's a convenient stop if you're shopping and sightseeing in the old city. A cheap, good dish is *chicharrones de pollo,* which is tasty fried bits of Dominican chicken. Or you might try curried baby goat in a sherry sauce. Sometimes the chef cooks lobster thermidor and Galician-style octopus. If you don't mind waiting half an hour, you can order the *sopa de ajo* (garlic soup). Many fans come here especially for the fricasséed pork chops.

La Baguette. Calle Gustavo Meija Ricart 126. ☎ **809/565-6432.** Snacks and pastries 25¢–$1.10. No credit cards. Mon–Sat 8:30am–8pm.

Don't expect fancy service and culinary chi-chi at this French bakery wanna-be. You'll stand up and place your order at the counter, then either carry your trove away or sit at the limited number of utilitarian tables in the corner. Menu items lean toward the snack-food and tasty morsel category, and include brochettes of pork, chicken, and beef; and turnovers (*pastelitos*) stuffed with cheese or meat. There's quite an array of sweets and pastries—flan, tarts, cookies, slices of cake, and the house version of mango mousse.

✪ **La Bahía.** Ave. George Washington 1. ☎ **809/682-4022.** Main courses RD$125–RD$250 ($9.40–$18.75). AE, MC, V. Daily 9am–2am. SEAFOOD.

You'd never know that this unprepossessing place right on the Malecón serves some of the best, and freshest, seafood in the Dominican Republic. One predawn morning as we passed by, fishermen were waiting outside to sell the chef their latest catch. Rarely in the Caribbean will you find a restaurant with such a wide range of seafood dishes. For your appetizer, you might prefer ceviche, sea bass marinated in lime juice, or lobster cocktail. Soups usually contain big chunks of lobster as well as shrimp. Specialties include kingfish in coconut sauce, sea bass Ukrainian style, baked red snapper, and seafood in the pot. Conch is a special favorite with the chef. Desserts are superfluous. The restaurant will stay open until the last customer departs.

✪ **La Canasta.** In the Sheraton Santo Domingo Hotel & Casino, Ave. George Washington 365. ☎ **809/221-6666.** Main courses RD$40–RD$200 ($3–$15). AE, DC, MC, V. Daily 8pm–6am. DOMINICAN.

The best late-night dining spot in the capital is set back from the Malecón, between the Omni Casino and the Omni Disco. It's not only economical but it also serves popular Dominican dishes culled from favorite recipes throughout the country, including *sancocho* (a typical stew with a variety of meats and yucca) and *mondongo* (tripe cooked with tomatoes and peppers). Other unusual dishes are goatmeat braised in a rum sauce and pigs' feet vinaigrette Créole style. Canasta is locally known for its *pollo a la plancha*, grilled chicken flavored with fresh Dominican herbs. The late-night dining hours are perfectly suited to the young Dominican clientele the restaurant serves, many of whom frequent the discos in the wee hours.

Scherezade. Calle Roberto Pastoriza 226 (at Calle Lope de Vega). ☎ **809/227-2323.** Reservations recommended. Main courses RD$175–RD$225 ($13.15–$16.90). AE, MC, V. Daily noon–midnight. ARABIC/ITALIAN/INTERNATIONAL.

Its name (heroine of the Arabic legend of *A Thousand and One Nights*) and decor (a simulation of a Moorish palace) evoke the Middle East better than anything else in town. A main dining room is divided into two sections. The bustling kitchen makes a roster of international dishes that are ambitious and for the most part successful. Menu items include pastas, osso bucco, fresh fish, Turkish-style shish kebabs, and well-flavored versions of Lebanese dishes such as tabouleh, tahini, and roast lamb with Mediterranean herbs. The staff is tactful, cosmopolitan, and better trained at their jobs than their colleagues at nearby competitors.

Toscana. Calle Erik Leonard Ekman 34, in Arroyo Hondo. ☎ **809/563-2777.** Main courses RD$95–RD$315 ($7.15–$23.65). AE, MC, V. Daily noon–midnight. ITALIAN/INTERNATIONAL.

Perpetually friendly srvice and hefty portions of good, fresh food continue to make this a popular spot. Set in the Arroyo Hondo district, north of the colonial zone, this Italian restaurant, with two dining rooms, serves flavorful versions of pastas, raviolis, lobster, fresh fish, and squid. Reminders of Créole and Caribbean food creep into the menu, thanks to such dishes as a cold ceviche of snapper or grouper; red snapper served with onions, capers, and herbs; and the selection of rum-based drinks with which to wash down your otherwise all-Italian meal.

✪ **Vesuvio I.** Ave. George Washington 521. ☎ **809/221-3333.** Reservations recommended Fri–Sat. Main courses RD$95–RD$325 ($7.20–$24.40). AE, DC, MC, V. Daily noon–1am. ITALIAN.

Along the Malecón, the most famous Italian restaurant in the Dominican Republic draws crowds of visitors and local businesspeople. What to order? That's always a problem here, as the Neapolitan owners, the Bonarelli family, have worked since 1954 to perfect and enlarge their menu. Their homemade soups are excellent. The restaurant prepares fresh red snapper, sea bass, and oysters in interesting ways. Recently, they have made some menu changes. They now offer *papardelle al Bosque* (with porcini mushrooms, rosemary, and garlic), kingfish carpaccio (thin-sliced cured fish, olive oil, chopped onion, and fresh ground black pepper), and black tallarini with shrimp à la crema. They also serve *agnollotti alla Salvia* (spinach and chicken in a creamy sage sauce), lobster Mediterráneo (chopped cold lobster with fresh tomatoes, onion, olive oil, and basil), and risotto tricolor (sun-dried tomatoes, basil, and mozzarella). Specialties include Dominican crayfish à la Vesuvio (topped with garlic and bacon).

The owner claims to be the pioneer of pizza in the Dominican Republic, and he makes a unique one next door in **Pizzeria Vesuvio**—a yard-long pizza pie! If you want to try his other Italian place, go to **Vesuvio II,** Ave. Tiradentes 17 (☎ **809/ 562-6060**).

ALL-YOU-CAN-EAT HOTEL LUNCH BUFFETS

✪ **Antoine's.** In the Sheraton Santo Domingo Hotel & Casino, ave. George Washington 361. ☎ **809/221-6666.** Reservations recommended. Lunch buffet RD$147.50–RD$175 ($11.05–$13.15). AE, DC, MC, V. Mon–Fri noon–3pm. INTERNATIONAL.

How this hotel set back from the Malecón makes any money on its all-you-can-eat buffets, we'll never know. Some locals seem to go hungry for a week before rushing in here to fill up at the groaning tables. The chefs seem versatile in all the kitchens of the world. Monday will be a French cuisine (not bad); Tuesday, Chinese (quite good); Wednesday, Dominican (they're much more at home here); and Thursday, Italian (only fair). Friday is the time to show up because, although you'll pay the top price (see above), it's still an amazing food value in that you can get your fill of fresh seafood.

✪ **El Alcázar.** In the Hotel Santo Domingo, Ave. Independencia at Ave. Abraham Lincoln. ☎ **809/221-1511.** Reservations required. Fixed-price lunch buffet RD$150 ($11.25). AE, DC, MC, V. Daily 11am–2pm. INTERNATIONAL.

The Dominican designer Oscar de la Renta created El Alcázar in a Moroccan motif, with aged mother-of-pearl, small mirrors, and lots of fabric. Dishes are always good, and sometimes excellent; well-made sauces add zest to the meals. The menu is likely to be Chinese one day, Mexican another day, Italian the next, although Monday is usually devoted to Dominican food. The presentation of the food and the service are two more reasons to dine here.

BEACHES & OUTDOOR ACTIVITIES

BEACHES   The Dominican Republic may have some great beaches, but they aren't in Santo Domingo. The principal beach resort near the capital is at **Boca Chica,** less than 2 miles east of the international airport and about 19 miles from Santo Domingo. Clear, shallow blue water laves the fine white-sand beach and a natural coral reef that protects the area from big fish. The east side of the beach, known as "St. Tropez," is popular with Europeans. Most of the major Santo Domingo hotels have swimming pools.

The great beaches are at **Puerto Plata,** but that's a rough 3-hour drive or an easy flight from the capital, and at **La Romana,** a 2-hour drive to the east (see sections 4 and 3, respectively, below).

GOLF   Serious golfers head for **Casa de Campo** with three 18-hole Pete Dye courses or the course that Robert Trent Jones designed at ✪ **Playa Dorada,** near Puerto Plata.

Golf is available in the capital at the **Santo Domingo Country Club;** it has an 18-hole course and often grants privileges to guests of some hotels. The rule here is members first, which means that it's impossible for weekend games. If your hotel doesn't have an arrangement with this club, you're out of luck.

TENNIS   Budget hotels rarely have courts, but you can often play on the courts of major hotels if you get your hotel desk to call in advance for you and make arrangements.

SPECTATOR SPORTS

BASEBALL   The national sport is baseball. The Dominican team is always a popular draw at the summer Olympics, and many of the country's native-born sons have gone on to the U.S. major leagues, including Yankee shortstop Tony Fernandez, Braves outfielder Luís Polonia, and perhaps the most famous, Tony Peña, a standout defensive catcher for many teams in the 1980s and 1990s. October to February, games are played at stadiums in Santo Domingo and elsewhere. Check the local newspaper for schedules and locations of the nearest game.

HORSE RACING   Santo Domingo's racetrack, **Hipódromo Peria Antillana,** on avenida San Cristóbal (☎ **809/565-3388**), schedules races on Tuesday, Thursday, and Saturday at 2pm. You can spend the day here and have lunch at the track's restaurant. Admission is free.

THE RELICS OF COLUMBUS & A COLONIAL ERA

Santo Domingo, a treasure trove of historic, sometimes-crumbling buildings, is undergoing a major government-sponsored restoration. The old town is still partially enclosed by remnants of its original city wall. The narrow streets, old stone buildings, and forts are like nothing else in the Caribbean, except Old San Juan. The only thing missing is the clank of the conquistadors' armor.

Old and modern Santo Domingo meet at the **Parque Independencia,** a big city square whose most prominent feature is its Altar de la Patria, a shrine dedicated to Duarte, Sanchez, and Mella, who are all buried here. These men led the country's fight for freedom from Haiti in 1844. As in provincial Spanish cities, the square is a popular family gathering point on Sunday afternoon. At the entrance to the plaza is **El Conde Gate,** named for the count (El Conde) de Penalva, the governor who resisted the forces of Admiral Penn, the leader of a British invasion. It was also the site of the March for Independence in 1844, and holds a special place in the hearts of Dominicans.

In the shadow of the Alcázar, **La Atarazana** is a fully restored section that centered around one of the New World's finest arsenals. It extends for a city block, a catacomb of shops, art galleries (both Haitian and Dominican paintings), boutiques, and some good regional and international restaurants.

Just behind river moorings is the oldest street in the New World, **Calle Las Damas** (Street of the Ladies). Some visitors assume that this was a bordello district, but actually it wasn't. Rather, the elegant ladies of the viceregal court used to promenade here in the evening. It's lined with colonial buildings.

Just north is the chapel of **Our Lady of Remedies,** where the first inhabitants of the city used to attend mass before the cathedral was erected.

Try also to see the **Puerta de la Misericordia.** Part of the original city wall, this "Gate of Mercy" was once a refuge for colonists fleeing hurricanes and earthquakes. To reach it, head 4 blocks west along Calle Padre Billini and turn left onto Calle Palo Hincado.

The **Monastery of San Francisco** is but a mere ruin, lit at night. That any part of it is still standing is a miracle; it was destroyed by earthquakes, pillaged by Drake, and bombarded by French artillery. To reach the ruins, go along Calle Hostos and across Calle Emiliano Tejera; continue up the hill and about midway along you'll see the ruins.

You'll see a microcosm of Dominican life as you head east along **Calle El Conde** from Parque Independencia to **Columbus Square,** which has a large bronze statue honoring the discoverer, made in 1882 by a French sculptor, and the **Catedral de Santa María la Menor** (see below).

Alcázar de Colón. Calle Emiliano Tejera (at the foot of Calle Las Damas). ☎ **809/689-4363.** Admission RD$10 (75¢). Mon and Wed–Fri 9am–5pm, Sat 9am–4pm, Sun 9am–1pm.

The most outstanding structure in the old city is the Alcázar, a palace built for the son of Columbus, Diego, and his wife, the niece of Ferdinand, king of Spain. Diego became the colony's governor in 1509, and Santo Domingo rose as the hub of Spanish commerce and culture in America. Constructed of native coral limestone, it stands on the bluffs of the Ozama River. For more than 60 years it was the center of the Spanish court and entertained such distinguished visitors as Cortés, Ponce de León, and Balboa. The nearly two dozen rooms and open-air loggias are decorated with paintings and period tapestries, as well as 16th-century antiques.

Casa del Cordón (Cord House). At Calle Emiliano Tejera and Calle Isabel la Católica. ☎ **809/ 682-4333.** Free admission. Tues–Sun 8am–4:30pm.

Near the Alcázar de Colón, the Cord House was named for the cord of the Franciscan order, which is carved above the door. Francisco de Garay, who came to Hispaniola with Columbus, built the casa in 1503–04, which makes it the oldest stone house in the Western Hemisphere. It once lodged the first royal audience of the New World, which performed as the Supreme Court of Justice for the island and the rest of the West Indies. On another occasion, in January 1586, the noble ladies of Santo Domingo gathered here to donate their jewelry as ransom demanded by Sir Francis Drake in return for his promise to leave the city.

✪ Catedral de Santa María la Menor. Calle Arzobispo Meriño (on the south side of Columbus Sq.). ☎ **809/682-6595.** Free admission. Cathedral, Mon–Sat 9am–4pm (Masses on Sun); Treasury, Mon–Sat 9am–4pm.

The oldest cathedral in the Americas was begun in 1514 and completed in 1540. With a gold coral limestone facade, it's a stunning example of the Spanish Renaissance style, with elements of Gothic and baroque. The cathedral, visited by Pope John Paul II in 1979 and again in 1984, was the center for a celebration of the 500th anniversary of the European Discovery of America in 1992. An excellent art collection of retables, ancient wood carvings, furnishings, funerary monuments, and silver and jewelry can be seen in the Treasury. On Sunday masses begin at 6am.

El Faro a Colón (Columbus Lighthouse). Ave. España (on the water side of Los Tres Ojos, near the airport in the Sans Souci district). ☎ **809/591-1492.** Admission RD$10 (75¢) adults, RD$5 (40¢) children 11 and under. Tues–Sun 10am–5pm.

Built in the shape of a pyramid cross, the towering El Faro a Colón monument is both a sightseeing attraction and a cultural center. In the heart of the structure is a chapel containing the Columbus tomb, and perhaps his mortal remains. The "bones" of Columbus were moved here from the Cathedral of Santa María la Menor (see above). (It should be pointed out that other locations, including the Cathedral of Seville, also claim to possess the remains of the explorer.) Adjacent to the chapel is a series of museums representing more than 20 countries, plus a museum dedicated to the history of Columbus and the lighthouse itself. The most outstanding and unique feature is the lighting system composed of 149 xenon Skytrack searchlights and a 70-kilowatt beam that circles out for nearly 44 miles. When illuminated, the lights project a gigantic cross in the sky that can be seen for miles beyond, even as far as Puerto Rico.

While the concept of the memorial dates back 140 years, the first stones were not laid until 1986 following the same design submitted in 1929 by J. L. Gleave, the winner of the worldwide contest held to choose an architect. The monumental lighthouse was inaugurated on October 6, 1992, the day Columbus's "remains" were transferred from the Santo Domingo cathedral, the oldest in the Americas. The multi-million-dollar monument stands 688 feet tall (taller than the Washington Monument) and 131 feet wide with sloping sides from 56 feet at the top to 109 feet at the bottom.

Museo de las Casas Reales (Museum of the Royal Houses). Calle Las Damas (at Calle Las Mercedes). ☎ **809/682-4202.** Admission RD$10 (75¢). Mon–Fri 9am–3pm, Sat 10am–5pm.

Through artifacts, tapestries, maps, and re-created halls, including a courtroom, this museum traces Santo Domingo's history from 1492 to 1821. Gilded furniture, arms and armor, and other colonial artifacts make it the most interesting of all museums of Old Santo Domingo. It contains replicas of the three ships commanded by Columbus, and one exhibit is said to hold part of the ashes of the famed explorer. You can see, in addition to pre-Columbian art, the main artifacts of two galleons sunk in 1724 on their way from Spain to Mexico, along with remnants of another 18th-century Spanish ship, the *Concepción.*

OTHER SIGHTS

In total contrast to the colonial city, modern Santo Domingo dates from the Trujillo era. A city of broad, palm-shaded avenues, its seaside drive is called **Avenida George Washington,** more popularly known as the **Malecón.** This boulevard is filled with restaurants, as well as hotels and nightclubs. Use caution at night—there are pickpockets galore.

We also suggest a visit to the **Paseo de los Indios,** a sprawling 5-mile park with a restaurant, fountain displays, and a lake.

About a 20-minute drive from the heart of the city, off the Autopista de las Américas on the way to the airport and the beach at Boca Chica, is **Los Tres Ojos** or "The Three Eyes," which stare at you across the Ozama River from Old Santo Domingo. There's a trio of lagoons set in scenic caverns, with lots of stalactites and stalagmites. One lagoon is 40 feet deep, another 20 feet, and yet a third—known as "Ladies Bath"—only 5 feet deep. A Dominican Tarzan will sometimes dive off the walls of the cavern into the deepest lagoon. The area is equipped with walkways.

Prieto Gray Line Tours of Santo Domingo, Ave. Francia 125 (☎ **809/ 685-0102**), the leading tour operator, will arrange a number of sightseeing excursions in the area. A daily 3-hour tour of the Colonial Zone costs $28. A more extensive 6-hour tour of the capital and its suburbs departs every Wednesday and Friday and costs $45. You can also take a 12-hour outing, by bus and boat, to the remote beaches of the Isla Saona, an island off the coast of La Romana, that departs every Saturday at 6:30am for $75.

Jardín Botánico. Ave. República de Colombia (at the corner of de los Proceres). ☎ **809/ 567-6211.** Admission RD$10 (75¢) adults, RD$5 (40¢) children. Tour by train RD$15 ($1.15) adults, RD$7 (55¢) children. Tues–Sun 9am–5pm.

Sprawled over 445 acres in the northern sector of the Arroyo Hondo, these are among the largest gardens of their kind in Latin America. They emphasize the flowers and lush vegetation native to the Dominican Republic, and require at least 2 hours to even begin to explore. A small, touristy-looking train makes a circuit through the park's major features, which include a Japanese Park, the Great Ravine, and a floral clock.

Museo de Arte Moderno. Plaza de la Cultura, Calle Pedro Henríquez Ureña. ☎ **809/ 685-2153.** Admission RD$10 ($1.50). Tues–Sat 9am–5pm.

The former site of the Trujillo mansion, plaza de la Cultura has been turned into a park and contains the Museum of Modern Art, which displays national and international works (the emphasis is, of course, on native-born talent).

Also in the center are the **National Library** (☎ **809/688-4086**) and the **National Theater** (☎ **809/687-3191**), which sponsors, among other events, folkloric dances, opera, outdoor jazz concerts, traveling art exhibits, classical ballet, and music concerts.

SHOPPING

The best buys are handcrafted native items, especially amber jewelry. Amber deposits, petrified tree resin that has fossilized over millions of years, are the national gem. Look for pieces of amber with trapped objects, such as insects and spiders, inside the enveloping material. Colors range from a bright yellow to black, but most of the gems are golden in tone. Fine-quality amber jewelry, along with lots of plastic fakes, is sold throughout the country.

A semiprecious stone of light blue (sometimes a dark-blue color), larimar is the Dominican turquoise. It often makes striking jewelry, and is sometimes mounted with wild boar's teeth.

Ever since the Dominicans presented John F. Kennedy with what became his favorite rocker, visitors have wanted to take home a rocking chair. To simplify transport, these rockers are often sold unassembled.

Other good buys include Dominican rum, hand-knit articles, macramé, ceramics, and crafts in native mahogany. Always haggle over the price, particularly in the open-air markets; no stallkeeper expects you to pay the first price asked. The best shopping streets are El Conde, the oldest and most traditional shop-flanked avenue, and avenida Mella.

In the colonial section, **La Atarazana** is filled with galleries and gift and jewelry stores, charging inflated prices. Duty-free shops are found at the airport, in the capital at the **Centro de los Héroes,** and at both the Hotel Santo Domingo and the Hotel Embajador. Shopping hours are generally 9am to 12:30pm and 2 to 5pm Monday to Saturday.

Ambar Marie. Caonabo 9, Gazcue. ☎ **809/682-7539.**

In case you're worried that the piece of amber you like may be plastic, you can be assured of the real thing at Ambar Marie, where you can even design your own setting for your choice gem. Look especially for the beautiful amber necklaces, as well as the earrings and pins.

Ambar Tres. La Atarazana 3. ☎ **809/688-0474.**

In the colonial section of the old city, Ambar Tres sells jewelry made from amber, black coral, mahogany carvings, watercolors, oil paintings, and other Dominican products.

✪ El Mercado Modelo. Ave. Mella.

Head first for the National Market, filled with stall after stall of crafts and spices, fruits, and vegetables. The merchants will be most eager to sell, so remember to bargain. You'll see a lot of tortoiseshell work here, but exercise caution, since many species, especially the hawksbill, are on the endangered-species list and could be impounded by U.S. Customs if discovered in your luggage. Rockers are for sale here, as are mahogany ware, sandals, baskets, hats, clay braziers for grilling fish, and so on.

Novo Atarazana. La Atarazana 21. ☎ **809/689-0582.**

At this well-established shop you can purchase amber, black coral, leather goods, wood carvings, and Haitian paintings.

Plaza Criolla. Ave. 27 de Febrero and ave. Anacaona.

Plaza Criolla is a modern shopping complex with a distinguished design theme. Shops are set in gardens with tropical shrubbery and flowers, facing the Olympic Center. The architecture makes generous use of natural woods, and a covered wooden walkway links the stalls together.

Tu Espacio. Ave. Cervantes 102. ☎ **809/686-6006.**

One of the most charming shops in the capital is crammed with all sorts of goodies, including Taíno art (hand-carved reproductions, of course), Dominican and European antiques, monumental bamboo furniture, and odds and ends that Victorians used to clutter their homes with. If you're looking for that special trinket, you're likely to find it here.

SANTO DOMINGO AFTER DARK
DANCING TO THE MERENGUE BEAT

La Guácara Taína. Calle Mirador, in Parque Mirador del Sur. ☎ **809/533-1051.** Cover (including your first drink) $7.50.

Merengue is king at the best *discoteca* in the Dominican Republic. This disco is in a cave, so you may have to duck the odd bat. It's located in a 4-mile-long park in a middle-class neighborhood. The rocky walls and arched ceilings reverberate with electronic music and live merengue shows.

Mesón de la Cava. Ave. Mirador del Sur 1. ☎ **809/533-2818.** Cover $1.50.

Behind El Embajador Hotel, this restaurant and nightclub built in a natural cave 50 feet under the ground provides live music for dancing. Shows with merengue music are offered, along with salsa, Latin jazz, and the blues. To reach it, you descend a perilous open-backed iron stairway.

At first we thought this was a mere gimmicky club, until we sampled the food and found it among the best in the capital. For an appetizer, you can choose from shrimp cocktail, onion soup, gazpacho, bisque of seafood, or red snapper chowder. Main courses include "gourmet" beefsteak, fresh sea bass in red sauce, tournedos, and coq au vin. You can finish with a sorbet. Meals average $18 per person, plus the cost of your drinks. Hot food is served daily from noon to 5pm and 6pm to 1am.

Neon Discotheque. In the Hispaniola Hotel, Ave. Independencia. ☎ **809/221-1511.** Cover RD$75 ($5.60); free for hotel guests.

One of the town's best-established dance clubs offers Latin jazz with different guest stars each week, although disco dancing under flashing lights is one of the main reasons for its popularity. The clientele tends to be very young, and includes many university students. The management reserves the right to accept only "well-behaved" guests.

Omni Disco / Diamante Bar. In the Sheraton Santo Domingo Hotel & Casino, Ave. George Washington 361. ☎ **809/221-6666.** Cover (Omni Disco) RD$100 ($7.50).

Anyone could while away an intriguing evening by dividing his or her time between these two watering holes, both of which lie on the premises of the Sheraton. The Omni Disco is one of the most artfully decorated discos in town, with mirrors and gray, green, and blue decor that functions as background for the throbbing, pulsating recorded music. If you consider yourself older and a bit more sedate (at least by D.R. standards), avoid the place on Tuesday nights, when it's slated as college night. After a while many visitors move on to the Diamante Bar, the showcase bar in the Sheraton's casino, in an annex building adjacent to the hotel itelf. Here, live bands perform merengue, salsa, and whatever might be popular in Latino circles in New York City, often with zest and flair. Both bars are open daily from 8pm to 4am.

PUBS & BARS

Most of the chic stops are in the big hotels.

Embassy Club. In the El Embajador Hotel, Ave. Sarasota 65. ☎ **809/221-2131.** Cover RD$100 ($7.50).

Outfitted with a sophisticated sound system, and decorated with bright colors and tropical motifs, this disco attracts the heirs and offspring of some of the capital's leading families, who dance to the live merengue and salsa music, flirt, and sometimes gossip with newcomers. Live music alternates with recorded music every evening, beginning at 8pm and continuing till 6am. Many patrons, just for a change of pace or else to find a bit younger clientele, eventually migrate the short distance over to the Guacara Taina disco and cave bar (recommended separately), whose entrance lies just behind the hotel.

Las Palmas. In the Hotel Santo Domingo, Ave. Independencia. ☎ **809/221-1511.**

This bar is adjacent to the lobby of the Hotel Santo Domingo, in premises that were originally decorated by Oscar de la Renta. Today it's best compared to a cross between a conventional bar and a disco, where the emphasis is on the bar trade between 6 and 9:30pm, and live music, such as salsa and merengue, from 9:30pm till closing time (4am). When someone isn't performing, large-screen TVs broadcast music videos beamed by satellite in from the U.S. mainland.

Merengue Bar. In the Jaragua Renaissance Resort & Casino, Ave. George Washington 367. ☎ **809/221-2222.**

The party atmosphere of this lively bar often spills out into the sophisticated Jaragua Casino. High-ceilinged and painted in dark, subtly provocative colors, it includes a sprawling bar area, a sometimes overcrowded dance floor, and rows of banquettes and tables that face a brightly lit stage. Here, animated bands from as far away as the Philippines crank out high-energy sounds daily beginning at 4pm and going strong until the wee hours of the morning. The joint really gets jumping around 10pm, when this bar/nightclub seems to forget that it operates in a jangling casino.

ROLLING THE DICE

Santo Domingo has several major casinos, all of which are open nightly till 4 or 5am. The most spectacular is the **Renaissance Jaragua Resort & Casino,** Ave. George

Washington 367 (☎ **809/221-2222**), whose brightly flashing sign is the most dazzling light along the Malecón at night. The most glamorous casino in the country is fittingly housed in the capital's poshest hotel, and offers blackjack, baccarat, roulette, and slot machines. You can gamble in either Dominican pesos or U.S. dollars.

Other casinos include **El Embajador Casino,** Ave. Sarasota 65 (☎ **809/221-2131**), where the popular games of blackjack, craps, and roulette are offered. In between gaming sessions, you can have a drink at La Fontana, the casual bar where hors d'oeuvres are served. Another casino is at the **Hispaniola Hotel,** Avenida Independencia (☎ **809/221-7111**).

One of the most stylish casinos is the **Omni Casino,** in the Sheraton Santo Domingo Hotel & Casino, Ave. George Washington 361 (☎ **809/221-1511**). Its bilingual staff will help you play blackjack, craps, baccarat, and keno, among other games. There's also a piano bar.

2 Barahona Peninsula

True bargain hunters are deserting the high-priced resorts such as Casa de Campo at La Romana and those sprawling megahotels at Punta Cana. Instead, they're heading for more remote parts of the island nation, where tourist structures are just developing. There is no more remote corner than the Barahona Peninsula, often called "a closely guarded secret" in the travel industry.

You're certainly off the beaten track here. This seldom-visited southwestern region is still unspoiled, unlike the overly developed north coast around Puerto Plata. It's a 3-hour drive west of Santo Domingo. The peninsula's chief city is Barahona, whose locals are called *Barahoneros*. Even more remote is the tiny fishing village of Baoruco, some 15 miles of coastal scenery southwest of Barahona.

GETTING THERE

If you don't have a car, call **Caribe Tours** (☎ **809/221-4422**) in Santo Domingo. This agency runs a minibus to the peninsula daily, charging $8 per person round-trip.

You can also call **Turinter** (☎ **809/686-4020**) or **Ecoturisa** (☎ **809/221-4104**), both in Santo Domingo; they conduct guided tours of the area's national parks and scenic wonderlands.

GETTING AROUND

Once here, if you came on your own by minibus, you can rent a car in Barahona from **Challenger Rent-a-Car** (☎ **809/524-2457**), which offers cars (often badly maintained) on a daily or weekly basis.

WHERE TO STAY & EAT

Hotel Caribe. Ave. Enriquillo, Barahona, República Dominicana. ☎ **809/524-4111.** Fax 809/524-4115. 24 rms. A/C TV TEL. Year-round, RD$250 ($18.75) single; RD$400 ($30) double. Rates Mon–Thurs include breakfast. AE, MC, V.

Painted a shade of pale blue both inside and out, this three-story hotel lies a few steps from the larger and better-accessorized Riviera Beach Hotel (see below). Unpretentious and carefully maintained by the Tesanos family, it occupies a strip of land near the sea, although anyone who wants to go swimming usually opts to walk for 5 minutes to a more hospitable stretch of sand nearby. There's no pool, no tennis courts, and few other vacation-oriented amenities. But the price represents extremely good value, the greeting is friendly, and the bedrooms offer comfortable retreats from the sun and sand. Although there's a restaurant and bar on the premises (Punta Inglés), the hotel does not cater to all-inclusive holidays, allowing you to pick where you want to dine and drink.

In Punta Inglés, main courses range from RD$90 to RD$175 ($6.75 to $13.15). Open daily from 7am to 11pm, it features grilled steaks, fried local fish, burgers, paella, and beer.

✪ **Riviera Beach Hotel.** Ave. Enriquillo 6, Barahona, República Dominicana. ☎ **809/524-5111.** Fax 809/524-5798. 108 rms. A/C TEL TV. Year-round, RD$830 ($62.25) single; RD$1,300 ($97.50) double. Rates include all meals and drinks. AE, DC, MC, V.

Partially financed by a local resident—a prosperous marble merchant of Lebanese descent—this is the largest and most mainstream hotel in Barahona. It's also one that encourages clients to check in as part of all-inclusive plans. Accented, as you'd expect, with touches of marble, it rises five stories above one of the best beaches in town. There's a generously proportioned swimming pool on the premises, a tennis court, and two restaurants, one (El Curro) specializing in à la carte dishes, the other (Mangall) featuring an almost endless roster of buffets. The bedrooms are simple, white-walled, and airy, each with a balcony but few other architectural pretensions.

A NEARBY PLACE TO STAY

Casa Bonita. Carretera de la Costa km 16, Baoruco (near Barahona), República Dominicana. ☎ **809/685-5184.** Fax 809/686-3940. 12 bungalows. Year-round, RD$885 ($66.40) bungalow for one; RD$1,120 ($84) bungalow for two. Rates include breakfast. AE, MC, V.

Built around 1990 as a low-slung cottage compound in the hamlet of Baoruco, a 15-minute drive south of Barahona, this low-key, slow-paced cottage colony has accommodations that consist of a dozen earth-toned *casitas* whose architecture emulates the natural, simple outdoor life favored in this obscure corner of the D.R. The setting here has been called Rousseau-esque. There's a swimming pool, a bar, a staff that speaks virtually no English, and both a river (the Baoruco) and a beach a short walk away. The food is a good reason to stay here. The chef, Miriam, who has been with the Schiffino family for a quarter of a century, has her own secret recipes and will feed you well.

PRISTINE BEACHES & UNTAMED NATURE

"The southwest," as it's known, is filled in part with small coffee plantations and weekend homes of the upper class of Santo Domingo. The beaches here are white sand, set against a terrain that looks rain foresty in parts. The beaches are all but deserted, although we did spot Oscar de la Renta here one time surveying the land for a fashion layout for *Vogue*.

Movie buffs, the type who knew how to read between the lines in Gore Vidal's outrageous *Myra Breckinridge*, will be happy to know (if they don't already) that the Barahona Peninsula was the birthplace of the glamorous Maria Montez, who has entered the legends of movie camp. Who can ever forget this temptress in *Tangier* or *The Siren of Atlantis*?

More alluring than the pristine beaches is a series of three government parks, among the most untamed in the Caribbean. One of these parks, **Parque Nacional Isla Cabritos,** is one of three islands in the **Lago Enriquillo,** bordering Haiti. This is the largest lake in the Caribbean, 21 miles in length. At 144 feet below sea level, it's also the lowest point in the Caribbean. Because of the lack of rain, it's a rather barren place with a few cacti and gnarled plants. However, people visit in hopes of getting a look at the American crocodile, which was imported to the lake in the early 1930s from Florida.

To visit, contact the **Dirección Nacional de Parques** (☎ 809/221-5340), which escorts visitors to the island twice a day. Nearly a dozen passengers are taken on a small launch for the 20-minute ride across a passage. The island is also home to wild goats, poisonous scorpions, and iguanas. If you want to spot a croc, it's best to take the first boat leaving at 7am.

Another national park, **Parque Nacional Bahoruco,** doesn't have adequate facilities for visitors. However, the most intrepid explore **Parque Nacional Jaragua,** named for a Taíno Indian chief. This very arid land covers some 520 square miles, the largest in the Dominican Republic. It's covered with desertlike vegetation, including many species of birds. Pink flamingos also live here. The park embraces Lago Oviedo, a saltwater lake east of the town of Oviedo. Pink flamingos frequent this lake. You'll really need to take a guided tour to reach this park on the Haitian border. Only trucks and Jeeps can get through, and there are no tourist facilities.

3 La Romana & Altos de Chavón

On the southeast coast of the Dominican Republic, La Romana was once a sleepy sugarcane town that also specialized in cattle raising, and unless one had business here with either industry, no tourist bothered with it. But when Gulf + Western opened (and later sold) a tropical paradise resort of refinement and luxury, Casa de Campo, on its outskirts, La Romana soon became known among the jet-set travelers. Just east of Casa de Campo is Altos de Chavón, a village built specially for artists.

GETTING THERE

BY PLANE   The easiest air routing to Casa de Campo from almost anywhere in North America is through San Juan, Puerto Rico (see "Getting There" in chapter 5). **American Eagle** (☎ 800/433-7300 in the U.S.) operates at least two (and in busy seasons, at three) daily nonstop flights to Casa de Campo / La Romana from San Juan. Each flight takes a little over an hour and departs late enough in the day to permit transfers from other flights.

BY CAR   If you're already in Santo Domingo, you can drive here in about an hour and 20 minutes from the international airport, along Las Américas Highway. (Allow another hour if you're in the center of the city.) Of course, everything depends on traffic conditions. (Watch for speed traps—low-paid police officers openly solicit bribes whether you were speeding or not.)

LA ROMANA
A SPECIAL SPLURGE

✪ **Casa de Campo.** La Romana, República Dominicana. ☎ **800/877-3643** or 809/523-3333. Fax 809/523-8548. 280 casitas, 150 villas. A/C MINIBAR TV TEL. Winter, $200–$225 casita for two; $445–$650 two-bedroom villa. Off-season, $145 casita for two; $260 two-bedroom villa. MAP $49 per person extra. AE, MC, V.

Translated as "House in the Country," Casa de Campo is one of the greatest resorts in the entire Caribbean area—and the competition is stiff. It brings a whole new dimension to a holiday. The ubiquitous Miami architect William Cox helped create it, and Oscar de la Renta provided the style and flair. Tiles, Dominican paintings, louvered doors, and flamboyant fabrics decorate the interior.

The accommodations consist of red-roofed, two-story casitas near the main building and more upscale villas that dot the edges of the golf courses, the gardens near the tennis courts, and the shores of the Atlantic. Some, within La Terrazza, are clustered in a semiprivate hilltop compound with views overlooking the meadows, the cane, and the fairways down to the distant sea. Villas, even off-season, are still very expensive. In winter, casitas for single or double occupancy costs $200 to $225, but off-season, the price for a casita drops to only $145 for a single or double—an amazing bargain!

WHERE TO EAT

El Patio. In Casa de Campo. ☎ **809/523-3333.** Main courses RD$85–RD$185 ($6.40–$13.90). AE, DC, MC, V. Daily 4pm–1am. CARIBBEAN/AMERICAN.

Originally designed as a disco, El Patio now contains a shield of lattices, banks of plants, and checkerboard tablecloths. Technically it's a glamorized coffee shop, but you can order some substantial daily specials such as shrimp or pork with rice, even goat stew. Meals might include ceviche, Cuban-style black-bean soup, sandwiches, salads, sirloin steaks, or pasta.

✪ **Lago Grill.** In Casa de Campo. ☎ **809/523-3333.** Buffet RD$250 ($18.75) at lunch, RD$350 ($26.25) at dinner. AE, DC, MC, V. Daily 7–11am, noon–4pm, and 7–11pm. CARIBBEAN/AMERICAN.

The Lago Grill is ideal for breakfast; in fact, it has one of the best-stocked morning buffets in the country. Your view is of a lake, a sloping meadow, and the resort's private airport, with the sea in the distance. At the fresh-juice bar, an employee in colonial costume will extract juices in any combination you prefer from 25 different tropical fruits. Then you can select your ingredients for an omelet and an employee will whip it up while you wait. The buffet includes sandwiches, burgers, *sancocho* (the famous Dominican stew), and fresh conch chowder. There's also a well-stocked salad bar. The hotel also presents a changing array of dinner buffets here, perhaps Chinese, Italian, or Dominican.

BEACHES & SPORTS GALORE AT CASA DE CAMPO

BEACHES   A large, palm-fringed sandy crescent, **Bayahibe** is a 20-minute launch trip or a 30-minute drive from La Romana. In addition, **La Minitas** is a tiny, but nice, immaculate beach and lagoon. Transportation is provided on the bus, or you can rent a horse-drawn buckboard. Finally, **Catalina** is a turquoise beach on a deserted island just 45 minutes away by motorboat.

GOLF   The **Casa de Campo** courses are known to dedicated golfers everywhere—in fact, *Golf* magazine called it "the finest golf resort in the world." The "Teeth of the Dog" course has also been called "a thing of almighty beauty"—and it is. The ruggedly natural terrain has seven holes skirting the ocean. "The Links" is the inland course, built on sandy soil away from the beach. Most golf passes are sold as 3-day memberships, priced at $165, which allows unlimited play; extra days cost $55 each. Rentals of golf carts are $20 per person per round. If anyone wants to play a mere 18 holes, the cost is $100 for "Teeth of the Dog" or $85 for "The Links." These prices include the use of a golf cart. Open daily from 7am to 7pm.

HORSEBACK RIDING   Trail rides at **Casa de Campo** cost $19 for 1 hour, $32 for 2.

SNORKELING   **Casa de Campo** has one of the most complete water-sports facilities in the Dominican Republic. Reservations and information on any seaside activity can be arranged through the resort's concierge. You can charter a boat for snorkeling. The resort maintains eight charter vessels, with a minimum of eight people required per outing. Wednesday to Monday, full-day snorkeling trips to Isla Catalina cost $30 per snorkeler.

TENNIS   A total of 13 clay courts at **Casa de Campo** are lit for night play. The courts are available daily from 7am to 10pm. Charges are $15 during the day or $18 at night.

ALTOS DE CHAVÓN: AN ARTISTS' COLONY

In 1976 a plateau 100 miles east of Santo Domingo was selected by Charles G. Bluhdorn, then chairman of Gulf + Western Industries, as the site for a remarkable project. Dominican stonecutters, woodworkers, and ironsmiths began the task that would produce Altos de Chavón, today a flourishing Caribbean art center set above the canyon of the Río Chavón and the Caribbean Sea.

A walk down one of the cobblestone paths of Altos de Chavón reveals at every turn architecture reminiscent of another era. Coral block and terra-cotta brick buildings house artists' studios, craft workshops, galleries, stores, and restaurants. Mosaics of black river pebbles, sun-bleached coral, and red sandstone spread out to the plazas. The **Church of St. Stanislaus** is centered on the main plaza, with its fountain of the four lions, colonnade of obelisks, and panoramic views.

The **School of Design** at Altos de Chavón has offered a 2-year Associate in Applied Science degree, in the areas of communication, fashion, environmental studies, product design, and fine arts/illustration since its inauguration in 1982. The school is affiliated with the Parsons School of Design in New York and Paris, providing local and international graduates with the opportunity to acquire the advanced skills needed for placement in design careers.

From around the world come artists-in-residence, the established and the aspiring. Altos de Chavón provides them with lodging, studio space, and a group exhibition at the culmination of their 3-month stay.

The **galleries** at Altos de Chavón offer a varied and engaging mix of exhibits. In three distinct spaces—the Principal Gallery, the Rincón Gallery, and the Loggia— the work of well-known and emerging Dominican and international artists is showcased. The gallery has a consignment space where finely crafted silk-screen and other multiple works are available for sale.

Altos de Chavón's *talleres* are craft ateliers, where local artisans have been trained to produce ceramic, silk-screen, and woven-fiber products. From the clay apothecary jars with carnival devil lids to the colored tapestries of Dominican houses, the richness of island myth and legend, folklore, and handcraft tradition is much in evidence. The posters, notecards, and printed T-shirts that come from the silk-screen workshops are among the most sophisticated in the Caribbean. All the products of Altos de Chavón's *talleres* are sold at **La Tienda,** the foundation village store.

Thousands of visitors annually view the Altos de Chavón **Regional Museum of Archaeology,** which houses the objects of Samuel Pion, an amateur archaeologist and collector of treasures from the vanished Taíno tribes, the island's first settlers. The timeless quality of some of the museum's objects makes them seem strangely contemporary in design—one discovers sculptural forms that recall the work of Brancusi or Arp. The museum is open daily from 9am to 9pm.

At the heart of the village's performing-arts complex is the 5,000-seat open-air **amphitheater.** Since its inauguration over a decade ago by Frank Sinatra and Carlos Santana, the amphitheater has hosted renowned concerts, symphonies, theater, and festivals, including concerts by Julio Iglesias and Gloria Estefan. The annual Heineken Jazz Festival has brought together such diverse talents as Dizzy Gillespie, Toots Thielmans, Tania Maria, and Randy Brecker.

WHERE TO EAT

Café de Sol. Altos de Chavón. ☎ **809/523-3333.** Pizza $8–$12. AE, MC, V. Daily 11am–11pm. ITALIAN.

The pizzas at this stone-floored indoor/outdoor cafe are the best on the south coast. The favorite seems to be *quattro stagioni,* made with tomato, mozzarella, mushrooms, artichoke hearts, cooked ham, and olives. You can also order such antipasti as a Mediterranean salad with tuna and ratatouille or a pasta primavera. The chef makes a soothing minestrone in the true Italian style, served with freshly made bread. To reach the cafe, climb a flight of stone steps to the rooftop of a building whose ground floor houses a jewelry shop.

El Sombrero. Altos de Chavón. ☎ **809/523-3333.** Reservations recommended. Main courses RD$135–RD$220 ($10.15–$16.50). AE, MC, V. Daily 6–11pm. MEXICAN.

In this thick-walled, colonial-style building, the jutting hand-hewn timbers and roughly textured plaster evoke a corner of Old Mexico. There's a scattering of dark, heavy furniture and an occasional genuine antique, but the main draw is the spicy cuisine. Most guests dine outside on the covered patio, within earshot of a group of wandering minstrels wearing sombreros. A margarita is an appropriate accompaniment to the nachos, enchiladas, black-bean soup, skillet-hot pork chops, grilled steaks, and brochettes.

La Piazzetta. Altos de Chavón. ☎ **809/523-3333.** Reservations required. Main courses RD$135–RD$220 ($10.15–$16.50). AE, MC, V. Wed–Mon 6–11pm. ITALIAN.

La Piazzetta snuggles in the 16th-century–style "village" set high above the Chavón River. Well-prepared Italian dinners might begin with an antipasto misto, followed with filet of sea bass with artichokes-and-black-olive sauce, chicken saltimbocca, or beef brochette with a walnut-and-arugula sauce. Your fellow diners are likely to be guests from the deluxe Casa de Campo nearby.

SHOPPING

Bugambilia. Altos de Chavón. ☎ **809/523-3333,** ext. 2355.

The staff will explain the origins of dozens of ceramic figures on display. Women have been sculpted in positions ranging from bearing water to carrying flowers to posing as brides; the female figures are crafted in the industrial city of Santiago as part of a long tradition of presenting peasant women without faces. Look, however, for an expression of dignity in the bodies of the figurines. The largest are packed but not shipped. The store also has a winning collection of grotesque papier-mâché carnival masks.

Everett Designs. Altos de Chavón. ☎ **809/523-3333,** ext. 8331.

The designs here are so original that many visitors mistake this place for a museum. Each piece of jewelry is handcrafted in a minifactory at the rear of the shop. Minnesota-born Bill Everett is the inspirational force for many of these pieces, which include Dominican larimar and amber, 17th-century Spanish pieces-of-eight from sunken galleons, and polished silver and gold.

Oscar de la Renta / Freya Boutique. Altos de Chavón. ☎ **809/523-3333,** ext. 2359.

With the exception of an outlet in Miami, this boutique is reputed to sell the creations of Señor de la Renta less expensively than anywhere else. Also for sale is a striking collection of purses and boxes cunningly fashioned from shell, bone, and cowhorn.

4 Puerto Plata

It was Columbus's intention to found a city at Puerto Plata and name it La Isabela. But a tempest detained him, and it wasn't until 1502 that Nicolás de Ovando founded Puerto Plata, or "port of silver," which lies 130 miles northwest of Santo Domingo. The port became the last stop for ships going back to Europe, their holds laden with treasures taken from the New World.

Puerto Plata appeals to vacationers who may shun more expensive resorts, and some hotels boast a nearly full occupancy rate almost year-round. It's already casting a shadow on business at longer-established resorts throughout the Caribbean, especially in Puerto Rico.

Most of the hotels are not actually in Puerto Plata itself but are in a special tourist zone called **Playa Dorada.** The backers of this usually sun-drenched spot have poured vast amounts of money into a flat area between a pond and the curved and verdant shoreline. (It rains a lot in Puerto Plata during the winter, whereas the south is drier.) There are major hotels, a coterie of condominiums and villas, a Robert Trent Jones–designed golf course, and a riding stable with horses for each of the major properties.

GETTING THERE

BY PLANE The international airport is actually not in Puerto Plata but is east of Playa Dorado on the road to Sosúa. For information about flights from North America, see "Getting There" at the beginning of this chapter.

BY CAR From Santo Domingo, the $3^1/2$-hour drive directly north on Autopista Duarte passes through the lush Cibao Valley, home of the tobacco industry and Bermudez rum, and through Santiago de los Caballeros, the second-largest city in the country, 90 miles north of Santo Domingo.

GETTING AROUND

For information on renting a car, see "Getting Around" at the beginning of this chapter. You might find that a motor scooter will be suitable for transportation in Puerto Plata or Sosúa, although the roads are potholed.

BY MOTOCONCHO The cheapest way of getting around is on a *motoconcho,* found at the major corners of Puerto Plata and Sosúa. This motorcycle *concho* (taxi) offers a ride to practically anywhere in town. You can also go from Puerto Plata to Playa Dorada (site of most of the hotels). Fares range from RD$10 to RD$25 (75¢ to $1.90).

BY MINIVAN Minivans are another means of transport, especially if you're traveling outside town. They leave from Puerto Plata's Central Park and will take you all the way to Sosúa. Determine the fare before getting in. Usually a shared ride between Puerto Plata and Sosúa costs RD$10 (75¢) per person. Service is daily from 6am to 9pm.

BY TAXI Agree with the driver on the fare before your trip starts, as the vehicles are not metered. You'll find taxis on Central Park at Puerto Plata. At night it's wise to rent your cab for a round-trip. If you go in the daytime by taxi to any of the other beach resorts or villages, check on reserving a vehicle for your return trip.

BY ORGANIZED TOUR One of the best-value local tour operators is **Apollo Tours,** Calle John F. Kennedy 15 (☎ **809/586-6610**). Operators of minivans or buses containing between 15 and 33 passengers, it conducts tours of Puerto Plata and the surrounding sites for RD$230 ($17.25) per person. More far-flung are the city tours of Santo Domingo, conducted every Wednesday and Friday for RD$600 ($45) per person.

ESSENTIALS

Round-the-clock drugstore service is offered by **Farmacía Deleyte,** Calle John F. Kennedy 89 (☎ **809/586-2583**). Emergency medical service is provided by **Clínica Dr. Brugal,** Calle José del Carmen Ariza 15 (☎ **809/586-2519**). To summon the **police** in Puerto Plata, call ☎ **809/586-2331.** Tourist information is available in Puerto Plata at the **Office of Tourism,** Playa Long Beach (☎ **809/586-3676**).

WHERE TO STAY
DOUBLES FOR LESS THAN $35

Hostal Jimessón. Calle John F. Kennedy 41, Puerto Plata, República Dominicana. ☎ **809/586-5131.** Fax 809/586-7313. 22 rms. A/C. Year-round, RD$300 ($22.45) single or double. Rates include morning coffee. AE, MC, V.

This is about as simple a hotel as this guide is willing to recommend. It lies in the commercial heart of downtown Puerto Plata, in what was originally a rather grand wood-sided house whose vestiges of gingerbread still remain. The public rooms have high ceilings, remnants of a faded grandeur, and some unusual antiques. The bedrooms, however, lack the charm of the front rooms. In a cinder-block addition in back, they're small, anonymous, and somewhat cramped. There are almost no resort-style amenities to speak off, but the staff is polite and the price really can't be beat. No more than two occupants are ever allowed in any bedroom. Only coffee is served in the morning, but there are several cafes in the neighborhood, as well as the many inexpensive restaurants in town.

Montemar. Ave. Las Hermanas Mirabal (Apdo. Postal 382), Puerto Plata, República Dominicana. ☎ **809/586-2800.** Fax 809/586-2009. 60 rms. A/C MINIBAR TV TEL. RD$450 ($33.75) double. AE, DC, MC, V.

Remodeled in 1995, the Montemar complex east of the airport plays a double role: It's one of the area's pioneer resorts, and it houses the local hotel school whose staff is well meaning but untrained. The distinctive lobby has large bamboo chandeliers and a mural behind the reception desk. Most of the accommodations have views of palms and the sea; some rooms are air-conditioned.

A lounge nearby engages a merengue band, which plays every night beside the illuminated palms. There are two tennis courts. Laundry, baby-sitting, and room service are provided. Three times a day a shuttle bus from the hotel takes guests to the beach. No meals are served.

THE BEST ALL-INCLUSIVE DEALS

Caribbean Village Club on the Green. Playa Dorada, Puerto Plata, República Dominicana. ☎ **809/320-1111.** Fax 809/320-5386. 336 rms, 144 suites. A/C TV TEL. Winter, $95 per person double or suite. Off-season, $75 per person double or suite. Rates are all-inclusive. AE, MC, V.

Upgraded in 1996 by a hotel chain, this modern low-rise property is near a cluster of competitors east of the airport. The hotel offers comfortable but simple bedrooms, and the all-inclusive rates include three meals a day, all beverages, and some water sports. Surprisingly, the so-called suites aren't much different from the regular doubles—and don't cost any more.

Standard Dominican and international food is offered at El Pilon, Italian pastas at Firenze, and fresh fish and seafood and local beef on the continental menu at La Miranda. At that last restaurant you may want to sample some of the excellent

Chilean vintages, all at reasonable prices. Facilities include water sports, seven all-weather tennis courts, a gym, sauna, and swimming pool with swim-up bar.

Villas Doradas Beach Resort. Playa Dorada (Apdo. Postal 1370), Puerto Plata, República Dominicana. ☎ **809/320-3000.** Fax 809/320-4790. 244 rms. A/C TV TEL. Year-round, $90 per person double. Rates are all-inclusive. AE, MC, V.

This collection of town houses east of the airport is arranged in landscaped clusters, usually around a courtyard. There's no beachfront here. Each unit is pleasantly furnished with louvered doors and windows. Personal service from the lackadaisical staff seems at a minimum here. A focal point of the resort is the restaurant Las Garzas, where shows entertain guests every evening beneath the soaring pine ceiling. The management also features barbecues around the pool area, where a net is sometimes set up for volleyball games. Of course, it would be tempting never to leave the shade of the cone-shaped thatch-roofed pool bar, which is one of the most popular parts of the whole resort. El Pescador is a fish restaurant open for dinner beside the beach, and Pancho serves Mexican dishes. For Chinese food, Jardín de Jade is another option. Facilities include a swimming pool, tennis, horseback riding, and kiddie pool, as well as sand beaches and golf facilities within walking distance.

WORTH A SPLURGE

✪ **Dorado Naco Resort Hotel.** Playa Dorada (Apdo. Postal 162), Puerto Plata, República Dominicana. ☎ **800/322-2388** or 809/320-2019. Fax 809/320-3608. 133 rms. A/C TV TEL. Winter, $107–$117 per person double. Off-season, $78–$93 per person double. Rates are all-inclusive. Third and fourth person $77 each in winter, $70 each off-season. Children 2–12 $32 a day; children under 2 stay free in parents' room. AE, DC, MC, V.

After registering, you'll be ushered past the poolside bar and restaurant complex, down a series of flowered walkways into your room. Each unit contains comfortable furniture, a kitchen, and a creative arrangement of interior space. You can spend some of your evenings cooking at home. Many units are clustered along parapets or around well-planted atriums, and some larger ones include duplex floor plans and enough spacious luxury to satisfy any vacationer. A wide array of entertainment is available, and a full range of activities is planned throughout the week in season. A beach bar and grill lie a short walk from every room. A nightly buffet is spread under a portico near the pool, and à la carte meals are available in the Flamingo Gourmet Restaurant and Valentino's Italian restaurant. Consider the Flamingo for dining even if you're not a hotel guest—it's one of the best in the area, serving a continental menu. The hotel has live music every night and live shows twice weekly. Facilities include a swimming pool, tennis court, and a water-sports center (for scuba diving, snorkeling, waterskiing, and sailing).

WHERE TO EAT

Another World / Otro Mundo. Km 7, Hwy. Puerto Plata–Sosúa. ☎ **809/320-4400** or 809/543-8019. Reservations recommended. Main courses RD$85–RD$275 ($6.40–$20.65). DC, MC, V. Daily 6pm–midnight. INTERNATIONAL.

This is the most prosperous and unusual independent restaurant in Puerto Plata; it attracts diners from the nearby all-inclusive hotels. About a mile east of the Playa Dorada tourist zone, in a green-sided Victorian building, it has a benign resident ghost that some readers claim to have spotted, an indoor/outdoor format accented with tropical touches, and an ersatz zoo whose residents (a tiger, monkeys, a honey bear, and wild birds) were all once abused before finding a home with the restaurant's kind-hearted owner. That owner is Stuart Ratner, a New York–born singer and actor who appeared in some productions during the 1970s with Barbra Streisand.

("I came here on holiday 14 years ago and never left.") Precede a meal here with the place's most popular drink, a "cocolobo, guaranteed to make you fly." It contains about four times the amount of alcohol in a "normal" cocktail. Follow with food that by local standards is almost incomprehensibly exotic, including frogs' legs, deep-water Caribbean crab, river prawns, chateaubriand, and beef Wellington. Also featured is fresh local fish, especially snapper. Live music is sometimes part of the entertainment.

Jardín de Jade. In the Villas Doradas Beach Resort, Playa Dorada. ☎ **809/586-3000.** Reservations recommended. Main courses RD$180–RD$275 ($6–$20.65). AE, DC, MC, V. Daily 7–11pm. CHINESE.

A high-ceilinged, airy, modern restaurant, Jardín de Jade offers the finest Chinese food in the area. Typical menu items include barbecued Peking duck, sautéed diced chicken in chile sauce, and fried crab claws. The chefs specialize in Cantonese and Szechuan cuisine. You've probably eaten these dishes before in better-prepared versions, but at least this restaurant provides a change of pace among other spots that tend to overcook food and overdo deep-frying. Because it's located in a solidly booked resort, it has a captive audience, yet it remains solid and reliable. Staff attitude and service continue to get low marks, however.

✪ **Porto Fino.** Ave. Las Hermanas Mirabal. ☎ **809/586-2858.** Main courses RD$45–RD$190 ($3.40–$14.25). AE, MC, V. Daily 10am–11pm. ITALIAN.

This popular Italian restaurant, just across from the entrance of the Hotel Montemar in Puerto Plata, serves up generous helpings of parmesan breast of chicken, eggplant parmesan, ravioli, and pizzas. You'll get off cheap if you order only pizza. Locals and visitors mingle freely here. This is a place to go for a casual meal in casual clothes, and not for some major gastronomic experience.

Roma II. Calle Beller at Emilio Prud'homme. ☎ **809/586-3904.** Main courses RD$60–RD$275 ($4.50–$20.65); pizza RD$50–RD$100 ($3.75–$7.50). AE, MC, V. Daily 11am–midnight. INTERNATIONAL.

This air-conditioned restaurant in the corner of town is staffed by an engaging crew of well-mannered young employees who work hard to converse in English. You can order from 13 varieties of pizza, such as cheese, shrimp, and garlic. Seafood dishes include paella and several preparations of lobster and sea bass. The menu is unfussy, as is the preparation. Don't look for any new taste sensations (except for octopus vinaigrette, one of the chef's specialties). The meat dishes, such as filet steak, are less successful than the fish offerings.

BEACHES, WATER SPORTS & OTHER OUTDOOR PURSUITS

The north coast is a water-sports scene, although the sea here tends to be rough. Snorkeling is popular, and the windsurfing is among the best in the Caribbean. The resort of **Cabarete,** east of Puerto Plata, hosts an annual windsurfing tournament.

BEACHES You'll find superb beaches to the east and west of Puerto Plata. Among the better known are Playa Dorada, Sosúa, Long Beach, Cofresi, Jack Tar, and Cabarete.

GOLF Robert Trent Jones Jr. designed the par-72, 18-hole **Playa Dorada championship golf course** (☎ **809/320-4362**), which surrounds the resorts and runs along the coast. Even nongolfers can stop at the clubhouse for a drink or a snack to enjoy the views. It's best to make arrangements at the activities desk of your hotel. Greens fees are RD$350 ($26.25) for 18 holes, RD$175 ($13.15) for 9 holes. You can hire a caddy for RD$135 ($10.15) for 18 holes, RD$75 ($5.65) for 9 holes. Cart rental costs RD$350 ($26.25) for 18 holes, RD$220 ($16.50) for 9 holes.

TENNIS   Nearly all the major resort hotels have tennis courts. If yours doesn't, there are seven all-weather tennis courts at the **Caribbean Village Club on the Green** (see previous recommendation), although guests at the resort come first, of course.

SEEING THE SIGHTS

Fort San Felipe, the oldest fort in the New World, is a popular attraction. Philip II of Spain ordered its construction in 1564, a task that took 33 years to complete. Built with 8-foot-thick walls, the fort was virtually impenetrable, and the moat surrounding it was treacherous—the Spaniards sharpened swords and embedded them in coral below the surface of the water to discourage use of the moat for entrance or exit purposes. The doors of the fort are only 4 feet high, another deterrent to swift passage. During Trujillo's rule Fort San Felipe was used as a prison. Standing at the end of the Malecón, the fort was restored in the early 1970s. Admission is RD$10 (80¢). It's open Thursday to Tuesday from 8am to 4pm.

Isabel de Torres (☎ **809/586-2325**), a tower with a fort built when Trujillo was in power, affords a panoramic view of the Amber Coast from a point near the top, 2,595 feet above sea level. You reach the observation point by cable car *(teleférico),* a 7-minute ascent. Once here, you are also treated to 7 acres of botanical gardens. The round-trip costs RD$80 ($6) for adults, RD$20 ($1.50) for children 12 and under. The aerial ride is operated Thursday to Tuesday from 8am to 5pm. There's often a long wait in line for the cable car, and at certain times it's closed for repairs, so check at your hotel before going there.

You can see a collection of rare amber specimens at the **Museum of Dominican Amber,** Calle Duarte 61 (☎ **809/586-2848**). The museum, open Monday to Saturday from 9am to 5pm, is near Puerto Plata's Central Park. Guided tours in English are offered. Admission is RD$20 ($1.50) for adults, RD$5 (40¢) for children.

The neoclassical house sheltering the Amber Museum also contains the densest collection of **boutiques** in Puerto Plata. Merchandise is literally packed into seven competing establishments. A generous percentage of the paintings is from neighboring Haiti, but the amber, larimar, and mahogany wood carvings are from the Dominican Republic. On the premises is a patio bar.

SHOPPING

The **Plaza Turisol Complex,** the largest shopping center on the north coast, has about 80 different outlets. Each week, or so it seems, a new store opens. You may want to head here to get a sampling of the merchandise available in Puerto Plata before going to any specific recommendation. The plaza lies about 5 minutes from the centers of Puerto Plata and Playa Dorada, on the main road heading east. Nearby is a smaller shopping center, **Playa Dorada Plaza,** with about 20 shops, selling handcrafts, clothing, souvenirs, and gifts. Both centers are open daily from 9am to 9pm.

The **Centro Artesanal,** Calle John F. Kennedy 3 (☎ **809/586-3724**), is a non-profit school for the training of future Dominican craftspeople, and it's also a promotion center for local crafts and jewelry. Selected student projects are for sale.

The **Plaza Isabela,** in Playa Dorada about 500 yards from the entrance to the Playa Dorada Hotel complex, is a collection of small specialty shops constructed in the Victorian gingerbread style, although much of its inventory has a Spanish inspiration and/or flair. Here you'll find the main branch of Dominican Republic's premier jeweler, **Harrison's,** Plaza Isabela, Playa Dorada (☎ **809/586-3933**). Established in 1980 by Boston-born Robert Harrison, it's a specialist in the application of their "trademark metal," platinum. Oddly, although there are almost two dozen branches of Harrison's in the Dominican Republic, the chain—at least as yet—has no outlets anywhere else in the world. Celebrities wearing the jewelry have included Madonna, Michael Jackson, Keith Richards of the Rolling Stones, and Patrick Swayze. There's another branch of this store in the Playa Dorada Shopping Plaza in the Playa Dorada Hotel complex.

CASINOS: THE HOT TICKET IN PUERTO PLATA AFTER DARK

These are both open daily until 5am.

Jack Tar Village. Playa Dorada. ☎ **809/320-3800.**

Jack Tar joins the gaming flock with a casino and disco, along with a European-style restaurant. It's built in Spanish Mediterranean colonial style with a terra-cotta roof. Between bouts at the gaming tables, guests quench their thirst at one of five bars. There's also an entertainment center that includes a 90-seat restaurant and a disco for 250 dancers.

Playa Dorada Casino. In the Playa Dorada Hotel, Playa Dorada. ☎ **809/586-3988.**

The casino's entrance is flanked by columns and leads to an airy garden courtyard. Inside, mahogany gaming tables are reflected in the silver ceiling. No shorts are permitted inside the premises after 7pm, and beach attire is usually discouraged.

DANCE CLUBS

The Playa Dorada Hotel complex contains about 20 hotels, 5 of which have discos that welcome anyone, resident or not, into their confines. None of them charges a cover, and the almost-universal drink of choice, Presidente Beer, costs around RD$40 ($3) a bottle. As in any disco in a holiday resort, the clientele includes off-hours hotel employees, some local residents, and tourists. Three of the best are in the Playa Dorado Hotel complex: **Andromeda,** in the Hotel Heaven (☎ **809/320-5250**), a high-voltage club off the hotel's lobby that opens nightly at 10pm; **Crazy Moon,** in the Paradise Hotel (☎ **809/320-3663**), outfitted in a colonial Caribbean style, with open-air balconies; and **Frankie's,** in the Playa Dorada Hotel (☎ **809/586-3988**), one of the most animated nightspots in Puerto Plata. You can also stop by **Vivaldi's,** a ground-floor disco at the corner of Avenida Las Hermanas Mirabel and the Malecón (☎ **809/586-3752**), which charges a cover of RD$50 ($3.70).

5 Sosúa

About 15 miles east of Puerto Plata is one of the finest beaches in the Dominican Republic, Sosúa beach, a strip of white sand more than half a mile wide in a cove sheltered by coral cliffs. The beach connects two communities, which together make up the town known as Sosúa. But, regrettably, you may not be allowed to enjoy a day on the beach in peace, as vendors and often beggars pursue visitors aggressively.

At one end of the beach is **El Batey,** an area with residential streets, gardens, restaurants, shops, and hotels that can be visited by those who can tear themselves away from the beach. Real-estate transactions have been booming in El Batey and its environs, where many streets have been paved and villas constructed.

At the other end of Sosúa beach lies **Los Charamicos,** a sharp contrast to El Batey. Here you'll find tin-roofed shacks, vegetable stands, chickens scrabbling in the rubbish, and warm, friendly people. This community is a typical Latin American village, recognizable through the smells, sights, and sounds in the narrow, rambling streets.

Sosúa was founded in 1940 by European Jews seeking refuge from Hitler, when Trujillo invited 100,000 of them to settle in his country on a banana plantation. Actually, only 600 or so Jews were allowed to immigrate, and of those, only about a dozen or so remained. However, there are some 20 Jewish families living in Sosúa today, and for the most part they are engaged in the dairy and smoked-meat industry the refugees began during the war. Many of the Jews intermarried with Dominicans, and the town has taken on an increasingly Spanish flavor; women of the town are often seen wearing both the Star of David and the Virgin de Altagracia. Nowadays many German expatriates are also found in the town.

GETTING THERE

Taxis, charter buses, and públicos from Puerto Plata and Playa Dorada let passengers off at the stairs leading down from the highway to Sosúa beach. Take the autopista east for about 30 minutes from Puerto Playa. If you venture off the main highway, anticipate potholes that fall all the way to China.

WHERE TO STAY

DOUBLES FOR LESS THAN $60

✪ **Hotel Sosúa.** Calle Dr. Alejo Martínez, El Batey, Sosúa, República Dominicana. ☎ **809/ 571-2683.** Fax 809/571-2180. 40 rms. A/C TV TEL. Year-round, $35 single; $50 double. Rates include continental breakfast. AE, MC, V.

Although this has been one of the best choices for affordable accommodations in Sosúa for at least a decade, it was made even better in 1994 after the owners completely renovated the interior. It's in a suburban community about a 2-minute drive from the center of town. Its simple and attractive layout includes a reception area designed to conceal a flagstone-rimmed pool from the street outside. The bedrooms are strung along a wing extending beside the pool and contain simple furniture that was for the most part crafted locally. The bedrooms contain ceiling fans, a minifridge, and an occasional pinewood balcony. On the premises is a restaurant (La Tortuga, recommended below), a minigym, a bar, and a boutique selling the day-to-day necessities that tourists might need.

Hotel Yaroa. El Batey, Sosúa, República Dominicana. ☎ **809/571-2651.** Fax 809/571-3814. 24 rms. A/C. Year-round, $30 single; $54 double. MAP $10 extra. AE, MC, V.

The Yaroa is named after a long-ago native village. It encompasses views of dozens of leafy trees that ring its foundations. Inside you'll find an atrium illuminated by a skylight, lots of exposed wood and stone, and a well-designed garden ringing a sheltered swimming pool. Each bedroom has a Spanish-style *mirador* (sheltered balcony) with a planter filled with local ferns, pine louvers for privacy, terra-cotta floors, and airy space. Two of the accommodations are designed like private cabañas at poolside. Breakfasts, light lunches, and dinners featuring French cuisine are served in the dining room, Yaroa (see "Where to Eat," below).

Villas los Coralillos. Alejo Martínez 1, Sosúa (Apdo. Postal 851), Puerto Plata, República Dominicana. ☎ **809/571-2645.** Fax 809/571-2095. 48 studios, 5 villas. A/C. Winter, $56 studio for one or two; $120 villa for four. Off-season, $40 studio for one or two; $100 villa for four. AE, DC, MC, V.

The well-furnished accommodations here are in a series of terra-cotta–tiled Iberian villas cantilevered over a bougainvillea-draped hillside. The action centers around the pool and main restaurant overlooking Sosúa Bay. Guests can request one- or two-bedroom villas, and the views from some of the villas are among the most panoramic in Sosúa. Each standard unit has twin beds and a small veranda. Villas have TVs; studios don't. Dining is at the hotel's El Coral Restaurant (see "Where to Eat," below). The hotel has added yet another restaurant directly on the beach, La Bahía, serving pizzas, and it's open daily from 8am to 3am. Los Coralillos is the only hotel in town with direct access to the main Sosúa beach; if you tire of the pool, you can stroll to the sea through century-old mahogany and almond trees.

THE BEST ALL-INCLUSIVE DEALS

Casa Marina / Club Marina. La Playita, Sosúa, República Dominicana. ☎ **809/571-3690.** Fax 809/571-3110. 344 rms. A/C TV TEL. Year-round, Casa Marina, $115 single; $160 double. Club Marina, $95 single; $140 double. Rates are all-inclusive. AE, MC, V.

These twin hotels were erected in 1987 as part of the building boom that swept over Sosúa. Originally conceived as different entities, with separate and unequal facilities, they were enlarged and combined in 1996 into a more seamless whole. What's the difference between the two? Residents of the Club Marina's 44 bedrooms have to walk about 3 minutes to reach the resort's main cluster of dining, drinking, entertainment, and water-sports facilities at Playita Beach, a short drive from the center of Sosúa. By far the larger hotel is the Casa Marina, with 300 units scattered among eight separate annexes. (Except for their views, over a pool or a garden, the 44 units at the Club Marina are equivalent in virtually every way, but cost less because of their relative isolation from the heart of the resort's action.) Throughout the complex, color schemes are brightly tropical, with locally made furniture and touches of rattan. Residents of both properties share access, all-inclusive, to three swimming pools, a medley of bars, a pair of restaurants specializing in Italian food and seafood, and an area that's devoted to an almost nonstop regiment of mass-produced buffets.

Punta Goleta Resort. Cabarete Rd., Cabarete, Sosúa, República Dominicana. ☎ **809/ 571-0700.** Fax 809/571-8707. 196 rms. A/C TV. Winter, $100 single; $170 double. Off-season, $85 single; $140 double. Rates include all meals. AE, MC, V.

Built in 1986, and set on about 100 acres of sandy, palm-dotted soil, this all-inclusive resort makes it a point to include enough distractions to keep a guest busy. The resort is designed in a neo-Victorian theme, with gingerbread trim and pastel colors. The location is private without being isolated, and in 1994 the management repainted and remodeled much of the hotel. There are two restaurants on the premises, one of which serves barbecued foods in a beachfront setting, and a disco, swimming pool, two tennis courts, and at least three different bars. Windsurfing is excellent in the waters offshore.

WORTH A SPLURGE

Sosúa by the Sea. Sosúa Beach, Sosúa (Apdo. Postal 361), Puerto Plata, República Dominicana. ☎ **809/571-3222.** Fax 809/571-3020. 46 studios, 35 apts. A/C MINIBAR TV TEL. Year-round, $75 studio; $92 apt. AE, MC, V.

The blue-and-white main building here is softened with inviting wooden lattices. The pool area opens onto Sosúa Bay, and the resort stands on a coral cliff above the beach. From the open-air rooftop lounge you have a view of Mount Isabel de Torres. The accommodations lie along meandering paths through tropical gardens. Reached by elevator, the airy but rather basic bedrooms are either studios or one-bedroom apartments, all with safes.

A formal restaurant serves both Dominican specialties and an international cuisine with live entertainment, and you can have lunch at the poolside bar and grill. The hotel has many amenities, including a massage parlor and a beauty salon.

WHERE TO EAT

✪ El Coral. El Batey. ☎ **809/571-2645.** Reservations recommended. Main courses RD$90–RD$300 ($6.75–$22.50). AE, DC, MC, V. Daily 7am–10:30pm. CARIBBEAN.

The best and arguably the most pleasant restaurant in town is El Coral, in a Spanish-style building set at the bottom of the garden near the end of the Sosúa beach. It offers a spacious area with terra-cotta tiles, wooden accents, and stark-white walls opening onto a panoramic view of the ocean. If you look out over the rear garden from one of the flowered terraces or through one of the big windows, you see a pool midway down the hill leading to the ocean. There's a bar adjoining the dining room. The specialties include conch or octopus Créole style, pork chops with pineapple, and shrimp with garlic. Dishes are tasty and filled with flavor. The cooks long ago fine-tuned their cooking, and they like to keep turning out the dishes they already know best without any experimentation.

La Puntilla de Pier Giorgio. Calle La Puntilla. ☎ **809/571-2215.** Main courses RD$135–RD$350 ($10.15–$26.25). AE, MC, V. Daily noon–4pm and 6pm–midnight. ITALIAN.

Set a 10-minute walk west of Sosúa's center, this establishment serves the best Italian food in town, and as such, attracts an animated clientele of Europeans looking for a change from too constant a diet of Créole and Dominican cuisine. Architecturally, the place might remind you of a garden-style veranda, permeated with Italian whimsy that's perched over low cliffs at the edge of the sea. Everybody's drink of choice here seems to be mimosas, a homemade version that delectably precedes such dishes as veal cutlets milanese, spaghetti with marinara or clam sauce (or prepared Sicilian style with eggplant and tomatoes). Also look for at least five different preparations of fresh fish, including a barbecued version that's especially succulent.

La Tortuga. In the Hotel Sosúa, Calle Dr. Alejo Martínez, El Batey, Sosúa. ☎ **809/571-2683.** Main courses $8–$18; fixed-price menu $10–$15. AE, MC, V. Daily 7am–11pm. DOMINICAN/ITALIAN.

Always known as a pleasant eatery, the restaurant in the Hotel Sosúa benefited from a radical upgrade in 1994. The result is La Tortuga (The Tortoise), whose dining room overlooks a swimming pool and a small but pleasant garden. It serves a medley of inexpensive Italian wines, which go well with such dishes as melon slices with Italian ham, shellfish salads, tortellini, spaghetti (with either meat or shellfish sauce), paella (for two diners only), and veal parmigiana. If you want to divide your meal into pasta for an appetizer and a meat dish for a main course, the staff will acquiesce. Main courses include four different preparations of chicken, and your choice of beef filet prepared with cognac, with peppers, with mushrooms, or with ham and cheese, Cordon Bleu style. These dishes are perfectly acceptable, even well prepared, but lack that spark of imagination that would elevate this restaurant to a loftier category.

Morua Mai. Pedro Clisante 5, El Batey. No phone. Main courses RD$85–RD$275 ($6.40–$20.65). AE, MC, V. Daily 8am–midnight. CONTINENTAL/DOMINICAN.

The patio here, which faces a popular intersection in the center of town, is the closest thing to a European sidewalk cafe in town. Inside, where occasional live entertainment is an important attraction, is a high-ceilinged, double-decked, and stylish space filled with touches of neo-Victorian gingerbread, upholstered banquettes, and wicker furniture. Consider this place for a sun-washed drink or cup of afternoon tea in the side courtyard, where a cabaña bar serves drinks from beneath a palm-thatched roof. Pasta, pizzas, and sandwiches, along with light meals, are served at lunch. Full dinners include such dishes as charcoal-grilled lobster, seafood platters, and lots of locally caught fish. An excellent paella is filled with lobster and shrimp. All meats and seafood are specially selected by the owner for freshness. The cookery isn't outstanding, but it's solidly good.

Restaurant Yaroa. In the Hotel Yaroa, El Batey. ☎ **809/571-2651.** Reservations recommended. Main courses RD$90–RD$225 ($6.75–$16.90). AE, MC, V. Daily 7am–11pm. DOMINICAN/ITALIAN.

This is the featured restaurant within a previously recommended hotel whose management (but not its owners) are Italian. The menu, which is not large, concentrates on a mixture of Dominican and Italian food that's likely to please the hotel's mostly Mediterranean clientele. Examples include lasagne with salad, many different preparations of fish, grilled beefsteak, vegetarian platters, and pastas. Filet steak might be prepared with Roquefort; poached kingfish, with a white-butter sauce. The setting is a land-locked garden adjacent to the resort's swimming pool, a 5-minute walk from Sosúa's beach.

6 Samaná

Another offbeat destination, where prices are still affordable, is Samaná, an undeveloped 30-mile-long peninsula located in the northeastern corner of the country. It has some of the finest white sandy beaches in the Dominican Republic. The main town, La Samaná, lies on the southern side of the peninsula overlooking a bay. The north coast of the peninsula is more accessible by boat. The roads are a bit of a joke, better suited for donkeys than cars.

In 1824 the *Turtle Dove,* a sailing vessel, was blown ashore at Samaná. Dozens of American slaves from the Freeman Sisters' underground railway escaped to these shores. They settled in Samaná and today their offspring are waiting to greet you. Although Spanish is the major language, you can still hear some form of 19th-century English, and you'll see villages with names such as Philadelphia or Bethesda.

GETTING THERE

To reach Samaná from Sosúa, you head east going through Cabarete, a windsurfing town 8 miles east of Sosúa. In some ways Cabarete evokes Malibu before it was overdeveloped. East of here lies Playa Grande, a long, nearly deserted stretch of beach strip, among the best in the West Indies. After leaving Playa Grande, you still have 120 miles to go east before reaching remote Samaná. Allow about 3 hours, unless you're tempted by one of the beaches along the way.

It's also possible to fly here from Santo Domingo, although there are no regularly scheduled flights. Many visitors to Samaná charter a small plane at Santo Domingo (dozens are available) and fly to El Portilo airport, the local airport at Samaná, in about 35 to 40 minutes. Prices vary but the airfare usually begins at $180 for two people.

WHERE TO STAY & EAT

Cayo Levantado. Lomo de Puerto Escondido, Samaná, República Dominicana. ☎ **809/538-3141.** Fax 809/538-2985. 42 rms. Year-round, RD$890 ($66.75) single; RD$1,380 ($103.50) double. Rates are all-inclusive. AE, MC, V.

Built in the mid-1990s, and consisting of a main building and a cluster of *casitas* (bungalows) in a landscaped garden at the edge of the sea, this informal and unpretentious resort includes all food and drinks within one price. Within a 30-minute drive west of Samaná, it has two bars and two restaurants, beside the beach and in the hotel's main building, respectively, and a lack-back, laissez-faire ambience conducive to quiet contemplation of garden, sea, and hillside. The accommodations are outfitted with wicker furniture and colorful, summery fabrics. Each has a writing desk. There's a swimming pool on the premises and a sandy beach within a 3-minute walk from the hotel. This is the more desirable of twin hotels charging the same rates for the same all-inclusive amenities. The affiliate is the **Hotel Cayacoa,** in Samaná (☎ **809/538-3131**), with 82 rooms that cost the same as those in the Levantado.

Hotel Tropic Banana. Las Terrenas, Provincia de Samaná, República Dominicana. ☎ **809/ 240-6110.** Fax 809/240-6112. 25 rms. Year-round, $40–$50 single; $50–$60 double. AE, MC, V.

On a pancake-flat 7-acre parcel of beachfront midway between the ocean and a range of rolling hills and mountains, this is one of the most escapist and otherworldly hotels in northeastern Hispaniola. Composed of an administrative headquarters and at least four green-and-and yellow annexes, the site was established in the mid-1970s by a French-born family (the Techers) whose Swiss, French, and Dominican staff cater to a "get away from it all" clientele from throughout Europe and the Americas. There's an unpretentious French restaurant on the premises, open daily from breakfast to around midnight, a bar, a swimming pool, a tennis court, a roster of horses for beachfront gallops, and a car-rental kiosk that's appreciated by clients who fly, rather than drive, to the hotels from other parts of the Caribbean. The accommodations have just enough furniture and amenities to be livable, but not enough to be plush. The rooms contain private porches and are cooled by ceiling fans and trade winds rather than air-conditioning.

The restaurant features Gallic/Caribbean food that's more stylish than you might have imagined. Try such creative dishes as fish carpaccio with passion fruit or squid salad flavored with fresh mint. It offers live music and merengue dancing at least 1 night a week.

The hotel lies in the hamlet of **Las Terrenas,** a hamlet with a population of around 8,000 people, set about 9 miles north of the larger town of Sánchez. From Sánchez, the drive is mountainous, requiring 30 minutes negotiating winding mountain roads. Las Terrenas lies 155 miles north of Santo Domingo. Despite that relatively short-sounding distance, the roads are awful, and require 5 hours of driving.

Villa Serena. Apdo. Postal 51-1, Las Galeras, Samaná. ☎ **809/696-0065.** Fax 809/538-2545. 11 rms. Year-round, $80–$100 single; $90–$110 double. Half board $21 extra. MC, V.

Some 26 miles east of the town of Samaná, beside the only road that runs along the edge of the peninsula, this hotel was built in the early 1990s along the lines of a rambling, two-story Victorian house with a wraparound balcony. Painted white with a blue-green roof and a large front garden, it sits above a rocky coastline, a 3-minute walk from a relatively uncrowded beach. The accommodations each have a private balcony and a decor that's different from its neighbors (Chinese, neoclassical gold-and-white, or Laura Ashley romantic). The more expensive rooms are air-conditioned; others have ceiling fans. Conceived for honeymooners and anyone looking for an escapist holiday far from urban life, the site is quiet, isolated, and low-key with little to do other than swim in the oval-shaped pool, visit the beach, read, and converse with other guests or the Croatia-born builders and owners, Dresimir Zovko and Natasha Despotovic. Many guests order lunch from operators of small charcoal grills set up on the beach (simple platters of pork or fish). The in-house restaurant, however, is the best of the three or four mainstream restaurants in Las Galeras, opening every day for breakfast, lunch, and dinner.

EXPLORING A RAIN FOREST & WATCHING WHALES

You can ask your hotel staff about arrangements for day trips to **Los Haitisses,** a national park in nearby Sánchez. Ancient Taíno inscriptions still adorn the cave walls here. This remote, unspoiled rain forest has crystal lakes, mangrove swamps, and limestone knolls. This karst region comprises some 100 miles of mangrove estuaries and land. You can also visit **Las Terrenas,** a remote stretch of coastline with nearly deserted beaches that are only now being discovered, although some German tourists have found them.

Sportfishing off the coast is among the finest in the entire Western Hemisphere. Nature lovers also flock here to see some 3,000 humpback whales off the coast in winter. Many whale-watching expeditions come here in January and February.

9

The British Leeward Islands

A string of islands that form a crescent, the British Leewards consist of Antigua and Barbuda, Montserrat, the twin state of St. Kitts and Nevis, and little Anguilla. Of them all, Antigua, with its many beaches and resort hotels, is the best equipped for mass tourism. However, more hotels and modern tourist facilities are drawing thousands to St. Kitts and Nevis.

1 Antigua & Barbuda

Antiguans boast that they have a different beach for every day of the year (which is a bit of an exaggeration). Most of these beaches are protected by coral reefs, and the sand is often sugar-white. For most visitors these beaches are reason enough to visit, but Antigua is also known for its sailing facilities centered at English Harbour. The principal "tourist zone" lies north of the capital of St. John in the northwest. Here you'll find some of the best hotels (but not *the* best) and an array of restaurants, beach bars, and water-sports facilities.

Old-timers claim that their island is trying to imitate Miami Beach with its sprawling resorts. To some extent that's true. Some of the Caribbean's largest resort hotels have opened in Antigua, which also means that the island boasts some of the most expensive places to stay in all the West Indies. The island's guest houses, small inns, and B&Bs just haven't kept pace with all the gigantic megaresorts that sometimes discount their packages dramatically to fill cavernous floors. There's a dearth of really good budget accommodations, but you'll find a number of small, less expensive restaurants, especially in St. John's.

Antigua, Barbuda, and Redonda form the independent nation of Antigua and Barbuda, within the Commonwealth of Nations. Redonda is an uninhabited rocky islet of less than a square mile located 20 miles southwest of Antigua. Sparsely populated Barbuda is covered as a day trip later in this section. Independence has come, but Antigua is still British in many of its traditions.

Rolling, rustic Antigua has as its highest point Boggy Peak, 1,360 feet above sea level. Stone towers, once sugar mills, dot the landscape; however, its inland scenery isn't as dramatic as on St. Kitts. But, oh, those beaches! Discovered by Columbus on his second voyage in 1493, Antigua has a population of about 67,000 and an area of 108 square miles.

The **summer carnival** takes place the week preceding the first Tuesday in August. Included in this festival are a beauty competition and calypso and steel-band competitions. Carnival envelops the streets in exotic costumes that recall the people's African heritage. The spring highlight is Antigua's annual **sailing week** in late April or May.

The capital is **St. John's,** a large, neatly laid out town, 6 miles from the airport and less than a mile from Deep Water Harbour Terminal. The port is the focal point of commerce and industry, as well as the seat of government and visitor shopping. Trade winds keep the streets fairly cool, as they were built wide just for that purpose. Protected in the throat of a narrow bay, the port city consists of cobblestone sidewalks, weather-beaten wooden houses, corrugated iron roofs, and louvered Caribbean verandas.

FAST FACTS: Antigua

Banking Hours Banks are usually open Monday to Thursday from 8am to 1pm and on Friday from 8am to 1pm and 3 to 5pm.

Currency The **Eastern Caribbean dollar (EC$)** is used on these islands. However, nearly all hotels bill you in U.S. dollars, and only certain tiny restaurants present their prices in EC dollars. Make sure you know which dollars are referred to when you inquire about a price. The EC dollar is worth about 37¢ in U.S. currency ($1 U.S. = EC$2.70). Unless otherwise specified, *rates quoted in this chapter are given in U.S. dollars.*

Customs Arriving visitors are allowed to bring in 200 cigarettes and 1 quart of liquor, plus 6 ounces of perfume.

Documents A valid passport is preferred when U.S. and Canadian nationals are visiting the island. However, an original birth certificate accompanied by a photo identification is also acceptable. Citizens of the United Kingdom need a passport, and all visitors must be in possession of an onward ticket, usually air.

Electricity Most of the island's electricity is 220 volts AC, 60 cycles (meaning that American appliances need transformers). The Hodges Bay area and some hotels are supplied with 110 volts AC, 60 cycles.

Emergencies In an emergency, contact the **police** (☎ **268/462-0125**), the **fire department** (☎ **268/462-0044**), or an **ambulance** (☎ **268/462-0251**).

Information Before you leave home, contact the **Antigua and Barbuda Department of Tourism,** 610 Fifth Ave., Suite 311, New York, NY 10020 (☎ **212/ 541-4117**); or 25 SE Second Ave., Suite 300, Miami, FL 33131 (☎ **305/ 381-6762**). In Canada, seek out the Antigua and Barbuda Department of Tourism & Trade, 60 St. Clair Ave. E., Suite 304, Toronto, ON M4T IN5 (☎ **416/ 961-3085**). In the United Kingdom, information is available at Antigua House, 15 Thayer St., London W1M 5LD (☎ **0171/486-7073**).

Language The official language is English.

Taxes and Service A departure tax of $11 U.S. is imposed, and an 8.5% government tax is added to all hotel bills. Most hotels also add a 10% service charge.

Time Antigua is on Atlantic standard time year-round, so it's 1 hour ahead of eastern standard time. When daylight saving time takes over, Antigua's time is the same as in the eastern United States.

Water   Water generally is safe to drink here, but many visitors prefer the bottled variety.

Weather   The average year-round temperature ranges from 75° to 85° Fahrenheit.

GETTING THERE

The major airline flying to Antigua's V. C. Bird Airport is **American Airlines** (☎ **800/433-7300** in the U.S.), which offers two daily nonstop flights to Antigua departing from San Juan; flight time is 1¹/₂ hours. Each of these flights departs late enough in the day to allow easy transfers from other flights. One of these flights from San Juan is the continuation of a nonstop flight from New York's JFK, which allows passengers originating in New York to remain on the same aircraft during the flight's brief touchdown on Puerto Rico. Most vacations on Antigua will cost less if you book your air transport simultaneously with a hotel reservation; American's tour desk will provide these arrangements for you.

Air Canada (☎ **800/268-7240** in Canada or **800/776-3000** in the U.S.) offers regularly scheduled flights from Toronto to Antigua on Saturday only.

BWIA (☎ **800/327-7401** in the U.S.) is an increasingly popular means of reaching Antigua. From Miami there are four flights weekly, and from Toronto there are two flights weekly. There are also five flights weekly from Kingston, Jamaica, plus connections from Europe—two flights weekly from both London and Frankfurt.

Passengers originating in Britain sometimes prefer to take advantage of the **British Airways** (☎ **800/247-9297** in the U.S. or 0345/22211 in Britain) four-times-per-week flights between London's Gatwick Airport and Antigua.

GETTING AROUND

BY BUS   Buses are not recommended for the average visitor, although they do exist and are cheap. Service seems erratic and undependable along impossibly bumpy roads. The official hours of operation between St. John's and the villages are 5:30am to 6pm daily—but don't count on it. In St. John's, buses leave from the West Bus Station for Falmouth and English Harbour, and from the East Bus Station for other parts of the island. Most fares are $1.

BY TAXI   Taxis meet every airplane and drivers wait outside the major hotels. In fact, if you're going to be on Antigua for a few days, you may find that a particular driver has "adopted" you. The typical one-way fare from the airport to St. John's is $12, but to English Harbour it's $25 and up. The government of Antigua fixes the rates and the taxis have no meters.

While it's costly, the best way to see Antigua is by private taxi as the drivers are also guides. Most taxi tours cost $16 and up per hour.

BY RENTAL CAR   Newly arrived drivers quickly (and ruefully) learn that the island's roads are among the worst, most potholed, and most badly marked in the Caribbean. Many visitors will prefer to hire one of the island's taxis whenever they want to go somewhere. (Hotels and restaurants on the island summon taxis for patrons.) Considering the need to *drive on the left* (a holdover from the British tradition), renting a car on Antigua is usually not worth it.

If you insist on driving, you must obtain an Antiguan driver's license, which costs $20. To be granted one, you must produce a valid driver's license from home. Most car-rental firms are authorized to issue you an Antiguan license, which they usually do without a surcharge.

Several different car-rental agencies operate on Antigua, although they're sometimes precariously financed local operations with cars best described as "battered." The best of them are affiliated with major car-rental companies in the United States. **Avis** (☎ **800/331-2112** in the U.S.) and **Hertz** (☎ **800/654-3131** in the U.S.) are represented on Antigua, both offering pickup service at the airport.

You can sometimes (but not always) get better deals at local car-rental places, including **Dollar Car Rental,** Nevis Street, St. John's (☎ **268/462-0362**), which rents cars year-round for $50 per day, although the rate might go down if you rent for a few days.

ESSENTIALS

Antigua is generally safe, but that doesn't mean that you should go wandering alone at night on the practically deserted streets of St. John's. Don't leave valuables unguarded on the beach.

The **Antigua and Barbuda Department of Tourism,** at Thames and Long streets in St. John's (☎ **268/462-0480**), is open Monday to Thursday from 8am to 4:30pm and on Friday from 8am to 3pm.

The principal medical facility is **Holberton Hospital,** on Queen Elizabeth Highway (☎ **268/462-0251**). Telephone calls can be made from hotels or from the office of **Cable and Wireless,** 42–44 St. Mary's St., in St. John's (☎ **268/462-0840**). Faxes and telegrams can also be sent from here.

WHERE TO STAY

Antigua's hotels are among the best and most plentiful in the eastern Caribbean, but you have to hunt for bargains. Check summer closings, which often depend on the caprice of the owners, who may decide to shut down if business isn't good. Incidentally, air-conditioning, except in first-class hotels, isn't as common as some visitors think it should be. Chances are, your hotel will be on a beach. You can also rent an apartment or cottage if you want to cook for yourself.

Remember that an 8.5% government tax and 10% service charge are added to your hotel bill, which makes quite a difference in your final tab.

DOUBLES FOR LESS THAN $55 (WINTER) / $35 (OFF-SEASON)

Joe Mike's Hotel. Nevis St., St. John's, Antigua, W.I. ☎ 268/462-1142. Fax 268/462-6056. 12 rms. A/C TEL. Year-round, $45 single; $55 double. AE, MC, V.

Only a 10-minute drive from the nearest good beach, this hotel is right in the heart of the capital. It's simplicity itself, but the welcome is warm and inviting. This peach-colored building with a porch around the second floor has standard rooms with furnishings that are a bit frayed. But it's a comfortable and cozy nest if you don't plan to spend most of your time in your room. There's a TV set in the lobby.

Murphy's Place. All Saints Rd. (P.O. Box 491), St. John's, Antigua, W.I. ☎ 268/461-1183. 6 units. Winter, $40 one-bedroom unit; $60 two-bedroom unit or studio. Off-season, $35 one-bedroom unit; $55 two-bedroom unit or studio. No credit cards.

This is one of those rare B&Bs on Antigua, and it's the island's best bargain. It's only 15 minutes from the airport, 10 minutes from a nearby beach, and a 10-minute walk into St. John's. Mrs. Murphy receives people from all over the world into her modern bungalow home. She works hard to keep everything clean, although all is admittedly simple in decor, with locally made mahogany furniture. You can cook your own meals or eat next door. Some units contain a double bed and shower, and others offer two bedrooms, with a spacious living room and a fully equipped kitchen. Each unit has a ceiling fan, and some have TVs.

DOUBLES FOR LESS THAN $90 (WINTER) / $80 (OFF-SEASON)

Antigua Sugar Mill Hotel. (P.O. Box 319, St. John's) Coolidge, Antigua, W.I. ☎ 268/462-3044. 22 rms. TV TEL. Winter, $70-99 single; $80-$100 double. Off-season, $50-$70 single; $60-$80 double. Extra person $10; children under 2 stay free in parents' room. MAP $30 per person extra. AE, DC, DISC, MC, V.

One mile from the nearest beach, an authentic 250-year-old sugar mill provides this unique hotel with colonial charm. In the hills above St. John's, it overlooks the airport and is surrounded on three sides by tropical foliage. The bedrooms are simply but comfortably furnished, and each has a patio and balcony; the superior accommodations come with TV and phone. Its most alluring feature is its swimming pool with a sunning deck and poolside bar. From an observation deck you can enjoy the most panoramic sunsets on island. The two-story white concrete building housing the rooms was constructed in 1960. A local on-site restaurant serves three meals a day, and room service is available.

✪ **The Catamaran Hotel & Marina.** Falmouth Harbour (P.O. Box 958, St. John's), Antigua, W.I. ☎ 800/223-6510 in the U.S., 800/424-5500 in Canada, or 268/460-1036. 16 units. Year-round, $55 single; $100 deluxe single; $65 double; $120 deluxe double; $70 efficiency for one; $80 efficiency for two; $150 Captain's Cabin for two. Children 9 and under $15 extra. AE, MC, V. Closed Sept.

This is a longtime favorite on Antigua. At Falmouth Harbour, a 2-mile drive from English Harbour, the Catamaran opens onto a palm-lined beach. When we first discovered the property years ago, a film crew had taken it over while making a movie about pirates of the West Indies. The management had to post a sign: TODAY'S "PIRATES" MUST WEAR BATHING SUITS ON THE BEACH. It's not as wild around here any more, and peace and tranquillity prevail.

On the second floor are eight self-contained rooms, each with a four-poster bed, a queen-size mattress, and a balcony opening onto the water. The most luxurious and spacious rental is called the Captain's Cabin. The standard rooms are quite small but well maintained and comfortable enough, and the efficiencies at water's edge can be rented by one person or two. Each efficiency has a balcony and an equipped kitchen. Boaters will like the hotel's location at the 30-slip Catamaran Marina. You can purchase supplies at a nearby grocery store, or else enjoy the hotel's own reasonably priced meals. Sportfishing and diving can be arranged, and the hotel offers Sunfish dinghies and rowboats.

Island Inn. Anchorage Rd. (P.O. Box 1218), St. John's, Antigua, W.I. ☎ **268/462-4065.** Fax 268/462-4066. 10 studios. A/C TV. Winter, $80 studio for one; $90 studio for two. Off-season, $75 studio for one; $80 studio for two. Extra person $10; children 11 and under stay free in parents' room. AE, DISC, MC, V.

A newly constructed hotel, this white concrete building trimmed in green enjoys a well-kept garden setting only a 10-minute walk from the beach at Dickenson Bay. It features self-contained air-conditioned one-bedroom studios with king-size or double beds, ceiling fans, individual balconies, or patios, plus fully equipped kitchenettes. Locals often use the inn for wedding receptions. There's a swimming pool and a simple restaurant serving low-cost breakfasts and dinners. Baby-sitting can be arranged, and room service is available.

Sand Haven Beach Hotel & Restaurant. Sand Haven, Runaway, St. John's, Antigua, W.I. ☎ and fax **268/462-4491.** 14 rms. Winter, $50 single; $75 double; $100 triple; $130 family room for up to six. Off-season, $40 single; $60 double; $85 triple; $95 family room. AE, MC, V.

Located on a secluded private beach in Dry Hill, this small hotel is a friend of the budget traveler. Although St. John's is only 3 miles away, the inn is in a secluded spot on its silvery stand of beachfront. It's the lazy life here, and you can see hotel patrons finding their favorite spot underneath the palms or ordering a cool rum punch at the beach bar. The hotel itself is flamboyantly painted in pink and turquoise, subdued with white. Each of the simply furnished rooms has a sea view, patio or balcony, and is cooled by ceiling fans. The furnishings are standard, with stone floors and rugs. A TV and phone are available in the lounge. Its beachside restaurant, Spice of Life, serves regional specialties and fresh seafood.

DOUBLES FOR LESS THAN $120(WINTER) / $85 (OFF-SEASON)

✪ **The Admiral's Inn.** English Harbour (P.O. Box 713, St. John's), Antigua, W.I. ☎ **800/223-5695** in the U.S. or 268/460-1027. Fax 268/460-1534. 14 rms, 1 suite. Winter, $86–$98 single; $104–$132 double; $144–$154 triple; $220 suite for two. Off-season, $64–$72 single; $78–$94 double; $104–$116 triple; $130 suite for two. MAP $44 per person extra. AE, MC, V. Closed Sept to mid-Oct. Take the road southeast from St. John's, following the signs to English Harbour.

Designed in 1785, the year Nelson sailed into the harbor as captain of the HMS *Boreas,* and completed in 1788, the building once here used to house dockyard services. Today this is the site of one of the most atmospheric inns on Antigua. In the heart of Nelson's Dockyard, and loaded with West Indian charm, the hostelry is constructed of weathered brick brought from England as ships' ballast and has a terrace opening onto a centuries-old garden. The ground floor, with brick walls, giant ship beams, and island-made furniture, has a tavern atmosphere, with decorative copper, boat lanterns, old oil paintings, and wrought-iron chandeliers.

There are three types of character-filled accommodations. The highest tariffs are charged for some ground-floor rooms in a tiny brick building—on the site of a provisions warehouse for Nelson's troops—across the courtyard from the main structure. Each of these spacious rooms has a little patio and a garden entry as well as optional air-conditioning. The same superior rate applies to front rooms on the first floor of the main building with views of the lawn and harbor. A medium rate applies to the back rooms on this floor, all of which have air-conditioning. The lowest rate is for smaller chambers on the top floor, which may get warm during the day in summer but are quiet, with dormer-window views over the yacht-filled harbor. All rooms have twin beds and ceiling fans. The Joiner's Loft is an upstairs suite adjacent to the annex rooms of the inn, with a large living room looking out over the water; there are two bedrooms, two baths, and a full kitchen. For the inn's restaurant, see "Where to Eat," below. On Saturday night a steel band plays. Amenities include room service, laundry, baby-sitting, free transportation to two nearby beaches, snorkeling equipment, and Sunfish craft.

✪ **Falmouth Harbour Beach Apartments.** English Harbour Village, Yacht Club Rd. (P.O. Box 713, St. John's), Antigua, W.I. ☎ **268/460-1094.** Fax 268/460-1534. 24 studios. Winter, $94–$98 studio for one; $120–$134 studio for two; $144–$158 studio for three. Off-season, $68–$72 studio for one; $88–$94 studio for two; $144–$158 studio for three. Children 15 and under stay for $15 when sharing their parents' studio. AE, MC, V. Free parking. Take the road southeast from St. John's and follow the signs to English Harbour.

This relatively simple place might be what you're looking for if you'd like to be near historic English Harbour. On, or just above, a small sandy beach, it offers an informal Antiguan atmosphere and rents twin-bedded studio apartments. Each studio has a ceiling fan, electric stove, refrigerator, oven, and terrace overlooking the water. However, the studios don't have air-conditioning, phones, or televisions. A dozen studios are directly on the beach, whereas the others lie on a hillside just behind. Nearby are restaurants, a supermarket, bank, post office, boutiques, and galleries. Temo Sports, with tennis and squash facilities, is just next door, and there's a dive operation in the dockyard, with many sailing and fishing boat charters. Bus service runs daily to and from St. John's, so you don't have to rent a car.

Lord Nelson Beach Hotel. Dutchman's Bay (P.O. Box 155, St. John's), Antigua, W.I. ☎ **268/ 462-3094.** Fax 268/462-0751. 17 rms. Winter, $80–$90 single; $100–$115 double. Off-season, $60–$70 single; $70–$80 double. Extra person $30 in winter, $25 off-season. AE, MC, V.

Built just before World War II on Antigua's northeast coast 5 miles east of St. John's as a single-story wood-sided beach club for American army officers, this establishment was acquired by the Fuller family in 1949. Today it's a more substantial concrete structure, with a dining room capped with timbers that were salvaged from warehouses destroyed during the hurricanes of 1950. Later a bar was added, using local stone and glass salvaged from an offshore lighthouse, as well as an annex containing two floors of simply furnished rooms. Today the place functions as a family-managed inn, set close to a white-sand beach and waters that are protected from ocean swells by a man-made reef, although it does show the wear and tear of the years.

Rex Blue Heron. Johnson's Point Beach (P.O. Box 1715, St. John's), Antigua, W.I. ☎ **800/ 255-5859** or 305/471-6170 in the U.S., or 268/462-8564. Fax 268/462-8005, or 305/471-9547 in the U.S. 40 rms. Winter, $120–$153 single or double; $202 triple. Off-season, $102–$136 single or double; $187 triple. MAP $50 per person extra. Children 11 and under stay free in parents' room. AE, DC, DISC, MC, V.

On the most beautiful beach on Antigua, about 15 miles from either St. John's or the airport, this hotel attracts tranquillity seekers. Casually comfortable, it crowns

Johnson's Point. This complex consists of two-story white stone buildings whose rooms overlook either well-kept gardens, the swimming pool, or the beachfront. In the lifetime of this edition the hotel might add two dozen more accommodations. The superior and beachfront units have air-conditioning, ceiling fans, TVs, and hair dryers, whereas the standard rooms offer only ceiling fans. Each room, however, has a patio or balcony. Along with two bars, there's an intimate on-site restaurant serving West Indian meals at affordable prices. A full range of water sports is available, including complimentary windsurfing, snorkeling equipment, and Sunfish sailing. Deep-sea and offshore scuba diving is also offered. There's live entertainment most evenings. The hotel appeals to couples and honeymooners.

BEST OFF-SEASON BETS

Antigua Village. Dickenson Bay (P.O. Box 649, St. John's), Antigua, W.I. ☎ **800/223-1588** in the U.S. or 268/462-2930. Fax 268/462-0375. 65 studios and apts. A/C. Winter, $170–$195 studio for two; $210–$245 one-bedroom apt for two; $380–$440 two-bedroom apt for four. Off-season, $95–$115 studio for two; $115–$140 one-bedroom apt for two; $210–$255 two-bedroom apt for four. AE, MC, V.

On a peninsula stretching out into turquoise waters 2 miles from St. John's, Antigua Village is more a self-contained condominium community than a holiday resort. A freshwater pool and minimarket are on the premises. You can use the neighboring tennis court, and there's an 18-hole golf course nearby, plus comprehensive water-sports facilities. The studio apartments and villas all have kitchenettes, patios and balconies, twin beds, and sofa beds in the living room.

WORTH A SPLURGE

✪ **The Copper and Lumber Store.** Nelson's Dockyard, English Harbour (P.O. Box 184, St. John's), Antigua, W.I. ☎ **268/460-1058.** Fax 268/460-1529. 3 rms, 11 suites. Winter, $160–$180 single; $195–$275 double; $215–$325 suite. Off-season, $80–$90 single; $85–$145 double; $95–$175 suite. AE, MC, V. From St. John's, follow the signs southeast to English Harbour.

This 18th-century building was originally occupied by purveyors of wood and sheet copper for building and repairing the British sailing ships that plied the waters of the Caribbean. The store and its adjacent harbor structures were built of brick brought from England in the holds of ships as ballast. These bricks imbue the building with 18th-century English charm and sometimes serve to conceal its necessary modern amenities.

Each of the brick-lined period units has its own design and is filled with fine Chippendale and Queen Anne reproductions, antiques, brass chandeliers, hardwood paneling, and hand-stenciled floors. Even the showers look like the cabinetry in a sailing vessel, lined with thick paneled slabs of mahogany accented with polished brass fittings. All suites have kitchens, private baths (with showers only), and ceiling fans. A traditional English pub adjoins the hotel and offers food daily from 10:30am to midnight. The Wardroom serves dinner nightly. The hotel also offers room service, laundry, and baby-sitting.

WHERE TO EAT

Many independently operated restaurants serve West Indian food not readily available in the hotel dining rooms. Some dishes, especially the curries, show an East Indian influence, and Caribbean lobster is a specialty.

IN ST. JOHN'S

✪ **Big Banana Holding Company.** Redcliffe Quay. ☎ **268/462-2621.** Main courses $7–$13. AE, DC, MC, V. Mon–Sat 8:30am–midnight. PIZZA.

Some of the best pizza in the eastern Caribbean is served in what used to be slave quarters, now amid the most stylish shopping and dining emporiums in town, a few steps from the Heritage Quay Jetty. With its ceiling fans and laid-back atmosphere, you almost expect Sydney Greenstreet to stop in for a drink. The frothy libations, coconut or banana crush, are practically desserts. In addition to the zesty pizza, you can order overstuffed baked potatoes, fresh-fruit salad, or conch salad. On Thursday a reggae band entertains from 10pm to 1am.

Calypso. Redcliffe St. ☎ **268/462-1965.** Reservations recommended. Lunch EC$25–EC$55 ($9.30–$20.40). AE, DC, MC, V. Mon–Fri 10am–4pm. WEST INDIAN.

This is an open-air restaurant located in the heart of St. John's just west of the library. There are remains of a brick kiln and tables have umbrellas. This little bistro serves a predominantly Caribbean cuisine with a touch of American. This establishment offers sandwiches, pizzas, steaks, and shrimp kebabs, but the local fare is the shining star, such as the cream of pumpkin soup, mackerel, and dumplings. A wide assortment of seafood is also served. Daily specials include pickled fish, fungi with seasoned rice, and a local specialty called ducune (grated sweet potato with sugar, coconut, and seasonings). The atmosphere seems inviting.

✪ **Curry House.** Redcliffe Way. ☎ **268/462-1895.** Main courses EC$10–EC$14 ($3.70–$5.20). No credit cards. Daily 9am–6pm. CARIBBEAN/INDIAN.

This is St. John's most reasonably priced restaurant, and it serves the best rôtis in town. These bread pockets are filled with all sorts of spicy meats and vegetables, and one is enough for a satisfying meal. Other savory dishes are offered as well, including curried conch with rice and various chicken and beef dishes, several of which have zesty flavors. The restaurant lies at the water end of Redcliffe, one building in a long line of shops and boutiques. Inside is a simple dining room with straw mats on the walls and just four tables. At the counter you can eat or else order take-away food items. The fresh fruity drinks hit the spot on a hot, dusty day in St. John's.

✪ **Hemingway's.** St. Mary's St. ☎ **268/462-2763.** Main courses $10–$25. AE, MC, V. Mon–Sat 8:30am–11pm. WEST INDIAN/INTERNATIONAL.

On the second floor of a building in the heart of St. John's, and accented with intricate gingerbread painted in bright tropical colors, this charming and bustling cafe attracts shoppers and sightseers. It's very busy when cruise ships dock. From its upper verandas, you can watch pedestrians in the street below and the dock where cruise-ship tenders land. Menu items include salads, sandwiches, burgers, sautéed filets of fish, pastries, ice creams, and many brightly colored tropical drinks.

Joe Mike's Restaurant. Nevis St. ☎ **268/462-1142.** Main courses $8–$10. AE, MC, V. Mon–Wed 7am–10pm, Thurs–Sat 7am–11pm. WEST INDIAN.

A popular eatery with the locals, this restaurant is on the ground floor of this previously recommended hotel. Hang out here if you'd like to connect with the bustling life of St. John's, at least during the day. Patrons show up for the good food, affordable prices, and happy times. Forget Caribbean haute cuisine as you peruse the menu. There are daily specials featuring local foods, including fresh fish. A specialty of the chef is ducana and saltfish; ducana is a kind of dumpling made with sweet potatoes, pumpkin, and coconut. Tuesday to Friday a one-man band entertains at lunchtime.

Pizzas in Paradise. Redcliffe St., Redcliffe Quay, St. John's. ☎ **268/462-2621.** Pizzas, pastas, and main courses $4–$30. AE, DC, MC, V. Mon–Sat 8am "until." PIZZA/CARIBBEAN.

The young people of the island, along with cruise-ship passengers and others, gravitate to this spot, which offers excellent pizzas and a satisfying assortment of seafood salads, fruit platters, pastas, and even grilled flying fish sandwiches. The older crowd usually opts for the grilled chicken with salad and baked potato. The most expensive item on the menu is a mammoth seafood pizza, and it's delectable. Situated in a historic building, this restaurant offers both indoor and outdoor dining. The deck has picnic tables with umbrellas overlooking the town's shops. A large selection of CDs provides background music except on Tuesday and Thursday night when there's live entertainment.

Redcliffe Tavern. Redcliffe Quay. ☎ **268/461-4557.** Reservations recommended. Main courses $10–$20; lunch from $6.90. AE, DISC, MC, V. Mon–Sat 8am–11pm. WEST INDIAN.

Owned by Ian Fraser, this waterside restaurant offers an unusual view of some of Antigua's artifacts of yesteryear, including machines used to pump water during the island's plantation era, the combination of which seems to enhance what was built by the British in the 18th century as a warehouse. Don't expect a quiet and isolated romantic evening here—the place is usually crowded.

Menu items include plantain-stuffed chicken breasts in a tomato or basil sauce, mozzarella wrapped in phyllo dough then served in a tomato-raspberry vinaigrette, and steaks with mushrooms or peppercorn sauce. A recommended dessert is Normandy-style apple tart.

AROUND THE ISLAND

✪ **The Admiral's Inn.** In Nelson's Dockyard, English Harbour. ☎ **268/460-1027.** Reservations recommended, especially for dinner in high season. Main courses $11–$27. AE, MC, V. Daily 7:30–10am, noon–2:30pm and 7–9:30pm. Closed Sept to mid-Oct. AMERICAN/CREOLE.

This historic building has already been reviewed as a hotel (see "Where to Stay," above). In a 17th-century setting, lobster, seafood, and steaks are served. The favorite appetizer is pumpkin soup, which is followed by a choice of four or five main courses daily—perhaps local red snapper, grilled steak, or lobster. Before dinner, have a drink in the bar, where you can read the names of sailors carved in wood more than a century ago. The service is agreeable, and the setting is heavy on atmosphere.

WORTH A SPLURGE

✪ **Coconut Grove.** In the Siboney Beach Club, Dickenson Bay. ☎ **268/462-1538.** Reservations required for dinner. Main courses $9.25–$24.95. AE, MC, V. Daily 7–11am, 11:30am–3:30pm, and 5:30–10:30pm. INTERNATIONAL/SEAFOOD.

Right on the beach are simple tables set on a flagstone floor beneath a thatch roof. North of St. John's, in a coconut grove (of course) and cooled by sea breezes, the restaurant is one of the best on the island. Each day a soup is prepared fresh from local ingredients. One appetizer is a seafood delight—scallops, shrimp, crab, lobster, and local fish with a mango-and-lime dressing. Lobster and shrimp dishes are strongly featured, and there's a catch of the day and a vegetarian specialty of the day. T-bone steak is regularly featured, as is Cajun chicken. Lighter fare is served at lunch. Also, during the bar's happy hour—from 3:30 to 7pm—all drinks are half price.

FUN ON & OFF THE BEACH

BEACHES Beaches, beaches, and more beaches—Antigua has some 365 of them.

However, because of crime it's unwise to have your fun in the sun at what appears to be a deserted beach. You could be the victim of a mugging in such a lonely setting. Increasingly, readers complain of vendors hustling everything from jewelry to T-shirts, disrupting their time on the beach. All beaches are public and open to all. Hotels can't restrain beach use—so be duly warned.

There's a lovely beach at **Pigeon Point,** in Falmouth Harbour, about a 4-minute drive from the Admiral's Inn. The beach at **Dickenson Bay,** near the Halcyon Cove Hotel, is also superior and a center for water sports; for a break, you can enjoy meals and drinks on the hotel's Warri Pier, built on stilts in the water. Chances are, however, you'll swim at your own hotel.

Other beaches are at the Curtain Bluff resort, with its long, sandy white **Carlisle Beach** set against a backdrop of coconut palms, and **Morris Bay,** which in addition to its strip of white sands, has waters attracting snorkelers, among others. The beach at **Long Bay** is on the somewhat-remote eastern coast, but the beach here is beautiful, and most visitors consider it worth the effort to reach it. **Half Moon Bay** is famous in the Caribbean and attracts what used to be called "blue bloods" to a stretch of sand that goes on for almost a mile. **Runaway Beach** is one of the most popular in Antigua, but because of its white sands it's worth fighting the crowds. **Five Islands** is actually a quartet of remote beaches with brown sands and coral reefs located near the Hawksbill Hotel.

GOLF   Antigua doesn't have the facilities of some of the other islands, but what it has is good. The 18-hole, par-69 course at the **Cedar Valley Golf Club,** Friar's Hill Road (☎ **268/462-0161**), is 3 miles east of St. John's, near the airport. Daily greens fees are $35 for 18 holes. Cart fees are also $35 for 18 holes, with club rentals going for $10.

PARASAILING   This sport is gaining in popularity on Antigua. Facilities are available during the day Monday to Saturday on the beach at **Dickenson Bay.** There are also facilities at the **Royal Antiguan Resort** at Deep Bay (☎ **268/462-3732**).

SAILING   All major hotel desks can book a day cruise on the 108-foot "pirate ship," the *Jolly Roger,* Redcliffe Quay (☎ **268/462-2064**). For $50 you're taken sightseeing on a fun-filled day, with drinks and a barbecued steak, chicken, or lobster. The *Jolly Roger* is the largest sailing ship in Antiguan waters. Lunch is combined with a snorkel trip. Dancing is on the poop deck, and members of the crew teach passengers how to dance calypso. Sailings are daily, lasting 5¹/₂ hours from 9:30am to 3pm. There's also a Saturday-night dinner cruise, going for $40 and leaving Heritage Quay in St. John's at 7pm, returning at 10pm.

SCUBA DIVING & OTHER WATER SPORTS   Scuba diving is best arranged through **Dive Antigua,** at the Rex Halcyon Cove Beach Resort, Dickenson Bay (☎ **268/462-3483**), Antigua's longest-established and most experienced dive operation. For $85 per person you can have instruction and a boat dive with all equipment provided.

The **Long Bay Hotel,** on the northeastern coast of the island at Long Bay (☎ **268/ 463-2005**), is a good location for various water sports—swimming, sailing, waterskiing, and windsurfing. The hotel also has complete scuba facilities. Both beginning snorkelers and experienced divers are welcomed. You're taken on snorkel trips by boat to Green Island and Great Bird Island (minimum of four). The shallow side of the double reef across Long Bay is ideal for the neophyte, and the whole area on the northeastern tip has many reefs of varying depths.

TENNIS   Tennis buffs will find courts at most of the major hotels, and some are lit for night games. We don't recommend playing tennis at noon—it's just too hot! If your hotel doesn't have a court, you can find them available at the **Rex Halcyon Cove,** the **Cedar Valley Golf Club,** and the **Royal Antiguan Hotel** (the last two have eight courts each). If you're not a guest, you'll have to book a court and pay charges that vary from hotel to hotel. Residents of a hotel usually play free.

WINDSURFING   The **High Wind Centre,** located at the Lord Nelson Beach Hotel, Dutchman's Bay (☎ **268/462-3094**), offers windsurfing for the absolute beginner, the intermediate sailor, and the advanced athlete. The outlet guarantees to get a neophyte up and enjoying the sport after a 2-hour introductory lesson. A lesson costs $45.

SEEING THE SIGHTS
ST. JOHN'S

In the southern part of St. John's, the **market,** at the lower end of Market Street, is colorful and interesting, especially on Saturday morning. Vendors busy selling their fruits and vegetables bargain and gossip.

Also in town, **St. John's Cathedral,** between Long Street and Newgate Street at Church Lane (☎ 268/461-0082), the Anglican cathedral, has had a disastrous history. Originally built in 1683, it was replaced by a stone building in 1745. That, however, was destroyed by an earthquake in 1843. The present pitch-pine interior dates from 1847. The interior was being restored when, in 1973, the twin towers and structure were badly damaged by another earthquake. The towers and the southern section have been restored, but restoring the northern part is estimated to cost thousands of dollars, for which contributions are gratefully received. At the entrance, iron gates were erected by the vestry in 1789. The figures of St. John the Baptist and St. John the Divine, at the south gate, were said to have been taken from one of the Napoleonic ships and brought to Antigua by a British man-of-war.

The **Museum of Antigua and Barbuda,** at Long and Market streets (☎ 268/462-1469), traces the history of the two-island nation—from geological birth to the present day. Housed in the old Court House building from 1750, exhibits include a wattle-and-daub house model, African-Caribbean pottery, and utilitarian objects of daily life. It's open Monday to Friday from 8:30am to 4:30pm, and on Saturday from 10am to 2pm. Admission is a $3 minimum donation for adults, free for children.

The **Antigua and Barbuda Botanical Gardens,** at Nevis and Temple streets (☎ 268/462-1007), was established in 1893 in the Green Belt of St. John's. As you enter the gardens you're captured by the unfolding majesty of the 80-year-old ficus tree, contrasted to the rolling lawns. The melodic sounds of tree frogs and birds emanate from the hollow, filled with lianas draped from branches of trees in the rain forest. Tropical blossoms, herbal plants, ferns, dripping philodendrons, rare bromeliads, and a colorful carpet of flowers await the visitor. Open daily from 9am to 6pm. Admission is by a minimum donation of $2.

AROUND THE ISLAND

After leaving St. John's, most visitors head southeast for 11 miles to ✪ **Nelson's Dockyard National Park** (☎ 268/460-1379), one of the biggest attractions of the eastern Caribbean. The dockyard is the only existing example of a Georgian naval dockyard in the world today, and is the centerpiece of the national park. One of the safest landlocked harbors in the world, the restored dockyard was used by Admirals Nelson, Rodney, and Hood, and was the home of the British fleet at the time of the Napoleonic Wars. From 1784 Nelson was the commander of the British navy in the Leeward Islands, and he made his headquarters at English Harbour. English ships used the harbor as early as 1671, finding it a refuge from hurricanes. The era of privateers, pirates, and great sea battles is recaptured in the dockyard's museum.

Restored by the Friends of English Harbour, the dockyard is sometimes known as a Caribbean Williamsburg. Its colonial naval buildings stand now as they did when Nelson was here (1784–87). However, Nelson never lived at Admiral House—it was built in 1855. The house has been turned into a museum of nautical memorabilia.

The park itself is worth exploring, filled with sandy beaches and much tropical vegetation, including various species of cactus and mangroves. The latter provides shelter for a migrating colony of African cattle egrets. The park is further enhanced by archaeological sites dating from well before the time of Christ. Nature trails have been cut through the park to expose the vegetation and coastal scenery. Tours of the dockyard are given, lasting 15 to 20 minutes, and hikes along nature trails can last anywhere from 30 minutes to 5 hours. The cost is $2.50 per person to tour the dockyard; children 12 and under are admitted free. The dockyard and its museum are open daily from 8am to 6pm.

Another major attraction is the **Dow's Hill Interpretation Center** (☎ 268/460-1053), lying just 2½ miles from the dockyard. The only one of its kind in the Caribbean, it offers multimedia presentations—a journey through six periods of the island's history, including the Amerindian hunters, the British military, and the struggles connected with slavery. A belvedere opens onto a panoramic view of the park. Admission to the center, including the multimedia show, is $5 per person, or $3 for children 15 and under. The center is open daily from 9am to 5pm.

A footpath leads to **Fort Barclay,** the fort at the entrance to English Harbour. The path starts just outside the dockyard gate, and the fort is about half a mile away. The interesting fort is a fine specimen of old-time military engineering.

If you're at English Harbour at sunset, head for **Shirley Heights** directly to the east, named after General Shirley, governor of the Leeward Islands in 1781, who fortified the hills guarding the harbor. Still standing are Palladian arches, once part of the barracks. The Block House, one of the main buildings, was put up as a stronghold in case of siege. The nearby Victorian cemetery contains an obelisk monument to the officers and men of the 54th Regiment.

On a low hill overlooking Nelson's Dockyard, **Clarence House** was built by English stonemasons to accommodate Prince William Henry, later known as the duke of Clarence, and even later known as William IV. The future king stayed here when he was in command of the *Pegasus* in 1787. At present it's the country home of the governor of Antigua and Barbuda and is open to visitors when His Excellency is not in residence. A caretaker will show you through (it's customary to tip, of course), and you'll see many pieces of furniture on loan from the National Trust. Princess Margaret and Lord Snowdon stayed here on their honeymoon.

On the way back, take ✪ **Fig Tree Drive,** a 20-some-mile circular drive across the main mountain range. It passes through lush tropical hills and fishing villages along the southern coast. You can pick up the road just outside Liberta, north of Falmouth. Winding through a rain forest, it passes thatched villages, and every hamlet has a church and lots of goats and children running about. However, don't expect fig trees—*fig* is an Antiguan name for bananas.

About half a mile before reaching St. John's you come to **Fort James,** begun in 1704 as a main lookout post for the port and named after James II.

Other places on the island worth seeking out include the following:

Parham Church, overlooking Parham Town, was erected in 1840 in the Italian style. Richly adorned with stucco work, it was damaged by an earthquake in 1843. Much of the ceiling was destroyed and very little of the stucco work remains, but the octagonal structure is still worth a visit.

The **Potworks Dam,** holding back the largest artificial lake on Antigua, is surrounded by an area of natural beauty. The dam holds back a billion gallons of water and provides protection for Antigua in case of a drought.

Indian Town, one of Antigua's national parks, is at a northeastern point on the island. Over the centuries Atlantic breakers have lashed the rocks and carved a natural bridge known as Devil's Bridge. It's surrounded by numerous blowholes spouting surf.

Megaliths, at Greencastle Hill, reached by a long climb, are said to have been set up by human hands for the worship of a sun god and a moon goddess. Some experts believe, however, that the arrangement is an unusual geological formation, a volcanic rockfall.

The **Antigua Rum Distillery,** at Rat Island (☎ 268/462-1072), turns out fine Cavalier rum. Check at the tourist office about arranging a visit. Established in 1932, the plant is next to Deep Water Harbour.

SHOPPING

Most of the shops except for the shopping centers are clustered on St. Mary's Street or High Street in St. John's. Some shops are open Monday to Saturday from 8:30am to noon and 1 to 4pm, but this rule varies greatly from store to store—Antiguan shopkeepers are an independent lot. Many of them close at noon on Thursday.

There are many duty-free items for sale, including English woolens and linens, and you can also purchase several specialized items made on Antigua, such as original pottery, local straw work, Antigua rum, and silk-screened, hand-printed local designs on fabrics, as well as mammy bags, floppy foldable hats, and shell curios.

If you want an island-made bead necklace, don't bother to go shopping; just lie on the beach—anywhere—and some "bead lady" will find you.

If you're in St. John's on a Saturday morning, you can attend the **fruit and vegetable market** at the West Bus Station. Handcrafts made locally are also offered for sale. One visitor said that "the incredibly sweet and juicy Antiguan black pineapple is worth the trip into town itself."

Harmony Hall. In Brown's Bay Mill, near Freetown. ☎ 268/460-4120.

Overlooking Nonsuch Bay, this old plantation-site house and sugar mill dates back to 1843—but now is much restored and is an ideal luncheon stopover or a shopping expedition. It displays an excellent selection of Caribbean arts and crafts, and in November plays host to the annual Caribbean Craft Fair. Lunch is served daily from noon to 4pm, featuring Green Island lobster, flying fish, and other specialties. Sunday is barbecue day. The entire complex is open daily from 10am to 6pm. To get here, follow the signs along the road to Freetown and Half Moon Bay.

Quin Farara's Liquor Store. Long St. and Corn Alley, St. John's. ☎ 268/462-0463.

Because the government has raised the duty on liquor, Antiguan alcohol isn't the bargain it once was. You can still buy liquor at discount prices, although because of heavy taxes liqueurs no longer offer much savings at all.

Shoul's Chief Store. St. Mary's St., St. John's. ☎ 268/462-1140.

Opposite Barclay's Bank is a cave of treasures. The store sells household items and appliances, a wide range of local and imported souvenirs, Antigua T-shirts, and fabrics of all colors, designs, and textures.

SHOPPING CENTERS

HERITAGE QUAY   Antigua's first shopping-and-entertainment complex is a multi-million-dollar center featuring some 40 duty-free shops and a vendors' arcade in which local artists and craftspeople display their wares. Restaurants in Heritage Quay offer a range of cuisine and views of St. John's Harbour, and a food court serves visitors who prefer to feast on local specialties in an informal setting. You could start your shopping with:

"Sunsneakers," 51 Heritage Quay (☎ 268/462-4523), established in 1989 when duty-free shopping was introduced on a large scale on Antigua. The outlet has one of the largest selections of swimwear available in the Caribbean.

Island Arts, upstairs at Heritage Quay (☎ 268/462-2787), was founded by Nick Maley, a makeup artist who worked on *Star Wars* and *The Empire Strikes Back.* You can purchase one of his own fine-art reproductions. Visitors are free to browse through everything from low-cost prints to works by artists exhibited in New York's Museum of Modern Art. You can also visit Nick's home and studio at Aiton Place, on Sandy Lane, directly behind the Hodges Bay Club 4 miles from St. John's. The residence is open Monday to Saturday from 10am to 4pm, but it's wise to call first (☎ 345/461-6324).

REDCLIFFE QUAY   This historic complex is one of the best centers for shopping (or dining) in St. John's. Once Redcliffe Quay was a slave-trading quarter, but after the abolition of slavery the quay was filled with grog shops and merchants peddling various wares. Now it has been redeveloped and contains a number of the most interesting shops in town, some in former warehouses.

A Thousand Flowers (☎ 268/462-4264) sells Indonesia batiks, crafted on the island into sundresses, knock-'em-dead shirts, sarongs, rompers, and various accessories such as necklaces and earrings. Many of the garments are designed into a one-size-fits-all motif of knots and flowing expanses of cloth appropriate for the tropics.

Caribelle Batik (☎ 268/462-2972) is an outlet for the Romney Manor workshop on St. Kitts. The Caribelle label consists of batik and tie-dye items such as beach wraps, scarves, and a range of casual wear for both women and men. The "Sensual Silk" label is also found here—these items are 100% silk in Caribbean colors, ranging from dresses and separates to accessories such as jewelry and scarves.

Jacaranda (☎ 268/462-1888) might tempt you with the art of local artists or placemats and prints by Jill Walker. The shop also stocks local clothing, cookbooks, pottery, and herbs and spices as well as gels, soaps, and salts for the bath.

Base (☎ 268/462-0920), the brainchild of Steven Giles, an English designer, is one of the best-known companies in the Caribbean. It carries an intriguing line of casual-comfort clothing in stripes, colors, and prints, all made at the company's world headquarters at Redcliffe Quay. The cotton and Lycra beachwear is eagerly sought out.

ANTIGUA AFTER DARK

Most nightlife revolves around the hotels, unless you want to roam Antigua at night looking for that hot native dive. If you're going out at night, make arrangements to have a taxi pick you up—otherwise you could be stranded in the wilds somewhere. Antigua has some of the best steel bands in the Caribbean, and they're usually hired by the megaresorts since the local dives can't compete financially for their talents.

The Royal Casino at the **Royal Antiguan Resort,** Deep Bay (☎ 268/462-3733), has American games, including blackjack, baccarat, roulette, craps, and slot machines. It's open nightly from 9pm "until," and there's no cover. The **King's Casino,** Heritage Quay (☎ 268/462-1727), is said to have "the world's largest slot machine." At Mamora Bay is **St. James's Club** (☎ 268/463-1113), which has a definite European flair.

BARS & NATIVE DIVES

Steel bands, limbo dancers, calypso singers, folkloric groups—there's always something going on every night on Antigua. You'd better check with your hotel to find out where "the heat" is on any given night. The following are usually reliable hot spots:

Locals flock to bars such as **The Verandah,** St. Mary's (☎ **268/462-5677**); **Millers by the Sea,** Runaway Beach (☎ **268/462-2393**); and **Russell's,** Fort James (☎ **268/462-5479**). Each has live entertainment at least 1 night a week. **The Jolly Roger,** Dickenson Bay (☎ **268/462-2064**), offers a 4-hour Saturday-night cruise that features a barbecue, dancing to a live band, and an open bar. A Sunday-afternoon barbecue hosted by **Shirley Heights Lookout,** Shirley Heights (☎ **268/463-1785**), often continues into the night as an energy-packed party.

Crazy Horse Saloon. Redcliffe Quay, St. John's. ☎ **268/462-7936.**

Taking its name from Paris's most fabled striptease club, this is actually a country-western hangout with a 30-foot bar, with memorabilia of the Wild West. There are five TV screens in case you find the local action boring. Monday night is Mexican with margaritas and tacos. Friday is party night with a live dance band, and Sunday is devoted to a jazz brunch and karaoke. Burgers, jerk pork, lobster (in at least 15 different ways), and Caribbean smoked fish round out the menu, along with seafood and grilled steaks. The club is open daily from 11am "until."

Ribbit Night Club. Green Bay. ☎ **268/462-7996.** No cover Thurs and Sun, $3 Fri, $8 Sat.

The nicest club on Antigua attracts mostly locals, ranging from the prime minister to young people who come here to dance. Overlooking Deep Water Harbour and St. John's, it's known for its hot music and its dancing 'til all hours. The club is open air with a DJ booth and one bar under a roof, the other alfresco. Two DJs keep the joint jumping on Friday and Saturday night. Sometimes special events are staged on Thursday and Sunday as well. Along with international music, you can hear reggae and some of the best steel bands in the Caribbean.

A DAY TRIP TO BARBUDA

Known by the Spanish as Dulcina, sparsely populated Barbuda, part of the independent nation of Antigua and Barbuda, is the last frontier of the Caribbean. Charted by Columbus in 1493, the island lies 26 miles to the north of Antigua and is about 15 miles long by 5 miles wide with a population of some 1,200 hardy souls, most of whom live around the unattractive village of **Codrington.**

Don't come here seeking lush, tropical scenery, as flat Barbuda consists of coral rock. There are no paved roads, few hotel rooms except for two super-expensive resorts, only a handful of restaurants, and pastel-colored beaches, the most famous of which stretches for more than 17 miles.

Since, for the most part, the accommodations available on Barbuda are super-expensive suites and villas offered by a pair of stratospherically expensive hotels (K-Club and Coco Point), we suggest visiting Barbuda as a day trip. While some less expensive so-called hotels have opened for business in recent years, these places have been known to open and close with alarming regularity. And there are some guest houses—some raffish, others very basic—but all seem to be rented on a first-come, first-served basis, where arriving on the island and addressing yourself to the landlord or landlady is about the only way to find a room.

GETTING THERE

The island is a 15-minute flight from Antigua's V. C. Bird Airport. Barbuda has two airfields: one at Codrington; the other a private facility, the Coco Point Airstrip, some 8 miles from Codrington at the Coco Point Lodge.

To reach Barbuda from Antigua, you can contact **LIAT** (☎ **268/462-0701**), which operates two daily flights (usually around 8am and again around 4pm) from

Barbuda

Airport ✈ Beach 🏖 Reef ||||

Goat Point

Atlantic Ocean

Cedar Tree Point

Hog Point

Codrington Lagoon

Two Foot Bay

Low Bay

Codrington ✈

■ **Martello Tower**

Palmetto Point

Pelican Bay

Coco Point 🏖

Caribbean Sea

Spanish Point

0 ———— 5 km
———— 3 mi

N

2-0191

Antigua to Barbuda's Codrington Airport. The cost is EC$120 ($44.40) for a day return ticket or EC$130 ($48.10) if you're staying over.

GETTING AROUND

Many locals rent small Suzuki four-wheel-drive Jeeps, which are the best way to get around the island. They meet incoming flights at the Codrington airport. Prices are negotiable. An Antiguan driver's license (see above) is needed if you plan to drive.

EXPLORING THE ISLAND

Hunters, anglers, and just plain beachcombers are attracted to the island, as it has some fallow deer, guinea fowl, pigeons, and wild pigs. Those interested in fishing for bonefish and tarpon can negotiate with the owners of small boats who rent them out.

Visitors over just for the day usually head for **Wa'Omoni Beach Park,** where they can visit the frigate bird sanctuary, snorkel for lobster, and eat barbecue.

Indeed, the most impressive sight on Barbuda is the **frigate bird sanctuary,** one of the largest in the world, where visitors can see the birds, *Fregata magnificens,* sitting on their eggs in the mangrove bushes. The mangroves stretch for miles in a long lagoon accessible only by a small motorboat. Tours to the sanctuary can be arranged at various hotels and resorts on Antigua. Besides the frigate bird, the island attracts some 150 species of birds, including pelicans, herons, and tropical mockingbirds.

Other curiosities of the island include a **"Dividing Wall,"** which once separated the Codrington family from the black people, and the **Martello Tower,** which predates the known history of the island. Tours also cover interesting underground

caves on the island. Stamp collectors might want to call at the **Philatelic Bureau** in Codrington.

2 Montserrat

If Montserrat were larger and wealthier, its recent troubles would have appeared as part of headlines around the world. This small pear-shaped island, some 27 miles southwest of Antigua, between Guadeloupe and Nevis, used to be viewed as the "unspoiled" Caribbean isle, a place where life continued the way it used to be.

But that all changed in 1995, when the island's Soufriére Hills volcano erupted, spewing tons of rocks and ash. Since its fateful eruption, the site has grown into a mountain range taller than any of the older hills dotting the face of the lushly verdant island. Fortunately, molten lava generated by the volcano has flowed more or less harmlessly into the sea, away from populated areas, although it caused great damage to the island's vegetation.

However, ash continues to spew from the volcano, with one of the heaviest ashfalls occurring on the morning of May 12, 1996. Another massive explosion occurred September 17, 1996, followed by more worrisome earthquake activities in October 1996. More of the same, it's feared, will follow. Volcano observers point to a frightening bulge in one side of the newly formed mountain, a bulge that might eventually explode. Motorists on the island have been warned to drive with due care and attention to slippery, ash-covered roads. Access routes to Plymouth, the once-thriving capital, are blocked by police barricades. And all sites of public affairs and commercial enterprise, as well as every home on the eastern, western, and southern sides of the island, have been relocated to the island's (relatively) stable northern tier. Fortunately for the tattered shreds of tourism that remain in place, the island's northern tier—its officially designated "safe zone"—was always known as the site of the best beaches and most of its tourist hotels.

How does a government evacuate an entire capital city? By placing banks, government offices, stores, and restaurants in a network of churches, schools, auditoriums, agricultural buildings, quonset huts, and once-private homes. More than at any time since colonial days, residents rely on word-of-mouth for directions to relocated homes and businesses. What will happen if Montserrat explodes into a Caribbean version of Krakatoa? The government has laid the groundwork to implement a mass evacuation to the United Kingdom if it should become necessary.

Currently it's anyone's guess as to the extent or duration of the crisis. But if things calm down and the homes and businesses of Plymouth are reclaimed by their former occupants, look for attempts to pick up the thread of an island culture that in the past has attracted such musical luminaries as Elton John, Paul McCartney, Sting, and Stevie Wonder. Regrettably, even the glory days of Montserrat's role in rock 'n' roll ended in 1989 when Air Studios, a state-of-the-art recording studio on the island's northern tier, went bankrupt after being devastated during Hurricane Hugo. Perhaps future development here might involve resettling Plymouth, or in a bolder move, erecting an all-new city in any of three possible locations in the island's northern tier. If this happens (and at this point, it's only speculation), possible sites would include St. Peters, St. Johns, and Salem.

If you opt for a visit to Montserrat, expect disruptions and limited facilities and activities (many of the hotels and restaurants, including all of them in Plymouth, are closed). Those geological oddities in the south and central part of the island that have attracted nature lovers and hikers for decades may be sealed off. Instead, you'll see a small, closely knit community as it struggles to relocate its primary places of business and government, and a population that's more or less coping gracefully under the strain.

Late-Breaking News: In the summer of 1997, the island was struck by another devastating eruption, which claimed several lives and prompted an evacuation. We strongly suggest that you call ahead to check on the status of the current situation before planning a trip.

GETTING THERE

At least 80% of the passengers flying into Montserrat transfer through Antigua. (For information on getting to Antigua, see section 1 of this chapter.) From Antigua, two different airlines run a flotilla of small planes. **LIAT** (☎ 268/462-0700 on Antigua) operates daily flights to Montserrat on planes holding between 19 and 37 passengers. For information about these flights, call LIAT on Antigua or dial LIAT's Montserrat-based sales representative, Montserrat Aviation (☎ 664/491-2533). Throughout the year, LIAT offers four flights a day, each requiring from 12 to 20 minutes each way, to Montserrat from Antigua. Aircraft are rarely larger than a Dash-8 or a Twin Otter to this island's recently renamed W. H. Bramble Airport.

Because of the recent collapse of a local competitor, LIAT has very few rivals in bringing visitors onto tiny Montserrat. Foremost among these is a charger outfit based on Antigua, **Carib Aviation** (☎ 268/462-3147 on Antigua), which can arrange charter flights from Antigua to fill in the gaps whenever LIAT fights aren't available or are sold out. A local travel agent that maintains a particularly good grip on alternative modes of transport in and out of Montserrat is **Carib World Travel,** officially located on Parliament Street in Plymouth (☎ 664/462-3147), although at this writing its temporary headquarters were in a private residence in the hamlet of Salem.

Most passengers coming from the North American mainland find it cheaper and more convenient to allow large carriers, such as **American** (☎ 800/433-7300) or **BWIA** (☎ 800/327-7401), to make bookings to Montserrat on the above-mentioned airlines as part of ongoing flights through Antigua.

GETTING AROUND

BY TAXI & BUS   Although the island contains 15 miles of surfaced roads, only those in the island's northern tier are currently accessible, and most of the island's vehicular traffic is limited to the route between the airport and the designated "safe zone" in the northern tier. The typical fare from the airport to any of the hotels in the northern tier, including the View Pointe, is EC$49 ($18.15). Sightseeing tours, when viable, cost around EC$30 ($11.10) per hour. The only regular bus service remaining on the island since the debut of volcanic activities runs between Corkhill, a once-northerly suburb of Plymouth, and the island's northern tip. Fares are EC$3 ($1.10) for as long as you want to ride in either direction.

BY BIKE   **Island Bikes,** Palm Loop, Woodlands (☎ 664/491-5552), offers a mobile way to see the lush scenery of Montserrat. You can ride on your own or ask Island Bikes to arrange a guide. Either way you'll see Montserrat from a different perspective. The cost is $25 per day.

BY RENTAL CAR   None of the major U.S.-based car-rental companies has an outlet on Montserrat, although you'll find a handful of private outlets. Before you rent, you'll be warned that volcanic ash, when filtered over one of the island's roads, contributes to slippery driving conditions. You'll also be required to buy a local Montserrat driver's license, priced at $12, that should accompany your valid U.S., British, Canadian, or other driver's license. These permits will usually be available from your car-rental agent; if not, you can get one from a police officer or from the immigration department at the island's airport.

Most island agencies stock a roster of battered Toyotas, Sentras, Daihatsus, and Mazdas, and rent for $25 to $35 a day, depending on the make and model. A collision-damage waiver costs $9 to $11 per day, but even if you buy it you'll still be liable for the cost of some of the repairs to your vehicle if you damage it, for any reason, during your rental. Two of the island's leading agencies are the **Neville Bradshaw Agency,** formerly in Plymouth but relocated to the northern suburb of Olveston since the crisis (☎ **664/491-5270**); and **Montserrat Enterprises,** formerly in Plymouth and also relocated to Olveston since the crisis (☎ **664/491-2431**).

Be warned that there are only two gasoline stations on Montserrat—not enough to service the petrol-related needs of the island. The foremost of these, Delta, is on the northern outskirts of Plymouth; the other operates with limited hours from a location near the island's airport.

FAST FACTS: Montserrat

Currency Most Leeward Islands use the **Eastern Caribbean dollar (EC$),** although most prices are given in U.S. dollars. Currently, the EC dollar is worth about 37¢ in U.S. currency ($1 U.S. = EC$2.70). Unless otherwise specified, rates quoted in this chapter are given in U.S. dollars.

Drugstores The leading pharmacy on the island, **Lee's Pharmacy** (☎ **664/491-3274**), fled from Plymouth and is operating in the island's northwestern hamlet of St. Peter's. It's open Monday to Saturday from 9am to 6pm.

Electricity You'll need an electrical transformer and adapter for all U.S.-made appliances, as the island supplies 220–230 volts AC, 60 cycles. Check with your hotel, though, to see if it has converted its circuitry.

Hospitals Montserrat's largest hospital, the **Glendon Hospital** (☎ 664/ 491-2880), has moved from Plymouth into what was a school in St. John's. It maintains a 24-hour emergency room, and although many delicate medical procedures are performed on-site, some difficult cases opt to be evacuated to medical facilities on Antigua, on Guadeloupe, or in Miami.

Information Although the official address of the **Montserrat Tourist Board** remains Marine Drive (P.O. Box 7), Plymouth, Montserrat, B.W.I. (☎ 664/ 491-2230), temporary headquarters have relocated the organization to Mayfield Estates, Olveston, in the northern suburbs of the former capital. It's open Monday to Friday from 8am to 4pm.

Police Call ☎ 664/491-2555.

Safety As in the Caymans and the British Virgins, crime is rare here. It would be wise, however, to take the usual precautions about safeguarding your valuables.

Taxes The government charges a hotel tax of 7% to 10%. In addition, there's an EC$25 ($9.25) departure tax when you leave the island.

Time Montserrat is on Atlantic standard time year-round. When it's 6am on the island, it's 5am in New York and Miami. However, island clocks match those of the eastern standard zone on the mainland when summer's daylight saving time is in effect in the United States.

Tips and Service Hotels and restaurants add a 10% surcharge to your final tab to cover tips. If they don't, it's customary to tip 10% to 15%.

Weather The mean temperature of the island ranges from a high of 86.5° to a low of 73.5° Fahrenheit.

WHERE TO STAY

Very few of Montserrat's already-limited hotels are still operating because of the volcanic activity. Since there are now a limited number of rooms available on the island, make sure you have a reservation before you arrive.

Belham Valley Hotel. P.O. Box 409, Old Towne, Montserrat, B.W.I. ☎ **664/491-5553.** 4 apts. TV TEL. Winter, $400 Jasmine studio apt; $500 one-bedroom apt; $500 Frangipani studio apt; $525 Mignonette two-bedroom apt. Off-season, $300 Jasmine studio; $375 one-bedroom apt; $375 Frangipani studio; $475 Mignonette apt. All rates are per week. AE, MC, V.

Despite its designation as a hotel, this place maintains and operates four apartments, each with kitchen, which are rented on a weekly basis. On a hillside 4 miles north of Plymouth, they overlook Belham Valley, its river, and the golf course. The beach is about a 7-minute walk, and you can also stroll over in the evening to the Vue Pointe Hotel (see below). The Frangipani studio cottage, surrounded by tropical shrubs and coconut palms, can accommodate two guests and consists of a bedroom, living area, fully equipped kitchen, private bath, and a balcony facing the golf course and the sea. The Jasmine studio apartment also accommodates two and contains a large bed-sitting room, a small dinette, a private bath, a fully equipped kitchen, and a small private patio with views of the sea or mountains. Another apartment, the Mignonette, accommodates four guests and has two bedrooms, a bath, and a living area with kitchen, plus a big patio facing the golf course and sea. There's also another modern apartment with one bedroom.

⭐ **Providence Estate House.** St. Peter's, Montserrat, W.I. ☎ **664/491-6476.** Fax 664/491-8476. 2 rms. TV. Winter, $77–$92 single or double. Off-season, $70–$85 single or double. Rates include breakfast. MC, V.

This B&B guest house is part of a turn-of-the-century plantation in the quiet countryside about 20 minutes north of Plymouth. Several acres of gardens can be viewed from the large veranda that encloses the swimming pool. From the veranda, at an elevation of 500 feet, there's a panoramic 180° view of the Caribbean, including the islands of Nevis and Redonda, as well as much of the northern coastline of Montserrat. A full breakfast is served against this backdrop. The house became locally famous when Sir Paul McCartney and his family rented it for several months some time ago. The guest rooms feature the original thick stone walls, heavy timbered ceilings, and tile floors. A kitchen is available on the veranda for drinks, snacks, and warm-up meals.

BEST OFF-SEASON BET

Vue Pointe Hotel. P.O. Box 65, Old Towne, Montserrat, B.W.I. ☎ **664/491-5210.** Fax 664/491-4813. 40 units. TV TEL. Winter, $170–$195 double; $225 triple. Off-season, $120–$135 double; $165 triple. MAP $40 per person extra. AE, DISC, MC, V.

This family-run cottage colony 4 miles north of Plymouth consists of hexagonal, shingle-roofed villas, plus some interconnected rooms. They're set on 5 acres of sloping land near a black-sand beach just 11 miles from the Montserrat airport and about 2 minutes from the challenging seaside Montserrat Golf Club. Most of the accommodations are constructed of natural lumber with open-beamed ceilings, and they're furnished with bamboo and modern pieces. Each has a private bath, a sitting-room area, and twin beds. A natural breeze sweeps through the accommodations in lieu of air-conditioning.

The cuisine is the best on the island, and everybody shows up for the West Indian barbecue on Wednesday night.

In winter, a single room costs $165 whereas a double goes for $120 to $160 and a triple for $180. Off-season, prices fall to $105 for a single, $135 for a double, and $165 for a triple. The hotel closes in sleepy September.

WHERE TO EAT

Many guests dine at their hotels. But since there are so few hotels and many people rent condos and villas, a number of independent restaurants exist, mainly cafes. Some of these are tiny local spots with a following.

Belham Valley Restaurant. Old Towne. ☎ **664/491-5553.** Reservations recommended, especially for dinner. Main courses $13–$30. AE, MC, V. Tues–Sun noon–2pm and 6:30–11pm. FRENCH/AMERICAN.

Near the Vue Pointe Hotel, 4 miles north of Plymouth, is the premier restaurant of Montserrat. You can enjoy a local creamy pumpkin soup, prime steaks, fettuccine with seafood, Montserrat conch fritters, or a combination of seafood served in a rich vermouth sauce. The kitchen always prepares Montserrat "mountain chicken" (frogs' legs). Desserts are likely to include coconut-cream cheesecake, mango mousse, and fresh coconut pie. The setting is tropical, and the restaurant occupies a former private home on a hillside overlooking the Belham River and its valley. It's convenient for guests at the Montserrat Golf Course. In winter live entertainment is offered Thursday to Saturday night.

Emerald Café. St. John's. ☎ **664/491-3821.** Reservations recommended for dinner in winter. Main courses EC$8–EC$68 ($2.95–$25.20). No credit cards. Daily 8am–11pm. CARIBBEAN/INTERNATIONAL.

Originally established in 1988, this was one of the first establishments to be relocated from unstable premises in Plymouth after the first volcanic activities in 1995. Its new location is in what was originally intended as a private house that was enlarged to contain its newest tenant. Set on the main highway in St. John's, near the island's busiest gas station (the A&F Service Centre), it mingles aspects of a Red Cross canteen with that of a simple luncheonette and West Indian restaurant. The menu items include several preparations of fish, lobster, tenderloin or sirloin steak, stewed beef or mutton, and barbecued spareribs. Although you won't find the touches of comfort and glamour that were the norm here before its relocation, the establishment provides a worthwhile site for meeting local residents and hearing about the often-bizarre situations the volcano has exposed.

Golden Apple. Main Rd., Cork Hill. ☎ 664/491-2187. Reservations required for dinner. Fixed-price dinner EC$40 ($14.80); lunch EC$16–EC$20 ($5.90–$7.40). No credit cards. Mon–Sat noon–2:30pm and 6:30–10pm. WEST INDIAN.

The Golden Apple is a 50-seat restaurant with a beautiful bougainvillea-filled garden out front. Guests are served huge portions of local cuisine, such as mountain chicken, stewed and curried conch, and, only on the weekends, goatwater stew. The atmosphere is welcoming and congenial even if they don't know you. The tables are covered with red-and-white-checked cloths. There's a large selection of fresh fruit including Montserrat coconut.

Mistress Morgan's. Airport Rd., St. John's. ☎ 664/491-5419. Reservations not required, but it's best to call anyway. Meals EC$10.50–EC$45 ($3.90–$16.65). No credit cards. Daily 7:30am–8pm. WEST INDIAN.

Luckily for Ann Morgan, owner of this laid-back, open-air restaurant, she was born and built her business on the island's north side. You can still enjoy what is known in the American South as "down home" cooking in the bare-bones atmosphere of the decidedly local eatery. There's not much, if anything, in the way of a menu. The owner gauges her cooking to meet requests. Some dishes are fairly West Indian standard; goatwater stew is served on Saturday.

Tina's. Lower Frith's, near Salem. ☎ 664/491-3538. Reservations recommended. Main courses EC$35–EC$70 ($12.95–$25.90); pizzas EC$23–EC$58 ($8.50–$21.45). No credit cards. Mon–Sat 10am–10:30pm, Sun 6–10pm. CREOLE.

Your congenial and hardworking hostess is Mrs. Tina Farrell, who welcomes guests into what was originally built as a private home, and which was configured into the premises of this unpretentious restaurant after the evacuation of other sections of Montserrat. You'll recognize the place by its cream-colored facade, a makeshift sign in front, and a string of colored lights that decorates its veranda long after Christmas is over. The cuisine is thoroughly Créole, usually prepared by Tina herself. Menu items vary according to whatever is available that day in the marketplace, but might include such dishes as baked chicken, West Indian–style fish, Tina's special spareribs, and different preparations of lobster and shrimp.

Vue Pointe Restaurant. In the Vue Pointe Hotel, Old Towne. ☎ 664/491-5211. Reservations recommended if you're not a hotel guest. Main courses EC$35–EC$55 ($12.95–$20.35). AE, MC, V. Daily 7am–11pm. FRENCH/CARIBBEAN.

Graciously elegant, this restaurant 4 miles north of Plymouth is surrounded by the lawns and shrubbery of the previously recommended hotel. It's the best-run restaurant on the island. The Wednesday-night barbecue, an island event, is enlivened by a steel band. The kitchen turns out "mountain chicken" (frogs' legs), filet of kingfish, Créole-style red snapper, West Indian curried chicken with condiments, and filet of sole, and does each dish admirably well. Dessert might be lime cheesecake or a tropical fruit salad. A Sunday beach barbecue is presented in winter only.

HIKING & OTHER OUTDOOR PURSUITS

BEACHES If you demand that your beaches on a Caribbean island be either white or pink sands, you'll have to look elsewhere. Perhaps you'll be drawn to the black-sand beaches (the soil is of volcanic origin) on the island's northern rim. If you prefer your beaches in beige tones, head for the northwest coast where you'll find the most frequented beaches: Carr's Bay, Little Bay, and Rendezvous Bay. The Vue Point Hotel can arrange day sails to these beaches.

GOLF The **Montserrat Golf Club,** Old Town (☎ 664/491-5220), has 18 tees but only 11 holes, which are combined into various configurations to create a conventional 18-hole game. Greens fees for a full day on the course are EC$60 to EC$70 ($22.20 to $25.90), depending on the season.

HIKING The verdant hills and vales of Montserrat have attracted hikers since the island was first colonized by the British. Regrettably, some of the most unusual geological features are in districts of the island that have been declared as dangerous by local authorities because of their proximity to smoldering, ash-spewing volcanos. The Galway Soufrière Hike and Great Alps Falls, until recently two of the premier geological sites in the Caribbean, aren't accessible at all until further notice.

Consequently, the Montserrat government has developed a network of panoramic, albeit less dramatic, hiking trails along the island's relatively safe northern tier. Foremost among these is a gentle uphill ramble from a clearly marked point just north of the hamlet of Salem to **The Cott.** Requiring 30 to 45 minutes each way, it presents sweeping views, elevations as high as 900 feet above the sea, and a visit to a ruined stone plantation house (more of a cottage, really) known as The Cott. Green-and-white signs indicate its location and the trails leading up to it.

Although you probably won't need a guide for this particular hike, Montserrat offers about a half-dozen government-trained guides who are willing to provide information about the status of more difficult climbs, including those in regions of the island presently designated as unfit or unsafe for hikers. For more information, contact the **Montserrat Tour Guides Association** (☎ 664/491-3160).

TENNIS Tennis buffs will find two asphalt courts at the previously recommended **Vue Pointe Hotel,** Old Towne. Residents play free, but nonresidents are charged EC$10 ($3.70) per hour. Two tennis courts are also available at the **Montserrat Golf Club** (see above) for those who pay court rental.

SCUBA DIVING The colossal seismic changes that have affected the topography of southern Montserrat have also affected the safety and accessibility of offshore dive sites that, until recently, were superlative. Consequently, at this writing, dive experts list about 30 sites as safe and worthy of underwater exploration. All but a handful of these lie off the island's northwestern coast, near zones that are officially designated as safe from volcanic activities.

Foremost among these is **Pinnacle (The Horn),** the underwater cone of an extinct volcano. It's a deep-water dive (from 65 to 300 feet below the waves) that's usually reserved only for experts. Colorful sponges, huge brain corals, and cavernous basket sponges, large enough to conceal a fully equipped diver, are abundant, along with prodigious numbers of fish. Spearfishing is illegal here. Other worthy sites include **Little Bay,** a relatively shallow dive that propels its participants into a cave filled with roosting and flying bats. Its entrance is open only at some intervals throughout the day, depending on the tides. Other areas known for their abundant underwater life include **Virgin Island** and **Lime Kiln Bay.**

The **Sea Wolf Diving School,** P.O. Box 289, Plymouth, Montserrat, W.I. (☎ 664/491-6859), is the most professional and safety-conscious dive outfit on

Montserrat, with a staff that has an intimate working knowledge of dive sites around the island. This PADI-registered school, with a pair of dive boats, has a policy of supervising only 10 divers at a time, and options that include dives designed for divers of all degrees of experience. At this writing, as a result of the volcanic crisis, the company operates out of the owner's private home in Woodlands. A snorkeling tour, lasting between 3 and 4 hours, costs $25 to $35 per person. Resort courses go for $70. A one-tank dive for experienced divers costs $50. Packages are available for stays on the island of a week or more, and the owners can arrange accommodations in private villas and guest houses throughout the island.

SEEING THE SIGHTS

The island is small, only 11 miles long and 7 miles across at its widest point. But seeing its former attractions is now a big problem. Virtually everything of geological or natural interest is off-limits or else covered in volcanic ash. For example, the former highest point, Chances Peak, which once rose to 3,000 feet, is now a minor bump (a local called it a "wart"), and lies on the side of the massive, all-new volcano known as the **Soufriére Hills volcano.**

About a 15-minute drive from Plymouth, the ruined **Fort St. George** dates from the 18th century and can still be visited as it lies in a "safe zone." The fort is 1,184 feet above sea level and offers panoramic views. At yet another fortification, **Bransby Point,** you can see restored cannons. The early earthworks date from 1640 to 1660.

SHOPPING

There is no duty-free shopping, but some interesting locally made handcrafts are for sale. Straw goods and small ceramic souvenirs predominate, along with Sea Island cotton fabrics. All the major shopping outlets have closed, but if you're interested you can ask around and be directed to makeshift locations.

Carol's Corner, in a public room of the Vue Pointe Hotel, Old Towne (☎ 664/491-5210), offers a concentrated collection of Montserrat-related memorabilia. It sells the famous stamps of Montserrat and copies of the difficult-to-obtain flag. There's also a collection of road maps, top-quality T-shirts, local jams and honey, and cosmetics and sundries.

MONTSERRAT AFTER DARK

Montserrat may be sleepy during the day, but it gets even quieter at night. The most activity is at the **Vue Pointe Hotel,** Old Towne (☎ 664/491-5210), where a steel band plays every Wednesday night, when you can order a barbecue dinner for EC$77 ($29) per person.

The Village Place, Salem (☎ 664/491-5202), is for nostalgic rock buffs. If you weren't looking for it, you might think that its encircling hibiscus fences concealed a private house. Set north of Plymouth and directly east of Old Towne, it's one of the most popular night bars and most enduring restaurants on Montserrat. Serving endless rounds of beer, and a lethal version of rum punch concocted by the owner Andy Lawrence, it enjoys some of the best-entrenched rock-related legends on the island. (Legend says that Elton John proposed to his wife here, and that Eric Clapton, Sting, members of Dire Straits and Deep Purple, and Mick Jagger have all enjoyed its raffish and occasionally rowdy charms.) Many visitors come just to drink, but if you want a meal, excellent versions of fried chicken and barbecued spareribs are served by Andy's hardworking wife, Sonia. Sonia is an island legend for her "Impossible Pie," its recipe known only to her, although we know that it requires patience, experience, and coconut juice. Snacks and main courses run EC$2 to EC$35 (75¢ to $12.95). It's open Tuesday to Sunday from 6pm to very late.

3 St. Kitts

A volcanic island of the British Leewards (although it's no longer British), St. Kitts has become a resort mecca in recent years. Its major crop is sugar, a tradition dating from the 17th century. But tourism may overwhelm it in the years to come, as its southeastern peninsula, site of the best white-sand beaches, has been set aside for massive hotel and resort development. Most of the island's other beaches are of gray or black volcanic sand.

Far more active and livelier than its companion island, Nevis, St. Kitts is still fairly sleepy itself. But go now before its inherent Caribbean character changes forever. However, the island doesn't offer a wide range of accommodations, particularly on the lower end of the price scale. One all-inclusive (Jack Tar) offers a good return on your money, and you might also get a good deal renting a condo with a kitchen. As for dining, if you avoid the high-priced resorts and eat at some of the little taverns where the locals go, you'll at least be able to keep food costs within reason.

At some point during your visit you should eat sugar directly from the cane. Any farmer will sell you a huge stalk, and there are sugarcane plantations all over the island—just ask your taxi driver to take you to one. You strip off the hard exterior of the stalk, bite into it, chew on the tasty reeds, and swallow the juice. It's best with a glass of rum.

The Caribs, the early settlers, called St. Kitts Liamuiga, or "fertile isle." Its mountain ranges reach up to nearly 4,000 feet, and in its interior are virgin rain forests, alive with hummingbirds and wild green vervet monkeys. The monkeys were brought in as pets by the early French settlers and were turned loose in the forests when the island became British in 1783. These native African animals have proliferated and can be seen at the Estridge Estate Behavioral Research Institute. Another import, this one British, is the mongoose, brought in from India as an enemy of rats in the sugarcane fields. However, the mongooses and rats operate on different time cycles—the rats ravage while the mongooses sleep. Wild deer are found in the mountains. Sugarcane climbs right up the slopes, and there are palm-lined beaches around the island. As you travel around St. Kitts, you'll notice ruins of old mills and plantation houses. You'll also see an island rich in trees and other vegetation.

St. Kitts, 23 miles long and 6½ miles wide, rides the crest of that arc of islands known as the northerly Leeward group of the Lesser Antilles. It's separated from the associated state of Nevis by a 2-mile-wide strait, and its administrative capital is Basseterre.

GETTING THERE

Dozens of daily flights on **American Airlines** (☎ 800/433-7300) land in San Juan, Puerto Rico. From there, **American Eagle** (same phone) makes four daily nonstop flights into St. Kitts.

If you're already on St. Maarten and want to visit St. Kitts (with perhaps a side trip to Nevis), you can do so aboard one of the most remarkable little airlines in the Caribbean. Known by its nickname, **Winair (Windward Islands Airways International)** (☎ 809/465-2186), it makes several flights a week from St. Maarten to St. Kitts and Nevis, with easy connections to or from such other Dutch islands as Saba, St. Eustatius, and about a dozen other destinations throughout the Caribbean.

Another possibility involves transfers into St. Kitts or Nevis through Antigua, St. Maarten, or San Juan on the Antigua-based carrier **LIAT** (☎ 268/462-0701). LIAT's one-way fares from each of those destinations to St. Kitts are $56, $61, and $130, respectively.

Reservations for ongoing flights from any of the above-mentioned hubs can most easily be made through the telephone networks of many of the U.S.-based carriers.

GETTING AROUND

BY PLANE Most visitors to St. Kitts or Nevis like to spend at least 1 day on the neighbor island. **LIAT** provides three daily flights to and from Nevis at a cost of EC$113 ($41.80) round-trip or EC$60 ($22.20) one-way. Make reservations at the LIAT office on Front Street in Basseterre (☎ **268/462-0701**) instead of at the airport.

BY FERRY The government passenger ferry **MV *Caribe Queen*** departs from each island, St. Kitts and Nevis, on Monday, Tuesday, Wednesday, Friday, and Saturday, and runs on a schedule (check the times at your hotel or the tourist office). It costs EC$10 ($3.70) each way.

BY BIKE If you're adventurous, head for **Cycle Crazy,** St. Mary's Street, St. John's (☎ **268/462-9253**), which rents bikes for $15 per day. But be warned that the roads are narrow, twisting, and potholed.

BY TAXI Most taxi drivers are also guides, so this is the best means of getting around. You don't even have to find a driver at the airport—one will find you. Drivers also wait outside the major hotels. Before heading out, however, you must agree on the price—taxis aren't metered. Also, ask if the rates quoted to you are in U.S. dollars or Eastern Caribbean dollars. To go from Robert L. Bradshaw International Airport to Basseterre costs about EC$16 ($5.90); to Sandy Point, EC$36 ($13.30) and up.

BY RENTAL CAR The only U.S.-based car-rental firm on St. Kitts is **Avis,** South Independence Square (☎ **800/331-2112** in the U.S., or 809/465-6507). It charges between $45 and $50 per day, or $270 and $300 per week, plus $10 per day for collision damage with a $250 deductible. Nine-seat vans are available at $70 per day or $240 per week. Tax is 5% extra, and a week's rental allows a seventh day for free. The company offers free delivery service to either the airport or any of the island's hotels. Drivers must be between ages 25 and 75.

Delisle Walwyn & Co., Liverpool Row, Basseterre (☎ **869/465-8449**), is a local company offering cars and Jeeps. Daily charges range from $30 to $55. This might be your best deal on the island.

Other local companies renting cars include **Sunshine Car Rental,** Cayon Street, Basseterre (☎ **869/465-2193**), which rents Suzuki Samurais at $40 per day (but with manual transmission). These are year-round rates. A final option is **TDC Rentals,** Fort Street, Basseterre (☎ **869/465-2991**), which often has a good selection of vehicles at competitive prices. This outfit seems to offer the best service.

Reflecting British tradition, *driving is on the left.* You'll need a local driver's license, which can be obtained at the Traffic Department, on Cayon Street in Basseterre, for EC$40 ($14.80). Usually a member of the staff at your car-rental agency will drive you to the Traffic Department to get one.

FAST FACTS: St. Kitts

Banking Hours Banks are open Monday to Friday from 8am to noon and on Friday also from 3 to 5pm.

Currency The local currency is the **Eastern Caribbean dollar (EC$),** exchanged at about EC$2.70 to the U.S. dollar (EC$1 = 37¢ U.S.). Many bills, however,

including those of hotels, are quoted in U.S. dollars. Always determine which "dollar" locals are talking about.

Customs   You're allowed in duty free with your personal belongings. Sometimes luggage is subjected to a drug check.

Drugstores   Skeritt's Drug Store, Fort Street, Basseterre (☎ **869/465-2008**), is open Monday to Saturday from 8am to 6pm. You can call for 24-hour prescription service at ☎ **869/465-2083**.

Electricity   St. Kitts's electricity is 230 volts AC, 60 cycles, so you'll need an adapter and a transformer for U.S.–made appliances.

Emergencies   Dial ☎ **911**.

Entry Requirements   U.S. and Canadian citizens can enter with proof of citizenship, such as a voter registration card or birth certificate. British subjects need a passport but not a visa.

Hospital   In Basseterre, there's a 24-hour emergency room at **Joseph N. France General Hospital,** Buckley Site (☎ **869/465-2551**).

Information   Tourist information is available from the tourist board's Stateside offices at 414 E. 75th St., New York, NY 10021 (☎ **212/535-1234**); or 1464 Whippoorwill Way, Mountainside, NJ 07092 (☎ **908/232-6701**). In Canada, an office is at 365 Bay St., Suite 806, Toronto, ON M5H 2V1

(☎ **416/368-6707**); and in the United Kingdom at 10 Kensington Court, London W8 5DL (☎ **0171/376-0881**).

On the island, the **local tourist board** operates at Pelican Mall, Bay Road, in Basseterre (☎ **869/465-4040**), open Monday and Tuesday from 8am to 4:30pm and Wednesday to Friday from 8am to 4pm.

Language   English is the language of the island, though it's spoken with a decided West Indian patois.

Police   In an emergency, call ☎ **911.**

Safety   This is still a fairly safe place to travel. Most crimes against tourists—and there aren't a lot—are robberies on Conaree Beach, so exercise the usual precautions. It would be wise to safeguard your valuables. Women should not go jogging along deserted roads.

Taxes   The government imposes a 7% tax on rooms and meals, plus another EC$27 ($10) airport departure tax (but not to go to Nevis).

Telecommunications   Telegrams and telexes can be sent from **Skantel,** Cayon Street, Basseterre (☎ **869/465-1000**), Monday to Friday from 8am to 6pm, on Saturday from 8am to 2pm, and on Sunday and public holidays from 6 to 8pm. International telephone calls, including collect calls, can also be made from this office.

Time   St. Kitts is on Atlantic standard time all year. This means that in winter when it's 6am in Basseterre, it's 5am in Miami and New York. When the United States goes on daylight saving time, St. Kitts and the U.S. East Coast are on the same time.

Tipping   Most hotels and restaurants add a service charge of 10% to cover tipping. If not, tip 10% to 15%.

Water   The water on St. Kitts and Nevis is so good that Baron de Rothschild's chemists selected St. Kitts as their only site in the Caribbean to distill and produce CSR (Cane Sugar Rothschild), a pure sugarcane liqueur.

Weather   St. Kitts lies in the tropics, and its warm climate is tempered by the trade winds. The average air temperature is 79° Fahrenheit and the average water temperature is 80°. Average rainfall is 55 inches. Dry, mild weather is usually experienced from November to April; May to October it's hotter and rainier.

WHERE TO STAY
DOUBLES FOR LESS THAN $45

Llewellyn's Haven. Adams Hill, Basseterre, St. Kitts, W.I. ☎ **869/465-2941.** 7 rms. Year-round, $35 single; $45 double. No credit cards.

The present owners have managed this place since the late 1980s. Family-oriented, it welcomes children. The bedrooms, all with bath (tub or shower), are off-white with a vaguely floral decor. It's in a residential suburb of Basseterre, about a 25-minute drive from the beach at Frigate Bay and about a 15-minute drive from the airport.

Windsor Guest House. 19 Cayon St. (P.O. Box 122), Basseterre, St. Kitts, W.I. ☎ **869/465-2894.** 7 rms, 2 with bath. Year-round, $20 single without bath; $30 single with bath; $25 double without bath; $35 double with bath. No credit cards.

This place is so peaceful it's almost dead. The staff doesn't show a lot of enthusiasm for their work, but it's the bargain of the island for those who don't mind roughing it. The quality of the rooms varies considerably, so ask to see your room before checking in. The bedrooms have off-white walls, two twin beds, a dresser, a night table, and not a lot else. The location, across from the Wesleyan Holiness Church, is about a 15-minute drive from Frigate Bay Beach and a 5-minute drive from the airport. There's no restaurant on the premises and no breakfast is served, but you do get maid service.

DOUBLES FOR LESS THAN $85 (WINTER) / $60 (OFF-SEASON)

Gateway Inn. Frigate Bay (P.O. Box 64, Basseterre), St. Kitts, W.I. ☎ 869/465-7155. Fax 869/465-9322. 10 apts. A/C TV TEL. Winter, $80 apt for two. Off-season, $60 apt for two. Extra person $15. AE, MC, V.

Built by local entrepreneurs in the early 1990s, this self-catering apartment complex has 10 apartments with a separate bedroom and living/dining area and a fully equipped kitchen. The furnishings include mostly mahogany pieces with upholstery and curtains sporting a floral Caribbean motif. The complex is in a secluded position about a 11-minute walk to either the beach or the island's public golf course. Although there's no restaurant or bar in the complex, each apartment includes maid service. Laundry, baby-sitting, and water sports can be arranged on-site, and guests can shop at the minimart convenience store within walking distance.

Morgan Heights Condominiums. Canada Estate (P.O. Box 735, Basseterre), St. Kitts, W.I. ☎ 869/465-8633. Fax 869/465-2972. 5 condos, 10 suites. AC MINIBAR TV TEL. Winter, $85 two-bedroom condo; $125–$175 suite. Off-season, $50 two-bedroom condo; $75–$105 suite. Extra person $20 in winter, $15 off-season. AE, DC, MC, V.

Set on a sandy offshore east coast island known as Canada Estate, this complex originally consisted of a quintet of two-bedroom apartments, each with its own kitchen with ceramic-tile floors, wicker furniture, and covered patios that overlook the Atlantic Ocean. After its initial construction, the complex was enlarged with 10 suites, each with its own kitchen. Although there's a view of the water, the beach is a 10-minute drive away. A swimming pool is on the grounds. In an open-sided outbuilding a short walk from the accommodations, you'll find a simple restaurant, the Atlantic Club (see "Where to Eat," below).

Palms Hotel. The Circus (P.O. Box 64), Basseterre, St. Kitts, W.I. ☎ 809/465-0800. Fax 809/465-5889. 10 suites. A/C TV TEL. Year-round, $75–$85 junior suite; $88–$105 one-bedroom suite; $110–$150 two-bedroom suite. AE, MC, V.

Occupying the upper floor of a two-story antique building surrounding the Circus, in the commercial heart of Basseterre, this hotel enjoys the most central location. Some of the rooms are accessible only via an outdoor veranda; others open off an enclosed hallway inside the much-restored, 200-year-old site. Although there's lots of hubbub in the square in the mornings, after 4pm it quiets down considerably. No meals are served, although there's a small bar and cafe on the premises. The accommodations are high-ceilinged, spacious, and simply but comfortably furnished, each named after a local bank or personality. The main drawback to this place is the slowness of the staff, whose laborious and langorous pace can be exasperating. But for clean and unpretentious lodgings in the heart of town, it's worth the delay. Swimming is an option at Frigate Bay, a 5-minute drive from the hotel.

BEST OFF-SEASON BET

Frigate Bay Resort. Frigate Bay (P.O. Box 137, Basseterre) St. Kitts W.I. ☎ 869/465-8935. Fax 869/465-7050. 40 rms, 16 suites. Winter, single or double $123–$173; $263–$373 suite. Off-season, $80–$113 single or double; $177–$220 suite. MAP $40 per person extra. Packages available. A/C TEL. AE, MC, V.

On a verdant hillside east of Basseterre, Frigate Bay has standard rooms and condo-minium suites administered as hotel units for their absentee owners. The central core of the resort contains a large swimming pool and a cabaña bar where you can enjoy a drink while partially immersed. An 18-hole golf course and tennis courts are within walking distance. The units are nicely furnished to the taste of the owners and painted in an array of pastel colors. They have cool tile floors, air-conditioning and ceiling fans, and private balconies. Many have fully equipped kitchens with breakfast bars.

AN ALL-INCLUSIVE RESORT

Jack Tar Village St. Kitts Beach Resort & Casino. Frigate Bay (P.O. Box 406, Basseterre), St. Kitts, W.I. ☎ **800-999-9182** in the U.S., or 869/465-8651. Fax 869/465-1031. 241 rms, 3 suites. A/C TV TEL. Winter, $170–$185 single; $280–$310 double; $380 suite. Off-season, $140–$150 single; $190–$220 double; $265 suite. Children 5–12 sharing parents' room $60 in winter, free off-season. Rates include meals, golf fees, drinks, and most water sports. AE, MC, V.

The largest hotel on St. Kitts, and certainly the showcase hotel of the much-touted Frigate Bay development, is 1 1/2 miles east of the airport on a flat, sandy isthmus be-tween the sea and a saltwater lagoon. It seems like a private country club, and the resort is almost completely self-contained. Each of the regular rooms has a patio or balcony and tropical furniture. Most visitors prefer the second-floor rooms because of the higher ceilings. When you check in, ID tags are issued in an effort to help you get acquainted with your fellow guests.

The resort has two restaurants, a number of bars, and the island's only casino. Organized activities include Scrabble and shuffleboard tournaments, scuba lessons, and toga contests. Services include laundry, baby-sitting, and activities for kids. Fa-cilities include two swimming pool areas (one for quiet reading, another for active sports), four tennis courts (lit at night), and a nearby golf course.

WORTH A SPLURGE

Fairview Inn. At the base of Ottley's Mountain(P.O. Box 212, Basseterre), St. Kitts, W.I. ☎ **800/223-9815** in the U.S., or 869/465-2472. Fax 869/465-1056. 30 rms. Winter, $120–$140 single or double; $170–$190 triple. Off-season, $70–$80 single or double; $100–$110 triple. MAP $35 per person extra. AE, DC, MC, V.

Built around the core of a much-restored 18th-century Great House, this is a simple and relaxed hotel whose rooms tend to be less standardized than those at other is-land hotels. Most are in individual cottages whose foundations flank the bottom of an awesomely steep hillside. Some units have air-conditioning and/or ceiling fans, with furnishings and amenities less elegant than those in the veranda-ringed Great House. There's a restaurant serving a well-prepared version of West Indian cuisine. The hotel lies a 20-minute drive from Frigate Bay Beach.

Fort Thomas Hotel. Fortlands (P.O. Box 407, Basseterre), St. Kitts, W.I. ☎ **800/851-7818** in the U.S. and Canada, or 869/465-2695. Fax 869/465-7518. 61 rms, 3 suites. A/C TV TEL. Winter, $110–$140 single; $130–$160 double; $245–$275 suite. Off-season, $100–$125 single; $115–$140 double; $245–$275 suite. MAP $35 per person extra. AE, MC, V.

On the northern side of Basseterre, a 10-minute drive from the airport, this tour-group favorite was constructed on the site of a historic fort. From its lookout perch, it commands a panoramic view of Great Bay, with Nevis in the far distance. It's not, of course, on a beach, but a shuttle is available to take guests to Frigate Bay. Secluded from the hustle and bustle of the capital, it offers a tranquil setting enlivened occa-sionally by local bands. The bedrooms are decorated in soothing tones, and couples, groups, families, and commercial travelers find refuge in them. Each unit has a small refrigerator. Life revolves around the swimming pool, and the restaurant serves sub-stantial fare at modest prices. Both international and Caribbean cuisine are offered.

Sun 'n Sand Beach Villas. Frigate Bay (P.O. Box 341,Basseterre), St. Kitts, W.I. ☎ **869/ 465-8037.** Fax 809/465-6745. 32 one-bedroom studios, 18 two-bedroom cottages. A/C TV TEL. Winter, $160 studio for one or two; $270 cottage for four. Off-season, $90 studio for one or two; $150 cottage for four. Extra person $20. MAP $35 per person extra. AE, DC, DISC, MC, V.

The low prices at this holiday apartment complex are partly a result of its location on the Atlantic side of the island, near a beach whose surf is sometimes troublesome. (Some beach aficionados opt for a somewhat inconvenient 15-minute walk to the calmer waters of a beach on the Caribbean side of the island.) Built in the mid-1980s, it offers a pool, two tennis courts illuminated for night play, an ice-cream parlor, and the availability, sometimes through outside purveyors, of all kinds of water sports. Each unit contains a kitchenette with a microwave and a full-sized refrigerator, and has tropical colors, simple rattan furniture, tile floors, breezy terraces, and sofas that convert into beds. You can stock the in-house kitchens at nearby grocery stores.

WHERE TO EAT

Most guests eat at their hotels; however, St. Kitts has a scattering of good restaurants where you're likely to have spiny lobster, crab back, pepperpot, breadfruit, and curried conch. The drink of the island is CSR (Cane Spirit Rothschild), a pure sugarcane liqueur developed by Baron Edmond de Rothschild. Islanders mix it with Ting, a bubbly grapefruit soda.

The Anchorage. Frigate Bay. ☎ **869/465-8235.** Main courses $13.50–$21.25. AE, MC, V. Mon–Thurs 11am–11pm, Fri–Sat 11am–midnight. WEST INDIAN / CONTINENTAL.

This isolated beachfront no-smoking restaurant on the rolling acres of Frigate Bay sits in the shadow of an enormous leafy tree. A roof shelters its concrete-slab floor from sudden showers. The owners prepare rum-based drinks and seafood, with a menu that offers four or five salads (lobster is the most expensive), broiled or thermidor lobster, sirloin, spareribs, hamburgers, a dozen kinds of sandwiches (much cheaper than the main courses), fresh fish, and ice cream. If you're looking for an unspoiled beach with a casual restaurant, you may want to head here.

Arlecchino. Cayon St., Basseterre. ☎ **869/465-9927.** Main courses EC$25–EC$45 ($9.25–$16.65); lunch EC$14–EC$20 ($5.20–$7.40). DISC, MC, V. Mon–Sat 9am–3pm and 5–10:30pm. WEST INDIAN / ITALIAN.

This favorite local hangout in the open air has some of the best-tasting and least expensive food in town. It's really like a trattoria Caribbean style. The waiters are friendly and helpful, and diners seem to take their time. At lunch try such specialties as braised pork, shrimp in garlic sauce, lobster with rice and peas, and most definitely the island-grown local vegetables. Dinner is more Italian in flavor with all the standard Mamma Mia offerings, including veal parmigiana, penne arrabratia (really hot), and such pastas as lasagne and spaghetti. Dessert is primarily ice-cream cake, and pizza can be ordered on Saturday only.

The Atlantic Club. At the Morgan Heights Condominiums, Canada Estate. ☎ **869/ 465-8633.** Reservations recommended for dinner. Main courses EC$15–EC$45 ($5.60–$16.70). AE, MC, V. Mon–Sat 11am–11pm. SEAFOOD / WEST INDIAN.

A Nevisian, Genford Gumbs, who worked at the deluxe Golden Lemon for 15 years, struck out on his own and opened this enterprise in the early 1990s next to his Morgan Heights Condominiums (recommended above). Lying on the east coast, a 5-minute drive from the center of Basseterre and a 3-minute drive from the airport, it overlooks the Atlantic Ocean. The cuisine is West Indian, with some seafood such as fresh fish, conch, and lobster usually available. The atmosphere is relaxed and casual, and the portions are large. A lot of locals show up on Saturday for the special, goatwater and souse. Some foreigners had rather skip this treat and order the burgers, soups, salads, and sandwiches, or even a Black Angus steak.

Chef's Place. Upper Church St., Basseterre. ☎ **869/465-6176.** Reservations recommended for dinner. Lunch or dinner EC$18–EC$55 ($6.65–$20.40). No credit cards. Mon–Sat 8am–11pm. WEST INDIAN.

This small air-conditioned eatery is located in the heart of Basseterre's business district. You can dine on the balcony overlooking the street. The breakfasts that include eggs, bacon, and pancakes are hearty. One of the specialties is the local version of jerk chicken. Another recommended dish, generally served on Saturday (a St. Kitts tradition), is goatwater stew and souse.

Coconut Cafe. In Colony's Timothy Beach Resort, Frigate Bay. ☎ **869/465-3020.** Reservations recommended for dinner. Main courses EC$32.50–EC$52 ($12–$19.20). AE, MC, V. Daily 7am–11pm. CARIBBEAN/AMERICAN.

Fronted with a garden, and ringed with trees, this establishment features a table-strewn open-air patio where most of the tables overlook the waters of Frigate Bay. Set in a hotel complex but operated independently, the place features Caribbean/American cuisine: steak, chicken, pork and lamb chops, seafood Créole style, as well as something they consider their best dish, "flying fish burgers." The staff is efficient and helpful. Many condo dwellers like to come here for their sundowner, often enjoying panoramic sunsets.

J's Place. Romney Grounds. ☎ **869/465-6264.** Main courses EC$20–EC$45 ($7.40–$16.65); lunch from EC$15 ($5.55). No credit cards. Daily 11am–7pm. CARIBBEAN.

Some of the best local food—cooked without fuss but filled with flavor—is found at this spot near the Brimstone Hill fortress. Most visitors to the fort stop off here for a reasonably priced lunch of burgers, sandwiches, and salads, including the "famous" lobster salad.

Although the restaurant closes at 7pm, many habitués stop off here for an early dinner. In the late afternoon the menu expands, offering such regional favorites as goat and conch "water" (actually a stew), mutton with rice and peas, fried or steamed kingfish, and grilled Caribbean lobster.

Pisces Restaurant & Bar. Cayon St., Basseterre. ☎ **869/465-5032.** Reservations recommended for dinner. Main courses EC$16.50–EC$55 ($6.10–$20.35). No credit cards. Daily 7am–2am. CARIBBEAN.

An immediate local favorite since it opened in 1993, Pisces is at the back of the Glimbara Guest House in Basseterre. It likes to think of itself as "your home away from home." The restaurant is owned and operated by Nerita Godfrey, or Rita, as she's affectionately known on the island. She specializes in seafood such as lobster, shrimp, and whelk. Each day she prepares some local dish, perhaps bullfoot soup with dinner rolls or a "cookup" (saltfish, pigtail, pig snout, chicken, and red peas, which is served on Tuesday). Her barbecued spareribs and conch stew are justly praised. On Saturday locals visit to sample her "goatwater." Lamb chops, pork chops, shrimp fried rice, and her special chicken are also favorites. Throughout the day you can order breakfast, sandwiches, and several forms of burgers, ranging from cheese to fish to veggie.

P.J.'s Pizza. Next to Island Paradise Condominiums, Frigate Bay. ☎ **869/465-8373.** Main courses EC$15–EC$50 ($5.60–$18.50). AE, MC, V. Daily 10am–11pm (times vary off-season). PIZZA/ITALIAN.

Set across from the Royal St. Kitts golf course, next to the Island Paradise Condominiums, this is an open-air, casual place where many members seem to arrive in their bathing suits throughout the day. On 5 acres a short walk from the beach, the place has been described even by its good-natured owner (Julie Dolma) as "a cinder-block gas station without the gas pumps." At night metal storm shutters complete the "industrial building" look, but many visitors appreciate the joint for its good pizza.

The owners are especially proud of the thin-baked spicy crust that comprises the base of the many kinds of pizzas they serve. Their specialty is a Mexican pizza with lettuce, tomatoes, refried beans, and sour cream. They also serve Italian onion soup, spicy sausage soup, and an array of made-at-home pastas.

Simple breakfasts (bagels with toast, muffins, and coffee) are also available.

Turtle Beach Bar & Grill. At the Ocean Terrace Inn, Turtle Beach. ☎ **869/469-9086.** Reservations recommended. Main courses $8.50–$18.50. AE, MC, V. Sun–Fri noon–5pm, Sat noon–5pm and 7:30–10pm. Take the Kennedy Simmonds Hwy. over Basseterre's Southeastern Peninsula, then follow the signs. SEAFOOD.

Set directly on the sand above Turtle Beach, this airy and sun-flooded restaurant is part of the Ocean Terrace Inn. Many patrons spend the hour before their meal swimming or snorkeling beside the offshore reef; others simply relax on the verandas or beneath shade trees (hammocks are available), perhaps with a drink in hand. Scuba diving, ocean kayaking, windsurfing, and volleyball are possible, and a flotilla of rental sailboats is moored nearby. Menu specialties might be stuffed broiled lobster, conch fritters, barbecued swordfish steak, prawn salads, and barbecued honey-mustard spareribs. The hotel runs a shuttle service between the restaurant and the hotel's reception area.

WORTH A SPLURGE

Fisherman's Wharf Seafood Restaurant and Bar. Fortlands, Basseterre. ☎ **869/ 465-2754.** Main courses $16–$26. AE, MC, V. Daily 6pm–midnight. SEAFOOD/CARIBBEAN.

At the west end of Basseterre Bay Road, the Fisherman's Wharf is between the sea and the white-picket fence surrounding the Ocean Terrace Inn. Its heart and soul lie near the busy buffet grill, where the hardworking chefs prepare fresh seafood. An employee will take your drink order, but you personally place your food orders at the buffet grill. Menu items are familiar fare, but prepared with often scrumptious flavor. Specialties are grilled lobster, shrimp in garlic sauce, grilled swordfish steak, and grilled catch of the day. The fish is caught locally and grilled to order over St. Kitts chosha coals.

Stone Walls Tropical Bar & Eating Place. Princess St., Basseterre. ☎ **869/465-5248.** Main courses $15–$22. AE, DC, MC, V. Dec–May, Mon–Sat 5pm "until." Off-season, Mon–Fri 5pm "until." INTERNATIONAL.

Newsweek in 1996 proclaimed this as one of the best bars in the world, and it's also a great place for good-tasting food served in a casual, open-air setting, with a lush garden surrounded by ancient stone walls, a few steps from The Circus. The constantly changing menu, written on a chalkboard, is innovative. Ben and Paulette Goldberg welcome you to sample their blackened snapper and a zesty gumbo, or an authentic, spicy Dhansak-style curry. Hot-off-the-wok stir-fries or hot-off-the-grill baby back ribs might tempt you, as will the barbecued salmon filets and sizzling, Jamaican-style jerk chicken. Begin with the piquant conch fritters or a robust homemade pâté. The restaurant was created by a journalist, Garry Steckles, of British Columbia, and his wife, Wendy.

BEACHES, WATER SPORTS & OUTDOOR PURSUITS

BEACHES You'll find the best swimming at the twin beaches of **Banana Bay** and **Cockleshell Bay, Conaree Beach** (2 miles from Basseterre), talcum-powder-fine

Frigate Bay (north of Banana Bay), and **Friar's Bay** (a peninsula beach that opens onto both the Atlantic and the Caribbean). The narrow peninsula in the southeast that contains the island's salt ponds also boasts the best white-sand beaches. All beaches, even those that border hotels, are open to the public. However, if you use the beach facilities of a hotel, you must obtain permission first and will probably have to pay a fee.

GOLF At Frigate Bay, there's the **Royal St. Kitts Golf Club** (☎ 869/465-8339), an 18-hole championship golf course designed by Peter Thomas. Greens fees are $35 per 18 holes.

TENNIS Daytime tennis is available for guests of the **Ocean Terrace Inn,** Fortlands (☎ 869/465-2754). Also downtown, at the **St. Kitts Lawn Tennis Club** (☎ 869/465-2938), you can arrange for a temporary membership; call for details.

WATER SPORTS Some of the best diving spots include **Nagshead,** at the southern tip of St. Kitts. This is an excellent shallow-water dive starting at 10 feet and extending to 70 feet. A variety of tropical fish, eagle rays, and lobster are found here. The site is ideal for certified divers. Another good spot for diving is **Booby Shoals,** between Cow 'n' Calf Rocks and Booby Island, off the coast of St. Kitts. Booby Shoals has abundant sea life, including nurse sharks, lobster, and stingrays. Dives—ideal for both certified and resort divers—are up to 30 feet in depth. A variety of activities is offered by **Pro-Divers** at Turtle Beach (☎ 869/465-3223). You can swim, float, paddle, or go on scuba-diving and snorkeling expeditions from here. A two-tank dive costs $50 if you have your own equipment or $60 if they provide the equipment. Night dives are $50. A PADI certification course is available for $300, with a resort course costing $75. Snorkeling trips lasting 3 hours are offered for $35 per person, and also day trips to Nevis, costing $25 per person.

SEEING THE SIGHTS

The British colonial town of **Basseterre** is built around the so-called **The Circus,** the town's round square. A tall green Victorian clock stands in the center of The Circus. After Brimstone Hill Fortress (see below), this **Berkeley Memorial Clock** is the most photographed landmark on St. Kitts. In the old days wealthy plantation owners and their families used to promenade here.

At some point, try to visit the **marketplace.** Here country people bring baskets brimming with mangos, guavas, soursop, mammy apples, and wild strawberries and cherries just picked in the fields. Tropical flowers abound.

Another major landmark is **Independence Square.** Once an active slave market, it's surrounded by private homes of Georgian architecture.

You can negotiate with a taxi driver to take you on a tour of the island for about $55 for a 3-hour trip, and most drivers are well versed in island lore. Lunch can be arranged at either the Rawlins Plantation Inn or the Golden Lemon. For more information, call the **St. Kitts Taxi Association,** The Circus, Basseterre (☎ 869/465-4253 during the day or 869/465-7818 at night).

The **Brimstone Hill Fortress,** 9 miles west of Basseterre (☎ 869/465-6211), is the major stop on any tour of St. Kitts. This historic monument, among the largest and best preserved in the Caribbean, is a complex of bastions, barracks, and other structures ingeniously adapted to the top and upper slopes of a steep-sided 800-foot hill.

The fortress dates from 1690 when the British armed the hill to aid in the recapture from the French of their Fort Charles below. In 1782 an invading force of 8,000

French troops bombarded the fortress for a month before its small garrison, supplemented by local militia, surrendered. The fortress was restored to the British the following year, and they thereupon embarked on an intense program of building and reconstruction that resulted in the imposing military complex that came to be known as "The Gibraltar of the West Indies."

Today the fortress is the centerpiece of a national park of nature trails and a diverse range of plant and animal life, including the green vervet monkey. It's also a photographer's paradise, with views of mountains, fields, and the Caribbean Sea. On a clear day, six neighboring islands can be seen.

Visitors will enjoy self-directed tours among the many ruined or restored structures, including the barrack rooms at Fort George, which comprise an interesting museum. At the gift shop, prints of rare maps and paintings of the Caribbean can be purchased. Admission is $5, half price for children. The Brimstone Hill Fortress National Park is open every day from 9:30am to 5:30pm.

At the hamlet of **Half-Way Tree,** a large tamarind marked the boundary in the old days between the British-held sector and the French half.

It was near the hamlet of **Old Road Town** that Sir Thomas Warner landed with the first band of settlers and established the first permanent colony to the northwest at Sandy Point. Sir Thomas's grave is in the cemetery of St. Thomas Church.

A sign in the middle of Old Road Town points the way to the **Carib rock drawings,** all the evidence that remains of the former inhabitants. The markings are on black boulders, and the pictographs date back to prehistoric days.

Two commercial tours might interest you. Get a taxi to take you to the **Sugar Factory,** which is best visited February to July, when you can see raw cane processed into bulk sugar. As mentioned, a very light liqueur, CSR, is now being produced at the factory, and it's enjoyed with a local grapefruit drink, Ting. You don't need a reservation.

Guests are also allowed to visit the **Carib Beer Plant,** an English lager beer-processing house. Carib Beer is the best in the West Indies, if sales are any indication. At the end of the tour through the plant, visitors are given a cold Carib in the lounge. Check with the tourist office before heading there to see if it's open.

SHOPPING

The good buys here are in local handcrafts, including leather items made from goatskin, baskets, and coconut shells. Some good values are also to be found in clothing and fabrics, especially Sea Island cottons. Store hours vary, but are likely to be 8am to noon and 1 to 4pm Monday to Saturday.

If your time is limited on the island, head first for the **Pelican Shopping Mall,** on Bay Road in Basseterre, containing some two dozen shops. Opened in 1991, it also offers banking services, a restaurant, and a philatelic bureau. Some major retail outlets in the Caribbean, including Little Switzerland, have branches at this mall. But don't confine all your shopping to the mall. Check out the offerings along the quaintly named **Liverpool Row,** which has some unusual merchandise. **Fort Street** is also worth traversing.

Ashbury's. The Circus / Liverpool Row, Basseterre. ☎ **869/465-8175.**

A local branch of a chain of luxury-goods stores based on St. Maarten, this well-respected emporium sells discounted luxury goods: fragrances, fine porcelain, crystal by Baccarat, handbags by Fendi, watches, and jewelry. Discounts range from 25% to 30% off what you might pay in retail stores in North America, although the selection is similar to dozens of equivalent stores throughout the Caribbean.

Into the Volcano

Mount Liamuiga was dubbed "Mount Misery" long ago, but it sputtered its last gasp around 1692. On the northeast coast, the dormant volcano is today one of the major highlights for hikers on St. Kitts. The peak of the mountain often lies under a cloud cover.

The ascent to the volcano is usually made from the north end of St. Kitts at Belmont Estate. The trail winds through a rain forest and travels along deep ravines up to the rim of the crater at 2,625 feet. The actual peak is at 3,792 feet. One intrepid hiker through the West Indies called this adventure "one of the most rewarding treks in the Caribbean." Figure on 5 hours of rigorous hiking to complete the round-trip walk, with 10 hours required from hotel pickup to return.

The caldera itself has a depth of some 400 feet from its rim to the crater floor. Many hikers climb—or should we say crawl—down into the dormant volcano. However, the trail is steep and slippery. Sometimes not always reliable roots and vines will be your only support. On the crater floor is a tiny lake along with volcanic rocks and various types of vegetation. Although many hikers go to the crater rim without a guide, it's absolutely necessary to have a guide to go into the volcano.

Greg's Safaris (☎ 869/465-4121) offers guided hikes to the crater for $60 per person (a minimum of four needed), including breakfast and a picnic at the crater's rim. The same outfit also offers half-day rain forest explorations, along with a picnic, for $40 per person.

Cameron Gallery. 10 N. Independence Sq. ☎ 869/465-1617.

In this gallery in the center of Basseterre, Britisher Rosey Cameron-Smith produces watercolors and limited-edition prints of scenes from St. Kitts and Nevis. She makes an effort to reproduce in art some of the essence of true West Indian life. Rosey is well known on the island for her paintings of Kittitian Carnival clowns. She also produces greeting cards, postcards, and calendars, as well as first-day covers of the Christmas stamps of Carnival clowns and masqueraders she painted for the government. She also displays the works of some 10 to 15 other artists.

Island Hopper. The Circus, Basseterre. ☎ 869/465-1640.

In The Circus, below the popular Ballahoo Restaurant, Island Hopper is one of St. Kitt's most patronized retail attractions. This store is worth a visit just to see the West Indian interior, and the owner goes to great lengths to provide items unavailable elsewhere. Island Hopper is the town outlet for Caribelle batik, selling everything from silks to pottery, from T-shirts to high fashion.

Kate Design. Mount Pleasant. ☎ 869/465-7740.

Set in an impeccably restored West Indian house, on a hillside below the Rawlins Plantation, this is the finest art gallery on St. Kitts. Virtually all the paintings on display are by Kate Spencer from England, whose work is well known throughout North America and Europe. Her still lifes, portraits, and paintings of island scenes range in price from $200, and have received critical acclaim from several different sources. Also for sale is a series of Ms. Spencer's silk-screened scarves, each crafted from extra-heavy stone-washed silk, priced from $84 each.

Lemonaid. At the Golden Lemon, Dieppe Bay. ☎ 869/465-7260.

This bazaar-style shop at the Golden Lemon specializes in local antiques, crafts, artwork, jewelry, and silverware, and carries a full line of elegant fragrances, plus spa products and skin-care lotions. Island clothes include those from John Warden's Island. The shop also sells Kisha batik fashions from Bali.

The Linen and Gold Shop. In the Pelican Shopping Mall, Bay Rd., Basseterre. ☎ **869/ 465-9766.**

There's a limited selection of gold and silver jewelry sold here, usually in bold modern designs, but the real appeal of this shop is the tablecloths and napery. Laboriously handcrafted in China from cotton and linen, they include everything from doilies to napkins to oversized tablecloths. The workmanship is as intricate as anything you'll find in the Caribbean.

Little Switzerland. In the Pelican Shopping Mall, Bay Rd., Basseterre. ☎ **869/465-9859.**

This is the most elaborate emporium of luxury goods on St. Kitts, with a medley of jewelry, wristwatches, porcelain, and crystal specifically selected for North American tastes. Lots of business is conducted when cruise ships pull up to the nearby wharves. Prices are set at about 25% to 30% less than what you might have paid for equivalent goods in North America, but the true bargains appear during the promotional sales. These continue almost without a break throughout the year, and although the individual pieces of jewelry change from sale to sale, discounts remain constant at around 40%.

The Palms. In the Palms Arcade, Basseterre. ☎ **869/465-2599.**

The Palms specializes in island "things": handcrafts; larimar, sea opal, and amber jewelry; West Indies spices, teas, and perfumes; tropical clothes by the Canadian designer John Warden; and Bali batiks by Kisha.

Romney Manor. Old Rd., 10 miles west of Basseterre. ☎ **869/465-6253.**

This is the most unusual factory on St. Kitts. It was built around 1625 as a manor house for the sugar baron Lord Romney, during the era when St. Kitts was the premier stronghold of British military might in the Caribbean. For years it was used as the headquarters and manufacturing center for a local clothier, Caribelle batiks.

In 1995, a tragic fire and the hurricanes completely gutted the historic building. Currently the manor is being slowly rebuilt. So you may just want to stop to admire the 5 acres of lavish gardens, where 30 varieties of hibiscus, rare orchids, huge ferns, and a 250-year-old saman tree still draw horticultural enthusiasts. Entrance to the gardens is free.

Rosemary Lane Antiques. 7 Rosemary Lane, Basseterre. ☎ **869/465-5450.**

This little nugget is housed in an early 19th-century Caribbean building painted purple and white so it'll stand out. The owner, Robert Cramer, has a choice collection of Kittitian, Caribbean, and international antiques, including furniture, paintings, silver, china, and glass. He'll ship anywhere in the world.

A Slice of the Lemon. Fort St., Basseterre. ☎ **869/465-2889.**

Decorated in a lemony-orange tone of sunshine colors, this store has the largest selection of perfumes on St. Kitts, but we're not sure that they're sold at the lowest prices available.

ST. KITTS AFTER DARK

The Ocean Terrace Inn's (O.T.I.) **Fisherman's Wharf,** Fortlands, (☎ **869/ 465-2754**), has a live band every Friday night from 8 to 10pm and a disc jockey from 10pm.

The **Turtle Beach Bar and Grill** (☎ 869/465-2754), on the southeast peninsula, has a popular seafood buffet on Sunday with a live steel band from 12:30 to 3pm. On Saturday, it's beach disco time.

If you're in the mood to gamble, St. Kitts's only casino is at the **Jack Tar Village, Frigate Bay** (☎ 869/465-8651). It's open to all visitors, who can try their luck at roulette, blackjack, craps, and slot machines. The casino is open daily from 10:30am to 2am. There's no cover charge.

4 Nevis

A local once said that the best reason to go to Nevis was to practice the fine art of *limin'*. To him, that meant doing nothing in particular. Limin' might still be the best reason to venture over to Nevis, a small volcanic island. If you want to go to the beach, then head for reef-protected Pinney's Beach, a 3-mile strip of dark-gold sand set against a backdrop of palm trees, with panoramic views of St. Kitts.

Like St. Kitts, Nevis appeals to the upmarket traveler and is known for one of the major deluxe resorts in the Caribbean (the Four Seasons) and for its plantation inns, which aren't cheap. Nevis has even fewer places to stay than St. Kitts, as it's smaller. So the options for the budget traveler are even fewer in terms of lodgings—a scattering of guest houses and a few bare-bones cottage colonies. There are a few acceptable West Indian eateries representing good value. But since Nevis is one of the most interesting destinations in the Caribbean, it's worth going anyway.

As you drive around the nostalgic island, through tiny villages such as Gingerland (named for the spice it used to export), you'll reach the heavily wooded slopes of Nevis Peak, which offers views of the neighboring islands. This beautiful island has remained relatively unspoiled. Its people, in the main, are descendants of African slaves.

On the Caribbean side, Charlestown, the capital of Nevis, was fashionable in the 18th century, when sugar planters were carried around in carriages and sedan chairs. Houses are of locally quarried volcanic stone, encircled by West Indian fretted verandas. A town of wide, quiet streets, this port only gets busy when its major link to the world, the ferry from St. Kitts, docks at the harbor.

GETTING THERE

BY PLANE   You can fly to Nevis on **LIAT** (☎ 869/469-9333), which offers scheduled service to the island. Flights from St. Kitts and Antigua are usually nonstop, while flights from St. Thomas, St. Croix, San Juan, Barbados, and Caracas, Venezuela, usually require at least one stop before reaching Nevis. The cost of taking one of LIAT's several daily flights between St. Kitts and Nevis—a 7-minute trip—is EC$113 ($41.90) round-trip.

Nevis Express Ltd. (☎ 869/469-9755) operates a daily shuttle service of six departures each way between St. Kitts and Nevis. A round-trip ticket from St. Kitts to Nevis costs $40. Call for reservations and information.

Any of North America's larger carriers, including **American Airlines** (☎ 800/433-7300), can arrange ongoing passage to Nevis on LIAT through such hubs as Antigua, San Juan, or St. Maarten, as part of through passage from virtually any major airport in North America.

The airport lies half a mile from Newcastle in the northern part of the island.

BY FERRY   You can also use the interisland ferry service from St. Kitts to Charlestown on Nevis aboard the government passenger ferry **MV *Caribe Queen.*** It departs Monday, Tuesday, Wednesday, Friday, and Saturday (check the time at

Atlantic Ocean

The Narrows

Newcastle

Oualie Beach

Long Haul Bay

Fort Ashby

Cotton Ground

Pinney's Beach

Eden Brown

Nevis Peak

Charlestown

Hermitage Village

New River

Bath

White Bay

Fig Tree

Montpelier

Gingerland

Saddle Hill

Caribbean Sea

Ferry to St. Kitts →

Airport ✈ Beach ⚲ Mountain ▲▲

0 — 2 km / 1.25 mi N

your hotel or the tourist office). Departure times from either island, we were told, are a bit erratic and must be confirmed on the day you plan to take the ferry. The cost is EC$10 ($3.70) each way.

GETTING AROUND

BY TAXI Taxi drivers double as guides, and you'll find them waiting at the airport at the arrival of every plane. A taxi ride between Charlestown and Newcastle Airport costs EC$30 ($11.10); from Charlestown to Pinney's Beach, EC$10 ($3.70). Between 10pm and 6am, 50% is added to the prices for Charlestown trips. A 3 1/2-hour sightseeing tour around the island will cost $75; the average taxi holds up to four people, so when the cost is sliced per passenger, it's a reasonable investment. No sightseeing bus companies operate on Nevis, but a number of individuals own buses that they use for taxi service.

BY RENTAL CAR If you're prepared to face the winding, rocky, potholed roads of Nevis, you can arrange for a rental car from a local firm through your hotel. Or you can check with **Skeete's Car Rental,** Newcastle Village, near the airport (☎ **869/469-9458**). Prices range from $45 per day.

Other local companies renting cars include **TDC Rentals,** Main Street, Charlestown (☎ **869/469-5690**), which rents vehicles costing from $30 daily. You can also try **Nisbett Rentals Ltd.,** Airport Road, Newcastle (☎ **869/469-9211**), which will rent you a Jeep or a Suzuki hatchback for $45 per day. Both companies charge the same prices year-round.

To drive on Nevis, you must obtain a permit from the Traffic Department, which costs EC$30 ($11.10) and is valid for 1 year. Remember, *drive on the left side of the road.*

FAST FACTS: Nevis

Language, currency, and entry requirements have already been discussed in the St. Kitts section. Most visitors will clear Customs on St. Kitts, so arrival on Nevis should not be complicated.

Banking Hours Banks are open Monday to Saturday from 8am to noon and most are also open on Friday from 3:30 to 5:30pm.

Drugstores Try **Evelyn's Drugstore,** Charlestown (☎ **869/469-5278**), open Monday to Friday from 8am to 5pm (closes at 4:30pm on Thursday), Saturday from 8am to 7pm, and Sunday for only 1 hour, from 7 to 8pm, to serve emergency needs.

Electricity An electrical transformer and adapter will be needed for most U.S. and Canadian appliances as the electricity is 230 volts AC, 60 cycles. However, check with your hotel to see if they have converted their voltage and outlets.

Emergencies For the police, call ☎ **911.**

Hospitals A 24-hour emergency room operates at **Alexandra Hospital** in Charlestown (☎ **869/469-5473**).

Information The best source is the **Tourist Bureau** on Main Street in Charlestown (☎ **869/469-1042**). For information before you go, refer to "Fast Facts: St. Kitts," in section 3 of this chapter.

Language English is the language of the island and is often accented with a lilting West Indian patois.

Post Office The post office, on Main Street in Charlestown, is open Monday to Wednesday and Friday from 8am to 3pm, and on Thursday from 8am to noon.

Safety Although crime is rare here, protect your valuables and never leave them unguarded on the beach, as so many visitors foolishly do.

Taxes The government imposes a 7% tax on hotel bills, plus a departure tax of EC$27 ($10) per person. You don't have to pay the departure tax on Nevis if you're returning to St. Kitts.

Telecommunications Telegrams and telexes can be sent from the **Cable and Wireless** office, Main Street, Charlestown (☎ **869/469-5000**). International telephone calls, including collect calls, can also be made there. It's open Monday to Friday from 8am to 5pm and on Saturday from 8am to noon.

Time As with St. Kitts, Nevis is on Atlantic standard time year-round, which means it's usually 1 hour ahead of the U.S. East Coast, except when the mainland goes on daylight saving time; then clocks are the same.

Tipping and Service A 10% service charge is added to your hotel bill. In restaurants, it's customary to tip 10% to 15% of the tab.

Water In the 1700s, Lord Nelson regularly brought his fleet to Nevis just to collect water, and Nevis still boasts of having Nelson spring water.

WHERE TO STAY

DOUBLES FOR LESS THAN $65 (WINTER) / $40 (OFF-SEASON)

Lindale's Guest House. Main St. (P.O. Box 463), Charleston, Nevis, W.I. ☎ 869/469-5412. 2 rms. Year-round, $40 single; $60 double. Extra person $10. Rates include continental breakfast. No credit cards.

If you don't mind just the bare essentials, then stay here. The house was built in 1963 and is a simple affair in the heart of Charlestown. The rooms are clean, with private baths and ceiling fans. Guests may use the telephone in the office and a TV is located in the main living room. Maude Cross owns and operates this tranquil abode, which was rebuilt after Hurricane Hugo wreaked its havoc. Children under 3 are not accepted.

Paradise Guest House. Paradise Estate, Charlestown, Nevis, W.I. ☎ 869/469-0394. 8 suites. Winter, $54.40 suite for one; $65.45 suite for two; $99.45 suite for three. Off-season, $32 suite for one; $38.50 suite for two; $58.50 suite for three. Children stay free in parents' suite. No credit cards.

This little whitewashed inn is basic but clean and comfortable, about a 5-minute ride from the beach. It's a two-story white concrete building on the outskirts of Charlestown, with blue trim and porches front and back surrounded by trees and flowers. The rooms have time-worn furnishings along with ceiling fans, a living room set, a dining table with two chairs, and a sink. A fridge and toaster oven can be requested. The triple unit is just for sleeping, with no facilities for preparing food. A phone and TV set are found in the seven-table restaurant, which serves local dishes three times a day. There's no room service, but baby-sitting is available.

Sea Spawn Guest House. Old Hospital Rd., Charlestown, Nevis, W.I. ☎ 869/469-5239. Fax 869/469-5706. 18 rms. Year-round, $35.10 single; $40.95–$58.50 double; $70.20 triple; $81.90 quad. Extra person $10. Children 11 and under stay free in parents' room. DISC, MC, V.

Only a 2-minute walk from Pinney's Beach, this is about the island's most no-frills entry, but, hey, you didn't come here to hang out in your hotel room. You're assured of cleanliness and reasonable comfort, though, in this simple white two-story concrete building with verandas all around the upper floor and ground floor. The hotel is close to the street. The bedrooms are a little bit grander than bunk style. Standing fans in the rooms attempt to keep you cool. Guests share a communal kitchen for $5 a day, although an on-site restaurant offers decent, inexpensive local fare three meals a day.

DOUBLES FOR LESS THAN $80 (WINTER) / $60 (OFF-SEASON)

Jonathan's Villa Hotel. Mount Lily, Nevis, W.I. ☎ 869/469-9148. Fax 809/469-9350. 10 units. TEL. Winter, $60–$125 unit for one or two. Off-season, $50–$100 unit for one or two. AE, MC, V.

On the slopes of Mount Lily, an 8-minute drive from the airport, this family-owned hotel offers cottage and villa rooms with ceiling fans, radios, telephones, and private baths. They're furnished in a tropical motif, with wicker and colorful island prints. The family-style villa also has a kitchenette. A restaurant specializes in West Indian cuisine. The front desk staff can arrange outings for you, including island and rainforest tours, nature hikes, and water sports. A 5-minute drive will take you to Herbert's Beach; other larger beaches such as Pinney's Beach and Jones Bay Beach are a 10-minute drive away.

Meadville Cottages. Craddock Road (P.O. Box 66, Charlestown), Nevis, W.I. ☎ 869/469-5235. 10 rms, 3 cottages. Winter, $60 single; $80 double; $80 cottage for four. Off-season, $40 single; $60 double; $70 cottage for four. V.

Housed in white concrete buildings on the outskirts of Charlestown in a commercial district, the Meadville cottages were opened in the mid-1980s with only four rooms and have expanded to 13 accommodations since that time. The amenities are few, but the prices are reasonable. The rooms are simple with wall-to-wall carpeting, mahogany furniture, and private baths. Some of the rentals have kitchenettes and L-shaped verandas. The cottages are near restaurants, shops, and Pinney's Beach.

DOUBLES FOR LESS THAN $100

Yamseed Inn. Newcastle, Nevis, W.I. ☎ **869/469-9361.** 4 rms. Year-round, $100 single or double. 3-night minimum stay. Rates include full breakfast. No credit cards.

Built as a private residence in 1964, this charming yellow bed-and-breakfast is located in the northernmost part of the island on a secluded beach offering panoramic views of St. Kitts. The spacious, airy bedrooms are well appointed with antiques, Oriental rugs (including some from Nepal), and locally crafted headboards. Each has its own bath and private entrance. Sybil Siegfried, who owns and operates the Yamseed, serves full breakfasts that include freshly baked multigrain and banana breads, homemade granola cereal, waffles, and fresh fruit. The Yamseed offers hammocks to laze away the days and beautiful surf to enjoy.

WHERE TO EAT

The local food is good. Suckling pig is roasted with many spices, and eggplant and avocado are used in a number of tasty ways. You may see turtle on some menus, but remember that this is an endangered species.

Beachcomber Restaurant & Bar. Pinney's Beach. ☎ **869/469-1192.** Reservations recommended for dinner. Burgers $7–$9; platters $15–$35. AE, MC, V. Daily 11:30am–4pm and 6:30–10pm. Closed Sun–Wed off-season. INTERNATIONAL.

This open-air restaurant on the beach offers some diversions with its pool table and dart boards. The veranda is an ideal place to enjoy the many grilled items served, including red snapper, wahoo, mahimahi, and swordfish. The Beachcomber also serves up burgers, salads, and soups. The atmosphere is casual.

Callaloo Restaurant. Main St., Charlestown. ☎ **869/469-5389.** Sandwiches and salads EC$6–EC$12 ($2.20–$4.40); platters EC$20 ($7.40). No credit cards. Mon–Sat 11am–10pm. WEST INDIAN / INTERNATIONAL.

This is a likable and unpretentious local restaurant set behind a tiny terrace on a street corner in Charlestown. Owned and operated by its Nevisian chef, Abdue Hill, it serves a loyal clientele in an air-conditioned, garden-inspired interior. Menu items include "the usual": sandwiches and salads, burgers, several preparations of steak and chicken, spareribs, stewed mutton, and grilled kingfish with rice, vegetables, and salad. No alcohol is served.

The Courtyard. Main St., Charlestown. ☎ **869/469-5685.** Platters EC$18–EC$35 ($6.65–$12.95). MC, V. Mon–Sat 7:30am–3:30pm. CARIBBEAN / INTERNATIONAL.

This is a simple restaurant whose charms aren't fully realized until you explore the various seating options. There's a West Indian bar on the ground floor and a dining room upstairs (which is used only when it threatens to rain). Most visitors head immediately for the garden in the rear, where palms, almonds, and sea grape push upward through holes in the crumbling concrete deck. The establishment sits on 18th-century foundations in the heart of Charlestown, near the main docks and the Customs House. Lunch platters include such items as sandwiches, burgers, and fish-and-chips. The proprietors boast that theirs is the best coffee on the island; you'll most likely see that it's definitely the most abundant. The restaurant will open for dinner, but only for reserved parties or special occasions.

✪ **Eddy's.** Main St., Charlestown. ☎ **869/496-5958.** Main courses EC$28–EC$35 ($10.35–$13). AE, MC, V. Mon–Wed and Fri–Sat 11:45am–3pm and 7–9:30pm. INTERNATIONAL.

Set on the upper floor of a plank-sided Nevisian house in the center of Charlestown, this local restaurant is open on three sides to the prevailing winds and offers an eagle's-eye view of street life in the island's capital. Its balcony juts out over the pedestrian traffic below, and the clean and airy interior contains a tuckaway bar, lattices and gingerbread, and lots of tropical color. The menu items, posted on one of several signs, are among the best prepared in Charlestown. Such dishes as Eddy's fish cioppino with roasted garlic-mayonnaise croûtons and juicy tandoori-sauced chicken are featured. For a new twist on a traditional favorite, try the lime-glazed seafood kebabs with black-bean salsa. No one will mind if you arrive only for a drink at the corner bar, but you'll be missing out on a tasty meal.

Muriel's Cuisine. Upper Happyhill Dr., Charlestown. ☎ **869/469-5920.** Reservations recommended. Main courses EC$25–EC$55 ($9.25–$20.35). AE, MC, V. Daily 8–10am, 11:30am–4pm, and 7–10pm. WEST INDIAN.

This Nevis-owned restaurant occupies the back of a concrete building whose front is devoted to a store. It's a 6-minute walk from Charlestown's waterfront, in a neighborhood of low-rise commercial buildings. Head here for an insight into island life, and for West Indian cuisine that might include three kinds of curries (goat, chicken, or lobster), chicken or seafood rôtis, lobster Créole, several preparations of conch (stewed or curried), saltfish, jerk pork or chicken, steamed fish, and (on Saturday night only) the inevitable goatwater stew.

Newcastle Bay Marina & Restaurant. Newcastle Marina, Charlestown. ☎ **869/469-9373.** Reservations recommended. Main courses $10–$20; lunch $7–$12. MC, V. Thurs–Tues 11am–10pm. Closed Mon–Thurs off-season. INTERNATIONAL.

This open-air restaurant on the water is part of the Mount Nevis Beach Club. The restaurant is housed in a concrete-block building with cathedral ceilings and the bar in the middle. From the deck, customers can take in the panoramic sea view while enjoying such fare as barbecued chicken and ribs along with burgers and sandwiches; highly recommended soups include pumpkin soup and conch chowder. Also try the pizza, some of the finest on Nevis.

Oualie Beach Club. Oualie Bay. ☎ **869/469-9735.** Reservations recommended for dinner. Main courses $20–$30. AE, MC, V. Daily 7–10am, noon–4pm, and 6–11pm. INTERNATIONAL/NEVISIAN.

This restaurant is the centerpiece of the only hotel that's adjacent to the second-most-famous swimming spot on Nevis, Oualie Beach. An airy, open-sided building with a pleasant staff and a setting a few steps from the ocean, it contains a bar area, a screened-in veranda, and a chalkboard menu featuring such dishes as broiled wahoo, several preparations of lobster, Créole conch stew, pastas, and spinach-stuffed chicken breast. There are many brightly colored rum drinks to accompany your meal.

Prinderella's. Tamarind Bay. ☎ **869/469-1291.** Main courses $7–$25. MC, V. Wed–Mon 10am–midnight. INTERNATIONAL.

With a name like Prinderella's, this place has to have some fun and whimsy. The name is an old joke based on spoonerisms. At its peak, as many as 60 diners can be accommodated here, enjoying this popular local spot with lattice walls 15 feet from the water on the wharf. The menu ranges from burgers to lobster, and you can count on freshly made salads, homemade soups, and pasta dishes. Even some English pub food, including shepherds pie and steak-and-kidney pie, appear on the menu, as does a homemade pâté. The safest bet? The fresh catch of the day, which somehow tastes better grilled—everything from flying fish to wahoo, mahimahi, or yellowfin tuna.

FUN ON & OFF THE BEACH

BEACHES   The best beaches on Nevis—in fact, one of the best beaches in the Caribbean—is the reef-protected **Pinney's Beach,** which has clear water, golden sands, and a gradual slope; its just north of Charlestown on the west coast. You'll have 3 miles of sand (often virtually to yourself) that culminates in a sleepy lagoon. It's best to bring your own sports equipment; while hotels are stocked with limited gear, it may be in use by other guests when you want it. You can go snorkeling or scuba diving among damselfish, tangs, grunts, blue-headed wrasses, and parrot fish, among other species.

GOLF   The **Four Seasons Golf Course,** Pinney's Beach (☎ **869/469-1111**), has a very challenging and visually dramatic golf course designed by Robert Trent Jones Jr. Greens fees are a steep $135 for nonguests.

HORSEBACK RIDING   Horseback riding is available at the **Nisbet Plantation Beach Club,** Newcastle (☎ **869/469-9325**). You can ride English saddle, and the cost is $40 per person for 1½ hours. With a guide, you're taken along mountain trails to visit sites of long-forgotten plantations.

MOUNTAIN CLIMBING   This is strenuous, and is recommended only for the stout of heart. Ask your hotel to pack a picnic lunch and arrange a guide (who will probably charge about $30 to $35 per person). Hikers can climb Mount Nevis, 3,232 feet up to the extinct volcanic crater, and enjoy a trek to the rain forest to watch for wild monkeys. The hike takes about 2½ hours, and once at the summit you'll be rewarded with views of Antigua, Saba, Statia, St. Kitts, Guadeloupe, and Montserrat. Of course, you've got to reach that summit, which means near-vertical sections of the trail requiring handholds on not-always-reliable vines and roots. It's definitely not for acrophobes. Guides usually can be found at the **Nevis Historical and Conservation Society,** based at the Museum of Nevis History on Main Street in Charlestown (☎ **869/469-5786**).

SNORKELING & DIVING   For **snorkeling,** head for Pinney's Beach. You might also try the waters of Fort Ashby, where the settlement of Jamestown is said to have slid into the sea; legend has it that the church bells can still be heard and the under-sea town can still be seen when conditions are just right. So far, no diver, to our knowledge, has ever found the conditions "just right."

For scuba divers, some of the best sites on Nevis include **Monkey Shoals,** lying 2 miles west of the Four Seasons resort. This is a beautiful reef starting at 40 feet, with dives up to 100 feet in depth. Angelfish, turtles, nurse sharks, and extensive soft coral can be found here. **The Caves** are on the south tip of Nevis, a 20-minute boat ride from the Four Seasons. A series of coral grottoes with numerous squirrel fish, turtles, and needlefish make this an ideal dive site for both certified and resort divers. **Champagne Garden,** a 5-minute boat ride from the Four Seasons, gets its name from bubbles emanating from an underwater sulfur vent. Because of the warm water temperature, large numbers of tropical fish are found here. Finally, **Coral Garden,** 2 miles west of the Four Seasons, is another beautiful coral reef with schools of Atlantic spadefish and large sea fans. The reef has a maximum of 70 feet and is suitable for both certified and resort divers.

Scuba Safaris Ltd., Oualie Beach (☎ **869/469-9518**), on the island's north end, offers scuba diving and snorkeling in an area rich in dive sites. It also features resort and certification courses, dive packages, and equipment rental. A one-tank scuba dive costs $45 while a two-tank dive goes for $80. Full certification courses cost $450 per person. Boat charters to Basseterre, Banana Bay, Cockleshell Bay, and other beaches are offered, as well as deep-sea fishing trips on request. Scuba Safaris operates on the premises of the Oualie Beach Club, to which it has no financial or managerial links.

TENNIS Most of the major hotels have tennis courts.

EXPLORING THE ISLAND

When you arrive at the airport, negotiate with a taxi driver to take you around Nevis. The distance is only 20 miles, but you may find yourself taking a long time if you stop to see specific sights and talk to all the people who'll want to talk to you.

The major attraction is the **Museum of Nevis History** at the Birthplace of Alexander Hamilton, on Main Street in Charlestown (☎ **869/469-5786**), overlooking the bay. Mr. Hamilton was the illegitimate son of a Scotsman, James Hamilton, and Rachel Fawcett, a Nevisian of Huguenot ancestry. The family immigrated to St. Croix and from there Alexander made his way to the North American colonies where he became the first secretary of the U.S. Treasury. His picture appears on the U.S. $10 bill. The lava-stone house by the shore has been restored, and a museum dedicated to the history and culture of Nevis has been established. The Archives of Nevis are housed there as well. The museum is open Monday to Friday from 8am to 4pm and on Saturday from 10am to noon. Admission is $2 for adults, $1 for children.

At Bath Village, about half a mile from Charlestown, stands the **Bath Hotel,** in serious disrepair, and its **Bath House,** which has been restored for use as a police garrison. Shortly after the Bath Hotel was completed on Nevis in 1778, its thermal baths attracted the elite from the United States, Canada, and Europe, who came to "take the waters." Temperatures rose as high as 108° Fahrenheit. They also drank and gambled in its casino with wealthy local residents who frequented the site. Some say that the Bath Hotel also housed a brothel for a short time. There are legends of entire plantation estates changing hands in the casino, as well as a fair share of bloody duels of honor.

Today the baths are in a stone and wood-sided outbuilding, a dim reminder of the site's earlier glamour. If you're interested in sampling the reputed health benefits of the waters, you'll be ushered down a flight of rough-sawn wooden steps to the reservoirs. Here, behind thin-walled partitions, five concrete-bottomed holding tanks contain shallow pools of the famous waters. No soap is allowed in the holding tanks, and no more than about 15 minutes of immersion is recommended, as serious health problems have resulted from too much time in the waters. The baths are open Monday to Friday from 8am to noon and 1 to 3:30pm and on Saturday from 8am to noon. Admission is free, although use of the baths costs $2.

Nearby, **St. John's Church** stands in the midst of a sprawling graveyard in Fig Tree Village. It's said to have been the parish church of Lady Nelson, wife of Horatio Lord Nelson. An 18th-century church of gray stone, it contains the record of Nelson's marriage to Frances Nisbet in the church register.

At Bellevue, Bath Plain, just beyond the Bath Hotel and next to Government House, stands the **Horatio Nelson Museum** (☎ **869/469-0408**). The vast collection of Nelson memorabilia gathered by Robert Abrahams, a Philadelphia lawyer, was given to the Nevis Historical and Conservation Society. A museum was opened on March 11, 1992, the 205th anniversary of the wedding of Nelson to Nevisian Frances

Nisbet. The exhibition, entitled "Nevis in the Time of Nelson," is the backdrop for the display of one of the largest collections of Horatio Nelson memorabilia in the Western Hemisphere. Fanny's Shoppe features Nelson memorabilia, island crafts, and books for both adults and children. The museum is open Monday to Friday from 9am to 4pm and on Saturday from 10am to 1pm. Admission is $2 for adults, $1 for children.

Fort Ashby, which overlooks what is thought to be the site of Jamestown, a settlement that slid into the sea around 1640, is now overgrown, but it was once used by Lord Nelson to guard his ships off Nevis while they took on fresh water and supplies. Nearby is **Nelson's Spring,** near Cotton Ground Village.

The **Eden Brown Estate,** about 1¹/₂ miles from New River, is said to be haunted. Once it was the home of a wealthy planter, whose daughter was to be married, but her husband-to-be was killed in a duel at the prenuptial feast. The mansion was then closed forever and left to the ravages of nature. A gray solid stone still stands. Only the most adventurous come here on a moonlit night.

Outside the center of Charlestown, the **Jewish Cemetery** was restored in part by an American, Robert D. Abrahams, the Philadelphia lawyer already mentioned. At the lower end of Government Road, it was the resting place of many of the early shopkeepers of Nevis. At one time, Sephardic Jews who had come from Brazil made up a quarter of the island's population. It's believed that Jews introduced sugar production into the Leewards. Most of the tombstones date from between 1690 and 1710.

An archaeological team from the United States believes that an old stone building in partial ruin on Nevis is probably the oldest **Jewish synagogue** in the Caribbean, according to the historian Dr. Vincent K. Hubbar, a resident of the island and author of *Swords, Ships and Sugar: A History of Nevis to 1900.* Preliminary findings in 1993 traced the building's history to one of the two oldest Jewish settlements in the West Indies, Hubbard noted, and current work at the site plus historic documents in England establish its existence prior to 1650.

The original function of the building site, located adjacent to the government administration building in Charlestown, had been forgotten perhaps as much as 150 or more years ago. However, because of Nevis's relatively large Jewish population in the 17th century and its well-known Jewish cemetery, many scholars and historians believed that a synagogue must have existed but didn't know exactly where.

SHOPPING

Normal store hours are Monday to Friday from 8am to noon and 1 to 4pm, but on Thursday some places close in the afternoon and on Saturday some stay open to 8pm.

Island Hopper. T.D.C. Shopping Mall, Main St., Charlestown. ☎ **869/469-5430.**

Hand-painted or tie-dyed cotton along with batik clothing are featured at this chain shop, which also has locations on St. Kitts and Antigua. From beach wraps to souvenirs, a wide selection of products is available, although most shoppers are here to look at the batiks.

Nevis Handicraft Cooperative Society Ltd. Cotton House, Charlestown. ☎ **869/469-1746.**

In a stone building about 200 feet from the wharf, near the marketplace, this handcraft shop contains locally made gift items, including unusual objects of goatskin, local wines made from a variety of fruits grown on the island, hot-pepper sauce, guava cheese, jams, and jellies.

Nevis Philatelic Bureau. Head Post Office, Market St., Charlestown. ☎ **869/469-5535.**

Those interested in stamp collecting can come here to see the wide range of colorful stamps. The postage stamps feature butterflies, shells, birds, and fish.

The Sandbox Tree. Evelyn's Villa, Charlestown. ☎ **869/469-5662.**

Housed in a clapboard house built in 1836, this is one of the most appealing gift shops on Nevis. It contains a collection of artworks from Haiti and Nevis, books for adults and children, hand-painted clothing, sheets, napkins, several pieces of antique furniture, and such culinary aids as spices, relishes, and exotic chutneys.

NEVIS AFTER DARK

Nightlife is not the major reason to visit Nevis. Summer nights are quiet, but there's organized entertainment in winter, often steel bands performing at the major hotels. Most action takes place at the **Four Seasons Resort,** Pinney's Beach (☎ **869/469-1111**), on Friday and Saturday nights. The **Old Manor Estate,** Gingerland (☎ **869/469-3445**), often brings in a steel band on Friday nights. On Saturday, the action swings over to the **Golden Rock,** Gingerland (☎ **869/469-3346**), where a string band enlivens the scene. Friday and Saturday nights can get raucous at **Eddy's** on Main Street (see "Where to Eat," above) when West Indian buffets are presented and live bands entertain.

10 The Dutch Windwards in the Leewards

Sint Maarten, Sint Eustatius (called "Statia"), and Saba—no more than dots in the Antilles—have long been dubbed "The Dutch Windwards." This is confusing to the visitor, but it makes sense in the Netherlands. The Dutch-associated islands of Aruba, Bonaire, and Curaçao, just off the coast of South America, go by the name of "The Dutch Leewards" (covered in chapter 16). The three Windward Islands, along with Bonaire and Curaçao, form the Netherlands Antilles. Aruba is now a separate entity.

The Dutch Windwards were once inhabited by the Carib peoples, who lent their name both to the Caribbean and, after a bit of linguistic corruption, to cannibalism—the Caribs believed that one acquired the strength of one's slain enemy by eating his flesh. Columbus, on his second voyage to America, is said to have sighted the group of small islands on the name day of San Martino (St. Martin of Tours), hence the present name of Sint ("Saint") Maarten.

Cooled by trade winds, the Windwards are comfortable to visit year-round. However, there's a history of unpredictable weather patterns during the hurricane season, so check the latest weather reports before you go.

1 St. Maarten

For an island that boasts a big reputation for its restaurants, hotels, and energetic nightlife, St. Maarten is small—only 37 square miles, about half the area of the District of Columbia. An island split between the Netherlands and France, St. Maarten is the Dutch half. The other half, St. Martin, is French. Legend has it that a gin-drinking Dutchman and a wine-guzzling Frenchman walked around the island to see how much territory each could earmark for his side in 1 day; the Frenchman outwalked the Dutchman, but the canny Dutchman got the more valuable piece of property.

Returning visitors who have been "off island" for a long time are often surprised and shocked at the St. Maarten greeting them today. No longer a sleepy Caribbean backwater, it has appeared like a boomtown in recent years. Many hotels and restaurants that sustained damage from Hurricane Luis in September 1995 have re-opened with freshly renovated facilities, new and better menu offerings, and an energized staff. A sense of newness and rejuvenation has come over the island.

The 100% duty-free shopping has turned the island into a virtual shoppers' mall, and the capital, Philipsburg, is bustling with cruise-ship passengers who often arrive by the hordes. Although Mother Nature rearranged them a bit, the 36 beaches of white sand remain unspoiled, and the clear turquoise waters are as enticing as ever. Sunshine is virtually guaranteed year-round, making all sorts of water sports and sailing possible. The nightlife is among the best in the Caribbean.

But much has been lost to the bulldozer as well. This is obviously not an island for people who don't like people—lots of them—so if "getting away from it all" is your aim, you'd better head over to the other nearby Dutch islands of Statia and Saba (see below). Nevertheless, in spite of its problems—including crime, traffic congestion, and corruption—St. Maarten continues to attract massive visitors. More and more, St. Maarten is more for those who like their Caribbean island Las Vegas in style.

The Dutch side of the island, for the most part, is cheaper than the French side, especially in its restaurants. Of course, they're not as good. And there's lots of deals, in package tours and villa rentals, so shop around and try never to pay the "rack" rate (off-the-street individual bookings). Stay out of the swank places, book a guest house or a small inn, and avoid the upmarket French-style restaurants, and you'll probably fare all right in both St. Maarten and St. Martin.

The divided island is the smallest territory in the world shared by two sovereign states (for more information on St. Martin, see chapter 12 on the French West Indies). The only way you know you're crossing an international border is when you see the sign BIENVENUE, PARTIE FRANÇAISE—attesting to the peaceful coexistence between the two nations on the island. The island was divided in 1648, and visitors still ascend Mount Concordia, near the border, where the agreement was reached. Even so, St. Maarten changed hands 16 times before it became permanently Dutch.

Northernmost of the Netherlands Antilles, St. Maarten lies 144 miles southeast of Puerto Rico. A lush island, rimmed with bays and beaches, it has a year-round temperature of 80° Fahrenheit. The Dutch capital, **Philipsburg,** curves like a toy village along Great Bay. The town lies on a narrow sand isthmus separating Great Bay and Great Salt Pond. The capital was founded in 1763 by Commander John Philips, a Scot in Dutch employ. To protect Great Bay, Fort Amsterdam was built in 1737.

The main thoroughfare is the busy Front Street, which stretches for about a mile and is lined with stores selling international merchandise, such as French designer fashions and Swedish crystal. More shops are along the little lanes, known as *steegijes,* that connect Front Street with Back Street, another shoppers' mart.

GETTING THERE

St. Maarten's **Queen Juliana International Airport** is the second busiest in the Caribbean, topped only by San Juan, Puerto Rico.

American Airlines (☎ **800/624-6262** in the U.S.) offers more frequent service into St. Maarten than any other airline. Daily nonstop flights travel to the island from New York's JFK and Miami. Several additional nonstop daily flights are offered into St. Maarten on either American Airlines or **American Eagle** (same number) from San Juan, Puerto Rico. Ask for one of the airline's tour operators, because you can usually save money by booking your airfare and hotel accommodation at the same time.

ALM Antillean Airlines (☎ **800/327-7230** in the U.S.) offers nonstop and some direct daily service to St. Maarten from the airline's home base on Curaçao.

GETTING AROUND

The budget traveler should stay in Philipsburg to avoid often high public transportation costs. In Philipsburg you'll be near the major shops, some of the most inexpensive restaurants, and gambling casinos, plus places to go at night. You can also walk to beaches. That way, you don't have to rent a car but can later take a tour of the island for a look. Taxis are expensive and minibuses are infrequent and often over-crowded. The taxi will save you time; the minibus, cold cash.

BY MINIBUS   This is a reasonable means of transport on St. Maarten if you don't mind inconveniences, and at times overcrowding. Buses run daily from 7am to mid-night and serve most of the major locations on St. Maarten. The most popular run is from Philipsburg to Marigot on the French side. Privately owned and operated, minibuses tend to follow specific routes, with fares ranging from $1.15 to $2.

BY BIKE   Of course, it's far cheaper to get around the island by scooter or bike than by rented car. The best deal on such rentals is found at **Rent 2 Wheels,** Low Lands Road, Nettle Bay (☎ 0590/87-20-59), just across the border on the French side. It rents scooters for $22 to $28 per day, with motorbikes beginning at $37.

BY TAXI   Taxis are unmetered, but St. Maarten law requires drivers to have a list that details fares to major destinations on the island. Typical fares from Juliana Air-port to the Maho Beach Hotel are $5; from Philipsburg to Juliana Airport, $10. There are minimum fares for two passengers, and each additional passenger pays an-other $2. Passengers are entitled to two pieces of luggage free, and each additional piece is assessed 50¢ extra. Fares are 25% higher between 10pm and midnight, and 50% higher between midnight and 6am. Even if you're renting a car, taxi regulations require you to take a cab to your hotel, where your car will be delivered. For late-night cab service, call ☎ 599/5-54317.

BY RENTAL CAR   Because of the island's size and diversity, car rentals on St. Maarten are practical, particularly if you want to experience both the Dutch and the French sides of the island. The taxi drivers' union strictly enforces a law that forbids anyone from picking up a car at the airport. As a result, every rental agency on the island is well equipped to deliver cars to a client's hotel, where an employee will com-plete all the necessary paperwork on the spot. If you prefer to rent your car upon ar-rival, head for one of the tiny rental kiosks that lie across the road from the airport, or take a taxi the short distance to where each company warehouses its cars.

The twin nationality of the island also causes complications with some rentals. In years gone by some rental companies, depending on their in-house policies, preferred not to rent a car on the Dutch side to a client staying on the French side. In recent years this injunction has been relaxed considerably and now depends on the indi-vidual discretion of the various companies.

All three major car-rental agencies require that renters be at least 25 years old to rent. Among the "big three" companies are **Budget** (☎ 800/527-0700 in the U.S., or 599/5-54030), **Hertz** (☎ 800/654-3131 in the U.S., or 599/5-54314), and **Avis** (☎ 800/331-2112 in the U.S., or 599/5-44316). An optional collision-damage waiver costs $9.50 to $15 extra per day at each of the three companies, but even if you purchase the waiver you might still be responsible for up to $600 of repairs to your car in the event of an accident. Your credit- or charge-card issuer may provide this coverage; check directly with the company before your trip.

It's sometimes cheaper to rent cars from local agencies, since these firms are highly competitive on St. Maarten. One firm we've gotten good deals from is **National Eurocar** (☎ 800/328-4567 in the U.S., or 599/4-42168 in Cole Bay, or 599/ 5-44268 at Queen Juliana Airport).

Drive on the right-hand side (on both the French and Dutch sides of the island), and don't drink and drive. Traffic jams are common near the island's

St. Maarten

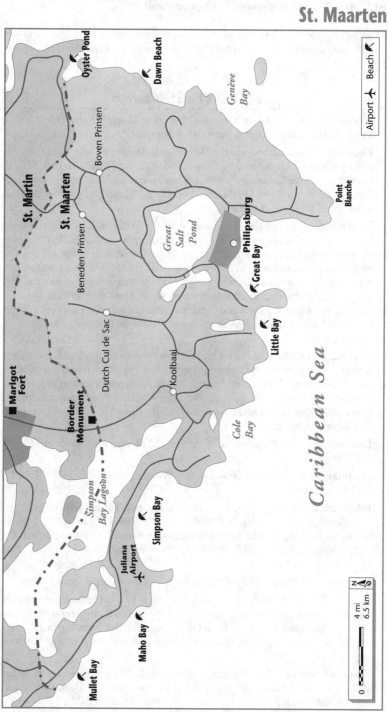

Oyster Pond

Dawn Beach

Genève Bay

Boven Prinsen

St. Martin

St. Maarten

Beneden Prinsen

Great Salt Pond

Philipsburg

Great Bay

Point Blanche

Little Bay

Dutch Cul de Sac

Koolbaai

Marigot Fort

Border Monument

Cole Bay

Caribbean Sea

Simpson Bay Lagoon

Simpson Bay

Juliana Airport

Maho Bay

Mullet Bay

Airport ✈ Beach ⬉

N

0   4 mi
    6.5 km

2-0207

major settlements, so be prepared to be patient. International road signs are observed, and there are no Customs formalities at the border between the island's political divisions.

FAST FACTS: St. Maarten

Banking Hours   Most banks are open Monday to Thursday from 8:30am to 1pm and on Friday from 8:30am to 1pm and 4 to 5pm.

Currency   The legal tender is the **Netherlands Antilles guilder (NAf),** and the official rate at which the banks accept U.S. dollars is 1.77 NAf for each $1 U.S. Regardless, U.S. dollars are easily, willingly, and often eagerly accepted in the Dutch Windwards, especially on St. Maarten. Prices in this chapter are given in U.S. currency unless otherwise designated.

Documents   To enter the Dutch-held side of St. Maarten, U.S. citizens should have proof of citizenship in the form of a passport (preferably valid, but not more than 5 years expired), an original birth certificate with a raised seal or a photocopy with a notary seal, or a voter's registration card with photo ID. Naturalized citizens may show their naturalization certificate, and resident aliens must provide the alien registration "green" card or a temporary card which allows them to leave and reenter the United States. British and Canadian visitors need valid passports. All visitors must have a confirmed room reservation before their arrival and a return or ongoing ticket.

Electricity   Dutch Sint Maarten uses the same voltage (110 volts AC, 60 cycles), with the same electrical configurations as the U.S., so adapters and transformers are not necessary. However, on French St. Martin transformers and adapters are definitely necessary. To simplify things, many hotels on both sides of the island have installed built-in sockets suitable for both the European and North American forms of electrical currents.

Emergencies   Call the **police** at ☎ **599/5-22222** or an **ambulance** at ☎ **599/5-22111**.

Hospitals   Go to the **Medical Center,** Welegen Road, Cay Hill (☎ **599/5-31111**).

Information   Before you go, contact the **St. Maarten Tourist Office,** 675 Third Ave., Suite 1806, New York, NY 10017 (☎ **800/786-2278** or 212/953-2084). Once on the island, go to the **Tourist Information Bureau,** in the Imperial Building at 23 Walter Nisbeth Rd. (☎ **599/5-22337**), open Monday to Friday from 8am to noon and 1 to 5pm.

Language   The language is officially Dutch, but most people speak English.

Safety   Crime is on the rise on St. Maarten and, in fact, has become quite serious. If possible, avoid night driving—it's particularly unwise to drive on remote, usually unlit, backroads at night. Also, let that deserted, isolated beach remain so. It's safer in a crowd, although under no circumstances should you ever leave anything unguarded on the beach.

Taxes and Service   A $5 departure tax is charged when you're leaving the island for St. Eustatius or Saba, and $10 is charged for international flights. A 5% government tax is added to hotel bills, and in general, hotels also add a 10% or 15% service charge. If service has not been added (unlikely), it's customary to tip around 15% in restaurants.

Telephone To call Dutch St. Maarten from the United States, dial 011 (the international access code), then 599 (the country code for the Netherlands Antilles), and finally 5 (the area code for all of St. Maarten) and the local number.

To make a call within Dutch St. Maarten, you need only the five-digit local number. But if you're calling "long distance" from the Dutch side of the island to the French side of the island, dial 00 (double zero), followed by 590 (the country code for French St. Martin), followed by the six-digit local number. If you're on the French side of the island and want to call anyone on the Dutch side, you'll have dial 00 (double zero), 599, then 5, followed by the five-digit local number. Know in advance that calls between the French and Dutch sides are considered long-distance calls and are quite expensive.

Time St. Maarten operates on Atlantic standard time year-round. Thus in winter, when the United States is on standard time, if it's 6pm in Philipsburg it's 5pm in New York. During daylight saving time in the United States, the island and the U.S. East Coast are on the same time.

Weather The island has a year-round temperature of about 80° Fahrenheit.

WHERE TO STAY

Remember, a government tax of 5% and a 10% to 15% service charge are added to your hotel bill. Ask about this when you book a room to save yourself a shock when you check out. See chapter 12 on the French West Indies for accommodations recommendations on French St. Martin.

DOUBLES FOR LESS THAN $70

Caribbean Hotel. 90 Front St. (P.O. Box 236), Philipsburg, St. Maarten, N.A. ☎ **599/ 5-22028.** 45 rms. A/C TV TEL. Year-round, $40 single; $60 double. AE, MC, V.

This is one of the most consistently booked hotels for business travelers from other Caribbean islands, as well as cost-conscious vacationers looking for inexpensive lodgings in the heart of the island's Dutch capital. It's in a three-story building with shops on the ground floor; climb a flight of steps to the second-floor reception area to register. The bedrooms, like the hotel's exterior, are outfitted in black and white with occasional touches of red and contain balconies with views over either the back (which is quieter) or over Front Street and the beach. At these great rates you don't get a lot of resort-type amenities—it's up to you to make your own fun! No meals are served on the premises, but many bars and cheap eateries are within walking distance.

Ernest's Guest House. Bush Rd., Cay Hill, St. Maarten, N.A. ☎ **599/5-22003.** 16 rms. A/C TV TEL. Year-round, $50–$70 single or double. No credit cards.

If transportation isn't a problem, this motel-style establishment is only 15 minutes from the beach. The unlikely location—above a pizza restaurant and a grocery store— along with the very simple accommodations, keeps the prices here rock-bottom. You're not far from restaurants and places to shop. The only drawback is that the bathing facilities are located directly inside each bedroom and are not separated by a partition or wall—so much for privacy.

Hotel Sylvia. 1 Leopard Rd., Cay Hill, St. Maarten, N.A. ☎ **599/5-23389.** 10 rms, 4 apts. TV. Year-round, $50–$60 single or double; $50 apt. No credit cards.

The rooms may be simple here, but they're spotlessly maintained. Near Philipsburg, and only a 10-minute walk from the nearest beach, this two-story white concrete building is also quite close to some of St. Maarten's best restaurants and shopping.

The rooms are decorated with somewhat-worn carpeting and have either queen- or king-size beds. Sylvia is more for adults; children are not encouraged. Second-floor rooms open onto balconies. The rooms have air-conditioning, whereas the apartments, which have kitchens, are equipped with ceiling fans. The on-site restaurant serves three meals a day, a rather standard but affordable fare, to guests only.

Joshua Rose Guest House. 7 Back St., Philipsburg, St. Maarten, N.A. ☎ **800/223-9815** in the U.S., or 599/5-24317. Fax 599/5-30080. 14 rms. TV. Winter, $50–$55 single; $70–$80 double. Off-season, $40–$50 single; $50–$60 double. Children under 12 $10. MC, V.

If you'd like to avoid transportation costs, you can stay in Philipsburg and walk wherever you need to go. This guest house on Back Street is perfect for that. It's only 1 block from the beach and within an easy walk of the island's leading entertainment, shopping, and restaurants. This family-owned facility rents small, clean rooms which have a vintage 1970s look. The superior rooms here have air-conditioning, whereas the standard units are cooled by ceiling fans. Some rooms open onto balconies with attractive mountain views. The hotel has a bar, plus a Chinese restaurant serving passable fare for lunch and dinner—at very low prices.

DOUBLES FOR LESS THAN $80 (WINTER) / $60 (OFF-SEASON)

Calypso Guest House. Simpson Bay (P.O. Box 112, Philipsburg), St. Maarten, N.A. ☎ **599/5-54233.** Fax 599/5-52881. 8 apts, all with kitchenette. A/C TV. Winter, $60–$80 apt for one; $80–$100 apt for two; $160 two-bedroom apt for four. Off-season, $50–$65 apt for one; $60–$80 apt for two; $100–$120 two-bedroom apt for four. Extra person $15. AE, MC, V.

This is one of the smallest hotels on the island's Dutch side—a welcome contrast to the massive hotels that otherwise dominate the island. A 5-minute drive from both the airport (whose loud noises usually stop around dusk) and Simpson Bay Beach, it contains a plain but worthwhile restaurant, a bar, and bedrooms that are somewhat bigger (considering the low costs) than you might have expected. The rooms have terra-cotta floor tiles, white walls, and simple—usually wicker—furnishings.

Hotel L'Esperance. 4 Tiger Rd., Cay Hill, St. Maarten, N.A. ☎ **599/5-25355.** Fax 599/5-24088. 21 one-bedroom apts, 2 two-bedroom apts. A/C TV TEL. Winter, $80 one-bedroom apt; $120 two-bedroom apt. Off-season, $60 one-bedroom apt; $90 two-bedroom apt. Children 11 and under stay free in parents' apt. AE, DISC, MC, V.

The management here exudes hospitality, as reflected by the bar which operates on the honor system. This two-story white Mediterranean-style building is found in a residential area about 10 minutes from Philipsburg. You're also a 10- to 15-minute walk from Belaire Beach, or about 10 to 15 minutes by car from the area's other good white sandy beaches. The lower apartments open onto patios, whereas the upper units have balconies. The one-bedroom apartments come with a living area, a dining area, and a refrigerator with a two-burner stove. The larger apartments have full kitchens where you can prepare your own meals, although there's a small restaurant on site serving mainly sandwiches and snacks. Guests often meet fellow guests at the bar. Because of its low cost and welcoming atmosphere, this is a haven for families, and baby-sitting can be arranged.

✪ **Sea Breeze Hotel.** 20 Cay Hill, St. Maarten, N.A. ☎ **599/5-26054.** Fax 599/5-26057. 30 rms. A/C TV TEL. Winter, $65 single; $75 double. Off-season, $45 single; $55 double. Extra person $15. AE, DISC, MC, V.

It'll be a Dutch treat—at least for your wallet—if you stay here, far removed from the high prices of the megaresorts. This simple white concrete building is only 5 minutes from Philipsburg. You're also about a 5-minute walk from Belaire Beach. The rooms are clean, comfortable, and decently maintained. To help you keep costs even lower, some accommodations have small kitchenettes; others contain just a refrigerator. The lower rooms have porches, whereas the upper units open onto balconies. Although small, this is a full-service hotel with a pool, a bar, and a simple restaurant serving three meals a day (other and better restaurants are within walking distance). Baby-sitting can be arranged.

BEST OFF-SEASON BETS

Divi Little Bay Beach Resort & Casino. Little Bay (P.O. Box 961), Philipsburg, St. Maarten, N.A. ☎ **800/367-3484** in the U.S., or 599/5-22333. Fax 599/5-23911. 130 rms. A/C TV TEL. Winter, $160–$300 double. Off-season, $130–$225 double. MAP $36 extra per person. AE, MC, V.

Set close to two other resorts along a strip of beachfront 10 minutes' drive east of the airport, this hotel was one of the island's first resorts. It opened in 1955 with only 20 rooms. The Netherlands' Queen Juliana and her husband, Prince Bernhard, were among the first guests, followed in later years by Queen Beatrix. Today, much altered and enlarged, and catering mostly to families, the resort occupies a series of buildings, none higher than three stories. Each accommodation has a veranda or patio and comfortable tropical-inspired furnishings. The single or double rate ranges from $160 to $300 in winter. However, the best off-season deal is $130 a night for two people in the less expensive units. Bigger rooms with better views go for $225. MAP is another $36 per person.

Café Divine offers informally elegant dining by candlelight with soft musical accompaniment. Facilities include water sports, three freshwater pools, and three tennis courts (lit at night).

Great Bay Beach Hotel and Casino. Front St. (P.O. Box 310), Philipsburg, St. Maarten, N.A. ☎ **800/223-0757** in the U.S., or 599/5-22446. Fax 599/5-23859. 285 rms, 10 suites. A/C TV TEL. Winter (all-inclusive), $330–$380 double; $405–$450 triple; $350–$410 suite for two. Off-season (EP), $95–$130 double; $125–$160 triple; $115–$155 suite for two. AE, DC, MC, V.

This deluxe all-inclusive resort at the southwestern corner of Great Bay lies within walking distance of Philipsburg, ideal for shopping trips. The hotel was given a complete $10-million renovation; all the guest rooms have been refurbished and now contain designer furniture, a terrace or patio, and a king-size bed or two full-size beds. The corner ocean rooms are the most expensive. The bathrooms have Valentino-designed tiles.

The all-inclusive rate in winter is $200 to $220 in a single or $330 to $380 in a double—pricey indeed. However, off-season you can book in here on the EP (no meals) getting a single for $85 to $120 or a double for $95 to $130. Opt for the least expensive rooms and go outside if you want to take in the view.

The hotel has a casino and disco, plus two restaurants, including a gourmet French dining room and a grill open nightly until 11pm. Facilities include one all-weather tennis court and two freshwater pools, which some prefer to the nearby beach.

WORTH A SPLURGE

Hotel La Chatelaine. Simpson Bay Beach (P.O. Box 2065, Philipsburg), St. Maarten, N.A. ☎ **599/5-54269.** Fax 599/5-53195. 12 apts, all with kitchenette. Winter, $160 one-bedroom apt for two; $235 two-bedroom apt for two. Off-season, $110 one-bedroom apt for two; $165 two-bedroom apt for two. Extra person $25–$30 each (up to four can stay in a one-bedroom apt and up to six in a two-bedroom apt). AE, MC, V.

This pink-sided, small-scale apartment complex lies on an idyllic strip of white-sand beach. The only drawback is its proximity to the roar of the jets arriving and departing from the nearby airport. (Luckily for light sleepers, air traffic is very light after

7pm at night.) The resort's focal point is a small but charming octagonal swimming pool with a gazebo. Most visitors forsake the pool in favor of a chaise lounge on the sands of nearby Simpson Bay. Each unit in this complex has a kitchen. Children 6 and under are not accepted.

✪ **Mary's Boon.** Simpson Bay (P.O. Box 2078, Philipsburg), St. Maarten, N.A. ☎ **599/ 5-54235.** Fax 599/5-53403. 14 apts. Winter, $125–$195 apt for two. Off-season, $90–$125 apt for two. MC, V. Take the first right turn from the airport toward Philipsburg.

This small, casual inn offers oversize stylish apartments with kitchenettes, designed as private villas. They're directly on a 3-mile sandy beach, just south of the Queen Juliana airport and 15 minutes from Philipsburg. It's near the airport—but big planes are rare, and only land in the daytime. The rooms are decorated in rattan and wicker, and louvered windows open to sea breezes. Most apartments are in separate cottages, but there are two in the main house. The efficiency apartments have ceiling fans. Note that children 15 and under are not accepted.

There's a dining gallery fronting Simpson Bay. The cuisine is West Indian/international and is served in a restaurant with a view of the sea. In the bar you fix your own drinks on the honor system. Dinners are not served in October.

✪ **Pasanggrahan.** 15 Front St. (P.O. Box 151), Philipsburg, St. Maarten, N.A. ☎ **599/5-23588.** Fax 599/5-22885. 30 rms. Winter, $128–$158 single or double. Off-season, $78–$95 single or double. AE, MC, V. Closed Sept.

Pasanggrahan is the Indonesian word for guest house, and this one is West Indian in style. A small, informal guest house, it's right on the busy, narrow main street of Philipsburg, toward the end of the mountain side of Front Street. It's set back under tall trees, with a white wooden veranda. The interior has peacock bamboo chairs, Indian spool tables, and a gilt-framed oil portrait of Queen Wilhelmina. So many guests asked to see the bedroom where the queen and her daughter, Juliana, stayed during World War II that the management turned it into the Sydney Greenstreet Bar. The renovated bedrooms have king-size beds and in some cases Saban bedspreads; some are in the main building and others are in an adjoining annex. All accommodations have ceiling fans, and all but six are air-conditioned. Set among the wild jungle of palms and shrubbery is the dining area, the Pasanggrahan Restaurant where service is from 7am to 11pm. The private beach is only 50 feet away.

Seaview Hotel & Casino. Front St. (P.O. Box 65), Philipsburg, St. Maarten, N.A. ☎ **599/ 5-22323.** Fax 599/5-24356. 45 rms. A/C TV TEL. Winter, $79–$99 single; $99–$130 double. Off-season, $46–$54 single; $55–$66 double. AE, MC, V.

In the commercial heart of Philipsburg, this hotel might be ideal for easy access to the shops, bars, and restaurants of the Dutch side's capital. Set behind an anonymous-looking masonry facade, this place offers simple but well-scrubbed accommodations, each of which contains a radio. It's a favorite of business travelers from other Caribbean islands, but is also a very good choice for a cost-conscious vacation on the beach. No meals are served other than breakfast, but all the restaurants of Philipsburg lie within a short walk.

WHERE TO EAT

See chapter 12 on the French West Indies for restaurant suggestions on French St. Martin. St. Maarten / St. Martin has dozens of good restaurants serving both the typical island fare and a wide selection of international cuisine. A favorite for the partying crowd is **Everyt'ing Cool,** Front Street in Philipsburg (☎ 599/5-31011), although many do come just to eat. The place is known for its 81 varieties of both alcoholic and nonalcoholic coladas. You can come here for the everyday party deal where you'll get a locker, a floating mattress, sports on the beach, a T-shirt, and of course, lunch and drinks, all for $25.

☺ **Cheri's Café.** 45 Cinnamon Grove, Shopping Centre, Maho Beach. ☎ **599/5-53361.** Reservations not accepted. Main courses $5.50–$16.75. No credit cards. Daily 11am–midnight. AMERICAN.

The island hot spot, Cheri's was winner of the *Caribbean Travel and Life* readers' pick for best bar in the West Indies. Known for its inexpensive food and live bands, it is by now an island institution. American expatriate Cheri Baston is the duenna of this open-air cafe serving some 400 meals a night.

The place is really only a roof without walls, and it's not on a beach. But people flock to it anyway, devouring 16-ounce steaks or a simple burger. It's also possible to get grilled fresh fish platters. You can dine under the canopy or on a terrace under the stars. Everybody from movie stars to rock bands, from high rollers at the casino to beach bums comprise the clientele. Some come for the inexpensive food, others for the potent drinks, and many to dance to the music. The bartender's special is a frozen "Straw Hat" made with vodka, coconut, tequila, both pineapple and orange juice, and strawberry liqueur. Maybe even one more ingredient, we suspect, although nobody's talking.

Chesterfields. Great Bay Marina, Pointe Blanche. ☎ **599/5-23484.** Reservations recommended. Main courses $7.95–$18.95. No credit cards. Mon–Sat 11:30am–5pm and 5:30–10pm, Sun 10:30am–2:30pm and 5:30–10pm. AMERICAN/CARIBBEAN.

Chesterfield's has a special attraction other than its good food—which, incidentally, is among the best on the Dutch side. It offers pierside dining with a view of the harbor, on a trade wind-swept veranda near Great Bay Marina, east of Philipsburg. The yachting set gathers here and everybody seems to know everybody else. The setting and the dress are both casual, and you dine on several international specialties, with fresh seafood and French-inspired cookery a highlight. Try the red snapper Créole or broiled, duck Chesterfield, or seafood pasta; on Wednesday nights, there's a special prime rib served with sautéed mushrooms. In season there's always some lively activity going on, such as champagne Sunday brunches with eggs Benedict or Florentine, or seafood omelets.

☺ **Crocodile Express Café.** Casino Balcony, at the Pelican Resort Club, Simpson Bay. ☎ **599/5-43021,** ext. 1127. Main courses $8.50–$15.75; sandwiches and salads $3.25–$9.50. DISC, MC, V. Daily 7:30am–11pm. DELI/GRILL/INTERNATIONAL.

Start the day overlooking Simpson Bay with extra-thick French toast made with homemade egg bread with fresh tropical fruits on top, or else order eggs any style. There's continuous service throughout the day, beginning with breakfast and followed by lunch, with snacks predominating in the afternoon. Many patrons file in for dinner as early as 6pm. Hearty deli fare includes well-stuffed sandwiches. At night you might prefer grilled local fish or tasty kebabs. A specialty is grilled chicken breast West Indian style, marinated in tropical fruit juices and served with grilled onions. On Thursday it's all you can eat of barbecued chicken and ribs, costing $12.95. Meals are followed by home-baked pies and other desserts, and drinks include fresh mango or frozen passion fruit.

On Wednesday on the beach from 5 to 9pm there's a beach-party barbecue and a limbo show, with nail-dancing, fire-eating, magic, and steel-pan music. The cost is $13.75 for the chicken-and-ribs dinner, and there's no cover either. This place represents exceptionally good value in food for St. Maarten.

Don Carlos Restaurant. Airport Rd., Simpson Bay. ☎ **599/5-53112.** Main courses $10.50–$28.50. AE, DC, DISC, MC, V. Daily 7:30am–10pm. MEXICAN/CARIBBEAN/INTERNATIONAL.

The restaurant is located just 5 minutes east of the airport with a view of arriving and departing planes from the floor-to-ceiling windows surrounded by international flags. The place serves breakfast, lunch, and dinner. The owners Shenny and Carl Wagner invite you for a drink in their Pancho Villa Bar before your meal in their hacienda-style dining room with a multilingual staff.

The Greenhouse. Bobby's Marina (off Front St.), Philipsburg. ☎ **599/5-22941.** Main courses $9–$16. AE, MC, V. Daily 11am–1am. AMERICAN.

Open to a view of the harbor, the Greenhouse is filled with plants, as befits its name. As you dine, breezes filter through the open-air eatery. The menu features the ever-popular catch of the day as well as burgers, pizza, and salads. Dinner specials might include fresh lobster thermidor, Jamaican jerk pork, or salmon in a light dill sauce. Happy Hour is daily from 4:30 to 7pm and features half-price appetizers and two-for-one drinks. The DJ not only spins out tunes but also gives prizes to Bingo champs and Trivia experts. There are also pool tables and video games to keep you entertained.

✪ Lynette's. Simpson Bay Blvd. ☎ **599/5-52865.** Reservations recommended. Main courses $6.95–$25. AE, MC, V. Winter, daily 11:30am–10:30pm; off-season, daily 6–10:30pm. WEST INDIAN.

This is the most noteworthy West Indian restaurant on St. Maarten. It's completely unpretentious, and rich in local flavors and understated charm. St. Maarten–born Lynette Felix, along with Clayton Felix, are the creative forces here, serving flavorful ethnic food from a location close to the airport. The setting is a concrete-sided, wood-trimmed building beside the highway, with a color scheme of pink, maroon, cream, and brown. The menu reads like a lexicon of tried-and-true Caribbean staples, including colombos (ragoûts) of goat and chicken, stuffed crab backs, curried seafood, and filet of snapper with green plantains and Créole sauce or garlic butter. An ideal lunch might be a brimming bowlful of pumpkin (squash) soup followed by one of the main-course salads. The one made from herbed lobster, when available, is particularly succulent. The dishes here have true island flavor.

Old Rock Café. Billy Foley Rd., Simpson Bay. ☎ **599/5-42369.** Main courses $10–$22.50; lunch $6–$10. AE, DISC, MC, V. Daily 11am–10pm. AMERICAN / WEST INDIAN.

The story goes that a large rock just couldn't be unearthed from the site where the restaurant was to be built; so came the name for this eatery set on the road leading to the Pelican Resort. The owners describe the place as having a "warm ski lodge" atmosphere, and the wood walls and floors and cathedral ceiling do evoke a bit of that feeling. However, the panoramic views that can be seen through the windows on all sides of the structure confirm firmly that you're in the islands. The menu is basic—burgers, soups, and salads. Two specialties are the baby back ribs and the chicken pot pie. A daily early-bird special is served between 5:30 and 6:30pm, and starts at about $10.

Shiv Sagar. 203 Front St., Philipsburg. ☎ **599/5-22299.** Reservations recommended. Main courses $14.75–$16.75. AE, DC, DISC, MC, V. Mon–Sat 11:30am–3pm and 6:30–10pm, Sun 11:30am–3pm. EAST INDIAN.

This restaurant opposite Barclay's Bank serves the island's only Indian cuisine. Because of its large selection of vegetarian dishes, it's also the best choice for noncarnivores. The cuisine roams freely through the East Indian kitchen, concentrating mainly on Mogul and Kashmiri specialties. The smell of coriander and cumin fill the air as you enter. Rôtis are prepared before diners here in a traditional tandoori oven, and the curries are appropriately zesty and spicy. You can also order a number of unusual specialties—perhaps red snapper cooked in a blend of hot spices. The open-air bar out front is one of the friendliest on the island.

Village Café. In the Village Shopping Center, Front St., Philipsburg. ☎ **599/5-20361.** Sandwiches and main courses $3–$10. No credit cards. Daily 8am–7pm. WEST INDIAN.

Although many restaurants are very expensive on St. Maarten, you can dine inexpensively without resorting to fast-food joints. This small restaurant on the waterfront is a case in point. You can eat on the patio or inside where the interior is white and graced with a number of plants. If you arrive for breakfast, you can order ample but standard fare; the fresh pastries are best. Throughout the day you can sample various hot local dishes, including a special such as chicken with rice and peas. Otherwise, there's an array of fresh salads and sandwiches served on fresh French bread. The ham-and-cheese special, for example, comes in a foot-long baguette that's ample enough for two, and it costs only $3.

BEST FIXED-PRICE MENUS

Pelican Reef Restaurant and Seafood House. Waterfront Marina, at the Pelican Resort & Casino, Simpson Bay. ☎ **599/5-42503,** ext. 1578. Reservations recommended. Main courses $14.50–$27.95; fixed-price menu $20.95–$21.95. AE, MC, V. Daily 6–10:30pm. STEAK/SEAFOOD.

This American steakhouse not only serves what are reputed to be the island's best steaks, but also offers tasty chops and seafood. The hosts, Marvin and Jean Rich, offer fine, friendly service, and present good-quality ingredients, artfully served with a view over Simpson Bay. Signature dishes include a hearty slab of prime rib on the bone, grilled Argentinian style on a charcoal grill; whole Caribbean lobster, baked and stuffed; grilled filet of fish, perhaps red snapper, from local waters; rack of baby lamb; or a thick veal chop. Mention should be made of El Gaucho steak, a chateaubriand cut from Argentina. It's a taste treat because of its leanness and is uniquely rich in flavor because the cattle were grass fed on the pampas. Served grilled on a wooden plank, it's accompanied by a cognac-and-peppercorn sauce, vegetables, and steak fries. Save room for the conch fritters with two sauces, and follow with a "chocolate island" or their frozen fantasy dessert. A special feature of the wine list is a "tasting" of fine armagnacs, unique because they're from single estates and both are made from 100% ugni blanc, a rare grape used only in the making of armagnacs and cognacs.

The Wajang Doll. 137 Front St., Philipsburg. ☎ **599/5-22687.** Reservations required. Dinner $18.90 with 14 dishes, $24.90 with 19 dishes. AE, MC, V. Mon–Sat 6:45–10pm. Closed Sept. INDONESIAN.

Housed in a wooden West Indian building on the main street of town, the Wajang Doll is one of the best Indonesian restaurants in the Caribbean. There's a low-slung front porch where you can watch the pedestrian traffic outside, and big windows in back overlook the sea. The restaurant is best known for its 19-dish dinner, a *rijstaffel* (rice table). The cuisine varies from West Java to East Java, and the chef crushes his spices every day for maximum pungency, according to an ancient craft. Other specialties include fried snapper in a chili sauce, marinated pork on a bamboo stick, and Javanese chicken dishes.

BEACHES, WATER SPORTS & OUTDOOR PURSUITS

BEACHES   St. Maarten has 36 beautiful white-sand beaches, and it's comparatively easy to find a part of the beach for yourself. But if it's too secluded, be careful. Don't carry valuables to the beach; there have been reports of robberies on some remote beaches.

Regardless of where you stay, you're never far from the water. If you're a beach-sampler, you can often use the changing facilities at some of the bigger resorts for a small fee. (Nudists should head for the French side of the island, although the Dutch side is getting more liberal about such things.)

On the west side of the island, west of the airport, **Mullet Bay Beach** is shaded by palm trees and can get crowded on weekends. Water-sports equipment rentals can be arranged through the hotel.

Great Bay Beach is preferred if you're staying along Front Street in Philipsburg. This mile-long beach is sandy, but since it borders the busy capital it may not be as clean as some of the more remote beaches. Immediately to the west, at the foot of Fort Amsterdam, **Little Bay Beach** looks like a Caribbean postcard, but it, too, can be overrun with visitors from the Little Bay Resort and Casino and the Belair Beach Hotel.

Stretching the length of Simpson Bay Village, **Simpson Bay Beach** is shaped like a half moon with white sands. It lies west of Philipsburg before you reach the airport. Water-sports equipment rentals are available here.

North of the airport, **Maho Bay Beach,** at the Maho Beach Hotel and Casino, is shaded by palms and is ideal in many ways, if you don't mind the planes taking off and landing. Palms provide shade, and food and drink can be purchased at the hotel.

The sands are pearly white at **Oyster Pond Beach,** near the Oyster Pond Hotel northeast of Philipsburg. Bodysurfers like the rolling waves here. In the same location, **Dawn Beach** is noted for its underwater tropical beauty (reefs lie offshore). The approach is through the Dawn Beach Hotel.

GOLF   The **Mullet Bay Resort** (☎ 599/5-52801, ext. 1851) has a challenging 18-hole course, designed by Joseph Lee. Greens fees are $105 for 18 holes. The course is very expensive, but it's the only game on island.

HORSEBACK RIDING   At **Crazy Acres,** Wathey Estate, Cole Bay (☎ 599/5-42793), riding expeditions invariably end on an isolated beach where the horses, with or without their riders, enjoy the cool waters in an after-ride romp. Two experienced escorts accompany a maximum of eight people on the outings, which begin at 9:30am and 2:30pm Monday to Saturday and last $2^1/_2$ hours. The price is $50 per person. Riders of all levels of experience are welcome, with the single provision that they wear bathing suits under their riding clothes for the grand finale on the beach. Reservations should be made at least 2 days in advance. Riding lessons are available.

PICNIC SAILS   A popular pastime is to sign up for a day of picnicking, sailing, snorkeling, and sightseeing aboard one of several boats providing this service. The sleek sailboats usually pack large wicker hampers full of victuals and stretch tarpaulins over sections of the deck to protect sun-shy sailors. Of all the trips offered, we've selected the following two for value. Some are overpriced—a rip-off, really. But those recommended below deliver—and at a fair price.

The ***Random Wind*** is a sailing boat that operates in conjunction with Fun in the Sun, Great Bay Marina (☎ 599/5-70210). It's a 47-foot traditional clipper making day trips that circumnavigate St. Maarten, carrying 15 passengers at a cost of $70. On Sunday a breakfast cruise is available at $30 per person, and dinner cruises (Wednesday only) cost $50. On Sunday Caribbean lunch cruises are also sold at $45 per head. Call for more information.

The *Gabrielle* (☎ 599/5-23170) sails from Bobby's Marina in Philipsburg year-round and offers either a full- or half-day trip, both of which include lunch, beer, French wine, and use of all equipment. The *Gabrielle* is a 46-foot ketch with a spacious shaded cockpit and large decks. A maximum of 14 people are taken to a secluded cove or small island where you can sunbathe, swim, and snorkel. You can make reservations at your hotel or by phone. The price is $65 per person for a full-day sail. A shorter sail is also offered, a coastal sail with lunch, priced at $45 per person, and held on designated days from 10:30am to 3pm. There's also a sunset sail, on designated days, priced at $30 per person, with drinks, from 5 to 7pm.

SAILING TO OTHER ISLANDS   Experienced skippers make 1-day voyages to St. Barts in the French West Indies and to Saba, another of the Dutch Windwards in the Leewards; they stop long enough for passengers to familiarize themselves with the island ports, shop, and have lunch. To arrange a trip, ask at your hotel or at the **St. Maarten Tourist Bureau,** 23 Walter Nisbeth Rd. in Philipsburg (☎ **599/ 5-22337**).

If you'd like to see some of the other islands nearby, the best deal is offered by *Voyager I* and *Voyager II.* There are daily sails to St. Barts costing $50 round-trip, or to Saba for $60 round-trip. Children 11 and under ride for half price. These are good-value trips well worth the time and money. For more details, call **Dockside Management** in Philipsburg (☎ **599/5-24096**).

TENNIS   If you're staying at one of our budget hotels, you'll regrettably find no tennis courts on land-scarce St. Maarten. However, the major resorts have courses, and will generally allow nonguests to play for an hourly fee providing their own guests haven't already booked the courts. It's best to have your hotel advise you of the nearest courts and place a call for you requesting court time.

WATER SPORTS   Windsurfing and **jetskiing** are especially popular on St. Maarten. The unruffled waters of Simpson Bay Lagoon, the largest in the West Indies, are ideal for these sports, as well as for **waterskiing.**

St. Maarten's crystal-clear bays and countless coves make for good **snorkeling and scuba diving.** Underwater visibility reportedly runs from 75 to 125 feet. The biggest attraction for scuba divers is the 1801 British man-of-war, HMS *Proselyte,* which came to a watery grave on a reef a mile off the coast. Most of the big resort hotels have facilities for scuba diving, and their staff can provide information about underwater tours, for photography as well as night diving.

The best water sports—and the best value—are found at **Pelican Watersports,** at the Pelican Resort & Casino, Simpson Bay (☎ 599/5-42640). Its PADI-instructed program features the most knowledgeable guides on the island, each one familiar with St. Maarten dive sites. Divers are taken out in custom-built 28- and 35-foot boats, and many return to claim that they've been led to some of the best reef diving in the Caribbean. A single-tank dive costs $45; a double-tank dive, $90. Snorkeling trips can also be arranged, as can trips to nearby islands, including Saba, Anguilla, and St. Barts.

SIGHTSEEING TOURS   The only outfits offering bus tours of the island are **Dutch Tours,** Cougar Road, 8 Unit One (☎ 599/5-23316), and **St. Maarten Sightseeing Tours** (☎ 599/5-22753), whose buses hold 22 to 52 people. They're only configured for large groups, and are very difficult to prearrange.

The alternative involves hiring a minivan from any of the taxi stands in Philipsburg where a 2¹/₂-hour tour encompassing both the French and Dutch sides of the island costs $30 for one or two passengers, and $7.50 for each additional passenger.

SHOPPING

St. Maarten is not only a free port, but there are no local sales taxes. Prices are sometimes lower here than anywhere else in the Caribbean; however, you must be familiar with the prices of what you're looking for to know what actually is a bargain. Many well-known shops on Curaçao have branches here, in case you're not going on to the ABC islands (Aruba, Bonaire, and Curaçao).

In spite of what various shopkeepers might tell you, the cost of merchandise is regulated on St. Maarten. Therefore, the difference among shops is in the selection they offer, not in the cost. You can on occasion save 25% off prices, especially in purchasing your favorite fragrance.

In general, the price marked on the merchandise is what you're supposed to pay. We're speaking of major retail outlets such as H. Stern, the jewelers, or Little Switzerland. At small, very personally run shops, some bargaining might be in order. Most shopkeepers will remind you that their merchandise is already discounted.

The main shopping center is in downtown Philipsburg. Most of the shops are on two leading streets, **Front Street** (called Voorstraat in Dutch), which is closer to the bay, and **Back Street** (Achterstraat), which runs parallel. Shopping hours in general are 8am to noon and 2 to 6pm Monday to Saturday. If a cruise ship is in port, many shops are also open on Sunday.

Antillean Liquors. Queen Juliana Airport. ☎ **599/5-54267.**

This duty-free shop has a complete assortment of liquor and liqueurs, as well as cigarettes and cigars. In general prices are lower here than in other stores on the island, and the selection is larger. Many bottles are priced anywhere from 30% to 50% lower than in the States. The only local product sold is an island liqueur called Guavaberry, which is made from rum (see the Guavaberry Company, below).

Caribbean Camera Centre. 79 Front St. ☎ **599/5-25259.**

The Caribbean Camera Centre has a wide range of merchandise, but it's always wise to know the prices charged back home. Cameras here may be among the lowest priced in the Dutch Windwards; however, we've discovered better deals on St. Thomas.

Colombian Emeralds International. Old St. ☎ **599/5-23933.**

Here you'll find stones ranging in style from collector to investment quality. Unmounted duty-free emeralds from Colombia as well as emerald, gold, diamond, ruby, and sapphire jewelry, will tempt you. The prices here are approximately the same as in other outlets of this famous chain throughout the Caribbean, and if you're seriously shopping for emeralds, this is the place. There are some huckster fly-by-night vendors around the island pawning fakes off on unsuspecting tourists; Colombian Emeralds offers the genuine item.

Guavaberry Company. 10 Front St. ☎ **599/5-22965.**

This place sells the rare island folk liqueur of St. Maarten that for centuries was made in private homes but is now available to everyone. Sold in square bottles, the product is made from rum that's given a unique flavor by use of rare local berries usually grown in the hills in the center of the island. Don't confuse guavaberries with guavas—they're very different. The liqueur is aged and has a fruity, woody, almost bittersweet flavor, and you can blend it with coconut for a unique guavaberry colada or pour a splash into a glass of icy champagne. Stop in at the shop and free-tasting house.

H. Stern Jewelers. 56 Front St. ☎ 599/5-23328.

This is the Philipsburg branch of a worldwide firm that engages in mining, designing, manufacturing, exporting, and retailing jewelry in all price ranges. If you're looking for quality jewelry, sometimes at 25% off Stateside prices, H. Stern is the place.

La Romana. In Royal Palm Plaza, 61 Front St. ☎ 599/5-22181.

Arguably the most interesting international specialty boutique on the island, this shop offers an excellent selection of the famous line of La Perla swimwear/beachwear for men and women, the La Perla fine lingerie collection, and the latest Fendi bags, luggage, accessories, and perfume. The management states that prices are sometimes up to 40% less than U.S. prices. Even if we lowered that to 25%, you'd still be getting a good bargain.

Little Switzerland. 42 Front St. ☎ 599/5-23530.

These fine-quality European imports are made even more attractive by the prices charged here, often 25% or more lower than Stateside. Elegant famous-name watches, china, crystal, and jewelry are for sale, plus perfume and accessories. Little Switzerland has the best overall selection of these items of any shop in the Dutch side.

Old Street Shopping Center. With entrances on Front St. and Back St. ☎ 599/5-24712.

The Old Street Shopping Center lies 170 yards east of the courthouse. Its lion's-head fountain is the most photographed spot on St. Maarten. Built in a West Indian–Dutch style, it features more that two dozen shops and boutiques, including branches of such famous stores as Colombian Emeralds. Dining facilities include the Philipsburg Grill and Ribs Co. and Pizza Hut.

Penny's Department Store. 48 Back St. ☎ 599/5-23349.

If you're looking for bargains, head here where the locals shop in a five-story building, the largest on the island. Penny's is a general department store similar to counterparts in the States. It carries a wide selection of clothing for men, women, and children, along with paper goods, gifts and souvenirs, small appliances, and linens. The stock is forever changing, and there is discounted merchandise from the basement on up.

Shipwreck Shop. Front St. ☎ 599/5-22962.

Here you'll find West Indian hammocks, beach towels, salad bowls, baskets, jewelry, T-shirts, postcards, books, and much more. It's also the home of wood carvings, native art, sea salt, cane sugar, and spices—in all, a treasure trove of Caribbean handcrafts. Indeed the shop lives up to the promise of its name—all the items that might have washed up in a shipwreck. If you're looking for gifts or handcrafts in general, this might be your best bet.

ST. MAARTEN AFTER DARK

On the Dutch side of St. Maarten there are few real nightclubs. After-dark activities begin early here, as guests select their favorite nook for a sundowner—perhaps the garden patio of **Pasanggrahan** (see "Where to Stay," above).

Visitors watch for the legendary **"green flash,"** an atmospheric phenomenon written about by Hemingway that sometimes occurs in these latitudes just as the sun drops below the horizon. Each evening guests wait expectantly, and have been known to break into a round of applause at a particularly spectacular sunset.

Many hotels sponsor **beachside barbecues** (particularly in season) with steel bands and native music and folk dancing. Outsiders are welcomed at most of these events, but call ahead to see if it's a private affair.

The most popular bar on the island is **Cheri's Café** (see "Where to Eat," above). For dancing and drinking, head to the **Coconuts Night Club** in the Maho Beach Hotel and Casino, Maho Plaza (☎ 599/5-52115). The club is open nightly from 9pm to 4am. Sometimes in season, comedy acts are booked here. But since the venue is forever changing, it's always best to call ahead to see what's happening.

CASINOS

Most of the casinos are in the big hotels. The **Casino Royale,** at the Maho Beach Hotel on Maho Bay (☎ 599/5-52115), opened in 1975. It has 16 blackjack tables, 6 roulette wheels, and 3 craps and 3 Caribbean stud-poker tables. The casino offers baccarat, mini-baccarat, and a large collection of more than 250 slot machines. It's open daily from 1pm to 4am. The Casino Royale Piano Bar is open nightly from 9:30pm, featuring the best of jazz, pop, and Caribbean music. There's no admission charge, and a snack buffet is complimentary.

A popular casino is at the **Pelican Resort & Casino,** Simpson Bay (☎ 599/ 5-42503), built to a Swiss design incorporating a panoramic view of Simpson Bay. The Las Vegas–style casino has 2 craps tables, 3 roulette tables, 9 blackjack tables, 2 stud-poker tables, and 120 slot machines. It's open daily from 1pm to 3am.

The Roman-themed **Coliseum Casino,** on Front Street in Philipsburg (☎ 599/ 5-32102), which opened in 1990, has taken several steps to attract gaming enthusiasts, especially "high rollers," and has the highest table limits ($1,000 maximum) on St. Maarten. The Coliseum features about 225 slot machines, 4 blackjack tables, 3 poker tables, and 2 roulette wheels. The Coliseum is open daily from 11am to 3am.

American breakfasts are served, and the action lasts at least until midnight daily.

One of the Caribbean's most spectacular casinos is the $20-million **Mont Fortune Casino,** Union Road (☎ 599/5-45222), a popular attraction at Port de Plaisance, ITT Sheraton's luxurious resort overlooking Simpson Bay. You'll be in the company of gaming devotees from across North and Latin America who are drawn to Mont Fortune as much for the ambience as for what the casino has to offer. This opulent gamer's paradise boasts 35,000 square feet of entertainment and gaming space.

Located at the Mullet Bay Resort, the **Grand Casino,** one of the Caribbean's largest, offers both Atlantic City– and Las Vegas–style rules and features a wide range of games, including baccarat, craps, double-deck 21, and progressive slots. The Grand is open daily from 1pm until 3am.

2 St. Eustatius

Called "Statia," this Dutch-held island is just an 8-square-mile pinpoint in the Netherlands Antilles, still basking in its 18th-century heritage as the "Golden Rock." One of the true backwaters of the West Indies, it's just awakening to tourism. It's located at a point 150 miles east of Puerto Rico, 38 miles south of St. Maarten, and 17 miles southeast of Saba.

Perhaps the island might best be visited on a day trip from St. Maarten to see if you like it for an extended stay. As Caribbean islands go, it's rather dull here, and its beaches of volcanic black sand aren't especially alluring. Some pleasant strands of beach exist on the Atlantic side, but the surf there is dangerous for swimming.

If you're a hiker or a diver, the outlook improves considerably. Hikes are possible around the base of the Quill, an extinct volcano on the southern end of the island. Wandering through a tropical forest, you encounter wild orchids, philodendron,

heliconia, anthurium, fruit trees, ferns, wildlife, and birds, with the inevitable oleander, hibiscus, and bougainvillea. The island's reefs are covered with corals and enveloped by marine life. At one dive site, known as Crack in the Wall or sometimes "the Grand Canyon," pinnacle coral shoots up from the floor of the ocean. Living among the reefs are barracudas, eagle rays, blacktip sharks, and other large ocean fish.

The good news for the budget traveler is that rates are often called "a steal." If you work it right, you can live in some places for the minimum dollar-a-day figure promised in the title of this guide.

Overlooking the Caribbean on the western edge of the plain, **Oranjestad** (Orange City) is the capital and the only village, consisting of both an Upper and Lower Town, connected by stone-paved, dogleg Fort Road.

GETTING THERE

St. Eustatius can be reached from Dutch St. Maarten's Queen Juliana Airport via Winair **(Windward Islands Airways International)** (☎ **599/5-52568** on St. Maarten). The flying time to Statia's Franklin Delano Roosevelt Airport is only 20 minutes from St. Maarten, with flights six times a day. Once on Statia, connections can also be made for flights to either Saba or St. Kitts. There are two flights a day to Saba and two flights a week to St. Kitts.

The little airline, launched in 1961, has an excellent safety record and has flown such passengers as David Rockefeller. Always reconfirm your return passage once you're on Statia.

GETTING AROUND

BY TAXI   Taxis are your best bet, as there are no buses and few visitors ever rent a car. Taxis meet all incoming flights, and on the way to the hotel, we assure you that your driver will offer himself as a guide during your stay on the island. Taxi rates are low, probably no more than $3.50 to $5 to your hotel from the airport. If you book a 2- to 3-hour tour (and in that time you should be able to cover all the sights on Statia), the cost is about $35 per vehicle.

BY RENTAL CAR   Avis (☎ **800/331-1212** in the U.S.) is your best bet if you want to reserve a car in advance. With unlimited mileage included, it rents a Honda Excel or similar vehicle for $40 a day or $240 a week, with a collision-damage waiver costing $8 a day. Drivers must be 21 years old and present a valid license and credit or charge card. Avis is at the airport (☎ **599/3-82421**) and in the center of Oranjestad at Lampeweg Building no. 1 (☎ **599/3-82421**).

FAST FACTS: St. Eustatius

Banks   **Barclay's Bank,** Wilhelminastraat, Oranjestad (☎ **599/3-82392**), the only bank on the island, is open Monday to Thursday from 8:30am to 3:30pm and on Friday from 8:30am to 12:30pm and 2 to 4:30pm. On weekends, most hotels will exchange money.

Currency   The official unit of currency is the **Netherlands Antilles guilder (NAf),** at 1.77 NAf to each $1 U.S., but nearly all places will quote you prices in U.S. dollars. Prices in this chapter are given in U.S. dollars unless otherwise stated.

Customs   There are no Customs duties since the island is a free port.

Documents   U.S. and Canadian citizens need proof of citizenship, such as a passport, voter registration card, or birth certificate, along with an ongoing ticket. If you're using a birth certificate or voter registration card, you'll also need some photo ID. British subjects need a valid passport.

Electricity   It's the same as in the United States, 100 volts AC, 60 cycles.

Information   The **Tourist Bureau** is at 3 Fort Oranjestraat (☎ **599/3-82433**), open Monday to Thursday from 8am to noon and 1 to 5pm and Friday from 8am to noon and 1 to 4:30pm.

Language   Dutch is the official language, but English is commonly spoken.

Medical Care   A licensed physician is on duty at the **Queen Beatrix Medical Center,** 25 Princessweg in Oranjestad (☎ **599/3-82211**).

Safety   Although crime is rare here, it's wise to secure your valuables and take the kind of discreet precautions you would anywhere. Don't leave valuables unguarded on the beach.

Taxes   There's no departure tax if you're returning to the Dutch-held islands of St. Maarten or Saba; if you're going elsewhere, the tax is $10. Hotels on Statia collect a 7% government tax and a 5% electricity tax.

Telephone and Telegraph   Ask at your hotel if you need to send a cable. St. Eustatius maintains a 24-hour-a-day telephone service—and sometimes it takes about that much time to get a call through!

To call Statia from the U.S., dial 011 (the international access code), then 599 (the country code for the Netherlands Antilles), and finally 3 (the area code for all of Statia) and the five-digit local number.

To make a call within Statia, only the five-digit local number is necessary.

Time   St. Eustatius operates on Atlantic standard time year-round. Thus in winter, when the United States is on standard time, if it's 6pm in Oranjestad it's 5pm in New York. During daylight saving time in the United States the island keeps the same time as the U.S. East Coast.

Tipping and Service   Tipping is at the visitor's discretion, and most hotels, guest houses, and restaurants include a 10% service charge.

Water   The water here is safe to drink.

Weather   The average daytime temperature ranges from 78° to 82° Fahrenheit. The annual rainfall is only 45 inches.

WHERE TO STAY

Don't expect deluxe hotels or high-rises—Statia is strictly for escapists. Sometimes guests are placed in private homes. A 15% service charge and 7% government tax are added to hotel bills. The **Talk of the Town Bar and Restaurant,** listed under "Where to Eat," below, also rents rooms.

DOUBLES FOR LESS THAN $60

Airport View Apartments. Golden Rock, St. Eustatius, N.A. ☎ **599/3-82474.** Fax 599/ 3-82517. 9 apts. A/C TV TEL. Year-round, $60 apt for one or two. AE, MC, V.

Airport View Apartments has two locations: Most units are in the Golden Rock area near the airport and four others are on Princessweg in Upper Town, Oranjestad. The accommodations in the Golden Rock area all have compact refrigerators, coffee-makers, and private baths. They consist of five one-bedroom apartments for one or two people and four two-bedroom apartments for up to four guests. On the premises are a bar/restaurant and an outdoor patio with a swimming pool and barbecue facilities.

In Upper Town, the accommodations consist of two three-bedroom units holding up to nine guests and two two-bedroom apartments for up to four people. They all have kitchens, living rooms, cable TV, dining rooms, and baths.

Country Inn. Concordia, St. Eustatius, N.A. ☎ **599/3-82484.** Fax 599/3-82484. 6 rms. A/C TV. Year-round, $35 single; $50 double. Rates include breakfast. No credit cards.

This is about as basic a hotel as this guidebook is willing to recommend. Established in the early 1990s about a 5-minute walk from the airport and a reasonable stroll to several well-recommended beaches, it's in a residential neighborhood of weathered concrete buildings. Some of your neighbors might be docile cows and goats belonging to the owners, Wendell and Iris Pompier. Breakfast is included as part of your experience here, as well as lunch or dinner if you make arrangements in advance. The bedrooms usually contain a radio, and a launderette and facilities for scuba diving are nearby.

DOUBLES FOR LESS THAN $95 (WINTER) / $75 (OFF-SEASON)

Golden Era Hotel. Lower Town, Oranjestad, St. Eustatius, N.A. ☎ **599/3-82345.** Fax 599/ 3-82445. 20 rms. Winter, $70 single; $88 double; $104 triple. Off-season, $60 single; $75 double; $90 triple. MAP $30 per person extra. AE, DC, MC, V.

Set directly on the water, this modern hotel is clean, serviceable, and comfortable. Built in stages between 1968 and 1975, the establishment, including its simply decorated bar and dining room, is operated by Hubert Lijfrock and Roy Hooker. Eight accommodations don't have a water view, but the remaining rooms offer a full or partial exposure to the sea; all are tasteful and spacious. Lunch and dinner are served daily. The fruit punch, with or without the rum, is delectable. The hotel also has a swimming pool.

Kings Well Resort. Oranje Bay, Oranjestad, St. Eustatius, N.A. ☎ **599/3-82538.** 8 rms. TV. Winter, $65–$86 single; $75–$112 double. Off-season, $50–$65 single; $65–$95 double. DISC, MC, V.

Set on the western (or Caribbean) side of the island, about half a mile north of Oranjestad, this simple, secluded hotel occupies about two-thirds of an acre of land that's perched on an oceanfront cliff. The surf is some 60 feet below. Construction on the place started in 1994 and has progressed slowly ever since. If you're looking for a laid-back, escapist vacation, this is your place. (Your nearest neighbors will be in the local cemetery.) Most views look out to the southwest, ensuring colorful sunsets that tend to be enhanced by drinks served from the bar of the in-house restaurant (reviewed below). There's no swimming pool, and the entire resort contains few amenities, other than the peace and calm that reign here. The owners are German-born Win Piechutzki, who designed the layout and many of the doors and windows, and his American wife, Laura.

La Maison sur la Plage. Zeelandia Beach, St. Eustatius, N.A. ☎ **599/3-82256.** Fax 599/3-82831. 10 rms. TV. Winter, $80 single; $95 double. Off-season, $60 single; $75 double. Rates include breakfast. AE, DISC, MC, V.

On the Atlantic side of the island, fronting Zeelandia Beach, this 10-room beachfront property lies only a mile from the airport. The waters of the Atlantic here can have an undertow, so swimming is risky. Severely damaged by hurricanes, the property hasn't quite bounced back yet. Guests are housed in a series of sparsely furnished cottages, each with two bedrooms and a little private porch where a continental breakfast is served. The place is simply furnished and clean, with no air-conditioning. Facilities include a pool.

Many visitors—especially day-trippers from St. Maarten—are drawn to the hotel's trellised French restaurant, which has ocean views and serves a classic French cuisine including such dishes as escargots, steak with pepper sauce, quiche Lorraine, and duck breast with a green-peppercorn sauce. The style is that of a classic bistro somewhere in the French countryside. The dessert specialty is orange crêpes.

WHERE TO EAT

Chinese Bar and Restaurant. Prinsesweg, Oranjestad. ☎ **599/3-82389.** Main courses $7–$10. No credit cards. Mon–Sat noon–3pm and 7:30–11pm. CHINESE.

This place caters to locals and offers the standard Chinese-restaurant fare, with a bit of local influence thrown in, including such dishes as curried shrimp. The atmosphere is very laid-back. For instance, even though the terrace is not set up for dining, you can request to have your table moved outside for an alfresco meal. The portions are hearty and range from the typical sweet-and-sour pork and a variety of shrimp dishes to chop suey and chow mein.

The Cool Corner. Emmaweg. ☎ **599/3-82523.** Main courses $8.75–$13.75. No credit cards. Daily noon–midnight (but call first to be sure). CHINESE.

This is another simple joint serving Chinese dishes in an unhurried manner. The specialty is Cantonese stir-fries along with standard Asian fare. Dishes offered include gingered beef, shrimp and broccoli, and beef with mushrooms. If you plan to dine here, call first—the chef has to leave the island to restock his larder, so the restaurant is only open 25 days each month.

King's Well Restaurant. Oranje Bay. ☎ **599/3-82538.** Reservations recommended. Main courses $5–$22. MC, V. Daily 11:30am–2pm and 5:30–9:30pm. INTERNATIONAL.

An open kitchen is the highlight of this restaurant owned by Win Piechutzki, who offers all his guests warm hospitality. If you want to splurge, try the prime steak seared in butter, flambéed in burgundy, and smothered with sautéed onions. Less expensive options are the sandwiches and burgers, which cost about $5. For dessert, you may want to try some of the homemade apple strudel served fresh daily.

L'Etoile. 6 Van Rheeweg (northeast of Upper Town, Oranjestad). ☎ **599/3-82299.** Reservations required. Main courses $8.50–$30. AE, MC, V. Mon–Fri 9am–1pm and 5–9pm, Sat 9am–1pm and 5–10pm. CREOLE.

Caren Henríquez has had this second-floor restaurant with a few simple tables for some time. She's well known on Statia for her local cuisine, but you don't run into too many tourists here. Favored main dishes include the ubiquitous "goatwater" (a stew), stewed whelks, mountain crab, and tasty spareribs. She also prepares Caribbean-style lobster. Caren is also known for her *pastechis*—deep-fried turnovers stuffed with meat. Expect a complete and very filling meal, down-home style.

Sonny's Place. Oranjestraat. ☎ **599/3-82609.** Main courses $10–$15. No credit cards. Wed–Mon 9:30am–12:30am. WEST INDIAN.

Housed in a green-and-white gazebo-like structure amid coconut and banana palms, this centrally located hangout offers patrons a taste of the local cuisine in a spirited atmosphere. Favorites here are the soups, such as oyster, goat meat, and for the culinary daring who want an authentic meal, bullfoot. For the less daring, try the kebabs of chicken or pork glazed with a peanut sauce or the grilled fish. Some nights you can enjoy Sonny's live entertainment ranging from DJs to local bands.

Stone Oven. 15 Faeschweg, Upper Town, Oranjestad. ☎ **599/3-82809.** Main courses $6–$12.50. No credit cards. Daily 10am–2pm and 5pm–"whenever." CREOLE.

A small house with a garden patio and a cozy Caribbean decor, this restaurant serves very simple food. To dine like many islanders do, you can try the bullfoot soup or the goatwater stew. For the less adventurous there are fried pork chops and chicken nuggets. Most of the dishes are served with your choice of rice and peas, french fries, fried plantains, and sweet potatoes. Many know this place as a bar where people sometimes dance when the mood and the music are right.

WORTH A SPLURGE

Talk of the Town Hotel. L. E. Sadlerweg, Golden Rock, St. Eustatius, N.A. ☎ **599/3-82236.** Reservations not required. Main courses $14.50–$19. AE, DISC, MC, V. Daily 7am–2pm and 5–9pm. (Bar, daily until 10:30pm.) AMERICAN/CREOLE.

At Golden Rock, a village in the center of the island, you'll get some of the best local food. The dishes are not spectacular, but they are well prepared and quite flavorful. Count on a soup of the day, or perhaps something more elegant, like shrimp cocktail or smoked salmon. Your best bet is usually filet of snapper broiled in a white-wine sauce. The chef will also prepare a 12-ounce T-bone steak or sautéed chicken breast with green peas and a béarnaise sauce. Lunches are the usual—tuna salad, burgers, or salads. Or else you can ask for chicken sate with a peanut-butter sauce.

The restaurant also rents 18 somewhat Spartan motel-like bedrooms, each with private bath, phone, air-conditioning, and TV. Including breakfast, singles range from $69 to $81, with doubles costing $86 to $98, year-round. There's a swimming pool.

BEACHES, WATER SPORTS & OUTDOOR PURSUITS

BEACHES Miles of golden sandy beaches are not the reason most visitors come to Statia. However, there are some, notably at **Oranje Baai,** which has lots of black sand and fronts the Caribbean side of the island, off Lower Town. Other beaches include **Zeelandia** and **Lynch.** On the southwestern shore of Statia are the best volcanic beaches for swimming. Ask a taxi driver to take you to what he or she thinks is the best spot.

CRAB CATCHING   We're perfectly serious. If you're interested, you can join Statians in a crab hunt. The Quill's crater is the breeding ground for these large crustaceans. At night they emerge from their holes to forage, and that's when they're caught. Either with flashlights or relying on moonlight, the "hunters" climb the Quill, catch a crab, and take the local delicacy home to prepare stuffed crab back.

HIKING   Perhaps this is the most popular sporting activity on the island. Those with the stamina can climb the slopes of the Quill. The highest point on the island, the Quill may be young in terms of geology (meaning 4,000 years old), but it's already extinct. Its volcanic cone harbors a crater filled with a dense tropical rain forest, containing towering kapok trees among other vegetation. A dozen or more wild orchids—some quite rare—grow here, and some 50 species of birdlife call it home. Islanders once grew cocoa, coffee, and cinnamon in the crater's soil, but today bananas are the only crop. The tourist office (see "Fast Facts: St. Eustatius," above) will supply you with a list of a dozen trails with varying degrees of difficulty and can also arrange for you to go with a guide whose fee is $20 or more (that has to be negotiated, of course).

TENNIS   Tennis can be played at the **Community Center** on Rosemary Lane (☎ 599/3-82249). The court has a concrete surface and is lit for night games. Changing rooms are available. The court fee is $2.80, and you must bring your own equipment.

WATER SPORTS   On the Atlantic side of the island, at Concordia Bay, the **surfing** is best. However, there's no lifeguard protection.

Snorkeling is available through the Caribbean Sea to explore the remnants of an 18th-century man-of-war and the walls of warehouses, taverns, and ships that sank below the surface of Oranje Bay more than 200 years ago.

Dive Statia is a full PADI diving center on Fishermen's Beach in Lower Town, Oranjestad (☎ 599/3-82435), offering beginning instruction to divemaster certifications. Its professional staff guides divers of all levels of experience to spectacular walls, untouched coral reefs, and historic shipwrecks. Dive Statia offers one- and two-tank boat dives, costing $40 to $75. Night dives and snorkel trips are also available.

SEEING THE SIGHTS

The capital, **Oranjestad,** stands on a cliff looking out on a beach and the island's calm anchorage, where in the 18th century you might have seen 200 vessels anchored offshore. **Fort Oranje** was built in 1636 and restored in honor of the U.S. Bicentennial celebration of 1976. Today, perched atop the cliffs, its terraced rampart is lined with old cannons. As mentioned, this fort may have been the first in the world to acknowledge the Stars and Stripes of the newly created republic of the United States of America. You'll see a bronze plaque honoring the fact that "Here the sovereignty of the United States of America was first formally acknowledged to a national vessel by a foreign official." The plaque was presented by Franklin D. Roosevelt. The fort is now used for government offices.

The **St. Eustatius Historical Foundation Museum,** Upper Town, Oranjestad (☎ 599/3-82288), is also called the de Graaff House in honor of its former tenant, Johannes de Graaff, who ordered the first-ever foreign salute to the Stars and Stripes at Fort Oranje (see above). After British Admiral Rodney sacked Statia for its tribute to the United States, he installed his own headquarters in this 18th-century house. Today a museum, the former governor's house stands in a garden, with a 20th-century wing crafted from 17th-century bricks. Exhibits demonstrate the process of sugar refining, shipping and commerce, defense, archaeological artifacts from the colonial period, and a pair of elegantly beautiful 18th-century antiques-furnished rooms. There's a section devoted to the pre-Columbian period. In the wing annex is a massive piece of needlework by an American, Catherine Mary Williams, showing the flowers of Statia. The museum is open Monday to Friday from 9am to 5pm and on Saturday and Sunday from 9am to noon; admission costs $2 for adults, $1 for children.

A few steps away, a cluster of 18th-century buildings surrounding a quiet courtyard is called **Three Widows' Corner.**

Nearby are the ruins of the first **Dutch Reformed church.** To reach it, turn west from Three Widows' Corner onto Kerkweg. Tilting headstones record the names of the characters in the island's past. The St. Eustatius Historical Foundation recently completed restoration of the church. Visitors may climb to the top level of the tower and see the bay as lookouts did many years before.

Once Statia had a large colony of Jewish traders, and **Honen Dalim,** the second Jewish synagogue in the Western Hemisphere, can be explored, although it's in ruins. It was begun about 1740 and was damaged by a hurricane in 1772; it fell into disuse at the dawn of the 19th century. The synagogue stands beside Synagogpad, a narrow lane whose entrance faces Madam Theatre on the square.

The walls of a *mikvah* (ritual bath) rise beside the **Jewish burial ground** on the edge of town. The oldest stone in the cemetery is that of Abraham Hisquiau de la Motta, who died in 1742. The inscription is in both Portuguese and Hebrew. The most recent marker is that of Moses Waag, who died February 25, 1825. Most poignant is the memorial of David Haim Hezeciah de Lion, who died in 1760 at the age of 2 years, 8 months, 26 days; carved into the baroque surface is an angel releasing a tiny songbird from its cage.

In addition, a short ride from Oranjestad takes you to the road's end at White Wall. Here on your left is **Sugarloaf,** a minireplica of Rio's famed cone. On the right is a panoramic view of St. Kitts.

At the base of the pink-gray cliff beneath Fort Oranje, **Lower Town** was the mercantile center of Statia in the 18th century. Bulging with sugar, rum, and tobacco, Lower Town was once filled with row upon row of brick warehouses. In some of these warehouses, slaves were held in bondage awaiting shipment to other islands in the Caribbean. You can wander at leisure through the ruins.

The Quill, an extinct volcano, called "the most perfect" in the Caribbean, shelters a lush tropical rain forest—a botanical wonderland—in its deep, wide crater. The Quill rises to 1,960 feet on the southern edge of the island. Hikers climb it, and birdwatchers come here for a glimpse of the blue pigeon, a rare bird known to frequent the breadfruit and cottonwood trees in the mountains. See "Hiking" under "Beaches, Water Sports & Outdoor Pursuits," above.

SHOPPING

Merchandise is very limited. Most shops, what few there are, are open Monday to Friday from 8am to noon and 1:30 to 5:30pm, and on Saturday from 10am to noon and 2:30 to 5:30pm; however, hours depend on local whims that day.

Mazinga Giftshop. Fort Oranje Straat, Upper Town, Oranjestad. ☎ **599/3-82245.**

Here you'll find an array of souvenirs—T-shirts, liquor, costume jewelry, 14-karat-gold jewelry, cards, drugstore items, beachwear, children's books, handbags, Delft from Holland, and paperback romances. You may have seen more exciting stores in your life, but this is the best Statia offers.

STATIA AFTER DARK

Dinner and drinks comprise most evenings, but if you're looking for more, perhaps on a weekend, you'll find something. Check to see if there's any action at **Talk of the Town** (see above), which occasionally has live music. The **Exit Disco,** at the Stone Oven Restaurant, 16A Feaschweg, Upper Town, Oranjestad (☎ **599/ 3-82543**), often has dancing on weekends. Sometimes a local band will appear here. You can also enjoy simple West Indian fare at this little spot. For a bar favored by locals, head for the **Cool Corner,** across from the St. Eustatius Historical Foundation Museum in the center of town (☎ **599/3-82523**). A lively crowd often gathers at **Franky's,** at Ruyterweg, also in the heart of town (☎ **599/3-82575**). Its cuisine is basic West Indian fare.

3 Saba

An extinct volcano, with no beaches or flat land, cone-shaped Saba is 5 square miles of rock carpeted in such lush foliage as orchids (which grow in profusion), giant elephant ear, and Eucharist lilies. At its zenith, Mount Scenery, it reaches 2,900 feet. Under the sea the volcanic walls that form Saba continue a sheer drop to great depths, making for some of the most panoramic dives in the Caribbean. Divers and hikers are increasingly attracted to the island, not the serious party person and casinogoer— and certainly not the beach buff.

Unless you're a serious hiker or diver, you might confine your look at Saba to a day trip from St. Maarten. If you're a self-sufficient type who demands almost no artificial amusement, then sleepy Saba might be your hideaway. If you can forgo those beaches and casinos, you can find reasonably priced lodgings and cut-rate meals all over the island. In other words, Saba is a bargain for those who appreciate its unique charms.

Saba is 150 miles east of Puerto Rico and 90 miles east of St. Croix. Most visitors fly over from the Dutch-held section of St. Maarten, 28 miles to the north.

GETTING THERE

BY PLANE   You can leave New York's JFK Airport in the morning and be at Captain's Quarters on Saba for dinner that night by taking a direct flight on either of the two airlines that currently fly from the United States to St. Maarten (see "Getting There" in section 1, above). From Queen Juliana Airport there, you can fly to Saba on **Winair (Windward Islands Airways International)** (☎ **599/5-52568** on St. Maarten). Flying time is 12 minutes, and the round-trip fare is $86.

Arriving by air from St. Maarten, the traveler steps from Winair's 20-passenger STOL (short takeoff and landing) plane onto the tarmac runway of the **Juancho Yrausquin Airport.** The airstrip is famous as one of the shortest (if not *the* shortest) landing strips in the world, stretching only 1,312 feet along the aptly named Flat Point, one of the few level areas on the island.

Many guests at hotels on St. Maarten fly over to Saba on the morning flight, spend the day sightseeing, then return to St. Maarten on the afternoon flight. Winair connections can also be made on Saba to both St. Kitts and Statia.

GETTING AROUND

BY TAXI   Taxis meet every flight. The cost of a 2-hour tour is about $10 per person if there are at least four passengers making the trip.

BY HITCHHIKING Hitchhiking has long been an acceptable means of transport on Saba, where everybody seemingly knows everybody else. On recent rounds, our taxi rushed a sick child to the plane and picked up an old man to take him up the hill because he'd fallen and hurt himself—all on our sightseeing tour! (We didn't mind.) By hitchhiking, you'll probably get to know everybody else, too.

ON FOOT The traditional means of getting around on Saba is still much in evidence. But we suggest that only the sturdy in heart and limb walk from the Bottom up to Windwardside. Many do, but you'd better have some shoes that grip the ground, particularly after a recent rain.

BY RENTAL CAR None of the "big three" car-rental companies maintains a branch on Saba. In the unlikely event that you should dare to drive a car on Saba, a locally operated company, **Johnson's Rental,** Windwardside (☎ **599/4-62269**), rents about six Mazdas, charging around $45 per day. Some insurance is included in the rates, but you might be held partly responsible for any financial costs in the event of an accident. Because of the very narrow roads and dozens of cliffs, it's crucial to exercise caution when driving in Saba.

FAST FACTS: Saba

Banks The main bank on the island is **Barclay's,** Windwardside (☎ **599/ 4-62216**), open Monday to Friday from 8:30am to 2pm.

Currency   Saba, like the other islands of the Netherlands Antilles, uses the **Netherlands Antilles guilder (NAf),** valued at 1.77 NAf to $1 U.S. However, prices given in this chapter are in U.S. currency unless otherwise designated, since U.S. money is accepted by almost everyone here.

Customs   You don't have to go through Customs when you land at Juancho E. Yrausquin Airport, as this is a free port.

Documents   The government requires that all U.S. and Canadian citizens show proof of citizenship, such as a passport or voter registration card with photo ID. A return or ongoing ticket must also be provided. Britishers must have a valid passport.

Drugstore   Try **The Pharmacy,** The Bottom (☎ 599/4-63289).

Electricity   Saba uses 110 volts AC, 60 cycles, so most U.S.-made appliances don't need transformers or adapters.

Information   Before you go, information can be obtained at the **Saba Tourist Board,** P.O. Box 6322, Boca Raton, FL 33427 (☎ **800/722-2394** or 407/394-8580). On the island, the **Saba Tourist Board** is at Lambees Place in the heart of Windwardside (☎ **599/4-62231**). It's open Monday to Thursday from 8am to noon and 1 to 5pm, and on Friday from 8am to noon and 1 to 4:30pm.

Medical Care   Saba's hospital complex is the **A. M. Edwards Medical Centre,** The Bottom (☎ **599/4-63289**).

Police   Call ☎ **599/4-63237.**

Safety   Crime on this island, where everyone knows everyone else, is practically nonexistent. But who knows? A tourist might rob you. It would be wise to safeguard your valuables.

Taxes   The government imposes a 5% tourist tax on hotel rooms. If you're returning to St. Maarten or flying over to Statia, you must pay a $5 departure tax. If you're going anywhere else, however, a $10 tax is imposed.

Telephone and Telegraph   Cables and international telephone calls can be placed at **Antelecon,** The Bottom (☎ 599/4-63211).

To call Saba from the United States, dial 011 (the international access code), then 599 (the country code for the Netherlands Antilles), and finally 4 (the area code for all of Saba) and the five-digit local number.

To make a call within Saba, only the five-digit local number is necessary.

Time   Saba is on Atlantic standard time year-round, 1 hour earlier than eastern standard time. When the United States is on daylight saving time, clocks on Saba and the U.S. East Coast read the same.

Tips and Service   Most restaurants and hotels add a 10% or 15% service charge to your bills to cover tipping.

Weather   You'll encounter a temperature of 78° to 82° Fahrenheit. The annual rainfall is 42 inches.

WHERE TO STAY
DOUBLES FOR LESS THAN $60

✪ **Cranston's Antique Inn.** The Bottom, Saba, N.A. ☎ **599/4-63203.** 6 rms. $40 single; $57 double; $65 triple. AE, MC, V.

Everyone congregates for rum drinks and gossip on the front terrace of this inn near the village roadway, on the west coast north of Fort Bay. It's an old-fashioned house, more than 100 years old, and every bedroom has antique four-poster beds. Mr. Cranston, the owner, will gladly rent you the same room where Queen Juliana once spent a holiday. Aside from the impressive wooden beds, the furnishings are mostly hit or miss.

Mr. Cranston has a good island cook, who makes use of locally grown spices. Island dishes are offered, including goat meat, roast pork from Saba pigs, red snapper, and broiled grouper. Meals begin at $12 and are served on a covered terrace in the garden or inside. The house is within walking distance of Ladder Bay.

DOUBLES FOR LESS THAN $95 (WINTER) / $75 (OFF-SEASON)

Cottage Club. Windwardside, Saba, N.A. ☎ **599/4-62486.** Fax 599/4-62476. 10 studio apts. TV TEL. Nov 15–Mar, $115 studio apt for one or two. Apr–Nov 14, $84 studio apt for one or two. Third and fourth person $20 extra. MC, V.

Small, intimate, and immersed in the architectural and aesthetic traditions of Saba, this hotel complex occupies about a half acre of steeply sloping and carefully landscaped terrain within a 2-minute walk of the center of the island's capital. Only its lobby evokes a historic setting. Designed of local stone, and set at an altitude above the other buildings of the complex, it's the focal point for a collection of island antiques, lace curtains, and a round-sided swimming pool. The studio apartments each contain a kitchenette, a semiprivate patio, ceiling fans, a living-room area, and a queen-size bed. They're contained in clapboard replicas of antique cottages—two studios per cottage—with red roofs, green shutters, white walls, and yellow trim. The interiors are breezy, airy, and comfortable. There's no bar or restaurant on the premises, but residents can buy groceries at a supermarket a short walk from the site that will deliver supplies if requested. The owners of the establishment are three Saban brothers (Gary, Mark, and Dean) whose extended families all seem to assist in the construction and maintenance of the place.

The Gate House. Hells Gate, Saba, N.A. ☎ **599/4-62416,** or 708/354-9641 for reservations only. Fax 599/4-62415. 6 rms. Winter, $85 single; $95 double. Off-season, $75 single or double. Rates include continental breakfast. MC, V. Closed Sept.

Its name derives from its position at the gateway to Saba, almost adjacent to the airport; it's the first hotel most visitors see on their way to other points around the island. Located on steeply sloping ground a 5-minute walk from the coast, it was built in 1990 as a concrete-sided replica of three two-story Saban town houses set adjacent one to another, and ringed with a wraparound veranda. There's an oval pool on the premises, a color scheme (red roofs, green shutters, white walls) that reflects traditional Saban themes, and an airy interior. Your hosts are the American-Dutch partnership of Jim Seigel and Manuela Doey, who devote much of their time and attention to administering the in-house restaurant (recommended below).

✪ **Scout's Place.** Windwardside, Saba, N.A. ☎ **599/4-62205.** Fax 599/4-62388. 14 rms, 1 apt. Winter, $65 single; $85 double; $100 apt for two. Off-season, discounts of around 20%. Rates include continental breakfast. MC, V.

Right in the center of the village, Scout's Place is hidden from the street. Set on the ledge of a hill, the place is owned by Diana Medora, who makes guests feel right at home. With only 15 accommodations, it's still the second-largest inn on the island. The old house has a large covered but open-walled dining room, where every table has a view of the sea. It's an informal place, with an individual decor that might include Surinam hand-carvings, peacock chairs in red-and-black wicker, and silver samovars. The rooms open onto an interior courtyard filled with flowers, and each has a view of the sea. The apartment with kitchenette is suitable for up to five occupants; an extra person is charged $20.

WORTH A SPLURGE

✪ Juliana's Apartments. Windwardside, Saba, N.A. ☎ **599/4-62269.** Fax 599/4-62389. 8 rms, 1 apt, 1 cottage. Winter, $90 single; $115 double; $135 apt or cottage. Off-season, $70 single; $90 double; $115 apt or cottage. Extra person $20. Dive packages available. AE, MC, V.

Built in 1985 near the Captain's Quarters, this hostelry is set on a hillside. Modern and immaculate, the accommodations here have balconies and access to a sun deck for lounging. Each room is simply but comfortably furnished and contains a radio. Juliana's offers a 2^1/$_2$-room apartment complete with kitchenette and Flossie's Cottage, a renovated original Saban cottage. The cottage is a two-bedroom home with a spacious living room, dining room, color TV, and fully equipped kitchen. There's also a recreation room and a swimming pool. The complex contains a simple restaurant, Tropics Café, that's open daily except Sunday for breakfast and lunch, and for dinner 4 nights a week.

WHERE TO EAT

Brigadoon Pub & Eatery. Windwardside. ☎ **599/4-62380.** Main courses $9.95–$20.95. AE, MC, V. Daily 6–9:30pm. INTERNATIONAL.

An array of Caribbean, American, and other international flavors combine to form a savory cuisine in this old colonial building with an open front. Whenever possible, fresh local ingredients are used, including herbs, spices, fruits, and vegetables. Fresh local fish is generally the preferred course, and you can also order live local lobster from the island's only live lobster tank (prices on this delicacy are likely to vary). Steaks are flown in weekly. You might also prefer the Saba fish pot, a variety of fresh catch from Saba's waters in a basil-and-tomato sauce. On Monday it's a Mexican fiesta with fajitas, tacos, burritos, and much more, priced from $3.50 each.

The Gate House. Hells Gate. ☎ **599/4-62416.** Reservations recommended. Fixed-price three-course meal $20. MC, V. Thurs–Tues 6:30–10:30pm. Closed Sept. CARIBBEAN.

Set on one of the upper floors of a previously recommended hotel, this popular and lively place lies closer to the island's only airport than any other restaurant on Saba. Views from its premises encompass the coastline, the hotel's swimming pool, and the arrival and departure of virtually every plane that lands on the island. Staff members might derive from the U.S. mainland, Holland, or St. Vincent, depending on whomever happens to be here on the night of your arrival. The menu changes every night, depending on what's available on-island and the inspiration of the chef. Staples that virtually always appear include curried conch, coconut shrimp, and grilled flanksteak, whereas items that come and go include pan-fried grouper, grilled mahimahi with jerk sauce or with lemon-butter-garlic sauce, and grilled chicken with Créole sauce.

Guido's Pizzeria. Windwardside. ☎ **599/4-62230.** Main courses $5.50–$15. MC, V. Daily 6pm–"whenever." AMERICAN.

Marcia and Bob Guido own this bustling little pizzeria where you can find basic familiar food. The pizzas come with all the standard toppings, even anchovies, served on crusts that are made fresh daily. There's also spaghetti and meatballs, burgers, and meatball sandwiches. As you wait for your meal, you may want to try your hand at the pool table. On Friday and Saturday nights about 9pm, dancing begins with DJs and occasionally a live band.

Lollipop's. St. John's. ☎ **599/4-63330.** Reservations recommended at dinner. Dinner (including soup/salad, main course, bread, dessert, coffee, and free transportation from/to your hotel) $18–$26; lunch $10–$14. MC, V. Daily 8am–11pm. WEST INDIAN.

Locals who gravitate here like the personality of the owner, Carmen Caines, so much that they've nicknamed her "Lollipop." She's warm and gracious and even has guests picked up at their hotel and delivered to her spot; you're also taken back to your hotel. She presents her West Indian fare on an outdoor terrace. She cooks whatever was good at the market that day, and that usually means fresh grilled fish. She's known for her land crab, and also prepares a wicked curried goat. Shrimp and lobster are also regularly featured. Lollipop is so sweet that after dinner you'll want to give her a kiss.

Saba Chinese Bar & Restaurant (Moo Goo Gai Pan). Windwardside. ☎ **599/4-62268.** Main courses $5–$17. MC, V. Tues–Sun 11am–midnight. CHINESE.

Amid a cluster of residential buildings on a hillside above Windwardside, this place is operated by a family from Hong Kong. It offers some 120 dishes, served in an unpretentious decor of plastic tablecloths and folding chairs. It's a real favorite with local residents. Meals include Cantonese and Indonesian specialties—lobster Cantonese, Chinese chicken with mushrooms, sweet-and-sour fish, chicken with cashew nuts, conch chop suey, several curry dishes, roast duck, and nasi goreng.

✪ Scout's Place. Windwardside. ☎ **599/4-62205.** Reservations required 2–3 hours in advance. Fixed-price dinner $16.50–$25; lunch $12. MC, V. Lunch daily at 12:30pm; dinner daily at 7:30pm. INTERNATIONAL.

Scout's Place is a popular dining spot for day-trippers to Saba; stop by early in the day to make a reservation for lunch. The food is simple and good, rewarding and filling, and the price is right, too. Dinner is more elaborate, with tables placed on an open-sided terrace, the ideal spot for a drink at sundown. Fresh seafood is a specialty, as is curried goat.

Sunset Bar & Restaurant. The Bottom. ☎ **599/4-63332.** Main courses $6–$14; lunch $4–$10. No credit cards. Daily 8am–2pm and 6pm–midnight. WEST INDIAN.

You'll enjoy West Indian specialties in a homelike atmosphere at this basic restaurant. For your main course you might want to go for something simple, such as the baked chicken served with rice and peas, potato salad, and your choice of local specialties. Other dishes include spareribs or pork chops with vegetables.

WATER SPORTS & OUTDOOR ACTIVITIES

HIKING   The island is as beautiful above the water as it is below. Mountain walking is the major sport, and the top of **Mount Scenery,** a volcano which erupted 5,000 years ago, is a wildlife reserve. Allow more than a day and take your time climbing the 1,064 sometimes-slippery concrete steps up the cloud-reefed mountain. You'll pass along a lush rain forest with palms, bromeliads, elephant ears, heliconia, mountain raspberries, lianas, and tree ferns. In her pumps, Queen Beatrix of the Netherlands climbed these steps and, upon reaching the summit, declared: "This is the smallest and highest place in my kingdom." One of the inns will pack you a picnic lunch. The higher you climb, the cooler it grows, about a drop of 1° Fahrenheit every 328 feet; on a hot day this can be an incentive. The peak is 2,855 feet high.

If you don't want to explore the natural attractions of the island on your own, the **Saba Tourist Board,** P.O. Box 527, Windwardside, Saba, N.A. (☎ **599/4-62322**), can put you in touch with a reputable guide for tours into the tropical rain forests that sheathe the sides of the island's vertiginous peak. Most of these will be conducted by **James ("Jim") Johnson** (☎ 599/4-63307), a fit and hardy Sabian in his 40s who knows the island's trails better than anyone else. Since Johnson has other occupations, you might have to work a bit to contact him for information about hikes to the top of Mount Scenery or Maskerhorn Hill. Depending on your priorities, a tour might include visits to terraced fields, the Big Rendezvous forest, and panoramas from various eyries throughout the island. Tours can be configured for between one and eight hikers, last about half a day, and cost between $50 and $100, depending on the distance covered and the number of people in your party. Actual prices, of course, are to be negotiated.

TENNIS   Tennis buffs will find a free concrete public court in The Bottom.

WATER SPORTS   Don't come here for beaches, as mentioned. Saba has only one sand beach, and it's about 20 feet long. Sports here are mostly do-it-yourself. Visitors, such as John F. Kennedy Jr., enjoy the underwater scenery and dark volcanic sands and coral formations.

The **Saba Deep Dive Center,** P.O. Box 22, Fort Bay, Saba, N.A. (☎ 599/4-63347), is a full-service dive center that offers scuba diving, snorkeling, equipment rental/repair, and tank fills. Whether 1 diver or 20, novice or experienced, Mike Myers and his staff of NAUI/PADI/ACUC/CMAS instructors/divemasters are concerned with personalized service and great diving. Dive sites around Saba, all protected by the Saba Marine Park, have permanent moorings and range from shallow to deep. Divers see pinnacles, walls, ledges, overhangs, and reefs—all with abundant coral and sponge formations and a wide variety of both reef and pelagic marine life. There's also a fully operational recompression chamber / hyperbaric facility located in the Fort Bay Harbor. The In Two Deep Restaurant and the Deep Boutique offer air-conditioned comfort, a view of the harbor area and the Caribbean Sea, good food and drink, and a wide selection of clothes, swimwear, lotions, and sunglasses. A certification course goes for $375. A single-tank dive costs $45; a two-tank dive, $90. Night dives are $65. The center is open daily from 8am to 6pm, with Saturday-night dinners.

The **Sea Saba Dive Center,** Windwardside (☎ 599/4-62246), has seven experienced instructors eager to share their knowledge of Saba Marine Park: famous deep- and medium-depth pinnacles, walls, spur and groove formations, and giant boulder gardens. Its two 40-foot uncrowded boats are best suited for a comfortable day on Saba's waters. Daily boat dives are made between the hours of 10am and 2pm, allowing a relaxing interval for snorkeling. Courses range from resort through divemaster. Extra day and night dives can be arranged. A two-tank dive costs $90; package prices are available with advance booking, starting at about $500 per person.

With **Saba Reef Divers,** Fort Bay Harbour, Windwardside (☎ 599/4-62541), you can explore the shoals, walls, shelves, reefs, pinnacles, and seamounts that surround the volcanic cone of the landmass of Saba. The owners—four Americans—take divers to the "Pinnacles," where they encounter unusual rock formations and reef sharks at 90 feet. Divers can maneuver their way around Diamond Rock, spotting barracuda, stingrays, grouper, and snapper lurking near the lush, sloping walls. Tent Reef, a long underwater fault crisscrossed with crevasses and drop-offs ranging from 40 to 130 feet, is another unusual option for divers with a sense of adventure. The outfit's boat is the *Mama,* a 40-foot vessel with plenty of shade. Packages are available, but otherwise a single-tank dive goes for around $50 and a two-tank dive for around $85.

Exploring an Underwater Wonderland

Circling the entire island to a depth contour of 200 feet, including four offshore underwater mountains (seamounts), the **Saba Marine Park,** Fort Bay (☎ **599/ 4-63295**), preserves the island's coral reefs and marine life. The park is zoned for various pursuits. The all-purpose recreational zone includes Wells Bay Beach, but it's seasonal—it disappears with the winter seas, only to reappear in late spring. There are two anchorage zones for visiting yachts plus Saba's only harbor. The five dive zones include a coastal area and four seamounts a mile offshore. In these zones are more than two dozen marked and buoyed dive sites and even a snorkeling trail. You plunge into a world of coral and sponges, swimming with parrot fish, doctorfish, and damselfish. The snorkel trail, however, is not for the neophyte—it can be approached from Wells Bay Beach but only May to October. Depths of more than 1,500 feet are found between the island and the seamounts, which reach a mini-mum depth of 90 feet. There's a $3-per-dive visitor fee and a $3-per-person, per week, yacht visitor fee. Funds are also raised through souvenir sales and donations. The Saba Marine Park also maintains a recompression chamber for diving accidents. The park office at Fort Bay is open Monday to Friday from 8am to 5pm, on Satur-day from 8am to noon, and on Sunday from 10m to 2pm.

SEEING THE SIGHTS

Tidy white houses cling to the mountainside, and small family cemeteries adjoin each dwelling. The lace-curtained gingerbread-trimmed cottages give a Disneyland aura.

The first Jeep arrived on Saba in 1947. Before that, Sabans went about on foot, climbing from village to village. Hundreds of steps had been chiseled out of rock by the early Dutch settlers beginning in 1640.

Engineers told them it was impossible, but Sabans built a single cross-island road by hand. Filled with hairpin turns, it zigzags from Fort Bay, where a deep-water pier accommodates large tenders from cruise ships, to a height of 1,600 feet. Along the way it has fortresslike supporting walls.

Past storybook villages, the road goes over the crest to The Bottom. Derived from the Dutch word *botte,* which means "bowl-shaped," this village is nestled on a pla-teau and surrounded by rocky volcanic domes. It occupies about the only bit of ground, 800 feet above the sea. It's also the official capital of Saba, a Dutch village of charm, with chimneys, gabled roofs, and gardens.

From The Bottom you can take a taxi up the hill to the mountain village of **Windwardside,** perched on the crest of two ravines at about 1,500 feet above sea level. This village of red-roofed houses, the second most important on Saba, is the site of the two biggest inns and most of the shops. From Windwardside you can climb steep steps cut in the rock to yet another village, **Hells Gate,** teetering on the edge of a mountain. However, there's a serpentine road from the airport to Hells Gate, where you'll find the island's largest church. Only the most athletic climb from here to the lip of the volcanic crater.

In Windwardside, the **Harry L. Johnson Memorial Museum** (no phone) is in an old sea captain's home, with antique furnishings, evoking an 1890s aura. Filled with family memorabilia, the house can be visited for an admission of $2. The surprise visit of the late Jacqueline Kennedy Onassis is still vividly recalled. It's open Monday to Friday from 10am to noon and 1 to 4pm.

SHOPPING

After lunch you can go for a stroll in Windwardside and stop at the boutiques, which often look like someone's living room—and sometimes they are. Most stores are open Monday to Saturday from 9am to noon and 2 to around 5:30pm, and some are also open shorter hours on Sunday.

The traditional **drawn threadwork** of the island is famous. Sometimes this work, introduced by a local woman named Gertrude Johnson in the 1870s, is called Spanish work, because it was believed to have been perfected by nuns in Caracas. Selected threads are drawn and tied in a piece of linen to produce an ornamental pattern. It can be expensive if a quality linen has been used.

Try to come home with some **"Saba Spice,"** an aromatic blend of 150-proof cask rum with such spices as fennel seed, cinnamon, cloves, and nutmeg, straight from someone's home brew. It's not for everyone (too sweet), but it will make an exotic bottle to show off at home.

Around the Bend. At Scout's Place, Windwardside. ☎ **599/4-62519.**

Housed in a charming little Saba cottage, this store is run by ex–New Yorker Jean Macbeth, whose taste is reflected in her hand-painted tops. The shop also features locally made oddments, such as Saba cottage wallplaques, and what Macbeth calls "pretties" of all kinds.

Frankly Freda's Nifty Gifties. Main Rd., Windwardside. ☎ **599/4-62259.**

Souvenirs in this shop include fish and parrot mobiles, amulets, island-made sterling and costume jewelry, sun visors, caps, and of course, T-shirts. The manager, Freda Johnson, creates the enchanting Saban drawn threadwork linens for sale as well.

Saba Artisan Foundation. The Bottom. ☎ **599/4-63260.**

In recent years the foundation has made a name for itself in the world of fashion with hand-screened resort fashions. The clothes are casual and colorful. Among the items sold are men's bush-jacket shirts, numerous styles of dresses and skirts, napkins, and placemats, as well as yard goods. Island motifs are used in many designs, and you might like a fern- or casava-leaf print. Also popular are the famous Saba drawn-lace patterns. The fashions are designed, printed, sewn, and marketed by Sabans.

Saba Tropical Arts. Windwardside. ☎ **599/4-62373.**

This is the place to go to watch hand silk-screening, and perhaps make a purchase. The designer Mieke Van Schadewijk has created some catchy patterns, all of which are displayed at his workshop boutique.

The Square Nickel. Windwardside. ☎ **599/4-62477.**

This is the island's variety store, a sort of five and dime. Douglas Johnson has accumulated a selection of clothing, housewares, jewelry, shoes, jeans, and just general knickknacks.

SABA AFTER DARK

Guido's Pizzeria (see "Where to Eat," above) is converted into the Mountain High Club Disco, with a mirrored disco ball suspended from the ceiling. This is on Friday and Saturday nights when dancing goes on until 2am or later, depending on the crowd. **Inner Circle,** The Bottom (☎ 599/4-62240), calls itself a "nightclub," attracting the locals. Most visitors simply drink into the night at either **Scout's Place** (see "Where to Eat," above), or at the **Captain's Quarters,** Windwardside (☎ 599/4-62377).

Jamaica

11

Most visitors already have a mental picture of Jamaica before they arrive: a boisterous culture of reggae and Rastafarianism, with white sandy beaches, tropical forests, rivers, mountains, and clear waterfalls. Jamaica's art, music, and cuisine are also remarkable.

Jamaica can be a tranquil and intriguing island, but there's no denying that it's plagued by crime, drugs, and muggings. There is also palpable racial tension here. But many visitors are unaffected; they're escorted from the airport to their heavily patrolled hotel grounds and venture out only on expensive organized tours. These vacationers are largely sheltered from the more unpredictable and sometimes dangerous side of Jamaica. Those who want to see "the real Jamaica," or at least to see the island in greater depth, had better be prepared for some hassle. Vendors on the beaches and in the markets can be particularly aggressive.

Most Jamaicans, in spite of their hard times, have unrelenting good humor and genuinely welcome visitors to the island. Others, certainly a minority, harm the tourism business, so that many visitors vow "never to return." Jamaica's appealing aspects have to be weighed against its poverty and problems, the legacy of traumatic political upheavals that have characterized the island in past decades, beginning in the 1970s.

Should you go? By all means, yes. Be prudent and cautious—just as if you were visiting New York, Miami, or Los Angeles. But Jamaica is worth it! The island has fine hotels and a zesty cuisine. It's well geared to couples who come to tie the knot or celebrate their honeymoon. As for sports, Jamaica boasts the best golf courses in the West Indies, and its landscape affords visitors lots of outdoor activities like rafting and serious hiking. The island also has some of the finest diving waters in the world, with an average diving depth of 35 to 95 feet. Visibility is usually 60 to 120 feet. Most of the diving is done on coral reefs, which are protected by underwater parks where fish, shells, coral, and sponges are plentiful. Experienced divers can also see wrecks, hedges, caves, drop-offs, and tunnels.

Jamaica is known for its all-inclusive resorts, most of which are expensive. But you can save money by staying at local B&Bs, small hotels, and various guest houses scattered throughout the island. And if you steer clear of the pricey restaurants catering almost exclusively to tourists, and eat where many of the Jamaicans themselves dine out, you'll cut your meal costs by two-thirds, maybe a lot less.

Every town from Kingston to Montego Bay to Negril has a "jerk center," and you almost can't go wrong patronizing one of these local dives for a true "taste of Jamaica." A jerk chicken or pork lunch runs about $6 in most places.

Jamaica lies 90 miles south of Cuba, with which it was chummy in the 1970s (when much of the world feared that Jamaica was going Communist). It's the third largest of the Caribbean islands, with some 4,400 square miles of predominantly green land, a mountain ridge peaking at 7,400 feet above sea level, and on the north coast, many white-sand beaches with clear blue sea.

GETTING THERE

There are two **international airports** on Jamaica: Donald Sangster in Montego Bay and Norman Manley in Kingston. The most popular routings to Jamaica are from New York and Miami. Remember to reconfirm all flights, going and returning, no later than 72 hours before departure. Flying time from Miami is 1¹/₄ hours; from Los Angeles, 5¹/₂ hours; from Atlanta, 2¹/₂ hours; from Dallas, 3 hours; from Chicago and New York, 3¹/₂ hours; and from Toronto, 4 hours.

Some of the most convenient and popular services to Jamaica are provided by **American Airlines** (☎ 800/433-7300 in the U.S.) through its hubs in New York and Miami. Throughout the year, a daily nonstop flight departs from New York's Kennedy Airport touching down in Montego Bay, and continuing on without a change of aircraft to Kingston. Return flights to New York from Jamaica usually depart from Montego Bay, touch down briefly in either Kingston or Miami, then continue nonstop back to Kennedy. From Miami, at least two daily flights depart for Kingston, and three daily flights for Montego Bay.

Air Jamaica (☎ 800/523-5585 in the U.S.), the national carrier, operates about 13 flights a week from New York's JFK, most of which stop at both Montego Bay and Kingston. More frequent are the flights that the airline operates to Jamaica from Miami. Some are nonstop to Kingston and others are nonstop to Montego Bay. The airline offers connecting service within Jamaica through its reservations network to a small independent airline, Air Jamaica Express, whose planes usually hold between 10 and 17 passengers. Air Jamaica Express flights depart from the country's international airports at Montego Bay and Kingston for small airports, including Port Antonio, Boscobel (near Ocho Rios), Negril, and Tinson Pen (a small airport near Kingston).

Continental (☎ 800/525-0280 in the U.S.) offers nonstop service from its hub at Newark, N.J., to Montego Bay, on Saturday and Sunday.

Air Canada (☎ 800/776-3000 in the U.S., or 800/268-7240 in Canada) flies to Jamaica from Toronto. In winter service is daily; off-season, flights are on Saturday and Sunday only. But all this is subject to change, depending on demand, so check with the airline.

In addition, **Northwest Airlines** (☎ 800/225-2525 in the U.S.) flies directly to Montego Bay from Minneapolis and Tampa.

British travelers usually take **British Airways** (☎ 800/247-9297 in the U.S., or 0345/222111 in Great Britain), which has three nonstop flights to Montego Bay and Kingston from London's Gatwick Airport.

GETTING AROUND

BY PLANE   Most travelers to Jamaica enter the country via Montego Bay. The island's domestic air service is provided by **Air Jamaica Express.** Reservations are handled by **Air Jamaica** (☎ 809/923-8680) in Kingston and Montego Bay (same phone for both cities), which has consolidated its reservation system. This service offers 30 scheduled flights daily, covering all the major resort areas. For example, there are 11 flights a day between Kingston and Montego Bay, and 3 flights a day between Negril and Port Antonio. Reservations can be made through overseas travel agents or through Air Jamaica. Incidentally, Tinson Pen Airport in the heart of downtown Kingston is for domestic flights only. Car-rental facilities are available only at the international airports at Kingston and Montego Bay.

BY TAXI & BUS Kingston has no city taxis with meters, so agree on a price before you get in. In Kingston and the rest of the island, special taxis and buses for visitors are operated by JUTA (Jamaica Union of Travellers Association) and have the union's emblem on the side of the vehicle. All prices are controlled, and any local JUTA office will supply a list of rates. JUTA drivers do nearly all the ground transfers, and some offer sightseeing tours.

BY BIKE & SCOOTER These can be rented in Montego Bay, and you'll need your valid driver's license. **Montego Honda / Bike Rentals,** 21 Gloucester Ave. (☎ 809/952-4984), rents Hondas for $35 a day, plus a $300 deposit. Scooters cost $35 per day. Deposits are refundable if the vehicles are returned in good shape. It's open daily from 7:30am to 5pm.

BY RENTAL CAR Jamaica is big enough, and public transportation is unreliable enough, that a car is a necessity if you plan to do much independent sightseeing. (In lieu of this, you can always take an organized tour to the major sights and spend the rest of the time on the beaches near your hotel.)

Depending on the road conditions, driving time for the 50 miles from Montego Bay to Negril is 1 1/2 hours; from Montego Bay to Ocho Rios, 62 miles and 1 1/2 hours; from Ocho Rios to Port Antonio, 60 miles and 2 1/2 hours; from Ocho Rios to Kingston, 60 miles and 2 hours; from Kingston to Mandeville, 65 miles and 1 1/2 hours; and from Kingston to Port Antonio, 68 miles and 2 hours.

It's best to stick to branches of U.S.-based rental outfits. Unfortunately, prices of car rentals in Jamaica have skyrocketed recently, making it one of the most expensive rental scenes in the Caribbean. There's also a 15% government tax on rentals. Equally unfortunate are the unfavorable insurance policies that apply to virtually every car-rental agency in Jamaica. You must be 25 years old to rent a car.

Avis (☎ 800/331-1084 in the U.S.) maintains offices at the international airports in both Montego Bay (☎ 809/952-4543) and Kingston (☎ 809/924-8013); the company's least expensive car requires a 24-hour advance booking and costs $330 per week, plus 15% tax. The company's collision-damage waiver (CDW) costs another $10 per day. **Budget Rent-a-Car** (☎ 800/527-0700 in the U.S.) has offices at the Montego Bay airport (☎ 809/952-3838) and in Kingston (☎ 809/938-2189). It rents cars for $252 and up per week with unlimited mileage, plus 15% government tax. A daily collision-damage waiver (CDW) costs another $15 and is mandatory. **Hertz** (☎ 800/654-3001 in the U.S.) operates branches at the airports at both Montego Bay (☎ 809/979-0438) and Kingston (☎ 809/924-8028). Its least expensive subcompact car rents for $300 per week, plus 15% tax, with unlimited mileage included. A collision-damage waiver costs $15 extra per day.

In Montego Bay, some local options are **United Car Rentals,** 49 Gloucester Ave. (☎ 809/952-3077), which rents Mazdas, Toyota Starlets, Hondas, and Suzuki Jeeps, all for around $50 per day for a two-door car without air-conditioning. You can also try **Jamaica Car Rental,** 23 Gloucester Ave. (☎ 809/952-5586), with a branch at the Sangster International Airport at Montego Bay (☎ 809/952-9496). Winter rates—a Suzuki Samurai, for example—begin at $65 per day, with a Toyota even cheaper at $60 per day.

Jamaica

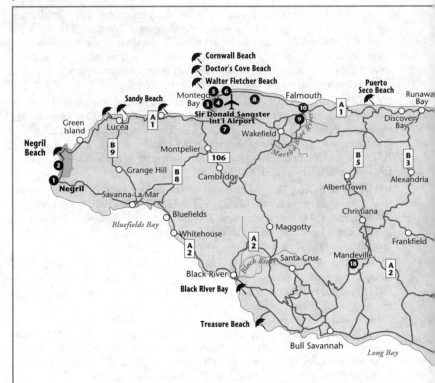

Cornwall Beach **3**
Doctor's Cave Beach **6**
Dunn's River Falls **11**
Falmouth **10**
Kingston **15**
Mandeville **18**
Martha Brae's Rafter's Village **9**

Montego Bay **5**
Negril **1**
Negril Beach **2**
Norman Manley
   International Airport **14**
Ocho Rios **12**
Port Antonio **13**

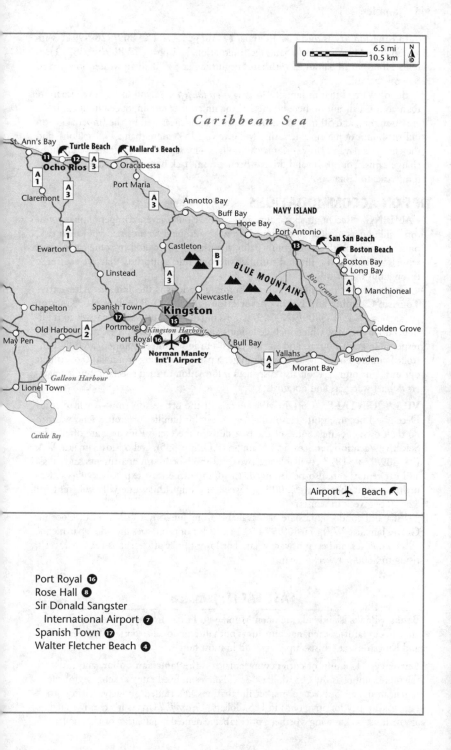

Port Royal ⓯
Rose Hall ⑧
Sir Donald Sangster
  International Airport ⑦
Spanish Town ⓱
Walter Fletcher Beach ④

In Kingston, try **Island Car Rentals,** 17 Antigua Ave. (☎ **809/926-5991**), with a branch at Montego Bay's Sangster International Airport (☎ **809/952-5771**). It rents Hondas and Samurais with rates beginning at $59 daily in winter, lowered to $49 off-season.

Be forewarned that in Jamaica *driving is on the left,* and you should exercise more than your usual caution here because of the unfamiliar terrain. Speed limits in town are 30 m.p.h., and 50 m.p.h. outside towns. Gas is measured by the Imperial gallon (a British unit of measurement that will give you 25% more than a U.S. gallon), and the charge is payable only in Jamaican dollars—most stations don't accept credit or charge cards. Your own valid driver's license from back home is acceptable for short-term visits to Jamaica.

TIPS ON ACCOMMODATIONS

CAMPING   Recent attacks against tourists have put a severe damper on many visitors' willingness to sleep in the Jamaican wild. Although you can, at your own risk, pitch a tent beneath any coconut palm, it's usually wiser (and in some cases *much* wiser) to stick to the limited number of bona-fide campsites that are scattered throughout the island.

One source of information about camping options is the **Jamaica Alternative Tourism Camping and Hiking Association (JATCHA),** P.O. Box 216, Kingston 7, Jamaica, W.I. (☎ **809/927-2097**). This organization offers alternatives to traditional luxury resorts, which include lodgings in old plantation houses, run-down but respectable guest houses, and in rare cases, outdoor camping under carefully controlled circumstances. For $15 you can get a pamphlet listing around 100 overnight options. The organization also dispenses information to such special-interest travelers as bird-watchers and botanists.

VILLA RENTALS   Certain villa rentals in the off-season (mid-April to mid-December) become quite reasonable, especially for families or groups who want to do their own cooking. Some of the best deals in the Ocho Rios area are offered by **Selective Vacation Services,** 154 Main St. (P.O. Box 335), Ocho Rios, Jamaica, W.I. (☎ **809/974-5187**). Available are two- and three-bedroom apartments and villas, and car rentals can also be arranged. In summer, the least expensive villa, a two-bedroom unit, begins at $2,000 per week, although this same villa will rent for $2,500 per week in winter.

Villa and condo rentals are also available from **Jamswi,** 135 Main St., Coconut Grove, Jamaica, W.I. (☎ **809/974-7114**). Its list of properties includes apartments, villa complexes, and even private villas. The lowest price off-season is $700 per week, rising to $800 per week in winter.

FAST FACTS: Jamaica

Banks   Banks islandwide are open Monday to Friday from 9am to 5pm. There are Bank of Jamaica exchange bureaus at both international airports (Montego Bay and Kingston), at cruise-ship piers, and in most hotels.

Currency   The unit of currency in Jamaica is the **Jamaican dollar,** and it uses the same symbol as the U.S. dollar, "$." There is no fixed rate of exchange for the Jamaican dollar. Subject to market fluctuations, it's traded publicly. Visitors to Jamaica can pay for any goods in U.S. dollars. *Be careful!* Unless it's clearly stated, always insist on knowing whether a price is being quoted in Jamaican or U.S. dollars.

In this guide we've generally followed the price-quotation policy of the establishment, whether in Jamaican dollars or U.S. dollars. For clarity, we have used the symbol "J$" to denote prices in Jamaican dollars; the conversion into U.S. dollars follows in parentheses. When dollar figures stand alone, they are always U.S. currency.

Jamaican currency is issued in banknotes of J$1, J$2, J$5, J$10, J$20, J$50, and J$100. Coins are 1¢, 5¢, 10¢, 20¢, 25¢, and 50¢. Currently (but subject to change), the exchange rate of Jamaican currency is J$35 to $1 U.S. (J$1 equals about 2.8¢ U.S.).

Customs   Do *not* bring in (or take out) illegal drugs from Jamaica. Your luggage is searched. *Ganja* (marijuana)-sniffing police dogs are stationed at the airport. Otherwise, you can bring in most items intended for personal use.

Documents   U.S. and Canadian residents do not need passports, but must have proof of citizenship (or permanent residency) and a return or ongoing ticket. In lieu of a passport, an original birth certificate or a certified copy, plus a photo ID, will do. A voter registration card is acceptable in some cases, but only if you have a notarized affidavit of citizenship, plus photo ID. Always double-check, however, with the airline you're flying. Sometimes *it* won't accept a voter registration card. Other visitors, including British subjects, need passports, good for a maximum stay of 6 months.

Immigration cards, needed for bank transactions and currency exchange, are given to visitors at the airport arrivals desks.

Drugs   Although commonly sold in Jamaica, drugs (including marijuana) are illegal and imprisonment is the penalty for possession. You will almost certainly be approached by people selling ganja, and though it's very common, you should still use common sense. Whatever you choose to do on your vacation, don't even think about trying to bring marijuana home. Customs agents patrol the airport with drug-sniffing dogs.

Drugstores   In Montego Bay, try **McKenzie's Drug Store,** 16 Strand St. (☎ **809/952-2467**); in Ocho Rios, **Great House Pharmacy,** Brown's Plaza (☎ **809/974-2352**); and in Kingston, **Moodie's Pharmacy,** in the New Kingston Shopping Centre (☎ **809/926-4174**). Prescriptions are accepted by local pharmacies only if issued by a Jamaican doctor. Hotels have doctors on call. If you need any particular medicine or treatment, bring evidence, such as a letter from your own physician.

Electricity   Most places have the standard electrical voltage of 110, as in the United States. However, some establishments operate on 220 volts, 50 cycles. If your hotel is on a different current from your U.S.-made appliance, ask for a transformer and adapter.

Embassies   The Embassy of the **United States** is at the Jamaica Mutual Life Centre, 2 Oxford Rd., Kingston 5 (☎ **809/929-4850**). The High Commission of **Canada** is in the Mutual Security Bank Building, 30–36 Knutsford Blvd., Kingston 5 (☎ **809/926-1500**), and there's a Canadian Consulate at 29 Gloucester Ave., Montego Bay (☎ **809/952-6198**). The High Commission of the **United Kingdom** is at 28 Trafalgar Rd., Kingston 10 (☎ **809/926-9050**). Calling embassies or consulates in Jamaica is a daunting challenge. Phones will ring and ring before being picked up—that is, if they're answered at all. Extreme patience is needed to reach a live voice on the other side.

Emergencies For the **police and air rescue,** dial ☎ **119;** to report a **fire** or call an **ambulance,** dial ☎ **110.**

Hospitals In Kingston, the **University Hospital** is at Mona (☎ **809/927-1620**); in Montego Bay, the **Cornwall Regional Hospital** is at Mount Salem (☎ **809/952-5100**); and in Port Antonio, the **Port Antonio General Hospital** is at Naylor's Hill (☎ **809/993-2646**).

Information Before you go, you can obtain information from the **Jamaica Tourist Board** at the following U.S. addresses: 500 N. Michigan Ave., Suite 1030, Chicago, IL 60611 (☎ **312/527-4800**); 1320 S. Dixie Hwy., Suite 1101, Coral Gables, FL 33146 (☎ **305/665-0557**); 3440 Wilshire Blvd., Suite 805, Los Angeles, CA 90010 (☎ **213/384-1123**); and 801 Second Ave., New York, NY 10017 (☎ **212/856-9727**). In Atlanta information can be obtained on the phone by dialing ☎ **770/452-7799**. In Canada, contact the tourist board at 1 Eglinton Ave. E., Suite 616, Toronto, ON M4P 3A1 (☎ **416/482-7850**). Britishers can contact the London office: 1–2 Prince Consort Rd., London SW7 4BZ (☎ **0171/224-0505**).

Once on Jamaica, you'll find tourist board offices at 2 St. Lucia Ave., Kingston (☎ **809/929-9200**); Cornwall Beach, St. James, Montego Bay (☎ **809/952-4425**); Shop no. 29, Coral Seas Plaza, Negril, Westmoreland (☎ **809/957-4243**); in the Ocean Village Shopping Centre, Ocho Rios, St. Ann (☎ **809/974-2582**); in City Centre Plaza, Port Antonio (☎ **809/993-3051**); and in the Hendriks Building, 2 High St., Black River (☎ **809/965-2074**).

Marriages You can get a marriage license after 24 hours' residence on the island, and then marry as soon as it can be arranged. You'll need your birth certificate, and, where applicable, divorce documents or death certificates. All documents must be properly certified—ordinary photocopies will not be accepted. Most Jamaican hotels will make arrangements for your wedding and license. Otherwise, the Jamaica Tourist Board can assist you in meeting and making arrangements with a government marriage officer.

Nudity Nude bathing is allowed at a number of hotels, clubs, and beaches (especially in Negril), but only where there are signs stating that swimsuits are optional. Elsewhere, the law will not even allow topless sunbathing.

Safety You can get into a lot of trouble on Jamaica or you can have a carefree vacation—much depends on what you do and where you go. The major hotels have security guards who protect the grounds. Mishaps have occurred when visitors have accepted invitations extended by strangers on the beach "to see the real Jamaica." Traveling around Jamaica calls for more precaution than on most islands in the West Indies. Many robberies occur when beach buffs leave their valuables unattended while they go for a swim. The second major form of robbery occurs when luggage or other valuables are left in a car, even the locked trunk of a vehicle.

The U.S. State Department, in a travel advisory, stated: "Crime in Kingston, Jamaica's capital, exceeds the level of criminal activity elsewhere in the Caribbean." Visitors are warned not to walk around alone at night. Caution is also advisable in many north-coast tourist areas, especially remote houses and isolated villas that can't afford to employ security forces. For the latest **travel advisories,** call the U.S. State Department (☎ **202/647-5225**).

Shopping Hours Hours vary widely, but as a general rule most business establishments are open Monday to Friday from 8:30am to 4:30 or 5pm. Some shops are open on Saturday until noon.

Taxes The government imposes a 12% room tax per night. You'll be charged a J$400 ($11.20) departure tax at the airport, payable in either Jamaican or U.S. dollars. There's also a 15% tax on rental cars and a 15% tax on all overseas telephone calls.

Time Jamaica is on eastern standard time year-round. However, when the U.S. is on daylight saving time, at 6am in Miami it's 5am in Kingston.

Tips and Service Many Jamaicans depend heavily on tips for their living. A general 10% or 15% is expected in hotels and restaurants on occasions when you would normally tip. Some places add a service charge to the bill. Tipping is not allowed in the all-inclusive hotels.

Water It's usually safe to drink piped-in water, islandwide, as it's filtered and chlorinated; however, it's more prudent to drink bottled water, if available.

Weather Expect temperatures around 80° to 90° Fahrenheit on the coast. Winter is a little cooler. In the mountains it can get as low as 40°. There's generally a breeze, which in winter is noticeably cool. The rainy periods in general are October through November (although this can extend into December) and May and June. Normally rain comes in short, sharp showers; then the sun shines.

1 Montego Bay

Montego Bay first attracted tourists in the 1940s when Doctor's Cave Beach was popular with the wealthy who bathed in the warm water fed by mineral springs. The town, now Jamaica's second-largest city, is on the northwestern coast of the island. In spite of the large influx of visitors, it still retains its own identity with a thriving business and commercial center, and it functions as the market town for most of western Jamaica. It has cruise-ship piers and a growing industrial center at the free port. The history of Mo Bay, as the islanders call it, goes back to 1494 when it was discovered as an Arawak settlement.

Because Montego Bay has its own airport, the Donald Sangster International Airport, those who vacation here have little need to visit Kingston, the island's capital, unless they're seeking its cultural pleasures. Otherwise, you have everything in Mo Bay, the most cosmopolitan of Jamaica's resorts.

WHERE TO STAY
DOUBLES FOR LESS THAN $50

Ocean View Guest House. 26 Sunset Blvd. (P.O. Box 210), Montego Bay, Jamaica, W.I. ☎ **809/952-2662.** 13 rms. Winter, $29.50 single; $36–$38 double. Off-season, $23.30 single; $29.50–$31.50 double. No credit cards.

Established in the 1960s when the grandparents of the present owners began to rent extra rooms in their home, this super-bargain is half a mile west of the airport and the same distance from the public beach. You'll need a taxi to reach this place, although the owner sometimes provides his own transportation to and from the airport. The simple bedrooms are supplemented with a small library and satellite TV room. All but two of the rooms are air-conditioned and all have fans, and most open onto a veranda or the spacious front porch. It's quietest at the back. The owner will arrange island tours, tennis, golf, and water sports for you. Dinners are offered only to guests, and reservations must be made by 2pm. T-bone steak, pork chops, roast chicken, and fresh fish are served. There are two major drawbacks here—cleanliness and service are minimal, and the hotel doesn't take advance reservations. This means,

Montego Bay

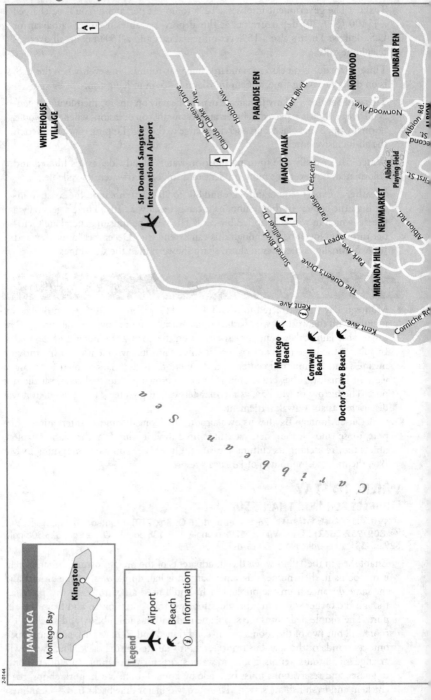

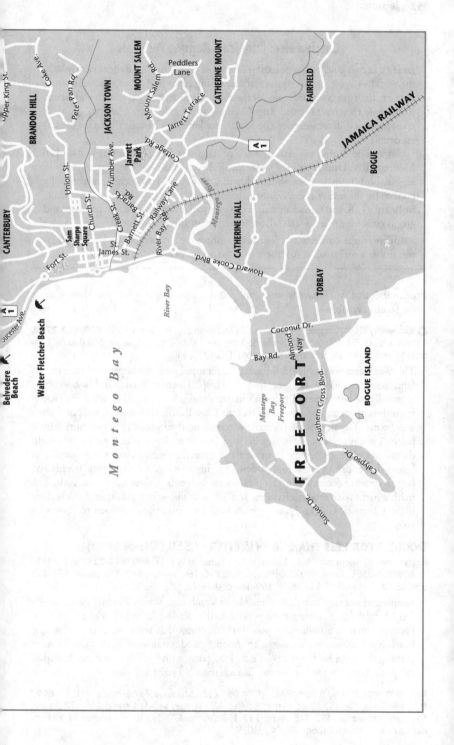

351

Catch a Fire: Jamaica's Reggae Festivals

Jamaica comes alive to the pulsating sounds of reggae during **Reggae Sunsplash,** the world's largest annual reggae festival, taking place in August. This week-long music extravaganza features some of the most prominent reggae groups and artists. In the past they have inclued Ziggy Marley, and the Melody Makers. Sunsplash takes place at different venues; check with the Jamaican Tourist Board for the latest details.

Some time during the second week of August a **Reggae Sunfest** is staged in Montego Bay. Usually this is a 4-day musical event. Some of the biggest names in reggae, both from Jamaica and worldwide, perform. Many local hotels are fully booked for the festivals, so advance reservations are necessary. The Jamaican Tourist Board's U.S. and Canadian offices can give you information about packages and group rates for the festivals. Call for information about Sumfest.

Other reggae concerts and festivals featuring top performers are held throughout the year on Jamaica. Ask the tourist board for details.

---

of course, that you'll have to wait until you're on the island before you know if there are rooms available.

✪ **Ridgeway Guest House.** 34 Queen's Dr., Montego Bay, Jamaica, W.I. ☎ **809/952-2709.** 10 rms. A/C TV TEL. Winter, $30 single; $50 double. Off-season, $25 single; $40 double. Children 11 and under stay free in parents' room. DC, DISC, MC, V.

This warm and hospitable B&B retreat, far removed from the impersonal megaresorts (and their megaprices), is a great find. The helpful owners, Brenda and Bryan (Bryan is actually his last name as he doesn't like to divulge his first name), offer free pickup from the airport and transport to Doctor's Cave Beach, a 15-minute walk or 5 minutes by car. The Bryans are constantly improving their property, a two-story white-painted building set among flowers and fruit trees from which guests may help themselves, perhaps having an orange and grapefruit salad. Guests may partake of before-dinner drinks in the roof garden, enjoying a view of the airport and ocean. The large rooms are decorated in a tropical motif with two or three queen-size beds. The marble baths have modern fixtures, and TV is available in a public area. Next door is the Chatwick Garden Hotel, with a pool and restaurant, all open to Ridgeway guests.

DOUBLES FOR LESS THAN $65 (WINTER) / $50 (OFF-SEASON)

Belvedere. 33 Gloucester Ave., Montego Bay, Jamaica, W.I. ☎ **800/814-2237** in the U.S., or 809/952-0593. Fax 809/979-0498. 27 rms. A/C TEL. Winter, $60–$70 single; $65–$75 double. Off-season, $45–$55 single; $50–$60 double. AE, DC, MC, V.

Simple and uncomplicated, this small hotel stands near Walter Fletcher Beach. Modestly furnished, its rooms have private baths, air-conditioning, and telephones. Facilities include a swimming pool and restaurant that serves breakfast only. The beach is a 5-minute walk away, with shopping and restaurants nearby. On Tuesday evening the hotel hosts a manager's cocktail party with live entertainment featuring calypso music. On the last Sunday of each month a jazz band plays.

Blue Harbour Hotel. 6 Sewell Ave. (P.O. Box 212), Montego Bay, Jamaica, W.I. ☎ **809/ 952-5445.** Fax 809/952-8930. 16 rms, 8 suites. A/C. Winter, $40–$64 single; $56–$72 double; $94 suite. Off-season, $29–$48 single; $42–$58 double; $70–$75 suite. Children 11 and under stay free in parents' room. AE, DC, MC, V.

On a hillside overlooking the harbor, midway between the airport and town off Route A1, this small hotel offers basic service in a friendly atmosphere. The rooms are simple with air-conditioning and full bathrooms, whereas the suites also contain TVs and kitchenettes. For dinner the hotel offers the option of a dine-around plan that includes 10 of Montego Bay's restaurants. (Transportation to and from the restaurants is provided.) The facilities include a swimming pool, an air-conditioned lounge, and a coffee shop serving breakfast and a light lunch. Tennis is nearby and arrangements can be made for golf, deep-sea fishing, scuba diving, and island tours. The beach is a 5-minute walk from the hotel, which provides free transportation to and from the shore.

Verney House Resort. 3 Leader Ave. (P.O. Box 18), Montego Bay, Jamaica, W.I. ☎ **809/ 952-2875.** Fax 809/979-2944. 25 rms. A/C. Winter, $45 single; $55 double; $75 triple; $95 quad. Off-season, $40 single; $50 double; $60 triple; $80 quad. MAP $18 per person extra. AE, MC, V.

In a verdant setting just far enough away from the urban congestion of Montego Bay, this hotel offers a feeling of remote calm. You can still get to where the action is by taking a short trek downhill, or head to one of several beaches, such as Cornwall Beach, that are only 5 minutes away on foot. The two-story structure was originally built on steeply sloping land in 1945. In 1995 the pastel-colored bedrooms were freshened up. Each accommodation has white walls, simple furnishings, and a sense that you're in a private home. The restaurant (the Kit-Kat) and bar overlook the swimming pool. The staff is usually gracious.

DOUBLES FOR LESS THAN $90 (WINTER) / $70 (OFF-SEASON)

✪ **Coral Cliff Hotel.** 165 Gloucester Ave. (P.O. Box 253), Montego Bay, Jamaica, W.I. ☎ **809/952-4130.** Fax 809/952-6532. 32 rms. A/C TEL. Winter, $67 single; $80–$90 double; $92–$112 triple. Off-season, $70 single; $60–$80 double; $80–$90 triple. MC, V.

For value received, the Coral Cliff Hotel may be your best bet in Montego Bay. The hotel grew from a colonial-style building that was once the private home of Harry M. Doubleday (of the famous publishing family). It's located about a mile west of the center of town but only 2 minutes from Doctor's Cave Beach. The Coral Cliff also offers its own luxurious swimming pool. Many of the light, airy, and spacious bedrooms open onto a balcony with a view of the sea. The rates are modest for what you get. The hotel's breeze-swept restaurant is appropriately called the Verandah Terrace, and it overlooks the bay. The food is good, too, featuring local produce and fresh seafood whenever available.

Royal Court Hotel. Sewell Ave. (P.O. Box 195), Montego Bay, Jamaica, W.I. ☎ **809/ 952-4531.** Fax 809/952-4532. 20 rms, 3 suites. A/C TEL. Winter, $70 single; $90 double; $135 suite. Off-season, $60 single; $70 double; $95 suite. AE, MC, V.

This reasonable accommodation is located on the hillside overlooking Montego Bay, above Gloucester Avenue and off Park Avenue. The rooms are furnished with bright, tasteful colors, and all have patios; the larger ones have fully equipped kitchenettes. Meals are served in the Pool Bar and Eatery. Its restaurant, Leaf of Life, specializes in vegetarian food among other selections. Free transportation is provided to the town, the beach, and the tennis club. This hotel is clean and attractive, has a charming atmosphere, and is a good value. New amenities and facilities include massage, gym, steamroom, Jacuzzi, TV room, conference room, and a doctor on the premises.

✪ **Toby Inn.** 1 Kent Ave. (P.O. Box 467), Montego Bay, Jamaica, W.I. ☎ **809/952-4370.** Fax 809/952-6591. 65 rms. A/C. Winter, $65 single; $75 double. Off-season, $55 single; $65 double. Extra person $25–$30. AE, MC, V.

Its location beside the busy main thoroughfare of downtown Montego Bay is either an advantage or a disadvantage, depending on how easy you want your access to the resort's inexpensive bars and restaurants. Despite the traffic and crowds around it, the almond, mango, and grapefruit trees that surround the two-story main building, a series of individual cottages, and the swimming pool, create a sense of rural isolation. You'll also find a restaurant serving Jamaican cuisine, a gift shop, a minigym, a bandstand for the rare concerts presented here, and a bar where a TV set provides at least some of the entertainment. The bedrooms have either a terrace or a balcony. The hotel is a 5-minute walk from Doctor's Cave Beach.

WORTH A SPLURGE

✪ **Richmond Hill Inn.** Union St. (P.O. Box 362), Montego Bay, Jamaica, W.I. ☎ **809/952-3859.** Fax 809/952-6106. 15 rms, 5 suites. A/C TEL. Winter, $80 single; $115–$118 double; $198 one-bedroom suite for up to four; $256 two-bedroom suite for up to four; $290–$350 three-bedroom penthouse suite for up to eight. Off-season, $75 single; $90 double; $168 one-bedroom suite for up to four; $220 two-bedroom suite for up to four; $250–$320 three-bedroom penthouse suite for up to eight. Extra person $27–$32; MAP $41–$48 per person extra. AE, MC, V.

Set high on a forested slope, 500 feet above the commercial center of Montego Bay, this is the much-restored site of what was originally built as the Dewar family (the scions of scotch) homestead. Very little of the original villa remains, but what you'll find is a hilltop eyrie ringed with urn-shaped concrete balustrades, a pool terrace suitable for sundowner cocktails, and comfortable, slightly fussy bedrooms with lace-trimmed curtains, homey bric-a-brac, and pastel colors. If you're an avid beachlover, know in advance that the nearest beach (Doctor's Cave Beach) is a 15-minute drive away. Maid and laundry service are included in the rates, and there's both a bar and a restaurant (featuring vistas over the blinking lights of Montego Bay).

Winged Victory Hotel. 5 Queen's Dr., Montego Bay, Jamaica, W.I. ☎ **809/952-3892.** Fax 809/952-5986. 16 rms, 8 suites. A/C. Winter, $90–$100 single or double; $175–$225 suite. Off-season, $60–$80 single or double; $110–$150 suite. MAP $35 per person extra. AE, MC, V.

On a hillside road in Montego Bay, in the Miranda Hill District, this tall and modern hotel delays revealing its true beauty until you pass through its comfortable public rooms into a Mediterranean-style courtyard in back. Here, urn-shaped balustrades enclose a terraced garden, a pool, and a veranda looking over the faraway crescent of Montego Bay. The veranda's best feature is the Calabash Restaurant. The owner, Roma Chin Sue, added hotel rooms to her already well-known restaurant in 1985. All but five have a private balcony or veranda, along with an eclectic decor that's part Chinese, part colonial, and part Iberian.

WHERE TO EAT

The Montego Bay area has some of the finest—and most expensive—dining on the island. But if you're watching your wallet and don't have a delicate stomach, you'll find that food is often sold right on the street. For example, on Kent Avenue you might try authentic jerk pork. Here you can get seasoned spareribs grilled over charcoal fires and sold with extra-hot sauce; order a Red Stripe beer to go with it. Cooked shrimp are also sold on the streets of Mo Bay; they don't look it, but they're very spicy, so be warned. If you have an efficiency unit with a kitchenette, you can cook fresh lobster or the "catch of the day" bought from Mo Bay fishers.

The Brewery. In Miranda Ridge Plaza, Gloucester Ave. ☎ **809/940-2433.** Main courses J$180–J$590 ($5.05–$16.50). AE, MC, V. Daily 11am–"until." AMERICAN/JAMAICAN.

This is more a bar than a full-scale restaurant, but lunch and dinner are both served. The basic hamburgers, salads, and sandwiches are available, and there's also a nightly

Jamaican dinner special, a bargain at about $6. You can enjoy drinks and your meal on the outside patio overlooking the ocean. The best time to come for drinks is during happy hour, from 4 to 6pm daily. Drinks made with local liquor are all half price. If you're really daring, you might want to try the bartender's specialty "fire water"; he won't disclose the ingredients, but promises that it lives up to its name. On Saturday night, live entertainment is offered, and the bar has karaoke on Tuesday and Friday.

Le Chalet. 32 Gloucester Ave. ☎ **809/952-5240.** Main courses $2.25–$16 at lunch, $4.50–$16 at dinner. AE, MC, V. Mon–Sat noon–10pm. INTERNATIONAL/CHINESE/JAMAICAN.

Set in the densest concentration of stores and souvenir shops of Montego Bay's "tourist strip," this high-ceilinged restaurant lies across Gloucester Avenue from the sea, and looks somewhat like a Howard Johnson's. Food is served in copious and well-prepared portions, and includes a lunchtime selection of burgers, sandwiches, platters of barbecued ribs, and salads, and a more substantial selection of evening platters. These might include chicken platters, steaks, fresh fish, and lobster, which seems to taste best here if prepared with Jamaican curry. The staff is articulate and helpful, and proud of their straightforward and surprisingly well-prepared cuisine.

The Native Restaurant. Gloucester Ave. ☎ **809/979-2769.** Reservations recommended. Main courses $9–$26. AE, MC, V. Daily 7:30am–10pm. JAMAICAN.

Open to the breezes, this casual restaurant with panoramic views serves some of the finest Jamaican dishes in the area. You can have a drink at the bamboo bar, with its extensive collection of international wines, and go for a swim in the restaurant pool between courses. Appetizers include jerk reggae chicken and ackee and saltfish, or smoked marlin. This can be followed by such old favorites as steamed fish, or fried or jerk chicken. The most tropical offering is "goat in a boat" (that is, a pineapple shell). A more recent specialty is Boononoonoos; billed as "A Taste of Jamaica," it's a big platter with a little bit of everything—meats and several kinds of fish and vegetables. Although fresh desserts are prepared daily, you may prefer to finish with a Jamaican Blue Mountain coffee.

The Pelican. At the Pelican, Gloucester Ave. ☎ **809/952-3171.** Reservations recommended. Main courses $5–$23. AE, DC, MC, V. Daily 7am–11pm. JAMAICAN.

A Montego Bay landmark, the Pelican has been serving good food at reasonable prices for more than a quarter of a century. It's ideal for families, as it keeps long hours. Many diners come here at lunch for one of the well-stuffed sandwiches, or they may order juicy burgers and barbecued chicken. You can also select from a wide array of Jamaican dishes, including stewed peas and rice, curried goat, Caribbean fish, fried chicken, and curried lobster. A "meatless menu" including such dishes as a vegetable plate or vegetable chili is also featured. Sirloin and seafood are also available, and the soda fountain serves old-fashioned sundaes with real whipped cream, making it about the best "cool for kids" recommendation at the resort.

✪ **Pork Pit.** 27 Gloucester Ave. ☎ **809/952-1046.** 1 pound of jerk pork $10. No credit cards. Daily 11am–11:30pm. JAMAICAN.

The Pork Pit is the best place to go for the famous Jamaican jerk pork and jerk chicken, and the location is right in the heart of Montego Bay, near Walter Fletcher Beach. In fact, many beach buffs come over here for a big lunch. Prices are reasonable. Picnic tables encircle the building, and everything is open-air and informal. The menu also includes steamed roast fish. A half-pound of jerk meat, served with a baked yam or baked potato and a bottle of Red Stripe, is usually sufficient for a meal.

WORTH A SPLURGE

Calabash Restaurant. In the Winged Victory Hotel, 5 Queen's Dr. ☎ **809/952-3892.** Reservations recommended. Main courses $6–$25. AE, MC, V. Daily noon–2:30pm and 6–10pm. INTERNATIONAL/JAMAICAN.

Perched on the hillside road in Montego Bay 500 feet above the distant sea, this well-established restaurant has amused and entertained Peter O'Toole, Robert McNamara, Leonard Bernstein, Francis Ford Coppola, and Roger Moore. More than 25 years ago the owner, Roma Chin Sue, established its Mediterranean-style courtyard and its elegantly simple eagle's-nest patio as a restaurant. The seafood, Jamaican classics, and international favorites include curried goat, lobster dishes, the house specialty of mixed seafood en coquille (served with a cheese-and-brandy sauce), and a year-round version of a Jamaican Christmas cake.

✪ Norma at the Wharfhouse. Reading Rd. ☎ **809/979-2745.** Reservations recommended. Main courses $26–$32. MC, V. Tues–Wed 6:30–10pm, Thurs–Sun noon–3:30pm and 6:30–10pm. Drive 15 minutes west of the town center along Rte. A1. NOUVELLE JAMAICAN.

Set in a coral-stone warehouse whose 2-foot-thick walls are bound together with molasses and lime, this is the finest restaurant in Montego Bay, a favorite of many of Jamaica's visiting celebrities. Built in 1780, it was restored by Millicent Rogers, heiress of the Standard Oil fortune, and now serves as the north-shore domain of Norma Shirley, one of Jamaica's foremost restaurateurs. You can request a table either on the large pier built on stilts over the coral reef (where a view of Montego Bay glitters in the distance) or in an elegantly formal early 19th-century dining room illuminated only with flickering candles. Before- or after-dinner drinks are served in the restaurant or in an informal bar in a separate building, much favored by local clients, the Wharf Rat. Service in the restaurant is impeccable and the food is praised throughout the island.

Menu specialties include grilled deviled crab backs, smoked marlin with papaya sauce, chicken breast with callaloo, nuggets of lobster in a mild curry sauce, and chateaubriand larded with pâté in a peppercorn sauce. Dessert might be a rum-and-raisin cheesecake or a piña-colada mousse.

Pier 1. Howard Cooke Blvd. ☎ **809/952-2452.** Main courses $15–$25. AE, MC, V. Mon–Fri 9:30am–11pm, Sat 1pm–midnight, Sun 4pm–midnight. SEAFOOD.

One of the major dining and entertainment hubs of Mo Bay was built on landfill in the bay. Fisherfolk bring fresh lobster to the restaurant, which the chef prepares in a number of ways, including Créole style or curried. You might begin with one of the typically Jamaican soups such as conch chowder or red pea (actually red bean). At lunch the hamburgers are the juiciest in town, or you might find the quarter-decker steak sandwich with mushrooms equally tempting. The chef also prepares such famous island dishes as jerk pork or chicken and Jamaican red snapper. Finish your meal with a slice of moist rum cake. You can drink or dine on the ground floor, open to the sea breezes, but most guests seem to prefer the more formal second floor. If you call, the staff can arrange to have you picked up in a minivan at most hotels (you're also returned). Although the place remains a local favorite and its waterfront setting is appealing, service is very laid-back.

BEACHES, GOLF, RAFTING & OTHER OUTDOOR PURSUITS

BEACHES   Cornwall Beach (☎ 809/952-3463) is a long stretch of white-sand beach with dressing cabañas. Admission to the beach is $2 for adults, $1 for children, for the entire day. A bar and cafeteria offer refreshments. It's open daily from 9am to 5pm.

Across from the Doctor's Cave Beach Hotel, **Doctor's Cave Beach,** on Gloucester Avenue (☎ **809/952-2566**), helped launch Mo Bay as a resort in the 1940s. Admission to the beach is $2 for adults, half price for children 12 and under. Dressing rooms, chairs, umbrellas, and rafts are available from 8:30am to 5:30pm daily.

One of the premier beaches of Jamaica, **Walter Fletcher Beach** (☎ **809/952-5783**), in the heart of Mo Bay, is noted for its tranquil waters, which makes it a particular favorite for families with children. Changing rooms are available, as is lifeguard service. You can have lunch here in a restaurant. The beach is open daily from 9am to 5pm, with an admission charge of $1 for adults, half price for children.

Frankly, you may want to skip all these public beaches entirely and head instead for the **Rose Hall Beach Club** (☎ **809/953-2323**), lying on the main road 11 miles east of Montego Bay. It's positioned on half a mile of secure, secluded white-sand beach with crystal-clear water. The club offers a full restaurant, two beach bars, a covered pavilion, an open-air dance area, showers, rest rooms, and changing facilities, plus beach volleyball courts, various beach games, and a full water-sports activities program. There's also live entertainment. Admission fees are $8 for adults and $5 for children. This beach club is far better equipped than any of the beaches previously recommended. The club is open daily from 10am to 6pm.

DIVING & OTHER WATER SPORTS   **Seaworld Resorts Ltd.,** whose main office is at the Cariblue Hotel, Rose Hall Main Road (☎ **809/953-2180**), operates scuba-diving excursions, plus many other water sports, including sailing and windsurfing. Its scuba dives plunge to offshore coral reefs, among the most spectacular in the Caribbean. There are three certified dive guides, one dive boat, and all the necessary equipment for either inexperienced or already-certified divers. Most dives begin at $35, $50 for night dives.

GOLF   The course at the **Wyndham Rose Hall Resort,** Rose Hall (☎ **809/953-2650**), is an unusual and challenging seaside and mountain course. The back 9 are the most scenic and interesting, rising into steep slopes and deep ravines on Mount Zion. A fully stocked pro shop, a clubhouse, and a professional staff are among the amenities. Nonresidents of the Wyndham pay $60 for 18 holes and $40 for 9 holes. Mandatory cart rental costs $33 for 18 holes, and the use of a caddy—also mandatory—is another $12 for 18 holes.

The ✪ **Ironshore Golf & Country Club,** Ironshore, St. James, Montego Bay (☎ **809/953-2800**), is another well-known 18-hole, 72-par golf course. Privately owned, it's open to all golfers who show up. Greens fees for 18 holes are $51.75.

HORSEBACK RIDING   A good program for equestrians is offered at the **Rocky Point Riding Stables,** at the Half Moon Club, Rose Hall, Montego Bay (☎ **809/953-2286**). Housed in what's the most beautiful barn and stables on Jamaica, built in the colonial Caribbean style in 1992, it offers around 30 horses and a helpful staff. A 90-minute beach or mountain ride costs $50, whereas a 2¹/₂-hour combination ride (including treks along hillsides, forest trails, beaches, and ending with a saltwater swim) goes for $70.

RAFTING   **Mountain Valley Rafting,** 31 Gloucester Ave. (☎ **809/956-0020**), offers rafting excursions on the Great River which depart from the Lethe Plantation, about 10 miles south of Montego Bay. Rafts are available for $36 for one or two participants as part of trips that last about an hour and operate daily from 8:30am to 4:30pm. Rafts are composed of bamboo trunks with a raised dais to sit on. In some cases a small child can accompany two adults on the same raft, although due caution should be exercised if you choose to do this. Ask about pickup by taxi at the end of the rafting run to return you to your rented car. Another option is available for guests of local hotels who want to be picked up by van at their hotels. For $45 per person, a half-day experience will include transportation to and from your hotel, an hour's rafting, lunch, a garden tour of the Lethe property, and a taste of Jamaican liqueur.

TENNIS The **Wyndham Rose Hall Resort,** Rose Hall (☎ **809/953-2650**), outside Montego Bay, offers six hard-surface courts, each lit for night play. As a courtesy, nonresidents are sometimes invited to play for free, but permission has to be obtained from the manager.

The **Half Moon Golf, Tennis, and Beach Club,** outside Montego Bay (☎ **809/953-2211**), has the finest tennis courts in the area—13 state-of-the-art courts, 7 of which are lit for night games. The pro shop, which accepts reservations for court times, is open daily from 7am to 8pm. If you want to play after those hours, you switch on the lights yourself. Non–hotel guests must purchase a day pass ($40 per person) at the front desk, which gives you access to the resort's tennis courts, gym, sauna, Jacuzzi, pools, and beach facilities.

The **Tryall Golf, Tennis, and Beach Club,** St. James (☎ **809/956-5660**), offers nine hard-surface courts—three lit for night play—near its Great House. Nonguests pay $25 per hour. You'll have to pay $12 per hour extra for lights at night.

SEEING THE SIGHTS
A BIRD-WATCHERS HAVEN

Rocklands Wildlife Station. Anchovy, St. James. ☎ **809/952-2009.** Admission J$320 ($8.95). Daily 2:30–5pm.

This sanctuary was established by Lisa Salmon, known as the Bird Lady of Anchovy, and it attracts nature-lovers and bird-watchers. It's a unique experience to have a Jamaican doctor bird perch on your finger to drink syrup, to feed small doves and finches millet from your hand, and to watch dozens of other birds flying in for their evening meal. Don't take children 5 and under, as they tend to worry the birds. Smoking and playing transistor radios are forbidden. Rocklands is about a mile outside Anchovy on the road from Montego Bay.

THE GREAT HOUSES

Occupied by plantation owners, the Great Houses of Jamaica were always built on high ground so that they overlooked the plantation itself and could see the next house in the distance. It was the custom for the owners to offer hospitality to travelers crossing the island by road. Travelers were spotted by the lookout, who noted the rising dust, and bed and food were then made ready for the traveler's arrival.

Barnett Estates and Bellfield Great House. Barnett Estates. ☎ **809/952-2382.** Admission $15. Daily 9:30am–5pm.

Once a totally private estate sprawled across 50,000 acres, this estate and Great House has hosted everybody from President Kennedy to Churchill and even Queen Elizabeth over the years. Now anybody who pays the entrance fee can come in and take a look. The domain of the Kerr-Jarrett family during 300 years of high society, this was once the seat of a massive sugar plantation. At its center is the Bellfield Great House, from the 18th century (not as ornate as Rose Hall, see below). Restored in 1994, it's a grand example of Georgian architecture. Guides in costumes offer narrated tours of the property. After the tour, drop in to the old Sugar Mill Bar for a tall rum punch.

Greenwood Great House. On Rte. A1 (14 miles east of Montego Bay). ☎ **809/953-1077.** Admission $10 adults, $5 children. Daily 9am–6pm.

Some people find Greenwood even more interesting than Rose Hall (see below). Erected between 1780 and 1800, the Georgian-style building was the residence of

Richard Barrett, who was of the same family as Elizabeth Barrett Browning. On display is the original library of the Barrett family, with rare books dating from 1697, along with oil paintings of the Barrett family, china made by Wedgwood for the family, and a rare exhibition of musical instruments in working order, plus a fine collection of antique furniture. The house today is privately owned but open to the public.

✪ **Rose Hall Great House.** On the Rose Hall Hwy. (9 miles east of Montego Bay). ☎ **809/953-2323.** Admission $15 adults, $10 children. Daily 9am–6pm.

Charging a very steep admission, the most famous Great House on Jamaica is the legendary Rose Hall. The subject of at least a dozen Gothic novels, Rose Hall was immortalized in the H. G. deLisser book *White Witch of Rosehall.* The house was built about two centuries ago by John Palmer. However, it was Annie Palmer, wife of the builder's grandnephew, who became the focal point of fiction and fact. Called "Infamous Annie," she was said to have dabbled in witchcraft. She took slaves as lovers, and then killed them off when they bored her. Servants called her "the Obeah woman" (*Obeah* is Jamaican for "voodoo"). Annie was said to have murdered several of her coterie of husbands while they slept, and eventually suffered the same fate herself in a kind of poetic justice. Long in ruins, the house has now been restored and can be visited by the public. Annie's Pub lies on the ground floor.

ORGANIZED TOURS & CRUISES

The **Croydon Plantation,** Catadupa, St. James (☎ 809/979-8267), is a 25-mile ride from Montego Bay. It can be visited on a half-day tour from Montego Bay (or Negril) on Tuesday, Wednesday, and Friday. Included in the price are round-trip transportation from your hotel, a tour of the plantation, a tasting of varieties of pineapple and tropical fruits in season, and a barbecued chicken lunch. Most hotel tour desks can arrange this tour. The cost is $50 for adults and $22.50 for children 12 and under.

Another plantation tour, the **Hilton High Day Tour,** has an office at Beach View Plaza (☎ 809/952-3343). Round-trip transportation on a scenic drive through historic plantation areas is included. Your day starts at an old plantation with a continental breakfast. You can roam around the 100 acres of the plantation and visit the German village of Seaford Town or St. Leonards village nearby. A Jamaican lunch of roast suckling pig with rum punch is served at 1pm. The charge for the day is $50 per person for the plantation tour, breakfast, lunch, and transportation. There's an additional charge of $10 for 30 minutes of horseback riding. Tour days are Tuesday, Wednesday, Friday, and Sunday.

Day and evening cruises are offered aboard the *Calico,* a 55-foot gaff-rigged wooden ketch that sails from Margaritaville on the Montego Bay waterfront. An additional vessel, the *Calico B,* also carries another 40 passengers per boat ride. You can be transported to and from your hotel for either cruise. The day voyage, which departs at 10am and returns at 3pm, provides a day of sailing, sunning, and snorkeling (with equipment supplied), plus a Jamaican buffet lunch served on the beach, all to the sound of reggae and other music. The cruise costs $50 per person and is offered daily. On the *Calico*'s evening voyage, which goes for $25 per person and is offered Wednesday to Saturday from 5 to 7pm, cocktails and wine are served as you sail through sunset. For information and reservations, call Capt. Bryan Langford, North Coast Cruises Ltd. (☎ 809/952-5860). A 3-day notice is recommended.

SHOPPING

When you go shopping in Montego Bay, be prepared for aggressive vendors. Since selling a craft item may mean the difference between whether or not they put something in the stove that night, there's often a feverish attempt to peddle goods to potential customers, all of whom are viewed as rich. Therefore, prepare yourself to be pursued persistently.

Warning: Some so-called "duty-free" prices are actually lower than Stateside prices, but then the government hits you with a 10% "General Consumption Tax" on all items purchased. But you can find good duty-free items here, including Swiss watches, Irish crystal, Italian handbags, Indian silks, and liquors and liqueurs. Appleton's rums are excellent value. Tía Maria (coffee-flavored) and Rumona (rum-flavored) are the best liqueurs. Khus Khus is the local perfume. Jamaican arts and crafts are available throughout the resort and at the Crafts Market (see below).

The main shopping areas are at **Montego Freeport,** within easy walking distance of the pier; the **City Centre** (where most of the duty-free shops are, aside from at the large hotels); and the **Holiday Village Shopping Centre.**

The **Old Fort Craft Park,** a shopping complex with 180 vendors (all licensed by the Jamaica Tourist Board), fronts Howard Cooke Boulevard (up from Gloucester Avenue in the heart of Montego Bay on the site of Fort Montego). A market with a varied assortment of handcrafts, it's ideal browsing country for both souvenirs and more serious purchases. You'll see a selection of wall hangings, hand-woven straw items, and hand-carved wood sculpture—and you can even get your hair braided. If you want some item, also be prepared for some serious negotiation. Persistent bargaining on your part will lead to substantial discounts.

At the **Crafts Market,** near Harbour Street in downtown Montego Bay, you can find a wide selection of handmade souvenirs of Jamaica, including straw hats and bags, wooden platters, straw baskets, musical instruments, beads, carved objects, and toys. That "jipijapa" hat is important if you're going to be out in the island sun.

One of the newest and most intriguing places for shopping is a mall, **Half Moon Plaza,** set on the coastal road about 8 miles east of the commercial center of Montego Bay. This upscale minimall caters to the shopping and gastronomic needs of the residents of one of the region's most elegant hotels, the Half Moon Club. (Residents of the 45 private villas which the hotel administers consider it a convenient boon to the success of their vacations.) On the premises are a bank and about 25 shops, all arranged around a flowering central courtyard, each selling a wide choice of carefully selected merchandise.

Ambiente Art Gallery. 9 Fort St. ☎ **809/952-7919.**

A 100-year-old clapboard cottage set close to the road houses this gallery. The Austrian-born owner, Maria Hitchins, is one of the doyennes of the Montego Bay art scene. She has personally encouraged and developed scores of local fine artworks and prints by local artists.

Blue Mountain Gems Workshop. At the Holiday Village Shopping Centre. ☎ **809/953-2338.**

Here you can take a tour of the workshops to see the process from raw stone to the finished product you can buy later. Wooden jewelry, local carvings, and one-of-a-kind ceramic figurines are also sold.

Golden Nugget. 8 St. James Shopping Centre, Gloucester Ave. ☎ **809/952-7707.**

The Golden Nugget is a duty-free shop with an impressive collection of watches for both women and men, and a fine assortment of jewelry, especially gold chains. The shop also carries leading brand-name cameras and a wide assortment of French perfumes.

Jolie Madame Fashions. 30 City Centre Bldg. ☎ **809/952-3126.**

The racks of clothing for women and girls here might contain evening dresses, casual clothes, and beach attire. Many garments range from $25. Norma McLeod, the designer and founder, is always on hand to arrange custom-made garments.

Klass Kraft Leather Sandals. 44 Fort St. ☎ **809/952-5782.**

Next door to Things Jamaican, this store offers sandals and leather accessories made on location by a team of Jamaican craftspeople. All sandals cost less than $35.

Neville Budhai Paintings. Budhai's Art Gallery, Reading Main Rd., Reading (5 miles east of town on the way to Negril). ☎ **809/979-2568.**

This is the art center of a distinguished artist, Neville Budhai, the president and cofounder of the Western Jamaica Society of Fine Arts. He has a distinct style and captures the special flavor of the island and its people in his artworks. The artist may sometimes be seen sketching or painting in Montego Bay or along the highways of rural Jamaica.

Things Jamaican. 44 Fort St. ☎ **809/952-5605.**

Affiliated with the government and set up to encourage the development of Jamaican arts and crafts, this place showcases the talents of Jamaican artisans. Displayed are a wealth of products, even food and drink, including rums and liqueurs along with jerk seasoning and orange-pepper jelly. Look for Busha Browne's fine Jamaican sauces, especially spicy chutneys or planters spicy piquant sauce. These recipes are prepared and bottled by the Busha Browne Company on Jamaica just as they were 100 years ago. Many items for sale are carved from wood, including sculpture, salad bowls, and trays. You'll also find large hand-woven Jamaican baskets.

Also look for reproductions of the Port Royal collection. Port Royal was buried by an earthquake and tidal wave in 1692. After resting underwater for 275 years, beautiful pewter items were recovered and are here reproduced. They include rat-tail spoons, a spoon with the heads of the monarchs William and Mary, and splay-footed lion rampant spoons. Many items were reproduced faithfully, right down to the pit marks and scratches.

MONTEGO BAY AFTER DARK

There's a lot more to do here at night than go to the discos, but the area certainly has those, too. Much of the entertainment is offered at the various hotels.

Pier 1, Howard Cooke Boulevard (☎ **809/952-2452**), already previewed for its Jamaican cookery (see "Where to Eat," above), might also be your entertainment choice for a night on the town. Friday night sees disco action from 10pm to 5am; the cover charge is J$100 ($2.80).

The Cricket Club, at the Wyndham Rose Hall (☎ **809/953-2650**), is more than just a sports bar. It's a place where people go to meet and mingle with an international crowd. Televised sports, karaoke sing-alongs, tournament darts, and backgammon are all part of the fun. The club is open daily from 7pm to 1am. There's no cover charge.

2 Negril

This once-sleepy village has turned into a tourist mecca, with visitors drawn to its beaches along three well-protected bays: Long Bay, Bloody Bay (now Negril Harbour), and Orange Bay. Negril became famous in the late 1960s when it attracted laid-back American and Canadian youths, who liked the idea of a place with no phones and no electricity; they rented modest digs in little houses on the West End where the local people extended their hospitality. But those days are long gone. Today more sophisticated hotels and all-inclusive resorts such as Hedonism II and Sandals Negril draw a better-heeled and less rowdy crowd, including Europeans.

On the western tip of the island, Negril is now famous for its Seven-Mile Beach. The town is 50 miles and about a 2-hour drive from Montego Bay's airport, along a winding road and past ruins of sugar estates and Great Houses.

At some point you'll want to explore **Booby Key** (or Cay), a tiny islet off the Negril coast. Once it was featured in the Walt Disney film *20,000 Leagues Under the Sea*, but now it's overrun with nudists from Hedonism II.

Chances are, however, you'll stake out your own favorite spot along Negril's ✪ **Seven-Mile Beach.** You don't need to get up for anything, as somebody will be along to serve you. Perhaps it'll be the "banana lady," with a basket of fruit perched on her head. Maybe the "ice cream man" will set up a stand right under a coconut palm. Surely the "beer lady" will find you as she strolls along the beach with a carton of Jamaican beer on her head, and hordes of young men will peddle illegal ganja whether you smoke it or not.

There are really two Negrils: The West End is the site of many little eateries, such as Chicken Lavish, and cottages that still receive visitors. The other Negril is on the east end, the first you approach on the road coming in from Montego Bay. Here are the upscale hotels, with some of the most panoramic beachfronts (such as Negril Gardens).

WHERE TO STAY
DOUBLES FOR LESS THAN $70 (WINTER) / $55 (OFF-SEASON)

Banana Shout. West End Rd. (P.O. Box 4), Negril, Jamaica, W.I. ☎ and fax **809/957-0384.** 7 cottages. Winter, $50–$95 cottage for one or two; $120 cottage for four; $200 cottage for eight. Off-season, $35–$55 cottage for one or two; $70 cottage for four; $160 cottage for eight. MC, V.

Set on 2¹/₂ acres of landscaped grounds with waterfalls, lily ponds, tropical flowers, and fruit trees, this property comprises seven cottages with three units poised on a cliff overlooking the sea. In front of the property is a series of tiered decks with concrete steps leading down the rocks to the surface of the water. The garden cottages are located across the road with private access to the beach. Each of the secluded units contains a kitchenette, ceiling fan, and private bath. The rooms are furnished with locally crafted pieces and artwork from Indonesia and Bali. The best deal at this hideaway is the cottage with the patio barbecue. For a group of eight, each person would only spend $20 to $25, depending on the time of year for your visit. Rick's Café is next door.

✪ **Blue Cave Castle.** Lighthouse Rd., Negril, Jamaica, W.I. ☎ **809/957-4845.** 10 rms. Winter, $50 single; $65 double. Off-season, $35 single; $45 double. Extra person $10. No credit cards.

Filled with a sense of whimsy and fun, this little mock castle has been touted by some wags as the best bargain in the Caribbean. It's been featured by the Jamaica Tourist Board in its TV ads, and the Dallas Cowboy cheerleaders calendar for 1997 was shot here. Battlements and turrets re-create medieval days, and the resort, covering an acre, is built over a cave. There are steps down to the cave from the garden, where local wedding receptions are held regularly. The guest rooms are decorated with handmade mahogany furniture and antique Turkish carpets covering the walls. Many of the objects decorating the "castle" were collected by the owner Susan Evanko during her globetrotting days. Three rooms are air-conditioned, although there are no room phones or TVs. There's no pool either, although you can swim off the cliffs in lieu of a beach. All rooms have sea views, refrigerators, ceiling fans, and balconies. A good restaurant in front is open to the public, but the dining area oceanside is reserved for guests only. You can take breakfast and lunch by the sea and enjoy a daily sunset barbecue.

Thrills. West End (P.O. Box 99, Negril Post Office), Westmoreland, Jamaica, W.I. ☎ **809/ 957-4390.** Fax 809/957-4153. 25 rms. Winter, $60 single; $65 double; $75 triple. Off-season, $45 single; $50 double; $65 triple. MAP $21 per person extra. MC, V.

Southwest of the center of Negril, on sloping, palm-dotted land that descends toward a rocky beach, this is a simple, but well-managed resort. Its centerpiece is a hexagonal tower set adjacent to a low-slung motel-like complex containing the bedrooms. Each room is simply decorated with white walls, island-made mahogany furniture and louvered doors, and tiled floors. An in-house restaurant serves international cuisine. Avid beachlovers negotiate a 10-minute drive (or a 20-minute walk) eastward to the famous sands of Negril's legendary beach. Snorkelers, however, find ample opportunities for pursuing their favorite sport off the low cliffs and caves along the coast. The resort has its own tennis courts, and a wide choice of dive shops and water-sports facilities are nearby.

DOUBLES FOR LESS THAN $90 (WINTER) / $65 (OFF-SEASON)

Devine Destiny. Summerset Rd., West End (P.O. Box 117), Negril, Jamaica, W.I. ☎ **809/ 957-9184.** Fax 809/957-3846. 40 rms, 4 suites. TEL. Winter, $77–$88 single or double; $180 suite. Off-season, $58–$69 single or double; $125 suite. AE, DC, MC. Children 11 and under stay free in parents' room. AE, DC, MC, V.

Lying about 550 yards from the West End cliffs, this funky retreat in a medley of a building styles lies about a 20-minute walk from the beach. There's a shuttle to Seven-Mile Beach if you don't want to walk. The resort is a two-story structure with a terracotta roof surrounded by gardens where wedding receptions are staged. The rooms are furnished in a standard style, and although some are small, all are quite comfortable and contain refrigerators. The suites are the best deal, of course, with ceiling fans, kitchens, living rooms with pull-out beds, TVs, and patios. The most expensive rooms are air-conditioned. All units, regardless of price, have patios or balconies. An on-site restaurant serves simple fare three times a day, and there's both a pool bar and a gazebo bar. Room service and baby-sitting are available, and the hotel has a TV room, sun deck, games room, gift shop, and tour desk.

Home Sweet Home. West End Rd., Negril, Jamaica, W.I. ☎ and fax **800/925-7418** in the U.S., or 809/957-4478. 14 rms. Winter, $90–$100 single or double. Off-season, $65–$80 single or double. Extra person $15; children 11 and under stay free in parents' room. AE, DC, DISC, MC, V.

On the cliff side, this is a cozy down-home place. At times it seems to re-create Negril's hippie heyday of the swinging sixties. You may find your groove here, as the writer Terry McMillan did when she visited many little inns while doing research for her hot seller, *How Stella Got Her Groove Back*. "Home" is a single pink concrete building with a garden with lots of greenery and flowering plants. There's also a pool and a Jacuzzi. When you see the bedrooms, you'll know that many visitors have slept here before you. All accommodations have ceiling fans, a radio and cassette player, and a balcony or veranda, but no TV or phone. There's a sun deck on the cliffs, and swimming, diving, and snorkeling are possible. A simple restaurant serves three inexpensive Jamaican-style meals a day.

Ocean Edge Resort Hotel. West End Rd. (P.O. Box 71), Negril, Jamaica, W.I. ☎ **809/ 957-4362.** Fax 809/957-4842. 23 rms, 4 villas, 1 suite. TV TEL. Winter, $80 single or double; $75 villa; $85 suite. Off-season, $65 single or double; $55 villa; $70 suite. Children 11 and under stay free in parents' unit. AE, MC, V.

Located on a cliff on West End Road across from Kaiser's Café, this hotel offers simple accommodations in a friendly atmosphere. The lodgings are modestly decorated in a tropical motif with hardwood furnishings and a few pictures on the walls. If you must have air-conditioning, don't stay in one of the villa rooms cooled only by ceiling fans. All the accommodations have TVs, telephones, and radios. The suite and villas have kitchenettes. Facilities include a swimming pool, Jacuzzi, and the Seven Seas restaurant, which specializes in fresh seafood. The hotel provides transportation to and from the beach, a 5-minute drive away.

DOUBLES FOR LESS THAN $120 (WINTER) / $85 (OFF-SEASON)

Drumville Cove Resort. West End Rd. (P.O. Box 72), Negril, Jamaica, W.I. ☎ **809/ 957-4369.** Fax 809/929-7291. 20 rms, 5 cottages. Winter, $90–$94 single; $103–$108 double; $85–$99 cottage. Off-season, $36–$49.50 single; $54–$58 double; $54–$63 cottage. AE, MC, V.

The rooms are housed in cream structures trimmed in brown overlooking the sea near the lighthouse, whereas the cottages are scattered throughout the property. All the rooms and cottages have radios, ceiling fans, and private baths, but only seven of the rooms and none of the cottages are air-conditioned; four rooms offer TVs. These basic lodgings are furnished with a mixture of wicker and hardwood and decorated with floral prints. Included on the property is a restaurant serving Jamaican specialties with a few American dishes. The nearest beach is a 5-minute car ride away (the hotel provides transportation), and there's a freshwater swimming pool for guest use.

Firefly Beach Cottages. Norman Manley Blvd. (P.O. Box 54), Negril, Jamaica, W.I. ☎ **800/ 477-9530** in the U.S., or 809/957-4358. Fax 809/957-3447. 19 units. Winter, $88–$115 single; $102–$160 double; $136 two-bedroom apt for four; $140 one-bedroom apt with three double beds for six; $170 two-bedroom apt for eight. Off-season, $44–$90 single; $75–$110 double; $91 two-bedroom apt for four; $92 one-bedroom apt with three double beds for six; $115 two-bedroom apt for eight. AE, MC, V.

With a lot of Jamaican flair, this laid-back hodgepodge of several white concrete and wooden buildings opens directly on the beach. There's even a so-called penthouse in the garden with sleeping lofts. In addition to these, there are various studios and cottages, including one large two-bedroom unit that can sleep up to eight in cramped conditions. Most of the units are cooled by air-conditioning and ceiling fans, and many beds are canopied. When they rent "rooms with a view" here, they mean it: The hotel opens onto a stretch of clothing-optional beach. All rooms have verandas and kitchens as well, but there's no restaurant, although many little eateries are within walking distance. No pool, but the beach is close at hand, and you don't even have to put on your bathing suit to enjoy it.

Jackie's on the Reef. West End Rd., Negril, Jamaica, W.I. ☎ **809/957-4997,** or 718/ 783-6763 in New York State. 3 rms, 1 cottage. Winter, $125 per person. Off-season, $115 per person. Rates include breakfast, dinner, and yoga class. No credit cards.

This is one of the most offbeat places to stay in all of Jamaica. It's like a counterculture "spa"—actually a holistic health retreat housed in a one-story gray stone building called "the temple." The bedrooms are generous in size with mosquito netting draped over the beds in the old plantation style. However, there are no TVs, phones, or air-conditioning (or even fans). But you'll find simple furnishings, such as twin beds and small tables. The yoga classes are conducted on a large porch; other services offered include massage, "scrubs," facials, and something known as "past-life regression and energy balancing." The food is Jamaican style and generous in quality. The hotel lies 7 miles from the nearest beach, but there's a small seawater pool and a ladder down to the reef for swimming. If nothing at the juice bar turns you on, you can always order a Red Stripe. The location is 2¹/₂ miles past the oldest lighthouse in Negril; just keep heading out the West End until you come to the sign. Note that children are not accepted.

Rock Cliff Hotel. West End Rd. (P.O. Box 67), Negril, Jamaica, W.I. ☎ **809/957-4331** or 809/957-4108. 29 rms, 2 suites. A/C. Winter, $100–$125 single; $115–$140 double; $290 suite for two. Off-season, $70–$80 single; $80–$90 double; $170–$190 suite for two. AE, MC, V.

This hotel is one of the better of the dozens of raffish guest houses that lie among the palms and sea grapes west of Negril's center. Set atop a low cliff overlooking the sea, and popular with divers, it features a restaurant, two bars, and a Sunday-night all-you-can-eat lobster buffet. There's a pool on the premises, and you can inch your way down the cliff for sea dips offshore from the rocks, but sea bathers usually trek 2 miles to the nearest beach. The suites (but not the conventional bedrooms) contain kitchenettes. The bedrooms have mahogany furniture, pastel-colored draperies, and off-white walls. Maid service is included, and baby-sitting and laundry can be arranged. There's a Jacuzzi, volleyball and basketball courts, a kiosk for sundries and souvenirs, and a well-recommended PADI-affiliated dive shop.

✪ **Rockhouse.** West End Rd. (P.O Box 24), Negril, Jamaica, W.I. ☎ and fax **809/957-4373.** 14 studios and villas (sleeping up to four). MINIBAR. Winter, $100 studio; $165 villa. Off-season, $85 studio; $120 villa. Extra person $25; children 11 and under stay free in parents' unit. AE, MC, V.

One of the special accommodations on Negril, this little inn stands in stark contrast to the hedonistic all-inclusive resorts. "On the rocks" here means not the way you like your drink but the way you prefer your vacation retreat: secluded and tranquil. A team of young Australians recently restored and expanded this retreat, with thatched roofs capping stone-and-pine huts. The rooms have minibars, ceiling fans, and refrigerators, but no TVs or phones. You'll really feel you're in Jamaica when you go to bed in a mosquito-draped four-poster bed or take a shower in the open air. Mercifully, the toilet facilities are inside, however. A quarter mile from the beach, Rockhouse has a ladder down to a cove where you can swim and snorkel; equipment is available for rent. After a refreshing dip in the pool, you can dine in the open-sided restaurant pavilion that serves spicy local fare three times a day. The restaurant and bar are quite fashionable. It's where you might have found Paul and Linda years ago before they got older and he was knighted Sir Paul McCartney by the queen.

WORTH A SPLURGE

Crystal Waters. Norman Manley Blvd. (P.O. Box 18), Negril Beach, Negril, Jamaica, W.I. ☎ **800/433-3020** in the U.S. and Canada or 809/957-4284. Fax 809/957-4889. 10 villas. A/C TEL. Winter, $125 one-bedroom villa; $170–$250 two-bedroom villa; $340 three-bedroom villa. Off-season, $95 one-bedroom villa; $130–$190 two-bedroom villa; $260 three-bedroom villa. Maximum of two people per room. MC, V.

Located on Negril Beach a 1¹/₂-hour drive from the international airport in Montego Bay, this hotel offers guests simple accommodations at reasonable prices. Nehru Caolsingh owns and operates these villas, which were opened in the mid-1960s. The accommodations are tropically decorated, furnished with a mixture of hardwoods and wicker. The villas include full kitchens, air-conditioning, ceiling fans, and baths. As a bonus, each villa is staffed with a housekeeper who will cook breakfast, lunch, and dinner for you. There's also a freshwater pool.

Foote Prints. Norman Manley Blvd. (P.O. Box 100), Negril, Jamaica, W.I. ☎ **809/957-4300.** Fax 809/957-4301. 30 rms, 1 apt. A/C. Winter, $135–$145 single or double, $165 single or double with kitchenette; $255 apt. Off-season, $85–$95 single or double, $115 single or double with kitchenette; $185 apt. Extra person $30 in winter, $20 off-season. AE, MC, V.

Dane and Audrey Foote started this enterprise with one building in the mid-1980s; it has since expanded to three. Located on Seven-Mile Beach next door to the Swept Away resort, this hostelry offers its best deals during the off-season (mid-April to mid-December). The rooms, four of which contain kitchenettes, are tropically decorated with hardwood furnishings, air-conditioning, and private baths. The hotel's restaurant, Robinson Crusoe's, serves breakfast, lunch, and dinner, specializing in a mix of Jamaican and American dishes. On Friday nights, a barbecue with local bands livens up the place.

Whistling Bird Resort. Norman Manley Blvd., Negril, Jamaica, W.I. ☎ **809/955-4403.** Fax 809/957-4933. 6 one-bedroom and 6 two-bedroom cabins. Winter, $108 cabin for one; $159 cabin for two; $238 cabin for four. Off-season, $81 cabin for one; $119.25 cabin for two; $178.50 cabin for four. Children stay free in parents' cabin. AE, MC, V.

This funky little resort offers a real Jamaican experience. A casual, laid-back, do-it-yourself place, the Whistling Bird offers separate wooden Jamaican-style cabins on the beach surrounded by plants and flowers, offering privacy. Each unit, except for one small cabin on the beach, has its own porch. Furnishings are in a real island style, with ceiling fans, wicker, and tropical prints. The resort is very family oriented, so children stay free here and cribs and high chairs are available, as is baby-sitting. There's an on-site chef preparing Jamaican-style dinners. No pool, no TV, but there's a phone in the office and at the bar where fellow guests—some in skimpy attire—get acquainted.

WHERE TO EAT

Café au Lait / Mirage Cottages. Lighthouse Rd., West End, Negril, Jamaica, W.I. ☎ **809/957-4471.** Fax 809/957-4414. Main courses $9–$30. MC, V. Daily 5–11pm. FRENCH/JAMAICAN.

Daniel and Sylvia Grizzle, a Jamaican/French couple, prepare the cuisine as well as direct the smooth operation of this place, located 2¹/₂ miles from the town center along the West End beach strip. Menu items include quiches, escargots, lobster, and an unusual crêpe made with cheese and callaloo. There are five kinds of pizza, roast lamb, fish steak, and curried shrimp, and a wine list stresses French products. Dessert may be lime tart with fresh cream.

The Grizzles also have seven cottages that they rent out to guests. Set in 4¹/₂ acres of tropical gardens, all the accommodations are well appointed. Above the restaurant are four units, each equipped with a kitchenette. The other units are closer to the ocean but have no kitchen facilities. The accommodations all have private baths and ceiling fans, and there are sunning areas, three access ladders to the sea, and a gazebo for relaxing in the shade. Winter rates are $98 for one; $110 for two, no matter what accommodations you choose. Off-season, tariffs drop to $55 for a single and $66 for a double.

✪ **Chicken Lavish.** West End Rd. ☎ **809/957-4410.** Main courses $5–$13. AE, CB, DC, DISC, MC, V. Daily 10am–10pm. JAMAICAN.

We've found that Chicken Lavish, whose name we love, is the best of the low-budget eateries. Just show up on the doorstep and see what's cooking. It's located along the West End beach strip. Curried goat is a specialty, as is fresh fried fish. The red snapper is caught in local waters. But the main reason we've recommended the place is because of the namesake. Ask the chef to make his special Jamaican chicken. He'll tell you, and you may agree, that it's the best on the island. What to wear here? Dress as you would to clean up your backyard on a hot August day.

Choices. West End Rd. ☎ **809/957-4841.** Main courses $4.20–$11.20. No credit cards. Daily 7am–11pm. JAMAICAN.

This no-frills open-air restaurant offers local food in a bustling atmosphere. The food is simple and the portions are hearty. You'll pay about $5 to $6 for breakfast, which includes ackee and salt codfish prepared with Jamaican spices, onions, green peppers, and tomatoes. Daily soup specials may include pumpkin or red pea. For a real island experience, try the spicy jerk chicken, fish, or pork. Other dishes might include stewed beef, curried goat, or a dish of oxtail. Most dishes come with salad and your choice of vegetable.

۞ Cosmo's Seafood Restaurant & Bar. Norman Manley Blvd. ☎ **809/957-4330.** Main courses J$150–J$500 ($4.20–$14). AE, MC, V. Daily 9am–10pm. SEAFOOD.

One of the best places to go for local seafood is centered around a Polynesian thatched bohío open to the sea and bordering the main beachfront. This is the dining spot of Cosmo Brown, who entertains locals as well as visitors. You can order his famous conch soup, or conch in a number of other ways, including steamed or curried. He's also known for his savory kettle of curried goat, or you might prefer freshly caught seafood or fish, depending on what the catch turned up. It's a rustic establishment, and prices are among the most reasonable at the resort.

Hungry Lion. West End Rd. ☎ **809/957-4486.** Main courses $7.50–$18. AE, MC, V. Daily 5–10pm. JAMAICAN/INTERNATIONAL.

Some of the best seafood and vegetarian dishes are found at this laid-back alfresco hangout on the cliffs. Instead of the usual Red Stripe beer, you can visit the juice bar and sample the tropical punches. This is a cozy, two-story, green-painted concrete and wood building. The first floor has an open-air section with booths inside, but on the second floor it's all windows. Menus change daily, depending on what's available in the local markets. About seven main courses are offered nightly, not only seafood and vegetarian platters, but many tasty chicken dishes as well, even shepherds pie, pasta primavera, grilled kingfish steak, and pan-fried snapper. Lobster is prepared in many different ways, and everything is accompanied by rice and peas along with steamed vegetables. The homemade desserts are luscious, especially the pineapple-carrot cake, our favorite.

Mariners Inn & Restaurant. West End Rd. ☎ **809/957-4348.** Pizzas J$120–J$300 ($3.35–$8.40); main courses J$120–J$300 ($3.35–$8.40). AE, MC, V. Daily 8am–10pm. JAMAICAN/AMERICAN.

Many guests escaping from their all-inclusive dining rooms head here for some authentic Jamaican flavor. The bar is shaped like a boat, and there's an adjoining restaurant, entered through a tropical garden. As you drink or dine, the sea breezes waft in, adding to the relaxed experience. The one appetizer is a bacon-wrapped banana—not everybody's favorite way to begin a meal, but the food picks up considerably after that. The chef knows how to use curry effectively in the lobster and chicken dishes, and even the goat. The coq au vin (chicken in wine) has never been to France, so you're better off sticking to such dishes as pan-fried snapper or fried chicken.

۞ Paradise Yard. White Hall Rd. ☎ **809/957-4006.** Main courses J$175–J$450 ($4.90–$12.60). V. Daily 8am–10pm. JAMAICAN.

Set on the verdant flatlands of downtown Negril, near the police station and a 10-minute walk from the beach, this simple but welcoming restaurant is the undisputed domain of the Jamaica-born chef and owner Lorraine Washington. Meals, served either on the outdoor terrace or in an airy and comfortable interior decorated with roughly textured boards and pink tiles, might include the house specialty, "Rasta Pasta" (defined as red and green "dreadlocks pasta" chosen in honor of the colors of the Jamaican flag, with tomatoes, pepper, and ackee), a succulent version of pasta with lobster, curried chicken (prepared either mild or in fiery degrees of hotness, depending on your taste), Mexican enchiladas, and some of the best pumpkin soup on Jamaica.

The Pickled Parrot. West End Rd. ☎ **809/957-4864.** Main courses $5.95–$23.95. AE, MC, V. Daily 9am–midnight. MEXICAN/JAMAICAN/AMERICAN.

With a name like the Pickled Parrot, you know you're heading for a night of fun here. It doesn't live up to the riotious times at Rick's (see below), but it's a serious rival for the sundowner market. The restaurant stands at the edge of a cliff and is open to the trade winds. There's a rope swing and a water slide for fun outside if you never grew up. Slot machines inside add to the funky ambience. The cook claims he serves the best lobster fajitas in town. You can also order the usual array of Stateside burgers, sandwiches, and freshly made salads at lunch. Actually, you can order the full dinner menu at lunch if you so desire. They prepare a predictable array of burritos, nachos, and even Mexican pizza (we prefer Italian). But you might also be tempted by the fresh fish, lobster Jamaican style (also shrimp in the same method), and the famous jerk chicken.

Sweet Spice. 1 White Hall Rd. ☎ **809/957-4621.** Reservations not accepted. Main courses $4.50–$14. MC, V. Daily 8:30am–11pm. JAMAICAN.

This is everybody's favorite mom-and-pop eatery, a real local hangout beloved by locals as well as scantily clad visitors to Negril. Next door to the more famous Paradise Yard (see above), it serves equally good food. The Whytes welcome guests warmly and serve them in an alfresco setting. The portions are large and most satisfying, and the cookery is home-style. Bring grandmother, mom and dad, and all the kids, as many Jamaican families do. You get what's on the stove that night or in the kettle, perhaps the fresh catch of the day or a conch steak. The grilled chicken is done to perfection, and shrimp is teamed and served with garlic butter or cooked in coconut cream. A number of curry dishes tempt, including concoctions made with goat, lobster, and chicken. Meals come with freshly cooked Jamaica-grown vegetables. The fruit juices served here (in lieu of alcoholic beverages) are truly refreshing, and the menu is the same at lunch or dinner.

✪ Tan-Ya's/Calico Jack's. In the Seasplash Resort, Norman Manley Blvd. ☎ **809/957-4041.** Reservations recommended. Main courses $6–$26. AE, MC, V. Daily 11am–3pm and 6:30–10pm. JAMAICAN/INTERNATIONAL.

Set within the thick white walls of a resort, these two restaurants provide well-prepared food and the charm of a small, family-run resort. Informal lunchtime food is served at Calico Jack's, whose tables are in an enlarged gazebo, near a bar and the resort's swimming pool. The resort's gastronomic showcase, however, is Tan-Ya's. Here, specialties include lemon-flavored shrimp, Tan-Ya's snapper with herb butter, three different preparations of lobster, smoked Jamaican lobster with a fruit salsa, and deviled crab backs sautéed in butter.

Tenby Beach Bar & Restaurant. West End Rd. ☎ **809/957-4372.** Reservations recommended. Main courses $6–$20. MC, V. Daily 8:30am–midnight. JAMAICAN/INTERNATIONAL.

This waterfront restaurant, decorated in cool tones of blue and white, is owned by the Lawrences, a native family who offer warm hospitality to all their patrons. You can get a variety of dishes at this local hangout, including stewed chicken with brown gravy (similar to chicken fricassée but a little spicier) or curried chicken and goat. The islanders recommend the seafood. You can order lobster in a variety of ways, including curried, grilled with a butter sauce, with garlic, or thermidor. If you don't see what you want on the menu, just ask—any reasonable request will be granted. The portions are huge and the atmosphere inviting.

WORTH A SPLURGE

✪ **Rick's Café.** Lighthouse Rd. ☎ **809/957-0380.** Main courses $11–$28. No credit cards. Daily 2–10pm. SEAFOOD/STEAK.

At sundown, everybody in Negril heads toward the lighthouse along the West End strip to Rick's Café—whether or not they want a meal. Of course, the name was inspired by the old watering hole of Bogie's *Casablanca;* the "Rick" in this case is the owner Carl Newman or his partner, Tom Martin. Actually a real "Rick" (Richard Hershman) first opened the bar back in 1974. Here the sunset is said to be the most glorious at the resort, and after a few fresh-fruit daiquiris (pineapple, banana, or papaya), you'll give whomever's claiming that no argument. "Casual" is the word in dress, and reggae and rock are heard on the sound track.

There are several Stateside specialties, including imported steaks, along with a complete menu of blackened dishes (Cajun style). The fish is always fresh, including red snapper, fresh lobster, or grouper, and you might begin with the smoked marlin platter.

Xtabi. West End Rd. ☎ **809/957-4336.** Main courses $10–$26; lunch $4.50–$15. AE, MC, V. Daily 8am–11pm. JAMAICAN/INTERNATIONAL.

The setting is formal and upmarket for laid-back Negril, although prices are most affordable—if you read from the right-hand side of the menu. Sitting on a cliff, near a series of caves where you can snorkel during daylight hours, the octagonal Xtabi has a patio facing the ocean where you can dine under the stars. The walls are painted aquamarine, a theme carried out in the matching cloths on the tables. Lunch is acceptable, if you're in the area. You get the usual grill items, an assortment of burgers, grilled cheee, steak or club sandwiches, and a series of salads ranging from fresh greens to avocado. But at night, the chefs try harder and the setting is more dramatic. The lobster thermidor is a sumptuous choice, as are the scampi grilled Jamaican style and the batter-fried shrimp. The catch of the day can be steamed, fried, or grilled as you wish, and steak and chicken are also prepared in a number of delectable ways. For dessert, opt for the fruit salad or—even better—one of the homemade cakes, perhaps chocolate, lemon, or marble.

A NEARBY PLACE TO STAY & EAT

Coconuts. Little Bay, Jamaica, W.I. ☎ **800/962-5548** in the U.S., or 809/997-5013. Fax 608/836-9391. 10 cottages. Winter, $695 per person per week cottage for two. Off-season, $595 per person per week cottage for two. Children 13–17, $395 extra; 6–12, $295 extra; 5 and under, $195 extra. Rates include three meals a day. MC, V.

In a fishing village on a quiet country road on the south coast, 8 miles east of Negril on the way to Savannah-La-Mar, this getaway offers a respite from the hustle and bustle of life. Guests stay in cedar-and-stone cottages that have their own private garden patios surrounded by flowers. Only two units have full baths; the rest have half baths. The philosophy here is, in a climate as beautiful as Jamaica's, why lather up in an indoor cubicle when you can enjoy the garden and ocean views offered by the four totally private coral stone showers located in the terraced gardens.

Your stay includes the use of the saltwater pool and sporting equipment, including snorkeling and fishing gear. Island tours and excursions into Negril or Savannah-La-Mar can be arranged. Your meals consist of freshly caught fish and lobster, chicken, fresh local vegetables, and local fruits and juices that you can enjoy at the seaside restaurant or on your private patio served by the staff. Price breaks are given to those traveling with a group. For four or more adults the weekly rate per person is $645, and for eight or more people the weekly rate is $595 per person.

SCUBA DIVING

The **Negril Scuba Centre,** in the Negril Beach Club Hotel, Norman Manley Boulevard (☎ **800/818-2963** in the U.S., or 809/957-4425), is the most modern, best-equipped scuba facility in Negril. A professional staff of internationally certified scuba instructors and divemasters teach and guide divers to several of Negril's colorful coral reefs. Beginner's dive lessons are offered daily, as well as multiple-dive packages for certified divers. Full scuba certifications and specialty courses are also available.

A resort course, designed for first-time divers with basic swimming abilities, includes all instruction, equipment, a lecture on water and diving safety, and one open-water dive. It begins at 10am daily and ends at 2pm. Its price is $75. A one-tank dive costs $30 per dive plus $20 for the rental of equipment (not necessary if divers bring their own gear). More economical is a two-tank dive, which includes lunch. It costs $55, plus the (optional) $20 rental of all equipment. This organization is PADI-registered, although it accepts all recognized certification cards.

One of the best-recommended dive facilities in Negril is **Scuba World,** a PADI-approved five-star dive shop located on the premises of the Poinciana Beach Hotel on Norman Manley Boulevard (☎ **809/957-5221**), near Sandals Negril. A 4-day certification course costs $300, a resort course for beginners is $75, and a one-tank dive for certified divers goes for $30, plus $20 for the rental of the necessary equipment. More than 20 dive sites, including coral reefs and caves are located at Poinciana.

3   Falmouth

This port town lies on the north coast of Jamaica, only about 23 miles east of Montego Bay. The Trelawny Beach Hotel originally put it on the tourist map (though we no longer recommend staying there). The town itself is interesting but ramshackle. There's talk about fixing it up for visitors, but no one has done it yet. If you leave your car at Water Square, you can explore the town in about an hour. The present Courthouse was reconstructed from the early 19th-century building, and fisherfolk still congregate on Seaboard Street. You'll pass the Customs Office and a parish church dating from the late 18th century. Later you can go on a shopping expedition outside town to Caribatik.

WHERE TO STAY

✪ **Good Hope.** P.O. Box 50, Falmouth, Jamaica, W.I. ☎ **800/OUTPOST** in the U.S., or 809/954-3289. Fax 809/954-3289. 10 rms. Winter, $100–$150 single; $150–$250 double. Off-season, $80–$125 single; $100–$175 double. Rates include continental breakfast. AE, MC, V.

Although this hotel is slightly more expensive than we would normally recommend in a budget guide, the beautifully restored 1755 Georgian Great House in the mountains of Cockpit Country exemplifies the romantic living that can be found in the more rural parts of Jamaica. Some 5 miles south of Falmouth and the beach, and set on a 2,000 acre plantation, the estate features lush gardens and country trails, horseback riding, tennis, and swimming. The Martha Brae River runs through. Like Strawberry Hill in Kingston, it, too, is owned by the music impresario Chris Blackwell, who not only helped promote the career of Bob Marley but has exquisite taste as well. This is the closest you get to enjoying the rich life of the grand planters of long ago. It's like walking back into Georgian days, but with all the modern conveniences.

Don't despair as you traverse the unmarked potholed road getting here (call for directions). The house at the end is worth the effort to reach it. The main house, which contains four guest rooms, is furnished with antiques, all evocative of the plantation era. The former coach house has five rooms and can be rented as a self-contained unit. In the rear is an antique guest house, ideal for a honeymoon with its wrought-iron canopy bed. Six rooms are air-conditioned. All meals, including after-noon tea, are prepared in the classic Jamaica style and served in the main house. Even if you can't stay here, call and see if you can come for dinner.

WHERE TO EAT

Glistening Waters Inn and Marina. Rock Falmouth (between Falmouth and the Trelawny Beach Hotel). ☎ **809/954-3229.** Main courses $7–$22. AE, MC, V. Daily 10am–10pm. SEAFOOD.

Residents of Montego Bay often make the 28-mile drive out here, along Route A1, just to sample the ambience of Old Jamaica. This well-recommended restaurant, with a veranda overlooking the lagoon, is housed in what was originally a private clubhouse of the aristocrats of nearby Trelawny. The furniture here may remind you of a stage set for *Night of the Iguana*. Menu items usually include local fish dishes, such as snapper or kingfish, served with bammy (a form of cassava bread). Other specialties are three different lobster dishes, three different preparations of shrimp, three different conch viands, fried rice, and pork served as chops or in a stew. The food is just what your mama would make (if she came from Jamaica).

The waters of the lagoon contain a rare form of phosphorescent microbe which, when the waters are agitated, glows in the dark. Ask about evening booze cruises, which cost $3 per person for diners. Departures are nightly at about 6:30pm.

RIVER RAFTING NEAR FALMOUTH

Rafting on the Martha Brae is an adventure. To reach the starting point from Falmouth, drive approximately 3 miles inland to **Martha Brae's Rafters Village** (☎ **809/952-0889**). The rafts are similar to those on the Río Grande, near Port Antonio, and cost $37 per raft, with two riders allowed on a raft, plus a small child if accompanied by an adult (but use caution). The trips last $1^1/_4$ hours and operate daily from 9am to 4pm. You sit on a raised dais on bamboo logs. Along the way you can stop and order cool drinks or beer along the banks of the river. There's a bar, a restaurant, and a souvenir shop in the village. Call for more information.

SHOPPING

Two miles east of Falmouth on the north-coast road is **Caribatik Island Fabrics,** at Rock Wharf on the Luminous Lagoon (☎ **809/954-3314**). You'll recognize the place easily, as it has a huge sign painted across the building's side. This is the private living and work domain of Keith Chandler, who established the place with his late wife, Muriel, in 1970. Today the batiks created by Muriel Chandler before her death in 1990 are viewed as stylish and sensual garments by the chic boutiques in the States.

In the shop is a full range of fabrics, scarves, garments, and wall hangings, some patterned after such themes as Jamaica's "doctor bird" and various endangered animal species of the world. Muriel's gallery continues to sell a selection of her original batik paintings. Either Keith or a member of the staff will be glad to describe the intricate process of batiking. The store is open Tuesday to Saturday from 9am to 4pm (closed in September).

4 Runaway Bay

Once this resort was a mere western satellite of Ocho Rios. However, with the opening of some large resort hotels, plus a colony of smaller hostelries, Runaway Bay is now a destination in its own right.

This part of Jamaica's north coast has several distinctions: It was the first part of the island seen by Columbus, the site of the first Spanish settlement on the island, and the point of departure of the last Spaniards leaving Jamaica following their defeat by the British.

Jamaica's most complete equestrian center is the **Chukka Cove Farm and Resort,** at Richmond Llandovery, St. Ann (☎ **809/972-2506**), less than 4 miles east of Runaway Bay. A 1-hour trail ride costs $30, and a 2-hour mountain ride costs $40. The most popular ride is a 3-hour beach jaunt where, after riding over trails to the sea, you can unpack your horse and swim in the surf. Refreshments are served as part of the $55 charge. A 6-hour beach ride, complete with picnic lunch, goes for $130. Polo lessons are also available, costing $50 for 30 minutes.

WHERE TO STAY & EAT
DOUBLES FOR LESS THAN $100 (WINTER) / $85 (OFF-SEASON)

Caribbean Isle Hotel. P.O. Box 119, Runaway Bay, St. Ann, Jamaica, W.I. ☎ **809/973-2364.** Fax 809/974-1706. 23 rms. A/C. Winter, $70 single; $100 double; $145 triple. Off-season, $70 single; $85 double; $120 triple. AE, MC, V.

This small hotel, a mile west of Runaway Bay, has 8 superior and 15 standard rooms, with personalized service in an informal atmosphere. The tattered rooms all have ocean views and private baths, and the so-called superior units all have private balconies. The hotel has a TV in the bar-lounge and a dining room leading onto a sea-view patio. Meals are served from 7:30am to 11pm daily. Dinner includes lobster, fish, shrimp, pork chops, chicken, and local dishes prepared on request. This hotel is located directly on the beach. Stay here only if you wish to save money—and don't get your hopes up too high.

✪ **Runaway H.E.A.R.T. Country Club.** Ricketts Ave. (P.O. Box 98), Runaway Bay, St. Ann, Jamaica, W.I. ☎ **809/973-2671.** Fax 809/973-2693. 20 rms. A/C TV TEL. Winter, $55 single; $123 double. Off-season, $50 single; $111 double. Rates include MAP. AE, MC, V.

Called "the best-kept secret in Jamaica," this place is located on the main road, and it practically wins hands down as the bargain of the north coast. One of Jamaica's few training and service institutions, the club and its adjacent academy are operated by the government to provide a high level of training for young Jamaicans interested in the hotel trade. The helpful staff made up of professionals and trainees offers the finest service of any hotel in the area.

The rooms are bright and airy and have either a king-size bed, a double bed, or twin beds. The accommodations open onto private balconies with views of well-manicured tropical gardens or vistas of the bay and golf course. Laundry is available, and there's a swimming pool and golf course.

Guests enjoy having a drink in the piano bar (ever had a cucumber daiquiri?) before heading for the dining room, the Cardiff Hall Restaurant, which has a combination of Jamaican and continental dishes. Nonresidents can also enjoy dinner, served nightly from 7 to 10pm; a well-prepared meal costs around $25. The academy has won awards for some of its dishes, including "go-go banana chicken" and curried codfish.

Tamarind Tree Hotel. P.O. Box 235, Runaway Bay, St. Ann, Jamaica, W.I. ☎ **809/973-4819.** Fax 809/973-2678. 16 rms, 3 three-bedroom cottages with kitchenette. A/C TV TEL. Winter, $62–$85 single; $73–$91 double. Off-season, $58–$80 single or double. Year-round, $165 cottage for up to six. AE, MC, V.

This small, family-style hotel was named after a lavishly blossoming tamarind tree (which has since been cut down) that grew near its entrance. Stuccoed, red-roofed buildings with awnings and pastel-trimmed balconies house cream-colored and carpeted bedrooms. There's a pool terrace, and the nearest beach (Cardiff Hall) is within a 5-minute walk. Although the occupants of the cottages usually cook their meals in their lodgings, there's a simple restaurant (The Bird Wing), which serves three meals a day, and a disco (The Stinger) whose drinks and recorded music relieve some of the evening monotony of this out-of-the-way hotel. The more appealing bedrooms are on the second floor, partly because of their greater access to cooling breezes.

A NEARBY PLACE TO STAY & EAT

Hotel and Gallery Joe James. Rio Bueno, Trelawny, Jamaica, W.I. ☎ **809/954-0048.** Fax 809/952-5911. 32 rms, 4 suites. Winter, $96 single; $120 double; $235 suite for one; $250 suite for two. Off-season, $70 single; $120 double; $200 suite for one; $225 suite for two. Rates include breakfast. AE, DC, MC, V.

For a 4- or 5-year period in the 1970s, Joe James was a bright flame on the arts scene of Jamaica, with exhibitions of his works in New York, Philadelphia, and Washington, D.C. Although his fame and press coverage have greatly diminished in recent years, the artist continues his endeavors in a concrete-sided compound of buildings set close to the shore of the sheltered harbor of Rio Bueno. Many visitors are fascinated by the showroom, which is loaded with large-scale paintings and wood carvings inspired by Jamaican and African themes. All the objects are for sale, and Mr. James is usually on the premises to explain his artistic theories.

Today, however, much of the establishment's income derives from the Lobster Bowl Restaurant, serving breakfast, lunch, and dinner daily. There's an outdoor terrace whose foundations were sunk into the waters of the harbor. The view encompasses the sea, the shore, and one of the neighborhood's largest industrial entities. Lunchtime platters include burgers, salads, sandwiches, and grilled fish. Evening meals are more copious and feature a choice of set menus comprised of grilled fish, broiled lobster, sirloin steak, or chicken, served with soup, salad, dessert, coffee, and Tía María as part of the all-inclusive price.

In the late 1980s, Mr. James built within a few steps of his showroom and the beach an angular two-story concrete building containing 32 simple and functional accommodations. All have ceiling fans; most have views over the bay and the massive industrial plant whose cranes and smokestacks rise on the opposite side of the harbor. Don't expect luxury here: The primary allure lies in the low cost, the proximity to the studio of one of Jamaica's better-known artists, and the complete lack of pretensions.

SEEING THE SIGHTS

Columbus Park Museum. Queens Hwy., Discovery Bay. ☎ **809/973-2135.** Free admission. Daily 9am–5pm.

This is a large, open area between the main coast road and the sea at Discovery Bay. You just pull off the road and then walk among the fantastic collection of exhibits, which range from a canoe made of a solid piece of cottonwood (the way Arawaks did it more than five centuries ago) to a stone cross that was originally placed on the Barrett estate at Retreat (9 miles east of Montego Bay) by Edward Barrett, brother of the poet Elizabeth Barrett Browning. You'll see a tally, used to count bananas carried on men's heads from plantation to ship, as well as a planter's strongbox with a weighted lead base to prevent its theft. Other items are 18th-century cannons, a Spanish water cooler and calcifier, a fish pot made from bamboo, a corn husker, and a water wheel. Pimento trees, from which allspice is produced, dominate the park.

Seville Great House. Heritage Park. ☎ **809/972-2191.** Admission $4. Daily 9am–5pm.

Built in 1745 by the English, the Seville Great House contains a collection of artifacts once used by everybody from the Amerindians to African slaves. In all you're treated to an exhibit of five centuries of Jamaican history. Modest for a Great House, it has a wattle-and-daub construction. A small theater presents a 15-minute historical film about the house.

5 Ocho Rios

This north-coast resort is a 2-hour drive east of Montego Bay or west of Port Antonio. Ocho Rios was once a small banana and fishing port, but tourism became the leading industry long ago. This resort—short on charm—is now Jamaica's cruise-ship capital. The bay is dominated on one side by a bauxite-loading terminal and on the other by a range of hotels with sandy beaches fringed with palm trees.

Ocho Rios and neighboring Port Antonio have long been associated with celebrities. Its two most famous writers are Sir Noël Coward, who invited the world to his doorstep, and Ian Fleming, creator of James Bond (see below, for details about their homes here).

Frankly, unless you're on a cruise ship, you may want to stay away from the major attractions on cruise-ship days. Even the duty-free shopping markets are overrun then, and the hustlers become more strident in promoting their crafts, often junk souvenirs. Dunn's River Falls becomes almost impossible to visit at those times.

However, Ocho Rios has its own unique flavor and offers the usual range of sports, including a major fishing tournament every fall, in addition to a wide variety of accommodations.

WHERE TO STAY
DOUBLES FOR LESS THAN $60

Little Pub Inn. 59 Main St. (P.O. Box 256), Ocho Rios, St. Ann, Jamaica, W.I. ☎ **809/ 974-2324.** Fax 809/974-5825. 22 rms. A/C TEL. Year-round, $44–$70 single or double. Extra person $20 in winter, $15 off-season; children 11 and under stay free in parents' room. Higher rates include full American breakfast. AE, MC, V.

If you don't mind a little noise, this place offers simple accommodations at sensible prices. Just next door to the Jamaica Grand Renaissance Resort, this hotel is in the Little Pub Complex containing a small nightclub, slot machines, and a restaurant that offers indoor and outdoor dining. The air-conditioned rooms have a tropical decor; some have small lofts that can be reached by ladder for extra bed space. The restaurant serves international cuisine and a few local specialties. Hotel guests receive a VIP card good for a 15% discount at the restaurant and nightclub. Although this is not the perfect place for peace and quiet, the hotel is located in the heart of Ocho Rios, offering easy access to Turtle Beach, shopping, restaurants, evening entertainment, and a variety of other activities.

Parkway Inn. Main St., Ocho Rios, St. Ann, Jamaica, W.I. ☎ **809/974-2667.** 21 rms. A/C. Year-round, $60–$65 single or double. AE, MC, V.

Its setting in the commercial heart of Ocho Rios appeals to any budget traveler who wants easy access to the town's inexpensive restaurants, shops, and bars. Built in the early 1990s, the hotel sports a bar on its third floor where patrons can enjoy a grand view over the lights of Ocho Rios. Although there aren't any resort-style facilities on site, guests are invited to use the pool, tennis courts, and water-sports facilities at the Jamaica Grand Hotel, next door, and any of the Ocho Rios beaches (the nearest is within a 10-minute walk). There's a Chinese/Jamaican restaurant on the premises serving simple meals. This hotel attracts a strong repeat business of business travelers hailing from other regions of Jamaica.

Pineapple Hotel. Pineapple Place (P.O. Box 263), Ocho Rios, St. Ann, Jamaica, W.I. ☎ **809/974-2727.** Fax 809/974-1706. 20 rms. A/C. Year-round, $60 single or double; $75 triple. Children 11 and under stay free in parents' room. AE, MC, V.

Next door to the Pineapple Place Shopping Centre, this hotel offers basic accommodations for reasonable prices. Expect no frills here. The tropically decorated quarters include private baths, tile floors, and air-conditioning, but if you want to make a phone call you must do it from the front desk. TVs are available for $2 extra per day. The Pineapple Pizza Pub is on the property, serving a combination of cuisines that include Italian, American, and Jamaican influences. Water sports can be arranged at the front desk, and there's a swimming pool on the premises. For a seaside romp, try Turtle Beach, a short walk away.

DOUBLES FOR LESS THAN $95

○ **Hibiscus Lodge Hotel.** 87 Main St. (P.O. Box 52), Ocho Rios, St. Ann, Jamaica, W.I. ☎ **809/974-2676.** Fax 809/974-1874. 27 rms. A/C TV. Winter, $92 double; $137 triple. Off-season, $81 double; $115 triple. Rates include breakfast. AE, CB, DC, MC, V.

The Hibiscus Lodge Hotel offers more value for your money than any resort at Ocho Rios. This intimate little inn, perched precariously on a cliff along the shore 3 blocks from the Ocho Rios Mall, has character and charm. All bedrooms, either doubles or triples, have private baths, ceiling fans, and verandas opening to the sea. Singles can be rented for the double rate.

After a day spent swimming in a pool suspended over the cliffs, with a large sundeck, guests can enjoy a drink in the unique swinging bar. On the 3-acre site are a Jacuzzi and tennis court, along with conference facilities. The owners also provide dining at the Almond Tree (see "Where to Eat," below). A piano bar, the Grotto, is open daily from 5pm to 2am.

WORTH A SPLURGE

Turtle Beach Towers. DaCosta Dr. (P.O. Box 73), Ocho Rios, St. Ann, Jamaica, W.I. ☎ **800/223-9815** in the U.S. and Canada, or 809/974-2801. 116 apts. A/C TEL. Winter, $110–$125 studio apt; $126–$155 one-bedroom apt; $198–$212 two-bedroom apt; $220 three-bedroom apt. Off-season, $82–$88 studio apt; $88–$112 one-bedroom apt; $132–$152 two-bedroom apt; $164 three-bedroom apt. Children 11 and under stay free in parents' apt (no children allowed in studio apts). AE, MC, V.

Located in a commercial district opposite the cruise-ship pier, these accommodations are housed in four high-rise towers offering apartment living with the added bonus of daily maid service. These air-conditioned lodgings contain private baths, fully equipped kitchenettes, and telephones. The property has a swimming pool and tennis courts equipped for night play, in addition to the beach. Water sports can also be arranged. Also on the premises is a restaurant serving both Jamaican and international specialties for breakfast, lunch, and dinner. On Tuesday evening, there's a manager's complimentary rum-punch party. The best deal is the three-bedroom apartments that sleep up to eight people. For a full group, the cost is only $27 per person.

A NEARBY PLACE TO STAY

✪ **Jamel Jamaica Hotel.** 2 Richmond Estate, Priory P.A., St. Anne, Jamaica, W.I. ☎ **809/ 972-1031.** Fax 809/972-0714. 22 rms, 2 suites. A/C TV TEL. Winter, $55 single; $88 double; $99 triple; $110 one-bedroom suite for two; $132 one-bedroom suite for three; $176 two-bedroom suite for four. Off-season, $44 single; $66 double; $88 triple; $88 one-bedroom suite for two; $99 one-bedroom suite for three; $132 two-bedroom suite for four. AE, DC, MC, V.

Some 7 miles west of Ocho Rios, this property lies on a windswept stretch of coastline, but despite its isolated locale its designers managed to infuse the grounds with some degree of drama, using hundreds of gallons of white paint, erecting urn-shaped balustrades separating pool terraces from the wild waterfront nearby, and landscaping with flowering shrubs and trees.

Each accommodation features a balcony with a sea view, lots of pastel colors, and floral fabrics. Although there's a restaurant and bar on the premises, many clients cook in their own kitchens or kitchenettes. (Cooking areas in the suites are larger and a bit better equipped than those in the conventional rooms.) The entertainment provided includes disco evenings and calypso parties with live musicians. Overall, the ambience is well managed and conducive to outings of large families or couples.

WHERE TO EAT

✪ **Almond Tree Restaurant.** In the Hibiscus Lodge Hotel, 87 Main St. ☎ **809/974-2813.** Reservations recommended. Main courses $12.50–$36. AE, DC, MC, V. Daily 7am–2:30pm and 6–9:30pm. INTERNATIONAL.

The Almond Tree is a two-tiered patio restaurant with a tree growing through the roof, overlooking the Caribbean at this previously recommended resort 3 blocks from the Ocho Rios Mall. Lobster thermidor is the most delectable item on the menu, but we also like the bouillabaisse (made with conch and lobster). Also excellent are the roast suckling pig, medallions of beef Anne Palmer, and a fondue bourguignonne. Jamaican plantation rice is a local specialty. The wine list offers a variety of vintages, including Spanish and Jamaican. Have an apéritif in the unique "swinging bar" (swinging chairs, that is).

✪ **Double V Jerk Centre.** 109 Main St. ☎ **809/974-5998.** Jerk pork or chicken J$300–J$460 ($8.40–$12.90) per pound. No credit cards. Mon–Sat 8:30am–1:30am. JERK/JAMAICAN.

When the moon is full and only a frosty Red Stripe beer can quench your thirst, or the fiery taste of Jamaican jerk seasonings ease your stomach growls, head here—and don't dress up. Set on Ocho Rios's main commercial boulevard, about a 3-minute drive east of the town center, this is viewed by almost everyone in town as the best outlet for jerk pork and chicken. Don't expect anything fancy, as it's one of the simplest restaurants in the region, with platters of meat that can be sold in quarter-pound or half-pound variations, depending on your appetite. Vegetables, salad, and fried breadfruit come with your main course. Although lots of local office workers and shopkeepers come here at lunch, the place is especially lively after 10pm, when live music transforms it into the closest approximation of a singles bar in town.

✪ **Evita's Italian Restaurant.** Eden Bower Rd. ☎ **809/974-2333.** Reservations recommended. Main courses $8.60–$23.10. AE, MC, V. Daily 11am–11pm. ITALIAN.

Located a 5-minute drive south of the commercial heart of Ocho Rios, in a hillside residential neighborhood that enjoys a panoramic view over the city's harbor and

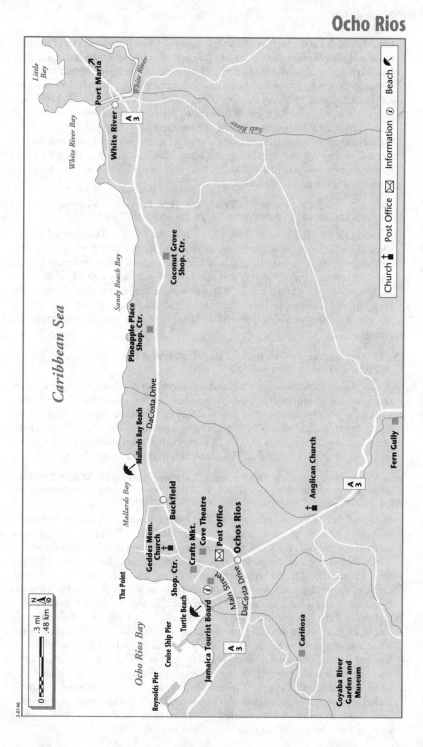

Ocho Rios

Caribbean Sea

Little Bay

White River Bay

Sandy Beach Bay

Mallards Bay

Ocho Rios Bay

The Point

Reynolds Pier

Cruise Ship Pier

Turtle Beach

Jamaica Tourist Board ⓘ

Mallards Bay Beach

White River

Port Maria

Buckfield

Geddes Mem. Church †

Shop. Ctr.

Crafts Mkt.

Cove Theatre

Post Office ⊠

Ochos Rios

Main Street

DaCosta Drive

Pineapple Place Shop. Ctr.

Coconut Grove Shop. Ctr.

DaCosta Drive

A 3

A 3

A 3

White River

Salt River

Anglican Church †

Fern Gully

Carifhosa

Coyaba River Garden and Museum

N

0   .3 mi
0   .48 km

Church †   Post Office ⊠   Information ⓘ   Beach ↙

2-0146

beachfronts, this is the premier Italian restaurant of Ocho Rios—and one of the most fun restaurants along the north coast of Jamaica. Its soul and artistic flair come from Eva Myers, the convivial former owner of some of the most legendary bars of Montego Bay, who established her culinary headquarters in this white gingerbread Jamaican house in 1990. An outdoor terrace adds additional seating and enhanced views. More than half the menu is devoted to pastas, and the selection includes almost every variety known in northern and southern Italy. If you don't want pasta, the fish dishes are excellent, especially the snapper stuffed with crabmeat and the lobster and scampi in a buttery white cream sauce. Italian (or other) wines by the bottle might accompany your menu choice. The restaurant lies a few steps from the Enchanted Gardens, an all-inclusive resort.

Little Pub Restaurant. 59 Main St. ☎ **809/974-2324.** Reservations recommended. Main courses $13–$28. AE, MC, V. Daily 7pm–midnight. JAMAICAN/INTERNATIONAL.

Located in a red-brick courtyard with a fountain and a waterfall surrounded by souvenir shops in the center of town, this indoor-outdoor pub's centerpiece is a restaurant in the dinner-theater style. Top local and international artists are featured, as are Jamaican musical plays. No one will mind if you just enjoy a drink while seated on one of the pub's barrel chairs. But if you want dinner, proceed to one of the linen-covered tables capped with cut flowers and candlelight. Menu items include barbecued chicken, stewed snapper, grilled kingfish, and the inevitable and overpriced lobster.

✪ **Parkway Restaurant.** 60 DaCosta Dr. ☎ **809/974-2667.** Main courses $8–$20. AE, MC, V. Daily 8am–11:30pm. JAMAICAN.

This popular establishment in the commercial center of town couldn't have a plainer facade. Inside, it continues to be unpretentious, but many local families and members of the business community know that they can get some of the best-tasting and least expensive local dishes here of any place in Ocho Rios. On clean napery, hungry diners are fed Jamaican-style chicken, curried goat, and filet of red snapper, and to top it off, banana-cream pie. Lobster and fresh fish are usually featured.

Ruins Restaurant, Gift Shop, and Boutique. Turtle River, DaCosta Dr. ☎ **809/974-2442.** Reservations recommended. Main courses $12–$32. AE, DC, MC, V. Mon–Sat noon–2:30pm and 6–9:30pm, Sun 6–9:30pm. CHINESE/INTERNATIONAL/JAMAICAN.

Here you dine in the center of town at the foot of a series of waterfalls that can be considered a tourist attraction in their own right. In 1831, a British entrepreneur constructed a sugar mill on the site, using the powerful stream to drive his water wheels. Today all that remains is a jumble of ruins, hence the restaurant's name. After you cross a covered bridge, perhaps stopping off for a drink at the bar in the outbuilding first, you find yourself in a fairyland where the only sounds come from the tree frogs, the falling water from about a dozen cascades, and the discreet clink of silver and china. Tables are set on a wooden deck leading all the way up to the pool at the foot of the falls, where moss and other vegetation line the stones at the base. At some point you may want to climb a flight of stairs to the top of the falls, where bobbing lanterns and the illuminated waters below afford one of the most delightful experiences on the island. However, the setting is more dramatic than the cuisine. Menu items include a wide range of Chinese food (more aptly—"Chinese-American"), including sweet-and-sour pork or chicken, several kinds of chow mein or chop suey, and a house specialty—lobster sautéed in a special sauce. International dishes include lamb or pork chops, chicken Kiev, steaks, and an array of fish.

BEACHES & SPORTS

BEACHES   Most visitors head for the beach. The most idyllic sands are found at the often-overcrowded **Mallards Beach,** shared by hotel guests and cruise-ship passengers, but locals may steer you to the white sands of **Turtle Beach** in the south.

GOLF   **Super Club's Runaway Golf Club,** at Runaway Bay near Ocho Rios on the north coast (☎ **809/973-2561**), charges no fee for residents who stay at any of Jamaica's affiliated "Super Clubs." For nonguests, the price is $58 for 18 holes year-round. Players can rent carts and clubs.

The **Manchester Country Club,** Rumalia Road (☎ **809/962-2403**), is Jamaica's oldest golf course, but has only nine greens. Greens fees are $12.50, and caddy fees run $4 for 18 holes. The course has a clubhouse.

The **Sandals Golf & Country Club,** at Ocho Rios (☎ **809/974-0119**), is free to residents of Sandals properties. If you're not staying at Sandals, you can still play for $50 for 9 holes or $70 for 18 holes, year-round. The golf course lies about 700 feet above sea level, a 5-minute drive from Ocho Rios.

TENNIS   **Ciboney Ocho Rios,** Main Street, Ocho Rios (☎ **809/974-1027**), offers three clay-surface and three hard-surface courts, all lit for nighttime play. Residents play free either day or night, but nonresidents must call and make arrangements with the manager.

SEEING THE SIGHTS

A pleasant drive south of Ocho Rios along Route A3 will take you inland through **Fern Gully.** This was originally a riverbed, but now the main road winds up some 700 feet among a profusion of wild ferns, a tall rain forest, hardwood trees, and lianas. For the botanist, there are hundreds of varieties of ferns, and for the less plant-minded, roadside stands offer fruit and vegetables, carved-wood souvenirs, and basketwork. The road runs for about 4 miles, and then at the top of the hill you come to a right-hand turn, onto a narrow road leading to Golden Grove.

Head west when you see the signs pointing to Lydford. You'll pass the remains of **Edinburgh Castle,** built in 1763, the lair of one of Jamaica's most infamous murderers, a Scot named Lewis Hutchinson, who used to shoot passersby and toss their bodies into a deep pit built for the purpose. The authorities got wind of his activities, and although he tried to escape by canoe, he was captured by the navy under the command of Admiral Rodney and was hanged. Rather proud of his achievements (evidence of at least 43 murders was found), he left £100 and instructions for a memorial to be built. It never was, but the castle ruins remain.

Continue north on Route A1 to **St. Ann's Bay,** site of the first Spanish settlement on the island, where you can see the **Statue of Christopher Columbus,** cast in his hometown of Genoa, erected near St. Ann's Hospital on the west side of town, close to the coast road. There are a number of Georgian buildings in the town. The **Court House** near the parish church, built in 1866, is most interesting.

Brimmer Hall Estate. Port Maria, St. Mary's. ☎ **809/974-2244.** Tours $15. Tours given Thurs at 2pm.

About 21 miles east of Ocho Rios, in the hills 2 miles from Port Maria, this 1817 estate is an ideal place to spend a day. You can relax beside the pool and sample a wide variety of brews and concoctions, including an interesting one called "Wow!" The Plantation Tour Eating House offers typical Jamaican dishes for lunch, and there's a souvenir shop with a good selection of ceramics, art, straw goods, wood carvings, rums, liqueurs, and cigars. All this is on a working plantation where you're driven around in a tractor-drawn jitney to see the tropical fruit trees and coffee plants, and learn from the knowledgeable guides about the various processes necessary to produce the fine fruits of the island.

Coyaba River Garden and Museum. Shaw Park. ☎ **809/974-6235.** Admission $4.50, free for children 12 and under. Daily 8:30am–5pm. Take the Fern Gully–Kingston road, turn left at St. John's Anglican Church, and follow the signs to Coyaba, just half a mile away.

A mile from the center of Ocho Rios, at an elevation of 420 feet, this park and museum were built on the grounds of the former Shaw Park plantation. The name *coyaba* comes from the Arawak name for paradise. Coyaba is a Spanish-style museum with a river and gardens filled with native flora, a cut-stone courtyard, fountains, an art gallery, and a crafts shop and bar. The museum boasts a collection of artifacts from the Arawak, Spanish, and English settlements in the area.

☼ Dunn's River Falls. Rte. A3. ☎ **809/974-2857.** Admission $6 adults, $3 children 2–12, free for children under 2. Daily 9am–5pm (8am–5pm on cruise-ship arrival days).

From St. Ann's Bay, follow the A3 east back to Ocho Rios and you'll pass Dunn's River Falls. There's plenty of parking space, and for a charge you can relax on the beach or climb with a guide to the top of the 600-foot falls. You can splash in the waters at the bottom of the falls or drop into the cool pools higher up between the cascades of water. The beach restaurant provides snacks and drinks, and dressing rooms are available. If you're planning to climb the falls, wear old tennis shoes to protect your feet from the sharp rocks and to prevent slipping. The falls can get quite crowded when the cruise ships are in port.

Firefly. Grants Pen, in St. Mary (20 miles east of Ocho Rios above Oracabessa). ☎ **809/997-7201.** Admission $10. Daily 9am–5:30pm.

Firefly was the home of Sir Noël Coward and his longtime companion, Graham Payn, who, as executor of Coward's estate, donated it to the Jamaica National Heritage Trust. The recently restored house is as it was on the day Sir Noël died in 1973, even to the clothes, including Hawaiian print shirts hanging in the closet in his austere bedroom with its heavy mahogany four-poster. The library contains a collection of his books, and the living room is warm and comfortable with big armchairs and two grand pianos (where he composed several famous tunes). When the English Queen Mother was entertained here, the lobster mousse Coward was serving melted, so he opened a can of pea soup instead. Guests—Coward's "bloody loved ones"—were housed in Blue Harbour, a villa nearer Port Maria where Sir Noël lived before building Firefly, and included Evelyn Waugh, Sir Winston Churchill, Errol Flynn and his wife (Patrice Wymore), Lord Laurence Olivier, Vivien Leigh, Claudette Colbert, Katharine Hepburn, and Mary Martin. Paintings by the noted playwright, actor, author, and composer adorn the walls. An open patio looks out over the pool and the sea, and across the lawn, on his plain, flat white marble grave, is inscribed simply: "Sir Noël Coward, born December 16, 1899, died March 26, 1973."

Goldeneye. Oracabessa (13 miles east of Ocho Rios). ☎ **809/974-5833.**

Coward was a frequent guest of Ian Fleming at Goldeneye, made fashionable in the 1950s. It was here that the most famous secret agent in the world, 007, was born in 1952. Fleming built the house in 1946, and wrote each of the 13 original Bond books in it. Through the large gates with bronze pineapples on the top came a host of international celebrities: Evelyn Waugh, Truman Capote, Graham Greene. The house was closed and dilapidated for some time after the writer's death, but its present owner, the British music publisher Christopher Blackwell, has restored the property. Although Fleming kept the place "just back to the basics," Blackwell sought the help of a designer to revamp the interior. With East Asia, including Timor, as the theme, the place now contains oversize bamboo sofas, totemlike Japanese obisps, and the like. Fleming's original desk, where 007 was born, remains, however. Unless you're a guest of the tenant, you aren't allowed to visit as it's private property. However, all 007 fans in this part of the world like to go by, hoping for a look. Look for the Esso (not Exxon) sign and take the narrow lane nearby going to the sea. Since you can't go inside, you might want to settle for a swim at James Bond Beach.

Harmony Hall / The Garden Café. Rte. A3, Tower Isle (4 miles east of Ocho Rios). ☎ **809/ 975-4222.** Free admission. Gallery, daily 10am–6pm; restaurant and cafe, Mon–Sat 10am– 10pm.

Harmony Hall was built near the end of the 19th century as the centerpiece of a sugar plantation. Today, after restoration it's the focal point of a restaurant and art gallery that showcases the painting and sculpture of Jamaican artists as well as a tasteful array of arts and crafts. Among the featured gift items are Sharon McConnell's Starfish Oils, with natural additives harvested in Jamaica. Sportswear that's sold includes "Reggae to Wear," designed and made on Jamaica.

The Garden Café, which is also known as Alexander's after the name of its co-owner, serves Jamaican cuisine as part of full evening meals priced at J$550 to J$900 ($15.40 to $25.20). The food is full of flavor, with an authentic taste—which may not be to everybody's liking. If you prefer to stop just for a cup of tea and a slice of homemade cake, it will cost about J$100 ($2.80).

Prospect Plantation. Rte. A3, St. Ann (3 miles east of Ocho Rios). ☎ **809/994-1058.** Tours $12 adults, free for children 12 and under; 1-hour horseback ride, $20. Tours given Mon–Sat at 10:30am, 2pm, and 3:30pm; Sun at 11am, 1:30pm, and 3pm.

Three miles east of Ocho Rios along Route A3, adjoining the 18-hole Prospect Mini Golf Course, is a working plantation. A visit to this property combines the opportunity to take an educational, relaxing, and enjoyable tour. On your leisurely ride by covered jitney through the scenic beauty of Prospect, you'll readily see why this section of Jamaica is called "the garden parish of the island." You can view the many trees planted by such visitors as Sir Winston Churchill, Dr. Henry Kissinger, Charlie Chaplin, Pierre Trudeau, Sir Noël Coward, and many others. You'll learn about and see growing pimento (allspice), bananas, cassava, sugarcane, coffee, cocoa, coconut, pineapple, and the famous leucaena "Tree of Life." You'll see Jamaica's first hydroelectric plant and sample some of the exotic fruit and drinks.

Horseback riding is available on three scenic trails at Prospect. The rides vary from 1 to $2^1/_4$ hours. Advance booking of 1 hour is necessary to reserve horses.

SHOPPING

For many, Ocho Rios provides an introduction to shopping Jamaica style. After surviving the ordeal, some visitors may vow never to go shopping again. Literally hundreds of Jamaicans pour into Ocho Rios hoping to peddle something, often something they made, to cruise-ship passengers and other visitors. Be prepared for aggressive vendors. Pandemonium greets many an unwary shopper, who must also be prepared for some fierce haggling. Every vendor asks too much for an item at first, which gives them the leeway to "negotiate" until the price reaches a more realistic level. Is shopping fun in Ocho Rios? A resounding no. Do cruise-ship passengers and land visitors indulge in it anyway? A decided yes.

THE CENTERS & MALLS

There are seven main shopping plazas. The originals are Ocean Village, Pineapple Place, and Coconut Grove. Newer ones include the New Ocho Rios Plaza, in the center of town, with some 60 shops. Island Plaza is another major shopping complex, as is the Mutual Security Plaza with some 30 shops. Opposite the New Ocho Rios Plaza is the Taj Mahal, with 26 duty-free stores.

OCEAN VILLAGE SHOPPING CENTRE   Here are numerous boutiques, food stores, a bank, sundries purveyors, travel agencies, service facilities—what have you. The **Ocho Rios Pharmacy** (☎ **809/974-2398**) sells most proprietary brands, perfumes, and suntan lotions, among its many wares. Call the shopping center at ☎ **809/974-2683.**

PINEAPPLE PLACE SHOPPING CENTRE   Just east of Ocho Rios, this is a collection of shops in cedar-shingle-roofed cottages set amid tropical flowers.

OCHO RIOS CRAFT PARK   At this complex of some 150 stalls, an eager seller will weave you a hat or a basket while you wait, or you can buy from the mixture of ready-made hats, hampers, handbags, placemats, and lampshades. Other stands stock hand-embroidered goods and will make up small items while you wait. Woodcarvers work on bowls, ashtrays, wooden-head carvings, and statues chipped from lignum vitae, and make cups from local bamboo. Even if you don't want to buy, this lively and colorful park is worth a visit.

COCONUT GROVE SHOPPING PLAZA   This collection of low-lying shops is linked by walkways and shrubs. The merchandise consists mainly of local craft items. Many of your fellow shoppers may be cruise-ship passengers.

ISLAND PLAZA   This shopping complex is right in the heart of Ocho Rios. Some of the best Jamaican art is to be found here, all paintings by local artists. You can also purchase local handmade crafts (be prepared to do some haggling over price and quality), carvings, ceramics, even kitchenware, and most definitely the inevitable T-shirts.

SPECIALTY SHOPS

The shopping, in general, is better at Montego Bay if you're going there. If not, wander the Ocho Rios crafts markets, although much of the merchandise has the same monotony. Among the few places that deserve special mentions are **Casa de Oro,** in Pineapple Place (☎ **809/974-2577**), which specializes in selling duty-free watches, fine jewelry, and the classic perfumes; and **Swiss Stores,** in the Ocean Village Shopping Centre (☎ **809/974-2519**), which sells all the big names in Swiss watches.

One of the best bets for shopping is **Soni's Plaza,** 50 Main St., the address of most of the shops recommended below. **Bollomongo** (☎ **809/974-7318**) has one of the island's widest selection of T-shirts, often in screen-printed designs. Bob Marley appears on many of them. You can even get Bob Marley on your beach towel. Swimwear such as "Sharkbite," is also sold. **Chulani's** (☎ **809/974-2421**) sells a goodly assortment of quality watches and brand-name perfumes, although some of the leather bags might tempt you as well. The **Taj Gift Centre** (☎ **809/974/9268**) has a little bit of everything: Blue Mountain coffee, film, Jamaican cigars, and hand-embroidered linen tablecloths. For something different, look for Jamaican jewelry made from hematite, a mountain stone.

Mohan's (☎ **809/974-9270**) offers one of the best selections of gold chains, rings, bracelets, and earrings in Ocho Rios. **Soni's** (☎ **809/974-2303**) dazzles here with gold, but also cameras, French perfumes, watches, china and crystal, linen tablecloths, and even the standard Jamaican souvenirs. **Tajmahal** (☎ **809/974-6455**) beats most competition in name brands in watches, jewelry, and fragrances.

If you'd like to avoid the hassle of the markets, but still find some local handcrafts or art, head for **Beautiful Memories,** 9 Island Plaza (☎ **809/974-2374**), which has a limited but representative sampling of Jamaican art, as well as an exhibit of local crafts, pottery, woodwork, and hand-embroidered items.

OCHO RIOS AFTER DARK

Boonoonoonoos is Jamaican for "very nice" or "super," and also stands for a "happening" on Jamaica.

Hotels often provide live entertainment to which nonresidents are invited. Ask at your hotel desk where the action is on any given night. Otherwise, you may want to look in on **Silks Discothèque,** in the Shaw Park Hotel, Cutlass Bay (☎ **809/ 974-2552**), which has a smallish dance floor and a sometimes-animated crowd of drinkers and dancers. Nonresidents of this well-known hotel can enter for an all-inclusive price of $25.

6 Port Antonio

Port Antonio is a verdant and sleepy seaport on the northeast coast of Jamaica, 63 miles northeast of Kingston, where Tom Cruise filmed *Cocktail*. It has been called the Jamaica of 100 years ago. Port Antonio is the mecca of the titled and the wealthy, including European royalty and such stars as Bruce Willis, Linda Evans, Raquel Welch, Whoopi Goldberg, Peter O'Toole, and Tommy Tune.

The small, bustling town of Port Antonio is like many on the island: clean and untidy, with sidewalks around a market filled with vendors; tin-roofed shacks competing with old Georgian and modern brick and concrete buildings; and lots of people shopping, talking, laughing, and some just loafing. The market is a place to browse among local craftwork, spices, and fruits.

In other days, visitors arrived by banana boat and stayed at the Tichfield Hotel (which burned down) in a lush, tropical, unspoiled part of the island. Captain Bligh landed here in 1793 with the first breadfruit plants, and Port Antonio claims that the ones grown in this area are the best on the island. Visitors still arrive by water—but now it's in cruise ships that moor close to Navy Island, and the passengers come ashore just for the day.

Navy Island and the long-gone Tichfield Hotel were owned for a short time by the film star Errol Flynn. The story is that after suffering damage to his yacht, he put into Kingston for repairs, visited Port Antonio by motorbike, fell in love with the area, and in due course acquired Navy Island (some say he got it in a gambling game). Later he either sold (or lost) it and bought a nearby plantation, Comfort Castle, still owned by his widow, Patrice Wymore Flynn, who spends most of her time there. He was much loved and admired by the Jamaicans and was totally integrated into the community. They still talk of him in Port Antonio—his reputation for womanizing and drinking lives on.

GETTING THERE

To reach Port Antonio from the capital, you can take Route A4 through Port Morant and up the east coast, or drive north on Route A3 through Castleton and travel east along the north coast.

WHERE TO STAY
DOUBLES FOR LESS THAN $40

✪ **De Montevin Lodge.** 21 Fort George St. (P.O. Box 85), Port Antonio, Jamaica, W.I. ☎ **809/993-2604.** 13 rms, 3 with bath. $26 single without bath; $39 double without bath; $52 single or double with bath. Rates include breakfast. AE.

This lodge, in the town center on Titchfield Hill, is the most ornate although still somewhat shabby version of a Victorian gingerbread house in town. It stands on a narrow backstreet whose edges are lined with architectural reminders (some of them not well preserved) of the colonial days. Originally built as a sea captain's house in 1881, the hotel is really worth a photograph. Cast-iron accents and elongated red-and-white balconies set a tone for the charm you find inside: cedar doors, art deco cupboards, a ceiling embellished with lacy plaster designs, and elaborate cove moldings. Don't expect modern amenities here; your room might be a study of another, not-yet-renovated era. A small beach, the Little Reef Beach, is a 5-minute walk from here. Frenchman's Cove and Boston Beach are a 15-minute drive away, and are a bit nicer.

DOUBLES FOR LESS THAN $100 (WINTER) / $85 (OFF-SEASON)

Bonnie View Plantation Hotel. Richmond Hill (P.O. Box 82), Port Antonio, Jamaica, W.I. ☎ **809/993-2752.** Fax 809/993-2862. 20 rms. Winter, $64–$72 single; $98–$102 double. Off-season, $54–$60 single; $82–$98 double. Rates include breakfast. MAP $24 per person extra. AE, MC, V.

The two-story house that contains this hotel is the subject of several local legends. Some claim that it was built by an expatriate Englishman as a holiday home around 1900; others maintain that it was the center of a large plantation and built around 1850. Other stories claim that Errol Flynn himself owned it briefly and used it as a place to carouse. Regardless of the details, it's obvious that this high-ceilinged, wood-framed building once boasted pretentions of grandeur and many of the grace notes of the Old World.

Today it's a battered remnant of its original self, with a white-painted exterior, a much-renovated dining room, and 15 rooms in the main house (another 5 bedrooms are in cabaña-style outbuildings in the garden). The accommodations contain Jamaica-made furniture and virtually no accessories, although a very limited number offer views of the sea. There's a smallish swimming pool in back, a restaurant and bar, and a vivid sense of small-town Jamaican values. The nearest beach (Frenchman's Cove) is about a 20-minute drive away.

WORTH A SPLURGE

Navy Island Marina Resort. Navy Island (P.O. Box 188), Port Antonio, Jamaica, W.I. ☎ **809/993-2667.** 1 rm, 9 villas. Year-round, $80 double; $100 one-bedroom villa for two; $140 one-bedroom villa for three; $180 two-bedroom villa for three; $200 two-bedroom villa for four. Rates include breakfast. Children 11 and under stay free in parents' villa. AE, MC, V.

Jamaica's only private island getaway, this resort and marina is on that "bit of paradise" once owned by the actor Errol Flynn. Today this cottage colony and yacht club is one of the best-kept travel secrets in the Caribbean. To reach the resort, you'll have to take a ferry from the dockyards of Port Antonio on West Street for a short ride across one of the most beautiful harbors of Jamaica. Hotel guests travel free.

Each accommodation is designed as a studio cottage or villa branching out from the main club. Ceiling fans and trade winds keep the cottages cool, and mosquito netting over the beds adds a plantation touch.

One of the resort's beaches is a secluded clothing-optional stretch of sand known as Trembly Knee Cove. You can leisurely explore the island, whose grounds are dotted with hybrid hibiscus, bougainvillea, and palms (many of which were originally ordered planted by Flynn himself).

At night, after enjoying drinks in the H.M.S. Bounty Bar, guests can dine in the Bounty. Facilities include a swimming pool, two beaches, and water sports (scuba diving and windsurfing).

A NEARBY PLACE TO STAY

✪ **Hotel Mocking Bird Hill.** Mocking Bird Hill (P.O. Box 254), Port Antonio, Jamaica, W.I.
☎ **809/993-7267.** Fax 809/993-7133. 10 rms. Winter, $140–$160 single or double. Off-season, $105–$125 single or double. AE, MC, V.

A 6-mile drive east of Port Antonio, this hotel occupies the much-renovated premises of what was originally built in 1971 as the holiday home of an American family. In 1993, two imaginative women transformed the place into a blue-and-white enclave of good taste, reasonable prices, and ecological consciousness. Set about 600 feet above the coastline, on a hillside laden with tropical plants, the place attracts a clientele of German and Dutch visitors, who seem to revel in the arts- and ecology conscious setting. The accommodations are simple but tasteful, and other than their ceiling fans, they're utterly devoid of the electronic gadgets that prevail in the urban world.

Much of the establishment's interior, including its restaurant (Mille Fleurs; see "Where to Eat," below), is decorated with Ms. Walker's artworks, and as this hotel grows, the gallery aspect will probably be expanded. On the premises is a bar, a lounge with TV, a public telephone, access to herbal massages, rafting tours, hiking treks, classes in painting and papermaking, and sweeping views out over the Blue Mountains and the Jamaican coastline. Don't expect four anonymous walls and a lack of contact with the environment—your experience will be steeped with consciousness-raising themes presented in a healthful and highly palatable setting.

WHERE TO EAT

Bounty. In the Navy Island Marina Resort, Navy Island. ☎ **809/993-2667.** Reservations recommended for dinner. Lunch or dinner $12–$20. AE, DC, DISC, MC, V. Daily 7am–10pm. JAMAICAN.

In Errol Flynn's former retreat (see our recommendation above), the Bounty, reached by ferry across the Port Antonio harbor, is the perfect place for a romantic tryst—all at budget-traveler prices. Where the former movie actor romped and eventually settled with Patrice Wymore Flynn (also an actor), the kitchen here is known for its convivial seafaring ambience, its fresh fish, and its down-home Jamaican cookery often appearing on the menu as daily specials. Come here early so you can enjoy a drink, taking in the view from the bar. (Flynn used to have quite a few, all recorded in *My Wicked, Wicked Ways,* his autobiography.) The lunch and dinner menus are the same. Steak is prepared delectably in a variety of ways, as are lobster, shrimp, chicken, and crayfish.

✪ **De Montevin Lodge Restaurant.** 21 Fort George St. ☎ **809/993-2604.** Reservations recommended a day in advance. Fixed-price meal $10–$19.50. AE. Daily 12:30–2:30pm and 7–9:30pm. JAMAICAN/AMERICAN.

At this previously recommended lodge, start with pepperpot or pumpkin soup, follow with curried lobster or chicken Jamaican style with local vegetables, and finish with coconut or banana-cream pie, perhaps bread pudding, washed down with coffee. We suggest an ice-cold Red Stripe beer with the meal, too. The menu changes according to the availability of fresh supplies, but the standard of cooking and the full Jamaican character of the meal are constant. Always call the day before to let them know you're coming, or just show up and take potluck. If you'd like a special dish cooked, you can request it at this time.

Yachtsman's Wharf. 16 West St. ☎ **809/993-3053.** Main courses $6–$13. No credit cards. Daily 7:30am–10pm. INTERNATIONAL.

Beneath a thatch roof at the end of an industrial pier near the departure point for the ferries to Navy Island, this rustic bar and restaurant is a favorite of the expatriate yachting set. Many of the ultra-expensive yachts whose crews have dined here have pinned their ensigns on the roughly textured planks and posts. It opens for breakfast and stays open all day. Menu items include the usual array of tropical drinks, burgers, seafood ceviche, curried chicken, and ackee with saltfish. Main dishes are served with vegetables.

WORTH A SPLURGE

✪ **Fern Hill Club.** Mile Gully Rd. ☎ **809/993-3222.** Reservations recommended. Fixed-price meal $10 at lunch, $30 at dinner. AE, MC, V. Daily 7:30am–9:30pm. Head east on Allan Ave. INTERNATIONAL/JAMAICAN.

One of the finest dining spots in Port Antonio has a sweeping view of the rugged coastline—the sunset-watching here is the best at the resort. Well-prepared specialties are served: jerk chicken, jerk pork, grilled lobster, and Créole fish. Depending on who's in the kitchen, the food here can be quite satisfactory, though once in a while, especially off-season, the cuisine might be a bit of a letdown. The club is also a venue for entertainment, with a calypso band and piano music during the week and disco music on weekends.

A NEARBY PLACE TO EAT

Mille Fleurs. In the Hotel Mocking Bird Hill, Port Antonio. ☎ **809/993-7267.** Reservations recommended. Fixed-price dinner $36; lunch platters $6.20–$17.90. MC, V. Daily 8:30am–10am, noon–3pm, and 7–9:30pm. INTERNATIONAL.

This restaurant (which is associated with the previously recommended hotel) is terraced into a verdant hillside about 600 feet above sea level with sweeping views over the Jamaican coastline and the faraway harbor of Port Antonio. Sheltered from the frequent rains, but open on the sides for maximum access to cooling breezes, it features candlelit dinners, well-prepared food, and great amounts of New Age charm. Menu items at lunch include sandwiches, salads, grilled fish platters, and soups. Evening meals are fixed-price three-course affairs featuring wholesome, healthful, and stylish dishes derived from around the world. The restaurant has been acclaimed by *Gourmet* magazine for its dishes. You may want to try the coconut-and-garlic soup, and the fish with spicy mango-shrimp sauce is a specialty. Breads and most jams are made on the premises. Some (but not all) of the dishes are designed for vegetarians.

BEACHES & OUTDOOR PURSUITS

BEACHES   Port Antonio has several white-sand beaches, including the famous **San San Beach,** which has recently gone private, although guests of certain hotels are admitted with a pass. Some beaches are free and others charge for use of facilities.

Boston Beach is free, and often has light surfing; there are picnic tables as well as a restaurant and snack bar. Before heading to this beach, stop nearby and get the makings for a picnic lunch at the most famous center for peppery jerk pork and chicken on Jamaica. These rustic shacks also sell the much rarer jerk sausage. The dish was said to originate with the Maroons who lived in the hills beyond and occasionally ventured out to harass plantation owners. The location is east of Port Antonio and the Blue Lagoon.

Also free is **Fairy Hill Beach** (Winnifred), with no changing rooms or showers. **Frenchman's Cove Beach** attracts a chic crowd to its white-sand beach combined with a freshwater stream. Non-hotel guests are charged a fee.

Navy Island, once Errol Flynn's personal hideaway, is a fine choice for swimming (one beach is clothing optional) and snorkeling (at **Crusoe's Beach**). Take the boat from the Navy Island dock on West Street across from the Exxon station. It's a

7-minute ride to the island, and a one-way fare is 30¢. The ferry runs 24 hours a day. The island is the setting for the Navy Island Marina Resort (see "Where to Stay," above).

✪ RAFTING   Rafting started on the Río Grande as a means of transporting bananas from the plantations to the waiting freighters. In 1871 a Yankee skipper, Lorenzo Dow Baker, decided that a seat on one of the rafts was better than walking, but it wasn't until Errol Flynn arrived that the rafts became popular as a tourist attraction. Flynn used to hire the craft for his friends, and he encouraged the drivers to race down the Río Grande, and bets were placed on the winner. Now that bananas are transported by road, the raft skipper makes one or maybe two trips a day down the waterway. If you want to take a raft trip, **Río Grande Attractions Limited,** c/o Rafter's Restaurant, St. Margaret's Bay (☎ **809/993-2778**), can arrange it for you.

The rafts, some 33 feet long and only 4 feet wide, are propelled by stout bamboo poles. There's a raised double seat about two-thirds of the way back for the two passengers. The skipper stands in the front, trousers rolled up to his knees, the water washing his feet, and guides the lively craft down the river, about 8 miles between steep hills covered with coconut palms, banana plantations, and flowers through limestone cliffs pitted with caves, through the Tunnel of Love, a narrow cleft in the rocks, then on to wider, gentler water.

The day starts at the Rafter's Restaurant, west of Port Antonio at Burlington on St. Margaret's Bay. Trips last 2 to 2½ hours and are offered from 8am to 4pm daily at a cost of $40 per raft, which is suitable for two people. From the Rafter's Restaurant, a fully insured driver will take you in your rented car to the starting point at Grants Level or Berrydale, where you board your raft. The trip ends at the Rafter's Restaurant, where you collect your car, which has been returned by the driver. If you feel like it, take a picnic lunch, but bring enough for the skipper too, who will regale you with lively stories of life on the river.

SEEING THE SIGHTS

Athenry Gardens and Cave of Nonsuch. Portland. ☎ **809/993-3740.** Admission (including guide for gardens and cave) $5 adults, $2.50 children 11 and under. Daily 9am–5pm (last tour at 4:30pm). From Harbour St. in Port Antonio, turn south in front of the Anglican church onto Red Hassel Rd. and proceed approximately a mile to Breastworks community (fork in road); take the left fork, cross a narrow bridge, go immediately left after the bridge, and proceed approximately 3½ miles to the village of Nonsuch.

These sights are 20 minutes south-southeast from Port Antonio. It's an easy drive and an easy walk to see the stalagmites, stalactites, fossilized marine life, and evidence of Arawak civilization. The cave is 1.5 million years old. From the Athenry Gardens, there are panoramic views over the island and the sea. The gardens are filled with coconut palms, flowers, and trees. Complete guided tours are given.

Crystal Springs. Buff Bay, Portland. ☎ **809/929-6280.** Admission J$100 ($2.80) adults, J$50 ($1.40) children. Daily 9am–5pm.

Crystal Springs is a tract of forested land whose borders were originally recorded in 1655. Then it was attached to a nearby plantation whose Great House is now under separate (and private) ownership. Visitors, however, can trek through the organization's 156 acres of forest whose shelter is much beloved by bird- and wildlife. A simple restaurant, usually open daily from 8am to 5pm, is on the premises, as well as a series of cottages erected in the early 1990s. These are usually rented to visiting ornithologists who don't care for the amenities or distractions of a traditional resort.

Folly Great House. Rte. A4 (on the outskirts of Port Antonio on the way to Trident Village). No phone. Free admission.

This house was reputedly built in 1905 by Arthur Mitchell, an American millionaire, for his wife, Annie, daughter of Charles Tiffany, founder of the famous New York store. Seawater was used in the concrete mixtures of its fondations and mortar, and the house began to collapse only 11 years after they moved in. Because of the beautiful location, it's easy to see what a fine Great House it must have been. The house is currently being restored, largely through fund-raising efforts.

Somerset Falls. Rte. A4 (8 miles west of Port Antonio, just past Hope Bay). ☎ **809/926-2952.** Tour $3. Daily 9am–5pm.

The waters of the Daniels River pour down a deep gorge through the rain forest, with waterfalls and foaming cascades. You can take a short ride in an electric gondola to the hidden falls. A stop on the daily Grand Jamaica Tour from Ocho Rios, this is one of Jamaica's most historic sites; the falls were used by the Spanish before the English captured the island. At the falls you can swim in the deep rock pools and buy sandwiches, light meals, soft drinks, beer, and liquor at the snack bar. The guided tour includes the gondola ride, a visit to a cave, and a visit to the freshwater fish farm.

7 Kingston

Kingston, with a population of more than 650,000 people, the largest English-speaking city in the Caribbean, is the capital of Jamaica. It sits on the plain between Blue Mountain and the sea.

The buildings are a mixture of very modern, graceful old, and plain ramshackle. It's a busy city, as you might expect, with a natural harbor that's the seventh largest in the world. The University of the West Indies has its campus on the edge of the city. The cultural center of Jamaica is here, along with industry, finance, and government. However, there's a terrible crime problem, and we recommend that you stay elsewhere.

WHERE TO STAY NEARBY

Remember to ask if the 12% room tax is included in the rate quoted when you make your reservation. The rates listed below are year-round, unless otherwise noted. All leading hotels in security-conscious Kingston have guards.

Pine Grove Mountain Chalets. Content Gap P.A., St. Andrew (for information, write Pine Grove Mountain Chalets, 62 Duke St., Kingston, Jamaica, W.I.). ☎ **809/977-8009.** Fax 809/977-8001. 17 rms. Year-round, $70 single or double. MAP $25 per person extra. MC, V.

This simple inn occupies a site originally developed in the 1930s as a coffee plantation. The setting includes a view over misty hills and the lights of faraway Kingston, landscaped brick walkways, topiary trees, and bedrooms that, although basic, are clean refuges after days spent walking or driving through the surroundings. The owners are Ronald and Marcia Thwaites, who deliberately avoided the installation of air-conditioning in favor of moisture-laden breezes. The accommodations are in low-slung, one-story motel-like units, each with basic amenities. There's a restaurant on site, and hiking trips into the nearby mountains can be arranged. Three of the rooms contain slightly battered kitchenettes, for which there's no additional charge.

Whitfield Hall. Contact John Allgrove, 8 Armon Jones Crescent, Kingston 6, Jamaica, W.I. ☎ **809/927-0986** (preferably from 7 to 9pm). 30 beds in 7 rms, none with bath; 1 cottage with kitchen and bath. $14 per person in communal rooms; $55 per night in cottage for up to four people (additional person, to a maximum of eight, $14). No credit cards. For directions, see below.

One of the most isolated and unusual hotels on Jamaica is Whitfield Hall, a high-altitude hostel and coffee estate about 6 miles from the hamlet of Mavis Bank. The main allure of this place is the opportunity to see Blue Mountain from a hillclimber's point of view. The accommodations are basic and there are no restaurant facilities. Be warned in advance that this is definitely an offbeat adventure.

Located more than halfway up Blue Mountain, Whitfield Hall is an old coffee plantation dating from 1776, and is the last inhabited house before you get to the peak at 7,402 feet above sea level. It offers accommodations for 30 guests. Blankets and linen are provided, but personal items (like towels, soap, and food) are not. There's a deep freeze and a refrigerator as well as good cooking facilities, crockery, and cutlery. All water comes from a spring, and lighting is by kerosene lamps called Tilleys. A wood fire warms the hostel and its guests, for it gets cold in the mountains at night. You bring your own food and share the kitchen and the two bathrooms.

Most visitors come to see the sunrise from the summit of Blue Mountain, which means getting up at around 2 or 3am to walk the final distance along a bridle path through the forest. The route is clearly marked, and you need a good flashlight and warm clothing, along with hiking boots or strong shoes. It's a 3-hour walk each way. It's also possible to hire a mule or a horse to make the jaunt, accompanied by a guide, for $42 round-trip for the 13-mile journey.

For reservations at the hostel, information, or a brochure, write or phone John Allgrove at the above address.

To get here, you can drive to Mavis Bank, about 20 miles from Kingston. Head northeast along Old Hope Road to the suburb of Papine, then proceed to Gordon Town. At Gordon Town, turn right over the bridge near the police station and drive into the hills for some 10 miles until you reach Mavis Bank. As alternatives, Whitfield Hall will send a four-wheel-drive for you, or you can walk. You can also get to Mavis Bank by bus from Kingston. Some people request that they be picked up in Kingston by a Land Rover for $46 each way for up to six passengers; extra passengers pay $5.50.

WHERE TO EAT

✪ **Chelsea Jerk Centre.** 7 Chelsea Ave. ☎ **809/926-6322.** Reservations recommended. A jerk chicken J$225 ($6.30); a pound of jerk pork J$180 ($5.05). AE, MC, V. Mon–Thurs 11am–11pm, Fri–Sat 11am–midnight, Sun 1–10pm. JAMAICAN.

Located between the New Kingston Shopping Centre and the Wyndham New Kingston Hotel, this is the city's most popular provider of the Jamaican delicacies jerk pork and jerk chicken. You can order food to take away or eat in the comfortably battered dining room. Though no appetizers are served here, you might order a side portion of what the scrawled chalkboard refers to as "Festival," which is fried cornmeal dumplings. The best bargain is Chelsea's Special, which is like an old-fashioned "blue plate" special at a U.S. roadside diner. It consists of rice, peas, and vegetables, along with jerk pork or chicken.

✪ **Devonshire Restaurant / The Grogg Shoppe.** In Devon House, 26 Hope Rd. ☎ **809/929-7046.** Reservations recommended for the Devonshire; not required for the Grogg Shoppe. Main courses J$205–J$825 ($5.75–$23.10). AE, MC, V. Mon–Fri noon–3pm and 6–10pm, Sat 6–10pm. JAMAICAN/SEAFOOD/STEAK.

These two restaurants near New Kingston are in what were originally the brick-sided servants' quarters of Kingston's most-visited mansion, Devon House. The more formal of the two is the Devonshire, which is a steak and seafood grill. You can eat on patios under the trees, in sight of the royal palms and the fountain in front of the historic Great House.

Appetizers include a "tidbit" of jerk pork or a bowl of soup (perhaps Jamaican red-pea—really bean—or pumpkin soup). Main dishes feature Jamaican ackee and saltfish, barbecued chicken, or steamed snapper. Also tasty are the unusual homemade ice creams made of local fruits, such as soursop. Blue Mountain tea or coffee is served. The bars for both restaurants serve 11 different rum punches and 10 fruit punches. Especially popular is the "Devon Duppy," which combines into one pastel-colored glass virtually every variety of rum in the bartender's inventory. Many aficionados opt for these drinks on one of the Grogg Shoppe's two different terraces.

The Hot Pot. 2 Altamont Terrace. ☎ **809/929-3906.** Reservations not required. Main courses $4–$6. MC, V. Daily 8am–10pm. JAMAICAN.

A short walk from both the first-class Pegasus and Wyndham hotels, this uncompli-cated Jamaican-run restaurant attracts an animated local clientele and serves simple but straightforward cuisine. In a red-and-white interior, near a view of a modest gar-den, you can drink Red Stripe beer or rum concoctions. Menu items include red-pea soup, beef stew, roast chicken, steaks, mutton, and fish.

Peppers. 31 Upper Waterloo Rd. ☎ **809/925-2219.** Main courses $11.20–$16.80. MC, V. Daily noon until ? (varies night to night). JAMAICAN.

The current hot spot for dining is this open-air spot near a shopping mall. It's espe-cially popular on Wednesday and Friday nights when half of Kingston seems to show up for dancing—and are these dancers ever hot! The food isn't neglected either. It's good and reasonable in price, specializing in jerk pork and chicken with french fries. The most elegant dish is grilled lobster, although more burgers and salads are sold instead. That's it—no vegetables, no other dishes. The Red Stripe flows like a river here.

WORTH A SPLURGE

El Dorado Room. In the Terra Nova Hotel, 17 Waterloo Rd. ☎ **809/926-9334.** Reservations recommended. Main courses $6.80–$23; brunch $16.80. AE, DC, MC, V. Daily 7am–11pm. INTERNATIONAL/JAMAICAN.

In one of the small and respectable hotels of New Kingston, off Hope Road, this res-taurant welcomes a crowd of local businesspeople and others at mealtimes into a for-mal dining room. Today the grandeur of the portico, the elaborate moldings of the hotel reception area, and the restaurant are souvenirs of the former affluent owners. There's an emphasis on fish and shellfish dishes, including mixed grill, pepper steak, seafood platters, and baked crab. The chef is also noted for his flambé dishes and his sirloin fondue. Wednesday is seafood buffet night, followed by a Jamaican buffet on Friday.

SEEING THE SIGHTS

Even if you're staying at Ocho Rios or Port Antonio, you may want to visit Kingston for brief sightseeing, and for trips to nearby Port Royal and Spanish Town.

IN TOWN

One of the major attractions, **Devon House,** 26 Hope Rd. (☎ 809/929-7029), was built in 1881 by George Stiebel, a Jamaican who became one of the first black millionaires in the Caribbean. He made his fortune mining in South America. A strik-ing classical building, the house has been restored to its original beauty by the Jamai-can National Trust. The grounds contain craft shops, boutiques, two restaurants (see

"Where to Eat," above), and shops that sell the best ice cream on Jamaica in exotic fruit flavors, and a bakery and pastry shop with Jamaican puddings and desserts. The main house also displays furniture of various periods and styles. Admission to Devon House is $3, and it's open Tuesday to Saturday from 9:30am to 5pm. Almost next door to Devon House are the sentried gates of **Jamaica House,** residence of the prime minister, a fine, white-columned building set well back from the road.

Continuing along Hope Road, at the crossroads of Lady Musgrave and King's House roads, turn left and you'll see a gate on the left with its own personal traffic light. This leads to **King's House,** the official residence of the governor-general of Jamaica, the queen's representative on the island. The outside and front lawn of the gracious residence, set in 200 acres of well-tended parkland, is sometimes open to view Monday to Friday from 10am to 5pm. The secretarial offices are housed next door in an old wooden building set on brick arches. In front of the house is a gigantic banyan tree in whose roots, legend says, duppies (as ghosts are called on Jamaica) take refuge when they're not living in the cotton trees.

Between Old Hope and Mona roads, a short distance from the Botanical Gardens, is the **University of the West Indies** (☎ 809/927-1660), built in 1948 on the Mona Sugar Estate. Ruins of old mills, storehouses, and aqueducts are juxtaposed with modern buildings on what must be the most beautifully situated campus in the world. The chapel, an old sugar-factory building, was transported stone by stone from Trelawny and rebuilt. The remains of the original sugar factory here are well preserved and give a good idea of how sugar was made in slave days.

The **National Library of Jamaica** (formerly the West India Reference Library), Institute of Jamaica, 12 East St. (☎ 809/922-0620), a storehouse of the history, culture, and traditions of Jamaica and the Caribbean, is the finest working library for West Indian studies in the world. It has the most comprehensive, up-to-date, and balanced collection of materials—including books, newspapers, photographs, maps, and prints. Exhibits highlight different aspects of Jamaican and West Indian life. There's also a special exhibit of Arawak artifacts, including drawings, pictures, and diagrams of their life, plus flints and other artifacts that help you understand the early history of Jamaica. It's open Monday to Thursday from 9am to 5pm and on Friday from 9am to 4pm.

The **Bob Marley Museum** (formerly Tuff Gong Studio), 56 Hope Rd. (☎ 809/927-9152), is the most-visited sight in Kingston, although unless you're a Bob Marley fan it may not mean much to you. The clapboard house with its garden and high surrounding wall was the famous reggae singer's home and recording studio until his death. The museum is open on Monday, Tuesday, Thursday, and Friday from 9am to 5pm and on Wednesday and Saturday from noon to 5:30pm. Admission is J$180 ($5.05) for adults, J$25 (70¢) for children 4 to 12, free for children 3 and under. It's reached by bus no. 70 or 75 from Halfwaytree.

IN PORT ROYAL

From West Beach Dock, Kingston, a ferry ride of 20 to 30 minutes will take you to Port Royal, which conjures up pictures of swashbuckling pirates led by Henry Morgan, swilling grog in harbor taverns. This was once one of the largest trading centers of the New World, with a reputation for being the wickedest city on earth (Blackbeard stopped here regularly on his Caribbean trips). But the whole thing came to an end at 11:43am on June 7, 1692, when a third of the town disappeared under water as the result of a devastating earthquake. Nowadays, Port Royal, with its memories of the past, has been designated by the government for redevelopment as a tourist destination.

Climbing the Blue Mountain

Jamaica has some of the most varied and unusual topography of any island in the Caribbean. Part of its allure to 18th-century mariners derived from its ample amounts of fresh water, which pours in the form of rivers, streams, and waterfalls from the heights of a mountain ridge appropriately named the Blue Mountains. These are now within the Blue Mountain–John Crow Mountain National Park (192,000 acres), which is maintained by the Jamaican government.

They're rich in the production of coffee, producing a blended version that's among the leading exports of Jamaica. But for the nature enthusiast, the mountains reveal an astonishingly complex series of ecosystems that change radically as you climb from sea level to the mountains' fog-shrouded peaks.

The most popular climb begins at Whitfield Hall, a high-altitude hostel and coffee estate about 6 miles from the hamlet of Mavis Bank. The summit of Blue Mountain Peak (7,402 feet above sea level) requires 3 hours each way. En route, hikers pass through acres of coffee plantations and forest, where temperatures are cooler (sometimes much cooler) than one might have expected, and where high humidity encourages the rampant growth of vegetation. Bird life en route includes hummingbirds, many species of warblers, rufus-throated solitaires, yellow-bellied sapsuckers, and Greater Antillean pewees.

The best preparation against the wide ranges of temperature that you'll encounter? Dress in layers, carry a soft-sided rucksack for storage, and bring some bottled water. If you opt for a 2am departure in anticipation of watching the sunrise from atop the peak, carry a flashlight as well. Sneakers are usually adequate, although many climbers bring their hiking boots to Jamaica solely in anticipation of their trek up Blue Mountain. Be aware that even during the "dry" season (December to March), rainfall is common. During the "rainy" season (the rest of the year), these peaks can receive up to 150 inches of rainfall a year, and fogs and mists are frequent.

Considering the social unrest on Jamaica, and the tendency for hiking paths to become obscured by vegetation and tropical storms, it's a very wise idea to hire a guide for your ascent of the mountain. Worthy contenders include **Sunventure Tours** (☎ 809/929-5694) and **SENSE Adventures** (☎ 809/927-2097). Depending on the time of departure (i.e., day or night), and the accoutrements included, the price of a guide for a trek up Blue Mountain ranges from $50 to $150 per person.

As you drive along the Palisades, you arrive first at **St. Peter's Church.** It's usually closed, but you may persuade the caretaker, who lives opposite, to open it if you want to see the silver plate, said to be spoils captured by Henry Morgan from the cathedral in Panama. In the ill-kept graveyard is the tomb of Lewis Galdy, a Frenchman swallowed up and subsequently regurgitated by the 1692 earthquake.

Fort Charles, the only one remaining of Port Royal's six forts, has withstood attack, earthquake, fire, and hurricane. Built in 1656 and later strengthened by Morgan for his own purposes, the fort was expanded and further armed in the 1700s, until its firepower boasted more than 100 cannons, covering both the land and the sea approaches. After subsequent earthquakes and tremors, the fort ceased to be at the water's edge and is now well inland. In 1779, Britain's naval hero, Horatio Lord Nelson, was commander of the fort and trod the wooden walkway inside the western parapet as he kept watch for the French invasion fleet. The fort is open daily from

9:30am to 4:30pm. There's an admission charge of $5. Part of the complex, **Giddy House,** once the Royal Artillery storehouse, is another example of what the earth's movements can do. Walking across the tilted floor is an eerie and strangely disorienting experience.

The **Buccaneer Scuba Club,** Morgan's Harbour, Port Royal, outside Kingston (☎ **809/967-8030**), is one of Jamaica's leading dive and water-sports operators. It offers a wide range of dive sites to accommodate various divers' tastes—from the incredible Texas Wreck to the unspoiled beauty of the Turtle Reef. PADI courses are also available. There's a wide array of water sports offered, including waterskiing, body-boarding, ring-skiing, and even a banana-boat ride. One-tank dives begin at $35, with a boat snorkel trip costing $15, including equipment, for 1 hour.

IN SPANISH TOWN

From 1662 to 1872, Spanish Town was the capital of the island. Originally founded by the Spaniards as Villa de la Vega, it was sacked by Cromwell's men in 1655 and all traces of papism were obliterated. The English cathedral, surprisingly retaining a Spanish name, **St. Jago de la Vega,** was built in 1666 and rebuilt after being destroyed by a hurricane in 1712. As you drive into the town from Kingston, the ancient cathedral, rebuilt in 1714, catches your eye with its brick tower and two-tiered wooden steeple, which was not added until 1831. As the cathedral was built on the foundation and remains of the old Spanish church, it's half-English, half-Spanish, showing two definite styles, one Romanesque, the other Gothic.

Of cruciform design and built mostly of brick, the cathedral is historically one of the most interesting buildings on the island. The black-and-white marble stones of the aisles are interspersed with ancient tombstones, and the walls are heavy with marble memorials that are almost a chronicle of Jamaica's history, dating back as far as 1662.

Beyond the cathedral, turn right and 2 blocks along you'll reach Constitution Street and the **Town Square.** This little square is surrounded by towering royal palms.

On the west side is old **King's House,** gutted by fire in 1925, though the facade has been restored. This was the residence of Jamaica's British governors until 1972 when the capital was transferred to Kingston, and many celebrated guests—among them Lord Nelson, Admiral Rodney, Captain Bligh of HMS *Bounty* fame, and William IV—have stayed here.

Beyond the house is the **Jamaica People's Museum of Craft & Technology,** Old King's House, Constitution Square (☎ **809/922-0620**), open Monday to Friday from 9:30am to 4pm. Admission is $4 for adults and $2 for children. The garden contains examples of old farm machinery, an old water mill wheel, a hand-turned sugar mill, a coffee pulper, an old hearse, and a fire engine. An outbuilding displays a museum of crafts and technology, together with a number of smaller agricultural implements. In the small archaeological museum are old prints, models (including one of King's House based on a written description), and maps of the town's grid layout from the 1700s.

The streets around the old Town Square contain many fine Georgian town houses intermixed with tin-roofed shacks. Nearby is the **market,** so busy in the morning that you'll find it difficult, almost dangerous, to drive through. It provides, however, a bustling scene of Jamaican life.

SHOPPING

Downtown Kingston, the old part of the town, is centered around Sir William Grant Park, formerly Victoria Park, a showpiece of lawns, lights, and fountains. North of the park is the Ward Theatre, the oldest in the New World, where the traditional Jamaican pantomime is staged from December 26 to early April. To the east is Coke Methodist Church, and to the south, the equally historic Kingston Parish Church.

Cool arcades lead off from King Street, but everywhere is a teeming mass of people going about their business. There are some beggars and the inevitable salespeople who sidle up and offer "hot stuff, mon," frequently highly polished brass lightly dipped in gold and offered at high prices as real gold. The hucksters do accept a polite but firm "no," but don't let them keep you talking or you'll end up buying—they're very persuasive! On King Street are the imposing General Post Office and the Supreme Court buildings.

For many years the richly evocative paintings of Haiti were viewed as the most valuable contribution to the arts in the Caribbean. There is on Jamaica, however, a rapidly growing perception of itself as one of the artistic leaders of the Third World. An articulate core of Caribbean critics is focusing the attention of the art world at large on the unusual, eclectic, and sometimes politically motivated paintings being produced on Jamaica.

Frame Centre Gallery. 10 Tangerine Place. ☎ **809/926-4644.**

This is one of the most important art galleries on Jamaica, and the founder and guiding force, Guy McIntosh, is widely respected today as a patron of the Jamaican arts. Committed to presenting quality Jamaican art, the gallery has three viewing areas and carries a varied collection of more than 300 works.

Kingston Crafts Market. At the west end of Harbour St., downtown.

A large, covered area of small stalls individually owned, the market is reached through such thoroughfares as Straw Avenue, Drummer's Lane, and Cheapside. All kinds of island crafts are on sale: wooden plates and bowls, trays, ashtrays, and pepperpots made from mahoe, the national wood of the island. Straw hats, mats, and baskets are also on display. Batik shirts and cotton shirts with gaudy designs are sold. Banners for wall decoration are inscribed with the Jamaican coat-of-arms, and wood masks often have elaborately carved faces. Apart from being a good place to buy worthwhile souvenirs, the market is where you can learn the art of bargaining and ask for a *brawta* (a free bonus). However, be aware that, unlike in Haiti, bargaining is *not* a Jamaican tradition. Vendors will take something off the price, but not very much.

Mutual Life Gallery. In the Mutual Life Centre, 2 Oxford Rd. ☎ **809/926-9025.**

One of the country's most prominent art galleries is in the corporate headquarters of a major insurance company. After you pass a security check, you can climb to the corporation's mezzanine level for an insight into the changing face of Jamaican art. Exhibitions change every 2 weeks.

The Shops at Devon House. At Devon House, 26 Hope Rd. ☎ **809/929-7029.**

Associated with one of the most beautiful and historic mansions on Jamaica, a building operated by the Jamaican National Trust, these shops ring the borders of a 200-year-old courtyard once used by slaves and servants. Although about 10 shops operate from these premises, four of the largest are operated by Things Jamaican, a nationwide emporium dedicated to the enhancement of the country's handcrafts. Shops include the Cookery, offering island-made sauces and spices, and the Pottery, selling crockery and stoneware. Look for pewter knives and forks, based on designs of pewter items discovered in archaeological digs in the Port Royal area in 1965. Other outlets include a children's shop, a leather shop, and a stained-glass shop as well as a gallery offering paintings, ceramics, and sculpture.

8 Mandeville

The "English Town," Mandeville lies on a plateau more than 2,000 feet above the sea in the tropical highlands. The commercial part of the town is small and is surrounded by a sprawling residential area popular with the large North American expatriate population mostly involved with the bauxite-mining industry. Much cooler than the coastal resorts, it's the best center from which to explore the entire island.

Shopping in the town is a pleasure, whether in the old center or in one of the modern complexes, such as Grove Court. The market in the center of town teems with life, particularly on weekends when the country folk bus into town for their weekly visit. The town has several interesting old buildings. The square-towered church built in 1820 has fine stained glass, and the little churchyard tells an interesting story of the past inhabitants of Mandeville. The Court House, built in 1816, is a fine old Georgian stone-and-wood building with a pillared portico reached by a steep, sweeping double staircase. There's also Marshall's Pen, one of the Great Houses, in Mandeville.

WHERE TO STAY & EAT

Hotel Astra. 62 Ward Ave., Mandeville, Jamaica, W.I. ☎ **809/962-3265.** 20 rms, 2 suites. TV TEL. Year-round, $65 single or double; $150 suite. Rates include continental breakfast. AE, MC, V.

Our top choice for a stay in this area is the family-run Hotel Astra, operated by Diana McIntyre-Pike, known to her family and friends as Thunderbird. She's always coming to the rescue of guests, happily picks up people in her own car and takes them around to see the sights, and organizes introductions to people of the island. The accommodations are mainly in two buildings reached along open walkways. There are a pool and a sauna, and the inn offers therapeutic massages. You can also spend the afternoon at the Manchester Country Club, where tennis and golf are available. Horses can be provided for cross-country treks.

The Country Fresh Restaurant offers excellent meals. Lunch or dinner is a choice of a homemade soup such as red pea or pumpkin, followed by local fish and chicken specialties. The kitchen is under the personal control of Diana, who's always collecting awards in Jamaican culinary competitions. Someone is on hand to explain the niceties of any Jamaican dish. A complete meal costs $10 to $20, with some more expensive items such as lobster and steak. Dinner is served from 6 to 9:30pm every day of the week. Thursday is barbecue night, when guests and townsfolk gather around the pool to dine.

The Revival Room is the bar, where everything including the stools is made from rum-soaked barrels. Try the family's own homemade liqueur and "reviver," a pick-me-up concocted from Guinness, rum, egg, condensed milk, and nutmeg. It's open daily from 11am to 11pm.

Mandeville Hotel. 4 Hotel St. (P.O. Box 78), Mandeville, Jamaica, W.I. ☎ **809/962-2138.** Fax 809/962-0700. 47 rms, 9 suites. TV TEL. Year-round, $65–$125 single or double; from $95 suite. AE, MC, V.

This ornate hotel was established around the turn of the century, and for a while housed part of the British military garrison. In the 1970s the venerable hotel was replaced with a modern peach-colored substitute, which was completely refurbished in

1982. It lies in the heart of Mandeville, across from the police station. It has an outdoor and indoor bar and a spacious lounge, and good food and service. Activity centers mainly around the pool and the coffee shop, where substantial meals are served at moderate prices. There are attractive gardens, and golf and tennis can be played at the nearby Manchester Country Club.

Popular with local businesspeople who use the coffee shop by the pool for a quick luncheon stop, the Mandeville Hotel offers a wide selection of sandwiches, plus milkshakes, tea, and coffee. The restaurant's à la carte menu offers Jamaican pepperpot soup, lobster thermidor, fresh snapper, and kingfish. Potatoes and vegetables in season are included in the main-dish prices. A full Jamaican breakfast begins at $6. From the restaurant's dining room, you'll have a view of the hotel's pool and the green hills of central Jamaica.

SEEING THE SIGHTS

Mandeville is the sort of place where you can become well acquainted with the people and feel like part of the community.

One of the largest and driest **caves** on the island is at Oxford, about 9 miles northwest of Mandeville. Signs direct you to it after you leave Mile Gully, a village dominated by St. George's Church, some 175 years old.

Among the interesting attractions, **Marshall's Pen** is one of the Great Houses, an old coffee plantation home some 200 years old, which has been restored and furnished in traditional style. The house is a history lesson in itself, as in 1795 it was owned by one of the governors of Jamaica—the earl of Balcarres. It has been in the hands of the Sutton family since 1939; they farm the 300 acres and breed Jamaican Red Poll cattle. This is very much a private home and should be treated as such. Guided tours can be arranged. A contribution of $10 per person is requested. For information or an appointment to see the house, contact Ann or Robert Sutton, Marshall's Pen Great House, P.O. Box 58, Mandeville, Jamaica, W.I. (☎ **809/ 904-5454**).

At **Marshall's Pen cattle estate and private nature reserve,** near Mandeville, guided bird-watching tours of the scenic property and other outstanding birding spots on Jamaica may be arranged in advance for groups of bird-watchers. Self-catering accommodation is sometimes available for bird-watchers only, but arrangements must be made in advance. Of Jamaica's 256 species of birds, 89 species (including 25 endemics and many North American migrants) may be seen in the wild at Marshall's Pen. For further information, contact Ann or Robert Sutton, Marshall's Pen, P.O. Box 58, Mandeville, Jamaica, W.I. (☎ **809/904-5454**). Sutton is the author of *Birds of Jamaica.*

The **Milk River Mineral Bath,** Milk River, Clarendon (☎ **809/924-9544;** fax 809/986-4962), lies 9 miles south of the Kingston–Mandeville highway. It boasts the world's most radioactive mineral waters, recommended for the treatment of arthritis, rheumatism, lumbago, neuralgia, sciatica, and liver disorders. These mineral-laden waters are available to guests of the Milk River Mineral Spa & Hotel, Milk River, Clarendon, Jamaica, W.I., as well as to casual visitors to the enclosed baths or mineral swimming pool. The baths contain water at approximate body temperature (90°) and are channeled into small tubs 6 feet square by 3 feet deep, each enclosed in a cubicle, where participants undress and dress again after their baths. The cost of a bath is J$50 ($1.40) for adults and J$25 (70¢) for children, and baths usually last about 15 minutes (it isn't good to remain in the waters too long). The restaurant offers fine Jamaican cuisine and health drinks in a relaxed old-world atmosphere. Some guests check into the adjacent hotel, where there are 25 rms (17 with bath), and many with air-conditioning, TV, and phone. About six of the rooms are in the main body of the hotel (a century-old Great House that was converted into a hotel in the 1930s). MAP rates for rooms with bath are $75 single and $102 double; for rooms without bath, $69 single and $96 double. American Express, MasterCard, and Visa are accepted.

9 The South Coast

Known as "Undiscovered Jamaica," the south coast attracts more foreign visitors every year and is a mecca for the budget traveler.

Local adventures are plentiful, too. Among the most popular is South Coast Safaris' boat tour up the Black River—once a major logging conduit (and still home to freshwater crocodiles). Another favorite is the trip to the Y. S. Falls, where seven spectacular cascades tumble over rocks in the foothills of the Santa Cruz Mountains, just north of the town of Middle Quarters (famed for its spicy freshwater shrimp).

The south coast has been called the sunniest on Jamaica, and that's true. It also means that the coast is the most arid. The Arawak lived here and were discovered by Columbus when he circumnavigated Jamaica in 1494. Five generations of Spaniards raised cattle on ranches on the broad savannas of St. Elizabeth when not repelling French pirates.

To reach the south coast, head east from Negril, following the signposts to Savanna-La-Mar. This is Sheffield Road and the highway isn't particularly good until it broadens into Route A2 at Savanna. After passing through the village of Bluefields, continue southeast to the small town of Black River, opening onto Black River Bay.

WHERE TO STAY

Invercauld Great House & Hotel. 66 High St. (P.O. Box 12), Black River, St. Elizabeth, Jamaica, W.I. ☎ **809/965-2750.** Fax 809/965-2751. 40 rms, 8 suites. TV TEL. Winter, $48–$51 per person double; $62 per person suite. Off-season, $44–$50 per person double; $54 per person suite.

In 1889, when Black River's port was one of the most important on Jamaica, a Scottish merchant imported most of the materials for the construction of this white-sided manor house. Today the renovated and much-enlarged house functions as a hotel. A few rooms are in the original high-ceilinged house; the rest, in a concrete outbuilding that was added in 1991. The rooms are clean, stripped down, and simple, usually with mahogany furniture made by local craftsmen. All are air-conditioned except for two single rooms that have ceiling fans. On the premises is a concrete patio and a swimming pool, plus a disco featuring live entertainment, a tennis court, and the conservatively dignified Willow restaurant. It's open daily for lunch and dinner, charging $20 to $24 for three-course meals of lobster, chicken, and fish.

✪ **Jake's.** Calabash Bay, Treasure Beach, St. Elizabeth, Jamaica, W.I. ☎ **800/OUTPOST** in the U.S., or 809/965-0552. Fax 809/965-0552. 6 rms, 1 suite. Year-round, $75 single or double; $95 suite. AE, MC, V.

In a setting of cactus-studded hills in the arid southwest (in total contrast to the rest of tropically lush Jamaica), this is a special haven, an ideal place for an off-the-record tryst. Perched on a cliffside overlooking the ocean, this complex of cottages is an explosion of colors, everything from funky purple to "toreador red." Each room is individually decorated, everything inspired by Sally Henzell, a Jamaican of British ancestry who is married to Perry Henzell, art director on *The Harder They Come*, that classic reggae film. Sally cites the controversial Catalán architect, Gaudí, as her mentor in the creation of Jake's—especially in the generous use of cracked mosaic tile so familiar to Barcelona devotees. The bedrooms could contain anything that Sally might have picked up at the flea market, or wherever. If it appealed to her, it's likely to be used to decorate one of the rooms. But be warned: There's no air-conditioning and days are hot here in the "desert." The fare is simple Jamaican, but it's tasty and good, made with fresh ingredients. Begin with the pepperpot soup and go on to the catch of the day, perfectly prepared.

Treasure Beach Hotel. Treasure Beach (P.O. Box 5), Black River, St. Elizabeth, Jamaica, W.I. ☎ **809/965-0110.** 28 rms, 8 suites. A/C TEL. Winter, $88–$99 single; $99–$110 double; $143 suite. Off-season, $77–$88 single; $88–$99 double; $110.30 suite. Full board $35 per person extra. AE, MC, V.

Set midway between Black River and Pedro Cross, on a steep but lushly landscaped hillside above Treasure Beach with an active surf, this white-sided hotel was built in the mid-1970s and renovated about a decade later. Although its staff is young and inexperienced, this is the largest and most elaborate hotel on Jamaica's south coast. Its centerpiece is a long and airy rattan-furnished bar whose windows look down the hillside to the beach and the hotel's 11 acres that flank it. Each outlying cottage contains two to six accommodations. Each has a ceiling fan and a veranda or patio. Amenities include a freshwater pool, a loosely organized array of such activities as volleyball and horseshoes, and live entertainment featuring calypso and reggae. Also on the property is the Yabo restaurant, a simple affair with slow and casual service open for breakfast, lunch, and dinner.

WHERE TO EAT

Bridge House Inn. 14 Crane Rd., Black River, St. Elizabeth, Jamaica, W.I. ☎ **809/965-2361.** Reservations recommended. Full meals $7–$18. MC, V. Daily 7:30am–3pm and 5–11pm. JAMAICAN.

This is an uncomplicated and very Jamaican restaurant in one of the town's few hotels, built in the early 1980s in a concrete beachfront motif in a grove of coconut palms and sea grapes. On the premises are 14 bedrooms, some air-conditioned and each with ceiling fan and simple furniture, but no TV and no telephone. Most clients appreciate this place, however, for its restaurant. Patrons include a cross section of the region, including the occasional conference of librarians or nurses. The menu includes complete dinners (fish, chicken, curried goat, oxtail, stewed beef, or lobster), served politely and efficiently by a staff of hardworking waiters. A separate bar area dispenses drinks. Main dishes include soup, salad, and your choice of vegetables.

THE ROAD TO ADVENTURE

The **Black River,** the longest stream on Jamaica, has mangrove trees, crocodiles in the wild, and the insectivorous bladderwort, plus hundreds of different species of bird including herons, ospreys, and many of the wading variety. You can indeed go on safari. The best tours are by **South Coast Safaris,** operating out of the town of Black River (☎ **809/965-2513** for reservations). The cost is $15; children 11 and under go for half price and those 2 and under go for free. Tours last about 1 1/2 hours and cover 12 miles (6 miles upstream, 6 miles back) with a running commentary on the ecology and history of the Black River. Tours are at 9am, 11am, 12:30pm, 2pm, and 4pm daily. Specialized tours can be arranged for any number of groups including bird-watchers, photographers, botanists, and natural-history buffs.

After leaving Black River, where you can find hotels and restaurants (see "Where to Stay," above), you can continue north along Route A2 to Mandeville or else go directly southeast to Treasure Beach.

Route A2 north takes you to **Middle Quarters,** a village on the plains of the Great Morass, through which runs the Black River. Day visitors often stop here and order a local delicacy, pepper shrimps.

Just north of the town of Middle Quarters is **Y. S. Falls,** where seven waterfalls form crystal pools. Guests take a jitney and go through grazing lands and a horse paddock on the way to the falls where they cool off in the waters and often enjoy a picnic lunch.

After Middle Quarters, the road cuts east toward Mandeville along Bamboo Avenue, a scenic drive along 2 miles of highway covered with bamboo. Here you'll see a working plantation, Holland Estate, growing sugarcane, citrus, papaya, and mango.

If you've decided to take the southern-coast route to **Treasure Beach,** follow the signs to Treasure Beach directly southeast of Black River. The treasures here are seashells in many shapes and sizes. This is the site of the Treasure Beach Hotel (see "Where to Stay," above).

To the east of Treasure Beach in Southfield is **Lovers' Leap,** a cliff plunging hundreds of feet into the sea. Two slave lovers reportedly jumped to their deaths here rather than be sold off to different masters.

12

The French West Indies

I t's France in the Caribbean, where Gallic charm combines with tropical beauty in the great curve of the Lesser Antilles. For most visitors, that's reason enough to visit. A long way from Europe, France's "western border" is composed mainly of Guadeloupe and Martinique, with a scattering of tiny offshore dependencies, such as the little Iles des Saintes.

Almond-shaped **Martinique** is the northernmost of the Windwards, whereas butterfly-shaped **Guadeloupe** is near the southern stretch of the Leewards. These are not colonies, as many visitors wrongly assume, but the westernmost of France, meaning that these *citoyens* are full-fledged citizens of *la belle France,* a status they have enjoyed since 1946.

Martinique has mountains dotted with lush vegetation, rain forests bursting with bamboo and breadfruit trees, and even a patch of desert in the south. But most visitors, including those from France, come just for the white-sand beaches.

In island boutiques you can purchase that Hermès scarf you've always wanted, certainly a bottle of Chanel perfume, or even some Baccarat crystal. For breakfast, freshly baked croissants will arrive on your plate. The French cheese is shipped in from Marseilles. The Créole cuisine is among the most distinctive in the West Indies.

Volcanic, tropically forested Guadeloupe, Martinique's companion island, is less favored by tourists but it has plenty to offer as well. It has even more recommendable Créole restaurants, and its landscape is dotted with pineapple groves, banana plantations, and sugarcane fields. The surf pounds hard against its Atlantic coast facing east, but the leeward bathing beaches on the west coast offer calmer seas.

Other islands in the French West Indies include **St. Martin** (which shares an island with the Dutch-held St. Maarten; see chapter 10), **St. Barthélemy, Marie-Galante,** and **La Désirade,** a former leper colony.

Unlike Barbados and Jamaica, the French West Indies are Johnny-come-latelies to tourism. Although cruise-ship passengers had arrived long before, mass tourism began in these islands only in the 1970s. Créole customs make these islands unique in the Caribbean. The inhabitants also serve some of the best food in the Caribbean, although one irate reader found it a "farcical version" of that offered in New Orleans. Don't be afraid if we've sent you to a dilapidated wooden shack. You may find the *New York Times* food editor there too, sampling a regional meal.

INFORMATION   For more information on these islands before you leave home, contact the **French West Indies Tourist Board,** 444 Madison Ave., New York, NY 10022 (☎ **212/838-7800**). You can also seek information at branch offices of the **French National Tourist Office** at 9454 Wilshire Blvd., Beverly Hills, CA 90212 (☎ **310/271-2358**), and 676 N. Michigan Ave., Chicago, IL 60611 (☎ **312/751-7800**). In Canada, visit 1981 ave. McGill College, Suite 480, Montréal, H3A 2W9 (☎ **514/288-4264**).

1 Martinique

Napoléon's Empress Joséphine was born on Martinique in 1763, the same year that France relinquished rights to Canada in exchange for the French West Indies. The mistress of Louis XIV, Madame de Maintenon, also lived here, in the small fishing village of Le Prêcheur.

Columbus was the first to chart Martinique. The French took possession in the name of Louis XIII in 1635, and subsequently established sugarcane plantations and rum distilleries. In spite of some intrusions by British forces, the French have remained here ever since.

In the beginning the French imported slaves from Africa to work the plantations, but at the time of the French Revolution the practice began to decline on Martinique. It wasn't until the mid–19th century, however, that Victor Schoelcher, a Paris-born deputy from Alsace, successfully lobbied to abolish slavery.

Martinique is part of the Lesser Antilles and lies in the semitropical zone; its western shore faces the Caribbean and its eastern shore faces the more turbulent Atlantic. The surface of the island is only 420 square miles—50 miles at its longest and 21 miles at its widest point.

The ground is mountainous, especially in the rain-forested northern part where Mount Pelée, a volcano, rises to a height of 4,656 feet. In the center of the island the mountains are smaller, with Carbet Peak reaching a 3,960-foot summit. The high hills rising among the peaks or mountains are called *mornes*. The southern part of Martinique has only big hills, reaching peaks of 1,500 feet at Vauclin, 1,400 feet at Diamant. The irregular coastline of the island provides five bays, dozens of coves, and miles of sandy beaches.

The climate is relatively mild, with the average temperature in the 75° to 85° Fahrenheit range. At higher elevations it's considerably cooler. The island is cooled by a wind the French called *alizé,* and rain is frequent but doesn't last very long. Late August to November might be called the rainy season; April to September are the hottest months.

The early Carib peoples, who gave Columbus such a hostile reception, called Martinique "the island of flowers," and indeed it has remained so. The vegetation is lush, and includes hibiscus, poinsettias, bougainvillea, coconut palms, and mango trees. Almost any fruit that can grow in the ground sprouts out of Martinique's soil—pineapples, avocados, bananas, papayas, and custard apples.

Bird-watchers are often pleased at the number of hummingbirds. The mountain whistler, the blackbird, the mongoose, and multicolored butterflies are also spotted. After sunset there's a permanent concert of grasshoppers, frogs, and crickets.

All this lushness, tropical beauty, and French/Créole food comes at a price. Martinique has a reputation for being one of the Caribbean's more expensive destinations, especially in the price of its food, a tradition it shares with mainland France. Its hotel and food prices are high.

To beat the high cost of dining out, we suggest picnicking during the day and then splurging at dinnertime. Grocery stores are loaded with choice tidbits from mainland France, and a bottle of French wine will cost you less here than on the non-French islands in the Caribbean.

Taxis and automobile rentals are high, so try to stay at a place on the beach (or near a beach) so you won't have long, expensive commutes every day. True budget hotels are hard to find on Martinique, but we have several suggestions below.

GETTING THERE

BY PLANE   Lamentin International Airport lies outside the village of Lamentin, a 15-minute taxi ride east of Fort-de-France and a 40-minute taxi ride northeast of the island's densest concentration of resort hotels (the Trois Islets peninsula). Most flights to Martinique and Guadeloupe require a transfer on a neighboring island—usually Puerto Rico, but occasionally Antigua. Direct or nonstop flights to the French islands from the U.S. mainland are rare: Air France (see below) offers only one flight per week, on Sunday, which leaves from Miami and stops at each of the two islands.

American Airlines (☎ 800/433-7300) flies into its busy hub in San Juan, and from here passengers transfer to one of usually two daily **American Eagle** (same phone number) flights heading to both Martinique and Guadeloupe. Taking off every day in the late afternoon, the Eagle flights usually arrive at their destinations between $1^1/_2$ hours and 2 hours later. Off-season, the evening flights to both islands are sometimes combined into a single flight, landing first on one island before continuing on to the next. Return flights to San Juan usually depart separately from both islands twice a day. Consult an American Airlines reservations clerk about booking your hotel simultaneously with your flight, since substantial discounts sometimes apply if you handle both tasks at the same time.

Air France (☎ 800/237-2747) flies from Miami to Martinique (sometimes with a touchdown on Guadeloupe en route) every Tuesday and Saturday throughout the year. The airline also operates separate ten-times-per-week nonstop flights from Paris's Charles de Gaulle Airport to both Martinique and Guadeloupe.

Antigua-based **LIAT** (☎ 809/462-0700, or through the reservations department of American Airlines) flies from Antigua to both Martinique and Guadeloupe several times a day, sometimes with connections on to Barbados. Both Antigua and Barbados are important air-terminus links for such transcontinental carriers as American Airlines (see above).

Another option for reaching Martinique and Guadeloupe involves flying **BWIA** (☎ 800/538-2942), the national airline of Trinidad and Tobago, from either New York or Miami nonstop to Barbados, and from there, transferring to a LIAT flight on to either of the French-speaking islands. **British Airways** (☎ 800/247-9297 in the U.S., or 0345/22211 in Britain) flies to both Antigua and Barbados from London's Gatwick Airport. From either of those islands connections are possible on LIAT onward to either Guadeloupe or Martinique.

BY FERRY   You can travel between Guadeloupe and Martinique by boat in a leisurely $3^3/_4$ hours with an intermediate stop on Dominica or the Saintes. The trip is made on modern, comfortable craft operated by **Trans Antilles Caribbean Express** (also known as **Exprés des Iles**). The Express schedule lists daily 8am departures from Pointe-à-Pitre and 1, 2, or 3pm departures from Fort-de-France. The adult fare is 345F ($69) one-way, 495F ($99) round-trip. For details and reservations, contact Exprès des Iles at 6 Immeuble Darse, quai Gatine, 97110 Pointe-à-Pitre, Guadeloupe, F.W.I. (☎ 590/82-12-45); or Exprès des Iles, Terminal Inter-Iles, Bassin de Radoub, 97200 Fort-de-France, Martinique, F.W.I. (☎ 596/63-12-11).

N

Atlantic Ocean

Macouba

Basse-Pointe

Grand Rivière

Leyritz

Le Lorrain

▲▲ **Montagne Pelée**

N1

Ajoupa-Bouillon

Le Marigot

Le Prêcheur

N1

Le Morne Rouge

Ste-Marie

Tartane

■ **Chateau Dubuc**

Morne des Esses

Caravelle Peninsula

St-Pierre

Trinité

■ **Musée Gaugin**

Le Carbet

Gros-Morne

N2

N3

Bellefontaine

Balata

Case-Pilote

N4

St-Joseph

N1

Fort-de-France

N1

Lamentin

Le François

✈ Lamentin International Airport

Pointe du Bout ⚓

Mt. Vauclin

N6

Anse Mitan ⚓

N5

Vauclin

Anse à l'Ane ⚓

Trois-Ilets

D7

Grande Anse

Anses-d'Arlets

D7

Rivière-Pilote

D37

Le Diamant

Ste-Luce

Le Marin

⚓ **Diamant**

D18A

■ **Diamond Rock**

Ste-Anne

Cap Chevalier

Petrified Forest ■

Plage des Salines

Caribbean Sea

Airport ✈   Beach ⚓   Mountain ▲▲

2-0197

GETTING AROUND

BY BUS & TAXI COLLECTIF There are two types of buses operating on Martinique. Regular buses, called *grands busses,* hold about 40 passengers and cost 5F to 10F ($1.25 to $5) to go anywhere inside the city limits of Fort-de-France. But to travel beyond the city limits, *taxis collectifs* are used. These are privately owned minivans that traverse the island and bear the sign TC. Their routes are flexible and depend on passenger need. A simple one-way fare is 30F ($5.70) from Fort-de-France to Ste-Anne. Taxis collectifs depart from the heart of Fort-de-France from the parking lot of Pointe Simon. There's no phone number to call for information about this unpredictable means of transport, and there are no set schedules. Traveling in a taxi collectif is for the adventurous tourist—they're crowded and not very comfortable.

BY TAXI Travel by taxi is popular but expensive. Most of the cabs aren't metered, and you'll have to agree on the price of the ride before getting in. Most visitors arriving at Lamentin Airport head for one of the resorts along the peninsula of Pointe du Bout. To do so costs about 160F ($32) during the day, about 260F ($52) in the evening. Night fares are in effect from 7:30pm to 6am, when 40% surcharges are added. You can call for a radio taxi (☎ **596/63-63-62**).

If you want to rent a taxi for the day, it's better to have a party of at least three or four people to keep costs low. Based on the size of the car, expect to pay 700F to 850F ($140 to $170) and up for a 5-hour trip, depending on the itinerary you negotiate with the driver.

BY RENTAL CAR Martinique has several local car-rental agencies, but some clients have complained of mechanical difficulties and billing irregularities. We recommend renting from either Hertz, Budget, or Avis. You must be 21 and have a valid local driver's license from your home country to rent a car for up to 20 days; after that, an International Driver's License is required.

Budget has offices at rue Félix-Eboué 12, in Fort-de-France (☎ **800/527-0700** in the U.S., or 596/63-69-00); **Avis,** at rue Ernest-Deproges 4, in Fort-de-France (☎ **800/331-2112** in the U.S., or 596/51-11-70); and **Hertz,** at rue Ernest-Deproges 24, in Fort-de-France (☎ **800/654-3001** in the U.S., or 596/60-64-64). Although each of these rental companies also maintains a kiosk at Lamentin Airport with staffs willing to transport prospective renters to pickup depots a short drive away, prices are usually lower if you reserve a car in North America at least 2 business days before your arrival.

Remember that regardless of which company you choose, you'll be hit with a value-added tax (VAT) of 9.5% on top of the final car-rental bill. (The VAT for some luxury goods, including jewelry, on Martinique can go as high as 14%.) Collision-damage waivers (CDWs), an excellent idea in a country where the populace drives somewhat recklessly, cost $11.60 to $20 per day.

BY FERRY The least expensive way to go between quai d'Esnambuc in Fort-de-France and Pointe du Bout is by ferry (*vedette*), which costs 19F ($3.80) per passenger. Ferry schedules are printed in the free visitor's guide, *Choubouloute,* which is distributed by the tourist office. However, if the weather is bad and/or the seas are rough, all the ferryboat services may be canceled.

There's also a smaller ferryboat that runs between Fort-de-France and the small-scale, unpretentious beach resorts of Anse Mitan and Anse-à-l'Ane, both across the bay and home to many two- and three-star hotels and several modest and unassuming Créole restaurants. A boat departs daily from quai d'Esnambuc in Fort-de-France at 30-minute intervals every day between 6am and 6:30pm. The trip takes only about

15 minutes, but the fare is the same as that for the above-mentioned ferryboat for Pointe du Bout.

BY BICYCLE & MOTORBIKE   You can rent motorscooters from **Funny,** rue Ernest-Deproges 80, in Fort-de-France (☎ **596/63-33-05**). The new 18-speed VTT (*velo tout terrain,* or all-terrain bike) is gradually making inroads from mainland France into the rugged countryside of Martinique, although there aren't many places to rent one. For tour information and possible rentals of these mountain bikes, as well as scooters, contact **Jacques-Henry Vartel,** VT Tilt, Anse Mitan (☎ **596/66-01-01**).

FAST FACTS: Martinique

Banking Hours   Banks are open Monday to Friday from 7:30am to noon and 2:30 to 4pm.

Consulate   The nearest U.S. consulate is on Barbados.

Currency   The **French franc (F)** is the legal tender here. Prices in this chapter are in both U.S. dollars and French francs. Currently, 1 franc is worth about 20¢ (4.98F = $1 U.S.). Banks give much better exchange rates than hotels, and there's a money-exchange service, **Change Caraïbes** (☎ **596/42-17-11**), available at Lamentin Airport. Its downtown branch is at rue Ernest-Deproge 4 (☎ **596/73-06-16**).

Customs   Items for personal use, such as tobacco, cameras, and film, are admitted without formalities or tax if not in excessive quantity.

Documents   U.S. and Canadian citizens need proof of identity (a voter registration card or birth certificate, plus a photo ID, or a passport) for stays of less than 21 days. After that, a valid passport is required. A return or ongoing ticket is also necessary. British subjects need a valid passport.

Drugstores   Try the **Pharmacie de la Paix,** at the corner of rue Perrinon and rue Victor-Schoelcher in Fort-de-France (☎ **596/71-94-83**), open Monday to Friday from 7:15am to 6:15pm and on Saturday from 7:45am to 1pm.

Electricity   Electricity here is 220 volts AC, 50 cycles, the same as that used on the French mainland. However, check with your hotel to see if they have converted the electrical voltage and outlets in the bathrooms (some have). If they haven't, bring your own transformer and adapter for U.S. appliances.

Emergencies   Call the **police** at ☎ **17,** report a **fire** at ☎ **18,** and summon an **ambulance** at ☎ **596/75-15-75.**

Hospitals   There are 18 hospitals and clinics on the island, and a 24-hour emergency room at **Hôpital Pierre Zobda Quikman,** Châteauboeuf, right outside Fort-de-France (☎ **596/55-20-00**).

Information   The **Office Départemental du Tourisme** (tourist office) is on boulevard Alfassa in Fort-de-France (☎ **596/63-79-60**), open Monday to Friday from 8am to 5pm and on Saturday from 8am to noon. The Information Desk at Lamentin Airport is open daily until the last flight comes in.

Languages   French, the official language, is spoken by almost everyone. The local Créole patois uses words borrowed from France, England, Spain, and Africa. In the wake of increased tourism, English is occasionally spoken in the major hotels, restaurants, and tourist organizations—but don't count on driving around the countryside and asking for directions in English.

Safety   Crime is hardly rampant on Martinique, yet there are still those who prey on unsuspecting tourists. Follow the usual precautions here, especially in Fort-de-France and in the tourist-hotel belt of Pointe du Bout. It's wise to protect your valuables and never leave them unguarded on the beach.

Telephone   To call Martinique from the United States, dial 011 (the international access code), then 596 (the country code for the Martinique), and finally the six-digit local number. When making a call from one place on Martinique to another on the island, you'll have to add a 0 (zero) to the country code (0596 for Martinique) and dial the four-digit country code plus the six-digit local number—in all, 10 digits for calls made on the island.

Time   Martinique is on Atlantic standard time year-round, 1 hour earlier than eastern standard time except when daylight saving time is in effect. Then Martinique time is the same as on the East Coast of the United States.

Water   Potable water is found throughout the island.

Weather   The climate is relatively mild—the average temperature is in the 75° to 85° Fahrenheit range.

TIPS FOR SAVING MONEY ON ACCOMMODATIONS

Family-run establishments are often called Relais Créoles. Although many of these are quite expensive, some are quite reasonable. However, don't expect the management to speak English, and also be prepared to find that your fellow guests may be French travelers on a budget. Nevertheless, some of the Relais Créoles—a sort of French West Indian B&B—represent some of the best accommodation values on Martinique.

Villa rentals, which can be arranged by the week or the month, are another option for families or groups traveling together. The **Villa Rental Service** of the Martinique Tourist Office (☎ 596/63-79-60) can arrange this type of vacation rental for you.

You can also contact **Gîtes de France,** B.P. 1122, 97209 Fort-de-France (☎ 596/73-67-92), which offers simple but comfortable studios and apartments in private homes. Also available are independent cottages as well as *chambres d'hôte* (B&B-style lodgings). Rates begin at 1,200F ($240) per week.

Camping can be done almost everywhere in the mountains, forests, and on the many beaches, although "indiscriminate" camping is not permitted. Only the French authorities can interpret what "indiscriminate" means. **Tropicamp at Gros Grisins Plage,** rue Schoelcher 6 (☎ 596/62-49-66), is one of several camps with full services, including hot showers. Other comfortable camps with showers and toilets are **Nid Tropical,** at Anse-à-l'Ane near Trois-Ilets (☎ 596/68-31-30); another one at **Vauclin,** on the southeast Atlantic coast (☎ 596/74-45-88), and yet another one at **Pointe Marin,** near the public beach of Ste-Anne (☎ 596/76-72-79). A nominal fee is charged for facilities. Between June and September camping is allowed in other areas that have no facilities whatsoever. For more details, contact the **Office National des Forêts,** km 3.5, route de Moutte, Fort-de-France (☎ 596/71-34-50).

Recreational vehicles are an ideal way of discovering the many natural and cultural riches found along Martinique's nearly 500 miles of roadway. One recommended camping car operation is **West Indies Tours,** which offers campers that are outfitted with beds for four, refrigerator, shower, sink, a 430-gallon water tank, dining table, stove, and radio-cassette player. Weekly rates are $565, $645, and $735, depending on the season. Contact Michel Toula at West Indies Tours, Le François (☎ 596/54-50-71).

You might also consider a package deal offered by **TourScan, Inc.,** P.O. Box 2367, Darien, CT 06820 (☎ **800/962-2080** or 203/665-8091). TourScan can inform you of package deals to more than 15 places on Martinique. Some best-value air-and-hotel packages begin at $508 per person for 3 nights, with extra days costing from only $30.

BEACHES & WATER SPORTS

BEACHES   The beaches south of Fort-de-France are white, whereas the northern strands are composed mostly of gray sand. Outstanding in the south is the $1^1/_2$ -mile **Plage des Salines,** near Ste-Anne, with palm trees and a long stretch of white sand, and the $2^1/_2$ -mile-long **Diamant,** with the landmark Diamond Rock offshore. Swimming on the Atlantic coast is for experts only, except at **Cap Chevalier** and **Presqu'île de la Caravelle Nature Preserve.**

The clean white sandy beaches of **Pointe du Bout,** site of the major hotels of Martinique, were created by developers. However, to the south the white-sand beaches at **Anse Mitan** have always been there welcoming visitors, including many snorkelers. Incidentally, nudist beaches are not officially sanctioned, although topless sunbathing is widely practiced at the big hotels, often around their swimming pools. Public beaches rarely have changing cabins or showers. Some hotels charge nonguests for the use of changing and beach facilities, and request a deposit for rental of towels.

SAILING   This popular pastime can cost quite a lot unless you have enough people in your party to split costs. Only a select few can afford yacht charters, either crewed or bareboat. If you want to see the waters around Martinique, it's better to go on one of the **sailboat excursions** in the bay of Fort-de-France and on the southeast coast of the island. Ask at your hotel desk what ships are taking passengers on cruises in Martinique waters. These vessels tend to change from season to season. On a smaller scale, many hotels, including the **Méridien** at Pointe du Bout (☎ **596/66-00-00**), will rent Hobie Cats and Sunfish to their guests, but only if sailing competence can be demonstrated.

SCUBA DIVING & SNORKELING   Scuba divers come here to explore the St-Pierre shipwrecks sunk in the 1902 volcano eruption and the Diamond Rock caves and walls. Small scuba centers operate at many of the hotels, but one of the major centers (open to all) is Bathy's Club in Pointe du Bout's Hôtel Méridien (see the Pointe du Bout section for details).

Snorkeling equipment is usually available free to hotel guests, who quickly learn that coral, fish, and ferns abound in the waters around the Pointe du Bout hotels.

WATERSKIING & WINDSURFING   Waterskiing is available at every beach near the large hotels. But windsurfing is the most popular sport in the French West Indies. Equipment and lessons are available at all hotel water-sports facilities, especially the **Hôtel Méridien.**

OUTDOOR PURSUITS FOR LANDLUBBERS

GOLF   The only golf course on the island is the Robert Trent Jones–designed 18-hole **Golf de l'Impératrice-Joséphine** at Trois-Ilets, a 5-minute drive from the leading resort area of Pointe du Bout and about 18 miles from Fort-de-France. See the Trois-Ilets section for details.

HIKING   Inexpensive guided excursions are organized year-round by the personnel of the **Parc Naturel Régional de la Martinique,** Excollège Agricole de Tivoli, B.P. 437, 97200 Fort-de-France (☎ **596/64-42-59**), and special excursions can be arranged for small groups.

Serious hiking excursions undertake to climb **Montagne Pelée** and explore the Gorges de la Falaise or the thick coastal rain forest between Grand' Rivière and Le Prêcheur. These are organized with local guides at certain times of the year by the park staff.

The **Presqu'île de la Caravelle Nature Preserve**, a well-protected peninsula jutting into the Atlantic Ocean, has safe beaches and well-marked trails to the ruins of historic Château Debuc and through tropical wetlands.

HORSEBACK RIDING The premier riding facility on Martinique, thriving since 1974, is **Ranch Jack,** Morne Habitué, Trois-Ilets. See the Trois-Ilets section for details.

TENNIS Each large hotel has courts. Residents play free during the day, and night games usually require a surcharge of around 15F ($3) per hour for illumination. Nonguests are charged about 50F ($10) per hour, although the tennis pros at Bathy's Club at the **Hôtel Méridien** (see below) in Pointe du Bout usually allow nonresidents to play for free if the courts are otherwise unoccupied—except at night.

You can also play at one of the three courts on the grounds of **Golf de l'Impératrice-Joséphine** at Trois-Ilets (see the Trois-Ilets section), a 5-minute drive from the major hotels at Pointe du Bout.

FORT-DE-FRANCE

A melange of New Orleans and Menton (French Riviera), Fort-de-France is the main town of Martinique. It lies at the end of a large bay surrounded by evergreen hills. Iron-grillwork balconies overflowing with flowers are commonplace here.

The proud people of Martinique are even more fascinating than the town, although today the Créole women are likely to be seen in jeans instead of their traditional turbans and Empress Joséphine–style gowns, and they rarely wear those massive earrings that used to jounce and sway as they sauntered along.

Narrow streets climb up the steep hills on which houses have been built to catch the overflow of the capital's more than 100,000 inhabitants.

WHERE TO STAY

Rates are sometimes advertised in U.S. dollars, sometimes in French francs, and sometimes in a combination of both.

Doubles for Less than $75

Hôtel Malmaison. Rue de la Liberté 7, 97200 Fort-de-France, Martinique, F.W.I. ☎ **596/ 63-90-85.** Fax 596/60-03-93. 20 rms. A/C TV TEL. Year-round, 250F–330F ($50–$66) single or double. AE, MC, V.

This cost-conscious inner-city hotel shows some of the battering it's received since it was built 60 years ago. It welcomes a clientele of local residents, business travelers from other parts of the Caribbean, and off-island musicians playing at any of Martinique's resorts. Despite the building's age, the bedrooms are outfitted with modern furniture, wooden tables, chairs, and armoires, and vague references to the French Empire style. The staff probably won't pay much attention to you after you've registered, but you'll have easy access to the bars and cheap restaurants of Fort-de-France.

Le Lafayette. Rue de la Liberté 5, 97200 Fort-de-France, Martinique, F.W.I. ☎ **596/73- 80-50.** Fax 596/60-65-79. 24 rms. A/C MINIBAR TV TEL. Year-round, 310F–340F ($62–$68) single; 370F–400F ($74–$80) double. AE, DC, MC, V.

You'll enter this modest downtown hotel, located right on La Savane, through rue Victor-Hugo; the reception hall is up a few terra-cotta steps. The dark-brown wooden doors are offset by soft beige walls. Japanese wall tapestries decorate the cramped and slightly dowdy bedrooms; most rooms contain twin beds, with pure-white bathrooms. The overall impression is neat but simple. The bedrooms at this unpretentious hotel were partially renovated in 1992. The inn is the oldest continuously operating hotel on Martinique, originally built in the 1940s with quasi–art deco hints that are now slightly dowdy. There's no on-site restaurant, but several eateries are within a short walk.

A Nearby Place to Stay
Martinique Cottages. B.P. 408, Jeanne d'Arc, Pays Mélé, 97232 Lamentin, Martinique, F.W.I. ☎ **596/50-16-08.** Fax 596/50-26-83. 8 cottages, all with kitchenette. TV TEL. Year-round, 290F ($58) cottage for one; 340F ($68) cottage for two. AE, MC, V.

Its only major drawback is that it's a 15-minute drive to reach the nearest beach, Plage Tartane or Plage de Ste-Luce. Other than that, you might be very happy in one of the eight pale-pink bungalows (all built in 1988) that comprise this pleasant resort. The resident owners are the brother-sister team of Peggy and Jean-Marc Arnaud, who deliberately painted the roofs of their bungalows in a different color (green, red, or white), and who work hard at maintaining the verdant garden around their buildings. Each bungalow contains one compact living unit with its own veranda, a ceiling fan, and locally made wooden furnishings. The establishment is a 5-minute drive from the island's international airport and a 15-minute drive from the cheap eateries of Fort-de-France.

The on-site restaurant (La Plantation) might be a bit more expensive than readers of this guide might prefer, but the food is well prepared and the setting is more stylish than the low cost of the accommodations might imply.

WHERE TO EAT
Abri-Cotier. Pointe-Simon. ☎ **596/63-66-46.** Main courses 50F–150F ($10–$30). AE, DC, MC, V. Daily noon–3pm and 7–11pm. (Bar, daily 10am–1am.) CREOLE.

It's little more than a wood-sided hut with Créole styling, with a wide veranda overlooking the harborfront and the parking lot. The management encourages cafe patrons to sit on the covered veranda and dining patrons to eat inside at cramped tables arranged bistro style in the darkly paneled interior. Don't expect grand cuisine—the venue is simple, raffish, and uncomplicated, but the service is fast and friendly. Menu items are predictably Créole and include a fricassée of shrimp, chicken with curry, rack of lamb, boudin Créole, and a brochette of seafood. Flavors are zesty, the taste is "of the island," and no one puts on airs here.

The Crew (L'Equipage). Rue Ernest-Deproges 42. ☎ **596/73-04-14.** Main courses 63F–105F ($12.60–$21). MC, V. Mon–Fri noon–3pm and 7–10pm, Sat noon–3pm. FRENCH/CREOLE.

Set in a wood-sided house that was erected near the port 150 years ago, this restaurant is outfitted in a nautical theme with wood trim. Styled after the kind of workaday brasserie you'd expect to find on the French mainland, it's in the heart of town, does a busy lunchtime trade with local office workers and shopkeepers, and specializes in unfussy but traditional French and grilled cuisine. A choice of appetizers is included in the price of a main course. Menu items feature large platters of such items as escargots, mussels in white-wine sauce, steak tartare, chunky pâtés, grilled chicken, fish, and steak, and—if you're interested—tripe.

♦ Le Second Souffle. Rue Blénac 27. ☎ **596/63-44-11.** Main courses 40F–50F ($8–$10); fixed-price four-course lunch or dinner 75F ($15). No credit cards. Mon–Fri 11am–3pm and 7–10pm. VEGETARIAN.

This restaurant prides itself on being the only vegetarian restaurant on Martinique that prepares its dishes exclusively from local ingredients. Set in a woodsy and rustic dining room very close to Fort-de-France's cathedral, it employs a staff of health-conscious local residents. You can admire a series of wall murals as you wait for medium- and large-sized platters of *crudités,* casseroles concocted from such vegetables as eggplant and christophine, vegetarian soups, and salads. Dessert might be a *filet de tinain* (miniature green bananas) served with chocolate sauce.

Early in 1995 the owners of this place opened a second branch, with very much the same price structure and format, at rue Albert-Camus 73, in the village of Lamentin (☎ **596/57-14-28**), near the airport. Unlike its main branch, however, it's open only for lunch Monday to Friday from 11am to 3:30pm. Both restaurants' names, incidentally, are references to the surges of energy (*les seconds souffles*) which anyone feels when refreshed with a healthy meal.

✪ **Marie-Sainte.** Rue Victor-Hugo 160. ☎ **596/70-00-30.** Fixed-price lunch 65F ($13). AE, V. Mon–Sat noon–4pm. CREOLE.

In its way this one of the most evocative restaurants in town, the kind of place that you'd expect in remote areas of the island, but not right in the capital. Your host is Agnés Marie-Sainte, a venerable Créole cook whose recipes for *boudin Créole, daube de poisson,* and *colombo* of mutton were derived from her ancestors. Continuing the maternal links that have propelled Créole food through the ages, she's assisted by her daughter Tézé. Together, in a simple dining room that's likely to be crowded with local residents, they offer fixed-price lunches with a strong emphasis on fresh fish (grilled or fried), and perhaps a fricassée of conch, always accompanied by a medley of such *legumes de pays* as fresh beans, dasheen, breadfruit, and christophine. This is about as authentic as it gets, and also as inexpensive as you're likely to find for meals of such quality and authenticity. Note that only lunch is served.

SEEING THE SIGHTS

At the center of the town lies a broad garden planted with many palms and mangos, **La Savane,** a handsome savanna with shops and cafes lining its sides. In the middle of this grand square stands a statue of Joséphine, "Napoléon's little Créole," made of white marble by Vital Debray. With the grace of a Greek goddess, the statue poses in a Regency gown and looks toward Trois-Ilets, where she was born.

If you like masquerades and dancing in the streets, you should attend ✪ **carnival,** or "Vaval" as this event of the year is known here. Carnival begins right after the New Year, as each village prepares costumes and floats. Weekend after weekend, frenzied celebrations take place, reaching fever pitch just before Lent.

Fort-de-France is the focal point, and the spirit of carnival envelops the island, as narrow streets are jammed with floats. On Ash Wednesday the streets of Fort-de-France are filled with *diablesses,* or she-devils (portrayed by members of both sexes). Costumed in black and white, they crowd the streets to form King Carnival's funeral procession. As devils cavort about and the rum flows, a funeral pyre is built at La Savane. When it's set on fire, the dancing of those "she-devils" becomes frantic (often because many are thoroughly drunk at this point). Long past dusk, the cortège takes the coffin to its burial, ending carnival until another year.

At any time of the year your next stop should be the **St. Louis Roman Catholic Cathedral,** on rue Victor-Schoelcher, built in 1875. Someone once likened this extraordinary iron building to "a sort of Catholic railway station."

A statue in front of the Palais de Justice is of the island's second main historical figure, Victor Schoelcher (you'll see his name a lot on Martinique). He worked to free the slaves more than a century ago. The **Bibliothèque Schoelcher,** rue de la Liberté (☎ **596/70-26-67**), also honors this popular hero. The elaborate structure was first displayed at the Paris Exposition of 1889. However, the Romanesque portal in red and blue, the Egyptian lotus-petal columns, even the turquoise tiles were imported piece by piece from Paris and reassembled here.

Guarding the port is **Fort St-Louis,** built in the Vauban style on a rocky promontory. In addition, **Fort Tartenson** and **Fort Desaix** stand on hills overlooking the port.

The **Musée Départemental de la Martinique,** rue de la Liberté 9 (☎ 596/71-57-05), the one bastion on Martinique that preserves its pre-Columbian past, has relics left from the early settlers, the peaceful Arawaks, and the cannibalistic Caribs. The museum faces the Savane and is open Monday to Friday from 8:30am to 5pm and on Saturday from 9am to noon and 2 to 5pm, charging 15F ($3) for adults and 5F ($1) for children.

The **Sacré-Coeur de Balata Cathedral,** at Balata, overlooking Fort-de-France, is a copy of the one looking down on Montmartre in Paris—and this one is just as incongruous, maybe more so. It's reached by going along route de la Trace (route N3). Balata is 6 miles north of Fort-de-France.

A few minutes away on route N3, the **Jardin de Balata (Balata Garden)** (☎ 596/64-48-73) is a tropical botanical park. The park was created by Jean-Philippe Thoze on land the jungle was rapidly reclaiming around a Créole house that belonged to his grandmother. He has also restored the house, furnishing it with antiques and engravings depicting life in other days, and with bouquets and baskets of fruit renewed daily. The garden contains flowers, shrubs, and trees growing in profusion and offering a vision of tropical splendor. Balata is open daily from 9am to 5pm. Admission is 35F ($7) for adults and 15F ($3) for children.

SHOPPING

Your best buys on Martinique are French luxury imports, such as perfumes, fashions, Vuitton luggage, Lalique crystal, or Limoges dinnerware. Sometimes (but don't count on it) prices are as much as 30% to 40% below those in the United States.

If you pay in dollars, store owners supposedly will give you a 20% discount; however, when you pay in dollars the exchange rates vary considerably from store to store, and almost invariably they're far less favorable than the rate offered at one of the local banks. The net result is that you received a 20% discount, but then they take away 9% to 15% on the dollar exchange, giving you a net savings of only 5% to 11%—not 20%. Actually, you're better off shopping in the smaller stores where prices are 8% to 12% less on comparable items and by paying in francs that you've exchanged at a local bank.

The main shopping street is **rue Victor-Hugo.** The other two leading shopping streets are **rue Schoelcher** and **rue St-Louis.** However, the most boutique-filled shopping streets are **rue Antione Siger, rue Lamartine,** and **rue Moreau-de-Jones.** Here you'll find the latest French designer fashions. Facing the tourist office and alongside **quai d'Esnambuc** is an open market where you can purchase local handcrafts and souvenirs. Many of these are tacky, however.

Far more interesting is the display of vegetables and fruit—quite a show—at the **open-air stalls along rue Isambert.** Don't miss it for its local ambience, and you can't help but smell the **fish market** alongside the Levassor River.

Gourmet chefs will find all sorts of spices in the open-air markets, or such goodies as tinned pâté or canned quail in the local *supermarchés.*

For the ubiquitous local fabric, madras, there are shops on every street with bolts and bolts of it, all colorful and inexpensive. So-called haute couture and resortwear are sold in many boutiques dotting downtown Fort-de-France.

Try to postpone your shopping trip if a cruise ship is in town, to avoid the stampede.

Cadet-Daniel. Rue Antoine-Siger 72. ☎ **596/71-41-48.**

Cadet-Daniel, which opened in 1840, offers the best buys in French china and crystal. It competes with Roger Albert in this respect, and which one offers the better deal changes from year to year, so it pays to compare before you buy. Cadet-Daniel sells Christofle silver, Limoges china, and crystal from Daum, Baccarat, and Lalique. Since the astronomical rise in prices of fine silver, porcelain, and crystal, however, the outfit has concentrated to an increasing degree on 18-karat-gold jewelry, crafted on Martinique into traditional Créole patterns.

La Case á Rhum. In the Galerie Marchande, rue de la Liberté 5. ☎ **596/73-73-20.**

Aficionados consider Martinique rum to be one of the world's finest distilled drinks. Hemingway in *A Moveable Feast* lauded it as the perfect antidote to a rainy day. This shop is the best place for browsing, offering all the brands of rum manufactured on Martinique (at least 12), as well as several others famous for their age and taste. Bottles range upward in price from $6. You can taste samples. We suggest that you try Vieux Acajou, a dark, mellow Old Mahogany, or a blood-red-brown liqueurlike rum bottled by Bally.

Centre des Métiers d'Art. Rue Ernest-Deproges. ☎ **596/70-25-01.**

This arts-and-crafts store is adjacent to the tourist office, fronting the town's waterfront. Inside is a mixture of valuable and worthless local, handmade artifacts, including bamboo, ceramics, painted fabrics, and patchwork quilts suitable for hanging. There's also a collection of original tapestries made by the store's charming owner, Yvonne Elima.

Galeries Lafayette. Rue Victor-Schoelcher 10 (near the cathedral). ☎ **596/71-38-66.**

This is a small-scale branch (a pale version) of what is the most famous department store in Paris, the world-class Galeries Lafayette. Specializing in fashion for men, women, and children, it also offers leather goods, jewelry, watches, and all the predictably famous names in French perfume and fashion. The store offers 20% off for purchases made with U.S.-dollar traveler's checks or a credit or charge card.

Nouvelles Galeries. Rue Lamartine 87. ☎ **596/63-04-60.**

This is another of the capital's large department stores, stocked with a downscale, not-very-glamorous assortment of products for the home and kitchen. Despite the many workaday items, it's also known for its toys, luggage, beauty accessories, china, crystal, and silver. Come here to look for occasional bargains. The emphasis is French with Caribbean overtones.

Paradise Island. Rue Ernest-Deproges 20. ☎ **596/63-93-63.**

It maintains the most stylish and upscale collection of T-shirts on Martinique, each displayed as a kind of couture-conscious art form. Whatever you like will probably be available in about a dozen different colors, and priced at 49F to 99F ($9.80 to $19.80) each.

Roger Albert. Rue Victor-Hugo 7–9. ☎ **596/71-71-71.**

This is by far the largest emporium of luxury goods on Martinique, a department store for locals and cruise-ship passengers. It's one of five different branches scattered throughout Martinique, although this one, a short walk from the waterfront, is by far the busiest. You'll find wristwatches, perfumes, sportswear by Lacoste and

Tacchini, Lladró and Limoges porcelain, and crystal by Swarovski and such other manufacturers as Daum and Lalique. For anyone with a non-French passport there are reductions of 20%, plus discounts of an additional 20%, depending on seasonal discounts and promotions. Even better, VAT (value-added tax) is not added to the price.

TROIS-ILETS

Marie-Josèphe-Rose Tascher de la Pagerié was born here in 1763. As Joséphine, she was to become the wife of Napoléon I and empress of France from 1804 to 1809. She'd been married before to Alexandre de Beauharnais, who'd actually wanted to wed either of her two more attractive sisters. Six years older than Napoléon, she pretended that she'd lost her birth certificate so he wouldn't find out her true age. Although many historians call her ruthless and selfish (certainly unfaithful), she is still revered by some on Martinique as an uncommonly gracious lady. Others have less kind words for her, because Napoléon is said by some historians to have "reinvented" slavery, and blame Joséphine's influence.

After 20 miles of driving south from Fort-de-France, you reach Trois-Ilets, a charming little village. One mile outside the hamlet, turn left to **La Pagerié,** where a small museum (☎ 596/68-33-06) of mementos relating to Joséphine has been installed in the former estate kitchen. Along with her childhood bed in the kitchen, you'll see a passionate letter from Napoléon. The collection was compiled by Dr. Robert Rose-Rosette. Here Joséphine gossiped with her slaves and played the guitar.

Still remaining are the partially restored ruins of the Pagerié sugar mill and the church (in the village itself) where she was christened in 1763. The plantation was destroyed in a hurricane. The museum is open Tuesday to Friday from 9am to 5:30pm and on Saturday and Sunday from 9am to 1pm and 2:30 to 5:30pm, charging 20F ($4) for admission.

A botanical garden, the **Parc des Floralies,** is adjacent to the golf course Golf de l'Impératrice-Joséphine, as is the museum devoted to Joséphine described above.

Maison de la Canne, Pointe Vatable (☎ 596/68-32-04), stands on the road to Trois-Ilets. (From Fort-de-France, you can take a taxi or shuttle bus to La Marina, Pointe du Bout; from here, a bus heads for Pointe Vatable.) It was created in 1987 to house a permanent exhibition that tells the story of sugarcane, with panels, models, tools, a miniature slave ship, an ancient plow tethered to life-size models of two oxen, and a restored carriage. Hostesses guide visitors through the exhibition. It's open Tuesday to Sunday from 9:30am to 5:30pm, with an admission fee of 15F ($3).

OUTDOOR PURSUITS

GOLF   The famous golf course designer Robert Trent Jones Sr. visited Martinique and left behind, in 1976, the 18-hole ✪ **Golf de l'Impératrice-Joséphine** at Trois-Ilets (☎ 596/68-32-81), a 5-minute drive from the leading resort area of Pointe du Bout and about 18 miles from Fort-de-France. At the only golf course on Martinique, the greens slope from the birthplace of Empress Joséphine (for whom it's named), across rolling hills with scenic vistas down to the sea. Amenities include a pro shop, a bar, a restaurant, and three tennis courts. Greens fees are 270F ($54) per person for 18 holes.

HORSEBACK RIDING   The premier riding facility on Martinique is **Ranch Jack,** Morne Habitué, Trois-Ilets (☎ 596/68-37-69). It offers morning horseback rides for both experienced and novice riders, for 340F ($68) per person for a 3½- to 4-hour ride. Jacques and Marlene Guinchard make daily promenades across the beaches and fields of Martinique, with a running explication of the history, fauna, and botany of the island. Cold drinks are included in the price, and transportation is usually free to and from the hotels of nearby Pointe du Bout. This is an ideal way to discover both botanical and geographical Martinique. Between 4 and 15 participants are required for a tour.

TENNIS   Play one of the three courts on the grounds of **Golf de l'Impératrice-Joséphine** at Trois-Ilets (☎ 596/68-32-81) for 50F ($10) per hour. No racquets are rented.

SHOPPING

Poterie de Trois-Ilets. Quartier Poterie, Trois-Ilets. ☎ **596/68-03-44.**

At Christmastime, many of the island's traditional foie gras and pastries are presented in crocks made by Martinique's largest earthenware factories, the Poterie de Trois-Ilets. At least 90% of its production is devoted to brickmaking. However, one small-scale offshoot of the company devotes itself to the production of earth-toned stoneware and pottery whose colors and shapes have contributed to the folklore of Martinique. In theory the studios are open Monday to Saturday from 7am to 4pm, but call before you set out to make sure they'll accept visitors.

POINTE DU BOUT

Pointe du Bout is a narrow peninsula across the bay from the busy capital of Fort-de-France. It's the best-accessorized resort area of Martinique, with at least four of the island's largest hotels, an impressive marina, about a dozen tennis courts, swimming pools, and facilities for horseback riding and all kinds of water sports. There's also a handful of independent restaurants, a gambling casino, and boutiques. Except for the hillside which contains the Hôtel Bakoua, most of the hotel district is flat and verdant, with carefully maintained gardens and rigidly monitored parking zones.

GETTING THERE   To drive there from Fort-de-France, leave by route 1, which takes you for a few minutes along the autoroute. You cross the plain of Lamentin, the industrial area of Fort-de-France and the site of the international airport. Very frequently the air is filled with the fragrance of caramel because of the large sugar-cane factories in the surrounding area.

After 20 miles of driving you reach Trois-Ilets, Joséphine's hometown. Three miles farther on your right, take D38 to Pointe du Bout.

For those who want to reach Pointe du Bout by sea, there's a ferry service (see "Getting Around," above), running all day long (until midnight) from Fort-de-France for a fare of 28F ($5.60) round-trip.

WHERE TO STAY

Auberge de L'Anse Mitan. Anse Mitan, 97229 Trois-Ilets, Martinique, F.W.I. ☎ **800/223-9815** in the U.S., or 596/66-01-12. Fax 596/66-01-05. 19 rms, 6 studios. A/C TEL. Winter, 330F ($66) single; 420F ($84) double; 400F ($80) studio for one or two. Off-season, 280F ($56) single; 330F ($66) double; 300F ($60) studio for one or two. Room (but not studio) rates include breakfast. AE, DC, MC, V.

Many of its guests like this hotel's location at the isolated end of a road whose more commercial side is laden with restaurants and a bustling nighttime parade. The hotel was built in 1930, but it has been renovated several times since then by the hospitable Athanase family. What you see today is a three-story concrete box–type structure. Six of the units are studios with kitchens and TVs; all have private shower. You don't get a lot that's special here, but few object to the price.

Rivage Hôtel. Anse Mitan, 97229 Trois-Ilets, Martinique, F.W.I. ☎ **596/66-00-53.** Fax 596/66-06-56. 18 rms, 9 with kitchenette. A/C. Year-round, 300F ($60) single; 350F ($70) double;

Begin the Beguine

The sexy and rhythmic beguine is *not* an invention of Cole Porter. It's a dance of the islands—though exactly which island depends on whom you ask. Popular wisdom and the encyclopedia give the nod to Martinique. Guadeloupeans claim it for their own, and to watch them dance it might convince you of their claim. Of course, calypso and the merengue move rhythmically along too—these islanders are known for their dancing.

On Guadeloupe, the folkloric troupe **Ballets Guadeloupeans** makes frequent appearances at the big hotels, whirling and moving to the rhythms of island music in colorful costumes and well-choreographed routines. Some resorts, including the Club Med–Caravelle, use their weekly visit to set the theme for the evening with the restaurant, La Beguine, serving up a banquet of traditional island dishes to accompany the dance, music, and costumes.

Ask at your hotel where the Ballets Guadeloupeans will be appearing during your stay, as their schedule tends to vary as they tour the island. You can catch them as they rotate through the hotels Arawak, Salako, L'Auberge de la Vieille Tour, and Callinago, as well as the Club Med–Caravelle. On the night of any of these performances, you can order a drink at the bar for 30F ($6) and witness the show, or partake of a hotel buffet for 250F ($50). Buffets usually start around 8pm, with the show beginning at 8:30pm. The troupe also performs on some cruise ships.

More famous than the dancers on Guadeloupe, however, is the touring group **Les Grands Ballets Martiniquais** on their sibling island. Everybody who goes to Martinique wants to see the show performed by this bouncy group of about two dozen dancers, along with musicians, singers, and choreographers. This most interesting program of folk dances in the Caribbean was launched in the early 1960s, and their performances of the traditional dances of Martinique have been acclaimed in both Europe and the States. With a swoosh of gaily striped skirts and clever acting, the dancers capture all the exuberance of the island's soul. The group has toured abroad with great success, but they perform best on their home ground, presenting tableaux that tell of jealous brides and faithless husbands, demanding overseers and toiling cane cutters. Dressed in traditional costumes, the island women and men dance the spirited mazurka, which was brought from the ballrooms of Europe, and, of course, the exotic beguine.

Les Grands Ballets Martiniquais perform Monday at the Hôtel Diamant-Novotel, Wednesday at the Novotel Carayou, Thursday at the Méridien Trois-Ilets, Friday at the Bakoua Beach, and Saturday at Hôtel La Bataliére—but this, too, can vary, so check locally. In addition, the troupe gives mini-performances aboard visiting cruise ships. The cost of dinner and the show is usually 200F ($40) per person. Most performances are at 8:30pm, with dinners at the hotels beginning at 7:30pm.

Whoever performs it for you, on whichever island, you'll soon realize that the beguine is more than a dance—it's a way of life. It's best to see it for yourself—or dance it, if you think you can.

400F ($80) triple. Kitchenette supplement 50F–60F ($10–$12). Extra person 100F ($20). MC, V.

Across the road from the beach, this small and simple hotel has units either with private kitchens or small refrigerators. There's a modest swimming pool on the premises, but many visitors prefer the nearby sea. (As you swim, the lights of Fort-de-France twinkle across the bay from the faraway shoreline.) A barbecue pit set up in the garden is used by guests for their own cookout parties. There aren't many amenities at this hotel, although the bars, restaurants, and sporting facilities of Anse Mitan are a short walk away. Despite its somewhat-bland format, the hotel offers good value for the money.

WHERE TO EAT

Au Poisson d'Or. L'Anse Mitan. ☎ **596/66-01-80.** Reservations recommended. Main courses 70F–150F ($14–$30); fixed-price menu 110F ($22). AE, MC, V. Tues–Sun noon–2:30pm and 7–10pm. Closed July. CREOLE.

Its position near the entrance of the resort community of Pointe du Bout makes it easy to find. There's no view of the sea and the traffic runs close to the edge of the veranda and terrace, but the reasonable prices and the complete change of pace make up for that. The rustic dining room offers such menu items as grilled fish, grilled conch, grilled seafood, scallops sautéed in white wine, poached local fish, and flan. These ordinary dishes are prepared with a certain flair and served with style.

Le Cantonnais. La Marina, Pointe du Bout. ☎ **596/66-02-33.** Main courses 55F–120F ($11–$24); fixed-price dinner 85F–130F ($17–$26). AE, MC, V. Wed–Mon 6:30–11pm. CHINESE.

Amid a classic Chinese decor of red and gold, this moderately priced restaurant across the road from the Méridien Hôtel offers Asian food whose flavors and colors are sometimes a welcome change from a constant diet of Créole and Caribbean food. Try broiled shark fin, chicken with salted-bean sauce, or steamed ribs with black-bean sauce. The restaurant's sliced duckling with plum sauce is excellent, too. Soups include braised bird's nest with minced chicken and a soothing version of egg drop.

Restaurant Les Châteaux. Pointe des Châteaux. ☎ **596/88-43-53.** Main courses 80F–325F ($16–$65). AE, DC, MC, V. Daily 11am–2:30pm and 7–10pm. CREOLE.

Many visitors make this gazebo-style restaurant the final destination of drives to the extreme eastern tip of Grande-Terre. Although some dishes are prohibitively expensive, many others cost under 110F ($22) each, and might comprise a meal in their own right. Lunches are informal affairs where at least some guests may dine in bathing suits. Dinners are a bit more formal but still permeated in a barefoot kind of charm that's heightened by the isolation you might feel on Guadeloupe's flat, sandy, and scrub-covered eastern tip. For savory local fare, try squid in Créole sauce, a court bouillon of fish (a version that's been simmering on the stove all day), several preparations of lobster, and an unusual *salade de coffre* that's concocted from the tenderized and grilled flesh of a local fish (*le coffre*) whose armor is so tough that local fishers compare it to a crustacean.

PLAYING IN THE WATER

DIVING   The Hôtel Méridien's **Bathy's Club** (☎ 596/66-00-00) is one of the major scuba centers for Pointe du Bout and welcomes anyone who shows up. Daily dive trips, depending on demand, leave from the Hôtel Méridien's pier. Prices include equipment rental, transportation, guide, and drinks on board. Dives are conducted twice daily, from 8am to noon and 2 to 6pm, and full-day charters can be arranged. The dive shop on the Méridien's beach stocks everything from weight belts and tanks to partial wet suits and underwater cameras. Dives cost 290F ($58) per person.

WINDSURFING   This is the most popular sport in the French West Indies. Equipment and lessons are available at all hotel water-sports facilities, especially at the **Hôtel Méridien,** Pointe du Bout (☎ 596/66-00-00), where 30-minute lessons cost 60F to 100F ($12 to $20). Board rentals are only 100F ($20) per hour.

SHOPPING

You'll find that the Marina complex has a number of interesting boutiques. Several sell handcrafts and curios from Martinique. They're sometimes of good quality, and are quite expensive, regrettably, particularly if you purchase some of the batiks of natural silk and the enameled jewel boxes.

La Belle Matadore. Immeuble Vermeil-Marina, Pointe du Bout. ☎ **596/66-04-88.**

The shop owner, Martinique-born Marie-Josée Ravenel, has carefully researched the history and traditions associated with the island's jewelry. Nearly all the merchandise sold here derives from models developed during slave days by the *matadores* (prostitutes), midwives, and slaves. The vivid and bold designs are for the most part crafted from 18-karat gold. Especially popular are the necklaces, brooches, and pendants popularized in the 18th and 19th centuries. Midway between the La Pagerié Hôtel and the Hôtel Méridien, the store carries baubles that range upward in price from 60F ($12) for a pendant shaped like Martinique.

THE SOUTH LOOP

We now leave Pointe du Bout and head south for more sun and beaches. Resort centers here include **Le Diamant** and **Ste-Anne.**

On the way to them from Trois-Ilets, you can follow a small curved road that brings you to **Anse-à-l'Ane, Grande Anse,** and **Anses d'Arlets.** At any of these places are small beaches, quite safe and usually not crowded.

ANSES D'ARLETS

This charming little village features a white-sand beach dotted with brightly painted *gommiers* (fishing boats), a good-size pier from which children swim and oldsters fish, a pretty steepled church, a bandstand for holiday concerts, and a smattering of modest little dining spots. A street—rue du Président-Kennedy—honors the slain American president.

The waters off Anses d'Arlets are a playground for scuba divers, with a wide variety of small tropical fish and colorful coral formations. The area itself has been for many years a choice spot for weekend "second homes," and is now beginning to develop touristically.

From Anses d'Arlets, route D37 takes you to Diamant. The road offers much scenery.

LE DIAMANT

Set on the island's southwestern coastline, this village offers a good beach, which is open to the prevailing southern winds. The village is named after one of Martinique's best-known geological oddities, Le Rocher du Diamant (Diamond Rock), a barren offshore island that juts upward from the sea to a height of 573 feet. Sometimes referred to as the Gibraltar of the Caribbean, it figured prominently in a daring British-led invasion in 1804, when British mariners carried a formidable amount of ammunition and 110 sailors to the top. Here, despite frequent artillery bombardments from the French-held coastline, the garrison held out for 18 months, completely dominating the passageway between the rock and the coastline of Martinique. Intrepid foreigners sometimes visit Diamond Rock, but the access across the strong currents of the channel is risky.

✪ **Diamond Beach,** on the Martinique mainland, offers a sandy bottom, verdant groves of swaying palms, and many different surf and bathing possibilities. The entire district has developed in recent years into a resort, scattered with generally small hotels, most of which consist of simple clusters of low-rise buildings with good land-scaping and access to the beach.

Where to Stay

Chambre d'Hôte Diamant Noir. Anse Cafard, Dizac, 97233 Diamant, Martinique, F.W.I. ☎ **596/76-41-25.** Fax 596/76-28-89. 9 rms. 311F ($62.20) single; 386F ($77.20) double. Rates include breakfast. No credit cards.

Much of the allure of this place derives from its charming owners, Dominique and Elléna Bertin. Their establishment consists of a 25-year-old main villa set in a sprawl-ing and well-maintained garden and a newer, 1-year-old annex immediately adjacent to the sea. It's about 1¹/₂ miles from Bourg Le Diamant, painted white with pink shutters, swathed in trailing strands of bougainvillea, and ringed with fruit trees. The beach lies within 100 yards of the place. Only breakfast is served, but at least two res-taurants are within an easy walk, and a communal kitchen is available for use by all guests.

Hôtel Relais Caraïbes. La Cherry, 97223 Diamant, Martinique, F.W.I. ☎ **596/76-44-65.** Fax 596/76-21-20. 3 rms, 12 bungalows. A/C TV TEL. Winter, 600F ($120) single; 700F ($140) double; 780F–1,190F ($156–$238) bungalow for two. Off-season, 350F–550F ($70–$110) single; 450F–650F ($90–$130) double; 600F–850F ($120–$170) bungalow for two. MC, V.

Despite its charm (some visitors define it as a tropical inn with an ocean view), the Caraïbes isn't as prohibitively expensive as you might think after an initial glance. It consists of a main building (which contains a trio of rooms above its restaurant) and a dozen bungalows scattered over carefully clipped lawns. Each bungalow offers a porch and a view from their clifftop location over the water to the jagged crags of Diamond Rock. (The bedrooms don't have ocean views.) Although privacy is assured by this inn's location about a mile from the main highway, the beach lies within a 5-minute walk. If you don't want to trek down to the beach, there's a pool perched along the clifftop, close to the resort's main building. Many different water sports are offered, including scuba.

L'Ecrin Bleu. Morne de la Croix, 97223 Le Diamant, Martinique, FWI. ☎ **596/76-41-92.** Fax 0596/76-41-90. 20 rms. A/C. Winter, 490F ($98) single; 525F ($105) double. Off-season, 380F ($76) single; 430F ($86) double. Rates include breakfast. AE, MC, V.

In the rocky hills above the hamlet of Bourg Le Diamant, this blue-and-white hotel was built in the early 1990s by a family (the Tosatos) from Marseilles. Isolated on virtually every side, and composed of three separate buildings, it offers clean, care-fully decorated bedrooms that each have views sweeping out over the sea and the lofty heights of Diamond Rock. The beach is a 5-minute downhill walk away, and there's access to all kinds of scuba-related activities. There's also a swimming pool and a res-taurant that's open only for dinner, every night from 7pm until at least 10:30pm. Here, French and Caribbean food, with an emphasis on different preparations of lob-ster from shellfish kept in a holding tank, cost between 85F and 135F ($17 and $27) for a fixed-price meal.

Where to Eat

Chez Christiane. Rue Principale, Bourg Le Diamant. ☎ **596/76-49-55.** Main courses 70F–300F ($14–$60). AE, DC, MC, V. Mon–Sat 7–11pm. CREOLE.

On the main street of Bourg Le Diamant, amid a dining room decorated with var-nished bamboo and slats of local hardwood, you can taste the Créole specialties of Christiane Ravin, a matron who has earned the respect of her colleagues after almost a dozen years at her trade. Every Friday night live music plays in the dining room with an ambience more like a nightclub than a restaurant. Otherwise, it's a worthy choice for such menu items as fricassée of chicken or conch, curried shrimp, octopus with Créole sauce, and well-seasoned filets of fish that include local, freshly caught snapper.

LE MARIN

As you follow the road south to Trois-Rivières you'll come to **Ste-Luce,** one of the island's most charming villages. Beautiful **beaches** surround the town, and it's the site of the Forêt Montravail. Continuing, you'll reach Rivière-Pilote, quite a large town, and **Le Marin,** at the bottom of a bay of the same name.

Long a popular stop en route south, Le Marin is the site of one of Martinique's most historic monuments, a Jesuit-style church built in 1766. In recent years the town has become a sailing center, its marina sheltering the island's single largest yacht charter fleet. Also of interest is Le Marin's biennial August fête, a cultural extravaganza. For overnighting, the Auberge du Marin (see below) is a good bet.

After passing Le Marin, you reach Vauclin, by going northeast; this is a fishing port and market town that's pre-Columbus. If you have time, stop in at the 18th-century **Chapel of the Holy Virgin.** Visitors like to make an excursion to **Mount Vauclin,** the highest point in southern Martinique, where you'll enjoy one of the most scenic panoramas in the West Indies.

Where to Stay

Auberge du Marin. Rue Osman-Duquesnay 21, 97290 Le Marin, Martinique, F.W.I. ☎ **596/ 74-83-88.** Fax 596/74-76-47. 5 rms, 2 with bath. Year-round, 180F ($36) single without or with bath; 200F ($40) double without or with bath. Rates include breakfast. MC.

This simple inn mimics the tradition of a *restaurant avec chambres,* which is well established in mainland France but not particularly common in the Antilles. Although most of the management's energies are devoted to running a restaurant (recommended below), it maintains two no-frills rooms with cramped but serviceable showers on the street level, and three somewhat larger rooms upstairs that share a communal bathtub, shower, and toilet. Don't expect luxury or resort amenities here, and the beach, Plage de Ste-Anne, is 6 miles away. The advantages of this place are the low rates, the view of the marina from some (but not all) of the bedrooms, a garden setting, and about the easiest access you can think of for a meal or a drink.

Where to Eat

Auberge du Marin. Rue Osman-Duquesnay 21, Le Marin. ☎ **596/74-83-88.** Main courses 55F–120F ($11–$24); lunch *plat du jour* 45F ($9); fixed-price 3-course lunch or dinner 78F ($15.60). MC. Mon–Tues and Thurs–Sat noon–1:30pm and 7:30–9:30pm, Wed and Sun 7:30–9:30pm. Closed Sept. FRENCH/CREOLE.

This restaurant is the focal point of an establishment that was recommended above for its quintet of simple bedrooms. It's on the site of a 19th-century police station (*gendarmerie*) whose position is still used as a reference by local residents despite its disappearance many decades ago. Its staff is gruff and somewhat blasé, but the place will probably grow more likable as your meal progresses, and the relatively low tab will more than make up for the rustic setting. Decorated with artifacts and carved masks from Venezuela, Haiti, and Brazil, the restaurant is in the heart of the hamlet of Le Marin, overlooking a garden and a marina. The lunchtime *plat du jour* is a meal in itself for many locals, and the fixed-price meal (soup or salad, a main platter of meat or grilled fish, and dessert), is a bargain. The chef does a noteworthy couscous and a magret or confit de conard (duckling).

STE-ANNE

From Le Marin, a 5-mile drive brings you to Ste-Anne, at the extreme southern tip of Martinique. This sleepy little village has **white-sand beaches.** It opens onto views of the Sainte Lucia Canal, and nearby is the Petrified Savanna Forest, which the French call **Savane des Pétrifications.** It's a field of petrified volcanic boulders in the shape of logs. The eerie, desertlike site, no-man's-land, is studded with cacti.

Where to Stay

La Dunette. 97227 Ste-Anne, Martinique, F.W.I. ☎ **596/76-73-90.** Fax 596/76-76-05. 18 rms. A/C TV TEL. Winter, 550F ($110) single; 600F–700F ($120–$140) double. Off-season, 350F ($70) single; 450F ($90) double. Rates include continental breakfast. MC, V.

A motel-like stucco structure directly beside the sea, this hotel appeals to guests who appreciate its simplicity and its isolation from the more built-up resort areas of other parts of Martinique. A three-story building originally constructed in the late 1960s, it's near the Club Med and the white-sand beaches of the Salines. Best defined as an unpretentious seaside inn with a simple, summery decor, the hotel is accented with a garden filled with flowers and tropical plants. The furnishings are casual and modern, and although some rooms are quite small, each benefited from a complete renovation in 1993. Drinks are served every night on the terrace above the sea. The in-house restaurant, open daily for lunch and dinner, is better than you might have expected, thanks to the culinary finesse of the Tanzania-born owner Gerard Kambona. Main courses may include a succulent version of red snapper stuffed with sea urchins, or a wide selection of shellfish plucked from local waters. The venue is the hotel's terrace overlooking the sea.

Where to Eat

✪ **Aux Filets Bleus.** Pointe Marin, Ste-Anne. ☎ **596/76-73-42.** Reservations required. Fixed-price menu 59F–240F ($11.80–$48). MC, V. Daily noon–3:30pm and 7:30–10:30pm. CREOLE/FRENCH.

This family-run blue-and-white restaurant is a 30-minute drive south of the airport. The seaside exposure of the alfresco dining room and its terrace makes you feel as if you're in an isolated tropical retreat, where the only sound is the splash of waves and the tinkling of ice in glasses. What appears to be a glass-covered reflecting pool set into the floor is actually a lobster tank, supposedly one of only a few on the island. The restaurant offers one of the island's cheapest fixed-price menus. Specialties include *bouillabaisse de la mer,* which is three types of fish covered with a tomato and onion sauce; crabmeat salad with a coulis of tomato, basil, and olive oil; *salade "filets bleues,"* with fresh crayfish, hearts of palm, avocados, fresh tomatoes, and whiskey-laden cocktail sauce; and *pavé de daurade aux senteurs des îles* (white fish with a coriander-and-fennel sauce). You can go for a swim before or after your meal.

Poï et Virginie. Place de l'Eglise, rue du Bord-de-Mer, Ste-Anne. ☎ **596/76-76-86.** Reservations recommended. Main courses 75F–200F ($15–$40). AE, DC, MC, V. Tues 7–9pm; Wed–Sun noon–2:30pm and 7–9pm. CREOLE.

From the outside this restaurant looks a bit like a ramshackle bungalow set beside the sands of the beach. Inside, the decor is much more substantial, with terra-cotta floor tiles, primitive Haitian paintings, slowly spinning ceiling fans, and lots of roughly textured wood. If it isn't too hot or rainy, you might sit on a wooden deck whose foundations are sunk directly into the seabed and hear the waves splashing beneath your table. Menu choices include fresh local lobster, marinated raw conch, stuffed crab back, raw marinated fish, local fresh oysters, and grilled fish from local waters. The restaurant's name, incidentally, was inspired by a 19th-century romantic novel,

Paul et Virginie, whose star-crossed protagonists were doomed to everlasting unrequited love.

THE NORTH LOOP

As we swing north from Fort-de-France, our main targets are Le Carbet, St-Pierre, Montagne Pelée, and Leyritz. However, we'll sandwich in many stops along the way.

From Fort-de-France there are three ways to head north to Montagne Pelée. The first way is to follow route N4 up to St-Joseph. Here you take the left fork for 3 miles after St-Joseph and turn onto D15 toward Marigot.

Another way to Montagne Pelée is to take N3 through the vegetation-rich *mornes* until you reach Le Morne Rouge. This road is known as "route de la Trace," and is now the center of the Parc Naturel de la Martinique.

Yet a third route to reach Montagne Pelée is to follow N2 along the coast. Near Fort-de-France, the first town you reach is Schoelcher.

Farther along route N2 you come to Case-Pilote, and then Bellefontaine. This portion, along the most frequented tourist route on Martinique—that is, Fort-de-France to St-Pierre—will remind many a traveler of the French Riviera. Bellefontaine is a small fishing village, with boats stretched along the beach. Note the many houses also built in the shape of boats.

LE CARBET

Leaving Bellefontaine, a 5-mile drive north will deliver you to Le Carbet. Columbus landed here in 1502, and the first French settlers arrived in 1635. In 1887 Gauguin lived here for 4 months before going on to Tahiti. You can stop for a swim at an Olympic-size pool set into the hills, or watch the locals scrubbing clothes in a stream. The town lies on the bus route from Fort-de-France to St-Pierre.

The **Centre d'Art Musée Paul-Gauguin,** Anse Turin, Le Carbet (☎ **596/78-22-66**), is near the beach represented in the artist's *Bord de Mer.* The landscape has not changed in 100 years. The museum, housed in a five-room building, commemorates the French artist's stay on Martinique in 1887, with books, prints, letters, and other memorabilia. There are also paintings by René Corail, sculpture by Hector Charpentier, and examples of the artwork of Zaffanella. Of special interest are faïence mosaics made of once-white pieces that turned pink, maroon, blue, and black in 1902 when the fires of Montagne Pelée devastated St-Pierre. There are also changing exhibits of works by local artists. The museum is open daily from 9am to 5:30pm, with an admission of 15F ($3).

ST-PIERRE

At the beginning of this century, St-Pierre was known as the "Little Paris of the West Indies." Home to 30,000 inhabitants, it was the cultural and economic capital of Martinique. On May 7, 1902, the citizens read in their daily newspaper that "Montagne Pelée does not present any more risk to the population than Vesuvius does to the Neapolitans."

However, on May 8, at 8am, the southwest side of Montagne Pelée exploded into fire and lava. At 8:02am all 30,000 inhabitants were dead—that is, all except one. A convict in his underground cell was saved by the thickness of the walls. When islanders reached the site, the convict was paroled and left Martinique to tour in Barnum and Bailey's circus.

St-Pierre never recovered its past splendor. Now it could be called the Pompeii of the West Indies. Ruins of the church, the theater, and some other buildings can be seen along the coast. A 50-passenger **submarine,** operated by the Companie de la Baie de St-Pierre, rue Victor-Hugo 76, St-Pierre (☎ **596/78-28-28**), enables visitors to explore the underwater wrecks of the ships destroyed in 1902 by the eruption of the volcano (until 1994 the wrecks had been accessible only to scuba divers). The cost of the submarine exploration is considerable, but worth it to many: 450F ($90) for adults and 225F ($45) for children.

The best way to visit this historic town is to take a little train, the **Cyparis Express** (☎ **596/78-31-41**), which departs on tours from the base of the Musée Volcanologique. Tours cost 50F ($10) for adults and 25F ($5) for children, and leave Monday to Thursday from 10:30am to 1pm and 2:30 to 7pm.

The **Musée Volcanologique,** rue Victor-Hugo, St-Pierre (☎ **596/78-15-16**), was created by the American volcanologist Franck Alvard Perret, who turned the museum over to the city in 1933. Here, in pictures and relics dug from the debris, you can trace the story of what happened to St-Pierre. Dug from the lava is a clock that stopped at the exact moment the volcano erupted. The museum is open daily from 9am to 5pm, with an admission of 15F ($3), free for children 7 and under.

Where to Eat

La Factorerie. Quartier Fort, St-Pierre. ☎ **596/78-12-53.** Reservations recommended. Main courses 70F–140F ($14–$28). AE, MC, V. Daily noon–2pm. CREOLE.

This budget eatery is midway between St-Pierre and Le Prêcheur, near the ruins of a 19th-century church, the Eglise du Fort. It's a ramshackle-looking cottage within a grove of mango trees and coconut palms. At least some of the staff will have been trained at Martinique's nearby agricultural training school. The restaurant is a bit battered and it only serves lunch, but if you're in the neighborhood around noontime, it makes a convenient stop. You'll enjoy such dishes as chicken with coconut, fricassée of conch, chicken with prawns, a freshwater crayfish served with a piquant tomato sauce, colombo with chicken, and a dessert flan made with fresh coconuts and sweet potatoes.

LE PRÊCHEUR

From St-Pierre you can continue along the coast north to Le Prêcheur. Once the home of Madame de Maintenon, the mistress of Louis XIV, it's the last village along the northern coast of Martinique. Here you can see hot springs of volcanic origin and the **Tombeau des Caraïbes (Tomb of the Caribs),** where, according to legend, the collective suicide of many West Indian natives took place after they returned from a fishing expedition and found their homes pillaged by the French.

MONTAGNE PELÉE

A panoramic and winding road (Rte. N2) takes you through a **tropical rain forest.** The curves are of the hairpin variety, and the road is twisty and not always kept in good shape. However, you're rewarded with tropical flowers, baby ferns, plumed bamboo, and valleys so deeply green you'll think you're wearing cheap sunglasses.

The village of **Morne Rouge,** right at the foot of Montagne Pelée, is a popular vacation spot for Martiniquais. From here on, a narrow and unreliable road brings you to a level of 2,500 feet above sea level, 1,600 feet under the round summit of the volcano that destroyed St-Pierre. Montagne Pelée itself rises 4,575 feet above sea level.

If you're a trained mountain climber and you don't mind 4 or 5 hours of hiking, you can scale the peak to Grand' Rivière. Realize that this is a mountain, that rain is frequent, and that temperatures drop very low. Tropical growth often hides deep crevices in the earth, and there are other dangers. So if you're really serious about this climb, you should hire an experienced guide. As for the volcano, its death-dealing rain in 1902 apparently satisfied it—at least for the time being!

Upon your descent from Montagne Pelée, drive down to **Ajoupa-Bouillon,** which some describe, with justification, as the most beautiful town on Martinique. Abounding in flowers and shrubbery with bright yellow and red leaves, this little village is the site of the remarkable Gorges de la Falaise. These are minicanyons on the Falaise River up which one can travel to reach a waterfall.

LEYRITZ

Continue east toward the coast, near the town of Basse-Pointe in northeastern Martinique. A mile before Basse-Pointe, turn left and follow a road that goes deep into sugarcane country to Leyritz, where you'll find one of the best-restored plantations on Martinique, and perhaps stop by for lunch.

Where to Stay & Eat

✪ **Hôtel Plantation de Leyritz.** 97218 Basse-Pointe, Martinique, F.W.I. ☎ **596/78-53-92.** Fax 596/78-92-44. 67 rms. A/C TV TEL. Winter, 450F–790F ($90–$158) single; 670F–825F ($134–$165) double. Off-season, 350F ($70) single; 495F ($99) double. Rates include continental breakfast. MC, V.

This hotel, which offers spa facilities, was built around 1700 by a plantation owner, Bordeaux-born Michel de Leyritz. It was the site of the "swimming pool summit meeting" in 1974 between Presidents Gerald Ford and Valéry Giscard d'Estaing. Today instead of these politicians you're likely to meet a stampede of cruise-ship passengers. It's still a working banana plantation, which has been restored to its original character. There are 16 acres of tropical gardens, and at the core is an 18th-century stone Great House. From the grounds the view sweeps across the Atlantic and takes in fearsome Montagne Pelée. The owners have kept the best of the old, such as the rugged stone walls (20 inches thick), the beamed ceilings, and the tile and flagstone floors. They have created a cozy setting of mahogany tables, overstuffed sofas, and gilt mirrors. About half the accommodations are in a series of small outbuildings scattered around the property; others are in a newer annex adjacent to the spa. Don't expect well-polished luxury—that's not the style here. Laundry service and an outdoor swimming pool are pluses, though.

The dining room is in a rum distillery, incorporating the fresh spring water running down from the hillside. Eating here is dramatic at night, and the cuisine is authentically Créole. Tour-bus crowds predominate at lunch. Your Créole lunch might be grilled chicken covered in coconut-milk sauce, along with *oussous*—a freshwater crayfish that comes in a herb sauce—sautéed breadfruit, and sautéed bananas. Dinner is more elaborate, with both French and Créole dishes, including duck with pineapple, a colombo of lamb, and *boudin* (blood pudding) Créole. Dinners are fixed-price affairs, costing 105F to 120F ($21 to $24) each. Lunch is served from 12:30 to 3pm and dinner is from 7:30 to 9pm daily.

BASSE-POINTE

At the northernmost point on the island, Basse-Pointe is a land of pineapple and banana plantation fields, covering the Atlantic-side slopes of Mount Pelée volcano.

Where to Eat

✪ **Chez Mally Edjam.** Route de la Côte Atlantique. ☎ **596/78-51-18.** Reservations required. Main courses 65F–180F ($13–$36). AE, MC, V. Daily noon–3pm; dinner by special arrangement only. Closed mid-July to mid-Aug. FRENCH/CREOLE.

This local legend operates from a modest house beside the main road in the center of town, 36 miles from Fort-de-France. Appreciating its exotic but genteel charm, many visitors prefer to drive all the way from Pointe du Bout to dine here instead of at the Leyritz Plantation. You sit at one of a handful of tables on the side porch, unless you prefer a seat in the somewhat more formal dining room.

Grandmotherly Mally Edjam (who is ably assisted by France-born Martine Hugé) is busy in the kitchen turning out her Créole delicacies. Both women know how to prepare all the dishes for which the island is known: stuffed land crab with a hot seasoning, small pieces of conch in a tart shell, and a classic *colombo de porc* (the Créole version of pork curry). Equally acclaimed are the establishment's lobster vinaigrette, the papaya soufflé (which must be ordered in advance), and the highly original confitures—tiny portions of fresh island fruits, such as pineapple and guava, that have been preserved in a vanilla syrup.

GRAND' RIVIÈRE

After Basse-Pointe, the town you reach on your northward trek is Grand' Rivière. From here you must turn back, but before doing so you may want to stop at a good restaurant right at the entrance to the town.

Where to Eat

Yva Chez Vava. Blvd. Charles-de-Gaulle. ☎ **596/55-72-72.** Reservations recommended. Main courses 60F–140F ($12–$28); fixed-price menu 80F ($16). AE, DC, MC, V. Daily noon– 6pm. FRENCH/CREOLE.

Directly west of Basse-Pointe, in a low-slung building painted the peachy-orange of a paw-paw fruit, Yva Chez Vava is a combination private home and restaurant. It represents the hard labor of three generations of Créole women. Infused with a simple country-inn style, it was established in 1979 by a well-remembered, long-departed matron, Vava, whose daughter, Yva, is now assisted by her own daughter, Rosy. Local family recipes are the mainstay of this modest bistro. A la carte menu items include Créole soup, a blaff of sea urchins, lobster, and various colombos or curries. Local delicacies have changed little since the days of Joséphine and her sugar fortune, and include *z'habitants* (crayfish), *vivaneau* (red snapper), *tazard* (kingfish), and *accras de morue* (cod fritters).

STE-MARIE

Heading south along the coastal road, you'll pass Le Marigot to reach a sightseeing stop in the little town of Ste-Marie. The **Musée du Rhum Saint-James,** route de l'Union at the Saint James Distillery (☎ **596/69-30-02**), displays engravings, antique tools and machines, and other exhibits tracing the history of sugarcane and rum from 1765 to the present. When inventories of rum are low and the distillery is functioning (February to July), guided tours of both the museum and its distillery are offered. Tours depart four times a day, at 90-minute intervals (10am, 11:30am, 1pm, and 2:30pm), cost 20F ($4) per person, and include a rum-tasting. Admission to the museum (open daily from 9am to 6pm, regardless of whether the distillery is functioning) is free. Samples of rum are available for purchase on site.

From here you can head out the north end of town and loop inland a bit for a stop at Morne des Esses, or continue heading south straight to Trinité.

MORNE DES ESSES

This is the *vannerie* (basket-making) capital of Martinique, and you can pick up a sturdy straw food basket in any of the small village shops.

Where to Eat

Le Colibri (The Hummingbird). Allée du Colibri. ☎ **596/69-91-95.** Main courses 120F– 200F ($24–$40). AE, DC, MC, V. Daily noon–3pm and 7–11pm. CREOLE.

One of the island's longest-runing restaurants, Le Colibri was established by Mme Clotilde Paladino, who is now assisted by her daughters. If the terrace fills up with weekenders from Fort-de-France, you'll be seated on another smaller veranda where you can survey the cooking. The place is decidedly informal, and it exudes the warmth of madame. The typically Créole cookery is first-class. You might begin with a calalou soup with crab or a sea-urchin tart. We recommend a *buisson d'écrevisses* (a stew of freshwater crayfish), stuffed pigeon, chicken with coconut, and roast suckling pig. For dessert, try a coconut flan. French wines accompany most meals.

TRINITÉ

If you're in Mornes des Esses, continue south then turn east, or from Ste-Marie head south along the coastal route (N1) to reach the small village of Trinité. The town is the gateway to the Carvalle peninsula, where the **Presqu'île de la Carabelle Nature Preserve** offers excellent hiking and one of the only safe beaches for swimming on the Atlantic coast. This town would hardly merit a stopover were it not for the Saint-Aubin Hôtel.

Where to Stay & Eat

✪ **Saint-Aubin Hôtel.** 97220 Trinité, Martinique, F.W.I. ☎ **596/69-34-77.** Fax 596/ 69-41-14. 15 rms. A/C TEL. Winter, 320F–360F ($64–$72) single; 420F–580F ($84–$116) double. Off-season, 300F–340F ($60–$68) single; 380F–450F ($76–$90) double. Rates include continental breakfast. AE, DC, MC, V.

A former restaurant owner, Normandy-born Guy Forêt has sunk his fortune into restoring this three-story Victorian house and turning it into a three-star hostelry, one of the loveliest inns in the Caribbean. The house was originally built in 1920 of brick and poured concrete as a replacement for a much older wood-sided house that had served as the seat of a large plantation. It was named after the uninhabited islet of St-Aubin, which lies offshore and is visible from the hotel. Painted a vivid pink with fancy gingerbread, it was once a plantation house. It sits on a hillside above sugarcane fields and Trinité's bay 14^1/$_2$ miles from the airport, 19 miles from Fort-de-France, and 2 miles from the seaside village of Trinité itself. There are 800 yards of public beach, plus there's a swimming pool on the grounds. All rooms sport wall-to-wall carpeting and modern (not antique) furniture. There are some family rooms as well. After dinner you can relax on the veranda on the first and second floors. The rooms have a view of either the garden or the sea. The hotel restaurant and bar are reserved for use by hotel guests. Meals are served only at dinnertime—never at lunch—Monday to Saturday. Meals might include avocado vinaigrette, Créole black pudding, grilled fresh fish, stuffed crab, and fish poached in court bouillon.

LE FRANÇOIS

Continuing your exploration of the east coast of Martinique, you can stop over in Le François to visit the **Musée Rhum Clement** at the Domaine de l'Acajou (☎ **596/ 54-62-07**), about 1^1/$_2$ miles south of the village center. It's open daily from 9am to 6pm, charging an admission of 38F ($7.60). The distillery lies in the cellar of an 18th-century mansion with period furnishings. The house commemorates the summit meeting of Presidents Mitterrand and Bush in 1992. A Christopher Columbus exhibit is set up in caves, and other exhibits trace the institution of slavery in the islands. The museum is located in a botanic park and you could easily spend 2 or 3 hours exploring the exhibits and grounds.

2 Guadeloupe

"The time is near, I believe, when thousands of American tourists will come to spend the winter among the beautiful countryside and friendly people of Guadeloupe." Or so Theodore Roosevelt accurately predicted on February 21, 1916. Guadeloupe isn't the same place it was when the Rough Rider himself rode through, but the natural beauty he observed is still here to be enjoyed.

Guadeloupe is formed by two different islands, separated by a narrow seawater channel known as the Rivière Salée. **Grande-Terre,** the eastern island, is typical of the charm of the Antilles, with its rolling hills and sugar plantations. **Basse-Terre,** to the west, is a rugged mountainous island, dominated by the 4,800-foot volcano La Soufrière, which is still alive. Its mountains are covered with tropical forests, impenetrable in many places. Bananas grown on plantations are the main crop. The island is ringed by beautiful beaches, which have attracted much tourism.

Like Martinique, Guadeloupe is not the least expensive island in the West Indies. As in all French islands, the cost of dining in restaurants is usually high, although we've found some suitable budget selections. The island has its big expensive resorts, but it also offers a number of budget Relais Créoles, really like West Indian B&Bs, charging reasonable rates. Some visitors prefer renting a villa, cottage, or apartment with a kitchenette.

GETTING THERE

Most flights into Guadeloupe are tied in with air connections to Martinique. See "Getting There" in the Martinique section, earlier in this chapter. Passengers originating in Toronto usually fly Air Canada to Miami, then transfer to flights on such other airlines as Air France on to Guadeloupe. There are no direct flights from anywhere in Canada to either Guadeloupe or Martinique.

GETTING AROUND

BY BUS   As on Martinique, there is no rail service. But buses link almost every hamlet to Pointe-à-Pitre. However, you may need to know some French to use the system. From Pointe-à-Pitre you can catch one of these jitney vans, either at the Gare Routière de Bergevin if you're going to Basse-Terre, or the Gare Routière de Mortenol if Grande-Terre is your destination. Service is daily from 5:30am to 7:30pm. The fare from the airport to Pointe-à-Pitre terminal on rue Peynier is 7F ($1.40).

BY TAXI   You'll find taxis when you arrive at the airport, but no limousines or buses. From 9pm until 7am, cabbies are legally entitled to charge you 40% more. In practice, either day or night, the taxi drivers charge you whatever they think the market will bear, although technically the fares are regulated by the government. Always agree on the price before getting in. Approximate fares are 120F ($24) from the airport to Gosier hotels, or 70F ($14) from the airport to Pointe-à-Pitre. Radio taxis can be called at ☎ **590/82-99-88.**

If you're traveling with people or are imaginative in putting a party together, it's possible to sightsee by taxi. Usually the concierge at your hotel will help you make this arrangement. Fares are usually negotiated.

BY RENTAL CAR   Your access to a car enables you to circumnavigate Basse-Terre, which many aficionados claim is one of the loveliest drives in the Caribbean. Car-rental kiosks at the airport are usually open to meet international flights. If you want to be sure to get a car when you arrive, it's often best—and also cheaper—to reserve one in advance through the nationwide toll-free numbers of North America's largest car-rental companies: **Hertz** (☎ **800/654-3001**), **Avis** (☎ **800/331-1084**), and **Budget** (☎ **800/527-0700**).

At all three, the best values are usually offered when you reserve at least 2 days in advance and keep the car for at least a week. If you decide to rent a car after your arrival on the island, each of the companies maintains its headquarters at the island's

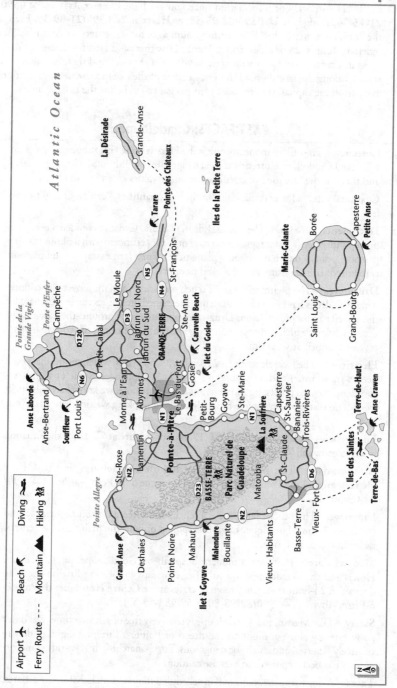

Le Raizet Airport. For information once you get here, contact **Avis** at ☎ **0590/ 21-13-54, Budget** at ☎ **0590/82-95-58,** or **Hertz** at ☎ **0590/21-09-35.** Each of the companies maintains different minimum ages for its renters: at Avis it's 25 or older; at Budget, 23 or older; and at Hertz, 21 with a valid credit or charge card.

As in France, *driving is on the right-hand side of the road,* and there are several gas stations along the island's main routes. Because of the distance between gas stations away from the capital, try not to let your gas gauge fall below the halfway mark.

FAST FACTS: Guadeloupe

Currency The official monetary unit is the **French franc (F),** although some shops will take U.S. dollars. Currently the exchange rate is 4.98F to $1 U.S. (1F = 20¢), and this was the rate used to calculate the dollar values given in this chapter.

Customs Items for personal use, "in limited quantities," can be brought in tax free.

Documents For stays of less than 21 days, U.S. and Canadian residents need only proof of identity (a voter registration card or birth certificate with a photo ID, or a passport), plus a return or ongoing plane ticket. For a longer stay, a valid passport is required. British visitors need a valid passport.

Drugstores The pharmacies carry French medicines, and most over-the-counter American drugs have French equivalents. Prescribed medicines can be purchased if the traveler has a prescription. Drugstores operate on an around-the-clock basis, the schedule of which is always changing. The tourist office can tell you what pharmacies are open at what time.

Electricity The local electricity is 220 volts AC, 50 cycles, which means that you'll need a transformer and an adapter for your U.S. appliances. Some of the big resorts lend these to guests, but don't count on it. One hotel we know had only six in stock (and of the six, two were broken!), and a long, long waiting list. Take your own.

Emergencies Call the **police** at ☎ **17,** or report a **fire** at ☎ **18.** If the situation is less urgent, call ☎ **0590/82-13-17.**

Information The major tourist office on Guadeloupe is the **Office Départemental du Tourisme,** square de la Banque 5, in Pointe-à-Pitre (☎ **590/ 82-09-30**).

Language The official language is French, and Créole is the unofficial second language. As on Martinique, English is spoken only in the major tourist centers, rarely in the countryside.

Medical Care There are 5 modern hospitals on Guadeloupe, plus 23 clinics. Hotels and the Guadeloupe tourist office can assist in locating English-speaking doctors. A 24-hour emergency room operates at the **Centre Hôpitalier de Pointe-à-Pitre,** Abymes (☎ **590/82-98-80** or 590/83-59-57).

Safety Like Martinique, Guadeloupe is relatively free of serious crime. But don't go wandering alone at night on the streets of Pointe-à-Pitre; by nightfall they're relatively deserted and might be dangerous. Purse-snatching by fast-riding motorcyclists has been reported, so exercise caution.

Taxes A departure tax, required on scheduled flights, is included in the airfares. Hotel taxes are included in all room rates.

Telephone To call Guadeloupe from the United States, dial 011 (the international access code), then 590 (the country code for Guadeloupe), plus the six-digit local number. However, once you're on Guadeloupe and are calling another place on the island, put a 0 (zero) before the 590 and dial all 10 digits of the number.

Time Guadeloupe is on Atlantic standard time year-round, 1 hour ahead of eastern standard time (when it's 6am in New York, it's 7am on Guadeloupe). When daylight saving time is in effect in the States, clocks in New York and Guadeloupe show the same time.

Tips and Service Hotels and restaurants usually add a 10% to 15% service charge, and most taxi drivers who own their own cars don't expect a tip.

SAVING MONEY ON ACCOMMODATIONS
GÎTES DE FRANCE

You might want to sty at any of the small-scale, unpretentious lodgings run by the **Gîtes de France,** a quasi-governmental body that administers more than 400 condominiums, bungalows, and cottages scattered across Guadeloupe. Don't expect a family-run bed-and-breakfast, or even a welcome that isn't anything except almost totally anonymous. Breakfast is not provided, and your landlord might be as far away as the Gîtes de France headquarters (Association Guadeloupéenne des Gîtes de France, Office du Tourisme, B.P. 759, 97172 Pointe-à-Pitre CEDEX, Guadeloupe; ☎ 590/91-64-33). The shortest rental you'll be allowed to arrange is for a week. Accommodations suitable for two people range from 1,650F to 2,200F ($330 to $440) for a week's stay. Most units contain kitchens.

CAMPING
Camping La Traverse. Anse de la Grande Plaine, 97116 Pointe Noire, Guadeloupe, F.W.I. ☎ 590/98-21-23. 20 tent sites; 13 cabins, none with bath. 50F ($10) tent site for one; 70F ($14) tent site for two; 180F–200F ($36–$40) cabin for one or two. No credit cards.

This campsite rents only the site, not the actual tents. (These, you supposedly bring on your own.) Still, if you bring the requisite equipment, a rental here includes free use of the site's showers and toilets, and easy access to a beach. (Although the beach is covered for the most part in gravel, you can usually wade out to deeper water along a sandy sea bottom.) The site also contains a few wood-sided cabins (bungalows), none of which have toilets or showers. They do, however, have rustic, very simple kitchens, mosquito netting, beds with sheets, a table, and chairs. There's also an on-site snack bar.

Camping Les Sables d'Or. Plage de Grand Anse, 97126 Deshaies, Guadeloupe, F.W.I. ☎ 590/28-44-60. 35 tent sites, 4 cabins. Year-round, 50F ($10) tent site for one; 80F ($16) tent site for two; 140F–150F ($28–$30) cabin for one or two without kitchenette, 180F ($36) with kitchenette. No credit cards.

Its amenities are about as basic as tried-and-true campers might have expected. They include showers, toilet facilities, tent sites raised a few inches above the soil level, and easy access to the sands of Grand Anse Beach. But you must bring your own tent. There are also barbecue pits and a communal kitchen reminiscent of a rather battered army canteen, which campers can use to cook. Accommodations that are a bit more upscale are available in half a dozen simple rooms strung motel-style beside the sands. Each have beds with sheets, a small refrigerator, a toilet, a ceiling fan, and mosquito nets. There's no on-site restaurant, but beach kiosks and simple nearby eateries sell food and beer.

A YOUTH HOSTEL

If you're looking for rock-bottom rates, consider staying in the closest thing on Guadeloupe to a youth hostel, the **Centre de Vacances de C.G.O.S.H.,** Rivières-Sens, 97113 Gourbeyre, Guadeloupe, F.W.I. (☎ **590/81-36-12**). These are 19 clapboard-covered bungalows built in the mid-1980s. You don't have to be a member of any special youth-hostel organization to stay here. These basic lodgings, partly subsidized by the French government, although far from luxurious, are somewhat better than you might have expected. Near the island's southern tip, the bungalows are within a 15-minute walk from the sleepy town of Basse-Terre. Each bungalow, which can hold up to six occupants, is 452F ($90.40) per night. They contain four beds in an air-conditioned bedroom, two more beds in a living area, a terrace, a private bathroom, and a kitchenette. There's a swimming pool on the premises, a nearby marina, a simple restaurant, and a bar. A sandy beach (Plage de Rivières Sens) is within a 5-minute walk. No credit or charge cards are accepted.

PACKAGE TOURS

To avoid the high cost of living on Guadeloupe, consider a package deal located by **TourScan, Inc.,** P.O. Box 2367, Darien, CT 06820 (☎ **800/962-2080** or 203/665-8091). TourScan can inform you of package deals at more than 40 places on Guadeloupe, ranging from luxury resorts to simple inns. Some best-value air-and-hotel packages begin at $524 per person for 3 nights, with an extra night costing from $24.

POINTE-À-PITRE

The port and chief city of Guadeloupe, Pointe-à-Pitre lies on Grande-Terre. Unfortunately, it doesn't have the old-world charm of Fort-de-France on Martinique, and what beauty it does possess is often hidden behind closed doors.

Having been burned and rebuilt so many times, the port has emerged as a town lacking in character, with modern apartments and condominiums forming a high-rise backdrop over jerry-built shacks and industrial suburbs. The rather narrow streets are jammed during the day with a colorful crowd creating a permanent traffic tie-up. However, at sunset the town becomes quiet again and almost deserted.

The real point of interest in Pointe-à-Pitre is shopping. It's best to visit the town in the morning—you can easily cover it in half a day—taking in the waterfront and outdoor market (the latter is livelier in the early hours). Be careful about walking alone on the nearly deserted streets of Pointe-à-Pitre at night.

The town center is **place de la Victoire,** a park shaded by palm trees and poincianas. Here you'll see some old sandbox trees said to have been planted by Victor Hugues, the mulatto who organized a revolutionary army of both whites and blacks to establish a dictatorship. In this square he kept a guillotine busy, and the death-dealing instrument still stood here (but not in use) until modern times.

With the recent completion of the **Centre St-Jean-Perse,** a $20-million project that had been on the drawing boards for many years, the waterfront of Pointe-à-Pitre, has been transformed from a bastion of old warehouses and cruise-terminal buildings into an architectural complex comprising a hotel, 3 restaurants, 80 shops and boutiques, a bank, and the expanded headquarters of Guadeloupe's Port Authority.

Named for Saint-John Perse, the 20th-century poet and Nobel laureate who was born just a few blocks away, the center is tastefully designed in contemporary French Caribbean style, which blends with the traditional architecture of Pointe-à-Pitre. It offers an array of French Caribbean attractions: duty-free shops selling Guadeloupean rum and French perfume; a renowned but expensive restaurant, La Canne à Sucre; small tropical gardens planted around the complex; and a location right near the open-air markets and small shops of this bustling port of call. For brochures, maps, and data on sightseeing, the Guadeloupe tourist office is just minutes away.

WHERE TO STAY

Hôtel St-John Anchorage. Centre Saint-John-Perse, rue Frébaut (at the harborfront), 97110 Pointe-à-Pitre, Guadeloupe, F.W.I. ☎ **590/82-51-57.** Fax 590/82-52-61. 44 rms. A/C TV TEL. Winter, 412F ($82.40) single; 512F ($102.40) double. Off-season, 362F ($72.40) single; 462F ($92.40) double. Rates include continental breakfast. MC, V.

This hotel rises four stories above the harborfront, near the quays. The bedrooms are clean, simple, and furnished with locally crafted mahogany pieces. Very few have views over the sea. Once you check in, the laissez-faire staff might leave you alone until the end of your stay. There's a simple coffee shop/cafe on the street level. Stay here if you want to be in the capital and don't have convenient transportation to go elsewhere. To reach a beach, you'll have to travel 2 miles to the east to Le Bas du Fort and the Grosier area (see below).

WHERE TO EAT

Le Big Steak House. rue Delgrès 2 (at quai Lardenoy). ☎ **590/82-12-44.** Main courses 85F–125F ($17–$25). AE, MC, V. Mon–Sat noon–3pm. STEAKS/SEAFOOD.

Virtually every shopkeeper and office worker in Pointe-à-Pitre is familiar with this two-fisted, well-managed restaurant, since it offers some of the best midday meals in town. Decorated with wood paneling and a cowboy-derived, Wild West format that evokes a steakhouse somewhere west of the Mississippi, it imports its meats twice a week from the mainland of France, and prepares them any way you prefer, usually with your choice of five different sauces. Anyone who wants more than one sauce as a garnish is cheerfully obliged—examples include versions with mustard, shallots, peppercorns, and chives. Fish culled from local waters is also popular, and includes red snapper cooked *en papillote,* or grilled daurade with Créole sauce. As you'd expect, a wide array of French wines is inventoried in the cellar. The site is especially suitable for cruise-ship day-trippers, as it lies virtually adjacent to the piers where cruise ships are tethered.

SHOPPING

Frankly, we suggest that you skip a shopping tour of Pointe-à-Pitre if you're going on to Fort-de-France on Martinique, as you'll find far more merchandise there, and perhaps friendlier service. If you're not, however, we recommend the following shops, some of which line rue Frébault.

Of course, your best buys will be anything French—perfumes from Chanel, silk scarves from Hermès, cosmetics from Dior, crystal from Lalique and Baccarat. Though they're expensive, we've found (but not often) some of these items discounted as much as 30% below U.S. or Canadian prices. While most shops will accept U.S. dollars, they'll give these discounts only for purchases made by traveler's check. Purchases are duty free if brought directly from store to airplane. In addition to the places below, there are also duty-free shops at Raizet Airport selling liquor, rums, perfumes, crystal, and cigarettes.

Most shops open at 9am, close at 1pm, then reopen between 3 and 6pm. They're closed on Saturday afternoon, Sunday, and holidays. When the cruise ships are in port, many eager shopkeepers stay open longer and on weekends.

One of the best places to buy French perfumes, at prices often lower than those charged in Paris, is **Phoenicia,** rue Frébault 8 (☎ 590/83-50-36). The shop also has a good selection of imported cosmetics. U.S. traveler's checks will get you further discounts.

Rosébleu, rue Frébault 5 (☎ **590/82-93-44**), sells fine crystal, fine porcelain, and tableware from all the grand chic names of Europe's leading porcelain manufacturers. These include Christofle, Kosta Buda, and Villeroy & Bosch, always at prices 20% less than on the French mainland.

Vendôme, rue Frébault 8–10 (☎ **590/83-42-84**), has imported fashions for both men and women, as well as a large selection of gifts and perfumes, including the big names. Usually you can find someone who speaks English to sell you a Cardin watch.

Tim-Tim, rue Henri-IV 15 (☎ **590/83-48-71**), is for nostalgia buffs. In the local Créole patois, Tim-Tim translates as "once upon a time." This little antique shop is run by the famous French author André Schwarz-Bart and his Guadeloupean wife, Simone, also a writer. They have assembled a sometimes-whimsical collection of Créole furnishings, baskets, madras table linens, and even dolls and maps.

The **Distillerie Bellevue,** rue Bellevue-Damoiseau, 97160 Le Moule (☎ **590/ 23-55-55**), caters to those who like to purchase "the essence of the island" wherever they shop. On Guadeloupe that essence is *rhum agricole,* a pure rum that's fermented from sugarcane juice. Once this rum was available in great abundance, but now only two distilleries still process it. On the island, savvy locals say that the rum there (whose brand name is Rhum Damoiseau) is the only rum you can drink without suffering the devastation of a rum hangover the next morning (comparable to a gin hangover). You're allowed to taste the product.

If you're adventurous, you may want to seek out some native goods in little shops along the backstreets of Pointe-à-Pitre. Collector's items are the straw hats or *salacos* made in Les Saintes islands. They look distinctly related to Chinese coolie hats and are usually well designed, often made of split bamboo. Native **doudou dolls** are also popular gift items.

Open-air stalls surround the **covered market** (Marché Couvert) at the corner of rue Frébault and rue Thiers. Here you can discover the many fruits, spices, and vegetables that are enjoyable just to view if not to taste. In madras turbans, local Créole women make deals over their strings of fire-red pimientos. The bright fabrics they wear compete with the rich tones of oranges, papayas, bananas, mangos, and pineapples, and the sounds of an African-accented French fill the air.

MOVING ON

Saint-John Perse once wrote about the fine times sailors had in Pointe-à-Pitre, as a stopover on the famous route du Rhum. But since that day is long gone, you may not want to linger; you can take a different route instead, this one to the "South Riviera," from Pointe-à-Pitre to Pointe des Châteaux. The hotels recommended below grew up on Grande-Terre because of the long stretches of white sands lying between Bas du Fort and Gosier (see below). These beaches, however, are not spectacular but often narrow and artificially created.

LE BAS DU FORT

The first tourist complex, just 2 miles east of Pointe-à-Pitre, is called Le Bas du Fort, near Gosier.

The **Aquarium de la Guadeloupe,** place Créole, Marina Bas-du-Fort (☎ **590/ 90-92-38**), is rated as one of the three most important of France and is the largest and most modern in the Caribbean. Just off the highway near Bas-du-Fort Marina, the aquarium is home to tropical fish, coral, underwater plants, huge sharks, and other sea creatures. Open daily from 9am to 7pm. Admission is 38F ($7.60) for adults, 20F ($4) for children 12 and under.

GOSIER

Some of the biggest and most important hotels of Guadeloupe are found at this holiday center, with its nearly 5 miles of beach, stretching east from Pointe-à-Pitre.

For an excursion, you can climb to **Fort Fleur-d'Epée,** dating from the 18th century. Its dungeons and battlements are testaments to the ferocious fighting between the French and British armies in 1794 seeking to control the island. The well-preserved ruins command the crown of a hill. From here you'll have good views over the bay of Pointe-à-Pitre, and on a clear day you can see the neighboring offshore islands of Marie-Galante and the Iles des Saintes.

WHERE TO STAY

Doubles for Less than $85 (Winter) / $75 (Off-Season)

✪ **Les Flamboyants.** Périnet, chemin des Phares et Balises, 97190 Gosier, Guadeloupe, F.W.I. ☎ **590/84-14-11.** Fax 590/84-53-56. 20 rms, 10 with kitchenette. A/C. Winter, 320F–380F ($64–$76) single; 360F–420F ($72–$84) double. Off-season, 260F–320F ($52–$64) single; 300F–360F ($60–$72) double. MC, V.

Small scale, and—at least in theory—more personalized than the massive hotels of Gosier that are in the same neighborhood, this inn was developed around the core of a pink-sided Créole house set in a pleasant garden. The main house was built just before World War II, and the various bungalows were constructed without much style in the mid-1970s. Although there's a small swimming pool on the premises, most residents opt for a 20-minute trek, past several bars and restaurants, to the nearest beach, Plage du Gosier. The accommodations are in bungalow-style outbuildings, many of which have views over the seacoast and the offshore island, Islet du Gosier. Those rooms with individual kitchenettes are the most expensive. The hotel offers discounts of around 15% for stays of a week or more.

Doubles for Less than $130 (Winter) / $100 (Off-Season)

L'Orchidée. Blvd. du Général-de-Gaulle 32, 97190 Gosier, Guadeloupe, F.W.I. ☎ **590/84-54-20.** Fax 590/84-54-90. 17 rms with kitchenette, 2 apts. A/C TV TEL. Winter, 450F ($90) single; 650F ($130) double; 700F ($140) apt for four; 750F ($150) apt for six. Off-season, 375F ($75) single or double; 500F ($100) apt for four; 550F ($110) apt for six. MC, V.

This four-story hotel rises adjacent to the town hall of Gosier. It's an easy walk to the beach, and close to the resort's restaurants and shops. In its pale-blue wicker-furnished bedrooms you'll find a kitchenette with dishes and cookware, and some of the feeling of an apartment in an urban resort. There's no restaurant, and no swimming pool, but considering the nearby beach and the many distractions nearby, it's still a good choice. The staff is warm-hearted.

Sud Caraïbes. Chemin de la Plage, Petit Havre, 97190 Gosier, Guadeloupe, F.W.I. ☎ **590/85-96-02.** Fax 590/85-80-90. 12 rms. A/C. Winter, 450F ($90) single; 600F ($120) double. Off-season, 350F ($70) single; 450F ($90) double. MC, V.

Part of its appeal to visitors (and the reason for its relatively low costs) derives from a location on the perimeter of the fishing village of Petit Havre, far removed from the shops, casinos, and touristic bustle of Gosier. Established in the mid-1980s, the resort has gradually developed a clientele of guests who don't care very much about its lack of resort amenities and who appreciate the individual attention they get from the owners. Although the bedrooms are brightly outfitted with rattan and private balconies, they don't contain any cooking facilities, and there's no restaurant on site. (A mom-and-pop grocery store is a 10-minute walk away.) There's a small swimming pool, but most visitors dip in the nearby sea instead.

Worth a Splurge

Canella Beach Residence. Pointe de la Verdure (B.P. 73), 97190 Gosier, Guadeloupe, F.W.I. ☎ **590/90-44-00.** Fax 590/90-44-44. 146 units, all with kitchenette. A/C TV TEL. Winter, 615F ($123) single; 800F ($160) double; 1,000F ($200) junior suite for two; 1,340F ($268) apt for four. Off-season, 420F ($84) single; 530F ($106) double; 710F ($142) junior suite for two; 900F ($180) apt for four. MC, V.

Near the tip of the Gosier peninsula, and built in 1990, this resort evokes an apartment or condominium complex more than a hotel, as virtually everyone opts to prepare at least some meals in the private kitchens. The accommodations are monochromatically outfitted in wicker and varnished hardwoods, and most open onto views of the sandy beach. The in-house restaurant, La Veranda, is good enough to be visited by residents of nearby hotels, who appreciate its flavorful Créole cuisine and hardworking staff. Main courses, served daily from 11:15am to 2:30pm and 7:15 to 9:30pm, begin at 80F ($16), and include Créole, French, and Asian platters. Most tables face a view of the water and the beach.

WHERE TO EAT

La Chaubette. Route de Ste-Anne. ☎ **590/84-14-29.** Reservations recommended. Main courses 50F–80F ($10–$16). AE, MC, V. Mon–Sat noon–4pm and 7–11. CREOLE.

This "front porch" Créole restaurant offers lots of local color and raffish charm. About a 12-minute ride east of Pointe-à-Pitre, it evokes a Guadeloupe version of a roadside inn, with its red-checked tablecloths and bamboo curtains. Mme Gitane Chavalin has dispensed food, drink, and good cheer since 1972, and she's known in the area for her Créole recipes and sense of humor. She uses the fish and produce of her island whenever possible. When it's available, her langouste is peerless, as is her hog's-head cheese with a minced-onion vinaigrette. Begin your meal here with a rum punch, made with white rum and served with a lime wedge and sugar. But don't order too much—it's lethal. Finish with coconut ice cream or a banana flaming with rum.

La Véranda. In the Hôtel/Résidence Canella Beach, Pointe de la Verdure, Gosier. ☎ **590/ 90-44-00.** Reservations recommended. Main courses 70F–120F ($14–$24). AE, DC, MC, V. Daily noon–2pm and 7–10pm. FRENCH/CREOLE.

On the grounds of a hotel and apartment complex in Grosier, though independently managed, this restaurant offers a refreshingly different array of food from the Créole specialties featured by many of its nearby competitors. Operated by a French-speaking émigré from South India, Bernard Sinniamourd, it's decorated in a pink-and-white tropical style that includes lots of potted palms, with access to an outdoor terrace. It prides itself on a creative menu that includes such dishes as grilled marlin with tamarind sauce, spicy versions of roast lamb inspired by the traditions of India, and a soupière of scallops with freshwater crayfish. One section of the restaurant is air-conditioned, the other open to breezes from the sea.

STE-ANNE

About 9 miles east of Gosier, little Ste-Anne is a sugar town and a resort offering many fine beaches and lodging facilities. In many ways it's the most charming of the villages of Guadeloupe, with its town hall in pastel colors, its church, and its principal square, place de la Victoire, where a statue of Schoelcher commemorates the abolition of slavery in 1848.

WHERE TO STAY & EAT

Doubles for Less than $60

La Barrière de Corail. Durivage, 97180 Ste-Anne, Guadeloupe, F.W.I. For information and reservations, write Mme Giroux, rue Bébian 4, 97110 Pointe-à-Pitre, Guadeloupe, F.W.I.

☎ **590/88-20-03.** 27 bungalows, all with kitchenette. Winter, 300F ($60) bungalow for one or two. Off-season, 280F ($56) bungalow for one or two. Air-conditioning 20F ($4) extra per night. No credit cards.

About three-quarters of a mile from the center of Ste-Anne, close to the Club Med Caravelle and clusters of roughly equivalent (but more expensive) competitors, this is a complex of white cottages with corrugated (usually red) roofs and brown trim. The nearest beach is the one shared by the permissive and somewhat topless crowd at Club Med adjacent to the hotel. Expect no frills here, but if you're looking for a woodsy, back-to-the-earth kind of ambience and don't need a list of amenities or maid service, one of these bungalows might be for you. The bedrooms are cramped, with tiny bathrooms and bare-bones kitchenettes, but few guests spend much time inside anyway. A handful of restaurants are within a brisk walk. No breakfast of any kind is served, and once you arrange for your rental you might not see any staff members for days at a time.

Worth a Splurge

Auberge du Grand Large. Route de la Plage, 97180 Ste-Anne, Guadeloupe, F.W.I. ☎ **590/88-20-06.** Fax 590/88-16-69. 10 bungalows, all with kitchenette. A/C TEL. Winter, 600F ($120) bungalow for one or two. Off-season, 380F ($76) bungalow for one or two. Extra person 100F ($20). MC, V.

Among the more unusual aspects of this cottage colony is the fact that each kitchenette is positioned under the sheltering eaves of an outdoor veranda. Thanks to the balmy climate and the privacy afforded by shrubberies and flowering vines, it allows you to cook meals in semisecluded retreats, which open to views of either the beach or a garden. There's no swimming pool on the premises, and only a moderate number of amenities, but the independent-minded travelers these bungalows attract don't seem to mind. The establishment is near the beachfront of Ste-Anne, close to the hamlet's center. Although most visitors cook their meals in-house, a restaurant on the premises serves simple platters of food inspired by Créole traditions. Cost-cutters should remember that if you opt to rent a bungalow here for a full week, and forgo the usual maid service, you'll pay 2,800F ($560) per week in high season, and 2,240F ($448) in low season, a price that works out to 160F ($32) per person per day, a genuine bargain.

Mini-Beach. B.P. 77, 97180 Ste-Anne, Guadeloupe, F.W.I. ☎ **590/88-21-13.** Fax 590/88-19-29. 6 rms, 3 bungalows with kitchenette. A/C TEL. Winter, 550F–700F ($110–$140) single or double or bungalow for one or two. Off-season, 300F–500F ($60–$100) single or double; 350F–450F ($70–$90) bungalow for one or two. Rates include breakfast. V.

Beneath a canopy of trees near the isolated northern edge of Ste-Anne's beach, this small hotel is personally managed by the resident-owner Nicole Poinard. Established in the early 1980s, it consists of a main building containing half a dozen rooms, a restaurant, and three one-room bungalows set close to the water's edge. Surprisingly, it's the rooms, not the bungalows, that sell out faster here. Each accommodation features a different decor, with tropical accents and mosquito nets. There's no pool, no tennis courts, and no other resort-type amenities, but many guests enjoy the blasé, vaguely permissive ambience of this very French hotel. The restaurant has an open kitchen where diners can watch the chef (Philippe) at work preparing lobsters from a holding tank.

ST-FRANÇOIS

Continuing east from Ste-Anne, you'll notice many old round towers named for Father Labat, the Dominican founder of the sugarcane industry. These towers were once used as mills to grind the cane. St-François, 25 miles east of Pointe-à-Pitre, used to be a sleepy fishing village, known for its native Créole restaurants. Then Air France discovered it and opened a Méridien hotel with a casino. That was followed by the promotional activities of J. F. Rozan, a native, who invested heavily to make St-François a jet-set resort. Now the once-sleepy village has first-class accommodations (also some budget choices), as well as an airport available to private jets, a golf course, and a marina.

WHERE TO STAY

Domaine de l'Anse des Rochers. L'Anse des Rochers, 97118 St-François, Guadeloupe, F.W.I. ☎ 590/93-90-00. 350 studio apts, all with kitchenette. A/C TEL. Winter, 530F–1,089F ($106–$217.80) studio apt for one or two. Off-season, 370F–765F ($74–$153) studio apt for one or two. AE, MC, V.

Except for the nearby presence of another hotel, this low-slung resort sits in an isolated position amid carefully landscaped grounds adjacent to the sea. Built in 1990, its accommodations are either in a network of detached bungalows or in a series of gingerbread-laced two-story annexes. Each building is painted a different Créole-inspired color (green, pink, red, or yellow), and paths leading from each of them seem to end up at the resort's swimming pool. The overall effect is that of a small, idealized, laid-back village, that rocks and rolls to disco music every night after dark. There's a restaurant on site, but many guests ignore its charms in favor of preparing their meals in their private kitchenettes.

Golf Marine Club Hôtel. Ave. de l'Europe (B.P. 204), 97118 St-François, Guadeloupe, F.W.I. ☎ 590/88-60-60. Fax 590/88-68-98. 74 rms. A/C TV TEL. Winter, 720F ($144) single; 900F ($180) double. Off-season, 450F–705F ($90–$141) single; 550F–882F ($110–$176.40) double. No credit cards.

Critics of this hotel claim that its name is deliberately misleading: The golf course it promises is a municipal golf course across the street, the docking facilities it promises are within walking distance but not associated with the hotel in any way, and the nearest beach requires a 5-minute walk. Despite these caveats, the hotel is a good bet for simple, cost-conscious bedrooms. Some have balconies, but those that face the rear garden are quieter than those that open onto the busy main street of St-François. The staff isn't the most organized on the island, but once you've checked into your lodging, you might appreciate this establishment's low-key attitude. There's a bar and a simple bistro on site, serving lunches and dinners.

WHERE TO EAT

✪ L'Oursin Blanc. Route de la République, St-François. ☎ 590/88-77-97. Main courses 55F–75F ($11–$15); fixed-price menu 70F–100F ($14–$20). No credit cards. Daily noon–2:30pm and 6–10:30pm. SEAFOOD/CREOLE.

Outfitted rustically with a mariner's theme, this simple restaurant is run by Frantz, who extends a hearty welcome. There's a bar attached to the place, if you feel like stopping in just for a thirst-quencher. The restaurant features fresh fish. After an apéritif, sit back and peruse the menu, including such dishes as a gratin de christophine (similar to a squash), a fricassée of conch, and a favorite local white fish caught off island, coffre, which is best grilled. You can also order grilled steaks and such classic French specialties as mussels in a white-wine-and-butter sauce. But most diners come here for the Créole dishes, including flavorful stuffed crab backs and boudin Créole or blood sausage. Fresh island vegetables are used whenever possible.

WHEN THE FIVE-IRON CALLS

Guadeloupe's only golf course is the well-known **Golf de St-François** (☎ 590/88-41-81), opposite the Hôtel Méridien. The golf course runs alongside an 800-acre lagoon where windsurfing, waterskiing, and sailing prevail. Designed by Robert Trent Jones, this 6,755-yard, par-71 course presents many challenges to the golfer, with water traps on 6 of the 18 holes, massive bunkers, prevailing trade winds, and a particularly fiendish 400-yard, par-4 ninth hole. Greens fees are 250F ($50) per day per person, which allows a full day of playing time. Golf clubs can be rented for 100F ($20) for the day, and an electric golf cart costs 220F ($44) for an 18-hole bout.

POINTE DES CHATEÂUX

Seven miles east of St-François is Pointe des Châteaux, the easternmost tip of Grand-Terre, where the Atlantic meets the Caribbean. Here, where crashing waves sound around you, you'll see a cliff sculpted by the sea into castlelike formations, the erosion typical of France's Brittany coast. The view from here is splendid. At the top is a cross put there in the 19th century.

You might want to walk to **Pointe des Colibris,** the extreme end of Guadeloupe. From here you'll have a view of the northeastern sector of the island, and to the east a look at La Désirade, another island, which has the appearance of a huge vessel anchored far away. Among the coved **beaches** found around here, Pointe Tarare is the *au naturel* one.

LE MOULE

To go back to Pointe-à-Pitre from Pointe des Châteaux, you can use an alternative route, N5 from St-François. After a 9-mile drive you reach the village of Le Moule, which was founded at the end of the 17th century and known long before Pointe-à-Pitre. It used to be a major shipping port for sugar. Now a tiny coastal fishing village, it never regained its importance after it was devastated in the hurricane of 1928, like so many other villages of Grand-Terre. Because of its more than **10-mile-long crescent-shaped beach,** it's developing as a holiday center. Modern hotels built along the beaches have opened to accommodate visitors.

Specialties of this Guadeloupean village are *palourdes,* the clams that thrive in the semi-salty mouths of freshwater rivers. Known for being more tender and less "rubbery" than saltwater clams, they often, even when fresh, have a distinct sulfur taste not unlike that of overpoached eggs. Local gastronomes prepare them with saffron and aged rum or cognac.

Nearby, the sea unearthed some skulls, grim reminders of the fierce battles fought among the Caribs, French, and English. It's called "the Beach of Skulls and Bones."

The **Edgar Clerc Archaeological Museum La Rosette,** Parc de la Rosette (☎ 590/23-57-57), shows a collection of both Carib and Arawak artifacts gathered from various islands of the Lesser Antilles. The museum is open Monday to Friday from 9am to 12:30pm and 2 to 5:30pm and on Saturday and Sunday from 9am to 12:30pm and 2 to 6pm. Admission is 10F ($2). The museum lies 3 miles from Le Moule heading toward Campêche.

To return to Pointe-à-Pitre, we suggest that you use route D3 toward Abymes. The road winds around as you plunge deeply into Grand-Terre. As a curiosity, about halfway along the way a road will bring you to **Jabrun du Nord** and **Jabrun du Sud.** These two villages are inhabited by Caucasians with blond hair, said to be survivors of aristocrats slaughtered during the Revolution. Those members of their families who escaped found safety by hiding out in Les Grands Fonds. The most important family here is named Matignon, and they gave their name to the colony known as "les Blancs Matignon." These citizens are said to be related to Prince Rainier of Monaco.

Pointe-à-Pitre lies only 10 miles from Les Grand Fonds.

A DRIVING TOUR NORTH FROM POINTE-À-PITRE

From Pointe-à-Pitre, head northeast toward Abymes, passing next through Morne à l'Eau; you'll reach **Petit Canal** after 13 miles. This is Guadeloupe's sugarcane country, and a sweet smell fills the air.

PORT LOUIS

Continuing northwest along the coast from Petit Canal, you come to Port Louis, well known for its beautiful **beach,** La Plage du Souffleur, which we find best in the spring, when the brilliant white sand is effectively shown off against a contrast of the flaming red poinciana. During the week the beach is an especially quiet spot. The little port town is asleep under a heavy sun, and it has some good restaurants.

Where to Eat

✪ **Le Poisson d'Or.** Rue Sadi-Carnot 2, Port Louis. ☎ **590/22-88-63.** Reservations required. Main courses 75F–150F ($15–$30); fixed-price menu 85F–150F ($17–$30). MC, V. Daily 11:30–3pm; dinner by reservation only. Drive northwest from Petit Canal along the coastal road. CREOLE.

You'll enter this white-sided Antillean house by walking down a narrow corridor and emerging into a rustic dining room lined with varnished pine. Despite the simple setting, the food is well prepared and satisfying. Don't even think of coming here at night without an advance reservation—you might find the place locked up and empty. The establishment's true virtue, however, is evident during the lunch hour, when, depending on the season, it's likely to shelter a mixture of local residents and tourists from the French mainland. Try the stuffed crabs or the court bouillon, topped off by coconut ice cream, which is homemade and tastes it. The place is a fine choice for an experience with Créole cookery, complemented by a bottle of good wine.

ANSE BERTRAND

About 5 miles from Port Louis lies Anse Bertrand, the northernmost village of Guadeloupe. What's now a fishing village was the last refuge of the Carib tribes, and a reserve was once created here. Everything now, however, is sleepy.

Where to Eat

✪ **Chez Prudence (Folie Plage).** Anse Laborde, 97121 Anse Bertrand, Guadeloupe, F.W.I. ☎ **590/22-11-17.** Reservations not required for lunch, recommended for dinner. Main courses 70F–153F ($14–$30.60); fixed-price menu 100F–160F ($20–$32). AE. Daily noon–3pm and 7–10pm. CREOLE.

About a mile north of Anse Bertrand at Anse Laborde, this place is owned by Prudence Marcelin, a *cuisinière patronne,* who enjoys much local acclaim for her Créole cookery. She draws people from all over the island, especially on Sunday when this place is its most crowded. Island children frolic in the saltwater pool, and in between courses diners can shop for handcrafts, clothes, and souvenirs sold by a handful of nearby vendors. Her court bouillon is excellent, as is either her goat or chicken colombo (curried). The *palourdes* (clams) are superb, and she makes a zesty sauce to serve with fish. The place is relaxed and casual. She also rents half a dozen very basic motel-style bungalows priced at 250F ($50) for single or double occupancy, for overnight stays.

CONTINUING THE TOUR

From Anse Bertrand, you can drive along a graveled road heading for **Pointe de la Grande Vigie,** the northernmost tip of the island, which you reach after 4 miles of what we hope will be cautious driving. Park your car and walk carefully along a narrow lane which will bring you to the northernmost rock of Guadeloupe. The view of the sweeping Atlantic from the top of rocky cliffs is remarkable—you stand at a distance of about 280 feet above the sea.

Afterward, a 4-mile drive south on quite a good road will bring you to the **Porte d'Enfer,** or "gateway to hell." Once here, you'll find the sea rushing violently against two narrow cliffs.

After this kind of awesome experience in the remote part of the island, you can head back, going either to Morne à l'Eau or Le Moule before connecting to the road taking you back to Pointe-à-Pitre.

AROUND BASSE-TERRE

Leaving Pointe-à-Pitre on route N1, you can explore the lesser windward coast. After a mile and a half you cross the Rivière Salée at Pont de la Gabarre. This narrow strait separates the two islands that form Guadeloupe. For the next 4 miles the road runs straight through sugarcane fields.

At the sign, on a main crossing, turn right on route N2 toward **Baie Mahault.** Leaving that town on the right, head for **Lamentin.** This village was settled by corsairs at the beginning of the 18th century. Scattered about are some colonial mansions.

STE-ROSE

From Lamentin, you can drive for 6½ miles to Ste-Rose, where you'll find several good beaches. On your left, a small road leads to **Sofaia,** from which you'll have a splendid view over the coast and forest preserve. The locals claim that a sulfur spring here has curative powers.

Where to Stay

La Sucrerie du Comté. Comté de Loheac, 97115 Ste-Rose, Guadeloupe, F.W.I. ☎ **590/ 28-60-17.** Fax 590/28-65-63. 52 rms. A/C. Winter, 510F ($102) single; 550F–660F ($110–$132) double. Off-season, 400F ($80) single; 440F ($88) double. Rates include breakfast. MC, V.

Although you'll see the ruins of a 19th-century sugar factory (including a rusting locomotive) on the 8 acres of forested land overlooking the sea, most of the resort is modern (it opened in 1991). The accommodations are in 26 rectangular, pink-toned bungalows. Each cozy bungalow comes with chunky and rustic handmade furniture and a bay window overlooking either the sea or a garden. (Each bungalow contains two units, both with ceiling fans; none has a TV or telephone.) Scuba diving, snorkeling, and fishing can be arranged. Partial renovations were made on this place in 1993–94, when it changed ownership. There's a restaurant on site, open daily for lunch and dinner, and a bar set beneath a veranda-style roof near a swimming pool. The nearest major beach is Grand Anse, a 10- to 15-minute drive from the hotel, but there's a small, unnamed beach within a 10-minute walk, although the swimming isn't very good.

Where to Eat

Restaurant Clara. Ste-Rose. ☎ **590/28-72-99.** Reservations recommended. Main courses 60F–140F ($12–$28). MC, V. Mon–Tues and Thurs–Sat noon–2:30pm and 7–10pm, Sun noon–2:30pm. CREOLE.

On the waterfront near the center of town is the culinary statement of Clara Lesueur and her talented and charming semiretired mother, Justine. Clara lived for 12 years in Paris as a member of an experimental jazz dance troupe, but she returned to Guadeloupe, her home, and set up her breeze-cooled restaurant, which she rebuilt in 1990 after hurricane damage. Try for a table on the open patio, where palm trees complement the color scheme.

Clara and Justine artfully meld the French style of fine dining with authentic, spicy Créole cookery. Specialties include *ouassous* (freshwater crayfish), brochette of sword-fish, *palourdes* (small clams), several different preparations of conch, sea-urchin om-elets, and *crabes farcis* (red-orange crabs with a spicy filling). The "sauce chien" that's served with many of the dishes is a blend of hot peppers, garlic, lime juice, and "se-cret things." The house drink is made with six local fruits and ample quantities of rum. Your dessert sherbet might be guava, soursop, or passionfruit.

DESHAIES/GRAND ANSE

A few miles farther along you'll reach Pointe Allegre, the northernmost point of Basse-Terre. At **Clugny Beach,** you'll be at the site where the first settler landed on Guadeloupe.

A couple of miles farther will bring you to **Grand Anse,** one of the best beaches on Guadeloupe. It's very large and still secluded, sheltered by many tropical trees.

At **Deshaies,** snorkeling and fishing are popular pastimes. The narrow road winds up and down and has a corniche look to it, with the blue sea underneath, the view of green mountains studded with colorful hamlets.

Some 9 miles from Deshaies, **Pointe Noire** comes into view. Its name comes from black volcanic rocks. Look for the odd polychrome cenotaph in town.

Where to Stay

Grand'Anse Hôtel. Grand Anse, 97114 Trois-Rivières, Guadeloupe, F.W.I. ☎ **590/92-92-21.** Fax 590/92-93-69. 16 bungalows. A/C TV TEL. Winter, 300F ($60) bungalow for one; 400F ($80) bungalow for two. Off-season, 250F ($50) bungalow for one; 300F ($60) bungalow for two. Rates include breakfast. MC, V.

Built in the 1970s but renovated in 1996, this secluded hotel is removed from all the tourist hordes. Although it's near the ferryboat piers of the hamlet of Trois-Rivières, you'll appreciate being away from the crowds. The hotel is made up of beige-sided interconnected bungalows set in a garden with a view of the mountains, and in some cases, the sea. The accommodations are mostly modern, with sliding glass doors, vague hints of French colonial styling, and mahogany furniture. Its bar and Créole restaurant are well recommended. The closest beach (a black volcanic sand one) is three-quarters of a mile away, but the hotel has a rectangular swimming pool. The staff is unpretentious and polite. The hotel's location close to the ferryboat departures for the Iles des Saintes makes day trips there both convenient and easy.

Where to Eat

Chez Jacky. Anse Guyonneau, Pointe Noire. ☎ **590/98-06-98.** Reservations recommended at dinner. Main courses 75F–130F ($15–$26); fixed-price menu 80F–130F ($16–$26); lunch plat-ters 45F–130F ($9–$26). V. Daily 9am–10pm. CREOLE.

Named after its owner, Jacqueline Cabrion, this establishment has gained a loyal cli-entele since it first appeared on the restaurant scene in 1981. In a French-colonial house about 30 feet from the sea, it features lots of exposed wood, verdant plants, tropical furniture, and a bar that sometimes does a respectable business in its own right. Menu items include colombo of conch, fricassée of conch, several preparations of grilled fish, lobster, ragoût of lamb, fried crayfish, and a dessert specialty of bananas flambé. Lighter fare includes a limited choice of sandwiches and salads, which tend to be offered only during daylight hours.

Le Karacoli. Grand Anse (1¼ miles north of Deshaies). ☎ **590/28-41-17.** Reservations recommended. Main courses 80F–150F ($16–$30). MC, V. Daily noon–2pm. CREOLE.

It's the best-signposted restaurant in town, with at least three large signs indicating its position at the edge of the region's most famous beach. The setting is as airy and tropical as you'd expect, with streaming sunlight, tables set outdoors in a garden, and a bar area that's sheltered from storms with a combination of poured concrete and clapboards. No one will mind if you drop in just for a drink, but if you want lunch, the only meal served, consider ordering any of such dishes as a boudin Créole, stuffed crab backs, scallops prepared "in the style of the chef," court bouillon of fish, a fricassée of octopus, and fried chicken. Sunday is usually more popular than most other days.

Les Gommiers. Rue Baudot, Pointe Noire. ☎ **590/98-01-79.** Main courses 60F–150F ($12–$30). AE, MC, V. Sun–Mon 11:30am–3pm, Tues–Sat 11:30am–3pm and 7–10pm. CREOLE.

Named after the large rubber trees (*les gommiers*) that grow nearby, this popular Créole restaurant serves up well-flavored platters that derive from the culinary experience of Mme Josette Besplan. She established her restaurant in the 1960s, in a wood and concrete house across the busy road from Pointe Noire's local *collège* (high school). In a dining room lined with plants, you can order such Créole staples as accras de morue, boudin Créole, fricassée of freshwater crayfish, seafood paella, and a custardlike dessert known as *flan coucou*. Dishes inspired by mainland France include filet of beef with Roquefort sauce and veal scallops.

ROUTE DE LA TRAVERSÉE

Four miles from Pointe Noire, you reach **Mahaut.** On your left begins the **route de la Traversée,** the Transcoastal Highway. This is the best way to explore the scenic wonders of **Parc Naturel de Guadeloupe,** passing through a tropical forest as you travel between the capital, Basse-Terre, and Pointe-à-Pitre.

To preserve the Parc Naturel, Guadeloupe has set aside 74,100 acres, or about one-fifth of its entire terrain. Reached by modern roads, this is a huge tract of mountains, tropical forests, and magnificent scenery.

The park is home to a variety of tame animals, including Titi (a raccoon adopted as the park's official mascot), and such birds as the wood pigeon, turtledove, and thrush. Small exhibition huts, devoted to the volcano, the forest, or to coffee, sugarcane, and rum, are scattered throughout the park. The Parc Naturel has no gates, no opening or closing hours, and no admission fee.

From Mahaut you climb slowly in a setting of giant ferns and luxuriant vegetation. Four miles after the fork, you reach **Les Deux Mamelles** (The Two Breasts), where you can park your car and go for a hike. Some of the trails are for experts only; others, such as the Pigeon Trail, will bring you to a summit of about 2,600 feet where the view is impressive. Expect to spend at least 3 hours going each way. Halfway along the trail you can stop at Forest House. From that point, many lanes, all signposted, branch off on trails that will last anywhere from 20 minutes to 2 hours. Try to find the **Chute de l'Ecrevisse** (Crayfish Waterfall), a little pond of very cold water that you'll discover after a quarter of a mile.

After the hike, the main road descends toward Versailles, a hamlet about 5 miles from Pointe-à-Pitre.

However, before taking this route, while still traveling between Pointe Noire and Mahaut on the west coast, you might consider the following luncheon stop.

Where to Eat

Chez Vaneau. Mahaut/Pointe Noire. ☎ **590/98-01-71.** Main courses 50F–150F ($10–$30). AE, MC, V. Mon–Wed and Fri–Sat noon–5pm and 7pm–midnight, Thurs and Sun noon–5pm. CREOLE.

Set in an isolated pocket of forest about 18 miles north of Pointe Noire, far from any of its neighbors, Chez Vaneau offers a wide, breeze-filled veranda overlooking a gully, the sight of neighbors playing cards, and steaming Créole specialties coming from the kitchen. This is the well-established domain of Vaneau Desbonnes, who is assisted by his wife, Marie-Gracieuse, and their children. Specialties include oysters with a piquant sauce, crayfish bisque, ragoût of goat, fricassée of conch, different preparations of octopus, and roast pork. In 1995 they installed a saltwater tank to store lobsters, which are now featured heavily on their menu.

BOUILLANTE

If you don't take the route de la Traversée at this time but wish to continue exploring the west coast, you can head south from Mahaut until you reach the village of Bouillante, which is exciting for only one reason: You might encounter the former French film star and part-time resident Brigitte Bardot.

Try not to miss seeing the small island called **Ilet à Goyave** or Ilet du Pigeon. Jacques Cousteau often explored the silent depths around it.

After a meal, you can explore around the village of Bouillante, the country known for its thermal springs. In some places if you scratch the ground for only a few inches you'll feel the heat.

Where to Eat near Bouillante

✪ **Chez Loulouse.** Malendure Plage. ☎ **590/98-70-34.** Reservations required for dinner. Main courses 80F–160F ($16–$32). AE, MC, V. Daily noon–3:30pm and 7–10pm. CREOLE.

A good choice for lunch is Chez Loulouse, a staunchly matriarchal establishment with plenty of offhanded charm, beside the sands of the well-known beach, opposite Pigeon Island. Many guests prefer their rum punches on the panoramic veranda, overlooking a scene of loaded boats preparing to depart and merchants hawking their wares. A quieter oasis is the equally colorful dining room inside, just past the bar. Here, beneath a ceiling of palm fronds, is a wraparound series of Créole murals that seem to go well with the reggae music emanating loudly from the bar.

This is the creation of one of the most visible and charming Créole matrons on this end of the island, Mme Loulouse Paisley-Carbon. Assisted by her children, she offers house-style Caribbean lobster, spicy versions of conch, octopus, accras, gratin of christophine (squash), and savory colombos (curries) of chicken or pork.

Le Rocher de Malendure. Malendure Plage, Pointe Batterie, 97125 Bouillante, Guadeloupe, F.W.I. ☎ **590/98-70-84.** Reservations recommended. Main courses 75F–135F ($15–$27). MC, V. Mon–Sat 11am–2pm and 7–10pm, Sun 11am–2pm. FRENCH/CREOLE.

Its position on a rocky peninsula 30 feet above the rich offshore reefs near Pigeon Island allows for panoramic views over the land and seascape. Each table is sheltered from too direct a contact with the sun (and the rain) with a shed-style roof, whose placement on sloping, terraced terrain allows for greater feelings of privacy. The establishment is the creative statement of Ghislaine and Franck Lesueur, both of whom were born on Guadeloupe of Breton parents. Much of the cuisine served here is seafood caught in offshore waters. Examples include grilled red snapper, fondues of fish, marinated marlin steaks, and different preparations of lobster and conch. Meat dishes include veal in raspberry vinaigrette and filet of beef with any of three different sauces.

Although most of the energy here is devoted to running the restaurant, the Lesueurs also maintain 11 bungalows. Single or double occupancy costs 350F ($70) per night. Each unit has a sea view and a simple kitchenette, so many visitors cook most of their meals in-house.

VIEUX HABITANTS

The winding coast road brings you to Vieux Habitants (Old Settlers), one of the oldest villages on the island, founded in 1636. The name comes from the people who settled it. After serving in the employment of the West Indies Company, they retired here. But they preferred to call themselves inhabitants, so as not to be confused with slaves.

BASSE-TERRE

Another 10 miles of winding roads brings you to Basse-Terre, the seat of the government of Guadeloupe. The town lies between the water and La Soufrière, the volcano. Founded in 1634, it's the oldest town on the island and still has a lot of charm; its market squares are shaded by tamarind and palm trees.

The town suffered heavy destruction at the hands of British troops in 1691 and again in 1702. It was also the center of fierce fighting during the French Revolution, when the political changes that swept across Europe caused explosive tensions on Guadeloupe. (As it did in the mainland of France, the guillotine claimed many lives on Guadeloupe during the infamous Reign of Terror.)

In spite of the town's history, there isn't much to see in Basse-Terre except for a 17th-century cathedral and Fort St-Charles, which has guarded the city (not always well) since it was established.

Where to Stay & Eat

Le Houëlmont. Rue de la République 34, 97120 Basse-Terre, Guadeloupe, F.W.I. ☎ **590/ 81-35-96.** Reservations recommended. Main courses 75F–200F ($15–$40); fixed-price meals from 95F ($19). MC, V. Mon–Sat noon–3pm and 7–10:30pm. INTERNATIONAL.

Set in the monumental heart of town, near the bus station, across a boulevard from a massive government building called the Conseil Général, is the oldest and best-established restaurant in the island capital, Le Houëlmont. The restaurant is named after an extinct volcano that can be viewed from the windows of the dining room. After climbing a flight of stairs to the paneled second story, diners enjoy a sweeping view over the hillside, sloping down to the sea a block away. Mme Boulon, the owner, an old-time Guadeloupienne restaurateur, offers fixed-price and à la carte meals. Specialties include a medley of Créole food, such as accras, court bouillon of fish, grilled fish, steaks, shellfish, and blood sausage, plus French and international dishes.

It's also possible to rent one of the eight bedrooms here, each with private bath and air-conditioning (some have TVs). Year-round, single rooms cost 280F ($56) and doubles run 280F to 300F ($56 to $60).

LA SOUFRIÈRE

The big attraction of Basse-Terre is the famous sulfur-puffing La Soufrière volcano, which is still alive, but dormant—for the moment at least. Rising to a height of some 4,800 feet, it's flanked by banana plantations and lush foliage.

After leaving the capital at Basse-Terre, you can drive to **St-Claude,** a suburb, 4 miles up the mountainside at a height of 1,900 feet. It has an elegant reputation for its perfect climate and tropical gardens.

Instead of going to St-Claude, you can head for **Matouba,** in a country of clear mountain spring water. The only sound you're likely to hear at this idyllic place is of birds and the running water of dozens of springs. The village was settled long ago by Hindus.

From St-Claude, you can begin the climb up the narrow, winding road the Guadeloupeans say leads to hell—that is, **La Soufrière.** The road ends at a parking area at La Savane-à-Mulets, at an altitude of 3,300 feet. That is the ultimate point to be reached by car. Hikers are able to climb right to the mouth of the volcano. However, in 1975 the appearance of ashes, mud, billowing smoke, and earthquakelike tremors proved that the old beast was still alive.

In the resettlement process, 75,000 inhabitants were relocated to Grande-Terre. However, no deaths were reported. But the inhabitants of Basse-Terre still keep a watchful eye on the smoking giant.

Even in the parking lot you can feel the heat of the volcano merely by touching the ground. Steam emerges from fumaroles and sulfurous fumes from the volcano's "burps." Of course, fumes come from its pit and mud caldrons as well.

Where to Eat en Route

Chez Paul de Matouba. Rivière Rouge. ☎ **590/80-29-20.** Main courses 50F–130F ($10–$26); fixed-price menu 100F ($20). No credit cards. Daily noon–4pm. Follow the clearly marked signs—it's beside a gully close to the center of the village. CREOLE/INTERNATIONAL.

You'll find good food in this family-run restaurant, which sits beside the banks of the small Rivière Rouge (Red River). The dining room on the second floor is enclosed by windows, allowing you to drink in the surrounding dark-green foliage of the mountains. The cookery is Créole, and crayfish dishes are the specialty. However, because of the influence of the region's early settlers, East Indian meals are also available. By all means, drink the mineral or spring water of Matouba. What one diner called "an honest meal" might include stuffed crab, colombo (curried) of chicken, as well as an array of French, Créole, and Hindu specialties. You're likely to find the place overcrowded in winter with the tour-bus crowd.

THE WINDWARD COAST

From Basse-Terre to Pointe-à-Pitre, the road follows the east coast, called the Windward Coast. The country here is richer and greener than elsewhere on the island.

To reach **Trois Rivières** you have a choice of two routes. One goes along the coastline, coming eventually to Vieux Fort, from which you can see Les Saintes archipelago. The other heads across the hills, Monts Caraïbes.

Near the pier in Trois Rivières you'll see the pre-Columbian petroglyphs carved by the original inhabitants, the Arawaks. They're called merely Roches Gravées, or "carved rocks." In this archaeological park, the rock engravings are of animal and human figures, dating most likely from A.D. 300 or 400. You'll also see specimens of plants, including cocoa, pimento, and banana, that the Arawaks cultivated long before the Europeans set foot on Guadeloupe. From Trois Rivières, you can take boats to Les Saintes.

After leaving Trois Rivières, you continue on route 1. Passing through the village of Banaier, you turn on your left at Anse St-Sauveur to reach the famous **Chutes du Carbet,** a trio of waterfalls. The road to two of them is a narrow, winding one, along many steep hills, passing through banana plantations as you move deeper into a tropical forest.

After 3 miles, a lane, suitable only for hikers, brings you to Zombie Pool. Half a mile farther along, a fork to the left takes you to Grand Etang, or large pool. At a point 6 miles from the main road, a parking area is available and you'll have to walk the rest of the way on an uneasy trail toward the second fall, Le Carbet. Expect to spend around 20 to 30 minutes, depending on how slippery the lane is. Then you'll be at the foot of this second fall where the water drops from 230 feet. The waters here average 70° Fahrenheit, which is pretty warm for a mountain spring.

The first fall is the most impressive, but it takes 2 hours of rough hiking to get there. The third fall is reached from Capesterre on the main road by climbing to Routhiers. This fall is less impressive in height, only 70 feet. When the Carbet water runs out of La Soufrière, it's almost boiling.

If you'd like to stop over along the Windward Coast before returning to Grande Terre, the area of Petit-Bourg, north of Ste-Marie and Goyave and directly southwest

Joe vs. the Volcano

The mountainous terrain of Guadeloupe's Basse-Terre is some of the most beautiful in the entire Caribbean. Although the coastline of Basse-Terre is lined with beach resorts and fishing villages, the mountainous interior (about 20% of the landmass of Guadeloupe) is devoted almost completely to the protected terrain of a French national forest, the Natural Park of Guadeloupe. Near the park's southernmost tip rise the misty heights of one of the island's most distinctive natural features, the 4,812-foot volcanic peak of La Soufrière. Since recorded history on Guadeloupe began, the volcano has erupted in 1560, 1797, 1975, and 1976–77. Dozens of lava flows along its slopes attest to the potential violence that reigns in the volcano's core. Today its many pits and craters offer the rare ability for geologists and hikers to gaze down into the rumbling and smoking primeval forces that shaped the planet Earth.

The park contains an intricate network of more than 200 miles of hiking trails, allowing physically fit hikers to visit a wealth of gorges, ravines, rain forests, rivers, and (at points north of La Soufrière) some of the highest waterfalls in the Caribbean. The watershed from the peak of La Soufrière pours rainwater down a ring of black sandy beaches along Basse-Terre's southern coastline.

Surprisingly, the trek up the mountainside is not considered particularly strenuous, although you should wear a hat or some other form of sun protection. Most of your walk is through scrubland and, at higher elevations, rocky plateaux covered with moss and lichens. Total time expended round-trip, without accounting for admiration of the views, is about 3 hours, although the experienced park rangers can usually reach the summit in about 20 minutes.

Begin your walking tour to the volcano's summit from one of the highest-altitude parking lots on Guadeloupe, Savane-à-Mulets. Savane-à-Mulets has no amenities of any kind. Set on the volcano's western slope at about 3,400 feet above sea level, 3 miles west of the village of St-Claude, it marks the farthest point a conventional vehicle can proceed along route de la Soufrière. (The road between St-Claude and Savane-à-Mulets is very steep—put your transmission in low gear en route.) Park your car in the parking lot, then hike along a network of carefully marked trails toward the summit. If a wind is blowing, it will probably clear away much of the mist that sometimes envelops the peak. Along the way you'll bypass a string of small craters and crevasses, many of them bubbling up mud and fumes. As you bypass each pit, the scent of sulfur and the radiant heat become very powerful. Of special note is the South Crater (Crader Sud), which spews lots of noise, steam, and sulfurous odors.

Be warned that a handful of hikers have had their valuables stolen during scattered incidents in this park. Lock anything extremely valuable in a safe back at your hotel, and carry minimal amounts of cash with you as you proceed on this itinerary. For more information about this and other hikes in the national park, contact the employees of the national park (☎ **590/80-24-25**).

of Pointe-à-Pitre, makes the best stopover. To reach Vernou from Petit-Bourg, cut inland (west) along route D23.

Where to Stay

Auberge de la Distillerie. Tabanon, C.D. 23, 97170 Petit-Bourg, Guadeloupe, F.W.I. ☎ **590/94-25-91.** Fax 590/94-11-91. 16 rms. A/C TV TEL. Winter, 450F ($90) single; 650F ($130) double. Off-season, 280F ($56) single; 450F ($90) double. MAP 120F ($24) per person extra. AE, MC, V.

This inn attracts more of a hiking crowd than a beachgoing one. Outfitted in a rustic and tropical-woodsy motif, it lies close to the entrance of the Parc National, near the hamlet of Vernou, in a luxuriantly verdant setting. You'll have to drive about 15 minutes to reach the black sands of the nearest beach (Plage de Viard), but hiking trails through the volcanic oddities of Basse-Terre are nearby. There's a bar (sometimes featuring live piano music) on the premises, and an unpretentious restaurant serving mostly Créole cuisine. Each accommodation contains a writing table, a balcony with a hammock, and a radio. Boating excursions can be arranged on the Lezard River where a waterfall (Cascade aux Ecrevisses) figures as one of the primary attractions.

BEACHES, WATER SPORTS & OTHER OUTDOOR PURSUITS AROUND THE ISLAND

BEACHES   Chances are, your hotel will be right on a beach, or no more than 20 minutes from a good one. Plenty of natural beaches dot the island, from the surf-brushed dark strands of western Basse-Terre to the long stretches of white sand encircling Grande-Terre. Public beaches are generally free, but some charge for parking. Unlike hotel beaches, they have few facilities. Hotels welcome nonguests, but charge for changing facilities, beach chairs, and towels.

Sunday is family day at the beach. Topless sunbathing is common at hotels, less so on village beaches. Nudist beaches also exist, including at **Ilet du Gosier,** off the shore of Gosier, site of many leading hotels.

Outstanding beaches of Guadeloupe include **Caravelle Beach,** a long, reef-protected stretch of sand outside Ste-Anne, about 9 miles from Gosier.

Another nudist beach, **Plage de Tarare,** lies near the tip of Grand-Terre at Pointe des Châteaux, site of many local restaurants.

On Basse-Terre, one of the best beaches is **Grande Anse,** a palm-sheltered beach north of Deshaies on the northwest coast.

Other good beaches are found on the offshore islands, Iles des Saintes and Marie-Galante (see below).

GOLF   Guadeloupe's only golf course is the well-known **Golf de St-François** (☎ **590/88-41-87**) at St-François, opposite the Hôtel Méridien, about 22 miles east of Raizet Airport (see "When the Five Iron Calls" in the St-François section, above, for details).

HIKING   The **Parc Naturel de Guadeloupe** is the best hiking grounds in the Caribbean (see the touring notes on route de la Traversée in "Around Basse-Terre," above). Marked trails cut through the deep foliage of rain forests until you come upon a waterfall or a cool mountain pool. The big excursion country, of course, is around the volcano, La Soufrière. Hiking brochures are available from the tourist office. Hotel tour desks can arrange this activity. For information about this and other hikes in the national park, contact **Organisation des Guides de Montagne de la Caraïbe,** Maison Forestière, Matouba (☎ **590/94-29-11**).

Warning: Hikers may experience heavy downpours. The annual precipitation on the higher slopes is 250 inches per year, so be prepared.

SAILING   Sailboats of varying sizes, crewed or bareboat, are plentiful. Information can be secured at any hotel desk. Sunfish sailing can be arranged at almost every beachfront hotel.

SCUBA DIVING   Scuba divers seem to be drawn more to the waters off Guadeloupe than to any other point in the French-speaking islands. Its allure derives from its lack of underwater currents, relatively calm seas, and the establishment of the **Cousteau Underwater Reserve,** a kind of French national park with many attractive dive sites, where the underwater environment is rigidly protected. Jacques Cousteau described the waters off Guadeloupe's Pigeon Island as "one of the world's 10 best diving spots." During a typical dive, sergeant majors become visible at a depth of 30 feet, spiny sea urchins and green parrot fish at 60 feet, and magnificent stands of finger, black, brain, and star coral come into view at depths of 80 feet.

Every year the specific sites favored by Guadeloupe's many dive aficionados range from one underwater locale to another. The most popular of these bear such names as Aquarium, Piscine, Jardin de Corail, Pointe Carrangue, Pointe Barracuda, and Jardin Japonais. Although scattered around the periphery of the island, many lie within the bay of Petit Cul-de-Sac Marin, south of Rivière Salée, the channel that separates the two halves of Guadeloupe. North of the Salée is another bay, Grand Cul-de-Sac Marin, where the small islets of Fajou and Caret also boast fine diving.

The **Centre International de la Plongée (C.I.P.),** B.P. 4, Lieu-Dit Poirier, Malendure Plage, 97125 Pigeon, Bouillante, Guadeloupe, F.W.I. (☎ **590/ 98-81-72**), is acknowledged as one of the most businesslike and professional dive operations on the island. Set in a wood-sided house on Malendure Plage, close to a well-known restaurant, Chez Loulouse, it benefits from a position at the edge of the above-mentioned Cousteau Underwater Reserve. Dive boats depart three times a day, usually at 10am, 12:30pm, and 3pm. A one-tank dive costs 200F ($40), whereas what Americans refer to as a "resort course" for first-time divers (the French refer to it as a *baptème*) goes for 230F ($46) and is usually conducted one-on-one with one participant and an instructor.

TENNIS   All the large resort hotels have tennis courts, many of which they light at night. The noonday sun is often too hot for most players. If you're a guest, tennis is free at most of these hotels, but you'll be charged for night play. If your hotel doesn't have a court, you might consider an outing to **Le Relais du Moulin,** Châteaubrun, near Ste-Anne (☎ **590/88-23-96**).

WINDSURFING & WATERSKIING   Windsurfing is the hottest sport on Guadeloupe today, and it's available with lessons at all the major beach hotels, at a cost of 130F ($26) and up. Most seaside hotels can arrange waterskiing at around 125F ($25) for 15 minutes' boating time.

GUADELOUPE AFTER DARK

Guadeloupeans claim that the beguine was invented here, not on Martinique, and they dance the beguine as if they truly did own it. Of course, calypso and the merengue move rhythmically along—the islanders are known for their dancing.

Ask at your hotel where the folkloric **Ballets Guadeloupeans** will be appearing. This troupe makes frequent appearances at the big hotels, although they don't enjoy the fame of the Ballets Martiniquais, the troupe on the neighbor island already described.

The **Casino de la Marina,** avenue de l'Europe (☎ **590/88-41-44**), stands near the Hôtel Méridien St-François. It's open daily from noon to 3am to persons 18 or older with proof of identity—a driver's license or valid passport. Once inside, you can play American roulette and blackjack. Dress is casual. A free buffet is served on Friday night. Admission is 69F ($13.80).

Another casino, **Gosier-les-Bains,** is in the resort community of Gosier (Bas du Fort), on the grounds of the Hôtel Arawak (☎ 590/84-79-68). Entrance is free, but an ID card with a photo, or a passport, is required for admission. Although dress tends to be casually elegant, coat and tie are not required. The casino is open Sunday to Thursday from 9pm to 3am and on Friday and Saturday from 7:30pm to 4am. (One room containing slot machines is open every night from 6pm until closing.) The most popular games are blackjack, roulette, and chemin de fer.

A SIDE TRIP TO THE ILES DES SAINTES

A cluster of eight islands off the southern coast of Guadeloupe, the Iles des Saintes are certainly off the beaten track. The two main islands and six rocks are Terre-de-Haut, Terre-de-Bas, Ilet-à-Cabrit, La Coche, Les Augustins, Grand Ilet, Le Redonde, and Le Pâté; only Terre-de-Haut ("land of high"), and to a lesser extent Terre-de-Bas ("land below"), attract visitors.

If you're planning a visit, **Terre-de-Haut** is the most interesting Saint to call upon. It's the only one with facilities for overnight guests.

Some claim that Les Saintes has one of the nicest bays in the world, a lilliput Rio de Janeiro with a sugarloaf. The isles, just 6 miles from the main island, were discovered by Columbus (who else?) on November 4, 1493, who named them "Los Santos."

The history of Les Saintes is very much the history of Guadeloupe itself. In years past the islands have been heavily fortified, as they were considered Guadeloupe's Gibraltar. The climate is very dry, and until the desalination plant opened, water was often rationed.

The population of Terre-de-Haut is mainly Caucasian, all fisherfolk or sailors and their families who are descended from Breton corsairs. The very skilled sailors maneuver large boats called *saintois* and wear coolielike headgear called a *salaco,* which is shallow and white with sun shades covered in cloth built on radiating ribs of thick bamboo. Frankly, the hats look like small parasols. If you want to take a photograph of these sailors, please make a polite request (in French, no less; otherwise they won't know what you're talking about). Visitors often like to buy these hats (if they can find them) for use as beach wear.

Terre-de-Haut is a place for discovery and lovers of nature, many of whom stake out their exhibitionistic space on the nude beach at Anse Crawen.

GETTING THERE

BY PLANE   The fastest way to get there is by plane. The "airport" is a truncated landing strip that accommodates nothing larger than 20-seat Twin Otters. **Air Guadeloupe** (☎ 590/82-47-00 on Guadeloupe, or 590/99-51-23 on Terre-de-Haut) has two round-trip flights daily from Pointe-à-Pitre, which take 15 minutes and cost around 150F ($30) per person, round-trip.

BY FERRY   Most islanders reach Terre-de-Haut via one of the several ferryboats that travel from Guadeloupe every day. Most visitors opt for one of the two boats that depart every day from Pointe-à-Pitre's Gare Maritime des Iles, on quai Gatine, across the street from the well-known open-air market. The trip requires 60 minutes each way, and costs 180F ($36) for round-trip passage. The most popular departure time for Terre-de-Haut from Pointe-à-Pitre is at 8am Monday to Saturday, and at 7am on Sunday, with returns scheduled every afternoon at 3:45pm. Be at the ferryboat terminal at least 15 minutes prior to the anticipated departure. Pointe-à-Pitre is not the only departure point for Terre-de-Haut: Other ferryboats (two per day) also depart from Trois Rivières, and one additional ferryboat leaves every day from the island's capital of Basse-Terre. Transit from either of these last two cities requires 25 minutes each way, and costs 100F ($20) for the round-trip passage.

For more information and last-minute departure schedules, contact **Frères Brudey** (☎ **590/83-12-99**) or **Trans Antilles Express,** Gare Maritime, quai Gatine, Pointe-à-Pitre (☎ **590/83-12-45**).

GETTING AROUND

On an island that doesn't have a single car-rental agency, you get about by walking or renting a **bike** or **motor scooter,** which can be rented at hotels and in town near the pier.

There are also minibuses called **Taxis de l'Ile** (eight in all), which take six to eight passengers.

WHERE TO STAY

Auberge Les Petits Saints aux Anacardiers. La Savane, 97137 Terre-de-Haut, Les Saintes, Guadeloupe, F.W.I. ☎ **590/99-50-99.** Fax 590/99-54-51. 12 rms, 6 with bath. A/C TV. Winter, 510F ($102) single without bath, 650F ($130) single with bath; 560F ($112) double without bath, 700F ($140) double with bath. Off-season, 350F ($70) single without bath, 450F ($90) single with bath; 400F ($80) double without bath, 500F ($100) double with bath. AE, MC, V.

This simple, cost-conscious guest house occupies a building that was erected in the 1970s as the private home of the island's mayor. Set in a hilltop garden a 5-minute walk from the nearest beach, it was transformed into a guest house in the early 1990s by expatriates from the French mainland. The rooms are simple but appealing and comfortable. On the premises is a restaurant, set up on a terrace surrounded with plants, that serves simple, health-conscious foods with an emphasis on fresh fish.

Hôtel La Saintoise. Place de la Mairie, 97137 Terre-de-Haut, Les Saintes, Guadeloupe, F.W.I. ☎ **800/423-4433** in the U.S., or 590/99-52-50. 8 rms. A/C. 260F ($52) single; 360F ($72) double. Rates include continental breakfast. MC, V.

Originally built in the 1960s, La Saintoise is a modern two-story building set near the almond trees and widespread poinciana of the town's main square, near the ferryboat dock, across from the town hall. As in a small French village, the inn places tables and chairs on the sidewalk, where you can sit out and observe what action there is. The owner will welcome you and show you through the uncluttered lobby to one of his modest, second-floor bedrooms, each of which is outfitted with a tile bath. This is a friendly and unpretentious place.

Kanao. 97137 Terre-de-Haut, Les Saintes, Guadeloupe, F.W.I. ☎ **800/221-4542** in the U.S., or 590/99-51-36. Fax 590/99-55-04. 19 rms, 3 bungalows with kitchenette. A/C TEL. Winter, 600F ($120) double; 700F–800F ($140–$160) bungalow for two. Off-season, 350F ($70) double; 450F ($90) bungalow for two. Rates include continental breakfast. MC, V.

Named after the open-sided log canoes originally used by the Arawaks, this modern concrete-sided structure erected on a little beach at Pointe Coquelet is about a 10-minute walk north of the town center. All accommodations have private showers and rather Spartan furnishings; five have views of the sea and Anse Mire cove. Very limited English is spoken and the staff might not be able to respond to many of your needs. Despite that, the hotel may be ideal for vacationers wanting to get away from it all. A garden with its own swimming pool is near the hotel, and the hotel restaurant serves breakfast, lunch, and dinner.

WHERE TO EAT

Many French-speaking guests used to come to Terre-de-Haut to eat roast iguana, the large but harmless lizard found on many of these islands. But now that the species is endangered, it is no longer recommended that this dish be consumed. Instead, you'll find conch (called *lambi*), Caribbean lobster, and fresh fish. For dessert, you can sample the savory island specialty, *tournament d'amour* (agony of love), a coconut pastry available in the restaurants but best sampled from the barefoot children who sell the delicacy near the boat dock.

✪ **Chez Jeannine (Le Casse-Croûte).** Fond-de-Curé, Terre-de-Haut. ☎ **590-99-53-37.** Reservations recommended for large groups only. Fixed-price three-course meal 70F ($14). V. Daily 9–10am, noon–3pm, and 7–10pm. CREOLE.

The creative statement of Mme Jeannine Bairtran, originally from Guadeloupe, this restaurant is a 3-minute walk south of the town center in a simple Créole house decorated with modern Caribbean accessories. Only a fixed-price meal is served, and it includes avocado stuffed with crabmeat, a *gâteau de poissons* (literally "fish cake"), and several different curry-enhanced stews (including one made with goat). Crayfish and grilled fish (the ubiquitous catch of the day) appear daily on the menu. Local vegetables are used. The ambience is that of a Créole bistro—in other words, a hut with nautical trappings and bright tablecloths.

Les Amandiers. Place de la Mairie. ☎ **590/99-50-06.** Reservations recommended. Fixed-price menu 65F–85F ($13–$17). AE, MC, V. Daily 8am–3pm and 6:30–9:30pm. CREOLE.

Across from the town hall on the main square of Bourg is perhaps the most traditional Créole bistro on Terre-de-Haut. A TV set (at loud volume) might be providing entertainment in the bar at the time of your visit. Monsieur and Madame Charlot Brudey are your hosts in this beige-painted building whose upper balconies sport tables and chairs for open-air dining. Conch (*lambi*) is prepared either in a fricassée or a colombo, a savory curry stew. Also available is a court bouillon of fish, a *gâteau* (terrine) of fish, and a seemingly endless supply of grilled crayfish, a staple of the island. The catch of the day is also grilled the way you like it. You'll find an intriguing collection of stews, concocted from fish, bananas, and christophine (chayote). A knowledge of French would be helpful around here.

EXPLORING THE ISLAND

On Terre-de-Haut, the main settlement is at **Bourg,** a single street that follows the curve of the fishing harbor. A charming hamlet, it has little houses with red or blue doorways, balconies, and Victorian gingerbread gewgaws. Donkeys are the beasts of burden, and everywhere you look are fish nets drying in the sunshine. You can also explore the ruins of **Fort Napoléon,** which is left over from those 17th-century wars, including the naval encounter known in European history books as "The Battle of the Saints." You can see the barracks and prison cells, as well as the drawbridge and art museum. Occasionally you'll spot an iguana scurrying up the ramparts. Directly across the bay, atop Ilet-à-Cabrit, sits the fort named in honor of Empress Joséphine.

You might also get a sailor to take you on his boat to the other main island, **Terre-de-Bas,** which has no accommodations, incidentally. Or you can stay on Terre-de-Haut and hike to **Le Grand Souffleur** with its beautiful cliffs, and to **Le Chameau,** the highest point on the island, rising to a peak of 1,000 feet.

Scuba-diving centers are not limited to mainland Guadeloupe. The underwater world off Les Saintes has attracted deep-sea divers as renowned as Jacques Cousteau, but even the less experienced may explore its challenging depths and multicolored reefs. Intriguing underwater grottoes found near Fort Napoléon on Terre-de-Haut are also explored.

SHOPPING

Few come here to shop but there is one offbeat choice at **Kaz an Nou Gallery** on Terre-de-Haut (☎ **590/99-52-29**), where a local artist, Pascal Fay, makes carved wooden house facades, all candy colored and trimmed in gingerbread. Naturally, they're in miniature. The most popular reproduction graces the cover of the best-selling picture book, *Caribbean Style.* Mr. Fay will point the way to the real house a few blocks away which has become a sightseeing attraction all on its own because of the book's popularity. The "houses" measure about 16 by 13 inches and sell for $100 to $400 each. His gallery ("Our House" in English) is open daily from 9am to noon and 2 to 6pm.

A SIDE TRIP TO MARIE-GALANTE

This offshore dependency of Guadeloupe is an almost-perfect circle of about 60 square miles. Almost exclusively French-speaking, it lies 20 miles south of Guadeloupe's Grand-Terre and is full of rustic charm.

Columbus noticed it before he did Guadelope, on November 3, 1493. He named it for his own vessel, but didn't land here. In fact, it was 150 years later that the first European came ashore.

The first French governor of the island was Constant d'Aubigne, father of the marquise de Maintenon. Several captains from the West Indies Company attempted settlement, but none of them succeeded. In 1674 Marie-Galante was given to the Crown, and from that point on its history was closely linked to that of Guadeloupe.

However, after 1816 the island settled down to a quiet slumber. You could hear the sugarcane growing on the plantations—and that was about it. Many windmills were built to crush the cane, and lots of tropical fruits were grown.

Now some 30,000 inhabitants live here and make their living from sugar and rum, the latter said to be the best in the Caribbean. The island's climate is rather dry, and there are many good beaches. One of these stretches of sand covers at least 5 miles—brilliantly white. However, swimming can be dangerous in some places. The best beach is at **Petite Anse,** 6½ miles from **Grand-Bourg,** the main town, with an 1845 baroque church. The 18th-century Grand Anse rum distillery can be visited, as can the historic fishing hamlet of Vieux Fort.

GETTING THERE & GETTING AROUND

Air Guadeloupe (☎ **590/82-74-00**) will bring you to the island in just 20 minutes from Pointe-à-Pitre, landing at Les Basse Airport on Marie-Galante, about 2 miles from Grand-Bourg. Round-trip passage costs 400F ($80).

Antilles Trans Express (Exprès des Iles), Gare Maritime, quai Gatine, Pointe-à-Pitre (☎ **590/83-12-45** or 590/91-13-43), operates boat service to the island with three daily round-trips between Point-à-Pitre and Grand-Bourg. The round-trip costs 160F ($32). Departures from Pointe-à-Pitre are daily at 8am, 12:45pm, and 5pm, with returns from Grand-Bourg at 6am, 9am, and 3:45pm.

A limited number of **taxis** are available at the airport, but the price should be negotiated before you drive off.

WHERE TO STAY

There are only a few little accommodations on the island, which, even if they aren't very up-to-date in amenities, are clean and hearty. At least the greetings are friendly. They may also be bewildering if you speak no French.

Auberge de l'Arbre à Pain. Rue Jeanne-d'Arc 34, 97112 Grand-Bourg, Marie-Galante, Guadeloupe, F.W.I. ☎ **590/97-73-69.** 7 rms. A/C. Year-round, 210F ($42) single; 250F ($50) double; 300F ($60) triple. V. At the harbor, take the first street going toward the church.

Set behind a clapboard facade close to the street, about a 5-minute stroll from the harborfront, this establishment was named after the half-dozen breadfruit trees (*les arbres á pain*) that shelter its courtyard and its simple but pleasant bedrooms from the blazing sun. You'll get a taste of Old France at this respectable auberge. Each room has uncomplicated furnishings, a private bath, and easy access to nearby beaches.

The hotel's restaurant is a favorite with many town residents. Meals are served daily from noon to 2pm and 7 to 11pm. Main courses cost 65F to 100F ($13 to $20), and include fresh fish and shellfish. Usually whatever's available includes a court bouillon of fish, a soufflé of sea urchins, and meat dishes derived from the conservative array of French culinary traditions. No reservations are required for the restaurant, although because the bedrooms are usually in demand throughout the winter, advance reservations for overnight stays are important.

WHERE TO EAT

Le Touloulou. Plage de Petite Anse, Marie-Galante. ☎ **590/97-32-63.** Main courses 65F–130F ($13–$26). MC, V. Tues–Sun 9am–4:30pm and 7–10:30pm. Closed 2 weeks in Oct. CREOLE.

Its French-speaking owners will tell you, if you ask them, about how during one of the recent hurricanes the relatively rare bamboo walls of this 30-year-old house were blown away and later replaced with conventional boards. Set adjacent to the beach, with a hardworking staff and a hyper-casual clientele, it specializes in shellfish and crayfish culled from local waters. If sea urchins or lobster is your passion, you'll find them here in abundance, prepared virtually any way you want. Other standbys include a savory, and highly ethnic, version of *bébelé* (cow tripe enhanced with breadfruit, dumplings, and plantains) and conch served either as fricassée or in puff pastry.

A SIDE TRIP TO LA DESIRADE

The ubiquitous Columbus spotted this *terre désirée* or "sought-after land" after his Atlantic crossing in 1493. Named La Désirade, the island is less than 7 miles long and about 1^1/$_2$ miles wide, and has a single potholed road running along its length. It lies just 5 miles off the eastern tip of Guadeloupe proper. This former leper colony is often visited on a day excursion.

The island has fewer than 1,700 inhabitants, including the descendants of Europeans exiled here by royal command. Tourism has hardly touched the place, if you can forget about those "day-trippers." Most visitors opt to spend only a day on La Désirade, sunning, or perhaps touring the island's barren expanses. There are, however, a handful of exceptionally simple guest houses charging around 300F ($60) for overnight accommodations for two. Don't expect anything grand.

The main hamlet is **Grande Anse,** which has a small church with a presbytery and flower garden, and the homes of the local inhabitants. **Le Souffleur** is a village where boats are constructed, and at **Baie Mahault** are the ruins of the old leper colony (including a barely recognizable chapel) from the early 18th century.

The best **beaches** are Souffleur, a tranquil oasis near the boat-building hamlet, and Baie Mahault, a small beach that's a Caribbean cliché with white sand and palm trees.

GETTING THERE & GETTING AROUND

From Pointe-à-Pitre, **Air Guadeloupe** (☎ 590/82-47-00) offers flights to La Désirade from Guadeloupe's Le Raizet Airport three times a week on aircraft containing between 9 and 19 passengers. The round-trip cost is 380F ($76) and trip time is between 15 and 20 minutes each way. Be warned in advance that unless a respectable number of passengers has shown up to share the flight with you, Air Guadeloupe might cancel the flight altogether. Because of this, some visitors opt to charter a three-passenger plane, suitable for daytime flights only, from **Ailes Guadeloupiennes** (☎ **590/83-02-65**) for a one-way fare of 600F ($120), the cost of which is divided among the three passengers.

Because of the infrequency of flights and the expense, most passengers opt for transit to La Désirade by **ferryboat,** which leaves St-François every day at 8am and 5pm (and sometimes at 3pm as well, depending on the season) from the wharves at St-François, near Guadeloupe's eastern tip. Returns from La Désirade to St-François include a daily departure every day at 3pm, allowing convenient access for daytrippers. Trip time is around 50 minutes each way, depending on conditions at sea. Round-trip passage on the ferryboat costs 120F ($24) per person.

If you'd like to spend the night, call **L'Oasis** (☎ **590/20-02-12**) or **Le Mirage** (☎ **590/20-01-08;** fax 590/20-07-45). Both are at Beauséjour, half a mile from the airport.

On La Désirade, three or four **minibuses** run between the airport and the towns. To get around, you might negotiate with a local driver. **Bicycles** are also available.

3 St. Martin

"Why French St. Martin?" you may ask. It hardly has the attractions of St. Thomas, Puerto Rico, or Jamaica. There are no dazzling sights, no spectacular nightlife. Even the sports program on St. Martin isn't as well organized as on many Caribbean islands, although the Dutch side has golf and other diversions.

Most people visit St. Martin just to relax on its many white sandy beaches. Mostly they come to sample "France in the tropics" on the smallest island in the world to be divided between two sovereign states, France and the Netherlands. France got the larger part, with 21 of the total of 37 square miles. The north is French, the south Dutch. The Dutch even spell the name of the island differently: Sint Maarten.

French St. Martin not only has some of the best cuisine in the Caribbean, but is filled with an extraordinary number of bistros and restaurants for such a small place. It has a distinctly French air. The policemen, for example, wear *képis*. The towns have names like Colombier and Orléans, the streets are called "rue de la Liberté" and "rue de la République," and the tricolor of France flies over the *gendarmerie* in Marigot, the capital.

Don't come here to escape the crowds, however. From a sleepy backwater in Caribbean tourism in 1970, the place has boomed, with a year-round population of 11,000, plus thousands of tourists, often tour groups and conventioneers, arriving weekly.

The island, both French and Dutch sides, is almost completely devoid of racial tensions, although crime, usually muggings and robberies of tourists, is on the rise.

Both French St. Martin and Dutch Sint Maarten are highly touted for their shopping bargains. Sometimes you can pick up a bargain, perhaps a French or Dutch import, but many goods such as electronics can be purchased much more cheaply on the U.S. mainland.

Although widely viewed as a high-priced island, as are all French islands, St. Martin is a far better bargain than St. Barts. Nevertheless, it has very expensive resorts, so you'll have to shop carefully for bargains, and we'll point out some of the best available. Food costs are high, even in simple restaurants, so it will be best to go on a picnic during the day, confining your main meal of the day to dinner.

The island has two jurisdictions, but there's complete freedom of movement between the two sectors. If you arrive on the Dutch side and clear Customs there, there'll be no red-tape formalities when crossing over to the French side—either for shopping, perhaps a hotel, or certainly for eating, as it has the best food (with some notable exceptions).

French St. Martin is governed from Guadeloupe and has direct representation in the government in Paris. Lying between Guadeloupe and Puerto Rico, the tiny island has been half French, half Dutch since 1648.

The principal town on the French side is **Marigot,** the seat of the subprefect and municipal council. Visitors come here not only for shopping, as the island is a free port, but also to enjoy the excellent cookery in the Créole bistros.

Marigot is not quite the same size as its counterpart, Philipsburg, in the Dutch sector. It has none of the frenzied pace of Philipsburg, which is often overrun with cruise-ship passengers. In fact, Marigot looks like a French village transplanted to the Caribbean. If you climb the hill over this tiny port, you'll be rewarded with a view from the old fort here.

About 20 minutes by car beyond Marigot is **Grand-Case,** a small fishing village that's an outpost of French civilization with many good restaurants and a few places to stay.

Note that the **map of St. Martin** is at the beginning of chapter 10. For a description of the facilities and attractions of Dutch St. Maarten, refer to chapter 10.

GETTING THERE

Most arrivals are at the Dutch-controlled **Queen Juliana International Airport,** St. Maarten. For a more detailed description of transportation on that side of the island, see "Getting There" for St. Maarten in chapter 10.

GETTING AROUND

BY BUS   It's cheapest to get around on one of the island's buses, which are operated by a sometimes-motley crew of local drivers, with a widely divergent armada of privately owned minivans and minibuses of every conceivable make and model. They run daily from 6am until midnight. One departs from Grand-Case for Marigot every 20 minutes. There's a departure every hour from Marigot to the Dutch side. A sample bus fare from Marigot to Grand-Case is between $1.50 and $2. Because they're sometimes difficult for a newcomer to spot, the best way to identify one is to ask a local resident.

BY TAXI   For visitors, the most common means of transport is a taxi. A **Taxi Service & Information Center** operates at the port of Marigot (☎ **590/87-56-54**). Always agree on the rate before getting into an unmetered cab. Here are some sample fares: from Marigot to Grand-Case, $10; from Queen Juliana Airport to Marigot, also $10. These fares are in effect from 7am to 10pm; after that, they go up by 25% until midnight, rising by 50% after midnight.

You can also book 2-hour sightseeing trips around the island, either through the organization listed above or at any hotel desk. The cost is $45 for one or two passengers, plus $10 for each additional passenger.

BY RENTAL CAR   The division of the island into dual political zones used to make car rentals on St. Martin rather complicated. Now rental companies on both sides of the Dutch-French border are cooperating more fully with one another. The main complication you'll face is a local law that forbids clients from picking up a rental car immediately upon arrival at Queen Juliana Airport. (This law was instigated

St. Martin

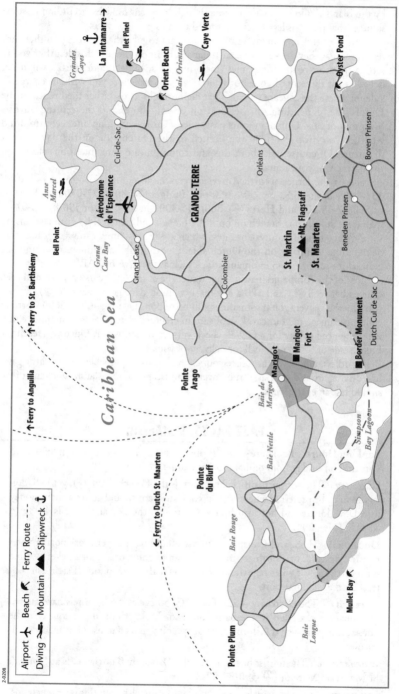

Airport ✈ Beach ⊀ Ferry Route - - -
Diving ⛵ Mountain ▲ Shipwreck ⚓

2-0208

← Ferry to Anguilla

← Ferry to St. Barthélemy

Caribbean Sea

Grandes
Cayes

La Tintamarre → ⚓

Ilet Pinel ⛵

Orient Beach ⊀

Caye Verte ◆

Baie Orientale

Oyster Pond ⚓

Cul-de-Sac ●

GRANDE-TERRE

Orléans ●

Boven Prinsen ●

Anse
Marcel ⛵

Bell Point

Aérodrome
de l'Espérance ✈

Grand
Case Bay

Grand Case ●

Colombier ●

Mt. Flagstaff ▲

St. Martin St. Maarten

Beneden Prinsen ●

Pointe
Arago

Baie de
Marigot

Marigot ■

Marigot
Fort ■

Border Monument ■

Dutch Cul de Sac ●

← Ferry to Dutch St. Maarten

Baie Nettle

Pointe
du Bluff

Simpson
Bay Lagoon

Baie Rouge

Pointe Plum

Baie
Longue

Mullet Bay ⊀

455

by the island's union of taxi drivers, although in recent months, according to some sources, that policy is less strictly enforced than in previous years.)

Because of this law, many visitors hire a taxi to take them directly to their hotels as soon as they arrive at Queen Juliana Airport on the Dutch side. After you're settled in, most rental companies (including Avis, Budget, and Hertz) will either deliver a car directly to your hotel, or a van will transport you without charge to a depot where the cars are stored. That depot might lie on either the French or the Dutch side, depending on the location of your hotel and the renting outfit's inventory of cars. Unlike in years past, once a car is rented, no one seems to mind whether you drop it off on the French or the Dutch side on the day of your departure. Of course, ask about this and communicate your intentions clearly on the first day of your rental.

Each of the largest North American car-rental companies—**Avis** (☎ **800/ 331-1084** in the U.S., or 590/87-50-60), **Budget** (☎ **800/527-0700** in the U.S., or 590/87-38-22), and **Hertz** (☎ **800/654-3001** in the U.S., or 590/87-73-01)— maintains at least one branch on both the French and Dutch sides of the island. All three charge roughly equivalent rates, which are usually similar to rates at branches of the same company on the Dutch side. Occasionally, additional discounts are granted for membership in organizations such as the AAA or AARP.

Most of the companies require that renters be at least 25 years or older, and each charges between $11 and $20 a day for a collision-damage waiver (CDW). Even if you buy the waiver, you'll sometimes still be responsible for $400 to $600 worth of collision damage to your car. Use of certain credit or charge cards sometimes eliminates the need to pay for a CDW; check with your card issuer. Once you reach the French side of St. Martin, call for delivery of your car.

Regardless of how you negotiate your car rental, you'll probably use very little gasoline driving around the flat, scrub-covered landscapes of the island. One tank of gas should last an entire week.

FAST FACTS: St. Martin

Banking Hours Banks are generally open Monday to Thursday from 8:30am to 1pm and on Friday from 8:30am to 1pm and 4 to 5pm.

Currency The currency, officially at least, is the **French franc (F),** yet U.S. dollars seem to be preferred wherever you go. Canadians should convert their money into U.S. dollars and not into francs. Currently, the exchange rate is 4.98F to $1 U.S. (1F = 20¢).

Documents U.S. and Canadian citizens should have either a passport, a voter registration card, or a birth certificate, plus an ongoing or a return ticket. With a birth certificate or voter registration card, you'll also need photo ID. British subjects need a valid passport.

Electricity The electricity is 220 volts AC, 50 cycles. Some hotels have altered the voltage and outlets in the bathrooms, so check. If not, don't count on the hotel; bring your own transformer and adapter if you plan to use U.S.-made appliances.

Information The tourist board, called the **Office du Tourisme,** is at Marie de St-Martin in Marigot (☎ **590/87-57-21**).

Language English is widely spoken on St. Martin, although this is a French possession. A patois is spoken only by a small segment of the local populace.

Medical Care   There's a hospital in Marigot (☎ 590/29-57-57), and hotels will help visitors in contacting English-speaking doctors.

Safety   The crime wave hitting Dutch-held St. Maarten also plagues French St. Martin. Travel with extreme caution here, especially at night. Avoid driving at night along the Lowlands road. Armed patrols have helped the situation somewhat, but hotel safes should be used to guard your valuables.

Taxes   There is no departure tax imposed for departures from Espérance Airport on the French side. However, for departures from Queen Juliana Airport on the Dutch side, a departure tax of between $12 and $15 is assessed, depending on the destination. This tax is *not* included in the price of most airline tickets.

Telephone   French St. Martin is linked to the Guadeloupe telephone system. To call French St. Martin from the United States, dial 011 (the international access code), then 590 (the country code for Guadeloupe), and then the six-digit local number.

To make a call within French St. Martin, add 0 (zero) to the country code (to make it 0590) and dial that code plus the six-digit local number, for a total of 10 digits. If you're calling "long distance" to the Dutch side of the island, dial 19, 599, 5, and then the five-digit Dutch number. To call French St. Martin from the Dutch side, dial 00 (double zero), 0590, and the six-digit local number. Local critics of this inefficient and expensive system complain that calling from the French to the Dutch side of the island, a distance of only a few miles, is the equivalent of dialing Holland from inside mainland France, and vice versa. Part of this is because of the fact that all calls are actually routed to Guadeloupe before being transferred back to the island's Dutch side. Such calls will usually be more (sometimes *much* more) expensive than you might have thought.

Time   St. Martin operates on Atlantic standard time year-round, 1 hour ahead of eastern standard time, which means that the only time the U.S. East Coast and St. Martin are in step is during the daylight saving time of summer.

Tips and Service   Your hotel is likely to add a 10% to 15% service charge to your bill to cover tipping. Likewise, most restaurant bills include the service charge.

Water   The water of St. Martin is safe to drink. In fact, most hotels serve desalinated water.

WHERE TO STAY

Hotels here are more continental in flavor than some of the beachside hotels outside Philipsburg on St. Maarten. On St. Martin, many little Antillean inns still exist, where English is definitely the second language if it's spoken at all.

Hotels on French St. Martin add a *taxe de séjour*, or government tax, and a 10% service charge. This visitors' tax on hotel rooms differs from hotel to hotel, depending on its classification, but the minimum is $3 a day.

You might consider a package deal offered by **TourScan, Inc.,** P.O. Box 2367, Darien, CT 06820 (☎ **800/962-2080** or 203/665-8091), which specializes in finding the best deals on the market. TourScan can inform you of package deals to more than 32 places on St. Martin. Some best-value air-and-hotel packages begin at $513 per person for 3 nights, with an extra night added on at prices that start at $34.

DOUBLES FOR LESS THAN $50

Le Cigalon. Rue Fichot, Marigot, 97150 St. Martin, F.W.I. ☎ **590/87-08-19.** Fax 590/87-79-84. 10 rms. A/C. Year-round, 200F ($40) single; 250F ($50) double; 300F ($60) triple. No credit cards.

This older, white-fronted Créole home with terraced pergolas lies in the heart of Marigot, on a quiet side street that somehow manages to avoid too much noise from nighttime traffic. The simple motel-like accommodations are nothing to write home about, but they're a great value on this expensive island. Each room is decorated with the utmost simplicity, usually with a handful of pictures, a bed, and a small modern writing table and chair. The beach (at Baie de la Potence) is a five-minute drive away. There's a verdant garden surrounding the building, and an in-house restaurant (Le Cigalon) serves Provençal-style dinners.

DOUBLES FOR LESS THAN $105 (WINTER) / $95 (OFF-SEASON)

Chez Martine. Blvd. de Grand-Case 140 (B.P. 637), 97150 St. Martin, F.W.I. ☎ 590/87-51-59. Fax 590/87-87-30. 6 rms. A/C. Winter, $85–$99 single; $99–$114 double. Off-season, $60–$70 single; $80 double. Extra person $15–$20. Rates include breakfast. AE, CB, DC, MC, V.

These are the simple bedrooms associated with one of Grand-Case's best-known restaurants (Chez Martine). Because the establishment is much better known for its dining rather than for its overnight accommodations, the format follows closely that of the *restaurant avec chambres* that's commonplace (and sometimes very appealing) in mainland France. The bedrooms occupy the upper floor of a white two-story building at the edge of the bay, within easy walking distance of many other restaurants and bars. Furnishings include two single or two double beds, wicker headboards, wicker chairs, a small desk, and in some cases, a sea view.

Jardins de Chevrise. Mont Vernon 52, 97150 St. Martin, F.W.I. ☎ 590/87-37-79. Fax 590/87-38-03. 25 efficiency apts with kitchenette. A/C. Winter, 485F ($97) efficiency apt for one; 520F ($104) efficiency apt for two. Off-season, 425F ($85) efficiency apt for one; 480F ($96) efficiency apt for two. MC, V.

These one-room apartments, each with a kitchenette, are in a series of two-story buildings, connected by a network of pergolas surrounding an outdoor swimming pool. The building is surrounded with palm trees and touched up with simple gingerbread trim. It's located on a hillside overlooking Orient Bay in a subdivision of other apartment building that are usually rented for weeks or months at a time, often by construction crews brought in from other parts of the Caribbean or Europe. The apartments are clean, bright, and well maintained, with rattan furnishings, earth-toned upholsteries in floral patterns, white walls, and tiled floors. There's a snack bar with limited offerings beside the pool, but most visitors either cook in their rooms or dine out. Access to the beach requires a rather steep descent down to the water.

La Résidence. Rue du Général-de-Gaulle (B.P. 679), Marigot, 97150 St. Martin, F.W.I. ☎ 800/423-4433 in the U.S., or 590/87-70-37. Fax 590/87-90-44. 21 rms. A/C MINIBAR TV TEL. Winter, $96–$116 single; $102–$122 double. Off-season, $74–$80 single; $92–$98 double. Rates include continental breakfast. AE, MC, V.

In the commercial center of town, La Résidence has a concrete facade enlivened with neo-Victorian gingerbread fretwork. Because of its location it's favored by business travelers. The rooms are arranged around a landscaped central courtyard with a fish-shaped fountain. A bar with a soaring tent serves drinks to clients relaxing on wicker and bentwood furniture. Each of the bedrooms contains minimalist decor, and all but a few have sleeping lofts and a duplex design of mahogany-trimmed stairs and balustrades. Room service is available. The hotel is known for its French and Créole restaurant (reviewed below).

Le Royale Louisiana. Rue du Général-de-Gaulle, Marigot, 97150 St. Martin, F.W.I. ☎ 590/87-86-51. Fax 590/87-96-49. 54 rms, 14 duplexes. A/C TV TEL. Winter, 350F ($70) single;

440F–490F ($88–$98) double; 610F–690F ($122–$138) duplex. Off-season, 300F ($60) single; 410F ($82) double; 640F ($128) duplex. Rates include continental breakfast. AE, DC, MC, V.

Occupying a prominent position in the center of Marigot, 10 miles north of Queen Juliana Airport, this hotel is designed in a hip-roofed French-colonial Louisiana style; its rambling balconies are graced with ornate balustrades. Each accommodation contains big sunny windows and modern furniture. Standard rooms have either king- or queen-size beds. Duplexes, ideal for families, have a bedroom and bath on the upper level and a sitting room with a foldout sofa on the lower floor. Duplex rates are not based on the number of occupants. The hotel's restaurant serves a simple breakfast, plus salads and sandwiches at lunchtime. A bar on the premises is open in the evening, but no meals are served.

Sol Hôtel Ambiance. Oyster Pond 38, 97150 St. Martin, F.W.I. ☎ 590/87-38-10. Fax 590/ 87-32-23. 9 bungalows. A/C. Winter, $115 bungalow for one; $130 bungalow for two; $150 bungalow for three. Off-season, $90 bungalow for one; $100 bungalow for two; $125 bungalow for three. Rates include continental breakfast and a one-way transfer either to or from the airport. AE, MC, V.

This pastel-ornamented building overlooks the yachts bobbing in the Oyster Pond right at the French-Dutch border. It's 8 miles east of Queen Juliana Airport and close to Captain Oliver's. Built in 1987 and remodeled in 1994, this remote outpost consists of bungalows done in traditional West Indian style. Although small, it aims to provide all the services of a large hotel, including a good-sized pool, daily maid service, and fax. Each unit, offering either a king-size bed or twin beds, has a kitchenette and a private terrace overlooking the ocean.

DOUBLES FOR LESS THAN $120

Hévéa. Blvd. de Grand-Case 163, 97150 St. Martin, F.W.I. ☎ 590/87-56-85. Fax 590/87-83-88. 2 rms, 3 studios with kitchenette. A/C. Winter, $76–$104 single or double; $118–$132 studio for two. Off-season, $55–$77 single or double; $88–$99 studio for two. MC, V.

Set on sloping land across the road from the white sands of Grand-Case Beach, this small but charming guest house has five accommodations all named after local flowers, shrubs, and trees. The setting is an old but much-renovated Créole house, with rooms surrounding a landscaped patio. The accommodations are small, but each contains ceiling beams and a carefully chosen assortment of antique artifacts. Although none has a view of the sea, the relatively modest prices make this hotel a worthy and sometimes colorful choice. There's an expensive restaurant on the premises (Hévéa), open only for dinner. The cafes and restaurants of Grand-Case are a short walk away.

Marina Royale Hôtel. Marina La Royale (B.P. 176), 97150 St. Martin, F.W.I. ☎ 590/ 87-52-46. Fax 590/87-92-88. 70 apts. A/C TV TEL. Year-round, $115.50 streetside apt for one or two; $163.80 marina-side apt for one to four; $268.80 marina-side apt for one to six. Off-season, discounts of 15%. AE, MC, V.

This large, long, two-story building sits at the edge of a marina at the seaward end of Marigot's rue du Général-de-Gaulle. It was originally built as a member of the Novotel chain. Since new owners took over the place in the 1990s, touches of rattan, floral curtains, white paint, and new carpeting have been added. Guests either cook in their apartments, or patronize any of the many restaurants and snack bars of Marigot. No food or beverage facilities are at the hotel, but the reception desk will give you a coupon for 35F ($7) to order an American breakfast at one of the nearby cafes.

WORTH A SPLURGE

✪ **Hôtel Pavillon Beach.** Plage de Grand-Case (B.P. 5133), 97070 St. Martin, F.W.I. ☎ 590/ 87-96-46. Fax 590/87-71-04. 6 studios, 11 suites with kitchenette. A/C TV TEL. Winter, $17

studio for one; $19 studio for two; $260 suite for two; $300 suite for three; $310 suite for four.
Off-season, $90 studio for one; $130 studio for two; $170 suite for two; $190 suite for three;
$210 suite for four. Rates include continental breakfast. AE, MC, V.

This two-story, small-scale hotel lies a few feet from the edge of the sea, adjacent to
the white sands of Grand-Case Beach. Built in 1990, it's well designed and stylish,
with decorative touches and amenities (tiles, urn-shaped balustrades, and kitchenettes)
that you might have expected in more expensive lodgings. The accommodations have
sliding glass doors with views over the water, wicker and rattan furnishings, pastel-
colored floral fabrics, cream-colored floors, a radio, and a private safe. The kitchenettes are compact, open-air affairs, set on each unit's veranda, each with a tiled
countertop and wooden cabinet doors. A short flight of masonry steps leads from the
rooms down to the beach. This place is for do-it-yourselfers, as it doesn't offer much
in the way of resort-type amenities. There's no pool, no bar, and no restaurant, but
access to tennis courts and water sports can be arranged, and the many bars and restaurants of Grand-Case lie within a short walk.

Laguna Beach Hôtel. Baie Nettle, 97150 St. Martin, F.W.I. ☎ **590/87-91-75.** Fax 590/
87-81-65. 63 rms. A/C TV TEL. Winter, $117–$176 single; $150–$182 double. Off-season,
$86–$116 single; $118 double. AE, MC, V.

On the road between Marigot and the Lowlands, the Laguna Beach Hôtel, which
opened in 1988, offers accommodations in a pair of two-level buildings. The rooms,
for the most part, are spacious and include radios, VCRs, terraces, private safes, refrigerators, and hair dryers. Laguna has a central freshwater swimming pool and three
tennis courts. Its dining room is open to the breezes. The public rooms are furnished
in part with rattan and decorated with Haitian art. Laundry and baby-sitting are
offered.

WHERE TO EAT
IN & AROUND MARIGOT

✪ **La Brasserie de Marigot.** Rue du Général-de-Gaulle 11. ☎ **590/87-94-43.** Main courses
50F–88F ($10–$17.60). AE, MC, V. Mon–Sat 7am–10pm, Sun 9am–4pm. FRENCH/CARIBBEAN.

This is where the real French eat. Opened in a former bank, it has a marble-and-brass
decor, a sort of retro 1950s style with green leather banquettes. Meals include
pot-au-feu, *choucroute* (sauerkraut) *garni*, blanquette de veau, cassoulet, even chicken
on a spit and steak tartare. Lobster is the most expensive item on the menu. You can
order interesting terrines here, and wine is sold by the glass, carafe, or bottle. The
kitchen also prepares a handful of Caribbean dishes such as red snapper in lobster
sauce. Located in the center of town, the brasserie is air-conditioned, with sidewalk
tables overlooking the pedestrian traffic outside. It also features the most glamorous
take-out service on St. Martin.

La Résidence / La Petite Bouffe. Rue du Général-de-Gaulle. ☎ **590/87-70-37.** Reservations
recommended for dinner. La Résidence, main courses 80F ($16); fixed-price dinner 140F ($28).
La Petite Bouffe, lunch platters 30F–50F ($6–$10). AE, MC, V. Mon–Sat noon–2pm and 6:30–
10pm. FRENCH.

This cost-conscious open-air restaurant is associated with a previously recommended
hotel. It opens onto a view over the quiet interior passageway of a complex of buildings near the Marina Royale. Lunches are served in an informal street-level annex,
La Petite Bouffe, and less formal and less expensive dinners are offered at La
Résidence upstairs. It's decorated with green-and-white tents and potted plants that
contribute privacy to the dining tables. The setting is intimate and friendly. The
menu includes a worthy version of an Antillean *soupe de poissons* (fish soup), with

many similarities to a Provençal bouillabaisse. You can also order a filet steak in a green-peppercorn sauce flambéed in cognac, or snapper or grouper baked with olive oil and spices, plus dessert soufflés flavored with either chocolate or Grand Marnier.

Le Bar de la Mer. Rue Felix-Eboué 2. ☎ **590/87-81-79.** Pizzas, burgers, pastas, and salads 42F–78F ($8.40–$15.60); platters 76F–125F ($15.20–$25). AE, MC, V. Daily 8am–2am. INTERNATIONAL.

Amid walls adorned with primitive Haitian paintings, at tables that overlook the food, vegetable, and handcrafts market of Marigot, this restaurant offers a menu of straight-forward and pleasant dishes that attract repeat customers. There's a dish for virtually every budget and taste, including pastas, pizzas, grilled local fish, burgers, lobster, and barbecued ribs. Breakfast anyone? Mornings attract local merchants and office work-ers who appreciate the croissants, steaming cups of tea and coffee, and a tipple of wine or two as a means of jump-starting their day.

Le Kontiki. Adjacent to the Hôtel La Plantation, Orient Bay Beach. ☎ **590/87-43-27.** Main courses $15–$23. AE, MC, V. Daily 8am–9:30pm. FRENCH/ASIAN/INTERNATIONAL.

Decorated like a low-slung replica of a wood-sheathed Créole house, this beachfront bar, cafe, restaurant, and water-sports kiosk functions as the centerpiece for many tourists' days at the beach. It's surrounded with about half a dozen thatch-covered cabañas for beach lovers, and serves potent versions of party-colored rum-runners. The ambience is low-key, relaxed, and Gallic. The food includes lots of seafood, grilled fish, and Chinese and Vietnamese dishes, as well as local versions of sushi— usually salmon, tuna, octopus, and squid—that's artfully arranged as an assortment on a platter. Prices for the water-sports aspects of this place? Jet skis and water scooters rent for $40 per half-hour session and parachute waterskiing goes for $50 for a 15-minute *ballade*. Looking for companionship on a weekend? The place hosts live music, often merengue or Caribbean jazz, every Saturday and Sunday from 4 to around 7pm.

Le Marocain. Rue de Hollande 147. ☎ **590/87-83-11.** Reservations recommended. Main courses 50F–98F ($10–$19.60). AE, DC, MC, V. Daily 7:30–10:30pm. MOROCCAN.

This is the only Moroccan restaurant in the Caribbean, the creative statement of a Casablanca-born, French-educated entrepreneur, Nordine Kadiri. Established in 1991 on the site of what was originally a Vietnamese restaurant, it contains a decor remi-niscent of North Africa, with mosaics, potted plants, and wood carved into the re-petitive geometrics for which Morocco is known. Even the restaurant's facade was inspired by the entrance to a casbah, with brick-red walls and a door of hammered copper. Dining is available indoors, as well as in the garden, where you'll be sheltered from rain and winds by a high-ceilinged tent imported from Morocco's southern deserts.

The restaurant offers a refreshing break from too constant a diet of Caribbean and French food. Menu items include the full array of traditional Moroccan cuisine, and include *tagines* (fire-baked clay pots with lids) containing chicken with olives or lem-ons, three kinds of couscous (lamb, chicken, or vegetarian), brochettes of lamb or chicken, *pastillas* (pastries) stuffed with sweetened lamb or chicken, and *mechouia* (spit-roasted lamb) served with desert herbs. A belly dancer performs twice a week (usually on Friday and Saturday).

BEACHES, WATER SPORTS & OUTDOOR PURSUITS

BEACHES   The island as a whole has 36 perfect white sandy beaches. The hotels, for the most part, have grabbed up the choicest sands, and usually for a small fee nonguests can use hotel beaches and changing facilities. Topless sunbathing is practiced commonly at the beaches on the French side. The **Club Orient Naturist Resort,** Baie Orientale 359 (☎ 590/87-33-85), has the only nudist beach on the island, but nude or mono-kini (as opposed to bikini) is relatively common, even though total nudity is not officially endorsed. The accommodations are in prefabricated red pine chalets imported from Finland. Some units are large enough to accommodate up to four people. The rooms are strictly no-frills at this back-to-nature sort of place. Many of the accommodations have large porches. There's no air-conditioning, but ceiling fans are adequate. That and the lack of clothing generally keep you cool. There's no pool, but the chalets are right on the beach.

Ilet Pinel, a tiny island off St. Martin, is perfect for beach recluses. You can get here by negotiating with a passing fisher to provide transport back and forth.

Beyond the sprawling Mullet Beach Resort on the Dutch side, **Cupecoy Bay Beach** lies just north of the Dutch-French border. On the western side of the island, it's a string of three white sandy beaches set against a backdrop of caves and sandstone cliffs that provide morning shade. The beach doesn't have facilities but is very popular. One section of the beach is "clothing optional."

Top rating on St. Martin goes to **Baie Longue,** a long beautiful beach that's rarely overcrowded. The location is to the north of Cupecoy Beach, reached by taking the Lowlands road. Don't leave any valuables in your car, as many break-ins have been reported. If you continue north along the highway, you reach the approach to another long and popular stretch of sand, **Baie Rouge.** Snorkelers are drawn to the rock formations at both ends of this beach. There are no changing facilities, but, for some, that doesn't matter as they prefer to get their suntan *au naturel.*

On the north side of the island, to the west of Espérance Airport, **Grand-Case Beach** is small but select. The sand is white and clean, but the first-class Grand-Case Beach Club takes up a huge hunk of the beach.

SCUBA DIVING   Scuba diving is excellent around St. Martin, with reef, wreck, night, cave, and drift diving; the depth of dives is 20 to 70 feet. Off the northeastern coast on the French side, dive sites include Ilet Pinel, for shallow diving; Green Key, a barrier reef; Flat Island, for sheltered coves and geologic faults; and Tintamarre, known for its shipwreck. To the north, Anse Marcel and neighboring Anguilla are good choices. Most hotels will arrange for scuba excursions on request. The island's premier dive operation is **Marine Time,** whose offices are based in the same building as L'Aventure, Chemin du Port in Marigot (☎ 590/87-20-28). Operated from in front of the Market Dock in downtown Marigot by England-born Philip Baumann and his Mauritius-born colleague, Corine Mazurier, it offers morning and afternoon dives in deep and shallow water, wreck dives, and reef dives at a cost of $45 per dive. A resort course for first-time divers with reasonable swimming skills costs $75, and includes 60 to 90 minutes of instruction in a swimming pool, then a one-tank dive above a coral reef. Full PADI certification costs $350 to $550, depending on the equipment used and past diving experience and requires 5 days.

You can also try the **Blue Ocean Watersport and Dive Center,** Baie Nettle (☎ 590/87-89-73). A certified dive costs $45, including equipment. A PADI certification course is available for $350 and takes 5 days. Three dives are offered for $120, five dives for $175.

SNORKELING   The calm waters ringing the shallow reefs and tiny coves found throughout the island make it a snorkeler's heaven. The waters off the northeastern shores of St. Martin have been classified as a regional underwater nature reserve, **Réserve Sous-Marine Régionale.** The area, comprising Flat Island (also known as

Tintamarre), Pinel Islet, Green Key, and Petite Clef, is thus protected by official government decree. The use of harpoons is strictly forbidden. Snorkeling can be enjoyed individually or on sailing trips. Equipment can be rented at almost any hotel.

One of the best-recommended sites for snorkeling lies on the beachfront of the Grand-Case Beach Club, where **Under the Waves** (☎ **590/87-51-87**) operates as a beachfront gift shop and clothing store, as a source of information for island activities, and as a point of departure for hour-long snorkeling trips to St. Martin's offshore reefs. The preferred spot for this is in the reefs that surround Créole Rock, an offshore clump of boulders ringed with reefs that, despite damage during the 1995 hurricanes, are rich in underwater fauna. Michigan-born Maria Welch operates hour-long supervised boat rides to the rock, priced at $25 per person with snorkeling gear included. Reservations are recommended.

TENNIS Tennis buffs heading for French St. Martin can play at most hotels. The **Méridien L'Habitation,** Anse Marcel (☎ **590/87-67-00**), has six courts, all lit for night play. The Omnisport (artificial grass) court at **Grand Anse Beach Club,** Grand Anse (☎ **590/87-51-87**), is also lit.

WATERSKIING & PARASAILING Most beachfront hotels have facilities for waterskiing as well as parasailing. Waterskiing averages $40 per half hour, and parasailing costs about $25 to $30 a ride.

WINDSURFING Aficionados of the sport recognize that, with one notable exception, winds and waves off most of the island's beaches are relatively unpredictable. Consequently, the island's windsurfing activities have tended to congregate on adjoining beaches near Grand-Case that include Orient Beach and Coconut Grove Beach, and to a lesser extend, Dawn Beach. Here relatively constant winds and (at least in the case of Coconut Grove Beach) reef-protected waters create a worthwhile spot for windsurfing.

Three outfits on these beaches that are known for the quality of their instruction are **Bikini Beach Watersports** (☎ **590/87-43-25**), **Kon Tiki Watersports** (☎ **590/ 87-46-89**), and **Tropical Wave** (☎ **590/87-37-25**). The last of the three, an outfit operated by American-born Pat Turner, is one of the island's leading sales agents for the Mistral brand of windsurfer. At any of the three above-mentioned outlets, boards rent for around $15 an hour, whereas instruction goes for $32 an hour.

SHOPPING

Many day-trippers come over to Marigot from the Dutch side just to look at the collection of boutiques and shopping arcades. Because it's a duty-free port, you'll find some of the best shopping in the Caribbean. There's a wide selection of French goods, including crystal, perfumes, jewelry, and fashions, sometimes at 25% to 50% less than in the United States and Canada. There are also fine liqueurs, cognacs, and cigars. Whether you're seeking jewelry, perfume, or St-Tropez bikinis, you'll find it in one of the boutiques along rue de la République and rue de la Liberté in Marigot.

Most of the boutiques on the French side are open Monday to Saturday from 9am to noon or 12:30pm and 2 to 6pm. When cruise ships are in port on Sunday and holidays, some of the larger shops open again.

Prices are often quoted in U.S. dollars and salespeople frequently speak English. Credit and charge cards and traveler's checks are generally accepted.

IN MARIGOT

At harborside in Marigot there's a frisky **morning market** where vendors sell spices, fruit, shells, and local handcrafts.

At **Port La Royale,** the bustling center of everything, mornings are even more alive: Schooners unload produce from the neighboring islands, boats board guests for picnics on deserted beaches, a brigantine sets out on a sightseeing sail, and the owners of a dozen different little dining spots are getting ready for the lunch crowd. The largest shopping arcade on St. Martin, it has many boutiques, some of which come and go with great rapidity.

Another shopping complex, the **Galerie Périgourdine,** facing the post office, is again a cluster of boutiques.

Act III. Rue du Général-de-Gaulle 3. ☎ **590/29-28-43.**

More than any other store on French St. Martin, this one is known for brand names for women's clothes that its designers refer to as *couture/prêt-à-porter.* Inside, you'll find what you need for whatever tropical cocktail party you might think of attending, made by such designers as Versace, Christian Lacroix, Cerruti, and Gaultier. Expect a bit of Gallic attitude, as well as an inventory more self-consciously upscale than that of any other women's boutique on the island. In winter we've found few bargains here, but if you visit off-season you'll often find good buys (the owners need to clear the shelves to make way for new merchandise).

Gingerbread Gallery. Marina Royale 14. ☎ **590/87-73-21.**

The owner Simone Seitre scours Haiti four times a year to secure the best works of a cross section of Haitian artists, both the "old master" and the talented amateur. One of the most knowledgeable purveyors of Haitian art in the Caribbean, this pan-European has promoted Haitian art at exhibits around the world. Even if you're not in the market for an expensive piece of art (the paintings come in all price ranges), you'll find dozens of charming and inexpensive handcrafts. The little gallery is a bit hard to find, on a narrow alleyway at the marina next to the Café de Paris, but it's worth the search.

Lipstick. Port La Royale, ave. Kennedy. ☎ **590/87-73-24.**

This is the leading purveyor of women's cosmetics and skin-care products on French St. Martin, with a beauty parlor one floor above street level that's devoted to an intelligent and tasteful use of the store's impressive inventories. For sale are cosmetics made by such manufacturers as Chanel, Lancôme, Guerlain, Yves St. Laurent, Dior, and an emerging brand from Japan known as Chiseido. Hair removals, massages, manicures, pedicures, facials, and hair styling are available upstairs. The outfit maintains another outlet a few storefronts away (Lipstick, rue de la République; ☎ **590/ 87-53-92**) that sells the cosmetics but has no beauty treatment facilities.

Maneks. Rue de la République. ☎ **590/87-54-91.**

Worth a stop, Maneks has a little bit of everything: video cameras, tobacco products, liquors, gifts, souvenirs, radio cassettes, Kodak film, watches, T-shirts, sunglasses, cameras, and pearls from Majorca. The shop also carries beach accessories.

Oro de Sol Jewelers. Rue de la République. ☎ **590/87-56-51.**

In this well-stocked store is one of the most imaginative selections on St. Martin, including an array of gold watches by Cartier, Ebel, Patek Philippe, and the like, as well as high-fashion jewelry studded with precious stones.

Paintings and Prints Gallery. Blvd. de France. ☎ **590/87-32-24.**

The local artist Roland Richardson welcomes visitors to his beautiful small gallery located on the waterfront in Marigot. A native of St. Martin, Mr. Richardson is recognized today as one of the Caribbean's premier artists. His works of art encompass many of the classic mediums including oil, watercolor, pastel, charcoal, and etching.

ST. MARTIN AFTER DARK

Some St. Martin hotels have dinner-dancing, piano-lounge music, and even discos. But the most popular after-dark pastime is leisurely dining.

Club l'Aventure, rue de la République (☎ 590/87-01-97), is still the most talked-about, most stylish, and most popular nightclub on the island's French side. Designed in a waterfront format that evokes an upscale yacht club, it contains two restaurants, one for pizza and snacks, and a more formal venue on its street level where meals cost around $25 per person. Upstairs is a high-energy multicultural disco, where even 40-year-olds feel comfortable mingling with the island's young and energetic. The cover is $5. It's open Monday to Saturday from 10:30pm until the management decides to close some time in the wee hours.

13 The British Windwards

These windward islands lie in the direct path of the trade winds, which swoop down from the northeast. British affiliated (now independent), they're Gallic in manner, Caribbean in outlook. French habits can be traced back to early Gallic invaders, as the islands changed hands many times before coming into Britain's orbit. On such islands as St. Lucia, and especially Dominica, you'll hear a Créole patois. English, however, is also spoken.

The British Windwards are made up of four main islands—St. Lucia, St. Vincent, Grenada, and Dominica—along with a scattering of isles or spits of land known as the Grenadines. Truly far-out islands, the Grenadines are a chain stretching from St. Vincent to Grenada. Some people group Barbados and Trinidad and Tobago in the British Windwards, but we have preferred to treat these independent island nations separately in the following chapters.

Topped by mountains and bursting with greenery, the British Windwards are still far enough off the main tourist circuit to make a visit to them something of an adventure. At some of the more remote oases, you'll have the sand crabs, iguanas, and seabirds to enjoy all by yourself.

For the most part, the islands are small and volcanic in origin. Most of the inhabitants used to live on their crops. There's little or no industry, except for tourism.

1 Dominica

The meager beaches aren't worth the effort, but the landscape and rivers are. Nature lovers who visit Dominica experience a wild Caribbean setting, as well as the rural life that has largely disappeared on the more developed islands. Dominica is, after all, one of the poorest and least developed islands in the Caribbean, where many of its citizens make a subsistence living from fishing or living off the land. Come to Dominica for the beauties of nature more than *la dolce vita.*

The cost of living here is the lowest of all the West Indies islands. Imported items, of course, carry high price tags, but if you stick to local produce, you can eat well for low prices. Hotel rates are very low, but the rooms will be quite basic—clean, albeit Spartan.

Untamed, unspoiled Dominica (pronounced Dom-in-*ee*-ka) is known for clear rivers and waterfalls, hot springs and boiling lakes.

Dominica

Airport ✈ Beach 🏖 Mountain ▲▲

Morne Aux Diables ▲▲
L'Anse Noire
Portsmouth ○ Calibishie ○
Woodford Hill ○
Picard Beach 🏖
Melville Hall Airport
Morne Diablotin ▲▲
Marigot ○

Caribbean Sea

Colihaut ○
Central Forest Reserve
Carib Indian Reservation ❸
Salisbury ○

Mero ○
Layou River
St. Joseph ○

Atlantic Ocean

Morne Trois Pitons ▲▲
Mahaut ○ Rosalie ○
Canefield Airport
Laudat ○
Trafalgar
Goodwill ○
La Plaine ○
Roseau ○ Reigate ○ Boiling Lake
Castle Comfort ○
Pointe Michel ○
Soufrière ○
Grand Bay

Botanical Gardens
National Park Office ❽
Cabrits National Park ❶
Carib Indian Reservation ❸
Emerald Pool Trail ❹
Morne Trois Pitons
National Park ❺
Portsmouth ❷
Sulphur Springs ❻
Titou Gorge and Valley
of Desolation ❾
Trafalgar Falls ❼

0 5 mi / 8 km N

2-0194

According to myth, it has 365 "rivers," one for each day of the year. This is the most rugged of Caribbean islands.

Dominica, with a population of 71,000, lies in the eastern Caribbean, between Guadeloupe to the north and Martinique to the south. English is the official language, but a French patois is widely spoken. The Caribs, the indigenous people of the Caribbean, live as a community on the northeast of the island. The art and craft of traditional basketry is still practiced and is unique to today's Carib community, whose numbers have dwindled to 3,000.

The mountainous island is 29 miles long and 16 miles wide, with a total land area of 290 square miles, many of which have never been seen by explorers.

Because of the pristine coral reefs, dramatic drop-offs, and shipwrecks found in the crystal-clear waters with visibility of 100 feet plus, scuba diving is becoming increasingly popular, particularly off the west coast, site of Dominica's two dive operations.

Yearly rainfall varies from 50 inches along the dry west coast to as much as 350 inches in the tropical rain forests of the mountainous interior, where downpours are not uncommon.

Clothing is casual, including light summer wear for most of the year. However, take along walking shoes for those trips into the mountains and a sweater for cooler evenings. Bikinis and swimwear should not be worn on the streets of the capital city, Roseau, or in the villages.

National Day celebrations on November 3 commemorate Columbus's discovery in 1493 and independence in 1978. Cultural celebrations of Dominica's traditional dance, music, song, and storytelling begin in mid-October and continue to Community Day, November 4, when people undertake community-based projects.

GETTING THERE

BY PLANE   There are two airports on Dominica, neither of which is large enough to handle a jetliner; therefore, there are no direct flights from North America. The **Melville Hall Airport** is on the island's northeastern coast, almost diagonally across the island from the capital, Roseau, on the southwestern coast. Should you land at Melville Hall, there's a 1¹/₂-hour taxi ride into Roseau, a tour across the island through the forest and coastal villages. The fare from Melville Hall to Roseau is $17 per person, and drivers have the right to gather up at least four passengers in their cabs. By private taxi the cost could be $50.

The newer **Canefield Airport** is about a 15-minute taxi ride to the north of Roseau. The 2,000-foot airstrip accommodates smaller planes than those that can land at Melville Hall. From here, the typical taxi fare into town is $8. There's also a public bus (with an "H" that precedes the number on the license plate). Charges are only $2 per person. They come every 20 minutes and hold 15 to 18 passengers.

For many Americans, the easiest way to reach Dominica is to take a daily **American Eagle** (☎ 800/433-7300) flight from San Juan. From Antigua, you can take one of the five daily **LIAT** (☎ 809/448-0275 or 809/448-2422) flights to Dominica. Another possibility would be to fly via St. Maarten. From here, LIAT offers one nonstop flight daily, and two other daily flights with intermediary stops. It's also possible to fly to Guadeloupe (see "Getting There" in section 2 of chapter 12). Once on Guadeloupe, you can make a connection to Dominica on **Air Guadeloupe** (☎ 809/448-2181).

BY BOAT   The *Caribbean Express* (☎ 596/60-12-38, or 809/448-2181 on Dominica), sailing from the French West Indies (see chapter 12), runs between Guadeloupe in the north to Martinique in the south, and Dominica is a port of call along the way. Call for exact schedules. Departures are twice a week.

In addition, the *Madikera* is a car-ferry sailing from Pointe-à-Pitre to Roseau five to seven times a week, depending on demand. For information about schedules, contact Trois Pitons Travel, 5 Great Marlborough St. in Roseau (☎ 809/448-6977).

GETTING AROUND

The capital of Dominica is Roseau, and many of the places to stay are found here or very close by.

BY MINIBUS   The public transportation system consists of private minibus service between Roseau and the rest of Dominica. These minibuses are filled mainly with schoolchildren, workers, and country people who need to come into the city. Taxis may be a more reliable means of transport for visitors, but there are hotels at which buses call during the course of the day. A typical minibus fare from Roseau to Portsmouth is EC$8 ($3).

BY TAXI   At either the Melville Hall or Canefield airport, you can rent a taxi, and prices are regulated by the government (see "Getting There," above). If you want to see the island by taxi, rates are about $18 per car for each hour of touring, and as many as four passengers can go along at the same time.

BY RENTAL CAR   If you rent a car, a fee of EC$30 ($11.10) is charged to obtain a driver's license, which is available at the airports. There are 310 miles of newly paved roads, and only in a few areas is a four-wheel-drive necessary. *Driving is on the left.*

Most U.S. vacationers reserve their car in advance from the local representative of **Budget Rent-a-Car,** headquartered near the island's major airport on the Main Highway, Canefield (☎ **800/527-0700** in the U.S., or 809/449-2080). Another option is the local office of **Avis,** 4 High St. in Rouseau (☎ **800/331-1212** in the U.S., or 809/448-2481), although we've found the service here poor.

There are also a handful of small, usually family-owned car-rental companies, the condition and price of whose vehicles vary widely. Their ranks include **Valley Rent-a-Car,** Goodwill Road, Roseau (☎ **809/448-3233**); **Wide Range,** 79 Bath Rd., Roseau (☎ **809/448-2198**); and **Auto Rentals,** Goodwill Road, Roseau (☎ **809/ 448-3425**).

FAST FACTS: Dominica

Banking Hours   Banks are open Monday to Thursday from 8am to 3pm and on Friday from 8am to 5pm.

Currency   Dominica uses the **Eastern Caribbean dollar (EC$),** worth about 37¢ in U.S. currency. Prices in this section are given in U.S. dollars unless otherwise indicated.

Customs   Dominica is lenient, allowing you personal and household effects, plus 200 cigarettes, 50 cigars, and 40 ounces of liquor or wine per person.

Documents   To enter, U.S. and Canadian citizens must have proof of citizenship, such as a passport, or a voter registration card or a birth certificate along with photo ID. In addition, an ongoing or return ticket must be shown. British visitors should have a valid passport.

Drugstores   The island's best-stocked drugstore is **Jolly's Pharmacy,** with two branches in Roseau at 37 Great George St. and 12 King George V St. Both branches share the same phone number and hours (☎ **809/448-3388**). They're open Monday to Thursday from 8am to 4:30pm, Friday from 8am to 5pm, and Saturday from 8am to 1:30pm.

Electricity   The electricity is 220–240 volts AC, 50 cycles, so both adapters and transformers are necessary for U.S.-made appliances. It's advisable to take a flashlight with you to Dominica, in case of power outages.

Emergencies   To call the **police,** report a **fire,** or summon an **ambulance,** dial ☎ **999.**

Hospitals   The island hospital is **Princess Margaret Hospital,** Federation Drive, Goodwill (☎ **809/448-2186**). However, those with serious medical complications may want to forgo a visit to Dominica, as island medical facilities are often inadequate.

Information   Before you leave home, contact the **Dominican Tourist Office,** 10 E. 21st St., Suite 600, New York, NY 10010 (☎ **212/475-7542**). In Canada, information is available at the **High Commission for the Eastern Caribbean States,** 112 Kent St., Suite 1610, Ottawa, ON K1P 5P2 (☎ **613/236-8952**), and in England at the **Caribbean Tourism Organization,** Vigilant House, 120 Wilton Rd., London SW1V 1JZ (☎ **0171/233-8382**).

The **Dominica Tourist Information Office** is on the Old Market Plaza, Roseau, with administrative offices at the National Development Corporation offices, Valley Road (☎ **809/448-2186**); it's open Monday from 8am to 5pm and Tuesday to Friday from 8am to 4pm. Also, information bureaus are at Melville Hall Airport (☎ **809/445-7051**) and Canefield Airport (☎ **809/449-1242**).

Language   English is the official language. Locals often speak a Créole-French patois.

Safety   Although crime is rare here, it would be wise to safeguard your valuables. Never leave them unattended on the beach or left alone in a locked car.

Taxes   A 10% government room tax is added to every hotel accommodation bill, plus a 3% tax on alcoholic drinks and food items. Anyone who remains on Dominica for more than 24 hours must pay an $10 departure tax.

Telecommunications   Dominica maintains phone, telegraph, teletype, Telex, and telefax connections with the rest of the world. International direct dialing (IDD) is available, as well as U.S. direct service through AT&T.

Time   Year-round, Dominica is on Atlantic standard time, 1 hour ahead of eastern standard time in the United States. When the United States changes to daylight savings time, clocks on Dominica and the U.S. East Coast tell the same time.

Tips and Service   Most hotels and restaurants add a 10% service charge to all bills. Where this charge has not been included, tipping is up to you.

Water   The water is drinkable from the taps and in the high mountain country. Pollution is hardly a problem here.

Weather   Daytime temperatures average between 70° and 85° Fahrenheit. Nights are much cooler, especially in the mountains. The rainy season is June to October, when there can be warnings of hurricane activity. Regrettably, Dominica lies in the "hurricane path," and fierce storms have taken their toll on the island over the years.

WHERE TO STAY

Don't forget that the government imposes a 10% tax on hotel rooms, and a 3% tax on beverages and food, which will be added to your hotel bill.

IN ROSEAU & CASTLE COMFORT

Doubles for Less than $35

Cherry's Lodge. 20 Kennedy Ave., Roseau, Dominica, W.I. ☎ **809/448-2366.** 6 rms, 3 with bath. Year-round, $13 single without bath, $22 single with bath; $25 double without bath, $35 double with bath. No credit cards.

Check into this simple, somewhat weather-beaten wooden house to experience the island's capital rather than for easy access to beaches or places to hike. Owned by Ms. Zena Tavernier, Cherry's Lodge prides itself on being the oldest hotel in Dominica, with a 100-year history. A wooden veranda sweeps around most of the building, allowing guests to sit on their porches and watch the mountain views and the lively street scene below. Although there are almost no amenities on site, the hotel is amid the island's densest concentration of bars and inexpensive restaurants. The accommodations are very plain, just a bed, a table, chairs, a washbasin, and a towel rack. Some visitors think the simplicity adds to the sense of tropical authenticity. The establishment's name, incidentally, derives from a long-ago cherry tree near the entrance. No meals are served.

Vena's Guest House. 48 Cork St., Roseau, Dominica, W.I. ☎ **809/448-3286.** 15 rms, 5 with bath. Year-round, $21 single without or with bath; $27 double without or with bath. No credit cards.

This boardinghouse, the former home of Jean Rhys, the Dominican author, is about as rock-bottom basic as they come. It occupies the upper stories of an old wooden building adjacent to a budget restaurant, Vena's World of Food. If your fellow guests are relatively quiet and well behaved, the place might suffice for cramped, ultra-basic lodgings. If there's a party going on, either in the lounge downstairs or in an adjacent room, you'll have to decide whether to participate or check out. Each room has a sink, a wood-framed bed, a wardrobe or cupboard, and a rather dim lighting fixture.

Doubles for Less than $75

✪ Hummingbird Inn. Morne Daniel (P.O. Box 1901, Roseau), Dominica, W.I. ☎ or fax **809/449-1042.** 9 rms, 1 suite. Winter, $55 single; $65 double; $110 suite. Off-season, $45 single; $55 double; $80–$92 suite. Extra person $20; children 11 and under stay free in parents' room. MAP $20 per person extra. AE, DC, DISC, MC, V.

A short drive from Roseau and the Canefield Airport, this hilltop retreat is a great little bargain. Opening onto panoramic views, the rooms are in two bungalows that are a 2-minute walk to the beach. Each has louvered windows and doors to capture the breezes in lieu of air-conditioning. Ceiling fans hum day and night, and you can also retreat to terraces with hammocks. Each accommodation has bedside tables and reading lamps (not always a guarantee on Dominica). The handmade quilts on the beds add a homey touch. One four-poster bed, a mammoth wooden affair, is 250 years old. This is a friendly, family-style place, and there are lovely gardens with exotic plants that attract both hummingbirds and iguanas. The local cook is one of the best on island, and she'll pack a picnic lunch for you during the day. The restaurant is open to nonguests without a reservation. Many diners come here to sample "mountain chicken" (frog).

✪ Reigate Hall Hotel. Mountain Rd. (P.O. Box 200, Reigate), Dominica, W.I. ☎ **809/448-4031.** Fax 809/448-4034. 17 rms, 2 suites. A/C TEL. Year-round, $65 single; $75 double; from $150 suite. Rates include breakfast. AE, MC, V.

On a steep hillside about a mile east of Roseau, this hotel was originally built in the 18th century as a plantation house. It was once one of the finest hotels on the island, but it faces increased competition now and has slipped a bit in terms of maintenance and service in recent years. It still has its admirers though, especially those drawn to its lofty setting and panoramic views. Some parts of the original structure are left, but the building has been substantially altered. The hotel has a comfortably airy design of hardwood floors and exposed stone. The guest rooms curve around the sides of a rectangular swimming pool and offer ocean vistas. The hotel has an outdoor tennis court, a good restaurant, laundry, baby-sitting, and room service.

Doubles for Less than $85

Anchorage Hotel. Castle Comfort (P.O. Box 34, Roseau), Dominica, W.I. ☎ **809/448-2638.** Fax 809/448-5680. 32 rms. A/C TV TEL. Winter, $65–$80 single; $85–$110 double. Off-season, $52–$64 single; $68–$88 double. MAP $35 per person extra. Children 11 and under granted 50% reductions. AE, DC, DISC, MC, V.

Having known better days, the Anchorage is at Castle Comfort, half a mile south of Roseau. The Armour family provides rooms with two double beds and a shower or bathtub, plus a balcony overlooking a pool. Try to see which room you're getting before checking in. Some rooms are quite passable; others are tired and worn. In spite of its location at the shore, there's little or no beach available, so guests spend their days around the pool. However, the hotel has its own jetty and a pebble beach for saltwater bathing, plus a squash court.

The hotel's French and Caribbean cuisine is simple, with an emphasis on fresh fish and vegetables. Nonresidents must ask permission to use the swimming pool, and they can also visit for meals. A West Indian band plays music twice a week for dancing. On

Thursday night, there's a buffet accompanied by a live band. Laundry, room service, and baby-sitting are provided.

Worth a Splurge

Castle Comfort Lodge. Castle Comfort (P.O. Box 2253, Roseau), Dominica, W.I. ☎ **800/ 544-7631** in the U.S., or 809/448-2188. Fax 809/448-6088. 15 rms. A/C. Year-round, $80–$85 single; $120 double. Rates include half board. Dive packages available. AE, MC, V.

No one at this diving lodge seems to mind that the setting doesn't include easy access to a sandy beach. Instead, you'll be able to easily go on dives off the calm, rock-fringed waters of Dominica's southwestern leeward shore. The lodge itself is a simple, rustic enclave devoted to enjoying the beauties both below and above the water's surface. Established by the mother of the present owner, Derek Perryman, it's centered around an open-air living and dining area, and a family-style living room where guests gather every evening to watch the superb sunsets off the island's southwestern coast. The well-scrubbed accommodations have white walls, wooden tables, chairs, and headboards. The dive operation here is certified by both NAUI and PADI, and cocktail cruises are offered as part of the entertainment. Derek, incidentally, is one of the leading divemasters on Dominica.

ELSEWHERE ON THE ISLAND

Floral Gardens. Concord Village (P.O. Box 192, Roseau), Dominica, W.I. ☎ **809/445-7636.** Fax 809/445-7636. 13 rms, 10 with bath; 3 apts. Year-round, $45 single or double without bath, $60 single or double with bath; $80 apt for two with kitchenette. AE, MC, V.

Everything about the place pays homage to the surrounding scenic jungles. Situated near the edge of the Carib Indian reservation adjacent to the Layou River, it appeals to hikers, naturalists, birders, and students of Indian culture. It was built on land owned by Roger and Lily Seraphin, and it's quietly proud of its allure as a funky, nonstandard hotel quite different from its larger and more anonymous competitors. The older part is designed vaguely like a tropical version of a Swiss chalet, with latticed windows and flowerboxes. The bedrooms in the newer section are preferable to those in the original house because they're larger, not as noisy, and get more sunlight. An on-site restaurant serves simple West Indian cuisine to residents and group tours, which sometimes stop in as part of guided jaunts through Dominica.

Layou River Hotel. Clarke Hall Rd., Layou (P.O. Box 8, Roseau), Dominica, W.I. ☎ **809/ 449-6281.** Fax 809/449-6713. 30 rms, 1 suite. A/C TEL. Year-round, $70 single; $82 double; $94 triple; $120 suite for two. Children 11 and under stay free in parents' room. MAP $20–$25 per person extra. AE, MC, V.

As its name implies, this is not a hotel devoted to beachgoing. Instead, its appeal derives from a landlocked location beside the swift waters of one of Dominica's most famous rivers, the Layou, about 10 miles north of Roseau. Built in 1973, the hotel's accommodations are in two symmetrical blocks of one and two stories each.

Although Castaway Beach and Portsmouth Beach are a 10-minute and 20-minute drive away, respectively, most visitors opt for freshwater swimming either in the hotel's pool or on a sandy beach near a slow-moving section of the river. The hotel has daily maid service and a decor grown a bit stale since the heyday of the hotel's construction. Still, the price is reasonable and the setting suitably verdant, with ample opportunities for exploring the ecological wealth of this very mysterious island.

Layou Valley Inn. Layou Rd. (P.O. Box 196), Roseau, Dominica, W.I. ☎ **809/449-6203.** Fax 809/448-5212. 8 rms, 7 with bath; 1 suite. Year-round, $56 single without bath; $60–$66 single or double with bath; $75 suite. AE, MC, V.

This isolated house is run by the charming and somewhat eccentric Greek-born, Russian-derived owner, Tamara Holmes. It lies on 16 acres of rain forest in the verdant foothills of the island's national park, 13 miles north of Roseau, virtually in the middle of nowhere. Although access to saltwater beaches is inconvenient from here, there are no fewer than five rivers—some with waterfalls, some with natural basins, some with hot springs—for freshwater swimming. You won't get fancy resort amenities here, and you'll have to provide your own transportation, but if you want to get back to nature, this place might be for you. It mainly appeals to botanists, bird-watchers, hikers, and anyone interested in playing the role of recluse in the jungles of Dominica. The rooms are simple and clean. Ms. Holmes prepares evening meals for $20 to $24 each, and serves drinks from a bar area with windows overlooking the garden.

✪ **Papillote Wilderness Retreat.** Trafalgar Falls Rd. (P.O. Box 2287), Roseau, Dominica, W.I. ☎ **809/448-2287.** Fax 809/448-2285. 7 rms, 1 suite, 1 cottage. Year-round, $65 single; $80 double; $90 suite; $95 cottage. MAP $30 per person extra. AE, MC, V. Closed Sept.

This hotel and restaurant is run by the Jean-Baptistes: Cuthbert, who handles the restaurant, and his wife, Anne Grey, who was a marine scientist. Their place, 4 miles east of Roseau, stands right in the middle of Papillote Forest, at the foothills of Morne Macaque. In this remote setting, they have created a unique rain-forest resort; you can lead an Adam and Eve life here, surrounded by exotic fruits, flowers, and herb gardens. The rooms have a rustic, log-cabin atmosphere. Laundry and room service are available.

Don't expect constantly sunny weather, since this part of the jungle is known for its downpours; their effect, however, keeps the orchids, begonias, and brilliantly colored bromeliads lush. The 12 acres of sloping and forested land are pierced with a labyrinth of stone walls and trails, beside which flows a network of freshwater streams, a few of which come from hot mineral springs. Natural hot mineral baths are available, and you'll be directed to a secluded waterfall where you can swim in the river. The Jean-Baptistes also run a boutique in which they sell Dominican products, including appliquéd quilts made by local artisans. Even if you don't stay here, it's an experience to dine on the thatch-roofed terrace.

Picard Beach Cottage Resort. Picard Beach, Portsmouth, Dominica, W.I. ☎ **800/223-6510** in the U.S., or 809/445-5131. Fax 809/445-5599. 8 cottages. TEL. Winter, $100–$120 cottage for one; $120–$140 cottage for two. Off-season, 50% reductions. Children 12 and under stay free in parents' room. MAP $30 per person extra. AE, MC, V.

This is the best deal on the island if you want to stay in a cozy West Indian cottage. Here you'll find eight Dominican-style, stained-wood cottages built in the 18th century. They're set on landscaped grounds opening on the beach. Each cottage has a veranda, kitchenette, ceiling fan, and phone. There's space in the living and dining area for two single beds. The decor is plain motel style, with flowery bed linens. There's a pool and a restaurant, plus such services as 24-hour security. A dive shop is about a 5-minute walk away. This is a good stop as you explore the northern part of the island.

WHERE TO EAT

It's customary to eat at your hotel, although Dominica has a string of independent eateries. Dress is casual. If you're going out in the evening, always call to make sure your dining choice is actually open and also that you have proper transportation there and back.

IN ROSEAU & CASTLE COMFORT

Calaloo Restaurant. 66 King George V St. ☎ **809/448-3386.** Reservations recommended. Main courses EC$45–EC$55 ($16.70–$20.40); lunch EC$12–EC$45 ($4.40–$16.70). AE, MC, V. Mon–Sat 8am–10pm, Sun 8am–9pm. WEST INDIAN.

When you enter this eatery, you'll be greeted by a collection of local art that adorns the walls, including straw mats, paintings, and maps of the route Christopher Columbus used when he sailed the Caribbean. Touted as one of the few remaining original Caribbean restaurants in the region, it offers patrons a taste of the island. Although the dinner prices include three courses, lunch is the best time to find a real bargain. The Calaloo's forte is the mountain chicken (frogs' legs) served in a variety of ways including fried, Créole style, and in a garlic-butter sauce. The menu also features calaloo soup, curried conch, and chicken, baked or fried. For a finale, try one of the homemade desserts.

✪ **Guiyave.** 15 Cork St. ☎ **809/448-2930.** Reservations recommended. Main courses EC$25–EC$45 ($9.25–$16.65). AE, MC, V. Mon–Fri 8:30am–3pm, Sat 9am–2:30pm. CREOLE.

This airy restaurant occupies the second floor of a wood-frame West Indian house. Rows of tables almost completely fill the narrow balcony overlooking the street outside. You can enjoy a drink at the stand-up bar on the second floor. It's open only for breakfast and lunch. Specialties include different preparations of conch and rabbit, octopus and lobster, spareribs, chicken, crab backs, and mountain chicken. On Saturday, they prepare rôtis and "goat water." The place is known for its juices, including refreshing glasses of soursop, tamarind, sorrel, cherry, and strawberry. One part of the establishment is a pâtisserie specializing in French pastries.

Ocean Terrace. In the Anchorage Hotel, Victoria St. ☎ **809/448-2638.** Reservations recommended. Burgers, pastas, soups, and sandwiches EC$6–EC$50 ($2.20–$18.50); three-course fixed-price meal EC$55 ($20.40). AE, DC, DISC, MC, V. Daily 7am–2:30pm and 7–10pm. INTERNATIONAL.

The menu here offers a marriage between international fare and local ingredients. The restaurant dining room serves lunch and dinner as a three-course meal, while à la carte items can be found in the bar downstairs. If you're in the mood to splurge a little, the fixed-price menu includes starters such as black-eyed pea and coconut soup, pâté of chicken and parsley served with a curried-cucumber vinaigrette, and a salad of local fruits and vegetables with fried shrimp in a garlic-wine sauce. For the main course, the selection includes chicken kebabs served with a fresh-fruit chutney and gingered barbecued lamb. Included in the fixed-price menu are a variety of desserts (fresh-fruit soups, served cold; and crêpes, served hot with vanilla ice cream). For a less expensive meal, it's best to try the bar menu—burgers, sandwiches, and pastas. Also a good bargain here are the breakfasts, which range from EC$3 to EC$27 ($1.10 to $10). You can have as little as a bowl of fresh local fruit or a fuller meal with eggs, bacon, and toast.

Orchard Restaurant. 31 King George St. ☎ **809/448-3051.** Main courses EC$20–EC$50 ($7.40–$18.50); snacks in fast-food restaurant EC$3–EC$9 ($1.10–$3.35). AE, MC, V (accepted only in restaurant). Restaurant, Mon–Fri 10am–9pm; snack bar, Mon–Sat 8am–6pm. CREOLE.

This clean, wood-lined oasis of calm lies on a busy street in the capital. It contains a fast-food outlet dispensing sandwiches, rôtis, hot pies, and chicken wings, as well as a more substantial restaurant that's favored by island businesspeople and foreign visitors. In a simple but tidy format that's clean and decent, you can order such menu items as "mountain chicken" (frogs' legs), callaloo soup with crabmeat, coconut shrimp, black pudding, blood sausage, several pumpkin dishes, and breadfruit puffs.

Friday night features barbecued meat dishes. The menu is familiar fare on Dominica, but the kitchen manages to put a unique stamp on all dishes, especially its lambi (conch) concoctions. Lobster is sometimes available. If you want home-cooking, island style, you'll get that hearty food here served with a smile, too.

✪ **World of Food Restaurant and Bar.** In Vena's Hotel, 48 Cork St. ☎ **809/448-3286.** Main courses EC$25–EC$58 ($9.25–$21.45). No credit cards. Daily 7:30am–10:30pm. CREOLE.

If you want to reach the restaurant without passing through Vena's Hotel (which is really a guest house), its entrance is on Field's Lane. In the 1930s, the garden containing this restaurant belonged to a well-known female novelist, Jean Rhys. Today it's the patio for one of the most charming Créole restaurants in Roseau. Some say that its owner, Vena McDougal, is the best Créole cook in town. You can have a drink at the stone-walled building at the far end of the garden if you want, but many guests select one of the tables in the shadow of a large mango tree. Specialties include steamed fish or fish steak, curried goat, chicken-filled rôti, black pudding, "mountain chicken" (frogs' legs), breadfruit puffs, crab backs, conch, and tee-tee-ree (fried fish cakes). She also makes the best rum punches on the island.

ELSEWHERE ON THE ISLAND

Almond Beach Restaurant & Bar. Calibishie. ☎ **809/445-7783.** Reservations required for dinner. Main courses EC$8–EC$25 ($3–$9.25). AE, DISC, MC, V. Mon–Sat 8am–10pm. WEST INDIAN.

At this restaurant, in Calibishie on the main road running from Portsmouth to Marigot, you can enjoy local favorites such as curries and calaloo soup. Mr. and Mrs. Joseph, the owners, offer hospitality to all who venture in, but serve dinner from 4 to 10pm only with arrangements made in advance. If you're the adventurous type and want to splurge a little, try the octopus or mountain chicken served as specials when in season. One of the special delights here is the rum, steeped in various herbs and spices until the Josephs feel it's just right, which can be several months. If you want fresh-squeezed fruit juice—papaya, soursop, grapefruit, tangerine, guava, and passionfruit—this is the place for you. For groups, the Josephs can arrange bélé dance exhibitions and will open on Sunday when there's a great demand.

The Almond Tree. In the Castaways Beach Hotel, Mero. ☎ **809/449-6244.** Main courses EC$25–EC$75. AE, MC, V. Daily, seatings at noon, 2pm, and 6:30pm. CREOLE.

If you're touring north along the coast, consider stopping in for a meal at the Castaways, 11 miles north of Roseau. In this resort setting, nonguests are welcome to eat in the hotel dining room with its waterfront setting. Guests dress in casual resortwear, and enjoy the hospitality of the staff. Here you get the standard cuisine for which Dominica is known, including *crapaud,* or mountain chicken. You can also get lambi (conch), as well as island crab mixed with a savory Créole stuffing. Fish and pork dishes are also served. All dishes are garnished with the fruits and vegetables of Dominica's rich soil, including passionfruit. Before dining, try a rum punch in the lounge or beach bar. The service is very laid-back and you can find better versions of many of these Créole dishes elsewhere, but if you're on this part of the island, a meal here should be generally satisfying.

Floral Gardens Restaurant. In the Floral Gardens Hotel, Concord Rd. ☎ **809/445-7636.** Reservations recommended. Main courses EC$20–EC$45 ($7.40–$16.70). AE, MC, V. Daily 7:30am–9pm. WEST INDIAN.

Located at the Floral Gardens Hotel about 10 miles from the Melville Hall Airport, this simple eatery specializes in Créole cuisine. For starters, try the pumpkin accras (grated pumpkin mixed with herbs and spices, then deep-fried and served with a pepper sauce) or the calaloo soup (puréed dasheen leaves seasoned with herbs, spices, coconut cream, and bits of crayfish). The main courses include chicken, mountain goat, mutton, rabbit, and seafood such as lobster, codfish, and crab. Save room for dessert such as the banana flambé lit up in Dominica's local rum.

✪ **Papillote Wilderness Retreat.** Trafalgar Falls Rd. ☎ **809/448-2287.** Reservations recommended for lunch, required for dinner. Main courses EC$25–EC$40 ($9.25–$14.80); fixed-price dinner EC$50 ($18.50). AE, DISC, MC, V. Daily noon–2pm and 7:30–8:30pm. CREOLE/CARIBBEAN.

Previously recommended for its lodgings, the Papillote is an alluring "Garden of Eden" type of restaurant. Even if you're not staying here, come by taxi for lunch—it's only 4 miles east of Roseau. For dinner, you'll need to make arrangements. Amid nature trails laced with exotic flowers, century-old trees, and filtered sunlight, you dine overlooking rivers and mountains. The array of healthful food includes flying fish and truly delectable river shrimp known as bookh. "Mountain chicken" (frogs' legs) inevitably appears, as does kingfish. Breadfruit or dasheen puffs merit a try if you've never ordered them, and tropical salads are flavor filled. Favorite dishes here include "the seafood symphony" and chicken rain forest (sautéed with orange, papaya, and banana, and wrapped in a banana leaf). Sturdy walking shoes and a bathing suit are often called for. Near the dining terrace is a Jacuzzi-size pool, which is constantly filled with the mineral-rich waters of a hot spring. Nonguests may use the pool for EC$5 ($1.85).

ENJOYING THE OUTDOORS

BEACHES   True beach buffs will look elsewhere for a good time—Dominica has some of the worst beaches in the Caribbean. There are some beaches in the northwest part of the island, around Portsmouth, and there are also secluded beaches in the northeast, along with spectacular coastal scenery. But these are all hard to reach, and you might settle instead for a freshwater swimming pool or river swimming.

The finest beach, lying on the northwestern coast, is **Picard.** It stretches for about 2 miles, a strip of grayish sand with palm trees in the background. The Castaways Beach Hotel opens onto this beach. Snorkelers like it a lot, and windsurfing is another sport practiced here. The finest swimming, however, is along the banks of the **Layou River.**

HIKING   Serious hikers find Dominica a major challenge. Guides should be used for all unmarked trails. You can arrange for a guide by going to the office of the **Dominica National Park** in the Botanical Gardens in Roseau (☎ **809/448-2732**) or the Dominica Tourist Board.

Wild and untamed Dominica offers very experienced and physically fit hikers some of the most bizarre geological oddities in the Caribbean. Sights include scalding lava covered with a hot, thin, and not-very-stable crust; a boiling lake where mountain streams turn to vapor as they come into contact with super-heated volcanic fissures; and a barren wasteland known as the Valley of Desolation.

All these attractions are in the 17,000 heavily forested acres of the ✪ **Morne Trois Pitons National Park,** in the island's south-central region. You should go with a guide, who are in plentiful supply waiting for your business in the village of Laudat. Few markers appear en route, but the trek, which includes a real assortment of geological oddities, stretches 6 miles in both directions from Laudat to the Boiling Lake. Hikers bring their lunch and walk cautiously, particularly in districts peppered with bubbling hot springs. Regardless of where you turn, you'll run into streams and waterfalls, the inevitable result of an island whose mountaintops receive up to 400 inches of rainfall a year. Winds on the summits are strong enough to have pushed one recreational climber to her death several years ago—so proceed with caution. Ferns, orchids, trees, and epiphytes create a tangle of underbrush, and insect, bird, and reptilian life is profuse.

Your trek should include a visit to the **Titou Gorge,** a deep and very narrow ravine whose depths were created as lava floes cooled and contracted. En route, there might be views of rare Sisserou and Jacquot parrots, monkeys, and vines whose growth seems to increase visibly on an hourly basis. The hill treks of Dominica have been described as "sometimes easy, sometimes hellish," and if it should happen to rain during your climb (and it rains very frequently on Dominica), your path is likely to become very slippery. But botanists and geologists agree with the assessment of experienced hikers, the climbs through the jungles of Dominica are the most rewarding in the Caribbean.

Locals warn that to proceed along the island's badly marked trails into areas that can be physically treacherous is not a good idea, and climbing alone or even in pairs is not advisable. Forestry officials recommend **Ken's Hinterland Adventure Tours & Taxi Service,** in the island capital of Roseau (☎ **809/448-4850**). Depending on their destination and the oddities they feature, treks cost $100 to around $150 for up to four participants, and require 5 to 8 hours round-trip. Transportation from Roseau in a minivan to the starting point of your hillclimb is usually included in the price.

SCUBA DIVING   The underwater terrain is spectacular, particularly on the island's southwestern end, with its dramatic drop-offs, walls, and pinnacles. An abundance of invertebrates, reef school fish, and unusual sea creatures such as seahorses, frogfish, batfish, and flying gunards attract the underwater photographer. You can discover diving on the island with **Dive Dominica Ltd.,** in the Castle Comfort Diving Lodge (P.O. Box 2253, Roseau), Castle Comfort, Dominica, W.I. (☎ **800/544-7631** in the U.S., or 809/448-2188). Open-water certification (both NAUI and PADI) instruction is given, costing $400 for 5 or 6 days of instruction. Two diving catamarans, 45 and 33 feet long, respectively, plus a handful of other, smaller boats that are used for groups of divers, get you to the dive sites in relative comfort. The dive outfit is closely linked to its on-site hotel, a 15-room lodge where at least 90% of the clientele check in as part of the outfit's dive packages. A 7-night dive package, double occupancy, where breakfasts and dinners are included as part of the price, along with five two-tank dives and one night dive, begins at $906 per person. The same package, geared to inexperienced divers not yet certified by PADI or NAUI, costs $605 per person, onto which is added the $400 certification fee described above.

Divers from all over the world patronize the **Dive Centre,** at the Anchorage Hotel in Castle Comfort (☎ **809/448-2188**). A fully qualified PADI and NAUI staff awaits divers there. A single-tank dive costs $45; a double-tank dive, $70; and a one-tank night dive, $50. A unique whale and dolphin watch from 2pm to sunset is a popular feature; the 3¹/₂-hour experience costs $50 per person. With a pool, classrooms, a private dock, and miniflotilla of dive boats, and a well-trained and alert staff, this is the most complete dive resort on Dominica.

SEEING THE SIGHTS

Those making day-trips to Dominica from other Caribbean islands will want to see the ✪ **Carib Indian Reservation,** in the northeast. In 1903, Britain got the Caribs to agree to live on 3,700 acres of land. Hence this is the last remaining turf of the once-hostile tribe for whom the Caribbean was named. Their look is Mongolian, and they're no longer "pure-blooded," as they have married outside their tribe. Today they survive by fishing, growing food, and weaving baskets and vertiver grass mats, which they sell to the outside world. They still make dugout canoes, too.

It's like going back in time when you explore ✪ **Morne Trois Pitons National Park,** a primordial rain forest—a "me Tarzan, you Jane" country. Mists rise gently over lush, dark-green growth, drifting up to blue-green peaks that have earned Dominica the title "Switzerland of the Caribbean." Framed by banks of giant ferns, rivers rush and tumble. Trees sprout orchids, and everything seems blanketed with some type of growth. Green sunlight filters down through trees, and roaring waterfalls create a blue mist.

One of the best starting points for a visit to the park is the village of Laudat, 7 miles from Roseau. Exploring the heart of Dominica is for serious botanists and only the most skilled hikers, who should never penetrate unmarked trails without a very experienced guide.

Deep in the park is the **Emerald Pool Trail,** a half-mile nature trail that forms a circuit loop on a footpath passing through the forest to a pool with a beautiful waterfall. Downpours are frequent in the rain forest, and at high elevations cold winds blow. It lies 3¹/₂ miles northeast of Pont Casse.

Five miles up from the **Roseau River Valley,** in the south-central sector of Dominica, **Trafalgar Falls** can be reached after you drive through the village of Trafalgar. Here, however, you have to approach by foot, as the slopes are too steep for vehicles. After a 20-minute walk past growths of ginger plants and vanilla orchids, you arrive at the base, where a trio of falls converge into a rock-strewn pool.

The **Sulphur Springs** are evidence of the island's volcanic past. Jeeps or Land Rovers get quite near. Not only Sulphur Springs but also the Boiling Lake are bubbling evidence of underground volcanic activity, north and east of Roseau. This seemingly bubbling pool of gray mud sometimes belches smelly sulfurous fumes—the odor is like a rotten egg. Only the very fit should attempt the 6-hour round-trip to ✪ **Boiling Lake,** the world's second-largest boiling lake. Go only with an experienced guide, as, according to reports, some tourists lost their lives in the **Valley of Desolation**— they stumbled and fell into the boiling waters!

Finally, **Titou Gorge** is a deep and narrow gorge where it's possible to swim under a waterfall. Later you can get warm again in a hot sulfur spring close by. Swimming here can be an "Indiana Jones experience." Again, you should only do this with an experienced guide (arranged at the tourist office). The guide will transport you to the gorge and will know if swimming is dangerous—which it is after heavy rainfall.

On the northwestern coast, **Portsmouth** is Dominica's second-largest settlement. Once here, you can row up the Indian River in native canoes, visit the ruins of old Fort Shirley in Cabrits National Park, and bathe at Sandy Beach on Douglas Bay and Prince Rupert Bay.

Cabrits National Park, on the northwestern coast, 2 miles south of Douglas Bay (☎ **809/448-2401,** ext. 415), is a 1,313-acre protected site containing mountain scenery, tropical forests, swampland, volcanic sand beaches, coral reefs, and the ruins of a fortified 18th-century garrison of British, then French construction. The park's land area is a panoramic promontory formed by twin peaks of extinct volcanoes, overlooking beaches, with Douglas Bay on one side and Prince Rupert Bay across the headland. Part of Douglas Bay forms the marine section of the park. Fort Shirley, the large garrison last used as a military post in 1854, is being wrested from encroaching vegetation. A small museum highlights the natural and historic aspects of the park. The name Cabrits comes from the Spanish-Portuguese-French word for goat, because of the animals left here by early sailors to provide fresh meat on future visits.

SHOPPING

Store hours are usually 8am to 5pm Monday to Friday and 9am to 1pm on Saturday. In Roseau, near the Old Market Plaza, of historical significance as a former slave-trading market and more recently the Wednesday-, Friday-, and Saturday-morning vegetable market, now house three craft shops, each specializing in coconut, straw, and Carib craft products.

Tropicrafts Island Mats, 41 Queen Mary St. at Turkey Lane (☎ 809/448-2747), offers the well-known grass rugs handmade and woven in several intricate patterns at Tropicrafts' factory. It also has for sale handmade bags, shopping bags, and placemats, all appliquéd by hand. The handmade dolls are popular with doll collectors. The Dominican vertivert-grass mats are known throughout the world.

Caribana, 31 Cork St. (☎ 809/448-7340), displays Dominica's art, craft, and culture. This is the latest manifestation of the old Caribana Handicrafts, established by the late Iris Joseph, who is credited with creating the straw-weaving industry on the island. Caribana is operated by her granddaughter. The staff is usually pleased to explain the dyeing processes that turn the straw into one of three different earth-related tones. When straw is buried in the earth, it turns black; when it's soaked in saffron, it turns yellow; and when it's boiled with the bark of the tang tree, it turns purple. The premises also contains a small cafe in the Irish Dangleben Gallery.

DOMINICA AFTER DARK

It's not very lively, but there is some evening activity. A couple of the major hotels, such as the **Castaways Beach Hotel** (☎ 809/449-6244) and **Reigate Hall Hotel** (☎ 809/448-4031), have entertainment on weekends, usually a combo or "jing ping" (traditional local music). In the winter season, the Castaways sponsors a barbecue on the beach on the weekends with live music. The **Anchorage Hotel** at Castle Comfort (☎ 809/448-2638) also has live entertainment and a good buffet on Thursday. Call for details.

The Warehouse, Checkhall Estate (☎ 809/449-1303), a 5-minute drive north of Roseau, adjacent to Canefield Airport, is the island's major disco, a social magnet open on Saturday for the island's night owls and disco lovers. It's owned and operated by Rosie and Cleve Royer, who converted a 200-year-old stone building once used to store rum. Recorded disco, reggae, and other music is played at loud volumes from 11pm to 4am. Entrance is EC$10 ($3.70).

If you're seeking more action, such as it is, head for **Wykie's Tropical Bar**, 51 Old St. (☎ 809/448-8015), in Roseau. This is little more than a cramped hole in the wall, yet it draws the movers and shakers of the island. Happy hour on Friday is the time to show up. With your local tropical drink, you might also be offered some black pudding or stewed chicken. A home-grown calypso band is likely to entertain. You'll definitely hear some "jing ping."

There's also **The Dominica Club,** 49 High St. (☎ 809/448-29925), in Roseau, with a lively bar, and live music on Wednesday night and Saturday afternoon. There are also two tennis courts here.

2 St. Lucia

In very recent years, St. Lucia (pronounced *Loo*-sha)—second largest of the Windward Islands—has become one of the most popular destinations in the Caribbean, with some of its finest resorts, both chain and independent. The heaviest tourist development is concentrated in the northwest, between the capital of Castries and the northern end of the island. Here is the string of white sandy beaches that put St. Lucia on world tourist maps.

The rest of the island remains relatively unspoiled, a checkerboard of green-mantled mountains, gentle valleys, banana plantations, a bubbling volcano, giant tree ferns, wild orchids, and fishing villages. There's a hint of the South Pacific about it, and a mixed French and British heritage.

In the 1990s, many luxurious and expensive all-inclusive resorts have been developed. Unfortunately, there are not that many inexpensive or even moderately priced properties, so you're going to have to search for bargains. Finding low-cost dining is also difficult. If you'd really like to see St. Lucia, contemplate an off-season visit when many hotels slash their prices by 40%.

St. Lucia lies some 20 miles from Martinique. This mountainous island of some 240 square miles has about 120,000 inhabitants. The capital, **Castries,** is built on the southern shore of a large, almost landlocked harbor surrounded by hills. The approach to the airport is very impressive.

Native son Derek Walcott was born in Castries. His father was an unpublished poet who died when Walcott was just a year old, and his mother was a former head-mistress at the Methodist school on St. Lucia. In 1992, Walcott won the Nobel Prize for literature. He prefers, however, not to tout the charms of St. Lucia and told the press, "I don't want everyone to go there and overrun the place." His warning has come too late.

GETTING THERE

BY PLANE   You'll probably have to change planes somewhere else in the Caribbean to get to St. Lucia. Both **American Airlines** (☎ 800/433-7300) and **American Eagle** (same phone number) service each of the island's two airports with nonstop service from the airline's hub in San Juan. The airline offers two daily nonstop flights from San Juan into Vigie Airport, and one daily nonstop flight from San Juan into the more remote and isolated Hewanorra Airport. Connections from all parts of the North American mainland to the airline's hub in San Juan are frequent and convenient.

Air Canada (☎ 800/268-7240 in Canada, or 800/776-3000 in the U.S.) has a nonstop flight that departs year-round on Saturday from Toronto.

LIAT (☎ 758/462-3142) has small planes flying from many points throughout the Caribbean into Vigie Airport, near Castries. Points of origin include such islands as Barbados, Antigua, St. Thomas, St. Maarten, and Martinique. The airline also offers less frequent service into Hewanorra Airport, mostly from St. Vincent and points to the south. Know in advance that LIAT flights tend to island-hop through many different touchdowns en route to St. Lucia, although some readers consider this part of their Caribbean adventure.

British Airways (☎ 800/247-9297 in the U.S., or 0345/22211 in Britain) offers three flights a week from London's Gatwick Airport to St. Lucia's Hewanorra Airport. All these touch down briefly on Antigua before continuing to St. Lucia. Service is available on Tuesday, Friday, and Sunday.

The island maintains two separate airports whose different locations cause endless confusion. Most international long-distance flights land at **Hewanorra International Airport** in the south, 45 miles from Castries. If you fly in here and you're booked into a hotel in the north, you'll have to spend about an hour and a half going along the potholed East Coast Highway. The average taxi ride costs $50 for up to four passengers. Once this airport was known as "Beane Field," when Roosevelt and Churchill agreed to construct a big air base here during the depths of World War II.

St. Lucia

Cape Moule-à-Chique **6**
Diamond Mineral Baths **3**
Forest Reserve **7**
Frigate Islands **8**
Gros Piton **5**
Morne Fortune **2**
Petit Piton **4**
Pigeon Island National Park **1**

Cariblue Beach
Pigeon Island **1**
Cap Estate
Rodney Bay
Anse Lavouette
Gros Islet
Redvit Beach
Choc Bay
Labrelotte Bay
Grande Anse Bay
Vigie Beach
Vigie Airport
Castries
La Toc
Graand Cul de Sac Bay
2
La Sorcière
Marigot Bay
Fort Charlotte
Roseau Bay
Atlantic Ocean
Anse-La-Raye
BARRE DE L'ISLE
Canaries
Dennery
Anse Chastanet
8
Soufrière
3
La Soufrière
7
Petit Piton
4
Fond St. Jacques
Micoud
5
Gros Piton
Choiseul
Savannes Bay
Hewanorra Airport
Vieux Fort
6
Maria Islands

0   5 mi / 8 km   N

Airport ✈ Beach ☛ Mountain ▲

200206

However, flights from other parts of the Caribbean usually land at the somewhat-antiquated **Vigie Field,** in the island's northeast, whose location just outside Castries is much more convenient to the capital and most of the island's hotels.

GETTING AROUND

BY LOCAL BUS   Minibuses (with names like "Lucian Love") and jitneys connect Castries with such main towns as Soufrière and Vieux Fort. They're generally over-crowded and often filled with produce on the way to market. However, since taxis are expensive, it might be a "last resort" means of transport. At least it's cheap. Buses for Cap Estate, in the northern part of the island, leave from Jeremy Street in Castries, near the market. Buses going to Vieux Fort and Soufrière leave from Bridge Street in front of the department store.

BY TAXI   Taxis are ubiquitous on the island, and most drivers are eager to please. The drivers have to be quite experienced to cope with the narrow, hilly, switchback roads outside the capital. Special programs have trained them to serve as guides. Their cars are unmetered, but tariffs for all standard trips are fixed by the government. Make sure you determine if the driver is quoting a rate in U.S. dollars or Eastern Caribbean dollars.

BY RENTAL CAR   First, *remember to drive on the left,* and try to avoid some of the island's more obvious potholes. You'll need a St. Lucia driver's license, which can easily be purchased at either airport when you arrive, or at the car-rental kiosks when you pick up your car. Present a valid driver's license from home to the counter attendant or government official and pay a fee of $12.

All three of the big U.S.-based car-rental companies maintain offices on St. Lucia: **Budget** (☎ 800/527-0700 in the U.S., or 758/452-0233), **Avis** (☎ 800/331-2112 in the U.S., or 758/452-2046), and **Hertz** (☎ 800/654-3001 in the U.S., or 758/ 452-0679). All three companies maintain offices at (or will deliver cars to) both of the island's airports. Each also has an office in Castries and, in some cases, at some of the island's major hotels.

You can sometimes get lower rates by booking through one of the local car-rental agencies. Try **C.T.L. Rent-a-Car,** Grosislet Highway, Rodney Bay Marina (☎ 758/ 452-0732), which rents Suzuki Muritis at $45 per day, and a Suzuki Samurai for $70 per day. In addition, **Cool Breeze Car Rental,** New Development, Soufrière (☎ 758/454-7898), and at the Hewanorra Airport (☎ 758/454-7898), rents cars from $60 a day in winter, with reductions of around $5 granted in summer.

FAST FACTS: St. Lucia

Banking Hours   Banks are open Monday to Thursday from 8am to 1pm and on Friday from 8am to noon and 3 to 5pm.

Currency   The official monetary unit is the **Eastern Caribbean dollar (EC$).** It's about 37¢ in U.S. currency. Most of the prices quoted in this section will be in American dollars, as they're accepted by nearly all hotels, restaurants, and shops.

Customs   At either airport, Customs may be a hassle if there's the slightest suspicion, regardless of how ill-founded, that you're carrying illegal drugs.

Documents   U.S. and Canadian citizens and British subjects need a valid passport, plus an ongoing or return ticket.

Drugstore   The best is **William Pharmacy,** Williams Building, Bridge Street, in Castries (☎ 758/452-3173), open Monday to Saturday from 8am to 4:30pm.

Electricity   Bring an adapter and transformer, as St. Lucia runs on 220–230 volts AC, 50 cycles.

Emergency   Call the **police** at ☎ **999.**

Hospitals   There are 24-hour emergency rooms at **St. Jude's Hospital,** Vieux Fort (☎ 758/454-6041), and **Victoria Hospital,** Hospital Road, Castries (☎ 758/ 452-2421).

Information   Before you leave home, you can contact the **St. Lucia Tourist Board** in the United States at 820 Second Ave., New York, NY 10017 (☎ 800/456-3984 or 212/867-2950). In Canada, information is available at 130 Spadina Ave., Suite 703, Toronto, ON 5V 2L4 (☎ 416/703-0141). In the United Kingdom, it's at 421A Finchley Rd., London NW3 6HJ (☎ 0171/431-3675).

Once on the island, you'll find the **St. Lucia Tourist Board** at Point Seraphine, Castries (☎ 758/452-4094).

Language   With its mixed French and British heritage, St. Lucia has interesting speech patterns. Although English is the official tongue, St. Lucians probably don't speak it as you do. Islanders also speak a French-Créole patois, similar to that heard on Martinique.

Post Office   The **General Post Office** is on Bridge Street (☎ 758/452-2671) in Castries. It's open Monday to Friday from 8:30am to 4pm.

Safety   St. Lucia has its share of crime, like everyplace else these days. Use common sense and protect yourself and your valuables. If you've got it, don't flaunt it! Don't pick up hitchhikers if you're driving around the island. Of course, the use of narcotic drugs is illegal, and possession or sale of such could lead to stiff fines or jail.

Service   Most hotels and restaurants add a 10% service charge.

Taxes   The government imposes an 8% occupancy tax on hotel-room rentals, and there's an $11 departure tax.

Telephone   On the island, dial all seven digits of the local number. Faxes may be handed in at hotel desks or at the offices of **Cable & Wireless** in the George Gordon Building on Bridge Street in Castries (☎ **758/452-3301**).

Time   St. Lucia is on Atlantic standard time year-round, placing it 1 hour ahead of New York and Miami. However, when the United States is on daylight saving time, St. Lucia's clocks match those of the U.S. East Coast.

Weather   This little island, lying in the path of the trade winds, has year-round temperatures of 70° to 90° Fahrenheit.

WHERE TO STAY

Most of the leading hotels on this island are pretty pricey—you have to really look for the bargains. Once you reach your hotel, chances are you'll feel pretty isolated, but that's what many guests want. Many St. Lucian hostelries have kitchenettes where you can prepare simple meals. Prices are usually quoted in U.S. dollars. Don't forget the 8% hotel tax and the 10% service charge added to your bill.

You might consider a package deal offered by **TourScan, Inc.,** P.O. Box 2367, Darien, CT 06820 (☎ **800/962-2080** or 203/655-8091). Some best-value air-and-hotel packages begin at $484 per person for 3 nights, with an extra night costing from $30.

DOUBLES FOR LESS THAN $55

Kimatrai. Vieux Fort (P.O. Box 238, Castries), St. Lucia, W.I. ☎ **758/454-6328.** 8 rms, 6 apts, 3 bungalows. A/C. Year-round, $30 single; $40 double; $200 2-week rental of one-bedroom apt for two; $250 2-week rental of two-bedroom apt for four; $400 2-week rental of two- or three-bedroom bungalow for four to six. No credit cards.

On the island's relatively undeveloped southeastern coast, just north of the hamlet of Vieux Fort, this hotel is about a quarter-mile from a beach whose surf is usually rougher than equivalent beaches on more sheltered regions of the island. But unless you'd planned to spend hours paddling in saltwater, that might not affect too closely your appreciation of this otherwise very acceptable hotel. The bedrooms are outfitted with pastel colors and simple accessories, and the staff is helpful. Since its establishment in the 1970s, it has built up a clientele who tend to return year after year. A car makes your stay at this place more appealing, especially because of its relative isolation, but if you're looking for privacy and an inexpensive haven from urban pressures, this is the kind of sleepy, no-frills place you want. Only the apartments and bungalow contain kitchenettes.

Seaview Apartel. John Compton Hwy. (P.O. Box 527, Castries), St. Lucia, W.I. ☎ **758/452-4359.** Fax 809/451-6690. 3 rms, 6 one-bedroom apts with kitchenette. A/C TV TEL. Year-round, $53 single or double; $59 apt for one or two. AE, MC, V.

Frankly, part of the low costs of this two-story motel-like building derive from its position adjacent to Vigie Field. Although noises from the airport are sometimes bothersome throughout the day (but not during the night, when air traffic is reduced), noises from the coastal road nearby might present a problem for light sleepers. Otherwise, you might grow accustomed to the relative spaciousness of these units, and if you're interested in cooking, you'll appreciate the kitchenettes in the half-dozen apartments. (Grocery stores, banks, laundries, shops, and a supermarket are a short walk from this location on the outskirts of Castries.) The accommodations have off-white walls, rattan furniture, a balcony, wall-to-wall carpeting that's moderately frayed, and easy access to the sea, just across the road. (Vigie Beach, a worthy place for swimming, is within a 10-minute walk.) This hotel tends to appeal to business travelers from other Caribbean islands, as well as cost-conscious travelers looking for inexpensive lodgings near the island's capital. On the premises is a simple eatery, the Seaview Restaurant, serving Créole and Caribbean cuisine.

DOUBLES FOR LESS THAN $70

Orange Grove Hotel. Grosislet Hwy. (P.O. GM 702), Castries, St. Lucia, W.I. ☎ 758/452-9040. Fax 758/452-8094. 51 rms, 11 suite. A/C TV. Year-round, $65 single; $70 double; $76–$82 suite. Children 11 and under stay free in parents' room. AE, MC, V.

This hilltop retreat, off the road leading to the super-expensive Windjammer Landing, has been recently renovated and improved, making it one of the island's most appealing choices. Formerly known as Bois d'Orange, it offers comfort and convenience—all at a good price. The beach is just 15 minutes away by car, and there's a shuttle bus daily. The suites are spacious and well furnished, although even the standard rooms are well appointed, each with West Indian rattan furnishings and tropical prints to enliven the scene. The accommodations also have separate living and sitting areas, along with patios or balconies overlooking the view. The rooms have a king-size bed or two twin beds. There's a pool and a simple restaurant serving both a Créole and international cuisine, and room service is available until 10pm.

The Still Plantation & Beach Resort. P.O. Box 246, Soufrière, St. Lucia, W.I. ☎ 758/459-7224. Fax 758/459-7301. 10 apts. Year-round, $65 studio apt; $80–$110 one-bedroom apt; $125 two-bedroom apt. MAP $25 per person extra. AE, MC, V.

The Still, a restaurant, has long been one of the most popular in the area, but in 1995, the owners opened a small inn right on the beach. Less than a mile east of Soufrière, the site is on the grounds of a plantation growing citrus, cocoa, and copra. A freshwater swimming pool landscaped into the lush tropical scene adds to the allure, and walks are possible in almost all directions. The cheapest rentals—four studio apartments—have no kitchen, but the others do. The most expensive one-bedroom units open onto a beach, and the site itself opens onto views of the towering Pitons nearby.

DOUBLES FOR LESS THAN $100 (WINTER) / $85 (OFF-SEASON)

Bay Gardens. Rodney Bay (P.O. Box 1892, Castries), St. Lucia, W.I. ☎ 758/452-8060. Fax 758/452-8059. 45 rms, 8 suites. A/C TV TEL. Winter, $77–$94 single; $94–$106 double; from $112 suite. Off-season, $65–$89 single; $77–$94 double; from $106 suite. Extra person $20; one child 11 and under stays free when sharing with two adults. AE, MC, V.

One of the newest small hotels of St. Lucia, this choice lies on Rodney Bay 7 miles north of Castries, within easy reach of Reduit Beach. The standard rooms are well furnished with many extras, such as an electric kettle for making tea or coffee, a minibar fridge, king-size or twin beds, radio, cable TV, and a balcony or terrace. The most expensive doubles have a Jacuzzi and shower, whereas the junior suites are the most elegant, with sitting areas and kitchenettes. There are two swimming pools and a heated Jacuzzi.

For such a small hotel, the Bay Gardens has a good restaurant, offering a variety of continental and French dishes, but with a dash of local herbs and spices. In fact, the restaurant is named Spices. Try the callaloo soup and other dishes. The chef even caters to special diets, such as vegetarian. Live music is presented for dancing Wednesday to Saturday evenings. A Caribbean buffet is offered on Wednesday night.

Green Parrot. Red Tape Lane, Morne Fortune, St. Lucia, W.I. ☎ **758/452-3399.** Fax 758/453-2272. 60 rms. A/C TEL. Winter, $90 single; $110 double. Off-season, $68 single; $80 double. AE, MC, V.

About 1½ miles east of Castries, this inn operates the most famous restaurant on St. Lucia. But savvy bargain hunters have known for years that it also offers some of the least expensive lodgings on the island. Built of stone and stucco, the complex overlooks Castries Harbour. The bedrooms are housed in units built up the hillside. The furnishings are your simple roadside motel style, but everything is clean and comfortable. Try for a spacious room with a patio or, better yet, a balcony that opens onto one of the most famous harbor views in the West Indies. The inn's shuttle takes guests on the 15-minute run between Castries and Vigie Beach. There's also a pool. Location and reasonable tariffs make this inn a favorite of commercial travelers to Castries.

✪ **Harmony Marina Suites.** Rodney Bay Lagoon (P.O. Box 155, Castries), St. Lucia, W.I. ☎ **758/452-0336.** Fax 758/452-8677. 30 one-bedroom suites. A/C TV TEL. Winter, $100–$125 suite for two. Off-season, $75–$100 suite for two. Extra person $20. MAP $46 per person extra. AE, MC, V.

Between 1992 and 1993 this cream-colored set of two-story buildings, a short walk from one of the island's finest beaches, was renovated and upgraded. Originally built in 1980, the complex now offers well-maintained accommodations. Ideal for families on a budget are four suites with kitchenettes and a wet bar. The suites sit adjacent to a saltwater lagoon where boats find refuge from the rough waters of the open sea. Each of the units offer a patio or balcony, views of moored yachts, the lagoon, and surrounding hills. The suites are decorated in rattan, wicker, and florals. All suites, except the VIP/honeymoon units (eight of these), have sofa sleepers folding out to make a double bed in the living room. The VIP suites feature a double Jacuzzi, a four-poster queen-size bed on a pedestal, and a sundeck, bidet, and white rattan furnishings. The on-site restaurant is Mortar & Pestle.

Marigot Beach Club. P.O. Box 101, Marigot Bay, St. Lucia, W.I. ☎ **800/2-STLUCIA** in the U.S., or 758/451-4974. Fax 758/451-4973. 22 units. Winter, $98 single or double; $129 studio for two; $155 cottage for two; from $180 villa. Off-season, $82.50 single or double; $103 studio for two; $129 cottage for two; from $155 villa. MAP $43 per person extra. AE, MC, V.

When it was known as Doolittle's Resort, it didn't build up a stellar reputation although its location at the northern edge of Marigot Bay was among the island's most scenic. However, under a new name and new management, the place has improved considerably. The rooms and the restaurant have been upgraded, and a gym and hair and beauty salon were added. The new owners even "resanded" the beach. To reach the resort, guests board "The Gingerbread Express," a quaint little ferry taking them on a 1-minute ride across this bay. A variety of accommodations are available, including standard studios with a kitchenette and king-size beds, ceiling fans, and screened-in patios with tables and chairs overlooking a small beach and bay. In addition, there are "Firefly Studios," recently refurbished in cool white in the West Indian gingerbread style. These are furnished in pickled wood, with mosquito nets draped over double beds. Each has a kitchen and patio. In addition, there are some one-, two-, and three-bedroom villas nestled on the hillside of the property, all self-contained with king-size beds, ceiling fans, and screened-in areas, but these may be too pricey for the budget traveler.

WORTH A SPLURGE

✪ **Islander Hotel.** Rodney Bay Marina (P.O. Box 907, Castries), St. Lucia, W.I. ☎ **800/ 223-9815** in the U.S., 800/468-0023 in Canada, 212/545-8469 in New York City, or 758/ 452-8757. Fax 758/452-0958. 40 rms, 20 studios, 4 two-room apts. A/C TV TEL. Winter, $110 single; $120 double; $120 studio for one; $130 studio for two; $240 two-bedroom apt for six. Off-season, $75 single; $85 double; $80 studio for one; $90 studio for two; $175 two-bedroom apt for six. Extra person $25 in winter, $20 off-season. MAP $28 per person extra. AE, DC, DISC, MC, V.

North of Castries, near the St. Lucian Hotel and Reduit Beach, this well-recommended hotel has an entrance festooned with hanging flowers. A brightly painted fishing boat serves as a buffet table near the pool, and there's a spacious covered bar area perfect for socializing with the owner, Greg Glace. Twenty of the accommodations are studios, with kitchenette and private bathtub or shower, whereas the rooms have private show-ers and small bars with minirefrigerators; the studios are slightly more expensive. Four two-bedroom apartments are in an annex across the street. Overlooking a grassy courtyard sheltered with vines and flowers, all rooms also have radios. A network of walkways leads to a convivial restaurant. Guests walk a few hundred feet to the beach or take a courtesy bus, a 3-minute ride.

The Moorings. Marigot Bay (P.O. Box 101, Castries), St. Lucia, W.I. ☎ **800/437-7880** in the U.S., or 758/451-4357. Fax 758/451-4353. 16 cottages. Winter, $135 one-bedroom cottage for one or two. Off-season, $85 one-bedroom cottage for one or two. Extra person $15. MAP $41 per person extra. AE, MC, V.

Operated by a company famous for chartering yachts, this resort lies at the south-ern edge of a symmetrically shaped lagoon that the author James Michener described as "the most beautiful bay in the Caribbean." The resort consists of a wood-sided, heavily timbered main building and a series of veranda-fronted accommodations that extend over a steeply sloping hillside above the bay. A ferryboat makes frequent runs across the bay to a neighboring resort.

Well known in yachting circles for the safe haven provided by Marigot Bay, the Moorings offers an opportunity to do very little except relax amid the palm and ba-nana groves, to swim and sail, perhaps to read. Some of the accommodations in the hotel are privately owned and rented while the owners are away. The decor varies according to the individual tastes of the owners but are usually inspired by the West Indian style, with lots of rattan, pastel colors, and open-sided verandas.

The Hurricane Hole (part of the Moorings) is recommended separately (see "Where to Eat," below). Facilities include a swimming pool, a PADI-approved scuba center, and the base for the Moorings Yacht Charter fleet.

WHERE TO EAT

As virtually every hotel on St. Lucia seems to be going all-inclusive, the independent restaurants have had to sail through rough waters. But there are quite a few, never-theless, of varying quality. Most restaurants are open for lunch and dinner, unless otherwise noted. The big problem about dining out at night, as it is on nearly all Caribbean islands, is getting to that special hideaway and back again with adequate transportation across the dark, potholed roads.

Bread Basket. Rodney Bay. ☎ **758/452-0647.** Breads and pastries EC$2.75–EC$6.50 ($1–$2.40); sandwiches EC$5.75–EC$7.50 ($2.10–$2.80); specials EC$15 ($5.60). No credit cards. Mon–Sat 7am–5pm, Sun 7am–noon. CONTINENTAL.

This small bakery offers homemade breads, pastries, and a wide selection of sand-wiches. Overlooking the marina, it features alfresco dining on the deck where patrons can view million-dollar yachts and Pigeon Island. The forte here are the baked goods from croissants to pies and cakes. This eatery serves full American breakfasts and light lunches with a few heartier specials such as stuffed crab backs and fish-and-chips. The sandwiches include roast beef, chicken, and tuna salad served on the freshly baked bread. To finish your meal, try the baked cheesecake; it's been called the best on the island.

Café Paradis (a.k.a. Doolittle's). At the Marigot Beach Club, Marigot Bay. ☎ **758/ 451-4974.** Reservations recommended. Main courses $8–$30; nightly barbecue $15. AE, MC, V. Daily 8am–10:30pm. For directions, see below. FRENCH/INTERNATIONAL.

This culinary showplace is the proud domain of a French-trained chef who was eager to escape to the Caribbean. With extended hours, the restaurant prepares award-winning rum punches. A view of the water beckons from the restaurant's veranda. Lunch items include rôtis, brochettes, burgers, salads, and grilled fish platters— nothing imaginative here. The dinner menu is enhanced with daily specials. Rack of lamb and lobster—prepared in about four different ways—are upscale staples. The linguine with king prawns and scallops is a great dish. The best deal here is the nightly barbecue, where for one price you get a soup or salad, a choice of baby back ribs, chicken, or steak, plus dessert. The barbecue starts at 6:30pm.

To reach the place, you'll have to take a ferryboat across Marigot Bay. Attached by a cable at either end of Marigot Bay, it makes the short run from its origin at the Moorings Marigot Bay Resort about every 10 minutes throughout the day and evening. Show a staff member the return half of your ferryboat ticket and you'll receive a $1 discount off your food or bar tab.

✪ Capone's. Rodney Bay. ☎ **758/452-0284.** Reservations required. Main courses EC$30– EC$40 ($11.10–$14.80). AE, MC, V. Tues–Sun 6:30–10:30pm. ITALIAN.

Capone's could have been inspired by the old Billy Wilder film *Some Like It Hot*, starring Marilyn Monroe. Actually, this is an art deco rendition of a speakeasy along Miami Beach in the 1930s. North of Reduit Beach, near the lagoon, it's brightly lit at night.

At the entrance is a self-service pizza parlor that also serves burgers and well-stuffed pita-bread sandwiches. However, we recommend that you go into the back for a really superb Italian meal, beginning with a drink, perhaps "Prohibition Punch" or a "St. Valentine's Day Massacre," served by "gangster" barmen. A player piano enlivens the atmosphere. You might begin with a pasta (the lasagne is a favorite, especially when accompanied by a "Little Caesar" salad). For your main course, try flame-grilled chicken breast with Dijon mustard (with ham and cream cheese), fresh local charcoal-grilled fish, or some of the best steaks on the island. Finish with an Italian espresso.

Chez Camille Guest House & Restaurant. 7 Bridge St., Soufrière, St. Lucia, W.I. ☎ **758/ 459-5379.** Main courses $9–$29. AE, MC, V. Mon–Sat 8am–10pm. WEST INDIAN.

One block inland from the waterfront and one floor above street level, this clean and decent Caribbean-style restaurant serves simple, unpretentious food. Operated by a local matriarch, Camilla Alcindor, it will welcome you for coffee, a soda, or Perrier, or for full-fledged dinners that include Caribbean fish Créole, lobster thermidor, and prime loin of beef with garlic sauce. The straightforward food is tasty. Opt for the fish and shellfish instead of the beef, and the chicken curry is savory. Lunches are considerably less elaborate, and include sandwiches, cold salads, omelets, and burgers. Our favorite tables are the pair that sit on a balcony overlooking the energetic activities in the street below. Otherwise, the inside tables can get a bit steamy on a hot night as there's no air-conditioning. This is the only really good place to eat in the village of Soufrière itself.

Camilla invites you to stay at her guest house, which has seven bedrooms, three bathrooms, two kitchens, and a living room. Winter rates are $35 single, $65 double, $85 triple, and $135 for a family of six. Off-season the charges drop to $30 single, $50 double, $75 triple, and $115 for a family of six. Chez Camille offers a fully modern kitchen that allows guests to cook their own meals, make arrangements for the maid to prepare meals for them, or eat at Camilla's Restaurant at a 10% discount.

Chak Chak. Beanfield, Vieux Fort. ☎ 758/454-6260. Main courses EC$17.50–EC$65 ($6.50–$24.10). AE, MC, V. Daily 9am–midnight. WEST INDIAN.

This simple restaurant, near the Hewanorra Airport, offers West Indian cuisine. Don't expect to be pampered here. The meals are basic, with most of the main courses served with rice, vegetables, and salad. The menu features an assortment of curried stews and Créole-style fish. You can find sirloin steaks, pork and lamb chops, and baked chicken as well. For a quick bite, the restaurant also serves burgers and sandwiches. All main dishes are served with locally grown vegetables, rice, and beans. Customers may eat outside on a small patio, and on Friday and Saturday nights there's disco dancing from 8pm until closing. Look for the weekend specials on the menu such as fish cakes or fish fingers. Want to go really local? Try the fish-head broth served with local green bananas.

Hurricane Hole. In the Moorings, Marigot Bay. ☎ 758/451-4357. Reservations recommended for nonguests. Main courses EC$17.50–EC$28 ($6.50–$10.35). AE, MC, V. Daily 7:30–10am, noon–2:30pm, and 6:30–10pm. INTERNATIONAL / ST. LUCIAN.

Cozy, candlelit, and nautical, this is the restaurant of the Marigot Bay Resort, which charters yachts to clients from around the hemisphere. The congenial bar does a brisk business before dinner, when the Marigot Hurricane (rum, banana, grenadine, and apricot brandy) is especially popular. Ceiling fans spin languidly as you peruse the menu, which is geared in part to surf-and-turf fans, although many dishes have genuine island flavor, especially at dinner. The callaloo soup with crab is given added zest by okra, although we're equally fond of the pumpkin soup blended with herbs and cream. A stuffed crab back is an alluring appetizer, followed by the freshest available fish of the day, which can be served in any number of ways, although we prefer *au naturel* with herbs, fresh butter, lemon, and garlic. Meats and poultry range from a spicy Indian curried chicken to smoked pork chops that are grilled to perfection.

J.J.'s. Marigot Bay Rd. ☎ 758/451-4076. Main courses EC$35–EC$60 ($13–$22.20). MC, V. Daily 8am–midnight. SEAFOOD.

Situated on a hill overlooking the bay, about a quarter mile from Marigot Bay Beach, this lively restaurant serves up seafood in many guises. The terrace provides outdoor dining with a view of the yachts as they come into the harbor. The starters include stuffed crab backs and fish cakes; the featured platter is the special mix of Créole-style squid and fish along with chicken. Of course there are other options, including curried chicken and grilled steaks. For a place to dance and mingle with the locals, try J.J.'s on Friday and Saturday nights when things get cranked up with live entertainment. The music is loud and the atmosphere is spirited.

Key Largo. Rodney Bay. ☎ 758/452-0282. Reservations not required. Salads EC$5–EC$20 ($1.90–$7.40); pizzas EC$15–EC$45 ($5.60–$16.70). MC, V. Daily 6am–11pm. ITALIAN.

This local hangout serves pizzas and salads only in a simple, casual environment. All pizzas come in one size (12 inches), served on a very thin crust with tomato sauce and mozzarella cheese. The house specialties include the Union Jack (bacon, egg, sausage, and tomato slices) and the signature Key Largo pizza (shrimp and artichokes). Featured on the salad menu are prawn and chicken options. Specialty coffees are served: espresso, cappuccino, and Key Largo coffee (with lime juice, dark rum, brown sugar, Kahlúa, and a frothy head of whipped milk). For a cooler, spirited drink, try the Caribbean punch.

Razmataz! Rodney Bay Marina. ☎ **758/452-9800.** Main courses EC$24–EC$55 ($8.90–$20.35). MC, V. Fri–Wed 4pm until the last customer leaves. INDIAN.

Across from the Royal St. Lucian Hotel, this welcome entry into the island cuisine features delectable tandoori dishes among other offerings. It's in an original Caribbean colonial timbered building with lots of gingerbread decorated in a medley of colors and lying in a garden, a 2-minute walk from the beach. There's live music on weekends, and the owner is often the entertainer. A tempting array of starters greets you, everything from pieces of fresh local fish marinated in spicy yogurt and cooked in the tandoor to mulligatawny soup (made with lentils, herbs, and spices). Tandoori delights include shrimp, fish, chicken, and mixed grill, and you get the best assortment of vegetarian dishes on the island.

The Still. Soufrière. ☎ **758/459-7224.** Main courses $10–$30. AE, V. Daily 8am–5pm. CREOLE.

The first thing you'll see as you drive up the hill from the harbor is a very old rum distillery set on a platform of thick timbers. The restaurant lies less than a mile east of Soufrière. The site is a working cocoa and citrus plantation that has been in the same St. Lucian family for four generations. The front blossoms with avocado and breadfruit trees, and a mahogany forest is a few steps away. The bar near the front veranda is furnished with tables cut from cross sections of mahogany tree trunks. A more formal and spacious dining room is nearby. St. Lucian specialties are served here, depending on what's fresh at the market that day. Try to avoid the place when it's overrun with cruise-ship passengers or tour groups. There are far better restaurants on St. Lucia, but if it's lunchtime and you're near Diamond Falls, you don't have a lot of choices.

Trou au Diable Beach Restaurant. Anse Chastanet Beach. ☎ **758/459-7000.** Reservations recommended. Fixed-price menu EC$35 ($13); lunch EC$15–EC$40 ($5.60–$14.80). AE, DC, MC, V. Daily 7am–11pm. WEST INDIAN.

This casual open-air restaurant is known for its tasty Créole cookery. Located beachside at the Anse Chastanet resort, this eatery's dining options are varied and many, ranging from light salads to robust curries. If you're in the mood for a light meal, try one of the salads, such as the local fruit-and-vegetable plate or an omelet. The sandwich assortment is diverse, from your basic grilled cheese to the more elaborate club. For heartier fare, try the St. Lucian chicken or one of the satay dishes, including lamb, pork, and beef. Vegetarian options include platters of fresh local vegetables, grilled kebabs, and rôtis served with a sweet mango chutney. On Tuesday night, the restaurant serves a barbecue buffet that includes soup, local salads, garlic bread, and your choice of chicken, ribs, steak, or fish. On Friday evening, a buffet is served with the same accompaniments as above, but with your choice of Créole-style beef, chicken, fish, and lamb.

BEACHES & OUTDOOR ACTIVITIES

BEACHES Since most of the island's hotels are built right on the beach, you won't have far to go for swimming. All beaches are open to the public, even those along

Rare Birds & Other Critters

The fertile volcanic soil of St. Lucia sustains a rich diversity of bird and animal life. Some of the richest troves for ornithologists are in protected precincts off the St. Lucian coast, in either of two national parks (Frigate Islands Nature Reserve and the Maria Islands Nature Reserve).

The **Frigate Islands** are a cluster of rocks a short distance offshore from Praslin Bay, midway up St. Lucia's eastern coastline. Barren except for tall grasses that seem to thrive in the salt spray, the islands were named after the scissor-tailed frigate birds (*Fregata magnificens*), which breed here every year between May and July. Then, large colonies of the graceful birds float in well-choreographed formations over islands that you can visit only under the closely supervised permission of government authorities. Many visitors believe that the best way to admire the Frigate Islands (and to respect their fragile ecosystems) is to walk along the nature trail that the St. Lucian government has hacked along the clifftop of the St. Lucian mainland, about 150 feet inland from the shoreline. Even without binoculars, you'll be able to see the frigates wheeling overhead. You'll also enjoy eagle's-eye views of the unusual geology of the St. Lucian coast, which includes sea caves, dry ravines, a waterfall (which flows only during rainy season), and a strip of mangrove swamp.

The **Maria Islands** are larger and more arid, and are almost constantly exposed to salt-laden winds blowing up from the equator. Set to the east of the island's southernmost tip, off the town of Vieux Fort, they contain a strictly protected biodiversity. The approximately 30 acres of cactus-dotted land comprising the two largest islands (Maria Major and Maria Minor) are home to more than 120 species of plants, lizards, butterflies, and snakes that are believed to be extinct in other parts of the world. These include the large ground lizard (*Zandolite*), and the nocturnal, non-venomous kouwes (*Dromicus ornatus*) snake.

The Marias are also a bird refuge, populated by such species as the sooty tern, the bridled tern, the Caribbean martin, the red-billed tropicbird, and the brown noddy, which usually builds its nest under the protective thorns of prickly pear cactus.

If permission is granted, visitors will set foot in either park only as part of a group that arrives by boat under the supervision of a qualified guide. The cost is $55 per person for the Frigates, and $70 per person for the Marias, for guided tours that last a full day and include lunch. These must be arranged through the staff of the **St. Lucia National Trust** (☎ 758/452-5005), who will supply further details.

hotel properties. However, if you use any of the hotel's beach equipment, you must pay for it. We prefer the beaches along the western coast, because a rough surf on the windward side makes swimming there potentially dangerous.

Leading beaches include **Pigeon Island,** off the northern shore, with white sand and picnic facilities. **Vigie Beach,** north of Castries Harbour, is one of the most popular on St. Lucia. It has fine sands, often a light beige in color. But for a novelty, you might try the black volcanic sand at Soufrière. The beach here is called **La Toc.**

Just north of Soufrière is that beach connoisseur's delight, the white sands of **Anse Chastanet,** set at the foothills of lush, green mountains. While here, you might want to patronize the facilities of the Anse Chastanet Hotel. **Reduit Beach** with its fine brown sands lies between Choc Bay and Pigeon Point.

GOLF   St. Lucia has a 9-hole golf course at the **Cap Estate Golf Club,** at the northern end of the island (☎ 758/450-8523). Greens fees are $27 for 18 holes and, there are no caddies. Hours are 8am to sunset daily. Another 9-hole course is now called **St. Lucia Sandals** (☎ 758/452-3081), although preference is given here to hotel guests.

HORSEBACK RIDING   North of Castries, you can hire a horse at **Cas-En-Bas** (to make arrangements, call René Trim; ☎ 758/450-8273). The cost is $30 per hour. A 2-hour ride costs $45. Ask about a picnic trip to the Atlantic, with a barbecue lunch and drink included for $55. Departures on horseback are at 8:30am, 10am, 2pm, and 4pm. Nonriders can be included—they're transported to the site in a bus and are charged nothing.

SCUBA DIVING   In Soufrière, **Scuba St. Lucia,** in the Anse Chastanet Hotel (☎ 758/459-7000), established in 1981, offers one of the world's top dive locations at a five-star PADI dive center. At the southern end of Anse Chastanet's quarter-mile-long, soft, secluded beach, it offers excellent diving and comprehensive facilities for divers of all levels. Some of the most panoramic coral reefs of St. Lucia—many only 10 to 20 feet below the surface of the water—lie a short distance from the beach and provide shelter for many denizens and a backdrop for schools of reef fish.

Many professional PADI instructors offer dive programs four times a day. Photographic equipment is available for rent (film can be processed on the premises) and instruction is offered in picture taking, the price depending on the time and equipment involved. Experienced divers can rent the equipment they need on a per-item basis. The packages include tanks, backpacks, and weight belts. Through participation in the "specialty" courses, divers can obtain PADI certification. A 2- to 3-hour introductory lesson, including a short theory session, equipment familiarization, development of skills in shallow water, and a tour of the reef, with all equipment included, costs $75. Single dives cost $35. Open daily from 8am to 5:45pm.

Rosemond Trench Divers Ltd., at the Marigot Beach Club, Marigot Bay (☎ 758/451-4761), is set adjacent to the waters of the most famous bay on St. Lucia. It'll take both novices and experienced divers to shallow reefs or to some of the most challenging trenches in the Caribbean. A resort course designed for novices (it includes theory, a practice dive in sheltered waters, and one dive above a reef) costs $75. A one-tank dive for certified divers, with all equipment included, costs $50; a two-tank dive is $70, and night dives cost $65. They also have a six-dive package for $190.

TENNIS   The best place for tennis on the island is the **St. Lucia Racquet Club,** adjacent to Club St. Lucia (☎ 758/450-0551). Its seven courts are maintained in state-of-the-art condition, and there's also a good pro shop on site. You must reserve 24 hours in advance. Hotel guests play for free; nonguests are charged $10 a day. Racquet rentals are $6 per hour.

WATER SPORTS   Unless you're interested in scuba (in which case you should head for the facilities at the Anse Chastenet Hotel), the best all-around water-sports center is **St. Lucian Watersports,** at the Rex St. Lucian Hotel (☎ 758/452-8351). Waterskiing costs $8 for a 10-minute ride. Windsurfers can be rented for $12 to $19 an hour; lessons go for $38 per person for a 3-hour course. Snorkeling is free for guests of the hotel; nonresidents pay $25, including equipment.

SEEING THE SIGHTS

Lovely little towns, beautiful beaches and bays, mineral baths, banana plantations— St. Lucia has all this and more. You can even visit a volcano.

Most hotel front desks will make arrangements for tours that take in all the major sights of St. Lucia. For example, **Sunlink Tours,** Reduit Beach Avenue, Castries (☎ 758/452-8232), offers many island tours, including full-day boat trips along the west coast of Soufrière, the Pitons, and the volcano for $75 per person. Plantation tours go for $55, and Jeep safaris can be arranged for $70. One of the most popular jaunts is a rain-forest ramble for $55 or a daily shopping tour at $15. The company has tour desks and/or representatives at most of the major hotels.

CASTRIES

The capital city has grown up around its harbor, which occupies the crater of an extinct volcano. Charter captains and the yachting set drift in here, and large cruise-ship wharves welcome vessels from around the world. Castries has been hit by several fires, most recently in 1948, which destroyed nearly all the old buildings of the capital. Because of those devastating fires, the town today has a look of newness, with glass-and-concrete (or steel) buildings replacing the French colonial or Victorian look typical of many West Indian capitals.

The **Saturday-morning market** in the old tin-roofed building on Jeremy Street in Castries is our favorite "people-watching" site on the island. The country women dress up in their traditional garb of cotton headdress; the number of knotted points on top reveals their marital status (ask one of the locals to explain it to you). The luscious fresh fruits and vegetables of St. Lucia are sold as weather-beaten men sit close by playing *warrie* (a fast game played with pebbles on a carved board). You can also pick up such St. Lucia handcrafts as baskets and unglazed pottery.

Government House is a late Victorian building. A Roman Catholic **cathedral** stands on Columbus Square, which has a few restored buildings.

Beyond Government House lies **Morne Fortune,** which means "Hill of Good Luck." No one had much luck here, certainly not the battling French and British fighting for Fort Charlotte. The barracks and guard rooms changed nationalities many times. You can visit the 18th-century barracks complete with a military cemetery, a small museum, the Old Powder Magazine, and the "Four Apostles Battery" (the apostles being a quartet of grim muzzle-loading cannons). The view of the harbor of Castries is spectacular. You can see north to Pigeon Island or south to the Pitons. To reach Morne Fortune, head east on Bridge Street.

PIGEON ISLAND NATIONAL LANDMARK

St. Lucia's first national park was originally an island surrounded on one side by the Caribbean and on the other by the Atlantic. It's now joined to the mainland by a causeway. On its west coast are two white-sand beaches. There's also a restaurant, Jambe de Bois, named after a wooden-legged pirate who once used the island as a hideout for his men.

Pigeon Island also offers an Interpretation Centre, equipped with artifacts and a multimedia display of local history, ranging from the Amerindian occupation of A.D. 1000 to the Battle of the Saints, when Admiral Rodney's fleet set out from Pigeon Island and defeated Admiral de Grasse in 1782.

The Captain's Cellar Olde English Pub lies under the center and is evocative of an 18th-century English bar. Pigeon Island, only 44 acres in size, got its name from the red-neck pigeon, or ramier, which once made this island home. It's ideal for picnics, weddings, and nature walks. The park is open daily from 9am to 5pm, charging an entrance fee of EC$10 ($3.70). For more information, call the **St. Lucia National Trust** (☎ 758/452-5005).

✪ MARIGOT BAY

Movie crews, formerly those for Rex Harrison's *Dr. Doolittle* and Sophia Loren's *Fire Power,* like to use this bay, one of the most beautiful in the Caribbean, for background shots. Just 8 miles south of Castries, it's narrow yet navigable by yachts of any size. Here Admiral Rodney camouflaged his ships with palm leaves while lying in wait for French frigates. The shore, lined with palm trees, remains relatively unspoiled, but some building sites have been sold. Again, it's a delightful spot for a picnic if you didn't take your food basket to Pigeon Island.

SOUFRIÈRE

This little fishing port, St. Lucia's second-largest settlement, is dominated by two pointed hills called **Petit Piton** and **Gros Piton.** These two hills, "The Pitons," have become the very symbol of St. Lucia. They're two volcanic cones rising to 2,460 and 2,619 feet. Formed of lava and rock, and once actively volcanic, they're now clothed in green vegetation. Their sheer rise from the sea makes them a landmark visible for miles around.

Near Soufrière lies the famous "drive-in" volcano. Called ✪ **Mount Soufrière,** it's a rocky lunar landscape of bubbling mud and craters seething with fuming sulfur. You walk into an old (millions of years) crater going between the sulfur springs and pools of hissing steam. A local guide is usually waiting beside them, shrouded with sulfurous fumes that are said to have medicinal properties. For a fee, he'll point out the blackened waters, among the few of their kind in the Caribbean. If you do hire a guide, agree—then doubly agree—on what that fee will be.

Nearby are the ✪ **Diamond Mineral Baths** (☎ 758/452-4759) surrounded by a tropical arboretum. Constructed on orders of Louis XVI in 1784, whose doctors told him that these waters were similar in mineral content to the waters at Aix-les-Bains, they were intended for recuperative effects for French soldiers fighting in the West Indies. Later destroyed, they were rebuilt after World War II. They have an average temperature of 106°F and lie near one of the geological attractions of the island, a waterfall that changes colors (from yellow to black to green to gray) several times a day. The different hues of the water result from a changing mixture of sulfur, iron oxides, and muds that are regurgitated from the super-heated earth core. As the mineral content of the waters change, so does the color. For EC$5 ($1.85), you can bathe and benefit from the recuperative effects yourself.

From Soufrière in the southwest, the road winds toward Fond St-Jacques where you'll have a good view of mountains and villages as you cut through St. Lucia's Cape Moule-à-Chique tropical rain forest. You'll also see the Barre de l'Isle divide.

CAPE MOULE-À-CHIQUE

At the southern tip of the island, Cape Moule-à-Chique is where the Caribbean Sea merges with the Atlantic. Here the town of Vieux Fort can be seen, as can the neighboring island of St. Vincent, 26 miles away.

BANANA PLANTATIONS

Bananas are the island's leading export. As you're being hauled around the island by taxi drivers, ask them to take you to one of the huge plantations that allow visitors to come on the grounds. We suggest a sightseeing look at one of the trio of big ones—the Cul-de-Sac, just north of Marigot Bay; La Caya, in Dennery on the east coast; and the Roseau Estate, south of Marigot Bay.

SHOPPING

Most of the shopping is in Castries, where the principal streets are William Peter Boulevard and Bridge Street. Many stores will sell you goods at duty-free prices (providing you don't take the merchandise with you but have it delivered to the airport or cruise dock). There are some good buys—not remarkable—in bone china, jewelry, perfume, watches, liquor, and crystal. Souvenir items include bags and mats, local pottery, and straw hats—again, nothing remarkable.

POINTE SERAPHINE

Built for the cruise-ship passenger, Pointe Seraphine, in Castries, has the best collection of shops on the island, together with offices for car rentals, organized taxi service (for sightseeing), a bureau de change, Philatelic Bureau, Information Centre, and international telephones. Cruise ships berth right at the shopping center. Under red roofs in a Spanish-style setting, the complex requires that you present a cruise pass or an airline ticket to the shopkeeper when purchasing goods. Visitors can take away their purchases, except liquor and tobacco, which will be delivered to the airport. All shops in the complex keep the same hours. The center is open in winter, Monday to Friday from 8am to 5pm and on Saturday from 8am to 2pm; off-season, Monday to Saturday from 9am to 4pm. It's also open when cruise ships are in port.

Benneton. Pointe Seraphine. ☎ **758/452-7685.**

Prices are about 20% lower than Stateside.

Colombian Emeralds. Pointe Seraphine. ☎ **758/453-7721.**

Colombian Emeralds's major competitor in this mall is Little Switzerland, but this store has a more diverse selection of watches and gemstones. There are two adjoining buildings, one of which sells only gold chains and wristwatches; the other features precious and semiprecious stones. Of special value are the wristwatches, which sometimes sell for up to 40% less than equivalent retail prices in North America.

The Gallery. Point Seraphine. ☎ **758/451-6116.**

This gallery of arts and crafts specializes in Haitian paintings and crafts that include bowls, local souvenirs, hand-carved serving trays, and picture frames. Many items, including the primitive paintings, cost $25. Some items look junky, but if you shop carefully you may find a special craft.

Images. Point Seraphine. ☎ **758/452-6883.**

Images operates two shops in Castries's wharfside shopping mall, but the more interesting of them sells the most exhaustive collection of enameled Indian jewelry on St. Lucia. Laboriously handcrafted with lots of exotic swirls, the ornaments (necklaces, bracelets, and earrings) range in price from $10. Also worthwhile are India-made evening bags lavishly adorned with sequins (a bargain at $24 each), and bags by Ted Lapidus. A few steps away, the establishment's second store specializes in perfumes that cost around 20% less than equivalent goods sold retail in North America.

The Land Shop. Pointe Seraphine. ☎ **758/452-7488.**

This store specializes in elegant handbags, garment bags, and briefcases. Some come with the English-made labels affixed. Prices are at least 25% less than for equivalent items sold in North America. Also available is a selection of shoes, and bags and briefcases range upward from $79.

Little Switzerland. Pointe Seraphine. ☎ **758/451-6799.**

Its inventory includes a broad-based but predictable array of luxury goods. Prices of the porcelain, crystal, wristwatches, and jewelry are usually around 25% less than those of equivalent goods bought on the North American mainland, but wise shoppers are usually alert to the special promotions (with savings of up to 40% below Stateside retail prices).

ELSEWHERE ON THE ISLAND

Gablewoods Mall, on Gros Islet Highway, 2 miles north of Castries, contains three restaurants and one of the densest concentrations of shops on the island. The best clothing and sundry shop is **Top Banana** (☎ 758/451-6389), which sells beachwear, scuba and snorkeling equipment, gifts, inflatable rafts, and casual resortwear.

Bagshaws. La Toc. ☎ 758/451-9249.

Just outside Castries, this is the leading island hand-printer of silk-screen designs. An American, Sydney Bagshaw, founded the operation in the mid-1960s, and today it's operated by his daughter-in-law, Alice Bagshaw. The family has devoted their considerable skills to turning out a high-quality line of fabric as colorful as the Caribbean. The birds (look for the St. Lucia parrot), butterflies, and flowers of St. Lucia are incorporated into their original designs. The highlights are an extensive household line in vibrant prints on linen, as well as clothing and beachwear for both men and women, and the best T-shirt collection on St. Lucia. At La Toc Studios, the printing process can be viewed 7 days a week.

There are **four other retail outlets:** in the Pointe Seraphine duty-free shopping mall (☎ 758/452-7570), in Marigot Bay (☎ 758/451-4378), in Rodney Bay (☎ 758/452-9435), and at the "Best of St. Lucia" at Hewanorra International Airport, Vieux Fort (☎ 758/454-7784).

Caribelle Batik. Howelton House, Old Victoria Rd., The Morne. ☎ 758/452-3785.

In this workshop, just a 5-minute drive from Castries, you can watch St. Lucian artists creating intricate patterns and colors through the ancient art of batik. You can also purchase batik in cotton, rayon, and silk, made up in casual and beach clothing, plus wall hangings and other gift items. Drinks are served in the Dyehouse Bar and Terrace in the renovated Victorian-era building.

Eudovic Art Studio. Goodlands, Morne Fortune. ☎ 758/452-2747.

Vincent Joseph Eudovic is a master artist and wood carver whose sculptures have gained increasing fame. He usually carves his imaginative free-form sculptures from local tree roots, such as teak, mahogany, and red cedar. Some of his carvings are from Laurier Cannelle trees, which have disappeared from the island, although their roots often remain in a well-preserved state. Native to St. Lucia, he teaches pupils the art of wood carving. In the main studio, much of the work of his pupils is on display. However, ask to be taken to his private studio, where you'll see his remarkable work.

Noah's Arkade. Jeremie St. ☎ 758/452-2523.

Many of the Caribbean gifts here are routine tourist items, yet you'll often find something interesting if you browse around. They sell local straw placemats, baskets, and rugs, wall hangings, maracas, shell necklaces, locally made bowls, dolls dressed in banana leaves, and warri boards. Branches are found at Hewanorra International Airport and the Pointe Seraphine duty-free shopping mall.

Sea Island Cotton Shop. Gablewoods Mall, Castries. ☎ 758/452-3674.

Catering almost exclusively to tourists, this is a large shop in the Gablewoods Mall. It carries T-shirts, Sunny Caribbee herbs and spices, hand-painted souvenirs, and beach- and swimwear.

ST. LUCIA AFTER DARK

There isn't much except the entertainment offered by hotels. In the winter, at least one hotel offers a steel band or calypso music every night of the week. Otherwise, check to see what's happening at **Capone's** (☎ 758/452-0284) and **The Green Parrot** (☎ 758/452-3167). There are other locations at the Rex St. Lucian Hotel, the Windjammer Landing Villa Beach Resort, duty-free Pointe Seraphine, and duty-free La Place Carenage.

Indies, at Rodney Bay (☎ 758/452-0727), is a split-floor, soundproof dance club with a large wooden dancing area and stage. There's also a trio of bars, with smoking and no-smoking sections. The DJs keep the joint jumping, with both West Indian and international sounds, often American. Surprise entertainment is occasionally featured to spice up the party. The action gets going Wednesday, Friday, and Saturday from 11pm. There's a cover charge of EC$20 ($7.40). Indies has opened a new bar around the side of the building called the Back Door, featuring alternative music and reggae. A sort of rock and sports bar, it serves snacks until 3am.

The Lime at Rodney Bay (☎ 758/452-0761) also operates **The Late Lime Night Club,** offering entertainment Wednesday to Saturday, beginning at 10pm and lasting until the crowd folds. Jazz, reggae, country/western—it's all here, even easy-listening music on Sunday. Wednesday, Friday, and Saturday are disco nights. The cover charge is EC$15 ($5.55).

3 St. Vincent

One of the major Windward Islands, sleepy St. Vincent is only now awakening to tourism, which hasn't yet reached massive dimensions the way it has on nearby St. Lucia. Sailors and the yachting set have long known of St. Vincent and its satellite bays and beaches in the Grenadines.

Visit St. Vincent for its botanical beauty and the Grenadines for the best sailing waters in the Caribbean. Don't come for the nightlife, the grand cuisine, and the fabled beaches. There are some white-sand beaches near Kingstown on St. Vincent, but most of the other beaches ringing the island are of black sand. The yachting crowd seems to view St. Vincent merely as a launching pad for the 60-mile string of the Grenadines, but there are enough attractions on the island to merit an exploration all on its own.

St. Vincent has any number of inexpensive inns and small West Indian taverns once you've paid the rather high airfare to reach it. The Grenadines, stamping ground of yachties, royalty, and high society (often British), are hardly what one thinks of first in contemplating a budget holiday in the sun. However, even here there are a few places to stay and keep costs affordable. If you'd like to visit the Grenadines, the one island in the chain that offers the widest range of affordable food and lodging is Bequia.

An emerald island 18 miles long and 11 miles wide, St. Vincent has fertile valleys, rich forests, lush jungles, rugged peaks, waterfalls, foam-whitened beaches, outstanding coral reefs (with what experts say is some of the world's clearest water), a volcano nestled in the sky and usually capped by its own private cloud, and 4,000 feet up, Crater Lake.

Unspoiled by the worst fallout that mass tourism sometimes brings, the islanders actually treat visitors like people: Met with courtesy, they respond with courtesy. British customs predominate, along with traces of Gallic cultural influences, but all with a distinct West Indian flair.

GETTING THERE

In the eastern Caribbean, St. Vincent—the "gateway to the Grenadines" (see section 4, later in this chapter)—lies 100 miles west of Barbados, where most visitors from North America fly first, and then make connections that will take them on to

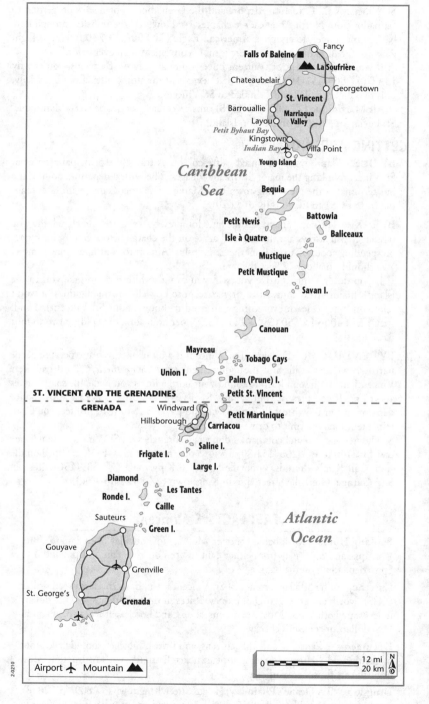

St. Vincent and the Grenadines

- Fancy
- Falls of Baleine
- La Soufrière
- Chateaubelair
- Georgetown
- St. Vincent
- Barrouallie
- Marriaqua Valley
- Layou
- *Petit Byhaut Bay*
- Kingstown
- *Indian Bay*
- Villa Point
- Young Island

Caribbean Sea

- Bequia
- Battowia
- Petit Nevis
- Baliceaux
- Isle à Quatre
- Mustique
- Petit Mustique
- Savan I.
- Canouan
- Mayreau
- Tobago Cays
- Union I.
- Palm (Prune) I.
- Petit St. Vincent

ST. VINCENT AND THE GRENADINES
GRENADA

- Windward
- Petit Martinique
- Hillsborough
- Carriacou
- Saline I.
- Frigate I.
- Large I.
- Diamond
- Les Tantes
- Ronde I.
- Caille
- Sauteurs
- Green I.
- Gouyave
- Atlantic Ocean
- Grenville
- St. George's
- Grenada

Airport ✈ Mountain ▲▲

0   12 mi / 20 km

N

2-0210

St. Vincent's **E. T. Joshua Airport** and the Grenadines. For details on getting to Barbados from North America, see chapter 14. However, the transfer through Barbados is no longer necessary, as **American Eagle** (☎ 800/433-7300) has one flight daily from San Juan, so getting here is more convenient than ever before.

If you decide to visit St. Vincent once you're already on Barbados, you can fly **LIAT** (☎ 809/457-1821) here, as that never-on-time airline offers five flights daily, plus two flights daily from Trinidad to St. Vincent.

Air Martinique (☎ 809/458-4528) runs twice-daily service between Martinique, St. Lucia, St. Vincent, and Union Island.

GETTING AROUND

BY BUS   Flamboyantly painted "alfresco" buses travel the principal arteries of St. Vincent, linking the major towns and villages. The central departure point is the bus terminal at the New Kingstown Fish Market. The price is low, with fares ranging from EC$1 to EC$6 (40¢ to $2.20).

BY TAXI   The government sets the rates for fares, but taxis are unmetered; the wise passenger will always ask the fare and agree on the charge before getting in. Figure on spending about $7 to go from the E. T. Joshua Airport to your hotel, maybe more. You should tip about 12% of the fare.

If you don't want to drive yourself, you can also hire taxis to take you to the island's major attractions. Most drivers seem to be well-informed guides (it won't take you long to learn everything you need to know about St. Vincent). You'll spend EC$40 to EC$50 ($14.80 to $18.50) per hour for a car holding two to four passengers.

BY RENTAL CAR   Driving on St. Vincent is a bit of an adventure because of the narrow, twisting roads and the requirement to *drive on the left*. To drive like a Vincentian, you'll soon learn to sound your horn a lot as you make the sharp curves and turns. If you present your valid U.S. or Canadian driver's license at the police department on Bay Street in Kingstown, and pay a EC$40 ($14.80) fee, you'll obtain a temporary permit to drive.

The major car-rental companies don't have branches on St. Vincent. Rental cars cost EC$140 to EC$200 ($51.80 to $74) a day, but that must be determined on the spot. Call **Kim's Rentals,** Grenville Street, in Kingstown (☎ 809/456-1884), or **Star Garage,** Grenville Street, also in Kingstown (☎ 809/456-1743).

FAST FACTS: St. Vincent

Banking Hours   Most banks are open Monday to Thursday from 8am to either 1 or 3pm and on Friday from either 8am to 5pm or from 8am to 1pm and 3 to 5pm, depending on the bank.

Currency   The official currency of St. Vincent is the **Eastern Caribbean dollar (EC$),** worth about 37¢ in U.S. money. Prices in this chapter are in U.S. dollars unless stated otherwise. Most restaurants, shops, and hotels will accept payment in U.S. dollars or traveler's checks.

Documents   Canadian and U.S. citizens, and British subjects, should have proof of identity and a return or ongoing airplane ticket. Passports, voter registration cards, or birth certificates are sufficient.

Drugstore   Try **Deane's Pharmacy,** Halifax Street, Kingstown (☎ 809/457-2056), open Monday to Friday from 8:30am to 4:30pm and on Saturday from 8:30am to 12:30pm.

Electricity   Electricity is 220 volts AC, 50 cycles, so you'll need an adapter and a transformer. Some hotels have transformers, but it's best to bring your own.

Information   Inquiries in the United States can be made to the **St. Vincent and Grenadines Tourist Office,** 801 Second Ave., 21st Floor, New York, NY 10017 (☎ **800/729-1726** or 212/687-4981), and 6505 Cove Creek Place, Dallas, TX 75240 (☎ **800/235-3029** or 214/239-6451).

The local **Department of Tourism** is in the Government Administrative Centre, on Bay Street, Kingstown (☎ **809/457-1502**).

Language   English is the official language.

Medical Care   There are two hospitals on St. Vincent, **Kingstown General Hospital,** Kingstown (☎ **809/456-1111**), and **Medical Associates Clinic,** Kingstown (☎ **809/457-2598**).

Post Office   The General Post Office on Halifax Street in Kingstown is open Monday to Friday from 8:30am to 3pm and on Saturday from 8:30 to 11:30am. There are sub-post offices in 56 districts throughout the state, and these include offices on the Grenadine islands of Bequia, Mustique, Canouan, Mayreau, and Union Island.

Safety   St. Vincent and its neighboring islands of the Grenadines are still safe islands to visit. In Kingstown, the capital of St. Vincent, chances are you'll encounter little serious crime. However, take the usual precautions and never leave valuables unguarded.

Taxes and Service   The government imposes an airport departure tax of EC$20 ($7.40) per person. A 7% government occupancy tax is charged for all hotel accommodations, and hotels and restaurants add a 10% to 15% service charge.

Telephone   Once on the island, dial all seven digits of the local number (not the 809 area code). The same is true for the Grenadines.

Time   Both St. Vincent and the Grenadines operate on Atlantic standard time year-round: When it's 6am on St. Vincent, it's 5am in Miami. During daylight saving time in the United States, St. Vincent keeps the same time as the U.S. East Coast.

Weather   The climate of St. Vincent is pleasantly cooled by the trade winds all year. The tropical temperature is in the 78° to 82° Fahrenheit range. The rainy season is May to November.

WHERE TO STAY

Don't expect high-rise resorts here, as everything is kept small. The places are comfortable, not fancy, and you usually get a lot of personal attention from the staff. Most hotels and restaurants add a 7% government tax and a 10% to 15% service charge to your bill; ask about this when you register.

You might want to consider a package deal offered by **TourScan, Inc.,** P.O. Box 2367, Darien, CT 06820 (☎ **800/962-2080** or 203/665-8091); some best-value air-and-hotel packages begin at $568 per person for 3 nights, with an extra night costing $24 and up.

DOUBLES FOR LESS THAN $60

Heron Hotel. Upper Bay St. (P.O. Box 226), Kingstown, St. Vincent, W.I. ☎ **809/457-1631.** Fax 809/457-1189. 12 rms. A/C TEL. Year-round, $44 single; $56.50–$62.50 double. Rates include full breakfast. MC, V.

This respectable but slightly run-down hotel is among the most historic buildings on St. Vincent. It was built of local stone and tropical hardwoods late in the

18th century as a warehouse, and later provided lodgings for colonial planters doing business along the then-teeming wharves of Kingstown. Operating in its present format since 1960, it occupies the second story of a building whose ground floor is devoted to shops. Some of the simple rooms overlook an inner courtyard; others face the streets. Overall, there's a sense of old-fashioned timelessness and dignified severity you'll almost never find in modern resorts, and it's hard to beat the establishment's low prices. It attracts a clientele of moderately eccentric guests, some of whom conduct business in the heart of the island's capital, whereas others want to be near the docks in time for early-morning departures. Room 15 is the largest of the lot. There's a restaurant whose busiest time of day is lunch. (The restaurant may close after dusk, so dinner reservations are important.)

Umbrella Beach Hotel. Villa Beach, East St. George (P.O. Box 530, Kingstown), St. Vincent, W.I. ☎ **809/458-4651.** Fax 809/457-4930. 9 rms, all with kitchenette. TEL. Year-round, $38–$48 single; $48–$58 double. AE, MC, V.

This is one of the simpler of several guest houses on the shoreline of St. Vincent opposite Young Island. Set in a garden, behind a green-and-white facade, the hotel charges more for the trio of rooms overlooking the water than it does for those that don't. The rooms are Spartan enough to justify their low costs, with varnished wood floors, wooden furnishings, and white walls. Maid service is included. While no meals other than breakfast are served, the hotel is next door to several inexpensive eateries. Although the Umbrella Beach is rather quiet, stiff drinks and live music are usually part of the program at the nearby Young Island Resort, which you can reach by taking any of the frequent ferryboats across the channel to an island.

DOUBLES FOR LESS THAN $75

✪ **Beachcombers Hotel.** Villa Beach (P.O. Box 126, Kingstown), St. Vincent, W.I. ☎ **809/458-4283.** Fax 809/458-4385. 14 rms. TEL. $75–$80 double. AE, MC, V.

This relative newcomer, established by Richard and Flora Gunn, immediately became a far more inviting choice than the traditional budget favorites, the Heron and Cobblestone. It's in a tropical garden right on the beach, adjacent to Sunset Shores. A pair of chaletlike buildings house the accommodations, all with private baths and tastefully decorated. They're cooled by ceiling fans, and each has a patio. The standard of cleanliness and maintenance is the finest on the island. Try for Room 1, 2 or 3, as they are not only the best but open onto the water. Some rooms have small kitchenettes. The hotel has a health spa (Mrs. Gunn is a massage and beauty therapist). And, astonishingly for a B&B, the Beachcombers offers a steam room, Turkish bath, sauna, and even facials, aromatherapy, and reflexology. The Beachbar & Restaurant, a favorite gathering place for locals, fronts an open terrace, and serves an excellent cuisine. Daughter Cheryl, who mastered her cookery skills in England, is the chef.

✪ **Cobblestone Inn.** Bax St. (P.O. Box 867, Kingstown), St. Vincent, W.I. ☎ **809/456-1937.** Fax 809/456-1938. 19 rms. A/C TEL. Year-round, $60 single; $72 double. Rates include breakfast. AE, DC, DISC, MC, V.

Originally built as a warehouse for sugar and arrowroot in 1814, the core of this historic hotel is made of stone and brick. Today it's one of the most famous hotels of St. Vincent, known for its labyrinth of passages, arches, and upper hallways. To reach the high-ceilinged reception area, you pass from the waterfront through a stone tunnel into a chiseled courtyard. At the top of a massive sloping stone staircase you're shown to one of the simple old-fashioned bedrooms. Some units contain TVs and some have windows opening over the rooftops of town. Meals are served on a third-floor eagle's eyrie high above the hotel's central courtyard. Rows of windows and thick mahogany tables in its adjacent bar create one of the most unusual hideaways in town. The hotel is convenient to town; however, you'll have to drive about 3 miles to the nearest beach.

Coconut Beach Inn. Indian Bay (P.O. Box 355, Kingstown), St. Vincent, W.I. ☎ **809/ 457-4900.** Fax 809/457-4900. 10 rms. Year-round, $45–$55 single; $65 double. Rates include breakfast. AE, MC, V.

This owner-occupied inn, restaurant, and bar lies 5 minutes (2 miles) south of the airport and a 5-minute drive from Kingstown. The hotel, which grew out of a villa constructed in the 1930s by one of the region's noted eccentrics, lies across the channel from the much more expensive Young Island. Its seaside setting makes it a choice for swimming and sunbathing. Island tours, such as sailing the Grenadines, can be arranged, as can diving, snorkeling, and mountain climbing. Each room is furnished in a straightforward modern style. The bedrooms vary widely from each other. A beach bar at water's edge serves tropical drinks, and an open-air restaurant opens onto a view of Indian Bay and features West Indian and Vincentian cooking prepared from local foods. Steaks, Cornish game hens, and hamburgers round out the fare.

Indian Bay Beach Hotel & Apartments. Indian Bay (P.O. Box 538, Kingstown), St. Vincent, W.I. ☎ **800/742-4276** or 809/458-4001. Fax 809/457-4777. 10 apts, some with kitchenette. A/C TEL. Winter, $65 one-bedroom apt for one; $75 one-bedroom apt for two; $90 two-bedroom apt for two to four. Off-season, $55 one-bedroom apt for one; $65 one-bedroom apt for two; $80 two-bedroom apt for two to four. MAP $25 per person extra. AE, MC, V.

This is a modestly priced, low-slung concrete building with white walls, blue trim, and awnings to deflect the sun's rays. Built in 1972 a few feet from the sea, in a residential neighborhood that's one of the most sought-after on St. Vincent, it's been renovated several times since then. Don't expect personalized forms of intimacy here; the setting is anonymous but serviceable, with easy access to many neighboring resorts whose bars, restaurants, and sports facilities can sometimes be made available to you. You can swim on a narrow beach near the hotel's foundation, although a more desirable site might be Indian Bay Beach, whose sands are a 5-minute walk away. If you don't feel inspired to cook, you'll find a lattice-ringed Caribbean bistro (A la Mer) on the premises, serving lunch from $10 and dinner from $15. The accommodations aren't frilly or fancy, but contain white walls, carpets, patterned draperies, wood furnishings, touches of rattan, and in some cases, views over the offshore upscale resort of Young Island. Every Friday night in winter a barbecue is featured, with chicken, pork, fish, and steak.

WHERE TO EAT

Most guests eat at their hotels on the Modified American Plan (half board). Unlike the situation on many Caribbean islands, many Vincentian hostelries serve authentic West Indian cuisine. There are also a few independent eateries.

Aggie's. Grenville St., Kingstown. ☎ **809/456-2110.** Reservations recommended. Main courses EC$15–EC$40 ($5.60–$14.80); lunch EC$15–EC$35 ($5.55–$12.95). AE, MC, V. Mon–Sat 9am–10pm, Sun 6–10pm (closing hours are approximate). WEST INDIAN / SEAFOOD.

Located on the island's southern end in Kingstown, this eatery provides a lively environment with warm hospitality. It's so relaxed that it remains open until the last customer leaves. This local hangout specializes in West Indian seafood at reasonable prices. What's in season determines which soups are offered (perhaps green pea, calaloo, or pumpkin); or try the fish or conch chowder. House specialties might include lobster, souse, conch, shrimp, fish, and whelk; or try the chicken, served baked or fried, or one of the curried beef and mutton dishes. A Créole buffet is featured at lunch from noon to 3pm on Friday with your choice of three meats such as pork, chicken, and fish. It's Créole day on Saturday serving specialties such as souse, Créole-style fish, and pilau.

Bounty. Egmont St., Kingstown. ☎ **809/456-1776.** Snacks and sandwiches EC$3.85–EC$6 ($1.40–$2.20); main courses EC$10–EC$13 ($3.70–$4.80). No credit cards. Mon–Fri 8am–5pm, Sat 8am–1:30pm. AMERICAN / WEST INDIAN.

Opposite Barclay's Bank in the center of Kingstown you'll find Bounty behind a green-and-white facade. A friendly local staff greets you, and people who work nearby frequent the place, making it their second home. An art gallery offers a variety of local works. Fill up on pastries of all kinds, rôtis, hot dogs, hamburgers, and sandwiches, along with homemade soups. Fish-and-chips is also served. The interesting collection of drinks includes passionfruit and golden apple.

Juliette's Restaurant. Egmont St., Kingstown. ☎ **809/457-1645.** Rôtis and sandwiches EC$3–EC$5 ($1.10–$1.85); fixed-price menu EC$10–EC$12 ($3.70–$4.45). No credit cards. Mon–Fri 8:30am–4:30pm, Sat 8:30am–2pm. WEST INDIAN.

Amid the capital's cluster of administrative buildings, across from the National Commercial Bank, this restaurant dispenses more lunches to office workers than any other establishment in town. It doesn't serve breakfast, although it opens early. It offers only snacks or lunch-type items in the morning. Meals are served in clean and respectable surroundings that are headed by a 27-year veteran of the restaurant trade, Juliette Campbell. (Ms. Campbell's husband is the island's well-known attorney general.) Menu items include soups, curried mutton, an array of fish, stewed chicken, stewed beef, and sandwiches. Many platters are garnished with fried plantains and rice. This is the type of cuisine you're likely to be served in a decent family-style boarding house on St. Vincent.

Pizza Party Chicken Roost. Arnos Vale. ☎ **809/456-4939.** Reservations not accepted. Main courses EC$15–EC$60 ($5.60–$22.20). No credit cards. Daily 9am–11pm. INTERNATIONAL.

Located across from the E. T. Joshua Airport, this fast-food restaurant offers a wide range of specialties from sandwiches and pizzas to steaks and lobster. Overlooking Mustique and Bequia, it's similar to a McDonald's with its counter service, but with a twist. The sandwiches extend from a simple egg and cheese to the more robust flying fish, and the burgers here are made with a quarter pound of freshly ground local beef. You can also find stuffed whelk, conch fritters, and shark on the menu. The specialty pizzas consist of the jump-up carnival (ground beef, bacon, tomato sauce, oregano, and three different cheeses), the Chicago tower (with everything, including sweet peppers and extra garlic), and the eastern special (curried chicken, pineapple, and mozzarella).

Rooftop Restaurants & Bar. Bay St., Kingstown. ☎ **809/457-2845.** Reservations not required for lunch, recommended for dinner. Main courses EC$25–EC$50 ($9.25–$18.50); lunch platters EC$18 ($6.70). AE, DISC, MC, V. Mon–Sat 11:30am–2pm and 7–10pm. WEST INDIAN/ INTERNATIONAL.

This restaurant does a thriving business because of its well-prepared food and its location three stories above the center of Kingstown. After you climb some flights of stairs, you'll see a bar near the entrance, an indoor area decorated in earth tones, and a patio open to the breezes. Lunches stress traditional Créole recipes using fish, chicken, mutton, beef, and goat. Dinners are more international, and include lobster, snapper with lemon-butter and garlic sauce, steak with onions and mushrooms, and several pork dishes. Every Friday a karaoke sing-along set-up is featured, and on Saturday evening there's a steel band in attendance after 6pm.

WORTH A SPLURGE

✪ **Basil's Bar & Restaurant.** Bay St., Kingstown. ☎ **809/457-2713.** Reservations recommended. Main courses EC$35–EC$55 ($12.95–$20.35); lunch buffet EC$30 ($11.10). AE, MC, V. Daily 8–11:30am, noon–2pm, and 7–10pm. SEAFOOD/INTERNATIONAL.

This brick-lined enclave is a less famous annex of the legendary Basil's Beach Bar on Mustique. It's inside the early 19th-century walls of an old sugar warehouse, on Kingstown's waterfront beneath the Cobblestone Inn. The air-conditioned interior is accented with exposed stone and brick, soaring arches, and a rambling mahogany bar, which remains open throughout the day. The menu could include lobster salad, shrimp in garlic butter, sandwiches, hamburgers, and barbecued chicken. Dinners feature grilled lobster, escargots, shrimp cocktail, grilled red snapper, and grilled filet mignon. You can order meals here throughout the day and late into the evening—until the last satisfied customer leaves. The lunch buffet is available daily from noon to 2pm.

Lime 'n' Pub. Villa Beach (opposite Young Island). ☎ **809/458-4227.** Main courses EC$30–EC$100 ($11.10–$37). AE, DC, MC, V. Daily noon–midnight. WEST INDIAN / INTERNATIONAL/ INDIAN.

This is one of the island's most popular restaurants, right on Young Island Channel opposite the super-expensive Young Island Hotel. It's the most congenial pub on the island, with a wide selection of pub grub, including pizzas. There's even a live lobster pond, but you'll pay dearly for this catch. A local band enlivens the atmosphere a few times every week in winter. In the more formalized section of this indoor and alfresco restaurant, you can partake of some good-tasting West Indian food, along with some dishes from India or the international kitchen. The rôtis win high praise, but we gravitate to the fresh fish and lobster dishes instead. The coconut shrimp is generally excellent. Service is among the most hospitable on the island.

FUN ON & OFF THE BEACH

BEACHES   All beaches on St. Vincent are public, and many of the best ones border hotel properties, which you can patronize for drinks or luncheons. Most of the resorts are in the south, where the beaches have white or golden-yellow sand. However, many of the beaches in the north have sands that look like lava ash in color. The safest swimming is on the leeward beaches; the windward beaches can be dangerous.

Some of the best beaches are the white sands of **Villa Beach** and the black sands of **Buccament Bay** or **Questelle's Bay,** all west-coast sites.

FISHING   It's best to go to a local fisherman for advice if you're interested in this sport, which your hotel will usually arrange for you. The government of St. Vincent doesn't require visitors to take out a license. If you arrange matters in time, it's sometimes possible to accompany the fishermen on one of their trips, perhaps 4 or 5 miles from shore. A modest fee should suffice. The fishing fleet leaves from the leeward coast at Barrouallie. They've been known to return to shore with everything from a 6-inch redfish to a 20-foot pilot whale.

HIKING   The best hikes are the **Vermont Nature Trails** if you don't want to face Soufrière, which blows its volcanic top on occasion. These marked trails (get a map at the tourist office) take you through a rain forest in the middle of the island. You'll pass long-ago plantations that nature has reclaimed, and enter a world of tropical fruit trees. You might even see the rare St. Vincent parrot with its flamboyant plumage.

Wear good hiking shoes and your antimosquito cologne. You can stop in at **T & M Ltd.** in Kingstown (☎ **809/456-1616**), which will provide directions and the provisions—everything from pâté to French cheese—for a picnic.

SNORKELING & SCUBA DIVING   The best area for snorkeling and scuba diving is the Villa/Young Island section on the southern end of the island.

Dive St. Vincent, on the Young Island Cut (☎ **809/457-4928**), has been owned and operated by a transplanted Texan, Bill Tewes, for more than 10 years. The oldest dive company in the country and the best, Dive St. Vincent now has two additional dive shops: Dive Canouan, at the Tamarind Beach Hotel on Canouan Island, and Grenadines Dive, at the Sunny Grenadines Hotel on Union Island. The shops have a total of six instructors and three divemasters, as well as seven dive boats. The chain of dive shops allows visitors to dive or be certified while sailing throughout St. Vincent and the Grenadines with a consistency of quality. All shops offer dive/snorkel trips as well as sightseeing day trips and dive instruction. Single-tank dives cost $50 and two-tank dives go for $90, including all equipment and instructors and/or divemaster guides. Dive packages are available.

TENNIS   Both the **Young Island Resort,** on Young Island (☎ **809/458-4826**), and the **Grand View Beach Hotel,** Villa Point (☎ **809/458-4811**), have courts open to nonguests, but you should call in advance to make arrangements.

EXPLORING KINGSTOWN

Special events include the week-long **Carnival** in early July, one of the largest in the eastern Caribbean, with steel-band and calypso competitions, along with the crowning of the king and queen of the carnival.

Lushly tropical, the capital isn't as architecturally fascinating as St. George's on Grenada. Some English-style houses do exist, many of them looking as if they belonged in Penzance, Cornwall, instead of the Caribbean. However, you can still meet old-time beachcombers if you stroll on Upper Bay Street. White-haired and bearded, they can be seen loading their boats with produce grown on the mountain, before heading to some secluded beach in the Grenadines. This is a chief port and gateway to the Grenadines, and you can also view the small boats and yachts that have dropped anchor here. The place is a magnet for charter sailors.

At the top of a winding road on the north side of Kingstown, **Fort Charlotte** (☎ **809/456-1165**) was built on Johnson Point, enclosing one side of the bay. Constructed about the time of the American Revolution, it was named after Queen Charlotte, the German consort of George III. The ruins aren't much to inspect; the reason to come here is the view. The fort sits atop a steep promontory some 640 feet above the sea. From its citadel you'll have a commanding sweep of the leeward shores to the north, Kingstown to the south, and the Grenadines beyond. A trio of cannons used to fight off French troops are still in place. You'll see a series of oil murals depicting the history of black Caribs. Admission is free, and it's open 24 hours.

The second major sight is the **Botanic Gardens** (☎ **809/457-1003**), on the north side of Kingstown about a mile from the center. Founded in 1765 by Gov. George Melville, they're the oldest botanic gardens in the West Indies. In this Windward Eden you'll see 20 acres of such tropical exotics as teak, almond, cinnamon, nutmeg, cannonball, and mahogany; some of the trees are more than two centuries old. One of the breadfruit trees was reputedly among those original seedlings brought to this island by Captain Bligh in 1793. There's also a large *Spachea perforata* (the Soufrière tree), a species believed to be unique to St. Vincent and not found in the wild since 1812. The gardens are open daily from 6am to 6pm.

Joe vs. the Volcano, Part II

Exploring St. Vincent's hot volcano, **La Soufrière,** is an intriguing adventure. As you travel the island, you can't miss its cloud-capped splendor. This volcano has occasionally captured the attention of the world. The most recent eruption was in 1979, when the volcano spewed ashes, lava, and hot mud that covered the vegetation on its slopes and forced thousands of Vincentians to flee its fury. Belching rocks and black curling smoke filled the blue Caribbean sky. Jets of steam spouted 20,000 feet into the air. About 17,000 people were evacuated from a 10-mile ring around the volcano.

Fortunately, the eruption was in the sparsely settled northern part of the island. The volcano lies away from most of the tourism and commercial centers of St. Vincent, and even if it should erupt again, volcanologists do not consider it a danger to visitors lodged at beachside hotels along the leeward coast. The last major eruption of the volcano occurred in 1902, when 2,000 people were killed. Until its 1979 eruption the volcano had been quiet since 1972. The activity that year produced a 324-foot-long island of lava rock jutting up from the water of Crater Lake.

At the rim of the crater you'll be rewarded with one of the most panoramic views in the Caribbean. That is, if the wind doesn't blow too hard and make you topple over into the crater itself! Extreme caution is emphasized. Inside, you can see the steam rising from the crater.

The trail back down is much easier, we assure you.

Even if you're an experienced hiker, don't attempt to explore this volcano without an experienced guide. Also, wear suitable hiking clothes and be sure that you're in the best of health before making the arduous journey. The easiest route is the 3-mile eastern route leaving from Rabacca. Some people attempt this on their own. The more arduous trail—longer by half a mile—is the western trail from Chateaubelair, which definitely requires a guide. The round-trip to the crater takes about 5 hours.

The **St. Vincent Forestry Headquarters,** in the village of Campden Park (☎ 809/457-8594), about 3 miles from Kingstown, along the west coast, offers a pamphlet giving hiking data to Soufrière. It's open Monday to Friday from 8am to noon and 1 to 4pm. **HAZECO Tours** (☎ 809/457-8634) offers guided hikes up to La Soufrière, costing $100 per couple, including lunch.

The **Archaeological Museum,** in the Botanic Gardens, houses a good collection of stone tools and other artifacts in both stone and pottery. In front of it are shrubs that might have been found in the compound of an early Carib home.

In the heart of town, you might pay a visit to **St. Mary's Catholic Church,** on Grenville Street, with its curious melange of architecture. Fancifully flawed, it was built in 1935 by a Belgian monk, Dom Carlos Verbeke. He incorporated Romanesque arches, Gothic spires, and almost Moorish embellishments. The result— a maze of balconies, turrets, battlements, and courtyards—creates a bizarre effect.

St. George's Cathedral has some beautiful stained-glass windows: The three on the east are by Kempe and the large one on the south is of Munich glass. The nave and lower part of the tower date from 1820, and the galleried interior is of late Georgian architecture. To reach the cathedral, follow Back Street (also known as Granby Street) west past the Methodist church.

SCENIC DRIVES

✪ **THE LEEWARD HIGHWAY**   The leeward or west side of the island has the most dramatic scenery. North from Kingstown, you rise into lofty terrain before descending to the water again. There are views in all directions. On your right you'll pass the Aqueduct Golf Course before reaching Layou. If you want to play golf, check its status, as it often opens and closes. Here you can see the massive **Carib Rock,** with a human face carving dating back to A.D. 600. This is one of the finest petroglyphs in the Caribbean.

Continuing north you reach **Barrouallie,** where there's another Carib stone altar. Even if you're not into fishing, you might want to spend some time in this whaling village, where some still occasionally set out in brightly painted boats armed with harpoons, Moby-Dick style, to seek the elusive whale. However, "Save the Whale" devotees need not harpoon their way here in anger. Barrouallie may be one of the last few outposts in the world where such whale-hunting is carried on, but Vincentians point out that it doesn't endanger an already endangered species since so few are caught each year. If one is caught, it's an occasion for festivities.

The leeward highway continues to **Chateaubelair,** the end of the line. Here you can swim at the attractive **Richmond Beach** before heading back to Kingstown. In the distance, the volcano, La Soufrière, looms menacingly in the mountains.

The adventurous set out from here to see the **Falls of Baleine,** $7^1/_2$ miles north of Richmond Beach on the northern tip of the island, accessible only by boat. Coming from a stream in the volcanic hills, Baleine is a freshwater fall. If you're interested in making the trip, check with the tourist office in Kingstown about a tour there.

THE WINDWARD HIGHWAY   This road runs along the eastern Atlantic coast from Kingstown. Waves pound the land, and all along the rocky shores are splendid seascapes. If you want to go swimming along this often-dangerous coast, stick to the sandy spots, as they offer safer sites. Along this road you'll pass coconut and banana plantations and fields of arrowroot.

North of Georgetown lies the **Rabacca Dry River,** which was the flow of lava from the volcano at its eruption at the beginning of the 20th century. The journey from Kingstown to here is only 24 miles, but it will seem like much longer. For those who want to go the final 11 miles along a rugged road to **Fancy,** the northern tip of the island, a Land Rover, Jeep, or Moke will be needed.

MARRIQUA VALLEY   Sometimes known as the Mesopotamia Valley, this area is one of the lushest cultivated valleys in the eastern Caribbean. Surrounded by mountain ridges, the drive takes you through a landscape planted with nutmeg, cocoa, coconut, breadfruit, and bananas. The road begins at Vigie Highway, to the east of the E. T. Joshua Airport runway. At Montréal you'll come upon natural mineral springs. Only rugged vehicles should make this trip.

Around Kingstown, you can also enjoy the **Queen's Drive,** a scenic loop into the high hills to the east of the capital. From here the view is panoramic over Kingstown and its yacht-clogged harbor to the Grenadines in the distance.

SHOPPING

You don't come to St. Vincent to shop, but once here, you might pick up some items in the Sea Island cotton fabrics and clothing that are specialties here. In addition, Vincentian artisans make pottery, jewelry, and baskets that have souvenir value at least. Most shops are open Monday to Friday from 8am to 4pm. Stores generally close from noon to 1pm for lunch. Saturday hours are 8am to noon.

Since Kingstown consists of about 12 small blocks, you can walk and browse and see about everything in a morning's shopping jaunt. Try to be in town for the colorful, noisy Friday-morning market. You might not purchase anything, but you'll surely enjoy the riot of color.

Juliette's Fashions. Back St., Kingstown. ☎ **809/456-1143.**

Owned and operated by the same entrepreneur as Juliette's Restaurant (see "Where to Eat," above), this is the best-stocked women's clothing store on St. Vincent. Beneficiary of its owner's frequent buying trips to New York and Miami, it sells women's sportswear, evening wear, beachwear, and costume jewelry.

Noah's Arkade. Bay St., Kingstown. ☎ **809/457-1513.**

Noah's sells gifts from the West Indies, including wood carvings, T-shirts, and a wide range of books and souvenirs. Noah's has shops at the Frangipani Hotel, Bequia, St. Vincent, and the Grenadines.

St. Vincent Handicraft Centre. Frenches St., Kingstown. ☎ **809/457-2516.**

Here you'll see a large display of the handcrafts of the island. On the site of an old cotton gin, this shop offers you a chance to view craftspeople at work, perhaps on macramé, pottery, textiles, or metalwork jewelry. Grass floor mats are a popular item.

St. Vincent Philatelic Services Ltd. Bonadie's Bldg., Bay St., Kingstown. ☎ **809/457-1911.**

This is the largest operating bureau in the Caribbean, and its issues are highly acclaimed around the world by stamp collectors. Stamp enthusiasts can visit or order by mail.

Sprott Brothers Ltd. Homeworks, Bay St., Kingstown. ☎ **809/457-1121.**

At this department store you can buy clothing designed by Vincentians, along with an array of fabrics, linens, and silk-screened T-shirts, even Caribbean-made furniture. In fact, there's a little bit of everything here.

Y. de Lima Ltd. Bay and Egmont sts., Kingstown. ☎ **809/457-1681.**

The familiar Y. de Lima Ltd. is well stocked with cameras, stereo equipment, toys, clocks, binoculars, and jewelry, the best selection on the island. Paragon bone china is sold, along with a selection of gift items. Caribbean gold and silver jewelry are also featured.

ST. VINCENT AFTER DARK

The focus is mainly on the hotels, and activities are likely to include nighttime barbecues and dancing to steel bands. In season at least one hotel seems to have something planned every night during the week. Inquire locally.

The Aquatic Club. Adjacent to the departure point of the ferryboat leading from St. Vincent's "mainland" to Young Island. ☎ **809/458-4205.**

During party nights when it rocks and rolls (usually Wednesday, Saturday, and Sunday), this is the loudest, most raucous, and most animated nightspot on St. Vincent, a source of giddy fun to its fans, and a sore bone of contention to nearby hotel guests who claim they can't sleep because of the noise. On these nights things get into a heat by 11pm and continue until as late as 3am. The other nights of the week the place functions just as a bar, with a spate of recorded music, but without the high-volume live bands that keep the three-times-per-week parties jumping. Centered around an open-sided veranda and an outdoor deck, the place is open every night from 9pm to 2 or 3am, and there's always a cover charge of EC$5 to EC$20 ($1.85 to $7.40).

The Attic. In the Kentucky Bldg., at Melville and Back sts., Kingstown. ☎ **809/457-2558.** Cover EC$5–EC$50 ($1.90–$18.50), depending on the entertainment.

The air-conditioned Attic features jazz and easy-listening music. Music is live only on Friday and Saturday; Tuesday and Thursday it's recorded. Wednesday is karaoke night. Fish and burgers are available.

Touch Entertainment Centre (TEC). Back St., Kingstown. ☎ **809/457-1825.**

Opposite Kentucky Fried Chicken on the top floor of the Cambridge Building, this is the best-known nightspot in the region. With advanced lighting, it's a soundproof (from the outside), air-conditioned environment, suitable for visitors. Every Wednesday night, in summer only, is disco night, especially for the young and the restless. Friday and Sunday nights there's a house party with a DJ. Surprisingly, it's not open on Saturday night.

4 The Grenadines

South of St. Vincent, this small chain of islands extends for more than 40 miles and offers the finest yachting area in the eastern Caribbean. The islands are strung like a necklace of precious stones. Here we'll explore Bequia, Union island, and Mayreau.

A few of the islands have accommodations, which we'll visit, but many are so small and so completely undeveloped and unspoiled that they attract only beachcombers and stray boaters.

Populated by the descendants of African slaves, the Grenadines, administered by St. Vincent, collectively add up to a landmass of 30 square miles. These bits of land, often dots on nautical charts, may lack natural resources, yet they're blessed with white sandy beaches, coral reefs, and their own kind of sleepy beauty. If you don't spend the night in the Grenadines, you should at least go over for the day to visit one of them and enjoy a picnic lunch (which your hotel will pack for you) on one of the long stretches of beach.

GETTING THERE

BY PLANE   Four of the Grenadines—Bequia, Mustique, Union Island, and Canouan—have small airports, the landing spots for flights on **Mustique Airways** (☎ **809/458-4380** on St. Vincent). Its planes are technically charters, although flights depart St. Vincent for Bequia on Monday, Wednesday, Friday, and Sunday at 8am. The cost is EC$80 ($29.60) round-trip.

BY BOAT   The ideal way to go, of course, is to rent your own yacht, as many wealthy visitors do. But a far less expensive method of transport for the budget traveler is to go on a mail, cargo, or passenger boat as the locals do—but you'll need time and patience. However, boats do run on schedules, and generally are punctual. The **government mail boat** MV *Baracuda* leaves St. Vincent on Monday and Thursday at 10:30am, stops at Bequia, Canouan, and Mayreau, and arrives at Union Island at about 3:45pm. On Tuesday and Friday the boat leaves Union Island at about 6:30am, stops at Mayreau and Canouan, reaches Bequia at about 10:45am, and makes port at St. Vincent at noon. One-way fares from St. Vincent are: to Bequia, EC$10 ($3.70) Monday to Friday and EC$12 ($4.45) on weekends; to Canouan, EC$13 ($4.80); to Mayreau, EC$15 ($5.55); and to Union Island, EC$20 ($7.40).

You can also reach Bequia Monday to Saturday on the *Admiral I* and *Admiral II*. For information on these sea trips, inquire at the Tourist Board, Bay Street, in Kingstown (☎ **809/457-1502**).

BEQUIA

Only 7 square miles of land, Bequia (pronounced "*Beck*-wee") is the largest of St. Vincent's Grenadines. It's the northernmost island in the Grenadines, offering quiet lagoons, reefs, and long stretches of nearly deserted beaches. Descended from seafarers and other early adventurers, its population of some 6,000 Bequians will give you a friendly greeting if you pass them along the road. Of the inhabitants, 10% are of Scottish ancestry, who live mostly in the Mount Pleasant region. A feeling of relaxation and informality prevails on Bequia.

The island lies 9 miles south of St. Vincent. There's a small airport, and you can also travel here by boat (see "Getting There," above).

GETTING AROUND   **Rental cars** owned by local people are available at the port, and you can hire a **taxi** at the dock to take you around or to your hotel if you're spending the night. Taxis are reasonably priced, but an even better bet are the so-called **dollar cabs,** which take you anywhere on the island for a small fee. They don't seem to have a regular schedule—you just flag one down. Before going to your hotel, drop in at the circular **Tourist Information Centre** (you'll see it right on the beach). Here you can ask for a driver who's familiar with the attractions of the island (all of them are). You should negotiate the fare in advance.

WHERE TO STAY

✪ **Frangipani Hotel.** P.O. Box 1, Bequia, The Grenadines, St. Vincent, W.I. ☎ **809/ 458-3255.** Fax 809/458-3824. 15 rms, 10 with bath. Winter, $35 single without bath, $120–$130 single with bath; $55 double without bath, $130–$150 double with bath. Off-season, $30 single without bath, $80–$100 single with bath; $40 double without bath, $90–$120 double with bath. Extra person $25. Children 12 and under $15. AE, MC, V.

The core of this pleasant guest house originated as the private, shingle-covered home of a 19th-century sea captain. Since it was transformed into a hotel it has added accommodations that border a sloping tropical garden in back. The complex overlooks the island's most historic harbor, Admiralty Bay, and is the preferred venue for many clients who return to it every year. The five rooms in the original house are smaller and much less glamorous (and cheaper) than the better-accessorized accommodations in the garden. The garden units are handcrafted from local stone and hardwoods, and have tile floors, carpets of woven hemp, wooden furniture (some of which was made on St. Vincent), and balconies. The in-house restaurant is designed in an open-sided format overlooking the yacht harbor. Guests can rent the tennis courts at a neighboring hotel, or arrange for scuba, sailboat rides, or other water sports nearby. (The nearest scuba outfitter, Sunsports, is fully accredited by PADI.) The hotel presents live music every Monday night in winter, and an outdoor barbecue every Thursday night at 7:30pm, with a steel band.

Julie's and Isola's Guest House. P.O. Box 12, Port Elizabeth, Bequia, The Grenadines, St. Vincent, W.I. ☎ **809/458-3304.** Fax 809/458-3812. 20 rms. Year-round, $36 single; $59 double. Rates include half board. MC, V.

These twin establishments are owned by two of the most kindhearted hoteliers on the island, Julie and Isola McIntosh. Julie, a mason, laid many of the bricks for both hotels, which lie across the street from one another about a block from the water in the center of Port Elizabeth. Isola's Guest House is the more modern; Julie's is slightly older. The rooms tend to be hot, small, and noisy at times, but it's an enduring favorite nonetheless. Good West Indian food is served in the dining room. The bill of fare is likely to include pumpkin fritters, very fresh fish, and curried dishes.

Keegan's Guest House. Lower Bay, Bequia, The Grenadines, St. Vincent, W.I. ☎ **809/ 458-3530.** Fax 809/457-3313. 8 rms, 1 apt. Year-round, $40–$50 single; $65–$80 double; $300–$425 per week apt for one to four. Room (but not apt) rates include breakfast and dinner. Extra person $30. No credit cards.

Ringed with white-painted picket fences that separate its sandy garden from the unpaved road outside, this is a simple but clean and respectable guest house adjacent to Lower Bay Beach. Built in the early 1980s, it presents an angular white-fronted facade, an uncomplicated interior, and well-swept verandas. Rates are low by almost anyone's standards, and include breakfast and dinner as part of the year-round price. All rooms have ceiling fans, tile-covered floors, off-white walls, maid service, and (on the upper floors) narrow balconies; the apartment has a kitchenette. There's a kiosk-style beach bar. The food is simple and based on West Indian traditions, with ample use of chicken, vegetables, conch, and local fish.

Kingsville Apartments. P.O. Box 41, Lower Bay, Bequia, The Grenadines, St. Vincent, W.I. ☎ **809/458-3404.** Fax 809/458-3000. 8 apts with kitchenette. Year-round, $65 one-bedroom apt for one or two; $95 two-bedroom apt for two to four. Extra person $20; children 9 and under stay free in parents' room. MC, V.

These cottage-style apartments on sunny flatlands near Lower Bay Beach are relatively isolated, but only a 5-minute walk from several restaurants. The interiors of each unit are simple but efficient, with ceiling fans. There are very few amenities (no pool, no outdoor barbecue, and no amusements other than what you arrange on your own), but the nearest beach is lined with almond trees whose screens contribute to sunbathers' sense of privacy, and the costs are low enough to permit almost anyone to stay within a budget. The owners are Kay King and her husband, both of whom are natives of nearby St. Vincent. Linens and towels are included with each rental, but after your initial check-in there's only very limited maid service.

WHERE TO EAT

The food is good and healthful here—lobster, chicken, and steaks from such fish as dolphin, kingfish, and grouper, plus tropical fruits, fried plantain, and coconut and guava puddings made fresh daily. Even the beach bars are kept spotless.

Frangipani. In the Hotel Frangipani, Port Elizabeth. ☎ **809/458-3255.** Reservations required for dinner. Main courses EC$20–EC$50 ($7.40–$18.50); fixed-price meal EC$42–EC$80 ($15.50–$29.60); Thurs barbecue EC$65 ($24.10). AE, MC, V. Daily 7:30am–5pm and 7–9pm. Closed Sept. CARIBBEAN.

This waterside dining room is one of the best restaurants on the island. The yachting crowd often comes ashore to dine here. With the exception of the juicy steaks imported for barbecues, only local food is used in the succulent specialties. Lunches, served throughout the day, include sandwiches, salads, and seafood platters. Dinner specialties include conch chowder, baked chicken with rice-and-coconut stuffing, lobster, and an array of fresh fish. A fixed-price menu is available, or you can order à la carte. A Thursday-night barbecue with live entertainment is an island event.

Friendship Bay Resort. Port Elizabeth. ☎ **809/458-3222.** Reservations required for dinner. Main courses EC$32–EC$75 ($11.85–$27.75); lunch EC$18–EC$45 ($6.65–$16.65). MC, V. Daily noon–3pm and 7:30–10pm. Closed Sept–Oct 15. INTERNATIONAL / WEST INDIAN.

Guests dine in a candlelit room high above a sweeping expanse of seafront on a hillside rich with the scent of frangipani and hibiscus. Lunch is served at the beach bar, but dinner is more elaborate. It might include grilled lobster in season, curried beef, grilled or broiled fish (served Créole style with a spicy sauce), shrimp curry, and charcoal-grilled steak flambé. Dishes are flavorsome and well prepared. An island highlight is the Friday- and Saturday-night jump-up and barbecue.

EXPLORING THE ISLAND

Obviously, the secluded beaches are tops on everyone's list of Bequia's attractions. As you walk along the beaches, especially near Port Elizabeth, you'll see craftspeople building boats by hand, a method they learned from their ancestors. Whalers sometimes still set out from here in wooden boats with hand harpoons, just as they do from a port village on St. Vincent.

Dive Bequia, Gingerbread House, Admiralty Bay (P.O. Box 16), Bequia, St. Vincent, W.I. (☎ 809/458-3504), specializes in diving and snorkeling. Scuba dives cost $50 for 1, $85 for 2 in the same day, and $400 for a 10-dive package. Introductory lessons go for $15 each per person. A 4-dive open-water certification course is $400. A snorkeling trip is $15 per person. These prices include all the necessary equipment.

The main harbor village, **Port Elizabeth,** is known for its safe anchorage, Admiralty Bay. The bay was a haven in the 17th century for the British, French, and Spanish navies, as well as for pirates. Descendants of Captain Kydd (a.k.a. Kidd) still live on the island. Today the yachting set "from anywhere" puts in here, often bringing a kind of excitement to the locals.

Frankly, after you leave Port Elizabeth there aren't many sights, and you might have a long, leisurely lunch and then spend some time on a beach. However, you'll pass a fort with a harbor view, and drive on to Industry Estates, which has a Beach House restaurant serving a fair lunch. At **Paget Farm** you can wander into an old whaling village, and maybe inspect a few jawbones left over from the catches of yesterday.

At Moonhole there's a vacation and retirement community built into the cliffs, really free-form sculpture. These are private homes, of course, and you're not to enter without permission. For a final look at Bequia, head up an 800-foot hill that the local people call **"The Mountain."** From that perch, you'll have a 360° view of St. Vincent and the Grenadines to the south.

SHOPPING

This is not a particularly good reason to come to Bequia, but there is some.

The Crab Hole. Next door to the Plantation House, Admiralty Bay. ☎ **809/458-3290.**

At shops scattered along the water you can buy hand-screened cotton made by Bequians. The best of these is the Crab Hole, where they invite guests to visit their silk-screen factory in back. Later you can make purchases at their shop in front, including sterling-silver and 14-karat-gold jewelry.

Noah's Arkade. In the Frangipani Hotel, Port Elizabeth. ☎ **809/458-3424.**

Island entrepreneur Lavinia Gunn sells Vincentian and Bequian batiks, scarves, hats, T-shirts, and a scattering of pottery. There are also dolls, placemats, baskets, and homemade jellies concocted from grapefruit, mango, and guava, plus West Indian cookbooks and books on tropical flowers and reef fish.

UNION ISLAND

Midway between Grenada and St. Vincent, Union Island is the southernmost of the Grenadines. It's known for its dramatic 900-foot peak, Mount Parnassus, which is seen by yachting people from miles away. For those cruising in the area, Union is the port of entry for St. Vincent. Yachters are required to check with Customs upon entry.

Perhaps you'll sail into Union on a night when the locals are having a "big drum" dance—costumed islanders dance and chant to the beat of drums made of goatskin.

GETTING THERE   The island is reached either by chartered or scheduled aircraft, by cargo boat, by private yacht, or by mail boat (see "Getting There" in section 3 on St. Vincent and at the beginning of this section). Both **Air Martinique** (☎ **809/ 458-4528**) and **LIAT** (☎ **809/457-1821**) fly onto Union Island.

WHERE TO STAY & EAT

Anchorage Yacht Club. Clifton, Union Island, The Grenadines, St. Vincent, W.I. ☎ **809/ 458-8221.** Fax 809/458-8365. 6 rms, 3 bungalows, 3 apts. A/C. Winter, $110 double; $150 bungalow or apt. Off-season, $90 double; $140 bungalow or apt. Rates include continental breakfast. Extra person $35. MC, V.

This club occupies a prominent position a few steps from the bumpy airplane landing strip that services at least two nearby resorts (Petit St. Vincent and Palm Island) and about a half-dozen small islands nearby. As a result, something of an airline hub aura permeates the place as passengers shuttle between their airplanes, boats, and the establishment's bar and restaurant. Although at least two other hotels are nearby, this is the most important. It combines a threefold function as a hotel, a restaurant, and a bar, with (under different management) a busy marine-service facility in the same scrubby, concrete-sided compound. Each bedroom is set between a pair of airy verandas and has white tile floors and simple, somewhat-sunbleached modern furniture. The most popular units are the bungalows and cabañas beside the beach.

The yachting club meets in the wood-and-stone bar, where you can order meals for EC$80 ($29.60) and up. The menu might include fish soup, a wide array of fresh fish, and Créole versions of lamb, pork, and beef. Try the mango daiquiri. The bar is open all day and into the night, but meals are served daily: breakfast from 7 to 10am, lunch from noon to 2:30pm, and dinner from 7 to 10:30pm.

MAYREAU

A tiny cay, 1½ square miles of land in the Grenadines, Mayreau is a privately owned island shared by super-expensive Saltwhistle Bay Club and a little hilltop village of about 170 inhabitants. It's on the route of the mail boat that plies the seas to and from St. Vincent, visiting also Canouan and Union Island.

WHERE TO STAY & EAT

Dennis' Hideaway. Saline Bay, Mayreau Island, The Grenadines, St. Vincent, W.I. ☎ and fax **809/458-8594.** 2 rms, neither with bath. Winter, $50 single; $70 double. Off-season, $40 single; $50 double. Rates include breakfast. AE, MC, V.

Most of the energy here goes into the restaurant and supermarket, although its bedrooms are available to overnight guests. All electricity is produced by the complex's own generator. The isolation contributes to a neighborly sense of raffish fun. The bedrooms have ceiling fans and simple but solid furniture. Dennis will charm and entertain you while you enjoy lunch or dinner here. On some nights he even plays the guitar. The view alone would justify coming here, but the West Indian food is another good reason. Since there's water in all directions, seafood is naturally the choice on the bill of fare. The selection might include lobster, shrimp, or conch. For those who want meat, Dennis usually has lamb or pork chops. A steel band plays on Wednesday and Saturday nights when bountiful buffets are featured.

5 Grenada

Its political troubles now over, this sleepy island is a good place to relax in the midst of fairly friendly people and the lovely and popular white sands of Grand Anse Beach. Exploring the lush interior, especially Grand Etang National Park, is worthwhile. Crisscrossed by nature trails and filled with dozens of secluded coves and sandy beaches, Grenada has moved beyond the 1980s and is now a safe and secure place to visit. It's not necessarily for the serious party person—and definitely not for those seeking action at the casino. Instead, it attracts visitors who like snorkeling, sailing, fishing, and doing nothing more invigorating than lolling on a beach under the sun.

Because it shelters so many elegant inns and hotels, Grenada has long been known as an upmarket target for well-heeled visitors, some of whom arrive on yachts. However, in recent years it has developed a number of at least moderately priced inns and small hotels, even guest houses, which make traveling here much more possible than ever for the budget traveler. Even cheaper is the offshore island of Carriacou, which is—until it's discovered—one of the major bargains of the Caribbean.

Grenada has any number of inexpensive places to eat, cheap eateries existing alongside the more expensive restaurants. Unlike many islands of the Caribbean, Grenada has abundant produce, so all the foodstuff doesn't have to be imported—hence, the lower costs in restaurants that rely on locally produced items.

The "Spice Island," Grenada is an independent three-island nation that includes Carriacou, the largest of the Grenadines, and Petit Martinique. The air on Grenada is full of the fragrance of spice and exotic fruits; the island has more spices per square mile than any other place in the world—cloves, cinnamon, mace, cocoa, tonka beans, ginger, and a third of the world's supply of nutmeg. "Drop a few seeds anywhere," the locals will tell you, "and you have an instant garden." The central area is like a jungle of palms, oleander, bougainvillea, purple and red hibiscus, crimson anthurium, bananas, breadfruit, birdsong, ferns, and palms.

The southernmost of the Windward Islands, Grenada (pronounced "Gre-*nay*-dah") lies 60 miles southwest of St. Vincent and about 90 miles north of Trinidad. An oval island, it's 21 miles long and about 12 miles wide, and is volcanic in origin.

Grenada has a **People to People** program that allows you to meet the doctor, the waiter, or the spice-basket maker. This free program matches visitors to the island with Grenadians who share similar interests. Just write to New Trends Tours (see below), requesting an introduction. Be sure to specify your interests and what you'd like to do on the island—play golf, have lunch, go to church—or specify the profession of the person you'd like to meet. If you're already on Grenada, stop by the New Trends Tours office. For more information on Grenada's "People to People" program, contact New Trends Tours, P.O. Box 797, St. George's, Grenada, W.I. (☎ 473/444-1236). Contact them directly by phone or send a self-addressed stamped envelope.

GETTING THERE

The **Point Salines International Airport** lies at the southwestern toe of Grenada. Most of the major hotels are only 5 to 15 minutes away by taxi.

American Airlines (☎ 800/433-7300) offers a daily morning flight from Kennedy in New York to San Juan, with connections to Grenada. If you live in many cities of the southeast, such as Atlanta, the better connection is via Miami.

BWIA (☎ 800/538-2942) has nonstop service from New York's Kennedy airport on Thursday and Sunday. The rest of the week it flies from Kennedy to Grenada with stopovers on either Antigua, St. Lucia, or Barbados.

LIAT (☎ 473/462-0700) also has scheduled service between Barbados and Grenada, as well as to the smaller neighboring island of Carriacou (see below). There are at least four flights daily between Barbados and Grenada, although flights are sometimes cancelled with little notice. We've often spent hours and hours waiting in the Barbados airport for a plane. Through either LIAT or BWIA you can connect on Barbados with several international airlines, including British Airways, Air Canada, American Airlines, and Air France.

In addition, **British Airways** (☎ 800/247-9297 in the U.S., or 0345/22211 in Britain) flies to Grenada every Thursday and Saturday from London's Gatwick Airport, making a single stop at Antigua en route.

GETTING AROUND

BY BUS　Minivans, charging EC$1 to EC$6 (35¢ to $2.20), are the most economical means of transport, although they're likely to be overcrowded and erratic in their schedules. The most popular run is between St. George's and Grand Anse Beach. Most minivans depart from Market Square or from the Esplanade area of St. George's.

BY TAXI　Rates are set by the government. Most arriving visitors take a cab at the Point Salines International Airport to one of the hotels near St. George's, at a cost of about $10. Add 33¹/₃% to the fare from 6pm to 6am. You can also use most taxi drivers as a guide for a day's sightseeing, and the cost can be divided among three or four passengers. The price is to be negotiated, depending on what you want to do.

BY RENTAL CAR　First, you must remember to *drive on the left.* A U.S., British, or Canadian driver's license is valid on Grenada; however, you must obtain a local permit, costing EC$30 ($11.10), before getting onto the roads. These permits can be obtained either from the car-rental companies or from the traffic department on the Carenage in St. George's. You can often do better renting a car from a local firm instead of one of the big three such as Hertz or Avis. Try **David's** (☎ 473/444-4404), with five locations on the island, including the main one at Point Salines International Airport. Cars are rented for $45 to $50 a day. Prices are competitive at **McIntyre Brothers,** True Blue area, in St. George's (☎ 473/444-2899).

A word of warning about local drivers: There's such a thing as a Grenadian driving machismo where the drivers take blind corners with abandon. An extraordinary number of accidents are reported in the lively local paper. Gird yourself with nerves of steel, don't drink and drive, and be extra alert for children and roadside pedestrians while driving at night. In fact, try to avoid night driving if possible.

FAST FACTS: Grenada

Banks　In St. George's, the capital, you'll find **Barclay's,** at Church and Halifax streets (☎ 473/400-3232); **Scotiabank,** on Halifax Street (☎ 473/440-3274); the **National Commercial Bank (NCB),** at the corner of Halifax and Hillsborough streets (☎ 473/440-3566); the **Grenada Bank of Commerce,** at the corner of Halifax and Cross streets (☎ 473/440-3521); and the **Grenada Cooperative Bank,** on Church Street (☎ 473/440-2111).

Currency　The official currency is the **Eastern Caribbean dollar (EC$),** worth about 37¢ U.S. Always determine which dollars—EC or U.S.—you're talking about when someone on Grenada quotes you a price. In this section we've cited prices in U.S. dollars unless otherwise indicated.

Grenada

Documents Proof of citizenship is needed to enter the country. A passport is preferred, but a birth certificate or voter registration card is accepted for American and Canadian citizens, and British subjects, providing they also have photo ID.

Electricity Electricity is supplied on the island by Grenada Electricity Services. It's 220–240 volts AC, 50 cycles, so transformers and adapters will be needed for U.S.–made appliances.

Embassies and High Commissions Grenada, unlike many of its neighbors, has a **U.S. Embassy,** at Point Salines at St. George's (☎ **473/444-1173**). It also has a **British High Commission,** on Church Street, St. George's (☎ **473/440-3536**).

Emergencies Dial ☎ **911** to summon the **police,** report a **fire,** or call an **ambulance.**

Information In the United States, the **Grenada Tourist Office** is at 820 Second Ave., Suite 900D, New York, NY 10017 (☎ **800/927-9554** or 212/687-9554). In Canada, contact the **Grenada Board of Tourism,** 439 University Ave., Suite 820, Toronto, ON M5G 1Y8 (☎ **416/595-1339**); and in London, contact the **Grenada Board of Tourism,** 1 Collingham Gardens, London, SW5 OHW (☎ **0171/370-5164**).

Once on the island, go to the **Grenada Board of Tourism,** The Carenage, in St. George's (☎ **473/440-2279**), open Monday to Friday from 8am to 4pm. Maps, guides, and general information are available.

Language   English is commonly spoken on this island of 100,000 people because of the long years of British influence. However, now and then you'll hear people speaking in a French–African patois handed down from long ago.

Medical Care   There's a general hospital, **St. George's Hospital,** Grand Etang Road (☎ 473/440-2051), with an x-ray department and operating theater. Private doctors and nurses are available on call.

Pharmacies   Try **Gittens Pharmacy,** Halifax Street, St. George's (☎ 473/440-2165), open Monday to Wednesday and Friday from 8am to 6pm, Thursday from 8am to 5pm, and Saturday from 8am to 3pm.

Post Office   The General Post Office in St. George's is open Monday to Thursday from 8am to 4pm, with a lunch break from 11:45am to 1pm, and on Friday from 8am to 5pm. It's closed on Saturday and Sunday.

Safety   Crime is on the rise on Grenada. Don't go walking on the beach at night. In fact, it's unwise to go walking anywhere after dark—take a taxi to where you're going. Tourists have been attacked by locals with machetes held at their throats while they were robbed. The island is generally safe during the day if the usual precautions are taken.

Service   A 10% service charge is added to most restaurant and hotel bills.

Taxes   A 10% VAT (value-added tax) is imposed on food and beverages, and there's an 8% room tax. Upon leaving Grenada, you must fill out an immigration card and pay a departure tax of EC$35 ($13).

Telecommunications   International telephone service is available 24 hours a day from pay phones. Public telegraph, Telex, and fax services are also provided from the Carenage offices of **Grenada Telecommunications Ltd.** (Grentel) in St. George's (☎ 473/440-1000 for all Grentel offices), open Monday to Friday from 7:30am to 6pm, on Saturday from 7:30am to 1pm, and on Sunday and holidays from 10am to noon. To call another number on Grenada, omit the 473 area code and dial all seven digits of the local number.

Weather   Grenada has two distinct seasons, dry and rainy. The dry season is January to May; the rest of the year is the rainy season, although the rainfall doesn't last long. The average temperature is 80° Fahrenheit. Because of constant trade winds, there's little humidity.

WHERE TO STAY

Don't forget that your hotel or inn will probably add a service charge to your bill—ask in advance about this. Also, there's an 8% government tax on food and beverage tabs.

DOUBLES FOR LESS THAN $40

Bailey's Inn. Spring (P.O. Box 82), St. George's, Grenada, W.I. ☎ **473/440-2912.** Fax 473/440-0532. 9 rms, 1 two-bedroom apt with kitchenette. Year-round, $20 single; $40 double; $68 two-bedroom apt for four. No credit cards.

This is about as simple a lodging as this guidebook is willing to recommend, but if you adjust your expectations accordingly, you might appreciate its position on a hillside above the wharves, shops, and cheap restaurants of St. George's. It's a two-story building painted in a medley of whites, browns, and golds, owned for four decades by Mrs. Muriel Bailey. The bedrooms have white walls, angular wooden furnishings, ceiling fans, and floors that are covered either in tiles or carpeting. The beach (Grand Anse) lies within a 15-minute drive.

Mamma's Lodge. Lagoon Rd. (P.O. Box 248), St. George's, Grenada, W.I. ☎ **473/440-1623.** Fax 473/440-4181. 18 rms. Year-round, $29.70 single; $42 double; $60 triple. Rates include breakfast. No credit cards.

This is the bargain of Grenada. Mamma's is named after the island's most celebrated cook (now deceased) who became famous in the press during the U.S. invasion of Grenada. Her restaurant, Mamma's (see "Where to Eat," below), became a hangout for U.S. service personnel. The lodge is about 5 minutes from Grand Anse Beach and about 3 minutes from St. George's. It's also only a 5-minute walk from Mamma's award-winning restaurant. Built in the typical two-floor motel style, it's locally owned and managed. The rooms are cooled by ceiling fans, and furnishings are rather sparse.

St. Ann's Guest House. Paddock, St. George's, Grenada, W.I. ☎ **473/440-2717.** 12 rms, 6 with bath. Year-round, $18 single without bath, $22 single with bath; $27 double without bath, $35 double with bath; $47 triple with bath. Rates include breakfast. No credit cards.

Family-owned and -operated, and lying on the outskirts of St. George's, this place is about as simple as you'd want to get. Yet, for some, it offers one of the bargains of the island. The atmosphere is homelike and inviting. A regular bus runs into the city or to Grand Anse Beach (public transportation tends to be very crowded). Close to the Botanical Gardens and the yacht harbor, the guest house is also near a cinema and a supermarket where you can find the makings of a picnic lunch. Guests also have use of a small bar and games room, and dinner can be provided upon request, although breakfast is included in the rates.

Doubles for Less than $65 (Winter) / $55 (Off-Season)

Camerhogne Park Hotel. Grand Anse (P.O. Box 378), St. George's, Grenada, W.I. ☎ **473/444-4587.** Fax 473/444-4847. 25 rms. A/C TV TEL. Winter, $55–$65 single or double. Off-season, $45–$65 single or double. Year-round, apt $90–$150. AE, DC, MC, V.

About a 5-minute stroll over to the fabled sands of Grand Anse Beach, this family-owned and -operated hotel lies about a 10-minute drive to the international airport at Point Salines. The rooms are simply but comfortably furnished and have more amenities than many comparably priced hotels, including both air-conditioning and ceiling fans. Most rooms have verandas as well. For stays of 6 or more nights, guests are granted a 10% discount. There's a restaurant on the premises that makes use of Grenadian produce when available. There's also a bar. The staff will help you arrange tours of the island and a car rental if you'd like to go exploring for the day.

Wave Crest Holiday Apartments. P.O. Box 278, Grand Anse, St. George's, Grenada, W.I. ☎ **473/444-4116.** Fax 473/444-4847. 18 apts with kitchenette. A/C TV TEL. Winter, $75 one-bedroom apt for two; $100 two-bedroom apt for four. Off-season, $65 one-bedroom apt for two; $90 two-bedroom apt for four. AE, MC, V.

Set amid a hilly landscape on the outskirts of St. George's, this small hotel and apartment compound was built in stages between 1980 and 1992. In 1994, what had become a complex of four independent buildings (all with white walls, red roofs, and vaguely Mediterranean styling) were completely renovated by the owners and founders, John and Joyce DaBreo. The bedrooms have white walls, mahogany furniture (much of it built on the island), carpets laid over tile floors, and—in some cases— views of the ocean. It's a 7-minute walk to Grand Anse Beach, and a handful of inexpensive diners and bars are nearby. No meals other than breakfast are served.

Doubles for Less than $90 (Winter) / $70 (Off-Season)

Cedars Inn. True Blue (P.O. Box 73), St. George's, Grenada, W.I. ☎ **800/223-6510** in the U.S., or 473/444-4641. Fax 473/444-4652. 20 rms and apts. A/C TV TEL. Winter, $80–$90 single or double; $95–$105 apt. Off-season, $60–$70 single or double; $65–$75 apt. Extra person $20; children 11 and under stay free in parents' room. MAP $30 per person extra. AE, DC, MC, V.

Conveniently located only minutes from both the international airport and Grenada's main attraction, Grand Anse Beach, this is a two-floor block of rooms and apartments. Each accommodation opens onto a private patio and contains a private bath. The setting is in a tropical landscape, although the rooms themselves are in a very simple motel-type style. West Indian meals are served in the hotel restaurant, and guests can also enjoy the pool bar. There's a free shuttle to take guests to the airport.

Hibiscus Hotel. Grand Anse (P.O. Box 279), St. George's, Grenada, W.I. ☎ **800/322-1753** in the U.S., or 473/444-4233. Fax 473/444-2873. 7 rms. A/C TV TEL. Year-round, $65 single; $80 double. Extra person $20; children 11 and under stay free in parents' room. MAP $25 per person extra. AE.

Right on Grand Anse Beach, near many of the super-expensive properties, this is one of the best of the small economical hotels on the island. In landscaped gardens, it lies only about a 2-minute stroll to Grand Anse. In about 7 minutes (by car) you'll be in the heart of St. George's; it's also convenient to the airport. Five cottages contain two rooms; and the other two rentals are in the building housing a bar.

✪ **La Sagesse Nature Center.** St. David's (P.O. Box 44), St. George's, Grenada, W.I. ☎ **473/444-6458.** Fax 473/444-6458. 3 apts, 1 honeymoon cottage. MINIBAR TV TEL. Winter, $70 apt for one; $80 apt for two; $90 cottage. Off-season, $50 apt for one; $60 apt for two; $75 cottage. AE, MC, V.

On a sandy, tree-lined beach 10 miles from Point Salines International Airport, La Sagesse consists of a seaside guest house, restaurant, bar, and art and pottery gallery, with water sports and satellite TV. Nearby are trails for hiking and exploring, a haven for wading and shore birds, hummingbirds, hawks, and ducks. Rivers, mangroves, and a salt pond sanctuary enhance the natural beauty of the place. The original Great House of what was once La Sagesse plantation contains three apartments, one with a fully equipped kitchen. The restaurant/bar specializes in lobster, fresh fish, and salads. You must book early in winter.

No Problem Apartment Hotel. True Blue (P.O. Box 280), St. George's, Grenada, W.I. ☎ **800/74-CHARMS** in the U.S., or 473/444-4634. Fax 473/444-2803. 20 suites. A/C TV TEL. Winter, $75–$85 single or double. Off-season, $55–$65 single or double. Extra person $20. MAP $30 per person extra. AE, MC, V.

An all-suite hotel 5 minutes from Point Salines Airport and Grand Anse Beach, these one-bedroom apartments are housed in a two-story motel unit. They offer one of the best deals on the island. The simply furnished suites open onto a swimming pool and bar area. Each is equipped with such amenities as a radio, satellite TV, phone, and alarm clock, as well as a fully equipped kitchenette. Baby-sitting can be arranged, and laundry service is provided. Thoughtful extras include a help-yourself coffee bar and free bicycles. There's also a reading room. The place has one of the most helpful staffs on the island.

BEST OFF-SEASON BET

Blue Horizons Cottage Hotel. P.O. Box 41, Grand Anse, Grenada, W.I. ☎ **473/444-4316.** Fax 473/444-4807. 36 cottages. A/C TV TEL. Winter, $160–$180 cottage for two. Off-season, $110–$120 cottage for two. Extra person $35–$50. AE, DC, DISC, MC, V.

The co-owners Royston and Arnold Hopkin purchased this place from a bankrupt estate. Sons of the famous Grenadian hotelkeepers Audrey and Curtis Hopkin, they transformed the neglected property into one of the finest on the island. The cottages are spread throughout a flowering garden of $6^1/4$ acres. Rates depend on the category of the cottage: standard, superior, or deluxe. Each has an efficiency kitchen and comfortable solid mahogany furniture. In winter, rates are $140 to $155 in a cottage for one and $160 to $180 in a cottage for two. However, off-season, prices drop to $105 for a cottage for one and $110 to $120 for a cottage for two. Children are welcome, and they can watch the 21 varieties of native birds said to inhabit the grounds.

Guests who prefer to cook in their rooms can buy supplies from a Food Fair at Grand Anse, a 10-minute walk away. Most important, Grand Anse Beach is only 5 minutes away on foot. On the grounds is one of the best restaurants on the island, La Belle Créole. Lunch is served around a pool bar. Laundry, baby-sitting, and room service are provided.

WORTH A SPLURGE

✪ **Flamboyant Hotel.** P.O. Box 214, Grand Anse Beach, St. George's, Grenada, W.I. ☎ 473/444-4247. Fax 473/444-1234. 32 rms, 8 suites. A/C MINIBAR TV TEL. Winter, $110 single; $125 double; $145 one-bedroom suite for two; $250 two-bedroom suite for four. Off-season, $80 single; $90 double; $100 one-bedroom suite for two; $150 two-bedroom suite for four. Extra person $35 each. MAP $40 extra per adult, $20 extra per child 11 and under. AE, DC, DISC, MC, V.

This hotel is a well-established staple on the island's touristic landscape, and until its room count was surpassed by better-funded rivals, it was one of the larger hotels on the island. It occupies a hillside that slopes down to Grand Anse Beach, a neighborhood peppered with other resorts. It was designed as a complex of modern, red-roofed buildings punctuated with an outdoor swimming pool. The management conscientiously arranges parties, crab races, barbecues, dinner dances, and reggae bands several nights a week. Each accommodation has a loggia-style balcony overlooking the beach, cream-colored walls, tile floors, and floral-patterned curtains and upholsteries; the suites contain kitchenettes. There's a minimart selling food supplies and a gift shop, and snorkeling equipment is lent free to residents.

True Blue Inn. Old Mill Ave., True Blue (P.O. Box 308), St. George's, Grenada, W.I. ☎ 800/742-4276 in the U.S., or 473/444-2000. Fax 473/444-1247. 5 apts, 2 cottages. A/C TV TEL. Winter, $135 one-bedroom apt; $180 two-bedroom cottage. Off-season, $90 one-bedroom apt; $125 two-bedroom cottage. MAP $35 per person extra. AE, DC, MC, V.

On the south coast of Grenada, about 5 minutes by car from the Point Salines airport and Grand Anse Beach, this resort takes its name "blue" from an old indigo plantation that once stood on this spot. It's appropriately named even for today's site, because of the panoramic views of the blue waters of Prickly Bay. You can select one-bedroom apartments with verandas overlooking the bay, or two-bedroom cottages nestled in tropical gardens. Children can stay in the two cottages (not the one-bedroom apartments). The accommodations are tastefully furnished in pastels and tropical rattan pieces. Each unit has a fully equipped kitchen with gas stove and large refrigerator. You can scuba dive or snorkel from the hotel's own private dock, and there's also an on-site pool. Boaters frequent the hotel's restaurant and bar, serving an international and Caribbean menu.

WHERE TO EAT

Bird's Nest. Grand Anse. ☎ 473/444-4264. Reservations recommended. Main courses EC$24–EC$55 ($8.90–$20.35). AE, MC, V. Daily 9am–11pm. CHINESE/CREOLE.

For change of pace, we suggest the Bird's Nest, in its own building with three palm trees at the entrance. It's 3 miles north of the airport, opposite the Grenada Renaissance. This family business offers Chinese food, mainly Szechuan and Cantonese, along with seafood and Caribbean cuisine. You'll see the familiar shrimp eggrolls along with eight different chow meins. Sweet-and-sour fish is a favorite, and daily specials are posted. A take-out service is available. This may not be the world's greatest Chinese restaurant, and some dishes are short on flavor, but it's generally satisfying and it's something different. Sandwiches can be ordered for lunch.

The Boatyard. L'Anse-aux-Epines, Prickly Bay. ☎ **473/444-4662.** Reservations recommended. Main courses EC$15–EC$70 ($5.60–$25.90). AE, MC, V. Mon–Sat 11am–11pm. INTERNATIONAL.

A favorite hangout of the island's medical students, this restaurant is situated on the water overlooking the marina where the yachts are moored. Lunch consists of a Caribbean daily special, and may include stewed pork or Créole chicken served in a tomato-based sauce with rice. Some of the featured dishes include stewed and barbecued chicken, Créole fish, and grilled steak; most are served with rice, salad, and ground vegetables. On Friday nights a steel-drum band plays, and when they're done the sound system is cranked up for indoor-outdoor dancing to the wee hours.

Delicious Landing. The Carenage. ☎ **473/440-9747.** Main courses EC$15–EC$28 ($5.55–$10.35). MC, V. Mon–Sat 8am–11pm. INTERNATIONAL / WEST INDIAN.

This place was originally built as a warehouse at the extreme tip of the northern edge of the Carenage, but when someone added a waterfront veranda to the boxy, unimaginative building, it was immediately transformed into the most desirable perch along the waterfront. The place is best suited for a midday pick-me-up, with or without alcohol, partly because of the cool breezes that blow in off the port. Cocktails include U.S. bombers, mango daiquiris, and an especially potent concoction the owners refer to as "navy grog." Menu items include such West Indian dishes as lambi (conch) chowder, sandwiches, and the most popular dish on the menu, lobster pando, a form of ragoût. We wouldn't say it's the best cooking in town, but it's quite competent and you get good value here.

Deyna's. Melville St., St. George's. ☎ **473/440-6795.** Main courses EC$15–EC$60 ($5.55–$22.20); lunch from EC$10.50 ($3.90). No credit cards. Mon–Sat 8am–9pm, Sun 10am–4pm. CREOLE.

This local dive has some true island flavor. It's not much on decor, but it has its faithful followers who come here often for lunch, at which time they can order well-stuffed sandwiches. Otherwise, the lunch and dinner menus are much the same. Although Mamma's might do it better, you can still dine well here eating as the islanders do. That means baked chicken, conch with breadfruit, and stewed fish, served with locally grown vegetables. Many dishes are given added zest by the use of various curries.

✪ **Mamma's.** Lagoon Rd., St. George's. ☎ **473/440-1459.** Reservations required a day in advance. Fixed-price meal EC$45 ($16.65). No credit cards. Daily 8am–midnight. CREOLE.

Mamma's lies on the road leading to Grenada Yacht Services. Every trip to the Caribbean should include a visit to an establishment like this. Serving copious meals, this Mamma became particularly famous during the U.S. intervention in Grenada, as U.S. servicepeople adopted her as their own island mama. Mamma (alias Insley Wardally) is now deceased, but her daughter, Cleo, carries on.

Meals, we were told, come in two sizes: "the usual" and "the special." (But we were later told that "the usual" and "the special" were the same.) Either way, meals include such dishes as callaloo soup with coconut cream, shredded cold crab with lime juice, freshwater crayfish, fried conch, and a casserole of cooked bananas, yams, and dasheen, along with ripe baked plantain, and rôtis made of curry and yellow chickpeas, followed by sugar-apple ice cream. Mamma's seafoods are likely to include crab backs, octopus in a hot-and-spicy sauce, and even turtle steak, although the latter could be an endangered species. Mamma is also known for her "wild meats," including armadillo, opossum, monkey (yes, that's right), game birds, and even the endangered iguana. However, "wild things" are only available when Cleo can obtain them. The specialty drink of the house is rum punch—the ingredients are a secret. Dinner here must be reserved a day in advance so you'll be sure of having a choice of 22 different foods from Grenada.

✪ **Morne Fendue.** St. Patrick's. ☎ **473/442-9330.** Reservations required. Fixed-price lunch EC$45 ($16.45). No credit cards. Mon–Sat 12:30–3pm. CREOLE.

As you're touring north from the beach at Grand Anse, one place is memorable. It's Betty Mascoll's Morne Fendue, 25 miles north of St. George's. This 1912 plantation house, constructed the year she was born, is her ancestral home. It was built of carefully chiseled river rocks held together with a mixture of lime and molasses, as was the custom in that day. Mrs. Mascoll and her loyal staff, two of whom have been with her for many years, always need time to prepare for the arrival of guests, so it's imperative to call ahead. Lunch is likely to include yam and sweet-potato casserole, curried chicken with lots of hot spices, and a hotpot of pork and oxtail. Because this is very much a private home, tipping should be performed with the greatest tact. Nonetheless, the hardworking cook and maid seem genuinely appreciative of a gratuity. Mrs. Mascoll is known for introducing her guests to her friends and neighbors on the long verandas beneath the hanging vines of her house. Mrs. Mascoll is now in her 80s and struggling to continue her long tradition of hospitality.

The Nutmeg. The Carenage, St. George's. ☎ **473/440-2539.** Main courses EC$18–EC$55 ($6.65–$20.35). AE, DISC, MC, V. Mon–Sat 8am–11pm, Sun 2–11pm. SEAFOOD/CREOLE.

Right on the harbor, the Nutmeg is over the Sea Change Shop where you can pick up paperbacks and souvenirs. Another rendezvous point for the yachting set and a favorite with just about everybody, it's suitable for a snack or a full-fledged dinner. Its drinks are very good; try one of the Grenadian rum punches made with Angostura bitters, grated nutmeg, rum, lime juice, and syrup. An informal atmosphere prevails, as you're served your filet of fish with potato croquettes and string beans. There's always fresh fish, and usually callaloo soup. Lambi (that ubiquitous conch) is also done very well here. Lobster thermidor is the most expensive item on the menu. There's a small wine list with some California, German, and Italian selections, and you can drop in just for a glass of beer to enjoy the sea view. Sometimes, however, you'll be asked to share a table.

Papa Hall's. At the Cot Bam Resort, Grand Anse. ☎ **473/444-2050.** Reservations recommended. Main courses EC$30–EC$50 ($11.10–$18.50); lunch EC$6–EC$30 ($2.20–$11.10). AE, MC, V. Daily 9am–11pm. CREOLE.

If you're looking for a casual atmosphere with lots of local color, then stop by for a drink and a bite to eat. If you order carefully, you can enjoy a meal at a sensible price especially when the chef decides to run specials. The breakfast choices range in price from EC$15 to EC$19 ($5.60 to $7) and include not only the standard fare of eggs and bacon, but also West Indian favorites such as smoked herring, codfish, and other local fish served with tomatoes, onions, and fresh local vegetables. The lunch and dinner menus include favored choices like Créole fish, calypso chicken, and various curried dishes including beef, lamb, and lobster. If you're looking for rôtis, the selection consists of beef, fish, chicken, shrimp, vegetable, and lamb. Beverages include specialty juices made from seamoss or the bark of the mauby tree and punches made from fresh local fruits and even one made with peanut butter.

Portofino. The Carenage, St. George's. ☎ **473/440-3986.** Reservations recommended. Pastas and pizzas EC$16–EC$40 ($5.90–$14.80); main courses EC$25–EC$59 ($9.25–$21.85). AE, MC, V. Mon–Sat 11am–11pm, Sat–Sun 6–11pm. ITALIAN/SEAFOOD.

The venue is Spartan and simple, with hints of Italy's Portofino. It's not a bad choice, with fine, unpretentious food like pastas, veal, chicken, and Italian-style beef. The restaurant serves the best pizzas in the capital, Italian-style antipasti such as eggplant parmesan, and a good bowl of minestrone. However, the fish and meat dishes are more ordinary, although the catch of the day—served with pasta and fresh vegetables—is usually available, as are shrimp and lobster. The finest pasta dish is the linguine with fresh fish. It also caters to vegetarians with choices like vegetarian lasagne. Live jazz is presented every Friday night, and on Sunday night a festival of Caribbean music is presented, along with candlelight dining and dancing—no cover.

Rick's Café. Grand Anse Shopping Center. ☎ **473/444-4597.** Reservations not accepted. Main courses EC$4.50–EC$30 ($1.70–$11.10). No credit cards. Tues–Thurs 11am–9:30pm, Fri–Sat 11am–10pm, Sun 4–9:30pm. AMERICAN.

The main dining area is bordered on one side by an open kitchen, containing a stone oven and barbecue, and a 30-foot counter complete with stools on the other. The diner-style atmosphere lacking table service offers relatively inexpensive meals. They're not preset; you mix and match items to suit your own taste. For example, if you order barbecued chicken or ribs, you could pair it with a side order of fries or a potato served with your choice of toppings, or if you're famished, a burger. The pizzas are served with a choice of the typical toppings; the most expensive option, a large with six toppings, costs EC$35 ($12.95). At the counter you can dine on banana splits, milkshakes, and 35 to 40 flavors of ice cream, including local favorites like passionfruit, coconut, rum raisin, and soursop.

BEACHES, WATER SPORTS & OTHER OUTDOOR PURSUITS

BEACHES   One of the best beaches in the Caribbean is ✪ **Grand Anse,** 2 miles of sugar-white sands extending into deep waters far offshore. You can also take off and discover dozens more beaches on your own, as they're all public.

DEEP-SEA FISHING   Fishers come here from November to March in pursuit of both blue and white marlin, yellowfin tuna, wahoo, sailfish, and other catches. Most of the bigger hotels have a sports desk that will arrange fishing trips for you. The **Annual Game Fishing Tournament,** held in January, attracts a number of regional and international participants.

Havadu is a 32-foot ocean-going pirogue, available for deep-sea-fishing offshore excursions and snorkeling. Various prices depend on the size of the group. For more information, contact **Best of Grenada,** The Carenage (☎ 473/440-4386).

GOLF   At the **Grenada Golf Course and Country Club,** Woodlands (☎ 473/444-4128), you'll find a nine-hole course, with greens fees of $12 for nine holes. The course is open Monday to Saturday from 8am to sunset and on Sunday from 8am to noon.

SCUBA DIVING & SNORKELING   Along with many other water sports, Grenada offers the diver an underwater world, rich in submarine gardens, exotic fish, and coral formations, sometimes with underwater visibility stretching to 120 feet. Off the coast is the wreck of the ocean liner *Bianca C,* which is nearly 600 feet long. Novice divers might want to stick to the west coast of Grenada, whereas more experienced divers might search out the sights along the rougher Atlantic side.

Daddy Vic's Watersports, in the Grenada Renaissance, Grand Anse Beach (☎ 473/444-4371, ext. 638), is directly on the sands. The premier dive outfit on the island, it offers night dives or two-tank dives for $45, and PADI instructors will offer an open-water certification program for $350 per person.

In addition, this is the best center for other water sports, offering snorkeling trips for $18 (1½ to 2 hours) or windsurfing with board rentals for $16 per hour. Sunfish rentals are $16 per half hour, parasailing is $30 per 10 minutes, jet-skiing runs $44 per half hour, and waterskiing is $15 per run. Even deep-sea-fishing arrangements can be made.

Giving the center serious competition is **Grand Anse Aquatics,** at the Coyaba Beach Resort on Grand Anse Beach (☎ 473/444-4129). A Canadian-run place, it's welcoming and inviting to divers, and there's a PADI instructor on site. The dive boat is well equipped with well-maintained gear. Both scuba diving and snorkeling jaunts to panoramic reefs and shipwrecks teaming with marine life are offered. A single dive costs $40, and a resort course or a night dive is $55. A snorkeling trip can be arranged for just $18. Diving instruction, including a resort course, is available.

If you'd rather strike out on your own, take a drive to Woburn and negotiate with a fisher for a ride to **Glovers Island,** an old whaling station, and snorkel away. Glovers Island is an uninhabited rock spit a few hundred yards offshore from the hamlet of Woburn.

Warning: Divers should know that Grenada doesn't have a decompression chamber. If you should get the bends, you'll have to take an excruciatingly painful air trip to Trinidad.

SAILING   Two large "party boats," designed for 120 and 250 passengers, respectively, operate out of St. George's harbor. The *Rhum Runner* and *Rhum Runner II,* c/o Best of Grenada, P.O. Box 188, St. George's, Grenada, W.I. (☎ 473/440-4FUN), make shuttle-style trips, three times a day, with lots of emphasis on strong liquor, steel-band music, and good times. Four-hour daytime tours, conducted every morning and afternoon, coincide with the arrival of cruise ships, but will carry independent travelers if space is available. Rides cost $20 per person and include snorkeling stops at reefs and beaches along the way. Evening tours are much more frequently attended by island locals, and are more bare-boned, louder, and usually less restrained. They cost $7.50 per person. Regardless of when you take it, your cruise will include rum, reggae music, and lots of hoopla.

TENNIS   Guests at the Secret Harbour, Grenada Renaissance, Calabash, Coyaba Beach Resort, and Twelve Degrees North can avail themselves of those well-kept courts; non-guests can play at these resorts, too.

EXPLORING ST. GEORGE'S & TROPICAL WATERFALLS

Carnival time on Grenada is the second weekend of August, with colorful parades, music, and dancing. The festivities begin on a Friday, continuing practically nonstop to Tuesday. Steel bands and calypso groups perform at Queen's Park. Jouvert, one of the highlights of the festival, begins at 5am on Monday with a parade of Djab Djab / Djab Molassi, devil-costumed figures daubed with a black substance. (*Be warned:* Don't wear your good clothes to attend this event—you may get sticky from close body contact.) The carnival finale, a gigantic "jump-up," ends with a parade of bands from Tanteen through the Carenage into town.

The capital city of Grenada, **St. George's** is one of the most attractive ports in the West Indies. Its landlocked inner harbor is actually the deep crater of a long-dead volcano—or so one is told.

In the town you'll see some of the most charming Georgian colonial buildings to be found in the Caribbean, still standing in spite of a devastating hurricane in 1955. The streets are mostly steep and narrow, which enhances the attractiveness of the ballast bricks, wrought-iron balconies, and red tiles of the sloping roofs. Many of the pastel warehouses date back to the 18th century. Frangipani and flamboyant trees add to the palette of color.

The port, which some have compared to Portofino, Italy, is flanked by old forts and bold headlands. Among the town's attractions is an 18th-century pink Anglican **church,** on Church Street, and the **Market Square** where colorfully attired farm women offer even more colorful produce for sale.

Fort George, on Church Street, built by the French, stands at the entrance to the bay, with subterranean passageways and old guardrooms and cells.

Everyone strolls along the waterfront of **The Carenage** or relaxes on its Pedestrian Plaza, with seats and hanging planters providing shade from the sun.

On this side of town, the **Grenada National Museum,** at the corner of Young and Monckton streets (☎ 473/440-3725), is set in the foundations of an old French army barrack and prison built in 1704. Small but interesting, it houses finds from archaeological digs, including the petroglyphs, native fauna, the first telegraph installed on the island, a rum still, and memorabilia depicting Grenada's history. The most comprehensive exhibit traces the native culture of Grenada. One of the exhibits shows two bathtubs—the wooden barrel used by the fort's prisoners and the carved marble tub used by Joséphine Bonaparte during her adolescence on Martinique. The museum is open Monday to Friday from 9am to 4:30pm and on Saturday from 10am to 1pm. Admission is $2.

The Outer Harbour is also called the **Esplanade.** It's connected to the Carenage by the Sendall Tunnel, which is cut through the promontory known as St. George's Point, dividing the two bodies of water.

You can take a drive up to Richmond Hill where **Fort Frederick** stands. The French began construction on the fort in 1779; however, after Grenada was returned to Britain, following the Treaty of Versailles in 1783, the English carried on the work until its completion in 1791. From its battlements you'll have a superb view of the harbor and of the yacht marina.

An afternoon tour of St. George's and its environs takes you into the mountains northeast of the capital. About a 15-minute drive delivers you to ✪ **Annandale Falls,** a tropical wonderland, where a cascade about 50 feet high falls into a basin. The overall beauty is almost Tahitian, and you can have a picnic surrounded by liana vines, elephant ears, and other tropical flora and spices. The **Annandale Falls Centre** (☎ 473/440-2452) houses gift items, handcrafts, and samples of the indigenous spices of Grenada. Nearby, an improved trail leads to the falls where you can enjoy a refreshing swim. Swimmers can use the changing cubicles at the falls free. The center is open daily from 8am to 4pm.

A SPECTACULAR RAIN FOREST & MORE AROUND THE ISLAND

The next day you can head north out of St. George's along the western coast, taking in beaches, spice plantations, and the fishing villages that are so typical of Grenada.

You pass through **Gouyave,** a spice town, the center of the nutmeg and mace industry. Both spices are produced from a single fruit. Before reaching the village, you can stop at the Dougaldston Estate, where you'll witness the processing of nutmeg and mace.

At the **Grenada Cooperative Nutmeg Association,** near the entrance to Gouyave, huge quantities of the spice are aged, graded, and processed. Most of the work is done within the ocher walls of the factory, which sport such slogans as "Bring God's peace inside and leave the Devil's noise outside." Workers sit on stools in the natural light from the open windows of the aging factory and laboriously sort the raw nutmeg and its by-product, mace, into different baskets for grinding, peeling, and aging. It's open Monday to Friday from 9am to 4pm.

Proceeding along the coast, you reach **Sauteurs,** at the northern tip of Grenada. This is the third-largest town on the island. It was from this great cliff that the Caribs leaped to their deaths instead of facing enslavement by the French.

To the east of Sauteurs is the palm-lined **Levera Beach,** an idyll of sand where the Atlantic meets the Caribbean. This is a great spot for a picnic lunch, but swimming can sometimes be dangerous. On the distant horizon you'll see some of the Grenadines.

Opened in 1994, the 450-acre **Levera National Park** has several white sandy beaches for swimming and snorkeling, although the surf is rough here where the Atlantic meets the Caribbean. It's also a hiker's paradise, and offshore are coral reefs and seagrass beds. The park contains a mangrove swamp, a lake, and a bird sanctuary. Perhaps you'll see a rare tropical parrot. Its interpretative center (☎ **473/ 442-1018**) is open Monday to Friday from 8am to 4pm, on Saturday from 10am to 4pm, and on Sunday from 10am to 5pm.

Heading down the east coast of Grenada, you reach **Grenville,** the island's second city. If possible, pass through here on a Saturday morning when you'll enjoy the hubbub of the native fruit-and-vegetable market. There's also a fish market along the waterfront. A nutmeg factory here welcomes visitors.

From Grenville, you can cut inland into the heart of Grenada. Here you're in a world of luxuriant foliage, passing along nutmeg, banana, and cocoa plantations.

In the center of the island, reached along the major interior road between Grenville and St. George's, is ✪ **Grand Etang National Park,** containing the island's spectacular rain forest, which has been made more accessible by hiking trails. Beginning at the park's forest center, the Morne LeBaye Trail affords a short hike along which you can see to the 2,309-foot Mount Sinai and the east coast. Down the **Grand Etang Road** trails lead to the 2,373-foot summit of Mount Qua Qua and the Ridge, and the Lake Circle Trail, taking hikers on a 30-minute trek along Grand Etang Lake, the crater of an extinct volcano lying in the midst of a forest preserve and bird sanctuary. Among the birds you're likely to see are the yellow-billed cuckoo and the emerald-throated hummingbird. The park is also a playground for Mona monkeys—those that didn't end up in Mamma's stewpot. Covering 13 acres, the water is a cobalt blue. All three trails offer the opportunity to see a wide variety of Grenada's flora and fauna. Guides for the park trails are available, but they must be arranged for in advance. After a rainfall the trails can be very slippery; hikers should wear sneakers or jogging shoes, and carry drinking water as well. Much of the rain falls on Grenada between June and November. The park's **Grand Etang Interpretation (Nature) Centre,** on the shores of Grand Etang Lake (☎ **473/442-7425**), is open Monday to Friday from 8am to 4pm, featuring a video show about the park. An admission of $1 is charged.

You'll then begin your descent from the mountains. Along the way you'll pass hanging carpets of mountain ferns. Going through the tiny hamlets of Snug Corner and Beaulieu, you eventually come back to the capital.

On yet another day you can drive south from St. George's to the beaches and resorts spread along the already much-mentioned **Grand Anse,** which is one of the most beautiful beaches in the West Indies. Water taxis can also take you from the Carenage in St. George's to Grand Anse.

Point Salines, where the airport is located, is at the southwestern tip of the island, where a lighthouse stood for 56 years. A sculpture of the lighthouse has been constructed on the grounds just outside the airport terminal building. A panoramic view ranging from the northwest side of Grenada to the green hills in the east to the undulating plains in the south can be seen from a nearby hill.

Along the way you'll pass through the village of Woburn, which was featured in the film *Island in the Sun,* and go through the sugar belt of Woodlands, with its tiny sugarcane factory.

SHOPPING

Everybody who visits Grenada comes home with a basket of spices, better than any you're likely to find in your local supermarket. These hand-woven panniers of palm leaf or straw are full of items grown on the island, including the inevitable nutmeg, as well as mace, cloves, cinnamon, bay leaf, vanilla, and ginger. The local stores also sell a lot of luxury-item imports, mainly from England, at prices that are almost (not quite) duty free. Store hours, in general, are 8 to 11:45am and 1 to 3:45pm Monday to Saturday.

Creation Arts & Crafts. The Carenage. ☎ 473/440-0570.

This is one of the only stores on Grenada selling handcrafts from off-island, which in this case includes Africa, Caribbean, and Latin America. You'll have to wander and drag answers out of the lethargic staff. Among the inventory are cinnamon-scented soaps and wooden bowls, painted masks made from calabash and sculptures of birds crafted by Grenadian artisans, plus casual wear.

Gift Remembered. Cross St., St. George's. ☎ 473/440-2482.

In the center of town a block from the water, Gift Remembered sells handcrafts, straw articles, jewelry, batiks, film, beachwear, postcards, good-quality T-shirts, books, and wood carvings. It's mainly for a sort of aimless shopping, but could come in handy if you promised to bring some remembrance back from the islands for a relative or friend.

Imagine. Grand Anse Shopping Centre. ☎ 473/444-4028.

If you're at the Grand Anse Beach area and would like to break up your time in the sun with some handcraft purchases, this is your best bet nearby. The resortwear isn't the most fashionable we've ever seen, but it's ideal if you're seeking some minor gift item. It offers excellent value in Caribbean handcrafts, all made of natural materials—dolls, ceramics, and straw items.

Sea Change Bookstore. The Carenage. ☎ 473/440-3402.

It's cramped, it's crowded, and the staff here might remind you of the dissatisfied teachers who used to punish you during elementary school. But despite these drawbacks, it's the largest repository of British and American newspapers on Grenada, piled untidily on overflowing shelves but pretty recent. There's also a collection of paperback books, island souvenirs, postcards, and film.

Spice Island Perfumes Ltd. The Carenage. ☎ 473/440-2006.

One of the most interesting shops in St. George's is this small store and workshop. It produces and sells perfumes, potpourri, and teas made from the locally grown flowers and spices. If you like, they'll spray you with a number of desired scents, including island flower, spice, frangipani, jasmine, patchouli, and wild orchid. The shop stands near the harbor entrance, close to the Ministry of Tourism, post office, and public library.

Tikal. Young St., St. George's. ☎ 473/440-2310.

This early 18th-century brick building is off the Carenage, next to the museum. You'll find an array of tastefully chosen handcrafts from around the world, as well as the finest selection of crafts made on Grenada, including batiks, ceramics, wood carvings, paintings, straw work, and clothing. The owner, Jeanne Fisher, is the designer of the local crafts.

Yellow Poui Art Gallery. Cross St., St. George's. ☎ 473/440-3001.

A 2-minute walk from Market Square, this is the most interesting shop for souvenirs and artistic items. Here you can see oil paintings and watercolors, sculpture, prints, photography, rare antique maps, engravings, and woodcuts, with prices beginning at $10 and going up. There's also a comprehensive display of newly acquired works from Grenada, the Caribbean area, and other sources, shown in three rooms.

GRENADA AFTER DARK

Regular evening entertainment is provided by the resort hotels and includes steel bands, calypso, reggae, folk dancing, and limbo, even crab racing. Ask at the hotels to find out what's happening at the time of your visit.

Cat Bam, Grand Anse Beach (☎ 473/444-2050), offers dancing and dining and stays open late (at least until 3am on Friday and Saturday). Next to the Coyaba Beach Resort, it sells Carib beer and rôtis on its open terrace. Or else try **The Boatyard,** Prickly Bay, L'Anse-aux-Epines (☎ 473/444-4662), down by the Marina. The time to show up is Friday night after 11pm when the action with a local DJ spins until dawn. Consider also the **Beachside Terrace** at the Flamboyant Hotel, Grand Anse (☎ 473/444-4247), a laid-back spot featuring crab races on Monday nights (you can bet on your "favorites"), a live steel band on Wednesday and, our pick, a beach barbecue with live calypso music on Friday nights. **Le Sucrier,** Sugar Mill, Grand Anse (☎ 473/444-1068), sees comedy acts, golden oldies, even the disco scene, but only Wednesday to Saturday nights. A young local crowd, both visitors and residents, shows up any time after 9pm.

For those seeking culture, the 200-seat **Marryshow Folk Theatre,** on Herbert Blaize Street near Bain Alley, St. George's (☎ 473/440-2451), offers performances of Grenadian, American, and European folk music, drama, and West Indian interpretative folk dance. This is a project of the University of the West Indies School of Continuing Studies. Check with the Marryshow Theatre or the tourist office to see what's on. Tickets cost EC$15 to EC$20 ($5.60 to $7.40).

The island's most popular nightspot is **Fantazia 2001,** at the Gem Holiday Beach Resort, Morne Rouge Bay, St. George's (☎ 473/444-2288). It's air-conditioned, with state-of-the-art equipment, good acoustics, and fantastic disco lights. The best in regional and international sounds is heard. Theme nights are frequent, ranging from "Oldie Goldies" to reggae nights. Live shows are presented on Friday and Saturday. The cover ranges from EC$10 to EC$35 ($3.70 to $12.95) per person, depending on the entertainment.

A SIDE TRIP TO CARRIACOU

Largest of the Grenadines, Carriacou, "land of many reefs," is populated by about 8,000 inhabitants, mainly of African descent, who are scattered over its 13 square miles of mountains, plains, and white-sand beaches. There's also a Scottish colony, and you'll see such names as MacFarland. In the hamlet of Windward, on the east coast, villagers of mixed Scottish and African descent carry on the tradition of building wooden schooners. Large skeletons of boats in various stages of readiness line the beach where workers labor with the most rudimentary of tools, building the West Indian trade schooner fleet. If you stop for a visit, a master boatbuilder will let you climb the ladder and peer inside the shell, and will explain which wood came from which island, and why the boat was designed in its particular way. Much of the population, according to reputation, is involved in smuggling; otherwise, they're sailors, fisherfolk, shipwrights, and farmers.

GETTING THERE   The fastest method of transport is on a 19-seat plane, which takes just 25 minutes from the Point Salines International Airport on Grenada to Carriacou's **Lauriston Airport. LIAT** (☎ 473/462-0700) makes the short takeoff and landing (STOL) flight in about 20 minutes. There are five flights a day from Grenada. It's also possible to fly **Airlines of Carriacou** (☎ 473/444-3549), which has daily scheduled service not only to Carriacou but to St. Vincent and the Grenadines as well. There are two flights per day on both Monday and Friday. For reservations, you can contact a travel agent, LIAT, or Airlines of Carriacou itself at the Point Salines airport.

   Boats leave from Grenada for Carriacou at 9am on Tuesday, Wednesday, Friday, Saturday, and Sunday, charging $7.50 for a one-way ticket or $12 round-trip. On Sunday there's a round-trip excursion boat. Otherwise, boats return from Carriacou to Grenada on Monday and Thursday. In addition, there's an express boat service between Grenada and Carriacou, taking 1 1/2 to 2 hours, as opposed to the 3 hours for the regular service. This express boat offers two round-trips on Monday, Tuesday, Thursday, and Friday, plus one round-trip on Saturday. The cost is EC$40 ($14.80) one-way or EC$75 ($27.75) round-trip. The tourist office will have the latest details. From Hillsborough, you can sail on to Petit Martinique. Carriacou has good places to stay; Petit Martinique doesn't.

ESSENTIALS   For information about the island, go to the **Carriacou Board of Tourism** in Hillsborough (☎ 473/443-7948), open Monday to Friday from 8am to noon and 1 to 4pm.

WHERE TO STAY

Ade's Dream Guest House. Hillsborough, Carriacou, Grenada, W.I. ☎ **473/443-7317.** Fax 473/443-8435. 7 rms, none with bath; 16 apts. Year-round, $21–$30 single or double; $40–$52 apt for two. Air-conditioning $5 per night extra. AE, MC, V.

   Pronounced "Oddy," these squeaky-clean rooms and apartments are above a grocery store in Carriacou's only town, Hillsborough. They're the bargain of the island, and could make a suitable overnight stop if you don't demand too much in the way of conveniences, although the apartments have phones and ceiling fans. The self-contained apartments are worth the extra money, and each has its own private balcony. You can watch the waves from these balconies and sleep to the sound of the surf. The bedrooms are basic, with shared bathing facilities similar to a school locker room. The facility lies at the edge of a good beach. A simple restaurant across the street serves three meals a day, and a water taxi is available for tours.

Cassada Bay Hotel. Belmont, Carriacou, Grenada, W.I. ☎ **473/443-7494.** Fax 473/443-7672. 16 cabins. Winter, $95 cabin for one or two. Off-season, $75 cabin for one or two. Rates include American breakfast. MC, V.

   Formerly a research study center for a university marine-biology department, this property has been converted into a comfortable, secluded hotel. It occupies a prime hillside with panoramic views of uninhabited islands. Two cabins are made of rough-cut timber and have all-white paneled rooms with simple furniture, double bedrooms, living rooms, and verandas, all serviced by a maid. The bedrooms have insect screens, louvered windows, and ceiling fans. The restaurant serves traditional West Indian food, and there's an open-air bar terrace to watch the sun go down (with a rum punch made with local limes and flavored with freshly ground nutmeg). The area is ideal for beach buffs and snorkelers, and local boats take picnic-bound passengers for trips to nearby islands. There are two dive operations within easy reach, and Jeep rentals can be arranged. It's a 5-minute ride from the airport.

Hope's Inn. L'Esterre, Carriacou, Grenada, W.I. ☎ **473/443-7457.** 6 rms, none with bath; 1 apt. Year-round, $25 single; $29 double; $40 one-bedroom apt for two; $50 one-bedroom apt for three. No credit cards.

This is one of the cheapest (acceptable) inns you're likely to find in all of Carriacou or Grenada, and although none of the bedrooms has a private bathroom, the raffishly informal place seems to suit its position on an island rarely visited by outsiders. It was built in 1992 with white walls, a red roof, and ultra-simple amenities such as curtained showers in the hall. The accommodations come with the use of a fan (set on a stand, not hung from the ceiling). Only the apartment has its own private kitchen; residents of the simple bedrooms share two communal cooking areas. (Guests usually prepare their own meals, but some hire cooks.) There's a modest grocery store nearby for purchases of liquor, supplies, soft drinks, cigarettes, and groceries. The beach (L'Esterre Beach) begins about 50 feet from the hotel's foundations.

Scraper's Bay View Holiday Cottages. Tyrrel Bay, Carriacou, Grenada, W.I. ☎ **473/443-7403.** 5 units. Year-round, $60 single or double. DISC, MC, V.

The administration of this 1970s hotel contributes a lot to its sense of raffish, and somewhat disorganized, fun. It consists of a main building and three white-sided outbuildings, flower gardens with picket fences and lots of hibiscus and oleander, and a restaurant that in its way is the best known on the island.

The rates can usually be negotiated downward, depending on business, from what's listed above. Regardless of what you eventually pay, you'll probably enjoy the bar (where rum punch is a specialty) and the rapid-fire dialogue of the owner, Scraper, whose real name is Stephen Gay. Scraper sometimes performs at his bar or restaurant. Don't expect the formality or services of a full-fledged resort here. If you appreciate nonstandard, aggressively informal hotels with a funky, strongly emphasized ethnic wit, this might be the place for you. The nearest beach is Tyrrel Bay, and the resort lies near the island's southern tip in the village of Harvey Vale.

VILLA RENTALS

Carriacou is a beautiful but remote island that hasn't yet experienced the onslaughts of hotel developments that have, in many cases, disfigured the landscapes of some other islands. Some of the island's most alluring accommodations are in privately owned houses, whose off-island owners surrender the keys to a local management company whenever they don't need access.

If the idea of a villa rental appeals to you, contact **Down Island Villa Rentals,** Hillsborough, Carriacou, Grenada, W.I. (☎ **473/443-8182;** fax 473/443-7086). It manages about 15 privately owned villas and apartments located in quiet residential spots. You need to book well ahead December to March. All the rentals are fully equipped homes with full kitchens and are built to take advantage of the trade winds. The minimum stay is 1 week and prices begin at $300 for two people off-season, rising to $400 and up in winter. Extra persons pay $75 to $100 per person weekly, and homes can accommodate up to six guests. Villas are either on, over, or within walking distance of coves and beaches. If four people share a top lodging in winter, this might bring your costs down to a surprisingly modest $35 or so per day. The smallest cottages off-season might be only $24 per person per day.

WHERE TO EAT

Scraper's. Tyrrel Bay. ☎ **473/443-7403.** Main courses EC$15–EC$60 ($5.55–$22.20); lunch from EC$15 ($5.55). DISC, MC, V. Daily 7am–midnight. SEAFOOD.

At this previously recommended guest house, you can order some of the island's finest cuisine in relaxed, friendly surroundings where everybody gets to know everybody else. The decor is hardly elegant, but no one comes here for that. They visit for the good food and the low prices. Scraper—actually Stephen Gay—makes the best conch on island, and it's served either Créole style or with curry. Lobster is occasionally featured on the menu. All these seafood delectables are freshly caught that day. Local seasonings add the right touch to bring out the fresh flavor in the food. Begin with Scraper's callaloo soup. The restaurant is right on the beach, and guests have a choice of places for dining, not only inside, but alfresco on the beach if they desire. Three times a week there's a steel band for entertainment.

EXPLORING THE ISLAND

The best time to visit Carriacou is in August in time for its **regatta,** which was begun by J. Linton Rigg in 1965 with the work boats and schooners for which the Grenadines are famous. Now work boats, three-masted schooners, and miniature "sailboats" propelled by hand join the festivities. Banana boats docking at the pier are filled with people rather than bananas, and sailors from Bequia and Union Island camp on tiny Jack-a-Dan and Sandy Isle, only 20 minutes away by outboard motor from Hillsborough. The people of the Grenadines try their luck at the greased pole, footraces, and of course the sailing races. Music fills the air day and night, and impromptu parties are held. At the 3-day celebration, Big Drum dancers perform in the Market Square.

The **Big Drum dance** is part of the heritage of Carriacou brought from Africa and nurtured here more purely than perhaps on any other Caribbean island. The "Go Tambo," or Big Drum, is an integral part of such traditional events as stone feasts (marking the setting of a tombstone) and the accompanying rites. The feast, called *saraca,* and setting of the tombstone may be as long as 20 years after a death. Another event involving the Big Drum and saracas is the *maroon.* This can involve a dream interpretation, but it seems actually to be just a regular festivity, held in various places during the dry season, with dancing and feasting. A boat launching may also be accompanied by the Big Drum and the saraca and usually draws crowds of participants.

The **Carriacou Parang Festival** is usually held on the weekend closest to December 25. The festival serves to maintain the indigenous culture of the people of Carriacou. Bands are formed out of guitar, cuatro, bass drum, and violin.

Hillsborough is the chief port and administrative center, handling the commerce of the little island, which is based mainly on growing limes and cotton. The capital bustles on Monday when the produce arrives, then settles down again until "mail day" on Saturday. The capital is nestled in a mile-long crescent of white sand.

The **Carriacou Museum,** on Paterson Street in Hillsborough (☎ **473/443-8288**), opposite Grentel, has a display of Amerindian artifacts, European china, glass shards, and exhibits of African culture. In two small rooms, it preserves the history of Carriacou, which parallels that of its neighbor island, Grenada. It's open Monday to Friday from 9:30am to 3:45pm and on Saturday from 10am to 2pm. Admission is EC$5 ($1.85) per person.

The largest and only inhabited island near Carriacou is 486-acre **Petite Martinique** (that's "pitty," not "petite"), with a population of about 600. The chief occupation, officially, is building and sailing fishing boats, but it's also infamous as the reputed center of the smuggling trade among the islands, dealing in cigarettes and liquor from St. Barts's and St. Maarten's duty-free ports.

Forgotten by time, this little island suddenly became prominent in the news in the fall of 1996 when the U.S. government announced that it planned to build a base here for the Grenada Coast Guard. The dockside site is intended to strengthen drug interdiction efforts in the Caribbean. In spite of strong local objection, plans are moving ahead to build the base. Petite Martinique would be the first of a series of such bases throughout the Caribbean, with other coast guard operations slated for Barbuda, Nevis, St. Vincent, Tobago, and St. Lucia.

14 Barbados

Bajans like to think of their island as "England in the tropics," but endless pink- and white-sand beaches are what really put Barbados on the map. Rich in tradition, Barbados has a grand array of hotels (many of them super-expensive). Although it doesn't offer casinos, it has more than beach life for travelers interested in learning about the local culture, and more sightseeing attractions than most islands of the West Indies.

Afternoon tea remains a tradition at many places, cricket is still the national sport, and many Bajans speak with a British accent. Crime has been on the rise in recent years, although Barbados is still viewed as a safe destination. The difference between the haves and the have-nots doesn't cause the sometimes-violent clash here that it does on some other islands, such as Jamaica.

Don't rule out Barbados if you're seeking a peaceful island getaway. Although the south coast is known for its nightlife and the west-coast beach strip is completely built up, some of the island remains undeveloped. The east coast is fairly tranquil, and you can often be alone here (but since it faces the Atlantic, the waters aren't tranquil as they are on the Caribbean side). Many escapists, especially Canadians seeking a low-cost place to stay in the winter, don't seem to mind the Atlantic waters at all.

Because it's so built-up with hotels and condos, Barbados offers more package deals than most islands. You can often get a steal in the off-season, which lasts from April until mid-December. You don't necessarily have to pay the "rack" rate (the walk-in rate for individual bookings) at hotels if you'll take the time to shop around. Barbados is filled with bargains, especially along its southern coast directly below Bridgetown. This strip of beachfront isn't the most glamorous, but it's the most reasonable in price.

GETTING THERE

More than 20 daily flights arrive on Barbados from all over the world. **Grantley Adams International Airport** is on Highway 7, on the southern tip of the island at Long Bay, between Oistins and The Crane (a village). From North America, the four major gateways to Barbados are New York, Miami, Toronto, and San Juan. Flying time to Barbados from New York is $4^1/_2$ hours; from Miami, it's $3^1/_2$ hours; from Toronto, 5 hours; and from San Juan, $1^1/_2$ hours.

American Airlines (☎ 800/433-7300) has dozens of connections passing through San Juan plus a daily nonstop flight from New York's JFK to Barbados and one from Miami to Barbados. U.S. passengers who do fly through San Juan can usually speed through U.S. Customs clearance in San Juan on their return flight rather than in their home cities, saving time and inconvenience.

Travelers via New York and Miami can opt for nonstop flights offered daily by **BWIA** (☎ 800/538-2942), the national airline of Trinidad and Tobago. BWIA also offers many flights from Barbados to Trinidad.

Canadians sometimes select nonstop flights to Barbados from Toronto. **Air Canada** (☎ 800/268-7240 in Canada, or 800/776-3000 in the U.S.) offers the most nonstop scheduled service from Canada to Barbados, with convenient evening departures. There are seven flights per week from Toronto in winter, plus one Sunday flight from Montréal year-round. In summer, when demand slackens, there will be fewer flights from Toronto.

Barbados is a major hub of the Caribbean-based airline known as **LIAT** (☎ 246/434-5428 for reservations, or 246/428-0986 at the Barbados airport), which provides generally poor service from Barbados to a handful of neighboring islands, including St. Vincent and the Grenadines, Antigua, and Dominica.

British Airways (☎ 800/247-9297 in the U.S., or 0345/22211 in Britain) offers nonstop service to Barbados from both of London's major airports (Heathrow and Gatwick).

GETTING AROUND

BY BUS   Unlike most of the British Windwards, Barbados has a reliable bus system fanning out from Bridgetown to almost every part of the island. On most major routes, there are buses running every 20 minutes or so. Bus fares are BD$1.50 (75¢) wherever you go. Exact change is required.

The nationally owned **buses** of Barbados are blue with yellow stripes. They're not numbered, but their destinations are marked on the front. Departures are from Bridgetown, leaving from Fairchild Street for the south and east; from Lower Green and the Princess Alice Highway, for the north going along the west coast. Call the **Barbados Tourist Board** (☎ 246/436-6820) for bus schedules and information.

Privately operated **minibuses** run shorter distances and travel more frequently. They're bright yellow, with their destinations displayed on the bottom left corner of the windshield. Minibuses in Bridgetown are boarded at River Road, Temple Yard, and Probyn Street. They, too, cost BD$1.50 (75¢).

BY TAXI   Taxis aren't metered, but rates are fixed by the government. Taxis on the island are identified by the letter "Z" on the license plates. One to five passengers can be transported at the same time, and can share the fare. Overcharging is infrequent; most drivers have a reputation for courtesy and honesty. Taxis are plentiful, and drivers will produce a list of standard rates, which is $16 per hour.

BY RENTAL CAR   If you don't mind *driving on the left*, you may find a rental car ideal on Barbados. A temporary permit is needed if you don't have an International Driver's License. The rental agencies listed below will all issue you a visitor's permit or you can go to the police desk upon your arrival at the airport. You're charged a registration fee of BD$10 ($5), and you must have your own license. The speed limit is 20 m.p.h. inside city limits, 30 m.p.h. elsewhere on the island. No taxes apply to car rentals on Barbados.

None of the major U.S.–based car-rental companies maintains an affiliate on Barbados, but a host of local companies rent vehicles, many of which are in bad shape.

Except in the peak of the midwinter season, cars are usually readily available without a prior reservation.

Most renters pay for a taxi from the airport to their hotel and then call for the delivery of a rental car. This is especially advisable because of frequent delays at airport counters.

Many local car-rental companies continue to draw serious complaints from readers, both for overcharging and for the condition of the rental vehicle. Proceed with rentals very carefully on this island. Check out the insurance and liability issues carefully when you rent.

The island's most frequently recommended car-rental firm is **National Car Rentals Ltd.,** Bush Hall, Main Road, St. Michael (☎ **246/426-0603**), which offers a wide selection of Japanese cars (note that it's not affiliated with the U.S. chain of the same name). Located near the island's national stadium (the only one on the island), its office is 3 miles northeast of Bridgetown. Cars will be delivered to almost any location on the island upon request, and the driver who delivers it will carry the necessary forms for the Bajan driver's license, which may be purchased for $5.

Other safe bets, charging approximately the same prices and offering the same services, include **Sunny Isle Motors,** Dayton, Worthing Main Road, Christ Church (☎ **246/435-7979**), and **P&S Car Rentals,** Pleasant View, Cave Hill, St. Michael (☎ **246/424-2052**). One company convenient to hotels on the remote southeastern end of Barbados is **Stoutes Car Rentals,** Kirtons, St. Philip (☎ **246/435-4456**). Closer to the airport than its competitors, it can theoretically deliver a car to the airport within 10 minutes of a call placed when you arrive.

BY SCOOTER OR BICYCLE In spite of the bad roads, a scooter or bike could be a viable option for some adventurous souls. The trouble is in finding a rental agency, as most outfitters have closed down. Call the tourist office (☎ **246/427-2623**) to see if a rental agency has opened.

FAST FACTS: Barbados

American Express The island's American Express affiliate is **Barbados International Travel Services, Inc.,** Horizon House, McGregor Street (☎ **246/431-2423**), in the heart of Bridgetown.

Business Hours Most **banks** on Barbados are open Monday to Thursday from 9am to 3pm and on Friday from 9am to 1pm and 3 to 5pm. **Stores** are open Monday to Friday from 8am to 4pm and on Saturday from 8am to noon. Most **government offices** are open Monday to Friday from 8:30am to 4:30pm.

Consulates and High Commissions Contact the **U.S. Consulate,** in the ALICO Building, Cheapside, Bridgetown (☎ **246/431-0225**); the **Canadian High Commission,** Bishop Court, Hill Pine Road (☎ **246/429-3550**); or the **British High Commission,** Lower Collymore Rock, St. Michael (☎ **246/436-6694**).

Currency The **Barbados dollar (BD$)** is the official currency, available in $5, $10, $20, and $100 notes, as well as 10¢ and $1 silver coins, plus 1¢ and 5¢ copper coins. The Bajan dollar is worth 50¢ in U.S. currency. Most stores take traveler's checks or U.S. dollars. However, it's best to convert your money at banks and pay in Bajan dollars.

Dentist **Dr. Derek Golding,** with two other colleagues, maintains one of the busiest practices on Barbados. Located at the Beckwith Shopping Mall in Bridgetown (☎ **246/426-3001**), he accepts most of the emergency dental

Barbados

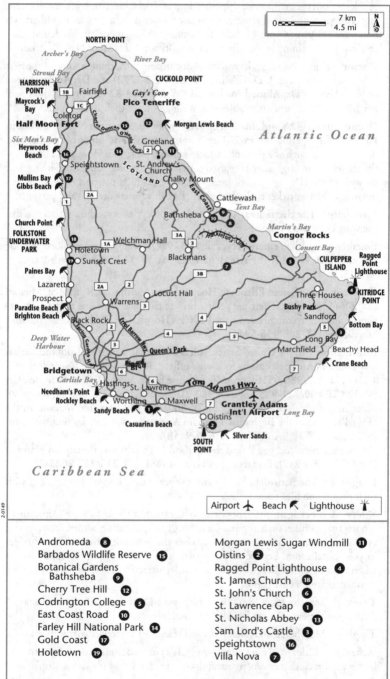

Scale: 0 — 7 km / 4.5 mi

N

Atlantic Ocean

NORTH POINT
Archer's Bay
River Bay
Stroud Bay
CUCKOLD POINT
HARRISON POINT
1B Fairfield
Gay's Cove
Maycock's Bay
Pico Teneriffe
1C Coleton
13
Half Moon Fort
12 Morgan Lewis Beach
Six Men's Bay
15
Heywoods Beach
16
14
Greenland
2
Speightstown
11
St. Andrew's Church
Mullins Bay
17
Chalky Mount
Gibbs Beach
2A
Cattlewash
Tent Bay
1
Church Point
Bathsheba
FOLKSTONE UNDERWATER PARK
18
Welchman Hall
3A
Martin's Bay
Congor Rocks
1A
10
Holetown
3
Consett Bay
19 Sunset Crest
Blackmans
CULPEPPER ISLAND
Paines Bay
2A
3B
7
5
Ragged Point Lighthouse
Lazarett
2
Locust Hall
KITRIDGE POINT
Prospect
Warrens
3
Three Houses
Paradise Beach
2
4
Bushy Park
Brighton Beach
Black Rock
3
Sandford
Bottom Bay
Deep Water Harbour
4
4B
5
5
3
Queen's Park
5
Long Bay
Bridgetown
6
Marchfield
Beachy Head
Carlisle Bay
6
Crane Beach
Needham's Point
Hastings St. Lawrence
7
Rockley Beach Worthing
Maxwell
7
Grantley Adams Int'l Airport
Long Bay
Sandy Beach
1
Casuarina Beach
2
Oistins
Silver Sands
SOUTH POINT

Caribbean Sea

2-0149

| Airport ✈ | Beach ⌐ | Lighthouse ☀ |

Andromeda ⑧
Barbados Wildlife Reserve ⑮
Botanical Gardens Bathsheba ⑨
Cherry Tree Hill ⑫
Codrington College ⑤
East Coast Road ⑩
Farley Hill National Park ⑭
Gold Coast ⑰
Holetown ⑲

Morgan Lewis Sugar Windmill ⑪
Oistins ②
Ragged Point Lighthouse ④
St. James Church ⑱
St. John's Church ⑥
St. Lawrence Gap ①
St. Nicholas Abbey ⑬
Sam Lord's Castle ③
Speightstown ⑯
Villa Nova ⑦

535

problems from the many cruise ships that dock off Barbados. This practice will accept any emergency and often remains open late for last-minute problems. Otherwise, hours are 8:30am to 4pm Monday to Saturday. All members of this dental team received their training in the United States, Britain, Canada, or New Zealand.

Doctor   Your hotel might have a list of doctors on call, although some of the best recommended are **Dr. J. D. Gibling** (☎ 246/432-1772) and **Dr. Adrian Lorde** or his colleague, **Dr. Ahmed Mohamad** (☎ 246/424-8236), any of whom will pay house calls to patients unable or unwilling to leave their hotel rooms.

Documents   A U.S. or Canadian citizen coming directly from North America to Barbados for a period not exceeding 3 months must have proof of identity and national status, such as a passport, which is always preferred. However, a birth certificate (either an original or a certified copy) is also acceptable, provided it's backed up with photo ID. For stays of longer than 3 months, a passport is required. An ongoing or return ticket is also necessary. British subjects need a valid passport.

Electricity   The electricity is 110 volts A.C., 50 cycles, so at most places you can use your U.S.–made appliances.

Emergencies   In an **emergency,** call ☎ **119.** Other important numbers include the **police** at ☎ **112,** the **fire** department at ☎ **113,** and an **ambulance** at ☎ **115.**

Hospitals   The **Queen Elizabeth Hospital** is on Martinsdale Road in St. Michael (☎ 246/436-6450). There are several private clinics as well; one of the most expensive and best recommended is the **Bayview Hospital,** St. Paul's Avenue, Bayville, St. Michael (☎ **246/436-5446**).

Information   In the United States, you can obtain information from the **Barbados Tourism Authority** at the following offices: 800 Second Ave., New York, NY 10017 (☎ **212/986-6516**), or 3440 Wilshire Blvd., Suite 1215, Los Angeles, CA 90010 (☎ **800/221-9831** or 213/380-2198). In Canada, there is no longer an office in Montréal, but you can call ☎ **800/268-9122** for information. In the United Kingdom, the **Barbados Tourism Authority** is at 263 Tottenham Court Rd., London W1P 9AA (☎ **0171/636-9448**).

Once on the island you'll find the **Barbados Tourism Authority** on Harbour Road (P.O. Box 242), Bridgetown, Barbados, W.I. (☎ **246/427-2623**).

Language   The Barbadians, or Bajans, as they're called, speak English, but with their own island lilt.

Safety   Crimes against tourists used to be rare, but the U.S. State Department reports rising crime, such as purse-snatching, pickpocketing, armed robbery, and even sexual assault upon women. It advises that you not leave cash or valuables in your hotel room, beware of purse snatchers when walking, exercise caution when walking on the beach or visiting tourist attractions, and be wary of driving in isolated areas of Barbados.

Taxes   When you leave, you'll have to pay a BD$25 ($12.50) departure tax. A 7¹/₂% government sales tax is added to hotel bills.

Tipping   Most hotels and restaurants add at least a 10% service charge to your bill.

Water   Barbados has a pure water supply. It's pumped from underground sources in the coral rock that covers six-sevenths of the island, and it's safe to drink.

Weather   Daytime temperatures are in the 75° to 85° Fahrenheit range throughout the year.

1 Bargain Places to Stay

Per square inch, Barbados has the best hotels in the Caribbean. Many are small and personally run. There are bargains to be found, but to find them you'll have to avoid the resorts on fashionable St. James Beach and instead head south from Bridgetown to such places as Hastings and Worthing. The best buys are often self-contained efficiencies or studio apartments where you can do your own cooking.

Prices cited in this section, unless otherwise indicated, are in U.S. dollars. Remember that the government hotel tax of 5% and a 10% service charge will be added to your final bill.

Some of the best and least expensive rental deals can be made through **Homar Rentals,** Europa, Sunset Crest, St. James (☎ 246/432-6750; fax 246/432-7229), which controls some 130 apartments. These accommodations are two-apartment bungalows, some on one floor, others in two-story buildings, all constructed from concrete. Furnishings for the most part are basic in a West Indian motif, with rattan pieces or leatherette. There are phones, and some bedrooms have ceiling fans, although TVs must be rented. Daily maid service is provided. Air-conditioning is token-operated at $4 for 10 hours. In winter, a single or double begins at $75 daily, with off-season prices lowered to $50. An extra person is charged $10, and one child 11 and under stays free in parents' room. Homar is one of several companies managing the Sunset Crest Resort, privately owned condos where apartments are rented when the owners are off-island. There's a network of three pools, plus a restaurant serving three standard meals a day. The nearby Beach Club also has a pool, a bar, and water-sports equipment for rent.

DOUBLES FOR LESS THAN $35 (WINTER) / $28 (OFF-SEASON)

✪ **Fairholme.** Maxwell, Christ Church, Barbados, W.I. ☎ **246/428-9425.** 11 rms, 20 studio apts. Winter, $30 single or double; $55 studio apt. Off-season, $28 single or double; $35 studio apt. No credit cards.

Fairholme is a converted plantation house that has been enlarged during the past 20 years with a handful of connected annexes. The main house and its original gardens are just off a major road 6 miles southeast of Bridgetown. The hotel is a 5-minute walk to the beach and across from its neighbor, the Sea Breeze, which has a waterfront cafe and bar that Fairholme guests may use. The older part has 11 double rooms, each with a living-room area and a patio overlooking an orchard and swimming pool. More recently added are 20 Spanish-style studio apartments, all with balcony or patio, built in the old plantation style, with cathedral ceilings, dark beams, and traditional furnishings. The restaurant has a reputation for home-cooking—wholesome, nothing fancy, but the ingredients are fresh. Air-conditioning is available only in the studios. At the reception desk you buy a brass token for $3 that you insert into your air conditioner for around 8 hours of cooling-off time.

Pegwell Inn. Welches, Christ Church Parish, Barbados, W.I. ☎ **246/428-6150.** 4 rms. Winter, $13 single; $26 double. Off-season, $11 single; $22 double. No credit cards.

This simple but respectable guest house in a one-story, wood-sided building was built during the early 1940s. Part of the energies of its owner, Rosemary Phillips, is devoted to running a kiosk-style minimart at the back of the house, and if you arrive during business hours it might pay to go around to the back, rather than to the front, of the house. There's a laundry across the street, a swimming area (Welches Beach, which can be seen across the road), and easy access to such nearby facilities as a bank, restaurants, and shops. Each accommodation is plain; two rooms have two single beds, two rooms have one double bed each, and all rooms have a toilet, a sink, and shower.

Rio Guest House. Paradise Village, St. Lawrence Gap, Christ Church, Barbados, W.I. ☎ **246/ 428-1546.** Fax 246/428-1546. 8 rms, 5 with bath; 1 studio. Winter, $25 single without bath; $35 single or double with bath; $75 studio. Off-season, $20 single without bath; $26 single or double with bath; $50 studio. No credit cards.

Built as a private home in the 1940s, this simple black-and-white–painted guest house is maintained by the resident owner, Mrs. Denise Harding. It features low rates, clean, no-frills bedrooms, and a two-story format of cost-efficient practicality. None of the single rooms has a private bathroom; there are no private kitchens, except in the studio. The minimarts, bars, nightclubs, and hamburger joints of St. Lawrence Gap are within walking distance, Dover Brach is within a 2-minute walk, and guests share a communal kitchen. In the kitchen, a large refrigerator is divided into compartments, each reserved more or less exclusively for one of the bedrooms, where residents can store their munchies.

DOUBLES FOR LESS THAN $65 (WINTER) / $60 (OFF-SEASON)

Atlantis Hotel. Bathsheba, St. Joseph, Barbados, W.I. ☎ **246/433-9445.** 15 rms. Winter, $35–$40 single; $65 double. Off-season, $30–$35 single; $60 double. Extra adult $35 each in winter, $30 each off-season; extra child 11 and under $17 each in winter, $15 each off-season. Rates include half board. AE.

This boxy, concrete-sided hotel offers virtues (and drawbacks) not associated with more modern resorts in better-developed regions of Barbados. It's one of the most durable establishments on the island, with a long history of feeding large numbers of lunchtime visitors (reviewed below). It's in an isolated position on Barbados's rocky and turbulent Atlantic coast, where strong currents, winds, and undertows usually make swimming a bad idea.

If that doesn't deter you, know that the scenery in St. Joseph is among the most beautiful on Barbados; many botanists and lovers of nature compare the district to the lowlands of Scotland. The establishment is respectable, well known by virtually everyone on the island, and if it's rejected at all, it's only because of its relative isolation from the more densely populated and convenient districts of the southwest. The accommodations are clean but simple affairs, with white walls, carpeted floors, wooden furniture, and (in many cases) views and balconies overlooking the surging Atlantic. Mrs. Enid Maxwell and members of her family are the well-established owners.

Chrizel's Guest House. Prospect, St. James, Barbados, W.I. ☎ **718/712-9567** in the U.S. for reservations, or 246/438-0207. 3 units. TV. Winter, $45–$55 single; $55–$65 double. Off-season, $35–$45 unit for one; $45–$55 unit for two. Extra person $25 in winter, $20 off-season; children 11 and under stay free in parents' unit. DISC, MC, V.

A 1-minute walk from Paradise and Morgan's Cove beaches, this is a real local guest house that some readers have hailed as "the best deal in the Caribbean." It's simple and plain, made more appealing by the warmth of its owner, Hazel Rice-Harper, who's on hand to offer advice and help. She even whipped up a breakfast for one Alaska couple of scrambled eggs, fried plantains, and guava jam. Guests have a choice of a suite, one standard apartment, and one so-called deluxe apartment, all sheltered in a white concrete building with direct access to a backyard, terraced with a lawn and plants. The apartments have wall fans and TVs, and those on the ground floor offer full kitchens. The suite upstairs shares a kitchen with Hazel who will make arrangements for baby-sitting. Once a week there's an in-house dinner for all guests.

Fleet View Apartments. Tent Bay, Bathsheba, St. Joseph, Barbados, W.I. ☎ **246/433-9445.** 6 apts. Winter, $40 studio apt for one or two; $45 one-bedroom apt for one or two. Off-season, $30 studio apt for one or two; $35 one-bedroom apt for one or two. AE.

These apartments are an annex of the Atlantis Hotel. They're simple, with little ornamentation, and cater to independent-minded guests who don't want the fussiness associated with a traditional hotel or resort. Be warned that since their last renovation occurred in 1980, the apartments are a bit battered. Their lack of every imaginable amenity, however, is offset by the surprisingly low rates, and if you have a bicycle or car you can compensate for the isolation. Although each unit has a modest kitchen, breakfast is served across the street in the dining room of the Atlantis Hotel, and if you grow tired of cooking, the Atlantis will happily feed you. For more information about the location, refer to the Atlantis listing, below.

Meridian Inn. Dover, Christ Church, Barbados, W.I. ☎ **246/428-4051.** Fax 246/420-6495. 12 studio apts. A/C. Winter, $59 studio apt for one or two. Off-season, $39 studio apt for one or two. Children under 3 stay free in parents' studio; children 4 and over, $12 per day. AE, MC, V.

Close to shopping, restaurants, and nightclubs, this four-story, white-painted building right on the street is about a minute's walk to a good beach. It offers some of the least expensive rooms on the island. Admittedly, although clean and comfortable, some of the accommodations evoke Miami motels of the 1960s. However, they're air-conditioned, with twin beds, kitchenettes, baths, and private balconies, along with daily maid service. Each has a ceiling fan and a small fridge; TVs can be rented. Phones are in the corridors. There's no room service. Baby-sitting can be arranged. On the ground floor a simple restaurant features fresh seafood at both lunch and dinner.

Southern Surf Beach Apartment. Rockley Beach, Christ Church, Barbados, W.I. ☎ **246/435-6672.** Fax 246/435-6649. 4 "Great House" rms, 12 studio apts. A/C. Winter, $50 single or double; $70 studio apt for two. Off-season, $40 single or double; $50 studio apt for two. Extra person in apartment $12. MC, V.

Close to the famous Accra Beach at Rockley, this is a good, serviceable choice in a centrally located complex with a swimming pool and garden. It's also convenient for nearby dining, shopping, and entertainment; this is a good choice if you don't want to rent a car. Four rooms are in the main or Great House, whereas the studio apartments are in a four-story concrete-block building. There are three apartments per floor, each simply but comfortably furnished, with a balcony and beach view. The rooms don't have phones, but there is one for public use in the apartment block, and the only TV is in the office reception area. Rooms in the main house, although not as large, have more of an old-time Bajan feeling, with ceiling fans overhead. Children are housed free in a studio apartment if an extra cot is not needed; otherwise a $12-per-day surcharge applies. Baby-sitting can also be arranged. Southern Surf owns the land between it and the ocean, so there's an unobstructed view of the beach.

Windsurf Village Hotel. Maxwell Main Rd., Christ Church, Barbados, W.I. ☎ **246/428-9095.** Fax 246/435-6621. 15 units. Winter, $45–$55 single or double; $55–$75 studio with kitchenette for two; $105–$150 two-bedroom apt for four. Off-season, $35 single or double; $45 studio with kitchenette for two; $95 two-bedroom apt for four. AE, MC, V.

Although this hotel assumes that windsurfers appreciate proximity to other windsurfers, many guests who don't have very much interest in the sport have been happy here, too. Designed in a two-story, white-walled format with balconies, with at least two patios for outdoor mingling of guests, it attracts a youngish crowd of sports enthusiasts, as well as older nonparticipants who appreciate the lighthearted setting. The bedrooms contain white-painted walls, wooden furnishings, ceiling fans, and tile-covered floors. Budgeteers like its location amid Barbados's densest concentration of nightclubs, supermarkets, and cheap eateries, all of which are in the same parish (Christ Church) within an easy walk or drive. It maintains a snack-style restaurant on the beach, with lunches priced at $4 to $6 and dinners beginning at $8.50.

Despite the establishment's name, it doesn't own or rent any Windsurfers. Instead, windsurfing enthusiasts are directed to the water-sports facilities at the nearby Club Mistral, where Windsurfer rentals are $20 per hour and lessons cost $20 per hour.

DOUBLES FOR LESS THAN $100 (WINTER) / $85 (OFF-SEASON)

Kingsley Club. Cattlewash-on-Sea (near Bathsheba), St. Joseph, Barbados, W.I. ☎ **246/ 433-9422.** Fax 246/433-9226. 7 rms. Winter, $92 single; $101 double. Off-season, $76 single; $84 double. MAP $43 per person extra. AE, MC, V. Take Hwy. 3 north of Bathsheba.

This little West Indian inn is far removed from the bustle of the tourist-ridden west coast. In the foothills of Bathsheba, opening onto the often-turbulent Atlantic, the Kingsley Club is on the northeast coast. This historic inn offers simply furnished and very modest but clean and comfortable bedrooms. At night you can sit back and enjoy a rum punch made from an old planter's recipe. The club enjoys a reputation for good cooking, and its Bajan food is recommended for those traveling to the east coast just for the day (see "Where to Eat," below). Cattlewash Beach is one of the longest, widest, and least crowded on Barbados. But be aware that swimming here can be extremely dangerous.

Little Bay Hotel. St. Lawrence Gap, Christ Church, Barbados, W.I. ☎ **246/435-7246.** Fax 246/435-8574. 7 studios, 3 one-bedroom apts. A/C TV TEL. Winter, $100 studio for one or two; $140 one-bedroom apt for up to four. Off-season, $65 studio for one or two; $85 one-bedroom apt for up to four. AE, MC, V.

This small apartment complex consists of an older core, which has been upgraded and renovated by its owners, the Patterson family, who took over in 1982. It's a peach-colored building with a tiled roof and pleasant, unfrilly accommodations with brick-tile floors, utilitarian furniture, and views over Barbados's well-developed southwestern coastline. There are ample opportunities for cost-conscious drinking, nightclubbing, and dining within a brisk walk (or short drive) of your room. If you cook your meals in-house, you'll have a private kitchenette and access to several grocery stores and minimarts nearby. No breakfast is served on site, but Italian dinners are served at Bellini's restaurant, which is vaguely associated with this hotel, for $13 to $25 per person.

Sunhaven Beach Apartment Hotel. Rockley Beach, Christ Church, Barbados, W.I. ☎ **246/ 435-8905.** Fax 246/435-6621. 9 rms, 26 apts. A/C. Winter, $65 single; $75 double; $90 triple; $80 one-bedroom apt for one, $95 one-bedroom apt for two, $110 one-bedroom apt for three, $125 one-bedroom apt for four. Off-season, $40 single; $50 double; $60 triple; $50 one-bedroom apt for one, $60 one-bedroom apt for two, $70 one-bedroom apt for three, $80 one-bedroom apt for four. Children 4 and under stay free in parents' unit; children 5–12, $10 each. MAP $25 per person extra. AE, DC, MC, V.

This small, rather innocuous-looking complex offers both conventional bedrooms and a larger number of one-bedroom apartments with kitchenettes. It's close to the sands of Rockley Beach, near many fast-food and inexpensive pub-style restaurants. The accommodations are small and a bit dowdy, with functional furniture and dour, floral-patterned carpeting, but if you're traveling with friends or children in tow, it's hard to beat the cost savings it represents. Each unit has a sea view and a balcony.

At one edge of the pool, overlooking the beach, is an open-air restaurant, The Lagoon, serving lunches for around $5 to $10 and dinners for $12.

Woodville Beach Apartments. Hastings, Christ Church, Barbados, W.I. ☎ **246/435-6694.** Fax 246/435-9211. 36 studios and apts. TEL. Winter, $98–$115 studio apt for one or two; $125 one-bedroom apt for one or two; $172 two-bedroom apt for up to four. Off-season, $65–$76 studio apt for one or two; $86 one-bedroom apt for one or two; $125 two-bedroom apt for up to four. AE, MC, V.

These apartments, last renovated in 1995, represent one of the best bargains on Barbados and are ideal for families. Directly on a rocky shoreline 2½ miles southeast of Bridgetown, the hotel is in the heart of the village of Hastings. The U-shaped apartment complex is built around a pool terrace overlooking the sea. Functional and minimalist in decor, it's clean and comfortable. The tiny kitchenettes in each accommodation are fully equipped, and a variety of rental units are offered. All have balconies or decks, and some units contain air-conditioning. There are supermarkets, stores, and banks within easy walking distance. Although some athletic guests attempt to swim off the nearby rocks, most walk 5 minutes to the white sands of nearby Rockley (Accra) Beach. A small restaurant is open on the property, serving American and Bajan fare.

BEST OFF-SEASON BETS

Casuarina Beach Club. St. Lawrence Gap, Christ Church, Barbados, W.I. ☎ **800/223-9815** in the U.S., or 246/428-3600. Fax 246/428-1970. 123 studios, 20 one-bedroom suites, 14 two-bedroom suites. A/C TEL. Winter, $165–$180 studio for two; $195 one-bedroom suite; $330 two-bedroom suite. Off-season, $90–$100 studio for two; $120 one-bedroom suite; $180 two-bedroom suite. MAP $32 per person extra. Children 11 and under stay free in parents' room. AE, MC, V.

You'll approach this resort, located midway between Bridgetown and Oistins, through a forest of palm trees swaying above a well-maintained lawn. Established in 1981, with substantial additions and improvements completed in 1991, the resort is pleasant, although the staff could afford to be a lot friendlier. Designed with red-tile roofs and white walls, the main building has a series of arched windows leading onto verandas, although to get to your accommodation you pass through the outlying reception building and beside the pair of swimming pools. These are separated from the wide sandy beach by a lawn area dotted with casuarina and bougainvillea. On the premises is an octagonal roofed open-air bar and restaurant, two floodlit tennis courts, a gift shop, a tiny store for the purchase of foodstuffs, and a fitness room. The front desk can arrange most seaside activities through outside agencies. Each accommodation is equipped with a ceiling fan and rattan furniture, and each suite contains a kitchenette. In winter a studio for two rents for $165, a one-bedroom suite for $195, and a two-bedroom suite for $330. However, off-season prices of only $95 for a studio for two make it more alluring. A one-bedroom suite off-season begins at a low of $125, a two-bedroom suite for $190, and children 11 and under sharing their parents' room are housed free. MAP is $10 per person extra. The hotel is decorated with local artwork, including paintings, terra-cotta pots, and sculptures.

Southern Palms. St. Lawrence, Christ Church, Barbados, W.I. ☎ **800/424-5500** in the U.S., or 246/428-7171. Fax 246/428-7175. 91 rms, 26 suites. A/C TV TEL. Winter, $185–$220 double; $270 suite. Off-season, $112–$140 double; $162 suite. MAP $40 per person extra. AE, DC, DISC, MC, V.

A seafront club with a distinct personality, Southern Palms lies on the Pink Beach of Barbados, midway between the airport and Bridgetown. The core of the resort is a pink-and-white manor house built in the Dutch style, with a garden-level colonnade of arches. Spread along the sands are multiarched two- and three-story buildings. Italian fountains and statues add to the Mediterranean feeling. In its more modern block, an eclectic mixture of rooms includes some with kitchenettes, some facing the ocean, others opening onto the garden, and some with penthouse luxury. Each room is a double, and the suites have small kitchenettes. The decor is the standard motel-like tropical motif. A cluster of straw-roofed buildings, the drinking and dining facilities, link the accommodations together.

Although in winter a single or double rents for $180, tariffs are slashed off-season to $112 to $140 double, one of the better bargains along the coast.

The Khus-Khus Bar and Restaurant serves both West Indian and continental cuisine. A local orchestra often entertains by providing merengue and steel-band music. Facilities include two beachside freshwater swimming pools, sailboat rentals, and two tennis courts. Snorkeling and scuba diving are available.

WORTH A SPLURGE

✪ **Bagshot House Hotel.** St. Lawrence, Christ Church, Barbados, W.I. ☎ **246/435-6956.** Fax 246/435-2889. 16 rms. A/C TEL. Winter, $85 single; $120 double. Off-season, $55 single; $80 double. Rates include breakfast. AE, CB, DC, DISC, MC, V.

Completely renovated in 1996, this small, family-managed hotel, which has been painted pink since the 1940s, has flowering vines tumbling over the railing of the balconies and an old-fashioned, unhurried kind of charm. The hotel was named after the early 19th-century manor house that once stood on this site. In front, a white-sand beach stretches out before you. Some of the well-kept rooms boast views of the water. A sunbathing deck, which doubles as a kind of living room for the resort, is perched at the edge of a lagoon. A deckside lounge is decorated with paintings by local artists, and a restaurant, Sand Dollar, is on the premises (see "Where to Eat," later in this chapter).

Sea Foam Haciendas. Worthing, Christ Church, Barbados, W.I. ☎ **800/8-BARBADOS** in the U.S. and Canada, or 246/435-7380. Fax 246/435-7384. 12 suites. A/C TEL. Winter, $115 single or double; $160 quad. Off-season, $77 single or double; $105 quad. Extra person $15 in winter, $12 off-season. July–Aug and Nov, only the quad rate is charged. MC, V.

Centrally located on Worthing Beach, this Spanish-designed property lies between the airport and Bridgetown. It's also convenient to supermarkets, banks, a post office, and a small shopping plaza. All the drinking and dining facilities of the St. Lawrence area are close at hand if you don't want to rent a car. Each suite is fully furnished, with two air-conditioned bedrooms, a modern kitchen with electric stove, and a large refrigerator with a microwave. Each suite also has its own private phone and radio, and there's a wall safe in the master bedroom. The open-style kitchen looks into the living and dining room area, which opens onto a large private balcony overlooking the ocean. Because of this place's good value, it enjoys a high repeat clientele.

Silver Sands Resort. Silver Sands, Christ Church, Barbados, W.I. ☎ **800/GO-BAJAN** in the U.S., 800/822-2077 in Canada, or 246/428-6001. Fax 246/428-3758. 41 rms, 45 studios, 20 one-bedroom suites. A/C TV. Winter, $130 single or double; $140 studio for two; $155 suite for two; $165 triple; $175 quad. Off-season, $65–$70 single or double; $75 studio for two; $80 suite for two; $90 triple; $100 quad. Extra person $10; children 12 and under stay free in parents' room. AE, DC, DISC, MC, V.

This is a beachfront resort of six mushroom-colored buildings on 6 acres of handsomely landscaped grounds. Each is well furnished, and, although not particularly stylish, all come with balconies and a number of conveniences, including pay-per-view

TV. All the studios have kitchenettes, and the suites come with full kitchens. Extra amenities include baby-sitting, and room service is also available. You can dine here or patronize several restaurants nearby. The Sands is a true resort, with two swimming pools, tennis courts, and a water-sports concession. The place may not be for the hopelessly romantic—it's too sterile for that. It's a good, all-around, reliable resort, one of the best in the area, and it charges only a fraction of the price of the megaresorts with their megatariffs.

2 Where to Eat

Angry Annie's Restaurant & Bar. First St., Holetown, St. James. ☎ **246/432-2119.** Main courses $15–$27.50. MC, V. Daily 6pm–10pm (or sometimes after midnight). INTERNATIONAL.

Don't ask "Annie" why she's angry. She might tell you! Annie and Paul Matthews, both of the U.K., run this restaurant in a new location. This cozy, 34-seat joint is decorated in tropical colors with a circular bar. Rock 'n' roll classics play on the excellent sound system. The dishes are tasty with lots of local flavor. The place is known for ribs, the most savory on the island. We also like their garlic cream potatoes, and their use of local vegetables whenever possible. Angry or not, Annie also turns out excellent pasta dishes, and you can also order fresh fish. Begin with a homemade soup or chicken wings, and then the night is yours, especially if you order such dishes as chicken Kiev or spaghetti bolognese. There's even a take-out service if you'd like to take something back to your studio or apartment.

✪ **Atlantis Hotel.** Bathsheba, St. Joseph. ☎ **246/433-9445.** Reservations required for Sun buffet and 7pm dinner, recommended at all other times. Two-course fixed-price lunch or dinner $16.50; Sun buffet $17.25. AE. Daily 11:30am–3pm, dinner at 7pm (and don't be late). BAJAN.

Harking back to the old-fashioned Barbados of several years ago, the slightly run-down Atlantis Hotel is often filled with both Bajans and visitors. It's located between Cattlewash-on-Sea and Tent Bay on the east coast (Atlantic Ocean). In the sunny, breeze-filled interior, with a sweeping view of the turbulent ocean, Enid I. Maxwell has been welcoming visitors from all over the world ever since she opened the place in 1945. Her copious buffets are one of the best food values on the island. From loaded tables, you can sample such Bajan foods as pumpkin fritters, peas and rice, macaroni and cheese, chow mein, souse, and a Bajan pepperpot. No one ever leaves here hungry.

Barbecue Barn. Rockley, Christ Church. ☎ **246/435-6602.** Reservations not accepted. Main courses BD$18.75–BD$23.50 ($9.40–$11.75). MC, V. Daily 11am–11pm. BAJAN.

This basic restaurant serves simple fare often to families staying in south-coast hotels. There's a fully stocked self-service salad bar. Try the barbecued chicken as a main course or in a sandwich. The menu also includes roast chicken, burgers, steak, and fried chicken nuggets. Most main courses are served with your choice of potato or spiced rice and garlic bread. A small selection of wines complements your meal.

Bombas. Paynes Bay, St. James. ☎ **246/432-0569.** Main courses $10–$16.50; lunch from $8. MC, V. Daily 11am–11pm. INTERNATIONAL.

Simple and unpretentious though it is, this place is "worth a detour," as Michelin always says. Right on the water at Paynes Bay, it's so inviting that you may adopt it as your local hangout. The avocados on Barbados are said to be "ethereal," and you can find out why here, along with sampling an array of other Bajan specialties and even dishes designed to appeal to the veggie market. The drinks here are made with fresh juices and not overly loaded with buckets of sugar. The owners Gaye and

Wayne, a Scottish/Bajan couple, are hospitable hosts, chalking up their latest offerings on a blackboard menu. You can visit just for a snack, perhaps enjoying ròti or seasoned flying fish. Their main dishes are certainly worth trying, including the catch of the day which can be blackened in the Cajun style or deep-fried in crispy batter and chips in the English style. They also make a wicked Bomba curry, or, for a taste of the Highlands of Scotland, will serve you sautéed chicken breast on a bed of saffron rice with a Drambuie-cream sauce.

Café Calabash. St. Nicholas Abbey, on the St. Peter / St. Lucy border. ☎ **246/422-8725.** Créole lunch, snacks, traditional English teas $4–$15. No credit cards. Mon–Fri 10am–4pm. BAJAN / AFTERNOON TEA.

On the site of this Jacobean plantation Great House, this is the most romantic place on Barbados to have afternoon tea or else to stop in for a Bajan lunch of Créole fare. Nick Hudson, a restaurateur who became famous islandwide when he operated the restaurant La Cage aux Folles, opened this cafe in 1997. Now you can eat or drink at one of the premier tourist attractions of Barbados. The cafe looks out onto one of the few remaining virgin rain forests in the Caribbean. A typical menu might include Bajan fish cakes, pepperpot stew, jerked pork chops, pickled bread fruit, and vegetarian somozas, followed by delectable desserts such as key lime pie or coconut meringue pie.

Café Sol. St. Lawrence Gap, Christ Church. ☎ **246/435-9531.** Main courses $11–$17. AE, MC, V. Daily 6–11pm. TEX-MEX.

Even though this cafe has a gringo section of the menu, designed for diehard meat-and-potatoes Yankees, most savvy foodies come to this St. Lawrence Gap eatery for some of the best Tex-Mex food on the island. The burritos and tacos don't get much bigger than here. If you're looking for flavorful and zesty meals, and at a good price with oversize portions and enthusiastic service, eat here. Feast on the tostados, fajitas, nachos, and all the good-tasting beef, shrimp, and chicken dishes, each served with rice and beans or fries. As for the non-Mexican burgers, barbecued chicken, hot dogs, and steaks, you can fare better elsewhere. This is a small, comfortable place with an outside bar and patio and a medley of recorded Italian and Mexican music to entertain you.

Crane Beach Hotel. Crane Bay, St. Philip. ☎ **246/423-6220.** Reservations required. Lunch BD$9–BD$45 ($4.50–$22.50); lunch buffet Wed and Fri (noon–3:30pm) BD$28 ($14); Sun brunch BD$40.25 ($20.10). AE, DC, MC, V. Daily 7:30am–9:30pm (Sun brunch 12:30–3pm). BAJAN.

On a remote hilltop opening onto the Atlantic Coast, this scenic restaurant serves traditional Bajan specialties as well as a few international dishes. The dinner, costing BD$42 to BD$60 ($21 to $30), is a little too pricey to be called a bargain, but lunches include burgers, sandwiches, and lighter fare kinder to your wallet. Sunday brunch is a real bargain. Served buffet-style, the brunch—"a good tuck-in"—includes soup of the day (hot or cold); Bajan and international dishes, including flying fish and a baked pie made of macaroni, cream, onions, and sweet peppers; a number of side items (rice and peas, candied sweet potatoes, and plantains); an assortment of desserts, including fresh fruit; and a beverage. Either before or after brunch, guests walk down the coral-hewn stairway from the hotel's cantilevered terrace to the pink sandy beach. The restaurant features live entertainment Tuesday and Friday until 10:30pm.

Ròti Hut. Worthing, Christ Church. ☎ **246/435-7362.** Snacks and plates $2–$4.60; picnic box $4.25. No credit cards. Mon–Thurs 11am–10pm, Fri–Sat 11am–11pm. ROTIS.

The island's best ròtis are served here at this little Worthing hut, an off-white concrete structure with an enclosed patio for dining. Count on these zesty pastries to be filled with good-tasting and spicy meats, or whatever. The crowd pleaser is the mammoth chicken or beef potato ròti. The locals like their ròtis with bone, but you can order yours without if you wish. You can also order other food items, including beef burgers, fried chicken, and beef or chicken curry with rice. This is also a good place to pick up a picnic box.

Shakey's Restaurant. Hastings Main Rd., Christ Church. ☎ **246/435-7777.** Main courses BD$10–BD$45 ($5–$22.50). AE, MC, V. Sat–Thurs 11am–11pm, Fri 11am–2am. INTERNATIONAL.

Housed in a white wooden structure, this family restaurant is a good bet if you're staying at a south-coast hotel. Pizzas are served here on thin and thick crusts starting at BD$10 ($5). Other menu options include spareribs, barbecued chicken, pastas, burgers, and sandwiches such as the hot hero with salami, pepperoni, and ham. Try the fried chicken served with mojo potatoes (mojo is a piquant sauce made with local herbs, vinegar, garlic, and oil). Throughout the week Bajan specials offered include flying fish, macaroni pie, and sweet-potato pie. Full take-out service is featured here, along with karaoke.

Taps on the Bay Tavern & Grill. St. Lawrence Gap, Christ Church. ☎ **246/435-6549.** Main courses $6–$20. AE, MC, V. Daily 6–10:30pm. (Bar, daily 5pm–2am.) CARIBBEAN/INTERNATIONAL.

This sea-view spot is a "hot" dining choice on the list of St. Lawrence eateries. It's known for its campy decor, such as a "shooter" chair (actually, an old dentist's chair). The victim sits in this chair and gets spun around after heavy drinking. The walls are covered with items sent back by tourists, including their photos, beer ads, currency, whatever. Visitors from almost anywhere can be seen at the canopied bar. If all this camp isn't a turn-off, you can get quite acceptable fare here, including grilled flying fish, a traditional Indian curry, crab Alfredo, and local fish prepared many ways. An extensive dessert menu features homemade pies and cakes, and you can finish off with a cappuccino or espresso. Bar snacks are also available, including steak on a bun or a cheese-cutter sandwich (cheese, lettuce, tomato, and cucumber on a bun). Thursday is karaoke night from 9pm "until," and on Friday there's a country-western band. Saturday is more Bajan authentic, as a steel band comes in to entertain.

T.G.I. Boomers. St. Lawrence Gap, Christ Church. ☎ **246/428-8439.** Main courses $9–$22.50; lunch specials $3.50–$7; American breakfast $6.50; daiquiris $3–$5. AE, MC, V. Daily 7:30am–11:30pm. AMERICAN/BAJAN.

Four miles south of Bridgetown near Rockley Beach along Highway 7, T.G.I. Boomers offers some of the best bargain meals on the island. An American/Bajan operation, it has an active bar and a row of tables where food is served, usually along with frothy pastel-colored drinks. The cook prepares a special catch of the day, and the fish is served with soup or salad, rice or baked potato, and a vegetable. You can always count on seafood, steaks, and hamburgers. For lunch, try a daily Bajan special or a jumbo sandwich. Be sure to try one of the 16-ounce daiquiris.

39 Steps. Chattel Plaza, Hastings, Christ Church. ☎ **246/427-0715.** Main courses $12.50–$16. MC, V. Mon–Fri noon–3pm and 6:30–9:30pm, Sat 6:30–10:30pm. Closed Sept. INTERNATIONAL.

This south-coast eatery, one of the area's most popular, is the best wine bar in Hastings. Diners walk the 39 steps (or whatever) to reach this convivial place where performers sometimes entertain on the sax and guitar. It's laid-back and casual, and the food and wine are not only good but affordable. Look to the chalkboard for the tasty favorites of the day. Whenever possible the cooks use fresh, local produce. They concoct dishes that appeal to a wide cross section, including English pub grub–style pies such as steak and kidney or chicken and mushroom. They also turn out lasagne and other pastas, along with seafood crèpes, shrimp and chicken curry, and blackened fish. The most famous dish of Barbados, flying fish, appears only on the lunch menu. They're not big on vegetables, however, serving only a mixed green salad. This pleasant restaurant and bar has lots of windows and a balcony for outdoor dining.

The Waterfront Cafe. The Careenage, Bridgetown. ☎ **246/427-0093.** Reservations required. Main courses BD$16–BD$28 ($8–$14). AE, MC, V. Mon–Sat 10am–midnight. INTERNATIONAL.

In a turn-of-the-century warehouse originally built to store bananas and freeze fish, this cafe serves international fare with a strong emphasis on Bajan specialties. Try the fresh catch of the day prepared Créole style, peppered steak, or the fish burger made with kingfish or dolphin. For vegetarians, the menu includes such dishes as pasta primavera, vegetable soup, and usually a featured special. This enterprise welcomes both diners and drinkers to its reverberating walls for Créole food, beer, and pastel-colored drinks. Live steel-pan music is presented, with a Bajan buffet featured on Tuesday from 7 to 9pm, costing BD$35 ($17.50). If you expect to see the Dixieland bands on Thursday night, you need to make reservations about a week in advance.

ALL-YOU-CAN-EAT PLACES

The Coach House. Paynes Bay, St. James. ☎ **246/432-1163.** Reservations recommended. Dinner BD$9–$45 ($4.50–$22.50); bar snacks BD$9–BD$25 ($4.50–$12.50); all-you-can-eat Bajan lunch buffet BD$22 ($11). AE, MC, V. Daily noon–2am. BAJAN.

The Coach House, named after a pair of antique coaches that stand outside, is a green-and-white house said to be 200 years old. The atmosphere is a Bajan version of an English pub, with an outdoor garden bar. Businesspeople and habitués of nearby beaches come here to order buffet lunches, where Bajan food is served Sunday to Friday from noon to 3pm. The price is $11 for an all-you-can-eat lunch including local vegetables and salads prepared fresh daily. The best deal here is the bar menu, which ranges from burgers and fries to fried shrimp and flying fish. Dinner is from an à la carte menu with steak, chicken, fish, curried dishes, fresh salads, and a wide range of desserts from cheesecake to banana flambé. Live music is available every night of the week, from top nightclub bands to steel bands. The pub is on the main Bridgetown–Holetown road, just south of Sandy Lane, about 6 miles north of Bridgetown.

The Ship Inn. St. Lawrence Gap, Christ Church. ☎ **246/435-6961.** Reservations recommended for the Captain's Carvery only. Main courses $8–$13; all-you-can-eat carvery meal $11 at lunch, $30 (plus $7.50 for appetizer and dessert) at dinner. AE, MC, V. Sun–Fri noon–3pm and 6:30–10:30pm (last order), Sat 6:30–10:30pm. ENGLISH PUB / BAJAN.

South of Bridgetown between Rockley Beach and Worthing, the Ship Inn is a traditional English-style pub with an attractive, rustic decor of nautical memorabilia. As an alternative, patrons may wish to drink and enjoy a tropical atmosphere in a garden bar. Many guests come for darts and to meet friends, and certainly to listen to the live music presented nightly by some of the island's top bands (see "Barbados After Dark," later in this chapter). The Ship Inn serves substantial bar food, such as homemade steak-and-kidney pie, shepherd's pie, and chicken, shrimp, and fish dishes. For more formal dining, visit the Captain's Carvery, where you can have your fill of succulent cuts from prime roasts on a nighttime buffet table, and an array of traditional Bajan food (filets of flying fish). Diners can enjoy their repast in a tropical garden. An additional attraction: Top local bands perform in the pub at no extra charge. The establishment stocks beers from Jamaica, Trinidad, and Europe.

WORTH A SPLURGE

✪ **Brown Sugar.** Aquatic Gap, St. Michael. ☎ **246/426-7684.** Reservations recommended. Main courses $14–$35; fixed-price buffet lunch $17.50. AE, DC, DISC, MC, V. Sun–Fri noon–2:30pm and 6–9:30pm (last order), Sat 6–9:30pm (last order). BAJAN.

Hidden behind lush foliage, Brown Sugar is an alfresco restaurant in a turn-of-the-century coral limestone bungalow south of Bridgetown. The ceiling is latticed, with slow-turning fans, and there's an open veranda for dining by candlelight below hanging plants. The chefs prepare some of the tastiest Bajan specialties on the island. Among the soups, we suggest hot gungo-peak soup (pigeon peas cooked in chicken broth and zested with fresh coconut milk, herbs, and a touch of white wine). Of the main dishes, Créole orange chicken is popular, or perhaps you'd like stuffed crab backs. Conch fritters and garlic pork are also spicy. A selection of locally grown vegetables is also offered. For dessert, we recommend the walnut-rum pie with rum sauce. The restaurant is known for its lunches—good value and served buffet style to local businesspeople.

Champers. Keswick Centre, Hastings, Christ Church. ☎ **246/435-6644.** Main courses $22–$25; lunch from $15. MC, V. Mon–Sat noon–3pm and 6–10pm. INTERNATIONAL.

The prices here are a bit higher than we like, but you're paying for some of the South coast's best seafood, served at this comfortable two-story restaurant on the ocean with picture windows. You can also eat at the four tables and the bar downstairs. On Saturday there's live guitar music in the lounge. Dinner includes an excellent and well-flavored shrimp-and-mango salad or a terrine made with dolphin and salmon. You can proceed to the chicken breast served in a spinach and bleu-cheese sauce or else opt for shrimp and scallops with a shellfish coulis. The lunch sandwiches are meals unto themselves, or you can order a shrimp-and-vegetable stir-fry, perhaps ravioli with fresh mushrooms and a walnut sauce.

Kingsley Club. Cattlewash-on-Sea (near Bathsheba), St. Joseph. ☎ **246/433-9422.** Reservations recommended for lunch, required for dinner. Main courses $8–$16; fixed-price four-course menu $25–$35. AE, MC, V. Daily noon–3pm and 6:30–7:30pm (last order). BAJAN.

A historic inn recommended previously for its rooms, the Kingsley Club also serves some of the best Bajan food on the island in a turn-of-the-century house cooled by Atlantic breezes. You're invited to "come tuck in" and enjoy your fill of split-pea and pumpkin soup, dolphin meunière, or planters of fried chicken, followed by one of the homemade desserts, perhaps coconut pie. The inn, on the northeastern coast a quarter mile northeast of Bathsheba, is about 15 miles from Bridgetown.

✪ **Koko's.** Prospect, St. James. ☎ **246/424-4557.** Reservations recommended. Main courses $17–$21. DISC, MC, V. Daily 6:30–10pm (last seating). Closed Mon May–Nov. BAJAN.

Koko's is an award-winning restaurant, known for its excellent Caribbean cookery, a kind of Bajan *cuisine moderne.* The location alone is appealing: It's in a charming once-private house, built on coral blocks on a terrace overlooking the sea. The appetizers are among the most appealing and innovative on Barbados, including "roots of the Caribbean," a traditional pepperpot meat stew flavored with cassareep. For the most typical starter, try "stamp & go"—actually, herbed conch fritters with a fiery dip. Hot pumpkin soup with goat cheese crumbles is another traditional favorite. Pastas and curries get a separate corner of the menu, ranging from Goan-style shrimp curry with toasted coconut to fusilli pasta tossed with a pink shrimp pesto. Main dishes have zesty flavors, none better than "Pick of the Pot"—flaky filet of barracuda crusted with black beans, ginger, garlic, and hot peppers, and given the final touch with a creamy crab sauce.

Witch Doctor. St. Lawrence Gap, Christ Church. ☎ **246/435-6581.** Reservations recommended. Main courses $11–$30. MC, V. Daily 6:15–9:45pm. BAJAN/AFRICAN.

The Witch Doctor hides behind a screen of thick foliage in the heart of the southern coast. The decor, in honor of its name, features African and island wood carvings of witch doctors. The place purveys a fascinating cuisine with some unusual concoctions that are tasty and well prepared, a big change from bland hotel fare. For an appetizer, try the split-pea and pumpkin soup. You'll also be offered ceviche (cold, soused in lime). Chef's specialties include various flambé dishes such as steak, shrimp Créole, fried flying fish, and chicken piri-piri (inspired by Mozambique).

3 Beaches, Water Sports & Other Outdoor Pursuits

You've probably come to swim and sunbathe, and both are far preferable on the western coast in the clear, buoyant waters, although you may also want to visit the surf-pounded Atlantic coast in the east, which is better for the views than for swimming.

BEACHES

Bajans will tell you that their island has a beach for every day of the year. If you're only visiting for a short time, however, you'll probably be happy with the ones that are easy to find. They're all open to the public—even those in front of the big resort hotels and private homes—and the government requires that there be access to all beaches, via roads along the property line or through the hotel entrance. The beaches on the west, the so-called **Gold Coast,** are the most popular.

WEST COAST Waters are calm here. Major beaches include **Paynes Bay,** with access from the Coach House. This is a good beach for water sports, especially snorkeling. There's also a parking area. The beach can get rather crowded, however, but the beautiful bay somehow makes it seem worth the effort to get here.

Directly south of Payne's Bay, at Fresh Water Bay, are three of the best west-coast beaches: **Brighton Beach, Brandon's Beach,** and **Paradise Beach.**

Church Point lies north of St. James Church, opening onto Heron Bay, site of the Colony Club Hotel. This is one of the most scenic bays on Barbados, and the swimming is ideal. The beach can get overcrowded, however. There are some shade trees when you've had enough sun. You can also order drinks at the beach terrace operated by the Colony Club.

Mullins Beach, a final west-coast selection, is also recommended. Its blue waters are glassy and attract snorkelers. There's parking on the main road. Again, the beach has some shady areas. At the Mullins Beach Bar you can order that rum drink.

SOUTH COAST Beaches here include **Casuarina Beach,** with access from Maxwell Coast Road, going across the property of the Casuarina Beach Hotel. This is one of the wider beaches of Barbados, and we've noticed that it's swept by trade winds even on the hottest days of August. Windsurfers are especially fond of this one. Food and drink can be ordered at the hotel.

Silver Sands Beach, to the east of Oistins, is near the southernmost point of Barbados, directly east of the South Point Lighthouse and near the Silver Rock Hotel. This white-sand beach is a favorite with many Bajans (who probably want to keep it a secret from as many tourists as possible). Drinks are sold at the Silver Rock Bar.

Sandy Beach, reached from the parking lot on the Worthing main road, has tranquil waters opening onto a lagoon, a cliché of Caribbean charm. This is a family favorite, with lots of screaming and yelling, especially on the weekends. Food and drink are sold here.

SOUTHEAST COAST   The southeast coast is the site of the big waves, especially at **Crane Beach,** the white-sand beach set against a backdrop of palms that you've probably seen in all the travel magazines. The beach is spectacular, as Prince Andrew, who has a house overlooking the beach, might agree. It offers excellent body surfing, but at times the waters might be too rough for all but the strongest swimmers. The beach is set against cliffs, and the Crane Beach Hotel towers above it. This is ocean swimming, not the calm Caribbean, so take precautions.

   Bottom Bay, north of Sam Lord's Castle Resorts, is one of our all-time Bajan favorites. You park on the top of a cliff, then walk down steps to this much-photographed tropical beach with its grove of coconut palms. There's even a cave. The sand is brilliantly white, a picture-postcard version of a beach with an aquamarine sea.

EAST COAST (ON THE ATLANTIC)   There are miles and miles of uncrowded beaches along the east coast, but this is the Atlantic side and swimming here is potentially dangerous. Many visitors like to visit the beaches here, especially those in the **Bathsheba** and **Cattlewash** areas, for their rugged grandeur. Waves are extremely high on these beaches, and the bottom tends to be rocky. The currents are also unpredictable. Otherwise, the beaches are ideal for strolling if you don't go into the water.

WATER SPORTS

SNORKELING & SCUBA DIVING   The clear waters off Barbados have a visibility of more than 100 feet most of the year. More than 50 varieties of fish are found on the shallow inside reefs. On night dives, sleeping fish, night anemones, lobsters, moray eels, and octopuses can be seen. On a mile-long coral reef 2 minutes by boat from Sandy Beach, sea fans, corals, gorgonias, and reef fish are plentiful. The *J.R.,* a dredge barge sunk as an artificial reef in 1983, is popular with beginners for its coral, fish life, and 20-foot depth. The *Berwyn,* a coral-encrusted tugboat that sank in Carlisle Bay in 1916, attracts photographers because of its variety of reef fish, shallow depth, good light, and visibility.

   The **Asta Reef,** with a drop of 80 feet, has coral, sea fans, and reef fish in abundance. It's the site of a Barbados wreck sunk in 1986 as an artificial reef. **Dottins,** the most beautiful reef on the west coast, stretches 5 miles from Holetown to Bridgetown and has numerous dive sites at an average depth of 40 feet and drop-offs of 100 feet. The SS *Stavronika,* a Greek freighter, is a popular site for advanced divers. Crippled by fire in 1976, the 360-foot freighter was sunk a quarter mile off the west coast to become an artificial reef in **Folkestone Underwater Park.** The mast is at 40 feet, the deck at 80 feet, and the keel at 140 feet. It's encrusted with coral.

   The Dive Shop, Pebbles Beach, Aquatic Gap, St. Michael (☎ **246/426-9947**), offers some of the best scuba diving on Barbados. Rates are $48 per one-tank dive or $70 for a two-tank dive. Two dive trips go out daily to the nearby reefs and wrecks. Snorkeling trips and equipment rentals are also possible. Visitors with reasonable swimming skills who have never dived before can sign up for a resort course. Priced at $60, it includes pool training, safety instructions, and a one-tank open-water dive. The establishment is NAUI and PADI certified. It's open daily from 9am to 5pm.

WINDSURFING   Experts say that the windsurfing off Barbados is as good as any this side of Hawaii. Judging from the crowds of 20- to 35-year-olds who flock here, it's true. Windsurfing on Barbados has turned into a very big business between

November and April. Thousands of windsurfers from all over the world now come here from as far away as Finland, Argentina, and Japan. The shifting of the trade winds between November and May and the shallow offshore reef off **Silver Sands** create unique conditions of wind and wave swells. This allows windsurfers to reach speeds of up to 50 knots and do complete loops off the waves. **Silver Sands** is rated the best spot in the Caribbean for advanced windsurfing (skill rating 5 to 6). In other words, one needs the skills similar to a professional downhill skier to master these conditions.

An outfit set up to handle the demand from windsurfers who derive from virtually everywhere, the **Barbados Windsurfing Club** maintains two branches on the island. Beginners and intermediates usually opt for the branch in Oistins (☎ **246/ 428-7277**), where winds are constant but where the sea is generally flat and calm. Advanced intermediates and expert windsurfers usually select the branch adjacent to the Silver Sands Hotel, in Christ Church (☎ **246/428-6001**), where stronger winds and higher waves allow surfers to combine aspects of windsurfing with conventional surfing as known in Hawaii. Boards and equipment used by both branches of this outfit are provided by Germany-based Club Mistral. Lessons at either branch cost between $40 and $55 per hour, depending on how many people are in your class. Equipment rents for between $25 and $35 per hour or $55 to $65 per half day, depending on where and what you rent. Budgeteers usually opt for the Oistins branch, as prices are lower than at the Silver Sands branch.

OTHER SPORTS

GOLF   The **Royal Westmoreland Golf & Country Club,** Westmoreland, St. James (☎ **246/422-4653**), is the island's premier golf course. But this $30-million, 27-hole course can only be played by guests of the Royal Pavilion, Glitter Bay, Colony Club, Tamarind Cove, Coral Reef, Crystal Cove, Cobblers Cove, Sandpiper Inn, and Sandy Lane.

Open to all is the 18-hole championship golf course of the **Sandy Lane Hotel,** St. James (☎ **246/432-1311**), on the west coast. Greens fees are $100 in winter and $75 in summer for 18 holes, or $65 in winter and $45 in summer for 9 holes. Carts and caddies are available.

HIKING   The **Barbados National Trust** (☎ **246/426-2421**) offers Sunday-morning hikes throughout the year. The program gives participants an opportunity to learn about the natural beauty of Barbados. It attracts more than 300 participants weekly. Led by young Bajans and members of the National Trust, the hikes cover a different area of the island each week. The tour escorts give brief talks on various aspects of the hikes, such as geography, history, geology, and agriculture. The hikes, free and open to participants of all ages, are divided into fast, medium, and slow categories. All the hikes leave promptly at 6am; each is about 5 miles long and takes about 3 hours to complete. There are also hikes at 3:30pm and 5:30pm, the latter conducted only on moonlit nights. For information or transportation, contact the Barbados National Trust.

HORSEBACK RIDING   A different view of Barbados is offered by the **Caribbean International Riding Centre,** Cleland Plantation, Farley Hill, St. Andrew (☎ **246/ 422-7433**). With nearly 40 horses, Mrs. Roachford or one of her daughters offers a variety of trail rides for any level of experience. Prices of various rides range from the 1-hour trek for $30 to a $2^{1}/_{2}$ hour jaunt for $65. You ride through some of the most panoramic parts of Barbados, especially the hilly terrain of the Scotland district. Wild ducks and water lilies, with the rhythm of the Atlantic as background music, are some of nature's sights viewed along the way.

TENNIS **Sandy Lane,** St. James (☎ 246/432-1311), has five courts open to nonguests. Two of the five courts—all of which are well maintained—are lit for night games. One of the courts simulates the feel of grass, while the other four are hard-surface. It's advised to play early or late, although the courts are wide open during the hot times between 10am and 3pm. Court rentals are $20 per hour or $10 per half hour. Lessons with a pro cost $25 per half hour or $50 per hour.

The **Barbados Hilton,** Needham's Point (☎ 246/426-0200), maintains four hard-surface courts, each lit for night play. The Hilton's courts are not nearly as clubby or gracious as those of Sandy Lane, but they're closer to Bridgetown and more convenient for many visitors. Guests play for free, while nonresidents pay $20 per half hour. At night all players are charged $10 per half hour for illumination of the courts.

4 Exploring the Island

TOURS & CRUISES

Barbados is worth exploring, either in your own car or with a taxi-driver guide. Unlike on so many islands of the Caribbean, the roads are fair and quite passable. They are, however, poorly signposted, and newcomers invariably get lost, not only once, but several times. If you get lost, the people in the countryside are generally helpful.

TAXI TOURS Nearly all Bajan taxi drivers are familiar with the entire island and like to show it off to visitors. If you can afford it, touring by taxi is far preferable to taking a standardized bus tour. The average day tour by taxi costs $50—but, of course, that figure has to be negotiated in advance.

ORGANIZED SIGHTSEEING TOURS Instead of a private taxi, you can also book a tour with **Bajan Tours,** Glenayre, Locust Hall, St. George (☎ 246/437-9389), a locally owned and operated tour company. Its best bet for the first-timer is the Exclusive Island Tour, which costs $56 per person and departs between 8:30 and 9am, returning between 3:30 and 4pm daily. It covers all the island highlights, including the Barbados Wildlife Reserve, the Chalky Mount Potteries, and the rugged east coast.

On Friday, for the same price, it conducts a Heritage Tour, mainly of the island's major plantations and museums. And Monday to Friday it offers an Eco Tour, which costs $56; it leaves at the same time as the above tours and takes in the natural beauty of the island. A full buffet lunch is included in all tours.

CRUISES Largest of the coastal cruising vessels, the *Bajan Queen* is modeled after a Mississippi riverboat and is the only cruise ship offering table seating and dining on local fare produced fresh from the on-board galley. There's also cover available from too much sun or rain. The *Bajan Queen* becomes a showboat by night, with local bands providing music for dancing under the stars. You're treated to a dinner of roast chicken, barbecued steak, and seasoned flying fish with a buffet of fresh side dishes and salads. Cruises are usually sold out, so you should book early to avoid disappointment. Each cruise costs BD$110 ($55) and includes transportation to and from your hotel. For reservations, contact Jolly Roger Cruises, Shallow Draft, Bridgetown Harbour (☎ 246/436-6424). Cruises are on Wednesday from 6 to 10pm and Saturday from 5 to 9pm.

The same company also owns two motorized replicas of pirate frigates, the *Jolly Roger I* and the *Jolly Roger II.* One or both of these, depending on demand, departs 5 mornings a week for daytime snorkeling cruises from 10am to 2pm. Included in the price of BD$123 ($61.50) is an all-you-can-eat buffet, complimentary drinks, and free use of snorkeling equipment, which requires a $20 refundable deposit. There's an on-board boutique on both of these boats, and lots of ho-ho-ho-ing. For information, call Jolly Roger Cruises or visit the berth at Bridgetown Harbour. They also operate a fourth boat, *Excellent,* a catamaran running on Monday, Wednesday, and Friday from 9am to 2pm and on Sunday from 10am to 3pm. The price of $55 includes a continental breakfast, a lunch buffet, free drinks, and free snorkeling gear (no deposit), plus inflatable water mattresses. Since it's a catamaran, there are fewer people, making the ambience more intimate.

The operator of **Limbo Lady Sailing Cruises,** 78 Old Chancery Lane, Christ Church (☎ 246/420-5418), Patrick Gonsalves himself skippers his classic 44-foot CSY yacht, *Limbo Lady,* and his wife, Yvonne, a singer and guitarist, serenades you on a sunset cruise. Daily lunch cruises are also possible, with a stop for swimming and snorkeling (equipment provided). Both lunch and sunset cruises offer a complimentary open bar and transportation to and from your hotel. Lunch cruises lasting 4¹/₂ hours cost $63, and 3-hour sunset cruises, including a glass of champagne, go for $52. Moonlight dinner cruises as well as private charters, both local and to neighboring islands, can also be arranged (call for more information).

SUBMERGED SIGHTSEEING You no longer have to be an experienced diver to see what lives 150 feet below the surface of the sea around Barbados. Now all visitors can view the sea's wonders on sightseeing submarines. The air-conditioned submersibles seat 28 to 48 passengers, and make several dives daily from 9am to 6pm. Passengers are transported aboard a ferryboat from the Careenage in downtown Bridgetown to the submarine site, about a mile from the west coast of Barbados. The ride offers a view of the west coast of the island.

The submarines have viewing ports. Besides the rainbow of colors, tropical fish, and plants, you'll see a shipwreck that lies upright and intact below the surface. You're taken aboard either *Atlantic I* or *Atlantic III* on two different trips: The Odyssey, costing $84.50 for adults and $42.25 for children, is a dive onto a reef where professional divers leave the vessel and perform a 15-minute dive show for the viewing passengers. The Expedition costs $73.50 for adults and $36.25 for children. For reservations, contact **Atlantis Submarines (Barbados), Inc.,** Shallow Draught, Bridgetown (☎ 246/436-8929). It's also possible to go cruising over one of the shore reefs to observe marine life. You sit in air-conditioned comfort aboard the *Atlantis Seatrec,* a semisubmersible boat, which gives you a chance to get a snorkeler's view of the reef through large viewing windows. You can also relax on deck as you take in the scenic coastline. The tour costs $29.50 for adults; children 4 to 12 are charged half fare (not suitable for those 3 or under). A second Seatrec tour explores wreckage sites. Divers go down with video cameras to three different wrecks in Carlisle Bay, and the video is transmitted to TV monitors aboard the vessel. The price is the same as for the first tour. For reservations, call the number above.

EXPLORING BRIDGETOWN

Often hot and traffic clogged, the capital, Bridgetown, merits no more than a morning's shopping jaunt. An architectural hodgepodge, it was founded by 64 settlers sent out by the earl of Carlisle in 1628.

Since some half a million visitors arrive on Barbados by cruise ship, the government has opened a $6-million terminal for them. It offers a variety of shopping options, including 20 duty-free shops, 13 local retail stores, and scads of vendors. Many of these reflect the arts and crafts of Barbados, or cruise passengers can choose among a range of products, including jewelry, liquor, china, crystal, electronics, perfume, and leather goods. Some shops sell Barbadian wood carvings and art, as well as locally made fashions. The interior was designed to re-create an island street scene, including storefronts appearing as traditional chattel houses in brilliant island colors with street lights, tropical landscaping, benches, and pushcarts.

Begin your tour at **The Careenage,** from the French word meaning to turn vessels over on their side for cleaning. This was a haven for the clipper ship, and even though today it doesn't have its yesteryear color, it's still worth exploring.

At **Trafalgar Square,** the long tradition of British colonization is immortalized. The monument here, honoring Lord Nelson, was executed by Sir Richard Westmacott and erected in 1813. The **Public Buildings** on the square are of the great, gray Victorian Gothic variety that you might expect to find in South Kensington, London. The east wing contains the meeting halls of the Senate and the House of Assembly, with some stained-glass windows representing the sovereigns of England. Look for the Great Protector himself, Oliver Cromwell.

Behind the Financial Building, **St. Michael's Cathedral,** east of Trafalgar Square, is the symbol of the Church of England transplanted. This Anglican church was built in 1655, but was completely destroyed in a 1780 hurricane. Reconstructed in 1789, it was also damaged by a hurricane in 1831, but was not completely demolished as before. George Washington is said to have worshiped here on his Barbados visit.

For years guides pointed out a house on Upper Bay Street where Washington allegedly slept during his only visit outside the United States. Beginning in 1910 the building was called "The Washington House," although historians seriously doubted the claim. Now, after a careful investigation, the house where Washington slept has been identified as the Codd House in Bush Hill, about half a mile south of the Upper Bay Street location. However, the building is privately owned and not open to the public.

The **synagogue,** Synagogue Lane (☎ 246/432-0840), is one of the oldest in the Western Hemisphere and is surrounded by a burial ground of early Jewish settlers. The present building dates from 1833. It was constructed on the site of an even older synagogue erected by Jews from Brazil in 1654. Sometime in the early 20th century the synagogue was deconsecrated and the structure has since served various roles. In 1983 the government of Barbados seized the deteriorating building, intending to raze it and build a courthouse on the site. An outcry went up from the small Jewish community on the island; money was raised for its restoration, and the building was saved and is now part of the National Trust of Barbados and a synagogue once again. It's open Monday to Friday from 8am to 4:30pm.

First made popular in 1870, **cricket** is the national pastime on Barbados. Matches can last from 1 to 5 days. If you'd like to see a local match, watch for announcements in the newspapers or ask at the Tourist Board, on Harbour Road (☎ 246/427-2623). From Bridgetown, you can hail a taxi if you don't have a car and visit **Garrison Savannah,** just south of the capital, which is a frequent venue for cricket matches and horse races.

The **Barbados Museum,** St. Ann's Garrison, St. Michael (☎ 246/427-0201), is housed in a former military prison. In the exhibition "In Search of Bim," extensive collections show the island's development from prehistoric to modern times. "Born of the Sea" gives fascinating glimpses into the natural environment. There are also fine collections of West Indian maps, decorative arts, and fine arts. The museum sells a variety of quality publications, reproductions (maps, cards, prints), and handcrafts. Its Courtyard Café is a good place for a snack or light lunch. The museum is open Monday to Saturday from 10am to 5pm and on Sunday from 2 to 6pm. Admission is $5 for adults, $2.50 for children.

Nearby, the russet-red **St. Ann's Fort,** on the fringe of the Savannah, garrisoned British soldiers in 1694. The fort wasn't completed until 1703. The Clock House survived the hurricane of 1831.

HEADING INLAND TO STROLL THROUGH TROPICAL GARDENS & TAKE A SPECTACULAR CAVE TOUR

Take Highway 2 from Bridgetown and follow it to **Welchman Hall Gully,** in St. Thomas (☎ **246/438-6671**), a lush tropical garden owned by the Barbados National Trust. You'll see some specimens of plants that were here when the English settlers landed in 1627. Many of the plants are labeled—clove, nutmeg, tree fern, and cocoa among others—and occasionally you'll spot a wild monkey. You'll also see a ravine and limestone stalactites and stalagmites, as well as breadfruit trees that are claimed to be descended from the seedlings brought ashore by Captain Bligh of the *Bounty.* Admission is $5, half price for children 6 to 12; kids 5 and under are admitted free. It's open daily from 9am to 5pm.

Also at Welchman Hall, St. Thomas, ✪ **Harrison's Cave** is the number-one tourist attraction of Barbados. Visitors view this beautiful, natural, underground world from an electric tram and trailer. Before the tour, a video show of the cave is shown in the presentation hall. During the tour, visitors see bubbling streams, tumbling cascades, and deep pools, which are subtly lit, while all around stalactites hang overhead like icicles; stalagmites rise from the floor. Visitors may disembark and get a closer look at this natural phenomenon at the Rotunda Room and the Cascade Pool. Tours are conducted daily from 9am to 4pm (closed Good Friday, Easter Sunday, and Christmas Day). You should reserve by calling ☎ **246/438-6640.** Admission is $8.75 for adults and $4.35 for children.

The **Flower Forest,** at Richmond Plantation (an old sugar plantation), St. Joseph (☎ **246/433-8152**), stands 850 feet above sea level near the western edge of the "Scotland district," a mile from Harrison's Cave. Set in one of the most scenic parts of Barbados, it's more than just a botanical garden—it's where people and nature came together to create something beautiful. After viewing the grounds, visitors can purchase handcrafts at Best of Barbados. Hours are 9am to 5pm daily, and admission is $7 for adults, $3.50 for children 5 to 16, and free for kids 4 and under.

HISTORIC SIGHTS IN ST. MICHAEL & ST. GEORGE PARISHES

Tyrol Cot Heritage Village. Codrington Hill, St. Michael. ☎ **246/424-2074.** Admission $5 adults, $2.50 children. Mon–Fri 9am–5pm.

If you arrived at the airport, you'll recognize the name of Sir Grantley Adams, the leader of the Bajan movement for independence from Britain. This was once his home, and his wife, Lady Adams, lived in the house until her death in 1990. Once you had to wangle a highly prized invitation to visit, but it's now open to all who pay admission. It was built sometime in the mid-1850s from coral stone, in a Palladian style. The grounds have been turned into a museum of Bajan life, including small chattel houses where potters and artists work.

Francia Plantation. St. George, Barbados. ☎ **246/429-0474.** Admission $4.50. Mon–Fri 10am–4pm. On the ABC Hwy., turn east onto Hwy. 4 at the Norman Niles Roundabout (follow the signs to Gun Hill); after going half a mile, turn left onto Hwy. X (follow the signs to Gun Hill and Francia Plantation); after another mile, turn right at the Shell gas station and follow Hwy. X past St. George's Parish Church and up the hill for a mile, turning left at the sign to Francia.

A fine family home, this house stands on a wooded hillside overlooking the St. George Valley and is still owned and occupied by descendants of the original owner.

You can explore several rooms, including the dining room with family silver and an 18th-century James McCabe bracket clock. On the walls are antique maps and prints, including a map of the West Indies printed in 1522.

Gun Hill Signal Station. Hwy. 4. ☎ **246/429-1358.** Admission $4 adults, $2 children 12 and under. Mon–Sat 9am–5pm. Take Hwy. 3 from Bridgetown and then go inland from Hwy. 4 toward St. George Church.

One of two such stations owned and operated by the Barbados National Trust, the Gun Hill Signal Station is strategically placed on the highland of St. George and commands a panoramic view from the east to the west. Built in 1818, it was the finest of a chain of signal stations and was also used as an outpost for the British army stationed here at the time. The old military cookhouse has been restored and houses a snack bar and gift shop.

A MEMORABLE DRIVE AROUND THE ISLAND

If you can afford it, the ideal way to take this tour is with a local taxi driver, who will generally negotiate a fair rate. An average full-day tour (4¹/₂ to 6 hours) averages $50 per person. Of course, you can tour on your own, although you'll have to rent an expensive car. Locals know the roads, which are often unmarked; visitors don't. If you do explore on your own, you can count on getting lost, at least several times. Although there are lots of signs, highway authorities will often leave you stranded at strategic junctions, and it's very easy to take a wrong turn if you don't know the way. Even people who live on Barbados often get confused. No clear, concise map of Barbados has yet been devised. Maps only help you with general directions; when you're looking for the route to a specific destination, they can often be most unhelpful.

That having been said, know that part of the fun of exploring Barbados is the discovery of the island. So if you do get lost a few times and miss an attraction or two, that's no great harm. The tour we've outlined below can be done in a day.

After leaving Bridgetown (see above), head south along Highway 7, passing through the resorts of Hastings, Rockley, Worthing, and St. Lawrence.

After going through Worthing, and providing you can find this badly marked road, turn right along **St. Lawrence Gap,** which is the restaurant row of Barbados, including such well-known places as the Witch Doctor and the Ship Inn. There are also several budget and medium-priced hotels located along this strip, which is generally lively both day and night.

At the end of St. Lawrence Gap, resume your journey along Highway 7 by taking a right turn. You'll bypass the town of **Oistins,** a former shipping port that today is a fishing village. Here the Charter of Barbados was signed at the Mermaid in 1652, as the island surrendered to Commonwealth forces. The Mermaid Inn, incidentally, was owned by a cousin of John Turner, who built the House of the Seven Gables in Salem, Massachusetts.

At the sign, take a left for Providence and the Grantley Adams Airport on a continuation of Highway 7 (you'll pass the airport on your right). After bypassing the airport, follow the signs to Sam Lord's Castle Resorts. At the hamlet of Spencers, leave Highway 7 and turn onto Rock Hall Road, going through the villages of St. Martins and Heddings until you come to the remote hilltop **Crane Beach Hotel** (☎ **246/423-6220**). Everyone touring the south coast stops here for the view of the Atlantic, and the hotel's much-photographed Roman-style swimming pool is beloved by all visiting cruise-ship passengers. There are two different entrance fees: $2.50 or $10. The $2.50 fee lets you hang out at the bar and is applied to your bar tab. A $10 pool package gives you greater access to the hotel's facilities, and $5 of this fee is applied to your bar tab.

After leaving the hotel, follow Crane Road east. Turn right at the sign and continue to the end of the road and **Sam Lord's Castle Resorts.** Although this is a hotel, it's also one of the major sightseeing attractions of Barbados; you can stop for a bite here if you didn't already stop at the Crane Beach Hotel. Built by slaves in 1820, and furnished in part with Regency pieces, the house is like a Georgian plantation mansion. Take note of the ornate ceilings, said to be the finest example of stucco work in the Western Hemisphere. At the entrance to the hotel are shops selling handcrafts and souvenirs. If you're not a guest, you'll have to pay BD$10 ($5) to enter.

After leaving Sam Lord's Castle, take a right onto Long Bay Road and continue east. Go right via the village of Wellhouse and continue along the main road, which skirts the coastline but doesn't touch the coast. On your right you'll see the **Ragged Point Lighthouse.** Turn right down a narrow road to the easternmost point of Barbados. Built in 1885, the lighthouse stands on a rugged cliff. Since that time its beacon has warned ships approaching the dangerous reef, called the Cobblers. The view from here is panoramic.

After leaving the lighthouse, continue straight along Marley Vale Road (don't expect proper signs). At the sign to Bayfield, go right and pass Three Houses Park. Take a right at the sign to Bridgetown onto Thickets Road. Take a right again at the sign to Bathsheba. When you come to another signpost, turn left toward Bathsheba and follow the signs to **Codrington College,** which opened in 1745. A cabbage palm–lined avenue leads to old coral-block buildings. Today the college is a training school for men and women from the entire Caribbean to enter the ordained ministry of the Anglican church. The college is under the auspices of the Dioceses of the West Indies. Entrance is $2.50.

After leaving the college, go right, then take the next left up the steep Coach Hill Road, where you'll have excellent views of the east coast and the lighthouse just visited. At the top of the hill, continue right and follow the signs to **St. John's Church,** perched on the edge of a cliff opening on the east coast some 825 feet above sea level. The church dates from 1836 and in its graveyard in the rear rests a descendant of Emperor Constantine the Great, whose family was driven from the throne in Constantinople (Istanbul) by the Turks. Ferdinando Paleologus, the royal relative, died on Barbados in 1678.

After leaving the church, go left and then take the next right onto Gall Hill Road. Stay on this road until you reach Four Roads Junction, go along Wakefield Road, and at the sign, turn left and then take the next right by **Villa Nova,** in St. John. Built in 1834 as a fine sugar-plantation Great House, it's surrounded by 6^1/$_2$ acres of landscaped gardens and trees. Its most famous association was with Sir Anthony Eden, former prime minister of Great Britain, who purchased it from the government in 1965. In 1966 the earl and countess of Avon entertained Queen Elizabeth and Prince Philip at the Great House. It has since been sold to private owners and so is currently closed to the public.

After leaving Villa Nova, turn left and pass through the hamlet of Venture. At the next intersection, continue left until you see the sign pointing right toward Easy Hall, another east-coast hamlet. At the next sign, pointing toward Flower Forest (described earlier in this section), go left along Buckden House Road. Take the next right and head down Highway 3, a steep, curvy road toward the ocean.

Turn right toward Bathsheba and follow the signs to the **Andromeda Botanic Gardens,** Bathsheba, St. Joseph (☎ **246/433-9261**). On a cliff overlooking Bathsheba on the rugged east coast, limestone boulders make for a natural 8-acre rock-garden setting, where thousands of orchids are in bloom every day of the year along with hundreds of hibiscus and heliconia. Many varieties of ferns, begonias, and other species grow here in splendid profusion. One section, a palm garden, has more than 100 species. A guide helps visitors to identify many of the plants. On the grounds you'll occasionally see frogs, herons, lizards, hummingbirds, and sometimes a mongoose or a monkey. With an admission of BD$10 ($5) for adults and BD$5 ($2.50) for children, the gardens are open daily from 9am to 5pm; children 5 and under enter free.

After leaving the gardens, turn right and follow the signs to the **Atlantis Hotel,** Bathsheba (☎ 246/433-9445), one of the oldest hotels on Barbados, where Enid Maxwell has been serving her favorite Bajan dishes, including flying fish and pickled breadfruit, for longer than she cares to remember. Tattered but respectable, this hotel was once a villa built by a wealthy planter in 1882. It's directly on the coast, just south of the "Scotland district."

Now continue north along the coast road to the town of **Bathsheba,** where ocean rollers break, forming cascades of white foam. This place has been called Cornwall in miniature. Today the old fishing village is a favorite low-cost resort for Bajans, although the waters of the Atlantic Ocean are dangerous for swimmers.

The trail north from Bathsheba takes you along the **East Coast Road,** which runs for many miles, opening onto dramatic views of the Atlantic. Chalky Mount rises from the beach to a height of 500 feet, forming a trio of peaks, and a little to the south, Barclays Park is a 15-acre natural wonder presented as a gift to the people of Barbados by the British banking family. There's a snack bar and a place to picnic here.

Farther north is the **Morgan Lewis Sugar Windmill,** in St. Andrew (☎ 246/426-2421). This is typical of the wind-driven mills that crushed the juice from the sugarcane from the 17th to the 19th century, producing the sugar that made Barbados Britain's most valuable possession in the Americas. It was from Barbados sugarcane that rum was first produced. Admission is $2.50 for adults, $1.25 children 13 and under, and its normal hours are 9am to 5pm Monday to Friday. At press time it was closed for renovations, so before coming here, please check to see if it has reopened.

Climb Morgan Lewis Hill to reach one of the panoramic sights of Barbados, **Cherry Tree Hill,** on Highway 1, offering magnificent views. You can look right down the eastern shore past Bathsheba to the lighthouse at Ragged Point, already described. The place is about 850 feet above sea level, and from its precincts you'll see out over the Scotland district. The cherry trees from which the hill got its name no longer stand here, having given way to mahogany.

On Cherry Tree Hill, signs point the way to **St. Nicholas Abbey** (☎ 246/422-8725), a Jacobean plantation Great House and sugarcane fields that have been around since about 1650. It was never an abbey—an ambitious owner in about 1820 simply christened it as such. More than 200 acres are still cultivated each year. The structure—at least the ground floor—is open to the public Monday to Friday from 10am to 3:30pm, charging an admission of $5; children 12 and under enter free. The house is believed to be one of three Jacobean houses in the Western Hemisphere, and is characterized by curved gables. Lt.-Col. Stephen Cave, the owner, is descended from the family that purchased the sugar plantation and Great House in 1810. You can lunch or take afternoon tea here (see Café Calabash in "Where to Eat," earlier in this chapter).

After leaving the abbey, follow the road to Diamond Corner, where you go left. Take another left onto the Charles Duncan O'Neal Highway to **Farley Hill National**

Park, in northern St. Peter Parish. Farley Hill House was used as a backdrop for the 1957 film *Island in the Sun,* starring Harry Belafonte. Unfortunately, it was gutted by fire. The park, dedicated by Queen Elizabeth in 1966, is open daily from 8:30am to 6pm. You pay a vehicular entrance fee of $1.50 for cars. After disembarking in the parking area, you can walk the grounds and enjoy the tropical flowers and lush vegetation.

Across the road from the park lies the **Barbados Wildlife Reserve** (☎ 246/422-8826), an operation set in a mahogany forest that's run by the Barbados Primate Research Center in St. Peter. From 10am to 5pm daily, for an admission charge of BD$20 ($10) for adults and BD$10 ($2.50) for children 12 and under, you stroll through what is primarily a monkey sanctuary and an arboretum. Aside from the uncaged monkeys, you can see wild hares, deer, tortoises, otters, wallabies (brought into Barbados from Australia), and a variety of tropical birds. Another attraction of the Wildlife Reserve is the **Grenade Hall Signal Station & Forest.** The signal station, which has been renovated from the original built in 1819, offers the island's most panoramic view of the east, west, and north coasts. Housed in the signal station are archaeological findings accompanied by a recorded commentary. Next to the signal station are 5 acres of indigenous woodland of whitewood, inkberry, liana vines, and other species. The forest is open to the public daily from 10am to 5pm.

From Farley Hill Park and the Wildlife Reserve, backtrack to the junction of Highways 1 and 2. From here, head west along Highway 1 and follow the signs to **Speightstown,** which was founded around 1635 and for a time was a whaling port. The "second city" of Barbados, the town has some colonial buildings constructed after the devastating hurricane of 1831. The parish church, rebuilt in a half-Grecian style after the hurricane, is one of the places of interest.

After exploring Speightstown, if you have time, turn left toward the **Gold Coast,** the protected western shoreline that opens onto the gentler Caribbean. Along the shoreline of the parishes of St. James and St. Peter are the island's plushest hotels.

On Highway 1, directly north of Holetown, lies **St. James Church,** an Anglican church rebuilt in 1872 on the site of the early settlers' church of 1660. On the southern porch is an old bell bearing the inscription "God Bless King William, 1696." Locals still recall the 1982 visit of Ronald and Nancy Reagan.

Continue south on Highway 1 to **Holetown,** the main center of the west coast; it takes its name from the town of Hole on the Thames River. Here the first English settlers landed in the winter of 1627. An obelisk marks the spot where the *Olive Blossom* landed the first Europeans. The monument, for some reason, lists the date erroneously as 1605. After Holetown, Highway 1 continues south taking you back to Bridgetown.

EXPLORING THE GREEN HILLS

Unless visitors make special efforts to explore the lush interior of this former British colony, most of their time on Barbados might be confined to the island's densely populated coastal plain. But much of Barbados's true beauty can only be appreciated through treks, tours, or hillclimbs through such rarely visited parishes as St. Thomas and St. George (both of which are landlocked) and the Atlantic-coast parishes of St. Andrews and St. John (where the rough surf of the Atlantic usually discourages the embarkation of sailing vessels). Until recently most visitors were requested to restrict their sightseeing in these relatively undeveloped parishes to the sides of the highways and roads. But a locally owned tour operator, **Highland Outdoor Tours,** Canefield, St. Thomas (☎ 246/438-8069), conducts a series of tours across privately owned land. With its verdant, rolling hills and many dramatic rock outcroppings, much of the terrain might remind you of a windswept but balmy version of Scotland.

You'll have the option of conducting your tour on horseback, on foot, or as a passenger in a tractor-drawn jitney. Horseback rides and walking tours last anywhere from 2 to 5 hours. As you traverse what used to be some of the most productive sugar plantations in the British Empire, your guide will describe the geology, architecture, and historical references you'll see en route.

All tours depart from the Highland Outdoor Tour Center in the parish of St. Thomas (in north-central Barbados). Transportation to and from your hotel is included in the price of horseback tours (from $25), hiking tours (from $50), and tractor-drawn jitney tours (from $25). Mountain-bike tours start at $32.50.

5 Shopping

Barbados merchants can sometimes treat you to duty-free merchandise at prices 20% to 40% lower than in the United States and Canada. But, of course, you've got to be a smart shopper to spot bargains and also be familiar with prices back in your hometown. Duty-free shops have two prices listed on merchandise, the local retail price and the local retail price less the government-imposed tax.

Some of the best duty-free buys include cameras (Leica, Rolex, and Fuji), watches (Omega, Piaget, Seiko), crystal (Waterford and Lalique), gold (especially jewelry), bone china (Wedgwood and Royal Doulton), cosmetics and perfumes, and liquor (including locally produced Barbados rum and liqueurs), along with tobacco products and cashmere sweaters, tweeds, and sportswear from Britain. If you purchase items made on the island of Barbados, you don't have to pay U.S. Customs duties if you're a citizen of the United States.

The outstanding item in Barbados handcrafts is black-coral jewelry. Clay pottery is another Bajan craft. We recommend a visit to the **Chalky Mount Potteries,** where this special craft originated. Potters turn out different products, some based on designs centuries old. The potteries (signposted) are found north of Bathsheba on the east coast in the parish of St. Joseph, near Barclay's Park. In the shops, you'll also find locally made vases, pots, pottery mugs, glazed plates, and ornaments.

From local grasses and dried flowers, wall hangings are made, and the island craftspeople also turn out straw mats, baskets, and bags with raffia embroidery. Still in its infant stage, leatherwork is also found now on Barbados, particularly handbags, belts, and sandals.

Cruise-ship passengers generally head for the **Bridgetown Cruise Terminal** at Bridgetown Harbour, with some 20 duty-free shops, 13 local and regional merchandise shops, and several vendors.

Shopping hours, in general, are 8am to 4pm Monday to Friday and 8am to noon on Saturday.

Articrafts. Broad St., Bridgetown. ☎ **246/427-5767.**

Here John and Roslyn Watson have assembled one of the most impressive displays of Bajan arts and crafts on the island. Roslyn's woven wall hangings are decorated with objects from the island, including sea fans and coral. They make a distinctive handcrafted design. Straw work, handbags, and bamboo items are also sold.

Best of Barbados. In the Southern Palms, St. Lawrence Gap, Christ Church. ☎ **246/428-7171.**

Part of an islandwide chain of seven stores, Best of Barbados sells only products designed and/or made on Barbados. It was established in 1975 by an England-born painter, Jill Walker, whose prints are best-sellers, and her husband, Jimmy. They sell articles celebrating aspects of island life, including coasters, mats, T-shirts, pottery, dolls and games, and cookbooks, among other items. This tasteful shop is in a pink-and-white building around the corner from the entrance to Southern Palms.

A more convenient location might be the outlet in Bridgetown at Mall 34, Broad Street (☎ **246/436-1416**).

Cave Shepherd. Broad St., Bridgetown. ☎ **246/431-2121.**

The best place to shop for duty-free merchandise on Barbados is Cave Shepherd, which has branches at Sunset Crest in Holetown, Speightstown, Grantley Adams International Airport, and the Bridgetown Harbour. Cave Shepherd is the largest department store on Barbados and one of the most modern in the Caribbean. The store offers perfumes, sweaters, cameras, swimwear, leather goods, batik, handcrafts, and souvenirs. More than 70 brands of liqueurs are sold as well as other spirits. After you finish shopping, relax on the top floor in the cool comfort of the Ideal Restaurant. Cave Shepherd has another restaurant, The Balcony, overlooking the street.

Colours of De Caribbean. In the Waterfront Marina, Bridgetown. ☎ **246/436-8522.**

Next to the Waterfront Café, on the Careenage, this unique store has a very individualized collection of tropical clothing—all made in the West Indies—and jewelry and decorative objects. Original hand-painted and -batiked clothing may hold the most interest.

Cotton Days. Bay St., St. Michael. ☎ **246/427-7191.**

Boutiques abound on Barbados, and Cotton Days is the best known and most stylish. It inventories casually elegant one-of-a-kind garments suitable for cool nights and hot climes. The collection has been called "wearable art." For inspiration, the in-house designers turn to the flora and fauna of the island and the underwater world. The sales staff is skilled at selecting whimsical accessories to accompany the dresses, blouses, and shifts sold here. Magazines such as *Vogue* and *Glamour* have praised this collection.

Earthworks Pottery / The Potter's House Gallery. Edgehill Heights 2, St. Thomas Parish. ☎ **246/425-0223.**

Some serious shoppers consider this one of the artistic highlights of Barbados. Deep in the island's central highlands, it's in a modern building erected in the 1970s by American-born Goldie Spieler. Her business, in her own words, is the result of "a hobby that got out of control." Trained as an art teacher and ceramic artist, Ms. Spieler and her son, David, create whimsical plates, cups, saucers, and serving vessels whose blues and greens emulate the color of the Bajan sea and sky. (Some of their fans claim that a morning bowl of corn flakes served on a snowy Stateside morning in a cerulean-blue porringer from Earthworks re-creates the warmth of a Caribbean holiday.) Many objects are decorated with the Antillean-inspired swirls and zigzags, and can be shipped virtually anywhere. On the premises is the studio where the slip-decorated objects are crafted; a showroom sells the output of at least a half-dozen other island potters. Prices per piece range from $3.

The Great House Gallery. At the Bagatelle Restaurant, Hwy. 2A, St. Thomas. ☎ **246/421-6767.**

On the airy upper floor of one of the most historic Great Houses on Barbados, this art gallery combines an inventory of artworks with West Indian graciousness. Pieces are displayed on high white walls amid the reflected glow of an antique mahogany floor: oils and watercolors by Caribbean, Latin American, and British artists priced from $10. Among them are the award-winning works of the owners themselves.

Harrison's. 1 Broad St., Bridgetown. ☎ **246/431-5500.**

In addition to this main shop, Harrison's has 14 branch stores, all selling a wide variety of duty-free merchandise, including china, crystal, jewelry, leather goods, and perfumes—all at fair prices. We've been able to find good buys here in the range of Baccarat, Lalique, Royal Doulton, and Waterford crystal. It also sells some state-of-the-art leather products handcrafted in Colombia. Harrison's is the major competitor to Cave Shepherd on the island, but we'd give the edge to Cave Shepherd.

Little Switzerland. In the Da Costas Mall, Broad St., Bridgetown. ☎ **246/431-0029.**

At this outlet you'll find a wide selection of fragrances and cosmetics from such famous houses as Giorgio, Chanel, Guerlain, Yves St. Laurent, La Prairie, and more. Fine china and crystal from European manufacturers such as Lladró are also sold, as is an array of goodies from Waterford, Lalique, Swarovski, Baccarat, and others. The shop also specializes in watches and jewelry, and also stocks Mont Blanc pens.

Mall 34. Broad St., Bridgetown. ☎ **246/435-8800.**

One of Bridgetown's most modern shopping complexes offers duty-free shopping in air-conditioned comfort at several outlets. You can find watches, clocks, china, jewelry, crystal, linens, sweaters, and liquor, together with souvenir items and tropical fashions.

Pelican Village. Princess Alice Hwy., Bridgetown. ☎ **246/426-1966.**

While in Bridgetown, go down to the Pelican Village on Princess Alice Highway leading down to the city's Deep Water Harbour. A collection of islandmade crafts and souvenirs is sold here in a tiny colony of thatch-roofed shops, and you can wander from one to the other. Sometimes you can see craftspeople at work. Some of the shops to be found here are gimmicky and repetitive, although interesting items can be found.

The Shell Gallery. Carlton House, St. James. ☎ **246/422-2593.**

For the shell collector, this is the best collection in the West Indies. Shells for sale come from all over the world. The outlet features the shell art of Maureen Edghill, who is considered the finest artist in this field. She founded this unique gallery in 1975. Also offered are hand-painted chinaware, shell jewelry, local pottery and ceramics, and batik and papier-mâché artwork depicting shells and aquatic life.

Walker's Caribbean World. St. Lawrence Gap. ☎ **809/428-1183.**

Close to the Southern Palms, it also offers many locally made items for sale, as well as handcrafts from the Caribbean Basin. Here you can buy the famous Jill Walker prints.

6 Barbados After Dark

Most of the big resort hotels feature entertainment nightly, often dancing to steel bands and occasional Bajan floor shows. Sometimes beach barbecues are staged.

Beach Club. Sunset Crest, St. James. ☎ **246/432-1309.** No cover Sun–Fri; free Sat for diners, $10 for nondiners.

This bar and restaurant serves as a social focal point for Sunset Crest, with many island residents happily hobnobbing with their friends and colleagues. Happy hour at the Beach Bar is 5 to 6pm nightly, when drinks are half price. Fish fries, barbecues, or buffets are offered from 7 to 10pm daily, priced from $10 to $12.50. There's live

---

The Joints Are Still Jumping at Dawn: Where to Find the Best Local Watering Holes

For the most authentic Bajan evening possible, head for **Baxters Road** in Bridgetown, a street that reaches its peak of liveliness on Friday and Saturday after 11pm. In fact, if you stick around until dawn, the joints are still jumping. The street is safer than it looks, because Bajans come here to have fun, not to make trouble. The entertainment tends to be spontaneous. Some old-time visitors have compared Baxters Road to the backstreets of New Orleans in the 1930s. If you fall in love with the place, you can "caf crawl" up and down the street, where nearly every bar is run by a Bajan mama. Each place has its own atmosphere.

The most popular "caf" on Baxters Road is **Enid's** (she has a phone, "but it doesn't work"), a little ramshackle establishment where Bajans come to devour fried chicken at 3 in the morning. Her place is open daily from 8:30pm to 8:30am, when the last satisfied customer departs into the blazing morning sun and Enid heads home to get some sleep before the new night begins. Stop in for a Banks beer.

---

entertainment every night, including bands and amateur talent shows. Sunday night is show night, when the entertainment is bigger and more theatrical than usual.

Coach House. Paynes Bay, St. James. ☎ **246/432-1163.** Cover from $5 (as soon as you pay it, you'll be given coupons worth $3 for drinks at the bar).

The Coach House, named after a pair of antique coaches that sometimes stand outside, is a green-and-white house 200 years old. The atmosphere is a Bajan version of an English pub with an outdoor garden bar. Businesspeople and habitués of nearby beaches come here to order buffet lunches, where Bajan food is served Monday to Friday from noon to 3pm. The price is $11 for an all-you-can-eat lunchtime assortment that includes local vegetables and salads prepared fresh daily. If you visit from 6 to 10:30pm, you can order bar meals, including flying-fish burgers, priced at $8 and up. Live music is presented most nights, featuring everything from steel bands to jazz, pop, and rock. The pub is on the main Bridgetown–Holetown road, just south of Sandy Lane, about 6 miles north of Bridgetown. An attentive crowd assembles together here for live music nightly from 9pm on.

Harbour Lights. Marine's Villa, Upper Bay St., Bridgetown. ☎ **246/436-7225.** Cover $6–$15, depending on the performers.

This is the most popular weekend venue for dancing, drinking, flirting, and "jiving to the music" on all of Barbados. In a modern seafront building whose oceanfront patio allows dancers the chance to cool off, the place plays reggae, soca, and just about anything else that happens to be popular in the Caribbean at the time. No one under 18 is allowed in. Grilled meats and hamburgers are available from a barbecue pit/kiosk on the premises. The location is beside the seacoast, about a mile southeast of Bridgetown. Live music is presented Friday to Monday.

✪ **John Moore Bar.** On the Waterfront, Weston, St. James Parish. ☎ **246/422-2258.**

Some visitors consider this the most atmospheric and least pretentious bar on Barbados. Established in 1958 in what had been a storefront, it was rebuilt in 1970 about 100 yards northwest of the town's only fire station. Its namesake (John Moore) died in 1987; the place is owned and managed by Lamont (Breedy) Addison, who began here as a teenager working for Mr. Moore. If you think that this bar functions only as a watering hole, think again: It's probably the most influential nerve center in this waterfront town, filled throughout the day and evening with one of the widest and most consistently congenial groups of residents in the neighborhood. Most visitors opt for a rum punch or beer, but if you're hungry, platters of local fish can be prepared, after a moderate delay, for between $5 and $7 each.

✪ Plantation Restaurant and Garden Theatre. Main Rd. (Hwy. 7), St. Lawrence, Christ Church. ☎ **246/428-5048.** Cover (including unlimited drinks) $52.50 for dinner and the show, $25 for the show only.

This is the island's most visible showcase for evening dinner theater and Caribbean cabaret. Dinner and a show are presented every Wednesday, Thursday, Friday, and Saturday. Dinner is served at 6:30pm, and one of two different shows (either *Barbados by Night* or the *Plantation Tropical Spectacular II*) is presented at 8pm. Both involve plenty of exotic costumes, and lots of reggae, calypso, limbo, and Caribbean exoticism. Advance reservations are recommended.

The Ship Inn. St. Lawrence Gap, Christ Church. ☎ **246/435-6961.** Cover $5 after 9pm.

Previously recommended for drinking and dining (see "Where to Eat," earlier in this chapter), this inn is now among the leading dining and entertainment centers on the south coast. Top local bands perform every night of the week, and patrons gather to listen to live reggae, calypso, and Top 40 music. The cover charge is redeemable in food or drink at any of the other bars or restaurants in the complex. That means that guests are actually only paying $2 for the live entertainment.

Waterfront Café. Cavan's Lane, The Careenage, Bridgetown. ☎ **246/427-0093.** No cover.

By anyone's estimate, this is the busiest, most interesting, and most animated nighttime watering hole in Bridgetown. In a turn-of-the-century warehouse originally built to store bananas and freeze fish, it welcomes both diners and drinkers to its reverberating walls for Créole food, beer, and pastel-colored drinks. Live music (reggae, ragtime, rock 'n' roll, or jazz) is presented Tuesday to Saturday from 8 to 11:30pm. Careenage Coffee, laced with various after-dinner potions, is an enduring favorite.

15 Trinidad & Tobago

Trinidad, birthplace of calypso and the steel pan, used to be visited only by business travelers in Port-of-Spain. The island was more interested in its oil, natural gas, and steel industries than in tourism. But all that has changed now. Trinidad is a serious tourist destination, with a spruced-up capital and a renovated airport.

The island's sophistication and cultural mélange, which is far greater than that of any other island in the southern Caribbean, is also a factor in increased tourist interest in Trinidad. Conversely, Tobago, its sibling island, is just as drowsy as ever—and that's its charm.

Charted by Columbus on his third voyage in 1498, Trinidad is named after the Holy Trinity that he saw represented in three massive peaks on the southern coast. Through the years the country has been peopled by immigrants from almost every corner of the world—Africa, the Middle East, Europe, India, China, and the Americas. It's against such a background that the island has become the fascinating mixture of cultures, races, and creeds that it is today.

Trinidad, which is about the size of Delaware, and its neighbor island, tiny Tobago, 20 miles to the northeast, together form a nation popularly known as "T&T." The islands of the new country are the southernmost outposts of the West Indies. Trinidad lies only 7 miles from the Paria Peninsula in Venezuela, to which in prehistoric times it was once connected.

The Spanish settled the island, which the Native Amerindians had called Iere, or "land of the hummingbird." The Spaniards made their first permanent settlement in 1592 and held onto it longer than they did any of their other real estate in the Caribbean. The English captured Trinidad in 1797, and it remained British until the two-island nation declared its independence in 1962. The Republic of Trinidad and Tobago is a parliamentary democracy, with a president and a prime minister. The British influence is still clearly visible today, from the strong presence of the British dialect to the islanders' fondness for cricket.

FAST FACTS: Trinidad & Tobago

Banking Hours   Most banks are open Monday to Thursday from 8am to 2pm and on Friday from 9am to noon and 3 to 5pm.

Currency   The **Trinidad and Tobago dollar (TT$)** is loosely pegged to the U.S. dollar at an exchange rate of about $1 U.S. = TT$6 (TT$1 = 16.6¢ U.S.). Ask what currency is being referred to when rates are quoted. We've used a combination of both in this chapter, depending on the establishment. U.S. and Canadian dollars are accepted in exchange for payment, particularly in Port-of-Spain. However, you'll do better by converting your Canadian or U.S. dollars into local currency. British pounds should be converted into the local currency. *Note:* Unless otherwise specified, dollar quotations appearing in this chapter are in U.S. currency.

Customs   Readers have reported long delays in clearing Customs on Trinidad. Personal effects are duty free, and visitors may bring in 200 cigarettes or 50 cigars plus 1 quart of "spirits."

Documents   Visitors arriving on Trinidad and Tobago should have an on-going or return ticket from their point of embarkation. You'll be asked to fill out an immigration card upon your arrival, and the carbon copy of this should be saved, as it must be returned to Immigration officials when you depart. Citizens of the United States and Canada, and British subjects, need passports to enter Trinidad and Tobago.

Electricity   The electricity is 110 or 220 volts AC, 60 cycles, but ask when making your hotel reservations so you'll know if you'll need transformers and/or adapters.

Embassies and High Commissions   In Port-of-Spain on Trinidad, the **U.S. Embassy** is at 7–9 Marli St. (☎ **868/622-6371**); the **Canadian High Commission** is at Maple House, 3 Sweet Briar Rd., St. Clair (☎ **868/622-6232**); and the **British High Commission** is at 19 St. Clair Ave., St. Clair (☎ **868/622-2748**).

Emergencies   Call the **police** at ☎ **999.** To report a **fire** or summon an **ambulance,** dial ☎ **990.**

Information   Contact the **Trinidad & Tobago Tourist Board** at 10–14 Philip St., Port-of-Spain, Trinidad, W.I. (☎ **868/623-1932**).

Language   English is the official language, although you'll hear it spoken with many different accents, including cultured British. Hindi, Chinese, French, and Spanish are also spoken.

Safety   As a general rule, Tobago is safer than its larger neighbor, Trinidad. Crime does exist, but it's not of raging dimensions. If you can, avoid the downtown streets of Port-of-Spain at night, especially those around Independence Square, where muggings have been reported. It would also be wise to safeguard your valuables and never leave them unattended at the beach or even in a locked car.

Taxes and Service   The government imposes a 15% value-added tax (VAT) on room rates. It also imposes a departure tax of TT$75 ($12.50) on every passenger more than 5 years old.

Time   Trinidad and Tobago time is the same as the U.S. East Coast. But when the States go on daylight saving time, Trinidad and Tobago doesn't; so when it's 6am in Miami, it's 7am in T&T.

Tipping   The big hotels and restaurants add a 10% to 15% service charge to your final tab.

Weather   Trinidad has a tropical climate all year, with constant trade winds maintaining mean temperatures of 84° Fahrenheit during the day, 74° at night, with a range of 70° to 90°. The rainy season runs from May to November, but it shouldn't deter a visit at that time; the rain usually lasts no more than 2 hours before the sun comes out again. However, carry along plenty of insect repellent if you visit then.

1 Trinidad

Trinidad is completely different from the other islands of the Caribbean, and that forms part of its charm and appeal. The island itself is 50 miles long and 40 miles wide. The limbo was born here, as was calypso, and steel-drum music. Visitors in increasing numbers are drawn to this island of many rhythms.

Trinidad is not for everyone, though. Because Port-of-Spain is one of the most bustling commercial centers in the Caribbean, more business travelers than tourists are drawn here. The island has beaches, but the best of them are far away from the capital. The city itself is hot, humid, and slightly on the dirty side, whereas the hilly suburbs are as charming as a southern city set in a tropical paradise.

Although Port-of-Spain, with its shopping centers, fast-food joints, modern hotels, and active nightlife, draws mixed reviews from readers, the countryside is calmer. Far removed from the traffic jams of the capital, you can explore the fauna and flora of the island. It's estimated that there are some 700 varieties of orchids alone, plus 400 species of birds.

Prices on Trinidad are often lower than on many other islands in the West Indies such as Barbados. Port-of-Spain abounds in inexpensive inns and guest houses. Since most of the dining establishments cater to locals, dining prices reflect the low wages.

The people are part of the attraction on this island, the most cosmopolitan in the Caribbean. Trinidad's polyglot population includes Syrians, Chinese, Americans, Europeans, East Indians, Parsees, Madrasis, Venezuelans, and the last of the original Amerindians, the early settlers of the island. You'll also find Hindustanis, Javanese, Lebanese, African descendants, and Créole mixtures. The main religions are Christianity, Hinduism, and Islam. In all there are about 1.2 million inhabitants, whose language is English, although you may hear speech in a strange argot, Trinibagianese.

Port-of-Spain, in the northwestern corner of the island, is the capital, with the largest concentration of the population, about 120,000. With the opening of its $2-million cruise-ship complex in Port-of-Spain, Trinidad now has become a major port of call for Caribbean cruise lines.

One of the most industrialized nations in the Caribbean, and the third-largest exporter of oil in the Western Hemisphere, Trinidad is also blessed with the huge 114-acre Pitch Lake from which comes most of the world's asphalt. Further, it's also the home of Angostura Bitters, the recipe for which is a closely guarded secret.

GETTING THERE

From North America, Trinidad is one of the most distant islands in the Caribbean. Because of the legendary toughness of Trinidadian Customs, it's preferable to arrive during the day (presumably when your stamina might be at its peak), if you can schedule it.

Trinidad is the transfer point for passengers heading to the beaches of Tobago. For information about getting to Tobago, refer to section 2 of this chapter.

Most passengers from the eastern half of North America opt for transit on **American Airlines** (☎ 800/433-7300), which has connections through New York. American also offers a daily nonstop flight to Trinidad from Miami, which is especially useful for transfers from the Midwest and the West Coast.

From New York, **BWIA** (☎ **800/538-2942**), Trinidad and Tobago's national airline, offers one to three daily flights into Port-of-Spain, depending on the day of the week and the season. Several of these are nonstop; most of them touch down en route, usually in Barbados, Antigua, or Guyana (and sometimes at all three) before continuing without a change of planes on to Trinidad, the airline's home base. From Miami, BWIA offers a daily nonstop flight to Port-of-Spain, departing every afternoon at 2:30pm and arriving in Trinidad in the early evening.

Air Canada (☎ **800/268-7240** in Canada, or 800/776-3000 in the U.S.) doesn't fly to Trinidad, but offers flights four or five times a week to Barbados, from which connecting flights are possible into Port-of-Spain.

GETTING AROUND

BY BUS   All the cities of Trinidad are linked by regular bus service from Port-of-Spain. Fares are low: from 50¢ (for runs within the capital). However, the old buses are likely to be very crowded. Always try to avoid them at rush hours. Beware of pickpockets.

BY TAXI   There are only unmetered taxis on Trinidad, and they're identified by their license plates, beginning with the letter *H*. There are also "pirate taxis" as well—private cars that cruise around and pick up passengers like a regular taxi. Maxi Taxis or vans can also be hailed on the street. A taxi ride from Piarco Airport into Port-of-Spain generally costs about $20.

You can rent taxis and local drivers for your sightseeing jaunts. A taxi tour alleviates the hassles of badly marked (or unmarked) roads and contact with the sometimes-bizarre local driving patterns; if a rented taxi is too expensive, you can take an organized tour. Most drivers will serve as guides. Their rates, however, are based on route distances, so get an overall quotation and agree on the actual fare before setting off. All fares are subject to 50% increases after midnight.

BY RENTAL CAR   Since the island is one of the world's largest exporters of asphalt, Trinidad's some 4,500 miles of roads are well paved. However, outback roads should be avoided during the rainy season as they're often narrow, twisting, and prone to washouts. Inquire about conditions, particularly if you're headed for the north coast. The fierce traffic jams of Port-of-Spain are legendary, and night driving anywhere on the island is rather hazardous.

If you're brave enough to set out on a venture via rental car, arm yourself with a good map and beware: The car will probably have a right-hand-mounted steering wheel, hence, *you'll drive on the left.* Visitors with a valid International Driver's License or a license from the United States, Canada, France, or the U.K. may drive without extra documentation for up to 3 months.

The major U.S.-based car-rental firms currently have no franchises on the island, so you have to make arrangements with a local firm (go over the terms and insurance of Trinidad/Tobago agreements carefully). Count on spending about $40 to $60 per day or more, with unlimited mileage included.

One of the island's leading local car-rental firms is **Bacchus Taxi & Car Rental Service,** 37 Tragarete Rd., Port-of-Spain (☎ 868/622-5588), which does not take reservations. You have to inquire if cars are available upon your arrival. Others include **Auto Rental,** Piarco Airport (☎ 868/669-2277), and **Singh's Auto Rental,** 7–9 Wrightson Rd., Port-of-Spain (☎ 868/625-4247).

ESSENTIALS

Medical care is sometimes limited and physicians and health-care facilities expect immediate cash payment for medical services. Don't expect to pay with a credit or charge card. Medical insurance from the United States is not always valid outside the country and supplemental medical insurance with specific overseas coverage is available. Contact the U.S. Embassy for updates. The **Port-of-Spain General Hospital** is on Charlotte Street (☎ 868/623-2951).

As for banks, the **Bank of Nova Scotia** has an office on Park Street at Richmond Street, Port-of-Spain (☎ 868/625-3566 or 868/625-5222). **Citibank** has offices at 12 Queen's Park E., Port-of-Spain (☎ 868/625-1046 or 868/625-1049), and at 18–30 High St., in San Fernando (☎ 868/652-3691 or 868/652-3293).

The main **post office** is on Wrightson Road, Port-of-Spain, and is open Monday to Friday from 8am to 4pm. You can send a cable or fax at the offices of **Textel,** 1 Edward St., Port-of-Spain (☎ 868/625-4431).

WHERE TO STAY

The number of hotels is limited, and don't expect your Port-of-Spain room to open directly on a white sandy beach—the nearest beach is a long, costly taxi ride away. Don't forget that a 15% government tax and 10% service charge will be added to your hotel and restaurant bills. All hotels raise their rates at Carnival (Monday and Tuesday preceding Ash Wednesday).

DOUBLES FOR LESS THAN $60

Alcazar Guest House. 13 Alcazar St., St. Clair, Port-of-Spain, Trinidad, W.I. ☎ 868/628-8612. 5 rms, 3 with bath. Year-round, $55 single or double without or with bath. Children stay free in parents' room. Rates include breakfast. No credit cards.

Lying in one of the better upmarket residential areas of Port-of-Spain, this well-run B&B was a private home when it was built in 1913. This is a colonial house with a veranda on two sides and a back porch set in a small garden. The rooms are spacious, reflecting the architectural style of the Edwardian era. Guests are encouraged to treat the place like home, and they gather around the communal TV on the back porch. The rooms are air-conditioned and also have ceiling fans. Baby-sitting can be arranged. Marcacas Beach is about half an hour away.

Alicia's House. 7 Coblentz Gardens, St. Ann's, Port-of-Spain, Trinidad, W.I. ☎ **868/623-2802.** Fax 868/623-8560. 17 rms. A/C TV TEL. Year-round, $38–$51 single; $57–$73 double; $90 triple; $120 quad. Rates include breakfast and are tripled during Carnival week. AE, MC, V.

This is a genteel, discreet guest house whose format in many ways was inspired by British models. It's in an upscale residential neighborhood (Coblentz Gardens), a short walk north of Queen's Park Savannah, the Botanical Gardens, and the dining and entertainment facilities of the Hilton Hotel. The setting is a flat-roofed, two- and three-story white-painted concrete building whose yard was neatly fenced in for privacy, with a ringaround garden and a pool in back. Ivan and Barbara Dara are your hosts (they named the place after their daughter, Alicia), who maintain a polite and rather discreet setting. The bedrooms contain wooden or rattan furniture, small refrigerators, ceiling fans, white walls, wooden floors, and touches of homey bric-a-brac. There's a swimming pool and Jacuzzi in the garden, and a lounge area for conviviality. Because of local zoning laws, no liquor is served on the premises, but guests are welcome to bring their own.

Carnetta's House. 28 Scotland Terrace, Andalusia, Maraval, Trinidad, W.I. ☎ **868/628-2732.** Fax 868/628-7717. 6 rms. A/C TV TEL. Year-round, $40–$50 single; $50–$60 double. AE, DC, MC, V.

This suburban home is set in the suburb of Andalusia in cool and scenic Maraval, about a 15-minute ride from the central business district and a 45-minute ride to Maracas Beach. In a natural setting on the Maraval River, the house is owned by Winston and Carnetta Borrell, both keen naturalists. He was the former director of tourism. Both are a wealth of information about touring the island, and Winston is a grand gardener, filling his property with orchids, ginger lilies, and anthuriums, among other plant life. Carnetta grows her own herbs to produce some of the finest meals around. The rooms have floral themes and are furnished in a tropical style.

Monique's Guest House. 114–116 Saddle Rd., Maraval, Trinidad, W.I. ☎ **868/628-3334.** Fax 809/622-3232. 20 rms. A/C TEL. Year-round, $45 single; $50 double; $55 triple. MC, V.

In the lush Maraval Valley just an 8-minute (3-mile) drive north of the center of Port-of-Spain, Monique's offers 20 newly rebuilt bungalow-style rooms, each with air-conditioning and phone. Some of the rooms can accommodate up to 4 people, and 10 rooms offer kitchenettes with their own porches and cable TVs. One room is designed for elderly travelers or those with disabilities. The air-conditioned dining room and bar offers a medley of local and international dishes, and Maracas Beach is only a 25-minute drive away. Mike and Monica Charbonné will be here to welcome you.

Surf's Country Inn. Blanchisseuse (P.O. Box 3429), Maraval, Trinidad, W.I. ☎ **868/669-2475.** 3 rms. Year-round, $50 single or double. Rates include breakfast. AE, MC, V.

This Spanish colonial inn overlooks the sea, and is set on a hillside a very short walk from the fishing village of Blanchisseuse. It's a small, friendly place whose dining and drinking facilities are popular with local residents. When he established it in 1989, the owner Andrew Hernandez conceived of it as only a restaurant, although over the years a trio of semidetached outbuildings, each with private patio and views of the sea, was added. Each accommodation is rustically outfitted with a ceiling fan, white walls, and red tile floors. L'Anse Martin Beach is one of several secluded swimming areas a short walk from the hotel, and the nearby hamlet contains a handful of raffish bars and snack bars. Seafood is invariably featured as part of meals, which are served more or less continuously every day from 9am to 10pm.

Zollna House. 12 Ramlogan Terrace, La Seiva, Maraval, Trinidad, W.I. ☎ **868/628-3731.** Fax 868/628-3737. 7 rms, 2 with bath. $30 single without bath, $45 single with bath; $50 double without bath, $65 double with bath. Rates include American breakfast. AE, MC, V.

On a hillside in the Maraval Valley with a view of Port-of-Spain and the Gulf of Paria, Zollna House is 2 miles from the capital. The two-story building has comfortably furnished bedrooms, two large porches, two indoor lounges, a beverage bar and games room, and dining areas on two floors, as well as a patio/barbecue set-up outdoors. The lush garden features flowering shrubs and fruit trees, home to a variety of birds. The house, white with black trim, is almost obscured by trees, but you can find it by going along Saddle Road, turning onto La Seiva Road, and going uphill for about a quarter of a mile.

The house is operated by Gottfried (Fred) Zollna, a German-American resident on Trinidad since 1965, and his Trinidadian wife, Barbara. They have a reputation for their easygoing hospitality and can advise on what to see and do. They also own a 35-foot yacht and often take their guests sailing in the Gulf of Paria. The Blanchisseuse Beach Resort on the north coast of Trinidad is also owned by the Zollnas.

DOUBLES FOR LESS THAN $70

✪ **Blanchisseuse Beach Resort.** Blanchisseuse, Trinidad, W.I. ☎ **868/628-3731.** Fax 868/628-3737. 15 rms. Winter, $45 single; $65 double. Off-season, $35 single; $55 double. Extra person $15. AE, MC, V.

On the north coast, this beachfront property, owned by Fred and Barbara Zollna, who also operate Zollna House (see above) outside Port-of-Spain, is set on 28 acres of rain forest at the Marianne River and its swimming lagoon. A place for those who seek solitude, it lures nature lovers with a free-flowing freshwater spring and natural swimming pools, along with tropical plants and flowers. Coconut palms, coffee, and cocoa are cultivated throughout the estate, and birds, butterflies, and other forest creatures are abundant. In nesting season, leatherback turtles come to lay their eggs in the loose soft sand of the beach. The Blanchisseuse area is well known for its fishing, and you can fish off the beach or in the river. The Cocos Hut Restaurant, with its sliding roof, was formerly used for drying copra, coffee, or coconut. Today it serves local and international food, and there are also barbecue pits and rafts. A campsite is also available.

✪ **La Maison Rustique.** 16 Rust St., St. Clair, Port-of-Spain, Trinidad, W.I. ☎ **868/622-1512.** 6 rms, 3 with bath; 1 studio cottage. Year-round, $40 single without bath, $50 single with bath; $70 double with bath; $95 cottage. Children 9 and under stay free in parents' room. Rates include full breakfast. MC, V.

A great little B&B, all trimmed in gingerbread, this choice recommendation enjoys an in-the-heart location near Queen's Park Savannah. A colonial Victorian house in a garden setting, La Maison Rustique (which is far from rustic) allows you to sit on the verandah for a daily high tea. The owner, Maureen Chin-Asiong, a delightful person, serves breakfast in a tea house, and will cater to special diets if asked. She's a baker supreme—just taste her croissants and popovers—and a graduate of the Wilton School of Cake Decorating in Chicago. She'll even pack you a picnic basket if you're going touring for the day. The bedrooms are neat and homey, very comfortably furnished and immaculately maintained. The nearest beach is a 45-minute drive away, but guests may be admitted to a nearby country club.

Tropical Hotel. 6 Rookery Nook, Maraval, Trinidad, W.I. ☎ **868/622-5815.** Fax 868/ 622-4249. 15 rms. A/C TEL. Winter, $50 single; $60 double; $85 triple. Off-season, $45 single; $55 double; $75 triple. Rates are doubled during Carnival week. AE, MC, V.

This hotel originated early in the 20th century as the centerpiece for the sugarcane plantation that surrounded it at the time. (The setting is a short drive northwest of Port-of-Spain in the Maraval Valley and is a 45-minute ride to Maracas Beach.) Don't expect soaring columns and architecture like *Gone with the Wind*. Its design is vaguely Iberian, its walls are made of stone, its roof is red, and most of the overnight accommodations lie on the second floor. Mr. Lennox Lake, the owner, maintains a tile-ringed swimming pool and restaurant. The bedrooms have white walls, carpeted floors, and nearly indestructible plastic chairs. The in-house restaurant features Créole cuisine, steaks, and lots of seafood, and prices both lunches and dinners at $15 to $25 each.

OFFBEAT NATURE RETREATS IN THE WILD

✪ **Asa Wright Nature Centre and Lodge.** Spring Hill Estate, Arima, Trinidad, W.I. ☎ **800/ 426-7781** in the U.S., or 868/667-4655. Fax 868/667-4655. 23 rms. Winter, $105 double. Off-season, $80 double. Rates include all meals, afternoon tea, and a welcoming rum punch. No credit cards.

There really isn't anything else like it in the Caribbean. Known to bird-watchers throughout the world, this center sits on 196 acres of protected land at an elevation of 1,200 feet in the rain-forested northern mountain range of Trinidad, 10 miles north of Arima, beside Blanchisseuse Road. Hummingbirds, toucans, bellbirds, manakins, several varieties of tanagers, and the rare oilbird are all on the property. Back-to-basics accommodations are available in the lodge's self-contained double rooms, in guest bedrooms in the 1908 Edwardian main house, or in one of the cottages built on elevated ground above the main house; all have private baths but no air-conditioning, TV, or phones.

Guided tours are available on the nature center's grounds, which contain several well-maintained trails, including a natural pool with a waterfall in which guests can swim in lieu of a beach (it's a 90-minute drive to the coast). Summer seminars are conducted with expert instructors in natural history, ornithology, and nature photography. The minimum age is 14 years if accompanied by an adult or 17 if unaccompanied.

For more information or to make reservations, call the above toll-free number or write Caligo Ventures, 156 Bedford Rd., Armonk, NY 10504.

Timberland Nature Resorts. Maracas Bay Rd. (8 miles from Maracas), Maracas, Trinidad, W.I. ☎ **868/638-2263** (phone answered only 6–8am Trinidad time). 2 rms. Year-round, $60 per person. Children under 12, $30. Rates include half board. MC, V.

Popular with scientists and bird-watchers, this retreat lies on the island's northern coast. Nature lovers are lured here by the best beach on the island. Birders can follow marked trails to take in some of Trinidad's wealth of tropical birds. The rooms are converted from a former cocoa estate known as La Bois Maison. The accommodations are plain but clean and comfortable—no air-conditioning, no phone, no TV. The restaurant is well known on Trinidad for its gourmet Créole seafood dishes. The setting is very rustic and very secluded, with ocean views of Tobago and Venezuela. The beach is reached after a 20-minute walk along a nature trail, or you can take an 8-minute drive to Maracas Beach. This place is for people who appreciate nature and the simplicity of life.

WHERE TO EAT

The food should be better than it is, considering all the different culinary backgrounds that have shaped the island, including West Indian, Chinese, French, and Indian.

Stick to local specials such as stuffed crabs or *chip-chip* (tiny clamlike shellfish), but skip the armadillo or opossum stewpots. Spicy Indian rôtis filled with vegetables or ground meat seem to be everyone's favorite lunch, and everyone's favorite drink is a fresh rum punch flavored with the home-produced Angostura Bitters. Except for a few fancy places, dress tends to be very casual.

La Fantasie. In the Normandie Hotel and Restaurant, 10 Nook Ave., St. Ann's Village. ☎ **868/624-1181,** ext. 2306. Reservations recommended. Main courses TT$40–TT$100 ($7–$17). AE, DC, MC, V. Daily noon–2pm and 6–10pm. FRENCH/CREOLE.

Off Queen's Park Savannah, and named after the 18th-century plantation that once stood here, La Fantasie is loaded with style and features a tempting modern Créole cuisine. Many dishes are given a light touch as opposed to the usually heavy, deep-fried food, a sort of *cuisine nouvelle* Créole. That alone would make it a winning choice. Since fresh ingredients are used and deftly handled, no false notes jar the senses. However, you're not exactly pampered here and the service has drawn complaints from readers. The changing menu might include filet mignon with a tamarind-flavored sauce, locally caught Trinidadian salmon in a wine-based sauce with sultana raisins and bananas, and shrimp with Créole sauce in a pastry shell flavored with cheese. "Fish walk up the hill" is grilled fish with chopped herbs. Meals might end with a Trinidadian fruitcake with a rum-flavored custard.

The Lounge. In the Chaconia Inn, 106 Saddle Rd., Maraval. ☎ **868/628-8603.** Main courses TT$30–TT$160 ($5–$27). AE, DC, MC, V. Daily 7am–10pm. INTERNATIONAL.

On the street level of a hotel, this conservatively decorated, modern dining room offers international cuisine to a busy crowd of lunch and dinnertime patrons, who appreciate its straightforward, uncomplicated cuisine. Dishes may not be innovative, but everything is market fresh. You can order several different preparations of fish, steak, shrimp, pork, and pasta dishes, as well as salads and a small choice of vegetarian dishes. On Saturday night the Roof Garden Restaurant, on the hotel's uppermost floor, serves barbecued meals.

Monsoon. 72 Tragarete Rd., Port-of-Spain. ☎ **868/628-7684.** Reservations recommended. Main courses TT$11–TT$35 ($1.80–$5.80). AE, MC, V. Mon–Sat 11am–10pm. INDIAN.

At this restaurant where East and West Indian cuisines combine, the walls are adorned with framed hand-painted fabrics from India and Trinidad. The menu's forte is curry, including chicken, lamb, vegetable, duck, pork, fish, shrimp, and conch. These curries are served with a chickpea mixture, chutney, and potatoes. Other items include *dhalpuri* (a flat bread spread with ground peas that's wrapped around meats and vegetables) and *paratha* (a flaky bread cooked on an open grill and served as a staple, much like potatoes or rice, with meats and vegetables).

✪ Rafters. 6A Warner St., Newtown. ☎ **868/628-9258.** Reservations required. Main courses TT$35–TT$125 ($6–$21); buffets from TT$95 ($16). AE, DC, MC, V. Mon–Thurs 11:30am–midnight, Fri 11am–3am, Sat 7pm–3am. SEAFOOD.

Rafters is housed in a century-old grocery shop in the central business district of a suburb of Port-of-Spain, a short walk off the Savannah. Wednesday to Saturday there are carvery buffets beginning at 7pm, and you can also order from an à la carte menu devoted mainly to local seafood items. The food is more plentiful than refined, but a very good value. On the regular menu, house specialties include seafood Créole. You can also order U.S. choice beef steaks. In the lounge, a snack-and-sandwich menu is offered daily, in a relaxed atmosphere attracting clients of all ages and occupations.

Restaurant Singho. Long Circular Mall, Level 3, Port-of-Spain. ☎ **868/628-2077.** Main courses TT$18–TT$60 ($3–$10). AE, MC, V. Daily 11am–11pm. CHINESE.

This restaurant contains an almost mystically illuminated bar and aquarium. The restaurant is on the second floor of one of the capital's largest shopping malls, midway between the commercial center of Port-of-Spain and Queen's Park Savannah. It's better than your typical chop suey and chow mein joint, and many dishes are quite tasty and spicy. For Trinidad, this Chinese cuisine isn't bad. Á la carte dishes include shrimp with oyster sauce, shark-fin soup, stewed or curried beef, almond pork, and spareribs with black-bean sauce. The take-away service is one of the best in town.

✪ Solimar. 6 Nook Ave. (opposite the Normandie Hotel and Restaurant, 3¹/₂ miles northwest of the city center), St. Ann's. ☎ **868/624-6267.** Reservations recommended. Main courses TT$55–TT$185 ($9.15–$30.80). AE, MC, V. Dec–Feb, Mon–Sat 6:30–10:30pm; Mar–Nov, Tues–Sat 6:30–10:30pm. Closed 1 week in mid-May and 2 weeks in mid-Aug (exact dates vary). INTERNATIONAL.

By some estimates this restaurant offers the most creative cuisine and most original format in Trinidad and Tobago. Established by an England-born chef (Joe Brown) who worked for many years in the kitchens of Hilton hotels around the world, it occupies a garden-style building whose open walls are cooled by ceiling fans. As you dine, you'll hear the sound of an artificial waterfall cascading into a series of fish ponds.

The menu, which changes every 6 weeks, presents local ingredients inspired by international cuisines. The chefs know some parts of the world better than others, but the results are usually very convincing, with tasty results. Dishes might include an English-inspired combination of grilled breast of chicken and jumbo shrimp dressed with a lobster sauce, and a Sri Lankan dish of herb-flavored chicken vindaloo. Choice aged U.S. meats such as ribeye are grilled. The restaurant's double-chocolate mousse is the highlight of the meal for many diners.

✪ Veni Mangé. 67A Ariapata Ave, Woodbrook. ☎ **868/624-4597.** Reservations recommended. Main courses $5–$10. AE, MC, V. Wed 7:30–10pm, Thurs and Sat–Tues 7–10am and 11:30am–3pm. (Bar, daily 3pm–midnight.) CREOLE.

Few other restaurants capitalize as successfully on the Créole sense of humor and sauciness that have always been part of the legend of Trinidad. It's located in an emerging business district that still retains a bit of the Caribbean look—that is, not too much concrete. Veni Mangé (whose name translates as "come and eat") was established by two of the best-known women on Trinidad, Allyson Hennessy and her sister, Rosemary Hezekiah. Allyson, the Julia Child of Trinidad, hosts a daily television talk show that's broadcast throughout Trinidad. Best described as a new generation of Créole women, both Allyson and Rosemary (whose parents were English/Venezuelan and Afro-Caribbean/Chinese) entertain with their humor and charm.

Start with the bartender's special, a coral-colored fruit punch—a rich, luscious mixture of golden papaya with guava, orange, and passion fruit. On some days they do an authentic callaloo soup, which, according to Trinidadian legend, can make a man propose marriage. Save room for one of the main courses, such as curried crab or West Indian hotpot (a variety of meat cooked Créole style), perhaps a vegetable lentil loaf. The helpings are large, and if you still have room, order their pineapple upside-down cake, unless you prefer a homemade version of soursop ice cream or a coconut mousse.

Dinner is served only on Wednesday night, and is something of a social event for the many regulars who make it part of their regular schedule. On Friday the place buzzes as a "celebrate the beginning of the weekend" bar. No formal food is served on Friday, but a roster of "cutters" (snacks and finger foods) is available.

BEACHES & ACTIVE SPORTS

For golf and tennis holidays, we recommend that you try another island.

BEACHES   Trinidad isn't thought of as beach country, yet it has more beach frontage than any other island in the West Indies. The only problem is that most of its beaches are undeveloped and found in distant, remote places, far removed from Port-of-Spain. The closest of the better beaches, **Maracas** (on the North Coast Road), is a full 18 miles from Port-of-Spain. Tobago (see section 2 of this chapter) has lovely, inviting, and more accessible beaches.

GOLF   The oldest golf club on the island, **St. Andrew's Golf Course,** Moka Estate (☎ **868/629-2314**), is in Maraval, about 2 miles from Port-of-Spain. This 18-hole course has a clubhouse that offers every facility to all visitors. Greens fees are $30. It's playable Monday to Friday from 7am to 7:30pm and on Saturday and Sunday from 6:30am to 8:30pm.

TENNIS   The **Trinidad Hilton,** Lady Young Road (☎ **868/624-3211**), has the best courts on the island. Two chevron courts are lit for night play. At the **Trinidad Country Club,** Champs-Elysées, Maraval (☎ **868/622-3470**), six courts are available, and lit at night. You have to become a member to play; a temporary membership costs TT$69 ($11). There are public courts in Port-of-Spain on the grounds of the Prince's Building (ask at your hotel for directions to these).

EXPLORING THE ISLAND

ORGANIZED TOURS   Sightseeing tours are offered by **The Travel Centre,** Uptown Mall, Edward Street, Port-of-Spain (☎ **868/623-5096**), in late-model sedans, with a trained driver-guide. Prices are quoted on a seat-in-car basis. Private arrangements will cost more.

A daily city tour, lasting 2 hours and costing $22 per person for two (but $16 per person for three or more) will take you past (but not inside) the main points of interest of Port-of-Spain: Whitehall, the President's House, Queen's Park Savannah, the Botanical Gardens, the National Museum and Art Gallery, the Emperor Valley Zoo, cathedrals, a mosque, temples, and through the commercial and residential centers, then to Lady Young Lookout for a view of the city.

You'll see tropical splendor at its best on a Port-of-Spain / Maracas Bay / Saddle Road jaunt leaving at 1pm daily, lasting 3¹/₂ hours. The tour begins with a drive around Port-of-Spain, passing the main points of interest listed above and then going on through the mountain scenery over the "Saddle" of the northern range to Maracas Bay, a popular beach. You return via Saddle Road, Santa Cruz Valley, the village of San Juan, and the Lady Young Road for the view of Port-of-Spain.

An Island Circle Tour is a 9- to 10-hour journey that includes a lunch stop (the tour price doesn't include lunch) and a welcome drink. Leaving at 9am daily, your car goes south along the west coast with a view of the Gulf of Paria, across the central plains, through Pointe-à-Pierre and San Fernando, and on eastward into rolling country overlooking sugarcane fields. Then you go down into the coconut plantations along the 14-mile-long Mayaro Beach for a swim and lunch before returning along Manzanilla Beach and back to the city. The cost is $75 per person for two, or $55 per person for three or more.

A Swirl of Color & Sound: The Carnival of Trinidad

Called "the world's most colorful festival," the Carnival of Trinidad is a spectacle of dazzling costumes and gaiety. Hundreds of bands of masqueraders parade through the cities on the Monday and Tuesday preceding Ash Wednesday, bringing traffic to a standstill. The island seems to explode with music, fun, and dancing.

Some of the Carnival costumes cost hundreds of dollars. For example, "bands" might depict the birds of Trinidad, such as the scarlet ibis and the keskidee; or a bevy of women might come out in the streets dressed as cats. Costumes are also satirical and comical.

Trinidad, of course, is the land of calypso, which grew out of the folk songs of the African–West Indian immigrants. The lyrics command great attention, as they're rich in satire and innuendo. The calypsonian is a poet-musician, and lyrics have often been capable of toppling politicians from office. In banter and bravado, the calypsonian gives voice to the sufferings and aspirations of his people. At carnival time the artist sings his compositions to spectators in tents. There's one show a night at each of the calypso tents around town, from 8pm to midnight. Tickets for these are sold in the afternoon at most record shops.

Carnival parties, or fêtes, with three or four orchestras at each one, are public and are advertised in the newspaper. For a really wild time, attend a party on Sunday night before Carnival Monday. To reserve tickets, contact the **National Carnival Committee,** Queen's Park Savannah, Port-of-Spain, Trinidad, W.I. (☎ **868/ 627-1358**). Hotels are booked months in advance, and most inns raise their prices—often considerably—at the time.

You can attend rehearsals of steel bands at their headquarters, called *panyards,* beginning about 7pm. Preliminary band competitions are held at the grandstand of Queen's Park Savannah in Port-of-Spain and at Skinner Park in San Fernando, beginning 2 weeks before Carnival.

An especially interesting trip is to the Caroni Swamp and Bird Sanctuary, a 4-hour trek by car and flat-bottomed boat into the sanctuary where you'll see rich Trinidad birdlife. The tour guides recommend long pants and long-sleeved, casual attire along with lots of insect repellent. The cost is $45 per person for two, or $30 per person for three or more.

PORT-OF-SPAIN

One of the busiest harbors in the Caribbean, Trinidad's capital, Port-of-Spain, can be explored on foot. Start out at ۞ **Queen's Park Savannah,** on the northern edge of the city. Called "The Savannah," it consists of 199 acres, complete with a racecourse, cricket fields, and vendors hawking coconut water. What is now the park was once a sugar plantation until it was swept by a fire in 1808 that destroyed hundreds of homes.

Among the Savannah's outstanding buildings is the pink-and-blue **Queen's Royal College,** containing a clock tower with Westminster chimes. Today a school for boys, it stands on Maraval Road at the corner of St. Clair Avenue. On the same road, the family home of the Roodal clan is affectionately called "**the gingerbread house**" by Trinidadians. It was built in the baroque style of the French Second Empire.

In contrast, the family residence of the Strollmeyers was built in 1905 and is a copy of a German Rhenish castle. Nearby stands **Whitehall,** which was once a private mansion but today has been turned into the office of the prime minister of Trinidad and Tobago. In the Moorish style, it was erected in 1905 and served as the U.S. Army headquarters in World War II. These houses, including Hayes Court, the residence of the Anglican bishop of Trinidad, and others form what is known as **"the magnificent seven"** big mansions standing in a row.

On the south side of the Memorial Park, a short distance from the Savannah and within walking distance of the major hotels, stands the **National Museum and Art Gallery,** 117 Frederick St. (☎ 868/623-5941), open Tuesday to Saturday from 10am to 6pm. The museum contains a representative exhibition of Trinidad artists, including an entire gallery devoted to Jean Michel Cazabon (1813–88), permanent collections of historical artifacts giving a general overview of the island's history and culture, Amerindian archaeology, British historical documents, and a small natural-history exhibition including geology, corals, and insect collections. There's also a large display filled with costumes dedicated to the colorful culture of Carnival.

At the southern end of Frederick Street, the main artery of Port-of-Spain's shopping district, stands **Woodford Square.** The gaudy **Red House,** a large neo-Renaissance building constructed in 1906, is the seat of the government of Trinidad and Tobago. Nearby stands **Holy Trinity Cathedral,** whose Gothic look may remind you of the churches of England. Inside, look for the marble monument to Sir Ralph Woodford made by the sculptor of Chantry.

Another of the town's important landmarks is **Independence Square,** dating from Spanish days. Now mainly a parking lot, it stretches across the southern part of the capital from the **Cathedral of the Immaculate Conception** to Wrightson Road. The Roman Catholic church was built in 1815 in the neo-Gothic style and consecrated in 1832.

The cathedral has an outlet that leads to the **Central Market,** on Beetham Highway on the outskirts of Port-of-Spain. Here you can see all the spices and fruits for which Trinidad is known. It's one of the island's most colorful sights, made all the more so by the wide diversity of people who sell their wares here.

At the north of the Savannah, the **Royal Botanical Gardens** (☎ 868/622-1221) covers 70 acres and is open daily from 6am to 6pm. Once part of a sugar plantation, the park is filled with flowering plants, shrubs, and rare and beautiful trees, including an orchid house. Seek out also the raw beef tree—an incision made in its bark is said to resemble rare, bleeding roast beef. Licensed guides will take you through and explain the luxuriant foliage to you. In the garden is the **President's House,** official residence of the president of Trinidad and Tobago. Victorian in style, it was built in 1875. Part of the gardens is the **Emperor Valley Zoo,** Royal Botanical Gardens (☎ 868/625-2264), in St. Clair, which shows a good selection of the fauna of Trinidad as well as some of the usual exotic animals from around the world. The star attractions are a family of mandrills, a reptile house, and open bird parks. You can take shady jungle walks through tropical vegetation. Admission is TT$4 (70¢) for adults, TT$1.50 (25¢) for children 3 to 12, and free for children under 3. It's open daily from 9:30am to 5:30pm.

AROUND THE ISLAND

For one of the most popular attractions in the area, the **Asa Wright Nature Centre,** see "Where to Stay," above.

On a peak 1,100 feet above Port-of-Spain, **Fort George** was built by Gov. Sir Thomas Hislop in 1804 as a signal station in the days of the sailing ships. Once it could be reached only by hikers, but today it's accessible by an asphalt road. From its citadel you can see the mountains of Venezuela. The drive is only 10 miles, but to play it safe, allow about 2 hours for the excursion.

At sundown, clouds of scarlet ibis, the national bird of Trinidad and Tobago, fly in from their feeding grounds to roost at the ✪ **Caroni Bird Sanctuary** (☎ 868/ 645-1305). The 40-square-mile sanctuary couldn't be more idyllic, with blue, mauve, and white lilies, oysters growing on mangrove roots, and caimans resting on mudbanks. The sanctuary lies about a half-hour drive (7 miles) south of Port-of-Spain.

Visitors are taken on a launch through these swamps to see the birds (bring along some insect repellent). For your exploration of this wonderland, the most reliable tour operator is **James Meddoo,** Bamboo Grove Settlement, 1 Butler Hwy. (☎ 868/ 662-7356). Meddoo has toured the swamps for some 25 years. His tour leaves daily at 4pm, lasts 2¹/₂ hours, and costs $10 per person.

The ✪ **Pitch Lake** lies on the west coast of Trinidad with the village of Le Brea on its north shore. To reach Pitch Lake from Port-of-Spain, take the Solomon Hocoy Highway. It's about a 2-hour drive, depending on traffic (which can be heavy around Port-of-Spain). At Le Brea, you'll find some bars and restaurants.

One of the wonders of the world, its surface like elephant skin, the lake is 300 feet deep at its center. It's possible to walk on its rough hide, but we don't recommend that you proceed far. Legend has it that the lake devoured a tribe of Chayma Amerindians, punishing them for eating hummingbirds in which the souls of their ancestors reposed. The bitumen mined here has been used for paving highways throughout the world. This lake was formed millions of years ago, and it's believed that at one time it was a huge mud volcano into which muddy asphaltic oil seeped. Churned up and down by underground gases, the oil and mud eventually formed asphalt. According to legend, Sir Walter Raleigh discovered the lake in 1595 and used the asphalt to caulk his ships. Some say that no matter how much is dug out, the lake is fully replenished in a day, but actually the level of the lake drops at the rate of about 6 inches a year. A tour of 120 miles around the lake lasts 5 hours.

The ✪ **Saddle** is a humped pass on a ridge dividing the Maraval Valley and the Santa Cruz Valley. Along this circular run, you'll see the luxuriant growth of the island, as reflected by grapefruit, papaya, cassava, and cocoa. Leaving Port-of-Spain by Saddle Road, going past the Trinidad Country Club, you pass through Maraval Village with its St. Andrew's Golf Course. The road rises to cross the ridge at the spot from which the Saddle gets its name. After going over the hump, you descend through the Santa Cruz Valley, rich with giant bamboo, into San Juan and back to the capital along Eastern Main Road or via Beetham Highway. You'll see splendid views in every direction. This tour takes about 2 hours and covers 18 miles.

Nearly all cruise-ship passengers are hauled along Trinidad's "Skyline Highway," the **North Coast Road.** Starting at the Saddle, it wends for 7 miles across the Northern Range and down to Maracas Bay. At one point, 100 feet above the Caribbean, you'll see on a clear day as far away as Venezuela in the west or Tobago in the east, a sweep of some 100 miles.

Most visitors take this route to ✪ **Maracas Beach,** one of the most splendid on Trinidad. Enclosed by mountains, it has the cliché charm of a Caribbean fantasy— white sands, swaying coconut palms, and crystal-clear water.

SHOPPING

One of the large bazaars of the Caribbean, Port-of-Spain has luxury items from all over the globe, including Irish linens, English china, Scandinavian crystal, French perfumes, Swiss watches, and Japanese cameras. More interesting than these usual items are the Asian bazaars where you can pick up items in brass. Reflecting the island's culture are calypso shirts (or dresses), sisal goods, woodwork, cascadura bracelets, silver jewelry in local motifs, and saris. For souvenir items, visitors often like to bring back figurines of limbo dancers, carnival masqueraders, or calypso singers.

Most stores are open Monday to Friday from 8am to 4pm (some shops remain open until 5pm). Liquor and food stores close at noon on Thursday, and nearly all shops, except liquor and food, close at noon on Saturday.

Art Creators and Suppliers. Apt. 402, Aldegonda Park, 7 St. Ann's Rd., St. Ann's. ☎ 868/624-4369.

It's in a banal apartment complex, but the paintings and sculptures sold inside are among the finest in the Caribbean. Clara De Lima Rosa Foster and Stella Beaubrun, the creative forces behind the gallery, are recognized for their knowledge of Trinidadian art. The works sold here are fairly priced examples of the best on Trinidad. Among the artistic giants are Glasgow, Robert Mackie, Boscoe Holder, Sundiata, Keith Ward, Jackie Hinkson, and many others.

Gallery 1-2-3-4. 10 Nook Ave., St. Ann's Village. ☎ 868/625-5502.

More iconoclastic and less conservative than any other gallery on the island, this art center displays its paintings in a space of minimalist walls and careful lighting. The gallery opened in 1985, and since then has attracted the attention of the art world because of its wide selection of Caribbean artists.

The Market. 10 Nook Ave., St. Ann's. ☎ 868/624-1181.

One of the most fashionable shopping complexes on Trinidad contains some 20 boutiques that represent some of the best jewelers, designers, and art dealers on the island. At this complex, you'll find a wide assortment of merchandise, including clothing, cosmetics, bags, shoes, china, decorative tableware, handcrafts, and designer jewelry and accessories. The complex forms an interconnected bridge among the Normandie Hotel and Restaurant, the restaurant La Fantasie, and Gallery 1-2-3-4.

Stecher's. 27 Frederick St. ☎ 868/623-5912.

For those luxury items we mentioned above, visit Stecher's, which sells crystal, watches, jewelry, perfumes, Georg Jensen silver, china (Lladró, Wedgwood, Royal Doulton, Royal Albert, Aynsley, Hutschenreuther), and other in-bond items that can be delivered to Piarco International Airport upon your departure. If you don't want to go downtown, you'll find branches at Long Circular Mall and West Mall, in residential areas of Port-of-Spain. You can also pay a last-minute call at the three tax-free airport branches: one outlet for famous perfumes and another for sunglasses, Cartier watches, lighters and pens, leather goods, Swarovski crystal, and local ceramics. A third branch sells tobacco and liquor. There's also a branch at the Cruise Ship Complex at the Port-of-Spain docks.

Y. de Lima. 83 Queen St. and 23 Frederick St. ☎ 868/623-1364.

This is another good store for duty-free cameras, watches, and local jewelry. Its third-floor workroom will make whatever you want in jewelry or bronze work. You may emerge with everything from steel-drum earrings to a hibiscus-blossom brooch.

TRINIDAD AFTER DARK

Chaconia Inn. 106 Saddle Rd., Maraval. ☎ 868/628-8603. No cover.

This place becomes a hot spot on Saturday night when a DJ enlivens the atmosphere. Open 24 hours, 7 days a week.

Mascamp Pub. French St. at Ariapata Ave. (on the western outskirts of Port-of-Spain).   ☎ **868/ 623-3745.** Cover $2–$5.

This is the only venue on Trinidad where calypso music from the island's greatest bands is presented continually throughout the year. (Many similar establishments offer the art form only during Carnival.) Set on the western outskirts of Port-of-Spain, it promotes a "rootsy," sometimes raucous, and generally high-energy format that's recommended only to adventurous readers who happen to love live musical performances with an ethnic slant.

Although simple lunches are served here every weekday from 11am to around 3pm, for a cost of around $7 the place is far more recommendable (and exciting) as a nightspot. Live music begins every night at 9pm and continues until as late as 4am, but calypso and its modern variations are the almost exclusive format every Friday, Saturday, and Sunday.

Trinidad Hilton. Lady Young Rd., Port-of-Spain. ☎ **868/624-3211.** Cover (including a buffet dinner with grills) TT$105 ($17).

The Hilton stages a Poolside Fiesta show, which happens every Monday night, with a folkloric performance beginning at 9pm and continuing live until 11pm. It features lots of live music, calypso, a steel band, and limbo. It's the most spectacular on Trinidad.

2 Tobago

Dubbed "the land of the hummingbird," Tobago lies 20 miles northeast of Trinidad, to which it's connected by frequent flights. It has long been known as a honeymooner's paradise. The physical beauty of Tobago is stunning, with its forests of breadfruit, mango, cocoa, and citrus, through which a chartreuse-colored iguana will suddenly dart.

Unlike bustling Trinidad, Tobago is sleepy, and Trinidadians come there, especially on weekends, to enjoy its wide sandy beaches. The legendary home of Daniel Defoe's Robinson Crusoe, Tobago is only 27 miles long and $7^1/_2$ miles wide. The people are hospitable, and their villages are so tiny that they seem to blend with the landscape.

Tobago's idyllic natural beauty makes it one of the greatest escapes in the Caribbean. It's for those who like a generous dose of sand, sun, and solitude in a mellow atmosphere.

Fish-shaped Tobago was probably sighted by Columbus in 1498 when he charted Trinidad, but the island was so tiny that he paid no attention to it in his log. For the next 100 years it lay almost unexplored. In 1628, when Charles I of England gave it to one of his nobles, the earl of Pembroke, the maritime countries of Europe suddenly showed a belated interest. From then on, Tobago was fought over no fewer than 31 times by the Spanish, French, Dutch, and English, as well as marauding pirates and privateers.

After 1803, the island settled down to enjoy a sugar monopoly unbroken for decades. Great Houses were built, and in London it used to be said of a wealthy man that he was "as rich as a Tobago planter." The island's economy collapsed in 1884, and Tobago entered an acute depression. The ruling monopoly, Gillespie Brothers, declared itself bankrupt and went out of business. The British government made Tobago a ward of Trinidad in 1889, and sugar was never revived.

The island's villagelike capital lies on the southern coast and provides a scenic setting with its bay surrounded by a mountainside. **Scarborough,** which is also the main port, is a rather plain town, however. The local market, the Gun Bridge, the Powder Magazine, and Fort King George will provide a good day's worth of entertainment. Most of the shops are clustered in the streets around the market.

GETTING THERE

BY PLANE   For many Americans, the easiest way to reach Tobago is to take an **American Eagle** (☎ 800/433-7300) flight from San Juan. The flight departs San Juan at 8:40pm and arrives in Tobago at 11:10pm Monday to Friday. A round-trip ticket costs $305, plus tax and fees.

BWIA (☎ 800/538-2942), the national airline of Trinidad and Tobago, links the two islands with shuttles, which run on Monday and Thursday. The flight times are mainly in the afternoon and evening, but there is one that leaves on those days at 6:30am. The flight lasts 20 minutes, and a round-trip costs $40 per person.

A recently established Trinidad-based airline, **Air Caribbean** (☎ 868/623-2500) maintains popular shuttle flights between Trinidad and Tobago, departing from Port-of-Spain every 2 hours daily between 6am and 8pm. The final return to Trinidad leaves from Tobago daily at 9pm. A round-trip ticket costs $50. Know in advance that since the beaches of Tobago are a favorite of vacationing Trinidadians, shuttle flights on any airline between the two islands are almost always crowded, and on weekends sometimes impossibly overbooked. Air Caribbean, however, operates extra flights on Friday, Sunday, and public holidays to meet traffic demands.

LIAT (☎ 868/462-0701) maintains one daily flight from Trinidad to Tobago. But there's a catch. You can only fly to Tobago on LIAT if you flew into Trinidad on this airline from some other island. If you'd like to skip Trinidad completely, you can book a LIAT flight with direct service to Tobago from either Barbados or Grenada.

Tobago's small airport lies at Crown Point, near the island's southwestern tip.

BY BOAT   It's possible to travel between Trinidad and Tobago by ferry service managed and operated by the **Port Authority of Trinidad and Tobago** (☎ 809/625-3055 in Port-of-Spain, or 868/639-2181 in Scarborough, Tobago). Call for departure times and more details. Ferries leave once a day (trip time is 5 hours). The round-trip fare is TT$60 ($10) in tourist class and TT$50 ($8) in economy class. Cabins are also available for TT$160 ($27).

GETTING AROUND

BY BUS   Inexpensive public buses travel from one end of the island to the other several times a day. Of course, expect an unscheduled stop at any passenger's doorstep, and never, never, be in a hurry.

BY TAXI   From the airport to your hotel, take an unmetered taxi, which will cost $8 to $32, depending on the location of your hotel. You can also arrange a sightseeing tour by taxi. Rates must be negotiated on an individual basis.

BY RENTAL CAR   Contact **Tobago Travel,** Milford Road, Store Bay (☎ 868/639-8778), where the average cost of a vehicle begins at $52 per day, with unlimited mileage, collision-damage coverage, value-added tax, and comprehensive insurance, plus delivery if you're housed in a hotel near the airport. An International Driver's License or your valid license from home entitles you to drive on the roads of Tobago. Islanders *drive on the left.*

ESSENTIALS

Most passengers arrive from Trinidad, where they have already cleared Customs.

The **Division of Tourism** has two offices providing information. The main office is at NIB Mall, Level 3, in Scarborough (☎ 868/639-2125), and a second office lies in the airport (☎ 868/639-0509).

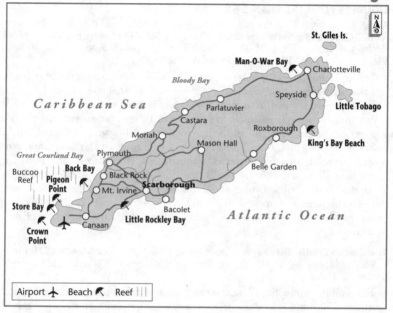

Scarborough offers three pharmacies: **Ross Budget Drugs** on Main Street (☎ 868/639-2658), **Scarborough Drugs** on Wilson Road (☎ 868/639-4161), and **Tobago Drugs** on Carrington Street (☎ 868/639-3930).

The **Tobago County Hospital** is on Fort George Street, Scarborough (☎ 868/639-2551). To reach the **police**, dial ☎ **999;** for a **fire or ambulance, ☎ 990.**

The **National Bank of Trinidad and Tobago** has an office on Main Street, Roxborough (☎ 868/660-4311).

WHERE TO STAY

The hotels of Tobago attract those who seek hideaways instead of high-rise resorts packed with activity. Sometimes to save money, it's best to take the MAP (breakfast and dinner) plan when reserving a room. There's a 15% value-added tax added to all hotel bills, and often a service charge of about 10%. Always ask if the VAT and service charge are included in the prices quoted to you.

DOUBLES FOR LESS THAN $45

Store Bay Holiday Resort. Store Bay Rd., Crown Point, Tobago, W.I. ☎ **868/639-8810.** Fax 809/639-8810. 15 rms. A/C. Winter, $40–$45 single or double. Off-season, $35–$40 single or double. Extra person $10. MC, V.

This is an L-shaped, motel-style building painted off-white with a green stripe; the clientele includes Caribbean business travelers who appreciate its proximity to the airport. The rooms have recently been painted and redecorated. Since there's a much-used kitchenette with new refrigerators in each room, you might be tempted to cook your own meals. The bedrooms flank a swimming pool, although you'll probably walk about 350 yards to reach the Store Bay Beach. No meals are served, but there are cafes and restaurants nearby.

DOUBLES FOR LESS THAN $65

Cocrico Inn. North St. at Commissioner St. (P.O. Box 287), Plymouth Village, Tobago, W.I. ☎ **800/223-9815** in the U.S., or 868/639-2961. Fax 868/639-6565. 16 rms. Winter, $50–$65 single; $60–$85 double; $105–$135 triple. Off-season, $40–$55 single; $50–$70 double; $85–$120 triple. MAP $22 extra per person. AE, MC, V.

This is an unpretentious, beige, L-shaped building with uncontroversial styling and a two-story format you might find in a motel. Built around 1978, it's best known for its popular bar and restaurant. There's a swimming pool, a paved-over sun terrace, and simple landscaping. Set in the center of Tobago's largest settlement, it's close to grocery stores, bars, and all the diversions of small-town life. Great Courtland Beach lies half a mile away, Turtle Beach is 1 mile away, and golf and tennis can be arranged within a reasonable distance for extra fees. The bedrooms aren't very large, but have clean, white-painted walls, wall-to-wall carpeting, wooden furnishings, standing fans or ceiling fans, and in the more expensive doubles, small kitchenettes.

The in-house restaurant is a respectable, diner-style place. Home-style cooking is prepared with lots of local seafood and fresh produce, and, though not fancy, is nutritious.

The Golden Thistle. Store Bay Rd., Crown Point, Tobago, W.I. ☎ **868/639-8521.** Fax 868/639-8521. 36 rms. A/C TV TEL. Winter, $40 single; $60 double. Off-season, $35 single; $50 double. AE, MC, V.

This simple, uncomplicated hotel is much appreciated by cost-conscious Europeans. Angela Williams, the kindly proprietor, welcomes a repeat clientele whose ages vary widely. The establishment lies on the island's western coast, about a 10-minute walk from Store Beach, in a well-tended garden perfumed with roses and flowering shrubs. The accommodations each have kitchenettes, terrazzo or tile floors, large bathtubs, and white walls. There's a swimming pool and a restaurant serving a simple fare.

Man-O-War Bay Cottages. Charlotteville Estate, Charlotteville, Tobago, W.I. ☎ **868/660-4327.** Fax 868/660-4328. 6 cottages. Year-round, $60 one-bedroom cottage; $80 two-bedroom cottage; $95 three-bedroom cottage; $140 four-bedroom cottage. For $12 a maid will clean the unit and prepare a meal. MC, V.

If you're seeking a Caribbean hideaway—that is, a cluster of beach cottages—then the Man-O-War might be for you. The cottages are a part of Charlotteville Estate, a 1,000-acre cocoa plantation. The entire estate is open to visitors, who may wander through at will. Pat and Charles Turpin rent several cottages on a sandy beach. Each unit is complete with a kitchen, a spacious living and dining room, a private bath, and a porch opening onto the sea.

Near the colony is a coral reef that's ideal for snorkelers. The couple will also arrange a boat rental if you want to explore Lovers' Beach. Bird-watchers often book these cottages, and scuba diving and guided nature tours are available. The Man-O-War Cottages are 36 miles from the airport. The ride follows a bumpy coastal road passing through many small villages en route.

Sandy Point Beach Club. Crown Point, Tobago, W.I. ☎ **868/639-8533.** Fax 868/639-8495. 9 studios, 35 suites. A/C TV TEL. Winter, $60 studio for one or two; $70–$80 suite. Off-season, $35 studio for one or two; $45–$55 suite. Extra person $10; children 11 and under $5 in room shared with parents. MAP $15 per person extra. MC, V.

Built in two different sections in 1977 and 1991, this miniature vacation village somewhat resembles a Riviera condominium. All but six of the units (those at poolside) contain a kitchenette. It's just a 3-minute run from the airport, but its shoreside position on the island's southwestern coast makes it seem remote. The little village of peaked and gabled roofs is landscaped all the way down to the sandy beach, where there's a rustic Steak Hut, which serves meals throughout the day and evening. The units are fully equipped, and each opens onto a patio, toward the sea, or onto a covered loggia. The studios contain living and dining areas with Jamaican wicker furniture, plus satellite color TV. Some of the studios have a rustic open stairway leading to a loft room with bunk beds, although there's a twin-bedded room on the lower level as well. There are two different swimming pools, plus a small gym and a disco in the basement.

DOUBLES FOR LESS THAN $95 (WINTER) / $75 (OFF-SEASON)

Harris Cottage. Bacolet, Scarborough, Tobago, W.I. ☎ **868/639-2111.** Fax 868/639-2226. 3 rms. A/C TV. Year-round, $35 single; $70 double. Rates include breakfast. MAP $15 per person extra. MC, V.

Its brick-sided construction marks this place as distinctly different from its many rather ramshackle guest house competitors. It lies about a mile from the center of Scarborough, in a fashionable residential neighborhood, a 4-minute walk from the white sands of Bacolet Beach. Built in the late 1980s, and owned by Roger Harris, it offers cozy and family-oriented accommodations with carpeted floors, separate dressing areas, and verandah-style morning breakfasts, which are both ritualized and pleasant. A garden surrounds the house, adding welcome touches of greenery. A rental car is available for $35 per day.

Kariwak Village. Store Bay (P.O. Box 27), Scarborough, Tobago, W.I. ☎ **868/639-8545.** Fax 868/639-8441. 24 rms. A/C TEL. Winter, $90 single or double. Off-season, $60 single or double. MAP $25 per person extra. AE, DC, DISC, MC, V.

A self-contained cluster of cottages evoking the South Pacific, this complex is about a 6-minute walk from the beach on the island's western shoreline and a 2-minute drive from the airport. During its construction in 1982, the builders made much use of Tobago's palm fronds, raw teak, coral stone, and bamboo.

Live entertainment is provided in season on weekends. The food served in the main restaurant is among the island's best, and you may want to come here for a meal even if you aren't staying here. A fixed-price meal, either à la carte or in the form of one of the weekend buffets, ranges from $20 to $24 per person.

Manta Lodge. Speyside (P.O. Box 433), Speyside, Tobago, W.I. ☎ **868/660-5268.** Fax 868/660-5030. 22 rms. Winter, $85–$125 single; $95–$150 double. Off-season, $65–$100 single; $75–$125 double. Extra person $15; children 5–12, $8; children 4 and under stay free in parents' room. MAP $30 per person extra. AE, DC, MC, V.

One of the newer properties on the island, this complex caters to serious bird-watchers and even more serious divers. It overlooks a beach named for the monster manta rays which islanders call "Tobago taxis." The mantas frequent the nearby dive sites. The lodge was built by Trinidad-born Sean Robinson. It's a colonial-style concrete building across the road from the beach with a garden in front. The loft rooms are especially popular with divers, containing air-conditioning and a sundeck. The superior and more expensive rooms have verandahs and air-conditioning, whereas the cheaper rooms are cooled by ceiling fans, although they have verandahs as well. Service and amenities are at a minimum here, but ice may be obtained on request. There's a pool as well as a restaurant and bar serving island food and drink. Room service and baby-sitting are also available.

WORTH A SPLURGE

Blue Waters Inn. Batteaux Bay, Speyside, Tobago, W.I. ☎ **800/742-4276** in the U.S., or 868/660-4341. Fax 868/660-5195. 38 rms, 4 efficiencies, 3 one- or two-bedroom suites. Winter, $108 single; $121 double; $150 efficiency; $275 one-bedroom suite; $400 two-bedroom suite. Off-season, $75 single; $85 double; $110 efficiency; $175 one-bedroom suite; $260 two-bedroom suite. AE, MC, V.

Attracting nature lovers, this property on the northeastern coast of Tobago extends into acres of tropical rain forest with myriad exotic birds, butterflies, and other wild-life. Managed by the MacLean family, the inn is about 24 miles from the airport and 20 miles from Scarborough. From the airport, it's a 1¼-hour drive along narrow, winding country roads. This is a very informal place, so leave your fancy resortwear at home.

All the basic, no-frills rooms have a private shower and ceiling fan, although several are air-conditioned as well. Meals are served in the casual restaurant, and there's also a bar dispensing tropical libations. Fishing, tennis, windsurfing, kayaking, and skin diving can be arranged, as can boat trips (including glass-bottom boats) to Little Tobago.

✪ **Richmond Great House.** Belle Garden, Tobago, W.I. ☎ **868/660-4467.** 7 rms, 3 suites. Winter, $135–$155 double; $175–$205 suite for two. Off-season, $120–$135 double; $155–$180 suite for two. Rates include half board. MC, V.

One of the most charming accommodations on the island is an 18th-century Great House set on 6 acres, part of a cocoa- and coconut-growing estate. Near Richmond Beach, it's owned by Dr. Hollis R. Lynch, a Tobago-born professor of African history at Columbia University. As befits his profession, he has decorated the mansion with African art along with a collection of island antiques. Guests are free to explore the garden and grounds and to enjoy the pool and the barbecue. It's not a bad choice for families. On the premises are two 19th-century tombs containing the remains of the original English founders of the plantation. All accommodations have a private bathroom and individualized decor. The hotel lies on the southern (windward) coast of Tobago, and the airport is within a 45-minute drive. Both a regional and an international cuisine are served. Since it's such a small place, the cook asks guests about their culinary preferences.

WHERE TO EAT

✪ **The Blue Crab.** Robinson St., Scarborough. ☎ **868/639-2737.** Reservations recommended for lunch, required for dinner. Main courses $17–$25; lunch platters $12–$20. AE, MC, V. Daily 11:30am–3:30pm and 7–10pm. CARIBBEAN/INTERNATIONAL.

One of our favorite restaurants in the capital, adjacent to the town's only Methodist church, this family-run spot occupies an Edwardian-era house with an oversize verandah. This is the domain of the Sardinha family, who returned to their native country after a sojourn in New York. They make the most of local ingredients and regional spices. Dinners might not always be available; when they are served, the menu will be dictated by whatever's available that day in the marketplace. The food is homemade and good. Menu items include fresh conch, stuffed crab backs, shrimp, an array of Créole meat dishes grilled over coconut husks, flying fish in a mild curry-flavored batter, shrimp with garlic butter or cream, and a vegetable-laced rice dish of the day. Lobster sometimes appears on the menu.

✪ **Jemma's Seaview Kitchen.** Speyside. ☎ **868/660-4066.** Reservations recommended. Main courses TT$55–TT$110 ($9–$18). No credit cards. Sun–Thurs 9am–9pm, Fri 9am–5pm. TOBAGONIAN.

A short walk north of the hamlet of Speyside, on Tobago's northeastern coast, this is one of the very few restaurants in the Caribbean designed as a tree house. Although the establishment's simple kitchen is firmly anchored to the shoreline, the dining area is set on a platform nailed to the massive branches of a 200-year-old almond tree that leans out over the water. Some 50 tables are available on a wooden deck that even provides a rooflike structure for shelter from the rain.

The establishment's owner is Mrs. Jemma Sealey, whose charming staff provides meals where soup or salad is usually included in the price of a main course. Lunch platters offer shrimp, fish, and chicken, whereas dinners feature more elaborate portions of each of those, as well as steaks, curried lamb, grilled or curried kingfish, lamb chops, and lobster served grilled or thermidor style. No liquor is served (only fresh orange or pineapple juice).

Kiskadee Restaurant. In the Turtle Beach Hotel, Courtland Bay. ☎ 868/639-2851. Reservations recommended for those not staying in the hotel. Main courses TT$65–TT$90 ($11–$15). AE, DC, DISC, MC, V. Daily 7:30–10am, 1–2:30pm, and 7–10pm. CREOLE/CARIBBEAN.

Five miles from Scarborough, the Kiskadee is casual. Its tables sit on an outdoor verandah whose edges overlook a tropical garden and the sea. Specialties include the catch of the day, steamed or grilled or in a curry. Other courses include baked chicken, sirloin steak, or Chinese-style stir-fry. The kitchen doesn't exactly extend itself in preparing these dishes, but flavors are zesty and spicy, and most diners leave having satisfied their tastes and appetites.

✪ **Le Beau Rivage.** In the Mount Irvine Bay Hotel, Tobago Golf Course, Buccoo Bay. ☎ 868/639-8871. Reservations required. Main courses $16–$28. AE, DC, MC, V. Daily 7–10pm. FRENCH/CARIBBEAN.

Run by the hotel, this restaurant resides in a former golf clubhouse 5 minutes northwest of the airport. From its windows, you'll have a sweeping view of one of Tobago's most historic inlets, Mount Irvine Bay. The cookery is more competent than exciting, but still quite good. Menu choices vary daily, but might include combinations of local ingredients with continental inspirations of *cuisine moderne,* including grilled Caribbean lobster, grilled filet of red snapper in a tomato purée, and rack of lamb. Dessert might include a fresh-fruit salad, coconut pie, coconut tart, or a fresh mango flan floating on a coulis of tropical fruits.

Man Friday. In the Sandy Point Beach Club, Crown Point, Tobago, W.I. ☎ 868/639-9547. Main courses TT$25–TT$60 ($4.15–$10); buffets and barbecues TT$65–TT$95 ($10.85–$15.85). AE, MC, V. Daily 7am–10pm. INTERNATIONAL.

What could be more Caribbean cliché than this, an open-air restaurant on the beach beside a small waterfall? If you can forgive the glaring purple-and-turquoise decor, you can enjoy a medley of dishes. The Thai dishes seem the most delectable, although fresh fish and a rather standard repertoire of pork, beef, and chicken dishes are also offered. Each day a different island specialty is featured. At lunch you can order "the usual": burgers, sandwiches, and shrimp and chicken dishes. The Saturday-night buffet is a well-attended event, and Monday and Thursday are devoted to barbecues. Live music is presented Monday and Wednesday to Friday. It's also a good place to head for your "sundowner."

✪ **Old Donkey Cart House.** Bacolet St., Scarborough, Tobago, W.I. ☎ 868/639-3551. Fax 868/639-6124. Reservations required. Main courses TT$50–TT$90 ($8–$15). AE, MC, V. Daily 8am–11pm. INTERNATIONAL.

This unusual and noteworthy restaurant occupies a green-and-white Edwardian house about half a mile south of Scarborough. Its entrepreneurial owner, Gloria Jones-Knapp, has been a fashion model in Europe. "Born, bred, and dragged up" on Tobago, she is today the island's leading authority on selected European wines, including Italian, French, Austrian, and German vintages. Her restaurant also serves freshly made fruit drinks laced with the local rum. Meals might include stuffed crab back, homemade pasta, shrimp and crabmeat cocktail, fresh fish, salads, homemade garlic bread, and callaloo soup with crab. Dining can be enjoyed either in the palm garden or on the verandahs of the Hibiscus Bar. If you're interested, ask about apartment suites for rent, costing $76 to $120 daily, double occupancy, including breakfast and taxes.

Papillon. Buccoo Bay Rd., Buccoo Bay. ☎ **868/639-0275.** Reservations recommended. Main courses TT$40–TT$130 ($7–$23); lunch TT$15–TT$55 ($2.50–$9.20). AE, MC, V. Daily 11:30am–12:30pm and 6:30–9:30pm. SEAFOOD/INTERNATIONAL.

Located near the Tobago Golf Club on the corner of Buccoo Bay Road and Mount Irvine, this restaurant offers international specialties with an emphasis on seafood, including kingfish steak, stuffed flying fish, and lobster Buccoo Bay (marinated in sherry wine and broiled with garlic, herbs, and butter sauce). The interior is adorned with pictures that refer to the novel and film *Papillon,* a story about a convict who settles in the Caribbean. For a change of pace, try curried goat, beef Stroganoff, or grilled lamb and beef. There's a patio for alfresco dining.

The Steak Hut. In the Sandy Point Beach Village, Crown Point. ☎ **868/639-8533.** Reservations recommended. Main courses TT$75–TT$95 ($12.50–$16). AE, MC, V. Daily 7–11:15am, 11:30am–5pm, and 7–9:15pm. STEAK.

On the island's southwestern side, the Steak Hut serves the best beef on the island, specializing in U.S. sirloin, T-bone, porterhouse, and tenderloin. The location, near the beach and swimming pool of this previously recommended hotel, is ideal, especially in the evening. The seafront restaurant also features local fish steaks—shark, flying fish, grouper, dolphin, barracuda, and kingfish. A steel band plays on Saturday night.

✪ Sugar Mill Restaurant. In the Mount Irvine Bay Hotel, Buccoo Bay. ☎ **868/639-8871.** Reservations required for those not staying at the hotel. Main courses TT$35–TT$45 ($6–$7.50); fixed-price meal TT$140 ($23). AE, DC, MC, V. Daily 7–10am, noon–3pm, and 7–10pm. INTERNATIONAL.

About a 5-mile drive northwest of the island's airport, this restaurant has at its core a 200-year-old sugar mill. Open-air, breezy, casually elegant, and permeated with the scent from nearby jasmine, this is the best restaurant on Tobago.

Lunch includes everything from salads and sandwiches to lamb chops provençal or sirloin steak. Dinner might include lobster bisque, a carbonade of beef, shrimp Newburg with rice pilaf, marinated grilled chicken, lobster sautéed in ginger, and filet of dolphin. Meals are usually accompanied by live music and entertainment, at least in season.

The Village Restaurant. At Kariwak Village, Store Bay. ☎ **868/639-8442.** Reservations recommended. Fixed-price meals TT$40–TT$65 ($7.10–$11.50) at lunch, TT$75–TT$100 ($13.30–$17.70) at dinner. AE, DC, MC, V. Daily 7:30am–9:30pm. INTERNATIONAL / WEST INDIAN.

At this restaurant where the menu changes daily, there are three eating areas including two open-air thatched huts where you can enjoy dining by candlelight. At lunch the meal generally consists of a vegetable, a starch, and meat such as steak or chicken. If you want lighter fare, there are sandwiches and salads. Sunday to Thursday the dinner menu consists of four courses, which might include fish broth, curried Caesar salad, baked chicken, and honey cake. On Friday and Saturday a buffet is served, costing TT$125 ($20.90); a band plays from 8:30 to 11pm.

BEACHES, WATER SPORTS & OUTDOOR ACTIVITIES

BEACHES If beach-fringed Tobago wasn't in fact the alleged location of Daniel Defoe's immortal story, the visitors who enjoy its superb beaches hardly seem to care. On Tobago sands, you can still feel like Robinson Crusoe in a solitary cove, at least for most of the week before the Trinidadians fly over to sample the sands on a Saturday.

A good beach, **Back Bay,** is within an 8-minute walk of the Mount Irvine Bay Hotel. Along the way, you'll pass a coconut plantation and an old cannon emplacement. Sometimes there can be dangerous currents here, but you can always enjoy exploring Rocky Point with its brilliantly colored parrot fish.

Try also **Man-O-War Bay,** one of the finest natural harbors in the West Indies, at the opposite end of the island. Once here, you'll come to a long sandy beach, and you can also enjoy a picnic at a government-run rest house.

The finest for last, **Pigeon Point,** on the island's northwestern coast, is the best-known bathing area with a long coral beach. Thatched shelters provide havens for changing into bathing attire, as well as tables and benches for picnics.

BOATING   The **Rex Turtle Beach Hotel,** Courland Bay (☎ **868/639-2851**), rents Aqua-finn sailboats and is a registered Mistral Sailing Centre.

FIELD TRIPS   Four different field trips offer close-up views of Tobago's exotic and often-rare tropical birds, as well as a range of other island wildlife and lush tropical flora. Naturalists of the Trinidad/Tobago area guide these excursions. The trips lead you on forest trails to coconut plantations, along rivers, and past waterfalls. Each trip lasts about 5 or 6 hours so you can take at least two per day if you like. One excursion goes to two nearby islands. The price per trip is $48 to $55 per person. For details, contact **Pat Turpin,** Man-O-War Bay Cottages, Charlottesville (☎ **868/660-4327;** fax 868/660-4328 or 868/660-4676).

GOLF   Tobago is the proud possessor of an 18-hole, 6,800-yard golf course at Mount Irvine called the **Tobago Golf Club** (☎ **868/639-8871**). Nonresidents pay $46 for 18 holes.

TENNIS   The **Rex Turtle Beach Hotel,** Courland Bay (☎ **868/639-2851**), has courts. The best courts, however, are at the **Mount Irvine Bay Hotel** (☎ **868/639-8871**), where two good courts are available.

WATER SPORTS—SNORKELING, DIVING & MORE   The unspoiled reefs off Tobago teem with a great variety of marine life. Divers can swim through rocky canyons 60 to 130 feet deep, and underwater photographers can shoot pictures they won't find anywhere else. Snorkeling over the celebrated Buccoo Reef is one of the specialties of Tobago. Hotels arrange for their guests to visit this underwater wonderland.

The **Rex Turtle Beach Hotel,** Courland Bay (☎ **868/639-2851**), is the best equipped for water sports. Sailing and windsurfing are available free, and waterskiing is offered at reasonable rates.

Dive Tobago Ltd., Pigeon Point (P.O. Box 53, Scarborough), Tobago, W.I. (☎ **868/639-0202;** fax 868/639-7275), operated by Jay Young, is the oldest and most established dive operation on Tobago. It offers easy resort courses, single dives, and dive packages. Equipment is available to rent. It caters to the beginner as well as to the experienced diver. A basic resort course, taking half a day and ending in a 30-foot dive, costs $55. Young is a certified PADI instructor. Jetbike rides and waterskiing are also available.

The **Tobago Dive Experience,** at the Rex Turtle Beach Hotel, Black Rock at Courtland Bay (☎ and fax **868/639-7034**), offers scuba dives, snorkeling, and boat trips. All dives are guided, with a boat following. Exciting drift dives are available for experienced divers. Manta rays are frequently seen 5 minutes from the shore, and there's rich marine life with zonal compaction. A one-tank dive costs $35 with no equipment or $42 with equipment.

Man Friday Diving, Charlotteville (☎ and fax **868/660-4676**), is a Danish-owned dive center with certified PADI and CMAS instructors along with PADI divemasters. The location is right on the beach of Man-O-War Bay at the northernmost tip of Tobago. With more than 40 different dive sites, they're always able to find suitable locations for diving, no matter what the water conditions are. Guided boat trips for certified divers, going out twice a day (except Sunday), leave at 9:30am and at 2pm. A resort course costs $75; a PADI open-water certification, $375. A one-tank dive costs $35, with a night dive going for $50. The outfitter also rents single or double kayaks.

EXPLORING THE ISLAND

In Tobago's capital, **Scarborough,** you can visit the local market Monday to Saturday morning and listen to the sounds of a Créole patois. Scarborough's stores have a limited range of merchandise, more to tempt the browser than the serious shopper.

The town need claim your attention only briefly before you climb up the hill to **Fort King George,** about 430 feet above the town. Built by the English in 1779, it was later captured by the French. After that it jockeyed back and forth among various conquerors until nature decided to end it all in 1847, blowing off the roofs of its buildings. The cannons still mounted had a 3-mile range, and one is believed to have come from one of the ships of Sir Francis Drake (you can still see a replica of the *Tudor Rose*). One building used to house a powder magazine, and you can see the ruins of a military hospital. Artifacts are displayed in a gallery on the grounds.

The **Tobago Museum,** Barrack Guard House, 84 Fort King George (☎ **868/639-3970**), on the grounds of the fort, displays numerous artifacts of the Amerindian culture, relics of the people who inhabited the island before the arrival of Columbus. There are original maps and documents, some going back as far as the 1600s. Also presented are documents related to the slave trade and military relics of the men who occupied the fortress in the 18th and 19th centuries. It's open Monday to Friday from 9am to 5pm, costing $5 for adults and $1 for children.

From Scarborough, you can drive northwest to **Plymouth,** Tobago's other town. In the graveyard of the little church is a tombstone dating from 1783 with a mysterious inscription: "She was a mother without knowing it, and a wife, without letting her husband know it, except by her kind indulgences to him."

Perched on a point at Plymouth is **Fort James,** which dates from 1768 when it was built by the British as a barracks. Now it's mainly in ruins.

From Speyside, you can make arrangements with a local fisherman to go to **Little Tobago,** a 450-acre offshore island where a bird sanctuary attracts ornithologists. Threatened with extinction in New Guinea, many birds, perhaps 50 species in all, were brought over to this little island in the early part of this century.

Off Pigeon Point lies ✪ **Buccoo Reef,** where sea gardens of coral and hundreds of fish can be seen in waist-deep water. This is the natural aquarium of Tobago. Nearly all the major hotels arrange boat trips to these acres of submarine gardens, which offer the best scuba diving and snorkeling. Even nonswimmers can wade knee-deep in the waters. Remember to protect your head and body from the tropical heat and to guard your feet against the sharp coral.

After about half an hour at the reef, passengers reboard their boats and go over to the **Nylon Pool,** with its crystal-clear waters. Here in this white-sand bottom, about a mile offshore, you can enjoy water only 3 or 4 feet deep. After a swim, you'll be returned to Buccoo Village jetty in time for a goat and crab race.

Cotton House Fashion Studio, Old Windward Road, in Bacolet (☎ **868/639-2727**), is one of the island's best choices for "hands-on" appreciation of the fine art of batik. Batik is an Indonesian tradition where melted wax, brushed onto fabric, resists dyes on certain parts of the cloth, thereby creating unusual colors and designs. This outlet contains one of the largest collections of batik clothing and wall hangings on Tobago. Dying techniques are demonstrated to clients, who can try their skills at the art form.

TOBAGO AFTER DARK

Your best bet for entertainment is at the **Mount Irvine Bay Hotel,** Mount Irvine (☎ 868/639-8871), where you might find some disco action, or else you can listen to the music of a steel band. The **Rex Turtle Beach Hotel,** Courtland Bay (☎ 868/639-2851), is the place to be on Wednesday night when it stages a Caribbean buffet dinner with cultural entertainment and dancing. You get a real West Indian flavor here. Every Saturday night, a steel band is brought in to entertain at a barbecue dinner from 7 to 10pm.

16 The Dutch Leewards

Cactus fences surround pastel-washed houses, divi-divi trees with their wind-blown look stud the barren countryside, free-form boulders are scattered about, and on occasion you'll come across an abandoned gold mine. Formerly Dutch possessions, the ABC group of islands—Aruba, Bonaire, and Curaçao—lie just off the northern coast of Venezuela. The islands, which only cover 363 square miles, have a widely diversified population of some 225,000 people, many of whom speak Papiamento, a language made up of Spanish, Portuguese, Dutch, African, and English elements. Dutch is the official tongue.

Duty-free shopping and gambling are promoted by the governments on all three islands. Curaçao has the most Dutch atmosphere, with a significant number of 18th-century buildings lining its streets. Curaçao, along with Aruba, boasts highly developed tourist centers, whereas Bonaire attracts the most dedicated scuba divers. Someone once said that there are more flamingos than people on Bonaire. Aruba, meanwhile, has the best beaches and a greater selection of hotel accommodations. The living is cheaper on Curaçao. Both Aruba and Bonaire are rather pricey.

In addition to Bonaire and Curaçao, the Netherlands Antilles encompasses Saba, St. Eustatius (Statia), and St. Maarten, already discussed in chapter 10, "The Dutch Windwards in the Leewards."

1 Aruba

Forget lush vegetation on Aruba—that's impossible with only 17 inches of rainfall annually. Aruba is dry and sunny almost year-round, with clean, exhilarating air like that found in the desert of Palm Springs, California. Its own Palm Beach, one of the best in the world, draws tourists in droves, as do its glittering casinos.

Aruba is not a chic address like St. Barts and Anguilla, but honeymooners, sun worshipers, snorkelers, sailors, and weekend gamblers find that it suits their needs just fine. As you lie back along the 7-mile stretch of white-sand beach, enjoying an 82° daytime temperature, you're not harassed by the locals peddling wares you don't want. There's almost no racial tension and, chances are, you won't get mugged. Trade winds keep the island from becoming uncomfortably hot, and there's very low humidity.

Aruba is not the best island for vacationers on a budget. In winter, the large resort hotels and time-share units are expensive; rates

Aruba

California
Lighthouse

Malmok Beach

California
Sand Dunes

Caribbean Sea

Fisherman's Hut Beach

Palm Beach

Eagle Beach

Noord

■ Altovista Chapel

Manchebo
Beach

Divi Beach

○ Bushiribana

Druif Bay

■ Natural Bridge

Oranjestad

Casibari

○ Ayó

○ Santa Cruz

✈ Queen Beatrix Airport

▲▲ Hooiberg

*Spanish
Lagoon*

■ Fontein Cave

Boca Prins

■ Guadarikiri Cave

■ Huliba Cave

○ Savaneta

Boca Grandi

Caribbean Sea

○ Sint Nicolas
(San-Nicolas)

Grapefield
Beach

Rodgers Beach

○ Seroe
Colorado

Baby Beach

Airport ✈ Beach ✔ Lighthouse ✵

2-0190

591

begin at around $150 a night. And Aruba does not have the number of inexpensive guest houses or small inns that many other islands do. However, there are numerous package deals, which a good travel agent can apprise you of. But you can always eat inexpensively at numerous fast-food franchises. We, of course, recommend some inexpensively and moderately priced restaurants where you'll get better food. Food tabs can be high since all food has to be imported onto desert-dry Aruba.

Aruba stands outside the hurricane path. Its coastline on the leeward side is smooth and serene, with sandy beaches; but on the eastern coast, the windward side, the look is rugged and wild, typical of the windswept Atlantic.

Many visitors come here for the annual pre-Lenten **Carnival,** a month-long festival with events day and night. With music, dancing, parades, costumes, and "jump-ups," Carnival is the highlight of Aruba's winter season.

GETTING THERE

On **American Airlines** (☎ 800/433-7300), Aruba-bound passengers can catch a daily nonstop $4^{1}/_{2}$-hour flight departing New York's JFK airport. From American's hub in San Juan, Puerto Rico, two nonstop flights depart every day for Aruba. American also offers a daily nonstop flight from Miami to Aruba. This service enables vacationers from Chicago, Los Angeles, San Francisco, and Seattle to fly directly to Aruba via the American Airlines Miami hub.

American's lowest fare is included in its "land package," whereby prearranged and prepaid accommodations at selected hotels are booked at the same time as the airfare through American's tour department. Contact an American Airlines reservations clerk or a travel agent for details.

ALM (☎ 800/327-7230) has good connections into Aruba from certain parts of the United States. There are direct flights to Aruba from Fort Lauderdale on Thursday and Sunday, from Atlanta on Sunday, and flights leave Miami daily and from Atlanta on Saturday via Curaçao.

Tiny **Air Aruba** (☎ 800/88-ARUBA), the country's national carrier, boasts Newark (N.J.), Baltimore, Tampa, and Miami as North American gateways. Air Aruba offers daily nonstop flights from Miami, daily flights from Newark, twice-weekly (Saturday and Sunday) nonstop flights from Baltimore, and five weekly flights from Tampa. Air Aruba also has links to Bonaire and Curaçao.

Air Canada (☎ 800/363-5440 in Canada, or 800/776-3000 in the U.S.) has good connections from Toronto and Québec to Miami. Once in Miami, Canadians and other passengers can fly Air Aruba to the island.

GETTING AROUND

BY BUS　Aruba has excellent bus service, with a round-trip fare between the beach hotels and Oranjestad of $1.75. Bus schedules are available at the Arubus Office at the central bus station on Zoutmanstraat. Your hotel reception desk will also know the approximate times the buses pass by where you're staying. There's regular daily service from 6am to midnight. Try to have the exact change. For **bus schedules and information,** call the Aruba Tourism Authority (☎ 297/8-23777).

BY MOTORCYCLE & MOPED　Since the roads of Aruba are good and the terrain flat, many visitors prefer this form of transport. Mopeds and motorcycles cost an average of $37 to $40 per day. They're available at **George's ScooterRental,** L. G. Smith Blvd. 136 (☎ 297/8-25975). **Nelson Motorcycle Rental,** Gasparito 10A, Noord (☎ 297/8-66801), rents scooters for $25 and motorcycles for $44 to $89.

Melcor Cycle Rental, Bubali 106B (☎ **297/8-75203**), in front of the Adventure Golf Club, rents scooters for $24 to $35 per day. You can also rent dirt bikes and street bikes beginning at $45 per day. These are cash prices; a 4% handling charge is assessed if you use a credit or charge card. You can also find rentals at **Semver Cycle Rental,** Noord 22 (☎ **297/8-66851**), where bikes begin at $25 per day.

BY TAXI In Aruba, the taxis are unmetered but rates are fixed, so tell the driver your destination and ask the fare before getting in. The main office is on Sands Street between the bowling center and Taco Bell. A **dispatch office** is located at the Bosabao (☎ **297/8-22116**). A ride from the airport to most of the hotels, including those at Palm Beach, costs about $8 to $14 per car, with a maximum of four passengers allowed. Some locals don't tip, although we suggest tipping, especially if the driver has helped you with luggage. Additionally, since it's next to impossible to locate a taxi on some parts of the island, it's a good idea to ask the taxi driver to return to pick you up at a certain time if you're going to a remote destination.

You'll also usually find the English-speaking drivers willing tour guides. Most seem well informed about their island and eager to share it with you. A 1-hour tour (and you don't need much more than that) costs $35 for a maximum of four passengers.

BY RENTAL CAR Unlike most Caribbean islands, Aruba makes it easy to rent a car. The roads connecting the major tourist attractions are excellent, and a valid U.S. or Canadian driver's license is accepted by each of the major car-rental companies. The three major U.S. car-rental companies maintain offices on Aruba, and also have airport branches and kiosks at the major hotels. No taxes are imposed on car rentals on Aruba, but insurance can be tricky. Even with the purchase of a collision-damage waiver, a driver is still responsible for the first $300 to $500 worth of damage. (Avis doesn't even offer this waiver, so in the event of an accident—unless you have private insurance—you'll be liable for up to the full value of damage to your car.) Rental rates range between $35 and $70 per day.

Try **Budget Rent-a-Car,** Kolibristraat 1 (☎ **800/472-3325** in the U.S., or 297/8-28600); **Hertz,** L. G. Smith Blvd. 142 (☎ **800/654-3001** in the U.S., or 297/8-24545), and **Avis,** Kolibristraat 14 (☎ **800/331-1084** in the U.S., or 297/8-28787). Budget requires that renters be at least 25; Avis, 23; and Hertz, 21.

For a better deal, consider **Hedwina Car Rental,** Bubali 93A (☎ **297/8-76442,** or 297/8-30880 at the airport). If you take a car for a week, you sometimes pay for only 5 days. Another agency to consider is **Thrifty Car Rental,** Balashi 65 (☎ **297/8-55300,** or 297/8-35335 at the airport), which offers good deals, with many rentals beginning at $45 to $50 per day. You can also rent Jeeps from $60 per day.

FAST FACTS: Aruba

Banking Hours Banks are open Monday to Friday from 8am to noon and 1:30 to 3:45pm.

Currency The currency is the **Aruba florin (AFl),** which is divided into 100 cents. Silver coins are in denominations of 5, 10, 25, and 50 cents and 1 and 2$\frac{1}{2}$ florins. The 50-cent piece, the square "yotin," is Aruba's best-known coin. The current exchange rate is 1.77 AFl to $1 U.S. (1 AFl is worth about 56¢). U.S. dollars, traveler's checks, and major credit and charge cards are widely accepted throughout the island. *Note:* Unless otherwise stated, prices quoted in this chapter are in U.S. dollars.

Documents To enter Aruba, U.S. and Canadian citizens, and British subjects, may submit a valid passport or a birth certificate (or, for U.S. citizens only, a voter registration card with a photo ID).

Electricity The electricity is 110 volts AC, 60 cycles, the same as in the United States.

Emergencies For the **police,** dial ☎ **11100.** For a **medical emergency,** dial ☎ **74300.** For the **fire** department, call ☎ **115.**

Information Before leaving home, you can contact the **Aruba Tourism Authority** at the following locations: 1000 Harbor Blvd., Weehawken, NJ 07087 (☎ **800/TO-ARUBA**); 2344 Salzedo St., Miami, FL 33144 (☎ **305/567-2720**); 199 14th St. NE, Suite 2008, Atlanta, GA 30309 (☎ **404/892-7822**); or 86 Bloor St. W., Suite 204, Toronto, ON M5S 1M5 (☎ **416/975-1950**).

Once on the island, for information go to the **Aruba Tourism Authority** at L. G. Smith Blvd. 172, Oranjestad (☎ **297/8-23777**).

Language The official language is Dutch, but nearly everybody speaks English. Spanish is also widely spoken.

Medical Care To receive medical care, go to the **Horacio Oduber Hospital** on L. G. Smith Boulevard (☎ **297/8-74300;** also the number to call in case of a medical emergency). It's a modern building near Eagle Beach, with excellent medical facilities. Hotels also have medical doctors on call, and there are good dental facilities as well (appointments can be made through your hotel).

Safety Aruba is one of the Caribbean's safer destinations, in spite of its numerous hotels and gambling casinos. Of course, pickpockets and purse-snatchers are around, but in no great numbers. However, it would be wise to guard your valuables. Never leave them unattended on the beach or even in a locked car.

Taxes and Service The government of Aruba imposes a 6.66% room tax, as well as a $20 airport departure tax. At your hotel, you'll have an 11% to 15% service charge added to charges for room, food, and beverages.

Telephones To call Aruba from the United States, dial 011 (the international access code), then 297 (the country code for Aruba), and then 8 (the area code) and the five-digit local number.

Once on Aruba, to call another number on the island only the five-digit local number is necessary.

Time Aruba is on Atlantic standard time year-round, so most of the year Aruba is 1 hour ahead of eastern standard time (when it's 10am on Aruba, it's 9am in New York). When daylight saving time is in effect in the United States, clocks in New York and Aruba show the same time.

Water The water, which comes from the world's second-largest desalination plant, is pure.

WHERE TO STAY

Most of Aruba's hotels are bustling and self-contained resorts. Unfortunately for the budget traveler, there's a dearth of family or budget hotels. The few guest houses tend to be booked up early in winter by faithful returning visitors. In season, you must make reservations well in advance; don't ever arrive expecting to find a room on the spot—you must have an address to give Immigration when you arrive on Aruba. Don't forget to ask if the 6.66% room tax and any service charge are included in the rates quoted when you make your reservation.

DOUBLES FOR LESS THAN $55 (WINTER) / $45 (OFF-SEASON)

Cactus Apartments. Matadera 5, Aruba. ☎ **297/8-22903.** Fax 297/8-20433. 13 apts.
A/C TV. Winter, $45 apt for one; $50 apt for two; $60 apt for three. Off-season, $35 apt for
one; $40 apt for two; $50 apt for three. AE, MC, V.

This is a small, inexpensive apartment complex whose mustard-colored exterior
blends into the surrounding arid, cactus-dotted landscape. Its oldest section was built
in the early 1980s. A car is recommended for anyone who wants to stay here, and
the owner Jacinto Tromp is well versed in the intricacies of the island's network of
buses and public transport. There's neither a bar nor restaurant on the premises, but
the bedrooms contain their own kitchenettes. The nearest beach is 2 miles away.
There's a small, on-site launderette, a single coin-operated telephone that's shared by
all the units, and maid service Monday to Saturday. A row of cactus plants forms a
hedge around several sides of the apartment block.

Mi Cielo Apartments. Italiesstraat 12, Aruba. ☎ **297/8-20021.** Fax 297/8-30076. 7 apts.
A/C TV. Winter, $55 studio apt for one or two; $75 one-bedroom apt. Off-season, $45 studio
apt for one or two; $65 one-bedroom apt. No credit cards.

Although these incredible rates—at least for Aruba—might not hold indefinitely, Mi
Cielo offers one of the island's lowest-priced places to stay. A local lawyer runs the
property and there's little on-site management, so the complex is more for self-
sufficient types. You're in a good location, however, between beach and town, about
a 10-minute walk each way. In this one-story property, the units are absolutely standard, with no frills or style, but each is reasonably comfortable and pleasantly furnished, with a patio and kitchenette. If your hopes aren't too high and you like saving
money, consider booking here.

DOUBLES FOR LESS THAN $75 (WINTER) / $60 (OFF-SEASON)

Andicuri Inn. De La Sallestraat 13, Oranjestad, Aruba. ☎ **297/8-21539.** Fax 297/8-29922.
18 apts. A/C TV TEL. Winter, $70 apt for one or two. Off-season, $60 apt for one or two. Two
children 11 and under stay free in parents' room. MC, V.

If you'd like to reside in the capital, just 5 minutes from the center and only 10 minutes from the nearest good beach, consider this affordable little entry. It offers fully
furnished and comfortable apartments, each with a king-size bed, cable TV, and walk-
in closet, plus a kitchen with a built-in stove. There's little style or grandeur here, but
you get reasonable comfort at a good price. The place is for independent types who
don't expect resort-style amenities. For your other diversions, you have to go outside
the property.

☼ Coconut Inn. Noord 31, Aruba. ☎ **297/8-62288.** Fax 297/8-65433. 34 studios, 6 apts.
A/C TV. Winter, $55 studio for one; $65 studio for two; $80 one-bedroom apt. Off-season, $40
studio for one; $55 studio for two; $70 one-bedroom apt. Extra person $15; children 2–17,
$7.50; children under 2 stay free in parents' room. Rates include breakfast. MC, V.

In the vicinity of the high-rises and the casinos, this is one of Aruba's few B&B accommodations. Considering what the nearby hotels are charging, this inn is a steal.
It's only a 3-minute drive from some of Aruba's best beaches, and the location is convenient to supermarkets, sundry stores, banks, restaurants, and even a pharmacy. A
public bus also stops a short walk away. Units come in an array of studios ranging
from rather plain and standard to deluxe, plus six one-bedroom apartments. The deluxe studios and the one-bedroom apartments can accommodate up to four guests,
a real savings. All rooms are fully furnished in a standard motel style, with private
baths, a private entrance, and a fully equipped kitchenette, as well as balconies or
patios. There's no maid service on Sunday. The hotel has a swimming pool and a
restaurant and bar where breakfast is served.

Turibana Plaza. Noord 124, Aruba. ☎ **297/8-67292.** Fax 297/8-62658. 19 apts. A/C TV TEL. Winter, $75 apt for two; $152.50 apt for four. Extra person, $15. Off-season, $50 apt for two; $95 apt for four. Extra person $10. AE, MC, V.

This modern complex of rather standard apartments is only minutes from the best white, sandy beaches of Aruba as well as some terrific restaurants near Oranjestad. And its prices are among the island's most affordable. For those cooking in, a supermarket is less than a mile away. Because of their low rates, the apartments are booked early in winter, so reserve as far in advance as possible. The bedrooms have wall-to-wall carpeting and plain, simple furnishings, with a full kitchenette. Some guests like the place so much that they check in for a month. On the ground level is an excellent restaurant. Although the Turibana Plaza isn't a full-service hotel, it does offer daily maid service and laundry facilities.

DOUBLES FOR LESS THAN $100 (WINTER) / $75 (OFF-SEASON)

✪ **Aruba Blue Village Suites.** Cunucu Abao 37, Aruba. ☎ **297/8-78618.** Fax 297/8-70081. 56 junior, one-bedroom, and two-bedroom suites. Winter, $85 junior suite; $95 one-bedroom suite; $120 two-bedroom suite. Off-season, $60 junior suite; $75 one-bedroom suite; $90 two-bedroom suite. AE, MC, V.

If you can forgo the beachfront location, you'll find one of Aruba's best deals here at this complex. Off-season, it's a sweet bargain if four people share a junior suite or six people share a two-bedroom suite: Only $16 per person a night. The accommodations are in the typical resort style, plain but comfortable, yet features include cable TV, a safety deposit box, a separate bath with shower, and a fully equipped kitchenette. Some 26 of the suites come with pull-out sofas. You're 5 minutes from the beach and close to casinos and nightlife. But many guests stay on the property, enjoying two spacious swimming pools, two large sun terraces, table tennis and other indoor and outdoor games, a children's playground, and bar and barbecue facilities at the pool. The complex of single-story apartments lies in a residential area removed from the hotel strip.

✪ **Stauffer Hotel Aruba.** J. E. Irausquin Blvd. 370, Aruba. ☎ **297/8-60855.** Fax 297/8-60856. 101 rms. A/C TV. Winter, $100 single or double. Off-season, $75 single or double. Extra person $10; children 11 and under stay free in parents' room. AE, DC, DISC, MC, V.

Although the accommodations are rather standard, the Stauffer (not to be confused with Stouffer) is a very good buy on high-priced Aruba. This plain, square three-story building is surrounded by high-rise hotels and a variety of restaurants and fast-food eateries. A bus stops in front, and the beach is across the street (the hotel provides free chairs and beach towels). The bedrooms are large, with two double beds, tables, and phones—there are no balconies. Although the hotel opened only in the mid-1990s, it has become well known and is already drawing a lot of repeat visitors. Services and facilities are very limited, however—no restaurant, no bar, and no pool.

✪ **Vistalmar Apartments.** Bucutiweg 28, Aruba. ☎ **297/8-28579.** Fax 297/8-22200. 8 one-bedroom apts. A/C. Winter, $100–$110 apt with a car. Off-season, $70 apt with a car. No credit cards.

An affordable and intimate place to stay on Aruba, this property doesn't have access to the celebrated beaches, but lies across from the water in a residential section near the airport. The complex of apartments is in two similar buildings, each with a balcony or courtyard offering water views. A little more stylish than some of the bleaker apartment units rented on the island, the accommodations here are spacious and furnished for comfort. Your hosts, among the island's more personable, are Aby and Katy Yarzagaray, a font of island information. Aby was born on Aruba and comes from a family who has lived on the island since 1805. Katy has resided here since the

1960s. The apartments have a master-size bedroom, a bathroom with a tub and shower, a separate dressing area, a fully equipped kitchen, and a living room with a sofa that can be turned into an extra bed. There's also a second sleeping room and a sun porch. The seaside sun deck in front of the complex is just 50 yards from the water, and guests can swim from the deck. Upon arrival, guests find complimentary food in the refrigerator. Daily maid service and such thoughtful touches as fresh flowers make this an inviting choice. The hosts offer complimentary use of boats, bikes, picnic coolers, snorkeling equipment, beach towels, and an outdoor grill. Not only that, but you also get a car!

BEST OFF-SEASON BETS

Amsterdam Manor Beach Resort. J. E. Irausquin Blvd. 252 (P.O. Box 1302), Oranjestad, Aruba. ☎ **297/8-71492.** Fax 297/8-71463. 73 apts. A/C TV TEL. Winter, $160–$310 unit for one or two persons. Off-season, $100–$230 unit for one or two persons. Additional person $20 extra. AE, DC, MC, V.

Opened in 1991, this hotel sports one of the two or three most interesting facades on the island. Inspired by the interconnected rows of canalfront houses in Amsterdam (or by a sprawling manor house on Curaçao), it lies amid an arid landscape across the street from Eagle Beach. Owned by a trio of Dutch investors, it has a series of inner courtyards, a swimming pool fed by a pair of splashing waterfalls, and a simple bar and restaurant. More than in any other hotel on the island, the accommodations draw from 19th-century Dutch models. The studios and one- or two-bedroom apartments have fully equipped kitchens. In winter, these units—for one or two people—cost $160 to $310. However, off-season one or two guests can book into an apartment for only $100, paying $20 for an extra person. Of course, even in summer some of the more luxurious units here cost up to $230, but the $100 accommodations are fine in every way, although not as spacious.

✪ **Aruba Palm Beach Resort and Casino.** J. E. Irausquin Blvd. 79, Oranjestad, Aruba. ☎ **800/345-2782** in the U.S. or Canada, or 297/8-23900. Fax 297/8-61941. 176 rms, 20 cabañas, 4 suites. A/C TV TEL. Winter, $194–$220 double; $225–$248 cabaña; $175 suite. MAP $41.98 per person extra. Additional adult $20 extra. Children stay free in parents' room. AE, DC, MC, V.

Built in 1966, during the earliest stages of Aruba's hotel boom, this seashell-pink high-rise palazzo stands in a choice location, in a beachside palm grove 6 miles north of the airport. Accented with coral stone and Moorish arches both inside and out, the place is sleek, stylish, and comfortable, with a polite staff and rooms that benefited from a complete overhaul back in 1988. Every unit has quality and character, with all the modern amenities, including small refrigerators.

In winter a single or double costs $194 to $220 and a cabaña is even more expensive at $225 to $248 for two. However, off-season (mid-April to mid-December) you can book in here in the least expensive double room for only $125, a terrific vacation deal. Even the most expensive single or double costs only $194, unless you opt for a more expensive cabaña or suite. An extra person can be tucked in for $20, and MAP is $42 per person.

You can enjoy the Las Vegas–inspired Palm Casino, nightly entertainment in the Oasis Lounge, fine dining in the Palm Garden Café, or cozy outdoor dining in the nautically inspired Seawatch Restaurant, which features U.S. beef and seafood. Live music is offered in the Players Club, open nightly until 3am. Room service, laundry, baby-sitting, and beauty salon are available. An Olympic-size freshwater swimming pool is the best on the island for swimming laps, and there's also a children's pool, plus two tennis courts.

WORTH A SPLURGE

Caribbean Palm Village Resort. Palm Beach Rd., Noord 43E, Aruba. ☎ **800/992-2015** in the U.S. and Canada, or 297/8-62700. Fax 297/8-62380. 140 units. A/C TV TEL. Winter, $160 single or double; $225 one-bedroom suite; $305 two-bedroom suite. Off-season, $100 single or double; $125 one-bedroom suite; $165 two-bedroom suite. Children stay free in parents' room. AE, DC, MC, V.

Although this low-rise charges more than we like to pay, it's still very good value as compared to the high-rise resorts. If you want a lot of resort-style amenities but don't want to pay $350 or beyond per day for the privilege, you might stay here. Off-season, this hotel becomes one of Aruba's better values. Attracting mainly families and couples from 30 to 60, it has an intimate atmosphere with welcoming Aruban hospitality. A three-story white and peach-colored building, it was built Spanish style around a pool (there's another pool as well). You walk to the rooms (no elevator), which have one double bed but no balcony. The suites, if you want to pay the extra money, have either a king- or queen-size bed, a pull-out sofa, a full kitchen with microwave and dishwasher, and a balcony. If you grow bored with the hotel's pools, the beach is a mile away. There are two restaurants serving both Aruban and international specialties, along with the Coco Loco pool bar. Other facilities include two Jacuzzis, two barbecue areas where guests cook their own dinners, and a tennis court. Baby-sitting is available, and you're conveniently located near a drugstore, supermarket, and sundries shopping.

The Mill Resort. L. G. Smith Blvd. 330, Palm Beach, Aruba. ☎ **297/8-67700.** Fax 297/8-67271. 200 units. A/C TV TEL. Winter, $155–$165 single or double with refrigerator; $185–$195 studio or minisuite with kitchenette for one or two. Off-season, $85–$95 single or double with refrigerator; $102–$112 studio or minisuite with kitchenette for one or two. AE, DC, MC, V.

Opened in 1990 and enlarged in 1994, this complex of two-story concrete buildings with red roofs is set in an arid, rather dusty location inland from the beach. It's adjacent to a large, modern re-creation of a Dutch windmill, whose Las Vegas sense of kitsch has become something of an Aruban landmark. Units ring a large swimming pool, and Eagle Beach (which is used by such megahotels as the Hilton) lies across the highway, within a 7-minute trek. The room decor is inspired by tropical models, with white rattan, carpeting or white floor tiles, and pastel-colored curtains and draperies.

This hotel is best for self-motivated visitors who aren't afraid to scour Aruba for alternative dining, drinking, and diversionary options. You'll find very limited bar and restaurant service here, but since most units have kitchenettes (or at least a refrigerator), many guests cook in. There's a launderette, a sauna, a fitness center, an exercise room, a beauty salon, and massage facilities. In many rooms you'll find king-size beds and Jacuzzi-style bathtubs.

Talk of the Town Resort. L. G. Smith Blvd. 2, Aruba. ☎ **800/223-1108** in the U.S., or 297/8-23380. Fax 297/8-33208. 62 units. A/C TV. Winter, $120–$145 single; $130–$145 double; $155 one-bedroom studio; $195 two-bedroom apt. Off-season, $88–$108 single; $98–$118 double; $118 one-bedroom studio; $128 two-bedroom apt. Extra person $10; children 11 and under stay free in parents' room. MAP $35 per person extra. AE, DC, MC, V.

Although it's seen the wear and tear of the years, this enduring favorite has long been known as one of the best moderately priced choices on Aruba. On the south side of Oranjestad, it's really like a motel, frequented by business travelers. A beach which has been upgraded and enlarged is 200 yards across the street. The bedrooms are a bit dark, and both standard and superior rooms have ceiling fans, balconies, room safes, refrigerators, and microwaves, whereas the studios and apartments offer fuller kitchenettes. Three meals a day are provided in the Moonlight Grill, and you can also patronize the open-air Surfside Bar and Grill. A daily happy hour with free snacks and live music draws the budget traveler, and at Friday night's carvery you can eat all the prime rib you want, one of Aruba's best food values. For years this resort sheltered Aruba's most famous restaurant, Talk of the Town, which has now closed. Room service and baby-sitting are available.

WHERE TO EAT

Boonoonoonoos. Wilhelminastraat 18. ☎ **297/8-31888.** Reservations recommended for dinner in winter. Main courses $15.75–$33.75. AE, DC, MC, V. Mon–Sat 11:30am–10:30pm, Sun 4–10:30pm. CARIBBEAN/INTERNATIONAL.

Named after the legendary beach parties of Jamaica (Boonoonoonoos), this restaurant in an old-fashioned Aruban house on the capital's main shopping street celebrates the widely divergent traditions of Caribbean cuisine. It offers a confectionery decor of blues, greens, and pinks, a bar outfitted with rows of hard-bottomed benches, and a crew of waiters in carnival-colored shirts. Even if you're not visiting the rest of the Caribbean, you can go on a culinary tour by wandering across the menu. Try an appetizer known as *ajaka,* an Aruban dish made with chicken and wrapped in banana leaves. The local callaloo soup and a homemade fish soup are also a good way to start. For a main dish, the most popular is actually Aruban: *keshi yena,* Aruban chicken casserole. You can also order Jamaican jerk ribs, based on a recipe dating back three centuries. You might also try a Bajan pepperpot or curried chicken Trinidad style. A small section of the menu is devoted to French cuisine including filet mignon and Dover sole meunière. This place continues to draw mixed reactions from readers, everything from raves to attacks. Slow service is one of the major complaints.

Brisas del Mar. Savaneta 222A. ☎ **297/8-44718.** Reservations required. Main courses $11–$32. AE, MC, V. Mon 6:30–9:30pm, Tues–Sun noon–2:30pm and 6:30–9:30pm. SEAFOOD.

A 15-minute drive east of Oranjestad, near the police station, Brisas del Mar is like a place you might encounter in some outpost in Australia. Here, in very simple surroundings right at water's edge, Lucia Rasmijn opened this little hut with an air-conditioned bar in front of which the locals gather to drink the day away. The place is often jammed on weekends with many of the same local people, who come here to drink and dance. In back the tables are open to the sea breezes, and nearby you can see the catch of the day, perhaps wahoo, being sliced up and sold to local buyers. Specialties include mixed seafood platter, baby shark, and broiled lobster; you can order meat and poultry dishes as well, including tenderloin steak and broiled chicken. Don't expect subtlety of cuisine, as this is the type of food Arubans enjoyed in the 1950s, and nothing much has changed since then.

Mama's & Papa's. Noord 41C. ☎ **297/8-67913.** Main courses $12.95–$28. AE, DC, MC, V. Mon–Sat 6:30–11pm. ARUBAN.

Located north of Oranjestad, this small eatery serves Aruban specialties and some West Indian dishes. Local favorites include *keshi yena,* a casserole of chicken and cheese, and *kreeft di cay reef,* broiled lobster. Fish selections are served in a variety of sauces including Créole and garlic butter. If you're in the mood for West Indian, try the curried chicken, stewed goat, or conch stew. Most nights a guitar player entertains with music from the 1960s. Desserts include carrot cake and sweet-potato pie.

Mi Cushina. In the La Quinta Beach Resort, J. E. Irausquin Blvd. 228. ☎ **297/8-72222.** Reservations recommended. Main courses $12–$30. AE, DC, MC, V. Tues–Sun noon–2pm and 6–10pm. ARUBAN/INTERNATIONAL.

For years in another and far more remote location, this little restaurant was known for serving some of the most authentic Aruban dishes on the island, maintaining a local tradition when nearly all other places had gone international. The world used to come to its door, but it was difficult to reach, especially at night. Mi Cushina decided to move right into the heart of the "hotel belt," to make itself more accessible. The decor isn't as quaint as it used to be, and the prices are a lot higher, but the old recipes were brought along to the new location. Yes, you'll find conch stir-fry, stewed goat, and slices of fish cooked Aruban style still on the new menu, but it also caters to a more international palate with its offering of such dishes as lobster thermidor and filet mignon. Those international dishes you can find better at other restaurants nearby, but here you can still order *funchi* (cornmeal), a fried concoction that accompanies many dishes, along with *pan bati* (a pancake), and other local fare.

Le Petit Cafe. Emmastraat 1, Strada Complex II. ☎ **297/8-26577.** Reservations recommended. Main courses $16.50–$32.50; lunch $5.30–$13. AE, DC, MC, V. Mon–Sat 11am–4:30pm and 6–11pm, Sun 6–11pm. CONTINENTAL.

This local hangout's specialty is called Romance on the Stone—meals cooked on hot stones, including steak, chicken, jumbo shrimp, fish, and lobster. Dinner is not for the price-conscious, but lunch offers a wide selection of dishes at reasonable prices. The menu spotlights chicken kebabs with peanut sauce and whatever happens to be the catch of the day. For a quick bite, try one of the salads (chicken, tuna, fruit, and chef) or a sandwich, such as a BLT, club, or steak. Le Petit Cafe offers indoor-outdoor dining with seating on two floors and also on the terrace.

The Waterfront Crabhouse. In the Seaport Market, L. G. Smith Blvd., Oranjestad. ☎ **297/8-35858.** Reservations recommended. Main courses $13.95–$24.95; continental breakfast $5.95; lunch from $12. AE, MC, V. Daily 8–11am, noon–4:30pm, and 5:30–10:30pm. SEAFOOD/STEAK.

Set at the most desirable end of a shopping mall in downtown Oranjestad, overlooking a manicured lawn, this restaurant evokes a dining room on the California coast. Amid painted murals of underwater life and rattan furniture, at tables placed both indoors and on a garden terrace, you can enjoy well-prepared seafood. Menu items include stuffed clams and fried squid with a marinara sauce, and linguine with white or red clam sauce, which can be ordered on the side or as a main course. The chef lists "crabs, crabs, crabs" as his specialty, including garlic crabs, Alaska crab legs, and (in season) soft-shell crabs; stuffed Maine lobster and Cajun grilled shrimp are also served. A wide range of other fish dishes, including yellowfin tuna and swordfish, are grilled over an open fire. All fish served are hook-and-line caught, never from drift nets. The restaurant's steak menu includes a 10-ounce Black Angus filet mignon, as well as the less expensive chopped sirloin smothered in onions.

BEACHES, WATER SPORTS & OUTDOOR PURSUITS

BEACHES   The western and southern shore, called the **Turquoise Coast,** attracts sun seekers to Aruba. **Palm Beach** and **Eagle Beach** (the latter closer to Oranjestad) are the best beaches. No hotel along the strip owns the beaches, all of which are open to the public (if you use any of the hotel's facilities, however, you'll be charged, of course). You can also spread your towel on **Manchebo Beach** or **Druif Bay Beach**— in fact, anywhere along 7 miles of uninterrupted sugar-white sands. In total contrast to the leeward side, the north or windward shore is rugged and wild.

CRUISES   Visitors interested in combining a boat ride with a few hours of snorkeling should contact **De Palm Tours,** which has offices in eight of the island's hotels and its main office at Lloyd G. Smith Blvd. 142, in Oranjestad (☎ **297/8-24400**). De Palm Tours offers a 1-hour glass-bottom-boat cruise that visits two coral reefs and the German shipwreck *Antilia* daily except Sunday and Thursday. It costs $17.50 per person.

GOLF   Visitors can play at the **Aruba Golf Club,** Golfweg 82 (☎ 297/8-42006), near San Nicolas on the southeastern end of the island. Although it has only 10 greens, they're played from different tees to simulate an 18-hole play. Greens fees are $10 for 18 holes and $7.50 for 9 holes. The course is open daily from 7:30am to 5pm, although anyone wishing to play 18 holes must begin the rounds before 1:30pm. Golf carts and clubs can be rented on site in the pro shop. On the premises is an air-conditioned restaurant and changing rooms with showers.

Aruba's long-awaited **Tierra del Sol** golf course (☎ 297/8-67800) opened in 1995. Designed by the Robert Trent Jones II Group, the 18-hole, par-71 course is on the northwest coast, near the California Lighthouse. Facilities include a restaurant and lounge in the clubhouse, two swimming pools, and eight tennis courts. The course is managed by Hyatt Resorts Caribbean. In winter greens fees are $120, including golf cart, or $72 after 3pm. Off-season, greens fees are $85, or $57 after 3pm. The course is open daily from 6am to 7pm.

TENNIS   Most of the island's beachfront hotels have tennis courts, often swept by trade winds. Many courts can also be lit for night games (we don't advise playing in Aruba's noonday sun), usually with a surcharge. The best tennis is at the **Aruba Racket Club** (☎ 297/8-60215), the island's first world-class tennis facility with eight courts, an exhibition center court, a pro shop, a swimming pool, aerobics center, a fitness center, and a shopping center. The location is part of the Tierra del Sol complex on Aruba's northwest coast, near the California Lighthouse. The club is open Monday to Saturday from 8am to 11pm and on Sunday from 8am to 6pm. Rates are $10 per hour per court.

WATER SPORTS   You can snorkel in rather shallow waters, and scuba divers find stunning marine life with endless varieties of coral as well as tropical fish in infinite hues; at some points visibility is up to 90 feet. Most divers want to see the German freighter *Antilia,* which was scuttled in the early years of World War II off the northwestern tip of Aruba, not too far from Palm Beach.

Red Sails Sports, in the Seaport Marketplace, Oranjestad (☎ 297/8-64500), is the best water-sports center on the island. The center has an extensive variety of activities, including sailing, windsurfing, waterskiing, and scuba diving. Scuba diving can be experienced in 1 day with Red Sail dive packages, including shipwreck dives as well as exploration of marine reefs. Guests are first given a poolside resort course where Red Sail's certified instructors teach procedures that ensure safety during the dives. For those who wish to become certified, full PADI certification can be achieved in as little as 4 days. One-tank dives cost $35 and up.

The **Divi Winds Center,** J. E. Irausquin Blvd. 41 (☎ 297/8-23300, ext. 623), near the Tamarind Aruba Beach Resort, is the windsurfing headquarters of the island. Equipment is made by Fanatic, Inc., and is rented for $15 to $18 per hour, $30 per half day, or $50 for a full day. The resort is on the serene (Caribbean) side of the island, and doesn't face the fierce Atlantic waves. Sunfish lessons can be arranged, and snorkeling gear can be rented for $10 per day.

SEEING THE SIGHTS

The capital of Aruba, **Oranjestad,** attracts shoppers rather than sightseers. The bustling city has a very Caribbean flavor, and it's part Spanish, part Dutch in architecture. Cutting in from the airport, the main thoroughfare, Lloyd G. Smith Boulevard, goes along the waterfront and on to Palm Beach, changing its name along the way to J. E. Irausquin Boulevard. But most visitors cross it heading for Caya G. F. Betico Croes, where they find the best free-port shopping.

After a shopping trip, you might return to the harbor where fishing boats and schooners, many from Venezuela, are moored. Nearly all newcomers to Aruba like to take a picture of the **Schooner Harbor.** Not only does it have colorful boats docked along the quay, but boatpeople display their wares in open stalls. The local patois predominates. A little farther along, at the fish market, fresh fish is sold directly from the boats. Also on the sea side of Oranjestad, **Wilhelmina Park** was named after Queen Wilhelmina of the Netherlands. A tropical garden has been planted along the water, and there's a sculpture of the Queen Mother.

Aside from shopping, the major attractions of Aruba are ✪ **Eagle Beach** and ✪ **Palm Beach,** among the finest in the Caribbean. Most of Aruba's high-rise hotels are stretched Las Vegas–strip style along these pure-white sand stretches on the leeward coast.

MUSEUMS

We know you didn't come to Aruba to look at museums, but just in case. . . .

Museo Arubano. Oranjestraat (just off L. G. Smith Blvd. behind the government buildings). ☎ **297/8-26099.** Admission $1.15. Mon–Fri 9am–noon and 1–4pm.

In the restored Fort Zoutman, the Museo Arubano (also called the King Willem III Tower and Fort Zoutman Museum) contains material on the culture and history of Aruba, with artifacts dating from the earliest times of the island through colonial days and up to the present. The 18th-century fort, the oldest building on Aruba, has at its entrance the King Willem III Tower, which served as a lighthouse for almost 100 years.

Archaeological Museum. Zoutmanstraat 1. ☎ **297/8-28979.** Admission free. Daily 8am–noon and 1–4pm.

Diagonally across the street from the Aruba Sonesta Resort & Casino, the Archaeological Museum contains on its first floor pre-Columbian artifacts found at numerous places on the island. You'll see agricultural and home equipment dating back 1,000 years, and even skeletons of people who were buried in big earthenware urns. In addition, there's a collection of skeletons and tools dating back 2,000 years.

OUT IN THE COUNTRY

If you can lift yourselves from the sands for one afternoon, you might like to drive into the *cunucu,* which in Papiamento means "the countryside." Here Arubans live in very modest but colorful pastel-washed houses decorated with tropical plants, which require expensive desalinated water to grow. Of course, all visitors venturing into the center of Aruba want to see the strangely shaped divi-divi tree with its trade wind–blown coiffure.

Rocks stud Aruba, and the most impressive ones are those found at **Ayo** and **Casibari,** northeast of Hooiberg. These stacks of diorite boulders are the size of buildings and puzzle geologists. On the rocks at Ayo are ancient Amerindian drawings. At Casibari, you can climb the boulder-strewn terrain to the top for a panoramic view of the island or wander around looking at rocks that nature has carved into seats and likenesses of prehistoric birds and animals. Casibari is open daily from 9am to 5pm. No admission is charged. There's a lodge at Casibari where you can buy souvenirs, snacks, soft drinks, and beer.

Guides can also point out drawings on the walls and ceiling of the **Caves of Canashito,** south of Hooiberg. While here, you may get to see the giant green parakeets.

Hooiberg is affectionately known as "The Haystack." It's Aruba's most outstanding landmark, and anybody with the stamina can take the steps all the way to the top of this 541-foot-high hill. One Aruban jogs up here every morning. From its precincts in the center of the island you can see Venezuela on a clear day.

On the jagged, windswept northern coast, the **Natural Bridge** has been carved out of the coral rock by the relentless surf. In a little cafe overlooking the coast you can order snacks. Here you'll also find a souvenir shop with a large selection of trinkets, T-shirts, and wall hangings.

You turn inland for the short trip to the **Pirate's Castle** at Bushiribana, which stands on a cliff on the island's windward coast. This is actually a deserted gold mill from the island's now-defunct industry. Another gold mill is in the old ghost town on the west coast, Balashi.

You can continue to the village of Noord, known for its **St. Anne's Church,** with a hand-carved, 17th-century Dutch altar.

EAST TO SAN NICOLAS

Driving along the highway more or less paralleling the south coast of Aruba toward the island's southernmost section, you may want to stop at the **Spaans Lagoen (Spanish Lagoon),** where legend says pirates used to hide out as they waited to plunder rich cargo ships in the Caribbean. Today this is an ideal place for snorkeling, and you can picnic at tables under the mangrove trees.

On to the east, you'll pass an area called **Savaneta,** where some of the most ancient traces of human habitation have been unearthed. You'll see along here the first oil tanks marking the position of the Lago Oil & Transport Company Ltd., the Exxon subsidiary around which the town of San Nicolas developed, although it had been an industrial center since the days of phosphate mining in the late 19th century. A "company town" until the refinery was closed in 1985, San Nicolas, 12 miles from Oranjestad, is called the Aruba Sunrise Side, and tourism has become its main economic factor. The town has a blend of cultures—customs, style, languages, color, and tastes. In the area are caves with Arawak artwork on the walls and a modern innovation, a PGA-approved golf course with sand "greens" and cactus traps.

Boca Grandi, on the windward side of the island, is a favorite windsurfing location; or if you prefer quieter waters, you'll find them at **Baby Beach** and **Rodgers Beach,** on Aruba's leeward side. Overlooking the latter two beaches is **Seroe Colorado (Colorado Point),** from which it's possible to see the coastline of Venezuela as well as the pounding surf on the windward side. You can climb down the cliffs and perhaps spot an iguana here and there; protected by law, the once-endangered saurians now proliferate in peace.

Other sights in the San Nicolas area are the **Guadarikiri Cave** and **Fontein Cave,** where you can see the wall drawings, plus the **Huliba** and **Tunnel of Love** caves, with guides and refreshment stands. Guadarikiri Cave is a haven for wild parrots.

AN UNDERWATER JOURNEY

One of the island's most diverting pastimes involves an underwater journey on one of the world's few passenger submarines, operated by ✪ **Atlantis Submarines,** in the Seaport Village Marina (opposite the Aruba Sonesta Resort & Casino), Oranjestad (☎ **800/253-0493** in the U.S., or 297/8-36090). An underwater ride offers one of the Caribbean's best opportunities for nondivers to witness firsthand the underwater life of a coral reef, with fewer obstacles and dangers than posed by a scuba expedition. In 1995 an old Danish fishing vessel was sunk to create a fascinating view for divers and submariners. Carrying 46 passengers to a depth of up to 150 feet, the submarine departs from the Oranjestad harborfront every hour on the hour, Tuesday to Sunday from 10am to 2pm (there are no departures on Monday). Each tour includes a 25-minute transit by catamaran to Barcadera Reef, 2 miles southeast of Aruba, a site chosen for the huge variety of its underwater flora and fauna. At the reef, participants transfer to the submarine for a 1-hour underwater lecture and tour.

Allow 2 hours for the complete experience. The cost is $69 for adults and $29 for children 4 to 16 (children under 4 are not admitted)—a splurge but perhaps the highlight of your vacation. Advance reservations are essential. In either event, a staff member will ask for a credit- or charge-card number (and give you a confirmation number) to hold the booking for you.

A SIGHTSEEING TOUR

De Palm Tours, L. G. Smith Blvd. 142, Oranjestad (☎ **297/8-24400**), has desks at all the major hotels. Its latest attraction is De Palm Island, a complete entertainment facility built on a private island just 5 minutes by ferry from Aruba. Their tours include a wide range of activities, featuring snorkeling, beach barbecues, and folklore shows. Its office is open Monday to Saturday from 8:30am to noon and 1 to 5pm. The cost of the organized jaunts ranges upward from $17.50, depending on what activity you select.

SHOPPING

Aruba manages to compress six continents into the half-mile-long **Caya G. F. Betico Croes,** in Oranjestad, the main shopping street of the capital. While this is not technically a free port, the duty is so low (3.3%) that articles are attractively priced—and Aruba has no sales tax. You'll find the usual array of Swiss watches; German and Japanese cameras; jewelry; liquor; English bone china and porcelain; Dutch, Swedish, and Danish silver and pewter; French perfume; British woolens; Indonesian specialties; and Madeira embroidery. Delft blue pottery is an especially good buy. More good buys include Dutch cheese (Edam and Gouda), as well as Dutch chocolate and English cigarettes in the airport departure area.

Philatelists interested in the wealth of colorful and artistic stamps issued in honor of the changed government status of Aruba can purchase a complete assortment, as well as other special issues, at the post office in Oranjestad.

In general, shops are open Monday to Saturday from 8am to noon and 2 to 6pm. Many stores are closed on Tuesday afternoon and some seem to keep irregular hours off-season, especially in the fall and spring.

SHOPPING CENTERS

Alhambra Moonlight Shopping Center. Adjacent to the Alhambra Casino, L. G. Smith Blvd. ☎ **297/8-35000.**

This is a blend of international shops, outdoor marketplaces, and cafes and restaurants. The merchandise ranges from fine jewelry, chocolates, and perfume to imported craft items, leather goods, clothing, and lingerie.

Seaport Village. L. G. Smith Blvd. 92. ☎ **297/8-36000.**

This complex of more than 130 boutiques consists of not only the Seaport Village Mall, but the Crystal Casino and the Aruba Sonesta Resort & Casino. It overlooks the harbor at Oranjestad. Here is a wide array of specialty shops, bars, and eateries, with prices for most budgets. Most shops are open Monday to Saturday from 9am to 6pm, and most eateries and bars are open daily, including Sunday.

One of the shops, the **Boulevard Book & Drugstore** (☎ 297/8-27358) has a complete range of goods from the latest paperback books to cosmetics, candies, gifts, toys, better-quality T-shirts and sweatshirts, swimwear, sportswear, and souvenirs. You can also buy stamps, road maps, current magazines, and newspapers.

SPECIALTY SHOPS

Aruba Trading Company. Caya G. F. Betico Croes 14. ☎ **297/8-22602.**

The Aruba Trading Company offers a complete range of tourist items: perfumes; cosmetics; souvenirs; gift items of porcelain, Delft, Hummel, and crystal ware; liquor; and cigarettes (the latter purchases can be delivered to your plane). Brand-name perfumes are often discounted here, but you'll have to search for the good buys.

D'Orsy's. In the Oranjestad Strada Complex II. ☎ **297/8-31233.**

At this parfumerie, Ralph Lauren's Safari fragrance is the best-selling item. But many other fragrances are also sold, including Lancôme, Cartier, Tiffany, and Estée Lauder. Although the selection is fairly standard, the merchandise is first rate, and the prices are somewhat less than on other islands such as Curaçao.

Gandelman Jewelers. Main St. 5A. ☎ **297/8-32121.**

Gandelman offers an extensive collection of fine gold jewelry and famous-name timepieces at duty-free prices. Go here if you're in the market for a Swatch watch. Prices are reasonable and the merchandise is the real thing.

Little Switzerland Jewelers. Caya G. F. Betico Croes 47. ☎ **297/8-21192.**

Famous for its duty-free 14- and 18-karat-gold jewelry and watches, Little Switzerland also carries a big variety of famous-name Swiss watches. Over the years we've gotten some very good buys here in their Omega and Rado watches, which are usually discounted handsomely from Stateside prices. Consider this a venue for fine tableware, Baccarat crystal, Lladró figurines, and Swarovski silver as well. This Curaçao-based store, with branches throughout the Caribbean, stands for dependability.

New Amsterdam Store. Caya G. F. Betico Croes 50. ☎ **297/8-21152.**

Aruba's leading department store is best for linens, with its wide selection of napkins, placemats, and embroidered tablecloths. It has an extensive line of other merchandise as well, from Delft blue pottery to beachwear and boutique items, along with assorted gift items, porcelain figures by Hummel, watches, French and Italian women's wear, and leather bags and shoes.

Penha. Caya G. F. Betico Croes 11–13. ☎ **297/8-24161.**

Penha offers one of the largest selections of top-name perfumes and cosmetics on the island. Long a household name on Aruba, it's one of the most dependable stores around. Prices are usually lower than in the States.

ARUBA AFTER DARK: ROLLING THE DICE

The casinos of the big hotels along Palm Beach are the liveliest nighttime destinations, and they stay open as long as business demands, often into the wee hours. In plush gaming parlors, you can try your luck at roulette, craps, blackjack, and the one-armed bandits. The **Americana Aruba Beach Resort & Casino,** J. E. Irausquin Blvd.

83 (☎ **297/8-24500**), opens daily at noon for slots, blackjack, and roulette, and at 8pm for all games. The **Holiday Inn Aruba Beach Resort & Casino,** J. E. Irausquin Blvd. 230 (☎ **297/8-67777**), wins the prize for all-around action, open from 9am to 4pm. The **Aruba Palm Beach Resort & Casino,** J. E. Irausquin Blvd. 79 (☎ **297/8-63900**), opens its slots at 9am and its other games at 1pm. The new **Casino Masquerade,** at the Radisson Aruba Caribbean Resort & Casino, J. E. Irausquin Blvd. 82, Palm Beach (☎ **297/8-66555**), is open from 10am to 4am daily. It offers blackjack, single deck, roulette, Caribbean stud, craps, and "Let It Ride."

Visitors have a tendency to flock to the newest casinos on the island, and these include those at the **Wyndham Hotel and Resort,** J. E. Irausquin Blvd. 77 (☎ **297/ 8-64466**), and at the **Hyatt Regency Aruba,** L. G. Smith Blvd. 85 (☎ **297/ 8-61234**). But outdrawing them all is the **Royal Cabana Casino,** J. E. Irausquin Blvd. 250 (☎ **297/8-79000**), at La Cabana All Suite Beach Resort & Casino. It's known for its multitheme three-in-one restaurant, but mainly for its showcase cabaret theater and nightclub, which features everything from Las Vegas–style revues to fe-male impersonators to comedy series on the weekend. You should call to find out what's happening here at the time of your visit and to reserve a table if the action in-terests you. The largest casino on Aruba, it offers 33 tables and games, plus 320 slot machines.

One of the island's best casinos is the Crystal Casino at the **Aruba Sonesta Resort & Casino,** L. G. Smith Blvd. 9 (☎ **297/8-36000**), open daily from 8am to 4am. The 14,000-square-foot casino offers 11 blackjack tables, 270 slot machines, 4 roulette tables, 3 Caribbean stud poker tables, 2 craps tables, a minibaccarat table, and 3 baccarat tables. The casino evokes European casinos with its luxurious furnish-ings, ornate moldings, marble, brass, gold leaf, and crystal chandeliers.

And one of the busiest casinos is **The Alhambra,** L. G. Smith Blvd. 47 (☎ **297/ 8-35000**). Designed like a neon-swathed update of a moghul's palace, this complex looks Moorish, with serpentine mahogany columns, arches, and domes. The casino is open from 10am till very late at night.

If you don't want to gamble or you tire of the casino scene, you can patronize a hotel's cocktail lounges and supper clubs. You don't have to be a guest of the hotel to see the shows, but you should make a reservation. Tables at the big shows, espe-cially in season, are likely to be booked early in the day. Usually you can go to one of the major hotel supper clubs and only order drinks.

2 Bonaire

Untrampled by hordes of tourists, unspoiled Bonaire is a scuba diver's delight. It also offers some of the Caribbean's best snorkeling. This sleepy island is devoid of the glitzy diversions of Aruba. Instead, powdery white sands and turquoise waters beckon.

Bonaire is also a bird-watcher's haven, with 135 different species. You'll spot fla-mingos (which nearly outnumber the sparse human population) as well as big-billed pelican, bright-green parrots, snipes, terns, parakeets, herons, and hummingbirds. Bring a pair of binoculars.

Bonaireans zealously treasure their precious environment and will go to great lengths to protect it. Although they eagerly seek tourism, they aren't interested in creating "another Aruba," with its high-rise hotel blocks. Spearfishing isn't allowed in its waters, nor is the taking or destruction of any coral or other living animal from the sea. Unlike some islands, Bonaire isn't just surrounded by coral reefs—it *is* the reef, sitting on the top of a dry, sunny underwater mountain. Its shores are thick with rainbow-hued fish.

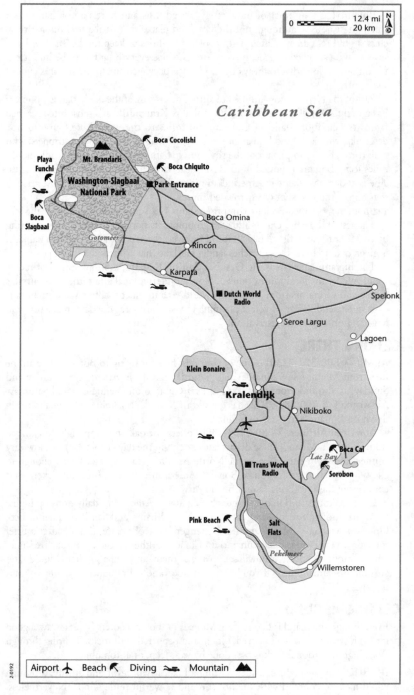

Bonaire

0 ————— 12.4 mi
20 km

N

Caribbean Sea

Boca Cocolishi

Boca Chiquito

Playa Funchi

Mt. Brandaris

Washington-Slagbaai National Park

Park Entrance

Boca Omina

Boca Slagbaai

Gotomeer

Rincón

Karpata

Dutch World Radio

Spelonk

Seroe Largu

Lagoen

Klein Bonaire

Kralendijk

Nikiboko

Boca Cai

Lac Bay

Sorobon

Trans World Radio

Pink Beach

Salt Flats

Pekelmeer

Willemstoren

Airport ✈ Beach ✎ Diving ≈ Mountain ▲▲

2-0192

Bonaire has a number of moderately priced inns and hotels and a handful of small guest houses, although not the fast-food places that Aruba has. Budget travelers should rent an apartment with cooking facilities to keep food costs low. Even so, you'll be shocked at grocery-store prices, since everything has to be imported. If you're a serious diver, always book in on a package tour to pursue this expensive sport.

Part of the Netherlands Antilles (an autonomous part of the Netherlands), Bonaire has a population of about 10,000. Its capital is **Kralendijk.** It's most often reached from its neighbor island of Curaçao, 30 miles to the west. Like Curaçao, it's desertlike, with a dry and brilliant atmosphere. Often it's visited by day-trippers, who rush through here in pursuit of the shy, elusive flamingo. Only 5 miles wide and 24 miles long, Bonaire is poised in the Caribbean close to the coast of South America. The island, whose name in Amerindian means "low country," attracts those seeking that out-of-the-way spot or uncrowded shore.

Boomerang-shaped Bonaire comprises about 112 square miles, making it the second largest of the ABC Dutch-affiliated grouping. Its northern sector is hilly, tapering up to Mount Brandaris, all of 788 feet. However, the southern half, flat as a flapjack, is given over to bays, reefs, beaches, and a salt lake that attracts the flamingos.

The big annual event is the **October Sailing Regatta,** a 5-day festival of racing sponsored by the local tourist bureau. Now an international affair, the event attracts sailors and spectators from around the world, as a flotilla of sailboats and yachts anchor in Kralendijk Bay. If you're planning to visit during regatta days, make sure you have an iron-clad hotel reservation.

GETTING THERE

ALM (☎ 800/327-7230) is one of your best bets for flying to Bonaire. The airline flies from Miami on Wednesday and Saturday and from Atlanta on Saturday and Sunday. It also flies from Newark, N.J., via Curaçao on Wednesday and Saturday. **Air Aruba** (☎ 800/882-7822) has links from Newark also, going via Aruba to touch down on Bonaire Thursday to Sunday.

American Airlines (☎ 800/433-7300) offers one daily nonstop flight to Curaçao from its hub in Miami. These depart late enough in the day (10:45 am) to allow easy connections from cities all over the Northeast. They reach Curaçao early enough to allow immediate transfers on to Bonaire. American will book (but not ticket) your connecting flight to Bonaire on Bonaire Airways.

Other routings to Bonaire are possible on any of American's daily nonstop flights to Aruba through American's hubs in New York, Miami, and San Juan, Puerto Rico. Once on Aruba, ALM will transfer passengers on to Bonaire, usually after a brief touchdown (or change of equipment) on Curaçao. Although these transfers are somewhat complicated, American will set up any of them, and will also offer reduced rates at some Bonairean hotels if you book your reservation simultaneously with your air passage.

GETTING AROUND

Even though the island is flat, renting Mopeds or motor scooters is not always a good idea. The roads are often unpaved, pitted, and peppered with rocks. Touring through Washington National Park is best done by van, Jeep, or automobile.

BY BIKE You might consider renting a bike, if you're fit and sturdy, although you'll have to contend with the hot sun and powerful trade winds. Nevertheless, much of the island is flat, and if you follow the main road you'll go along the water's edge. The best deals are at **Cycle Bonaire,** Kaya L. D. Gerjharts (☎ 599/7-7558), where you can rent a 21-speed or an 830 Trek for $15 per day, or $75 for 6 days (in that case, it can become your cheap means of transport around Bonaire). Rental includes a water bottle, lock, helmet, repair kit, and pump. A map is provided free for a 6-day rental; otherwise, you're charged $5.

BY TAXI   Taxis are unmetered, but the government has established rates. All taxi-cabs carry a license plate with the letters *TX*. Each driver should have a price list to be produced upon request. As many as four passengers can go along for the ride unless they have too much luggage. A trip from the airport to your hotel should cost about $10 to $12. From 8pm to midnight fares are increased by 25%, and from 11pm to 6am they go up by 50%.

Most taxi drivers can take you on a tour of the island, but you'll have to negoti-ate a price according to how long a trip you want and what you want to see. For more information, call **Taxi Central Dispatch** (☎ **599/7-8100**).

BY RENTAL CAR   In car rentals, it pays to shop around. Sometimes—but not always—you can make a better deal with a local agency. Try **Avanti Rentals,** Kaya Herman Pop 2 (☎ **599/7-5661**), which offers year-round rentals beginning at $45 per day, including tax and insurance. He'll also rent you a Suzuki Samurai for $56 a day, which is ideal for touring this desertlike island. Make reservations well in advance.

Flamingo Car Rental, Kaya Grandi 86, in Kralendijk (☎ **599/7-8888**), also has a kiosk at the airport for your convenience. Its stock of Japanese-made cars, usually a type of Nissan, costs $38 to $40 daily.

Avis (☎ **800/331-1084**) is at Flamingo Airport. Weekly arrangements are cheaper, but daily rates range from $39 to $64, with unlimited mileage.

Your valid U.S., British, or Canadian driver's license is acceptable for driving on Bonaire. *Driving on Bonaire is on the right.*

FAST FACTS: Bonaire

Banking Hours   Banks are usually open Monday to Friday from 8:30am to noon and 2 to 4pm.

Currency   Like the other islands of the Netherlands Antilles (Curaçao, St. Maarten, St. Eustatius, and Saba), Bonaire's coin of the realm is the **Netherlands Antillean florin (NAf),** sometimes called a guilder, equal to 56¢ in U.S. currency. However, U.S. dollars are widely accepted.

Customs   There are no Customs requirements for Bonaire.

Documents   U.S. and Canadian citizens don't need a passport to enter Bonaire, although a birth or naturalization certificate, alien registration card, or a voter's registration card will be required, plus a return ticket. British subjects may carry a British Visitor's Passport, obtainable at post offices on Bonaire, although a valid passport issued in the United Kingdom is preferred, especially if they plan to visit other countries in the area.

Electricity   The electricity on Bonaire is slightly different from that used in North America (110–130 volts, 50 cycles, as opposed to U.S. and Canadian voltages of 110 volts, 60 cycles). Adapters and transformers are necessary for North American appliances, but you should still proceed with caution in using any appliance on Bonaire and try to avoid usage if possible because of the erratic current. Be warned, further, that electrical current used to feed or recharge finely calibrated diving equip-ment should be stabilized with a specially engineered electrical stabilizer. Every dive operation on the island has one of these as part of its standard equipment for visiting divers to use.

Information Before you go, you can contact the **Bonaire Government Tourist Office** at Adams Unlimited, 10 Rockefeller Plaza, Suite 900, New York, NY 10020 (☎ **800/U-BONAIR** or 212/956-5911).

For tourist information on Bonaire, go to the **Bonaire Government Tourist Bureau,** Kaya Libertad Simón Bolivar 12, Kralendijk (☎ **599/7-8322**), open Monday to Friday from 7:30am to noon and 1:30 to 5pm.

Language English is widely spoken, but you'll hear Dutch, Spanish, and Papiamento.

Medical Care The **St. Francis Hospital** is in Kralendijk (☎ **599/7-8900**). A plane on standby at the airport takes seriously ill patients to Curaçao for treatment.

Safety "Safe, safe Bonaire" might be the island's motto in this crime-infested world. But remember, any place that attracts tourists also attracts people who prey on them. Safeguard your valuables.

Taxes and Service The government requires a $5.50-per-person daily room tax on all hotel rooms. Most hotels and guest houses add a 10% service charge in lieu of tipping. Restaurants generally add a service charge of 15% to the bill. Upon leaving Bonaire, you'll be charged an airport departure tax of $10, so don't spend every penny. There's also an interisland departure tax of $5.75.

Telecommunications Service for telephone, Telex, telegraph, radio, and TV is available in English. To call Bonaire from the United States, dial 011 (the international access code), then 599 (the country code for Bonaire), and then 7 (the area code) and the four-digit local number.

Once on Bonaire, to call another number on the island only the four-digit local number is necessary.

Time Bonaire is on Atlantic standard time year-round, 1 hour ahead of eastern standard time (when it's noon on Bonaire, it's 11am in Miami). When daylight saving time is in effect in the United States, clocks in Miami and Bonaire show the same time.

Water Drinking water is pure and safe. It comes from distilled seawater.

Weather Bonaire is known for its climate, with temperatures hovering at 82° Fahrenheit. The water temperature averages 80°. It's warmest in August and September, coolest in January and February. The average rainfall is 22 inches, and December to March are the rainiest months.

WHERE TO STAY

Hotels, all facing the sea, are low-key, hassle-free, and personally run operations where everybody gets to know everybody else rather quickly.

Taxes and service charges are seldom included in the prices you're quoted, so ask about them when making your reservations.

DOUBLES FOR LESS THAN $75

Avanti Bungalows. Punt Vierkant, Belnem, Bonaire, N.A. ☎ and fax **599/7-8405.** 13 bungalows. A/C TV. Winter, $70 one-bedroom bungalow; $95 two-bedroom bungalow; $125 three-bedroom bungalow. Off-season, $65 one-bedroom bungalow; $90 two-bedroom bungalow; $120 three-bedroom bungalow. Extra person $15. AE, MC, V.

A block in from Bachelor's Beach, this complex of bungalows, south of the airport, is managed by a family business, Happy Holiday Homes. The basic units are comfortable, with the usual amenities including air-conditioning, cable TV, an on-site washer, and a living/dining-room area. There aren't a lot of grace notes around here; it's pretty much a do-it-yourself affair. The bungalows are in rows of two or three units each, and all have front terraces and gardens. The area is heavily planted for more privacy. Each unit is furnished differently with a sofa, Venetian blinds, just-adequate tables and chairs, and color-coordinated curtains and bed linens. The bed-rooms are air-conditioned and the living/dining areas are cooled by ceiling fans. The kitchens are fully furnished, with refrigerators and microwaves. There's no swimming pool.

Black Durgon Inn. Gobernador De Groot Blvd., Kralendijk, Bonaire, N.A. ☎ **800/526-2370** in the U.S., or 599/7-5736. Fax 599/7-8846. 9 rms. A/C TV. Year-round, $60 single; $75 double. Children 12 and under $10. No credit cards.

From the front it looks like a typical roadside motel of no special interest. However, once you go through the gate you'll come upon a parklike setting with palm trees and other plants, and shore access to Small Wall, one of Bonaire's most dramatic vertical wall dives. The rooms are in a single one-story concrete building, with the water-facing rooms containing a patio. The furnishings are in the simple, uncompli-cated, totally functional format, but the low prices (for Bonaire) compensate for any lack of style. There's a communal kitchen with a barbecue area, and several refrig-erators are available for those who like to cook in. A sandy beach is on site, with a private wharf and dive shop. Restaurants are about a 5-minute drive away. There's daily maid service, and baby-sitting can be arranged.

Blue Iguana. Kaya Prinses Marie 6, Kralendijk, Bonaire, N.A. ☎ and fax **599/7-6855**. 7 rms, none with bath. Year-round, $55 single; $70 double. Rates include breakfast. No credit cards.

This is the most amusing, funky, offbeat, and arts-oriented guest house on Bonaire. It occupies a bright-yellow century-old building about 2 blocks north of the center of Kralendijk, separated from the dusty road by a screen of cactus. The allure is artsy, appealingly battered, and—if it suits your sense of bohemian adventure—fun. It's *chatelaine* is the Curaçao-born, New York–derived artist Laurie Dovale.

The furnishings include a mishmash of family antiques, a mixture of tropical and North European kitsch, and old photographs. Friends of the owner drop in through-out the day offering sightseeing advice, homemade brownies, and handmade souve-nirs. No meals are served other than breakfast, although guests have the run of a communal kitchen whose old-fashioned allure reached its peak around 1940. A rear garden is a haven for land turtles, squirrels, seedlings sprouting from coffee cans, and a quartet of iguanas that search out the fruit and table scraps Ms. Dovale prepares for them. Each accommodation has a ceiling fan, old furniture chosen as much for its nostalgia value as for its solidity, and thin doors that might transmit noises from the comfortably cluttered public rooms. The bars and restaurants of Kralendijk are a very short walk away from this appealingly eccentric hotel.

Bonaire Caribbean Club. Tourist Rd., Kralendijk, bonaire, N.A. ☎ **800/748-8733** or 599/7-7901. Fax 599/7-7900. 20 apts. A/C. Year-round, $55–$75 one-bedroom apt; $110 two-bedroom apt. Apr–July 1 and Nov–Dec 15, guests receive 7th night free. Extra person $9; chil-dren 4 and under stay free in parents' apt. AE, MC, V (5% extra fee for use of charge card).

A mile north of the hotel strip, this Dutch-owned complex rents bungalow apart-ments, some with their own porches. Some good dive sites lie about a block away, although the property fronts a coral beach. The nearest good sandy beach, however, is about 1¹/₂ miles away. The apartments are two to a unit in a park setting with gardens and flowering vines around the porches. The furnishings are simple, with colorful seat cushions and curtains in a vague tropical motif. All have kitchens and air-conditioning, and some offer ceiling fans as well, although there are no phones or TVs. A pool with a mural of underwater life is the big on-site attraction, and there's a simple restaurant serving breakfast and dinner. Daily maid service is provided except on Sunday, and baby-sitting can be arranged with advance notice.

Leeward Inn. Kaya Grandi 60, Kralendijk, Bonaire, N.A. ☎ **599/7-5516.** Fax 599/7-5517. 5 rms. Year-round, $55 single; $60 double. AE, MC, V.

This is a simple, masonry-built hotel with pastel-colored bedrooms, tile floors, louvered Dutch-style windows, and white Formica furnishings. Three are air-conditioned; the others make do with a ceiling fan. Although it was built as a private home in 1915, the inn is too anonymous to be considered cozy or quaint, but it's hard to beat the prices. There's a simple indoor-outdoor restaurant, the Harthouse Café (reviewed below). Downtown Kralendijk, with its bars and diners, lies within 3 blocks. Guests appreciate the hammocks and lounge chairs, and the presence of expatriate New Yorkers Don and Ditta Balstra, who sometimes offer live music in their bar.

DOUBLES FOR LESS THAN $90

Buddy Dive Center. Kaya Gob. N.E. Debrot (P.O. Box 231, Kralendijk), Bonaire, N.A. ☎ **800/786-3483** or 599/7-5080. Fax 599/7-8647. 4 rms, 30 apts with kitchen. Winter, $97 single or double; $167.70 one-bedroom apt for one; $173.70 one-bedroom apt for two; $62.92 per person two-bedroom apt for up to four; $52.57 per person three-bedroom apt for up to six. Off-season, $93 single or double; $152.30 one-bedroom apt for one; $158.30 one-bedroom apt for two; $57.70 per person two-bedroom apt for up to four; $48.53 per person three-bedroom apt for up to six. AE, MC, V.

On the island's western edge amid a strip of other hotels, many of which are more expensive, this hotel consists of three buildings. The oldest contains bedrooms but not apartments. The pair of newer buildings (circa 1992–93) have white concrete walls, red roofs, and apartments with kitchens, air-conditioning, and TV. As its name implies, most visitors check in here for the diving opportunities, abundant off the nearby coast. (If that's your intention, ask about the dive packages.) The accommodations are ultra-simple and not particularly large, each outfitted with rattan furniture and white walls; the apartments also have balconies. There's a pool, although most visitors swim at Buddy Beach, a few steps away. Maid service is offered only twice a week; arrangements for rental cars and all the usual PADI and NAUI dive options are available on-site. Each apartment has its own kitchen, and there's also an in-house restaurant, Buddy's Reef.

Carib Inn. J. A. Abraham Blvd. (P.O. Box 68), Kralendijk, Bonaire, N.A. ☎ **599/7-8819.** Fax 599/7-5295. 10 apts. A/C TV. Winter, $89 studio apt; $99 efficiency apt; $119 one-bedroom apt; $139 two-bedroom apt; $159 three-bedroom apt. Off-season, $79 studio apt; $89 efficiency apt; $109 one-bedroom apt; $129 two-bedroom apt; $149 three-bedroom apt. AE, MC, V.

On the water, this hotel—owned and managed by the American diver Bruce Bowker—is occupied with dedicated scuba divers drawn to its five-star PADI dive facility. This is the most intimate little dive resort on Bonaire and remains one of Bonaire's best values. Eight of its ten rooms have kitchens. All units are equipped with refrigerators, and maid service is provided daily. The accommodations are furnished in a tropical rattan. The baths have been enlarged and refurbished. There's no restaurant or bar. Repeat guests are likely to book this place far in advance in winter.

The Great Escape. Blvd. Europese Economische Gemeenschap 97 Belnem, Bonaire, N.A. ☎ and fax **599/7-7488.** 10 rms, 2 suites. A/C. Winter, $90–$100 single or double; $115 suite. Off-season, $75–$85 single or double; $100 suite. Extra person $30 in winter, $20 off-season. Children stay free in parents' room. Rates include full breakfast. AE, MC, V.

About half a mile south of the airport, near Bachelor's Beach, this is one of the newest B&Bs on the island, a welcoming and homey two-story white stone building. The lobby is large and open, and guests gather to watch TV in a lounge on the wide up-stairs balcony. Although not noted for any particular style, except for the flowery courtyard with a freshwater swimming pool, the accommodations range from stan-dard through deluxe to the most expensive of all, a suite. Special budget honeymoon arrangements can be made. The rooms are pleasantly furnished and well maintained and offer a double bed or two twins. The suites have two double beds and a pull-out sofa, although all accommodations have both a ceiling fan and air-conditioning. This place is family friendly, with a small playground with a tiny zoo. Children stay free, and baby-sitting can be arranged. A simple restaurant serves three meals a day.

Sunset Inn. Kaya C. E. B. Hellmund 29 (P.O. Box 333, Kralendijk), Bonaire, N.A. ☎ **800/ 344-4439** in the U.S., or 599/7-8448. Fax 599/7-8118. 5 rms. A/C TV. Winter, $80 single or double; $100 suite. Off-season, $55 single or double; $75 suite. Extra person $10. AE, DC, MC, V.

This small-scale hotel complex overlooks the bay of Kralendijk. A shared kitchen is used (sometimes energetically) as a communal gathering place. Each unit has an elec-tronic safe, a small refrigerator, and simple, rustic, slightly battered furnishings. A narrow beach (Sunset Beach) is within about 50 feet of the hotel's entrance.

BEST-VALUE DIVE PACKAGES

✪ **Captain Don's Habitat.** Kaya Gob. N. Debrot 103, Pier 7, Bonaire, N.A. ☎ **599/7-8290.** Fax 599/7-8240. For all reservations and business arrangements, contact Captain Don's Habi-tat, 903 South America Way, Miami, FL 33132 (☎ **800/327-6709;** fax 305/371-2337). 62 units. A/C. Winter, $926–$1,411 per person. Off-season, $696–$973 per person. Rates for 8-day/7-night stays include breakfast, airport transfers, tax, service, equipment, 12 boat dives, and unlimited 24-hour shore dives. AE, MC, V.

Built on a coral bluff overlooking the sea about 5 minutes north of Kralendijk, this unique diving, snorkeling, and nature-oriented resort, with an air of congenial infor-mality, has a philosophy and lifestyle for those whose souls belong to the sea. The infrastructure and staff are devoted to the many different possibilities for diving off the coast of Bonaire. Habitat and its accompanying dive shop are the creation of Capt. Don Stewart, Caribbean pioneer and "caretaker of the reefs," a former Cali-fornian who sailed his schooner from San Francisco through the Panama Canal, ar-riving on a reef in Bonaire in 1962—he's been here ever since. Called the "godfather of diving" on the island, Captain Don was instrumental in the formation of the Bonaire Marine Park, whereby the entire island became a protected reef.

More than 90% of the guests here opt for one of the packages, which incorporate a variable number of dives with accommodations in settings ranging from standard double rooms to oceanfront villas. The most popular arrangement is the 8-day/ 7-night package (rates are listed above).

This resort has an oceanfront restaurant and two seaside bars. A casual, laid-back crowd gathers for meals at Rum Runners, the social hub. Theme nights are staged weekly, which divert guests from the rather standard fare served here. Services include laundry and baby-sitting. There's a boutique, an ocean-bordering pool, and a com-plete diving program.

WHERE TO EAT

If you're striking out for Washington Slagbaai or one of the island's more remote beaches, you can stop at the **Sand Dollar Grocery** at Kaya Gob. N. Debrot (☎ **599/ 7-5490**), and rent a cooler for $5.60, plus a $9.80 deposit. Later, you can head for **The Sandwich Factory,** Princess Plaza in Kralendijk(☎ **599/7-7369**). Here you can purchase foot-long hoagies for $8 or pizza, hot and spicy chili, hot dogs, and draft beer—in other words, your picnic!

China Garden. Kaya Grandi 47. ☎ **599/7-8480.** Reservations recommended. Main courses $6–$12. AE, MC, V. Wed–Mon 11:30am–2pm and 4:30–10pm. ASIAN.

Good-tasting Eastern dishes, with some Indonesian specialties, are served to West Indians and visitors in this restored Bonairean mansion between the Divi Flamingo and Sunset Beach hotels. Portions are enormous and prices are low considering what you get. The chefs from Hong Kong also cook Chinese, American, and local dishes, including a variety of curries ranging from beef to lobster. Seafood dishes, prepared in a variety of styles, including lobster in black-bean sauce, are also served. Special culinary features include a Java rijstaffel and the nasi goreng special. We don't want to oversell this place, as you'll find far better Chinese dining elsewhere in the Caribbean, especially on Puerto Rico. A lot of the Cantonese fare is on the bland side. However, there's a warmth and conviviality about the place, and the reasonable prices are a find on Bonaire. The place is air-conditioned and seats 60 guests.

Green Parrot Restaurant. In the Sand Dollar Condominiums & Beach Club, Kaya Gob. N. Debrot 79. ☎ **599/7-8738.** Reservations recommended. Main courses $8–$28.50; lunch $4.85–$9.25. AE, MC, V. Daily 8–10:30am and 11am–10pm. CONTINENTAL.

On a breeze-filled pier, this place is part of the complex of a resort a 15-minute drive from the airport. It serves burgers, pasta, sandwiches, and seafood dishes. You can gaze at the waves, enjoy a frozen tropical fruit drink, and watch the sunset. On Saturday night there's a barbecue buffet with entertainment. The food consistently ranks as some of the island's best, especially the charcoal-grilled fish (based on the catch of the day). You might also try the barbecued chicken and ribs, and various U.S. beef cuts (from T-bone to filet mignon), as well as garlic shrimp and the highly favored onion strings (like an onion loaf). Go here for the fun and good times.

Harthouse Café. In the Leeward Inn, Kaya Grande 60. ☎ **599/7-5516.** Main courses $10–$25. AE, DISC, MC, V. Wed–Mon 5–11pm. (Bar, Wed–Mon 4–11pm.) PIZZA/INTERNATIONAL.

This cafe, part of the Leeward Inn, serves the island's best pizza. It also makes the best coffee in Bonaire. The decor centers around a mural of a Bonairean scene, and the funky bar is cute and cozy with various knickknacks placed about. The pizzas are worth the trip, especially the mushrooms with pepperoni, although you may opt for "the works," not only mushrooms and pepperoni, but onions, sausage, and peppers. In addition the menu features the usual sandwiches and burgers. The best items, however, are the daily specials, usually a local Dutch dish or perhaps a fresh fish main course. The chef's salad is a meal unto itself. For dessert, try one of the giant cookies, a brownie, or banana walnut bread.

Je-Mar Health Shop. Kaya Grandi 5., Kralendijk. ☎ **599/7-5012.** Main courses $3–$6. MC, V. Daily 7am–3pm. CONTINENTAL.

Don't expect any frills here. This basic restaurant, located in the heart of Kralendijk, specializes in healthy cuisine. This is the place to go if you're a vegetarian—for tofu burgers, salads, and specials such as eggplant served with noodles and mixed vegetables. The menu also includes steak, baked chicken, and garlic shrimp. There are two specials daily—one vegetarian. If you're in the mood for dining alfresco, try the plant-strewn terrace that overlooks Kaya Grandi, the town's main road.

Old Inn. J. A. Abraham Blvd. ☎ **599/7-6666.** Reservations recommended. Main courses $12.50–$18. MC, V. Daily 5–10pm. INDONESIAN/INTERNATIONAL.

Formerly Toys Grand Café, this restaurant has lost much of its eccentricity under its new ownership. The wild murals on the walls are gone, replaced with a basic

Dutch-Indonesian decor that's common to the island. However, many of the Indonesian dishes that were popular remain, including the nasi goreng, an Indonesian fried-rice special. The prices are still fairly reasonable and you'll most likely receive good service and a filling meal.

✪ **Richard's Waterfront Dining.** J. A. Abraham Blvd. 60. ☎ **599/7-5263.** Reservations recommended for groups of six or more. Main courses $12.50–$19.90. DC, MC, V. Tues–Sun 6:30–10:30pm. STEAK/SEAFOOD.

On the airport side of Kralendijk, within walking distance of the Divi Flamingo, this restaurant, with its large covered terrace, was once a private home. Reasonable in price, it's the favorite of many locals who have sampled every restaurant on the island. Boston-born Richard Beady and his Aruban partner, Mario, operate a welcoming oasis and begin a happy hour at 5pm, an hour before dinner. Gathered around the coral bar, guests speculate on the offerings that night. From a chalkboard menu, you're likely to be offered grilled wahoo or the fresh catch of the day, filet mignon béarnaise, U.S. sirloin with green-peppercorn sauce, or shrimp scampi. It's best to begin with the fish soup, if featured. Pastas are also an item here. On a recent visit, we had our best meal on Bonaire at this restaurant. The menu is wisely kept small so that dishes every night can be given the attention they deserve. The style of the kitchen is to deliver all the natural goodness of a dish without overwhelming it with sauces or too many seasonings. The fact that all diners are welcomed with such a warm hospitality contributes to the enjoyment of an evening. Seating is on a first-come, first-served basis.

t'ankertje. Ceb Hallmund. ☎ **599/7-5216.** Main courses $8–$14. No credit cards. Mon–Fri 5–10pm. INTERNATIONAL.

A winning little eatery, this inviting establishment (pronounced "tan-*ker-jay*") is across the street from the water in Kralendijk. Open-air tables are set near the ocean. For inspiration, the cooks roam the world—everything from Italian-style pizza to Mexican tacos. Our favorite dish is their Indonesian sate with marinated chicken and a delectable peanut-butter sauce. The "Arabian sandwich," similar to a gyro, appears on pita bread stuffed with pork. Your best bet? Look for the daily specials chalked up on a blackboard menu. If it's fresh fish, go for it; otherwise, you can sample what's frozen from the larder—perhaps a blackened sirloin steak or a Wiener schnitzel.

Zeezicht Restaurant. Kaya Corsow 10. ☎ **599/7-8434.** Reservations not required. Main courses $8–$26. AE, MC, V. Daily 8am–11pm. INTERNATIONAL.

This is the best place in the capital to go for a sundowner. You join the old salts or the people who live on boats to watch the sun go down, and you try to see the "green flash" that Hemingway wrote about. Zeezicht (pronounced "*Zay*-zict" and meaning "sea view"), has long been popular for its excellent local cookery. A two-story operation, it serves a small rijstaffel as well as fresh fish from the nearby fish market. Lobster is occasionally offered, and there's always steak.

BEACHES, DIVING & OUTDOOR PURSUITS

The true beauty on Bonaire is under the sea, where visibility is 100 feet 365 days of the year, and the water temperatures range from 78° to 82° Fahrenheit. Many dive sites can be reached directly from the beach, and sailing is another pastime. The bird-watching is among the best in the Caribbean, and for beachcombers there are acres and acres of driftwood, found along the shore from the salt flats to Lac Bay.

BEACHES   Bonaire has some of the whitest sand beaches in the West Indies. The major hotels have beaches, but you may want to wander down to the southeast coast for a swim at the "clothes-optional" **Sorobon** or **Boca Cai** on Lac Bay. In the north,

Coastal Reef Diving

One of the richest reef communities in the entire West Indies, Bonaire has plunging walls that descend to a sand bottom at 130 or so feet. The reefs are home to various coral formations that grow at different depths, ranging from the knobby brain coral at 3 feet to staghorn and elkhorn up to about 10 feet deeper, and gorgonians, giant brain, and others all the way to 40 to 83 feet. Swarms of rainbow-hued tropical fish inhabit the reefs, and the deep reef slope is home to a range of basket sponges, groupers, and moray eels. Most of the diving is done on the leeward side where the ocean is lake flat. There are more than 40 dive sites on sharply sloping reefs.

The water off the coast of Bonaire received an additional attraction in 1984. A rust-bottomed general cargo ship, 80 feet long, was confiscated by the police along with its contraband cargo, about 25,000 pounds of marijuana. Known as the *Hilma Hooker* (familiarly dubbed "The Hooker" by everyone on the island), it sank unclaimed (obviously) and without fanfare one calm day in 90 feet of water. Lying just off the southern shore near the capital, its wreck is now a popular dive site.

The ✪ **Bonaire Marine Park** was created to protect the coral-reef ecosystem off Bonaire. The park incorporates the entire coastline of Bonaire and neighboring Klein Bonaire. Scuba diving and snorkeling are all popular here. The park is policed, and services and facilities include a Visitor Information Center at the Karpata Ecological Center, lectures, slide presentations, films, and permanent dive-site moorings.

Bonaire has a unique program for divers in that the major hotels offer personalized, close-up encounters with the island's fish and other marine life under the expertise of Bonaire's dive guides at the marine park and other locations around the island.

Dive I and **Dive II,** at opposite ends of the beachfront of the Divi Flamingo Beach Resort & Casino, J. A. Abraham Boulevard (☎ **599/7-8285**), north of Kralendijk, are among the island's most complete scuba facilities. They're open

you may want to swim at **Playa Funchi,** on the coastline of the Washington/Slagbaai National Park.

BIRD-WATCHING   Bonaire is home to 190 species of birds, 80 of which are indigenous to the island. But most famous are its flamingos, which can number 15,000 during the mating season. For great places to bring your binoculars, see "Seeing the Sights," below.

BOATING   Every visitor to Bonaire wants to take a trip to uninhabited Klein Bonaire. The **Flamingo Beach Hotel** (☎ 599/7-8285) and **Sunset Beach Hotel** at Playa Lechi (☎ 599/7-5300) offer trips daily. You'll be left in the morning for a day of snorkeling, beachcombing, and picnicking, then picked up later that afternoon. Other hotels will also arrange a trip to the islet for you, including a barbecue.

HORSEBACK RIDING   Spend part of a day or all day at one of Bonaire's fine horse ranches, where private lessons and trail rides are available. You can usually arrange a day in the saddle through your hotel.

MOUNTAIN BIKING   Explore more than 186 miles of trails and dirt roads where you can venture off the beaten path to enjoy the scenery and contrasting geography. Check with your hotel about arranging a trip.

Monday to Saturday from 8:30am to noon and 1:30 to 5pm. Both operate out of well-stocked beachfront buildings, rent diving equipment, charge the same prices, and offer the same type of expeditions. A resort course for first-time divers costs $88; for experienced divers, a one-tank dive goes for $38.50.

Captain Don's Habitat Dive Shop, Kaya Gob. N. Debrot 103 (☎ 599/7-8290), is a PADI five-star training facility. The open-air, full-service dive shop includes a classroom, photo/video lab, camera-rental facility, equipment repair, and compressor rooms grouped around spacious seafront patios. Habitat's slogan is "Diving Freedom," and divers can take their tanks and dive anywhere any time of day or night, most often along "The Pike," half a mile of protected reef right in front of the property. The highly qualified staff is here to assist and advise but not to police or dictate dive plans. Diving packages include boat dives, unlimited off-shore diving (24 hours a day), unlimited air, tanks, backpack, weights, and belt. Some dive packages also include accommodations and meals (see "Where to Stay," above).

At the **Bonaire Scuba Center,** in the Black Durgon Inn, Gobernador de Groot Boulevard (☎ 599/7-5736), some of the island's best diving is available from the doorstep of this inn. A living reef just 50 feet from shore quickly drops to 150 feet. Snorkeling is also possible from the property. The center caters to both novice and advanced divers, and offers both resort and certification courses.

Sand Dollar Dive and Photo, at the Sand Dollar Condominium & Beach Club, Kaya Gobernador N. Debrot (☎ 599/7-5252), is open daily from 8:30am to 5:30pm. It offers dive packages, PADI and NAUI instruction, and equipment rental and repairs; boat and shore trips are available with an instructor by appointment. The photo shop offers underwater photo and video shoots, PADI specialty courses by appointment, E-6 processing, print developing, and equipment rental and repair.

SCUBA DIVING   Bonaire is internationally known for its beautiful reefs and dive sites, and many hotels cater almost exclusively to scuba divers. See the "Coastal Reef Diving" box for details, descriptions of dive sites, and outfitters.

SEA KAYAKING   Paddle the protected waters of Lac Bay, or head for the miles of flats and mangroves in the south (the island's nursery) where baby fish and wildlife can be viewed. Kayak rentals are available at **Bonaire Windsurfing,** Lac Bay (☎ 599/7-5363), for $15 per hour or $25 per half day.

SNORKELING   Snorkeling equipment can be rented (see the "Coastal Reef Diving" box).

TENNIS   The **Sunset Beach Hotel** at Playa Lechi (☎ 599/7-5300) has two good tennis courts, illuminated for night play. Use of the courts is free to both hotel guests and nonguests during the day, although any night games will bring a small charge for illumination. A tennis instructor is available, and racquets and balls can be borrowed without charge.

WINDSURFING   Consistent conditions—enjoyed by windsurfers with a wide range of skill levels—make the shallow, calm waters of Lac Bay the island's home to the sport. Call **Bonaire Windsurfing** (☎ 599/7-5363) for details.

SEEING THE SIGHTS
KRALENDIJK

The capital, Kralendijk, means "coral dike" and is pronounced "*Kroll*-en-dike," although most denizens refer to it as Playa, Spanish for "beach." A dollhouse town of some 2,500 residents, it's small, neat, pretty, and Dutch-clean. Its stucco buildings are painted pink and orange, with an occasional lime green. The capital's jetty is lined with island sloops and fishing boats.

Kralendijk nestles in a bay on the west coast, opposite **Klein Bonaire,** or Little Bonaire, an uninhabited, low-lying islet a 10-minute boat ride from the capital.

The main street of town leads along the beachfront on the harbor. A Protestant church was built in 1834, and St. Bernard's Roman Catholic Church has some stained-glass windows.

At **Fort Oranje** you'll see a lone cannon dating from the days of Napoleon. If possible, try to get up early to see the **Fish Market** on the waterfront, where you'll see a variety of strange and brilliantly colored fish.

THE TOUR NORTH

The road north is one of the most beautiful stretches in the Antilles, with turquoise waters on your left, and coral cliffs on your right. You can stop at several points along this road where you'll find paved paths for strolling or bicycling.

After leaving Kralendijk, and passing the Sunset Beach Hotel and the desalination plant, you'll come to **Radio Nederland Wereld Omroep (Dutch World Radio).** It's a 13-tower, 300,000-watter. Opposite the transmitting station is a lovers' promenade, built by nature and an ideal spot for a picnic.

Continuing, you'll pass the storage tanks of the Bonaire Petroleum Corporation, the road heading to **Gotomeer,** the island's loveliest inland sector, with a saltwater lake. Several flamingos prefer this spot to the salt flats in the south.

Down the hill the road leads to a section called **"Dos Pos"** (Two Wells), which has palm trees and vegetation in contrast to the rest of the island, where only the drought-resistant kibraacha and divi-divi trees, tilted before the constant wind, can grow, along with forests of cacti.

Bonaire's oldest village is **Rincón.** Slaves who used to work in the salt flats in the south once lived here. There are a couple of bars, including the Amstel and the Tropicana, and the Rincón Ice Cream Parlour makes homemade ice cream in a variety of interesting flavors. Above the bright roofs of the village is the crest of a hill called Para Mira or "stop and look."

A side path outside Rincón takes you to some Arawak inscriptions supposedly 500 years old. The petroglyph designs are in pink-red dye. At nearby **Boca Onima** you'll find grotesque grottoes of coral.

Before going back to the capital, you might take a short bypass to **Seroe Largu,** which has a good view of Kralendijk and the sea. Lovers frequent the spot at night.

✪ Washington/Slagbaai National Park

Washington/Slagbaai National Park (☎ **599/7-8444**) is concerned with the conservation of the island's fauna, flora, and landscape, and is a changing vista highlighted by desertlike terrain, secluded beaches, caverns, and a bird sanctuary. Occupying 15,000 acres of Bonaire's northwesternmost territory, the park was once plantation land, producing divi-divi, aloe, and charcoal. It was purchased by the Netherlands Antilles government, and since 1967 part of the land, formerly the Washington plantation, has been a wildlife sanctuary. The southern part of the park, the Slagbaai plantation, was added in 1978.

The park can be seen in a few hours, although it takes days to appreciate it fully. Touring the park is easy, with two routes: a 15-mile "short" route, marked by green arrows, and a 22-mile "long" route, marked by yellow arrows. The roads are well marked and safe, but somewhat rugged, although they're gradually being improved. Tickets cost $5 for adults and $1 for children 11 and under, and can be purchased at the gate. The park is open daily except holidays from 8am to 5pm. The gates close at 3pm.

Whichever route you take, there are a few important stops to make. Just past the gate is **Salina Mathijs,** a salt flat that's home to flamingos during the rainy season. Beyond the salt flat on the road to the right is **Boca Chikitu,** a white-sand beach and bay. A few miles up the beach lies **Boca Cocolishi,** a two-part black-sand beach. Its deep, rough seaward side is separated from the calm, shallow basin by a ridge of coralline algae. Hermit crabs walk the beach and shallow water.

The main road leads to **Boca Bartol,** a bay full of living and dead elkhorn coral, sea fans, and reef fish. A popular watering hole good for bird-watching is **Poosdi Mangel. Wajaca** is a remote reef where many sea creatures live, including turtles, octopuses, and triggerfish. Immediately inland towers 788-foot **Mount Brandaris,** Bonaire's highest peak, at whose foot is **Bronswinkel Well,** a watering spot for pigeons and parakeets. Some 130 species of birds live in the park, many with such exotic names as banana quit and black-faced grassquit. Bonaire has few mammals, but you'll see goats and donkeys, perhaps even a wild bull.

HEADING SOUTH

Leaving the capital again, you pass the **Trans World Radio antennas,** towering 500 feet in the air, transmitting with 810,000 watts. This is one of the hemisphere's most powerful medium-wave radio stations, the loudest voice in Christendom and the most powerful nongovernmental broadcast station in the world. It sends out interdenominational Gospel messages and hymns in 20 languages to places as far away as Eastern Europe and the Middle East.

Later, you come on the ✪ **salt flats,** where the brilliantly colored pink flamingos live. Bonaire shelters the largest accessible nesting and breeding grounds in the world. The flamingos build high mud mounds to hold their eggs. The birds are best viewed in spring when they're usually nesting and tending their young. The salt flats were once worked by slaves, and the government has rebuilt some primitive stone huts, bare shelters little more than waist high. The slaves slept in these huts during the week and returned to their homes in Rincón in the north on weekends. The centuries-old salt pans have been reactivated by the International Salt Company. Near the salt pans you'll see some 30-foot obelisks in white, blue, and orange built in 1838 to help mariners locate their proper anchorages.

Farther down the coast is the island's oldest lighthouse, **Willemstoren,** built in 1837. Still farther along, **Sorobon Beach** and **Boca Cai** come into view. They're at landlocked Lac Bay, which is ideal for swimming and snorkeling. Conch shells are stacked up on the beach. The water here is so vivid and clear you can see coral 65 to 120 feet down in the reef-protected waters.

A SIGHTSEEING TOUR

Bonaire Sightseeing Tours (☎ 599/7-8778) transports you on tours of the island, both north and south, taking in the flamingos, slave huts, conch shells, Goto Lake, the Amerindian inscriptions, and other sights. Each of these tours last 2 hours and costs $17 per person. You can take a half-day "City and Country Tour," lasting 3 hours and costing from $22 per person, allowing you to see the entire northern section and the southern part as far as the slave huts.

SHOPPING

Kralendijk features an assortment of goods, including gemstone jewelry, wood, leather, sterling, ceramics, liquors, and tobacco at 25% to 50% less than in the United States and Canada. Prices are often quoted in U.S. dollars, and major credit and charge cards and traveler's checks are usually accepted. Most shops are open Monday to Saturday from 8am to noon and 2 to 6pm; they might open for a few hours on Sunday if a cruise ship is in port. Walk along Kaya Grandi in Kralendijk to sample the merchandise.

Ki Bo Ke Pakus "What Do You Want." In the Divi Flamingo Beach Resort & Casino, J. A. Abraham Blvd. ☎ **599/7-8239.**

This place has some of the most popular merchandise on the island—T-shirts, handbags, dashikis, locally made jewelry, batiks from Indonesia, and Delft blue items.

Littman Jewelers. Kaya Grandi 35. ☎ **599/7-8160.**

Steve and Esther Littman have restored this old house to its original state. They sell Tag Heuer dive watches. The shop also carries Daum French crystal and Lladró Spanish porcelain. Next door, the Littmans have a shop called **Littman's Gifts,** selling T-shirts from standard to hand-painted, plus sandals, hats, Gottex swimsuits, gift items, costume jewelry, and toys.

Things Bonaire. Kaya Grandi 38C. ☎ **599/7-8423.**

Things Bonaire carries many gift items, including black-coral jewelry, sunglasses, postcards, and locally made shell and driftwood items. It also stocks men's and women's swimsuits, shorts, T-shirts, beach towels, guayaberas, caps, hats, and visors.

United Colors of Benetton. Kaya Grandi 49. ☎ **599/7-5107.**

This worldwide chain with its multicolored clothing and controversial (to some) ads has invaded Bonaire. Directly imported from Italy, the clothing is often priced 30% lower than in Europe or the United States—or so they claim.

BONAIRE AFTER DARK

Underwater **slide shows** provide entertainment for both divers and nondivers in the evening. The best shows are at **Captain Don's Habitat** (☎ 599/7-8290; see the "Coastal Reef Diving" box, above). Check when you get to Bonaire about times.

Divi Flamingo Beach Resort & Casino. J. A. Abraham Blvd. ☎ **599/7-8285.**

A casino opened here in 1984 in a former residence adjoining the property. Promoted as the "World's First Barefoot Casino," it offers blackjack, roulette, poker, wheel of fortune, video games, and slot machines. Gambling on the island is regulated by the government. Entrance is free. Open Monday to Saturday from 8pm to 2am.

Fantasy Disco. Kaya L. Z. Gerharts 1 (at Kaya Grandi). ☎ **599/7-7345.** Cover $6.

Near the heart of town, in a landlocked, two-story modern building that seems to encourage wandering by clients from one level to the next, this is the island's busiest, most popular, and most deeply entrenched disco. The musical theme will vary, depending on the night of the week, and may focus on merengue, reggae, or American-style rock 'n' roll, depending on whatever the DJ's in the mood for that night. Wednesday night is ladies' night, when women drink for reduced prices.

✪ **Karel's Beach Bar.** On the waterfront. ☎ **599/7-8434.**

Almost Tahitian in its high-ceilinged, open-walled design, this popular bar is perched above the sea on stilts. You can sit at the long rectangular bar with many of the island's dive and boating professionals or select a table near the balustrades overlooking the illuminated surf. On weekends local bands entertain.

3 Curaçao

Just 35 miles north of the coast of Venezuela, Curaçao, the "C" of the Dutch ABC islands of the Caribbean, is the most populous in the Netherlands Antilles. It attracts visitors because of its distinctive culture, warm people, duty-free shopping, lively casinos, and water sports. Fleets of tankers head out from its harbor to bring refined oil to all parts of the world.

The largest of the Netherlands Antilles, Curaçao is 37 miles long and 7 miles across at its widest point. Because of all that early Dutch building, Curaçao is the most important island architecturally in the entire West Indies, with more European flavor than anywhere else in the Caribbean. After leaving the capital, **Willemstad,** you plunge into a strange, desertlike countryside that evokes the American Southwest. The landscape is an amalgam of browns and russets, studded with three-pronged cactus, spiny-leafed aloes, and the divi-divi trees, with their coiffures bent by centuries of trade winds. Classic Dutch-style windmills are in and around Willemstad and in some parts of the countryside. These standard farm models pump water from wells to irrigate vegetation.

Curaçao, together with Bonaire, St. Maarten, St. Eustatius, and Saba, is in the Kingdom of the Netherlands as part of the Netherlands Antilles. Curaçao has its own governmental authority, relying on the Netherlands only for defense and foreign affairs. Its population of 171,000 represents more than 50 nationalities.

Only in the 1990s did tourism become the biggest money earner for this island. As a result, a number of inexpensive or moderately priced hotels, inns, and apartment complexes have opened.

GETTING THERE

The air routes to Curaçao International Airport, Plaza Margareth Abraham (☎ 599/9-682288), are still firmly linked to those leading to nearby Aruba. In recent years, however, developments at such airlines as American have initiated direct or nonstop routings into Curaçao from such international hubs as Miami.

American Airlines (☎ 800/433-7300) offers a daily nonstop flight to Curaçao from its hub in Miami, which departs late enough in the day to permit easy connections from cities all over the Northeast. Fortunately, it arrives early enough in the day (around 3pm) to allow guests to unpack and enjoy a leisurely dinner the same evening. American also offers flights to Curaçao's neighbor, Aruba, from New York, Miami, and San Juan, Puerto Rico. Once on Aruba, many clients transfer on to Curaçao on any of ALM's many shuttle flights. An American Airlines sales representative can also sell discounted hotel packages if you book your airfare and overnight accommodations simultaneously.

Air Aruba (☎ 800/882-7822) flies daily from Newark, N.J., to Aruba, with two flights on Saturday and Sunday (one of the Sunday flights stops in Baltimore to pick up passengers). The same airline also offers daily nonstop flights to Aruba from Miami and Tampa, and direct service from Baltimore. On Aruba, regardless of their points of origin, Curaçao-bound passengers either remain on the same plane for its continuation on to Curaçao, or transfer to another aircraft after a brief delay.

Another choice is **ALM** (☎ 800/327-7230), Curaçao's national carrier. It flies 15 times a week from Miami to Curaçao. Although 10 of these flights stop in either Aruba, Bonaire, or Haiti, three are nonstop. ALM also flies two times a week to

Curaçao from Atlanta, usually with a stop on Bonaire en route. Finally, ALM has inaugurated flights to Curaçao from Fort Lauderdale on Tuesday and Sunday.

GETTING AROUND

BY BUS   Some hotels operate a free bus shuttle that will take you from the suburbs to the shopping district of Willemstad. A fleet of DAF yellow buses operates from Wilhelmina Plein, near the shopping center, to most parts of Curaçao. Some limousines function as "C" buses. When you see one listing the destination you're heading for, you can hail it at any of the designated bus stops.

BY TAXI   Since taxis don't have meters, ask your driver to quote you the rate before getting in. Drivers are supposed to carry an official tariff sheet, which they'll produce upon request. Charges go up by 25% after 11pm. Generally there's no need to tip, unless a driver helped you with your luggage. The charge from the airport to Willemstad is about $15, and the cost can be split among four passengers. If a piece of luggage is so big that the trunk lid won't close, you'll be assessed a surcharge of $1.

In town, the best place to get a taxi is on the Otrabanda side of the floating bridge. To summon a cab, call ☎ **599/9-690747.** Cabbies will usually give you a tour of the island for around $20 per hour for up to four passengers.

BY RENTAL CAR   Since all points of touristic interest on Curaçao are easily accessible by paved roads, you may want to rent a car. U.S., British, and Canadian visitors can use their own licenses, if valid, and *traffic moves on the right.* International road signs are observed.

Avis (☎ **800/331-2112**) and **Budget** (☎ **800/527-0700**) offer some of the lowest rates. Budget usually offers the best deal if it has compact cars with manual transmission and no air-conditioning in stock. The rate begins at $192 per week with unlimited mileage, whereas the lowest rate you're likely to be quoted at Avis is $309 a week with unlimited mileage. The cheapest car at **Hertz** (☎ **800/654-3001** in the U.S., or 599/9-681182) rents for $283 per week, and represents especially good value because it includes air-conditioning. Rentals are often cheaper if you reserve from North America at least a week before your departure.

Local car-rental firms include **Rent a Yellow,** Santa Rosa 9 (☎ **599/9-673777**), whose cars are painted like a yellow cab. The lowest rates are for vehicles without air-conditioning, costing from $33.50 daily, rising to $36.35 with air-conditioning. Tariffs include tax and insurance.

FAST FACTS: Curaçao

Banks   Banking hours are Monday to Friday from 8:30am to noon and 1:30 to 4:30pm. However, the Banco Popular and the Bank of America remain open during the lunch hour, doing business Monday to Friday from 9am to 3pm.

Currency   Whereas Canadian and U.S. dollars are accepted for purchases on the island, the official currency is the **Netherlands Antillean florin (NAf),** also called a guilder, which is divided into 100 NA (Netherlands Antillean) cents. The exchange rate is $1 U.S. to 1.77 NAf (1 NAf = 56¢ U.S.). Shops, hotels, and restaurants usually accept most major U.S. and Canadian credit and charge cards.

Documents   To enter Curaçao, U.S. or Canadian citizens need proof of citizenship, such as a birth certificate or a passport, along with a return or continuing airline ticket out of the country. British subjects need a valid passport.

Curaçao

0   5 km
     3 mi
N

Noordpunt

Westpunt
Playa
Abao
Knip
Bay

○ Westpunt
■ Boca Tabla

Caribbean Sea

Christoffel National Park

▲▲
St. Christoffelberg

Santa
Marta
Bay
○ Soto   ○ Barber

San Juan Bay

○ St. Willibrordus

Daaibooi

Boca St.
Marie

Curaçao International Airport

Boca Hato

■ **Hato Caves**

○ St. Michiel   ○ Julianadorp

Blauwbaai

Piscadera Bay

Brienvegat

○ Santa Catarina

● Emmastad

St. Anna Bay

● Santa Rosa

St. Joris Bay

Willemstad

○ Montagne

Seaquarium ■

Jan Thiel Bay

Spanish
Water

Santa Barbara Beach

Caribbean Sea

Curaçao Underwater Marine Park

Oostpunt

Airport ✈   Beach ☂   Diving ⌐   Mountain ▲▲

2-0193

Electricity   The electricity is 110–130 volts AC, 50 cycles, the same as in North America, although many hotels will have transformers if your appliances happen to be European.

Information   In the United States, contact the **Curaçao Tourist Board** at 400 Madison Ave., Suite 311, New York, NY 10017 (☎ **800/270-3350** or 212/ 683-7660); or 330 Biscayne Blvd., Suite 330, Miami, FL 33132 (☎ **305/ 374-5811**).

For tourist information on Curaçao, go to the **Curaçao Tourist Board,** Pietermaai (☎ **599/9-616000**).

Language   Dutch, Spanish, and English are spoken on Curaçao, along with Papiamento, a patois that combines the three major tongues with Amerindian and African dialects.

Medical Care   Medical facilities are well equipped, and the 534-bed **St. Elisabeth Hospital,** Breedestraat 193 (☎ **599/9-624900**), near Otrabanda in Willemstad, is one of the most up-to-date facilities in the Caribbean.

Police   The police emergency number is ☎ **114** or ☎ **444444.**

Safety   While Curaçao is not plagued with crime, it would be wise to safeguard your valuables.

Taxes and Service   Curaçao levies a room tax of 7% on accommodations, and most hotels add 12% for room service. There's a departure tax of $12.50 for international flights, or $5.65 for flights to other islands in the Netherlands Antilles.

Telephones   To call Curaçao from the United States, dial 011 (the international access code), then 599 (the country code for Curaçao), and then 9 (the area code) and the local number (the number of digits in the local number varies).

Once on Curaçao, to call another number on the island only the local number is necessary; to make calls to an off-island destination, dial 021 and then the area code and number.

Time   Curaçao is on Atlantic standard time year-round, 1 hour ahead of eastern standard time and the same as eastern daylight saving time.

Water   The water comes from a modern desalination plant and is safe to drink.

Weather   Curaçao has an average temperature of 81° Fahrenheit. Trade winds keep the island fairly cool, and it is flat and arid, with an average rainfall of only 22 inches per year—hardly your idea of a lush, palm-studded tropical island.

WHERE TO STAY

Your hotel will be in Willemstad or in one of the suburbs, which are 10 to 15 minutes from the shopping center. The bigger hotels often have free shuttle buses running into town, and most of them have their own beaches and pools.

Remember that Curaçao is a bustling commercial center, and the downtown hotels often fill up fast with business travelers and visitors from neighboring countries on a shopping holiday. Therefore, reservations are always important.

When making reservations, ask if the 7% room tax and 12% service charge are included in the price you're quoted.

DOUBLES FOR LESS THAN $55

Bahia Inn. Lagun Beach (P.O. Box 3501, Willemsted), Curaçao, N.A. ☎ **599/9-641000.** Fax 599/9-690888. 6 studios, 1 apt. A/C TV. Year-round, $55–$60 single or double; $90 apt for up to four. Extra person $16; children 5 and under, $5. AE, DISC, MC, V.

In the countryside west of town, this resort has been popular with Europeans who know a good bargain when they find one. They've been coming back for years, and don't want to share their "secret" with you. Nevertheless, word about Bahia Inn on lovely Lagun (as opposed to Laguna) Beach has spread, so early bookings in winter are needed. Simply but comfortably furnished studios are in one building—three upstairs, three downstairs. Each has a double bed, table and bench, along with a kitchenette. Cooling is both by ceiling fan and air-conditioning. The rooms open onto a small front balcony or one in the rear facing the beachfront. The apartment is in a separate building, also fronting the beach. There's a common terrace, facing the waters, and here's where fellow patrons meet and mingle. A simple restaurant is nearby. With advance notice, baby-sitting can be arranged.

Limestone Resort. Spanish Water Bay (P.O. Box 3521, Willemsted), Brakke Put Areba, Curaçao, N.A. ☎ and fax **599/9-673007.** 7 cottages. A/C TV TEL. Year-round, $45–$64 cottage for one or two; $95 cottage for four. Extra person $20; children 11 and under, $10. No credit cards.

This resort is on Spanish Water Bay, with its own beach. This is a somewhat ritzy part of the island. Within walking distance is a restaurant on the beach partially afloat like a boathouse. There's also a dinghy available which you can use to visit the underwater marine park, 10 minutes away. The rooms are rather standard, but are quite comfortable, with both double or twin beds, each with a living room and porch plus a kitchenette. Each unit is in a separate building in a setting of palm trees. There is an on-site dive shop offering daily lessons, plus a sail school. Car rentals can be arranged.

DOUBLES FOR LESS THAN $80

Hotel Holland. F. D. Rooseveltweg 524, Curaçao, N.A. ☎ **599/9-688044.** Fax 599/9-688114. 40 rms, 5 suites. A/C TV TEL. Year-round, $66 single; $79 double; from $117 suite. AE, DC, MC, V.

A 5-minute drive from the airport, the Hotel Holland contains the Flying Dutchman Bar, a popular gathering place, plus a small casino that opened in 1991. For a few brief minutes of every day you can see airplanes landing from your perch at the edge of the poolside terrace, where well-prepared meals from the Cockpit Restaurant are served during good weather. The restaurant offers breakfast, lunch, and dinner. This property is the domain of ex-navy frogman Hans Vrolijk and his family. Hans still retains his interest in scuba and arranges dive packages for his guests. The comfortably furnished accommodations have VCRs, refrigerators, and balconies. Laundry, baby-sitting, and room service are available.

DOUBLES FOR LESS THAN $105

Hotel Seru Coral. Koraal Partier 10, Curaçao, N.A. ☎ **599/9-678499.** Fax 599/9-678256. 30 studios, 34 one-bedroom suites, 14 bungalows, 4 two-bedroom suites, 4 villas. A/C TV TEL. Year-round, $113.15 studio for one or two; $144.58 one-bedroom suite for one or two; $197.72 bungalow for four; $233.15 two-bedroom suite for four; $297.72 villa for up to six. Children 12 and under stay free in parents' room. The hotel resists more than the number of occupants listed above, but they will set up an extra bed for one additional occupant for $9 per day. AE, DC, MC, V.

Built in the early 1990s, this is a landscaped hotel complex whose white-walled buildings are clustered around the edges of a very large circular pool terrace. It lies on Curaçao's eastern edge, about 4 miles from the nearest beach (Santa Barbara Beach), but the inconvenience of reaching the beach is offset by the lavish size of the round swimming pool, the largest freshwater pool on Curaçao. At least five room configurations are available, allowing groups of travelers to cut their costs to very reasonable levels. But regardless of which type of accommodation you select, each has white walls with pastel trim, white tile floors, and a mixture of rattan and wooden furniture. Water sports, boat trips, and tennis can be arranged nearby, and families are welcome. On the premises is a child's wading pool and easy availability of baby-sitters, as well as a launderette, a minimart for grocery shopping, and a bar.

Otrabanda Hotel & Casino. Breedestraat, Otrabanda, Curaçao, N.A. ☎ **599/9-627400.** Fax 599/9-627299. 45 rms, 3 suites. A/C TV TEL. Winter, $105 single; $115 double; $150 suite. Off-season, $95 single; $105 double; $140 suite. Rates include breakfast. AE, DISC, MC, V.

This six-story, somewhat anonymous hotel occupies a position in the heart of Willemstad. Although the nearest beach is a 15-minute drive away, there's a modern pool and most diversions, shopping opportunities, bars, and inexpensive restaurants of the island's capital are within an easy stroll. The bedrooms are simple, Spartan, and clean, with white walls, carpets, wooden furniture, and a format favored equally by business travelers and tourists. On the premises is the newly refurbished Bay Sight Terrace restaurant and the Pontoon Bar. The ground-floor casino, although not particularly memorable, seems relatively busy.

Van der Valk Plaza. Plaza Pier (P.O. Box 229), Willemstad, Curaçao, N.A. ☎ **800/447-7462** in the U.S., or 599/9-612500. Fax 599/9-618347. 232 rms, 18 suites. A/C TV TEL. Winter, $91–$124 single or double; $141 suite. Off-season, $57–$95 single or double; $118 suite. Rates include breakfast. AE, MC, V.

Standing guard over the Punda side of St. Anna Bay, the Plaza is nestled in the ramparts of an 18th-century waterside fort on the eastern tip of the entrance to the harbor, a 20-minute drive south of the airport. In fact, it's one of the harbor's two "lighthouses." (The hotel has to carry marine collision insurance, the only hostelry in the Caribbean with that distinction.) The original part of the hotel was built in 1954, long before the wave of touristic interest swept the island, and followed the style of the arcaded fort. However, now there's a tower of rooms stacked 15 stories high. Each of the bedrooms—your own crow's nest—is comfortably furnished and contains a personal safe, although the room decor strikes many as garish. The pool, with a bar and suntanning area, is inches away from the parapet of the fort. In the hotel's Waterfort Grill, you can order American and continental dishes. A second restaurant, Tournesol, is more formal. It's located on the top floor of the hotel and offers a panoramic view to diners. The more gourmet of the two restaurants, Tournesol, is open for dinner only, Tuesday to Sunday, and features French cuisine. The hotel offers laundry, baby-sitting, and room service (from 7:30am to 11pm), and has a small casino.

BEST OFF-SEASON BET

Holiday Beach Hotel & Casino. Pater Euwensweg 31 (P.O. Box 2178), Willemstad, Curaçao, N.A. ☎ **599/9-625400.** Fax 599/9-624397. 200 rms. A/C TV TEL. Winter, $150–$165 double. Off-season, $110–$120 double. MAP $33 per person extra. AE, DC, MC, V.

Along a sandy beach dotted with palm trees, this establishment sits near a grassy peninsula jutting out to sea about a mile from the capital and boasts all the facilities of a resort hotel. The main part of the complex houses the Casino Royale, one of the largest casinos on the island, and a handful of tennis courts. Local entertainment is offered in the hotel's nightclub. After dinner you can enjoy a drink in the Tropic Lounge, perhaps before heading to the roulette tables.

The sleeping quarters are in two four-story wings, centering around a U-shaped garden with a large freshwater swimming pool. The modern bedrooms are well furnished, with private balconies overlooking the water. Wall-to-wall carpeting and big tile baths are just part of the comforts. Laundry, baby-sitting, and room service are available.

In winter, a single rents for $135 to $150, while a double goes for $150 to $165. Off-season, prices are slashed to $110 for a single and $110 to $120 for a double, plus tax.

WORTH A SPLURGE

Lion's Dive Hotel & Marina. Bapor Kibra, Willemstad, Curaçao, N.A. ☎ **599/9-618100.** Fax 599/9-618200. 72 rms. A/C TV TEL. Winter, $135 single; $150 double. Off-season, $115 single; $130 double. AE, DC, MC, V.

On the island's largest white sandy beach, a 30-minute taxi ride southeast of the airport, is a complete dive resort with programs supervised by the Underwater Curaçao staff. Most of its comfortable accommodations have a sea view, as well as a balcony or terrace and two queen-size beds. Other facilities include a freshwater pool and three restaurants specializing in Italian and American cuisine plus seafood. Introductory dives and resort and certification courses are offered, and on the premises is a fully equipped rental dive shop. Two boat dives are conducted daily. Massage facilities are available, as are laundry and baby-sitting services. The hotel also has a health club.

WHERE TO EAT

The Cockpit. In the Hotel Holland, F. D. Rooseveltweg 524. ☎ **599/9-688044.** Reservations required. Main courses $10–$25. AE, DC, MC, V. Daily 7am–10pm. DUTCH/INTERNATIONAL.

The restaurant's decor has an aeronautical flavor with the nose of an airplane cockpit as the focal point. Located on the scrub-bordered road leading to the airport, a few minutes from the landing strips, this restaurant serves international cuisine with an emphasis on Dutch and Antillean specialties. Guests enjoy fresh fish in season (served according to Curaçao style), Dutch-style steak, Caribbean curried chicken, split-pea soup, and various pasta dishes, such as shrimp linguine della mama served in a lobster sauce and topped with melted cheese. All dishes are accompanied by fresh vegetables and Dutch-style potatoes. No one pretends that the food is gourmet fare—it's robust, hearty, and filled with good country flavor, nothing else. But on some occasions nothing else is what's called for, and it's also one of the best dining values on this island where food prices often climb to dizzying heights. Guests can enjoy their meals outside around the pool or in the cockpit-inspired dining room.

✪ **Golden Star.** Socratesstraat 2. ☎ **599/9-654795.** Main courses $7.50–$25.70. AE, DC, MC, V. Daily 9am–1am. CREOLE.

The best place to go on the island for *criollo* (local) food is inland from the coast road leading southeast from St. Anna Bay, at the corner of Dr. Hugenholtzweg and Dr. Maalweg, southeast of Willemstad. Evoking a roadside diner, the air-conditioned restaurant is very simple, but it has a large menu of very tasty Antillean dishes, such as *carco stoba* (conch stew), *bestia chiki* (goatmeat stew), *bakijauw* (salted cod), and *concomber stoba* (stewed meat and marble-size spiny cucumbers). Other specialties include criollo shrimp *(kiwa)* and *sopi carni* (meat stew). Everything is served with a side order of funchi, the cornmeal staple. The place has a large local following with an occasional tourist dropping in.

The Grill King. Water Foort 2–3. ☎ **599/9-616870.** Main courses $4.50–$26. AE, DC, DISC, MC, V. Mon–Thurs noon–midnight, Fri–Sat noon–12:30am, Sun 5:30pm–midnight. GRILLED MEATS / FISH.

This casual eatery draws a medley of locals and visitors to an open-air site near the harbor with a panoramic view of the passing ships. It's a lively, bustling place, specializing in grilled meats and fish, although there are other choices as well. The grilled steaks are succulent, as is the fresh catch of the day. You can also order pepper steak, a platter full of seafood (shrimp, calamari, conch, and lobster). Savvy foodies often gravitate to the mixed grill with pork, beef, conch, and chicken, all served with fresh vegetables. Burgers are also available, and there's not only a soup of the day but a daily special, often regional. The bar often stays open until 1am, attracting a convivial crowd.

Herbie's Pizza. Santa Rosaweg, Van Engelen. ☎ **599/9-67533.** Main courses and pizzas $3.25–$19. AE, DC, MC, V. Daily 11am–11pm. PIZZA/ITALIAN.

This is the local family favorite—in fact they like families so much here that the owners have dubbed their eatery "The Family Restaurant." East of town on Santa Rosaweg, both locals and visitors flock here for their pizza fix. In the front is a counter for ordering takeout along with some tables. Behind this is an open-air dining area and a two-story hut. Upstairs is the bar. To the left is an area for children, with a minizoo with monkeys, ducks, rabbits, and parrots. Children's parties are held here every day. In addition to pizza, the menu offers a standard repertoire of chicken, fish, and meat dishes, all prepared Italian style from family recipes. There are a number of freshly made pastas, salads, and soups, the menu rounded off nicely with such desserts as egg custards, pies, and tiramisù. Live music is presented on Friday and Saturday nights, so Herbie's becomes a cheap way to spend an evening.

Il Barile. Hanhi Sna 12, Punda. ☎ **599/9-613025.** Main courses $6–$15. AE, DC, DISC, MC, V. Mon–Sat 8am–8pm. ITALIAN.

Many Italian meals in Curaçao are very expensive, but this winning little two-story trattoria-style place not only offers affordable prices, but serves a very good cuisine. It's really only an informal cafe with an outdoor terrace on the ground floor. Many locals, including some Italians, cite it for its good food. You can drop in for breakfast, stick around for such lunch offerings as burgers and sandwiches, and definitely stay for dinner. It's in the evening when the kitchen shines, turning out a number of pasta dishes, such as linguine al pesto. The fresh basil in the pesto sauce is grown at the owner's home. You can also order an excellent grilled red snapper or shrimp in garlic butter.

Jaanchi's. Westpunt 15. ☎ **599/9-640126.** Main courses $12–$16; lunch from $10. AE, DC, MC, V. Daily noon–8pm. SEAFOOD.

In the village of Westpunt, on the island's western tip, this local dive has made a name for itself by its fried fresh fish. Many locals drive out here for a feast that ranges from shrimp to conch and octopus—each dish prepared according to time-tested traditional recipes. For those with real exotic palates, the menu offers a number of very rare regional dishes, even iguana soup! If the spicy local goat doesn't interest you, you can always opt for a good steak instead. Platters are served with rice, french fries, fried bananas, salad, and funghi polenta (a cornmeal bread). The restaurant is built ranch style offering open-air dining. Birds looking for handouts (breadcrumbs) will often join you at table. On Sunday and holidays there's live music when Jaanchi's becomes rather festive.

Martha Koosje Café. Martha Koosje Weg 10. ☎ **599/9-648235.** Reservations recommended. Main courses $12.90–$28. AE, DC, DISC, MC, V. Daily 6–10:30pm. CARIBBEAN.

In a 160-year-old estate on the west side of the island, this is a discovery. It's an alfresco dining room decorated with antique furnishings and in full bloom with tropical flora. The place deserves to be better known, lying at the narrowest part of the island.

A Curaçao/Dutch couple, Errol and Simone Caprino, recently took over from the long-established owners and plan changes. Errol is an actor, so he's going to offer dinner theater–type entertainment. The bar opens at 5pm, so you can come early for a leisurely drink, enjoying pre-entertainment entertainment by watching the iguanas on the roof being fed. The food has been improved. Today you can begin with pumpkin soup or, even better, fish soup, perhaps a seafood cocktail. Locals like the grilled steaks served with various sauces, or you can sample conch, shrimp, or grilled red snapper (delectable). For the truly regional palate, there's a savory goat stew or, for an occasional treat, octopus vinaigrette.

Pinocchio. Schottegatweg 82, Salinja. ☎ **599/9-376784.** Main courses $12.30–$21.50. AE, DC, MC, V. Mon–Sat 10am–10pm, Sun 6–10pm. INTERNATIONAL.

Set in the suburb of Salinja, a short drive south of Willemstad, this plant-filled restaurant caters to couples and families. Decorated in a tropical medley of bright colors, it maintains an active bar area. Menu items are simple and flavorful, including burgers, sandwiches, salads, steaks, fish dishes, buffalo-style chicken wings, and pita pockets filled, Lebanese style, with spiced lamb (shwarma). Eat here when you want something simple and fast.

❂ **Rijstaffel Restaurant Indonesia and Holland Club Bar.** Mercuriusstraat 13, Salinja. ☎ **599/9-612999.** Reservations recommended. Main courses $12.70–$21.20; rijstaffel $22 for 16 dishes, $24.30 for 20 dishes, $37.15 for 25 dishes; all vegetarian $21 for 16 dishes. AE, DC, MC, V. Mon–Sat noon–2pm and 6–9:30pm, Sun 6–9:30pm. INDONESIAN.

This is the best place on the island to sample the Indonesian rijstaffel, the traditional rice table with all the zesty side dishes. You must ask a taxi to take you to this villa in the suburbs near Salinja, near the Princess Beach Resort & Casino southeast of Willemstad. You're allowed to season your plate with peppers rated hot, very hot, and palate-melting. At lunchtime the selection of dishes is more modest, but for dinner Javanese cooks prepare the specialty of the house, a rijstaffel consisting of 16, 20, or 25 dishes. There's even an all-vegetarian rijstaffel. Warming trays are placed on your table and the service is buffet style. It's best to go with a party so that all of you can share in the feast. The spicy food is a good change of pace when you tire of seafood and steak.

Rodeo Ranch Saloon & Steakhouse. At the Curaçao Seaquarium, in Bapor Kibra. ☎ **599/9-615757.** Reservations recommended. Main courses $13.70–$34.30. AE, MC, V. Mon–Sat 6pm–midnight, Sun noon–2pm and 6pm–midnight. (Bar, daily 5pm–midnight.) STEAK/AMERICAN.

East of Willemstad, the Rodeo Ranch is a lot of fun. The owners have created a touch of the Old West with a replica of a covered wagon over the entrance and an interior decor of rough-sawn planking, dark woods, and antique wagon wheels. A "sheriff," wearing a 10-gallon hat and a silver star, greets visitors at the door. You'll be presented with a cowhide-covered menu by a cowgirl/waitress. To the sounds of country-western music, you can order dishes such as soup from the kettle, a chuckwagon choice of potato specials, steak, roast prime rib, and seafood. All steaks are U.S. prime beef, and there's a serve-yourself soup-and-salad bar. You don't have to dress up, and you'll enjoy your meal in air-conditioned comfort. Hot snacks are served at the happy hour from 5 to 7pm.

BEACHES, WATER SPORTS & OUTDOOR PURSUITS

BEACHES   Its beaches are not as good as Aruba's 7-mile strip of sand, but Curaçao does have some 38 of them, ranging from hotel sands to secluded coves. About

30 minutes from town, in the Willibrordus area on the west side of Curaçao, **Daaibooi** is a good beach. It's free, but there are no changing facilities. A good private beach on the eastern side of the island is **Santa Barbara Beach,** on land owned by a mining company. Its between the open sea and the island's primary water-sports and recreational area known as Spanish Water. On the same land are Table Mountain, a remarkable landmark, and an old phosphate mine. The natural beach has pure-white sand and calm water. A buoy line protects swimmers from boats. Rest rooms, changing rooms, a snack bar, and a terrace are among the amenities. You can rent water bicycles and small motorboats. The beach, open daily from 8am to 6pm, has access to the Curaçao Underwater Park.

Blauwbaai (Blue Bay) is the largest and most frequented beach on Curaçao, with enough white sand for everybody. Along with showers and changing facilities, there are plenty of shady places to retreat from the noonday sun. To reach it, take the road that goes past the Holiday Beach Hotel, heading toward Julianadorp. Follow the sign that tells you to bear left for Blauwbaai and the fishing village of San Michiel.

Other beaches include **Westpunt,** known for the gigantic cliffs that frame it and the Sunday divers who jump from the cliffs into the ocean below. The public beach is located on the northwestern tip of the island. **Knip Bay,** just south of Westpunt, is a beach at the foot of beautiful turquoise waters. On weekends, live music and dancing make the beach a lively place. Changing facilities and refreshments are available. **Playa Abao,** with crystal turquoise water, is a beach at the northern tip of the island.

A Word of Caution to Swimmers: The sea water remains an almost-constant 76° Fahrenheit year-round, with good underwater visibility, but beware of stepping on spines of the sea urchins that sometimes abound in these waters. To give temporary first aid for an embedded urchin's spine, try the local remedies of vinegar or lime juice, or as the natives advise, a burning match if you're tough. Whereas the urchin spines are not fatal, they can cause several days of real discomfort.

BOATING TOURS   Taber Tours, Dokweg (☎ 599/9-376637), offers a handful of seagoing tours, such as a snorkel/barbecue trip to Port Marie, which includes round-trip transportation to excellent reef sites, use of snorkeling equipment, and a barbecue, for $60 per person. No children under 10 are allowed.

A less ambitious tour involves a sunset cruise with wine, cheese, and French bread served on board. The 2-hour sailing trip leaves at dusk on Saturday only, for a cost of $30 per adult and $20 for children 11 and under.

Travelers looking for a seagoing experience similar to the sailing days of yore should book a trip on the *Insulinde,* Handelskade (☎ 599/9-601340; beware, this is a cellular phone so the connection may be muffled). This 120-foot traditionally rigged sail logger is available for day trips and chartering. Every Thursday (or by special arrangement) the ship sails north from its berth beside Willemstad's main pier to the island's northwestern shore. Here, at Porto Marie (also referred to as Boca St. Marie), guests disembark onto the white sands of a beach, beside a private beach house. Included in the $55-per-person charge is lunch and use of snorkeling equipment. Round-trip transport from some of the island's hotels is also included in the price. Advance reservations are necessary. Outbound transit is by sail; the engines are used on the return. Departure from the pier is at 9am every Thursday; return to the pier is around 6pm the same day. Longer trips to Bonaire or Venezuela are also available.

GOLF   The Curaçao Golf and Squash Club, Wilhelminalaan, in Emmastad (☎ 599/9-373590), is the place to go for a round of golf. Greens fees are $20, and both clubs and carts can be rented upon demand. The nine-hole course (the only one on the island) is open to nonmembers Friday to Wednesday only in the morning, from 8am to noon. (Afternoon tee-offs are reserved for members and for tournaments.) Thursday hours for nonmembers are 10:30am until sundown.

TENNIS   There are tennis courts at the Curaçao Caribbean Hotel & Casino, Princess Beach Resort & Casino, and Holiday Beach Hotel & Casino. These courts are open to non-guests.

WATER SPORTS   Most hotels offer their own programs of water sports. However, if your hotel isn't equipped, head for one of the most complete water-sports facilities on Curaçao, **Seascape Dive and Watersports,** at the Curaçao Caribbean Hotel (☎ **599/9-625000,** ext. 6056). Specializing in snorkeling and scuba-diving trips to reefs and underwater wrecks, it operates from a hexagonal kiosk set on stilts above the water, just offshore from the hotel's beach.

Open from 8am to 5pm daily, the company offers snorkeling excursions for $25 per person in an underwater park offshore from the hotel, waterskiing for $50 per half hour, and rental of jet skis for $50 per half hour. A Sunfish rents for $20, and an introductory scuba lesson, conducted by a competent dive instructor with PADI certification, goes for $45; packages of four dives cost $124.

One trip enthusiastically endorsed by some readers departs from the hotel at 7am (when participation warrants). The destination is Little Curaçao, midway between Curaçao and Bonaire. Clothes are optional once you get to the sugar-white sands of the island. Fishing, snorkeling, and the acquisition of a "topless tan" are highlights. The price is $70 per person, and the excursion lasts all day.

Underwater Curaçao, in Bapor Kibra (☎ **599/9-618131**), has a complete PADI-accredited underwater sports program. A fully stocked modern dive shop has retail and rental equipment. Individual dives and dive packages are offered, costing $33 per dive for experienced divers. An introductory dive for novices is priced at $65 and a snorkel trip costs $20, including equipment.

Scuba divers and snorkelers can expect spectacular scenery in waters with visibility often exceeding 100 feet at the ✪ **Curaçao Underwater Park,** which stretches along 12¹/₂ miles of Curaçao's southern coastline. Although its premises technically begin at Princess Beach and extend all the way to East Point, the island's southeasternmost tip, some scuba aficionados and island dive operators are aware of other, excellent dive sites outside the official boundaries of this park. Lying beneath the surface of the water are steep walls, at least two shallow wrecks, gardens of soft corals, and more than 30 species of hard corals. Although access from shore is possible at Jan Thiel Bay and Santa Barbara Beach, most people visit the park by boat. For easy and safe mooring, the park has 16 mooring buoys, placed at the best dive and snorkel sites. A snorkel trail with underwater interpretive markers is laid out just east of the Princess Beach Resort & Casino and is accessible from shore. Spearfishing, anchoring in the coral, and taking anything from the reefs except photographs are strictly prohibited.

SEEING THE SIGHTS

Most cruise-ship passengers see only Willemstad—or, more accurately, the shops of Willemstad—but you may want to get out into the *cunucu* (countryside) and explore the towering cacti and rolling hills topped by *landhuizen* (plantation houses) built more than three centuries ago.

✪ WILLEMSTAD

Willemstad was originally founded as Santa Ana by the Spanish in the 1500s. Dutch traders found a vast natural harbor, a perfect hideaway along the Spanish Main, and they renamed it Willemstad in the 17th century. Not only is Willemstad the capital of Curaçao, it's also the seat of government for the Netherlands Antilles.

The city grew up on both sides of the canal. Today it's divided into the **Punda** and the **Otrabanda,** the latter literally meaning "the other side." Both sections are connected by the **Queen Emma Pontoon Bridge,** a pedestrian walkway. Powered by a diesel engine, it swings open many times every day to let ships from all over the globe pass in and out of the harbor.

The view from the bridge is of the old **gabled houses** in harmonized pastel shades, such as deep earth-toned golds, mustards, and greens. The bright pastel colors, according to legend, are a holdover from the time when one of the island's early governors is said to have had eye trouble and flat white gave him headaches.

The colonial-style architecture, reflecting the Dutch influence, gives the town a "storybook" look. The houses, built three or four stories high, are crowned by "step" gables and roofed with orange Spanish tiles. Hemmed in by the sea, a tiny canal, and an inlet, the streets are narrow, and they're crosshatched by still narrower alleyways. Except for the pastel colors, Willemstad may remind you of old Amsterdam. It has one of the most intriguing townscapes in the Caribbean. The city can be rather dirty, however, in spite of its fairy-tale appearance.

A **statue of Pedro Luis Brion** dominates the square known as Brionplein right at the Otrabanda end of the pontoon bridge. Born on Curaçao in 1782, he became the island's favorite son and best-known war hero. Under Simón Bolívar, he was an admiral of the fleet and fought for the independence of Venezuela and Colombia.

In addition to the pontoon bridge, the **Queen Juliana Bridge** opened to vehicular traffic in 1973. Spanning the harbor, it rises 195 feet, which makes it the highest bridge in the Caribbean and one of the tallest in the world.

The waterfront originally guarded the mouth of the canal on the eastern or Punda side, but now it has been incorporated into the Plaza Hotel. The task of standing guard has been taken over by **Fort Amsterdam,** site of the Governor's Palace and the 1769 Dutch Reformed church. The church still has a British cannonball embedded in it. The arches leading to the fort were tunneled under the official residence of the governor.

A corner of the fort stands at the intersection of Breedestraat and Handelskade, the starting point for a plunge into the island's major shopping district.

A few minutes' walk from the pontoon bridge, at the north end of Handelskade, is the **Floating Market,** where scores of schooners tie up alongside the canal, a few yards from the main shopping section. Docked boats arrive from Venezuela and Colombia, as well as other West Indian islands, to sell tropical fruits and vegetables—a little bit of everything, in fact. The modern market under its vast concrete cap has not replaced this unique shopping expedition, which is fun to watch.

Between I. H. (Sha) Capriles Kade and Fort Amsterdam, at the corner of Columbusstraat and Kerkstraat, stands the **Mikve Israel–Emanuel Synagogue** (☎ **599/9-611633**), one of the oldest synagogue buildings in the Western Hemisphere. Consecrated on the eve of Passover in 1732, it antedates the first U.S. synagogue (in Newport, Rhode Island) by 31 years and houses the oldest Jewish congregation in the New World, dating from 1651. A fine example of Dutch colonial architecture, covering about a square block in the heart of Willemstad, it was built in a Spanish-style walled courtyard, with four large portals. Sand covers the sanctuary floor following a Portuguese Sephardic custom, representing the desert where Israelites camped when the Jews passed from slavery to freedom. The *theba* (pulpit) is in the center, and the congregation surrounds it. The highlight of the east wall is the Holy Ark, rising 17 feet, and a raised banca, canopied in mahogany, is on the north wall.

The synagogue has services every Friday at 6:30pm and Saturday at 10am, as well as similar holiday service times. Visitors are welcome to all services, with appropriate dress required.

Adjacent to the synagogue courtyard is the **Jewish Cultural Historical Museum,** Kuiperstraat 26–28, housed in two buildings dating back to 1728. They were originally the rabbi's residence and the bathhouse. On display are a great many ritual, ceremonial, and cultural objects, many of which date back to the 17th and 18th centuries and are still in use by the congregation for holidays and life-cycle events.

The synagogue and museum are open to visitors Monday to Friday from 9 to 11:45am and 2:30 to 4:45pm; if there's a cruise ship in port, also on Sunday from 9am to noon. There's a $2 entrance fee to the museum.

WEST OF WILLEMSTAD

You can walk to the **Curaçao Museum,** Van Leeuwenhoekstraat (☎ 599/ 9-626051), from the Queen Emma Pontoon Bridge. Furnished with paintings, objects d'art, and antique furniture made in the 19th century by local cabinetmakers, it re-creates the atmosphere of an era gone by. A novelty is the polka-dot kitchen. The museum contains a large collection from the Caiquetio tribes, the early inhabitants described by Amerigo Vespucci as giants 7 feet tall. In the gardens are specimens of the island's trees and plants. There's also a reconstruction of a traditional music pavilion in the garden where Curaçao musicians give regular performances. It's open Monday to Friday from 9am to noon and 2 to 5pm, and on Sunday from 10am to 4pm. Admission is $2.50 for adults, $1.25 for children 13 and under.

The **Curaçao Seaquarium,** off Martin Luther King Boulevard at a site called Bapor Kibra (☎ 599/9-4616666), has more than 400 species of fish, crabs, anemones, and other invertebrates, sponges, and coral displayed and growing in a natural environment. A rustic boardwalk connects the low-lying hexagonal buildings comprising the Seaquarium complex, which sits on a point off which the *Oranje Nassau* broke up on the rocks and sank in 1906 (the name of the site, Bapor Kibra, means "sunken ship"). Located a few minutes' walk along the rocky coast from the Princess Beach Resort & Casino, the Seaquarium is open daily from 8:30am to 11pm. Admission is $13.25 for adults, $7.50 for children 14 and under.

A special feature of the aquarium is an "animal encounter." Divers, snorkelers, and experienced swimmers are able to feed, film, and photograph sharks, which are separated from them by a large window with feeding holes. In the animal encounter section, swimmers are able to swim among sharks, stingrays, lobsters, sabalo, parrot fish, and other marine life, feeding and photographing these creatures in a controlled environment where safety is always a consideration. For the nonswimmer, a 46-foot semisubmarine (underwater observation tower) is in the middle. Sharks as well as other species are "called" to the windows of the semisubmarine for a close-up view. The Seaquarium is also home to Curaçao's only full-facility, white-sand, palm-shaded beach.

The newest attraction at the Seaquarium is the *Seaworld Explorer,* a semisubmersible submarine that departs daily at 4:30pm on hour-long journeys into the deep. You're taken on a tour of submerged wrecks off the shores of Curaçao and are treated to close encounters of coral reefs with their rainbow-hued tropical fish. The *Explorer* has a barge top that submerges only 5 or so feet under the water. But the submerged section has wide glass windows allowing passengers underwater views which can extend for 110 feet or so. Reservations must be made a day in advance by calling ☎ 599/9-628986. Adults pay $30.75; children 11 and under are charged $20.15.

The **Curaçao Underwater Marine Park** (☎ 599/9-624242), established in 1983 with the financial aid of the World Wildlife Fund, stretches from the Princess Beach

Resort & Casino to the east point of the island, a strip of about 12½ miles of untouched coral reefs. For information on snorkeling, scuba diving, and trips in a glass-bottom boat to view the park, see "Beaches, Water Sports & Outdoor Pursuits," above.

The **Country House Museum,** Doktorstuin 27 (☎ **599/9-642742**), 12 miles west of Willemstad, is a small-scale restoration of a 19th-century manor house that boasts thick stone walls, a thatched roof, and artifacts that represent the antique methods of agriculture and fishing of long ago. It's open Tuesday to Friday from 8am to 4pm, and Saturday and Sunday from 8am to 6pm. Admission is $1.50.

Also en route to Westpunt, you'll come across a seaside cavern known as **Boca Tabla,** one of many such grottoes on this rugged, uninhabited northwest coast.

In the Westpunt area, a 45-minute ride from Punda in Willemstad, **Playa Forti** is a stark region characterized by soaring hills and towering cacti, along with 200-year-old Dutch land houses, the former mansions that housed the slaveowner plantation heads.

Out toward the western tip of Curaçao, a high wire fence surrounds the entrance to the 4,500-acre, ✪ **Christoffel National Park,** Savonet (☎ **599/9-640363**), about a 45-minute drive from the capital. A macadam road gives way to dirt, surrounded on all sides by abundant cactus and bromeliads. In the higher regions you can spot rare orchids. Rising from flat, arid countryside, 1,230-foot-high St. Christoffelberg is the highest point in the Dutch Leewards. Donkeys, wild goats, iguanas, the Curaçao deer, and many species of birds thrive in this preserve, and there are some Arawak paintings on a coral cliff near the two caves. A folk legend surrounds Piedra di Monton, a rockheap accumulated by African slaves who worked on the former plantations. According to the legend passed down through the generations, any worker would be able to climb to the top of the rockpile, jump off, and fly back home across the Atlantic. If, however, the slave had at any time in his life tasted a grain of salt, the magic would not work and he would crash to his death below.

The park has 20 miles of one-way trail-like roads, with lots of flora and fauna along the way. The shortest trail is about 5 miles long, and because of the rough terrain, takes about 40 minutes to drive through. Various walking trails are available also. One of them will take you to the top of St. Christoffelberg in about 1½ hours. (Come early in the morning when it isn't so hot.) The park is open Monday to Saturday from 8am to 4pm and on Sunday from 6am to 3pm. Admission is $9 for both adults and children. The park also has a museum with varying exhibitions year-round set in an old storehouse left over from plantation days. Phone to arrange a guided tour. Next door, the park has opened the **National Park Shete Boka** (Seven Bays). It's a turtle sanctuary and contains a cave with pounding waves off the choppy north coast. Admission to this park is $1.50 per person.

NORTH & EAST OF WILLEMSTAD

Just northeast of the capital, **Fort Nassau** was completed in 1797 and christened by the Dutch as Fort Republic. Built high on a hill overlooking the harbor entrance to the south and St. Anna Bay to the north, it was fortified as a second line of defense in case Waterfront gave way. When the British invaded in 1807, they renamed it Fort George in honor of their own king. Later, when the Dutch regained control, they renamed it Orange Nassau in honor of the Dutch royal family. Today diners have replaced soldiers.

Along the coast to the southeast of town, the oddly shaped **Octagon House** on Penstraat was where the liberator, Simón Bolívar, used to visit his two sisters during the wars for Venezuelan independence. This landmark used to be a museum, but is currently closed.

From the house you can head north, going along the eastern side of the water, to the intersection of Rijkseenheid Boulevard and Fokkerweg. Here you'll see the **Autonomy Monument,** a vibrant 20th-century sculpture representing the Dutch islands.

In the area, the **Amstel Brewery** (☎ 599/9-612944) allows visitors to tour its plant where Curaçao beer is brewed from desalinated seawater. Tours are given only on Tuesday and Thursday at 9:30am.

In addition, the **Curaçao Liqueur Distillery,** in the Salinja area (☎ 599/ 9-613526), offers free tours and tastes at Chobolobo, the 17th-century landhuis where the famous liqueur is made. The cordial, named after the region where it originated, is a distillate of dried peel of a particular strain of orange found only on Curaçao. Several herbs are added to give it an aromatic bouquet. It's made by a secret formula handed down through generations. One of the rewards of a visit here is a free snifter of the liqueur at the culmination of the guided tours, offered Monday to Friday from 8am to noon and 1 to 5pm.

On Schottegatweg West, northwest of Willemstad, past the oil refineries, lies the **Beth Haim Cemetery,** the oldest Caucasian burial site still in use in the Western Hemisphere. Meaning "House of Life," the cemetery was consecrated before 1659. On about 3 acres are some 2,500 graves. The carving on some of the 17th- and 18th-century tombstones is exceptional.

Landhuis Brievengat, Brievengat (☎ 599/9-378344), gives visitors a chance to visit a Dutch version of an 18th-century West Indian plantation house. This stately building, in a scrub-dotted landscape on the eastern side of the island, contains a few antiques, high ceilings, and a frontal gallery facing two entrance towers, said to have been used to imprison slaves and even for romantic trysts. The plantation was originally used for the cultivation of aloe and cattle, but an 1877 hurricane caused the plantation to cease operation. The building was pulled down, but around 1925 the remains of the structure were donated to the Society for the Preservation of Monuments, which rebuilt and restored it. It's open daily from 9:30am to noon and 3 to 6pm; admission is $1.

The **Hato Caves,** F. D. Rooseveltweg (☎ 599/9-680379), have been called "mystical." Every hour, professional local guides take visitors through this Curaçao world of stalagmites and stalactites, found in the highest limestone terrace of the island. Actually, they were once old coral reefs, which were formed when the ocean water fell and the landmass was uplifted over the years. Over thousands of years limestone formations were created, some mirrored in an underground lake. After crossing the lake, you enter the "Cathedral," an underground cavern. The largest hall of the cave is called La Ventana or "The Window." Also displayed are samples of ancient Indian petroglyph drawings. The caves are open Tuesday to Sunday from 10am to 5pm, charging $6.25 for adults and $4.50 for children 4 to 11 (free for kids 3 and under).

SIGHTSEEING TOURS

Taber Tours, Dokweg (☎ 599/9-376637), offers several tours, both day and night, to points of interest on Curaçao. The tour through Willemstad, to the Curaçao liqueur distillery, through the residential area and the Bloempot shopping center, and to the Curaçao Museum (admission fee included in the tour price) costs $12.50 for adults, $6.25 for children 11 and under.

The easiest way to go exploring is to take a 1 1/4-hour **trolley tour,** visiting the highlights of Willemstad. The open-sided cars, pulled by a silent "locomotive," makes two tours each week: Monday at 11am and Wednesday at 4pm. The tour begins at Fort Amsterdam near the Queen Emma Pontoon Bridge. It costs $15 for adults or $10 for children 2 to 12 (free for kids 1 and under). Call ☎ **599/9-628833** for more information.

SHOPPING

Curaçao is a shopper's paradise. Some 200 shops line the major shopping malls of such wooden-shoe-named streets as Heerenstraat and Breedestraat. Right in the heart of Willemstad, the Punda shopping area is a 5-block district. Most stores are open Monday to Saturday from 8am to noon and 2 to 6pm (some from 8am to 6pm). When cruise ships are in port, stores are also open for a few hours on Sunday and holidays. To avoid the cruise-ship crowds, do your shopping in the morning.

Look for good buys in French perfumes, Dutch Delft blue souvenirs, finely woven Italian silks, Japanese and German cameras, jewelry, silver, Swiss watches, linens, leather goods, liquor, and island-made rum and liqueurs, especially Curaçao liqueur, some of which has a distinctive blue color. The island is famous for its 5-pound "wheels" of Gouda or Edam cheese. It also sells wooden shoes, although we're not sure what you'd do with them. Some of its stores also stock some good buys in intricate lacework imported from everywhere between Portugal and China. If you're a street shopper and want something colorful for a back bathroom, consider one of the wood carvings or flamboyant paintings from Haiti or the Dominican Republic. Both are hawked by street vendors at any of the main plazas.

Incidentally, Curaçao is not technically a free port, but its prices are low because of its low import duty.

Benetton. Madurostraat 4. ☎ **599/9-614619.**

This member of a worldwide casual sportswear chain based in Italy has invaded Curaçao with all its many colors. In July you can stock up on winter wear, and in December make summer purchases. Some items are marked down by about 20% off Stateside prices.

Bert Knubben Black Koral Shop. In the Princess Beach Resort & Casino, Dr. Martin Luther King Blvd. ☎ **599/9-367888.**

Bert Knubben is a name synonymous with craftsmanship and quality. Although collection of black coral has been made illegal by the Curaçao government, an exception was made for Bert, a diver who has been harvesting corals from the sea and fashioning them into fine jewelry and objets d'art for more than 35 years. Collectors avidly seek out this type of coral, not only because of the craftsmanship in the work, but because it's becoming increasingly rare and one day may not be offered for sale at all. The black coral jewelry is rivaled only by Bernard I. Passman's "Black Coral and . . ." shops in George Town in the Cayman Islands and in Charlotte Amalie on St. Thomas.

Boolchand's. Heerenstraat 4B, Punda. ☎ **599/9-612262.**

In business since 1930, Boolchand's stands for reliability in electronic equipment. Electronics are a good buy on Curaçao because the government of Curaçao has declared that these can be sold duty-free.

Galdelman Jewelers. Breedestraat 35, Punda. ☎ **599/9-611854.**

This is the island's best and most reliable choice for the jewelry collector. The store is well stocked with a large selection of fine jewelry—often exquisitely designed. If you want something local, ask to see the selection of Curaçaoan gold pieces. Here you'll find timepieces by Piaget, Corum, Concord, Baume & Mercier, Tag Heuer, Gucci, Swiss Army, Fendi, Swatch, and many others. Exclusive here is the unique line of Prima Classe leathergoods with the world map. Gandelman Jewelers has eight other stores in the Dutch Caribbean.

Obra di Man. Bargestraat 57. ☎ **599/9-612413.**

The best selection for authentic local handcraft items, especially handmade dolls, is Obra di Man. Most of the dolls here represent island folkloric characters. The store also sells hand-screened fabrics, black coral jewelry, and souvenirs. You can also purchase posters of Curaçao's architecture.

Palais Hindu. Heerenstraat 17. ☎ **599/9-616897.**

To satisfy your audio and video needs, Palais Hindi sells a wide range of video and cassette recorders. They also stock a lot of photographic equipment, along with cameras and watches.

Penha & Sons. Heerenstraat 1. ☎ **599/9-612266.**

In the oldest building in town, constructed in 1708, this traditional outlet has a history going back to 1865. It has been long known for its perfumes and brand-name clothes, one of the finest collections in the ABC islands. It's the distributor of such names as Boucheron, Calvin Klein, Yves Saint Laurent, and other perfumes and cosmetics of Elizabeth Arden, Clinique, Clarins, and Estée Lauder, among others. The collection of merchandise at this prestigious store is quite varied—Hummel figurines and Delft blue souvenirs. Their men's and women's boutiques feature travel and sportswear. The firm has 10 other stores in the Caribbean.

CURAÇAO AFTER DARK

Most of the action spins around the island's **casinos,** at the Sonesta Beach Hotel & Casino Curaçao, the Curaçao Caribbean Hotel & Casino, the Holiday Beach Hotel & Casino, and the Princess Beach Resort & Casino. The Emerald Casino at the Sonesta is especially popular, designed to resemble an open-air courtyard. It features 143 slot machines, 6 blackjack tables, 2 roulette wheels, 2 Caribbean stud poker tables, a craps table, a baccarat table, and 1 for minibaccarat. The casino at the Princess Beach Hotel is the liveliest on the island. These hotel gaming houses usually start their action at 2pm, and some of them remain open until 4am. The Princess Beach serves complimentary drinks.

The landlocked, flat, and somewhat dusty neighborhood of **Salinja** is now the nightlife capital of Curaçao, with many drinking and dancing outlets.

The historic **Landhuis Brievengat** (see "Seeing the Sights," above), in addition to being a museum with artifacts of the island, is also the site of Wednesday- and Friday-night rijstaffel parties. They begin at 7pm, require an admission fee of $8 (which includes the first drink), and feature heaping portions of rijstaffel that begin at $16 each. Although the landhuis itself is not directly connected with the dancing and drinking, there's a platform set up amid the flamboyant trees nearby, and two bands that alternate with one another to provide a happy ambience. It's wise to phone before going, but the event—especially on Friday night—is very popular. Tables and chairs for the event are folded and stored between presentations.

Club Facade. Lindbergweg 8. ☎ **599/9-614640.** Cover $10.

In the Salinja district, this is one of the most popular discos on the island. Spread over several different levels of a modern building, it has a huge bar and three dance floors, and is sometimes filled with balloons. There's live music Wednesday to Sunday from 8pm to 3am.

Club Safari. Lindergweg, Salinja. ☎ **599/9-655453.** Cover $6–$7.

In a sprawling and much-renovated low-slung building set inland from the coast, in the heart of the Salinja district, this is the leading and most attractive disco on Curaçao. The jungle motif is enhanced with masses of coconut palms, a dance floor where rhythms seem to pulsate out of the floor, and a copious bar area where more than a usual number of drinks seem to be tinted blue. Although hours vary with the season and according to the number of foreign visitors on island, it's usually open Wednesday to Sunday from 9:30pm to 2am.

Notes

Notes

WHEREVER YOU TRAVEL, *H*ELP IS NEVER FAR AWAY.

From planning your trip to providing travel assistance along the way, American Express® Travel Service Offices are always there to help you do more.

Caribbean

ANTIGUA
St. John's

ARUBA
Oranjestad

BAHAMAS
Freeport
Nassau

BARBADOS
Bridgetown

BRITISH VIRGIN ISLANDS
Tortola
Virgin Gorda

CAYMAN ISLANDS
Grand Cayman

CURAÇAO
Willemstad

DOMINICA
Roseau

DOMINICAN REPUBLIC
Santo Domingo

FRENCH WEST INDIES
St. Barthelemy

GRENADA
St. George's

GUADELOUPE
Pointe-à-Pitre

HAITI
Port-au-Prince

JAMAICA
Kingston
Montego Bay
Negril
Ocho Rios
Port Antonio

MARTINIQUE
Fort de France

MONTSERRAT
Plymouth

PUERTO RICO
Mayagüez
San Juan

ST. KITTS
Basseterre

ST. LUCIA
Castries

ST. MAARTEN
Philipsburg

ST. VINCENT
Kingstown

TURKS & CAICOS
Providenciale

U.S. VIRGIN ISLANDS
St. Croix
St. Thomas

do more AMERICAN EXPRESS

Travel

http://www.americanexpress.com/travel

American Express Travel Service Offices are found in central locations throughout the Caribbean.